Contents

The MILEPOST®
All-The-North Travel Guide®

(© Beth Davidow)

(© Harry M. Walker)

(© Robin Brandt)

Bear in the tall grass, Kodiak Island.
(© Tom Bol)

The MILEPOST®

PUBLISHER
William S. Morris III

EDITOR
Kris Valencia Graef

EDITORIAL AND ART DIRECTION
Art Director, David L. Ranta
Asst. Art Director, Pat Penisten
Asst. Editor, Carol Phillips
Page Design, Pam Smith
Field Editors, Earl Brown, Blake Hanna,
Marion Nelson, Lynn Owen,
Stephanie Olness, Marion Stirrup

ADVERTISING SALES
Director, Lea Cockerham
Alaska Manager, Sharon Athas Coté
Southeast, Lisa Dallas
Kenai Peninsula, Marion Nelson
Anchorage/Fairbanks/Kodiak, Lynn Owen
Interior/Southcentral Alaska, Stephanie Olness
*Yukon Territory/Northern British Columbia/
Northwest Territories*, Earl L. Brown
Southern British Columbia/Alberta, Blake Hanna
National, Fatima Mulholland

ADVERTISING COORDINATOR
Paige Stephenson

FULFILLMENT
Manager, Jill Kaniut
Assistant, Jaime Klosterman

ADMINISTRATION
Director of Magazines, Matthew H. Brown
General Manager, David C. Foster
Director of Circulation, Gail Weaverling
Controller, Frank Chandler
Business Manager, Dean Nelson

EDITORIAL, ADVERTISING SALES AND
FULFILLMENT OFFICES:
619 E. Ship Creek Ave, Suite 329
Anchorage, AK 99501
Phone (907) 272-6070; fax (907) 258-5360

ADMINISTRATIVE OFFICES
735 Broad Street
Augusta, GA 30901
Phone (706) 722-6060

To order *THE MILEPOST®* and related products, phone 1-800-726-4707; e-mail books@themilepost.com; or visit our book catalog at www.themilepost.com

The MILEPOST® is an annual publication of Morris Communications Corporation, 735 Broad Street, Augusta, GA 30901.

ISSN 0361-1361 ISBN 1-892154-00-5
Key title: The Milepost
Printed in U.S.A.

A PUBLICATION OF THE MAGAZINE DIVISION
OF MORRIS COMMUNICATIONS CORPORATION

Wish I was going with you . . .

Dear Fellow Adventurer:

We are proud at Morris Communications Corporation to bring you this, the 51st edition, of *The MILEPOST®*. In many very real ways, the highly experienced editorial staff of *The MILEPOST®* are your traveling companions as you make an incredible journey through western Canada and Alaska. You are on your way to one of the most beautiful—and exciting—vacations in the world. And *The MILEPOST®* will keep you informed on everything from fuel stops to side trips every mile of the way.

I made my first trip to Alaska back in 1968 and have returned there—often several times a year—every year but one. Only people who have never experienced Alaska and western Canada ask me why I love it so passionately. But once you have experienced this vast and wild country, seen the wildlife, enjoyed a lingering sundown, experienced life in a Native village, explored a glacier, sailed down a deep fjord, panned for your own gold, hiked along the original Iditarod Trail, enjoyed fresh salmon you caught yourself from a clear, cold rushing stream, there is no way not to love what Alaskans call The Last Great Place, because it surely is.

Once again, *The MILEPOST®* staff have logged every mile of every main highway and by-way from Seattle, Washington and Great Falls, Montana to Prudhoe Bay at the north of Alaska and Homer, the last town on the connected Alaska highway system at the southern tip of the Kenai Peninsula. And every year, things change while they stay the same. You can not purchase a better planner for your western Canada/Alaska vacation and, as I said above, your copy of *The MILEPOST®* will prove itself invaluable "on the road."

Have a great time on your Alaska vacation and thank you so much for investing in *The MILEPOST®*. I only wish I was going along with you.

Sincerely,

William S. Morris III
Publisher

Photography credits: Cover—Howling wolf. (Michael DeYoung/Alaska Stock). Insets—View of Lion Head. (© Ken Graham). Glacier viewing. (Courtesy Glacier Bay Tours & Cruises). Column insets: Alyeska Resort, page 566; Gladys Blyth, pages 230, 233; Alisha A. Brown, page 300; Earl L. Brown, pages 47, 52, 53, 73, 75–78, 81–83, 95–97, 100, 112, 113, 114, 118, 120, 121, 128, 132, 133, 137, 152, 157, 159, 160, 164, 168, 188, 200, 201, 203, 207–209, 211, 213, 214, 216, 217, 224, 228, 261, 264, 265, 268, 278, 279, 284, 299, 300, 450, 451, Kris Graef, pages 176, 199, 311, 319, 320, 330, 332, 355, 358, 366, 368, 372, 385, 391, 392, 394, 406, 407, 419, 443, 489, 492, 495, 498, 499, 501, 502, 504, 505, 514, 515, 521, 523, 526, 532, 533; Stephen Graef, page 492; Great Northern Arts Festival, page 302; Blake Hanna, pages 36, 38, 39, 41, 44, 69, 229, 244; Leslie Leong, page 215; Judy Parkin, pages 61, 64, 65, 68, 75, 219, 229, 234, 237, 249, 253; Tom Parkin, pages 63, 236; David Ranta, pages 557, 561; Jill Shepherd, page 563; Tetlin NWR, page 175; Evelyn Trabant (UAF), page 446; Harry M. Walker, page 286

Photo submissions: Copies of photo submission guidelines must be requested before submitting photos. Send request and postpaid return envelope to the Editor. *The MILEPOST®* assumes no responsibility for unsolicited materials.

Advertising and Editorial Policy: *The MILEPOST®* does not endorse or guarantee any advertised service or facility, although we trust that our advertisers will live up to their promises. A sincere effort is made to give complete, accurate and annually up-to-date travel information for this immense segment of North America. However, between the time of our field surveys and the time of the readers' trip, many things may change. In all such cases, the publisher will not be held responsible.

Thank you: *The MILEPOST®* appreciates the assistance of the many individuals, agencies and associations—too numerous to list here—that review editorial copy each year and help provide up-to-date information.

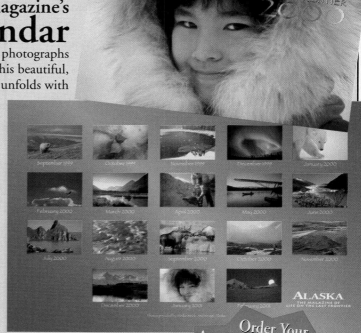

Key to Highways in *The MILEPOST* ®

Circled letters on map
identify highways as listed below:

How to Use *The MILEPOST*

The MILEPOST provides mile-by-mile descriptions of all major highways and roads in Alaska and northwestern Canada; detailed information on all major destinations (cities, communities, national parks and other attractions) in the North; and how-to help for various modes of transportation (air, ferry, railroads, etc.). Refer to the Contents page and Index for subjects and destinations.

The MILEPOST will work for you regardless of how you plan to travel—whether by car, by plane, on a tour bus, or by bicycle. It will help you plan your trip, as well as acting as a valuable guide during your trip.

The backbone of *The MILEPOST* is the highway logs. The Key to Highways map on the opposite page shows you what highways are covered in *The MILEPOST*. In these mile-by-mile descriptions of the highways and byways of the North, you will find campgrounds; businesses offering food, lodging, gas and other services; attractions; fishing spots; road conditions; descriptions of the geography and history of the land and communities; and much more.

To the right is an abbreviated version of part of the Parks Highway log, keyed to help you understand how to read all highway logs in *The MILEPOST*.

1. A boldface paragraph appears at the beginning of each highway log in *The MILEPOST* that explains what beginning and ending destinations are used, and what boldface letters represent those destinations. In this log A represents **Anchorage**, F is **Fairbanks**.

2. The boldface numbers represent the distance in miles from the beginning and ending destinations, and the lightface numbers are the metric equivalent in kilometers (unless otherwise noted). For example, the entrance to Denali National Park and Preserve is 237.3 miles, or 381.9 kilometers, from Anchorage.

3. **Junctions** with other logged roads are indented and color-coded. And the cross-referenced section is always uppercased. In this example, the DENALI NATIONAL PARK section is referenced. Refer to the Contents page to quickly find other sections.

4. "Log" advertisements are classified-type advertisements that appear in the text. These are identified by the boldface name of the business at the beginning of the entry and "[ADVERTISEMENT]" at the end. These log advertisements are written by the advertisers.

5. Display advertisements are keyed in the log by a boldface entry at their highway locations, followed by the words "See display ad." Their advertisement will appear near this entry or a page or section will be referenced.

It may also help you to know how our field editors log the highways. *The MILEPOST* field editors drive each highway, taking notes on facilities, features and attractions along the way and noting the mile at which they appear. Mileages are measured from the beginning of the highway, which is generally at a junction or the city limits, to the end of the highway, also usually a junction or city limits. Most highways in *The MILEPOST* are logged either south to north or east to west. If you are traveling the opposite direction of the log, you will read the log back to front.

To determine driving distance between 2 points, simply subtract the first mileage figures. For example, the distance from Crabb's Crossing at **Milepost A 231.3** to the park entrance at **Milepost A 237.3** is 6 miles.

Look for these symbols throughout *The MILEPOST*:

▲ Campground   ♿ Wheelchair accessible
← Fishing   **MP** On-line advertiser

Parks Highway Log

Distance from Anchorage (A) is followed by distance from Fairbanks (F). **①**

ALASKA ROUTE 1

A 231.3 (372.2 km) **F 126.7** (203.9 km) Crabb's Crossing, second bridge northbound over the Nenana River. Boundary of Denali National Park and Preserve.

A 234.1 (376.7 km) **F 123.9** (199.4 km) Double-ended turnout with litter barrels to east; scenic viewpoint.

A 235.1 (378.4 km) **F 122.9** (197.8 km) *CAUTION: Railroad crossing.*

A 237.2 (381.7 km) **F 120.8** (194.4 km) Riley Creek bridge.

② **A 237.3** (381.9 km) **F 120.7** (194.2 km) Turnoff to east for entrance to **DENALI NATIONAL PARK AND PRESERVE** (formerly Mount McKinley National Park) to west. Visitor Center is 0.5 mile/0.8 km from the highway junction.

> **Junction** with Park Road. See DENALI NATIONAL PARK section for log of Park Road and details on the park. **③**

Clusters of highway businesses north and south of the park entrance offer a variety of services to the highway traveler and park visitor.

A 238 (383 km) **F 120** (193.4 km) Third bridge northbound over the Nenana River.

④ **A 238.1** (383.2 km) **F 119.9** (193 km) **Denali Raft Adventures.** Come with the original Nenana River rafters! Paddleboats too! Age 5 or older welcome, 7 departures daily. Whitewater or scenic floats. Get away to untouched wilderness! 2-hour, 4-hour, full-day and overnight trips are available. See display ad in DENALI NATIONAL PARK section. Phone (907) 683-2234. Internet: www.alaskaone.com/denraft. VISA, Master Card accepted. [ADVERTISEMENT]

A 238.4 (383.6 km) **F 119.6** (192.5 km) **Denali Bluffs Hotel.** See display ad this section. **⑤**

The introduction to each highway logged in *The MILEPOST* includes a chart of mileages between major points (see below).

Maps also accompany each highway logged in *The MILEPOST*. Consult the map key for an explanation of abbreviations (see example at bottom). Mileage boxes at communities and junctions on the highway map reflect the rounded off mileage in the highway log at the corresponding point.

	Anchorage	Denali Park	Fairbanks	Talkeetna	Wasilla
Anchorage		237	358	113	42
Denali Park	237		121	153	195
Fairbanks	358	121		245	316
Talkeetna	113	153	245		71
Wasilla	42	195	316	71	

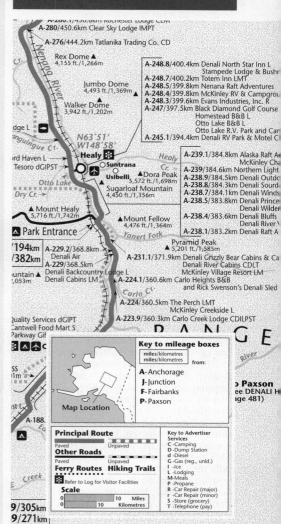

Welcome to the North Country

The North Country is the land north of 51° 16' latitude. Geographically, it encompasses Alaska, Yukon Territory, western Northwest Territories, northern British Columbia and Alberta. Following are some facts and figures about each of these areas.

Alaska

Population: 621,400
Capital: Juneau
Largest City: Anchorage
Area: 587,878 square miles/ 1,522,486 square km
Coastline: 33,904 miles/ 54,562 km
Highest Point: Mount McKinley, 20,320 feet/6,194m
Lowest Point: Pacific Ocean, sea level
State Flower: Forget-me-not
State Tree: Sitka spruce
State Bird: Willow ptarmigan
State Motto: "North to the Future"
Major Industries: Tourism, petroleum, fishing, lumber
Drinking age: 21. The sale and/or importation of alcoholic beverages is prohibited in some 50 bush communities.

Top Ten Attractions:
1. Glaciers
2. Inside Passage
3. Native Arts and Culture
4. Wildlife Viewing
5. Historic Mining Towns and Areas
6. Museums
7. Sportfishing
8. Trans-Alaska Pipeline
9. Russian Heritage
10. National Parks and Monuments

Fish & Game: Alaska Dept. of Fish and Game, Box 25526, Juneau, AK 99802; phone (907) 465-4180, fax (907) 465-2772; Internet www.state.ak.us/local/akpages/FISH.GAME/ adfghome.htm
Visitor Information: Alaska Division of Tourism, Box 110801, Juneau, AK 99811-0801; phone (907) 465-2010; Internet www.travelalaska.com and www.state.ak.us /tourism

Alaska was purchased by the U.S. from Russia in 1867. It became the 49th state on January 3, 1959. Alaska is the largest state in the union in area (twice the size of Texas), but ranks 49th in population, based on the 1990 census. (Only Wyoming has fewer residents.) Approximately 15 percent of the population is Native: Eskimo, Aleut and Indian (Athabascan, Tlingit, Haida, Tsimshian).

Alaska has 17 of the 20 highest mountains in the United States, including the highest peak in North America—Mount McKinley (Denali). Geographically, the state falls into roughly 6 distinct natural regions: Southeastern, Southcentral, the Interior, Southwestern, Western and the Brooks Range/Arctic.

Southeastern Alaska is a moist, luxuriantly forested panhandle extending some

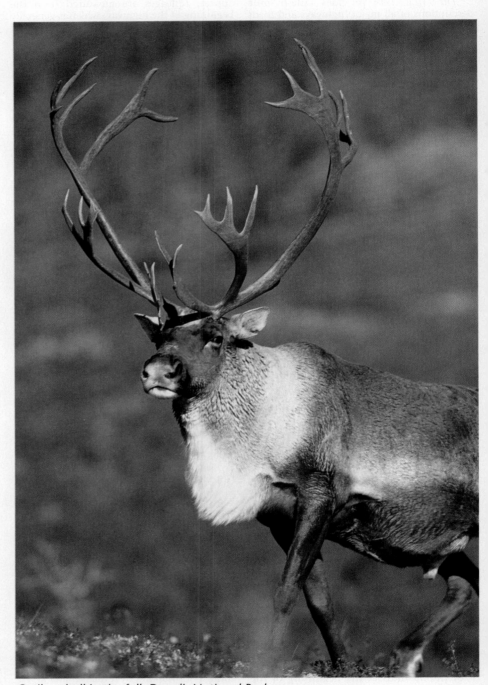

Caribou bull in the fall, Denali National Park. (© Robin Brandt)

500 miles/805 km from Dixon Entrance south of Ketchikan to Icy Bay on the Gulf of Alaska coast. This narrow strip of coast, separated from the mainland and Canada by the Coast Mountains and the hundreds of islands of the Alexander Archipelago, form the Inside Passage water route used by ships and ferries. Cruise ships bring thousands of passengers through the Inside Passage each summer.

The Southcentral region of Alaska curves

650 miles/1,046 km north and west from the Gulf of Alaska coast to the Alaska Range. This region's tremendous geographic variety includes the Matanuska–Susitna river valleys, the Chugach and Wrangell–St. Elias mountain ranges, the Kenai Peninsula and the glaciers of Prince William Sound. Anchorage, the state's largest city, is the hub of Southcentral.

Interior Alaska lies cradled between the Brooks Range to the north and the Alaska

Detail of totem at Sitka National Historical Park. (© Loren Taft)

Range to the south, a vast area that drains the Yukon River and its tributaries. It is a climate of extremes, holding both the record high (100°F at Fort Yukon) and the record low (-80°F at Prospect Creek). Fairbanks is the hub of the Interior and a jump-off point for bush communities in both the Interior and Arctic.

Southwestern Alaska takes in Kodiak Island, the Alaska Peninsula and Aleutian Islands. Kodiak, less than an hour's flight from Anchorage and about 10 hours by ferry from Homer, is the largest island in Alaska. Kodiak was Russian Alaska's first capital city. Brown bear viewing is an attraction on Kodiak and at Katmai National Park and Preserve near King Salmon. The Southwest ferry system provides service from Kodiak to Unalaska/ Dutch Harbor.

Western Alaska stretches from the head of Bristol Bay north along the Bering Sea coast to the Seward Peninsula near the Arctic Circle. This region extends inland from the coast to encompass the Yukon–Kuskokwim Delta. Nome is one of the best known destinations in Western Alaska.

Arctic Alaska lies above the Arctic Circle (latitude 66°33'), between the Brooks Range

to the south and the Arctic sea coast to the north, and from the Canadian border to the east westward to Kotzebue. Day and overnight trips to Kotzebue, Barrow and Prudhoe Bay are popular packages offered out of both Anchorage and Fairbanks.

If you include the Marine Highway, all regions of Alaska are connected by highway with the exception of Western Alaska. And that region's hub cities—Bethel and Nome—are less than 2 hours from Anchorage by air.

Bush travel in all regions of Alaska is covered in detail in our companion book, *The Alaska Wilderness Guide.*

Yukon Territory

Population: 27,800
Capital: Whitehorse
Largest City: Whitehorse
Area: 186,661 square miles/ 483,414 square km
Highest Point: Mount Logan, 19,545 feet/5,957m
Lowest Point: Beaufort Sea, sea level
Territorial Flower: Fireweed
Territorial Bird: Raven
Drinking age: 19. Packaged liquor, beer and wine are sold in government liquor stores.
Major Industries: Tourism, mining

Top Ten Attractions:
1. SS *Klondike*, Whitehorse
2. MacBride Museum, Whitehorse
3. Northern Lights Centre, Watson Lake
4. Diamond Tooth Gerties, Dawson City
5. Palace Grand Theatre, Dawson City
6. Beringia Interpretive Centre, Whitehorse
7. Dredge #4, Dawson City
8. Kluane National Park
9. Whitehorse Fish Ladder
10. Robert Service Cabin, Dawson City

Fish & Game: Yukon Government, Dept. of Renewable Resources, Fish and Wildlife Branch, Box 2703, Whitehorse, YT Y1A 2C6, phone (867) 667-5221
Visitor Information: Tourism Yukon, Box 2703, Whitehorse, YT Y1A 2C6; phone (867) 667-5340; Internet www.touryukon. com; E-mail info@touryukon.com

Shaped somewhat like a right triangle, Yukon Territory is bordered on the west by Alaska at 141° longitude; on the north by the Beaufort Sea/Arctic Ocean; on the south by British Columbia at latitude 60°; and on the east by the western Northwest Territories.

Yukon Territory is larger than all the New England states combined. Canada's highest peak, Mount Logan (elev. 19,545

feet/5,957m), is located in Yukon's St. Elias Mountains.

First Nations peoples of the Yukon belong to the Athabascan and Tlingit language families. These are Gwitchin, Han, Northern Tutchone, Southern Tutchone, Kaska, Tagish, Tlingit and Upper Tanana.

The Yukon was made a district of the Northwest Territories in 1895, and became a separate territory in June of 1898. The territory's first capital was Dawson City, site of the great Klondike gold rush, which brought thousands of gold seekers to the Yukon and Alaska in 1897–98. The Klondike gold rush began celebrating its centennial in 1996—marking the discovery of gold on Bonanza Creek on August 16, 1896—and continued the celebration through 1998.

At the height of the gold rush, an estimated 40,000 people lived in Dawson City. By 1903, as other gold stampedes drew off much of Dawson's population, the city's boom days were over, although mining continued to support the community for many years. On March 31, 1953, Whitehorse—on the railway and the highway, with a large airport—replaced Dawson City as capital.

Western Northwest Territories

Population: 57,600
Capital: Yellowknife (until 1999)
Largest City: Yellowknife
Area: 550,000 square miles/1.4 million square km
Highest Point: Cirque of the Unclimbables Mountain, 9,062 feet/2,762m
Lowest Point: Beaufort Sea, sea level
Territorial Flower: Mountain avens
Drinking age: 19. Packaged liquor, beer and wine are sold in government liquor stores. Sale and possession of alcohol is prohibited in several communities.
Major Industries: Mining, manufacturing, fishing

Top Ten Attractions:
1. Nahanni National Park Reserve
2. Wood Buffalo National Park
3. Canol Heritage Trail Park Reserve
4. Dempster Highway
5. Pingos (cone-shaped hills) of the Tuktoyaktuk Peninsula
6. Roman Catholic "Igloo" Church, Inuvik
7. Twin Falls Gorge Territorial Park
8. Prince of Wales Northern Heritage Center, Yellowknife
9. Northwest Territories Legislative Assembly Building, Yellowknife
10. Wildcat Cafe, Yellowknife

Motorist on the Dempster Highway to Inuvik, NWT. (© Leslie Leong)

Fish & Game: Dept. of Economic Development and Tourism, Tourism Development and Marketing, Box 1320, Yellowknife, NT X1A 2L9; phone (800) 661-0788
Visitor Information: NWTAT (MP), Box 610, Yellowknife, NT X1A 2N5; phone (800) 661-0788; Internet www.nwttravel.nt.ca

On April 1, 1999, Northwest Territories will be divided into 2 territories. Passed by popular vote in 1982 and approved by the Canadian Parliament in 1993, this division will create Nunavut and its capital, Iqaluit on Baffin Island, in what is now the eastern half of Northwest Territories.

Northwest Territories comprises about a third of Canada. Western Northwest Territories is about the size of Alaska. Western Northwest Territories' Wood Buffalo National Park is the second largest national park in the world.

A majority of the population of Northwest Territories is Native. Aboriginal groups are the Dene, Inuvialuit, Inuit, Gwich'in, Dogrib and Metis.

Access to western Northwest Territories is from Alberta via the Mackenzie Highway system, from British Columbia via the Liard Highway, and from Yukon Territory via the

Dempster Highway. A major road-building project in the 1960s constructed most of the highway system in western Northwest Territories. Road improvement is ongoing, with most roads now paved.

British Columbia

Population: 3,764,200
Capital: Victoria
Largest City: Vancouver
Area: 365,900 square miles/947,608 square km
Highest Point: Mount Fairweather, 15,295 feet/4,662m
Lowest Point: Pacific Ocean, sea level
Provincial Flower: Pacific dogwood
Provincial Tree: Western red cedar
Provincial Bird: Settler's jay
Provincial Motto: *Splendor Sine Occasu* (Splendour Without Diminishment)
Drinking age: 19. Packaged liquor, beer and wine are sold in government liquor stores.
Major Industries: Forestry, mining and energy, tourism, agriculture, seafood products, food

Top Attractions:
1. Royal BC Museum, Victoria
2. Butchart Gardens, Victoria
3. Vancouver Aquarium
4. Capilano Suspension Bridge, North Vancouver
5. Barkerville Historic Town
6. Fort Steele Heritage Town
7. Grist Mill and Gardens, Keremeos
8. Grouse Mountain, North Vancouver
9. Ksan Historical Indian Village Museum, Hazelton

Fish & Game: Fish and Wildlife Branch, Ministry of Environment, Parliament Buildings, Victoria, BC V8V 1X4
Visitor Information: Tourism British Columbia, Dept. TG, Box 9830, Stn. Prov. Govt., Victoria, B.C. V8W 9W5 Canada; phone (800) 663-6000; Internet www.travel.bc.ca

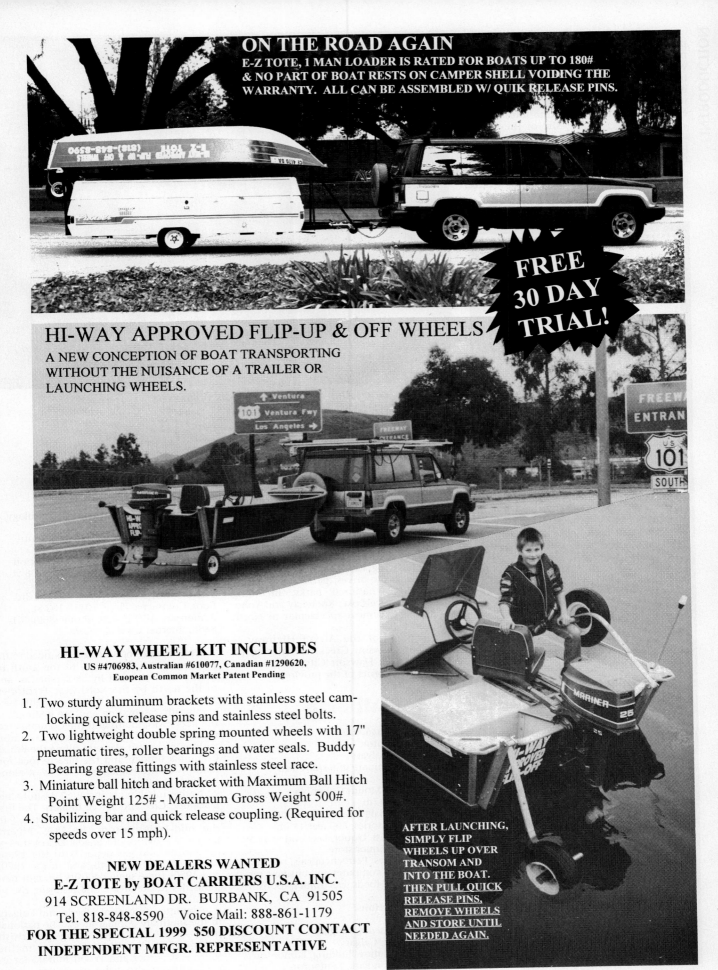

Canada's most westerly—and 3rd largest—province, British Columbia stretches 813 miles/1,300 km from its southern border with the United States to the northern boundary with Yukon Territory. It is bounded on the east by Alberta and on the west by the Pacific Ocean. The province encompasses the Queen Charlotte Islands and Vancouver Island, site of the capital city of Victoria. Approximately half the province's population resides in the Victoria–Vancouver area.

British Columbia entered the Dominion of Canada on July 20, 1871, as the 6th province.

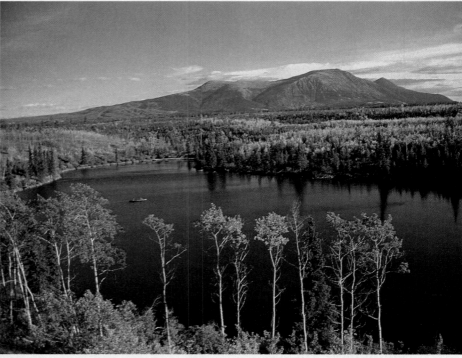

Falls colors along Atlin Road in British Columbia. (© Earl L. Brown, staff)

The region was important in early fur trade, and expansion of the province came with the 1860s Cariboo gold rush, followed by the completion of Canada's first transcontinental railway—the Canadian Pacific.

The cities of Vancouver and Victoria are popular tourist areas, as are Vancouver Island and the Gulf and San Juan island groups. The Sunshine Coast, along the shores of British Columbia facing Vancouver Island, is popular for its scenic drives, parks and beaches. The region's national parks, including Glacier, Mt. Revelstoke, Kootenay and Yoho, are among the most spectacular in North America.

Mile Zero of the Alaska Highway is located in Dawson Creek, BC (not to be confused with Dawson City, YT), in the northeastern corner of the province.

Alberta

Population: 2,545,600
Capital: Edmonton
Largest City: Calgary
Area: 255,287 square miles/661,142 square km
Highest Point: Mount Columbia, 12,293 feet/3,747m
Lowest Point: Salt River at the border with Northwest Territories, 600 feet/183m
Drinking age: 18. Liquor, beer and wine are sold in private liquor stores.
Major Industries: Petrochemicals, plastics, forest products, computer and business services, processed foods, electronics, tourism

Top Ten Attractions:
1. Calgary Zoo
2. Glenbow Museum, Calgary
3. Heritage Park, Calgary
4. Alberta Legislature Building, Edmonton
5. Fort Edmonton Park, Edmonton
6. Muttart Conservatory, Edmonton
7. Provincial Museum of Alberta, Edmonton
8. Storyland Valley Zoo, Edmonton
9. Royal Tyrrell Museum of Palaeontology, Drumheller
10. Edmonton Space and Science Centre

Fish & Game: Environmental Protection Branch, Information Centre, 9920 108 St., Edmonton, AB T5K 2M4
Visitor Information: Travel Alberta, 3rd floor, Commerce Place, 10155 102 St., Edmonton, AB T5J 4G8; phone (800) 661-8888; Internet www.atp.ab.ca

The Province of Alberta is bounded to the west by British Columbia, to the south by Montana, to the east by Saskatchewan and to the north by the Northwest Territories. Among the dramatic features of this geographically fascinating area are a stretch of the Rocky Mountains and the Columbia Icefield—source of the Athabasca, Columbia and Saskatchewan glaciers—along the British Columbia border, and the bizarre rock formations of the badlands to the west along the Red Deer River.

Native inhabitants included Assiniboine, Blackfoot, Cree and Sarcee Indians. The first European settlers—fur traders—arrived in the mid-18th century. In 1875 Alberta became a province of Canada. Discoveries of oil and natural gas deposits in the 1930s caused economic growth, and in the 1970s and 1980s these same deposits brought new industries to the area and a resulting rise in population.

Edmonton in central Alberta and Calgary to the south are popular areas. The national parks—Banff and Jasper along the British Columbia border, Waterton Lakes in the southwest corner and Wood Buffalo far in the north—are also major attractions.

Travel Planning

Sunset over Chilkat Inlet near Haines, AK. (© Bruce M. Herman)

Air Travel

Slightly more than half of all visitors to Alaska arrive by air. Air travel is also one of the most common forms of transportation in the North. You can fly just about anywhere. If there is no scheduled service, you can charter a plane.

About 10 domestic airlines and 2 dozen small scheduled carriers provide scheduled service within Alaska. In addition to scheduled air service, there are more than 200 certified charter/air taxi operators in Alaska.

Air taxi operators conduct their business from a specific base of operations, primarily through the charter of aircraft, and offer a wide variety of options: drop-off and pickup for hunters, sport fisherman and river runners; photo safaris to see wildlife or glaciers; round-trip flights to remote communities which may include an overnight.

Check the advertisements for scheduled and charter air service in the communities covered in *The MILEPOST®*. There are many to choose from.

Air taxi rates may vary from carrier to carrier. Most operators charge an hourly rate either per plane load or per passenger; others may charge on a per-mile basis. Flightseeing trips to area attractions are often available at a fixed price per passenger.

Sample per-hour fares for charter planes with varied wheel, float and ski capabilities (luggage space limited and dependent on number of passengers): Piper Archer (3 passengers), $175; Piper Cherokee 6 (5 passengers), $230; Islander (9 passengers), $430; Chieftain (9 passengers), $650.

Any pilot flying for hire is required to hold a commercial or airline transport pilot certificate. The customer can and should be protected by having the pilot show his/her credentials. A pilot with the necessary credentials will be glad to show them. Do not fly with a pilot who cannot produce certification.

The MILEPOST® highway logs include the location of most airstrips along the highways and in the communities in Alaska and northwestern Canada. Aircraft symbols corresponding to airstrip locations are included on the highway strip maps. The map symbol (✈) is the same for airports with scheduled service, as for airstrips with no scheduled service and limited facilities.

Accommodations

Accommodations in the North—as anywhere else—can range from luxurious to utilitarian. You'll find lodging in fine lodges and major-chain hotels/motels; in bed and breakfasts; in rustic log cabins; and in mobile homes. Considering the comparative remoteness of many communities, and the seasonal nature of Northern travel, visitors are often surprised at the wide variety of lodging available.

The larger cities (Anchorage, Fairbanks, etc.) have more to choose from than the smaller, more remote communities. But in midsummer, even those locations with greater numbers of rooms available can fill up quickly. You should consider making reservations ahead of time during the busy summer season, whether your destination is a major city or a small highway community.

Some facilities along highways of the North may be a bit on the rustic side compared to what you're used to. This is, after all, the Last Frontier. You'll also find some first-class establishments in surprisingly remote locations. Sometimes the frills of city travel may be missing, but the hospitality of the North more than makes up for it.

Paid advertisements for accommodations appearing in *The MILEPOST®*—whether display ads or "log ads" placed in the highway log—are written by the advertisers themselves. We do not endorse or guarantee any of these facilities or services, although we trust the advertisers will live up to their promises. If they don't, please write us, phone us or e-mail us. Keep in mind that businesses may close, ownership may change, and rates may increase. As rates often change, it's a good idea to contact the particular lodging you are interested in and inquire about their current rates.

FLIGHT TIMES BETWEEN SELECTED CITIES					
Between	**Time**	**Between**	**Time**	**Between**	**Time**
Anchorage—Bethel	1 hr. 15 min.	Anchorage—Valdez	40 min.	Juneau—Haines	35 min.
Anchorage—Cordova	45 min.	Anchorage—Wrangell	2 hrs. 20 min.	Juneau—Ketchikan	50 min.
Anchorage—Dutch Harbor	2 hrs. 5 min.	Fairbanks—Barrow	1 hr. 20 min.	Juneau—Seattle, WA	2 hrs. 10 min.
Anchorage—Fairbanks	50 min.	Fairbanks—Delta Junction	35 min.	Juneau—Sitka	35 min.
Anchorage—Juneau	1 hr. 35 min.	Fairbanks—Kotzebue	2 hrs. 10 min.	Juneau—Skagway	45 min.
Anchorage—King Salmon	1 hr.	Fairbanks—Nome	2 hrs. 20 min.	Juneau—Whitehorse, YT	1 hr.
Anchorage—Kodiak	55 min.	Fairbanks—Northway	1 hr.	Juneau—Yakutat	45 min.
Anchorage—Kotzebue	1 hr. 30 min.	Fairbanks—Prudhoe Bay	1 hr. 25 min.	Ketchikan—Sitka	50 min.
Anchorage—Nome	1 hr. 30 min.	Fairbanks—Whitehorse, YT	3 hrs. 35 min.	Nome—Kotzebue	40 min.
Anchorage—Petersburg	2 hrs.	(1 stop in Dawson City)		Whitehorse—Dawson City	1 hr. 40 min.
Anchorage—Seattle, WA	3 hrs. 15 min.	Juneau—Glacier Bay	25 min.	Yakutat—Cordova	45 min.

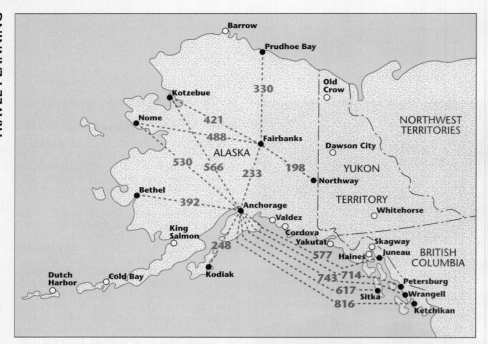

Air Mileage Between Major Points In Alaska

Private aircraft information in these logs includes only the name and location of the airstrip, the elevation, length and surface material of the longest runway and the availability of fuel. Many Northland pilots fly jet craft. Jet and other fuel is available at many airports. Fuel sold in Alaska and Canada is almost exclusively 100LL; 80 octane fuel is no longer available, though some airports offer car gasoline. *NOTE: The brief description of airstrips given in* The MILE-POST® *is in no way intended as a guide.* Pilots should have a current copy of the *Alaska Supplement*. For a packet of free brochures including *Flight Tips for Pilots in Alaska*, write the Federal Aviation Administration, 222 W. 7th Ave., Anchorage, AK 99513.

Pilots may also get in touch with the Alaska Airmen's Assoc., Inc., P.O. Box 241185, Anchorage, AK 99524-1184, phone (907) 245-1251, fax (907) 245-1259, to order a copy of the *Alaska Airmen's Logbook for Alaska, Northwest Canada and Russia*. A new edition with updated information will be available in late spring 1999.

Two free Canadian publications of interest are *Air Tourist Information—Canada* (TP771) and *Flying the Alaska Highway in Canada* (TP2168). Both are available from the Civil Aviation Publications Office, phone (800) 305-2059.

Arctic Circle

The Arctic Circle is the latitude at which the sun never sets on the day of the summer solstice (June 20 or 21) and never rises on the day of the winter solstice (December 21 or 22). For about 2 months during summer, the sun shines continually; during winter there are 2 months of darkness. The only light is that of the moon and the aruroa borealis (northern lights).

The northern third of Alaska lies within the Arctic Circle—the only true polar region

in the state. The Brooks Range separates the Arctic region from the Interior of Alaska and, surprisingly, the temperature in the Interior is often more severe, as the Arctic Ocean has an ameliorating effect on temperatures in the Far North.

Motorists will cross the Arctic Circle in Alaska at **Milepost J 115.3** on the Dalton Highway, where there is a BLM Wayside and interpretive display about the Arctic Circle. In Canada, motorists cross the Arctic Circle at **Milepost J 252** on the Dempster Highway in Yukon Territory. A sign and turnout mark this crossing.

Aurora Borealis

The aurora borealis, or northern lights, are one of the North's greatest attractions. They range from simple arcs to drapery-like forms of light in green, red, blue and purple hues in northern night skies. In Alaska, auroras occur most often in the spring and fall months because of the tilt of the planet in relation to the sun's plane.

The Geophysical Institute at the University of Alaska Fairbanks predicts aurora displays on their web site at www.gi.alaska.edu. The Institute suggests the best time to view auroras is around the equinox (March and late September–October). They also answer most frequently asked questions about auroras at their web site. Fairbanks is a good place to see auroras.

The auroras are natural phenomena caused by the presence of charged particles in the earth's magnetic field. Electrons and protons released through sun spot activity emanate into space, a few drift to Earth where the planet's magnetic forces pull them to the most northern and southern latitudes. Regardless of the subtleties of scientific analysis, this spectacular light show produced by nature is high on the list of "must see" features for many visitors to the Northland.

Photographers delight in pursuing these

elusive phenomena, and visitors sometimes luck into photo and/or video displays devoted to the aurora, e.g. at Northern Lights Theatre at Denali Park.

The Aurora Borealis Monument is in Fairbanks at the International Airport. Made of laser light reflective material, the "Solar Borealis" sculpture changes color as you pass beneath it.

Bears

There are 3 types of bears found in Alaska: the black bear, brown/grizzly bear and polar bear. Black bears range throughout most of the state, with highest densities in Southeast, Prince William Sound and Southcentral. Black bears can be brown in color, and may be confused with a grizzly, although they are normally smaller than a grizzly, with a more pointed head. Brown/grizzly bears range in color from black to blond, and range over most of the state. Alaska's coastal brown/grizzly bear is the world's largest carnivorous land mammal. (While polar bears are as large or larger, they actually live at sea on the ice, rather than on land.) Grizzlies have a distinct shoulder hump and larger head than black bears.

Formal bear viewing areas include: Pack Creek bear observatory on Admiralty Island (permit required, fly-in or boat-in from Sitka or Juneau); Anan Bear Observatory (fly-in or boat-in from Wrangell); McNeil River State Game Sanctuary (permit required, fly-in from Homer or Anchorage); and Brooks Falls/Katmai National Park (fly-in from Homer and Anchorage). Visitors are most likely to see brown/grizzly bears in Denali National Park and on Kodiak Island.

Bears may be encountered anywhere in Alaska, from a remote campground to a city park in Anchorage. Pay attention to bear alerts posted at trailheads and in campgrounds detailing recent bear activity in the area. Keep a clean campsite. When hiking, make a lot of noise and avoid dense brush. Avoid surprising bears. Avoid close encounters. Let the bears know where you are. Bears will normally avoid people. Even though their vision is poor, their senses of smell and hearing are excellent. Make noise by talking, singing or ringing a bell.

Bicycling

Road conditions vary throughout the North, from paved highways to unimproved dirt roads. Read the highway logs in *The MILEPOST®* for details on road conditions, grades and highway shoulders.

According to the Alaska Dept. of Transportation, of the more than 1,500 miles of paved highway along the Alaska, Glenn/Tok Cut-off, Haines, Klondike, Parks, Richardson, Seward and Sterling highways, a little over 1,000 miles have 4 foot or wider paved shoulders. And there are nearly 100 miles of shared-use pathway along these highways currently. With the TRAAK initiative—Trails and Recreation Access for Alaska—more shared-use paths along Alaska's highways and byways are planned. These paths are intended for use by pedestrians, bicyclists, joggers, in-line skaters, etc., in summer, and cross-country skiers, dog sledders and others in winter. For current information on this program, look at the TRAAK homepage at www.dot.state.ak.us/external/state_wide/planning/traakhome.html

Anchorage, Fairbanks and Juneau have extensive bike trail systems. Maps showing these pathways are available locally.

Boating

Whether traveling by sailboat, cruiser, rowboat, canoe, inflatable raft or kayak, the North offers thousands of miles of challenging and scenic waterways.

For marine sailors, the Inside Passage and Southcentral Alaska's Prince William Sound provide scenic recreational boating and a sheltered transportation route. There are numerous marine charter services (most skippered, some bare-boat) along the Inside Passage from Prince Rupert, BC, to Haines and Skagway, AK, and in Southcentral Alaska ports. See the advertisements appearing in the communities. Marine facilities and transient moorage are also noted in the community descriptions.

Sea kayaking is popular in many coastal communities in Alaska. Rentals and/or guided kayak tours are available out of the following ports: Homer (for Kachemak Bay); Seward (Resurrection Bay, Kenai Fjords National Park); Valdez and Whittier (Prince William Sound); and in Southeastern Alaska out of Juneau, Sitka and Ketchikan. South-

east has hundreds of miles of sheltered waterways that are ideal for sea kayaking. Favorite destinations include: Gastineau Channel and Tracy Arm (out of Juneau); Glacier Bay National Park and Preserve; Point Adolphus in Icy Strait (out of Hoonah); Misty Fiords (out of Ketchikan); Sitka Sound and Outer Chichagof Island (from Sitka); Tebenkof Bay and Kuiu Island (from Kake); Yakutat Bay and Russell Fiord (from Yakutat); and Seymour Canal on Admiralty Island (from Juneau).

Outstanding sea kayaking opportunities are also available on the west coast of Prince of Wales Island. Canoe trails have been established on Prince of Wales Island along the Honker Divide and at Sarkar Lakes. Contact Craig Ranger District, Tongass National Forest, Box 145, Craig, AK 99921, phone (907) 826-3271. For maps and information contact the Thorne Bay Ranger District, Tongass National Forest, Box 19001, Thorne Bay, AK 99919, phone (907) 828-3304.

Inland boaters will find hundreds of river and lake systems suitable for traveling by boat, raft, kayak or canoe. In Alaska and Yukon Territory, the Yukon River system provides many of these waterways. In western Northwest Territories, it is the Mackenzie River system.

Guided float trips are found on most major runnable rivers in the North, and many of these operators advertise in *The MILEPOST*. Some of those with scheduled daily departures are: the Kenai River (Cooper Landing); Nenana River (Denali National Park entrance area, Parks Highway); and the Mendenhall River (Juneau). For the independent river runner, there are an even greater

Exploring Prince William Sound by kayak. *(© Tom Bol)*

number of opportunities.

The Bureau of Land Management maintains 6 rivers that are part of the National Wild and Scenic Rivers System: Birch Creek, Beaver Creek, Fortymile River, Delta River, Gulkana River and Unalakleet River. These rivers offer a variety of float trips. The Fortymile River is accessible from the Taylor Highway; the Gulkana River is accessible from the Richardson and the Denali high-

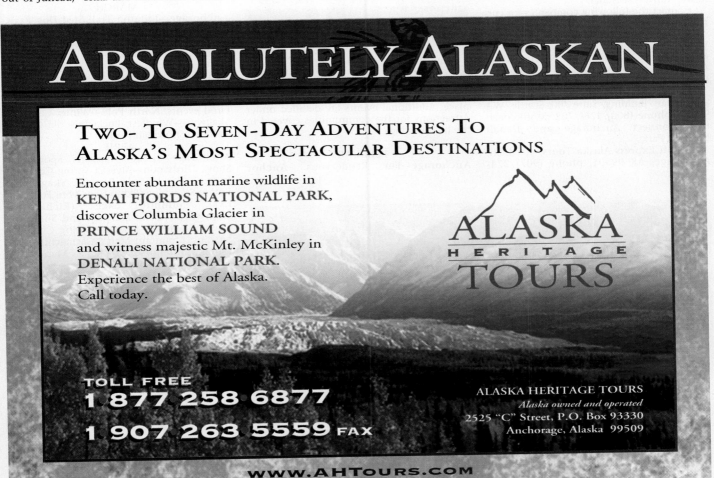

ways. The BLM offers brochures on the river trails, including access points, portages and scale of difficulty. Write the Bureau of Land Management, 1150 University Ave., Fairbanks, AK 99709-3899; phone (907) 474-2251.

Canoeing on the Kenai Peninsula's Swan Lake and Swanson River canoe trails starts about late May and continues until late October. For details on the trails write the Refuge Manager, Kenai National Wildlife Refuge, Box 2139, Soldotna, AK 99669. These canoe trails are accessible from the Swanson River road off the Sterling Highway.

Northern rivers pass through wild country and help is a long way off. Follow safety guidelines and prepare a float plan. For more information on Alaska's wild rivers, see *The Alaska Wilderness Guide*, available from *The MILEPOST®*.

Bus Lines

Independent travelers wishing to travel by public bus within Alaska and Yukon Territory will generally find routes and services much more limited than in the Lower 48. Scheduled bus service is available within Alaska and Yukon Territory, but scheduled direct bus service to Alaska from the Lower 48 is not available, unless you wish to join an escorted motorcoach tour. If your schedule allows, you can travel from the Lower 48 to Alaska via public bus service by using several carriers. Most scheduled bus service in the North is seasonal.

Contact the following companies for current schedules:

Alaska Direct Bus Line, 2191 2nd Ave., Whitehorse, YT Y1A 2E3, phone (800) 770-6652 or (867) 668-4833. Service from Anchorage to Fairbanks, Tok, Whitehorse, Dawson City, Skagway and Denali.

Alaska Sightseeing/Cruise West, 4th and Battery Building, Suite 700, Seattle, WA 98121, phone (800) 426-7702. Motorcoach trips connect Anchorage and Denali National Park.

Denali Express Alaska Tours, 405 L St., Anchorage, AK 99501, phone (907) 274-

0696. Service between Anchorage and Denali Park; group tours and special itineraries.

Gray Line of Alaska/Alaskon Express, 300 Elliott Ave. W., Seattle, WA 98119, phone (800) 544-2206 or fax (206) 281-0621. Scheduled service to Anchorage, Fairbanks, Skagway, Whitehorse, Haines and most communities en route. Motorcoach tours to Anchorage, Denali National Park, Fairbanks, Prudhoe Bay, Prince William Sound, Seward and Portage Glacier.

Greyhound Lines of Canada, 2191 2nd Ave., Whitehorse, YT Y1A 3T8, phone (867) 667-2223, fax (867) 633-6858. Scheduled service to Whitehorse from all U.S.–Canada border crossings; also the Whitehorse depot has carriers to Dawson City and Alaska destinations.

Norline Coaches (Yukon) Ltd., 34 MacDonald Rd., Whitehorse, YT Y1A 4I2, phone (867) 668-3355 for scheduled service, (867) 633-3864 for charter lines. Service between Whitehorse, Mayo, Carmacks and Dawson City. Daily service to Skagway.

Parks Highway Express, Box 82884, Fairbanks, AK 99708, phone (907) 479-3065, (888) 600-6001. Service between Anchorage, Denali Park and Fairbanks.

Princess Tours®, 2815 2nd Ave., Suite 400, Seattle, WA 98121, phone 1-800-835-8907. Motorcoach tours include the Klondike in Canada's Yukon, Anchorage, the Kenai Peninsula, Denali National Park, Fairbanks and Prudhoe Bay.

Seward Bus Line, Box 1338, Seward, AK 99664, phone (907) 224-3608, fax (907) 244-7237. Daily, year-round service between Anchorage and Seward.

Calendar of Events

Travelers may wish to take into account some of the North's major celebrations when planning their visit. Following are some of these events by month and by place. Additional events are detailed under Attractions for the communities covered in the highway logs.

FEBRUARY
Anchorage—Fur Rendezvous. **Anchor**

A booth at the Southeast Alaska State Fair at Haines in August. (© Ruth von Spalding)

Point—Snow Rondi. **Cordova**—Iceworm Festival. **Fairbanks/Whitehorse, YT**—Yukon Quest Sled Dog Race; Yukon Sourdough Rendezvous. **Homer**—Winter Carnival. **Whitehorse, YT**—Sourdough Rendezvous. **Willow**—Winter Carnival.

MARCH
Anchorage—Iditarod Trail Sled Dog Race. **Bethel**—Camai Native Dance Festival. **Dawson City, YT**—Thaw-Di-Graw Spring Carnival. **Fairbanks**—Winter Carnival; North American Sled Dog Championships. **Kodiak**—Pillar Mountain Golf Classic. **Nenana**—Tripod Raising. **Nome**—Bering Sea Ice Classic Golf Tournament; month of Iditarod events. **North Pole**—Winter Carnival. **Skagway**—Windfest; Buckwheat Ski Classic. **Valdez**—Snowman Festival.

APRIL
Anchorage—Great Alaskan Sportsman Show. **Girdwood**—Alyeska Spring Carnival. **Juneau**—Alaska Folk Festival. **Skagway**—Rotary Snowplow Exhibition; Mini Folk Festival. **Summit Lake (Richardson Highway)**—Arctic Man Ski and Snow Go Classic. **Valdez**—Extreme Skiing Championships; Mountain Man Snowmachine Hill Climb. **Whitehorse, YT**—Rotary Music Festival. **Wrangell**—Garnet Festival.

MAY
This month is a busy one for fishing derbies for halibut (Homer, Seldovia and Valdez) and salmon (Ketchikan, Petersburg, Seldovia and Sitka). **Cordova**—Copper River Delta Shorebird Festival. **Dawson City, YT**—International Gold Show. **Delta Junction**—Buffalo Wallow Square Dance Jamboree. **Haines**—Great Alaska Craft Beer & Homebrew Festival. **Haines Junction, YT**—Kluane Mountain Festival. **Homer**—Kachemak Bay Shorebird Festival. **Kodiak**—Crab Festival. **Nome**—Polar Bear Swim. **Petersburg**—Little Norway Festival.

JUNE
Anchorage—Mayor's Midnight Sun Marathon. **Anchor Point**—Kids All-American Fishing Derby. **Fairbanks**—Midnight Sun Baseball Game. **Fairbanks/Galena**—Yukon 800.

Haines Junction, YT—Alsek Music Festival; Kluane Chilkat Bike Relay to **Haines, AK.** **Nome**—Midnight Sun Festival. **Palmer**—Colony Days. **Sitka**—Summer Music Festival. **Whitehorse, YT**—Yukon International Storytelling Festival.

JULY
Anderson—Bluegrass Festival. **Chugiak/ Eagle River**—Bear Paw Festival. **Dawson City, YT**—Canadian Airlines International Midnight Dome Race; Dawson City Music Festival; Yukon Gold Panning Championships. **Delta Junction**—Deltana Fair. **Fairbanks**—Golden Days; World Eskimo–Indian Olympics. **Girdwood**—Forest Fair. **Haines Junction, YT**—Canada Day celebration; Pine Lake Regatta. **Seward**—Mount Marathon Race. **Skagway**—International Softball Tournament; Ducky Derby; Soapy Smith's Wake. **Soldotna**—Progress Days. **Stewart-Hyder**—International Rodeo. **Talkeetna**—Moose Dropping Festival. **Watson Lake, YT**—Watson Lake Rodeo.

AUGUST
Dawson City and Watson Lake, YT—Discovery Days. **Fairbanks**—Tanana Valley State Fair. **Haines**—Southeast Alaska State Fair; Bald Eagle Music Fest. **Ketchikan**—Blueberry Arts Festival. **Kodiak**—State Fair and Rodeo. **Ninilchik**—Kenai Peninsula State Fair. **Palmer**—Alaska State Fair. **Seward**—Silver Salmon Derby. **Skagway**—Flower & Garden Show. **Whitehorse/ Dawson City, YT**—Annual Sourdough Rendezvous Bathtub Race; Klondyke Harvest Fair.

SEPTEMBER
Dawson City, YT—Great Klondike Outhouse Race and Bathroom Wall Limerick Contest. **Fairbanks**—Equinox Marathon. **Nome**—Great Bathtub Race. **Skagway/ Whitehorse**—Klondike Trail of '98 Road Relay.

OCTOBER
Anchorage—Oktoberfest. **Kodiak**—Oktoberfest. **Sitka**—Alaska Day Festival.

NOVEMBER
Anchorage—Great Alaska Shootout. **Fairbanks**—Athabascan Old-Time Fiddling Festival; Top of the World Classic . **Haines**—Bald Eagle Festival. **Ketchikan**—Winter Arts Fair.

DECEMBER
Cordova—Community Tree Lighting. **Fairbanks**—Winter Solstice Festival. **North Pole**—Candle-lighting. **Talkeetna**—Winterfest.

JANUARY 2000
Seward—Polar Bear Jump-Off Festival.

Camping

Alaska and Canada offer both government and private campgrounds. With few exceptions, government and private campgrounds are located along the road system and most roadside campgrounds accommodate both tents and RVs. Wilderness camping is also available in most state, federal and provincial parklands. *The MILEPOST®* logs all public roadside campgrounds and includes facilities (water, firewood, etc.) and camping fees, length of vehicle or length of stay limits. *The MILEPOST®* highway logs also include private campgrounds. Keep in mind that government campgrounds do not maintain dump stations (except some British

Motorhome camping at Mosquito Lake campground on the Haines Highway.
(© Roger Holden)

Columbia provincial parks) and few offer electrical hookups. Season dates for most campgrounds in the North depend on weather.

NOTE: Campers are urged to use established campgrounds. Overnighting in rest areas and turnouts is illegal unless otherwise posted, and may be unsafe.

The MILEPOST® indicates both private and public campgrounds with ▲ tent symbols in the highway logs and on the strip maps.

ALASKA
Federal agencies offering recreational campsites are the Bureau of Land Management (BLM), the National Park Service (NPS), the U.S. Forest Service (USFS) and the U.S. Fish and Wildlife Service (USF&WS). Alaska State Parks, the largest state park system in the United States, maintains more than 3,000 campsites within its 120-unit park system.

Camping is available at 40 state recreation sites, 5 state parks (Chugach, Denali, Chilkat, Kachemak Bay and Wood-Tikchik), 14 state recreation sites and a state historic park. Reservations are not accepted at any state campgrounds. Camping rates (subject to change) range from $6 to $15. An annual pass, good for unlimited camping in a calendar year, is available for $75 for Alaska residents and $200 for nonresidents. The pass is a windshield decal and is not transferable. There is a day-use parking fee of $3 or $5 per vehicle at a small number of state park facilities, including some picnic sites, trailheads and fishing access sites. A full-year parking pass may be purchased for $25. To obtain camping or parking passes, send check or money order payable to the State of Alaska. Mail to Alaska Camping Pass, Division of Parks and Outdoor Recreation, 3601 C Street, Suite 200, Anchorage, AK 99503-5929.

BLM maintains about 12 campgrounds; fees are charged at some. Unless otherwise posted, all undeveloped BLM public lands are open to free camping, usually for a maximum of 14 days per stay. Write the Bureau of Land Management, 1150 University Ave., Fairbanks, AK 99709-3899, phone (907) 474-2251.

The National Park Service maintains 7 campgrounds in Denali National Park and Preserve (see DENALI NATIONAL PARK section). There are established hike-in campgrounds at Glacier Bay and Katmai national parks and preserves, and wilderness camping in other national parks and preserves in Alaska. For more information, contact any of the Alaska Public Lands Information Centers or access on-line information for the national parks (see "National Parks" on page 29).

Most USFS campgrounds charge a fee of under $10 per night depending on facilities. There is a 14-day limit at most campgrounds; this regulation is enforced. For further information write the Office of Information, USDA Forest Service, Box 21628, Juneau, AK 99802.

U.S. Fish & Wildlife Service manages several camping areas within Kenai National Wildlife Refuge. Contact the Refuge Manager, Kenai National Wildlife Refuge, Box 2139, Soldotna, AK 99669, phone (907) 262-7021.

Campgrounds in the Chugach National Forest are operated under permit by Alaska Recreational Management, Inc. For information phone (907) 522-8368; fax: (907) 522-8383.

The Alaska Department of Natural Resources, Division of Parks & Outdoor Recreation, rents out public use cabins located throughout the state. Contact the nearest State Park office or DNR public information centers in Anchorage or Fairbanks for information about reservation and fees. Detailed cabin information and availability can be found on the Internet at: http://www.state.ak.us

Two special passes for federal recreation areas are available to U.S. citizens. The Golden Age Passport is for persons 62 and older and costs a one time fee of $10. The Golden Access Passport is free for persons with blindness or other permanent disability. Both provide lifetime admittance to federally operated parks, monuments, historic sites, recreation areas and wildlife refuges that charge entrance fees. Accompanying passengers in a private car enter without charge as well. The passport bearer also receives a 50 percent discount on federal use fees charged for facilities and services such as camping, boat launching and parking (exceptions to the 50 percent discount may apply in government facilities operated by concessionaires, such as the Russian River ferry). These passes must be obtained in person by showing proof of age for a Golden Age Passport, or proof of being medically diagnosed with blindness or another permanent disability for the Golden Access Passport. The passports are available at most of the federal recreation areas where they may be used, so travelers do not need to obtain them in advance. They also can be obtained at Alaska Public Lands Information Centers in Anchorage and Fairbanks.

CANADA

Territorial campgrounds in Northwest Territories charge $12 or $15 per night, depending upon the site, in attended campgrounds and parks with facilities. Campground-use firewood is available for a fee.

Yukon Territory has 43 Yukon government campgrounds located along its road system. There is a per night fee of $8 charged for nonresidents. These well-maintained campgrounds often have kitchen shelters (which may not be used as sleeping accommodations) and free firewood for use at the campground. There is a 14-day limit.

Provincial park campgrounds and private campgrounds are readily available along Alaska Highway connecting routes in British Columbia and Alberta. Provincial park camping fees range from $10 to $20 a night depending on facilities.

National park campgrounds in Canada generally have a per-night fee ranging from $12 for a tent site to $25 for a full-hookup site. A park motor-license sticker is required for motorists staying overnight in the national parks. Electrical service is standard 60 cycle. Wood for campfires is supplied free to all camping and picnicking grounds. Bring your own ax to split kindling. "Serviced" campgrounds have caretakers.

Crossing the Border

Travel between the United States and Canada is usually a fairly straightforward procedure. However, travelers are reminded that all persons and their vehicles are subject to search and seizure at the border according to the laws of whichever country they are entering. Vehicles may be searched at the discretion of the customs officials, whether or not the traveler feels that he or she has complied with customs requirements.

Customs agents in both Canada and the U.S. are charged with enforcing a daunting number of regulations pertaining to agricultural products, commercial goods, alcohol, tobacco and firearms. Canada vigorously enforces its firearms importation laws, and border officials may—at their discretion—search any vehicle for handguns.

Certain items, mainly crafts and souvenirs made from parts of wild animals, have caused some problems for travelers to the North in recent years. An item which may be purchased legally in Alaska, for example carved ivory, can be brought back into the Lower 48 but may not be permitted transit through Canada without a permit. Some items which may be purchased legally in parts of Canada may not be allowed into the United States. For example, a seal-fur doll purchased in Inuvik, NWYT, would be

confiscated by the U.S. Fish and Wildlife Service or U.S. customs because the import of seal products is prohibited except by special permit.

For information on Canadian customs, contact Customs Border Services, Regional Information Unit, 333 Dunsmuir St., Main Floor, Vancouver, BC V6B 5R4; phone (604) 666-0545.

For further U.S. customs information, contact the nearest U.S. customs office or write U.S. Customs Service, P.O. Box 7407, Washington, DC 20044. In Seattle, WA, phone (206) 553-4676. Also try the internet at www.customs.ustreas.gov/

Following are the locations and hours of operation for highway customs offices located along the southern border of Alberta and British Columbia. Stations are open year-round unless otherwise noted.

Border Crossing	Open
Aden, AB–Whitlash, MT	9 A.M.–5 P.M.
Aldergrove, BC–Lynden, WA	8 A.M.–midnight
Boundary Bay, BC–Point Roberts, WA	24 hours
Carson, BC–Danville, WA	8 A.M.–midnight
Carway, AB–Piegan, MT	7 A.M.–11 p.m.
Cascade, BC–Laurier, WA	8 A.M.–midnight
Chief Mountain, AB–MT (June 1–Sept. 22)	7 A.M.–10 P.M.
Chopaka, BC–Nighthawk, WA	9 A.M.–5 P.M.
Coutts, AB–Sweetgrass, MT	24 hours
Del Bonita, AB–MT (Sept. 16–May 31)	9 A.M.–6 P.M.
Douglas, BC–Blaine, WA	24 hours
Flathead, BC–Trail Creek, MT (June 1–Oct. 31)	9 A.M.–5 P.M.
Huntingdon, BC–Sumas, WA	24 hours
Kingsgate, BC–Eastport, ID	24 hours
Midway, BC–Ferry, WA	9 A.M.–5 P.M.
Nelway, BC–Boundary Dam, WA	8 A.M.–midnight
Osoyoos, BC–Oroville, WA	24 hours
Pacific Highway	24 hours
Paterson, BC–Frontier, WA	24 hours
Roosville, BC–Port of Roosville, MT	24 hours
Rykerts, BC–Porthill, ID (October–April)	8 A.M.–midnight
(May–September)	7 A.M.–midnight
Waneta, BC–Boundary, WA	9 A.M.–5 P.M.
Wildhorse, AB–MT (October–May 14)	8 A.M.–5 P.M.
(May 15–September)	8 A.M.–9 P.M.

Entry into Canada from the U.S. (non-residents)

Identification: Citizens or permanent residents of the United States do not require passports or visas to enter Canada. However, native-born U.S. citizens should carry some identifying paper that shows their citizenship, in case they are asked for it. This could include a driver's license and voter's registration (together), passport with photo, or some employment cards with description and photo. Social security cards or driver's licenses alone are not positive identification. Birth certificates of children are sometimes required. Proof of residence may also be required. Naturalized U.S. citizens should carry a naturalization certificate or some other evidence of citizenship. Permanent residents of the United States who are not U.S. citizens are advised to have their Resident Alien Card (U.S. Form 1-151 or Form 1-551).

Officials at Canadian customs are concerned about child abductions. If you are traveling with children, remember to bring identification for them. A divorced parent traveling with his or her young child, *without the other parent,* should be able to present a notarized statement of custody; a copy of divorce/custody papers is recommended. When traveling with children who are not your own, have proper identification *and* written permission from a parent or guardian.

Persons under 18 years of age who are not accompanied by an adult should bring a letter with them from a parent or guardian giving them permission to travel into Canada. Proof of sufficient funds to travel within—and back out of—Canada may be required.

Motorists: U.S. motorists are advised to obtain a Canadian Nonresident Interprovincial Motor Vehicle Liability Insurance Card, which provides evidence of financial responsibility. This card is available only in the United States through U.S. insurance companies or their agents. All provinces in Canada require visiting motorists to produce evidence of financial responsibility should they be involved in an accident. Financial responsibility limits vary by province.

All national driver's licenses are valid in Canada. (See also Driving Information this section.)

Entry by private boat or plane: Report to Canada Customs by phoning (888) 226-7277. Provide the names, dates of birth and citizenships of all people on board, the purpose of trip, and declare any firearms or other goods. You will then be given a reporting number for your records. Upon arriving at the designated customs reporting site, you must call Canada Customs a second time to be advised either to wait for a customs officer or to proceed with your travels.

Baggage: The necessary wearing apparel and personal effects in use by the visitor are admitted free of duty. Up to 50 cigars, 200 cigarettes (1 carton) and 14 ounces of manufactured tobacco, 200 tobacco sticks, and up to 40 ounces of spiritous liquor or wine or 24 12-ounce cans or bottles of beer or ale may be allowed entry in this manner. Additional quantities of alcoholic beverages up to a maximum of 2 gallons may be imported into Canada (except the Northwest Territories) on payment of duty and taxes plus charges for a provincial permit at port of entry. To import tobacco products a person must be 18 years of age or over, and to import alcoholic beverages the importer must have reached the legal age established by authorities of the province or territory into which the alcoholic beverages are being entered.

Gifts: Be prepared to provide receipts for gifts, in case you are asked to show the dollar value. Gifts are duty- and tax-free when each gift is valued at $60 (Canadian) or less. If the value of a gift exceeds $60, you may have to pay duties and taxes on the excess amount.

Firearms: Firearms are divided into 3 categories—prohibited, restricted and long guns. The *only* category of gun a U.S. visitor may bring into Canada is a long gun, which is a regular hunting rifle or shotgun with a barrel at least 18 1/2 inches/47 cm, and an overall length of 26 inches/66 cm, and which does not fall into the category of a prohibited or restricted firearm. Non-restricted firearms may be imported only for sporting or hunting use while in Canada, for use in competitons, for in-transit movement through Canada or for a person's protection against wildlife in remote regions of Canada (exclud-

ing national parks) as long as the customs officer is satisfied that the circumstances warrent the importation of the firearm. Restricted weapons may only be imported for the purpose of attending an approved shooting competition in Canada. A temporary permit to carry is required.

Nonresidents arriving at a Canada customs port must declare all their firearms, including long guns. Anyone who illegally carries a firearm into Canada is subject to a number of penalties, including seizure of the weapon and the vehicle in which it is carried. It is against the law for visitors to bring handguns into Canada. Personal protection devices such as stun-guns, mace or pepper spray are also prohibited. Specific questions on importing guns should be directed to the Regional Information Unit; phone (604) 666-0545.

Plants, fruit and vegetables: House plants may be imported without a permit. Some fruits and vegetables may be restricted or prohibited entry into Canada and all are subject to inspection at the border.

Meat and dairy products: You can import some meat and dairy products from the United States. There are limits on the quantity or dollar value of certain food products you can bring into Canada at the low rates of duty or that you can include in your personal exemption. If you bring in quantities of these products over and above the limits, you will have to pay a high rate of duty (from 150 to 350 percent). You may also need an agricultural inspection certificate.

Animals: Dogs and cats (over 3 months of age) from the United States must be accompanied by a certificate issued by a licensed veterinarian of Canada or the United States certifying that the animal has been vaccinated against rabies during the preceding 36 months; such a certificate shall describe the animal and date of vaccination and shall be initialed by inspectors and returned to the owner.

Up to 2 pet birds per family may be imported into Canada. Birds of the parrot family and song birds may be admitted when accompanied by the owner, if the owner certifies in writing that, upon entering the country, the birds have not been in contact with any other birds during the preceding 90 days and have been in the owner's possession for the entire period. All birds of the parrot family, except budgies, cockatiels and Rose-ringed parakeets, are on the CITES endangered species list and require special permits.

GST Refund: You can claim a Goods and Services Tax (GST) refund of the GST paid on most goods and on accommodation of less than one month. For more information, phone (800) 668-4748 when in Canada.

Re-entry into the U.S. (residents)

It is the responsibility of the traveler to satisfy U.S. immigration authorities of his right to re-enter the United States. Canadian immigration officers may caution persons entering from the United States if they may have difficulty in returning.

Re-entry to the United States can be simplified if you list all your purchases before you reach the border, keep sales receipts and invoices handy, and pack purchases separately.

Within 48 hours: Residents of the United States visiting Canada for less than 48 hours may bring in for personal or household use merchandise to the fair retail value

of $200, free of U.S. duty and tax. Any or all of the following may be included, as long as the total value does not exceed $200: 50 cigarettes, 10 cigars (non-Cuban in origin), 4 ounces/150 ml of alcoholic beverages or alcoholic perfume.

If any article brought back is subject to duty or tax, or if the total value of all articles exceeds $200, no article may be exempted from duty or tax. Members of a family household are not permitted to combine the value of their purchases under this exception.

Persons crossing the international boundary at one point and re-entering the United States in order to travel to another part of Canada should inquire at U.S. customs regarding special exemption requirements.

After more than 48 hours: Residents may bring back, once every 30 days, merchandise for personal or household use to the value of $400 free of U.S. duty and tax. The exemption will be based on the fair retail value of the article acquired and goods must accompany the resident upon arrival in the United States. Members of a family household traveling together may combine their personal exemptions—thus a family of 5 could be entitled to a total exemption of $2,000. Up to 100 cigars (non-Cuban in origin) per person may be imported into the United States by U.S. residents, and up to 200 cigarettes, and 1 liter of alcoholic beverages if the resident has reached the age of 21 years.

Animals: Your pets, including those taken out of the country and being returned, must have a valid veterinarian health certificate. Particularly, dogs must have proof of rabies vaccination. If you are traveling with pet birds, check with customs about specific requirements. Wildlife and fish are subject to certain import and export restrictions, prohibitions, permits or certificates, and quarantine requirments. Endangered species of wildlife and products made from them are generally prohibited from being imported or exported.

Trademarked items: Foreign-made trademarked items may be limited as to the quantity which can be brought into the U.S. The types of items usually of interest to tourists are lenses, cameras, binoculars, optical goods, tape recorders, musical instruments, jewelry, precious metal-ware, perfumes, watches and clocks. Returning residents are allowed an exemption, usually one article of a type bearing a protected trademark. The item must be for your personal use and not for sale.

Plants: Plants, cuttings, seeds, unprocessed plant products and certain endangered species either require an import permit or are prohibited from entering the U.S. Every single plant or plant product must be declared to the customs officer. Call Quarantines at (303) 436-8645 for information on current plants and import permits.

Entry into the U.S. from Canada (non-residents)

Exemptions: Non-residents of the U.S. may bring in for personal or household use merchandise to the fair retail value of $200, free of U.S. duty and tax. In addition to $200 in items, some articles may be brought in free of duty and tax. They must be for your personal use and not for others or for sale. These exemptions include personal effects (wearing apparel, articles of personal adornment, toilet articles, hunting, fishing and photographic equipment); one liter of alcoholic beverages (wine, beer or liquor) if you are an adult non-resident; 200 cigarettes, or 50 cigars, or 2 kilograms (4.4 lb.) of smoking tobacco, or proportionate amounts of each; and vehicles for personal use if imported in connection with your arrival.

Gifts: Articles up to $100 in total value for use as bona fide gifts to other persons may be brought in free of duty and tax, if you will be in the U.S. for at least 72 hours and have not claimed this gift exemption in the past 6 months. This gift exemption may include up to 100 cigars.

Restricted or Prohibited Items: Some items must meet certain requirements, require a license or permit, or may be prohibited entry. Among these are: liquor-filled candy (prohibited); fruits, plants and endangered species of plants, vegetables and their products; firearms and ammunition, if not intended for legitimate hunting or lawful sporting purposes; hazardous articles (fireworks, dangerous toys, toxic or poisonous substances); lottery tickets; meats, poultry and products (sausage, pate); narcotics and dangerous drugs; pets (cats, dogs and birds); pornographic articles and publications; switchblade knives; trademarked items (certain cameras, watches, perfumes, musical instruments, jewelry and metal flatware); vehicles and motorcycles not equipped to comply with U.S. safety or clean air emission standards if your visit is for more than one year; wildlife (birds, fish, mammals, animals) and endangered species, including any part or product (pheasants, articles from reptile skins, whalebone or ivory, mounted specimens and trophies, feathers or skins of wild birds).

If you require medicine containing habit-forming drugs, carry only the quantity normally needed and properly identified, and have a prescription or written statement from your personal physician that the medicine is necessary for your physical well-being. Other pharmaceuticals and/or medicinal devices other than for the personal use of the traveler must be approved by the U.S. Food and Drug Administration.

Re-entry into Canada (residents)

When returning to Canada, residents must declare all of the goods they acquired abroad and are bringing back, as purchases, gifts, prizes or awards. Residents need to include goods still in their possession that they bought at a Canadian or foreign duty-free shop. They must also declare any repairs or modifications made to their vehicle, vessel or aircraft while they were out of the country. If unsure about whether an article is admissible or if it should be declared, residents should always declare it first and then ask a customs officer.

Absence of 24 hours or more: Residents can claim goods worth up to $50 as a personal exemption. This does not apply to tobacco products and alcoholic beverages. Residents may have to make a written declaration. If the goods they bring in are worth more than $50, they cannot claim this exemption and must pay duties on the full value.

Absence of 48 hours or more: Residents can claim goods worth up to $200 in total. These goods can include tobacco products and alcoholic beverages. They may have to make written declaration.

After any trip of 48 hours or longer, you are entitled to a special duty rate on goods worth up to $300 more than your personal exemption. The current special duty rate under the United States Tariff treatment, when combined with GST, is 8 percent.

Absence of 7 days or more: Residents can claim goods up to $500 in total. These goods can include tobacco products and alcoholic beverages. Residents may have to make a written declaration.

To claim tobacco products and alcoholic beverages, residents must meet the age requirements set by the province or territory where they enter Canada. Tobacco products may include up to 200 cigarettes, 50 cigars or cigarillos, 200 tobacco sticks and 200 grams of manufactured tobacco. Alcoholic beverages may include up to 1.14 litres (40 ounces) of wine or liquor, or 24 355 ml (12-ounce) cans or bottles (8.5 liters) of beer or ale. If you bring in more than the free allowance, the cost may be high, since you will have to pay both customs and provincial or territorial assessments.

Gifts: Under certain conditions, residents may send gifts from outside Canada duty- and tax-free to friends in Canada. Each gift must be worth $60 or less and cannot be an alcoholic beverage, a tobacco product or advertising matter. If the gift is worth more than $60, the recipient will have to pay regular duties on the excess amount. It is always a good idea to include a gift card to avoid any misunderstanding. Gifts brought back with the resident do not qualify for the gift exemption.

In most cases, you have to pay regular duties on prizes and awards you receive outside Canada. ♿

Cruise ships offer swimming pools and other amenities. (© Lee Foster)

Cruise Ship Travel

Cruises to Alaska are primarily available from May through September on board more than 30 ships—ranging from large luxury cruise ships to small explorer-class ships. Most ships depart from Vancouver, BC (some from San Francisco and Seattle) and cruise to Alaska via the Inside Passage.

The Inside Passage is the route north along the coast of British Columbia and through southeastern Alaska that uses the protected waterways between the islands and the mainland. (Inside Passage is also commonly used to refer to Southeast Alaska and its communities, which are the ports of call for the cruise ships.) The water passage travels along hundreds of miles of forested coastline, passing deep fjords and the steep, snow-capped peaks of the Coast Range. Other ports of call include:

College Fjord, an 18-mile-long estuary that extends northeast off Port Wells, another estuary, in the northwest corner of Prince William Sound, near Whittier. Glaciers cascade down the west side of College Fjord. At the north end of College Fjord, where a large black island of rock divides Harvard Arm from Yale Arm, are the "twin" tidewater glaciers— named Yale Glacier and Harvard Glacier by members of the Harriman Alaska Expedition in 1899.

Hubbard Glacier, about 34 miles northeast of Yakutat, has become a popular port of call with cruise ships crossing the Gulf of Alaska between Southeast Alaska's Inside Passage and Southcentral Alaska's Prince William Sound. Framed by snow-covered mountains, Hubbard Glacier rolls toward the sea like a blue-white breaking wave. The glacier made headlines in June 1986, when it surged, damming Russell Fiord. The ice dam eventually weakened and broke..

Misty Fiords, a national monument encompassing more than 2 million acres of Southeast Alaska. Large cruise ships sail Behm Canal, a more than 100-mile-long, deepwater canal that is the major waterway through the monument. The scenery is dramatic: thick rainforest, vertical granite cliffs and snowy peaks. Waterfalls plunge to salt water along the steep-walled waterways, fed by lakes and streams which absorb an annual rainfall in excess of 14 feet.

Tracy Arm, and adjoining *Endicott Arm,* both long, deep, narrow fjords that extend more than 30 miles into the heavily glaciated Coast Mountain Range, about 50 miles southeast of Juneau. At the head of each arm are active tidewater glaciers, which continually calve icebergs into the fjords: Sawyer and South Sawyer glaciers at the head of Tracy Arm; Dawes Glacier at the head of Endicott Arm.

Cruise Lines

Following is a list of cruise lines serving Alaska in 1999. Included are the names of the line's ships (passenger capacity is shown in parentheses) and proposed Alaska ports of call. Not all ships have the same itinerary. Contact the cruise line directly or your travel agent for more details.

There's a bewildering array of travel options connected with cruise ship travel. Both round-trip and one-way cruises are available, or a cruise may be sold as part of a packaged tour that includes air, rail and/or motorcoach transportation. Various shore excursions may be included in the cruise price or offered to passengers for added cost. Ports of call may depend on length of cruise, which ship you choose, time of sailing or debarkation point. Because of the wide variety of cruise trips available, it is wise to work with your travel agent.

Alaska Sightseeing/Cruise West, 4th & Battery Bldg., Suite 700, Seattle, WA 98121-1438; phone 1-800-426-7702 or (206) 441-

8687, fax (206) 441-4757. *Spirit of Glacier Bay* (58 passengers); *Spirit of Alaska* (82 passengers); *Spirit of Discovery* (84 passengers); *Spirit of '98* (101 passengers); *Spirit of Endeavor* (107 passengers); and *Spirit of Columbia* (90 passengers). Ports of call: Anchorage, Cordova, Glacier Bay, Haines, Juneau, Ketchikan, Misty Fiords, Petersburg, Sitka, Skagway, Tracy Arm, Valdez, Wrangell.

Carnival Cruise Line, Carnival Place, 3655 NW 87th Ave., Miami, FL 33178-2428; phone (305) 599-2600. *Jubilee* (1,486 passengers). Ports of call: College Fjord, Haines, Hubbard Glacier, Juneau, Ketchikan, Seward, Sitka, Skagway, Tracy Arm, Valdez.

Celebrity Cruises, Inc., 5201 Blue Lagoon Dr., Miami, FL 33126; phone (305) 262-6677. *Mercury* (1,870 passengers) and *Galaxy* (1,870 passengers). Ports of call: College Fjord, Glacier Bay, Haines, Hubbard Glacier, Inside Passage, Juneau, Ketchikan, Misty Fiords, Seward, Sitka, Skagway, Valdez.

Clipper Cruise Lines, Windsor Bldg., 7711 Bonhomme Ave., St. Louis, MO 63105-1956; phone 1-800-325-0010 or (314) 727-2929, fax (314) 727-6576. *Yorktown Clipper* (138 passengers). Ports of call: Glacier Bay, Haines, Juneau, Ketchikan, Misty Fiords, Petersburg, Sitka, Skagway, Tracy Arm, Wrangell.

Crystal Cruises, 2121 Avenue of the Stars, Los Angeles, CA 90067; phone 1-800-446-6620, (310) 785-9300. *Crystal Harmony (960 passengers)*. Ports of call: Glacier Bay, Hubbard Glacier, Juneau, Ketchikan, Misty Fiords, Seward, Sitka, Skagway, Tracy Arm.

Glacier Bay Tours & Cruises, 520 Pike St., Suite 1400, Seattle, WA 98101; phone 1-800-451-5952 or (206) 623-2417, fax (206) 623-7809; Internet: www.glacierbaytours.com. *Executive Explorer* (49 passengers), *Wilderness Discoverer* (86 passengers), *Wilderness Explorer* (36 passengers) and the *Wilderness Adventure* (74 passengers). Glacier Bay, Haines, Juneau, Kake, Ketchikan, Misty Fiords, Tracy Arm, Sitka, Skagway.

Holland America Westours, 300 Elliot Ave. W., Seattle, WA 98119; phone (206) 281-3535, fax (206) 281-0351; Internet: www.hollandamerica.com. *Statendam* (1,266 passengers), *Nieuw Amsterdam* (1,214 passengers), *Noordam* (1,214 passengers), *Ryndam* (1,266 passengers), *Westerdam* (1,494 passengers); and Veendam (1,266 passengers). Ports of call: College Fjord, Glacier Bay, Hubbard Glacier, Skagway, Juneau, Ketchikan, Seward, Sitka, Valdez.

Norwegian Cruise Lines, 95 Merrick Way, Coral Gables, FL 33134; phone 1-800-327-7030, (305) 436-4000. *Norwegian Dynasty* (800 passengers); *Norwegian Wind* (1,246 passengers). Ports of call: Cordova, Glacier Bay, Haines, Hubbard Glacier, Juneau, Ketchikan, Prince William Sound, Seward, Sitka, Skagway.

Princess Cruises, 10100 Santa Monica Blvd., Los Angeles, CA 90067; phone (310) 553-1770, fax (310) 277-6175. *Regal Princess* and *Crown Princess* (1,590 passengers); *Dawn Princess* and *Sea Princess* (2,000 passengers); *Sky Princess* (1,200 passengers); *Sun Princess* (1,950 passengers). Ports of call: College Fjord, Glacier Bay, Hubbard Glacier, Juneau, Ketchikan, Seward, Sitka, Skagway.

Royal Caribbean Cruise Line, 1050 Caribbean Way, Miami, FL 33132; phone 1-800-327-6700. *Rhapsody of the Seas* (2,400 passengers); *Vision of the Seas* (passenger capacity not available). Ports of call: Haines, Hubbard Glacier, Glacier Bay, Juneau, Ketchikan, Misty Fiords, Skagway.

Society Expeditions, 2001 Western Ave., Suite 710, Seattle, WA 98121; phone (206) 728-9400. *World Discoverer* (138 passengers). Ports of call: College Fjord, Hubbard Glacier, Misty Fiords, Seward, Sitka, Tracy Arm.

Special Expeditions Marine, 1415 Western Ave., Suite 700, Seattle, WA 98101; phone (206) 382-9593. *Sea Bird* and *Sea Lion* (70 passengers). Ports of call: Althorp Rocks, Glacier Bay, Haines, Juneau, Ketchikan, Le Conte Bay, Point Adolphus, Sitka, Tracy Arm, Petersburg.

World Explorer Cruises, 555 Montgomery St., Suite 1400, San Francisco, CA 94111; phone 1-800-854-3835, (415) 393-1565. *Universe Explorer* (550 passengers). Ports of call: Glacier Bay, Hubbard Glacier, Juneau, Ketchikan, Seward, Sitka, Skagway, Valdez, Wrangell.

The Seward Highway, a National Scenic Byway, near Jerome Lake. (© Loren Taft)

Daylight Hours

An advantage to Northern summer travel are the long hours of daylight at these latitude. Following are sunrise and sunset times for June 21, 1999 (summer solstice) and December 21, 1999 (winter solstice), representing the longest and shortest days in the North in Anchorage, Fairbanks, Barrow and Juneau. You can get sunrise and sunset times for any location, for any day or year, from the U.S. Naval Observatory website at www.usno.navy.mil

SUMMER MAXIMUM DAYLIGHT
(June 21, 1999)

	Sunrise	Sunset
Anchorage	4:20 A.M.	11:42 P.M.
Barrow	sun does not set	
Fairbanks	2:59 A.M.	12:47 A.M. following day
Juneau	3:51 A.M.	10:08 P.M.

WINTER MINIMUM DAYLIGHT
(December 21, 1999)

	Sunrise	Sunset
Anchorage	10:14 A.M.	3:41 P.M.
Barrow	sun does not rise	
Fairbanks	10:58 A.M.	2:40 P.M.
Juneau	8:44 A.M.	3:07 P.M.

Driving North

Driving to the North is no longer the ordeal it was in the early days. Those old images of the Alaska Highway with vehicles stuck in mud up to their hubcaps are far removed from the asphalt-surfaced Alaska Highway of today.

Motorists can still expect road construction and some rough road, but have patience! Ongoing projects like the Shakwak Highway Reconstruction Project on the Alaska Highway between Beaver Creek, YT, and the Alaska border, for example, are helping to improve severely deteriorated sections of road.

Roads in the North range from multi-lane freeways to 1-lane dirt and gravel roads. The more remote roads are gravel. Motorists are much farther from assistance and more preparation is required for these roads.

Major highways in Alaska are paved with the exception of the following highways that are at least partially gravel: Steese Highway (Alaska Route 6), Taylor Highway (Alaska Route 5), Elliott Highway (Alaska Route 2), Dalton Highway (Alaska Route 11) and Denali Highway (Alaska Route 8).

In Yukon Territory, the Alaska Highway, the Haines Highway and the Klondike Highway from Skagway to Dawson City are asphalt-surfaced. All other roads are gravel.

Major routes through Alberta and British Columbia are paved, with the exception of the Cassiar Highway (BC Highway 37).

Highways within western Northwest Territories are mostly gravel roads, although paving continues on many routes. Paving is almost completed on NWT Highway 3 to Yellowknife, and NWT Highway 1 is paved from its junction with Highway 3 to the Alberta border.

RV owners should be aware of the height of their vehicles in metric measurements, as bridge heights in Canada are noted in meters.

Know your vehicle and its limitations. Some Northern roads may not be suitable for a large motorhome or trailer, but most roads will present no problem to a motorist who allots adequate time and uses common sense.

Also safeguard against theft while at

campgrounds, rest stops or in the cities. Always lock your vehicle, be sure valuables are out of sight in an unattended vehicle and report any thefts to the authorities.

NOTE: Driving with the headlights on at all times is the law in Yukon Territory and on posted roads in Alaska.

ROAD CONDITIONS

General road conditions are noted in the introduction to each highway in *The MILE-POST*. Specific areas of concern are also called out in the log.

Keep in mind the variable nature of road conditions. Some sections of road may be in poor condition because of current construction or recent bad weather. Other highways—particularly gravel roads closed in winter—may be very rough or very smooth, depending on when maintenance crews last worked on the road.

Asphalt surfacing for most Northern roads is Bituminous Surface Treatment (BST), an alternative to hot-mix pavement which involves application of aggregates and emulsified asphalt. Also known as "chip seal," recently applied or repaired BST is as smooth as any Lower 48 superhighway. However, weather and other factors can lead to failures in the surfacing which include potholes and loss of aggregate.

Also watch for "frost heaves" caused by subsidence of the ground under the road.

Many gravel roads in the North (such as the Dalton Highway) are treated with calcium chloride as a dust-control measure. Because calcium chloride tends to eat into paint and metal parts on your vehicle, be sure to thoroughly wash your vehicle.

Gravel road is treated with calcium chloride to keep the dust down. This substance corrodes paint and metal; Wash your vehicle as soon as possible. In heavy rains, calcium chloride and mud combine to make a very slippery road surface; drive carefully! Keep in mind that many highways in the Yukon and some highways in Alaska are gravel.

PLANNING YOUR TRIP

Depending on where you want to stop and how much time you have to spend, you can count on driving anywhere from 150 to 500 miles a day. On most roads in the North, you can figure on comfortably driving 250 to 300 miles a day.

Log mileages are keyed on the highway strip maps which accompany each highway section in *The MILEPOST*. Use the mileage boxes on these maps to calculate mileages between points (or refer to the mileage box at the beginning of the highway).

Once you have figured the number of driving miles in your itinerary, you can calculate approximate gas cost using the Gas Price Averages chart. (Keep in mind that 1999 prices will vary from 1998 summer averages.) U.S. motorists factor in the exchange rate for Canadian prices using the accompanying conversion chart.

Normally, May through October is the best time to drive to Alaska. A severe winter or wet spring may affect road conditions and there may be some rough road until road maintenance crews get out to upgrade and repair. Motels, hotels, gas stations and restaurants are open year-round in the cities and on many highways. On more remote routes, such as the Cassiar Highway, not all businesses are open year-round. Check ahead for accommodations and gas if traveling these roads in winter.

VEHICLE PREPARATION

There are some simple preparations that motorists can make for their trip North to make driving easier. First make sure your vehicle and tires are in good condition. An inexpensive and widely available item to include is a set of clear plastic headlight covers (or black metal matte screens). These protect your headlights from flying rocks and gravel. You might also consider a wire-mesh screen across the front of your vehicle to protect paint, grill and radiator from flying rocks. The finer the mesh, the more protection from flying gravel. For those hauling trailers, a piece of quarter-inch plywood fitted over the front of your trailer offers protection.

There is practically no way to protect the windshield, although some motorists have experimented with screen shields that do not seriously impair their vision. These are not recommended nor do you see many of them in the North, but it is, of course, up to the individual motorist whether these are worthwhile.

Crankcases are seldom damaged, but gas tanks can be harmed on rough gravel roads. Sometimes rocks work their way in between the plate and gas tank, wearing a hole in the tank. However, drivers maintaining safe speeds should have no problems with punctured gas tanks. A high vehicle clearance is best for some of the rougher gravel roads.

Also keep in mind the simple precautions that make driving easier. A visor or tinted glass helps when you're driving into the sun. Good windshield wipers and a full windshield washer (or a bottle of wash and a squeegee) make life easier. Many motorists

GAS PRICE AVERAGES SUMMER 1998

Alaska Location	Per Gallon U.S. Funds	Canada Location	Per Liter Canadian Funds*
Anchorage	$1.22	Atlin, BC	$.77
Cantwell	1.49	Contact Creek, BC	.65
Eagle	1.72	Dawson City, YT	.79
Fairbanks	1.26	Dawson Creek, BC	.58
Glennallen	1.46	Destruction Bay, YT	.73
Prudhoe Bay	1.89	Fort Nelson, BC	.68
Soldotna	1.40	Fort St. John, BC	.60
Tok	1.48	Grande Prairie, AB	.56
Valdez	1.49	Watson Lake, YT	.69
		Whitehorse, YT	.66

*See chart below for equivalent cost in U.S. funds for 1 gallon

LITERS TO U.S. GALLONS

Liters	Gallons	Liters	Gallons	Liters	Gallons
1	.3	21	5.5	41	10.8
2	.5	22	5.8	42	11.1
3	.8	23	6.1	43	11.4
4	1.1	24	6.3	44	11.6
5	1.3	25	6.6	45	11.9
6	1.6	26	6.9	46	12.2
7	1.8	27	7.1	47	12.4
8	2.1	28	7.4	48	12.7
9	2.4	29	7.7	49	12.9
10	2.6	30	7.9	50	13.2
11	2.9	31	8.2	51	13.5
12	3.2	32	8.5	52	13.7
13	3.4	33	8.7	53	14.0
14	3.7	34	9.0	54	14.3
15	4.0	35	9.2	55	14.5
16	4.2	36	9.5	56	14.8
17	4.5	37	9.8	57	15.0
18	4.8	38	10.0	58	15.3
19	5.0	39	10.3	59	15.6
20	5.3	40	10.6	60	15.9

For more precise conversion: 1 liter equals .2642 gallons; 1 gallon equals 3.785 liters.

GAS COST IN U.S. FUNDS PER GALLON

If the Canadian Exchange rate is: $1.00 U.S. equals Canadian funds:	25% $1.25	30% $1.30	35% $1.35	40% $1.40	45% $1.45
$.56	$1.70	$1.63	$1.57	$1.51	$1.46
.57	1.73	1.66	1.60	1.54	1.49
.58	1.76	1.69	1.63	1.57	1.51
.59	1.79	1.72	1.65	1.60	1.54
.60	1.82	1.75	1.68	1.62	1.57
.61	1.85	1.78	1.71	1.65	1.59
.62	1.88	1.81	1.74	1.68	1.62
.63	1.91	1.83	1.77	1.70	1.64
.64	1.94	1.86	1.79	1.73	1.67
.65	1.97	1.89	1.82	1.76	1.70
.66	2.00	1.92	1.85	1.78	1.72
.67	2.03	1.95	1.88	1.81	1.75
.68	2.06	1.98	1.91	1.84	1.78
.69	2.09	2.01	1.93	1.87	1.80
.70	2.12	2.04	1.96	1.89	1.83

(left label: Canadian Price Per Liter)

For example: If gas costs $0.60 Canadian per liter and the current exchange rate is 30% ($1.00 U.S. equals $1.30 Canadian), using the above chart, the equivalent to 1 U.S. gallon of gas costs $1.75 U.S. Or cost per liter X 3.785 divided by exchange rate (1.30)=U.S. cost per gallon.

also find bug screens to be a wise investment.

Dust and mud are generally not a major problem on Northern roads, though you may run into both. Heavy rains combined with a gravel road or roadbed torn up for construction make mud. Mud flaps are suggested. Dust can seep into everything and it's difficult if not impossible to keep it out. Remember to close the windows on your trailer or camper when on a dusty road. It also helps to keep clothes, food and bedding in sealed plastic bags. Also check your air filter periodically.

Driving at slow, safe speeds not only keeps down the dust for drivers behind you, it also helps prevent you from spraying other vehicles with gravel.

Drive with your headlights on at all times. This allows you to be seen easier, especially in dusty conditions, or when approaching vehicles are driving into the sun. It is also the law in the Yukon and posted roads in Alaska.

NOTE: If driving on a paved surface, it is still necessary to observe "Loose Gravel" signs. Drive slowly.

Although auto shops in Northern communities are generally well-stocked with parts, carry the following for emergencies and on-the-spot repairs: flares; first-aid kit; trailer bearings; bumper jack with lug wrench; electrician's tape; assortment of nuts and bolts; fan belt; 1 or 2 spare tires (2 spares for remote roads); and a tool set including crescent wrenches, socket and/or open-end wrenches, hammer, screwdrivers, pliers, wire, and prybar for changing the fan belt.

If you are driving a vehicle which may require parts not readily available up North, add whatever you think necessary. You may wish to carry an extra few gallons of gas, water, and fluid for brakes, power steering and automatic transmissions.

If your vehicle should break down on the highway and tow truck service is needed, normally you will be able to flag down a passing motorist. Travelers in the North are generally helpful in such situations (traditionally, the etiquette of the country requires one to stop and provide assistance). If you are the only person traveling in the disabled vehicle, be sure to leave a note on your windshield indicating when you left the vehicle and in what direction you planned to travel.

GASOLINE

Unleaded gas is widely available in Alaska and is the rule in Canada. Diesel fuel is also commonly available. Good advice for Northern travelers: gas-up whenever possible.

In the North, as elsewhere, gas prices vary (see chart at right). Generally, gas prices are slightly higher in Canada and Alaska than the Lower 48, but this is not a hard and fast rule. You may find gas in Anchorage or elsewhere at the same price—or even lower—than at home. A general rule of thumb is the more remote the gas station, the higher the price. Gas prices may vary considerably from service station to service station within the same community.

It is a good idea to carry cash, since some gas stations in Alaska are independents and do not accept credit cards. Most Chevron, Texaco and Tesoro stations will accept VISA or MasterCard. Also watch for posted gas prices that are for *cash*, but not noted as such. Besides double-checking the posted

price before filling up, also ask the attendant which pump is for unleaded, regular or diesel, depending on what you want.

Keep in mind that Canadian gas stations have converted to the metric system; quantity and price are based on liters (see Gas Cost in U.S. Funds Per Gallon chart opposite page). There are 3.785 liters per U.S. gallon, 4.5 liters per imperial gallon. See also Liters to U.S. Gallons conversion chart.

INSURANCE

Auto insurance is mandatory in all Canadian provinces and territories. Drivers should carry adequate car insurance before entering the country. Visiting motorists are required to produce evidence of financial responsibility should they be involved in an accident. There is an automatic fine if visitors are involved in an accident and found to be uninsured. Your car could be impounded for this. Your insurance company should be able to provide you with proof of insurance coverage (request a Canadian Nonresident Interprovincial Motor Vehicle Liability Insurance Card) that would be accepted as evidence of financial responsibility.

The minimum liability insurance requirement in Canada is $200,000 Canadian, except in the Province of Quebec where the limit is $50,000 Canadian. Further information regarding automobile insurance in Canada may be obtained from The Insurance Bureau of Canada, 151 Young St., 18th floor, Toronto, ON M5C 2W7; phone (416) 362-2031 or fax (416) 361-5952.

TIRES

On gravel, the faster you drive, the faster your tires will wear out. So take it easy and you should have no tire problems, provided you have the right size for your vehicle, with the right pressure, not overloaded, and not already overly worn. Belted bias or radial ply tires are recommended for gravel roads.

Carry 1 good spare. Consider 2 spares if you are traveling remote gravel roads such as the Dempster or Dalton highways. The space-saver doughnut spare tires found in some passenger cars are not adequate for travel on gravel roads.

WINTER DRIVING

In addition to the usual precautions taken when driving in winter, such as keeping the windshield clear of ice, checking antifreeze and reducing driving speeds on icy pavement, equip your vehicle with the following survival gear: traction material (ashes, kitty litter, wood chips); chains (even with snow tires); first-aid kit; shovel, ice scraper, flashlight, flares; fire extinguisher; extra warm clothing (including gloves and extra socks), blankets or sleeping bags; food; tools; and an extension cord to plug car into block heater. Other items which may be added to your survival gear are a tow rope or cable, ax, jumper cables and extra gas.

Extremely low temperatures occur in the North. A motorist may start out in -35° to -40°F weather and hit cold pockets along the road where temperatures drop to -60°F or more. If you do become stranded in weather like this, do not leave your vehicle; wait for aid. DO NOT attempt to drive unmaintained secondary roads or highways in winter (i.e. Denali Highway, Top of the World Highway), even if the roads look clear of snow.

Call ahead for road conditions and weather reports.

RULES AND REGULATIONS

Regulations common to Alaska, Alberta, British Columbia, Northwest Territories and Yukon Territory include: Right turn on red permitted after complete stop, unless prohibited by sign; transporting open alcoholic beverage containers within a motor vehicle is prohibited.

Following are rules and regulations in effect in Alaska and northwestern Canada at our presstime:

ALASKA

Division of Motor Vehicles, Dept. of Public Safety, 5700 E. Tudor Rd., Anchorage, AK 99507; phone (907) 269-5551.

Road Condition Report: For summer road construction advisories, phone 24-hour recorded daily reports hot line (907) 273-6037 for Anchorage and Southcentral Alaska; phone (907) 456-7623 for Fairbanks, Tok and Valdez areas. Or toll-free (in Alaska) 1-800-478-7675. Or visit the home page of the Alaska Dept. of Transportation: www. dot. state.ak.us. "Navigator" reports on road construction are available from visitor centers; also check local newspapers.

Headlight use: One-half hour after sunset to one-half hour before sunrise. Driving with headlights on during all hours of the day is permitted. Headlights required at all times on designated roadways where speed is in excess of 45 mph.

Minimum driver's age: 16 years; 14 with driver's permit if accompanied by a licensed driver 19 years or older.

Rest area camping: Permitted as posted.

Seat belts: Seat belts are mandatory for all drivers and passengers. Child restraints are mandatory for children under 7 years. Applies to out-of-state drivers.

Studded tires: Permitted from Sept. 15 to May 1 (Sept. 30 to April 15 south of 60°N).

Motorcycles: Protective glasses, goggles or windscreen required. Reflectorized helmet required if under 19 and for passenger.

CB Radio: The following channels may be monitored: 2,9,11,14,19, 21 and 22.

Firearms: Permitted. Unlawful to discharge firearm on, from or across the driveable portion of any roadway including roadway shoulders.

Trailers: Independent braking system not required for trailers where gross weight is less than 3,000 lbs. Riding in trailer is prohibited, but riding in pickup/camper is permitted.

ALBERTA

Alberta Registries, Municipal Affairs, 9th floor, 10365 97th St., Edmonton, AB T5J 3W7; phone (403) 427-4095.

Road Condition Report: 1-800-642-3810 (in Alberta).

Headlight use: When light conditions restrict visibility to 500 feet/150m or less. Driving with headlights on during all hours of the day is permitted.

Minimum driver's age: 16 years; 14 to receive learner's permit.

Rest area camping: Prohibited unless otherwise designated.

Seat belts: Seat belts are mandatory for all drivers. Child restraints are mandatory for children under 6 years or 18kg (40 lbs.). Applies to out-of-province drivers.

Studded tires: Permitted year-round but only where marked or posted within federal parks.

Motorcycles: Safety helmet required.

CB Radio: Channel 9 is monitored for emergencies.

Firearms: Rifles must be unloaded and safely stored in trunk. Pistols must be carried in a secure storage box, unloaded, trigger locked and safely stored in trunk.

Trailers: Independent braking system not required for trailers where gross weight is less than 909 kg (2,000 lbs.) and is less than half that of towing vehicle. Riding in trailer prohibited.

BRITISH COLUMBIA

Licensing Operations Insurance Corp. of British Columbia, 2631 Douglas St., Victoria, BC V8T 5A3; phone (250) 387-3140 or (800) 950-1498.

Road Condition Report: Province-wide operator information (604) 660-9770; province-wide recorded information, 75¢/minute (VISA or Mastercard) 1-800-550-4997; province-wide recorded information, 75¢/min. (900) 565-4997; Vancouver-area recorded information, 75¢/min. (604) 420-4997; province-wide recorded information from the U.S., $1/min. (900) 288-4997. Free cellular call at *4997. Or call Talking Yellow Pages in Victoria (250) 953-9000 ext. 7623; Vancouver (604) 299-9000 ext. 7623. Internet address: www.th.gov.bc.ca/bchighways.

Minimum driver's age: Driver's license divided into 6 classes—age 19 for class 1, 2 and 4; 18 for class 3; 16 for classes 5 and 6.

Rest area camping: Prohibited.

Seat belts: Seat belts are mandatory for driver and all passengers. Child restraints are mandatory for children under 6 years. Applies to out-of-province drivers.

Studded tires: Permitted from Oct. 1 to April 30.

Motorcycles: Safety helmet required.

CB Radio: Not monitored for emergencies.

Firearms: All rifles and shotguns must be declared at the border. Pistols are prohibited; strictly enforced.

Trailers: Independent braking system not required for trailers where gross weight is less than 2,000 kg (4,400 lbs.) and is less than 40 percent of licensed weight of towing vehicle. Riding in trailer prohibited.

NORTHWEST TERRITORIES

Motor Vehicle Division, P.O. Box 1320, Yellowknife, X1A 2L9; phone (867) 873-7406, fax (867) 873-0120.

Road Condition Report: For the South Mackenzie, phone 1-800-661-0750 in NWT; for the North Mackenzie, 1-800-661-0752 in NWT.

Minimum driver's age: 16 years, 15 with learner's permit.

Rest area camping: Prohibited.

Seat belts: Seat belts are mandatory for driver and all passengers. Child restraints are mandatory for children less than 18 kg (40 lbs.). Applies to out-of-territory drivers.

Studded tires: Tires that are manufactured as studded tires are permitted year-round for passenger vehicles.

Motorcycles: Safety helmet required for driver and passenger.

CB Radio: Channel 9 or 19 is monitored for emergencies.

Firearms: Contact the Canadian Firearms Centre, phone 1-800-731-4000.

Trailers: Independent braking system not required for trailers where gross weight is less than 1,360 kg (2,992 lbs.) and is less than half of licensed weight of towing vehicle. Riding in trailer prohibited, but riding in pickup/camper is permitted.

YUKON TERRITORY

Dept. of Motor Vehicles, Box 2703, Whitehorse, YT Y1A 2C6; phone (867) 667-5315, fax (867) 393-6220.

Road Condition Report: (867) 456-7623; toll free in YT only 1-877-456-7623. Internet: www.yukonweb.wis.net/tourism /roads .html.

Minimum driver's age: 16 years, 15 with learner's permit.

Rest area camping: Prohibited.

Seat belts: Seat belts are mandatory for driver and all passengers. Child restraints are mandatory for children 6 and under weighing less than 18 kg (40 lbs.). Applies to out-of-territory drivers.

Studded Tires: No restrictions.

Motorcycles: Safety helmet required.

CB Radio: Channel 9 may be monitored for emergencies.

Firearms: No regulations on firearms in vehicles.

Trailers: Independent braking system not required for trailers where gross weight is less than 910 kg (2002 lbs.) and is less than half of licensed wieght of towing vehicle. Riding in trailer prohibited.

Ferry Travel

Ferry travel to and within Alaska is provided by the Alaska Marine Highway, which is the name of the Alaska state ferry system and also refers to the water route the ferries follow from Bellingham, WA, up the Inside Passage to Skagway, AK.

The Inside Passage is the route north along the coast of British Columbia and through southeastern Alaska that uses the protected waterways between the islands and the mainland. (Inside Passage is also commonly used to refer to Southeast Alaska and its communities.)

BC Ferries also serves the Inside Passage, providing marine transportation for passengers and vehicles between Port Hardy and Prince Rupert, BC. Port Hardy is located at the north end of Vancouver Island. Prince Rupert is the western terminus of Yellowhead Highway 16 and the southern port for 3 Alaska state ferries serving southeastern Alaska. Prince Rupert is also the farthest north of the 46 ports served by BC Ferries.

If traveling to Alaska by ferry, visitors may make their way up the Inside Passage to any Southeast Alaska community via the Inside Passage/Southeast ferry system. Motorists often use the Alaska Marine Highway northbound or southbound as an alternative to driving all of the Alaska Highway and its access routes. By using the Alaska state ferry one way to transport themselves and their vehicles between Bellingham or Prince Rupert and Skagway or Haines, travelers can eliminate between 700 and 1,700 miles of highway driving (depending on their itinerary), avoid covering the same ground twice, and have the opportunity to take in the magnificent scenery and picturesque communities of the Inside Passage.

The MV *Kennicott's* Southeast/Southwest Inter-Tie Trips between Juneau, Valdez and Seward save additional highway mileage.

The Alaska Marine Highway also provides marine access for passengers and vehicles to various communities in Southcentral/Southwest Alaska. Complete details on the Alaska

state ferry system are given here. See also the ALASKA STATE FERRY SCHEDULES beginning on page 747.

Alaska State Ferries

The main office of the Alaska Marine Highway is in Juneau. Write 1591 Glacier Ave., Juneau, AK 99801-1427; phone toll free 1-800-642-0066, TDD 1-800-764-3779; fax (907) 277-4829. Or via the Internet: www.dot.state.ak.us/amhshome.html.

Local ferry reservation numbers are: Juneau (907) 465-3941; Anchorage (907) 272-7116; Homer terminal (contract agent) 1-800-382-9229 or (907) 235-8449, fax (907) 235-6907, internet www.akms.com/ferry; Kodiak terminal (contract agent) 1-800-526-6731 or (907) 486-3800, fax (907) 486-6166, internet www.akferry.com.

The Alaska Marine Highway actually operates 2 ferry systems, one in Southeast Alaska and one in Southcentral/Southwest Alaska. The MV *Kennicott* connects the 2 systems with a once-a-month round-trip between Juneau, Valdez and Seward in summer. (See the MV *Kennicott* Southeast/Southwest Inter-Tie Trips schedule.)

The Alaska state ferries on the Southeast system depart from Bellingham, WA (85 miles north of Seattle on Interstate 5, Exit 250), or Prince Rupert, BC (450 miles/724 km west of Prince George, BC, or approximately 1,000 miles/1,609 km by highway from Seattle, WA) for Southeast Alaska communities.

Bellingham is accessible by Amtrak and bus. Fairhaven Station transportation center, next to the Bellingham Cruise Terminal at 401 Harris Ave. in south Bellingham, provides a central location for rail, bus, airporter, taxi and ferry services.

Motorists should keep in mind that only 2 major Southeast communities are connected to the Alaska Highway: Haines, via the Haines Highway; and Skagway, via Klondike Highway 2. (See the HAINES HIGHWAY and KLONDIKE HIGHWAY 2 sections.)

The Southeast system also includes feeder service between Ketchikan and Stewart/Hyder; Ketchikan and Hollis; Ketchikan and Metlakatla; and Juneau and Pelican. See Inside Passage/Southeast Alaska schedules in the ALASKA STATE FERRY SCHEDULES section beginning on page 747.

The Southcentral/Southwest ferry system of the Alaska Marine Highway serves coastal communities from Prince William Sound to the Aleutian Islands. Southcentral communities on the ferry system that are also accessible by highway are Valdez, Seward and Homer. Southcentral communities accessible only by ferry are Cordova, Seldovia and Kodiak. Whittier is accessible only via shuttle train (see "Railroads" this section). All communities on the Southwest system are accessible only by ferry or by air.

Travel on the Alaska state ferries is at a leisurely pace, with observation decks, food service (hot meals, snacks and beverages) and vehicle decks on all ferries. Cabins are available only on 5 Southeast ferries (the *Columbia, Malaspina, Matanuska, Taku* and *Kennicott*) and 1 Southwest ferry (the *Tustumena*).

Keep in mind that the state ferries are not cruise ships: They do not have beauty salons, gift shops, deck games, telephones and the like. The small stores on the larger ferries are open limited hours and sell a limited selection of items.

FERRY ROUTES *Washington and British Columbia from Puget Sound to Hecate Strait*

© 1999 The MILEPOST®

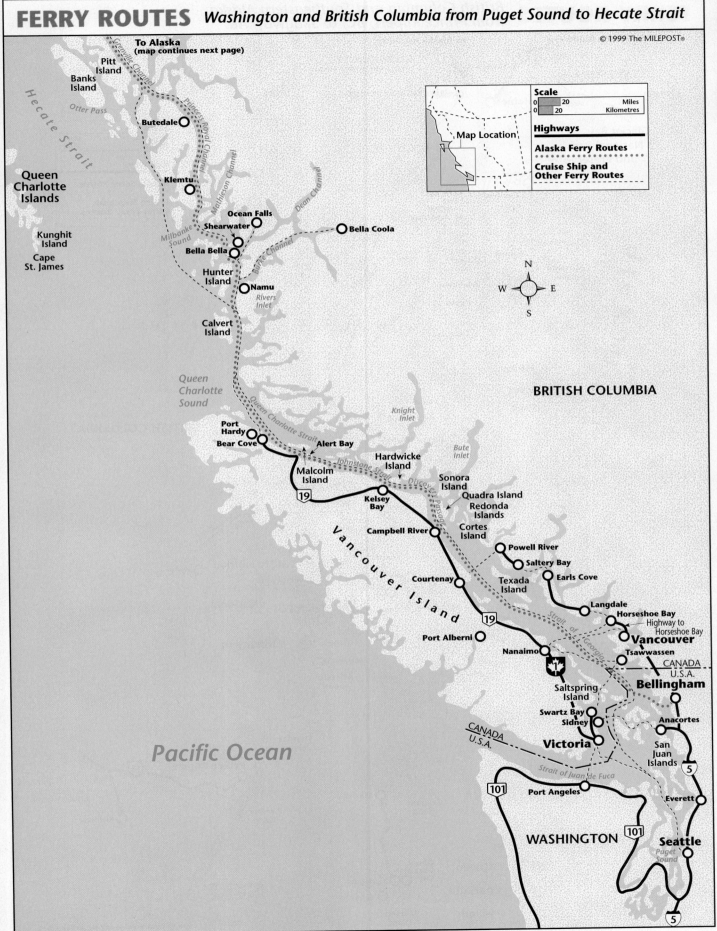

Scale

0   20   Miles
0   20   Kilometres

Highways

······· **Alaska Ferry Routes**

- - - - **Cruise Ship and Other Ferry Routes**

Map Location

To Alaska
(map continues next page)

Pitt Island
Banks Island

Hecate Strait

Otter Pass

Butedale

Queen Charlotte Islands

Klemtu

Kunghit Island

Cape St. James

Princess Royal Channel

Grenville Channel

Mathieson Channel

Ocean Falls

Shearwater

Bella Bella

Milbanke Sound

Hunter Island

Namu

Rivers Inlet

Calvert Island

Dean Channel

Burke Channel

Bella Coola

Queen Charlotte Sound

Knight Inlet

BRITISH COLUMBIA

Bute Inlet

Port Hardy

Bear Cove

Alert Bay

Malcolm Island

Queen Charlotte Strait

Johnstone Strait

Hardwicke Island

Sonora Island

Quadra Island

Redonda Islands

Cortes Island

Discovery Passage

19

Kelsey Bay

Campbell River

Powell River

Saltery Bay

Earls Cove

Vancouver Island

Courtenay

Texada Island

Langdale

Horseshoe Bay

Highway to Horseshoe Bay

19

Strait of Georgia

Vancouver

Port Alberni

Nanaimo

Tsawwassen

CANADA
U.S.A.

Bellingham

1

Saltspring Island

Swartz Bay

Sidney

Anacortes

San Juan Islands

5

Victoria

CANADA
U.S.A.

Strait of Juan de Fuca

Pacific Ocean

101

Port Angeles

Everett

101

WASHINGTON

Seattle

Puget Sound

5

FERRY ROUTES

British Columbia and Southeastern Alaska from Prince Rupert, BC, to Skagway, AK

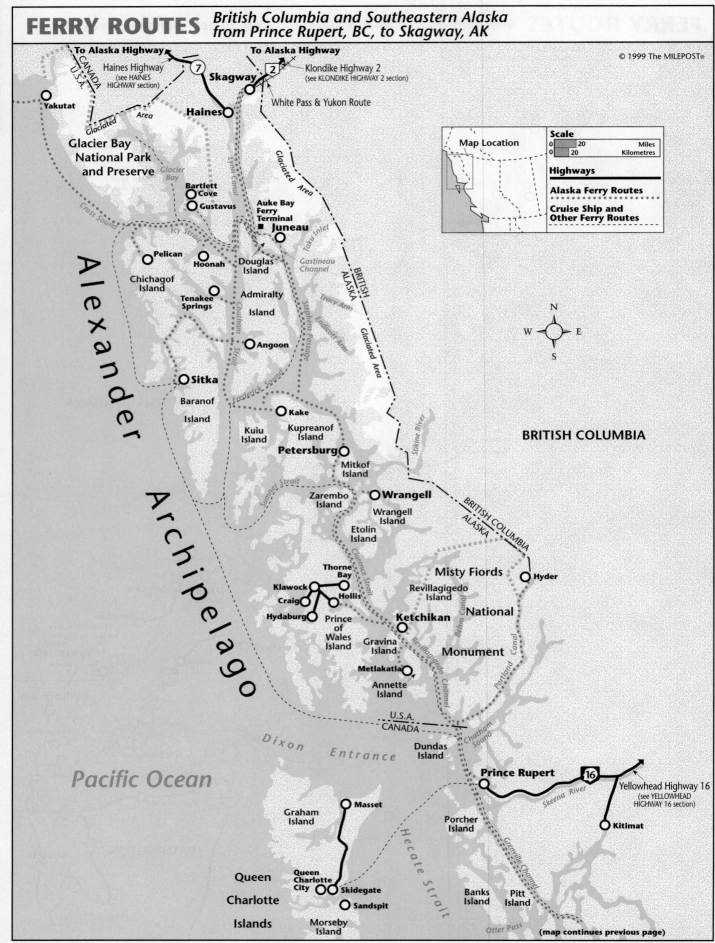

© 1999 The MILEPOST®

To Alaska Highway

Haines Highway (see HAINES HIGHWAY section)

⑦

To Alaska Highway

② Klondike Highway 2 (see KLONDIKE HIGHWAY 2 section)

Skagway

White Pass & Yukon Route

Haines

Yakutat

CANADA
U.S.A.

Glaciated   Area

Glacier Bay National Park and Preserve

Glacier Bay

Lynn Canal

Glaciated Area

Bartlett Cove

Gustavus

Auke Bay Ferry Terminal

Icy Strait

Juneau

Taku Inlet

Pelican

Hoonah

Douglas Island

Gastineau Channel

Chichagof Island

Alexander

Tenakee Springs

Admiralty Island

Chatham Strait

Stephens Passage

Tracy Arm

Endicott Arm

Glaciated Area

BRITISH
ALASKA

Angoon

Sitka

Baranof Island

Frederick Sound

Archipelago

Kake

Kuiu Island

Kupreanof Island

BRITISH COLUMBIA

Petersburg

Mitkof Island

Sumner Strait

Zarembo Island

Wrangell

Wrangell Island

Stikine River

BRITISH COLUMBIA
ALASKA

Etolin Island

Misty Fiords

Hyder

Clarence Strait

Thorne Bay

Klawock

Hollis

Craig

Revillagigedo Island

National

Behm Canal

Hydaburg

Prince of Wales Island

Ketchikan

Gravina Island

Revillagigedo Channel

Monument

Portland Canal

Metlakatla

Annette Island

U.S.A.
CANADA

Dixon   Entrance

Dundas Island

Chatham Sound

Pacific Ocean

Prince Rupert

⑯

Yellowhead Highway 16 (see YELLOWHEAD HIGHWAY 16 section)

Skeena River

Masset

Graham Island

Porcher Island

Grenville Channel

Kitimat

Hecate Strait

Queen Charlotte City

Skidegate

Sandspit

Queen Charlotte Islands

Banks Island

Pitt Island

Morseby Island

Otter Pass

(map continues previous page)

Map Location

Scale
| 0 | 20 | Miles |
| 0 | 20 | Kilometres |

Highways

Alaska Ferry Routes

Cruise Ship and Other Ferry Routes

N
W   E
S

SOUTHCENTRAL/SOUTHWEST FERRY ROUTES

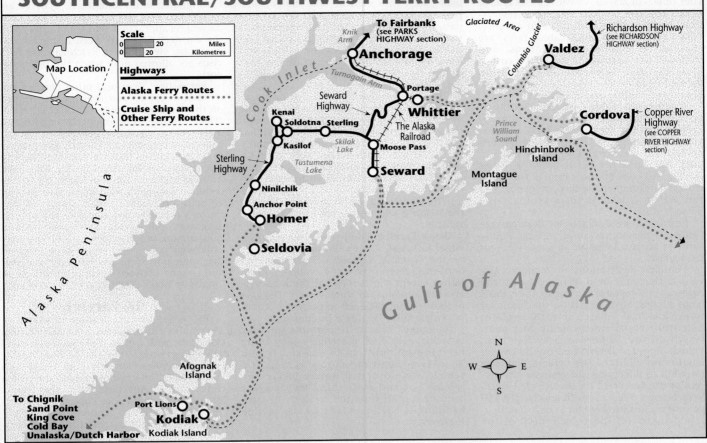

It's a good idea to bring your own snacks, books, games and toiletries, since these are not always available on board.

Season: The Alaska ferry system has 2 seasons—May 1 to Sept. 30 (summer), when sailings are most frequent, and Oct. 1 to April 30 (fall/winter/spring). Summer schedules for 1999 appear in the ALASKA STATE FERRY SCHEDULES section beginning on page 747.

Contact the Alaska Marine Highway office for fall/winter/spring schedules, fares and information. In winter, departures are somewhat less frequent on the Inside Passage/Southeast Alaska routes. On the Southcentral system, the MV *Bartlett* is out of service from September through March, resuming sailings between Cordova and Valdez in April. The port of Whittier is not on the winter schedule. The MV *Tustumena* continues service in winter to Seldovia, Homer, Kodiak, Seward, Cordova, Valdez and the Aleutian Chain. The MV *Kennicott* departs Juneau March 1, 1999, for Valdez and Seward.

Reservations: Required on all vessels for passengers, vehicles and cabins. For reservations write the Alaska Marine Highway, 1591 Glacier Ave., Juneau, AK 99801-1427; phone toll free 1-800-642-0066, or fax (907) 277-4829; TDD 1-800-764-3779. Or via the Internet: www.dot.state.ak.us/amhshome.html.

Local ferry reservation numbers are: Juneau (907) 465-3941; Anchorage (907) 272-7116; Homer terminal (contract agent) 1-800-382-9229 or (907) 235-8449, fax (907) 235-6907, internet www.akms.com/ferry; Kodiak terminal (contract agent) 1-800-526-

6731 or (907) 486-3800, fax (907) 486-6166, internet www.akferry.com.

The Alaska state ferries are very popular in summer. Reservations should be made as far in advance as possible to get the sailing dates you wish. Cabin space on summer sailings is often sold out quickly on the Bellingham sailings. Requests for space are accepted year-round and held until reservations open. (See also "Call or Fax Reservations" and "Getting on our Waitlist" in the ALASKA STATE FERRY SCHEDULES section begining on page 747.)

Deck Passage: If cabin space is filled, or you do not want a cabin, you may go deck passage. This means you'll be sleeping in one of the reclining lounge chairs or rolling out your sleeping bag in an empty corner or even out on deck. There is a limited number of recliner chairs and spaces to roll out sleeping bags. Small, free-standing tents are permitted on the solarium deck (but not under the heated covered area) and on the stern of the cabin deck if space allows (except on the *Kennicott*). Beware of wind; some campers duct-tape their tents to the deck. Pillows and blankets are available for rent from the purser on most sailings. Public showers are available on all vessels except the *Bartlett*.

Fares and fare payment: See information regarding fares and payment in the ALASKA STATE FERRY SCHEDULES section beginning on page 747.

Vehicle tariffs depend on the size of vehicle. You are charged by how much space you take up, so a car with trailer is measured from the front of the car to the end of the trailer, including hitch space. Bicycles,

kayaks and inflatables are charged a surcharge.

Passenger tariffs are charged as follows: adults and children 12 and over, full fare; children 2 to 11, approximately half fare; children under 2, free. Passenger fares do not include cabins or meals. Senior citizen (over 65) discount of 50 percent off the passenger fare between Alaskan ports only; restrictions may apply. Special passes and travel rates are also available to persons with disabilities. Contact the Alaska Marine Highway System for more on these fares and restrictions.

Surcharges are assessed on pets ($25 to/from Bellingham, $10 to/from Prince Rupert and to/from Stewart/Hyder) and unattended vehicles ($50 to/from Bellingham, $20 to/from Prince Rupert and to/from Stewart/Hyder, and $10 to/from other ports).

Check-in times: Summer check-in times for reserved vehicles prior to departure are: Bellingham and Prince Rupert, 3 hours; Ketchikan, Juneau, Haines, Skagway, Homer, Seward, Kodiak, 2 hours; Petersburg, 1 1/2 hours; all other ports, 1 hour. Call the Sitka terminal for check-in time (907/747-3300). Passengers without vehicles must check in 1 hour prior to departure at all ports except Bellingham, where check-in is 2 hours prior to departure. For MV *Bartlett* departures from Whittier, check-in time at the Portage train loading ramp is 1 hour prior to train departure.

Stopovers: In-port time on all vessels is only long enough to unload and load. You may go ashore while the ferry is in port, but you must have your ticket receipt with you to reboard. A stopover is getting off at any port between your point of origin and final destination and taking another vessel at a later time. For travelers with vehicles and/or cabins this can be done as long as reservations to do so have been made in advance. Passenger, vehicle and cabin fares are charged on a point-to-point basis, and stopovers will increase the total ticket cost.

NOTE: Check the schedules carefully. Ferries do *NOT* stop at all ports daily, and northbound and southbound routes vary.

Cabins: All cabins on the Southeast system ferries have a toilet and shower. Linens (towels, sheets, blankets) are provided. Pick up cabin keys from the purser's office when you board. Cabins are sold as a unit, not on a per berth basis. In other words, the cost of the cabin is the same whether 1 or more passengers occupy it. You can get on a waitlist for a cabin at the purser's office.

Restrooms are available for deck-passage (walk-on) passengers on all vessels. Public showers are available on all vessels except the *Bartlett*.

Vehicles: Reservations are required. Any vehicle that may be driven legally on the highway is acceptable for transport on the 4 larger vessels. Most vessels on the Southeast system can load vehicles up to 70 feet/21m long with special arrangements. Maximum length on the *Tustumena* is 40 feet/12m. Vehicle fares are determined by the overall length and width of the vehicle. Vehicles from 8¹/₂ to 9 feet wide are charged 125 percent of the fare listed for the vehicle length. Vehicles over 9 feet in width are charged 150 percent of the fare listed for vehicle length.

Once you on the vehicle deck of the vessel, a crew member will direct you to your parking location. Park, set your hand brake, lock your vehicle, take the personal possessions you will need and proceed to a passageway leading to the passenger areas. If the vehicle you are putting on board will not be accompanied, lock the vehicle and leave the keys with the loading officer.. RVs cannot be used as dining or sleeping facilities while on the ferries.

Hazardous materials may not be transported on the ferries. The valves on propane or similar type tanks must be turned off and sealed by a ferry system employee. If this has not been done by the time you board, notify the purser when surrendering your ticket for boarding. Portable containers of fuel are permitted but must be stored with vessel personnel while en route.

The state assumes no responsibility for the loading and unloading of unattended vehicles.

Food Service: Food service varies from vessel to vessel. There's dining room service on the *Kennicott, Columbia, Tustumena* and *Bartlett*. Cafeteria service is available on all ferries except the *Bartlett*. Alcoholic beverages are available on some vessels. The cost of meals is not included in passenger, cabin or vehicle fares. Tipping is prohibited.

Luggage: You are responsible for your own luggage! Foot passengers may bring hand luggage only (not to exceed 100 lbs.). There is no limit on luggage carried in a vehicle. Coin-operated storage lockers are available aboard most ships, and baggage carts are furnished on the car deck. Baggage handling is NOT provided by the Marine Highway.

Vehicle deck restrictions: Periodic "car deck calls" are made 3 times a day between Bellingham and Ketchikan. These are announced over the loudspeaker and allow passengers approximately 15 minutes to visit the car deck and walk pets, retrieve items from cars, etc. North of Ketchikan, car deck visits are allowed only when the ferry is in port.

Pet policy: Dogs and other pets are not allowed in cabins and must be transported on the vehicle deck only—*NO EXCEPTIONS.* (There are special accommodations for animals aiding disabled passengers. Proper paperwork is required.) Animals and pets are to be transported inside a vehicle or in suitable containers furnished by the passenger. Animals and pets must be cared for by the owner. Passengers who must visit pets or animals en route should apply to the purser's office for an escort to the vehicle deck. (On long sailings the purser periodically announces "cardeck calls.") You may walk your pet at port stops. Keep in mind that some port stops are very brief and that sailing time between some ports will be as long as 36 hours (Bellingham to Ketchikan).

BC Ferries

BC Ferries provides year-round service on 25 routes throughout coastal British Columbia, with a fleet of 40 passenger- and vehicle-carrying ferries. BC Ferries' "Inside Passage" service between Port Hardy and Prince Rupert offers Alaska-bound travelers a convenient connection with the Alaska Marine Highway at Prince Rupert.

Port Hardy is approximately 307 miles/494 km north of Victoria via Trans-

Experience the beauty inside. Experience the Inside Passage.

Take a summer day cruise between Port Hardy and Prince Rupert aboard our ferry-liner *Queen of the North*. Join us on this remarkable voyage with or without your vehicle, as we journey through calm inlets, evergreen covered islands and majestic coastal mountains. Sail with us return or make it part of your own unforgettable tour of British Columbia and Alaska. The abundant wildlife, the rich native culture, and the spectacular scenery remind you that you're part of something larger. Slip away. And experience the beauty inside.

(250) 386-3431 1112 Fort Street, Victoria, B.C. Canada V8V 4V2 **www.bcferries.bc.ca**

BC FERRIES Inside PASSAGE
❀ BC FERRIES

Canada Highway 1 and BC Highway 19. From Nanaimo it is 236 miles/380 km—or about 5 hours' driving time—to Port Hardy. If you are driving from Victoria, allow at least 8 hours (the route is almost all 2-lane highway between Victoria and Campbell River). The Port Hardy ferry terminal is located at Bear Cove, 4 miles/7 km south of downtown Port Hardy.

Prince Rupert is located 450 miles/724 km west of Prince George via the Yellowhead Highway (see YELLOWHEAD HIGHWAY 16 section).

Positioning cruises for 1999 are: northbound, *Queen of the North*, leaving Tsawwassen on May 13 at 9:30 A.M., arriving Port Hardy 10:30 P.M.; southbound, *Queen of the North*, leaving Port Hardy on October 21 at 7:30 A.M., arriving Tsawwassen 8:30 P.M.

Summer service between Port Hardy and Prince Rupert is aboard the *Queen of the North*, which carries 750 passengers and 157 vehicles. The ferry has a cafeteria, buffet dining room, news/gift shop, elevator, facilities for passengers with special needs, video arcade, licensed and view lounges, children's playroom, day cabins and staterooms (for round-trip use). Summer service (May 14 to September 28, 1999) on this route is during daylight hours to make the most of the scenery, so cabins are not necessary. Fall/winter/spring service is an overnight trip on the *Queen of Prince Rupert*.

Or travel the Discovery Coast Passage between Port Hardy and Bella Coola. Summer service only from June 15 to Sept. 13, 1999. The *Queen of Chilliwack* features a cafeteria, gift shop, licensed lounge, reclining seats, showers and a lively and sociable atmosphere.

Reservations: Strongly recommended for passengers and required for vehicles on the Inside Passage and Discovery Coast Passage routes. For reservations (7 A.M. to 10 P.M. daily) and recorded schedule information (24-hours) phone (250) 386-3431 in Victoria, or long distance from outside B.C.; or 1-888-223-3779 in British Columbia outside the Victoria dialing area. Or fax (250) 381-5452. Reservations may also be made on-line at www.bcferries.bc.ca. The Internet site also has rates, schedules and fleet profiles. Or contact BC Ferries at 1112 Fort St., Victoria, BC V8V 4V2.

Schedules and fares: The 1999 Inside Passage sailing schedule is shown here. Schedules are subject to change without notice. Rates current at time of printing (subject to change) are as follows (1-way, in Canadian funds): Adult passenger, $104; child (5 to 11 years), $52; car, $214; camper/RV (up to 20 feet in length, over 6 feet 8 inches in height), $356; additional

length, $17.80 per foot; motorcycle, $107; bicycle, $6.50. Service during the fall, winter and spring is less frequent and fares are reduced. Contact BC Ferries for details.

Check-in time is 1 hour before sailing. Cancellations made less than 30 days prior to departure are subject to a cancellation fee.

Fishing

The biggest challenge for fishermen visiting Alaska and northwestern Canada is the sheer number and variety of fishing opportunities available. The following information is designed to help figure out the what, when, where and how of your fishing trip.

Fishermen are advised to first identify whether they want to fish fresh water or salt water and their desired species. Salmon are the most popular sport fish in Alaska, with all 5 species of Pacific salmon found here: King (chinook), silver (coho), pink (humpy), chum (dog) and red (sockeye). Salmon are anadromous, spawning in fresh water and maturing in the sea. King salmon fishing in Southeast is restricted to salt water. Silver and pink salmon can be taken in fresh water and salt water. Reds are taken in freshwater streams. Large landlocked lakes have populations of kokanee (landlocked red salmon).

Other sport fish include halibut, rainbow trout and steelhead, Dolly Varden and Arctic char, cutthroat and brook trout, northern pike, and lake trout.

Halibut, a saltwater fish that can weigh more than 300 pounds, is the largest fish in Alaska that a fisherman is likely to catch. The Pacific halibut is also the best known member of the "bottomfish" family, a catch-all term for non-salmon fish that includes lingcod, rockfish and a variety of other species.

Rainbows are a freshwater trout, the sea-run of which is the steelhead. Cutthroat are common on the mainland and every major island in Southeastern Alaska, occurring in both fresh water (non-seagoing) and salt water (sea-going). Dolly Varden and Arctic char also both have populations that go to sea and do not, which spawn in streams and migrate to sea in the spring to feed, and may be either a saltwater or freshwater sportfish. Eastern brook trout is an introduced species to freshwater lakes.

Northern pike (also called pike, jack fish and pickerel) are widely distributed throughout most of Alaska except southeastern. The northern pike is the most sought-after indigenous sport fish in Interior Alaska after the Arctic grayling. Alaska's Interior also has

Grayling caught in the Chena River outside Fairbanks. (© Robin Brandt)

the largest Arctic grayling fishery in North America. These popular game fish are the main sport fish species in the Tanana River drainage.

If you know what kind of fish you want, that may also determine when to go. Although most fishing enthusiasts focus their trips between April and October, when the weather is generally more mild, the fish have something to say about timing. The Alaska Dept. of Fish and Game Sportfish Division gives a run timing for all fisheries by region.

Where to fish is probably the most difficult choice, with the number of fishing destinations available well beyond the capability of most anglers to visit. The list of possible fishing spots is also beyond our capability to list here, although many favorite fishing spots are mentioned under Area Fishing in the Attractions section of each community covered in *The MILEPOST*®. The Alaska Dept. of Fish and Game is the source for much of this information, and they have literally hundreds of pamphlets on fishing regional waters. Particularly helpful is their "Sportfishing Alaska" brochure, which shows run times and also lists area office phone numbers. Or write the Sport Fish Division, Box 25526, Juneau, AK 99802-5526; phone (907) 465-4180; Internet address: www.state.ak.us/local/akpages/FISH.GAME/adfghome.htm.

While you may fish any body of water with fish in it, local knowledge greatly increases your chances of success. Many fishing guides and charter operators advertise in *The MILEPOST*®. It is possible to fly out of almost any Alaskan community, fish a remote body of water, and fly back to town, all within 3 hours. Charter planes charge an hourly rate, either per plane load or per passenger, or may offer a fixed-rate fishing charter that may or may not include guide services and fishing gear. Fly-in fishing operators may offer lodge accommodations or only provide drop-off and pickup service, with the client either camping or overnighting at a U.S. Forest Service cabin. (Many of these cabins are located on fishing lakes with skiffs available.)

Charter boats are available for half-, full- or multi-day fishing trips out of most South-central, Southeast and Southwestern Alaska port communities. Multi-day fishing boat

BC FERRIES 1999 INSIDE PASSAGE SCHEDULE
PORT HARDY TO PRINCE RUPERT • May 14 – October 20, 1999

NORTHBOUND	SOUTHBOUND
Departs: Port Hardy 7:30 A.M.	**Departs:** Prince Rupert 7:30 A.M.
Arrives: Prince Rupert 10:30 P.M.	**Arrives:** Port Hardy 10:30 P.M.
Dates: May 14, 16, 18, 20, 22, 24, 26, 28, 30 only.	**Dates:** May 15, 17, 19, 21, 23, 25, 27, 29, 31 only.
June, July (odd-numbered days)	June, July (even-numbered days)
August (even-numbered days)	August (odd-numbered days)
September (odd-numbered days except Sept. 29)	September (even-numbered days except Sept. 30)
October 1, 3, 5, 7, 9, 11, 13, 15, 17, 19 only.	October 2, 4, 6, 8, 10, 12, 14, 16, 18, 20 only

charters may overnight on board yachts or in floating lodges. Boat charters for saltwater sportfishing average $185 per person per day, based on a shared charter boat. Rates often include gear, license, bait, fish processing and land transportation, but ask ahead of time. Clients may have a destination in mind, or depend on the charter boat operator for guiding services.

There are also numerous fishing lodges in the North. Full-service lodges generally offer food and lodging, guide service, boats for saltwater fishing and daily fly-outs for freshwater fishing. Rates range anywhere from $300 to $800 per person per day, and include transportation to the lodge, accommodations, meals, guide services, fishing license and equipment, and fish processing. Refreshments, gratuities and personal items are extra.

When, where and how you fish requires some careful thought and planning, but the rewards are well worth it. Throughout *The MILEPOST®* you will find this ⤙ friendly little symbol. Wherever you see one, you will find a description of the fishing at that point.

Contact fish and game offices (listed in the "Welcome to the North Country" section) for current license fees and regulations.

GPS

GPS stands for global positioning system, which is a satelllite-based navigation system consisting of 24 orbiting satellites transmitting various data. GPS receivers translate this data into coordinates to help you determine your position. There are several manufacturers of GPS receivers and each has several models.

Latitudes and longitudes for most major communities have been included on the highway strip maps for GPS users. These coordinates were supplied by a variety of sources, including individual GPS receivers and the National Imagery and Mapping Agency's GEOnet Names Server (www.nima.mil).

Making *The MILEPOST®* user-friendly for GPS receivers is a pilot project for us. We would appreciate feedback from GPS users as to how best to serve your needs. Please contact the Editor, 619 E. Ship Creek Ave., Suite 329, Anchorage, AK 99501; or e-mail kris@themilepost.com with your comments.

Hiking

Alaska State Parks, the U.S. Forest Service, and Bureau of Land Management maintain most of the established trails within Alaska. *The MILEPOST®* notes all trailheads along roads and highways in the highway logs, and popular hiking trails accessible from a major city are usually noted under Attractions in that community. Check trail conditions locally before hiking.

Within the Alaska state park system, Chugach State Park outside of Anchorage has the most extensive trail system, with more than 200 miles of hiking trails (see page 376 in the ANCHORAGE section). Kachemak Bay State Park, across the water from Homer, also has a fairly extensive trail system.

Tongass National Forest in Southeast Alaska has almost 600 miles of trails.

Chugach National Forest offers some 200 miles of trail, including an extensive system of hiking trails on the Kenai Peninsula, maintained by the Glacier and Seward Ranger districts. The most popular trail is the Resurrection Pass trail, a 38.6-mile/62.1-km trail that follows Resurrection Creek from Hope up Resurrection Pass then down Juneau Creek to the Sterling Highway.

Other popular Kenai Peninsula trails are Johnson Pass USFS Trail (which follows a portion of the Iditarod National Historic Trail), Crow Pass (a Chugach State Park trail that also follows a portion of the Iditarod National Historic Trail), Russian Lakes and Ptarmigan Creek USFS trails. There are USFS public-use cabins along many of the trails; these must be reserved in advance. See the STERLING HIGHWAY and SEWARD HIGHWAY for trailhead locations.

The Alaska Public Lands Information Center, 605 W. 4th, Anchorage, AK 99501, has general information on hiking in all public lands in Alaska. The USDA Forest Service Supervisor and District Ranger offices have trail maps and detailed information on hiking trails in Tongass and Chugach national forests.

Most national parklands in Alaska have no established trail systems, instead offering cross-country hiking or—depending on the terrain—bushwacking. An exception is the 33-mile Chilkoot Trail out of Skagway, managed by the National Park Service. See "National Parks" this section.

The BLM's White Mountains National Recreation Area north of Fairbanks has more than 200 miles of winter trails and 20 miles of summer hiking trails. The BLM also manages the 27-mile Pinnell Mountain National Recreation Trail—the first national recreation trail established in the state—located within Steese National Conservation Area outside Fairbanks. See both the ELLIOTT HIGHWAY and STEESE HIGHWAY sections.

Yukon Territory has established wilderness trails, too. Information about hiking in Kluane National Park Reserve is available from Parks Canada, Canadian Heritage, 300 Main St., Room 105, Whitehorse, YT Y1A 2B5. For other hiking trails in the Yukon, contact Tourism Yukon, Box 2703, Whitehorse, YT Y1A 2C6, phone (867) 667-5340.

Holidays

The following list of observed holidays for 1999 in Alaska and Canada can help you plan your trip. Keep in mind that banks and other agencies may be closed on these holidays and traffic may be heavier.

ALASKA

New Year's Day	Jan. 1
Martin Luther King Day	Jan. 18
Presidents' Day	Feb. 15
Seward's Day	March 29
Easter Sunday	April 4
Memorial Day	May 31
Independence Day	July 4
Labor Day	Sept. 6
Columbus Day	Oct. 11
Alaska Day	Oct. 18
Veterans Day	Nov. 11
Thanksgiving Day	Nov. 25
Christmas Day	Dec. 25

CANADA

New Year's Day	Jan. 1
Good Friday	April 2
Easter Monday	April 5
Victoria Day	May 24
Canada Day	July 1
Civic Holiday	Aug. 2
Labour Day	Sept. 6
Thanksgiving Day	Oct. 11
Remembrance Day	Nov. 11
Christmas Day	Dec. 25
Boxing Day	Dec. 26

Internet

The MILEPOST® includes Internet addresses when available. You may also visit our website at www.themilepost.com for updates and more information on travel in the North Country.

Many of our print advertisers also advertise on our website, where more information is available on their businesses as well as links to other homepages. Look for this symbol in advertisements in *The MILEPOST®*

and then visit www.themilepost.com for more information.

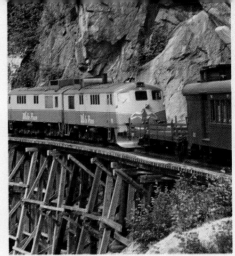

National Parks

Denali National Park and Preserve is one of 15 national park units in Alaska. Parklands range from the remote Bering Land Bridge National Preserve on the Bering Sea to Skagway's Klondike Gold Rush National Historical Park, one of the state's most visited attractions.

The MILEPOST® has detailed information on Denali National Park (see page 462) and Glacier Bay National Park (see page 711). Road-accessible national parks in Alaska also covered in *The MILEPOST®* include Wrangell-St. Elias National Park (see page 534 in the EDGERTON HIGHWAY/McCARTHY ROAD section), Kenai Fjords National Park (see the description under Seward Attractions in the SEWARD HIGHWAY section); Sitka National Historical Park (see Sitka on page 694 in the INSIDE PASSAGE section); and Klondike Gold Rush National Historial Park (see Skagway on page 725 in the INSIDE PASSAGE section). There's also a description of Yukon–Charley Rivers National Park, accessible via the Yukon River from Eagle (see page 286 in the TAYLOR HIGHWAY section).

On-line information is available on the National Park Service's World Wide Web pages (www.nps.gov) for the following national parks in Alaska: Aniakchak (/ania); Bering Land Bridge (/bela); Cape Krusenstern (/cakr); Denali (/dena); Gates of the Arctic (/gaar); Glacier Bay (/glba); Katmai (/katm); Kenai Fjords (/kefj)/ Klondike Gold Rush (/klgo); Kobuk Valley (/kobu); Lake Clark (/lacl); Noatak (/noat); Sitka (/sitk); Wrangell-St. Elias (/wrst) and Yukon–Charley Rivers (/yuch).

Or contact the Alaska Public Lands Information Centers in Anchorage, AK at 605 W. 4th Ave., Suite 105, Anchorage 99510, phone (907) 271-2737; Fairbanks, AK at 250 Cushman St., Suite 1A, Fairbanks 99701, phone (907) 456-0527; or Ketchikan at 50 Main St., Ketchikan, AK 99901, phone (907) 228-6214.

Photography

Many lodges and tour outfitters promote the spectacular photography opportunities in their area by offering special photo tours to photograph wildlife or landscapes. And a great many visitors to the North bring along a 35mm camera hoping to take home unique photographs of their experiences. Many actually purchase a new camera specifically for their trip, but wonder whether or not they will have the right type of film or equipment to effectively capture Alaska's scenery and wildlife. (For photographing the aurora borealis, for example, the Geophysical Institute in Fairbanks recommends a tripod and exposures of 10 seconds or more.)

If you are wondering about photography equipemnt, here are a few tips that may be useful.

Point and shoot cameras are those that can be defined as those small enough to fit into a small case or a purse. They are relatively inexpensive and most models are capable of recording extremely nice quality images. All of them offer fully automatic functions, making them ideal for everyone. They load the film automatically and also set the film speed for you (also known as "ISO" or "ASA."). They auto-focus and auto-flash so all you have to do is compose a picture and press the button. They even rewind the film after the last photo is taken and offer many features for individual creativity.

As for brand names and models, Canon, Nikon, Olympus and Fuji are leaders in this field, although there are many other excellent camera manufacturers. All of them come with a standard wide-angle lens, usually set at 38mm. Many models offer zoom lenses that range from wide-angle to medium telephoto (38mm-130mm range) and afford much more versatility. These range in price from about $225-$325.

SLR's (Single Lens Reflex) are those that allow the user to choose from a wide variety of lenses. Average travelers do not want to be inconvenienced by the size and weight of a large camera bag nor do they want to be burdened by having to change the lens frequently. Most people choose an SLR system because they either want the ability to use more powerful lenses for wildlife photography or would like the ability to be creative with the control features these cameras provide.

Both Kodak and Fuji make fine films whether you wish to shoot print film or slide film. For most photography in Alaska, ASA 200 film offers the best overall quality and versatility for the majority of weather and lighting situations. It can be argued that ASA 100 films are sharper, but unless you plan to do extreme enlargements (11x14 to 20x30), you are unlikely to notice the difference. Finally, for very poor weather conditons, you might consider bringing a few rolls of higher speed film, such as Fujichrome Sensia 400 (if you want slides) or Fuji's ASA 800 print film.

Railroads

Although no railroads connect Alaska or the Yukon with the Lower 48, there are 2 railroads in the North: the Alaska Railroad and the White Pass & Yukon Route.

The Alaska Railroad

The Alaska Railroad operates year-round passenger and freight service between Anchorage, Fairbanks, Portage and Whittier. In summer, passenger service is available daily between Anchorage and Fairbanks via Talkeetna and Denali Park; Portage and Whittier; Anchorage and Whittier; and between Anchorage and Seward. For more information on the Alaska Railroad, write Passenger Services Dept., Box 107500, Anchorage 99510. Phone 1-800-544-0552 or (907) 265-2494; fax 265-2323; e-mail reservations@akrr.com. Homepage: http://www.alaska.net/~akrr.

Construction of the railroad began in 1915 under Pres. Woodrow Wilson. On July 15, 1923, Pres. Warren G. Harding drove the golden spike at Nenana, signifying completion of the railroad. The main line extends from Seward to Fairbanks, approximately 470 miles/756 km.

The Alaska Railroad accommodates visitors with disabilities. Six coaches feature wheelchair lifts. Coaches have provisions for occupied wheelchairs, and restrooms are accessible. With advance notice, sign language interpreters are available.

The White Pass & Yukon Route Railway out of Skagway. (© Lee Foster)

Following are services, schedules and fares available on Alaska Railroad routes. Keep in mind that schedules and fares are subject to change without notice.

Anchorage–Talkeetna–Denali–Fairbanks: Passenger service between Anchorage, Talkeetna, Denali Park and Fairbanks is offered daily on the *Denali Star* from May 15 to Sept. 12, 1999. The express service operates with full-service dining, a vista-dome for all passengers to share and coaches with comfortable reclining seats. Travel along the 350-mile/563-km route between Anchorage and Fairbanks at a leisurely pace with comfortable window seats and good views of the countryside. Packages including sightseeing tours, hotels, river rafting, hiking and flightseeing are available in Talkeetna, Denali, Fairbanks and Anchorage from Alaska Railroad Scenic Tours.

Luxury railcars are available on the Anchorage–Denali Park–Fairbanks route through Gray Line of Alaska (Holland America Lines/Westours) and Princess Tours. These tour companies operate (respectively) the *McKinley Explorer* and *Midnight Sun Express*. These luxury railcars, which are coupled onto the end of the regular Alaska Railroad train, are glass-domed and offer gourmet cuisine along with other amenities. Tickets are priced higher than those for the regular Alaska Railroad cars, and are sold on a space-available basis. Packages with a Denali Park overnight are also available. Phone Princess Tours at (800) 835-8907, or Gray Line of Alaska at (800) 544-2206 for details.

During the summer, northbound express trains depart Anchorage at 8:15 A.M., arrive Talkeetna at 11:25 A.M., arrive Denali Park at 3:45 P.M., and arrive Fairbanks at 8:15 P.M. Southbound express trains depart Fairbanks at 8:15 A.M., arrive Denali Park at noon, and arrive Anchorage at 8:15 P.M.

One-way fares are as follows: Anchorage–Denali Park, $102; Anchorage–Talkeetna, $60; Fairbanks–Denali Park, $54; Anchorage–Fairbanks, $154. Children ages 2 through 11 ride for 50 percent of adult fare; under 2 ride free.

During fall, winter and spring, weekend-only rail service is provided between Anchorage and Fairbanks on the *Aurora*. The train travels from Anchorage to Fairbanks on Saturday and returns on Sunday. The *Aurora* is a "flag stop" train and will stop wherever people want to get on or off.

Reservations should be made more than 40 days prior to travel. Include the dates you plan to travel, points of departure and destination, the number of people in your party and your home phone number. Tickets may be purchased in advance by mail if you desire. Checks, Visa, MasterCard, Discover and Diners Club are accepted.

Each adult is allowed 2 pieces of luggage with a maximum combined weight of 100 lbs. Children are allowed 2 pieces of baggage with a maximum combined weight of 75 lbs. Excess baggage may be checked for a nominal fee. Bicycles are accepted for a charge of $20 per station, on a space-available basis on the day of travel. Keep in mind that baggage, including backpacks, must be checked before boarding, and it is not accessible during the trip. Canoes, motors, motorcycles, items weighing over 150 lbs., etc., are not accepted for transportation on passenger trains. These items are shipped via freight train.

Local Service: Local rural service between Talkeetna and Hurricane Gulch operates Thursday, Friday, Saturday and Sunday each week between May 15 and Sept. 12, 1999. This 1-day trip aboard the *Hurricane* takes you past breathtaking views of Mount McKinley (weather permitting), into some remote areas and provides an opportunity to meet local residents who use the train for access. Local service uses self-propelled rail diesel cars and provides vending-machine snacks. The *Hurricane* is a "flag stop" train and will stop wherever people want to get on or off.

Portage–Whittier: The Portage–Whittier shuttle train carries passengers and vehicles between Portage on the Seward Highway and Whittier on Prince William Sound. Portage, which has no facilities other than the railroad's vehicle loading ramp, is 47 miles/76 km south of Anchorage at **Milepost S 80.3** on the Seward Highway. Whittier, on Prince William Sound, is port to the Alaska Marine Highway's ferry MV *Bartlett*, which provides passenger and vehicle service to Cordova and Valdez. The Portage–Whittier railway line is 12.4 miles/20 km long, includes 2 tunnels (one 13,090 feet/3,990m long, the other 4,910 feet/1,497m long). Called the Whittier Cutoff, the line was constructed in 1942–43 as a safeguard for the flow of military supplies. It is a 35-minute train ride.

The shuttle makes several round trips daily between Portage and Whittier, from mid-May through mid-September, connecting with Alaska Marine Highway ferry sailings and other vessels which operate between Whittier and Valdez. (Remember that ferry tickets are purchased separately from train tickets.)

Train tickets for the Whittier shuttle may be purchased from ticket sellers at Portage. Reservations are not accepted for the shuttle train, although passengers with confirmed ferry connections are given priority boarding on the 1:20 P.M. shuttle between Portage and Whittier, if vehicles are at Portage by no later than 12:30 P.M. Standard vehicles under 23 feet/7m in length are charged $72, round-trip, between Portage and Whittier; this includes driver fare. Other adult passengers in the vehicle, $20 round-trip; children (2—11 years of age), $10 round-trip. Vehicle rates are based on length. Some height and width restrictions apply.

During fall, winter and spring, service to

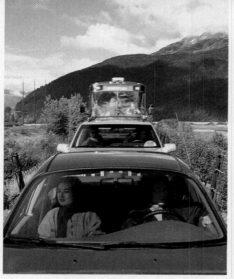

Alaska Railroad's Whittier shuttle pulls out of Portage. (© Kris Graef, staff)

Whittier is provided on Wednesday, Friday, Saturday and Sunday.

Anchorage–Seward: Rail passenger service between Anchorage and Seward operates daily on the *Coastal Classic* between May 15 and Sept. 6, 1999. (Weekend service to Seward is available May 8–9 and Sept. 11–12.) The 230-mile/370-km round-trip excursion follows Turnagain Arm south from Anchorage and passes through some of the most beautiful scenery to be found along the railroad. Travel is aboard classic passenger coaches. Food service is available in the bar/deli car. Departs Anchorage at 6:45 A.M., arrives Seward at 11:05 A.M. The return trip departs Seward at 6 P.M., arriving Anchorage at 10:25 P.M. Reservations are recommended. The round-trip fare is $86 for adults; 50 percent fare for children 2 through 11. Overnight tours which include hotel and Resurrection Bay boat excursions, Exit Glacier and Alaska SeaLife Center are available from the railroad ticket office.

Anchorage–Whittier: Rail passenger service between Anchorage and Whittier operates daily on the *Glacier Discovery* between May 15 and Sept. 12, 1999. The 50-mile/80-km excursion follows the Turnagain Arm of the Cook Inlet, passes through 2 tunnels, and arrives in Whittier, located on the Prince William Sound. Food service is available in the bar/deli car. Departs Anchorage at 9 A.M. and arrives Whittier at 11:30 A.M. The return trip departs Whittier at 5:45 P.M. and arrives Anchorage at 8:15 P.M. Reservations are recommended. The round-trip fare is $52 for adults; children ages 2-11 pay 50 percent of adult fare. Tours are available, including one-day connecting cruises of Prince William Sound and cruises offering overnight accommodations.

White Pass & Yukon Route

The White Pass & Yukon Route (WP&YR) is a narrow-gauge (36-inch) privately owned railroad built in 1898 at the height of the Klondike Gold Rush. Between 1900 and 1982, the WP&YR provided passenger and freight service between Skagway, AK, and Whitehorse, YT. The WP&YR no longer offers rail service the entire way to Whitehorse.

The WP&YR now operates a 3-hour round-trip train excursion between Skagway

and the White Pass Summit, an 8-hour steam excursion between Skagway and Lake Bennett, and a combination train and bus trip between Skagway and Whitehorse, as well as other special trips.

Construction of the WP&YR began in May 1898. The railroad reached White Pass in February 1899 and Whitehorse in July 1900. It was the first railroad in Alaska and at the time the most northern of any railroad in North America. The White Pass & Yukon Route was declared an International Historic Civil Engineering Landmark, one of only 22 in the world, in 1994.

The railroad follows the old White Pass trail. The upper section of the old "Deadhorse" trail near the summit (Mile 19 on the WP&YR railway) is visible beside the tracks. During the Klondike Gold Rush, thousands of men took the 40-mile/64-km White Pass trail from Skagway to Lake Bennett, where they built boats to float down the Yukon River to Dawson City and the goldfields.

The WP&YR has one of the steepest railroad grades in North America. From sea level at Skagway the railroad climbs to 2,885 feet/879m at White Pass in only 20 miles/32 km of track. Currently, the railroad offers daily train service between Skagway and Fraser, BC, mid-May to mid-September, and a limited number of rail trips to Carcross and steam trips to Lake Bennett in summer.

Following are services, schedules and fares (U.S. funds) for White Pass & Yukon Route in 1999. All times indicated in schedules are local times (Skagway is on Alaska Time, which is 1 hour earlier than Whitehorse, which is on Pacific Time.) Children 12 and under ride for half fare when accompanied by an adult. Children under 2 years ride free if not occupying a seat; half fare for separate seat. Reservations are required. (Tuesdays, Wednesdays and Thursdays are especially busy days.) For reservations and information, contact the White Pass & Yukon Route, Box 435, Skagway, AK 99840. Phone toll free in the U.S. and Canada (800) 343-7373 or (907) 983-2217 in Skagway. Internet: www.whitepassrailroad.com.

Summit Excursion: This approximately 3-hour round-trip excursion features the most spectacular part of the WP&YR railway, including the steep climb to White Pass Summit, Bridal Veil Falls, Inspiration Point and Dead Horse Gulch. Offered twice daily from May 13 to Sept. 23, 1999; the morning train departs Skagway at 8:30 A.M. and returns at 11:45 A.M.; the afternoon train departs Skagway at 1 P.M. and returns at 4:15 P.M. On Tuesdays and Wednesdays another trip departs Skagway at 4:30 P.M. and returns at 7:45 P.M. Fares are $78 for adults and $39 for children 12 and under.

Skagway to Whitehorse: Through-service between Skagway, AK, and Whitehorse, YT, is offered daily from May 19 to Sept. 12, 1999. Through passengers travel 28 miles/45 km by train between Skagway, AK, and Fraser, BC, and then 87 miles/140 km by bus between Fraser and Whitehorse, YT. The train portion of this trip takes passengers over historic White Pass Summit. Northbound service departs Skagway at 12:40 P.M. and arrives Whitehorse at 5:30 P.M. Southbound service departs Whitehorse at 8 A.M. and arrives Skagway at noon. One-way fares are $95 for adults and $47.50 for children 12 and under.

Special Steam Excursions: Steam travel returns to the White Pass & Yukon Route with limited summer runs to beautiful Lake

Bennett. This 80-mile/128.7-km round-trip takes 8 hours and includes a layover at a restored 1903 station. Six steam trips are scheduled for these Saturdays: June 12 and 26, July 10 and 24, and August 7 and 21, 1999. Departs Skagway at 8 A.M. Fares are $156 for adults and $78 for children 12 and under; includes lunch.

Lake Bennett Adventure: Travel 20 miles/32 km beyond the Summit to historic Bennett, BC, the end of the Chilkoot Trail. A two-hour layover allows time to explore the area and tour historic displays in the restored 1903 station. The 8 1/2-hour, 80-mile/129 km round-trip is every Monday, Thursday, Friday and Saturday, in June, July and August, departing Skagway at 8 A.M.. Fares are $128 for adults and $64 for children 12 and under; includes lunch.

Chilkoot Trail Hikers Service: Service between Bennett and Fraser, BC, offered on Mondays, Thursdays, Fridays and Saturdays in June, July and August. Hikers who have completed the 33-mile/53 km Chilkoot Trail can be picked up at Lake Bennett twice daily and transported back to Skagway, or with bus connections on to Whitehorse. $25 to Fraser, BC; $65 to Skagway.

Private Red Caboose Charter: A 4-hour round-trip adventure to Fraser, B.C. in an authentic Red Caboose. Charter only, May 19—September 12, 1999, departing Skagway at 8 A.M. or 12:40 P.M. Six round-trip tickets included in the $650 fare. Advance reservations required.

Renting An RV

An increasingly popular way to explore Alaska and northwestern Canada is through the big, wide windows of an RV. The good news is you don't have to own an RV to take an RV vacation. You can rent one!

Across the North, dealers offer every type of rig, from modest tent trailers to top-of-the-line, self-contained motorhomes. In between, you have a choice of trailers, converted vans or truck campers. Amenities vary from luxurious to utilitarian, and some dealers have specially-equipped wheelchair-accessible units. Many RV rental companies advertise in The MILEPOST®. Check advertisements in Anchorage, Fairbanks and other cities.

How do you decide what to rent? The most popular are Class C units, measuring 20 to 29 feet in length. Laura Bly of "USA Today," in an article on her RV rental experience, wrote: "When estimating how much space you'll need, err on the liberal side. In our case, a 29-footer for a family of 3. What had initially seemed like a palace grew smaller with each passing mile, and I was grateful we didn't need to fold the dinette table into an extra bed each evening." And she and her family were gone only 3 nights.

Further evidence of that point comes from the Recreational Vehicle Renters Association (www.rvamerica.com): "Most families will want the space and comfort of a full-size motorhome. Smaller units are ideal for smaller parties or those who want to 'rough it'."

Inside a Class C, you'll find almost every convenience of home. Some larger units include 2 queen-size beds, air conditioning, a microwave, dinette seating 4, even a bathroom with a shower stall. On the other hand, you can choose a trimmed-down RV for much less money and still have your shower by using the campground facilities.

What will it cost? The basic rule is: The more space, privacy and comfort you want, the more the RV costs to rent. How much depends on the size of the RV you rent and the length of your vacation. Depending on the season, motorhomes generally rent from about $70 to $170 per day plus mileage. Truck campers and travel trailers average $50 to $120 per day. Weekly rates offer a savings over daily rates. Keep in mind that some RVs come fully equipped with all the necessities so you need only your own personal items. Others provide linens and kitchen gear, but for an additional charge. Or you can pack your own bedding (sleeping bags work well) and cooking supplies. Ask what your RV rental includes.

The "early bird gets the worm" adage applies here, so make reservations as soon as possible. That way you will get exactly the model and size you want. One experienced renter suggests getting the reservation in writing, so you won't encounter any last-minute disappointments. With nothing on paper to prove confirmation, you might end up with a smaller unit than the one you requested.

What's more, you need to know exactly what's inside the unit before you confirm. Are kitchen supplies (cookware, dinnerware, utensils) included? Bed and bath linens? Maps? Are airport transfers provided? At a charge or no charge? Be sure to know the fee for dropping the RV at a destination other than your pick-up point. Fees can be extremely high.

If you see a sign that states a small unit sleeps 6, be advised that even the larger ones claim sleeping room for no more than 6 or 7 people. Also find out when seasonal rates change. You could save a significant amount of money or rent a larger vehicle for about the same price just by scheduling your trip to coincide with the off-season. Many consider May off-season, June peak time, which means mid-to-late May could be an ideal time for your holiday.

A deposit of about $200 holds your reservation. The majority of rental agencies accept major credit cards, cash or traveler's checks. As a rule, they don't take personal checks. The reservationist will inform you of payment options.

You don't need a special license to rent an RV, yet it is a bit more complicated than renting a car. Most dealers include comprehensive insurance coverage, but with a high deductible. To lower it, some offer a waiver for a daily fee. Talk to your own insurance agent; your policy may or may not cover rentals.

You may be eager to get on the road right away, but take the advice of some renters who regretted they didn't learn more about their new traveling companion before driving off. Here are some things to remember:

When the dealer demonstrates how to operate the rental, pay close attention. This is for your safety and convenience. Ask questions. For example, how to extinguish the propane pilot light (necessary when you add gas) and how to re-ignite it. Critical areas are maintenance and operation: filling fresh water tanks, emptying waste, using appliances, hooking up. The more you know about your home on wheels, the more likely you'll enjoy a trouble-free trip.

On your rental agreement, note any dents, rips or other damage you see in or on the RV. Keep a log of anything that goes wrong with the RV which is not your fault. You may be able to negotiate a discount at the end of your trip.

Make a backup set of keys if the dealer doesn't give you one.

Ask for a written statement about the fee structure. Will your reservation deposit be applied to your total charges? Are you required to prepay the rental including mileage charges? Does the rental agency require a security deposit? Is it refundable? Is there a prep charge? Are you required to fill the gas tank to avoid additional charges? Propane? How much do additional days and miles cost? Will you be charged if you don't clean the interior and/or wash the exterior?

Know exactly what procedures to follow if you encounter mechanical problems or an emergency. What if you get a ding in the windshield? Is the unit equipped with a spare tire? Write down emergency phone numbers and be sure you have a thorough understanding of all of the agency's policies.

Ask the dealer about any restrictions for RV travel due to the size or weight of the vehicle, or conditions of the roads you plan to travel. Don't overload the RV. Factor in full gas, water and waste tanks to allowable load.

Be sure you understand the papers required should you cross the border between Alaska and Canada.

Know what time the vehicle must be returned to avoid another day's charge.

Shipping

Whether you are moving to Alaska, or plan to ship your vehicle North rather than drive one or both ways, there is a shipper to accommodate your needs.

Vehicles: Carriers that will ship cars, campers, trailers and motorhomes from Anchorage to Seattle include: Alaska Railroad, Box 107500, Anchorage, AK 99510-7500, phone (907) 265-2490; Alaska Vehicle Transport, Inc., phone 1-800-422-7925; Sea–Land Freight Service, Inc., 1717 Tidewater Ave., Anchorage, AK 99501, phone 1-800-478-2671 or (907) 274-2671; and Totem Ocean Trailer Express (TOTE), 2511 Tidewater, Anchorage, AK 99501, phone (907) 276-5868 or toll free 1-800-234-8683.

In the Seattle, WA, area, contact A.A.D.A. Systems, Box 2323, Auburn 98071, phone (206) 762-7840 or 1-800-929-2773; Alaska Railroad, 2203 Airport Way S., Suite 215, Seattle, WA 98134, phone (206) 624-4234; Sea–Land Service, Inc., 3600 Port of Tacoma Road, 4th floor, Tacoma, WA 98424, phone (206) 593-8100 or 1-800-426-4512 (outside the Tacoma area); or Totem Ocean Trailer Express (TOTE), 500 Alexander Ave., Tacoma, WA 98421, phone (206) 628-9280 or 1-800-426-0074.

Vehicle shipment between southeastern Alaska and Seattle is provided by Alaska Marine Lines, 5615 W. Marginal Way SW, Seattle, WA 98106, phone (206) 763-4244 or toll free (800) 950-4AML or (800) 326-8346 (direct service to Ketchikan, Wrangell, Prince of Wales Island, Kake, Petersburg, Sitka, Juneau, Haines, Skagway, Yakutat, Excursion Inlet and Hawk Inlet). Boyer Alaska Barge Line, 7318 4th Ave. S., Seattle, WA 98108,

Moose are commonly seen along roads in Alaska. (© Robin Brandt)

phone (206) 763-8575 (serves Ketchikan, Metlakatla, Prince of Wales Island and Wrangell).

Persons shipping vehicles between Seattle/Tacoma and Anchorage are advised to shop around for the carrier that offers the services and rates most suited to the shipper's needs. Not every carrier offers year-round service, and freight charges vary greatly depending upon the carrier and the length and height of the vehicle. Rates increase frequently and the potential shipper is cautioned to call carriers' rate departments for those rates in effect at shipping time. An approximate sample fare from Seattle/Tacoma to Anchorage to ship a 4-door sedan one-way is $1,141; for a truck, you might pay $1,332. From Anchorage to Seattle/Tacoma, it is approximately $738 for a vehicle and $919 to ship a truck.

Not all carriers accept rented moving trucks and trailers, and a few of those that do, require authorization from the rental company to carry its equipment to Alaska. Check with the carrier and your rental company before booking service.

Book your reservation at least 2 weeks in advance and 3 weeks during summer months, and prepare to have the vehicle at the carrier's loading facility 2 days prior to sailing. Carriers differ on what non-vehicle items they allow to travel inside, from nothing at all to goods packaged and addressed separately. Coast Guard regulations forbid the transport of vehicles holding more than one-quarter tank of gas, and none of the carriers listed above allow owners to accompany their vehicles in transit. Remember to have fresh antifreeze installed in your car or truck prior to sailing!

Household Goods and Personal Effects: Most moving van lines have service to and from Alaska through their agency connections in most Alaska and Lower 48 cities. To initiate service contact the van line agents nearest your origin point.

Northbound goods are shipped to Seattle and transferred through a port agent to a water vessel for carriage to Alaska. Few shipments go over the road to Alaska. Southbound shipments are processed in a like manner through Alaska ports to Seattle, then on to destination.

U-Haul provides service into the North Country for those who prefer to move their goods themselves. There are 53 U-Haul dealerships in Alaska and northwestern Canada for over-the-road service. In Alaska, there are 8 dealerships in Anchorage, 6 in Fairbanks, 2 in Soldotna and Juneau and 1 in each of the following communities: Eagle River, Glennallen, Homer, Ketchikan, Delta Junction, Kenai, Palmer, Petersburg, Seward, Tok, Valdez, Wasilla, Sitka and North Pole. In Canada, there are dealerships and ready stations in Dawson City (summer only), Fort St. John, Fort Nelson, Whitehorse and at other locations along the Alaska Highway. There are also breakdown stations for service of U-Haul vehicles in Beaver Creek, Swift River and the Kluane Wilderness Area.

It's also possible to ship a rented truck or trailer into southeastern Alaska aboard the water carriers that accept privately owned vehicles (see Shipping Vehicles). A few of the water carriers sailing between Seattle and Anchorage also carry rented equipment. However, shop around for this service, for this has not been common practice in the past, and rates can be very high if the carrier does not yet have a specific tariff established for this type of shipment. You will not be allowed to accompany the rented equipment. Be aware, however, that U-Haul allows its equipment to be shipped on TOTE or Sea-Land, resulting in a 30 percent savings over the price of driving it between Seattle and Anchorage.

When to go

One of the most often asked questions is "when is the best time to travel?" The high season is June through August, generally the warmest and sunniest months in the North, although July is often one of the wettest months in some regions. The weather is as variable and unpredictable in the North as anywhere else. Go prepared for sunny hot days and cold rainy days. Waterproof footwear is always a good idea, as are a warm coat and rain gear. Generally, dress is casual. Comfortable shoes and easy-care clothes are best. There are stores in the North—just like at home—where you can buy whatever you forgot to bring along. There are laundromats (some with showers) in most communities and dry cleaners in the major cities and some smaller towns.

Because most people travel in the summer, filling up hotels, motels, campgrounds and ferries, you might consider an early spring (April or May) or fall (late August into October) trip. There's usually more room at the lodges and campgrounds and on the ferries in these shoulder seasons. The weather can also be quite beautiful in early spring and in the fall. Keep in mind that some tours, attractions, lodges and other businesses operate seasonally. Check the advertisements in *The MILEPOST* for details on months of operation or call ahead if in doubt.

While June through August are the warmest months, weather can be really beautiful—clear, sunny and mild—in spring and fall. (Record highs for summer are generally in the 90s with record winter lows to minus 60 degrees.) Precipitation is normally heaviest in August and September in Anchorage; July and August in Fairbanks; and September and October in Juneau. But it can be a dry or a wet summer, depending on El Niño and other variable factors.

The landscape "greens up" in late May, and June has the longest days (21 hours and 49 minutes of daylight on June 21 in Fairbanks). Wildflowers peak in July. The trees and tundra are especially colorful in the fall; they start turning in late August. The days are short in winter (3 hours and 42 minutes of daylight is the winter solstice minimum in Fairbanks), but people who choose to live in the North feel that the winter has a special beauty all its own, and there are many popular events in winter (Fur Rendezvous and the Iditarod, for example).

The following numbers provide recorded weather information: Anchorage, (907) 936-2525; Fairbanks, (907) 452-3553; Alaska Highway in BC, (250) 774-6461; Alaska Highway in Yukon Territory, (867) 668-6061; Dawson Creek, BC, (250) 784-2244. The Alaska region National Weather Service Internet address is www.alaska.net/~nwsar/.

Wildlife

The opportunity to observe and photograph birds and mammals is a major attraction for visitors to the North. *The MILEPOST* road logs point out wildlife viewing spots along the highways where travelers have a good chance of seeing Dall sheep, moose, caribou, mountain goats, eagles, sandhill cranes, and other mammals and birds.

Besides the chance encounter with wildlife along the roads or in the parks, Alaska offers several opportunities for planned wildlife viewing, such as bear observatories (see "Bears" on page 12), bird festivals (Copper River Delta Shorebird Festival in Cordova, and Kachemak Bay Shorebird Festival in Homer, both in May, and the Haines Bald Eagle Festival in November), custom bird-watching trips, and sightseeing cruises.

The privately operated summer sightseeing cruises to view Alaska's glaciated coastline provide a great opportunity to see wildlife: sea otters, Steller sea lions, dolphins, harbor seals, Dall porpoises, whales (minke, gray, fin, humpback), puffins, eagles, black-legged kittiwakes, common murres, cormorants, parakeet and rhinoceros auklets, among others. Some of these popular destinations—such as Kenai Fjords, Glacier Bay, Prince William Sound, Kachemak Bay—as well as other inland lake and river cruises offer unique opportunities to see wildlife.

Visitors may not see North America's largest rodent while traveling in Alaska, but they probably will see its work: Beaver dams reaching 15 feet in height and hundreds of feet in length are not uncommon.

Much more visible are 2 members of the squirrel familiy: the arctic ground squirrel and the hoary marmot. There's also a good chance of seeing snowshoe hare, especially during cyclical population highs.

Moose and caribou are commonly spotted from the road. Moose can be aggressive; never approach them.

Best rules for observing all wildlife, especially the larger mammals: Keep your distance and do not feed them. Contact the Alaska Dept. of Fish and Game for more information on wildlife watching.

Alaska Highway via
EAST ACCESS ROUTE ⑮ ② ③ ④ ㊸

Connects: Great Falls, MT, to Dawson Creek, BC   **Length:** 866 miles
Road Surface: Paved   **Season:** Open all year
Major Attractions: Waterton Lakes National Park, Head-Smashed-In Buffalo Jump, Royal Tyrrell Museum, Fort Edmonton Park

(See maps, pages 34–35)

	Calgary	Dawson Creek	Edmonton	Great Falls	Lethbridge	Valleyview
Calgary		548	181	318	140	395
Dawson Creek	548		367	866	688	153
Edmonton	181	367		499	321	214
Great Falls	318	866	499		178	713
Lethbridge	140	688	321	178		535
Valleyview	395	153	214	713	535	

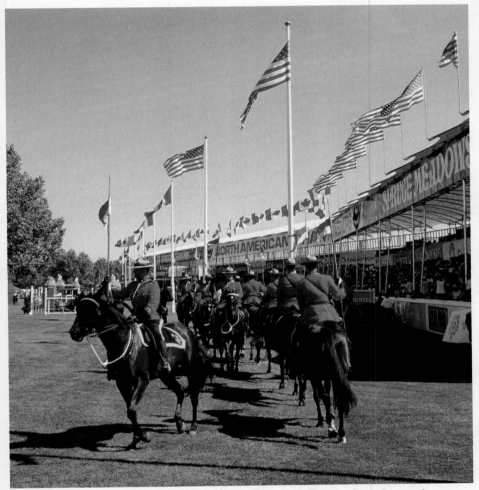

Royal Canadian Mounted Police Musical Ride at Spruce Meadows Equestrian Center south of Calgary. (Blake Hanna, staff)

The East Access Route is logged in *The MILEPOST®* as one of the 2 major access routes (the other is the West Access Route) to the Alaska Highway. When the Alaska Highway opened to civilian traffic in 1948, this was the only access route to Dawson Creek, BC, the start of the highway.

Highways on this route are all paved primary routes, with visitor services available along the way. Total driving distance from Great Falls, MT, to Dawson Creek, BC, is 867 miles/1,394 km.

The East Access Route log is divided into 3 sections: Great Falls to Sweetgrass, MT, at the Canadian border; Coutts, AB, at the Canadian border to Edmonton; and Edmonton to Dawson Creek, BC.

East Access Route Log

This section of the log shows distance from Great Falls (GF) followed by distance from Sweetgrass (SG). Physical mileposts and exit numbers reflect distance from Idaho–Montana border.

INTERSTATE HIGHWAY 15

GF 0 SG 117.5 (189 km) Exit 280 to **GREAT FALLS** (pop. 55,100; elev. 3,333 feet/1,016m), Montana's second largest city, located at the confluence of the Sun and Missouri rivers, Great Falls is home to the Charles M. Russell Museum. Giant Springs State Park on the north edge of the city has one of the largest springs in the world. The Roe River, which flows out of the springs, is 201 feet long and recognized by the Guiness Book of Records as the world's shortest river.

GF 10.5 (16.9 km) **SG 107** (172.2 km) Exit 290 west to U.S. Highway 89/Choteau.

GF 33.5 (53.9 km) **SG 84** (135.2 km) **Junction** with MT Highway 221 and exit 313 to Dutton; services.

GF 38.5 (61.9 km) **SG 79** (127.1 km) Rest areas near Teton River bridge.

GF 47 (75.6 km) **SG 70.5** (113.4 km) Exit 328 to Brady; services.

GF 54.5 (87.7 km) **SG 63** (101.4 km) Exit 335 to Midway Road.

GF 58.5 (94.1 km) **SG 59** (94.9 km) Exit 339 to **CONRAD** (pop. 3,074); 3 motels, 2 private campgrounds. ▲.

GF 68.5 (110.2 km) **SG 49** (78.9 km) Exit 348 to **junction** with MT Highway 44 west to Valier and Lake Frances Recreation Area.

GF 73.5 (118.3 km) **SG 44** (70.8 km) Exit 352 to Bullhead Road and Marias River picnic area.

GF 81.5 (131.2 km) **SG 36** (57.9 km) Exit 363 to **SHELBY** (pop. 3,000); all visitor services available, inlcuding several private campgrounds. Marias Museum of History and Art located across from city park. ▲

Junction with U.S. Highway 2 to Cut Bank and Glacier National Park.

GF 98.5 (158.5 km) **SG 19** (30.5 km) Exit 379 to Kevin/MT highway 215 and Oilmont/MT Highway 343; services.

GF 109.5 (176.2 km) **SG 8** (12.9 km) Exit 389 to **SUNBURST** (pop. 520); all services.

GF 117.5 (189 km) **SG 0** Exit 397 to rest area at **SWEETGRASS** at U.S.–Canada border; food, gas, and lodging. Duty-free shop. Customs and immigration open 24 hours a day.

This section of the log shows distance from the Canadian border (CB) followed by distance from Edmonton (E).

ALBERTA HIGHWAY 4

CB 0 E 382.2 (615 km) U.S.–Canada border, **COUTTS** border crossing; customs and immigration open 24 hours a day. Food, *(Continues on page 36)*

EAST ACCESS ROUTE Great Falls, MT, to Edmonton, AB

© 1999 The MILEPOST®

(map continues next page)

To Slave Lake

Edmonton
N53°33' W113°30'

To Jasper ←
(see YELLOWHEAD
HIGHWAY 16 section)

To Saskatoon →

Chip Lake

43

16

16

60

Wabamun Lake

J-10.2/16.4km Devon Lions Club Campground C

Devon

19

Leduc

DC-367/591km
E-0
CB-382/615km
PG-450/724km

39

River

Saskatchewan

2

North

Ponoka

Lacombe

E-91/146km
CB-291/469km

Red Deer

Innisfail

Bowden

Olds

N

W — E

S

Red

Deer

River

Red

Deer

River

ROCKY

BRITISH COLUMBIA

ALBERTA

Carstairs

Crossfield

72

Drumheller
J-60.1/96.8km Drumheller Regional Chamber
of Development and Tourism

Airdrie

Balzac

N51°05' W114°05'

To Jasper

To Revelstoke ←

Golden

95

93

Banff

1

Bow River

Calgary

CB-188.6/303.5km Pine Creek RV
Campground C

E-181/292km
CB-201/323km

1 → To Regina

Bow River

Columbia River

Kootenay River

M O U N T A I N S

Columbia Lake

Sheep River

High River

Willow Creek

Nanton

E-286/460km
CB-96/155km

95

93

Stavely

Claresholm

CB-111.2/179km Granview
RV Park CDT

E-319/514km
CB-63/101km

Keho Lake

N49°42' W112°50'

Crowsnest Pass
4,534 ft./1,3825m

Frank

Head-Smashed-In Buffalo
Jump World Heritage Site

3

785

Oldman R.

Monarch

3

3 → To Regina

Lethbridge

4

Stirling

New Dayton

Cranbrook

6

Fort
Macleod

Oldman R.

5

52

Warner

Waterton Lakes
National Park

Raymond

2

Milk River

To Hope ←

3

Kingsgate

BRITISH COLUMBIA
IDAHO

Eastport

CANADA
UNITED STATES

Waterton
Park

5

Cardston

501

Coutts

N49°00' W111°57'

ALBERTA
MONTANA

Sweetgrass

E-382/615km
CB-0
GF-118/189km

89

Lake Koocanusa

Glacier
National
Park

2

To Medicine Hat →

To Spokane ←

95

2

37

93

2

Browning

Shelby

2

Sandpoint

2

Kalispell

Lake
Francis

Conrad

Brady

To Medicine Hat →

89

GF-0
SG-118/189km

15

87

N47°5' W111°3'

Great Falls

15

To Helena

87

To Billings

Principal Route

Paved ▬▬▬▬
Unpaved ▭▭▭▭

Other Roads

Paved ▬▬
Unpaved ▭▭

Ferry Routes
Hiking Trails

Refer to Log for Visitor Facilities

Scale

0 ___ 20 Miles
0 ___ 20 Kilometres

Key to Advertiser
Services

C - Camping
D - Dump Station
d - Diesel
G - Gas (reg., unld.)
I - Ice
L - Lodging
M - Meals
P - Propane
R - Car Repair (major)
r - Car Repair (minor)
S - Store (grocery)
T - Telephone (pay)

Map Location

Key to mileage boxes

miles/kilometres
miles/kilometres
from:

GF- Great Falls
SG- Sweetgrass
PG- Prince George
CB- Canadian Border
E- Edmonton
DC- Dawson Creek

EAST ACCESS ROUTE
Edmonton, AB, to Dawson Creek, BC

© 1999 The MILEPOST®

Key to mileage boxes from:
CB-Canadian Border
E-Edmonton
DC-Dawson Creek
PG-Prince George
Y-Yellowhead Hwy. Jct.
GP-Grande Prairie

miles/kilometres
miles/kilometres

Map Location

To Fort McMurray

Northern Woods & Waters Route

Lesser Slave Lake

Winagami Lake

To Yellowknife
(see MACKENZIE ROUTE section)

Northern Woods & Waters Route

To Fort St. John
(see ALASKA HIGHWAY section, page 83)

To Chetwynd
(see WEST ACCESS ROUTE section, page 55)

Heritage Highway

DC-0
E-367/591km
PG-250/402km
Dawson Creek

N55°46'
W120°14'

Pouce Coupe

Tupper

E-342/550.4km Last Chance Bi-Lo dG

E-311/500.5km Town of Beaverlodge

Demmitt

Hythe

Beaverlodge

Wembley

DC-83/134km
E-284/457km
GP-0
Y-207/333km

Woking

Bear River

Spirit River

Rycroft

Dunvegan

Fairview

Hines Creek

Grimshaw

Y-88/142km
GP-119/191km

Sexsmith

Bezanson

E-262/421.6km West Smoky RV Campsite CD

Grande Prairie
N55°10' W118°48'

Nampa

Peace River

Donnelly

McLennan

Triangle

High Prairie

Joussard

Slave Lake

Smith

Athabasca
N54°43'
W113°16'

Clyde

Westlock

Onoway

Spruce Grove
Stony Plain

DC-367/591km
E-0
CB-382/615km
PG-450/724km

Edmonton
N53°33' W113°30'

(map continues previous page)

E-10/16km Glowing Embers Travel Centre CDiST

E-19.3/31km Bears & Bedtime Mfg.

Wabamun Lake

North Saskatchewan River

E-47.3/76.1km Gunn General Store RV & Campground CDdGiMPST

E-74/119.2km Ol'Pembina River Ferry Crossing RV Park CDiT

Sangudo

Mayerthorpe

E-79.3/127.7km Rochfort Bridge Trading Post M

Whitecourt
N54°08' W115°41'

DC-255/411km
E-112/180km

DC-205/330km
E-162/261km

Fox Creek

E-192/309km Little Smoky Motel, Restaurant & Campground CDLMT

Little Smoky

E-186.4/300km Sands Wilderness Campground & RV Park CD

Iosegun L.

Smoke Lake

Swan Hills

Grizzly Trail

Edson

Y-0
GP-207/333km

To Jasper
(see YELLOWHEAD HIGHWAY 16 section)

Forestry Trunk Road

DC-153/246km
E-214/344km
Valleyview
N55°04' W117°17'

Calais

Crooked Creek

Debolt

E-230/370.1km Cosy Cove Campground & Marina CDiST

Surgeon R.

Grande Cache

Big Horn Highway

ROCKY MOUNTAINS

Little Smoky River

Smoky River

Wapiti River

BRITISH COLUMBIA
ALBERTA

Peace River

Smoky River

Key to Advertiser Services
C-Camping
D-Dump Station
d-Diesel
G-Gas (reg., unld.)
I-Ice
L-Lodging
M-Meals
P-Propane
R-Car Repair (major)
r-Car Repair (minor)
S-Store (grocery)
T-Telephone (pay)
Refer to Log for Visitor Facilities

Principal Route
Paved
Unpaved
Other Roads
Paved
Unpaved
Ferry Routes **Hiking Trails**

Scale
Miles
Kilometres

(Continued from page 33)

gas and lodging at border. Duty-free shop.

NOTE: Watch for road construction at the border in 1999.

CB 9.9 (15.9 km) **E 372.3** (599.1 km) **Junction** with Secondary Road 501, which leads west 67 miles/108 km to **CARDSTON** (pop. 3,502), located at the **junction** of Highways 2, 5 and 501. Established in 1887 by Mormon pioneers from Utah, Cardston's **Remington–Alberta Carriage Centre** features one of the world's foremost collections of horse-drawn vehicles.

Waterton Park, 25 miles/40.2 km west of Cardston, is the tourist centre for **Waterton Lakes National Park.** Known for its dramatic lake and mountain scenery, Waterton Lakes is actually one large lake broken into 3 sections—Lower, Middle and Upper Waterton lakes. Lower Waterton Lake extnds down into Montana. Park adjoins Glacier National Park in Montana, and the 2 parks together are known as the Waterton–Glacier International Peace Park. Both parks are also noted for their grand old hotels. The Prince of Wales Hotel, just north of the townsite, was built in 1927 by the Great Northern Railway.

CB 10.4 (16.7 km) **E 371.8** (598.3 km) Turnout with litter barrels.

CB 11.9 (19.1 km) **E 370.3** (595.9 km) Milk River Travel Information and Interpretive Centre; picnic tables, dump station and travel information. The large dinosaur model on display here makes a good photo subject. Advanced bookings for Alberta adventures and attractions available here, open mid-May to Labour Day weekend for tickets.

CB 13 (21 km) **E 369.2** (594.1 km) **MILK RIVER** (pop. 926) has food, gas, stores, lodging and a small public campground (6 informal sites; no hookups). The 8 flags flying over the campground represent 7 countries and the Hudson's Bay Co., all of which once laid claim to the Milk River area. Grain elevators are on the west side of the highway, services are on the east side.▲

CB 13.5 (21.7 km) **E 368.7** (593.3 km) **Junction** with Secondary Road 501 east to **Writing-on-Stone Provincial Park**, 26 miles/42 km; camping, Indian petroglyphs.

CB 23.6 (38 km) **E 358.6** (577.1 km) Road west to **WARNER** (pop. 434); store, gas, restaurant. Warner is the gateway to **Devil's Coulee Dinosaur Egg Site**, where dinosaur eggs, and fossilized fish and reptiles were discovered in 1987. Visits to Devil's Coulee are by tour bus only, as the site is still under excavation. The tour buses leave the Dinosaur Egg Interpretive Centre in Warner from June to mid-September.

CB 23.8 (38.3 km) **E 358.4** (576.8 km) **Junction** with Highway 36A north to Taber, centre of Alberta's sugar beet industry.

CB 36.3 (58.5 km) **E 345.9** (556.6 km) Small community of New Dayton.

CB 41 (66 km) **E 341.2** (549.1 km) **Junction** at Craddock elevators with Highway 52 west to Raymond (10 miles/16 km), site of the annual Stampede and Heritage Days; Magrath (20 miles/32 km); Cardston (46 miles/74 km); and Waterton Lakes National Park (74 miles/119 km).

CB 44.4 (71.4 km) **E 337.8** (543.6 km) Small community of Stirling to west; municipal campground with 15 sites, some with power and water, dump station, showers and tennis court. Grain elevators and rail yards alongside highway. Stirling is the oldest, best-preserved Mormon settlement in Canada and a National Historic Site. ▲

CB 46.1 (74.2 km) **E 336.1** (540.9 km) **Junction** with Highway 61 east to Cypress Hills.

CB 62.7 (100.9 km) **E 319.5** (514.2 km) **Junction** with Highway 5 south to Cardston (48 miles/77 km south) and Waterton Park (81 miles/131 km). Mayor Magrath Drive to north provides access to Lethbridge motels, hotels and Henderson Lake Park (see city description following). Continue west on Scenic Drive for access to Indian Battle Park (via Whoop-Up Drive) and junction with Crowsnest Highway 3.

Chinook Country Tourist Information Centre, on the north side of the intersection of Highways 4, 5 and Mayor Magrath Drive, has RV parking, restrooms, picnic shelter, dump station and dumpster; open year-round.

Lethbridge

CB 63 (101.4 km) **E 319.2** (513.7 km) At junction of Highways 3, 4 and 5. **Population:** 66,000. **Elevation:** 3,048 feet/929m. **Emergency Services:** Phone 911 for police, ambulance and fire department. **Hospital:** Lethbridge Regional Hospital, phone (403) 382-6111.

Visitor Information: Chinook Country Tourist Association, on the north side of the intersection of Highways 4, 5 and Mayor Magrath Drive, has souvenirs, RV parking, restrooms, picnic shelter, dump station and dumpster; open year-round. Phone (800) 661-1222 and ask for operator 48 (while in

---

LETHBRIDGE ADVERTISERS

Chinook Country Tourist
   Assoc. ....Ph. (800) 661-1222
Best Western Heidelberg
   Inn ....Ph. (800) 791-8488
Lethbridge R.V. Parks ....2 locations—see ad
Quality Inn Lethbridge ....Ph. (800) 561-9815

the area call 320-1222) for information on attractions and facilities in southwest Alberta. A tourist information centre is also located at Highway 3 at the west entrance to the city next to the Brewery Gardens; open March 1 to Oct. 31. **Newspaper:** *The Lethbridge Herald* (daily).

Private Aircraft: Airport 4 miles/6.4 km southeast; elev. 3,047 feet/929m; length 6,500 feet/1,981m; paved, fuel 100, jet. FSS.

The Lethbridge region was home to 3 Indian nations: the Sik-si-kah (Blackfoot), Kai'nah (Many Chiefs, now called Bloods), and Pi-ku'ni (Scabby Robes, now called Peigans). Collectively, they formed the Sow-ki'tapi (Prairie People). Because European fur traders along the North Saskatchewan River first came into contact with the Blackfoot, that tribal name came to be applied to the entire confederacy.

In 1869, the American Army decided to stop trade in alcohol with Indians on reservations across Montana. In December 1869, 2 American traders, John Jerome Healy and Alfred Baker Hamilton, built a trading post at the junction of the St. Mary and Belly (now Oldman) rivers, near the future site of Lethbridge. The post became known as Fort Whoop-Up, the most notorious of some 44 trading posts built in southern Alberta from 1869 to 1874. An important trade commodity was "whiskey," a concoction of 9 parts river water to 1 part pure alcohol, to which was added a plug of chewing tobacco for colour and a can of lye for more taste. The mixture was boiled to bring out its full flavour, and well deserved the Indian name "firewater."

Alarmed by the activities of the whiskey

traders, Prime Minister Sir John A. Macdonald formed the North West Mounted Police (NWMP), now the Royal Canadian Mounted Police, to bring law and order to the West. The NWMP reached Fort Whoop-Up on Oct. 9, 1874, and immediately put a stop to the whiskey trade.

Early development of Lethbridge commenced in 1874 with the arrival of Nicholas Sheran in search of gold. The gold, in fact, turned out to be black gold—coal—and by the late 1870s a steady coal market and permanent settlement had developed. Elliot Galt, working with his father, Sir Alexander

Galt, helped pioneer coal shipments on the Oldman River and later a narrow-gauge railway that connected to the mainline of the Canadian Pacific Railway.

The climax of the early development of Lethbridge came with the CPR construction in 1909 of the high level rail bridge that today carries freight shipments by rail westward through Crowsnest Pass to Vancouver, and onward by ship to the Pacific Rim. The "Bridge"—with a mile-long span and 300-foot elevation—is still the longest and highest bridge of its kind in the world.

Today, Lethbridge is Alberta's third largest city. It has a strong agricultural economy. In late June and early July, bright yellow fields of canola surround the highways leading into the city. Other fields, both irrigated and dryland, produce wheat, sugar beets, potatoes, corn and a variety of other crops.

Lethbridge is southwest Alberta's service and shopping centre, with several malls and a variety of retail businesses. There is a wide choice of restaurants, hotel/motel accommodations, and bed and breakfasts.

There are 2 campgrounds in the city: Henderson Lake campground and Bridgeview campground. ▲

Henderson Lake Park also holds several of the city's attractions, including the **Nikka Yuko Japanese Garden**, a golf course, swimming pool, picnic area and rose gardens. The Lethbridge Black Diamonds professional baseball team also plays at the park.

An extensive trail system leads to **Indian Battle Park** in the beautiful Oldman River valley. Indian Battle Park showcases a replica of **Fort Whoop-Up**, the Helen Schuler Coulee Centre, the Sir Alexander Galt Museum and the High Level Bridge.

Lethbridge hosts the Ag–Expo in March and the Lethbridge International Airshow and Whoop-Up Days in August.

The Alberta Birds of Prey Centre, a 10-minute drive east of Lethbridge, is a 70-acre working conservation centre featuring hawks, falcons, eagles and owls from around rld. Live flying shows with hawks and falcons are presented, weather permitting.

Open May 1 to early October, 10:30 A.M. to 5 P.M.; admission fee charged.

Best Western Heidelberg Inn offering 66 immaculate rooms in modern 9-story building. On-site facilities include J.B.'s Restaurant, Hi Pub, and sauna and fitness room. AAA Three Diamond rating. Awards points for: Gold Crown Club, Canadian Plus, American Advantage, Alaska Airlines, American West Airlines and Petro Points. Top exchange on U.S. funds. 1303 Mayor Magrath Dr., Lethbridge, AB. Reservations 1-800-791-8488; fax (403) 328-8846.
[ADVERTISEMENT]

Lethbridge R.V. Parks. Lethbridge has 2 beautiful RV parks. Bridgeview, on the banks of the Oldman River, has 100 serviced sites, a brand new 10,000-square-foot clubhouse which includes a registration office, large laundromat and bright, clean washrooms. A new Olympic-sized heated pool, lots of pull-throughs, shade and easy access from Highway 3. Phone (403) 381-2357. Henderson Lake RV Park is centrally located in the city, has 100 sites, close to shopping, restaurants, golf. Phone (403) 328-5452. At both parks you will receive a sampling of friendly Alberta hospitality. See display ad this section. [ADVERTISEMENT] ▲

East Access Route Log
(continued)

CB 66.6 (107.2 km) E 315.6 (507.9 km) **Junction** with Crowsnest Highway 3. Tourist information centre beside Brewery Gardens.

CROWSNEST HIGHWAY 3

CB 69.5 (111.8 km) E 312.7 (503.2 km) **Junction** with Highway 25. Access to **Park Lake Provincial Park** (9 miles/14 km north); 53 campsites, swimming, boat launch, fishing, playground. ◄▲

CB 71.9 (115.7 km) E 310.3 (499.4 km) Rest area with litter barrels and historical information sign about Coalhurst.

CB 72.4 (116.5 km) E 309.8 (498.6 km) Community of Coalhurst just north of highway; gas station.

CB 73.8 (118.9 km) E 308.4 (496.3 km) CPR marshalling yards at Kipp.

CB 77.5 (124.7 km) E 304.7 (490.3 km)

Large turnout with litter barrels and information sign about Coalhurst Mine Disaster.

CB 78.8 (126.8 km) E 303.4 (488.3 km) **Junction** with Highway 23 north. Continue west on Highway 3 for Fort Macleod.

CB 81.5 (131.2 km) E 300.7 (483.9 km) Westbound, the highway enters Oldman River valley. Good view west of the Rockies on a clear day.

CB 82.9 (133.4 km) E 299.3 (481.7 km) **Junction** with Highway 3A.

CB 95.7 (154 km) E 286.5 (461.1 km) **Junction** with Highway 2 south to Cardston and the U.S. border, with access to Waterton Lakes and Glacier national parks. Continue on Highway 3.

Fort Macleod

CB 96.1 (154.7 km) E 286.1 (460.4 km) Turn south for tourist services and town centre. **Population:** 3,100. **Elevation:** 3,300 feet/1,006m. **Visitor Information:** Tourist office adjacent replica of Fort Macleod north of highway.

There are several hotels and motels, campgrounds, restaurants, shopping facilities and gas stations. This community's Main Street is a designated historic site; walking tours are offered.

The main attraction in Fort Macleod is the **Fort Macleod Museum**, a replica of Fort Macleod, which features the history of the Mounted Police, local Native cultures and early pioneers, in a fort setting. The original fort, named for Colonel J.F. Macleod, was built in 1874 and was the first outpost of the North West Mounted Police (later the RCMP) in western Canada.

During July and August, the museum features a local re-creation of the official RCMP Musical Ride: Youth in NWMP uniforms execute drills on horseback in a colorful display. The museum is open daily from May to mid-October; open weekdays the rest of the year (closed Dec. 24 to March 1). ▲

The Sunset Motel, winner of 11 Travel Alberta Housekeeping Awards, 2 Diamond AAA/CAA rated, and an Alberta Best property, emphasizes clean, comfortable rooms, friendly service and reasonable prices. They offer air-conditioned 1-, 2-, and 3-room units, free toast and coffee, refrigerators, kitchenettes, remote control cable televisions, free movies, direct dial touch-tone phones, free local calls and Native crafts shop. Laundromat, convenience store, gas and fast food adjacent. Full U.S. exchange. Off-season rates Oct. 1 to May 15. Easy access to Highways 2 and 3. Closest motel to Head-Smashed-In Buffalo Jump World Heritage Site. 104 Highway 3 West. Phone (403)553-4448. Toll-free reservations 1-888-554-2784. E-mail: sunsetmo@telusplanet.net. [ADVERTISEMENT]

East Access Route Log
(continued)

CB 99 (159.4 km) E 283.2 (455.8 km) **Junction** with Highway 2 north to Calgary and Edmonton. Highway 3 (Crowsnest) continues 600 miles/965.6 km west to Hope, BC. The highway takes its name from Crowsnest Pass (elev. 4,534 feet/1,382m), one of the lowest passes in the Rockies, which Highway 3 crosses 65.5 miles/105.5 km west of here.

ALBERTA HIGHWAY 2
CB 100 (160.8 km) E 282.2 (454.1 km)

Escarpment at Head-Smashed-In Buffalo Jump, the oldest, largest and best preserved buffalo jump in North America. *(Blake Hanna, staff)*

Oldman River bridge. Alberta government campground to southwest with 10 campsites, dump station, playground, fishing and swimming. North of the river is the largest turkey farm in Alberta. ●◄▲

CB 100.4 (161.6 km) **E 281.8** (453.5 km) **Junction** with Highway 785, which leads 10 miles/16 km to **Head-Smashed-In Buffalo Jump**, a UNESCO World Heritage Site. The 1,000-foot/305-m-long cliff, where Plains peoples stampeded buffalo to their deaths for nearly 6,000 years, is one of the world's oldest, largest and best-preserved buffalo jumps. The site was named, according to legend, for a young brave whose skull was crushed when he tried to watch the stampede from under a protective ledge which gave way. An interpretive centre houses artifacts and displays describing the buffalo hunting culture. First Nations interpretive guides available on site. Guided walks available twice daily during July and August. Open year-round; 9 A.M. to 7 P.M., June 1 to Labour Day; 9 A.M. to 5 P.M., Labour Day through May; closed major holidays. Admission fee charged.

CB 111.2 (179 km) **E 271** (436.1 km) **Junction** with Highway 519 east to small settlement of **GRANUM**. Private RV park with 27 campsites.

Granview RV Park. Easy access off Highway 2, 1/2 mile east on Highway 519. 17 large, fully-serviced sites, some pull-through, plus 10 unserviced sites. Firepits, free hot showers. Swimming and fishing lake adjacent to park. 2-minute walk to 9-hole par 3 golf course and driving range. Short drive to Head-Smashed-In Buffalo Jump World Heritage Site and other prime tourist attractions. Reservations phone 1-888-788-2222 or (403) 687-3830. ▲

CB 116.2 (187 km) **E 266** (428 km) Community of Woodhouse.

CB 121.8 (196 km) **E 260.4** (419.1 km) **CLARESHOLM** (pop. 3,427), a prosperous ranching centre with all visitor facilities. The old railway station houses a museum and tourist infocentre. Camping at Centennial Park; 17 sites, dump station, playground. ▲

CB 125.5 (201.9 km) **E 256.7** (413.1 km) Turnout with litter cans and historical information sign about Stavely.

CB 131.3 (211.3 km) **E 250.9** (403.8 km) Community of Stavely to the east.

CB 132.1 (212.6 km) **E 250.1** (402.5 km) Access road west to **Willow Creek** Provincial Park; 150 campsites, swimming, fishing. ●◄▲

CB 138.4 (222.8 km) **E 243.8** (392.3 km) Small settlement of Parkland.

CB 145.9 (234.8 km) **E 236.3** (380.3 km) Nanton campground (75 sites) at **junction** with Secondary Road 533, which leads west to Chain Lakes Provincial Park. ▲

CB 146.8 (236.3 km) **E 235.4** (378.8 km) **NANTON** (pop. 1,665); all visitor facilities. Nanton is famous for its springwater, which is piped from Big Spring in the Porcupine Hills, 6 miles/10 km west of town, to a large tap located in town centre. Springwater tap operates mid-May to September. WWII Lancaster bomber on display at **Lancaster Air Museum** on Highway 2 South.

CB 151.1 (243.2 km) **E 231.1** (371.9 km) **Junction** with Highway 2A, which parallels Highway 2 northbound.

CB 162.8 (262 km) **E 219.4** (353.1 km) **Junction** with Highway 23 west to **HIGH RIVER** (pop. 6,893) located on Highway 2A. All visitor facilities. Once the centre of a harness-making industry, High River has elegant sandstone buildings and the Museum of the Highwood (open in summer).

CB 164 (264 km) **E 218.2** (351.1 km) Stop of interest commemorating Spitzee Post, built in 1869.

CB 171.6 (276.1 km) **E 210.6** (338.9 km) **Junction** at Aldersyde with Highways 2A and 7 to Okotoks, Black Diamond and Turner Valley (18.5 miles/30 km). Stop of interest commemorating the Turner Valley oil fields.

CB 173.3 (278.9 km) **E 208.9** (336.2 km) Sheep Creek bridge. **Sheep Creek** Provincial Park has a picnic area, playground, swimming and fishing. ●

CB 183 (294.5 km) **E 199.2** (320.6 km) **Junction** with Highway 2A to **OKOTOKS** (5 miles/8 km west), which has a general store, RV repair and a tea room. Near Okotoks is **Spruce Meadows Equestrian Center**, which

hosts the International Horse Show, June to September; phone (403) 974-4200.

CB 184.6 (297.2 km) **E 197.6** (318 km) Restaurant and gas station with diesel and propane to east.

CB 188.6 (303.5 km) **E 193.6** (311.6 km) Calgary southern city limits. Private RV park to east. ▲

Pine Creek R.V. Campground. See display ad this section. ▲

NOTE: To bypass downtown Calgary, exit at Marquis of Lorne Trail and continue to Highway 2 (Deerfoot Trail) north.

CB 196.5 (316.2 km) **E 185.7** (298.8 km) Exit for Glenmore Trail, the southwest bypass route that connects with Trans-Canada Highway 1 west to Banff and Vancouver, BC.

Calgary

CB 200.8 (323.1 km) **E 181.4** (291.9 km) Located at the confluence of the Bow and Elbow rivers. **Population:** 767,059. **Elevation:** 3,440 feet/ 1,049m. **Emergency Services:** Phone 911 for emergency services. **Hospitals:** Bow Valley Centre, 841 Centre Ave. NE; Foothills, 1403 29th St. NW; Rockyview, 7007 14th St. SW; Peter Lougheed Center, 3500 26th Ave. NE.

Visitor Information: In the downtown area at the base of Calgary Tower, and at the Calgary Airport; both are open year-round. A visitor centre at Canada Olympic Park is open in summer only. Or call Calgary Convention & Visitors Bureau at (403) 263-8510 or (800) 661-1678 (toll-free in North America).

Private Aircraft: Calgary International Airport, 4 miles/6.4 km northeast; elev. 3,557 feet/1,084m; 3 runways. See Canadian Flight Supplement.

This bustling city is one of Alberta's 2 major population and business centres. A great influx of homesteaders came to Calgary with the completion of the Canadian Pacific Railway in 1883. It grew as a trading centre for surrounding farms and ranches. Oil and gas discovered south of the city in 1914 contributed to more growth.

Perhaps the city's best-known attraction is the annual **Calgary Stampede**, which takes place at the Exhibition Grounds, July 9–18, 1999. The 10-day event includes a parade and daily rodeo; phone (800) 661-1260 for Stampede information and tickets.

Some other major attractions are: Calgary Science Centre, 11th Street and 7th Avenue; the Glenbow Museum, which presents a lively journey into the heritage of the Canadian West, 130 9th Avenue SE; the Eau Claire Market, adjacent to Prince's Island in the downtown area; the Calgary Chinese Cultural Centre, 197 1st St. SW; the Energeum, at the Energy Resources Bldg., 640 5th Ave. SW; Fort Calgary Interpretive Centre, 750 9th Ave. SE; Calgary Zoo

MILEPOST® *field editor Blake Hanna relaxing in a pot of dinosaur soup at Drumheller RV park.* (Blake Hanna, staff)

Botanical Garden and Prehistoric Park, off Memorial Drive, featuring a prehistoric park with life-sized replicas of dinosaurs; and Heritage Park, west of 14th Street and Heritage Drive SW, a re-creation of Calgary's pioneer eras. Visitors may recognize the distinctive Saddledome, located at the Exhibition Grounds, which was the site of the 1988 Winter Olympics skating and hockey events. Canada Olympic Park (site of ski jumping, luge and bobsled) is on Trans-Canada Highway 1, west of Sarcee Trail.

Calgary has large shopping malls, department stores, restaurants, and many hotels and motels. Most lodging is downtown or on Highway 2 south (Macleod Trail), Trans-Canada Highway 1 north (16th Avenue) and Alternate 1A (Motel Village). There are several campgrounds in and around the city. ▲

East Access Route Log
(continued)

CB 211.3 (340 km) E 170.9 (275 km) Calgary northern city limits.

Highway 2 from Calgary to Edmonton bypasses most communities. Except for a few service centres built specially for freeway traffic, motorists must exit the freeway for communities and gas, food or lodging.

CB 212.8 (342.6 km) E 169.4 (272.6 km) Exit to community of BALZAC. Private RV park with dump station. ▲

CB 214.2 (344.8 km) E 168 (270.4 km) Pay phone at vehicle inspection site.

CB 216.9 (349.1 km) E 165.3 (266 km) Road west to AIRDRIE (pop. 14,506). Visitor facilities include hotels and motels.

CB 224.5 (361.4 km) E 157.7 (253.8 km) Dickson–Stephensson Stopping House on Old Calgary Trail; rest area and tourist information on west side of highway.

CB 224.9 (361.9 km) E 157.3 (253.1 km)

Junction with Highway 2A west to Crossfield and Highway 72 east to Drumheller, 60 miles/97 km, site of Alberta's Badlands. Turn to Side Trip to Alberta's Badlands this section for log.

The Badlands are famous for the dinosaur fossils found there. Fossil displays at world-renowned Royal Tyrrell Museum of Paleontology in Drumheller.

CB 226.8 (365.1 km) E 155.4 (250.1 km) Gas and restaurant at turnout.

Side Trip to Alberta's Badlands

Alberta Highways 72 and 9 lead 60 miles/97 km east to Drumheller in Alberta's Badlands—a region characterized by scanty vegetation and intricate erosional features. Besides its fantastic scenery, the Badlands is also famous for its dinosaurs. It is one of the best places in the world to recover the fossilized remains of dinosaurs, many of which are displayed at the world-famous Royal Tyrrell Museum of Paleontology in Drumheller. **Distance from Highway 2 junction (J) is shown.**

J 0 Junction with Alberta Highway 2 at **Milepost CB 224.9** (approximately 25 miles/40 km north of Calgary).

J 7.5 (12.1 km) **Junction** with Highway 791, which leads to the Fairview Colony.

J 13.8 (22.2 km) Rosebud River.

J 14 (22.6 km) Beiseker Colony.

J 20.7 (33.4 km) **BEISEKER** (pop. 640); all services available. Highway 72 becomes Highway 9 eastbound.

J 33.2 (53.5 km) **Junction** with Highway 21 to Three Hills and Trans-Canada Highway 1.

J 37.3 (60.1 km) **Junction** with Highway 836. Food and gas available.

J 50.6 (81.5 km) Horseshoe Canyon Viewpoint; restrooms and picnic tables. Canyon tours available.

J 45.1 (72.6 km) **Junction** with Highway 840 to Rosebud and Standard.

J 60.1 (96.8 km) **DRUMHELLER** (pop. 6,277); all visitor facilities available, including bed and breakfasts, motels, campgrounds, restaurants and gas. **Visitor**

Information: Drumheller Regional Chamber of Development and Tourism, Box 999, Alberta T0J 0Y0; phone (403) 823-8100.

The first dinosaur fossil found in the badlands was an Albertosaurus (a slightly smaller version of the Tyrannosaurus), unearthed in 1884 by Joseph Burr Tyrrell pronounceds TEER-ell) just east of what is today Drumheller. His find sparked the "Great Canadian Dinosaur Rush," as famous fossil hunters Barnum Brown, Joseph Sternberg and others vied for trophies. Today, the major attraction in Drumhbeller is the **Royal Tyrrell Museum of Paleontology**, located in Midland Provincial Park just outside the city limits. The museum boasts an outstanding fossil collection presented in stunning displays. More than 30 complete dinosaur skeletons, as well as flying reptiles, prehistoric mammals and marine invertebrates, are displayed in a huge walk-through diorama exhibit. A tropical plant conservatory with more than 100 species of plants simulates the botan-

ical world of the dinosaurs. A viewing window in the main laboratory allows visitors a watch scientists at work. Park rangers lead visitors on 90-minute interpretive hikes into the badlands around the museum, and there are special programs for children. The museum has a restaurant and gift shop. Summer hours are 9 A.M. to 9 P.M. daily. Admission is free. For more information, contact the museum at Box 7500, Drumheller, AB T0J 0Y0; phone (403) 823-7707; http://tyrrell.magtech.ab.ca.

An annual event in Drumheller is the Canadian Badlands Passion Play, presented in a natural bowl amphitheatre each summer. Phone (403) 823-7750 for dates.

Scenic drives in the area include the Dinosaur Trail and East Coulee Drive. Highlights along the Dinosaur Trail, a 30-mile/50-km driving loop through the Red Deer River Valley from Drumheller, are the Dinosaur Burial Grounds; the Homestead Antique Museum; the West Drumheller Oil Field; Horse Thief Canyon; and Midland Mine office in Midland Provincial Park. The East Coulee Drive includes the much-photographed hoodoos; the swinging bridge at Rosedale; East Coulee School Museum and Tea Room; and the Atlas Coal Mine.

Drumheller Regional Chamber of Development and Tourism. See display ad this section.

Return to Milepost CB 224.9
East Access Route

CB 231.2 (372 km) **E 151** (243 km) Exit to **CROSSFIELD**; gas, hotel, food.

CB 237 (381.5 km) **E 145.2** (233.7 km) Exit west for **CARSTAIRS** (pop. 1,796), a farm and service community with tourist information centre and campground. The campground has 28 sites, electric hookups,

hot showers and dump station. Services here include groceries, liquor store, banks, a motel, propane and gas stations. ▲

CB 253.7 (408.3 km) **E 128.5** (206.8 km) **Junction** with Highway 27 west to **OLDS** (pop. 5,542); all visitor facilities, museum and information booth.

CB 258.2 (415.6 km) **E 124** (199.5 km) Turnout with litter barrels.

CB 263.6 (424.2 km) **E 118.6** (190.9 km) **Junction** with highway west to Bowden and Red Lodge Provincial Park (8.5 miles/14 km); 110 campsites, playground, swimming and fishing. **BOWDEN** (pop. 936) is the site of a

Devonian Way Bypass

This bypass route circles the southwest edge of Edmonton, connecting Highway 2 and Highway 16 via Secondary Highway 19 (Devonian Way) and Highway 60. **Distance from Highway 2 and Devonian Way junction (J) is shown.**

J 0 Junction with Highway 19, Devonian Way, at **Milepost CB 367.4**. Follow Devonian Way west.

J 0.4 (0.7 km) Rest area to south.

J 2.1 (3.4 km) Capital Raceway to south, Amerlea Meadows equestrian facility to north.

J 5.2 (8.3 km) Rabbit Hill Ski area to west.

J 8.2 (13.2 km) **Junction** with Highway 60 (Edmonton truck bypass). Turn north on Highway 60 for Devon and Yellowhead Highway; turn south at intersection and drive 0.6 mile/1 km for **Leduc No. 1 Well Historic Site.** The Leduc Well was drilled on Feb. 13, 1947, before an invited asssembly of businesspeople, government officials and reporters. It was the 134th try for Imperial Oil after drilling 133 dry wells, and it was wildly successful, making Edmonton the "Oil Capital of Canada." A 174-foot/53-m derrick marks the site. Visitors may climb to the drilling floor to view drilling equip-

Leduc No. 1 Well was Alberta's first oil well and is now a historic site.
(Blake Hanna, staff)

ment and tools.

J 9.2 (14.8 km) Dump station.

J 10.2 (16.4 km) Turn east on Athabasca Avenue for downtown **DEVON**; all visitor services. Camping at Devon Lions Club Campground, 180 sites on North Saskatchewan River; follow signs for Patrick O'Brien Memorial Park. The campground is adjacent to Devon Golf & Country Club.

Devon Lions Club Campground. See display ad this section.▲

J 10.6 (17 km) Bridge over North Saskatchewan River.

J 13.8 (22.2 km) **University of Alberta Devonian Botanic Garden;** alpine garden, 5-acre Kurimoto Japanese Garden, and other special collections gardens set in natural landscape. Live exotic butterfly showhouse with 30 species of butterflies. Open daily, 10 A.M. to 7 P.M. in summer, shorter hours rest of year. Fee charged.

J 16.9 (27.2 km) **Junction** with Secondary Highway 627; turn east for Edmonton.

J 22.7 (36.6 km) **Junction** with Yellowhead Highway 16; turn to **Milepost E 10.**

Return to Milepost E 10 or CB 367.4 East Access Route

---

large oil refinery and Alberta Nurseries and Seeds Ltd., a major employer. Most visitor services available. Heritage rest area with 24 campsites, dump station and tourist information booth at junction. ▲

CB 271 (436.2km) **E 111.2** (179 km) **Junction** with Highway 54 west to **INNISFAIL** (pop. 6,064); all visitor facilities. South

of Innisfail 3 miles/5 km is the RCMP Dog Training Centre, the only one in Canada; open to the public daily year-round from 9 A.M. to 4 P.M.

CB 273 (440.7 km) **E 109.2** (175.7 km) Turnout with pay phone and litter cans.

CB 285.5 (459.5 km) **E 96.7** (155.6 km) Tourist service area with gas stations and restaurants.

CB 286.6 (461.3 km) **E 95.6** (153.8 km) **Junction** with Highway 2A (Gaetz Avenue) east to **RED DEER** (pop. 59,834). **Emergency Services:** Phone 911. **Visitor Information:** At Heritage Ranch, adjacent Highway 2 (watch for signs). Heritage Ranch has a staffed visitor centre (open daily year-round) with a gift shop and snack bar, ample parking and access to Waskasoo Park. Phone (800) 215-8946.

Red Deer has all visitor facilities, including major chain motels and retail outlets. Camping at Lions Municipal Campground on Riverside Drive; from Highway 2 exit to 67th Street or 32nd Street. Open May to September.

CB 289.3 (465.6 km) **E 92.9** (149.5 km) Large turnout with pay phone and litter barrels.

CB 291.6 (469.3 km) **E 90.6** (145.8 km) **Junction** with Highway 11 west to Sylvan Lake (10 miles/16 km), a popular watersports destination for Red Deer residents, with swimming beach and marina. **Sylvan Lake Provincial Park** has picnicking and swimming. Private campgrounds and waterslide nearby. ▲

CB 304 (489.6 km) **E 78.2** (125.8 km) **Junction** with Highway 12. Exit east for **LACOMBE** (pop. 7,580); all visitor facilities. Camping at Michener Park; 21 sites. Site of the Federal Agricultural Research Station; open to the public weekdays, 8 A.M. to

4:30 P.M. Exit west on Highway 12 for **Aspen Beach Provincial Park** at Gull Lake (6 miles/10 km); camping, swimming. ▲

CB 321.3 (517.1 km) E 60.9 (98 km) **Junction** with Highway 53 east to **PONOKA** (pop. 5,861); all visitor facilities. Camping at Ponoka Stampede Trailer Park, May to October. Ponoka's Stampede is held June 29 to July 3 at Stampede Park. ▲

CB 325.4 (523.7 km) E 56.8 (91.4 km) Turnout with pay phone.

CB 336.7 (541.8 km) E 455 (73.2 km) Northbound-only access to Wetaskiwin rest area with picnic tables and information centre (open May to September); restrooms, gas service, dump station and groceries.

CB 340.5 (548 km) E 41.7 (67.1 km) **Junction** of Highway 13 east to Wetaskiwin, site of the Reynolds–Alberta Museum and Aviation Hall of Fame.

CB 351.2 (565.2 km) E 31 (49.9 km) Turnout to east with litter barrels and pay phone.

CB 362.4 (583.2 km) E 19.8 (31.9 km) Exit to **LEDUC** (pop. 14,117); all visitor facilities. Founded and named for the Leduc oil field. The 200-million barrel Leduc oil field was the first in a series of post-war oil and natural gas finds that changed the economy of Alberta.

CB 367.4 (591.3 km) E 14.8 (23.8 km)

Junction with Highway 19 west and Edmonton Bypass route (see DEVONIAN WAY BYPASS ROUTE this section).

Access to Leduc No. 1 well historic site.

NOTE: Northbound motorists wishing to avoid heavy traffic through Edmonton may exit west on Highway 19 (Devonian Way) for Devon Bypass route. Drive 8.2 miles/13.2 km west on Highway 19, then 14.5 miles/23.3 km north on Highway 60 to junction with Yellowhead Highway 16, 10 miles/16 km west of Edmonton (see Milepost E 10 this section).

Highway 2 northbound becomes Calgary Trail. Access to Edmonton International Airport.

CB 377.2 (607.1 km) E 5 (8 km) Gateway Park Visitor InfoCentre; pay phones, restrooms, dump station.

CB 377.9 (608.2 km) E 4.3 (6.9 km) Stoplight at Ellerslie (grain elevator). Access to golf course and private campground; follow Ellerslie west to 127th and turn south to 41st Avenue SW. ▲

CB 382.2 (615 km) E 0 **Junction** with Whitemud Drive/Highway 2. Turn west for Highway 16A West (see YELLOWHEAD HIGHWAY 16 section) and for continuation of Highway 2 north to Athabasca and the Northern Woods and Waters Route.

When the Alaska Highway opened to civilian traffic in 1948, the original access route to Dawson Creek, BC, from Edmonton was north 91 miles/147 km via Highway 2 to the historic fur-trading post of **ATHABASCA** (today's population: 2,300). Motorists then headed west along today's Northern Woods & Waters Route to High Prairie, then turned either north to McLennan and Peace River, or south via Valleyview to Grande Prairie, AB. In late 1955, Highway 43 was completed connecting Edmonton and Valleyview via Whitecourt.

Continue north for Edmonton city centre (description follows).

Whitemud Drive west continues as Highway 2, crossing the North Saskatchewan River, then turns north to become 170th

Edmonton

Street. Access to West Edmonton Mall on 170th Street.

Edmonton

E 0 DC 367 (590.6 km) Capital of Alberta, 1,853 miles/2,982 km from Fairbanks, AK. **Population:** 627,000; area 890,000. **Elevation:** 2,182 feet/668m. **Emergency Services:** Phone 911 for all emergency services. **Hospitals:** Grey Nuns Community Health Centre, 3015–62 St., phone (780) 450-7000; Misericordia, 16940 87th Ave., phone (780) 484-8811; Royal Alexandra, 10240 Kingsway Ave., phone (780) 477-4111; University, 8440–112 St., phone (780) 492-8822.

EDMONTON ADVERTISERS

Comfort Inn ....17610–100th Ave.
Edmonton Queen ....Rafters Landing
Rainbow Valley Campground
& RV Park....................Ph. (888) 434-3991

Alberta is on Mountain Time.

Visitor Information: Edmonton Tourism operates visitor information centres downtown and on Highway 2 south. Or contact Edmonton Tourism, 9797 Jasper Ave., Edmonton, AB T5J 1N9; phone (780) 496-8400 or (800) 463-4667; web site www.ede.org.

Private Aircraft: Edmonton International Airport (phone 780/890-8382) 14 miles/22.5 km southwest and Edmonton City Centre Airport (780/496-2836) north side of downtown. See Canadian Flight Supplement.

The North Saskatchewan River winds through the centre of Edmonton, its banks lined with public parks. Riverboat tours depart from Rafter's Landing, located on 98th Avenue, across from the distinctive glass pyramids of Muttart Conservatory.

Muttart Conservatory houses plants from the temperate, tropical and arid climates of the world; 9626 96 A Street, phone 496-8755.

Other major attractions include the **Edmonton Space & Science Centre**, which has the largest planetarium dome in North America and an IMAX theatre, at 1121–142 St., phone 451-3344 (www.edmonton science.com); the architectural highlight of the city, the **Alberta Legislature Building**, at 10800–97 Ave. (www.assembly.ab.ca); the **Alberta Aviation Museum**, 11410 Kingsway Ave., phone 453-1078; and the **Provincial Museum of Alberta**, 12845–102 Ave., phone 453-9100 (www.pma.edmonton.ab.ca).

Fort Edmonton Park, Canada's largest living history park, features more than 60 period buildings on 158 acres. Costumed interpreters bring history to life on 1885 Street, 1905 Street, 1920 Street and in the Hudson's Bay Co. fort (1846). Activities and attractions at the park include a steam train ride, stagecoach and streetcar rides; blacksmithing and rope- making demonstrations; retail shops and food outlets. Open 10 A.M. daily, May to September; special events year-round. Contact Fort Edmonton Park, Box 2359, Edmonton, AB T5J 2R7; phone (780) 496-8787 (www.gov.edmonton.ab.ca/fort/).

Also on the list of major attractions for visitors to Edmonton is the world's largest shopping mall—**West Edmonton Mall**. The mall features some 800 stores and services, a waterpark, ice arena, aquariums and 100 restaurants. Located on 87 Avenue at 170 Street, the shopping mall is open 7 days a week; www.westedmontonmall.com).

Edmonton Coliseum is home to the Edmonton Oilers NHL hockey team. The Edmonton Trappers baseball team play at Telus Field.

Known as Canada's Festival City, Edmonton hosts a number of events throughout the year. These events include Jazz City International Music Festival (June 25–July 14, 1999); International Street Performers Festival (July 9–18, 1999); Klondike Days (July 22–31, 1999); Heritage Festival (July 31–Aug. 2, 1999), Edmonton Folk Music Festival (Aug. 5–8, 1999); and the Fringe Theatre Event (Aug. 13–22, 1999).

There are 80 hotels and motels in Edmonton and some 2,000 restaurants. Within the Edmonton vicinity there is camping at Rainbow Campground on Whitemud Drive, and at Glowing Embers Travel Centre, at the Devon Overpass. ▲.

East Access Route Log

(continued)

This section of the log shows distance from Edmonton (E) followed by distance from Dawson Creek (DC).

HIGHWAY 16A WEST

E 0 DC 367 (590.6 km) Downtown Edmonton. Jasper Avenue westbound (becomes Yellowhead 16A.

E 10 (16 km) **DC 357** (574.5 km) **Junction** of Highways 16A West and 60 (Devon Overpass); access to private campground. ▲

Glowing Embers Travel Centre. See display ad this section. ▲

NOTE: Southbound travelers may bypass Edmonton by taking Highway 60 south, then Highway 19 east to Highway 2 (see DEVONIAN WAY BYPASS log this section).

E 16 (26 km) **DC 351** (564.9 km) **SPRUCE GROVE** (pop. 14,123). All visitor facilities including motels, restaurants, gas and service stations, grocery stores, farmer's market, shopping malls and all emergency services. Recreational facilities include a golf course, swimming pool, skating and curling rinks, parks, and extensive walking and cycling trails. The chamber of commerce tourist information booth, located on Highway 16A, is open year-round; phone (403)

Colorful murals decorate more than a dozen buildings in Stony Plain. *(Blake Hanna, staff)*

962-2561.

E 19.3 (31 km) DC 347.7 (559.5 km)
STONY PLAIN (pop. 7,405). All visitor facilities including hotels, restaurants, supermarkets, shopping mall and gas stations with major repair service; RCMP and hospital; outdoor swimming pool, tennis courts and 18-hole golf course. The Multicultural Heritage Centre here has historical archives, a craft shop and home-cooked meals. Other attractions include 16 outdoor murals; Oppertshauser Art Gallery; the Andrew Wolf Winery; and the Pioneer Museum at Exhibition Park. Visitor information centre at Rotary Park rest area. Camping at Lions RV Park and Campground; 26 sites.

Bears and Bedtime Mfg. features handmade, limited-edition collectable teddy bears, bear-making supplies, teddy bear books, Cherished Teddies, Boyd's Bearstones, Beanie Babies and other gift items. Hours: Monday–Friday 9 A.M.–6 P.M., Saturday 10 A.M.–6 P.M. Visit our website at www.bearsandbedtime.com. Phone 1-800-461-BEAR(2327). See ad in the YELLOWHEAD HIGHWAY section. [ADVERTISEMENT]

E 23.9 (38.5 km) DC 343.1 (552.1 km)
Edmonton Beach turnoff to south; campground. ▲

E 24.2 (39.4 km) DC 342.8 (551.7 km)
Hubbles Lake turnoff to north.

E 25.5 (41.1 km) DC 341.5 (549.6 km)
Restaurant, gas station and store to north.

E 29.8 (47.9 km) DC 337.2 (542.6 km)

Junction of Yellowhead Highway 16 and Highway 43. If you are continuing west on Yellowhead Highway 16 for Prince George or Prince Rupert, BC, turn to **Milepost E 25** in the YELLOWHEAD HIGHWAY section.

Turn north onto Highway 43 and continue with this log for Dawson Creek, BC.
HIGHWAY 43
E 31.7 (51 km) DC 335.3 (539.6 km)
Turnout to east with litter barrel and historical information sign about construction of the Alaska Highway.

E 33.7 (54.3 km) DC 333.3 (536.4 km)
Gas station to east.

E 38 (61.1 km) DC 329 (529.5 km) Highway 633 west to Alberta Beach Recreation Area on Lac Ste. Anne. Facilities include a

municipal campground (open May 15 to Sept. 15) with 115 sites. ▲

E 40.7 (65.5 km) DC 326.3 (525.1 km)
ONOWAY (pop. 681) has a medical clinic, dentist and veterinary clinic. Other services include gas, propane, banks and bank machine, grocery stores, laundromat, restaurants, motel, car wash, post office, pharmacy, RV park with hookups and dump station. Information booth and Elks campground with 8 sites. ▲

E 46.8 (75.3 km) DC 320.2 (515.3 km)
Junction of Highways 43 and 33 (Grizzly Trail). Continue on Highway 43.

Alberta government campground with dump station, water, toilets and stoves. ▲

E 47.3 (76.1 km) DC 319.7 (514.5 km)
Restaurant and gas station. Campground south on **Lac Ste. Anne**; fishing. ◄▲

Gunn General Store & Campground. See display ad this section.

E 49.1 (79 km) DC 317.9 (511.6 km)
Lessard Lake county campground; water, stoves, boat launch, fishing for pike and perch. Golf course to west. ◄▲

E 72.7 (117 km) DC 294.3 (473.6 km)
SANGUDO (pop. 405) is on a 0.3-mile/0.4-km side road. Restaurants, motel and hotel accommodations; gas station with garage open 7 days a week; grocery, clothing and liquor stores; antique shop; banks, post office, pharmacy, laundromat and car wash. Oval race car track with racing in summer; shale baseball diamonds; elk farm tours. A public campground with 14 sites, showers and flush toilets, is located at the sportsground. ▲

E 73.1 (117.7 km) DC 293.9 (473 km)
Pembina River bridge.

E 74 (119.2 km) DC 293 (471.5. km)
Ol' Pembina River Ferry Crossing RV Park. "Peaceful camping along the Pembina River, where history surrounds the RV park." 5 landscaped acres with 15 spacious sites. One cozy motel unit. Walking/history trails. Old ferry site. Water and electrical sites. Pull-throughs, sewer dump, showers and flush toilets, coin washer and dryer. Evening appointments for hair stylist and massage therapist. 1 km off Highway 43, turn south at RV park sign, flying 3 flags. Phone (780) 785-2379 with answering machine. [ADVERTISEMENT] ▲

E 74.1 (119.3 km) DC 292.9 (471.3 km)
Gas station and restaurant to south.

E 78.3 (126 km) DC 288.7 (464.6 km)
Second longest wooden railway trestle in the world crosses highway and Paddle River. The C.N.R. Rochfort Bridge trestle is 2,414 feet/736m long and was originally built in 1914.

E 80.6 (129.7 km) DC 286.4 (460.9 km)
ROCHFORT BRIDGE. Trading post (open daily, year-round) with gas, convenience store, gift shop, restaurant and Lac Ste. Anne Pioneer Museum. Camping.

Rochfort Bridge Trading Post—A fun stop. Fresh bread and pies baked from scratch: rhubarb, blueberries, sour-cream and raisin pies, and more. Home-style meals. Licensed. Verandah. One of the largest all-Canadian gift stores. Distinctive items, including rare First Nations art: birch bark biting, fish scale art and moose tufting. Par 3 golf course with rentals. And you can photograph our cute donkeys. See display ad this section. [ADVERTISEMENT]

E 83.1 (133.7 km) DC 283.9 (456.1 km)
Paved turnouts with litter barrels both sides of highway.

E 85 (136.8 km) DC 282 (453.8 km)
MAYERTHORPE (pop. 1,692). One mile/1.6 km from the highway on a paved access road. Hotel, motel, restaurant, grocery store, gas stations with repair service, car wash, hospital, laundromat, post office, RCMP and banks. A public campground with 30 sites (no hookups, pit toilets) and 9-hole golf course are located 1 mile/1.6 km south of town. Airstrip located 2 miles/3.2 km southwest of town; no services. (Most northbound air travelers use Whitecourt airport, which has fuel.) ▲

E 87 (140 km) DC 280 (450.6 km) Gas station and restaurant at junction with

Highway 658 north to Goose Lake.

E 109 (175.4 km) DC 258 (415.2 km) Lions Club Campground; 74 sites, flush toilets, showers, water, tables and firepits. Fee charged. ▲

Whitecourt

E 111.8 (179.9 km) DC 255.2 (410.7 km). Located two hours from Edmonton. **Population:** 7,800. **Emergency Services: Police,** phone (780) 778-5454. **Fire Department,** phone (780) 778-2311. **Hospital** located on Hilltop, phone (780) 778-2285. Ambulance service available.

Visitor Information: Tourist information booth on Highway 43 west at the traffic lights. The helpful staff will assist with

WHITECOURT ADVERTISERS

Boston Pizza ....Ph. (780) 778-2500
Gateway Esso...................................Hwy. 43
Glenview Motel ....Ph. (780) 778-2276
McDonald's ....Hwy. 43
Quality Inn ....Ph. (800) 228-5151
Renford Inn......................Ph. (780) 778-3133
Sagitawah Tourist Park....Ph. (780) 778-3734
Tags Food & Gas/A&W ....3711 Highway St.
Whitecourt Lions Club
    Campground ....Ph. (780) 778-6782

travel plans and directions to Whitecourt sights and activities. The booth is fully stocked with pamphlets and brochures. Open daily, 9 A.M. to 6 P.M., May 1 to Sept. 1; weekdays only, 9 A.M. to 5 P.M., September through April. Free dump station and freshwater fill-up adjacent tourist booth. Information is also available from the Chamber of Commerce, P.O. Box 1011, Whitecourt, AB T7S 1N9; phone (780) 778-5363, fax 778-2351.

Elevation: 2,567 feet/782m. **Radio:** 96.7 CJYR-FM, 107.5 SKUA-FM. **Television:** 10 channels. **Newspaper:** *Whitecourt Star* (weekly); *Whitecourt Advertiser* (biweekly).

Private Aircraft: Airport 4 miles/6.4 km south on Highway 32; elev. 2,567 feet/782m; length 5,800 feet/1,768m; paved; fuel 80, 100, jet (24-hour, self-serve). Aircraft maintenance, 24-hour flight service station, all-weather facility.

Transportation: Air—Local charter air service available; helicopter and fixed-wing aircraft. **Bus**—Greyhound service to Edmonton, Grande Prairie, Peace River and points north.

Located at the junction of Highways 43 and 49, Whitecourt dubs itself the "Gateway to the Alaska Highway and the fabulous North." Established as a small trading, trapping and forestry centre, Whitecourt became an important stop for Alaska Highway travelers when a 106-mile section of Highway 43 connecting Whitecourt and Valleyview was completed in October 1955. This new route was 72 miles shorter than the old Edmonton to Dawson Creek route via Slave Lake.

Several major forest industries operating

in and around Whitecourt offer tours. Visitors may observe state-of-the-art technologies at sawmills, medium-density fiberboard production and pulp plants. Check with the tourist information booth or chamber of commerce for tour times.

The Eric S. Huestis Demonstration Forest, northwest of town on Highway 32 (see **Milepost E 117.1**), has 4.3 miles/7 km of self-guided trails with interpretive sites and information signs describing forest management techniques and the forest life-cycle; phone (780) 778-7165.

Recreational activities include an excellent 18-hole public golf course and fishing in area creeks, rivers and lakes (boat rentals at Carson–Pegasus Provincial Park). Swimming, in-line skating, tennis, gold panning, walking trails, beach volleyball and river boating are also enjoyed in summer. In the fall, big game hunting is very popular. During the winter there is ice fishing, snowmobiling and cross-country skiing on area trails, downhill skiing at a local facility, skating and curling, bowling and swimming at the indoor pool.

There are 15 hotels/motels, a bed and breakfast, 23 restaurants, 14 gas stations, several laundromats, 2 malls, 6 liquor stores and 5 banks. Most services are located on the highway or 2 blocks north in the downtown business district. Some gas stations and restaurants are open 24 hours.

This full-service community also supports a library and 7 churches. The Legion, located in the business district, is open year-round. Service clubs (Lions, Kinsmen) and community organizations (Masons, Knights of Columbus) welcome visitors.

A popular wilderness area nearby is Carson–Pegasus Provincial Park, located 14.6 miles/23.5 km west and north of town on Highway 32 (paved). The park has 182 campsites, electrical hookups, dump station, boat launch, boat rentals, concession, convenience store, hot showers and laundry facilities. Powered sites and showers are open year-round. There are 2 lakes at the park: **McLeod (Carson) Lake**, stocked with rainbow trout, has a speed limit of 12 kmph for boaters; **Little McLeod (Pegasus) Lake** has northern pike and whitefish, electric motors and canoes only. Eagle River Outfitting (phone 780/778-3251), located 7 miles/11.3 km south of town via Highway 32, offers camping and wilderness activities. ◄▲

East Access Route Log

(continued)

E 111.9 (180.1 km) DC 255.1 (410.5 km) Beaver Creek bridge.

CAUTION: The highway between Whitecourt and Valleyview is known locally as "Moose Row" and "Moose Alley." Several moose–vehicle accidents occur yearly. Northbound travelers, watch for moose on road, especially at dusk and at night.

E 112.4 (180.9 km) DC 254.6 (409.7 km) McLeod River.

E 112.6 (181.2 km) DC 254.4 (409.4 km) Railroad crossing.

E 112.7 (181.4 km) DC 254.3 (409.2 km) **Junction** with Highway 32 South (paved). Access to Eagle River Outfitting, 7 miles/11.3 km south; camping, wilderness activities. Highway 32 leads 42 miles/68 km to Yellowhead Highway 16 (see **Milepost E 97.5** in the YELLOWHEAD HIGHWAY section). ▲

E 112.9 (181.7 km) DC 254.1 (408.9 km) Gas stations both sides of highway.

E 113.4 (182.5 km) DC 253.6 (408.1 km) Turnoff to north for **Sagitawah Tourist Park** (RV camping) and Riverboat Park, both at the confluence of the McLeod and Athabasca rivers. Riverboat Park has a boat launch, picnic area and toilets. ▲

E 113.6 (182.8 km) DC 253.4 (407.8 km) Athabasca River bridge.

E 115.6 (186 km) DC 251.4 (404.6 km) Vehicle inspection station to north.

E 117.1 (188.4 km) DC 249.9 (402.2 km) **Junction** with Highway 32 North (paved). Access to Eric S. Huestis Demonstration Forest (self-guided trails and information signs on forest life-cycle) and **Carson–Pegasus Provincial Park**. The provincial park, 9.3 miles/15 km north, has 182 campsites, electrical hookups, group camping area, tables, flush toilets, showers, water, dump station, firewood, store, laundromat and playground. (Powered sites and showers open year-round.) Boat launch, boat rentals and rainbow trout fishing are available. ◄▲

E 117.6 (189.2 km) DC 249.4 (401.4 km) Alberta Newsprint Co. to south.

E 122 (196.3 km) DC 245 (394.3 km) Turnout with litter barrel.

E 122.5 (197.1 km) DC 244.5 (393.5 km) Chickadee Creek government campground; 7 sites, pit toilets, water, tables and firepits. ▲

E 124.3 (200 km) DC 242.7 (390.6 km) Chickadee Creek.

E 131.8 (212.1 km) DC 235.2 (378.5 km) Turnouts with litter barrels both sides of highway.

E 140.5 (226.1 km) DC 226.5 (364.5 km)

Two Creeks government campground; 8 campsites, pit toilets, water, picnic tables and firepits. ▲

E 142.5 (229.3 km) DC 224.5 (361.3 km) Turnout with litter barrel to south.

E 143 (230.1 km) DC 224 (360.5 km) Turnout with litter barrel to north.

E 152 (244.6 km) DC 215 (346 km) Iosegun Creek government campground; 12 sites, pit toilets, water, tables and firepits. ▲

E 159 (255.9 km) DC 208 (334.7 km) Fox Creek airport.

Fox Creek

E 162 (260.7 km) DC 205 (329.9 km) **Population:** 2,600. **Elevation:** 2,800 feet/853m. **Emergency Services:** RCMP, phone (780) 622-3740. **Ambulance,** phone (780) 622-3000. **Hospital,** phone (780) 622-3545. **Visitor**

Information: Tourist Information Centre at the Rig Earth Resource Park, open in summer; gift shop, coffee area and selection of informational videos to view; phone (780) 622-2000. Off-season contact the Town Office at (780) 622-3896 for information.

Private Aircraft: Fox Creek airport, 3 miles/4.8 km south on Highway 43; elev. 2,840 feet/866m; length, 2,950 feet/899m; paved; no fuel. Unattended.

Fox Creek is in the centre of oil and gas exploration and production. (A Jomax 4, 150-foot/46m drilling rig is on display at Rig Earth Resource Park.) North America's largest known natural gas field is here.

All visitor facilities including 2 hotels, 3 motels and gas stations with repair service. Grocery store open daily until midnight. Convenience stores, pharmacy, laundromats, liquor stores, restaurants and banks.

Fox Creek R.V. Campground, located near the visitor information centre, is a municipal campground with 17 sites, full hookups, showers and dump station   ▲

Fox Creek is also a popular outdoor recreation area. Two local lakes popular with residents and visitors are **Iosegun** and **Smoke lakes,** which are located within 10 miles/16 km on either side of the townsite on good gravel road. Camping, boat launch and fishing for northern pike, perch and pickerel are favorites for this area.   ◆▲

East Access Route Log
(continued)

E 167 (268.7 km) DC 200 (321.9 km) Turnout with litter barrel.

E 169.5 (272.8 km) DC 197.5 (317.8 km) Turnouts with litter barrels both sides of highway.

E 172 (276.8 km) DC 195 (313.8 km)

Pines government campground; 25 sites, shelter, firewood, pump water, tables and pit toilets.

E 182.1 (293 km) DC 184.9 (297.6 km) Turnout with litter barrel.

E 186.4 (300 km) DC 180.6 (290.6 km) Turnoff for RV park and bed-and-breakfast.

Sands Wilderness Campground & R.V. Park. 24-hour security campground. Large full-service, power and unserviced sites, tenting area. Spacious pull-throughs with power. Water fill-up and dump station. Laundromat, showers. Concession. Horseshoe pits, 9-hole par 3 golf, and mini-golf. Hiking trail. Children's playground. Free firewood. Guests have said, "One of the nicest campgrounds in Canada." Trail rides and raft trips. Your host—"Wild Bill" Sands, Box 511, Valleyview, AB T0H 3N0. Phone/fax: (780) 524-3757. [ADVERTISEMENT]   ▲

E 192 (309 km) DC 175 (281.6 km) **LITTLE SMOKY** (pop. about 50). Motel, RV park, antique shop, gift shop, pay phone, propane, grocery store, service station and post office.   ▲

Little Smoky Motel, Restaurant & Campground. See display ad this section. ▲

E 192.2 (309.3 km) DC 174.8 (281.3 km) Little Smoky River bridge.

E 193.5 (311.4 km) DC 173.5 (279.2 km) Waskahigan (House) River bridge at confluence with Smoky River. Government campground with 24 sites, pit toilets, water, tables and firepits.   ▲

E 197 (317 km) DC 170 (273.6 km) Turnout.

E 206.7 (332.6 km) DC 160.3 (258 km) Turnout with litter barrel.

E 208.5 (335.5 km) DC 158.5 (255.1 km) Peace pipeline storage tanks.

E 210.8 (339.2 km) DC 156.2 (251.4 km) Valleyview Riverside golf course.

E 213.2 (343.1 km) DC 153.8 (247.5 km) Valleyview tourist information centre (phone 780/524-2410); pay phone, postal service, souvenirs, picnic tables, water, flush toilets, dump station. Open daily in summer, 8 A.M. to 8 P.M.

E 213.4 (343.4 km) DC 153.6 (247.2 km) Valleyview airport to west.

Private Aircraft: Valleyview airport; elev. 2,434 feet/742m; length, 3,300 feet/1,006m; paved; no fuel. Unattended.

CAUTION: The highway between Valleyview and Whitecourt is known locally as "Moose

Row" and "Moose Alley." Several moose–vehicle accidents occur yearly. Southbound travelers, watch for moose on road, especially at dusk and at night.

Valleyview

E 214.1 (344.4 km) DC 152.9 (246.1 km) Approximately 4 hours drive time from Edmonton. **Population:** 1,906. **Emergency Services:** RCMP, phone (780) 524-3343. **Fire Department,** phone (780) 524-3916. **Ambulance,** phone (780) 524-3211. **Hospital,** Valleyview General, 45 beds, phone (780) 524-3356.

Visitor Information: Major tourist information centre and rest stop located 0.9 mile/1.5 km south of Valleyview on Highway 43. Open daily, 8 A.M. to 8 P.M. from May through Labour Day weekend; phone (780) 524-2410, fax (780) 524-2727, e-mail valvadm@vvw-TEQ.Net. Postal service, souvenirs and refreshments, as well as regional travel and community events and services information. For information on small business opportunities, contact the Valleyview Regional Economic Development Board office at (403) 524-5051.

Elevation: 2,400 feet/732m. **Newspaper:** *Valley Views* (weekly). **Transportation: Air**—Airport 0.7 mile/1.1 km south (see **Milepost E 213.4**). **Bus**—Greyhound.

Valleyview, known as the "Portal to the Peace Country" of northwestern Alberta, is located at the junction of Highways 43 and 49. From Valleyview, Highway 43 continues west to Grande Prairie and Dawson Creek. Highway 49 leads north to connect with Highway 2 east to Athabasca and north to Peace River. From Peace River, travelers may follow the Mackenzie Highway to Northwest Territories (see the MACKENZIE ROUTE section for details).

Originally called Red Willow Creek when it was homesteaded in 1916, Valleyview boomed with the discovery of oil and gas in the 1950s, and services grew along with the population. Today, Valleyview's economy has diversified to include the oil and gas industry, forestry, tourism, agriculture and government services. Farming consists mainly of grain, oilseed, beef cattle and forage production.

The community has a full range of services including banks, automatic teller machines, post office, a library, several churches and a veterinary clinic.

All visitor facilities available, including 5 motels and hotels, several restaurants, gas stations (many with major repair service, propane and diesel), laundromat, grocery, liquor store, clothing and hardware stores, a bakery, gift shops and a golf course. Some gas stations and restaurants open 24 hours a day.

The area boasts many lakes and streams, abundant wildlife, and lush vegetation, including berries. Summer travelers can take advantage of the long summer days here by attending local rodeos, fairs and festivals;

playing a round of golf on one of the local golf courses; visiting one of the provincial parks along Sturgeon Lake; taking a dip in the outdoor swimming pool in town; or exploring the wilderness by all-terrain vehicle, horse, canoe or hiking trail.

Horizon Motel, Restaurant & Gift Shop. At the Horizon, we have built our business on loyalty and customer satisfaction. An Alberta Best property, clean, well-appointed rooms, several nonsmoking and deluxe family suites available, reasonable rates. Our Westside Cafe, "where to turn when you simply must have a good meal...," tastefully decorated, featuring Western and Chinese menu. Open daily 6 A.M. to 10 P.M. Tour buses welcome. Quality souvenirs and gifts. Bank rate of exchange paid on U.S. funds. We take pride in our service; stop in and experience for yourself! Phone (780) 524-3904. Fax (780) 524-4223. [ADVERTISEMENT] ▲

Lion's Den Campground, west end of town, has 19 sites with hookups, tables, showers and toilets. Full-service private campground (Sherk's RV Park) with 56 sites, close to town. ▲

East Access Route Log
(continued)

E 216 (347.6 km) **DC 151** (243 km) Highways 49/2 lead north 86 miles/138.4 km to Peace River and **junction** with the Mackenzie Highway 12 miles/19 km west of Peace River. See the MACKENZIE ROUTE section for a description of Peace River and the log of the Mackenzie Highway to western Northwest Territories.

Continue on Highway 43 west for Dawson Creek.

E 222.6 (358.2 km) **DC 144.4** (232.4 km)

24-hour convenience store and gas.

E 224.7 (361.6 km) **DC 142.3** (229 km) Access north to **Sturgeon Lake**; fishing and camping. **Williamson Provincial Park** (1.2 miles/2 km); 60 campsites, boat launch, showers, dump station. Fishing for perch, pickerel, northern pike and whitefish. ◆▲

E 227 (365.3 km) **DC 140** (225.3 km) **CALAIS** (pop. about 550); post office and grocery store.

E 230 (370.1 km) **DC 137** (220.5 km) Private campground and marina on **Sturgeon Lake**; fishing, boat rentals. ◆▲

Cosy Cove Campground & Marina. See display ad this section. ▲

E 232 (373.3 km) **DC 135** (217.3 km) Sturgeon Heights. Turnoff for **Youngs Point Provincial Park**, 6 miles/10 km northeast; 97 campsites (some with electrical hookups), firewood, showers, playground, hiking trails, dump station, boat launch, fish cleaning station, beach, fishing in **Sturgeon Lake**. ◆▲

E 235 (378.2 km) **DC 132** (212.4 km) Turnouts both sides of highway; historic marker.

E 240 (386.2 km) **DC 127** (204.4 km) **CROOKED CREEK** (pop. 10); gas station, grocery, ice cream store (with giant cones), post office and pay phone.

E 246 (395.9 km) **DC 121** (194.7 km) DeBOLT, a small farming community north of highway with a general store and district museum. Garage with gas on highway.

E 253.8 (408.7 km) **DC 113.2** (181.9 km) **Junction.** Forestry Trunk Road leads 632 miles/1,017 km south, intersecting Yellowhead Highway 16 and Trans-Canada Highway 1, to Highway 3.

E 255.2 (410.7 km) **DC 111.8** (179.9 km) Microwave towers to east.

E 259.5 (417.6 km) **DC 107.5** (173 km)

Smoky River bridge and government campground; 30 sites, shelter, firepits, firewood, tables, pit toilets, water pump and boat launch. ▲

E 264 (424.9 km) **DC 103** (165.7 km) **BEZANSON.** Post office, gas station with diesel, cafe, liquor store, grocery, general store, propane.

E 269 (432.9 km) **DC 98** (157.7 km) Kleskun Hills Park to north 3 miles/5 km. The park features an ancient sea bottom with fossils of dinosaurs and marine life.

E 270.6 (435.5 km) **DC 96.4** (155.1 km) Turnout to north with historical sign about the Kleskun Hills.

E 283.5 (456.2 km) **DC 83.5** (134.4 km) Weigh scales to north.

E 283.8 (456.7 km) **DC 83.2** (133.9 km) Railroad crossing.

E 284 (457 km) **DC 83** (133.6 km) **Junction** with Highway 2. Dawson Creek-bound travelers continue on Highway 43.

Turn north on Highway 2 for Sexsmith (8.5 miles/13.7 km) and Grimshaw (105 miles/169 km), Mile 0 of the Mackenzie Highway to Northwest Territories (see MACKENZIE ROUTE section).

To reach Grande Prairie city centre, keep straight ahead on Highway 43 (Clairmont Road) as it becomes 100th Street and follow it downtown. To skirt the downtown area, take the Highway 43 Bypass. Highway 43 becomes 100th Avenue (Richmond Avenue) on the west side of Grande Prairie.

Bighorn Highway 40 (paved) connects Grande Prairie with Grande Cache and Yellowhead Highway 16. To reach the Bighorn Highway, follow Wapiti Road (108th Street) south from Highway 43 on the west side of Grande Prairie. See BIGHORN HIGHWAY log page 52.

Grande Prairie

E 288 (463.5 km) **DC 79** (127.1 km). Located at **junction** of Highways 43 and 40. **Population:** 33,500. **Emergency Services: RCMP,** phone (780) 538-5700. **Fire Department,** phone (780) 532-2100. **Ambulance,** phone (780) 532-9511. **Hospital,** Queen Elizabeth, 10409 98th St., phone (780) 538-7100.

Visitor Information: Chamber of Commerce office at 10632 102nd Ave, T8V 6J8; open weekdays 8:30 A.M. to 8:30 P.M. Visitor service center located off Highway 43 Bypass on 106th Street at Bear Creek Reservoir, open 9 A.M. to 9 P.M. in July and August, shorter hours in June; phone (780) 539-7688. The Grande Prairie Rotary Club operates a free bus tour of the city Monday,

GRANDE PRAIRIE ADVERTISERS

Camp Tamarack RV Park ..Ph. (780) 532-5856
Country Roads R.V. Park...Ph. (780) 532-6323
Grande Prairie Museum
   and Gift Shop ....Ph. (780) 532-5482
GrapeVine Wine &
   Spirit Emporium ....Ph. (780) 538-3555
Igloo Inn ....Ph. (780) 539-5314
Lodge Motor Inn, The ......Ph. (780) 539-4700
Parkside Inn ....Ph. (780) 532-3702
Wee Links Golf &
   Campground ....Ph. (780) 538-4501

Cosy Cove Campground & Marina

Boat Rentals - Camping - Groceries - Ice
Fishing Tackle, Bait & Licenses
Power Hookups - Grassy Tent Sites - Shower
Laundry - Dump Station - 24-Hour Security

Located on the shores of Sturgeon Lake (23km west of Valleyview)
CALL (780) 957-2400 for information
VISA   MasterCard

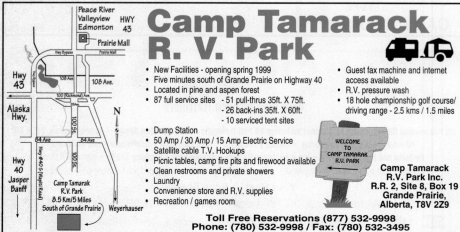

Camp Tamarack R. V. Park

- New Facilities - opening spring 1999
- Five minutes south of Grande Prairie on Highway 40
- Located in pine and aspen forest
- 87 full service sites - 51 pull-thrus 35ft. X 75ft.
   - 26 back-ins 35ft. X 60ft.
   - 10 serviced tent sites
- Dump Station
- 50 Amp / 30 Amp / 15 Amp Electric Service
- Satellite cable T.V. Hookups
- Picnic tables, camp fire pits and firewood available
- Clean restrooms and private showers
- Laundry
- Convenience store and R.V. supplies
- Recreation / games room

- Guest fax machine and internet access available
- R.V. pressure wash
- 18 hole championship golf course/ driving range - 2.5 kms / 1.5 miles

WELCOME TO CAMP TAMARACK R.V. PARK

Camp Tamarack R.V. Park Inc.
R.R. 2, Site 8, Box 19
Grande Prairie, Alberta, T8V 2Z9

Toll Free Reservations (877) 532-9998
Phone: (780) 532-9998 / Fax: (780) 532-3495

Tuesday and Thursday at 7 P.M. Check with the infocentre for details.

Private Aircraft: Airport 3 miles/4.8 km west; elev. 2,195 feet/669m; length 6,500 feet/1,981m; paved; fuel 80, 100, jet. 24-hour flight service station.

Elevation: 2,198 feet/670m. **Transportation: Air**—Scheduled air service to Vancouver, BC, Edmonton, Calgary, and points north. **Bus**—Greyhound.

Grande Prairie was first incorporated as a village in 1914, as a town in 1919, and as a city in 1958, by which time its population had reached nearly 8,000.

With a strong and diverse economy based on agriculture (cereal grains, fescue, honey, livestock), forestry (a bleached kraft pulp mill, sawmill and oriented strand board plant), and oil and gas, Grande Prairie is a regional centre for much of northwestern Alberta and northeastern British Columbia. The trumpeter swan is the symbol of Grande Prairie and is featured throughout the city.

A variety of shopping is available at 2 major malls, several strip malls and a well-developed downtown area. Visitor facilities include several restaurants, hotels, motels, and bed and breakfasts. Recreation facilities include 2 swimming pools, 3 18-hole golf courses, a par 3 golf course, ball diamonds, amusement park, tennis courts, public library, a public art gallery and 3 private galleries. Churches representing almost every denomination are located in Grande Prairie. There are several public schools and a regional college.

Area attractions include Muskoseepi Park, which follows the Bear Creek corridor. The park includes 9 miles/15 km of paved walking and biking trails, a bird sanctuary at Crystal Lake, picnic areas, swimming pool, lawn bowling, mini-golf, a stocked pool, playground and canoe, paddleboat and bike rentals. Visitor services are available in the Pavilion. Nearby is the **Grande Prairie Museum & Pioneer Village** and the Regional College, a unique circular facility designed by Douglas Cardinal. Several of the downtown buildings have murals by local artists.

Weyerhaeuser offers tours of their pulp mill and sawmill in summer; phone (780) 539-8213 for details.

The area has prime hunting for both migratory birds and big game. Area lakes are the nesting sites of the trumpeter swan. Hiking, camping and fishing are popular outdoor activities.

Annual events include the Stompede the first weekend in June, several smaller rodeos,

Canada Games, Highland Games, pari-mutuel racing during July, the County Fair, Heritage Day and the Dinosaur Festival. Contact the visitor information centre for

Visit www.themilepost.com

Bighorn Highway 40 Log

This 207-mile/333.2-km paved highway connects Yellowhead Highway 16 and Highway 43, and the communities of Hinton, Grande Cache and Grande Prairie.

Distance from Yellowhead Highway 16 junction (Y) is followed by the distance from Grande Prairie (GP).

Y 0 GP 207 (333.2 km) **Junction** of Highways 16 and 40. (See **Milepost E 177** in the YELLOWHEAD HIGHWAY 16 section.) Log follows Highway 40 northbound.

Y 2.1 (3.4 km) **GP 204.9** (329.8 km) Community of **ENTRANCE** (pop. 79) to west.

Y 3 (4.8 km) **GP 204** (328.4 km) Athabasca River bridge.

Y 3.7 (5.9 km) **GP 203.3** (327.3 km) Access road to west leads 10 miles/16 km to the community of **BRULE** (pop. 161), which has a guest ranch with trail riding, fishing and cross-country skiing in winter. 🐟

Y 8.5 (13.6 km) **GP 198.5** (319.6 km) Access road leads west 4 miles/7 km to Athabasca Lookout Nordic Centre; cross-country and biathlon skiing, hiking trails and day lodge.

Y 8.9 (14.3 km) **GP 198.1** (318.9 km) Turnout to east with litter barrels and information sign about William A. Switzer Provincial Park.

Y 9.8 (15.8 km) **GP 197.2** (317.4 km) Access road leads east to Jarvis Lake day-use area; pump water, public phone, beach and boat launch.

Y 12.8 (20.5 km) **GP 194.2** (312.7 km) Kelley's Bathtub day-use area to west; hiking trail, public phone, swimming.

Y 15.2 (24.5 km) **GP 191.8** (308.7 km) Winter Creek.

Y 15.3 (24.7 km) **GP 191.7** (308.5 km) Side road to east leads 1.2 miles/2 km to Cache Lake and 2.4 miles/4 km to Graveyard Lake. Cache Lake campground has 14 sites, sewer hookups, water pump, picnic tables, shelter, children's playground, camping fee $9. Graveyard campground has 16 sites, sewer hookups, water available at Cache Lake campground, camping fee $9. ▲

Y 16.8 (27 km) **GP 190.3** (306.2 km) Access road to east leads to **Gregg Lake** day-use area and campground; 164 sites, sewer hookups, tap water, picnic tables, shelter, children's playground, fish-cleaning stand, beach, hiking trails, public phone. Camping fee $13. 🛶▲

Y 17.6 (28.4 km) **GP 189.4** (304.8 km) Turnout to west with litter barrels and information sign about William A. Switzer Provincial Park for southbound travelers.

Y 22.9 (36.9 km) **GP 184.1** (296.3 km) Wildhay River bridge.

Y 25.6 (41.2 km) **GP 181.4** (292 km) Side road to west leads 20 miles/32 km to Rock Lake campground on Rock Lake; 96 sites, sewer hookups, water pump, picnic tables, shelter, hiking trails, boat launch, camping fee $9. ▲

Y 28.9 (46.5 km) **GP 178.1** (286.7 km) Entering Grande Cache ranger district northbound.

Y 30.6 (49.3 km) **GP 176.4** (283.9 km) Fred Creek.

Y 36.3 (58.5 km) **GP 170.7** (274.7 km) Pinto Creek.

Y 40.5 (65.2 km) **GP 166.5** (268 km) Bridge over the Little Berland River.

Y 43.2 (69.6 km) **GP 163.8** (263.6 km) Fox Creek.

Y 48.4 (77.9 km) **GP 158.6** (255.3 km) Bridge over the Big Berland River. Big Berland River government campground at north end of bridge to west has 12 sites, sewer hookups, water pump, picnic tables, shelter, camping fee $9. ▲

Y 52.9 (85.2 km) **GP 154.1** (248 km) Hendrickson Creek.

Y 56.4 (90.7 km) **GP 150.6** (242.5 km) Access road to east leads 1.8 miles/3 km to Hucklebury Tower.

Y 57.4 (92.3 km) **GP 149.6** (240.9 km) Shand Creek.

Y 61.3 (98.6 km) **GP 145.7** (234.6 km) Burleigh Creek.

Y 65.2 (105 km) **GP 141.8** (228.2 km) Pierre Grey's Lakes government campground to east; 83 sites, sewer hookups, pump water, picnic tables, shelter, fireplaces, firewood (for sale), hiking trails, boat launch, camping fee $9. ▲

Y 66.1 (106.4 km) **GP 140.9** (226.8 km) Entering **MUSKEG RIVER** (pop. 22) northbound; pay phone.

Y 67.9 (109.3 km) **GP 139.1** (223.9 km) **Junction** with Highway 734 (Forestry Trunk Road, gravel) which leads north 116 miles/187 km to Highway 34. There are no services along the highway.

Y 69.4 (111.7 km) **GP 137.6** (221.5 km) Turnout to south.

Y 70 (112.6 km) **GP 137** (220.6 km) Veronice River bridge.

Y 74.1 (119.3 km) **GP 132.9** (213.9 km) Muskeg River bridge.

Y 74.9 (120.6 km) **GP 132.1** (212.6 km) Mason Creek day-use area; picnic facilities and hiking trail to the Muskeg River.

Y 75.1 (120.8 km) **GP 131.9** (212.3 km) Mason Creek.

Y 75.7 (121.8 km) **GP 131.3** (211.4 km) Grande Cache airport to south.

Y 80.8 (130.1 km) **GP 126.2** (203.1 km) Susa Creek.

Y 82 (132 km) **GP 125** (201.2 km) Washy Creek.

Y 84.1 (135.3 km) **GP 122.9** (197.9 km) Carconte Creek.

Y 84.5 (136 km) **GP 122.5** (197.2 km) Grande Cache Lake to south; picnic area, swimming, boat launch.

Y 85.3 (137.3 km) **GP 121.7** (195.9 km) Allen Creek.

Y 86.7 (139.5 km) **GP 120.3** (193.7 km) **Victor Lake** to south; canoeing, fishing.

Y 88.1 (141.7 km) **GP 118.9** (191.5 km) Entering Grande Cache northbound. Visitor information and interpretive centre to east. Wildlife displays, rest area, the Bighorn Gallery and souvenirs.

Grande Cache

Y 88.2 (142 km) **GP 118.8** (191.2 km) Located 116 miles/188 km south of Grande Prairie. **Population:** 5,000. **Emergency services:** RCMP, phone (780) 827-2222. **Hospital,** phone (780) 827-3701. **Ambulance,** phone (780) 827-3600. **Fire department,** phone (780) 827-3600.

Visitor information: Tourist information centre is located on 100th Street (Highway 40) at the south entrance into town, open 9 A.M. to 7 P.M. daily, May–September; 9 A.M. to 5 P.M. Monday–Friday the rest of the year. Phone (888) 827-3790.

Elevation: 4,200 feet/1,280m. **Private Aircraft:** Grande Cache airport, 12 miles/19 km east on Highway 40; elev. 4,117 feet/1,255m; length 5,000 feet/1,524m; asphalt; no fuel available.

Grande Cache was established in 1969 in conjunction with resource development by McIntyre Porcupine Coal Ltd. In 1980 a sawmill was constructed by British Columbia Forest Products Ltd. and in 1984 a medium security correctional centre was built.

Historically, the location was used as a staging area for fur trappers and Natives prior to their departure to trap lines in the valleys and mountain ranges now known as Willmore Wilderness Park. Upon their return, they stored large caches of furs while waiting for transportation opportunities to trading posts.

Visitor facilities include hotel, bed and breakfast, 4 motels, 2 banks, restaurants, laundromats, service stations with repair facilities, car washes and a library. Shopping facilities include several small shopping centres, 2 supermarkets, a bakery, sporting goods store and department store.

Recreational facilities include a recreation centre which houses a curling rink, swimming pool, skating rink, fitness rooms and saunas. Grande Cache Golf and Country Club, located in the northeast part of town, has 9 holes, grass greens, clubhouse and pro shop.

Camping at Marv Moore municipal campground on the south side of the highway, at the north end of town just past the golf course. There are 55 sites, full hookups, showers, flush toilets, public phone, children's playground. Camping fee from $10 (dry camping) to $15 (hookups). ▲

Big Horn Highway Log

(continued)

Y 91.3 (146.9 km) GP 115.7 (186.3 km) Smoky River campground to south has 22 sites, sewer hookups, no water, shelters, firewood, firepits, tables, pit toilets, boat launch. Camping fee $8. Trail access to Willmore Wilderness Park. ▲

Y 91.5 (147.2 km) GP 115.5 (186 km) **Smoky River** bridge, fishing for arctic grayling, Dolly Varden and whitefish. ☙

Y 92.3 (148.6 km) GP 114.7 (184.6 km) Turnoff to south for Willmore Wilderness Park and Hell's Gate campground (4 miles/6.4 km south); 10 sites, sewer hookups, horse holding areas, camping fee $8. ▲

Y 95.3 (153.4 km) GP 111.7 (179.8 km) Grande Cache gun range to east. Northbound, the highway parallels the Northern Alberta Resource Railroad and the Smoky River.

Y 100.8 (162.2 km) GP 106.2 (171 km) Turnout to east overlooks Smoky River Coal Ltd. and H.R. Milner Generating Station.

Y 104.8 (168.7 km) GP 102.2 (164.5 km) Entering Grande Prairie Forest northbound, entering Edson Forest southbound.

Y 106.7 (171.7 km) GP 100.3 (161.5 km) Turnoff to east for Sheep Creek day-use area; shaded picnic tables, water pump, firepits, firewood, litter barrels, outhouses and gravel parking areas. Boat launch on the Smoky River.

Y 107.1 (172.4 km) GP 99.9 (160.8 km) Sheep Creek. Sheep Creek campground to east; 9 sites, water pump, camping fee $8.

Y 108.4 (174.5 km) GP 98.6 (158.7 km) Entering Game Country Tourist Zone northbound, Evergreen Tourist Zone southbound.

Y 110.1 (177.2 km) GP 96.9 (156 km) Wayandie Road. Highway ascends steep hill northbound, some sections of 7 percent grade.

Y 125.1 (201.3 km) GP 81.9 (131.9 km) Southview recreation area to east; gravel parking area, shaded picnic tables, litter barrels, outhouses, highbush cranberries in season.

Y 128.5 (206.8 km) GP 78.5 (126.4 km) *CAUTION: Logging trucks next 36 miles/60 km northbound.*

Y 130.4 (209.8 km) GP 76.6 (123.4 km) 16th base line sign marks north–south hunting boundary.

Y 145.6 (234.3 km) GP 61.4 (98.9 km) Kakwa River bridge.

Y 145.9 (234.8 km) GP 61.1 (98.4 km) Turnoff for **Kakwa River** campground and day-use area; 14 sites, sewer hookups, picnic tables, firewood, firepits, water pump, litter barrels, outhouses, gravel parking area. Camping fee $5.50. Fishing for arctic grayling. ☙▲

Y 159.1 (256.1 km) GP 47.9 (77.1 km) Access road to east leads 3.6 miles/6 km to **Musreau Lake** campground and day-use area. There are 50 picnic sites, 69 campsites, picnic tables, firewood, firepits, water pump, litter barrels, outhouses, equestrian trails, boat launch and fishing. ☙▲

Y 161.8 (260.4 km) GP 45.2 (72.8 km) Steep Creek.

Y 164.3 (264.4 km) GP 42.7 (68.8 km) Cutbank River bridge. River access at north end of bridge. Area historic sites and museums sign.

Y 165.6 (266.5 km) GP 41.4 (66.7 km) Elk Creek.

Y 165.8 (266.8 km) GP 41.2 (66.4 km) *CAUTION: Logging trucks next 36 miles/60 km southbound.*

Y 179.5 (288.9 km) GP 27.5 (44.3 km) Canfor Road leads east to Gold Creek Gas Plant and Highway 734.

Y 180.9 (291.1 km) GP 26.1 (42.1 km) Big Mountain Creek.

Y 182.8 (294.1 km) GP 24.2 (39.1 km) Bald Mountain Creek.

Y 189.4 (304.5 km) GP 17.6 (28.5 km) Access road leads west 0.1 mile/0.2 km to picnic area and 7 miles/11 km to Grovedale.

Y 191.1 (307.5 km) GP 15.9 (25.7 km) Bent Pipe Creek.

Y 194.1 (312.4 km) GP 12.9 (20.8 km) Ainsworth O.S.B. Plant.

Y 199.7 (321.3 km) GP 7.3 (11.8 km) **Junction** with Highway 666 which leads southwest to O'Brien Provincial Park and day-use area; water pump, firewood, playground, hiking trails. Also access to Nitehawk ski resort. Highway 666 continues from this junction 5 miles/8 km to Grovedale. ▲

Y 199.8 (321.5 km) GP 7.2 (11.6 km) Wapiti River bridge.

Y 200.1 (322 km) GP 6.9 (11.1 km) Entering Grovedale ranger district southbound.

Y 201.6 (324.4 km) GP 5.4 (8.7 km) Turnoff for Camp Tamarack RV Park. Also access to Dunes golf and winter club (15 miles/25 km east); 18 holes, grass greens, driving range, pro shop. ▲

Y 207 (333.2 km) GP 0 Entering Grande Prairie northbound. Turn east on 100th Avenue for **Grande Prairie Museum.**

Return to Milepost E 284
East Access Route

more information.

Camping within the city limits at Rotary Park public campground, located off the Highway 43 Bypass at the northwest edge of town near the college; Wee Links Golf and Campground at the south end on 100 Avenue; Country Roads R.V. Park near the junction of Highway 43 and 2; and Camp Tamerack RV Park south on Highway 40. ▲

Grande Prairie Museum And Gift Shop. Dinosaurs once roamed the Grande Prairie area long before aboriginal tribes arrived some 8,000 years ago. Explorers, trappers and fur traders came, to be followed by missionaries and pioneer families. Grande Prairie Museum presents these fascinating stories and much, much more. Check the Internet or phone (780) 532-5482. [ADVERTISEMENT]

GrapeVine Wine & Spirit Emporium. We carry the largest selection of wine in the Peace Country. Check out our "Fine Wine Room" with old vintages and large bottles of rare and hard to find wine. On the liquor side of our store, we carry over 60 different single-malt scotches. In the beer department, we specialize in microbreweries and still have room for all your old favorites. The "GrapeVine" a must stop in Grande Prairie. See us at 9506 100 Street. The big pink building on 100 Street. (780) 538-3555. [ADVERTISEMENT]

Wee Links Golf & Campground. Campground, Pitch & Putt Golf Course (grass greens) and driving range at a secluded setting within Grande Prairie city limits. Clean washrooms, hot coin showers, pay phone, water and power at sites, firepits, snacks, hiking/biking trails. 68 Avenue and 100 Street. VISA and MasterCard. Reservations (780) 538-4501. [ADVERTISEMENT] ▲

East Access Route Log

(continued)

E 298 (479.6 km) DC 69 (111 km) **Saskatoon Island Provincial Park** is 1.9 miles/3 km north on park road; 96 campsites, dump station, boat launch, swimming, playground; Saskatoon berry picking in July; game preserve for trumpeter swans. ▲

E 299 (481.2 km) DC 68 (109.4 km) **WEMBLEY** (pop. 1,463) has a hotel (banking service and liquor store at hotel), post office, grocery store, gas stop, car wash and restaurants. Picnicking and camping at Sunset Lake Park in town (dump station).

Camping May 1 to Oct. 15 at Pipestone Creek County Park, 9 miles/14.5 km south; 99 sites, showers, flush toilets, dump station, boat launch, firewood, fishing, playground, fossil display and an 18-hole golf course with grass greens nearby. Bird watching is good here for red-winged blackbirds and yellow-headed blackbirds.　　　　◄▲

Beaverlodge

E 311 (500.5 km) DC 56 (90.1 km) **Population:** 1,997. **Elevation:** 2,419 feet/737m. **Emergency Services:** RCMP, phone 911. **Ambulance**, phone 911. **Hospital**, Beaverlodge Municipal Hospital, phone (780) 354-2136.

Visitor Information: Located in the restored Lower Beaver Lodge School at Pioneer Campsite on the north side of Highway 43 at the west end of town.

Private Aircraft: DeWit Airpark 2 miles/3.2 km south; elev. 2,289 feet/1,698m; length 3,000 feet/914m; paved; no fuel.

Beaverlodge is a service centre for the area with RCMP, hospital, medical and dental clinic. There are 9 churches, schools, a swimming pool and tennis courts.

Visitor services include 3 motels, 8 restaurants and gas stations. There are supermarkets, banks, a drugstore, car wash and sporting goods store. **Beaverlodge Area Cultural Centre**, at the south end of town, features local arts and crafts as well as a tea room. South Peace Centennial Museum is west of town (see **Milepost E 312**). Camping is available at **Pioneer Campsite**, a municipal campground with 19 sites, showers, dump station, electrical hookups, tourist information. The Beaverlodge Airpark, 2 miles/3.2 km south of town, is becoming a popular stopover on the flying route to Alaska.　　　　▲

Beaverlodge is the gateway to Monkman Pass and Kinuseo Falls. Beaverlodge is also home to Canada's most northerly Agricultural Research Station (open to the public), and serves as regional centre for grain transportation, seed cleaning and seed production. Cereal grains, such as wheat, barley and oats, are the main crops in the area. The PRT Alberta Inc. reforestation nursery here, visible from the highway as you enter town, grows about 8 million seedlings a year. Tours are available; phone (780) 354-2288.

Town of Beaverlodge. See display ad this section.

East Access Route Log

(continued)

E 312 (502.1 km) DC 55 (88.5 km) **South Peace Centennial Museum** to east, open daily in summer; phone (780) 354-8869. Well worth a stop, the museum features vintage vehicles and working steam-powered farm equipment from the early 1900s. Open 10 A.M. to 8 P.M., mid-May through mid-October. The annual Pioneer Day celebration, held here the third Sunday in July, attracts several thousand visitors.

E 312.4 (502.7 km) DC 54.6 (87.9 km) Turnoff for Driftwood Ranch Wildlife Haven, 14.3 miles/23 km west, a private collection of exotic and endangered animals. Opens May 1 for season; phone (780) 356-3769 for more information.

E 314.3 (505.8 km) DC 52.6 (84.8 km) Golf course. This joint project of Hythe and Beaverlodge residents has a clubhouse that was once an NAR station. The 9-hole par 35 course has grass greens. Visitors are welcome; rentals available.

E 320 (515 km) DC 47 (75.6 km) **HYTHE** (pop. 623) is an agricultural service community and processing center for fruit and berry crops, especially saskatoon berries. Canola is also a major crop. The town has a motel, a bed and breakfast, restaurant, laundromat, gas station, tire repair, car wash, outdoor covered heated swimming pool, complete shopping facilities and a hospital. Municipal campground in town with 17 sites, showers, dump station and playground. The information centre is housed in the Tags Food and Gas store. Inquire locally for directions to Riverside Bison Ranch. An old 1910 tack shop, staffed by volunteers in summer, is located between the highway and railroad tracks.　　　　▲

E 329 (529.4 km) DC 38 (61.1 km) **Junction** with Highway 59 east to Sexsmith.

E 337 (542.3 km) DC 30 (48.3 km) **DEMMITT**, an older settlement, site of a sawmill (worth a visit), postal service, cafe and gas.

E 340 (547.2 km) DC 27 (43.4 km) Railway crossing.

E 341 (548.8 km) DC 26 (41.8 km) Public campground to east; 15 sites, shelter, firewood, tables, pit toilets, pump water and playground.　　　　▲

E 341.3 (549.2 km) DC 25.7 (41.3 km) Vehicle inspection station to west.

E 342 (550.4 km) DC 25 (40.2 km) Gas, diesel and convenience store.

E 343.3 (552.5 km) DC 23.7 (38.1 km) Alberta–British Columbia border. Turnout

with litter barrels and pay phone.

TIME ZONE CHANGE: Alberta is on Mountain time; most of British Columbia is on Pacific time.

E 345.1 (555.4 km) DC 21.9 (35.2 km) **Junction** with Heritage Highway 52 (gravel surface) which leads 18.5 miles/30 km south to **One Island Lake Provincial Park** (30 campsites, fee charged, rainbow and brook trout fishing) and 92 miles/148 km southwest from Highway 2 to Tumbler Ridge townsite, built in conjunction with the North East Coal development. Monkman Provincial Park, site of spectacular Kinuseo Falls, lies south of Tumbler Ridge. A campground with viewing platform of falls is accessible via a 25-mile/40-km road from Tumbler Ridge. Heritage Highway loops north 59.5 miles/96 km from Tumbler Ridge to join Highway 97 just west of Dawson Creek (see **Milepost PG 237.7** in the WEST ACCESS ROUTE section).

E 345.7 (556.3 km) DC 21.3 (34.3 km) Tupper Creek bridge.

E 347 (558.5 km) DC 20 (32.1 km) Swan Lake Provincial Park, with 41 campsites, picnic area, playground and boat launch, is 1.2 miles/2 km north of the tiny hamlet of **TUPPER**, which has a general store.　　▲

E 347.9 (559.9 km) DC 19.1 (30.7 km) Sudeten Provincial Park day-use area; 8 picnic tables. Plaque tells of immigration to this valley of displaced residents of Sudetenland in 1938–39.

E 348.9 (561.5 km) DC 18.1 (29.1 km) Tate Creek bridge.

E 349.7 (562.7 km) DC 17.3 (27.8 km) Side road west to community of Tomslake.

E 356.3 (573.4 km) DC 10.7 (17.2 km) Turnout to east with litter barrel.

E 358 (576.1 km) DC 9 (14.5 km) Historic sign tells of Pouce Coupe Prairie.

E 359.4 (578.4 km) 7.6 (12.2 km) Railway crossing.

E 360 (579.3 km) DC 7 (11.2 km) Weigh scales to east.

E 360.4 (580 km) DC 6.6 (10.6 km) Bissett Creek bridge. Regional park located at south end of bridge.

E 361 (581 km) DC 6 (9.6 km) **POUCE COUPE** (pop. 904; elev. 2,118 feet/646m). **Visitor Information:** Tourist Bureau Office located in Pouce Coupe Museum, 5006 49th Ave. (1 block south of Highway 2). Open 8 A.M. to 5 P.M., May 15 to Sept. 15. Phone (250) 786-5555.

The Pouce Coupe area was first settled in 1898 by a French Canadian, Hector Tremblay, who set up a trading post in 1908. The Edson Trail, completed in 1911, brought in the main influx of settlers from Edmonton in 1912. Historical artifacts are displayed at the **Pouce Coupe Museum**, located in the old NAR railroad station. 1998 marks the 100th anniversary of Tremblay's arrival and the 25th anniversary of the museum.

The village has a motel, hotel, restaurant, post office, gas station, dump station, car wash, municipal office, library, schools and food store. Camping at Regional Park, open May to September; hookups.　　▲

E 364.5 (586.6 km) DC 2.5 (4 km) Dawson Creek airport.

E 367 (590.6 km) DC 0 **DAWSON CREEK**, the beginning of the Alaska Highway.

Turn to the ALASKA HIGHWAY section, page 83, for description of Dawson Creek and log of the Alaska Highway.

Alaska Highway via
WEST ACCESS ROUTE (5) (🍁) (97)

Connects: Seattle, WA, to Dawson Creek, BC   **Length:** 817 miles
Road Surface: Paved   **Season:** Open all year
Highest Summit: Pine Pass, 3,068 feet
Major Attractions: Fraser River Canyon/Hell's Gate, Barkerville
(See maps, pages 56–57)

	Cache Creek	Dawson Creek	Prince George	Seattle
Cache Creek		527	277	290
Dawson Creek	527		250	817
Prince George	277	250		567
Seattle	290	817	567	

Bijoux Falls Provincial Park, between Prince George and Dawson Creek at Milepost PG 115.3, makes a pleasant picnic stop. (© Earl L. Brown, staff)

The West Access Route links Interstate 5, Trans-Canada Highway 1 and BC Highway 97 to form the most direct route to Dawson Creek, BC, for West Coast motorists. This has been the major western route to the start of the Alaska Highway since 1952, when the John Hart Highway connecting Prince George and Dawson Creek was completed.

Travelers may also continue on I-5 to the international border at Blaine (22 miles/35.4 km beyond Exit 256), the more direct route if you are bound for Vancouver, BC.

The West Access Route junctions with Yellowhead Highway 16 at Prince George. This east–west highway connects with the Alaska State Ferry System and BC Ferries at Prince Rupert, and with the East Access Route to the Alaska Highway at Edmonton. Turn to the YELLOWHEAD HIGHWAY 16 section for a complete log of that route.

Distances via this 817-mile route between Seattle, WA, and Dawson Creek, BC, are: Seattle to Abbotsford, 120 miles; Abbotsford to Cache Creek, 170 miles; Cache Creek to Prince George, 277 miles; and Prince George to Dawson Creek, 250 miles.

The West Access Route log is divided into 4 sections: Seattle to the Canadian border; Abbotsford to Cache Creek; Cache Creek to Prince George; and Prince George to Dawson Creek.

West Access Route Log

This section of the log shows distance from Seattle (S) followed by distance from the Canadian border (CB) at Sumas.

INTERSTATE HIGHWAY 5

S 0 CB 116 (186.7 km) Exit 165 northbound (165B southbound) to downtown **SEATTLE** (pop. 532,900), the Alaska gateway city since the Klondike Gold Rush days, when it became the major staging and departure point for most of the gold seekers.

S 12 (19.3 km) **CB 104** (167.4 km) Exit 177 east to **LAKE FOREST PARK** (pop. 3,402) and west 4.5 miles to **EDMONDS** (pop. 30,341). Food, gas, diesel east off exit.

S 28 (45 km) **CB 88** (141.6 km) Exit 193 to **EVERETT** (pop. 76,685); all services.

S 34 (54.7 km) **CB 82** (132 km) Exit 199 to **MARYSVILLE** (pop. 11,714); food, gas and lodging either side of freeway.

S 41 (66 km) **CB 75** (120.7 km) Exit 206 to Twin Lakes Park day-use area 1 mile west, Wenberg State Park 6.2 miles west. Arlington Airport 2.3 miles east. 24-hour gas, food and shopping east off exit.

S 42 (67.6 km) **CB 74** (119.1 km) Rest area northbound.

S 43 (69.2 km) **CB 73** (117.5 km) Exit 208; food, 24-gas and diesel east off exit.

S 56 (90.1 km) **CB 60** (96.5 km) Exit 221 to **La CONNER** (pop. 751), 11 miles northwest; gas station east off exit.

S 61 (98.2 km) **CB 55** (88.5 km) Exit 226 to **MOUNT VERNON** (pop. 20,680); all services.

S 65 (104.6 km) **CB 51** (82 km) Exit 230 to **BURLINGTON** (pop. 4,854) to east, and **ANACORTES** (pop. 12,871, 16 miles/20 km west. Food, gas and lodging at exit.

S 66 (106.2 km) **CB 50** (80.5 km) Exit 231 to Chucaknut Drive scenic route and access to Bay View State Park.

S 67 (107.8 km) **CB 49** (78.9 km) Exit 232 to diesel, 24-hour gas, food and camping.

S 73 (117.5 km) **CB 43** (69.2 km) Rest area.

S 81 (130.3 km) **CB 35** (56.3 km) Exit to North Lake Samish and Lake Padden Recreation Area; diesel, gas and groceries west off exit.

S 85 (136.8 km) **CB 31** (50 km) Exit 250 to **Bellingham's Fairhaven Transportation Center** and **Bellingham Cruise Terminal**, departure point for Alaska State Ferries.

S 88 (141.6 km) **CB 28** (45.1 km) Exit 253 to **BELLINGHAM** (pop. 57,830); all services.

S 91 (146.4 km) **CB 25** (40.2 km) Exit 256 to Washington Highway 539 north to Lynden and the Canadian border; access to Bellis Fair Mall parkway, food, gas and lodging at this exit.

Follow Highway 539 North 12 miles to **junction** with Highway 546. Continue on
(Continues on page 58)

WEST ACCESS ROUTE

Lac La Hache, BC, to Dawson Creek, BC (includes Hudson's Hope Loop)

© 1999 The MILEPOST®

To Wonowon
(see ALASKA HIGHWAY section)

BRITISH COLUMBIA | ALBERTA

C-74.2/119.4km Pine Ridge Campground C

Hudson's Hope Loop Road

Fort St. John

C-40/65km
AH-47/75km

Hudson's Hope

C-87/140km
AH-0

DC-0
E-367/591km
PG-250/402km
CC-527/848km

W.A.C. Bennett Dam

C-40.4/65km Hudson's Hope Museum

N55°46' W120°14'

Williston Lake

Peace River

ROCKY

Big Lake

Dawson Creek

49 → To RYCROFT

Moberly L.

PG-178.4/287.1km Caron Creek RV Park CD

Chetwynd

East Pine

East Pine River

Groundbirch

2

PG-144.3/232.2km Silver Sands Lodge CGILM

Pine River

DC-62/100km
PG-188/302km
C-0

29

Heritage Highway

To GRANDE PRAIRIE
(see EAST ACCESS ROUTE section)

97 LeMoray

Azouzetta L.

Mackenzie

Murray R.

J-18/29km Mackenzie Chamber of Commerce

39

Pine Pass
2,868 ft./874m

Bullmoose Creek

J-55.9/90km District of Tumbler Ridge

DC-155/249km
PG-95/153km

Pack River

Misinchinka River

Tudyah Lake

MOUNTAINS

Tumbler Ridge

J-56/90km

McLeod R.

McLeod Lake
Fort McLeod

PG-71.8/115.5km Whiskers Bay Resort CILMS

Key to mileage boxes

| miles/kilometres |
| miles/kilometres from: |

CC- Cache Creek
PG- Prince George
DC- Dawson Creek
J- Junction
AH- Alaska Highway
PR- Prince Rupert
E- Edmonton
C- Chetwynd

Map Location

McLeod's Lake

Bear Lake

PG-44.8/72.1km Grizzly Inn Restaurant, Motel and RV Park CDdGILMT

Carp Lake

Crooked River

Tacheeda Lakes

Parsnip R.

Davie Lake

Salmon River

Summit L.

John Hart Highway

DC-250/402km
PG-0
CC-277/446km
PR-448/720km
E-450/724km

97

PG-26.9/43.3km Historic Huble Homestead

PG-14.7/23.6km Salmon Valley Resort & Campground CDIST

PG-9.5/15.3km Hart Highway Campground CT
PG-6.4/10.3km Hartway RV Park & Antiques CDIT

Principal Route

Paved / Unpaved

Other Roads

Paved / Unpaved

Ferry Routes | **Hiking Trails**

Refer to Log for Visitor Facilities

Scale
0 — 20 Miles
0 — 20 Kilometres

Key to Advertiser Services

C -Camping
D -Dump Station
d -Diesel
G -Gas (reg., unld.)
I -Ice
L -Lodging
M -Meals
P -Propane
R -Car Repair (major)
r -Car Repair (minor)
S -Store (grocery)
T -Telephone (pay)

To Prince Rupert
(see YELLOWHEAD HIGHWAY 16 section)

16

Nechako River

Prince George

Purden Lake

Fraser River

Cluculz L.

Bednesti L.

N53°55' W122°46'

CC-274/440.9km Sintich Trailer & RV Park CDT
CC-273/439.3km Southpark RV Park CIT

97

CC-268.3/431.8km Bee Lazee RV Park CDIST

CC-258.3/415.7km Fraser River RV Park CT

CARIBOO

To Tete Jaune Cache
(see YELLOWHEAD HIGHWAY 16 section)

BRITISH COLUMBIA

ALBERTA

COLUMBIA

Hixon

CC-241/387.8km Hixon Fireplace Inn M

Cariboo Highway

J-46.7/75.2km Cariboo Tourism Association

Bowron Lake

Bowron Lake Provincial Park

MOUNTAINS

CC-226/363.7km Cinema 2nd Hand CIST

CC-209.5/337.2km Lazy Daze Resort CDILST

Cottonwood

26

Wells

Barkerville

J-50/80.5km Becker's Lodge Ltd. CLM

Glaciated Area

N52°59' W122°29'

Quesnel

Cottonwood R.

Cottonwood Dragon L.

Jack of Clubs Lake

J-51/82km

PG-74/119km
CC-203/327km
J-0

CC-197.5/317.8km Valhalla Motel L

CC-196/315.4km Robert's Roost Campsite CDILT

CC-195.8/315.1km Dragon Lake Golf Course & Campsite CDM

Fraser River

Likely

MOUNTAINS

Quesnel R.

Quesnel Lake

Wells Gray Provincial Park

McLeese Lake

CC-166/267km The Castle
CC-164/263.9km Cariboo Wood Shop

McLeese L.

CC-141.8/228.2km Whispering Willows Outpost Campground and Store CDS

Horsefly

Horsefly Lake

Soda Creek

CC-128/206km Super 8 Motel L

Hendrix Lake

INTERIOR PLATEAU

Williams Lake

150 Mile House

CC-96/154.5km Crystal Springs (Historical) Resort Ltd. CDILST

PG-149/240km
CC-128/206km

CC-93.4/150.3km Kokanee Bay Motel and Campground CDILST
CC-93.3/150km Clancy's dGMPST
CC-92/148.1km Fir Crest Resort CDILST

Eagle Creek

Canim L.

Mahood L.

FRASER PLATEAU

To Bella Coola

20

97

Williams Lake

N52°07' W122°09'

Lac La Hache

PG-189/304km
CC-88/142km

(map continues previous page)

(Continued from page 55)
Highway 546 for 13 miles to **junction** with Highway 9.

S 116 (186.7 km) **CB 0** U.S.–Canada International border at Sumas, WA. The Sumas, WA–Huntingdon, BC, border crossing is open 24-hours.

Follow BC Highway 11 north 4 miles/6.4 km to Abbotsford.

This section of the log shows distance from Abbotsford (A) followed by distance from Cache Creek (CC).

TRANS-CANADA HIGHWAY 1

A 0 CC 170 (273.6 km) Exit 92. **Junction** of Trans-Canada Highway 1 and Highway 11 south to the international border crossing at Sumas–Huntingdon. Highway 11 north to **ABBOTSFORD** (pop. 105,403), all visitor services. Abbotsford is the "Raspberry Capital of Canada" and is the home of the Abbotsford International Airshow in August. **Visitor Information:** Abbotsford Chamber of Commerce, 2462 McCallum Road; phone (604) 859-9651.

Highway 11 north crosses the bridge over the Fraser River to Mission (7.2 miles/11.9 km north), and connects with Highway 7 to Harrison Hot Springs (41 miles/66 km). This 2-lane highway traverses the rural farmland on the north side of the Fraser River, rejoining Trans-Canada Highway 1 at Hope (56 miles/90 km).

A 1.9 (3 km) **CC 168.1** (270.5 km) Exit 95 to Whatcom Road and westbound exit to Sumas River rest area. Access to Sumas Mountain Provincial Park; hiking.

A 5.3 (8.5 km) **CC 164.7** (265.1 km) Exit 99 to Sumas River rest area (eastbound only); tables, toilet, pay phones.

A 8.8 (14.2 km) **CC 161.2** (259.4 km) Exit 104 to small farming community of Yarrow and road to Cultus Lake. The Lower Fraser Valley is prime agricultural land.

CAUTION: Watch for farm vehicles crossing freeway.

A 15 (24.1 km) **CC 155** (249.4 km) Exit 116 to Lickman Road; access south to Visitor Infocentre, open daily in summer, and Cottonwood Meadows RV park. Chilliwack Antique Powerland museum located behind the infocentre. ▲

Cottonwood Meadows RV Country Club. Exit 116. Highly rated and recommended by Good Sam, Woodalls, Tourism B.C. New, secure, clean, well-maintained, full service park. Easy access, electronic gates, well lit and well managed. Lazy stream, full hookups, cable TV, wide level sites, paved roadways. Nicest washrooms, laundromat, clubhouse, Jacuzzi, pay phone. Near U.S. border crossing, shopping centers, golf courses. Pets on leash only. Open end of March to early November. VISA, MasterCard. 44280 Luckakuk Way, Chilliwack, BC V2R 4A7. Phone (604) 824-PARK (7275).
[ADVERTISEMENT]

A 16.8 (27.1 km) **CC 153.2** (246.5 km) Highway 119B to Chilliwack Airport.

A 17 (27.4 km) **CC 153** (246.2 km) Exit 119 north to Chilliwack (all services, description follows) and south to Sardis (all services) and Cultus Lake Provincial Park.

Cultus Lake Provincial Park has 300 campsites; water, flush and pit toilets, showers, firewood, water, boat launch, swimming, fishing, canoeing, kayaking, and hiking and walking trails. Cultus Lake resort area also offers water slides, go-carts and other activities. 🐟▲

CHILLIWACK (pop. 60,186) has motels, restaurants, shopping malls, banks, gas stations, RV parks and other services. There is a library, 2 movie theatres and an arts centre. Recreational attractions include golf and the popular Cultus Lake area with water park, boat rentals, horseback riding and camping. **Visitor Information:** Chilliwack Chamber of Commerce, phone (604) 858-8121. ▲

A 18 (29 km) **CC 152** (244.6 km) Exit 123 Prest Road north to Rosedale, south to Ryder Lake.

A 23.2 (37.4 km) **CC 146.8** (236.2 km) Exit 129 for Annis Road and RV park. ▲

Chilliwack RV Park and Campground. See display ad this section. ▲

A 26.5 (42.5 km) **CC 143.5** (230.9 km) Exit 135 to Highway 9 east to Harrison Hot Springs and alternate route Highway 7 to Hope and Vancouver. Westbound exit for Bridal Veil Falls. Also exit here for access

to Minter Gardens, which rivals Victoria's famous Butchart Gardens for beauty. The 27 acres of floral displays feature 11 themed gardens, topiary figures and a rare collection of Chinese Penjing Rock Bonsai. Opens 9 A.M. daily, April through October. Entertainment is scheduled Sundays and holidays, weather permitting. Internet: www.minter.org.

Exit north for Cheam Lake Wetlands Regional Park. Once mined for its marl deposits, Cheam Lake is now a wildlife habitat; interpretive trails, good bird watching.

Minter Gardens. See display ad this section.

Bridal Falls Camperland. If you are heading to Alaska using the western route, spending a day or two in the beautiful Bridal Falls area is a must. Camperland is a full-facility, 5-star RV resort featuring a huge heated pool, hot tubs, clubhouse, licensed restaurant and large sites (50-amp) that will accommodate the largest RVs. Within 1 mile are numerous tourist attractions, restaurants, museums, golf. Phone (604) 794-7361. See display ad this section. [ADVERTISEMENT] ▲

A 27.3 (43.9 km) **CC 142.7** (229.6 km) Exit 138 to Popkum Road. Eastbound access to **Bridal Veil Falls Provincial Park** to south; picnicking, trail to base of falls. Also access to small community of Popkum and various roadside attractions, including water slide, Sandstone Gallery rock and gem museum, and prehistoric-themed amusement park. Food, gas and lodging.

A 34.5 (55.5 km) **CC 135.5** (218.1 km) Exit 146 Herrling Island, a cottonwood tree farm (no access or services), visible from highway.

A 40.5 (65.2 km) **CC 129.5** (208.4 km) Exit 153 to Laidlaw and access to Jones (Wahleach) Lake. Country store on Laidlaw.

A 42.5 (68.4 km) **CC 127.5** (205.2 km) Truck weigh scales; public phone.

A 44.7 (71.9 km) **CC 125.3** (201.6 km) Exit 160 to Hunter Creek rest area; tables, toilet, pay phone, information kiosk.

A 45.5 (73.2 km) **CC 124.5** (200.4 km) Exit 165 to Flood–Hope Road (eastbound); access to private RV park. ▲

Wild Rose Good Sampark.. See display ad this section. ▲

A 48.5 (78.1 km) **CC 121.5** (195.5 km) Exit 168 to Flood–Hope Road (westbound); access to private RV park. ▲

A 48.7 (78.4 km) **CC 121.3** (195.2 km) Silver Creek, Flood–Hope Road exit.

A 50 (80.5 km) **CC 120** (193.1 km) **Junction** of Trans-Canada Highway 1, Highway 3 (Crowsnest Highway) and Highway 5 (Coquihalla Highway). Use Exit 170 northbound for Trans-Canada Highway 1 to Hope.

Hope

A **50.2** (80.8 km) CC **119.8** (192.8 km) Located on the Fraser River near Mount Hope (elev. 6,000 feet/1,289m). **Population:** 6,247. **Elevation:** 140 feet/43m. **Emergency Services:** RCMP, Fire Department, Ambulance, phone 911. Hospital, 1275 7th Ave., phone (604) 869-5656. **Visitor Information:** Visitor Info-Centre and museum building, corner of Hudson Bay Street and Water Avenue, on the right northbound as you enter town. Open daily 8 A.M. to 8 P.M. in July and August, 9 A.M. to 5 P.M. in May, June and September; weekdays only, 10 A.M. to 4 P.M., rest of the year.

Hope is a convenient tourist stop with complete services. About 30 motels and resorts are in Hope or just outside town on Trans-Canada Highway 1 and on Highway 3.

The major attraction in the Hope area is the Coquihalla Canyon Provincial Recreation Area, the focus of which is the Othello Quintette Tunnels. The 5 rock tunnels which cut through the tortuous canyon were part of the Kettle Valley Railway. This stretch of railway has been restored as a walking trail through the tunnels and across bridges. The tunnels are accessible from downtown Hope via Kawkawa Lake Road and Othello Road, about a 10-minute drive.

The Coquihalla Highway, completed in 1987, connects Hope with the Trans-Canada Highway just west of Kamloops, a distance of 118 miles/190 km. This is a 4-lane divided highway; toll charged.

There are several private campgrounds in Hope. ▲

West Access Route Log

(continued)

A **50.7** (81.6 km) CC **119.3** (191.9 km) Bridge over Fraser River. Turnout at north end, access to pedestrian bridge across the Fraser.

A **51.5** (82.8 km) CC **118.5** (190.7 km) **Junction** with Highway 7, which leads west to Harrison Hot Springs (22.5 miles/36 km) and Vancouver.

A **53.1** (85.5 km) CC **116.9** (188.1 km) Rest area (westbound access only) with picnic tables to west by Lake of the Woods.

A **60.8** (97.8 km) CC **109.2** (175.7 km) Easy-to-miss turnoff (watch for sign 1,320 feet/400m before turn) for Emory Creek Provincial Park east of highway; 34 level gravel sites in trees, water, fire rings, picnic tables, firewood, flush and pit toilets, and litter barrels. Camping fee April to October. Hiking and walking trails. Gold panning and fishing in Fraser River. ◄▲

Very much in evidence between Hope and Cache Creek are the tracks of the Canadian National and Canadian Pacific railways. Construction of the CPR—Canada's first transcontinental railway—played a significant role in the history of the Fraser and Thompson river valleys. Begun in 1880, the CPR line between Kamloops and Port Moody was contracted to Andrew Onderdonk.

A **64.8** (104.3 km) CC **105.2** (169.3 km) YALE (pop. 500; elev. 250 feet/76m). **Emergency Services:** Police, Fire Department, Ambulance, phone 911. **Visitor Information:** In the museum, phone (604) 863-2324. Visitor facilities include motels, stores, gas stations and restaurants.

Yale was the head of navigation for the Lower Fraser River and the beginning of the overland gold rush trail to British Columbia's goldfields. The Anglican Church of Saint John the Divine here was built for the miners in 1859 and is the oldest church still on its original foundation in mainland British Columbia. Next to the church is Yale Museum and a bronze plaque honouring Chinese construction workers who helped build the Canadian Pacific Railway. Walking around town, look for the several plaques relating Yale's history. Daily guided walking tours of historic Yale are offered in summer; fee charged, includes admission to museum and church. Phone (604) 863-2428 for more information.

A **65.6** (105.5 km) CC **104.5** (168.2 km) Entering **Fraser Canyon** northbound. The Fraser River and canyon were named for Simon Fraser (1776–1862), the first white man to descend the river in 1808. This is the dry forest region of British Columbia, and it can be a hot drive in summer. The scenic Fraser Canyon travelers drive through today was a formidable obstacle for railroad engineers in 1881.

A **66** (106.2 km) CC **104** (167.4 km) Yale Tunnel, first of several northbound through the Fraser Canyon.

A **67.3** (108.3 km) CC **102.7** (165.2 km) Turnout to east with plaque about the Cariboo Waggon Road, which connected Yale with the Cariboo goldfields near Barkerville. Built between 1861 and 1863 by the Royal Engineers, it replaced an earlier route to the goldfields—also called the Cariboo Waggon Road—which started from Lillooet.

A **68.4** (110.1 km) CC **101.6** (163.5 km) Saddle Rock Tunnel. This 480-foot-/146-m-long tunnel was constructed from 1957–58.

A **72.1** (116 km) CC **97.9** (157.5 km) Private campground. ▲

A **72.3** (116.3 km) CC **97.7** (157.2 km) Sailor Bar Tunnel, nearly 984 feet/300m long. There were dozens of bar claims along the Fraser River in the 1850s bearing colourful names such as Sailor Bar.

A **76.5** (123.1 km) CC **93.5** (150.5 km) Spuzzum (unincorporated), gas station and food.

A **77.1** (124.1 km) CC **92.9** (149.5 km) Stop of interest at south end of Alexandra Bridge, built in 1962, the second largest fixed arch span in the world at more than 1,640 feet/500m in length.

A **77.5** (124.8 km) CC **92.5** (148.9 km) **Alexandra Bridge Provincial Park**, picnic areas and interpretive displays on both sides of highway. Hiking trail down to the old Alexandra Bridge, still intact. This suspension bridge was built in 1926, replacing the original built in 1863.

A **77.8** (125.2 km) CC **92.2** (148.4 km) Historic Alexandra Lodge (closed), is the last surviving original roadhouse on the Cariboo Waggon Road.

A **79.5** (128 km) CC **90.5** (145.6 km) Alexandra Tunnel.

A **80.5** (129.5 km) CC **89.5** (144 km) Rest area by Copper Creek to east.

A **82.6** (133 km) CC **87.4** (140.7 km) Hells Gate Tunnel (328 feet/100m long).

A **83.3** (134 km) CC **86.7** (139.5 km) Ferrabee Tunnel (328 feet/100m long).

A **83.6** (134.5 km) CC **86.4** (139 km) **Hells Gate**, the narrowest point on the Fraser River and a popular attraction. (Northbound traffic park at lot immediately south of attraction on east side of road; southbound traffic park on west side of road at attraction.) Two 25-passenger airtrams take visitors some 500 feet down across the river to a restaurant and shop complex. Footbridge across river to view fishways through which some 2 million salmon pass each year. A display details the life cycle of the salmon, the construction of the International Fishways and the history of Hells Gate. From the foodbridge, visitors may also see rafters running Hells Gate. The trams operate daily, April 1 to Oct. 30, 1999. There is also a steep trail down to the fishways; strenuous hike.

Hells Gate was well named. It was by far the most difficult terrain for construction of both the highway and the railway. To haul supplies for the railway upstream of Hells

Canadian National and Canadian Pacific railways cross over the Fraser River.
(© Roger Pickenpaugh)

Gate, Andrew Onderdonk built the stern-wheel steamer *Skuzzy*. The *Skuzzy* made its way upstream through Hells Gate in 1882, hauled by ropes attached to the canyon walls by bolts.

Hell's Gate Airtram. See display ad this section.

A 83.8 (134.9 km) **CC 86.2** (138.7 km) Hells Gate turnaround for travelers who miss the Hells Gate parking lot.

A 85.7 (137.9 km) **CC 84.3** (135.7 km) China Bar Tunnel, built in 1960. It is almost 2,300 feet/700m long, one of the longest tunnels in North America. Point of interest sign at south end about Simon Fraser.

A 88 (141.6 km) **CC 82** (132 km) **Anderson Creek Campground.** Quiet, secluded, some riverfront locations. Try fishing or view the rafters. Easy turnaround at bottom of hill. Pull-throughs, shaded parking, washrooms and coin-operated showers. 30-amp service, sani-station, reasonable rates. In season, help yourself to fresh fruit off the old orchard trees. Phone (604) 867-9005. [ADVERTISEMENT] ▲

A 91 (146.5 km) **CC 79** (127.1 km) **BOSTON BAR** (pop. 885; elev. 400 feet/122m). **Emergency Services:** Phone 911. Services include gas stations, cafes, grocery stores, motels and private RV parks. Site of the J.S. Jones Timber Mill; tours may be available in summer, phone (604) 867-9214 for information. Boston Bar was the southern landing for the steamer *Skuzzy*, which

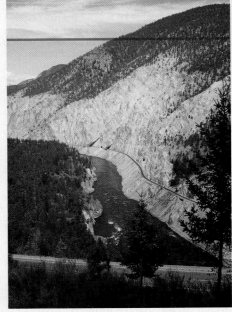

View of precipitous railway route from picnic area at Skihist Provincial Park, Milepost A 122.8. (© Judy Parkin)

plied the Fraser River between here and Lytton during construction of the CPR.

North Bend, located across the river from Boston Bar, is a former railway community. Old cable cage from the aerial car ferry that once served North Bend is on display at the CN station in Boston Bar.

North Bend is the access point for the Nahatlatch River and lakes via a logging road. River rafting trips are available on the Nahatlatch River.

A 94 (151.3 km) **CC 76** (122.3 km) **Canyon Alpine RV Park & Campground.** Still the best-kept secret in the Fraser Canyon, but quickly being discovered and described as "...one of the nicest parks on the Alaskan route." Secure RV parking and tenting 3 miles north of Boston Bar. 31 level, pull-through sites, fully serviced with 30 amp, water, sewer and cable TV. Easy access and turnarounds for rigs over 35 feet. 14-foot entrance gate clearance. Away from traffic noise and railroads. Clean washrooms. Hot showers. Shaded sites. Fire rings. Firewood. 50 yards south of restaurant, store, laundromat and telephones. Pets on leash welcome. 10 minutes from world-famous Hell's Gate Airtram. Open April 15 to Oct. 15. 50490 Trans-Canada Highway. Toll free (800) 644-PARK. Your friendly hosts, Jay and Maggie. See display ad this section. [ADVERTISEMENT] ▲

A 101 (162.5 km) **CC 69** (111 km) Turnoff for Blue Lake, 0.6 mile/1 km gravel road.

A 112.8 (181.5 km) **CC 57.2** (92.1 km) Viewpoint to west overlooking the Fraser River.

A 113.6 (182.9 km) **CC 56.4** (90.7 km) Canadian National and Canadian Pacific railways cross over the Fraser River here; a favorite spot for photos. Gravel turnout to east.

A 114.6 (184.5 km) **CC 55.4** (89.2 km) Skupper rest area (northbound only); toilets, tables, litter barrels.

A 117.8 (189.6 km) **CC 52.2** (84 km)

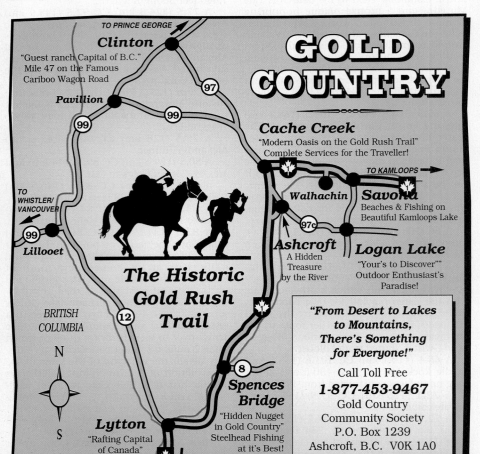

Junction with Highway 12 to Lillooet (see description at **Milepost CC 7**). Turn west here for community of Lytton (description follows).

LYTTON (pop. 322; elev. 561 feet/171m). **Emergency Services: RCMP,** phone (250) 455-2225. **Fire Department,** phone (250) 455-2333. **Ambulance,** phone (250) 374-5937. **Hospital,** St. Bartholomew's, phone (250) 455-2221. **Visitor Information:** Visitor Infocentre, 400 Fraser St., phone (250) 455-2523. Located at the confluence of the Thompson and Fraser rivers, Lytton acts as headquarters for river raft trips. All visitor facilities are available. Sand bars at Lytton yielded much gold, and river frontage has been set aside for recreational gold panning. Lytton has recorded the highest temperature in British Columbia, 111°F/44°C.

Watching rafters on the Thompson River at Goldpan Provincial Park, Milepost A 134.7. (© Blake Hanna, staff)

Lytton. Rafting capital of British Columbia. Whitewater on the Thompson, and Hells Gate on the Fraser. Hiking is great in our interior dry climate, amid beautiful scenery. Enjoy the Stein Valley, Native and Gold Rush history in our museums. Sawmill tours arranged at the Visitor Infocentre, 400 Fraser St., phone (250) 455-2523, fax (250) 455-6669. [ADVERTISEMENT]

A 122.8 (197.6 km) **CC 47.2** (76 km) **Skihist Provincial Park** to east; 58 campsites on east side of highway with water, flush and pit toilets, firewood and dump station. Picnic area on west side of highway (good place to watch the trains go by); wheelchair-accessible restrooms. &▲

A 134.7 (216.8 km) **CC 35.3** (56.8 km) **Goldpan Provincial Park** to west alongside river; 14 campsites, picnic area, water, firewood, canoeing, kayaking, fishing. ◄▲

A 136 (218.9 km) **CC 34** (54.7 km) In summer, watch for fruit stands selling locally grown produce along the highway. Watch for bighorn sheep on the hillsides in the fall.

A 137 (220.5 km) **CC 33** (53.1 km) **BIG HORN;** trading post, fuel, tire shop and 24-hour towing.

Big Horn, BC. Bring your binoculars! Depending on month and season, you may see eagles, osprey, bears, deer or bighorn sheep on our mountain face. Large viewing windows in our cafe. Enjoy our extra-deep-dish pies, custom burgers. We also sell fishing tackle, fishing licenses. Fresh fruit (June–September), local rocks and minerals, fireworks, souvenirs. Trading post. Fuel. 24-hour towing BCAA. Tire shop. Family operated. Box 98, Spences Bridge, BC V0K 2L0. (250) 458-2333. [ADVERTISEMENT]

A 140 (225.3 km) **CC 30** (48.3 km) Junction with Highway 8 to Merritt and south access to Spences Bridge. Plaque here about the great landslide of 1905.

A 141.2 (227.2 km) **CC 28.8** (46.3 km) North access to **SPENCES BRIDGE** (pop. 300; elev. 760 feet/231m) located at the confluence of the Thompson and Nicola rivers. Services include lodging, camping, restaurant,

pub and grocery with tackle and fishing licenses. A record 30-lb., 5-oz. steelhead was caught in the Thompson River in 1984. Look for an osprey nest atop the hydroelectric pole on the east side of the river. ▲

Acacia Grove. One block off Highway 1. RV park, cabins with kitchen units, tenting. Serene river valley setting overlooking the Thompson River, famous for steelhead, salmon, rainbow trout fishing and rafting. Visit with the mountain sheep August to May. Horseshoes, croquet, darts, walking trails to river. Pull-throughs, full service, laundromat, free hot showers, flush toilets, groceries and gift shop. Your hosts Ed and Gayleen Streifel. Phone/fax (250) 458-2227. Box 69, Spences Bridge, BC V0K 2L0. [ADVERTISEMENT] ▲

Log Cabin Pub. You will appreciate this unique log structure. The logs were specially selected and prepared locally, some spanning 50 feet. This pub combines the rustic charm of a turn-of-the-century roadhouse with all the amenities of a neighborhood pub. Excellent food and hospitality by your hosts John and Laurie Kingston. [ADVERTISEMENT]

A 153.4 (246.9 km) **CC 16.6** (26.7 km) Viewpoint overlooking Thompson River with plaque about the Canadian Northern Pacific (now the Canadian National Rail-

way), Canada's third transcontinental railway, completed in 1915.

A 158.4 (255 km) **CC 11.6** (18.7 km) Red Hill rest area to east; tables, toilets, litter barrels, pay phone.

A 164.3 (264.4 km) **CC 5.7** (9.2 km) Stop of interest sign to east describes **Ashcroft Manor Historic Site,** a roadhouse on the Cariboo Waggon Road. Small museum (no charge).

Ashcroft Manor & Tea House. See display ad this section.

Summer temperatures in this dry and desert-like region typically reach the high 80s and 90s (26°C to 32°C). Fields under black plastic mesh tarps—which may be seen as the highway descends northbound—are ginseng, an Asian medicinal root crop. The world supply of North American ginseng, which takes 4 years to mature, is grown in the southern Cariboo.

A 164.5 (264.7 km) **CC 5.5** (8.9 km) **Junction** with road to **ASHCROFT,** a small village on the Thompson River with full tourist facilities just east of the highway. Historic Ashcroft supplanted Yale as gateway to the Cariboo with the arrival of the Canadian Pacific Railway in 1885. There are a number of original buildings with distinctive architectural details. Ashcroft Museum

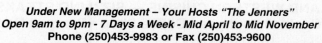

houses a fine collection of artifacts tracing the history of the region. Logan Lake, east of Ashcroft, is the site of the second largest open-pit copper mine in North America (tours available).

Also **junction** with Highway 97C to Logan Lake and Merritt.

A 168.2 (270.7 km) **CC 1.8** (2.9 km) Second turnoff northbound for Ashcroft and road to Logan Lake.

Cache Creek

A 170 (273.6 km) **PG 277** (445.8 km) Located at the junction of Trans-Canada Highway 1 and Highway 97. **Population:** 1,115. **Elevation:** 1,508 feet/460m. **Emergency Services:** RCMP, phone (250) 453-2216. **Ambulance**, phone (250)-374-5937. **Hospital**, phone (250) 453-5306.

Visitor Information: Write Box 460, Cache Creek, BC V0K 1H0; fax (250) 457-9669.

Cache Creek has ample facilities for the traveler (most located on or just off the main highways), including motels, restaurants,

Irrigating hay fields near Cache Creek. The area's agriculture includes ginseng farming and cattle ranching as well. (© Liz Bryan)

service stations and grocery store. Private campgrounds are available east of Cache Creek on Trans-Canada Highway 1 (across from the golf course) and just north of town on Highway 97.

A post office and bus depot are on Todd Road. Nearby, Cariboo Jade Shoppe offers free stone-cutting demonstrations in summer. On display out front is a 2,850-lb. jade boulder. Public park and swimming pool on the Bonaparte River, east off Highway 97 at the north edge of town.

The settlement grew up around the confluence of the creek and the Bonaparte River. The Hudson's Bay Co. opened a store here, and Cache Creek became a major supply point on the Cariboo Waggon Road. Today, hay and cattle ranching, ginseng farming, mining, logging and tourism support the community. Area soils are dry but fertile. Residents claim that with irrigation nearly anything can be grown here.

From the junction, Highway 97 leads north 277 miles/445.8 km to Prince George. Kamloops is 52 miles/83.7 km east via Trans-Canada Highway 1. Traveling north from Cache Creek the highway generally follows the historic route to the Cariboo goldfields.

Brookside Campsite. 1 km east of Cache Creek on Highway 1, full (30 amp) and partial hookups, pull-throughs, tent sites, super- clean heated wash and laundry rooms, free showers, sani-stations, store, playground, nature path, heated pool, golf course adjacent, pets on leash, pay phones. VISA, MasterCard, C.P. two days. Box 737, Cache Creek, BC V0K 1H0. Phone/fax: (250) 457-6633. [ADVERTISEMENT]　　　&▲

West Access Route Log
(continued)

From Cache Creek, continue north on BC Highway 97 for Dawson Creek. Kilometre-posts on this section of highway are located on the east side of the highway facing west, so that they may be seen by traffic traveling in either direction. Highway 97 between Cache Creek and Prince George is called the **Cariboo Highway,** and the region is locally referred to as "Super, Natural Cariboo Country." Contact the Cariboo Tourist Assoc., P.O. Box 4900, Williams Lake, BC V2G 2V8; phone toll free (800) 663-5885.

This section of the log shows distance from Cache Creek (CC) followed by distance from Prince George (PG).

BC HIGHWAY 97/CARIBOO HIGHWAY

CC 0 PG 277 (445.8 km) Cache Creek, **junction** of Trans-Canada Highway 1 and Highway 97.

CC 2.5 (4 km) **PG 274.5** (441.8 km) **Cache Creek Campground,** 3 km north of Cache Creek on Highway 97 north. Full hookups, pull-throughs and tenting, sani-station, store, country kitchen restaurant, laundromat, coin showers, heated washrooms. Outdoor pool and whirlpool (no charge). 18-hole mini-golf, horseshoes, seasonal river swimming and fishing. P.O. Box 127, Cache Creek, BC V0K 1H0. For reservations, phone (250) 457-6414. See display ad

this section. [ADVERTISEMENT]　　▲

CC 7 (11.3 km) **PG 270** (434.5 km) **Junction** with Highway 99 to Hat Creek Ranch, Marble Canyon Provincial Park (descriptions follow) and to **LILLOOET** (pop. 2,984), a 46.5-mile/75-km drive west from here. Lillooet boasts high summer temperatures, rockhounding, gold panning and 15 historic points of interest from the gold rush days.

Drive 0.4 mile/0.7 km west on Highway 99 for Hat Creek Heritage Ranch, a restored Cariboo Trail roadhouse and farm with reconstructed barn, working blacksmith shop, wagon and trail rides and tours.

Historic Hat Creek Ranch. Explore the history of this 326-acre attraction. Tour the 1861 travelers' roadhouse, over 25 rooms each with a unqiue story to share. Visit the native Shuswap Vilage. See their summer and winter homes. Learn about the foods they ate, the gates they played and the life they led. Relax in the heritage apple orchard. Cool off in the air-conditioned gift shop and coffee shop. Open daily 10 A.M. to 6 P.M. June to September. 1-800-782-0922. [ADVERTISEMENT]

Marble Canyon Provincial Park, 17.5 miles/28 km west on Highway 99, has 34 campsites, picnicking, swimming and hiking trails.　　　▲

This route, formerly Highway 12, was designated as part of Highway 99 when the logging road between Lillooet and Pemberton was paved, making it possible to drive to the Cariboo from Vancouver (209 miles/336.5 km from here) via Whistler and Blackcombe ski areas. Highway 99, promoted as the "Sea to Sky Highway," is a scenic route with many winding sections and steep (to 13 percent) grades. Sea to Sky Highway is logged in *Northwest Mileposts®.*

CC 10 (16 km) **PG 267** (430 km) Gravel turnout with plaque about the BX stage-coaches that once served Barkerville. Formally known as the BC Express Company, the BX served the Cariboo for 50 years.

CC 13.6 (21.9 km) **PG 263.4** (423.9 km) Paved road leads east to Loon Lake, rainbow fishing, boat launch. Camping at **Loon Lake Provincial Park** (16 miles/26 km); 14 sites, water, pit toilets, firewood.　　⊷▲

CC 16.6 (26.7 km) **PG 260.4** (419.1 km) Carguile rest area.

CC 25 (40.2 km) **PG 252** (405.5 km) **Junction** with Pavilion Mountain Road west to Pavilion via Kelly Lake. Camping at **Downing Provincial Park** (11 miles/18 km); 25 sites, swimming, fishing.　　⊷▲

CC 25.5 (41 km) **PG 251.5** (404.7 km) **CLINTON** (pop. 729, area 4,000; elev. 2,911 feet/887m). **Visitor Information:** Available at various local businesses; look for signs. All visitor facilities are available, including 3 motels, campground, gas stations, 24-hour towing and stores. Originally the site of 47 Mile Roadhouse, a gold-rush settlement on the Cariboo Waggon Road from Lillooet, today Clinton is called the "guest ranch capital of British Columbia." The museum,

housed in a building of local, handmade red brick that once served as a courthouse, has fine displays of pioneer tools and items from the gold rush days, and a scale model of the Clinton Hotel. Clinton pioneer cemetery just north of town. Clinton boasts the oldest continuously held event in the province, the Clinton Ball (in May the weekend following Victoria Day), an annual event since 1868.

Clinton has its own sign forest. Visitors may sign a wooden slab (donated by the local sawmill) and add it to the sign forest.

Gold Trail RV Park. Fully serviced sites, 30-amp power. Pull-throughs. Immaculate. Washrooms with flush toilets, handicap-equipped. Free hot showers for guests. On highway in town; easy walking to all amenities. Well-lit level sites. Grassed and landscaped. Sani-station. 1640 Cariboo Highway North, Clinton, BC V0K 1K0. Phone (250) 459-2519.　　　&▲

CC 31 (49.9 km) **PG 246** (395.9 km) Dirt and gravel road leads 21 miles/34 km west to **Big Bar Lake Provincial Park**; 33 campsites, water, pit toilets, firewood, swimming, fishing and boat launch.　　　⊷▲

Clinton Lookout and Big Bar rest area to east just north of turnoff; toilets, tables, litter barrels.

CC 35 (56.3 km) **PG 242** (389.5 km) Loop road leads east 3 miles/5 km to Painted Chasm geological site and **Chasm Provincial Park** picnic area. This 1-mile/1.6-km-long bedrock box canyon was cut by glacial meltwaters.

CC 36.9 (59.4 km) **PG 240.1** (408.9 km) Restaurant, bed-and-breakfast and art gallery.

59 Mile Bed & Breakfast and Arctic Artists Gallery. Original Eskimo art by award-winning carver Iyak. Visit this fine gallery and meet the artist. Iyak uses soapstone, whalebone, musk ox horn and cariboo antler. Also available are paintings by arctic artist Lyle R. Trimble. Compare prices before you go North. Iyak, Laurie and family offer a warm and friendly bed and breakfast. Come and stay with this Eskimo family and relax and enjoy the Gallery. Phone/Fax (250) 459-7076. P.O. Box 518, Clinton, BC V0K 1K0. [ADVERTISEMENT]

59 Mile Restaurant. The place where the German and Canadian homestyle cooking is at home in a great and cozy western atmosphere. We use only fresh, in-season vegetables and fruits. Breakfast served all day. Daily lunch and dinner specials. We are well-known for our delicious schnitzels and homemade pies, cakes, and buns. Licensed 45-seat restaurant with a 20-seat German beer garden/patio. Located on Highway 97 with easy RV access, fully handicap accessible. Overnight parking available. Open year-round. Bus tours and group bookings welcome. Phone (250) 459-7750. Fax (250) 459-7782. [ADVERTISEMENT]　　　&

CC 45 (72.4 km) **PG 232** (373.4 km) **70 MILE HOUSE** (unincorporated), originally a stage stop named for its distance from Lillooet, Mile 0. General store, post office, restaurant, motel, gas station with diesel and bus depot.

North Bonaparte Road leads east 7.5 miles/12 km to **Green Lake Provincial Park**; 121 campsites, water, toilets, firewood, dump station, swimming and boat launch. Rainbow and kokanee fishing at Green Lake. Paved road leads north to Watch Lake, east to Bonaparte Lake, and northeast to join Highway 24 at Bridge Lake.　　⊷▲

CC 58.8 (94.7 km) **PG 218.2** (351.1 km)

The 108 Heritage Site at Milepost CC 80.5 has several original log buildings from local pioneer ranches. (© Brian Stein)

83 MILE HOUSE; restaurant, gas, propane, store, public phone. Turnoff for Green Lake (7 miles/11 km).

CC 60 (96 km) PG 217 (347.2 km) Lookout Road to forestry tower on summit of Mount Begbie (elev. 4,186 feet/1,276m); great views.

CC 66 (106.2 km) PG 211 (339.6 km) **Junction** with Highway 24 East to Lone Butte Bridge Lake and Little Fort (60 miles/96.5 km) on Yellowhead Highway 5. Highway 24 provides access to numerous fishing lakes and resorts, including **Bridge Lake Provincial Park** (31 miles/50 km east) with 20 campsites. 🐟▲

100 Mile House

CC 72 (115.9 km) PG 205 (329.9 km) **Population:** 2,600. **Elevation:** 3,050 feet/930m. **Emergency Services:** Police, phone (250) 395-2456. **Ambulance**, phone (250) 395-3288. **Hospital**, phone (250) 395-2202. **Visitor Information:** At the log cabin by 100 Mile House Marsh (a bird sanctuary at the south edge of town); phone (250) 395-5353, fax 395-4085. Look for the 39-foot-/12-m-long skis! Or contact the Cariboo Tourist Assoc., P.O. Box 4900, Williams Lake, BC V2G 2VB; phone toll free (800) 663-5885. Also the South Cariboo Chamber of Commerce, Box 2312, 100 Mile House, BC V0K 2E0; phone (250) 395-5353; Internet: www.netshop.net/-100mile/sccofc.html.

This large, bustling town was once a stop for fur traders and later a post house on the Cariboo Waggon Road to the goldfields. In 1930, the Marquess of Exeter established the 15,000-acre Bridge Creek Ranch here. Today, 100 Mile House is the site of 2 lumber mills, and an extensive log home building industry.

Visitor services include restaurants, motels, a campground, gas stations with repair service, stores, a post office, 2 golf courses, a government liquor store, 2 supermarkets and banks. Shopping malls and the downtown area are located east of the highway. Centennial Park in town has picnic

sites and walking trails. ▲

Horse Lake Road leads east from 100 Mile House to **Horse Lake** (kokanee) and other fishing lakes of the high plateau.

99 Mile Motel. Air-conditioned sleeping and housekeeping units. Fridges in all units, housekeeping units with microwave ovens. DD touchtone phones, remote control cable TV, super channel and TSN, courtesy in-room coffee and tea. Carports, winter plug-ins, freezer available for guests, bowling, legion; supermarket and cross-country ski trails. Senior citizens discount, commercial rates, partially wheelchair accessible, small dogs only. Highway 97, 100 Mile House, BC V0K 2E0. (250) 395-2255 (call collect), or fax (250) 395-2243. [ADVERTISEMENT] ♿

West Access Route Log

(continued)

CC 74 (119 km) PG 203 (326.7 km) **Junction** with road east to **Ruth, Canim** and **Mahood** lakes; resorts and fishing. Camping at **Canim Beach Provincial Park** (27 miles/43 km); 16 sites, water, pit toilets, swimming. Access to Canim Falls. 🐟▲

CC 78.2 (125.8 km) PG 198.8 (319.9 km) **108 Mile Ranch**, a recreational community built in the 1970s, was once a cattle ranch. Motel and golf course.

CC 80.5 (129.5 km) PG 196.5 (316.2 km) Rest area to west beside 108 Mile Lake. Alongside is **108 Heritage Site** with some of the original log buildings from 108 Mile Ranch, and others relocated from 105 Mile. Guided tours; open May to early September.

CC 85 (136.8 km) PG 192 (309 km) **Lac La Hache KOA.** Located on 60 acres of rolling ranchland 3 miles south of Lac La Hache. Heated swimming pool, free showers, store, gift shop, laundromat, games room. Extra-long shady pull-throughs; shaded grassy tent sites; camping cabin. Full hookup facilities, sani-dump, phone. Pets welcome. VISA, MasterCard. (250) 396-4181. Box 68, Lac La Hache, BC V0K 1T0. [ADVERTISEMENT] ▲

CC 88 (141.6 km) PG 189 (304.2 km) **LAC LA HACHE** (pop. 400; elev. 2,749 feet/838m); motels, stores, gas stations and a museum. The community holds a fishing derby in July and a winter carnival in mid-February. Lac La Hache is French for "Ax

Lake." There are many stories of how the lake got its name, but local historian Molly Forbes says it was named by a French–Canadian *coureur de bois* (voyageur) "because of a small ax he found on its shores."

Lac La Hache, lake char, rainbow and kokanee; good fishing summer and winter (great ice fishing). 🐟

CC 92 (148.1 km) PG 185 (297.7 km) **Fir Crest Resort** (Good Sam). Open all year. Quiet parklike setting just 2 minutes from Highway 97, but away from traffic noise. Full hookups including pull-throughs, 50 amp, camping and cabins on the lakeshore. Sandy beach, swimming, games room, groceries, sani-dump, laundromat. Full marina with boat, motor, canoe and tackle rentals. Show this ad for a 10 percent discount. Phone (250) 396-7337. [ADVERTISEMENT] ▲

CC 93.3 (150.1 km) PG 183.7 (295.6 km) **Clancys'** restaurant, truck stop (full-serve gas, diesel, propane), convenience store and gifts. Open 7 A.M.–12 A.M. 2 acres, paved parking, air-conditioned, licensed with home cooking and homemade desserts. Very easy access to pumps for any length of vehicle. American exchange. Clancys', located Mile 122, Highway 97 at Kokanee Bay. [ADVERTISEMENT]

CC 93.4 (150.3 km) PG 183.6 (295.4 km) **Kokanee Bay Motel and Campground.** Relaxation at its finest right on the lakeshore. Fish for kokanee and char or take a refreshing dip. We have a modern, comfortable motel, cabins. Full trailer hookups, grassy tenting area, hot showers, laundromat. Aquabike, boat and canoe rentals. Fishing tackle and ice. Phone (250) 396-7345. Fax (250) 396-4990. [ADVERTISEMENT] ▲

CC 96 (154.5 km) PG 181 (291.3 km) **Crystal Springs (Historical) Resort Ltd.** Visit the Cariboo's best. We honour Good Sam, AAA and are a Good Neighbor Park, senior rates. 8 miles north of Lac La Hache. Parklike setting on lakeshore. Showers, flush toilets, laundromat, full (20- and 30-amp pull-throughs) and partial hookups, boat rentals. New chalets. Groceries, tackle, camping supplies, handicrafts. Games room, playground, picnic shelter. Pets on leash. Public

FREE MILEPOST® BUMPER STICKER

Just complete the attached questionnaire and return the postage-paid card or fax to

1-907-258-5360

FREE

"I Drove the Alaska Highway with The Milepost"

B U M P E R   S T I C K E R !

To receive a free "I Drove the Alaska Highway with The Milepost" bumper sticker, simply complete our questionnaire and return this postage-paid card, or fax copy of card to us at the number below. Offer good while supplies last. Remember to include your name and address on the bottom of the card.

First 50 surveys returned, receive a FREE one-year subscription to Alaska Magazine.

1. Your age group is:
   - ❏ 18 -25
   - ❏ 26 -29
   - ❏ 30 - 39
   - ❏ 40-49
   - ❏ 50 - 54
   - ❏ 55 - 64

2. Your annual household income range is:
   - ❏ Under $50,000
   - ❏ $50,000 - $75,000
   - ❏ $100,000 - $125,000
   - ❏ Over $150,000

3. The mode(s) of transportation used on your Alaska trip:
   - ❏ Recreational Vehicle/Camper
   - ❏ Car
   - ❏ Motorcycle
   - ❏ Rental Car
   - ❏ Airplane
   - ❏ Ferry
   - ❏ Cruise Ship
   - ❏ Railroad
   - ❏ Bus

4. The number of persons in your Alaska travel party was (or will be):
   - ❏ 1
   - ❏ 2
   - ❏ 3 or more

5. The duration of your Alaska trip was (or will be):
   - ❏ Under 2 weeks
   - ❏ 2 - 3 weeks
   - ❏ 3 - 4 weeks
   - ❏ 4 - 5 weeks
   - ❏ More than 5 weeks

6. Please check the activities in which you plan to (or did) participate:
   - ❏ Fishing
   - ❏ Hunting
   - ❏ Boating
   - ❏ Camping
   - ❏ Hiking
   - ❏ Cycling
   - ❏ Photography
   - ❏ Tours/Sightseeing
   - ❏ Other Activities _____

7. On average, how many meals a day did you eat out:
   - ❏ 1
   - ❏ 2
   - ❏ 3
   - ❏ Rarely or never ate out

8. Did you purchase goods or services from a MILEPOST advertiser?
   - ❏ Yes
   - ❏ No

9. The number of vacation trips you usually take each year is:
   - ❏ 1
   - ❏ 2
   - ❏ 3
   - ❏ 4 or more

10. Have you traveled to Alaska within the past two years?
   - ❏ Yes
   - ❏ No

11. Do you plan to visit Alaska in the next two years?
   - ❏ Yes
   - ❏ No

12. The number of vacation trips you usually take each year is:
   - ❏ 1
   - ❏ 2
   - ❏ 3
   - ❏ 4 or more

13. Which of the following items did you take on your last Alaska trip, or plan to take on your next trip?
   - ❏ Digital Camera
   - ❏ Camcorder
   - ❏ Sleeping bag
   - ❏ Camp stove
   - ❏ Tent
   - ❏ Backpack
   - ❏ Fishing Tackle
   - ❏ Fishing Electronics
   - ❏ Hunting/target shooting equipment
   - ❏ 35mm Camera
   - ❏ Binoculars
   - ❏ Boat
   - ❏ Power boat
   - ❏ Kayak
   - ❏ Videocassette recorder
   - ❏ Recreational Vehicle/Type/Brand _____
   - ❏ Bicycle
   - ❏ Off-road vehicle

14. Did you use the guide to help select:
   - ❏ Places to eat and sleep
   - ❏ Places to visit
   - ❏ Routes to take on your trip
   - ❏ Charters or tour to take

15. Where did you learn about the Milepost?
   - ❏ Magazine _____
   - ❏ Catalog _____
   - ❏ Book Review
   - ❏ Friend/ Relative
   - ❏ Word of Mouth
   - ❏ Travel Agent
   - ❏ Other (specify)_____

Name_____

Address_____

City_____ State_____ Zip_____

Phone_____ Fax_____

E-mail_____

Please fax completed card to 1-907-258-5360 or tear card out at perforation and mail.
Fold the card along the panels, tape, and mail.

Fold this panel and tape so that the return address below is on the outside.

Fold this panel before mailing.

beach and boat launch adjacent, fishing. Your hosts, Doug and Lorraine Whitesell. Phone (250) 396-4497. [ADVERTISEMENT]

CC 96 (154.5 km) **PG 181** (291.3 km) **Lac La Hache Provincial Park**; 83 campsites, lakeshore picnic area, water, flush and pit toilets, firewood, dump station, boat launch, swimming, hiking trail and fishing. Camping on east side of highway, picnicking and boat launch on west side of highway.

CC 97 (156.1 km) **PG 180** (289.7 km) San Jose River parallels highway to west. Canadian artist A.Y. Jackson painted in this valley.

CC 104.4 (168 km) **PG 172.6** (277.7 km) Stop of interest sign commemorating the miners, traders and adventurers who came this way to the Cariboo goldfields in the 1860s.

CC 116.6 (187.6 km) **PG 160.4** (258.1 km) 148 Mile Ducks Unlimited conservation area. This is an important waterfowl breeding area in Canada and offers good bird watching for bald eagles, osprey, great horned owls, American kestrels and pileated woodpeckers.

CC 118.5 (190.7 km) **PG 158.5** (255.1 km) **150 MILE HOUSE**, so named because it was 150 miles from Lillooet on the old Cariboo Waggon Road. The post office, which serves about 1,200 people in the area, was established in 1871. Hotel, restaurant, pub, gas station with repair service and a store open daily. Hunting and fishing licenses available at the store.

CC 119.1 (191.7 km) **PG 157.9** (254.1 km) **Junction** with road to Quesnel and Horsefly lakes. **Horsefly Lake Provincial Park** (40 miles/65 km) has 22 campsites. Fishing for rainbow and lake trout.

Williams Lake

CC 128 (206 km) **PG 149** (239.8 km) Located at the junction of Highway 97 and Highway 20 to Bella Coola. **Population:** 36,737. **Elevation:** 1,922 feet/586m. **Emergency Services: Police,** phone (250) 392-6211. **Hospital,** phone (250) 392-4411. **Ambulance,** phone (250) 392-5402.

Visitor Information: Visitor Infocentre located on east side of highway just south of the junction of Highways 97 and 20, open year-round; phone (250) 392-5025, fax (250) 392-4214. Write 1148 S. Broadway, Williams Lake, BC V2G 1A2. Or contact the Cariboo Tourism Association, P.O. Box 4900, Williams Lake, BC V2G 2V8; phone toll free (800) 663-5885.

Williams Lake has complete services, including hotels/motels, restaurants, an 18-hole golf course and par-3 golf course, a twin sheet arena and pool complex. Highway 97 northbound bypasses the business and shopping districts of downtown Williams Lake, which are situated to the west of the highway. Motels, gas stations and fast-food restaurants are located on frontage roads paralleling Highway 97 on the south side of town.

The famous **Williams Lake Stampede**, British Columbia's premier rodeo, is held here annually on the July 1 holiday. The 4-day event draws contestants from all over Canada and the United States. The rodeo grounds are located in the city.

At the north end of Williams Lake is Scout Island Nature Center. This island is

reached by a causeway, with boardwalks providing access to the marshes. A nature house is open May to August.

Located on the shore of the lake of the same name, the town was named for Shuswap Indian Chief Willyum. It grew rapidly with the advent of the Pacific Great Eastern Railway (now B.C. Railway) in 1919, to become a major cattle marketing and shipping centre for the Cariboo–Chilcotin.

Highway 20, the Chilcotin Highway, heads west from Williams Lake 282 miles/454 km (paved and gravel) to Bella Coola. Highway 20 is logged in *Northwest Mileposts®*.

Super 8 Motel. See display ad this section.

West Access Route Log
(continued)

CC 136.4 (219.5 km) **PG 140.6** (226.3 km) Wildwood Road; gas station, store, access to private campground.

C 141.3 (227.3 km) **PG 135.7** (218.4 km) Turnout with litter barrel.

CC 141.8 (228.2 km) **PG 135.2** (217.6 km) **Whispering Willows Outpost Campground and Store.** RV pull-throughs, sanidump. Power and water hookups, free hot showers, flush toilets. Level, spacious treed area for camping. Safe firepits, wood available. Teepee for rent. Play area. Confectionary store. Pets and horse trailers welcome, corrals available. Deep Creek runs by Whispering Willows Campground, RR 4, Site 12, Comp. 46, Williams Lake, BC V2G 4M8. (250) 989-0359. [ADVERTISEMENT]

CC 145.3 (233.9 km) **PG 131.7** (211.9 km) Turnout with litter barrel.

CC 147.8 (237.9 km) **PG 129.2** (207.9 km) Replica of a turn-of-the-century roadhouse (current status of services unknown) at junction with side road which leads west 2.5 miles/4.5km to the tiny settlement of **SODA CREEK**. The original wagon road to the goldfields ended here and miners went the rest of the way to Quesnel by river steamboats. Soda Creek became an important transfer point for men and supplies until the railway went through in 1920. Soda Creek was so named because the creek bed is carbonate of lime and the water bubbles like soda water.

CC 155 (249.4 km) **PG 122** (196.4 km) **McLEESE LAKE**, small community with gas stations, cafe, post office, store, pub, private campground and motel on McLeese Lake. The lake was named for a Fraser River steamboat skipper. **McLeese Lake**, rainbow to 2 lbs., troll using a flasher, worms or flatfish lure.

Junction with road to Beaver Lake and on to Likely. Historic **Quesnelle Forks**, a heritage site with a Forestry campsite, is located near Likely. Travelers may continue north from Likely to Barkerville and rejoin Highway 97 at Quesnel.

CC 155.5 (250.2 km) **PG 121.5** (195.5

km) Rest area to west overlooking McLeese Lake.

CC 160 (257.5 km) **PG 117** (188.3 km) Turnout with litter barrel to west with plaque about Fraser River paddle-wheelers.

CC 164 (263.9 km) **PG 113** (181.8 km) **Cariboo Wood Shop.** A gift shop you must stop at. We specialize in Canadian-made gifts and souvenirs. Our woodshop produces quality furniture and accessories. Also many other great gifts—pottery, wheat weaving, art calendars, note pads, easy listening music on tapes and CDs—to name a few. Best of all our famous homemade fudge. 20 flavors to choose from: Maple nut, amaretto, Heavenly Goo and many more! Ask for a free taste. Come in for a visit and treat yourself to a relaxing atmosphere and friendly staff. Easy access drive-through loop for every size of RV. Open 7 days a week 8:30 A.M.–5:30 P.M. Groups welcome. Phone (800) 986-WOOD. [ADVERTISEMENT]

CC 166 (267 km) **PG 111** (178.6 km) Glass sculpture museum and rock shop. **the Castle.** See display ad this section.

CC 166.5 (267.9 km) **PG 110.5** (177.8 km) Marguerite rest area. View upriver to Marguerite reaction cable ferry across the Fraser River. Ferry crossing takes 10 minutes, operates 7 A.M. to 6:45 P.M.; 2 cars and 10 passengers, no charge.

CC 168.5 (271.2 km) **PG 108.5** (174.6 km) Basalt columns to east create a formation known as the Devil's Palisades. Cliff swallows nest in the columns.

CC 169.8 (273.2 km) **PG 107.2** (172.5 km) Stone cairn commemorates **Fort Alexandria**, the last North West Co. furtrading post established west of the Rockies, built in 1821. The actual site of the fort is across the river. Cairn also marks the approximate farthest point reached by Alexander Mackenzie in his descent of the Fraser in 1793.

CC 180 (289.7 km) **PG 97** (156.1 km) Australian rest area to west with toilets, tables and litter barrels. Private campground to east.

CC 188.5 (303.4 km) **PG 88.5** (142.4 km) Kersley (unincorporated), gas and food.

CC 188.6 (303.6 km) **PG 88.4** (142.3 km) Restaurant, gas and private campground.

CC 195.8 (315.1 km) **PG 81.2** (130.6 km) **Dragon Lake Golf Course & Campsite.** Situated on edge of Dragon Lake. RV and campsites at $10 per night. Flush toilets, showers, sani-dump, wharf, trout fishing.

Canada is on the metric system.
10 miles equal roughly 16 kilometres.

Located off Hwy 97 just 10 minutes south of city centre. 9-hole golf course with driving range. Snack bar, lounge. Campers register at golf club pro shop. Phone (250) 747-1358. 1692 Flint Avenue, Quesnel, BC, V2J 2M6. [ADVERTISEMENT] ▲

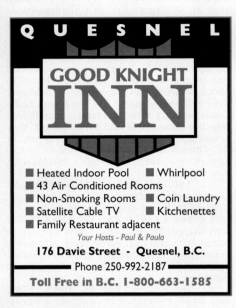
CC 196 (315.4 km) **PG 81** (130.4 km) South end of loop road east to **Dragon Lake**, a small, shallow lake popular with Quesnel families. Camping and fishing for rainbow.

CC 196 (315.4 km) **PG 81** (130.4 km) **Robert's Roost Campsite** located 6 km south of Quesnel and 2 km east of Highway 97 in a parklike setting on beautiful Dragon Lake. Partial and fully serviced. 15- and 30-amp service. Sani-dump, fishing, boat rental, swimming, horseshoes, playground, shower$, flush toilets and laundromat. Can accommodate any length unit. Limited accommodation. Approved by Tourism BC. Hosts: Bob and Vivian Wurm, 3121 Gook Road, Quesnel, BC V2J 4K7. Phone (250) 747-2015 or (888) 227-8877. [ADVERTISEMENT] ▲

CC 197.5 (317.8 km) **PG 79.5** (127.9 km) **Valhalla Motel**. Quietly situated at the top of Dragon Hill. All rooms have air conditioning, individual electric heat, colour televisions, direct dial telephones, queen beds, refrigerators. Nonsmoking rooms available. Complimentary coffee. Guest laundry. Winter plug-ins. Close to fairgrounds, recreation centre, racing oval, shopping centre. Senior discount. Pets welcome. Major credit cards. 2010 Valhalla Rd., Quesnel, BC V2J 4C1. (250) 747-1111. See display ad this section. [ADVERTISEMENT]

Quesnel

CC 203 (326.7 km) **PG 74** (119.1 km). Located at the confluence of the Fraser and Quesnel rivers. **Population**: 10,000. **Elevation**: 1,789 feet/545m. **Emergency Services**: Emergency only, phone 911. **RCMP**, phone (250) 992-9211. **Ambulance**, phone (250) 992-3211. **Hospital**, phone (250) 992-2181.

Visitor Information: Located on the west side of the highway just north of Quesnel River bridge, in LeBourdais Park. Open year-round. Write Quesnel Visitor Infocentre, Stn. A, 703 Carson Ave., Quesnel, BC V2J 2B6; phone (250) 992-8716, or toll free (800) 992-4922. For information on the Cariboo Tourist Region, contact the Cariboo Tourist Assoc., P.O. Box 4900 Williams Lake, BC V2G 2V8; phone toll free (800) 663-5885.

Quesnel (kwe NEL) began as a supply town for the miners in the gold rush of the 1860s. The city was named after the Quesnel River, which in turn was named after fur trader Jules Maurice Quesnel, a member of Simon Fraser's 1808 expedition down the Fraser River and later a political figure in Quebec. Today, forestry is the dominant economic force in Quesnel, with 2 pulp mills, a plywood plant, and 5 sawmills and planer

QUESNEL ADVERTISERS

CARIBOO COUNTRY

Quesnel, Wells and Barkerville...

Rich in culture, history and recreational activities, the North Cariboo has it all: gold panning, fishing, walking and hiking trails, wildlife, and horseback riding. Canoe the Bowron Lake circuit or try white water rafting in the summer. Great snow invites skiing, snowmobiling, and snow shoeing in the winter.

Annual activities in the region include Billy Barker Days and the Quesnel Fall Fair. See our galleries and museums or walk back in time over a hundred years with a visit to Cottonwood House or Barkerville Historic Town. Attend the summer art school in Wells or drop in for an evening performance.

The North Cariboo: where the goldrush began.

more than just Gold!

City of Quesnel, 405 Barlow Avenue, Station A, Quesnel, B.C. V2J 4C3 1-800-992-4922 *the "Tomato House" in Wells, B.C.*

Highway 26 Log

This 51-mile/82-km paved road leads to Barkerville Historic Town in the historic Cariboo gold fields (active mining under way). Gas available in Wells.

The Barkerville gold strike was made in 1861. Today, Highway 16 follows the route of the original Cariboo wagon road built to serve the boom towns.

Distance from Highway 97 junction (J) is shown.

J 0 Junction with Highway 97 at **Milepost CC 206.** Visitor Infocentre on southeast side of junction.

J 0.8 (1.3 km) Barlow Creek residential area; grocery, food and fuel. Eastbound, Highway 26 accesses local roads. Watch for deer.

J 13 (21 km) Rest area and interpretive trails to south. Wooden rail "snake" and wire fences with wooden top rail allow deer and moose to safely jump them, while penning domestic livestock.

J 15.2 (24.5 km) Cottonwood River bridge. The river is named for the black cottonwood trees growing alongside it.

J 16.7 (26.9 km) **Cottonwood House Historic Site**, a restored and furnished log roadhouse built in 1864. Gift shop, coffee shop, picnicking and guided tours by costumed docents. Open May to September.

J 20.1 (32.4 km) Swift River Forest Road leads 0.2 mile/0.3 km to Lightning Creek Forest Service recreation site (first turn on left); free camping, 14-day limit. *CAUTION: Active logging road, drive with headlights on.* ▲

J 21.4 (34.5 km) Lover's Leap viewpoint and Mexican Hill Summit, one of the steepest grades on the original Cariboo Waggon Road, to the south.

J 27.1 (43.6 km) Historical stop of interest marker for Charles Morgan Blessing's grave. Blessing, from Ohio, was murdered on his way to Barkerville in 1866. His killer, John Barry, was caught when he gave Blessing's keepsake gold nugget stickpin, in the shape of a skull, to a Barkerville dance-hall girl. John Barry was the only white man hanged in the Cariboo during the gold rush.

J 37.3 (60.1 km) Stanley Road and Boulder Gold Mines (active claim). Stanley Road is a 1.9-mile/3-km loop road that leads past the gold-rush ghost towns of Stanley and VanWinkle, the old Lightning Hotel, and gold rush-era gravesites. A worthwhile sidetrip.

J 38.6 (62.2 km) Stanley (Loop) Road, Chisholm Creek. Remnants of Stanley townsite and cemetery dating back to 1800's. The authentic Stanley Trail leads from the townsite through the remnants of Van Winkle, ending at the Richfield Courthouse in Barkerville.

J 40.2 (64.7 km) Devil's Canyon paved turnout to south. This was the highest point on the Cariboo Waggon Road.

J 42.9 (69 km) Slough Creek, site of much hydraulic mining activity after Joe Shaw discovered gold here in 1870.

J 44.9 (72.2 km) Paved turnout to litter barrel to south. **Jack o' Clubs Lake**; fishing for rainbows, lake trout and Dolly Varden. ◄

J 45.2 (72.7 km) Rest area on peninsula to south with picnic tables, pit toilets and boat launch.

J 45.7 (73.6 km) Paved turnout with litter barrels to south.

J 46.1 (74.2 km) Lakeshore turnout with area information sign.

J 46.7 (75.2 km) **WELLS** (pop. 300, elevation 4,200 feet/1280m) dates back to the 1930s when the Cariboo Gold Quartz Mine, promoted and developed by Fred Wells, brought hundreds of workers to this valley. The mine closed in 1967, but the town has continued as a service centre and attraction for tourists, with numerous art galleries and gift shops, some housed in refurbished buildings from the 1930's.

Wells businesses include: Wells Service Station (BCAA) (250) 994-3224; Northwoods Restaurant (250) 994-3325; W&J Getaway rental home (250) 249-5474; White Cap Motor Inn (250) 994-3489; Hubs Motel (250) 994-3313; Wells Hotel (250) 994-3427; Amazing Space Studio and Art Gallery (250) 994-2332; Tree House Arts (250) 994-3264; and Marie Nagel's Art Studio (250) 994-3492.

Guided and self-guided tours of the town are available. A museum with displays of local mining history is open daily from June to September.

Recreation in the area is centered around some 30 miles/50 km of marked trails leading into alpine country. Summer activities include hiking historical trails, mountain biking (rentals available), gold panning, llama trekking and fishing. In winter, trails are groomed for skiing, snowmobiling and dogsledding, and there are scheduled snow machine races.

The local Legion hosts horseshoes and bocci tournaments, has a pub and offers potluck suppers throughout the year.

J 49.6 (79.8 km) Barkerville Provincial Park Forest Rose Campground to north. Lowhee Campground to south; 170 campsites, picnic areas and dump stations. ▲

J 50 (80.5 km) Gravel road leads north 18 miles/29 km to **Bowron Lakes Provincial Park**, noted for its interconnecting chain of lakes and the resulting 72-mile/116-km canoe circuit which takes from 7 to 10 days to complete. Visitor information available at registration centre next to main parking lot where canoeists must register and pay circuit fees. Reservations recommended in July and August (required for 7 or more people); phone (250) 992-3111.

Airfield at junction with 2,500-foot/762-m paved runway, elev. 4,180 feet/1,274m.

There are 2 private lodges at the

north end of the lake with restaurants, camping (at Becker's Lodge), a general store and canoe rentals. Provincial park campground has 25 sites, water, pit toilets, firewood and a boat launch. Swimming, fishing, canoeing, kayaking and hiking. ⇔▲

Becker's Lodge. Overlooking Bowron Lake and the snowcapped Cariboo Mountains from our beautifully restored lodge restaurant, open for breakfast, lunch and dinner. We also offer cabins, chalets and bungalows, campsites with firepits and picnic tables. Hot showers, flush toilets, coin laundry. Licensed canoe outfitter for the Bowron Lake Wilderness Park. Canoe/kayak day-rentals. Store. Reservations: (800) 808-4761. Local calls: (250) 992-8864. [ADVERTISEMENT] ▲

J 50.1 (80.7 km) Entrance to Barkerville; admission charged. Admission fees in 1997 for a 2-day pass were: Adults, $5.50; youth and seniors, $3.25; children, $1; and families, $10.75.

J 50.3 (81.7 km) Former site of Cameronton, named for John A. "Cariboo" Cameron who found gold in this area. Also in this area is Williams Creek, the richest gold-producing creek during the gold rush.

J 50.9 (81.9 km) Turnoff on 1.8-mile/2.9-km side road for gold rush cemetery and Government Hill Campground (0.2 mile/0.4 km), New Barkerville (0.4 mile/0.7 km) and Grubstake Store (0.7 mile/1.1 km). ▲

J 51 (82.1 km) **BARKERVILLE**, a provincial historic town; open year-round, phone (604) 994-3332. Visitor information at Reception Centre.

Barkerville was named for miner Billy Barker, who struck gold on Williams Creek. The resulting gold rush in 1862 created Barkerville. Virtually a ghost town when the provincial government began restoration in 1958, today Barkerville's buildings and boardwalks are faithful restorations or reconstructions from the town's heyday. Visitors can pan for gold, shop at the old-time general store, watch a blacksmith at work, or take in a show at the Theatre Royal. Restaurants and food service available. It is best to visit between June 1 and Labour Day, when the Theatre Royal offers performances and all exhibits are open.

The Theatre Royal is extremely popular with visitors. The half-hour spring show plays daily (except Saturdays) from 12:45 to 1:15 P.M. between May and June. Regular season begins mid-June and continues until Labour Day. Admission is charged at all shows.

History comes alive at Barkerville thanks to interpreters and street performers who represent actual citizens of the town in 1870, discuss "current" events with visitors, conduct tours and stage daily dramas throughout the summer.

Beyond Main Street, the Cariboo Waggon Road leads on (for pedestrians only) to Richfield, 1 mile/1.6 km, to the courthouse of "Hanging" Judge Begbie.

Return to Milepost CC 206
West Access Route

mills. Check with the Tourist Infocentre about tours.

Accommodations include 4 hotels, 15 motels, 5 bed and breakfasts and 8 campgrounds. There are gas stations (with diesel and propane), 2 shopping malls and 45 restaurants offering everything from fast food to fine dining. Golf and a recreation centre with pool are available.

Visitors can take a walking tour of the city along the **Riverfront Park** trail system. The 3.1-mile/5-km north Quesnel trail starts at Ceal Tingley Park at the confluence of the Fraser and Quesnel rivers. The west Quesnel trail is a 2.7-mile/4.3-km walk through a residential area. Trail information is available at the Visitor Infocentre.

Quesnel & District Museum and Archives. The best-kept secret in the Cariboo. Exhibits from farming, logging and mining. Artifacts used by our pioneers in their homes. Coins from all over the world; 1911 White car; a famous Centennial quilt. First Nations exhibit and a collection of some of the rarest Chinese artifacts found in western Canada. Mystery surrounds our museum with Mandy, our "haunted doll," and for a chuckle and a smile see the 80-year-old prophylactic. Considered one of the top 10 British Columbia museums! Admission fee $2 per person; 12 and under free. Located across from BC Rail amongst the famous rose garden and adjacent to the Tourist Information Centre on Highway 97. Open year-round. Phone 1-250-992-9580. [ADVERTISEMENT]

There are some interesting hoodoo formations and scenic canyon views at nearby **Pinnacles Provincial Park**, 5 miles/8 km west of Highway 97; picnicking. It is a 1.1-mile/1.8-km walk round-trip from the parking area to the pinnacle viewpoints.

Quesnel offers gold panning tours, guided hiking tours and Voyager canoe trips on the Fraser River. Boat tours are also available on other area rivers. Contact the Visitor Infocentre for more information.

A worthwhile side trip is Highway 26, which intersects Highway 97 at **Milepost CC 206**. This 51-mile/82-km paved highway leads to Wells, Bowron Lake and **Barkerville Provincial Historic Park**, a reconstructed and restored Cariboo gold rush town. (See HIGHWAY 26 side road log pages 68-69.) Gold Pan City Stage Lines offers charter and scheduled tours of Barkerville and surrounding area from Quesnel.

The Hudson's Bay 1881 Heritage House Restaurant. Located on Highway 97 and Carson Avenue, is housed in Quesnel's oldest building: a log structure dating back to the 1860s. Delicious homemade meals, fresh-baked buns and pies are served in this friendly, historic atmosphere. Scheduled and impromptu entertainment features local and visiting performers. Licensed. Open 7 A.M.–9 P.M. Phone (250) 992-2700. [ADVERTISEMENT]

Billy Barker Days, a 4-day event held the

third full weekend in July, commemorates the discovery of gold at Barkerville in 1862. Held in conjunction with the Quesnel Rodeo, Billy Barker Days is the third largest outdoor family festival in the province. For more information, write Box 4441, Quesnel, BC V2J 3J4. The Barlow Creek Music Festival takes place on Highway 26 the weekend after Billy Barker Days.

Country Haven Family Restaurant. Home-style cooking. Breakfast served all day. Fully licensed. Located 1/2 block from Quesnel Tourist Infocentre on Highway 97 North (490 Carson Ave.). Open year-round. Summer hours Monday–Saturday 6 A.M.–8 P.M. Sundays and holidays 7 A.M.–8 P.M. Tour groups welcome. Please phone ahead. (250) 992-9654. [ADVERTISEMENT]

West Access Route Log
(continued)

CC 206 (331.5 km) **PG 71** (114.3 km) Quesnel airport.

Junction with Highway 26 to Wells, Barkerville and Bowron Lake. See HIGHWAY 26 side road log this section.

CC 209.5 (337.2 km) **PG 67.5** (108.6 km) **Lazy Daze Resort.** RV sites, cabins and tenting only 3 minutes off highway. Pull-throughs, hookups. 30 amp service. Free hot showers for guests. Located on Ten Mile Lake; boat rentals, convenience store, laundry, play area and picnic shelter. (250) 992-3282. RR8, Box 29, Best site, Quesnel, BC, V2J 5E6. [ADVERTISEMENT] ▲

CC 210 (338 km) **PG 67** (107.8 km) Paved side road leads 0.6 mile/1 km to **Ten Mile Lake Provincial Park**; 142 campsites, flush toilets, showers, picnic area, playground, boat launch, good swimming beach, hiking and mountain bike trails, dump station. Security gates closed 11 P.M.–7 A.M. Self-guided trail to beaver colony, good bird watching (pileated woodpeckers, warblers, snowy owls), naturalist programs. Good fishing for rainbow to 3 lbs. ⇔▲

CC 214.2 (344.7 km) **PG 62.8** (101.1 km) Cottonwood River bridge. Turnout with litter barrels and stop-of-interest sign at south end of bridge describing railway bridge seen upriver.

CC 218.7 (352 km) **PG 58.3** (93.8 km) Hush Lake rest area to west; toilets, tables, litter barrels.

CC 226 (363.7 km) **PG 51** (82 km) **Cinema 2nd Hand.** General store, groceries. Movie rentals, souvenirs. Local artwork, circle drive. 9 A.M.–9 P.M. every day. Free camping, picnic tables, firepits and wood, toilet, some long pull-throughs, some shady sites, fireworks, phone. Welcome to friendly Cinema, BC. Vic and Theresa Olson, RR 1 Box 1, Site 10, Hixon, BC V0K 1S0. (250) 998-4774. [ADVERTISEMENT] ▲

CC 229.6 (369.5 km) **PG 47.4** (76.3 km) Strathnaver (unincorporated), no services.

CC 241 (387.8 km) **PG 36** (58 km) **HIXON** (pop. 1,500) has a post office, 2 motels, gas stations, grocery stores, 2 restaurants (1 with licensed premises), a pub and private campground. Hixon is the Cariboo's most northerly community. Extensive placer mining took place here in the early 1900s. Southbound motorists watch for roadside display about points of interest in the Cariboo region located just north of Hixon. ▲

Hixon Fireplace Inn. Excellent cuisine. Food preparation on the premises. Soups and chowders. In-season specialties. Try our delicious pies. Easy RV access, ample parking. Monday to Saturday 7 A.M. to 8 P.M., Sunday noon to 8 P.M. Your hosts, Dave and Fran Krieger. Most major credit cards, Interac. Wir sprechen Deutsch. (250) 998-4518. [ADVERTISEMENT]

CC 247.6 (398.5 km) PG 29.4 (47.3 km) Woodpecker rest area to west; toilets, tables, litter barrels.

CC 257.7 (414.7 km) PG 19.3 (31 km) Stoner (unincorporated), no services.

CC 258.3 (415.7 km) PG 18.7 (30.1 km) Fraser River RV Park. See display ad this section. ▲

CC 261.8 (421.3 km) PG 15.2 (24.5 km) Red Rock (unincorporated); ice; gas station with diesel; pay phone.

CC 268.3 (431.8 km) PG 8.7 (14 km) Bee Lazee RV Park, Campground & Honey

RV PARK, CAMPGROUND
& HONEY FARM
• Heated Pool •
• Coin RV-Car Wash •
Hi-Pressure with Soap
(All Facilities on Premises)
- Long Pull Thrus - Full Hookups - Tenting
-Large Clean Heated Washrooms, FREE
HOT SHOWERS - Play Area - Laundry
Rates $13 - $17
All Tax Included
Prince George
X
Bee Lazee
X
9 Miles (South)
Good Sampark
Phone or Fax (250) 963-7263
e-mail: drone @computime.bc.ca

Farm. See display ad this section. ▲

CC 270.6 (435.5 km) PG 6.4 (10.3 km) Junction with bypass road to Yellowhead 16 East. Keep left for Prince George; continue straight ahead for Jasper and Edmonton. If you are headed east on Yellowhead Highway 16 for Jasper or Edmonton, turn to **Milepost E 450** in the YELLOWHEAD HIGHWAY 16 section and read the log back to front.

CC 273 (439.3 km) PG 4 (6.4 km) Southpark RV Park. See display ad this section. ▲

CC 273.4 (440 km) PG 3.6 (5.8 km) Access to Prince George airport to east.

CC 274 (440.9 km) PG 3 (4.8 km) Sintich Trailer Park. See display ad this section. ▲

CC 275.2 (442.8 km) PG 1.8 (2.8 km) Bridge over the Fraser River. Turn right at north end of bridge then left at stop sign for city centre via Queensway. This is the easiest access for Fort George Park; follow Queensway to 20th Avenue and turn east.

Continue straight ahead for Highway 16 entrance to city.

CC 276 (444.1 km) PG 1 (1.6 km) Junction of Highway 97 with Yellowhead 16 West. Description of Prince George follows.

If you are headed west on Yellowhead Highway 16 for Prince Rupert, turn to Milepost PG 0 in the YELLOWHEAD HIGHWAY 16 section. Prince Rupert is port of call for Alaska state ferries and BC Ferries.

Prince George

CC 277 (445.8 km) Population: 76,500, area 160,000. **Emergency Services: RCMP,** phone (250) 562-3371, emergency only, phone 911. **Fire Department,** phone 911. **Ambulance,** 24-hour service, phone 911. **Poison Control Centre,** phone (250) 565-2442. **Hospital,** Prince George Regional, phone (250) 565-2000; emergency, phone (250) 565-2444.

Visitor Information: Tourism Prince George, Dept. MP, 1198 Victoria St., phone (250) 562-3700 or fax 563-3584, or toll free (800) 668-7646. Open year-round, 8:30 A.M. to 5 P.M. weekdays Monday through Saturday. Visitor centre, junction Yellowhead 16 and Highway 97; open daily late-May to Labour Day, phone (250) 563-5493.

Elevation: 1,868 feet/569m. **Climate:** The inland location is tempered by the protection of mountains. The average annual frost-free period is 85 days, with 1,793 hours of bright sunshine. Dry in summer; chinooks off and on during winter which, accompanied by a western flow of air, break up the cold weather. Summer temperatures average 72°F/22°C with lows to 46°F/8°C. **Radio:** CKPG 550, CJCI 620, BC-FM 94.3, CBC-FM 91.5, C-101 FM. **Television:** 36 channels via cable. **Newspaper:** *The Citizen* (daily except Sunday); *Prince George This Week* (Sunday); *Free Press* (Thursday and Sunday).

Prince George is located at the confluence of the Nechako and Fraser rivers, near the geographical centre of British Columbia. It is the fourth largest city in British Columbia. Hub of the trade and travel routes of the province, Prince George is located at the junction of Yellowhead Highway 16—linking Prince Rupert on the west coast with the Interior of Canada—and Highway 97, which runs south to Vancouver and north to Dawson Creek.

In the early 1800s, Simon Fraser of the North West Trading Co. erected a post here which he named Fort George in honour of the reigning English monarch. In 1906, survey parties for the transcontinental Grand Trunk Pacific Railway (later Canadian National Railways) passed through the area,

FRASER RIVER RV PARK

**Quiet & Relaxing / Spacious Treed RV Sites on the Fraser River
Easy access with large turn around at the bottom of the hill
Phone (250) 330-4453**

- 30 Amp Service
- Hot Showers, Flush Toilets
- Tenting
- Space To Turn Around

Southpark RV Park

In a peaceful setting south of Prince George on Hwy 97

- Xtra Long Full Service Pull-Throughs • Laundry • Hot Showers
- Store/Gas & Golf Nearby   Pets On Leash - PLEASE!
- Caravans Welcome - Auto Storage

9180 Caribou Hwy. • Prince George B.C. V2N 6E2

30 & 50 AMP SERVICES

Good Sam Club

PHONE: (250) 963-7577 FAX: (250) 963-9222

SINTICH TRAILER & R.V. PARK

"AN ADULT COMMUNITY"

- Large Pull-throughs • Large RV Lots
- Up to 50-amp Service
- Free Hot Showers • Laundromat
- Cable T.V. • RV Storage

Good Sampark

GROCERY STORE & SERVICE
STATION NEARBY

South of Prince George on Hwy 97

Box 1022, Prince George, BC V2L 4V1

For Reservations: **Phone and FAX (250) 963-9862**
CAA Approved • VISA • Master Card
e-mail: gudrun-schmidt@bc.sympatico.ca.

Wir sprechen auch deutsch.

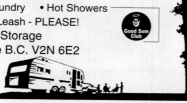

P.G. HI-WAY MOTEL

45 Comfortable Budget & Deluxe Units
1 Mile N.E. of Highways 97/16

※ 31 Brand New, Well Appointed Rooms
※ 12 Full Size Kitchens
※ Barrier-Free Suite • Quiet Location
※ Close to Laundromat and Shopping Mall
※ Restaurants Nearby • Cable TV
※ Direct Dial Phones • Major Credit Cards
※ Air-Conditioning • Winter Plug-Ins

1737 - 20th Avenue, Prince George, BC
Telephone (250) 564-6869 • FAX (250) 562-5687
Toll Free Reservations: 1-888-557-4557

DELUXE FAMILY FACILITIES

Blue Spruce R.V. Park and Campground

Owners & Hosts: Ted & Reina McAfee

Store • Ice • Heated Pool • Mini Golf
128 Sites • Long Pull-Throughs
Full Hook-ups • Sani-Dump
Camping Cabins • Grassy Tenting
Laundromat • Free Showers
Playground • Pay Phones
Postal Services • 24-Hour Security

P.O. Box 3040 STN. B
Prince George, BC V2N 4T8

*3 Miles West of Highway 97 on
Highway 16 West Yellowhead
Route to Prince Rupert*

Good Sam Club

FAX (250) 964-7274

(250) 964-7272

PRINCE GEORGE
~ BC's Northern Capital ~

**For Information Contact: Tourism Prince George, 1198 Victoria Street, Prince George, BC V2L 2L2
Phone: (250) 562-3700 Fax: (250) 563-3584 1-800-668-7646 e-mail: information@tourismpg.bc.ca**

To Dawson Creek

Prince George

and with the building of the railroad a great land boom took place. The city was incorporated in 1915 under the name Prince George. Old Fort George is now a park and picnic spot and the site of Fort George Museum.

Prince George is primarily an industrial centre, fairly dependent on the lumber industry, with 3 pulp mills, sawmills, planers, dry kilns, a plywood plant and 2 chemical plants to serve the pulp mills. Oil refining, mining and heavy construction are other major area industries. The Prince George Forest Region is the largest in the province.

Prince George is the focal point of the central Interior for financial and professional services, equipment and wholesale firms, machine shops and many services for the timber industry. Canada's newest university opened here in the fall of 1994. The campus of the University of Northern British Columbia is located at the top of Cranbrook Hill.

Agriculture in central British Columbia is basically a forage-livestock business, for which the climate and soils are well suited. Dairying and beef are the major livestock enterprises, with minor production in sheep and poultry.

ACCOMMODATIONS/VISITOR SERVICES

Prince George offers 5 hotels, 17 motels, 9 RV parks, and more than 3 dozen bed and breakfasts. Most accommodations are within easy reach of the business district. There are

PRINCE GEORGE ADVERTISERS

A-1 Bed & Breakfast..........Ph. (877) 562-2626
Anco Motel ....Ph. (250) 563-3671
Arctic RV Service Centre...Ph. (250) 962-9631
Blue Spruce RV Park &
   Campground ....Ph. (250) 964-7272
Celeste's R.V. Center Ltd..Ph. (250) 962-2049
Downtown Motel ....Ph. (250) 563-9241
Dutch Maid Laundromat ..Ph. (250) 564-1260
Econo Lodge ....Ph. (250) 563-7106
Esther's Inn ....Ph. (250) 562-4131
Fraser-Fort George
   Regional Museum........Ph. (250) 562-1612
Goldcap Motor Inn...........Ph. (250) 563-0666
Grama's Inn Ltd. ....Ph. (250) 563-7174
Inland Spring
   and Axle Ltd. ....Ph. (250) 562-9090
Northwood Pulp and
   Timber Limited ....Ph. (250) 562-3700
Pine Centre Mall ....Ph. (250) 563-3681
P.G. Hi-Way Motel..................1737 20th Ave.
Prince George
   Art Gallery ....Ph. (250) 563-6447
Prince George Native
   Art Gallery ....Ph. (250) 614-7726
Prince George Railway &
   Forestry Museum.........Ph. (250) 563-7351
Ricky's Pancakes & Family
   Restaurant ....Ph. (250) 564-8114
Tourism Prince George.....Ph. (250) 562-3700

Camping in rest areas is prohibited in British Columbia. See "Driving North" in the TRAVEL PLANNING section.

www.themilepost.com

more than 80 restaurants in the city. Most stores are open 7 days a week. The usual hours of operation are: Sunday, noon to 5 P.M.; Saturday and Monday through Wednesday, 9:30 A.M. to 6 P.M.; Thursday and Friday, 9:30 A.M. to 9 P.M.

TRANSPORTATION

Air: Prince George airport is southeast of the city, serviced by Canadian Airlines International, Air BC and Central Mountain Air. Limousine service to and from the airport.

Railroad: VIA Rail connects Prince George with Prince Rupert and Jasper, AB. Passenger service south to Vancouver via British Columbia Railway 3 days a week.

Bus: Greyhound. City bus service by Prince George Transit & Charter Ltd.

ATTRACTIONS

City Landmarks: Centennial Fountain at the corner of 7th Avenue and Dominion Street depicts the early history of Prince George in mosaic tile. A cairn at Fort George Park commemorates Sir Alexander Mackenzie.

Connaught Hill Park offers colorful flower gardens and a panoramic view of the city. Follow Connaught Drive to the park.

Fort George Park is the largest park in Prince George and a good stop for travelers with its playgrounds, picnic tables, barbecue facilities and museum. The Fort George Railway operates on weekends and holidays at the park from a railway building patterned after the original Grand Trunk Pacific stations.

Fraser Fort George Regional Museum. Located in Fort George Park at 333 20th Avenue, the museum includes an explorations gallery focusing on the region's natural history and environment. A history hall provides an overview of the area's developmental history and includes an interactive multimedia film display. Open daily in summer, 10 A.M. to 5 P.M. Wheelchair accessible. Admission fee charged. For more information phone (250) 562-1612. &

Giscome Portage Regional Park, next to the scenic Fraser River, includes the Huble Homestead, which dates from 1912. These original and reconstructed buildings are surrounded by grazing land and forest. Picnic tables and snackbar. Guided interpretive tours during peak season; admission free. Located north of Prince George on Highway 97; turn east off the highway at **Milepost PG 26.9** and drive 3.7 miles/ 6 km.

Cottonwood Island Park, located on the Nechako River (see city map), has picnic facilities and extensive nature trails.

Prince George Railway and Forestry Museum features a dozen original railway buildings, including 2 stations. Among the 50 pieces of rolling stock are 5 locomotives, a 1903 snow plow, a 1913 100-ton steam wrecking crane and a 90-foot 100-ton turntable. Items from 8 past and present rail-

Prince George visitor centre is located at the junction of Highways 97 and 16.
(© Brian Stein)

The John Hart Highway is a good paved highway that crosses the Canadian Rockies between Prince George and Dawson Creek. (© Earl L. Brown, staff)

way companies are displayed. There is also a small collection of forestry, mining and agricultural machinery. Located at 850 River Road next to Cottonwood Island Nature Park. Open May to September daily from 9:30 A.M. to 5 P.M. For more information phone (250) 563-7351.

Golf Courses. Aspen Grove Golf Club is 9 miles/14.5 km south of the city; Yellowhead Grove Golf Club, Pine Valley Golf Club, and Prince George Golf and Curling Club are on Yellowhead Highway 16 West.

Swimming. Four Seasons Swimming Pool at the corner of 7th Avenue and Dominion Street has a pool, water slide, diving tank and fitness centre. Open to the public afternoons and evenings.

Rockhounding. The hills and river valleys in the area provide abundant caches of Omineca agate and Schmoos. For more information, contact Prince George Rock and Gem Club, phone (250) 562-4526; or Spruce City Rock and Gem Club, phone (250) 562-1013.

Tennis Courts. A total of 20 courts currently available to the public at 3 places: 20th Avenue near the entrance to Fort George Park; at Massey Drive in Carrie Jane Gray Park; and on Ospika Boulevard in the Lakewood Secondary School complex.

Industrial Tours are available from mid-May through August by contacting Tourism Prince George at (250) 562-3700. Tours, which are on weekdays only, include Northwood Pulp and Timber, Prince George Sawmill and North Central Plywoods. Tours of Prince George Pulp and Intercon Pulp are available June–August, Monday–Friday; reservations required.

Tours of the Pacific Western Brewery are available; reservations required. Phone (250) 562-2424 or (800) 663-8002, Monday through Friday.

Special Events: Elks May Day celebration; Prince George Regional Forest Exhibition in May (even years); Folkfest on July 1, Canada Day; Prince George Live, Sunday through Thursday during July and August; International Food Festival in August; Annual Sandblast Skiing in August; Prince George Airshow in July; Prince George Exhibition in August; Oktoberfest in October;

and the winter Mardi Gras Festival in mid-February. Details on these and other events are available from Tourism Prince George; phone (250) 562-3700.

Side Trips: Prince George is the starting point for some of the finest holiday country in the province. There are numerous lakes and resorts nearby, among them: Bednesti Lake, 30 miles/48 km west of Prince George; Cluculz Lake, 44 miles/71 km west; Purden Lake, 42 miles/68 km east; and Tabor Lake, 6 miles/10 km east.

AREA FISHING: Highways 16 and 97 are the ideal routes for the sportsman, with year-round fishing and easy access to lakes and rivers. Hunters and fishermen stop over in Prince George as the jumping-off place for some of North America's finest big game hunting and fishing. For more information contact Fish & Wildlife at (250) 565-6145, or Tourism Prince George, phone (250) 562-3700.

West Access Route Log

(continued)
The John Hart Highway, completed in 1952, was named for the former B.C. premier who sponsored its construction. The highway is a 2-lane paved highway with both straight stretches and winding stretches.

This section of the log shows distance from Prince George (PG) followed by distance from Dawson Creek (DC).

BC HIGHWAY 97/HART HIGHWAY

PG 0 DC 250 (402.3 km) John Hart Bridge over the Nechako River. The 4-lane highway extends 6.5 miles/10.5 km northbound through the commercial and residen-

tial suburbs of Prince George.

PG 1.5 (2.4 km) **DC 248.5** (399.9 km) Truck weigh scales. 24-hour gas station with diesel and propane; lube and oil service.

PG 2.5 (4 km) **DC 247.5** (398.3 km) RV service centre.

PG 6.4 (10.3 km) **DC 243.6** (392 km) **Hartway RV Park.** Shaded, fully-serviced sites. Pull-throughs. Free hot showers, laundromat, 30-amp, cable TV. Groceries nearby.

Phone. On-site antique and gift shop. On south Kelly Road adjacent to highway. Access at stop light (Handlen Road Junction); south of RV park. 7729 South Kelly Rd., Prince George, BC V2K 3H5. Phone (250) 962-9724. [ADVERTISEMENT] ▲

PG 6.5 (10.5 km) **DC 243.5** (391.9 km) Two-lane highway (with passing lanes) begins abruptly northbound.

PG 9.5 (15.3 km) **DC 240.5** (387 km) **Northland RV Park.** See display ad this section. ▲

PG 14.6 (23.5 km) **DC 235.4** (378.8 km) Salmon River bridge. Litter barrel and river access to west at north end of bridge.

PG 14.7 (23.6 km) **DC 235.3** (378.7 km) **Salmon Valley RV Park and Campground** and convenience store, on over 27 acres along the scenic Salmon River. All facilities are wheelchair accessible, including showers. 50 treed sites, 12 pull-throughs, all with fire

rings, tables, laundry. Limited water and power 15–30 amp. Swimming and camping on the Salmon that's second to none. Fair fishing for rainbows, grayling and spring salmon. "Home of the Happy Camper." Phone (250) 971-2212. Fax (250) 971-2212. Good Sam discounts. [ADVERTISEMENT] ♿▲

PG 16.4 (26.4 km) **DC 233.6** (375.9 km) Highway overpass crosses railroad tracks.

PG 22 (35.4 km) **DC 228** (366.9 km) Gravel turnouts both sides of highway.

PG 26.5 (42.6 km) **DC 223.5** (359.7 km) Paved turnout to east with litter barrels and point-of-interest sign about Crooked River Forest Recreation Area.

PG 26.9 (43.3 km) **DC 223.1** (359 km) Access east 3.7 miles/6 km to Giscome Portage regional park via Mitchell Road. Site of historic Huble Homestead; guided tours, picnicking. Free admission.

Historic Huble Homestead. Relax and visit a historic Northern BC settlement. Scenic location next to the mighty Fraser River. Original furnished log buildings. Includes the Huble's house—the oldest home in the region. Farm animals. Numerous picnic tables. Guided interpretive tours. Free admission. Just 6 km east of Highway 97. Phone (250) 960-4400. [ADVERTISEMENT]

PG 28.2 (45.4 km) **DC 221.8** (356.9 km) Turnoff to west for **Summit Lake,** a resort area popular with Prince George residents; lake char and rainbow fishing spring and fall.

PG 29.3 (47.2 km) **DC 220.7** (355.2 km) Westcoast Energy compressor station.

PG 30.7 (49.4 km) **DC 219.3** (352.9 km) Second turnoff to west for Summit Lake.

PG 36.6 (58.9 km) **DC 213.4** (343.4 km) Cottonwood Creek.

PG 38.8 (62.4 km) **DC 211.2** (339.9 km) Paved turnout with litter barrel.

PG 40.6 (65.3 km) **DC 209.4** (337 km) Railroad crossing.

PG 42 (67.6 km) **DC 208** (334.7 km) Slow down for sharp turn across railroad tracks.

PG 43.9 (70.6 km) **DC 206.1** (331.7 km) Turnoff to west for **Crooked River Provincial Park;** 90 campsites, picnic area, flush toilets, tables, firepits, dump station. Camping fee charged. Also horseshoe pits, volleyball, playground, trails, swimming and paddleboat rentals. Powerboats prohibited. Picnic shelter with wood stove. Crooked River and area lakes have fair fishing for rainbow, Dolly Varden, grayling and whitefish.

Highway 97 follows the Crooked River north to McLeod Lake.

PG 44.8 (72.1 km) **DC 205.2** (330.1 km) **BEAR LAKE** (unincorporated). Population 300; gas, diesel, propane, grocery, restaurant, motel, RV park, gift shop, post office and ambulance station. Highway maintenance camp.

The 2 lumber mills in town are the main industry of the area, employing approximately two-thirds of the community. Information on area fishing, hiking, hunting and swimming may be obtained from the Bear Lake Community Commission; phone (250) 972-4488, or write general delivery, Bear Lake, BC V0J 3G0.

Grizzly Inn, Restaurant, Motel & RV Park. See display ad this section.

PG 50.7 (81.6 km) **DC 199.3** (320.7 km) Angusmac Creek.

PG 54.2 (87.2 km) **DC 195.8** (315.1 km) Tumbler Ridge branch line British Columbia Railway connects Tumbler Ridge with the B.C. Railway and Canadian National Railway, allowing for shipments of coal from Tumbler Ridge to Ridley Island near Prince Rupert.

PG 55.6 (89.5 km) **DC 194.4** (312.8 km) Large gravel turnout with litter barrel to west.

PG 56.1 (90.3 km) **DC 193.9** (312 km) Large gravel turnout with litter barrel to west.

PG 57 (91.7 km) **DC 193** (310.6 km) Large gravel turnout with litter barrel to west.

PG 60.8 (97.8 km) **DC 189.2** (304.5 km) Turnout with litter barrel to east.

PG 62.4 (100.4 km) **DC 187.6** (301.9 km) Large gravel turnout with litter barrel to east.

PG 65.2 (104.9 km) **DC 184.8** (297.4 km) Lomas Creek.

PG 67.9 (109.3 km) **DC 182.1** (293 km) Large, double-ended, paved rest area to west beside small lake; litter barrels, picnic tables and pit toilets.

PG 68.8 (110.7 km) **DC 181.2** (291.6 km) 42 Mile Creek.

PG 71.8 (115.5 km) **DC 178.2** (286.8 km) **Whiskers Bay Resort** has beautiful lakeside camping spots on a quiet bay, some with electricity and water. Hot showers. Cabins with showers, fridges and cooking facilities. Fishing is right off our dock or in the many surrounding lakes. Sunsets are sensational and hummingbirds are bountiful. The cafe offers breakfast, lunch, wonderful burgers, homemade pies, soups, the best coffee on the highway and real northern hospitality. Come visit us! [ADVERTISEMENT]

PG 76.6 (123.3 km) **DC 173.4** (279.1 km) First view northbound of McLeod Lake and view of Whisker's Point.

PG 77.7 (125 km) **DC 172.3** (277.3 km) Turnoff to west for **Whisker's Point Provincial Park** on McLeod Lake. This is an exceptionally nice campground with a paved loop road, 69 level gravel sites, a dump station, tap water, flush toilets, boat ramp, fire rings, firewood and picnic tables. Also horseshoe pits, volleyball, playground and picnic shelter. Camping fee charged. Boat launch, swimming, sandy beach and fishing.

McLeod Lake has fair fishing for rainbow, lake char and Dolly Varden, spring and fall, trolling is best.

PG 84 (135.2 km) **DC 166** (267.1 km) Food, gas, camping and lodging.

PG 84.5 (136 km) **DC 165.5** (266.3 km) **FORT McLEOD** (unincorporated) has a gas station, grocery, motel and cafe. A monument here commemorates the founding of Fort McLeod, oldest permanent settlement west of the Rockies and north of San Francisco. Founded in 1805 by Simon Fraser as a trading post for the North West Trading Co., the post was named by Fraser for Archie McLeod.

PG 84.7 (136.3 km) **DC 165.3** (266 km) **McLEOD LAKE** (unincorporated), post office, store, lodging and liquor store.

PG 84.8 (136.5 km) **DC 165.2** (265.8 km) McLeod lake Lodge; food, gas, lodging.

PG 85 (136.8 km) **DC 165** (265.5 km) Turnoff for **Carp Lake Provincial Park,** 20 miles/32 km west via a gravel road; 105 campsites on Carp and War lakes, limited island camping, picnic tables, firepits, boat launch, fishing and swimming. Also tap water, dump station, horseshoe pits, playground and picnic shelter with wood stove. Ten-minute walk to scenic War Falls. Camping fee charged. Park access road follows the McLeod River to Carp Lake. Carp Lake, rainbow June through September; special restrictions in effect, check current posted information. **McLeod River,** rainbow from July, fly-fishing only.

PG 85.6 (137.8 km) **DC 164.4** (264.6 km) Paved turnout with litter barrel to west.

PG 87.6 (141 km) **DC 162.4** (261.4 km) Westcoast Energy compressor station and McLeod Lake school.

PG 89.8 (144.5 km) **DC 160.2** (257.8 km) Turnoff to west for **Tudyah Lake Provincial Park;** 36 campsites, picnic tables, fire rings, firewood, pit toilets, drinking water. Also swimming, boat ramp, fishing. Camping fee charged.

Tudyah Lake, shore access, rainbow, Dolly Varden and some grayling in summer and late fall. **Pack River** (flows into Tudyah Lake), fishing for grayling (catch-and-release only), June 1 to July 1; rainbow, June 10 to November; large Dolly Varden, Sept. 15 to Oct. 10, spinning.

PG 89.9 (144.7 km) **DC 160.1** (257.6 km) Bear Creek bridge.

PG 93.9 (151.1 km) **DC 156.1** (251.2 km) Gas, food and lodging (open year-round).

PG 94.7 (152.4 km) **DC 155.3** (249.9 km) Parsnip River bridge. This is the Rocky Mountain Trench, marking the western boundary of the Rocky Mountains. Northbound motorists begin gradual climb through the Misinchinka then Hart ranges of the Rocky Mountains.

Parsnip River, good fishing for grayling and Dolly Varden, some rainbow, best from August to October; a boat is necessary.

PG 95.2 (153.2 km) **DC 154.8** (249.1 km) **Junction** with Highway 39 (paved), which leads 18 miles/29 km to the community of Mackenzie (description follows). Food, gas, lodging, camping and **tourist information caboose** at junction. Signed trailheads along Highway 39 are part of the Mackenzie Demonstration Forest. There are 8 self-guiding trails in the demonstration forest, each focusing on an aspect of forest management.

Interpretive signs are posted along each trail.

Mackenzie

J 18 (29 km) Located 18 miles/29 km northwest of the John Hart Highway 97 via Highway 39. **Population:** 6,000. **Emergency Services:** Emergency only, phone 911. **RCMP,** phone (250) 997-3288. **Hospital,** 12 beds. Ambulance, phone 911.

Visitor Information: Visitor/tourist information booth in the railway caboose located at the junction of Highways 97 and 39. Or write the Chamber of Commerce, Box 880, Mackenzie, BC V0J 2C0; phone (250) 997-5459.

Elevation: 2,300 feet/701m. **Radio:** CKMK 1240, CKPG 1240; CBC-FM 990. **Television:** Channels 3, 13 and cable.

A large, modern, planned community, Mackenzie was built in 1965. The city was named after Alexander Mackenzie, early explorer. It lies at the south end of Williston Lake, the largest manmade reservoir on the continent. Construction of the new town in what had been just wilderness was sparked by the Peace River Dam project and the need to attract skilled employees for industrial growth. Mackenzie was incorporated in May 1966 under "instant town" legislation; the first residents moved here in July 1966. Industry here includes mining and forestry, with 4 sawmills, a paper mill and 2 pulp mills. Inquire about mill tours at the Infocentre.

On display in Mackenzie is the "world's largest tree crusher." The 56-foot-long electrically powered Le Tourneau G175 tree crusher was used in clearing land at the Peace River Power Project in the mid-1960s.

Attractions include swimming, waterskiing, fishing and boating at **Morfee Lake**, a 10-minute walk from town. There are boat launches on both Morfee Lake and Williston Lake reservoir. Good view of Mackenzie and Williston Lake reservoir from the top of Morfee Mountain (elev. 5,961 feet/1,817m); check with Infocentre for directions. There are self-guided hiking trails at John Dahl Regional Park, located behind the recreation centre. Check at the infocentre for additional hiking information. Local businesses offer llama trekking.

The Mackenzie and District Museum, located at the Ernie Bodin Community Centre, offers exhibits on early settlers, area wildlife and lakes, and the birth of the town; phone (250) 997-3021. The Mackenzie Community Arts Council displays new shows of local artists monthly at the Mountain Gifts and Gallery, (250) 997-5818, located at the Mackenzie Arts Centre in the Ernie Bodin Bldg.

Mackenzie has all visitor facilities, including motels, restaurants, shopping malls, gas stations, swimming pool, tennis courts, 9-hole golf course and other recreation facilities. There is also a paved 5,000-foot/1,524-m airstrip.

There is a municipal RV park with 20 sites, flush toilets, showers and sani-dump. Fee only for electrical hookups ($10–$16). Fishing for rainbow, Dolly Varden, arctic char and grayling in **Williston Lake**.　�▲

District of Mackenzie. See display ad this section.

West Access Route Log

(continued)

PG 95.2 (153.2 km) **DC 154.8** (249.1 km) **Junction** with Highway 39 to Mackenzie; food, gas, lodging and tourist booth.

PG 95.5 (153.7 km) **DC 154.5** (248.6 km) Highway crosses railroad tracks.

PG 98.9 (158.2 km) **DC 151.1** (243.2 km) Gravel turnout with litter barrel to east.

PG 106 (170.6 km) **DC 144** (231.7 km) Turnout with litter barrel to east.

PG 108.4 (174.4 km) **DC 141.6** (227.9 km) Highway maintenance yard.

PG 108.5 (174.6 km) **DC 141.5** (227.7 km) Bridge over Honeymoon Creek.

PG 109.6 (176.4 km) **DC 140.4** (225.9 km) Powerlines crossing highway carry electricity south from hydro dams in the Hudson's Hope area (see **Milepost PG 187.9**).

PG 110.5 (177.8 km) **DC 139.5** (224.5 km) Slow down for sharp curve across railroad tracks.

PG 112.3 (180.7 km) **DC 137.7** (221.6 km) Bridge over Rolston Creek; dirt turnout by small falls to west.

PG 115.3 (185.6 km) **DC 134.7** (216.8 km) **Bijoux Falls Provincial Park**; pleasant picnic area adjacent falls on west side of highway. This day-use area has paved parking for 50 cars, pit toilets and picnic tables. Good photo opportunity.

Misinchinka River, southeast of the highway; fishing for grayling, whitefish and Dolly Varden.

PG 116.3 (187.2 km) **DC 133.7** (215.2 km) Highway crosses under railroad.

PG 119.3 (191.8 km) **DC 130.8** (210.5 km) Crossing **Pine Pass** (elev. 2,868 feet/874m), the highest point on the John Hart-Peace River Highway, and the lowest pass breaching the Rocky Mountains in Canada. Beautiful view of the Rockies to the northeast. Good highway over pass; steep grade southbound.

View of scenic Azouzetta Lake from Milepost PG 121.4. The lake is just east of Pine Pass, highest point on the Hart Highway. (Earl L. Brown, staff)

PG 119.4 (192.2 km) **DC 130.6** (210.2 km) Turnoff to Powder King Ski Village. Skiing November to late April; chalet with ski shop, cafeteria, restaurant and lounge, hostel-style hotel. This area receives an annual average snowfall of 495 inches.

PG 121.4 (195.4 km) **DC 128.6** (207 km) Paved viewpoint to east with point-of-interest sign about Pine Pass and view of Azouzetta Lake. Pit toilet and litter barrels.

PG 122.4 (197 km) **DC 127.6** (205.3 km) Pine Valley Park, open year-round; cafe, lodge, campground on **Azouzetta Lake**. Very scenic spot. Spectacular hiking on Murray Mountain Trail; inquire at lodge for details. A scuba diving school operates at Azouzetta Lake in summer. Fishing for rainbow (stocked lake) to 1¹/₂ lbs., flies or lures, July to October. Boat launch. ◄▲

PG 125.5 (202 km) **DC 124.5** (200.3 km) Microwave station and receiving dish to west.

PG 125.7 (202.3 km) **DC 124.3** (200 km) Westcoast Energy compressor station.

PG 128.7 (207.1 km) **DC 121.3** (195.2 km) Power lines cross highway.

PG 131.1 (211 km) **DC 118.9** (191.3 km) Turnout with litter barrel. Watch for moose northbound.

PG 140.6 (226.3 km) **DC 109.4** (176.1 km) Bridge over Link Creek.

PG 141.4 (227.5 km) **DC 108.6** (174.8 km) Gravel turnout with litter barrels.

PG 142.3 (229 km) **DC 107.7** (173.3 km) Bridge over West Pine River.

PG 142.8 (229.8 km) **DC 107.2** (172.5 km) Bridge over West Pine River.

PG 143 (230.1 km) **DC 107** (172.2 km)

Large, double-ended paved rest area with picnic tables, litter barrels and pit toilets beside Pine River. Across the road is **Heart Lake** Forestry campground with toilets, picnic tables, firepits and garbage containers; fishing for stocked trout. ◄▲

PG 143.4 (230.8 km) **DC 106.6** (171.6 km) Bridge over West Pine River, B.C. Railway overpass. Private RV park.

PG 144.3 (232.2 km) **DC 105.7** (170.1 km) Food, gas, towing, lodging and camping; autotel 784-9443. ▲

Silver Sands Lodge. See display ad this section. ▲

PG 146.1 (235.1 km) **DC 103.9** (167.2 km) Cairns Creek.

PG 146.9 (236.4 km) **DC 103.1** (165.9 km) Gravel access road to Pine River to south.

PG 148.2 (238.5 km) **DC 101.8** (163.8 km) LeMoray (unincorporated). Lodge to north of highway was closed in 1998, current status unknown. Highway maintenance camp.

PG 148.3 (238.7 km) **DC 101.7** (163.7 km) Gravel turnout to south.

PG 148.8 (239.5 km) **DC 101.2** (162.9 km) Lillico Creek.

PG 149.7 (240.9 km) **DC 100.3** (161.4 km) Marten Creek.

PG 150.4 (242 km) **DC 99.6** (160.3 km) Big Boulder Creek.

PG 156.2 (251.4 km) **DC 93.8** (151 km) Fisher Creek.

PG 156.9 (252.5 km) **DC 93.1** (149.8 km) Large gravel turnout with litter barrel to south beside Pine River.

PG 159.9 (257.3 km) **DC 90.1** (145 km) Crassier Creek. Watch for moose in area, especially at dusk and night.

PG 161.7 (260.2 km) **DC 88.3** (142.1 km) Westcoast Energy compressor station.

PG 163.6 (263.3 km) **DC 86.4** (139 km) Pull-off to south.

PG 169.5 (272.8 km) **DC 80.5** (129.5 km) Turnout with picnic tables, pit toilets and litter barrel to south at Jack Pine Point overlooking the beautiful Pine River valley. Chetwynd area map.

PG 172.4 (277.4 km) **DC 77.6** (124.9 km) Westcoast Energy (natural gas), Pine River plant. View of the Rocky Mountain foothills to the south and west.

PG 177.4 (285.5 km) **DC 72.6** (116.8 km) Turnout with litter barrel.

PG 178.4 (287.1 km) **DC 71.6** (115.2 km) **Caron Creek RV Park.** See display ad this section. ▲

PG 181.9 (292.7 km) **DC 68.1** (109.6 km) Bissett Creek.

PG 183.6 (295.5 km) **DC 66.4** (106.9 km) Turnout with litter barrels at Wildmare Creek.

PG 184.1 (296.3 km) **DC 65.9** (106 km) Truck stop; gas, diesel, food and lodging.

PG 187 (300.9 km) DC 63 (101.4 km) Chetwynd Infocentre in red-roofed log chalet; phone (250) 788-3345. Trailhead for 50-mile/80-km Chetwynd area hiking and biking trail system. Forestry Interpretive Centre adjacent.

PG 187.2 (301.3 km) DC 62.8 (101.1 km) Little Prairie Heritage Museum. Features the region's pioneer days, and is well worth a visit. The museum is open from the first Tuesday in July to the last Saturday in August. Phone (250) 788-3358.

Chetwynd

PG 187.6 (301.9 km) DC 62.4 (100.4 km) Located on Highway 97 at the junction with Highway 29 north to the Alaska Highway via Hudson's Hope, and south to Tumbler Ridge. **Population:** 3,200, area 8,000. **Emergency Services:** RCMP, phone (250) 788-9221. Hospital, Poison Control Centre and Ambulance, phone (250) 788-3522. **Fire Department,** phone (250) 788-2345.

Visitor Information: Chamber of Commerce, open 8 A.M. to 5 P.M. in summer, 9 A.M. to 4 P.M. weekdays rest of year. Write Box 1000, Chetwynd V0C 1J0, or phone (250) 788-3345 or 788-3655; fax 788-7843.

Elevation: 2,017 feet/615m. **Radio:** CFGP 105, CISN-FM 103.9, CJDC 890, CKNL 560, CBC 1170, CFMI-FM 102, CHET-FM 94.5. **Television:** 7 channels (includes CBC, BCTV, ABC, CBS and NBC) plus pay cable.

The town was formerly known as Little Prairie and is a division point on the British Columbia Railway. The name was changed to honour the late British Columbia Minister of Railways, Ralph Chetwynd, who was instrumental in the northward extension of the province-owned railway.

In recent years, Chetwynd's collection of chain saw sculptures has earned it the title, "Chain Saw Sculpture Capital of the World."

The Infocentre has a map showing locations of the 2 dozen sculptures in town.

Chetwynd lies at the northern end of one of the largest known coal deposits on earth. Access from Chetwynd south to Tumbler Ridge and the resource development known as the North East Coal is via Highway 29 south, a 56-mile/90-km paved road (see HIGHWAY 29 SOUTH side road log this section). Forestry, mining, natural gas processing, ranching and farming are the main industries in Chetwynd. Louisiana Pacific has a modern non-polluting pulp mill here.

Chetwynd is a fast-growing community with several large motels, fast-food outlets, restaurants, banks and 4 bank machines, post office, 2 laundromats, gas stations, supermarkets and 2 9-hole golf courses. Good traveler's stop with easy access to all services. (Heavy commercial and industrial traffic often fill up local motels and campgrounds; reserve ahead.)

Recreation includes a skate park, hockey arena, curling rink and ball diamonds. Chetwynd & District Leisure Pool has a wave machine, whirlpool, sauna and weight room; open daily 6 A.M. to 10 P.M., visitors welcome.

There's a dump station at the 51st Avenue car/truck wash. There are private RV parks in town and on Highway 97. **Moberly Lake Provincial Park** is 12 miles/19.3 km north of Chetwynd via Highway 29 north (see **Milepost PG 187.9**) and 1.9 miles/3 km west via a gravel road. The park has 109 campsites, beach, picnic area, playground, nature trail, boat launch and a private marina next door with boat rental and concession. There's good swimming at huge Moberly Lake on a warm summer day. Worth the drive. ▲

Westwind RV Park. Good Sam. Area's newest and most modern. On Highway 97 North towards Dawson Creek. 50 large pull-through sites with full hookups. New, immaculate, restrooms and showers. Laundry facility. Wheelchair access. Walking distance to leisure pool and hiking trails. Your perfect stopping point for your Northern travels ... ask about our area attractions. Your hosts, David and Laurie Gayse. Phone (250) 788-2190, fax (250) 788-2086. See our display ad for more. [ADVERTISEMENT] ♿▲

West Access Route Log

(continued)

PG 187.8 (302.2 km) DC 62.2 (100.1 km) Highway crosses railroad tracks.

PG 187.9 (302.4 km) DC 62.1 (99.9 km)

Junction with Highway 29 north to Moberly Lake, Peace River Provincial Recreation Area and Peace Canyon Dam and Hudson's Hope. Highway 29 north connects with the Alaska Highway 53.7 miles/86.4 km north of Dawson Creek. Turn to HUDSON'S HOPE LOOP section for log of this route.

Highway climbs next 12 miles/19 km for Dawson Creek-bound motorists.

PG 189.4 (304.8 km) DC 60.6 (97.5 km)

Junction with Highway 29 (paved) south to Gwillim Lake and Tumbler Ridge (see HIGHWAY 29 SOUTH side road log this section).

Tumbler Ridge is also accessible from **Milepost PG 237.7** via the Heritage Highway.

Highway 29 South Log

Highway 29 South is a paved road that leads 55.9 miles/90 km from **Milepost PG 189.4** to the community of Tumbler Ridge. Travelers may return to Highway 97 via Highway 29, or via the Heritage Highway, a paved road that leads 59.5 miles/95 km from Tumbler Ridge to junction with Highway 97 at **Milepost PG 237.7**.
Distance from Highway 97 junction (J) is shown.

J 0 Junction with Highway 97 at **Milepost PG 189.4.**

J 0.1 (0.2 km) Turnout with litter barrels to east.

Highway 29 climbs next 2.3 miles/3.7 km southbound.

J 1.9 (3.1 km) Distance marker indicates Tumbler Ridge 88 km.

J 2.8 (4.5 km) Sign: Trucks check brakes, steep hill ahead.

J 3 (4.8 km) Large gravel turnouts with litter barrels both sides of highway.

J 5.5 (8.8 km) Twidwell Bend bridge.

J 5.6 (9 km) Access road east to Long Prairie (8 miles/12.9 km).

J 6.6 (10.6 km) Highway parallels Sukunka River to west.

J 8.2 (13.2 km) Zonnebeke Creek.

J 8.5 (13.7 km) Natural Springs Resort; 9-hole golf course.

J 9 (14.5 km) Kilometrepost 15.

J 10.6 (17 km) Bridge over Dickebush Creek.

J 11 (17.7 km) Sanctuary River.

J 13.7 (22 km) **Junction** with Sukunka Forest Road, which leads west 11 miles/17.7 km to Sukunka Falls. *NOTE: Radio-controlled road, travelers must monitor channel 151.325 MHz.*

J 13.8 (22.2 km) Highway climbs next 3 miles/4.8 km southbound.

J 16.7 (26.9 km) Turnouts with litter barrels both sides of highway.

J 21.6 (34.8 km) Turnout with litter barrels to east.

J 26.9 (43.3 km) Turnouts with litter barrels both sides of highway.

J 28.4 (45.7 km) Paved road leads east 1.2 miles/1.9 km to **Gwillim Lake Provincial Park** (gate closed 11 P.M. to 7 A.M.); 49 campsites, picnic tables, firewood and firepits. Day-use area and boat launch. Fishing for lake trout, grayling and pike. Camping fee $7 to $12. ⊷▲

J 40.8 (65.6 km) Access road leads west 9 miles/14.5 km to Bullmoose Mountain and mine. Mine tours may be available; phone (250) 242-5221 for current information.

J 41.1 (66.1 km) Turnout to east.

J 41.5 (66.8 km) Bridge over Bullmoose Flats River.

J 46.1 (74.2 km) Turnout with litter barrels to east. Phillips Way Summit, elev. 3,695 feet/1,126m.

J 51.4 (82.7 km) Bullmoose Creek bridge.

J 52.6 (84.3 km) Wolverine River bridge.

J 54.1 (87 km) Murray River bridge.

J 54.8 (88.2 km) Flatbed Creek bridge.

J 54.9 (88.3 km) Flatbed Creek Campground; 28 sites, hookups, water,

flush toilets, showers, dump station, picnic tables and playground. Camping fee $10. ▲

J 55.9 (90 km) Turnoff for community of Tumbler Ridge (description follows).

Tumbler Ridge

Located 116.5 miles/187.5 km southwest of Dawson Creek via Highways 97 and 29. **Population:** 3,775. **Emergency Services: RCMP**, phone (250) 242-5252. **Medical Centre**, phone (250) 242-5271. **Ambulance**, phone (800) 461-9911. **Fire Department**, phone (250) 242-5555.

Visitor Information: Located in town at Southgate Road and Front Street, across from the hospital. Open year-round. Write the Chamber of Commerce, Box 606, Tumbler Ridge, BC V0C 2W0, or phone (250) 242-4702, fax 242-5159.

Elevation: 3,000 feet/914m. **Private Aircraft:** 9 miles/15 km south; elev. 3,150 feet/960m, length 4,000 feet/1,218m; asphalt; fuel 80, 100, Jet B.

Tumbler Ridge was built in conjunction with development of the North East Coal resource. Construction of the townsite began in 1981. It is British Columbia's newest community, incorporated June 1, 1984.

Visitor facilities include a motel, restaurants, retail and grocery outlets, service stations with major repairs and propane and a car wash. Camping at Flatbed Creek Campground just outside of town and at Monkman RV Park in town. Recreational facilities include a community centre with arena, curling rink, weight room, indoor pool and a library. Outdoor facilities include tennis courts and a 9-hole golf course. ▲

The Visitor Infocentre provides a free slide presentation on Tumbler Ridge history and development. The Grizzly Valley Days Maritime West Festival, held Aug. 18–24, 1998, includes a parade, cod barrel race, Mr. Grizzly Valley contest, craft fair, lobster boil and other activities for the whole family.

Major attraction in the area is Monkman Provincial Park, site of spectacular 225-foot/69-m Kinuseo (keh-NEW-see-oh or Keh-NEW-soh) Falls. The falls and a 42-site campground are accessible from Tumbler Ridge via a 37-mile/60-km dirt road (watch for trucks) south from town. Viewing platform of falls is a short walk from the campground. For more information on the park, contact BC Parks in Fort St. John, phone (250) 787-3407.

The Quintette Mine is the World's largest computerized open pit mine. Coal mine tours are available at Quintette Mine south of town and at Bullmoose Mine (see **Milepost J 40.7** on Highway 29).

District of Tumbler Ridge. See display ad page 80.

Return to Milepost PG 189.4 West Access Route

District of Tumbler Ridge. See display ad this section.

PG 199.3 (320.7 km) **DC 50.7** (81.6 km) Gravel turnouts with litter barrels both sides of highway.

PG 201.2 (323.8 km) **DC 48.8** (78.5 km) Slow down for sharp curve across railroad tracks.

PG 204.3 (328.8km) **DC 45.7** (73.5km) Access to Louisianna Pacific Pulp Mill to north.

PG 205.6 (330.9 km) **DC 44.4** (71.5 km) Turnout with litter barrel and a commanding view of the East Pine River valley to the south.

PG 206.5 (332.3 km) **DC 43.5** (70 km) Sharp curves approximately next 2 miles/3.2 km as highway descends toward Dawson Creek. View of Table Mountain.

PG 207.9 (334.6 km) **DC 42.1** (67.7 km) Highway crosses under railroad.

PG 208.1 (334.9 km) **DC 41.9** (67.4 km) East Pine River bridge.

Sharp turn to south at west end of bridge for **East Pine Provincial Park** (0.5 mile on gravel road); picnicking and boat launch on Pine River. Turnout with litter barrel at park entrance.

From East Pine Provincial Park, canoeists may make a 2-day canoe trip down the Pine River to the Peace River; take-out at Taylor Landing Provincial Park (at **Milepost DC 34** on the Alaska Highway).

PG 208.2 (335.1 km) **DC 41.8** (67.3 km) Bridge across East Pine River. Railroad also crosses river here.

PG 208.3 (335.2 km) **DC 41.7** (67.1 km) Turnout with litter barrel to south.

Night view of Tumbler Ridge's fanciful City Hall. The community is south of the Hart Highway. (© Earl L. Brown, staff)

PG 209.8 (337.6 km) **DC 40.2** (64.7 km) East Pine (unincorporated) has a store and gas station.

PG 211.7 (340.7 km) **DC 38.3** (61.6 km) Turnout with litter barrel to north. Westbound brake-check area.

PG 221.5 (356.5 km) **DC 28.5** (45.9 km) Turnouts with litter barrels both sides of highway.

PG 222 (357.3 km) **DC 28** (45 km) Groundbirch (unincorporated); store, liquor outlet, gas, propane, diesel, post office and camping. ▲

PG 230.7 (371.3 km) **DC 19.3** (31.1 km) Progress (unincorporated), highway maintenance yard, cairn and pay phone.

PG 234.4 (377.2 km) **DC 15.6** (25.1 km) Turnout with litter barrels to north.

PG 237.7 (382.5 km) **DC 12.3** (19.8 km) **Junction** with Heritage Highway, which leads 59.5 miles/96 km (paved) south to the community of Tumbler Ridge and access roads to the North East Coal Development. (Tumbler Ridge is also accessible via Highway 29 south from Chetwynd. See side road log this section.)

From Tumbler Ridge, the Heritage Highway continues 92 miles/148 km east and north to connect with Highway 2 southeast of Dawson Creek. Inquire locally about road conditions.

PG 238 (383 km) **DC 12** (19.3 km) Kiskatinaw River bridge.

PG 240.7 (387.4 km) **DC 9.3** (15 km) Arras (unincorporated), cafe and gas station.

PG 247.9 (398.9 km) **DC 2.1** (3.4 km) Small turnout with litter barrel and point of interest sign to south.

PG 248 (399.1 km) **DC 2** (3.2 km) Private RV Park. ▲

PG 249.9 (402.2 km) **DC 0.1** (0.2 km) Entering Dawson Creek. Private campground on south side of highway; Rotary Lake Park and camping on north side of highway. ▲

PG 250 (402.3 km) **DC 0 Junction** of the Hart Highway and Alaska Highway; turn right for downtown Dawson Creek, Mile Zero of the Alaska Highway.

Turn to the ALASKA HIGHWAY section on page 83 for description of Dawson Creek and log of the Alaska Highway.

HUDSON'S HOPE LOOP

Connects: Chetwynd, BC, to Alaska Hwy.   **Length:** 87 miles
Road Surface: Paved   **Season:** Open all year
Steepest Grade: 10 percent
Major Attraction: W.A.C. Bennett and Peace Canyon Dams

(See map, page 57)

	Alaska Hwy	Chetwynd	Hudson's Hope
Alaska Hwy		87	47
Chetwynd	87		40
Hudson's Hope	47	40	

Visitor photographs scenic Peace River farmland on Hudson's Hope Loop.

(Earl L. Brown, staff)

The Hudson's Hope Loop links the John Hart Highway (Highway 97) with the Alaska Highway (also Highway 97). This 86.9-mile/139.8-km paved loop road provides year-round access to the town of Hudson's Hope, W.A.C. Bennett Dam, Peace Canyon Dam and Moberly Lake. As a shortcut bypassing Dawson Creek, the Hudson's Hope Loop saves 28.9 miles/46.5 km. Highway 29 is a good, scenic 2-lane road but is steep and winding in places.

Hudson's Hope Loop Log

Distance from Chetwynd (C) is followed by distance from Alaska Highway junction (AH).

BC HIGHWAY 29

C 0 AH 86.9 (139.8 km) **Junction** of Highways 29 and 97 at Chetwynd.

> Turn to **Milepost PG 187.6** in the WEST ACCESS ROUTE section for description of Chetwynd and log of BC Highway 97.

C 0.5 (0.8 km) **AH 86.4** (139 km) Truck weigh scales to west. Highway climbs next 4.3 miles/7 km westbound.

C 2.3 (3.7 km) **AH 84.6** (136.1 km) Jackfish Road to east.

C 5 (8 km) **AH 81.9** (131.8 km) Turnout with litter barrel to west.

C 12 (19.3 km) **AH 74.9** (120.5 km) Gravel access road leads 2 miles/3.2 km west to **Moberly Lake Provincial Park** on south shore; 109 campsites, swimming, waterskiing, picnicking, drinking water, dump station, boat launch, $9.50 camping fee. This beautiful 9-mile-/14.5-km-long lake drains at its east end into Moberly River, which in turn runs into the Peace River. Fishing for lake trout, Dolly Varden and whitefish. ◄▲

C 12.2 (19.6 km) **AH 74.7** (120.2 km) Moberly River bridge; parking area with litter barrel at south end.

C 15.9 (25.6 km) **AH 71** (114.3 km) High-way cairn is memorial to John Moberly, fur trader and explorer who first landed here in 1865.

C 16.4 (26.4 km) **AH 70.5** (113.5 km) Spencer Tuck Regional Park; picnic tables, swimming, fishing and boat launch. ◄►

C 17.4 (28 km) **AH 69.5** (111.8 km) Camping resort. ▲

C 18.3 (29.5 km) **AH 68.6** (110.4 km) **MOBERLY LAKE.** Post office, cafe, store and pay phone.

C 18.5 (29.8 km) **AH 68.4** (110.1 km) Moberly Lake and District Golf Club, 0.7 mile/1.1 km from highway; 9 holes, grass greens, rentals, clubhouse, licensed lounge. Open May to September.

C 25.4 (40.9 km) **AH 61.5** (99 km) Cameron Lake camping area; tables, water, toilets, firewood, playground, horseshoe pits, boat launch (no motorboats) and swimming. Camping fee by donation. ▲

C 30.7 (49.4 km) **AH 56.2** (90.4 km) Gravel turnout with litter barrel to east. Highway descends northbound to Hudson's Hope.

C 35.9 (57.8 km) **AH 51** (82.1 km) Suspension bridge over Peace River; paved turnouts at both ends of bridge with concrete totem pole sculptures. View of Peace Canyon Dam.

C 36.5 (58.7 km) **AH 50.4** (81.1 km) Turnoff to west for Dinosaur Lake Campground and B.C. Hydro **Peace Canyon Dam.** The dam's visitor centre, 0.6 mile/1 km on paved access road, is open from 8 A.M. to 4 P.M. daily from late May through Labour Day; Monday through Friday the rest of the year (closed holidays). Self-guided tour includes a full-scale model of duck-billed dinosaurs and a tableau portraying Alexander Mackenzie's discovery of the Peace River canyon. A pictorial display traces the construction of the Peace Canyon Dam. Phone (250) 783-5211 for a guided tour (groups of 8 or more).

Dinosaur Lake Campground, on Dinosaur Lake, has 30 campsites with firepits, water, toilets and tables. Boat launch and swimming area. Camping fee by donation. ▲

C 38.3 (61.6 km) **AH 48.6** (78.2 km) Alwin Holland Memorial Park (0.5 mile/0.8 km east of highway) is named for the first teacher in Hudson's Hope, who willed his property, known locally as The Glen, to be used as a public park. There are 17 campsites, picnic grounds, barbecues and water. Camping fee by donation. ▲

C 39 (62.8 km) **AH 47.9** (77.1 km) King Gething Park; small campground with 15 grassy sites, picnic tables, cookhouse, flush toilets, showers and dump station east side

Hudson's Hope Museum has a collection of dinosaur fossils. (Earl L. Brown, staff)

of highway. Camping fee by donation. ▲

Hudson's Hope

C 40.4 (65 km) AH 46.5 (74.8 km) **Population:** 1,122. **Emergency Services: RCMP,** phone (250) 783-5241. **Fire Department,** phone (250) 783-5700. **Ambulance,** phone (800) 461-9911. **Medical Clinic,** phone (250) 783-9991.

Visitor Information: A log building houses the tourist information booth at Beattie Park. Open daily mid-May to the end of August, hours are 8 A.M. to 5:30 P.M. Phone (250) 783-9154 or write Box 330, Hudson's Hope, BC V0C 1V0. (Off-season, phone the District Office at 250/783-9901.)

Elevation: 1,707 feet/520m. **Climate:** Summer temperatures range from 60°F/16°C to 90°F/32°C, with an average of 135 frost-free days annually. **Radio:** CBC, CKNL 560, CJDC 870. **Television:** Channels 2, 5, 8, 11 and cable.

Private Aircraft: Hudson's Hope airstrip, 3.7 miles/6 km west; elev. 2,200 feet/671m; length 5,200 feet/1,585m; asphalt.

Visitor services in Hudson's Hope include a motel, hotel, 2 bed and breakfasts, 3 restaurants, 2 service stations, a laundromat, bank, post office, supermarket, bakery, and convenience and hardware stores.

Hudson's Hope is the third oldest permanently settled community in British Columbia. The site was first visited in 1793 by Alexander Mackenzie. In 1805 a Hudson's Bay trading post was established here by Simon Fraser. In 1916, after the fur-trading days were over, a major influx of settlers arrived in the area. It was the head of navigation for steamboats on the lower Peace River until 1936, the year of the last scheduled steamboat run. Area coal mines supplied Alaska Highway maintenance camps during the 1940s.

Modern development of Hudson's Hope was spurred by construction of the Peace Power project in the 1960s. Today the area's principal claim to fame is the 600-foot-/183-m-high **W.A.C. Bennett Dam** at the upper end of the Peace River canyon, 15 miles/24.1 km west of Hudson's Hope. The 100-million-ton dam is one of the largest earth-fill structures in the world, and Williston Lake, behind it, is the largest body of fresh water in British Columbia. The dam provides about 20 percent of British Columbia's hydroelectricity. Tours of the Gordon M. Shrum generating station are available daily from mid-May to the end of September, weekdays only the remainder of the year (closed holidays). Phone (250) 783-5211 for information. Tours are available each hour on the half hour from 9:30 A.M. to 4:30 P.M.

Also of interest is the Hudson's Hope Museum on Highway 29 in town. The museum has a fine collection of artifacts and dinosaur fossils from the Peace District. It offers hands-on paleontology and dinosaur activities, and is well worth a visit. Souvenir shop in the museum; (250) 783-5735; admission by donation. Historic log-constructed St. Peter's Anglican United Church adjacent museum.

Hudson's Hope Museum. See display ad this section.

Hudson's Hope Loop Log

(continued)

C 41.2 (66.3 km) AH 45.7 (73.5 km) Turnout to north with Hudson's Hope visitor map.

CAUTION: Watch for deer between here and the Alaska Highway, especially at dusk and at night.

C 44 (70.8 km) AH 42.9 (69 km) Lynx Creek bridge.

C 48.4 (77.9 km) AH 38.5 (62 km) Turnout to south for view of the Peace River.

C 50.9 (81.9 km) AH 36 (57.9 km) Farrell Creek bridge and picnic site.

C 56.6 (91.1 km) AH 30.3 (48.8 km) Pull-through turnout with litter barrels. View of Peace River valley. *CAUTION: Watch for frost heaves and rough spots next 10 miles/16 km.*

C 57.1 (91.9 km) AH 29.8 (48 km) Turnout to south with litter barrels and view of Peace River valley.

C 59.3 (95.4 km) AH 27.6 (44.4 km) Turnout to south with litter barrels.

C 64.7 (104.1 km) AH 22.2 (35.7 km) Halfway River.

C 67.2 (108.1 km) AH 19.7 (31.7 km) Rest area to south with point of interest sign, litter barrel and toilet. A slide occurred here on May 26, 1973, involving an estimated 10 million to 15 million cubic yards of overburden. Slide debris completely blocked the river channel for some 12 hours, backing up the river an estimated 24 feet/7.3m above normal level.

C 71.1 (114.4 km) AH 15.8 (25.4 km) Turnout to north.

C 73.5 (118.3 km) AH 13.4 (21.6 km) Beaver dam to north.

C 74.2 (119.4 km) AH 12.7 (20.4 km) Pine Ridge Campground. A relaxing owner-operated campground, halfway between Fort St. John and Hudson's Hope. 100 spacious sites, some with power. Showers, washer and dryer, spring water and confectionery. Cooking shelter, firepits and firewood, horseshoe pits, ping pong, ball diamonds, child-proof fence. Very reasonable rates. Gates open 7 A.M.–9 P.M. (Pets on a leash please.) Your hosts, the Bentleys, (250) 262-3229 mid-May to mid-September. [ADVERTISEMENT] ▲

C 74.6 (120.1 km) AH 12.3 (19.8 km) Cache Creek 1-lane bridge. Turnout to north at east end of bridge for picnic area with litter barrels.

C 76.6 (123.3 km) AH 10.3 (16.6 km) Turnout with litter barrel to north overlooking Bear Flat in the Peace River valley. Highway begins climb eastbound. *CAUTION: Switchbacks.*

C 78.1 (125.7 km) AH 8.8 (14.2 km) Highest point on Highway 29 (2,750 feet/838m) overlooking Peace River Plateau. Highway descends on a 10 percent grade westbound. *CAUTION: Switchbacks.*

C 86.9 (139.8 km) AH 0 Truck stop at junction with gas, diesel, propane, tire repair, restaurant and convenience store.

Junction with the Alaska Highway, 6.7 miles/10.8 km north of Fort St. John; turn to **Milepost DC 53.7** in the ALASKA HIGHWAY section for log.

CAUTION: Watch for deer on the highway between here and Hudson's Hope, especially at dusk and at night.

Connects: Dawson Creek, BC, to Delta Junction, AK **Length:** 1,390 miles
Road Surface: Paved   **Season:** Open all year
Highest Summit: Summit Lake 4,250 feet
Major Attractions: Muncho Lake, Liard Hotsprings, Watson Lake
Signforest, SS *Klondike*, Kluane Lake, Trans-Alaska Pipeline Crossing

(See maps, pages 84–88)

	Dawson Cr.	Delta Jct.	Fairbanks	Ft. Nelson	Haines Jct.	Tok	Watson Lk.	Whitehorse
Dawson Cr.		1390	1488	283	985	1282	613	895
Delta Jct.	1390		98	1107	405	108	777	495
Fairbanks	1488	98		1205	593	206	875	593
Ft. Nelson	283	1107	1205		702	999	330	612
Haines Jct.	985	405	593	702		297	372	90
Tok	1282	108	206	999	297		669	387
Watson Lk.	613	777	875	330	372	669		282
Whitehorse	895	495	593	612	90	387	282	

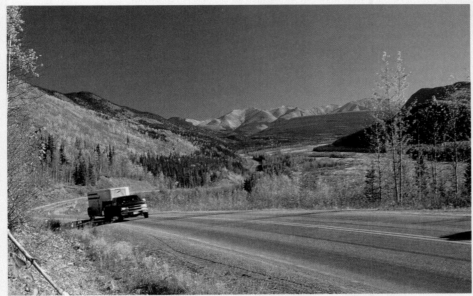

The Alaska Highway winds through the MacDonald River Valley near Milepost DC 381. (© Earl L. Brown, staff)

The Alaska Highway begins as BC Highway 97 at **Mile 0** in Dawson Creek, BC. The Alaska Highway then travels 613 miles/987 km in a northwesterly direction from Dawson Creek to the Yukon Territory border near Watson Lake, YT, **Historical Mile 635**, where it becomes Yukon Highway 1. The highway then crosses 577 miles/929 km of Yukon Territory to reach Port Alcan on the Alaska border, entering Alaska at **Historical Mile 1221.8**, where it becomes Alaska Route 2. From this international border, it is 200 miles/322 km to Delta Junction, AK, **Historical Mile 1422**, the official end of the Alaska Highway.

From Delta Junction to Fairbanks, a distance of 98 miles/158 km, travelers will be on the Richardson Highway, Alaska Route 4. Although often treated as a natural extension of the Alaska Highway (and logged as such in previous editions of *The MILE-POST®*), the highway between Delta Junction and Fairbanks is designated as Alaska Route 4, the Richardson Highway. Originally known as the Richardson Trail, this route predates construction of the Alaska Highway by some 50 years. (Turn to the RICHARDSON HIGHWAY section for a log of that route.)

Road Conditions

All of the Alaska Highway is asphalt surfaced. Repaving and highway improvement are ongoing. Surfacing of the Alaska Highway ranges from poor to excellent.

There are still some stretches of poor surfacing with many chuckholes, gravel breaks (sections of gravel ranging from a few feet to several miles), hardtop with loose gravel, deteriorated shoulders and bumps.

CAUTION: Loose gravel patches are common on the Alaska Highway and are often signed. Slow down for loose gravel! Excessive speeds can lead to loss of control of your vehicle.

Surfacing on much of the highway is fair, with older patched pavement and a minimum of gravel breaks and chuckholes. There are also sections of excellent surfacing where highway maintenance crews have recently upgraded the road.

On the northern portion of the highway—in Yukon Territory and on into Alaska—watch for frost heaves. This rippling effect in the pavement is caused by the freezing and thawing of the ground. Drive slowly in sections of frost heaves to avoid breaking an axle or trailer hitch.

Keep in mind that road conditions are subject to change! Weather and traffic may cause deterioration of newer pavement, while construction may improve older sections. Always be alert for bumps and holes in the road and for abrupt changes in highway surfacing. There are stretches of narrow, winding road without shoulders. Also watch for soft shoulders. Dust and mud are generally only a problem in construction areas.

Always watch for construction crews along the Alaska Highway. Extensive road construction may require a detour, or travelers may be delayed while waiting for a pilot car to guide them through the construction. Motorists may encounter rough driving at construction areas, and muddy roadway if there are heavy rains while the roadbed is torn up.

For current road conditions, see Road Condition Report sources listed under Driving Information in the TRAVEL PLANNING section of this book.

Detailed weather information for the Canadian portion of the Alaska Highway is available from Atmospheric Environment Service of Environment Canada. For 24-hour recorded weather information between Dawson Creek and Sikanni Chief, phone (250) 784-2244 or (250) 785-7669; for detailed weather information, phone the weather office at (250) 785-4304 between 6:15 A.M. and 4:45 P.M.; or for weather broadcasts, tune to 580 AM. Between Sikanni Chief and the BC–YT border, phone (250) 774-6461 for 24-hour recorded message; for detailed weather information phone (250) 774-2302 between 3 A.M. and 6:15 P.M.; or tune your radio to 590 AM for weather broadcasts. Between the BC–YT border and the YT–AK border, phone (867) 668-6061 for 24-hour recorded message; for detailed weather information phone (867) 667-8464 (24 hours a day); or tune your radio to CBC Yukon (570 AM) for weather broadcasts. Regional weather forecasts are also supplied to local visitor information centres, local

(Continues on page 89)

ALASKA HIGHWAY Dawson Creek, BC, to Milepost DC 409

© 1999 The MILEPOST®

Muncho Lake Provincial Park

DC-409/655km
DJ-981/1579km

Toad River (Historical Mile 422)
DC-407.5/652km The Poplars Campground CDdGILMrST
DC-404.6/647.4km Toad River Lodge CDdGILMPrT
Stone Mountain Safaris L
DC-378.6/605.7km Rocky Mountain Lodge CGILr

(map continues next page)

Summit (Historical Mile 392)

F-1115/1794km
DC-373/597km

Stone Mountain Provincial Park

ROCKY MOUNTAINS

To Fort Simpson, NWT
(see LIARD HIGHWAY section)

DC-301/484km
DJ-1089/1753km
FL-109/175km

N58°54' W123°07'

DC-283/454km
DJ-1107/1782km
F-1205/1939km

DC-333/532.5km Steamboat CdGIMrT

Steamboat (Historical Mile 351)

DC-278.4/448km Trapper's Den

Fort Nelson (Historical Mile 300)
N58°49' W122°32'
DC-277.9/447.2km Husky 5th Wheel Truck Stop & RV Park CDdGIMPRST

97

Prophet River (Historical Mile 233)
DC-226.9/365.2km Neighbours Inn CdGIST

Trutch Mountain Bypass

DC-173.4/279km Buckinghorse River Lodge CdGILMT

Sikanni Chief (Historical Mile 162)
DC-159.4/256.5km Sikanni River RV Park CDdGILPT

DC-144.5/232.5km Mae's Kitchen dGLMT

DC-140.4/225.9km Pink Mountain Campsite & RV Park CDdGILPST
Pink Mountain Motor Inn CDdGILMPT

Pink Mountain (Historical Mile 143)

DC-140/226km
DJ-1250/2011km

DC-101/162km
DJ-1289/2074km

97

Wonowon (Historical Mile 101)

DC-71.7/115.4km The Shepherd's Inn CGILMPT

DC-47/76km
DJ-1343/2161km

N56°15' W120°50'

Charlie Lake

Fort St. John

DC-53.7/86.4km Mile 54 Shell Truck Stop dGIMPrST
DC-51.5/82.9km Ron's RV Park CDT
DC-51.2/82.4km Rotary RV Park CDT
DC-50.6/81.4km Charlie Lake General Store dGIPST
DC-50.4/81.1km Paradise Lane Bed & Breakfast L

DC-42.3/68.1km The Honey Place

DC-35/56.3km Redwood Esso and Taylor Lodge dGILPST

Taylor

Hudson's Hope Loop

29

Hudson's Hope

DC-43.7/70.3km Sourdough Pete's RV Park & Troy's Amusement Park CDIST

W.A.C. Bennett Dam

29

DC-9.5/15.3km Farmington Fairways Golf & Camping CDMT

97

N55°46' W120°14'

Chetwynd

97

DC-0
DJ-1390/2237km
PG-250/402km
E-367/591km
F-1488/2395km

Dawson Creek

To Prince George
(see WEST ACCESS ROUTE section, page 55)

John Hart Highway

To Grande Prairie
(see EAST ACCESS ROUTE section, page 33)

Map Location

Key to mileage boxes
miles/kilometres
miles/kilometres
from:
DC- Dawson Creek
DJ- Delta Junction
E- Edmonton
F- Fairbanks
FL- Fort Liard
PG- Prince George

Principal Route
Paved   Unpaved
Other Roads
Paved   Unpaved
Ferry Routes   Hiking Trails

Refer to Log for Visitor Facilities

Key to Advertiser Services
C - Camping
D - Dump Station
d - Diesel
G - Gas (reg., unld.)
I - Ice
L - Lodging
M - Meals
P - Propane
R - Car Repair (major)
r - Car Repair (minor)
S - Store (grocery)
T - Telephone (pay)

Scale
0   20 Miles
0   20 Kilometres

DC-409/655km
DJ-981/1579km

DC-436/698km
DJ-954/1535km

Muncho Lake
(Historical
Mile 456)

N59°00' W125°46'

(map
continues
previous
page)

DC-477.7/764.7km Liard
River Lodge CDdGILMST

Liard River
Hotsprings
Provincial Park

DC-477/764km
DJ-913/1469km

Liard River
(Historical Mile 496)

DC-477.8/764.9km Trapper Ray's
Liard Hotsprings Lodge CdGILMrT

DC-443.7/710.3km J & H Wilderness Resort CDdGILMST
DC-443.6/710.1km Muncho Lake Lodge CDGILMrT
DC-442.7/707.9km Northern Rockies/Highland Glen Lodge CDdGILMST
DC-436.6/698.7km Double G Service DdGILMrST

Muncho Lake
Provincial Park

ROCKY   MOUNTAINS

Kechika River

Fireside (Historical
Mile 543)

DC-568/910km
DJ-822/1322km

Contact Creek (Historical Mile 590)

Hilgren
Lakes

DC-570/912.9km
Contact Creek
Lodge dGILMPrT

DC-575.9/922km Iron
Creek Lodge CDdGILMrT

DC-613/1021km
DJ-777/1251km
RR-239/385km
F-875/1408km

N60°07' W128°48'

Watson Lake
(Historical Mile 635)

Lower Post
(Historical
Mile 620)

DC-610.5/1017.7km Campground
Services CDdGIPrST

DC-619.6/1032km

Green Valley
RV Park CDlST

DC-626.2/1043km
Junction 37 Services
CDdGILMPrST

DC-626/1043km
DJ-764/1229km
DL-145/234km

Upper Liard
Village

(Historical
Mile 642)

DC-627/1043.9km The Northern
Beaver Post CDLMT

To Ross River
(see CAMPBELL HIGHWAY section)

To Dease Lake
(see CASSIAR HIGHWAY section)

Albert Cr.

DC-751/1249km
DJ-638/1027km

DC-698.4/1161.6km Walker's
Continental Divide CDdGILMT

Swift River
(Historical
Mile 733)

DC-710/1180.9km Swift River
Lodge dGILMrT

CASSIAR   MOUNTAINS

DC-776/1294km
DJ-614/988km

Teslin
(Historical Mile 804)

N60°10' W132°42'

DC-776.3/1294km Yukon Motel Lakeshore Resort CDdGILMPT

DC-769.6/1282.5km Dawson Peaks
Resort & RV Park CDGLM

DC-752.9/1252km Morley
River Lodge CDdGILMT

(map
continues
next page)

www.themilepost.com

ALASKA HIGHWAY
Teslin, YT, to Milepost DC 1136

© 1999 The MILEPOST®

To Ross River
(see CANOL ROAD section)

6

Nisutlin River

Quiet Lake

Johnson's Crossing
(Historical Mile 836)

DC-808.9/1346km Johnson's Crossing
Campground Services CDdGIST

Cr. Lone Tree
Deadman

Teslin
(Historical Mile 804)

(map continues previous page)

DC-836.8/1392.5km
Jake's Corner Inc. Teslin
dCLIMPT

Jake's Corner
(Historical Mile 866)

DC-784.3/1306.7km Muktuk
Annie's Salmon Bake CDLM
N60°410' W132°42'

DC-776/1294km
DJ-614/988km

To Atlin
(see ATLIN ROAD section)

7

Little — Squanga Cr.
Little — Squanga L.

Tagish

Little Atlin L.

Marsh L.

Tagish Road
(see TAGISH ROAD section)

DC-837/1393km
A-58/93km
S-101/163km
W-47/76km

Atlin Lake

BIG SALMON RANGES

Teslin River

Teslin Lake

M'Clintock River

Whitehorse
(Historical Mile 918)

DC-884/1470.2km Hi-Country RV Park CDdPST
DC-883.2/1468.9km Whitehorse Shell DdGIPST
DC-882.6/1468km Philmar RV Service and Supply RT
DC-881/1465.5km Pioneer RV Park CDdGIPrST
DC-880/1464km Fireweed RV Service R
DC-873.5/1453.3km Sourdough Country Campsite
RV Park CDIT

Carcross Corner DdGIMPST
Yukon Rock Shop

Carcross

2

DC-874.4/1455km

White Pass & Yukon Route

Lake Bennett

To Skagway
(see KLONDIKE HIGHWAY section)

8

Tutshi Lake

YUKON TERRITORY
BRITISH COLUMBIA

DC-887/1476km
DJ-503/809km

M'Clintock River

N60°43' W135°03'

DC-885.8/473.1km Yukon
Transportation Museum
DC-882.9/1468.5km Mountain
Ridge Motel & RV Park CDIT

Wolf Cr.

Fish L.

DC-874/1455km
W-13/21km
S-99/159km

Fox Lake

Lake Laberge

To Dawson City
(see KLONDIKE LOOP section)

2

Yukon River

Yukon River

D-327/527km
W-8/13km

1

Takhini River

Takhini River

Stony Cr.

Mendenhall R.

Champagne
(Historical Mile 974.6)

Taye

DC-944/1568km
DJ-447/719km

DC-964.6/1602.2km
Otter Falls Cutoff CdGIST

Cracker Cr.

DAWSON RANGE

Aishihik Lake

Sekulmun Lake

Aishihik River

West Aishihik River

Aishihik

DC-985/1635km
DJ-405/652km
H-152/246km

Dezadeash R.

N60°45' W137°30'

Sixmile Lake

Kusawa Lake

Kasawa Lake

Dezadeash Lake

To Haines
(see HAINES HIGHWAY section)

3

Mush Lake

Bates Lake

Alsek River

Kathleen Lake

Marshall Cr.

Pine L.

Kloo L.

Sulphur L.

Christmas Cr.

Haines Junction
(Historical Mile 1016)

DC-1023.7/1698.5km Trans North Helicopters
DC-1020.3/1693km Kluane Bed and Breakfast T
DC-991.6/1645.9km Bear Creek
Lodge CdGILMrT

Slims R.

Kaskawulsh R.

Kluane
National
Park

Mount Hubbard
15,015 ft./4,577m

DC-1062/1759.8km Dalan Campground CD
DC-1061.6/1759.2km Burbilly Hill
DC-1061.5/1759km Burwash Landing Resort & RV Park CDdGLMT
Destruction Bay Fishing Charters
Kluane Museum of Natural History T
Burwash Landing (Historical Mile 1093)

DC-1084.6/1797.2km Kluane Wilderness
Village CDdGILMPRrST

DC-1034.9/1717km Cottonwood RV
Park & Campground CDIS

Kluane Lake

Burwash Landing

DC-1113.8/1844.8km Pine Valley Motel & Cafe CdGILMrT

DC-1051.7/1743.3km Destruction Bay Lodge
DC-1051.5/1743km Talbot Arm Motel CDdGILMPrST

Soldier's Summit
3,293 ft./1,003m

Boutillier Summit
3,291 ft./1,004m

Destruction Bay
(Historical Mile 1083)

DC-1052/1743km
DJ-339/545km

N61°15' W138°48' Destruction Bay

Bear Creek Summit
3,294 ft./1,004m

Donjek River

Kluane Wilderness Village
(Historical Mile 1118)

DC-1135/1880km White River RV Park CDdGT

Tincup Lake

Pickhandle Lake

Koidern R.

White R.

DC-1084.6/1797.2km

DC-1136/1881km
DJ-254/409km

(map continues next page)

ST. ELIAS MOUNTAINS

Glaciated
Area

▲ Mount Logan
19,520 ft./5,950m

▲ Mount Steele 16,644 ft./5,073m
▲ Mount Luciana 17,147 ft./5,226m

Kluane

Mount Vancouver
15,840 ft./4,828m

Key to mileage boxes

miles/kilometres
miles/kilometres

from:
DC–Dawson Creek
DJ–Delta Junction
A–Atlin
D–Dawson City
H–Haines
S–Skagway
W–Whitehorse

Map Location

Key to Advertiser Services

C –Camping
D –Dump Station
d –Diesel
G –Gas (reg., unld.)
I –Ice
L –Lodging
M–Meals
P –Propane
R –Car Repair (major)
r –Car Repair (minor)
S –Store (grocery)
T –Telephone (pay)

🏕 Refer to Log for Visitor Facilities

Principal Route
Paved
Unpaved

Other Roads
Paved
Unpaved

Ferry Routes   Hiking Trails

Scale
0   20   Miles
0   20   Kilometres

© 1999 The MILEPOST®

ALASKA HIGHWAY Milepost DC 1378 to Delta Junction, AK

© 1999 The MILEPOST®

To Livengood
(see ELLIOTT HIGHWAY section)

To Circle
(see STEESE HIGHWAY section)

The Alaska Railroad

To Chena Hot Springs
(see STEESE HIGHWAY section)

V-364/586km
F-0

Fairbanks

3

To Anchorage
(see PARKS HIGHWAY section)

V-356./572.9km Road's End RV Park C

N64°08' W147°03'

North Pole

V-349/561.6km Santa Claus House
V-348.7/561.2km Santaland RV Park CDIT

Moose Creek

V-346.7/557.9 km North Pole VFW Post 10029

Eielson Air Force Base

N64°06' W147°01'

Piledriver Slough

Salcha River

V-332.3/534.8km The Knotty Shop

Little Salcha R.

V-328.3/528.3km Salcha Store and Service dGIPST

Salcha

V-326/524km
F-39/62km

V-322.2/518.5km Salcha River Lodge GILMST

Harding Lake

Shaw Creek

V-314.8/506.6km Midway Lodge ILMT

Birch Lake

Trans-Alaska Pipeline

Richardson Highway
(see Richardson HIGHWAY section)

Tanana River

Quartz Lake

V-275.4/443.2km The Fur Shack

Big Delta

V-275/442.6km Rika's Roadhouse at Big Delta State Historical Park CDM
Tanana Trading Post dGI

V-273.9/440.8km Big D B&B L

V-270.3/435km Alaska 7 Motel

V-268/431.3km Smith's Green Acres RV Park & Campground CDLT

Little Delta Creek

N64°00' W145°07' Delta Junction

DC-1422/2288km
DJ-0
V-266/428km
G-151/242km
F-98/158km

DC-1420.9/2286.7km Bergstad's Travel and Trailer Court CD

Tanana River

DC-1412.5/2273.1km Cherokee Lodge & RV Park CDILMT

Clearwater Creek

DC-1403.3/2258.3km Farm Tours

West Fork

Delta Creek

4

Sawmill Creek

Gerstle River

Little Gerstle River

Johnson River

Clearwater Creek

Dry Cr.

Moosehead L.

Lisa L.

Glaciated Area

Mount Deborah ▲
12,339 ft./3,639m

▲ Hess Mountain
11,940 ft./3,761m

▲ Mount Hayes
13,832 ft./4,216m

Glaciated Area

2

(map continues previous page)

DC-1380/2221km
DJ-42/67km

Sears Cr.

Berry Cr.

Bear Creek

Glaciated Area

To Valdez
(see RICHARDSON HIGHWAY section)

ALASKA RANGE

Principal Route

Paved — Unpaved

Other Roads

Paved — Unpaved

Ferry Routes — Hiking Trails

Refer to Log for Visitor Facilities

Scale

0 ——— 10 Miles
0 ——— 10 Kilometres

Key to Advertiser Services
C -Camping
D -Dump Station
d -Diesel
G -Gas (reg., unld.)
I -Ice
L -Lodging
M -Meals
P -Propane
R -Car Repair (major)
r -Car Repair (minor)
S -Store (grocery)
T -Telephone (pay)

Map Location

Key to mileage boxes

miles/kilometres
miles/kilometres from:

DC- Dawson Creek
DJ- Delta Junction
V- Valdez
F- Fairbanks
G- Glennallen

(Continued from page 83)
hotels and motels, and lodges along the highway.

Driving the Alcan

Although not really called the ALCAN anymore, quite a few people still refer to the Alaska Highway by its original military acronym. What visitors don't know—and what some Northerners may remember—is that ALCAN (which stood for Alaska-Canada military highway) was the military name for the pioneer road at its completion in 1942. Because civilian traffic was restricted on the new highway during the war years, and many residents did not take kindly to the restriction, the military name for the road was not popular. The pioneer road was officially named the Alaska Highway in March 1943.

Today's Alaska Highway is a 2-lane highway that winds and rolls across the wilderness. The best advice is to take your time; drive with your headlights on at all times; keep to the right on hills and corners; watch for wildlife on the road; and—as you would on any highway anywhere else—drive defensively.

There are relatively few steep grades or high summits on the Alaska Highway, with most occurring as the Alaska Highway crosses the Rocky Mountains between Fort Nelson, BC, and Watson Lake, YT. The highest summit on the highway is at Summit Lake, elev. 4,250 feet/1,295m. The few steep grades are generally short stretches from 6 to 10 percent.

Gas, food and lodging are found along the Alaska Highway on an average of every 20 to 50 miles. (The longest stretch without services is about 100 miles.) Not all businesses are open year-round, nor are most services available 24 hours a day. There are dozens of government and private campgrounds along the highway.

Remember that you will be driving in 2 different countries that use 2 different currencies: For the best rate, exchange your money at a bank. There are banks in Dawson Creek, Fort St. John, Fort Nelson, Watson Lake, Whitehorse, Tok, Delta Junction and Fairbanks. Haines Junction has banking service at the general store.

Mileposts and Kilometreposts

Mileposts were first put up at communities and lodges along the Alaska Highway in the 1940s to help motorists know where they were in this vast wilderness. Today, those original mileposts remain a tradition with communities and businesses on the highway and are still used as mailing addresses and reference points, although the figures no longer accurately reflect driving distance.

When Canada switched to the metric system in the mid-1970s, the mileposts were replaced by kilometreposts. These posts are located on the right-hand side of the highway (Alaska-bound). Kilometreposts, consisting of reflective white numerals on green signs, are up along the British Columbia portion of the Alaska Highway every 3 miles/5 km. In Yukon Territory, white posts with black numerals are up along the highway every 1.2 miles/2 km.

The kilometerage of the British Columbia

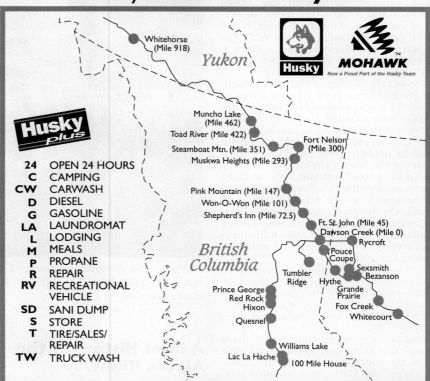

portion of the Alaska Highway was recalibrated by the government in the fall of 1990, with kilometreposts corrected to reflect current driving distances. As of our press time, kilometreposts along the Yukon Territory portion of the Alaska Highway still reflected the metric equivalent of the historical mileposts. Thus, at the BC–YT border (**Historical Mile 627**) the kilometerage from Dawson Creek is given as 967.6 km on the BC side and 1009 km on the YT side.

The MILEPOST® log of the Alaska Highway gives distance from Dawson Creek to the AK–YT border as actual driving distance in miles from Dawson Creek followed by kilometre distance based on the kilometreposts. Use our mileage figure from Dawson Creek to figure correct distance between points on the Alaska Highway in Canada. Use our kilometre figure from Dawson Creek to pinpoint location in reference to physical kilometreposts on the Alaska Highway in Canada. On the Alaska portion of the highway, mileposts are based on historical miles, so distance from Dawson Creek in the log is given according to the historical mileposts up along the road.

NOTE: Due to road reconstruction, many kilometreposts and mileposts are missing. Missing kilometreposts south from Beaver Creek were scheduled to be replaced for in late 1998, so their location in 1999 may differ from The MILEPOST® log

Traditional milepost figures in Canada are indicated in the text as **Historical Mile**. Where the governments of British Columbia, Yukon and Alaska have installed commemorative mileposts, the text reads **Historic Milepost**. Restored in 1992 to commemorate the 50th anniversary of the construction of the Alaska Highway, many of these historic markers are accompanied by signs and interpretive panels. These mileposts reflect the original or traditional mileage and do not reflect actual driving distance.

Milepost 0 in downtown Dawson Creek has been a landmark since the 1940s.
(© Earl L. Brown, staff)

A Brief History of the Alaska Highway

Construction of the Alaska Highway officially began on March 9, 1942, and ended eight months and 12 days later on Oct. 25, 1942. But an overland link between Alaska and the Lower 48 had been studied as early as 1930 under President Herbert Hoover's authorization. It was not until the bombing of Pearl Harbor in December 1941 that construction of the highway was deemed a military necessity. Alaska was considered vulnerable to a Japanese invasion. On Feb. 6, 1942, approval for the Alaska Highway was given by the Chief of Staff, U.S. Army. On Feb. 11, President Roosevelt authorized construction of the pioneer road.

The general route of the highway, determined by the War Department, was along a line of existing airfields from Edmonton, AB, to Fairbanks, AK. This chain of airfields was known as the Northwest Staging Route, and was used to ferry more than 8,000 war planes from Great Falls, MT, to Ladd Air Force Base in Fairbanks, AK, as part of the Russian–American Lend Lease Program. The planes were flown from Fairbanks to Nome, then on to Russia.

In March 1942, rights-of-way through Canada were secured by formal agreement between the 2 countries. The Americans agreed to pay for construction and turn over the Canadian portion of the highway to the Canadian government after the war ended. Canada furnished the right-of-way, waived import duties, sales taxes, income taxes and immigration regulations, and provided construction materials along the route.

A massive mobilization of men and equipment began. Regiments of the U.S. Army Corps of Engineers were moved north to work on the highway. By June, more than 10,000 American troops had poured into the Canadian North. The Public Roads Administration tackled the task of organizing civilian engineers and equipment. Trucks, road-building equipment, office furniture, food, tents and other supplies all had to be located and then shipped north.

Road work began in April, with crews working out of the 2 largest construction camps, Whitehorse and Fort St. John. The highway followed existing winter roads, old Indian trails, rivers and, on occasion, "sight" engineering.

For the soldiers and civilian workers, it was a hard life. Working 7 days a week, they endured mosquitoes and black flies in summer, and below zero temperatures in winter. Weeks would pass with no communication between headquarters and field parties. According to one senior officer with the Public Roads Administration, "Equipment was always a critical problem. There never was enough."

In June 1942, the Japanese invaded Attu and Kiska islands in the Aleutians, adding a new sense of urgency to completion of the road. Crews working from east and west connected at Contact Creek on Sept. 25. By October, it was possible for vehicles to travel the entire length of the highway. The official opening of the Alaska Highway was a ribbon-cutting ceremony held Nov. 20, 1942, on Soldier's Summit at Kluane Lake. (A rededication ceremony was held Nov. 20, 1992, as part of the 50th anniversary celebration of the Alaska Highway.) The Alaska Highway was named an International Historical Engineering Landmark in 1996.

Dawson Creek

Milepost 0 of the Alaska Highway. **Population:** 11,125, area 27,000. **Emergency Services:** RCMP, phone (250) 782-5211. **Fire Department,** phone (250) 782-5000. **Ambulance,** phone (250) 782-2211. **Hospital and Poison Centre,** Dawson Creek and District Hospital, 11000 13th St., phone (250) 782-8501.

Visitor Information: At NAR (Northern Alberta Railway) Park on Alaska Avenue at 10th Street (one block west of the traffic circle), in the building behind the railway car. Open year-round, 8 A.M. to 7 P.M. daily in summer, 10 A.M. to 4 P.M. Tuesday through Saturday in winter. Phone (250) 782-9595, or e-mail dawsoncrk@pris.bc.ca. Trained visitor-information counselors can answer questions about weather and road conditions, local events and attractions. Plenty of public parking in front of the refurbished grain elevator that houses the Dawson Creek Art Gallery and Museum.

Elevation: 2,186 feet/666m. **Climate:** Average temperature in January is 0°F/-18°C; in July it is 60°F/15°C. The average annual snowfall is 72 inches with the average depth of snow in midwinter at 19.7 inches. Frost-free days total 97, with the first frost of the year occurring about the first week of September. **Radio:** CJDC 890. **Television:** 13 channels via cable including pay TV. **Newspapers:** *Peace River Block News* (daily); *The Mirror* (weekly).

Private Aircraft: Dawson Creek airport, 2 SE; elev. 2,148 feet/655m; length 5,000 feet/1,524m and 2,300 feet/701m; asphalt; fuel 100, jet. Floatplane base parallels runway.

Dawson Creek lies 367 miles/591 km northwest of Edmonton, AB, and 250 miles/402 km northeast of Prince George, BC.

Dawson Creek (like Dawson City in the Yukon Territory) was named for George Mercer Dawson of the Geological Survey of Canada, whose geodetic surveys of this region in 1879 helped lead to its development as an agricultural settlement. The open, level townsite is surrounded by rolling farmland, part of the government-designated Peace River Block.

Dawson Creek

DAWSON CREEK ADVERTISERS

Alahart RV Park.................Ph. (250) 782-4702
Alaska Hotel Cafe & Dew Drop
   Inn Pub ....55 paces south of Mile 0 Post
Dawson Creek Art Gallery ....NAR Park
Dawson Creek Coin
   Laundry Ltd.........5 blocks S. of traffic circle
Dawson Creek Tourist
   Information Bureau .....Ph. (250) 782-9595
Farmington Fairways &
   Campground ....Ph. (250) 843-7774
Handy Crafters Corner
   Co-op ....Ph. (250) 782-6470
Husky Oil ....See ad for locations
Joy Propane......................Ph. (888) 782-6008
King Koin Laundromat .....Ph. (250) 782-2590
Lodge Motor Inn &
   Cafe, The ....Ph. (250) 782-4837
Mile "0" RV Park &
   Campground ....Adjacent Walter
                 Wright Pioneer Village
Northern Lights RV Park Ltd.........1 mile from
         Alaska Hwy. Jct. on Hwy. 97 S.
Northwinds Lodge ....1 block E. of Co-op Mall
Organic Farms Bakery.......Ph. (250) 782-6533
Peace Villa Motel....................1641 Alaska Ave.
Rocking Horse Antiques &
   Collectables...........1 block E. of Mile 0 Post
Rowland House
   Bed & Breakfast ....Ph. (250) 782-5654
TLC Car Wash.................Across from Northern
                 Lights College
Trail Inn.............................Ph. (250) 782-8595
Tubby's RV Park......................1913 Hart Hwy.
United Spring &
   Brake Ltd........Directly behind McDonald's

The Peace River Block consists of 3.5 million acres of arable land in northeastern British Columbia, which the province gave to the Dominion Government in 1883 in return for financial aid toward construction of the Canadian Pacific Railway. (While a route through the Peace River country was surveyed by CPR in 1878, the railroad was eventually routed west from Calgary through Kicking Horse Pass.) The Peace River Block was held in reserve by the Dominion Government until 1912, when some of the land was opened for homesteading. The federal government restored the Peace River

Farmland around Dawson Creek. (© Earl L. Brown, staff)

Block to the province of British Columbia in 1930.

Today, agriculture is an important part of this area's economy. The fields of bright yellow flowers (in season) in the area are canola, a hybrid of rapeseed that was developed as a low cholesterol oil seed. Raw seed is processed in Alberta and Japan. The Peace River region also produces most of the province's cereal grain, along with fodder, cattle and dairy cattle. Other industries include the production of honey, hogs, eggs and poultry. Some potato and vegetable farming is also done here.

On the British Columbia Railway line and the western terminus of the Northern Alberta Railway (now Canadian National Railway), Dawson Creek is also the hub of four major highways: the John Hart Highway (Highway 97 South) to Prince George; the Alaska Highway (Highway 97 North); Highway 2, which leads east to Grande Prairie, AB; and Highway 49, which leads east to Spirit River and Donnelly.

The Northern Alberta Railway reached Dawson Creek in 1931. As a railhead, Dawson Creek was an important funnel for supplies and equipment during construction of the Alaska Highway in 1942. Some 600 carloads arrived by rail within a period of five weeks in preparation for the construction program, according to a report by the Public Roads Administration in 1942. A "rutted provincial road" linked Dawson Creek with Fort St. John, affording the only approach to the southern base of operations. Field headquarters were established at Fort St. John and Whitehorse. Meanwhile, men and machines continued to arrive at Dawson Creek. By May of 1942, 4,720 carloads of equipment had arrived by rail at Dawson Creek for dispersement to troops and civilian engineers to the north.

With the completion of the Alaska Highway in 1942 (and opening to the public in 1948) and the John Hart Highway in 1952, Dawson Creek expanded both as a distribution centre and tourist destination. Dawson Creek was incorporated as a city in 1958.

The development of oil and natural gas exploration in northeastern British Columbia, and related industries such as pipeline construction and oil storage, has contributed to the economic expansion of Dawson Creek. The city is also one of the major

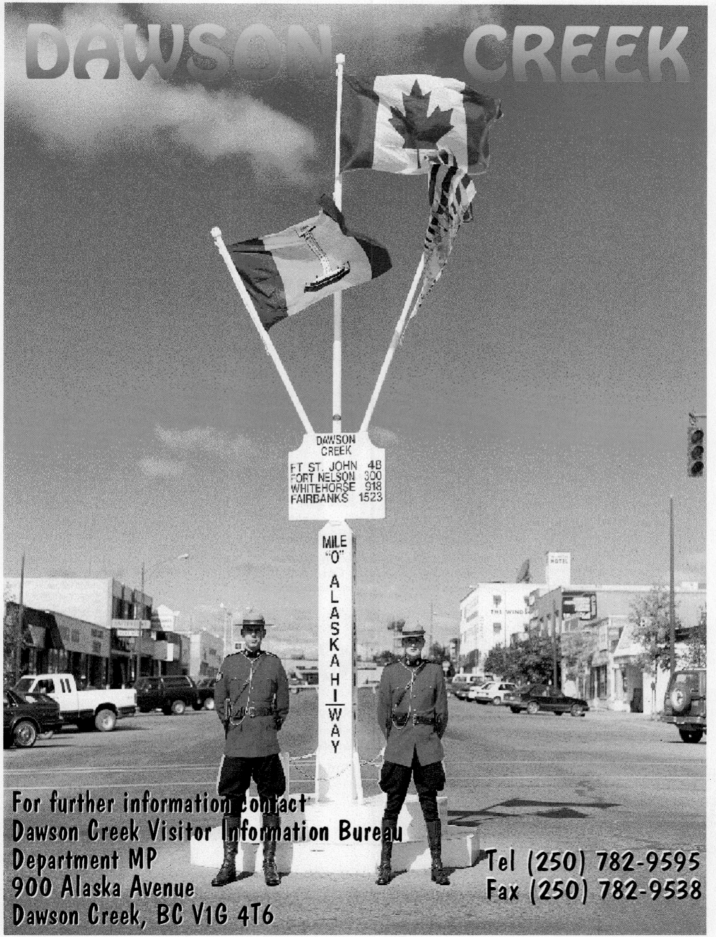

DAWSON CREEK

DAWSON
CREEK

FT. ST. JOHN 48
FORT NELSON 300
WHITEHORSE 918
FAIRBANKS 1523

MILE
"0"
ALASKA HIWAY

For further information contact
Dawson Creek Visitor Information Bureau
Department MP
900 Alaska Avenue
Dawson Creek, BC V1G 4T6

Tel (250) 782-9595
Fax (250) 782-9538

supply centres for the massive resource development known as North East Coal, southwest of Dawson Creek. Access to the coal development and the town of Tumbler Ridge is via the Heritage Highway, which branches off the John Hart Highway just west of Dawson Creek and also branches off Highway 2 southeast of the city. Highway 29 extends south from Chetwynd to Tumbler Ridge.

Provincial government offices and social services for the South Peace region are located in Dawson Creek. City Hall is located on Ben Heppner Way, a street recently renamed in honor of the famous opera tenor, who comes from this area.

The city has a modern 100-bed hospital, a public library and a college (Northern Lights, associated with the University of Northern BC in Prince George). There are also an

indoor swimming pool, 2 skating arenas, a curling rink, bowling alley, golf course, art gallery, museum, tennis and racquetball courts. There are numerous churches in Dawson Creek. (Check at the Visitor Infocentre for location and hours of worship.)

ACCOMMODATIONS/VISITOR SERVICES

There are 14 hotels/motels, several bed and breakfasts, and dozens of restaurants. Department stores, banks, grocery, an organic bakery, drug and hardware stores, antique shop and other specialty shops. Shopping is downtown and in the 2 shopping centres, Co-op Mall and Dawson Mall. Visitors will also find laundromats, car washes, gas stations and automotive repair shops. The liquor store is adjacent the NAR Visitor Infocentre on Alaska Avenue.

There are 4 campgrounds in Dawson

Creek, 2 located on either side of the Hart Highway at its junction with the Alaska Highway and 2 located on Alaska Avenue. There is a private campground on the Hart Highway, 2 miles/3.2 km west from the Alaska Highway junction. There are also campgrounds (both private and provincial) north of Dawson Creek on the Alaska Highway. ▲

The Alaska Hotel Cafe & Dew Drop Inn Pub combines the spirit of Northern Adventure with Old World charm. Where to Eat in Canada, which lists the 500 top restaurants, suggests, "It is a good idea to start out on the Alaska Highway with a good meal under your belt, and there's no better place than the Alaska Cafe." The cafe also holds membership in World Famous Restaurants International. The pub features live entertainment nightly, a hot spot in town. The building, having 15 "rooms with charm," provides a perfect backdrop for the Kux-Kardos collection of antiques and works of art (tours available). At the Alaska, our philosophy is Deluxe Evolutionary ... "Always changing for the better." Phone (250) 782-7998 to reserve. Pets welcome. Located 55 paces south of the mile "0" post. A definite must to experience. [ADVERTISEMENT]

Northern Lights RV Park welcomes you! Enjoy peaceful surroundings just 1.5 miles from Dawson Creek. Spacious, level pull-throughs with your own lawn and picnic table. Check out our souvenir shop or try fly fishing in our trout pond. Come to see the attractions in our area? Day trips to the WAC Bennett Dam, Kinuseo Falls and the Kiskatinaw Bridge all offer gorgeous scenery and abundant wildlife. Or, just sit back and relax while we pamper you and your rig to prepare you for your Alaska Highway adventure! Your hosts—the Bates Family. Phone (250) 782-9433. E-mail: lbates@pris.bc.ca. Internet address: www.pris.bc.ca\rvpark\. [ADVERTISEMENT]

Organic Farms Bakery. Using grain crops from our family farm, 100 percent certified organic stoneground flour. Specializing in German-style rye, spelt and whole wheat breads, buns, pretzels and delicious pastries. Flours and spelt pastas. Taste the difference!

1425 97th Ave., Dawson Creek (look for our colourful bakery), just off Alaska Ave. Phone (250) 782-6533. [ADVERTISEMENT]

TRANSPORTATION

Air: Scheduled service from Dawson Creek airport to Prince George, Vancouver, Edmonton, Grande Prairie and Calgary via Air BC. The airport is located 2 miles/3.2 km south of the Alaska Avenue traffic circle via 8th Street/Highway 2; there is a small terminal at the airport. There is also a floatplane base.

Railroad: Canadian National Railroad and British Columbia Railway provide freight service only. B.C. Railway provides passenger service from Vancouver to Prince George.

Bus: Greyhound service to Prince George and Vancouver, BC; Edmonton, AB; and Whitehorse, YT. Dawson Creek also has a city bus transit system.

ATTRACTIONS

NAR Park, on Alaska Avenue at 10th Street (near the traffic circle), is the site of the Visitor Infocentre, which is housed in a restored railway station; phone (250) 782-9595. The Visitor Infocentre offers a self-

guided historical walking tour with descriptions of Dawson Creek in the early 1940s during construction of the Alaska Highway.

Also at the station is the Dawson Creek Station Museum, operated by the South

Peace Historical Society, which contains pioneer artifacts and wildlife displays. Be sure to leave enough time to view the hour-long video about the building of the Alaska Highway. Souvenirs and restrooms at the museum.

In front of the station is a 1903 railway car, called "The Blue Goose Caboose." Adjacent to the station is a huge wooden grain elevator, which has been refurbished; its annex now houses an art gallery with art shows throughout the summer; admission by donation. Good display of Alaska Highway construction photos; restroom, gift shop. The last of Dawson Creek's old elevators, it was bought and moved to its present location through the efforts of community organizations. Every Saturday in summer there is an outdoor farmer's market featuring flowers, produce, baked goods and crafts for sale.

Inquire at the Visitor Infocentre for the location of Bear Mountain Community Forest. This Ministry of Forests recreation area features interpretive trails on the flora and fauna of the area. It is located 6 miles/10 km south of the city.

Recreational facilities in Dawson Creek include a bowling alley, miniature golf, indoor pool, 2 ice arenas, curling rink, 18-hole golf course, tennis courts and an outdoor pool at Rotary Lake Park.

Walter Wright Pioneer Village and Mile 0 Rotary Park. The entrance to the village is highlighted by Gardens North, consisting of 9 separate gardens, including a

memorial rose garden. Bring a camera to capture the amazing variety of perennials and annuals that grow in the North. The pioneer village contains an impressive collection of local pioneer buildings, including a teahouse; antiques and collectibles shop; and a general store. Souvenirs and Gardens North seeds are available. Admission is $1. Food service available at the Mile 1 Cafe. Check at the infocentre for summer tours of the gardens.

Adjacent to the village is the Sudeten Memorial Hall. "A Mile Zero Welcome," a presentation about Dawson Creek, then and now, by Marilyn Croutch, is held either in Sudeten Hall or the old Dawson School in summer; phone (250) 782-7144. Check with the Visitor Infocentre for details on entertainment offerings. Also located here is Rotary Lake, an outdoor man-made swimming facility; restrooms and picnic areas are found throughout Rotary Park.

Dawson Creek Walking Path, a community project to restore the creek, provides a peaceful path for travelers to stretch their legs and take in some local scenery. When complete, the path will connect Rotary Park with Kinsmen Park on 8th Street. Pick up a brochure at the visitor centre.

Special Events. Mile Zero Celebration Days held in May. July 4th festivities take place at Sudeten Hall. The Fall Fair and Stampede in August features the largest amateur rodeo in North America.

Tumbler Ridge Side Trip. To reach Tumbler Ridge, drive west from Dawson Creek 12 miles/20 km on Highway 97 to junction with the Heritage Highway (see **Milepost PG 237.7** in the WEST ACCESS ROUTE section), or drive west 60.6 miles/97.5 km to junction with Highway 29 South (see **Milepost PG 189.4** in the WEST ACCESS ROUTE section). Heritage Highway 52 (paved) leads south 59.5 miles/96 km to the community of Tumbler Ridge. Highway 29 South is a paved maintained road all the way to Tumbler Ridge. Tumbler Ridge is the townsite for Quintette Coal Limited's large-scale surface mines, and also serves workers of the Bullmoose Mine. Tours of Quintette and Bullmoose mines are available; inquire at the Visitor Infocentre in Tumbler Ridge. The huge coal processing plant and overhead conveyor are visible from the road. Monkman Provincial Park, site of spectacular 225-foot/69-m Kinuseo (Keh-NEW-see-oh) Falls, lies south of Tumbler Ridge. Contact BC Parks in Fort St. John (phone 250/787-3407) or Tumbler Ridge Infocentre (250/242-4702) for more information.

At Tumbler Ridge, motorists have a choice: return to Highway 97 via Highway 52; return to Highway 97 via Highway 29 South to Chetwynd; or continue on the Heritage Highway loop, 76 miles/123 km via all-gravel road and 16 miles/25 km via paved road, to Highway 2 southeast of Dawson Creek. (Highway 29 South offers the best road surface.) There are no services on the Heritage Highway except at Tumbler Ridge, which has a motel, campgrounds, restaurants, a bank and shopping. On gravel stretches of the road, watch for poor road conditions in wet weather.

Alaska Highway Log

Distance from Dawson Creek (DC) is followed by distance from Delta Junction (DJ). Original mileposts are indicated in the text as Historical Mile.

In Canada, mileages from Dawson Creek are based on actual driving distance, not historical mileposts, and kilometres are based on physical kilometreposts. Mileages from Delta Junction are also based on actual driving distance, not historical mileposts, but are followed by the metric conversion to kilometres.

BC HIGHWAY 97

DC 0 DJ 1390 (2236.9 km) **Mile 0** marker of the Alaska Highway on 10th Street in downtown Dawson Creek.

Northbound: Good pavement approximately next 284 miles/457 km (through Fort Nelson). Watch for road construction and surface changes from Pink Mountain north.

DC 1.2 (1.9 km) DJ 1388.8 (2235 km) **Junction** of the Alaska Highway and John Hart Highway.

Prince George-bound travelers turn to the end of the WEST ACCESS ROUTE section and read log back to front. Alaska-bound travelers continue with this log.

DC 1.5 (2.4 km) DJ 1388.5 (2234.5 km) Mile 0 Rotary Park (picnicking and swimming), Walter Wright Pioneer Village and Mile 0 Campground to west. ▲

DC 1.7 (2.7 km) DJ 1388.3 (2234.2 km) **Historic Milepost 2.** Sign about Cantel Repeater Station. Cantel telephone–teletype lines stretched from Alberta to Fairbanks, AK, making it one of the world's longest open-wire toll circuits at the time.

DC 2 (3.2 km) DJ 1388 (2233.7 km) Recreation centre and golf course to west. Louisiana Pacific waferboard plant to east.

DC 2.7 (4.3 km) DJ 1387.3 (2232.6 km) Truck scales and public phone to east. Truck stop to west; gas, cafe.

DC 2.9 (4.7 km) DJ 1387.1 (2232.3 km) Northern Alberta Railway (NAR) tracks.

DC 3.3 (5.3 km) DC 1386.7 (2231.6 km) Turnout with litter barrel to east. **Historic Milepost 3**; historic sign marks Curan & Briggs Ltd. Construction Camp, U.S. Army Traffic Control Centre.

DC 3.4 (5.5 km) DJ 1386.6 (2231.4 km) **Historical Mile 3.** The Trading Post to east.

DC 9.5 (15.3 km) DJ 1380.5 (2221.6 km) Golf course, driving range and RV park. ▲

Farmington Fairways Golf and Camping. See display ad this section.

DC 11.2 (18 km) DJ 1378.8 (2218.9 km) Turnout with litter barrels to west.

DC 11.5 (18.5 km) DJ 1378.5 (2218.4 km) Turnout with litter barrels to east.

DC 13.1 (21.1 km) DJ 1376.9 (2215.8 km) **Historic Milepost 13** "Start of Storms Contracting Co. Ltd. contract."

DC 14.8 (24 km) DJ 1375.2 (2213.1 km) Farmington (unincorporated).

DC 15.8 (25.4 km) DJ 1374.2 (2211.5 km) Farmington store to west; gas, groceries, phone.

DC 17.3 (27.8 km) DJ 1372.7 (2209.1

km) Exit east for loop road to **Kiskatinaw Provincial Park**. Follow good 2-lane paved road (old Alaska Highway) 2.5 miles/4 km for provincial park; 28 campsites, drinking water, firewood, picnic tables, fire rings, outhouses and garbage containers. Camping fee $7 to $12. ▲

This interesting side road gives travelers the opportunity to drive the original old Alaska Highway and to cross the historic curved wooden **Kiskatinaw River Bridge**. A sign at the bridge notes that this 531-foot-/162-m-long structure is the only original timber bridge built along the Alaska Highway that is still in use today.

DC 17.5 (28.2 km) DJ 1372.5 (2208.8 km) Distance marker indicates Fort St. John 29 miles/47 km.

CAUTION: Watch for deer.

DC 19.4 (31.2 km) DJ 1370.6 (2205.7 km) Large turnout to east.

DC 19.8 (31.9 km) DJ 1370.2 (2205.1 km) Highway descends northbound to Kiskatinaw River.

DC 20.9 (33.6 km) DJ 1369.1 (2203.3 km) Kiskatinaw River bridge.

CAUTION: Strong crosswinds on bridge.

Turnout with litter barrel and picnic tables to east at north end of bridge. View of unique bridge support.

DC 21.6 (34.5 km) DJ 1368.4 (2202.2 km) Loop road to Kiskatinaw Provincial Park and Kiskatinaw River bridge (see **Milepost DC 17.3**).

DC 25.4 (41 km) DJ 1364.6 (2196.1 km) NorthwesTel microwave tower to east. Alaska Highway travelers will be seeing many of these towers as they drive north. The Northwest Communications System was constructed by the U.S. Army in 1942–43. This land line was replaced in 1963 with the construction of 42 microwave relay stations

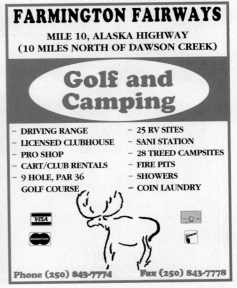

by Canadian National Telecommunications (Cantel, now NorthwesTel) between Grande Prairie, AB, and the YT–AK border.

DC 30.5 (49.1 km) DJ 1359.5 (2187.8 km) Turnout to east with litter barrels. Turnout to west with litter barrels, pit toilet and historical marker about explorer Alexander Mackenzie.

Highway begins steep winding descent northbound to the Peace River bridge. Good views to northeast of Peace River valley and industrial community of Taylor.

Some wide gravel shoulder next 4 miles/6.4 km for northbound traffic to pull off.

CAUTION: Trucks check your brakes.

DC 32.1 (51.6 km) DJ 1357.9 (2185.3 km) Large turnout with litter barrels.

DC 33.8 (54.4 km) DJ 1356.2 (2182.5 km) Pingle Creek.

DC 34 (54.7 km) DJ 1356 (2182.2 km) Access to **Taylor Landing Provincial Park**; boat launch, parking and fishing. Jet boat outfitter. Also access to Peace Island Regional Park, 0.5 mile/0.8 km west of the highway, situated on an island in the **Peace River** connected to the south shore by a causeway. Peace Island has 35 shaded campsites with gravel pads, firewood, fire rings, picnic tables, picnic shelter, toilets, potable water, playground and horseshoe pits. There are also 4 large picnic areas and a tenting area. Camping fee. Open Memorial Day to Labour Day. Nature trail, good bird watching and good fishing in clear water. Boaters should use caution on the Peace River since both parks are downstream from the W.A.C. Bennett and Peace Canyon dams and water levels may fluctuate rapidly.

DC 34.4 (55.4 km) DJ 1355.6 (2181.6 km) **Peace River Bridge**. Bridging the Peace was one of the first goals of Alaska Highway engineers in 1942. Traffic moving north from Dawson Creek was limited by the Peace River crossing, where 2 ferries with a capacity of 10 trucks per hour were operating in May. Three different pile trestles were constructed across the Peace River, only to be washed out by high water. Work on the permanent 2,130-foot suspension bridge began in December 1942 and was completed in July 1943. One of 2 suspension bridges on the Alaska Highway, the Peace River bridge collapsed in 1957 after erosion undermined the north anchor block of the bridge. The cantilever and truss-type bridge that crosses the Peace River today was completed in 1960.

Gas pipeline bridge visible to east.

DC 35 (56.3 km) DJ 1355 (2180.6 km) **Historic Milepost 35** at TAYLOR (pop. 1,031; elev. 1,804 feet/550m), located on the north bank of the Peace River. **Visitor Information**: On left northbound (10114 100 St.); phone (250) 789-9015. Inquire here about industrial tours of Canadian Forest Products, Fiberco Pulpmill and Greenhouse Complex. Taylor is an industrial community clustered around a Westcoast Energy Inc. gas-processing plant and large sawmill. Established in 1955 with the discovery and development of a natural gas field in the area, Taylor is the site of a pulp mill and plants that handle sulfur processing, gas compressing, high-octane aviation gas production and other byproducts of natural gas. The Westcoast Energy natural gas pipeline reaches from here to Vancouver, BC, with a branch to western Washington.

The fertile Taylor Flats area has several market gardens and roadside stands in summer. A hotel, motels, cafes, grocery store, private RV park, gas station and post office are located here. Free municipal dump station and potable water located behind the North Taylor Inn. Recreation facilities include a championship 18-hole golf course, a motorcross track and a recreation complex with swimming pool, curling rink and district ice centre for skating (open year-round). Gold Panning Championship held in August. ▲

Redwood Esso and Taylor Lodge. See display ad this section.

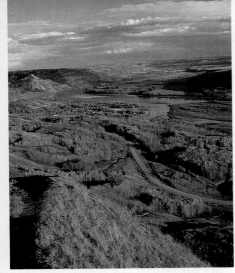

View of Peace River Valley near Fort St. John. (© Earl L. Brown, staff)

DC 36.3 (58.4 km) **DJ 1353.7** (2178.5 km) Railroad tracks.

DC 40 (64.5 km) **DJ 1350** (2172.6 km) **Historical Mile 41.** Post office.

DC 40.3 (64.9 km) **DJ 1349.7** (2172.1 km) Exit east for Fort St. John airport.

DC 40.4 (65 km) **DJ 1349.6** (2171.9 km) B.C. Railway overhead tracks.

DC 40.9 (65.8 km) **DJ 1349.1** (2171.1 km) **Historic Milepost 42** Access Road to Fort St. John Airport.

DC 42.3 (68.1 km) **DJ 1347.7** (2168.9 km) World's largest glass beehive at the Honey Place to west. Well worth a visit. The Peace Country produces several tons of high quality honey annually.

The Honey Place. See display ad this section.

DC 43.7 (70.3 km) **DJ 1346.3** (2166.6 km) Miniature golf, driving range and RV park. ▲

Sourdough Pete's RV Park and Troy's Amusement Park. See display ad this section. ▲

DC 44.6 (71.7 km) **DJ 1345.4** (2165.2 km) Access to Fort St. John via 86th Street. Private RV park. ▲

DC 45.7 (73.5 km) **DJ 1344.3** (2163.4 km) **Historic Milepost 47,** Fort St. John/"Camp Alcan" sign. In 1942, Fort St. John "exploded." What had been home to 200 became a temporary base for more than 6,000.

DC 45.8 (73.7 km) **DJ 1344.2** (2163.2 km) South access to Fort St. John via 100th Street. Exit east for Visitor Infocentre and downtown Fort St. John.

DC 47 (75.6 km) **DJ 1343** (2161.3 km) **Historical Mile 48.** North access to Fort St. John via 100th Avenue to downtown. Truck stop with 24-hour gas and food.

Fort St. John

DC 47 (75.6 km) **DJ 1343** (2161.3 km) Located approximately 236 miles/ 380 km south of Fort Nelson. **Population:** 15,021; area 45,000. **Emergency Services: RCMP,** phone (250) 787-8100. **Fire Department,** phone (250) 785-2323. **Ambulance,** phone (250) 785-2079. **Hospital,** on 100th Avenue and 96th Street, phone (250) 785-6611.

Visitor Information: Visitor Infocentre is located at 100th St. and 96th Ave., beside Centennial Park and next to the leisure pool, in the same building as the chamber of commerce and the Northern Rockies Alaska Highway Tourist Assoc. Open year-round: 8 A.M. to 8 P.M. in summer, 8:30 A.M. to 5 P.M. the rest of the year. Write 9923 96th Ave.,

Fort St. John, BC V1J 4K9; phone (250) 785-6037, fax (250) 785-7181, e-mail fsjchof-com@awink.com; web site www.gbsweb.net/fortstjohnchamber.

Visitors may also contact the Ministry of Environment & Parks, Parks and Outdoor Recreation Division, regarding wilderness hiking opportunities along the Alaska Highway. The Ministry is located at 10003 110 Ave., Room 250, Fort St. John, BC V1J 6M7; phone (250) 787-3407.

Elevation: 2,275 feet/693m. **Climate:** Average high temperature in July, 71/11 C, average low 50 F/10 C. In January, average high is 12 F/-11 C; low if -2 F/-19 C. **Radio:** CKNL 560. **Television:** Cable. **Newspaper:** *Alaska Highway News* (daily), *The Northerner* (weekly).

Private Aircraft: Fort St. John airport, 3.8 E; elev. 2,280 feet/695m; length 6,900 feet/2,103m and 6,700 feet/2,042m; asphalt; fuel 100, Jet. Charlie Lake airstrip, 6.7 NW; elev. 2,680 feet/817m; length 1,800 feet/549m; gravel; fuel 100.

Visitor services are located just off the Alaska Highway and in the city centre, several blocks north of the highway. Fort St. John is a large modern city with all services available.

Fort St. John is set in the low, rolling hills of the Peace River Valley. The original Fort St. John was established in 1806 on the muddy banks of the Peace River, about 10 miles south of the present townsite, as a trading post for the Sikanni and Beaver Indians. The earlier Rocky Mountain Fort site, near the mouth of the Moberly River, dates from 1794. A granite monument, located on Mackenzie Street (100th Street) in Fort St. John's Centennial Park, is inscribed to Sir Alexander Mackenzie, who camped here on his journey west to the Pacific Ocean in 1793. Mackenzie was looking for trade routes for the North West fur company. He reached Bella Coola on July 22, 1793.

The Peace region was homesteaded in the early 1900s. The town's early commercial development centered around a store established by settler C.M. Finch. His stepson, Clement Brooks, carried on Finch's entrepreneurship, starting several businesses in Fort St. John after WWII.

In 1942, Fort St. John became field headquarters for U.S. Army troops and civilian engineers working on construction of the Alaska Highway in the eastern sector. It was the largest camp, along with Whitehorse (headquarters for the western sector), of the dozen or so construction camps along the highway. Much of the field housing, road building equipment and even office supplies were scrounged from old Civilian Conservation Corps camps and the Work Projects Administration.

As reported by Theodore A. Huntley of the Public Roads Administration, "A narrow winter road from Fort St. John to Fort Nelson, 256 miles north, provided the only access to the forest itself. From Fort St. John

PETRO-CANADA TRUCK STOP
OPEN 24 HOURS

On The Alaska Highway
(North End of Town)

* Convenience Store *
- Subs & Sandwiches
- Cold Drinks • Ice Cream
- Novelties • Bank Machine
- Lotto Centre

AUTO PROPANE OILS • REGULAR & PREMIUM GAS - DIESEL
FREE SANI DUMP WITH FILLUP
Restaurant Adjacent

(250) 787-6066
11724 Alaska Highway
Fort St. John, B.C.

Four Seasons Motor Inn
(FORMERLY FORT ST. JOHN TRAVELODGE)

TELEPHONE (250) 785-6647
Reservations 1-800-523-6677
9810 - 100th St. Fort St. John, BC
V1J 3Y1 Canada

FORT ST. JOHN ADVERTISERS

Best Western
  Coachman Inn ....Ph. (250) 787-0651
City of Fort St. John ....Ph. (250) 785-6037
Fort St. John–North Peace
  Museum.................1 blk. N. of Alaska Hwy.
Four Seasons Motor Inn ...Ph. (250) 785-6647
Husky Car and Truck
  Wash.....................Across from McDonald's
North Peace Cultural
  Centre.......................Ph. (250) 785-1992
Northgate Inn..................Ph. (250) 787-8475
Petro-Canada Truck Stop..............Alaska Hwy.
Rapid Lube & Wash.............11204 100th Ave.
Tirecraft ....Ph. (250) 785-2411
Totem Mall...................................Alaska Hwy.

HUSKY CAR AND TRUCK WASH
10 BAY CAR AND TRUCK WASH
Able to Handle the Largest R.V.'s • High Pressure Pumps Foam Brush Wash • 3 Vacuum Cleaners
Across From McDonald's Restaurant

- **HUSKY UNLEADED GAS & DIESEL FUEL**
Free Coffee With Fill-Up
Mile 48, Alaska Highway, Fort St. John, BC

Phone (250) 785-3121

NORTHGATE INN
10419 Alaska Road, Fort St. John, BC V1J1B1

Come Experience Our Great Northern Hospitality
- Pub • Restaurant • Coffee Shop •

- 24-Hour Front Desk
- Lots of Parking
- Children and Pets Welcome
- 43 Air Conditioned Rooms
- Meeting Room

(250) 787-8475
FAX (250) 787-0533

Derrick outside North Peace Museum.
(© Earl L. Brown, staff)

Peace region raise grain and livestock, such as sheep and cattle. Bison are also raised locally. The fields of clover and alfalfa have also attracted bees, and honey is produced for both local markets and export.

TRANSPORTATION

Air: Served by Canadian Regional Airlines and Central Mountain Air. Connecting flights to Fort Nelson, Whitehorse, Vancouver, Grande Prairie, Edmonton and Prince George. **Bus**: Coachways service to Prince George, Vancouver, Edmonton and Whitehorse; depot at 10355 101st Ave., phone (250) 785-6695.

ACCOMMODATIONS/VISITOR SERVICES

Numerous major motels, hotels, restaurants, fast-food outlets and full-service gas stations are located on the Alaska Highway and in town. Other services include supermarkets, laundromats, several banks (automatic teller machines at Totem Mall and downtown at Charter Banks), a car wash and shops. The Totem Mall is located on the Alaska Highway.

North Peace Recreation Centre, located behind Centennial Park at 98th and 96th Ave., has indoor tennis, skating and curling. A Farmer's Market is held in the centre lobby on Saturdays, 9 A.M. to 4 P.M., May through December. North Peace Leisure Pool, next to the centre, has a waterslide, wave pool, lap pool, swirl pool, sauna and steam rooms; phone (250) 787-8178.

Fresh water fill-up and dump station located at the northwest corner of 86th Street and the Alaska Highway. Private

north and west for almost 1,500 miles the wilderness was broken only by dog and pack trails or short stretches of winter road, serviceable only until made impassable by the spring thaw. Within 6 months the first vehicle to travel overland to Alaska would roll into Fairbanks. Thus was a highway born."

The Alaska Highway was opened to the traveling public in 1948, attracting vacationers and homesteaders. An immense natural oil and gas field discovered in 1955 made Fort St. John the oil capital of British Columbia. "Energetic City," referring to the natural energy resources and the city's potential for positive growth, became the slogan for the region.

An extension of the Pacific Great Eastern Railway, now called British Columbia Railway, from Prince George in 1958 (continued to Fort Nelson in 1971), gave Fort St. John a link with the rail yards and docks at North Vancouver.

Today, Fort St. John is booming as a support centre for the province's oil and natural gas industry. A natural gas pipeline is under construction. Other industries include forestry and agriculture. Farms in the North

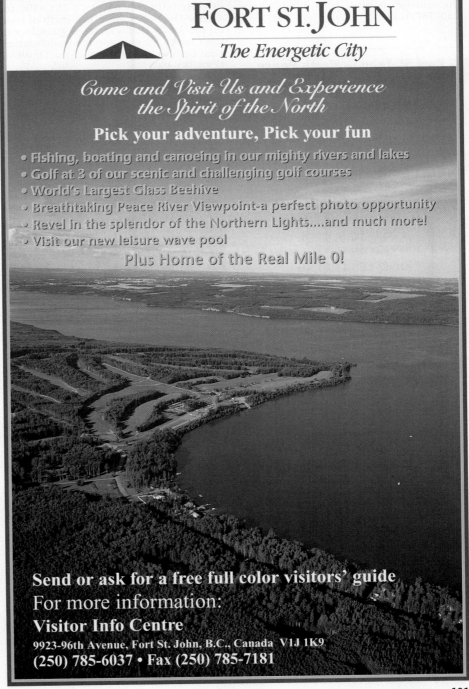

campground south of town at **Milepost DC 43.7**. Camping north of the city at Beatton and Charlie Lake provincial parks, and at private and Rotary campgrounds at Charlie Lake. ▲

ATTRACTIONS

Centennial Park, located on 100th Street, has picnic tables, volleyball net, horseshoe pits and a playground. The Info-centre and the North Peace Museum are also located in Centennial Park. Inquire at the Visitor Infocentre about local hiking trails, fishing, boat tours, trail rides and the lily farm. The visitor centre is open 8 A.M. to 8 P.M. daily in summer.

North Peace Museum features more than 6,000 artifacts from the region, including items from Finch's Store, an 1806 Fort St. John post, a trapper's cabin and early-day schoolroom. The museum gift shop offers a good selection of local and Northwest books. The museum is open year-round; phone (250) 787-0430.

Outside the museum is a 136-foot-high oil derrick, presented to the North Peace Historical Society and the people of Fort St. John. Check with the North Peace Museum about summer entertainment at the derrick.

North Peace Cultural Centre, at 10015 100th Ave., has a library, a 413-seat theatre, an art gallery, cafe and gift shop. Phone 785-1992.

Play golf. Fort St. John's only in-town golf course is Links Golf Course, just off the Bypass Road at 86 Street; 9 holes, pro shop and lounge. Phone (250) 785-9995. The Lakepoint Golf Course, on Golf Course Road at Charlie Lake, is rated one of the nicest courses in British Columbia. Open 8 A.M. to 9 P.M. daily; 18 holes, pro shop, lounge and restaurant. Phone (250) 785-5566.

Industry and agriculture of the area are showcased for the public at various places. Check with the Infocentre for directions and details. Canada Forest Products offers tours of their mills, phone (250) 785-8906 for details. The Honey Place, just south of town on the Alaska Highway, offers guided tours, fresh honey for sale, and the world's largest glass beehive for viewing year-round; phone (250) 785-4808.

Fish Creek Community Forest, adjacent to Northern Lights College, has 3 interpretive trails to view forest management activities and learn more about the forest. Cross-country ski trails in winter. From the Alaska Highway follow 100th Street north 1.2 miles/2 km to parking area at college.

W.A.C. Bennett Dam is a major attraction in the area. For an interesting side trip, drive north from Fort St. John on the Alaska Highway to **Milepost DC 53.7** and take Highway 29 west 46.5 miles/74.8 km to Hudson's Hope. Highway 29 follows the original Canadian government telegraph trail of 1918. Hudson's Hope, formerly a pioneer community established in 1805 by explorer Simon Fraser, grew with construction of the W.A.C. Bennett Dam, which is located 13.5 miles/21.7 km west of town. B.C. Hydro's Peace Canyon dam is located approximately 4 miles/6.4 km south of Hudson's Hope. Turn to the HUDSON'S HOPE LOOP section for more information.

Alaska Highway Log

(continued)

Distance from Dawson Creek (DC) is followed by distance from Delta Junction (DJ). Original mileposts are indicated in the text as Historical Mile.

In Canada, mileages from Dawson Creek are based on actual driving distance, not historical mileposts, and kilometres are based on physical kilometreposts. Mileages from Delta Junction are also based on actual driving distance, not historical mileposts, but are followed by the metric conversion to kilometres.

DC 45.8 (73.7 km) **DJ 1344.2** (2163.2 km) South access to Fort St. John via 100th Street.

DC 47 (75.6 km) **DJ 1343** (2161.3 km) **Historical Mile 48.** North access to Fort St. John via 100th Avenue.

DC 48.6 (78.2 km) **DJ 1341.4** (2157.3 km) **Historic Milepost 49** commemorates "Camp Alcan."

DC 49.5 (79.6 km) **DJ 1340.5** (2157.3 km) Exit for **Beatton Provincial Park**, 5 miles/8 km east via paved road; 37 campsites, picnic shelter, wood stove, horseshoe pits, volleyball net, playground, baseball field, sandy beach, swimming and boat launch. Camping fee $7 to $12. Fishing for northern pike, walleye (July best) and yellow perch in **Charlie Lake**. ◀━━✦

DC 50.4 (81.1 km) **DJ 1339.6** (2155.8 km) **Paradise Lane Bed and Breakfast.** See display ad this section.

DC 50.6 (81.4 km) **DJ 1339.4** (2155.5 km) **CHARLIE LAKE** (unincorporated), gas, diesel and propane, grocery, pub, post office, bed and breakfast, private RV parks and Ministry of Energy, Mines and Petroleum. Access to lakeshore east side of highway; boat launch, no parking. At one time during construction of the Alaska Highway, Charlie Lake was designated Mile 0, as there was already a road between the railhead at Dawson Creek and Fort St. John, the eastern sector headquarters for troops and engineers.

Charlie Lake General Store. See display ad this section.

DC 51.2 (82.4 km) DJ 1338.8 (2154.5 km) **Historic Milepost 52.** Charlie Lake Mile 0 Army Tote Road. Site of a major distribution camp for workers and supplies heading north. 12 American soldiers also drowned here in 1942 while crossing the lake aboard pontoon barges.

Rotary R.V. Park. See display ad this section. ⅙▲

DC 51.5 (82.9 km) DJ 1338.5 (2154 km) **Ron's R.V. Park. Historical Mile 52.** Treed sites with complete RV hookups, shaded lawned tenting areas, picnic tables, firepits, firewood provided. Walking trails, playground, flush toilets, hot showers, laundromat, pay phone, ice. Shaded full-hookup pull-throughs, good drinking water. Large boat launching facilities nearby. Boat rentals. Quiet location away from hectic city confusion. Post office, golf course, fishing licenses. Charlie Lake, world famous for walleye and northern pike fishing. Phone (250) 787-1569.
[ADVERTISEMENT]   ▲

DC 52 (83.7 km) DJ 1338 (2153.2 km) Exit east on Charlie Lake Road for lakeshore picnicking.

DC 53.6 (86.3 km) DJ 1336.4 (2150.7 km) Truck weigh scales east side of highway.

DC 53.7 (86.4 km) DJ 1336.3 (2150.5 km) Truck stop with restaurant, gas and diesel (open year-round).

Mile 54 Shell Truck Stop. See display ad this section.

> **Junction** with Highway 29, which leads west 47 miles/75.6 km to Hudson's Hope and the W.A.C. Bennett Dam, then south to connect with the Hart Highway at Chetwynd (see HUDSON'S HOPE LOOP section).

Turn east for **Charlie Lake Provincial Park**, just off highway; paved loop road (with speed bumps) leads through campground. There are 58 shaded sites, picnic tables, kitchen shelter with wood stove, firepits, firewood, outhouses, dump station, water and garbage. Level gravel sites, some will accommodate 2 large RVs. Camping fee $9.50 to $12. Playfield, playground, horseshoe pits, volleyball net and a 1.2-mile/2-km hiking trail down to lake. Watch for wildflowers. Because of the wide variety of plants here, including some that may not be seen elsewhere along the Alaska Highway, Verna E. Pratt's *Wildflowers Along the Alaska Highway* includes a special list of species for this

From Fort St. John the Alaska Highway heads north towards Wonowon and Pink Mountain. *(© Earl L. Brown, staff)*

park. Fishing in Charlie Lake for walleye, northern pike and yellow perch. Access to the lake for vehicles and boats is from the Alaska Highway just east of the park entrance. Boat launch and picnic area at lake.   ◄▲

DC 62.4 (100.4 km) DJ 1327.6 (2136.5 km) A 30-foot/9-m statue of a lumberjack marks Clarke Sawmill to west. (The statue wears a Santa suit at Christmas.)

DC 63.6 (102 km) DJ 1326.4 (2134.6 km) Microwave tower to east.

DC 65.4 (105 km) DJ 1324.6 (2131.7 km) Turnout with litter barrel to west.

DC 71.7 (115.4 km) **DJ 1318.3** (2121.5 km) **Historical Mile 72.** Food, gas, camping, lodging and crafts store. ▲

The Shepherd's Inn. We specialize in making folks at home, offering regular and breakfast specials, complete lunch and dinner menu. Low-fat buffalo burgers. Our specialties: homemade soups, home-baked sweet rolls, cinnamon rolls, blueberry and bran muffins, bread, biscuits and trappers bannock. Delicious desserts, rhubarb-strawberry, Dutch apple and chocolate dream pie, cherry and strawberry cheesecake. Hard ice cream. Specialty coffees: Norwegian Mint, Swiss Almond. Herb teas. Refreshing fruit drinks from local fruits: blueberry and raspberry coolers. Caravaners and bus tours ... a convenient and delightful stop on your Alaska Highway adventure! You may reserve your stop–break with us. Full RV hookups, motel service 24 hours. NOTE: Highway 29 traffic from Hudson's Hope northbound entering Alaska Highway ... your first motel stop. Southbound ... your last motel selection. Quality Husky products. Your "Husky Buck" is a great traveling idea. Phone (250) 827-3676. An oasis on the Alcan at Mile 72. [ADVERTISEMENT] ▲

DC 72.7 (117 km) **DJ 1317.3** (2119.9 km) Cafe and private campground. ▲

DC 72.8 (117.1 km) **DJ 1317.2** (2119.8 km) **Historic Milepost 73** commemorates Beatton River Flight Strip, 1 of 4 gravel airstrips built for American military aircraft during WWII. Road to Prespetu and Buick Creek.

DC 79.1 (127.3 km) **DJ 1310.9** (2109.6 km) **Historical Mile 80** paved rest area to west with litter barrels, picnic tables, water and flush toilets. Information panel on Alaska Highway parks.

DC 91.4 (147.1 km) **DJ 1298.6** (2089.8 km) **Historical Mile 92.** Westcoast Energy compressor station to west.

DC 94.6 (152.2 km) **DJ 1295.4** (2084.7 km) Oil pump east of highway behind trees.

DC 95 (152.9 km) **DJ 1295** (2084 km) Access west to Crystal Springs Ranch (32 miles/52 km).

DC 101 (161.7 km) **DJ 1289** (2074.4 km) **Historic Milepost 101. WONOWON** (pop. 150), unincorporated, has 3 gas stations (gas, diesel, propane), 2 restaurants, 2 motels, camping, a food store, pub and post office. Formerly known as Blueberry, Wonowon was the site of an official traffic control gate during WWII. Wonowon Horse Club holds an annual race meet and gymkhana at the track beside the highway, where the community club holds its annual snowmobile rally in February. ▲

The historic sign and interpretive panel here commemorate Blueberry Control Station, "site of the Blueberry Control Gate, a 24-hour military checkpoint operated by U.S. Army personnel through the war years."

The Alaska Highway follows the Blueberry and Prophet river drainages north to Fort Nelson. The Blueberry River, not visible from the highway, lies a few miles east of Wonowon.

DC 101.5 (163.3 km) **DJ 1288.5** (2073.6 km) Food, diesel, gas, camping and lodging to east; open year-round. ▲

DC 103.5 (166.5 km) **DJ 1244** (2002 km) **Historic Milepost 104** marks start of Adolphson, Huseth, Layer & Welch contract during Alaska Highway construction.

DC 114 (183.2 km) **DJ 1276** (2053.5 km) Paved turnout with litter barrel to east.

DC 122.9 (197.8 km) **DJ 1267.1** (2039.1 km) Townsend Creek.

DC 124.1 (199.7 km) **DJ 1265.9** (2037.2 km) Turnout to east with dumpster.

DC 124.3 (200 km) **DJ 1265.7** (2036.9 km) The Cut (highway goes through a small rock cut). Relatively few rock cuts were necessary during construction of the Alaska Highway in 1942–43. However, rock excavation was often made outside of the roadway to obtain gravel fill for the new roadbed.

DC 135.3 (217.7 km) **DJ 1254.7** (2019.2 km) Gravel turnout to east.

CAUTION: Northbound travelers watch for moose next 15 miles/24 km, especially at dusk

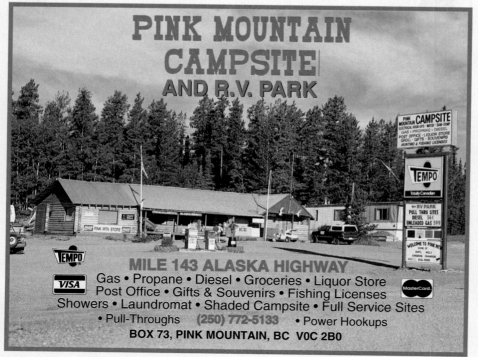

and at night.

DC 140.4 (225.9 km) **DJ 1249.6** (2011 km) **Historical Mile 143. PINK MOUNTAIN** (pop. 99, area 300; elev. 3,600 feet/1,097m). Post office, grocery, motels, restaurant, campgrounds, gas stations (gas, diesel, propane) with minor repair service. Bus depot at Pink Mountain Motor Inn east side of highway. Pink Mountain is home to Darryl Mills, Canadian champion bullrider. ▲

Pink Mountain Campsite & R.V. Park, on the left northbound. Take it easy folks, you've arrived at one of the nicest campgrounds on the highway … coffee's always on. Unleaded Tempo gas, diesel, metered propane for RVs and auto. Post office, general store, liquor store, fishing and hunting licenses. Souvenirs—you'll like our prices. Shaded campsites, picnic tables, firepits and firewood. Tents and RVs welcome. Full hookups, power hookups, water and sani-

dump. Pull-throughs. Something for everyone. Cabins starting at $20 (weekly rates available). Laundromat and clean showers. Open year-round. VISA and MasterCard. Phone and fax (250) 772-5133. Your hosts, Cliff and Judy. [ADVERTISEMENT] ▲

Pink Mountain Motor Inn. Mile 143, a welcome stopping point for all travelers. 34 rooms, gift shop, and licensed restaurant with pies and pastries and home-cooked meals. The perfect lunch break stop for bus tours. For RVs, electric hookups, gravel sites. Treed camping and picnic tables. Water, hot showers, laundromat. Dump station. Caravans welcome, reservations recommended. Full line of Esso products. Fax (250) 774-1071. Phone (250) 772-3234. Your hosts, Jimmy and Grace. [ADVERTISEMENT] ▲

DC 144.1 (231.9 km) **DJ 1245.9** (2005 km) **Historical Mile 147.** Food, gas, lodging and camping. ▲

DC 144.5 (232.5 km) **DJ 1245.5** (2004.4 km) **Historical Mile 147.** Mae's Kitchen restaurant, motel, gas and diesel; open year-round.

Mae's Kitchen. See display ad this section.

DC 144.7 (232.9 km) **DJ 1245.3** (2004. km) **Historic Milepost 148** commemorates **Suicide Hill**, one of the most treacherous hills on the original highway, noted for its ominous greeting: "Prepare to meet thy maker." Beatton River bridge. The Beatton River was named for Frank Beatton, a Hudson's Bay Co. employee. The Beatton River flows east and then south into the Peace River system.

DC 146 (234 km) **DJ 1244** (2002 km) **Private Aircraft:** Sikanni Chief flight strip to east; elev. 3,258 feet/993m; length, 6,000 feet/1,829m; gravel, current status unknown. Well-known local pilot Jimmy "Midnight" Anderson used the Sikanni Chief airstrip, which was the southernmost airfield in the Northwest Staging Route used during WWII.

DC 150.3 (241.9 km) **DJ 1239.7** (1995 km) *CAUTION: Southbound travelers watch for moose next 15 miles/24 km, especially at dusk and at night.*

DC 155.6 (250.4 km) **DJ 1234.4** (1986.5

km) Large double-ended, gravel turnout with litter barrels. *CAUTION: Slow down! Watch for loose gravel.*

DC 156.6 (252 km) **DJ 1233.4** (1984.9km) Sikanni Hill. *CAUTION: Slow down for hill.*

DC 159.2 (256.2 km) **DJ 1230.8** (1980.9 km) Sikanni Chief River bridge (elev. 2,662 feet/811m). To the west you may see steel stanchions, all that remains of the historic wooden Sikanni bridge, which was destroyed by arson July 10, 1992. The original timber truss bridge built across the Sikanni Chief

River in the spring of 1943 was the first permanent structure completed on the Alaska Highway. Highway construction crews rerouted much of the pioneer road built in 1942 and replaced temporary bridges with permanent structures in 1943. The Sikanni Chief River flows east and then north into the Fort Nelson River, which flows into the Liard River and on to the Mackenzie River, which empties into the Arctic Ocean. Check at the lodge for information on Sikanni River Falls (see **Milepost DC 168.5**).

Sikanni Chief River, fair fishing at

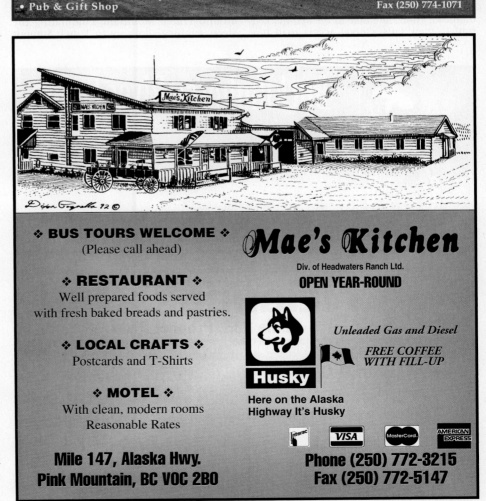

mouth of tributaries in summer for pike; grayling to 2½ lbs.; whitefish to 2 lbs.

DC 159.4 (256.5 km) DJ 1230.6 (1980.4 km) Historical Mile 162. SIKANNI CHIEF. Food, gas, lodging and camping.

Sikanni River RV Park. This riverside RV park offers a beautiful, natural setting for your enjoyment, with easy access to well

graveled, long sites. Its reputation for both cleanliness and beauty has made it a popular destination. Make it a must on your list. Reservations recommended. Resident owners. Clean, safe, secure. Recommended as a fueling stop in "Alaska Highway—An Insiders Guide" for 6 years. Located at the bottom of Sikanni River Hill. Phone (250) 774-1028. [ADVERTISEMENT] ▲

DC 160 (257.5 km) DJ 1230 (1979.4 km) "Drunken forest" on hillside to west is shallow-rooted black spruce trees growing in unstable clay-based soil that is subject to slide activity in wet weather.

DC 160.4 (258.1 km) DJ 1229.6 (1978.8 km) Section of the old Alaska Highway is visible to east; no access.

DC 168.5 (271.2 km) DJ 1221.5 (1965.7 km) Gravel road west to Sikanni River Falls. This private road is signed "Travel at own risk." Drive in 10.5 miles/16.9 km to parking area with picnic tables at B.C. Forest Service trailhead; 10-minute hike in on well-marked trail to view falls. Gravel access road has

some steep hills and a single-lane bridge. *CAUTION: Do not travel in wet weather. Not recommended for vehicles with trailers.*

IMPORTANT: Watch for moose on highway northbound to **Milepost DC 200,** *especially at dusk. Drive carefully!*

DC 172.5 (277.6 km) DJ 1217.5 (1959.3 km) Polka Dot Creek.

DC 173.1 (278.6 km) DJ 1216.9 (1958.3 km) Buckinghorse River bridge; access to river at north end of bridge.

DC 173.2 (278.7 km) DJ 1216.8 (1958.2 km) Historical Mile 175. Inn with gas and camping to east at north end of bridge. Also turnoff east for **Buckinghorse River Provincial Park.** Follow the narrow gravel road past the gravel pit 0.7 mile/1.1 km along river to camping and picnic area. The park has 30 picnic tables, side-by-side camper parking, fire rings, water pump, outhouses and garbage containers; unmaintained, no camping fee. Fishing for grayling in Buckinghorse River. Swimming in downstream pools. ☛▲

DC 173.4 (279 km) DJ 1216.6 (1957.9 km) Historical Mile 175. Buckinghorse River Lodge, on left northbound. Motel, cafe with home cooking, ice cream and ice cream novelties. Bed and breakfast available. Service station, large parking area, free camping. Pets welcome, corrals available. Look forward to our friendly atmosphere. Picnic tables and beautiful scenery. A great spot to take a break for fishing or walking. Phone (250) 773-6468. [ADVERTISEMENT] ▲

DC 176 (283.2 km) DJ 1214 (1953.7 km) South end of 27-mile/43-km **Trutch Mountain Bypass.** Completed in 1987, this section of road rerouted the Alaska Highway around Trutch Mountain, eliminating the steep, winding climb up to Trutch Summit

(and the views). Named for Joseph W. Trutch, civil engineer and first governor of British Columbia, Trutch Mountain was the second highest summit on the Alaska Highway, with an elevation of 4,134 feet/1,260m. The new roadbed cuts a wide swath through the flat Minaker River valley. The river, not visible to motorists, is west of the highway; it was named for local trapper George Minaker. Trutch Mountain is to the east of the highway. Motorists can see part of the old highway on Trutch Mountain.

DC 182.8 (294.2 km) DJ 1207.2 (1942.7 km) Large gravel turnout to west with dumpster.

DC 199.1 (320 km) DJ 1190.9 (1916.5 km) Large gravel turnout with litter barrels.

DC 202.5 (325.5 km) DJ 1187.5 (1911 km) Turnout with dumpster at north end of Trutch Mountain bypass (see **Milepost DC 176**).

CAUTION: Southbound travelers watch for moose on highway, especially at dusk, to Sikanni Chief. Drive carefully!

DC 204.2 (328 km) DJ 1185.8 (1908.3 km) Beaver Creek; fishing for grayling to 2½ lbs. ☚

DC 217.2 (349.3 km) DJ 1172.8 (1887.4 km) Turnoff to west for **Prophet River Park,** formerly a provincial park; current status unknown. Drive in 0.4 mile/0.6 km via gravel road; side-by-side camper parking (36 sites, some pull-throughs), picnic tables, fire rings, water pump, outhouses and garbage containers. Unmaintained; no camping fee. The park access road crosses an airstrip (originally an emergency airstrip on the Northwest Air Staging Route) and part of the old Alaska Highway (the Alcan). This park is also the first stop on the self-guided Forest Ecology Tours (Ecotours) established by the Fort Nelson Forest District. A pamphlet, available from their office in Fort Nelson (phone 250/774-5511), describes the forests at various sites along the Alaska Highway. This Ecotour stop is noted for its trembling aspen stands and mature white spruce. ▲

The Alaska Highway roughly parallels the Prophet River from here north to the Muskwa River south of Fort Nelson.

Private Aircraft: Prophet River emergency airstrip; elev. 1,954 feet/596m; length 6,000 feet/1,829m; gravel; no services.

DC 218.2 (350.7 km) DJ 1171.8 (1885.8 km) View of Prophet River to west.

DC 222.3 (357.2 km) DJ 1167.7 (1879.2 km) Bougie Creek bridge; turnout with litter barrel beside creek at south end of bridge. At this Ecotour stop, note the typical climax white spruce stand and trees of a variety of ages.

CAUTION: Watch for rough road approaching Bougie Creek bridge from either direction.

DC 224.8 (360.6 km) DJ 1165.2 (1875.2 km) Microwave tower to east.

DC 226.2 (363.4 km) DJ 1163.8 (1872.9 km) Prophet River Indian Reserve to east.

DC 226.5 (363.9 km) DJ 1163.5 (1872.4 km) St. Paul's Roman Catholic Church to east.

DC 226.9 (365.2 km) DJ 1163.1 (1871.8 km) Gas, diesel, food and camping to east at Neighbors Inn.

Neighbors Inn. See display ad this section. ▲

DC 227 (364.7 km) DJ 1163 (1871.6 km) Historical Mile 233. PROPHET RIVER, gas, diesel, propane, food, camping and lodging. Southbound travelers note: Next service 68 miles/109 km. ▲

DC 227.6 (366.3 km) DJ 1162.4 (1870.6

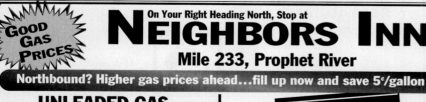

km) **Historic Milepost 234**, Adsett Creek Highway Realignment. This major rerouting eliminated 132 curves on the stretch of highway that originally ran between Miles 234 and 275. Double-ended turnout with dumpster.

DC 227.7 (366.4 km) DJ 1162.3 (1870.5 km) Adsett Creek.

DC 230.7 (371.3 km) DJ 1159.3 (1865.7 km) Natural gas pipeline crosses beneath highway.

DC 232.9 (374.8 km) DJ 1157.1 (1862.1 km) Turnout to west with dumpster.

DC 235.5 (378.4 km) DJ 1154.5 (1857.9 km) Mesa-like topography to the east is Mount Yakatchie.

DC 241.5 (388 km) DJ 1148.5 (1848.3 km) Parker Creek.

DC 245.9 (395.7 km) DJ 1144.1 (1841.2 km) Gravel turnout with dumpster.

DC 261.1 (420.2 km) DJ 1128.9 (1816.7 km) Turnout to east with dumpster.

DC 264.6 (425.2 km) DJ 1125.4 (1811.1 km) Jackfish Creek bridge. Ecotour stop; note the variety of trembling aspen stands and the white spruce seedlings under them.

DC 265.5 (426.5 km) DJ 1124.5 (18.09.6 km) Turnoff to east for **Andy Bailey Lake Provincial Park** (day use only) via 6.8-mile/11-km dirt and gravel access road. (Large RVs and trailers note: only turn-around space on access road is approximately halfway in.) The park is located on Andy Bailey Lake (formerly Jackfish Lake); picnic tables, fire rings, firewood, water, out-houses, garbage containers, boat launch (no powerboats), swimming and fair fishing for northern pike. Bring insect repellent!

DC 270.8 (435.1 km) DJ 1119.2 (1801.1 km) Gas pipeline crosses highway overhead.

DC 271 (435.4 km) DJ 1119 (1800.8 km) Westcoast Energy gas processing plant to east. Petrosul (sulfur processing) to west.

DC 272.4 (437.6 km) DJ 1117.6 (1798.6 km) Access to downhill skiing to east.

DC 276.2 (443.8 km) DJ 1113.8 (1792.4 km) Rodeo grounds to west. The rodeo is held in August.

DC 276.7 (444.6 km) DJ 1113.3 (1791.6 km) Railroad tracks. Microwave tower.

DC 277.5 (446.2 km) DJ 1112.5 (1790.3 km) **Muskwa Heights** (unincorporated), an industrial area with rail yard, plywood plant, sawmill and bulk fuel outlet.

DC 277.9 (447.2 km) DJ 1112.1 (1789.7 km) 24-hour truck stop with gas, diesel, propane, major repair, grocery, restaurant and RV campground. ▲

Husky 5th Wheel Truck Stop and RV Park. See display ad this section. ▲

DC 278.1 (447.5 km) DJ 1111.9 (1789.4 km) Truck scales to west.

DC 278.4 (448 km) DJ 1111.6 (1788.9 km) **Trapper's Den. Historic Mile 293.** Owned and operated by a local trapping family. Moose horns, diamond willow, Northern novelties, books, artwork. Fur hats, headbands, earmuffs. Birchbark baskets,

moose-hair tuftings. Mukluks, moccasins, mits and gloves. Professionally tanned furs. See our "Muskwa River Pearls." Photographers welcome. Located 1/2 mile north of

Husky 5th Wheel RV Park on the Alaska Highway. VISA, MasterCard. Mail orders. Open 10 A.M. to 6 P.M. daily or phone for appointment. John, Cindy and Mandy Wells. Box 1164, Fort Nelson, BC V0C 1R0. (250) 774-3400. Recommended. [ADVERTISEMENT]

DC 279 (448.6 km) DJ 1111 (1787.9 km) Site of oriented strand board plant processing aspen and balsam poplar. This 400,000-square-foot building is the largest industrial building of its kind in the province.

DC 281 (451.4 km) DJ 1109 (1784.7 km) **Muskwa River** bridge, lowest point on the Alaska Highway (elev. 1,000 feet/305m). The Muskwa River flows to the Fort Nelson River. Fair fishing at the mouth of tributaries for northern pike; some goldeye. The Fort Nelson River is too muddy for fishing. The Muskwa River valley exhibits typical river-bottom balsam poplar and white spruce stands, according to the Fort Nelson Forest District's Forest Ecology Tours pamphlet. ◄

The Alaska Highway swings west at Fort Nelson above the Muskwa River, winding southwest then northwest through the Canadian Rockies.

DC 283 (454.3 km) DJ 1107 (1781.5 km) Entering Fort Nelson northbound. Fort Nelson's central business district extends along the highway from the private camp-ground at the east end of the city to the pri-

Always watch for wildlife along the Alaska Highway. (© Earl L. Brown, staff)

Fort Nelson's Most Resourceful Location

vate campground at the west end. Businesses and services are located both north and south of the highway.

Fort Nelson

DC 283 (454.3 km) DJ 1107 (1781.5 km) **Historical Mile 300. Population:** 4,401; area 6,000. **Emergency Services:** RCMP, phone (250) 774-2777. **Fire Department,** phone (250) 774-2222. **Hospital,** 35 beds, phone (250) 774-6916. **Ambulance,** phone (250) 774-2344. Medical, dental and optometric clinics. Visiting veterinarians and chiropractors.

Visitor Information: Located in the Recreation Centre at the west end of town, open 8 A.M. to 8 P.M. Inquire here about local attractions, industrial tours and information about the Liard Highway. Fort Nelson Heritage Museum across the highway from the Infocentre. Contact the Town of Fort Nelson by writing Bag Service 399M, Fort Nelson, BC V0C 1R0; phone (250) 774-6400 (seasonal) or (250) 774-2541 (all year).

Elevation: 1,383 feet/422m. **Climate:** Winters are cold with short days. Summers are hot and the days are long. In mid-June (summer solstice), twilight continues throughout the night. The average number of frost-free days annually is 116. Last frost occurs about May 11, and the first frost Sept. 21. Average annual precipitation of 17.7 inches. **Radio:** CBC 88.3-FM. **Television:** Channels 8 and cable. **Newspaper:** *Fort Nelson News* (weekly).

Transportation: Air—Scheduled service to Edmonton, Calgary, Grande Prairie, and Vancouver via Canadian Regional Airlines. Charter service available. **Bus**—Greyhound service. **Railroad**—B.C. Railway (freight service only).

Private Aircraft: Fort Nelson airport, 3.8 ENE; elev. 1,253 feet/382m; length 6,400 feet/1,950m; asphalt; fuel 100, Jet.

FORT NELSON ADVERTISERS

Ardendale
    Bed & Breakfast ....Ph. (250) 774-2433
Bluebell Inn, The..............Ph. (800) 663-5267
Dan's Neighbourhood Pub ......S. end of town
Dixie Lee ....Ph. (250) 774-6226
Fabric Fun......................New Landmark Plaza
Fort Nelson Heritage
    Museum ....Across from Travel Infocentre
Fort Nelson Hotel ....Ph. (250) 774-6971
Fort Nelson
    Service Centre ....Ph. (250) 774-7950
KaCee's Koin Kleaners ..Next to IGA Foodstore
Mini-Price Inn ....Ph. (250) 774-2136
Northern Deli...................Ph. (250) 774-3311
Northern Husky...........................Downtown
Northern Vision Health
    Foods ....New Landmark Plaza
Pioneer Motel ....Ph. (250) 774-6459
Provincial Motel...............Ph. (250) 774-6901
Red Rose Convenience Store ...S. end of town
Subway.........................Main St., next to Esso
Sukhi's Coin-Op
    Laundromat ....Ph. (250) 774-7786
Tirecraft ....Ph. (250) 774-6372
Town of Fort Nelson........Ph. (250) 774-2541
Woodlands Inn ....Ph. (250) 774-6669
Westend R.V.
    Campground ....Ph. (250) 774-2340

Fort Nelson is located in the lee of the Rocky Mountains, surrounded by the Muskwa, Fort Nelson and Prophet rivers. The area is heavily forested with white spruce, poplar and aspen. Geographically, the town is located about 59° north latitude and 122° west longitude.

Flowing east and north, the Muskwa, Prophet and Sikanni Chief rivers converge to form the Fort Nelson River, which flows into the Liard River, then on to the Mackenzie River, which empties into the Arctic Ocean. Rivers provided the only means of transportation in both summer and winter in this isolated region until 1922, when the Godsell Trail opened, connecting Fort Nelson with Fort St. John. The Alaska Highway linked Fort Nelson with the Outside in 1942.

In the spring, the Muskwa River frequently floods the low country around Fort Nelson and can rise more than 20 feet/6m. At an elevation of 1,000 feet/305m, the Muskwa (which means "bear") is the lowest point on the Alaska Highway. There was a danger of the Muskwa River bridge washing out every June during spring runoff until 1970, when a higher bridge—with piers arranged to prevent log jams—was built.

Fort Nelson's existence was originally based on the fur trade. In the 1920s, trapping was the main business in this isolated pioneer community populated with less than 200 Indians and a few white men. Trappers still harvest beaver, wolverine, weasel, wolf, fox, lynx, mink, muskrat and marten. Other area wildlife includes black bear, which are plentiful, some deer, caribou and a few grizzly bears. Moose remains an important food source for the Indians.

Fort Nelson aboriginal people are mostly Slave (slay-vee), who arrived here about 1775 from the Great Slave Lake area and speak an Athabascan dialect.

Fort Nelson was first established in 1805 by the North West Fur Trading Co. The post, believed to have been located about 80 miles/129 km south of Nelson Forks, was named for Lord Horatio Nelson, the English admiral who won the Battle of Trafalgar.

A second Fort Nelson was later located south of the first fort, but was destroyed by fire in 1813 after Indians massacred its 8 residents. A third Fort Nelson was established in 1865 on the Fort Nelson River's west bank (1 mile from the present Fort Nelson airport)

by W. Cornwallis King, a Hudson's Bay Co. clerk. This trading post was built to keep out the free traders who were filtering in from the Mackenzie River and Fort St. John areas. The free traders' higher fur prices were a threat to the Hudson's Bay Co., which in 1821 had absorbed the rival North West Fur Trading Co. and gained a monopoly on the fur trade in Canada.

This Hudson's Bay Co. trading post was destroyed by a flood in 1890 and a fourth Fort Nelson was established on higher ground upstream and across the river, which is now known as Old Fort Nelson. The present town of Fort Nelson is the fifth site.

Fort Nelson saw its first mail service in 1936. Scheduled air service to Fort Nelson—by ski- and floatplane—also was begun in the 1930s by Yukon Southern Air (which was later absorbed by CPAir, now Canadian Airlines International and Canadian Regional Airlines). The Canadian government began construction of an airport in 1941 as part of the Northwest Air Staging Route, and this was followed by perhaps the biggest boom to Fort Nelson—the construction of the Alaska Highway in 1942. About 2,000 soldiers were bivouacked in Fort Nelson, which they referred to as Zero, as it was the beginning of a road to Whitehorse and another road to Fort Simpson. Later Dawson Creek became Mile 0 and Fort Nelson Mile 300.

Fort Nelson expanded in the 1940s and 1950s as people came here to work for the government or to start their own small businesses: trucking, barging, aviation, construction, garages, stores, cafes, motels and sawmills. It is surprising to consider that as recently as the 1950s Fort Nelson was still a pioneer community without power, phones, running water, refrigerators or doctors. Interesting recollections of Fort Nelson's early days may be found in Gerri Young's book *The Fort Nelson Story*, available at the museum.

Fort Nelson was an unorganized territory until 1957 when it was declared an Improvement District. Fort Nelson took on village status in 1971 and town status in 1987.

Forestry is a major industry here with a veneer plant, plywood plant, oriented strand board plant and sawmill complex. Check with the Infocentre about scheduled industrial tours.

Forestry products are shipped south by truck and rail. Fort Nelson became a railhead in 1971 with the completion of a 250-mile extension of the Pacific Great Eastern Railway (now British Columbia Railway) from Fort St. John.

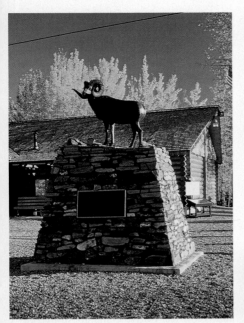

Chadwick Ram bronze sculpture outside Fort Nelson Heritage Museum.

(© Earl L. Brown, staff)

Agriculture is under development here with the establishment of the 55,000-acre McConachie Creek agricultural subdivision.

Northeastern British Columbia is the only sedimentary area in the province currently producing oil and gas. Oil seeps in the Fort Nelson area were noted by early residents. Major gas discoveries were made in the 1960s when the Clarke Lake, Yoyo/Kotcho, Beaver River and Pointed Mountain gas reserves were developed. The Westcoast Energy natural gas processing plant at Fort Nelson, the largest in North America, was constructed in 1964. This plant purifies the gas before sending it south through the 800-mile-long pipeline that connects the Fort Nelson area with the British Columbia lower mainland. Sulfur, a byproduct of natural gas processing, is processed in a recovery plant and shipped to outside markets in pellet form.

In 1997, the BC government set aside more than 4.4 million hectares of Northern Rockies wilderness near Fort Nelson. The Muskwa–Kechika area preserves critical wildlife habitat while allowing logging, mining, oil and gas exploration, and is designed to balance resource management with conservation. For more information contact the Land Use Coordination Office; phone (250) 953-3471, www.luco.gov.bc.ca.

ACCOMMODATIONS/VISITOR SERVICES

Fort Nelson has 10 hotels/motels, 3 bed and breakfasts, several gas stations and restaurants, a pub, fast food, deli and health food outlets; laundromat; an auto supply store, department stores and other services, most located north and south just off the Alaska Highway. The post office and liquor store are on Airport Drive. There are 2 banks, both with ATMs, on the business frontage road north of the highway. Fresh water fill-up and free municipal dump station adjacent to the blue chalet near the museum. Inquire at the Infocentre for location of local churches and their hours of worship.

Ardendale Bed & Breakfast. Welcome to our large log home. Comfortable rooms, spa, cable TV, guest lounge. Excellent breakfast of your choice. Sleigh, buggy and wagon rides available. Close to the golf course and cross-country skiing. Laundry facilities. Smoking outdoors on deck. Phone (250) 774-2433. Fax (250) 774-2436. VISA. Frank and Gail Parker, Box 427, Fort Nelson, BC V0C 1R0. [ADVERTISEMENT]

Fort Nelson has 2 campgrounds: one is located at the north (or west) end of town near the museum; the other is at Muskwa

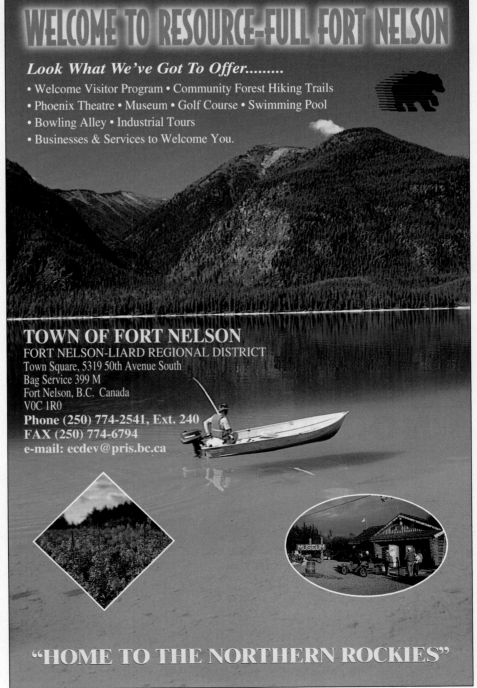

Heights south of Fort Nelson.

Westend RV Campground and Mini Golf welcomes RVs, caravans and tenters. Located in town next to the Museum, only a

few minutes from stores and downtown. Over 140 sites, lots of shade, full hookups, pull-throughs. Town water, coin-op showers

and laundry, playground. Free RV wash and firewood. Open April 1–Nov. 1. We hope you enjoy our Northern hospitality. VISA, MasterCard, American Express. Cash accepted with identification. Under new management. Your hosts, Craig and Theresa Hess. Phone (250) 774-2340. [ADVERTISEMENT] ▲

ATTRACTIONS

Fort Nelson offers travelers a free "Welcome Visitor Program" on summer evenings (Monday through Thursday in 1998) at 6:45 P.M. at the Phoenix Theatre. These interesting and entertaining presentations are put on by local residents and range from slide shows to talks on items of local

interest. Check with the Visitor Infocentre or at the Town Square for details.

The **Fort Nelson Heritage Museum**, across the highway from the Travel Infocentre, has excellent displays of pioneer arti-

facts, Alaska Highway history, wildlife (including a white moose), a spruce bark canoe, and souvenirs and books for sale. Outside the museum is the Chadwick Ram, a bronze sculpture by Rick Taylor. The statue commemorates the world record stone sheep taken in the Muskwa Valley area in 1936. This nonprofit museum charges a modest admission fee. Native crafts are displayed at the Fort Nelson–Liard Native Friendship Centre, located on 49th Avenue.

The recreation centre, across from the museum, has tennis courts; hockey and curling arena for winter sports. There is also a sportsplex with bowling alley. Swimming pool, swirl pool, sauna and gym located in the Aqua Centre on Simpson Trail. For golfers, the **Poplar Hills Golf and Country Club**, just north of town on the Old Alaska Highway, has grass greens; open daily.

A community demonstration forest is open to the public. There is a forest trail (0.6 mile/1 km, half-hour walk), a silviculture trail (1.9 miles/3 km, 45-minute walk) and a Native trail. Located off the Simpson Trail via Mountainview Drive; check at the Infocentre for trail guide.

Fort Nelson hosts a number of annual benefits, dances, tournaments and exhibits. Check locally for details and dates on all events. Summer events include a rodeo in August. Winter events include a big cash prize curling bon spiel in February, Trapper's Rendezvous in March and the Canadian Open Sled Dog Races in December (with local racers from the well-known Streeper Kennels). Terry Streeper is a four-time World Champion (Anchorage) and also an Open North American Champion (Fairbanks) sled dog racer, and won more than 30 major races in 6 countries during the 1990s. Streeper Kennels is located on Radar Road.

The Northern Rockies Toastmasters Club meets at Town Square every second Thursday (check with the Visitor Infocentre). Travelling Toastmasters are welcome to join the meeting, according to Earl Brown, *The MILEPOST* field editor and president of the local club.

Alaska Highway Log

(continued)

Distance from Dawson Creek (DC) is followed by distance from Delta Junction (DJ). Original mileposts are indicated in the text as Historical Mile.

In Canada, mileages from Dawson Creek are based on actual driving distance, not historical mileposts, and kilometres are based on physical kilometreposts. Mileages from Delta Junction are also based on actual driving distance, not historical mileposts, but are followed by the metric conversion to kilometres.

DC 284 (456.4 km) **DJ 1106** (1779.9 km) **Historic Milepost 300**, historic sign and interpretive panel at west end of Fort Nelson. Visitor information in the Recreation Centre north side of highway, log museum south side of highway. Private campground adjacent museum. ▲

Northbound: Watch for sections of rough, narrow, winding road and breaks in surfacing between Fort Nelson and the BC–YT border (approximately next 321 miles/516.5 km). Road reconstruction may still be underway at Steamboat Mountain in summer 1998.

Southbound: Good pavement, wider road, next 284 miles/457 km (to Dawson Creek).

DC 284.5 (457.5 km) **DJ 1105.5** (1779.1 km) Fort Nelson Forest District Office to north provides a pamphlet of self-guided Forest Ecology Tours on the Alaska and Liard highways; phone (250) 774-5511.

DC 284.7 (458.2 km) **DJ 1105.3** (1778.8 km) **Junction** with south end of Old Alaska Highway (**Mile 301–308**). The Muskwa Valley bypass between Mile 301 and 308 opened in 1992.

DC 287.9 (462.6 km) **DJ 1102.1** (1773.6 km) Access to Poplar Hills Golf and Country Club, located on Old Alaska Highway; 9-hole

golf course, driving range, grass greens, clubhouse (licensed), golf club rentals. Open 8 A.M. to dusk, May to October.

DC 291 (467.6 km) **DJ 1099** (1768.6 km) Parker Lake Road. **Junction** with north end of Old Alaska Highway (**Mile 308–301**).

DC 292 (469.9 km) **DJ 1098** (1767 km) Private airstrip alongside highway; status unknown.

DC 301 (483.5 km) **DJ 1089** (1752.5 km)

> **Junction** with Liard Highway (BC Highway 77) north to Fort Liard, Fort Simpson and other Northwest Territories destinations. See LIARD HIGHWAY section.

DC 304.1 (489.4 km) **DJ 1085.9** (1747.4 km) **Historic Milepost 320**. Sign marks start of Reese & Olson contract during construction of the Alaska Highway.

DC 308.2 (495.3 km) **DJ 1081.8** (1740.9 km) Raspberry Creek. Turnout with dumpster to south.

DC 316.6 (506.2 km) **DJ 1073.4** (1727.4 km) Turnout with dumpster to south.

DC 318.4 (509.1 km) **DJ 1071.6** (1724.5 km) Kledo Creek bridge. The Kledo River is a tributary of the Muskwa River. This is a popular hunting area in the fall.

DC 318.7 (509.5 km) **DJ 1071.3** (1724 km) Kledo Creek wayside rest area to north (unmaintained).

View of the Muskwa River Valley from turnout at Milepost DC 334.3.

(© Earl L. Brown, staff)

field editor Earl Brown used a 500mm lens to get this shot.)

DC 322.7 (516 km) **DJ 1067.3** (1717.6 km) Steamboat Creek bridge. *NOTE: Highway begins climb northbound up Steamboat Mountain; some 10 percent grades.*

DC 329 (526.1 km) **DJ 1061** (1707.5 km) Pull-through turnout with dumpster to south.

DC 333 (532.5 km) **DJ 1057** (1701 km) **Historic Milepost 351. STEAMBOAT** (unincorporated), lodge with food, gas, diesel and camping to south; open year-round. Historical sign marks start of Curran & Briggs Ltd. contract during construction of the Alaska Highway.

Steamboat at **Historical Mile 351**. Cafe with fresh-baked bread, pies and pastry. Husky gas, diesel and oil products. Level pull-throughs, full hookups, RV parking with a view. Public phone. Picnic area (pets on a leash, please). Ice, souvenirs and handicrafts. Your hosts, Ed and Carol Paynter. Open year-round. Phone (250) 774-3388. [ADVERTISEMENT] ▲

DC 333.7 (533.5 km) **DJ 1056.3** (1699.9 km) Winding road ascends Steamboat Mountain westbound. Views of the Muskwa River valley and Rocky Mountains to the southwest from summit of 3,500-foot/1,067-m Steamboat Mountain, named because of its resemblance to a steamship.

DC 334.3 (534.5 km) **DJ 1055.7** (1698.9 km) Turnout with view and dumpster to south.

DC 336.7 (538.5 km) **DJ 1053.3** (1695.1 km) Large turnouts both sides of highway with dumpsters, payphones and toilets.

Highway descends for westbound travelers. *NOTE: 1998 road reconstruction has improved and shortened the highway in this area. Kilometreposts and driving distances have not been recalibrated in* The MILEPOST® *log.*

DC 342.8 (548 km) **DJ 1047.2** (1685.2 km) Turnout with dumpster and point of interest sign to south. View of **Indian Head Mountain**, a high crag resembling the classic Indian profile. *IMPORTANT: DO NOT FEED BEARS!*

DC 345 (551.5 km) **DJ 1045** (1681.7 km) **Teetering Rock** viewpoint with dumpster and outhouses to north. Teetering Rock is in the distance on the horizon. (*MILEPOST®*

Fort Nelson Forest District (phone 250/774-5511) has developed a 7.6-mile-/12.3-km-long trail to Teetering Rock; steep climbs. Stay on well-marked trails, keep pets on leash; it is easy to get lost in this country.

DC 346.4 (553.9 km) **DJ 1043.6** (1679.5 km) Mill Creek, which flows into the Tetsa River. The highway follows the Tetsa River westbound. The Tetsa heads near Summit Lake in the northern Canadian Rockies.

Tetsa River, good fishing for grayling to 4 lbs., average $1^1/_2$ lbs., flies or spin cast with lures; Dolly Varden to 7 lbs., average 3 lbs., spin cast or black gnat, coachman, Red Devils, flies; whitefish, small but plentiful, use flies or eggs, summer. 🐟

DC 346.5 (554 km) **DJ 1043.5** (1679.3 km) Turnoff to south for **Tetsa River Provincial Park**, 1.2 miles/1.9 km via gravel road. Grass tenting area, 25 level gravel sites in trees, picnic tables, fire rings, firewood, outhouses, water and garbage containers. Camping fee $7 to $12. ▲

DC 351 (561.2 km) **DJ 1039** (1672.1 km) *CAUTION: Slow down, dangerous curve! Watch for road construction next 2 miles/3.2 km northbound in 1999.*

DC 357.5 (571.5 km) **DJ 1032.5** (1661.6 km) **Historical Mile 375**. Gas, store, cabins and private campground. ▲

DC 358.6 (573.3 km) **DJ 1031.4** (1659.8 km) Highway follows Tetsa River westbound. Turnouts next 0.2 mile/0.3 km south to river.

DC 360.2 (575.9 km) **DJ 1029.8** (1657.2 km) Turnout with dumpster, picnic site. Ecotour stop: Note the aspen-dominated slopes on the north side of the Tetsa River, and the white spruce on the south side.

DC 364.4 (582.6 km) **DJ 1025.6** (1650.5 km) Gravel turnout to south.

DC 365.6 (584.6 km) **DJ 1024.4** (1648.6 km) Tetsa River bridge No. 1, clearance 17 feet/5.2m.

DC 366 (585.4 km) **DJ 1024** (1647.9 km) Pull-through turnout with dumpster to north.

DC 367.3 (587.3 km) **DJ 1022.7** (1645.8 km) Tetsa River bridge No. 2.

The high bare peaks of the central Canadian Rockies are visible ahead westbound.

DC 371.5 (594.2 km) **DJ 1018.5** (1639.1 km) South boundary of **Stone Mountain Provincial Park** (the north boundary is at **Milepost DC 380.7** on the highway). Stone Mountain Park encompasses the Summit Pass area and extends south to include Wokkpash Recreation Area. Access is via MacDonald Creek hiking trail and by 4-wheel drive from 113 Creek (see **Milepost DC 382.2**) to Wokkpash Creek trail. Contact the Parks District Office in Fort St. John; phone (250) 787-3407.

Stone sheep are frequently sighted in this area. Stone sheep are indigenous to the mountains of northern British Columbia and southern Yukon Territory. They are

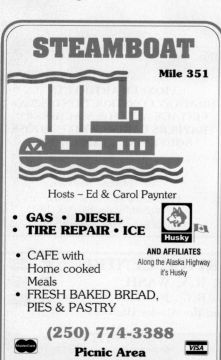

darker and somewhat slighter than the bighorn sheep found in the Rocky Mountains. Dall or white sheep are found in the mountains of Yukon, Alaska and Northwest Territories.

CAUTION: Northbound, watch for caribou and stone sheep along the highway. DO NOT FEED WILDLIFE. DO NOT STOP VEHICLES ON THE HIGHWAY TO TAKE PHOTOS; use shoulders or turnouts. You are now in bear country ... a fed bear is a dead bear—don't feed bears!

DC 372.7 (596 km) DJ 1017.3 (1637.1 km) Pull-through turnout with dumpster to north.

DC 373.3 (597 km) DJ 1016.7 (1636.2 km) **Historical Mile 392. SUMMIT LAKE** (unincorporated), lodge with gas, diesel, propane, cafe, camping and lodging. The peak behind Summit Lake is Mount St. George (elev. 7,419 feet/2,261m) in the Stone Mountain range. The Summit area is known for dramatic and sudden weather changes. ▲

DC 373.5 (597.4 km) DJ 1016.5 (1635.9 km) Rough gravel side road leads 1.5 miles/2.5 km to Flower Springs Lake trailhead, 4.3 miles/7 km to microwave tower viewpoint. Not suitable for motorhomes, trailers or low clearance vehicles. (This road was closed beyond Flower Springs Lake in 1998; current status unknown.)

DC 373.6 (597.6 km) DJ 1016.4 (1635.7 km) **Historic Milepost 392 Summit Pass** (elev. 4,250 feet/ 1,295m); gravel turnout, sign and interpretive panel at the highest summit on the Alaska Highway. A very beautiful area of bare rocky peaks (which can be snow-covered anytime of the year). Summit Lake provincial campground to south at east end of lake; 28 level gravel sites; camping fee $7 to $12; picnic tables; water and garbage containers; information shelter; boat launch. Hiking trails to Flower Springs Lake and Summit Peak. Fair fishing for lake trout, whitefish and rainbows. ◄▲

DC 375.6 (600.8 km) DJ 1014.4 (1632.5 km) Turnout to north.

DC 375.9 (601.3 km) DJ 1014.1 (1632 km) Picnic site to south with tables and dumpster on Rocky Crest Lake. Nice spot for photos; good reflections in lake when calm.

DC 376 (601.5 km) DJ 1014 (1631.8 km) Erosion pillars (hoodoos) north of highway (0.6-mile/1-km hike north); watch for caribou. Northbound, the highway winds through a rocky limestone gorge before descending into the wide and picturesque MacDonald River valley.

Turnouts next 2.5 miles/4 km northbound with views of the valley. Watch for Stone sheep along the rock cut; they are frequently sighted along this stretch of road.

DC 378.2 (605.1) DJ 1011.8 (1628.3 km) Baba Canyon to north. Popular with hikers (strenuous).

DC 378.6 (605.7 km) DJ 1011.4 (1627.6 km) **Historical Mile 397.** Rocky Mountain Lodge to south; food, gas, lodging and camping. ▲

Rocky Mountain Lodge. See display ad this section. ▲

DC 379.7 (607.4 km) DJ 1010.3 (1625.9 km) Turnout to south.

DC 380.7 (609 km) DJ 1009.3 (1624.3 km) North boundary of **Stone Mountain Provincial Park** (see description at the south boundary of the park at Milepost DC 371.5).

CAUTION: Southbound, watch for wildlife alongside and on the road. DO NOT FEED

Wide rocky MacDonald River Valley vista opens for northbound travelers.
(© Earl L. Brown, staff)

WILDLIFE.

DC 381.2 (611.2 km) DJ 1008.8 (1623.5 km) Highway winds along above the wide rocky valley of MacDonald Creek. MacDonald Creek and river were named for Charlie McDonald, a Cree Indian credited with helping Alaska Highway survey crews locate the best route for the pioneer road.

DC 382.2 (612.8 km) DJ 1007.8 (1621.8km) Trail access via abandoned Churchill Copper Mine Road (4-wheel drive only beyond river) to **Wokkpash Recreation Area**, located 12 miles/20 km south of the highway, which adjoins the southwest boundary of Stone Mountain Provincial Park. This remote area features extensive hoodoos (erosion pillars) in Wokkpash Gorge, and the scenic Forlorn Gorge and Stepped Lakes. Wokkpash Creek hiking trai follows Wokkpash Creek to Wokkpash Lake: 9 miles/15 km. Contact the Parks District Office in Fort St. John before venturing into this area; phone (250) 787-3407.

DC 383.3 (614.6 km) DJ 1006.7 (1620.1 km) 113 Creek. The creek was named during construction of the Alaska Highway for its distance from Mile 0 at Fort Nelson. While Dawson Creek was to become Mile 0 on the completed pioneer road, clearing crews began their work at Fort Nelson, since a rough winter road already existed between Dawson Creek and Fort Nelson. Stone Range to the northeast and Muskwa Ranges of the Rocky Mountains to the west.

DC 384.2 (615.4 km) DJ 1005.8 (1618.6 km) 115 Creek provincial campground to southwest, adjacent highway; double-ended entrance. Side-by-side camper parking (8 sites), water, garbage containers, picnic tables. Camping fee $7 to $12. Access to the riverbank of 115 Creek and **MacDonald Creek.** Beaver dams nearby. Fishing for grayling and Dolly Varden. ◄▲

DC 385.4 (616.6 km) DJ 1004.6 (1616.7 km) 115 Creek bridge. Turnout to south at east end of bridge with tables and dumpster. Like 113 Creek, 115 Creek was named during construction of the Alaska Highway for its distance from Fort Nelson, Mile 0 for clearing crews.

DC 390.5 (624.8 km) DJ 999.5 (1608.5 km) **Historical Mile 408.** MacDonald River

Services (closed in 1998; current status unknown).

DC 392.5 (627.8 km) DJ 997.5 (1605.3 km) MacDonald River bridge, clearance 17 feet/ 5.2m. Highway winds through narrow valley.

MacDonald River, fair fishing from May to July for Dolly Varden and grayling. ◄

DC 394.8 (631.8 km) DJ 995.2 (1601.6 km) Turnout with litter barrel to east.

DC 396.1 (633.8 km) DJ 993.9 (1599.5 km) Folding rock formations on mountain face to west. The Racing River forms the boundary between the Sentinel Range and the Stone Range, both of which are composed of folded and sedimentary rock.

DC 399.1 (638.6 km) DJ 990.9 (1594.7 km) Stringer Creek.

DC 400.7 (641.1 km) DJ 989.3 (1592.1 km) Racing River bridge, clearance 17 feet/5.2m. River access to north at east end of bridge. Ecotour stop: Note the open south-facing slopes on the north side of the river that are used as winter range by stone sheep, elk and deer. Periodic controlled burns encourage the growth of forage grasses

Farmland in the picturesque Toad River Valley at Historical Mile 422.
(© Earl L. Brown, staff)

and shrubs, and also allow chinook winds to clear snow from grazing grounds in winter.

Racing River, grayling to 16 inches; Dolly Varden to 2 lbs., use flies, July through September.

DC 404.6 (647.4 km) DJ 985.4 (1585.8 km) **Historical Mile 422. TOAD RIVER** (unincorporated), situated in a picturesque valley. Popular artist Trish Croal makes her home here. Highway maintenance camp, school and private residences on north side of highway. Toad River Lodge on south side of highway with cafe, gas, tire repair, propane, camping and lodging. Ambulance service. Toad River Lodge is open year-round. The lodge is known for its collection of hats, which numbers more than 4,500. Also, inquire at the lodge about good wildlife viewing locations nearby. ▲

Toad River Lodge. See display ad this section. ▲

Stone Mountain Safaris. New 4-bedroom cedar log lodge with queen bed and single bed per room. Two shared baths. Hot tub, snooker table, wildlife displays. Experience our bed and breakfast or our "all inclusive" package. Horseback rides and adventure trips available. Mountain views and wildlife viewing. Located halfway between Dawson Creek and Whitehorse. So why not get off the highway and experience our quiet, private ranch setting. From Toad River go west 6 miles on Alaska Highway and turn right for 1 mile, then right again for 2 miles. Reservations required. Your hosts Dave and Ellie Wiens, Box 7870, Toad River, B.C. V0C 2X0. Phone (250) 232-5469; fax (250) 232-5801. [ADVERTISEMENT]

Private Aircraft: Toad River airstrip; elev. 2,400 feet/732m; length 3,000 feet/914m. Unattended; no fuel; prior permission to land required.

DC 405.5 (648.8 km) DJ 984.5 (1584.4 km) Turnout to south with **Historic Milepost 422.** Sign and interpretive panel commemorate Toad River/Camp 138 Jupp Construction.

DC 406.3 (650.1 km) DJ 983.7 (1583.1 km) Turnout with dumpster to north.

DC 407.5 (652 km) DJ 982.5 (1581.1 km) Historical Mile 426. Food, gas, propane, tire repair, cabins and camping south side of highway. Inquire here about local hiking trails and riverboat tours. ▲

The Poplars Campground. See display ad this section. ▲

DC 409.2 (654.6 km) DJ 980.8 (1578.4 km) South boundary of **Muncho Lake Provincial Park.** (The north boundary is at **Milepost DC 460.7** on the highway.) Muncho Lake Park straddles the Alaska Highway, encompassing the alpine peaks and valleys surrounding Muncho Lake. There are no signed trails. Guides and outfitters offers trips into the backcountry.

DC 410.6 (656.8 km) DJ 979.4 (1576.1 km) Turnout with information panel on area geology. Impressive rock folding formation on mountain face, known as Folded Mountain.

DC 411 (657.4 km) DJ 979 (1575.5 km) Beautiful turquoise-coloured Toad River to north. The highway now follows the Toad River westbound.

Toad River, grayling to 16 inches; Dolly Varden to 10 lbs., use flies, July through September. 🐟

DC 415.5 (664.7 km) DJ 974.5 (1568.3 km) 150 Creek bridge. Creek access to south at east end of bridge.

DC 417.6 (668.2 km) DJ 972.4 (1564.9 km) Centennial Falls to south. (Waterfall dries up in summer, unless it is raining.)

DC 419.8 (671.7 km) DJ 970.2 (1561.3 km) Toad River bridge. Turnout with dumpster to south at west end of bridge; fishing. 🐟

DC 422.6 (676.2 km) DJ 967.4 (1556.8 km) Watch for moose in pond to north; morning or evening best.

DC 423 (676.8 km) DJ 967 (1556.2 km) Double-ended turnout with dumpster to north. Excellent wildlife viewing area; watch

NORTHERN ROCKIES
Highland Glen Lodge Ltd.
Hotel & Licensed Dining Room • RV Park
Mile 462 • Alaska Highway • Box 8-M, Muncho Lake, B.C. V0C IZO
— **Open Year Round** —
TOLL FREE RESERVATION LINE 1-800-663-5269
PHONE (250) 776-3481 FAX (250) 776-3482
★ ★ BUS TOURS WELCOME ★ ★

➢ New Hotel, Lakeshore Chalets and Motel Rooms, Restaurant, Bakery, Lakeshore RV-Park, Children's Playground.

➢ To avoid disappointment please make reservation by phoning ahead.

➢ Owned and operated by "bush pilot" Urs and wife Marianne.

➢ On beautiful Muncho Lake, Northern Rockies Lodge offers modern facilities in a natural setting.

➢ Newest and largest Lodge on Muncho Lake, featuring 45 ft. high fire place in the vaulted ceiling log dining room. European trained chef.

Spacious Lakeshore and Pull-Through RV Sites
- Discount gas for registered guests -

LIARD AIR LTD.
– Outpost cabins on remote mountain lakes
– Fly-in fishing and Northern Rockies Sightseeing Tours
– Nahanni National Park excursions
– Air Tax Service

for Stone sheep, caribou, bear and moose.

CAUTION: Watch for Stone sheep along the highway (or standing in the middle of the highway). DO NOT FEED WILDLIFE. Do not stop vehicles on the highway to take photos; use shoulders or turnouts.

DC 423.1 (677 km) **DJ 966.9** (1556 km) The highway swings north for Alaska-bound travelers. Highway climbs next 6 miles/9.7 km northbound. For Dawson Creek-bound travelers, the highway follows an easterly direction.

DC 424.1 (678.7 km) **DJ 965.9** (1554.4 km) **Historic Milepost 443** at Peterson Creek No. 1 bridge. The creek was named for local trapper Pete Peterson, who helped Alaska Highway construction crews select a route through this area. Historic sign marks start of Campbell Construction Co. Ltd. contract during construction of the Alaska Highway.

DC 424.3 (679 km) **DJ 965.7** (1554.1 km) The Village (closed in 1998; current status unknown).

DC 429.5 (688.9 km) **DJ 960.5** (1545.7 km) Viewpoint to east with information shelter and dumpster. Information panel on geology of "Sawtooth Mountains."

DC 436.5 (698.5 km) **DJ 953.5** (1534.5 km) **Historic Milepost 456.** Entering **MUNCHO LAKE** (pop. 26; elev. 2,700 feet/823m). Muncho Lake businesses extend from here north along the east shore of Muncho Lake to approximately **Milepost DC 443.7.** Businesses in Muncho Lake include 4 lodges, gas stations with towing and repair, restaurants, cafes and campgrounds. The post office is located at Double G Service; open year-round.

A historic sign and interpretive panel mark Muncho Lake/Refueling Stop, Checkpoint during Alaska Highway construction. The road around the lake was a particular challenge. Workers had to cut their way through the lake's rocky banks. Horses were used to haul away the rock.

The Muncho Lake area offers hiking in the summer and cross-country skiing in the winter. Boat rentals are available from J&H Wilderness Resort and Northern Rockies

Lodge. MV *Sandpiper* boat tours of the lake available from Double G Service. Flightseeing and fly-in fishing service available at Northern Rockies Lodge. An annual lake trout derby is held in June; inquire locally for dates.

CAUTION: Watch for Stone sheep and caribou on the highway north of here. Please DO NOT FEED WILDLIFE. Please do not stop on the highway to take photos; use shoulders or turnouts.

DC 436.6 (698.7 km) **DJ 953.4** (1534.3 km) Double G Service; post office, lake tours, gas, diesel, store, food and lodging.

Double G Service, located at the south end of beautiful Muncho Lake, offers you

"one stop" service. For your vehicle, full-service unleaded gas and diesel, oils, welding and licensed mechanic. Towing. For you—a convenience store with cold drinks, ice cream novelties, local crafts and souvenirs. Comfortable motel rooms, playground, post office. Our cozy cafe has delicious homemade bread and pastries, hearty soups, stews and chili. Excellent area hiking just out the back door. Pick up your tickets for the Muncho lake tour aboard the M.V. *Sand-*

piper for a personally guided and narrated 1-hour cruise in our comfortable 32-foot, 20-passenger, all enclosed cabin. Bring your camera! We look forward to meeting you. VISA, MasterCard. Phone (250) 776-3411. [ADVERTISEMENT]

DC 436.9 (699.2 km) **DJ 953.1** (1533.8 km) Gravel airstrip to west; length 1,200 feet/366m. View of Muncho Lake ahead northbound. The highway along Muncho Lake required considerable rock excavation by the Army in 1942. The original route went along the top of the cliffs, which proved particularly hazardous. (Portions of this hair-raising road can be seen high above the lake.) The Army relocated the road by benching into the cliffs a few feet above lake level.

Muncho Lake, known for its beautiful deep green and blue waters, is 7 miles/11 km in length, and 1 mile/1.6 km in width; elevation of the lake is 2,680 feet/817m. The colours are attributed to copper oxide leaching into the lake. Deepest point has been reported to be 730 feet/223m, although recent government tests have not located any point deeper than 400 feet/122m. The lake drains the Sentinel Range to the east and the Terminal Range to the west, feeding the raging Trout River in its 1,000-foot/305-m drop to the mighty Liard River. The mountains surrounding the lake are approximately 7,000 feet/2,134m high.

Muncho Lake, fishing for Dolly Varden; some grayling; whitefish to 12 inches; lake trout (record to 50 lbs.), use spoons, spinners, diving plug or weighted spoons, June and July best. The lake trout quota is 3 trout per person; minimum size 15¾ inches. Make sure you have a current British Columbia fishing license and a copy of the current regulations. Also rainbow trout.

DC 437.7 (700.5 km) **DJ 952.3** (1532.5 km) Strawberry Flats Campground, Muncho Lake Provincial Park; 15 sites on rocky lakeshore, picnic tables, outhouses, garbage containers. Camping fee $7 to $12. ▲

CAUTION: Watch for bears in area.

DC 442.2 (707.9 km) **DJ 947.8** (1525.3 km) **Historical Mile 462.** Northern Rockies/Highland Glen Lodge (open year-round) with lodging, restaurant, gas and camping west side of highway. Flying service for sightseeing and fly-in fishing. ▲

Northern Rockies/Highland Glen Lodge, Mile 462, Muncho Lake, BC. Toll-free reservation line: (800) 663-5269. Phone (250) 776-3481, fax (250) 776-3482. New hotel, lakeshore chalets and motel rooms. The newest and largest log building in BC. Featuring a 45-foot-high fireplace in vaulted ceiling dining room. Restaurant with European-trained chef and bakery. Spacious lakeshore RV sites, power and water hookups, dump station for guests. Children's playground. Fly-in fishing trips into the Arctic and Pacific watersheds for arctic grayling, Dolly Varden, rainbow trout, lake trout, northern pike and walleye. Outpost fishing cabins. Air taxi service, glacier and Northern Rocky Mountain local sightseeing flights. [ADVERTISEMENT] ▲

DC 442.9 (709 km) **DJ 947.1** (1524.2 km) Turnoff to west for MacDonald campground, Muncho Lake Provincial Park; 15 level gravel sites, firewood, picnic tables, outhouses, boat launch, information shelter, pump water, on Muncho Lake. Camping fee $7 to $12. *CAUTION: Watch for bears in area.* ▲

DC 443.6 (710.1 km) **DJ 946.4** (1523 km)

Historical Mile 463. Muncho Lake Lodge; gas, propane, food, camping and lodging. ▲

Muncho Lake Lodge. See display ad this section. ▲

DC 443.7 (710.3 km) **DJ 946.3** (1522.9 km) **Historical Mile 463.1.** J&H Wilderness Resort; food, gas, store, boat rentals, tackle, rafting trips, lodging and camping available. Muncho Lake businesses extend south to **Milepost DC 436.5.** ▲

J&H Wilderness Resort. See display ad this section. ▲

DC 444.9 (712.2 km) **DJ 945.1** (1520.9 km) Muncho Lake viewpoint to west with information panel, large parking area, picnic tables, dumpster and outhouses. View of Peterson Mountain at south end of lake.

CAUTION: Watch for Stone sheep on highway next 10 miles/16 km northbound.

DC 453.3 (725.6 km) **DJ 936.7** (1507.4 km) Turnout with dumpster to east.

DC 454 (726.7 km) **DJ 936** (1506.3 km) Mineral lick; watch for Stone sheep. There is a trailhead 0.2 mile/0.3 km off the highway; a 5- to 10-minute loop hike takes you to viewpoints overlooking the Trout River valley and the steep mineral-laden banks frequented by sheep, goats, caribou and elk. Good photo opportunities, early morning best. *CAUTION: Steep banks, slippery when wet. Bring insect repellent.*

DC 455.5 (729.2 km) **DJ 934.5** (1503.9 km) Turnout with dumpster and message board to west.

DC 457.7 (732.7 km) **DJ 932.3** (1500.4 km) Trout River bridge. The Trout River drains into the Liard River. The highway follows the Trout River north for several miles.

Trout River, grayling to 18 inches; whitefish to 12 inches, flies, spinners, May, June and August best. ➤

DC 458.9 (734.6 km) **DJ 931.1** (1498.4km) Gravel turnout to east.

DC 460.7 (737.4 km) **DJ 929.3** (1495.5 km) Prochniak Creek bridge. The creek was named for a member of Company A, 648th Engineers Topographic Battalion, during construction of the Alaska Highway. North boundary of Muncho Lake Provincial Park.

DC 463.3 (741.6 km) **DJ 926.7** (1491.3 km) Watch for curves next 0.6 mile/1 km northbound.

DC 465.6 (745.3 km) **DJ 924.4** (1487.6 km) Turnout with dumpster to east.

DC 466.3 (746.3 km) **DJ 923.7** (1486.5 km) *CAUTION: Dangerous curves next 3 miles/5 km northbound. Watch for road construction between Kilometreposts 750 and 762 in 1999.*

DC 468.9 (749.5 km) **DJ 921.1** (1482.3 km) Pull-through turnout with dumpster to east. This Ecotour stop shows the extent of the 1959 fire that swept across the valley bottom. Lodgepole pine, trembling aspen and paper birch are the dominant species re-establishing this area.

DC 471 (754.1 km) **DJ 919** (1478.9 km) First glimpse of the mighty Liard River for northbound travelers. Named by French-Canadian voyageurs for the poplar ("liard") that line the banks of the lower river. The Alaska Highway parallels the Liard River from here north to Watson Lake. The river offered engineers a natural line to follow during routing and construction of the Alaska Highway in 1942.

DC 472.2 (756 km) **DJ 917.8** (1477 km) Washout Creek.

DC 474.3 (759.5 km) **DJ 915.7** (1473.6 km) Turnout with dumpster to west.

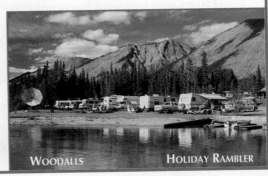

DC 476.7 (763 km) DJ 913.3 (1469.8 km) Lower Liard River bridge. This is the only remaining suspension bridge on the Alaska Highway. The 1,143-foot suspension bridge was built by the American Bridge Co. and McNamara Construction Co. of Toronto in 1943.

The **Liard River** flows eastward toward the Fort Nelson River and parallels the Alaska Highway from the Lower Liard River bridge to the BC–YT border. The scenic Grand Canyon of the Liard is to the east and not visible from the highway. Good fishing for Dolly Varden, grayling, northern pike and whitefish.

DC 477.1 (763.8 km) DJ 912.9 (1469.1 km) **Historical Mile 496. LIARD RIVER**

(unincorporated), lodge with gas, store, pay phone, food, camping and lodging to west; open year-round. ▲

Liard River Lodge. See display ad this section.

DC 477.7 (764.7 km) DJ 912.3 (1468.2 km) **Historic Milepost 496.** Turnoff to north for **Liard River Hotsprings Provincial Park**, long a favorite stop for Alaska Highway travelers. The park has become so popular in recent years that the campground fills up very early each day in summer. Overflow day-parking area across highway from park entrance. The park is open year-round. This well-developed provincial park has 53 large, shaded, level gravel sites (some will accommodate 2 RVs), picnic tables, picnic shelter,

water, garbage containers, firewood, fire rings, playground and heated restrooms at the hot springs with wheelchair-accessible toilet. Camping fees to $15.50. Pay phone at park entrance. &▲

Excellent interpretive programs and nature walks in summer; check schedule posted at park entrance and at information shelter near trailhead. Emergency phone at park headquarters. *CAUTION: BEWARE OF BEARS!*

A boardwalk leads to the pools, crossing a wetlands environment that supports more than 250 boreal forest plants, including 14 orchid species and 14 plants that survive at this latitude because of the hot springs. Also watch for moose feeding in the pools. There are 2 hot springs pools with water temperatures ranging from 108° to 126°F/42° to 52°C. Nearest is the Alpha pool with a children's wading area. Beyond the Alpha pool is Beta pool, which is larger and deeper. Both have changing rooms. Beta pool is about a 0.4-mile/0.6-km walk. Plenty of parking at trailhead.

DC 477.8 (764.9 km) DJ 912.2 (1468 km) **Historical Mile 497.** Liard Hotsprings Lodge (open year-round) with food, gas, lodging and camping. Fishing, sightseeing charter trips and jetboat tours available. ➤▲

Trapper Ray's Liard Hotsprings Lodge. See display ad this section. ▲

DC 482.8 (772.9 km) DJ 907.2 (1460 km) Teeter Creek. A footpath leads upstream; 10-minute walk to falls. Grayling fishing. ➤

DC 485.4 (777 km) DJ 904.6 (1455.8 km) Small turnout overlooking the Liard River.

DC 489 (783.6 km) DJ 901 (1450 km) **Private Aircraft:** Liard River airstrip; elev. 1,400 feet/427m; length 4,000 feet/1,219m; gravel; no fuel.

DC 495 (792.3 km) DJ 895 (1440.3 km) **Historic Milepost 514.** Smith River bridge, clearance 17 feet/5.2m. The historic sign here commemorates Smith River Airport Road. The old airstrip, part of the Northwest Staging Route, is located in a burned-over area about 25 miles/40 km from the highway (accessible by 4-wheel drive only).

Access to **Smith River Falls** via 1.6-mile/2.6-km gravel road; not recommended for large RVs or trailers or in wet weather. There is a hiking trail down to 2-tiered Smith River Falls from the parking area. Grayling fishing. ✄

DC **509.4** (815.6 km) DJ **880.6** (1417.1 km) Large turnout with dumpster to east.

DC **513.9** (822.8 km) DJ **876.1** (1409.9 km) **Historical Mile 533. COAL RIVER**, lodge with gas, diesel, food, camping and lodging. ▲

DC **514.2** (823.2 km) DJ **875.8** (1409.4 km) **Historical Mile 533.2.** Coal River bridge. The Coal River flows into the Liard River south of the bridge.

DC **519.5** (831.4 km) DJ **870.5** (1400.9 km) Sharp easy-to-miss turnoff to west for undeveloped "do-it-yourself campsite" (watch for sign). Small gravel parking area with outhouse, dumpster, and beautiful view of the Liard River (not visible from the highway). Although signed "Whirlpool Canyon," this scenic stretch of the Liard River has been identified by one astute reader as **Mountain Portage Rapids**, with Whirlpool Canyon being located farther downriver. ▲

DC **524.2** (839.2 km) DJ **865.8** (1393 km) **Historical Mile 543.** Fireside (unincorporated). Highway maintenance camp and truck stop.

DC **524.7** (840 km) DJ **865.3** (1392.5 km) Good view of Liard River and Cranberry Rapids to west.

DC **530** (848.7 km) DJ **860** (1384 km) Gravel turnout with dumpster to south.

DC **540.4** (865.3 km) DJ **849.6** (1367.3 km) North end of rerouting of Alaska Highway (see **Milepost DC 527.7**).

DC **545.9** (874.2 km) DJ **844.1** (1358.4 km) Turnout with litter barrel to west overlooking the Liard River.

DC **550.9** (882.2 km) DJ **839.1** (1350.4 km) **Historical Mile 570, Allen's Lookout.** Very large pull-through turnout with picnic tables, outhouse and dumpster to west overlooking the Liard River. Goat Mountain to west. Legend has it that a band of outlaws took advantage of this sweeping view of the Liard River to attack and rob riverboats.

DC **555** (888.8 km) DJ **835** (1343.8 km) Good berry picking in July among roadside raspberry bushes; watch for bears.

DC **556** (890.4 km) DJ **834** (1342.2 km) Highway swings west for Alaska-bound travelers.

NOTE: *Watch for road construction between Kilometreposts 895 and 906 in 1999.*

DC **562.5** (900.8 km) DJ **827.5** (1331.7 km) Large gravel turnout with dumpster.

DC **567.9** (909.4 km) DJ **822.1** (1323 km) Historic **Milepost 588, Contact Creek** bridge. Turnout. Contact Creek was named by soldiers of the 35th Regiment from the south and the 340th Regiment from the north who met here Sept. 24, 1942, completing the southern sector of the Alaska Highway. Historic sign and interpretive panel.

NOTE: *New road construction between Contact Creek and Iron Creek in 1998 is scheduled for seal coating in 1999.*

DC **568.3** (910.2 km) DJ **821.7** (1322.4 km) First of 7 crossings of the BC–YT border. Large gravel turnout to north with point of interest sign about the Yukon Territory. "The Yukon Territory takes its name from the Indian word *Youcon*, meaning 'big river.' It was first explored in the 1840s by the Hudson's Bay Co., which established several trading posts. The territory, which was then considered a district of the Northwest Territories, remained largely untouched until the Klondike Gold Rush, when thousands of people flooded into the country and communities sprang up almost overnight. This sudden expansion led to the official formation of the Yukon Territory on June 13, 1898."

DC **570** (912.9 km) DJ **820** (1319.6 km) **Historical Mile 590. CONTACT CREEK**, lodge open year-round; food, gas, diesel, car repair, towing and pay phone.

Contact Creek Lodge. See display ad this section.

DC **573.9** (918.9 km) DJ **816.1** (1313.3 km) Irons Creek culbert, completed in 1998, is the largest culvert in the world at 25 feet high, 135 feet long and 62 feet wide. Turnout with litter barrel.

According to the folks at Iron Creek Lodge, Irons Creek was named during construction of the Alaska Highway for the trucks that stopped here to put on tire irons

View of Liard River from turnout at Milepost DC 545.9. (© Earl L. Brown, staff)

(chains) in order to make it up the hill.

DC **575.9** (922 km) DJ **814.1** (1310.1 km) **Historical Mile 596.** Iron Creek Lodge; food, gas, diesel, dump station, lodging, camping

Visit us on the internet at www.themilepost.com

British Columbia–Yukon border crossing at Milepost DC 605.1.
(© Earl L. Brown, staff)

and fishing at private stocked lake.

Iron Creek Lodge. See display ad this section.

DC 582 (931.8 km) **DJ 808** (1300.3 km) NorthwesTel microwave tower.

DC 585 (937 km) **DJ 805** (1295.5 km) **Hyland River** bridge; good fishing for rainbow, Dolly Varden and grayling.

NOTE: Watch for logging trucks northbound to Watson Lake.

DC 585.3 (937.2 km) **DJ 804.7** (1295 km) **Historical Mile 605.9.** Hyland River bridge. The Hyland River is a tributary of the Liard River. The river was named for Frank Hyland, an early-day trader at Telegraph Creek on the Stikine River. Hyland operated trading posts throughout northern British Columbia, competing successfully with the Hudson's Bay Co., and at one time printing his own currency.

DC 598.7 (957.5 km) **DJ 791.3** (1273.4 km) Access to Lower Post (unincorporated), at **Historical Mile 620,** via short gravel road.

DC 605.1 (967.6 km) **DJ 784.9** (1263.1 km) **Historic Milepost 627** marks official BC–YT border; Welcome to the Yukon sign. Monitor CB Channel 9 for police. The Alaska Highway (Yukon Highway 1) dips back into British Columbia several times before making its final crossing into the Yukon Territory near Morley Lake (**Milepost DC 751.5**).

NOTE: Kilometreposts on the Yukon Territory portion of the highway reflect historical mileposts. Kilometreposts on the British Columbia portion of the highway reflect actual driving distance. There is approximately a 40-kilometre difference at the BC–YT border between these measurements.

Northbound: Good paved highway with wide shoulders next 380 miles/611.5 km to Haines Junction, with the exception of some short sections of narrow road and occasional gravel breaks.

Southbound: Good sections of reconstructed road. Watch for more construction and rough, narrow, winding road and breaks in surfacing between border and Fort Nelson (approximately 321 miles/516.6 km).

DC 606.9 (1011.9 km) **DJ 783.1** (1260.2 km) Lucky Lake picnic area to south; ball diamond and 1.2-mile/2-km hiking trail to Liard River Canyon (watch for signs), observation platform with information panels at river. **Lucky Lake** is a popular local swimming hole for Watson Lake residents, who installed a water slide here. Relatively shallow, the lake warms up quickly in summer, making it one of the few area lakes where swimming is possible. Stocked with rainbow trout.

According to R. Coutts in *Yukon Places & Names,* Lucky Lake was named by American Army Engineer troops working on construction of the Alaska Highway in 1942: "A young woman set up a tent business and clients there referred to transactions as 'a change of luck.'"

DC 609.2 (1015.5 km) **DJ 780.8** (1256.5 km) Paved drive-through rest area with litter barrel and outhouses to north.

DC 610.4 (1017.5 km) **DJ 779.6** (1254.6 km) Weigh station.

DC 610.5 (1017.7 km) **DJ 779.5** (1254.4 km) **Mile 632.5. Campground Services** at Mile 632.5 is the largest and best equipped RV park in Watson Lake, the gateway to the Yukon. The park features 140 full or partial hookups and pull-throughs, tent sites, playground, firepits and a screened kitchen.

Coin-op showers, laundry and car wash. Good Sam Park. A food market stocks groceries, "chester fried" chicken, convenience items, movie rentals, fishing tackle, licenses and ice. Gasoline and diesel and ICG propane are available at the self-serve pumps. A licensed mechanic is available for repairs, alignments, tire changes, etc. Agents for Western Union money transfers. Open for business year-round, serving the traveler's needs for over 25 years! Phone (867) 536-7448. [ADVERTISEMENT]

Watson Lake

DC 612.9 (1021 km) **DJ 777.1** (1250.6 km) **Historic Milepost 635.** "Gateway to the Yukon," located 330 miles/531 km from Fort Nelson, 275 miles/443 km from Whitehorse. **Population:** 1,794. **Emergency Services: RCMP,** phone (867) 536-5555 (if no answer call 867/667-5555). **Fire Department,** phone (867) 536-2222. **Ambulance,** phone (867) 536-4444. **Hospital,** phone (867) 536-4444.

Visitor Information: Located in the Alaska Highway Interpretive Centre behind the Signpost Forest, north of the Alaska Highway; access to the centre is from the Campbell Highway. Open 8 A.M. to 8 P.M. daily, mid-May to September. Phone (867) 536-7469; fax (867) 536-2003. The town of Watson Lake provides a toll-free number (Lower 48 only) for information on local tractions; phone (800) 663-5248.

Elevation: 2,265 feet/690m. **Climate:** Average temperature in January is -16°F/-27°C, in July 59°F/15°C. Record high temperature 93°F/34°C in June 1950, record low -74°F/-59°C in January 1947. Annual snowfall is 90.6 inches. Driest month is April, wettest month is September. Average date of last spring frost is June 2; average date of first fall frost is Sept. 14. **Radio:** CBC 990. **Television:** Channel 8 and cable.

Private Aircraft: Watson Lake airport, 8 miles/12.9 km north on Campbell Highway; elev. 2,262 feet/689m; length 5,500 feet/1,676m and 3,530 feet/1,076m; asphalt; fuel 100, jet. Heliport and floatplane bases also located here. The Watson Lake airport terminal building was built in 1942. The log structure has been designated a Heritage Building.

In the late 1800s, Watson Lake was known as Fish Lake. The lake was later renamed Watson, for Frank Watson of Yorkshire, England. He gave up on the gold rush in 1898 to settle here on its shores with his Indian wife. Today, Watson Lake is an important service stop on the Alaska and Campbell highways (Campbell Highway travelers, fill your gas tanks here!); a communication and distribution centre for the southern Yukon; a base for trappers, hunters and fishermen; and a supply point for area mining and mineral exploration.

Watson Lake businesses are located along either side of the Alaska Highway. The lake itself is not visible from the Alaska Highway. Access to the lake, airport, hospital and Ski Hill is via the Campbell Highway (locally referred to as Airport Road). The ski area is about 4 miles/6.4 km out the Campbell Highway from town.

Watson Lake was an important point during construction of the Alaska Highway in 1942. The airport, built in 1941, was one of the major refueling stops along the Northwest Staging Route, the system of airfields through Canada to ferry supplies to Alaska and later lend-lease aircraft to Russia. Of the nearly 8,000 aircraft ferried through Canada, 2,618 were Bell P–39 Airacobras.

The Alaska Highway helped bring both people and commerce to this once isolated settlement. A post office opened here in July 1942. The economy of Watson Lake is based on services and also the forest products industry. White spruce and lodgepole pine are the two principal trees of the Yukon and provide a forest industry for the territory. White spruce grows straight and fast wherever adequate water is available, and it will grow to extreme old age without showing decay. The lodgepole pine developed from the northern pine and can withstand extreme cold, grow at high elevations and take full advantage of the almost 24-hour summer sunlight of a short growing season.

ACCOMMODATIONS/VISITOR SERVICES

There are several hotels/motels, restaurants and gas stations with unleaded, diesel and propane, automotive and tire repair. Dump stations available at local campgrounds and service stations. There are department, variety, grocery and hardware stores. The RCMP office is east of town centre on the Alaska Highway. There is 1 bank in Watson Lake—Canadian Imperial

---

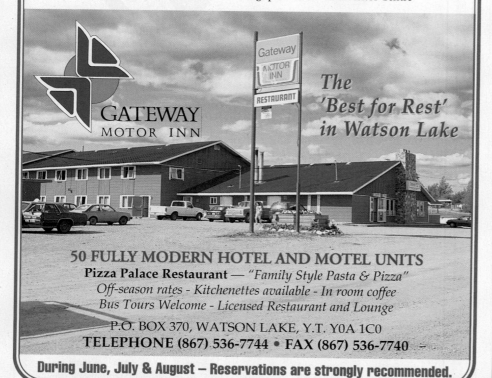
Bank of Commerce; it is open Monday through Thursday from 10 a.m. to 3 p.m., Friday 10 a.m. to 6 p.m., closed holidays. ATM available 24 hours.

Check at the Visitor Information Centre for locations of local churches. Dennis Ball Memorial Swimming Pool is open weekdays in summer. Lucky Lake waterslide is open on weekends in summer from 1–4 P.M.

Belvedere Motor Hotel, located in the centre of town, is Watson Lake's newest and finest hotel. It offers such luxuries as Jacuzzi tubs in the rooms, waterbeds and cable TV, and all at competitive prices. Dining is excellent, whether you decide to try the superb dining room menu or the coffee shop menu. Phone (867) 536-7712, fax (867) 536-7563. [ADVERTISEMENT]

Big Horn Hotel. New in 1993. 29 beautiful rooms. Centrally located on the Alaska Highway in downtown Watson Lake, YT. Our rooms are quiet, spacious, clean and they boast queen-size beds and complimentary coffee. You get quality at a reasonable price. Available to you are king-size motionless waterbeds, Jacuzzi rooms, kitchenette suites. We know you'll enjoy staying with us. Book ahead. Phone (867) 536-2020, fax

Welcome to North 60° Country!

NORTH 60° PETRO

Your Mileage Guide to Shell Stations Throughout the Yukon

Shell products are distributed by North 60° Petro at the following stations:

Alaska Hwy.

KM	MI	
1022	635	Watson Lake Shell
1294	804	Teslin Lake Motors
1345	836	Johnson's Crossing Lodge
1464	910	McCrae Shell
1465	911	Pioneer RV Park
1469	913	Whitehorse Shell
1477	918	Second Ave. Shell
		Yukon Tire Centre
		Granger Shell
1635	1016	Haines Junction
1743	1083	Talbot Arm Motel
1879	1168	White River Lodge
1931	1202	1202 Motor Inn

Atlin Road

KM	MI	
98	61	Pine Tree Services

Robert Campbell Hwy.

KM		
427	258	Faro Shell
364	220	Ross River

Silver Trail Hwy.

KM		
53	33	Heartland Services–Mayo

Klondike Hwy.

KM	MI	
105	65	Montana Services
116	73	Spirit Lake Resort
538	334	Stewart Crossing Shell
720	447	Central Shell

NORTH 60° PETRO

FINE FUELS. SUPER SERVICE. QUALITY LUBRICANTS.

Watson Lake Signpost Forest has more than 41,000 signs. (© Earl L. Brown, staff)

reservations (867) 536-7781; fax (867) 536-2724. [ADVERTISEMENT]

The turnoff for Watson Lake Yukon government campground is 2.4 miles/3.9 km west of the Signpost Forest via the Alaska Highway; see description at **Milepost DC 615.3**. There is a private campground at **Milepost DC 619.6**, 4.3 miles/6.9 km past the turnoff for the government campground; a private campground 2.4 miles/3.9 km east of the Signpost Forest on the Alaska Highway (see **Milepost DC 610.5**); and an RV park located downtown. ▲

Downtown R.V. Park, situated in the centre of town. 71 full-hookup stalls, 19 with pull-through parking; showers; laundromat. Town water. Free truck/trailer, motorhome wash with overnight stay. Easy walking distance to stores, garages, hotels, restaurants, liquor store, banking, churches, information centre and the world-famous Signpost Forest. Just across the street from Wye Lake Park. Excellent hiking trails. Phone (867) 536-2646 in summer, phone/fax (867) 536-2224 in winter. [ADVERTISEMENT] ▲

TRANSPORTATION

Air: No scheduled service. Helicopter charters available from Frontier Helicopters and Trans North Helicopters.

Bus: Scheduled service to Edmonton and Whitehorse via Coachways.

Taxi and **Car Rental:** Available.

ATTRACTIONS

The **Alaska Highway Interpretive Centre**, operated by Tourism Yukon, is well worth a visit. Located behind the Signpost Forest, north of the Alaska Highway, the centre offers a video on Yukon history and the Alaska Highway. Excellent slide presentation and displays, including photographs taken in the mid-1940s showing the construction of the Alaska Highway in

(867) 536-2021. [ADVERTISEMENT]

Watson Lake Hotel. The historic Watson Lake Hotel. We're right in the heart of Watson Lake's historical Signpost Forest. Enjoy northern hospitality at its finest. Ample parking on our 6 acres of property. Quiet outside modern units (renovated May 1993), boardwalk gift shops and espresso bar. Senior, government, military and corporate discounts. Phone for this area. The centre is open daily, May to mid-September. Free admission. Phone (867) 536-7469.

Northern Lights Centre. The only planetarium in North America featuring the myth and science of the northern lights. Using advanced video and laser technology, the centre offers 2 different presentations on the aurora borealis inside a 110-seat "Electric Sky" theatre environment. Also interactive displays. Afternoon and evening showings daily from May to September. Admission charged. Located across from the Signpost Forest. Get your Yukon Explorer's Passport stamped here. Phone (867) 536-STAR; Internet www.yukon.net/northern-lights.

The Watson Lake Signpost Forest, seen at the north end of town at the junction of the Alaska and Robert Campbell highways, was started by Carl K. Lindley of Danville,

IL, a U.S. Army soldier in Company D, 341st Engineers, working on the construction of the Alaska Highway in 1942. Travelers are still adding signs to the collection, which numbered 41,602 in September 1998. Visitors are encouraged to add a sign to the Signpost Forest. **Historic Milepost 635** is located at the Signpost Forest.

Special Events. The annual Watson Lake Rodeo (NRA-approved) is held at Lucky Lake in July. A parade, 8 main events and junior events are featured.

Wye Lake Park offers a picnic area and boardwalk trails for viewing birds. There is also a bandshell, kitchen shelter and wheelchair-accessible restrooms. The lake attracts both migrating birds (spring and fall) and resident species, such as nesting grebes. Native plants and flowers are identified by plaques. The development of this park was initiated by a local citizens group.

St. John the Baptist Anglican Church has a memorial stained-glass window designed by Yukon artist Kathy Spalding. Titled "Our Land of Plenty," the window features a scene just north of Watson Lake off the Campbell Highway.

Drive the Campbell Highway. This good gravel road offers an excellent wilderness highway experience. Motorists can travel the entire 373 miles/600 km of the Campbell Highway, stopping at Ross River and Faro en route, to junction with the Klondike Highway at Carmacks. Or drive north 52 miles/83 km from Watson Lake to Simpson Lake for picnicking, fishing and camping. (See CAMPBELL HIGHWAY section for details.)

Play golf at Upper Liard, 6 miles/9.6 km north of Watson Lake on the Alaska High-

way. The 9-hole, par-35 course has grass greens and is open daily May through September. Phone (867) 536-2477.

Explore the area. Take time to fish, canoe a lake, take a wilderness trek or sightsee by helicopter. Outfitters in the area offer guided fishing trips to area lakes. Trips can be arranged by the day or by the week. Check with the visitor information centre.

AREA FISHING: Watson Lake has grayling, trout and pike. McKinnon Lake (walk-in only), 20 miles/32 km west of Watson Lake, pike 5 to 10 lbs. Toobally Lake, string of lakes 14 miles/23 km long, 90 air miles/145 km east, lake trout 8 to 10 lbs.; pike 5 to 10 lbs.; grayling 1 to 3 lbs. Stewart Lake, 45 air miles/72 km north northeast; lake trout, grayling.

Alaska Highway Log

(continued)

Distance* from Dawson Creek (DC) is followed by distance from Delta Junction (DJ). Original mileposts are indicated in the text as Historical Mile.

*In Canada, mileages from Dawson Creek are based on actual driving distance, not historical mileposts, and kilometres are based on physical kilometreposts. Mileages from Delta Junction are also based on actual driving distance, not historical mileposts, but are followed by the metric conversion to kilometres.

YUKON HIGHWAY 1

DC 612.9 (1021 km) DJ 777.1 (1250.6 km) Watson Lake Signpost Forest at the junction of the Campbell Highway (Yukon

Route 4) and Alaska Highway. The first 6 miles/9.7 km of the Campbell Highway is known locally as Airport Road; turn here for access to visitor information (in the Alaska Highway Interpretive Centre), airport, hospital and ski hill.

The Campbell Highway leads north to Ross River and Faro (see CAMPBELL HIGHWAY section), to junction with the Klondike Highway to Dawson City. Campbell Highway travelers should fill gas tanks in Watson Lake.

DC 615.3 (1025 km) DJ 774.7 (1246.7 km) Turnoff to north for Watson Lake Recreation Park. Drive in approximately 2 miles/3 km for Watson Lake Yukon government campground; 55 gravel sites, most level, some pull-through, drinking water, kitchen shelters, outhouses, firepits, firewood and litter barrels. Camping fee $8. ▲

There is a separate group camping area and also a day-use area (boat launch, swimming, picnicking at Watson Lake). Follow signs at fork in access road. Trails connect all areas.

DC 618.5 (1030 km) DJ 771.5 (1241.6 km) Watch for livestock.

DC 619.6 (1032 km) DJ 770.4 (1239.8 km) Green Valley R.V. Park. Phone (867) 536-2276. Just 7 miles west of Watson Lake, quiet greenbelt area along Liard River. Friendly service, clean facilities. Pay phone. Serviced and unserviced sites, dump station, grassy tent sites, riverside camping, firepits, car wash, laundry, showers, grocery, coffee, pastries, ice, souvenirs, free gold panning, game room, fishing licenses and tackle. Fish for grayling and dollies. Pick wild strawberries and raspberries in season. Cold beer and off sales. Bikers welcome. Your hosts: Ralph and Marion Bjorkman. [ADVERTISEMENT] ▲

DC 620 (1032.4 km) DJ 770 (1239.2 km) Upper Liard River bridge. The Liard River heads in the St. Cyr Range in southcentral Yukon Territory and flows southeast into British Columbia, then turns east and north to join the Mackenzie River at Fort Simpson, NWT.

Liard River, grayling, lake trout, whitefish and northern pike.

DC 620.2 (1032.7 km) DJ 769.8 (1238.8 km) Historical Mile 642. UPPER LIARD VILLAGE, site of Our Lady of the Yukon Church. Food, lodging and camping. ▲

DC 620.3 (1033 km) DJ 769.7 (1238.7 km) Greenway's Greens golf course to south with 9 holes, par 35, grass greens, open daily in summer.

DC 620.8 (1033.7 km) DJ 769.2 (1237.9 km) Albert Creek bridge. Turnout with litter barrel to north at east end of bridge. A sign near here marks the first tree planting project in the Yukon. Approximately 200,000 white spruce seedlings were planted in the Albert Creek area in 1993.

DC 626.2 (1043 km) DJ 763.8 (1229.2 km) **Historic Milepost 649. Junction 37 Services.** See display ad this section.

Services here include gas, store with souvenirs, propane, car repair, car wash, laundromat, cafe, camping and lodging. ▲

Junction with the Cassiar Highway, which leads south to Yellowhead Highway 16. See CASSIAR HIGHWAY section.

DC 627 (1043.9 km) DJ 763 (1227.9 km) **Historic Mile 650. The Northern Beaver Post.** As with trading posts of the past, The Northern Beaver Post is an essential stop for any traveler. Here you will find quality 90 percent Canadian-made gifts and souvenirs which are as useful as they are decorative. In the friendly atmosphere of the Post, discover the largest inventoried family gift shop on the Alaska Highway. Enjoy Native and Eskimo arts and crafts, porcelain dolls, furs, wildflower books, cards and stamps. Licensed Beanie Baby dealer and Bradford plate dealer. Present this ad to receive a 10 percent discount on regular priced Ts and sweatshirts. Shipping available. Caravans and buses call for special early morning openings. 7 days a week, April–Oct., extended summer hours. Winter 9-8. Limited free RV parking. New, clean, nonsmok-

ing cabins with private washrooms. (Ask about our new Jacuzzi suites). Great food next door at newly built Wolfit Down Restaurant. On-site bakery; fresh breads and pastries. Homemade, full-course meals (just like Gramma's). Espresso, lattes, cappuccino. Licensed dining room and deck. Liquor to go. Clean washrooms. Caravans and bus tours welcome (reservations requested). For all your souvenir wolf collections. Also, Baby Nuggett RV Park Inc. currently being constructed. Peaceful, quiet and level 60–100 foot treed pull-through sites. Dry parking available in the beginning of the season. Some fully-serviced sites available later in the season. Phone for progress report (867) 536-2307; (867) 536-7666 after hours. ▲
[ADVERTISEMENT]

DC 627.3 (1044.5 km) DJ 762.7 (1227.4 km) Large double-ended gravel turnout and rest area with litter barrels, pit toilets and Watson Lake community map.

DC 630 (1050.8 km) DJ 760 (1223.1 km) Several hundred rock messages are spelled out along the highway here. The rock messages were started in summer 1990 by a Fort Nelson swim team.

DC 633 (1055.6 km) DJ 757 (1218.2 km) Gravel turnout to north.

DC 637.8 (1063.3 km) DJ 752.2 (1210.5 km) Microwave tower access road.

DC 639.8 (1066.5 km) DJ 750.2 (1207.3 km) *NOTE: Hill and sharp curve.*

DC 647.2 (1078.5 km) DJ 742.8 (1195.4 km) Turnout with litter barrel on Little Rancheria Creek to north.

Rancheria Falls at Milepost DC 695.2. The recreation site has a boardwalk trail to the falls. (© Beth Davidow)

DC 647.4 (1079 km) **DJ 742.6** (1195.1 km) Little Rancheria Creek bridge. Northbound winter travelers put on chains here.

DC 650.6 (1084 km) **DJ 739.4** (1189.9 km) Highway descends westbound to Big Creek.

DC 651.1 (1084.8 km) **DJ 738.9** (1189.1 km) Big Creek bridge, clearance 17.7 feet/5.4m. Turnout at east end of bridge.

DC 651.2 (1085 km) **DJ 738.8** (1189 km) Turnoff to north for Big Creek Yukon government day-use area, adjacent highway on Big Creek; gravel loop road, outhouses, firewood, kitchen shelter, litter barrels, picnic tables, drinking water.

DC 652.5 (1087.3 km) **DJ 737.5** (1186.8 km) Sign reads: "Northbound winter travelers chains may be removed."

DC 658.4 (1096.7 km) **DJ 731.6** (1177.4 km) Pull-through turnout south side of highway.

DC 662.3 (1102.9 km) **DJ 727.7** (1171.1 km) NorthwesTel microwave tower road to north.

NOTE: Recent highway reconstruction and straightening in this area has resulted in the displacement of many kilometreposts.

DC 664.1 (1105.8 km) **DJ 725.9** (1168.2 km) Double-ended turnout to north to Lower Rancheria River.

DC 664.3 (1106.2 km) **DJ 725.7** (1167.9 km) Bridge over Lower Rancheria River. For northbound travelers, the highway closely follows the Rancheria River west from here to the Swift River. Northern bush pilot Les Cook was credited with helping find the best route for the Alaska Highway between Watson Lake and Whitehorse. Cook's Rancheria River route saved engineers hundreds of miles of highway construction.

Rancheria River, fishing for Dolly Varden and grayling. ✦

DC 665.1 (1110.4 km) **DJ 724.9** (1166.6 km) Scenic viewpoint.

DC 667.2 (1113.7 km) **DJ 722.8** (1163.2 km) Turnout to south.

DC 667.6 (1114.3 km) **DJ 722.4** (1162.5 km) Large double-ended turnout with litter barrel to south.

DC 671.9 (1118.7 km) **DJ 718.1** (1155.6 km) Spencer Creek.

DC 673.4 (1121 km) **DJ 716.6** (1153.2 km) Improved highway and view of Cassiar Mountains westbound.

DC 677 (1126.9 km) **DJ 713** (1147.4 km) Turnout with litter barrel to south overlooking the Rancheria River. Trail down to river.

According to R.C. Coutts, author of *Yukon: Places & Names,* the Rancheria River was named by Cassiar miners working Sayyea Creek in 1875, site of a minor gold rush at the time. Rancheria is an old Californian or Mexican miners' term from the Spanish, meaning a native village or settlement. It is pronounced Ran-che-RI-ah.

DC 678.5 (1129.3 km) **DJ 711.5** (1145 km) George's Gorge, culvert.

DC 683.2 (1137 km) **DJ 706.8** (1137.4 km) NorthwesTel microwave tower to south.

DC 684 (1138.4 km) **DJ 706** (1136.2 km) Turnout with litter barrel overlooking Rancheria River. *CAUTION: Watch for livestock on or near highway in this area.*

DC 687.2 (1143.8 km) **DJ 702.8** (1131 km) **Historic Milepost 710.** Rancheria Hotel–Motel to south; gas, food, camping and lodging. Historic sign and interpretive panel on highway lodges. ▲

DC 687.4 (1143.9 km) **DJ 702.6** (1130.7 km) Turnoff to south for private campground (formerly Rancheria Yukon government campground) adjacent highway overlooking Rancheria River. The Rancheria is a tributary of the Liard River. ▲

DC 689.2 (1146.6 km) **DJ 700.8** (1127.8 km) Canyon Creek.

DC 690 (1148 km) **DJ 700** (1126.5 km) Highway follows the Rancheria River.

DC 692.5 (1152 km) **DJ 697.5** (1122.5 km) Young Creek.

DC 694.2 (1155 km) **DJ 695.8** (1119.7 km) **Historical Mile 717.5.** Abandoned building.

DC 695.2 (1156.5 km) **DJ 694.8** (1118.1 km) **Rancheria Falls** recreation site has a good gravel and boardwalk trail to the falls; easy 10-minute walk. Large parking area with toilets and litter barrels at trailhead.

DC 697.4 (1160 km) **DJ 692.6** (1114.6 km) Beautiful view of the Cassiar Mountains.

DC 698.4 (1161.6 km) **DJ 691.6** (1113 km) **Historical Mile 721.** Walker's Continental Divide; gas, food, camping and lodging. ▲

Walker's Continental Divide. Fresh baking daily, mouth-watering cinnamon rolls, rhubarb pie, muffins and tarts. Breakfast served all day—try our sourdough pancakes. Gift shop, hard ice cream. New motel, clean, comfortable, cozy rooms (nonsmoking rooms available). RV park with water and power hookups, pull-throughs, showers and trailer dump. Clean washrooms. Hospitality spoken here, free of charge. Phone/fax (867) 851-6451. [ADVERTISEMENT] ▲

DC 698.7 (1162 km) **DJ 691.3** (1112.5 km) Upper Rancheria River bridge, clearance 17.7 feet/5.4m. For northbound travelers, the highway leaves the Rancheria River.

DC 699.1 (1162.8 km) **DJ 690.9** (1111.9 km) Large gravel turnout to north with point of interest signs, outhouses and litter barrels. This 3,300-foot/1,000-m pass marks the Continental Divide, the water divide between rivers that drain into the Arctic Ocean via the Mackenzie River system (the Rancheria and Liard) and those that drain into the Pacific Ocean via the Yukon River system (the Swift and Teslin rivers). All rivers crossed by the Alaska Highway between here and Fairbanks, AK, drain into the Yukon River system.

DC 699.6 (1163.3 km) **DJ 690.4** (1111.1 km) **Historic Milepost 722. Private Aircraft:** Pine Lake airstrip 3 miles/4.8 km north; deserted WWII emergency airstrip; elev. 3,250 feet/991m; length 6,000 feet/1,829m; gravel, status unknown.

DC 702.2 (1168 km) **DJ 687.8** (1106.9 km) Swift River bridge. For northbound travelers, the highway now follows the Swift River west to the Morley River.

DC 706.2 (1174.5 km) **DJ 683.8** (1100.4 km) *Steep hill for westbound travelers.*

DC 709.7 (1180 km) **DJ 680.3** (1094.8 km) Seagull Creek.

DC 710 (1180.9 km) **DJ 680** (1094.3 km) **Historic Milepost 733, SWIFT RIVER.** Lodge with food, gas, lodging, car repair, pay phone and highway maintenance camp. Open year-round.

Swift River Lodge. Friendly haven in a beautiful mountain valley. Tasty cooking with a plentiful supply of coffee. Mouthwatering homemade pies and pastries fresh daily. Wrecker service, welding and repairs. Reasonable rates. Gas and diesel at some of the best prices on the highway. Clean restrooms; gifts; and public phone. [ADVERTISEMENT]

DC 710.5 (1181.5 km) **DJ 679.5** (1093.5 km) **Historical Mile 733.5.** The highway re-enters British Columbia for approximately 42 miles/68 km northbound.

DC 712.7 (1185 km) **DJ 677.3** (1090 km) Partridge Creek.

DC 716 (1190.3 km) **DJ 674** (1084.7 km) Gravel turnout with litter barrels.

DC 718.5 (1194.2 km) **DJ 671.5** (1080.6 km) Screw Creek.

DC 719.6 (1196 km) **DJ 670.4** (1078.9 km) **Historical Mile 743.** Turnout with litter barrel to south on **Swan Lake.** Fishing for trout and whitefish. The pyramid-shaped mountain to south is Simpson Peak. 🐟

DC 724.2 (1203.7 km) **DJ 665.8** (1071.5 km) Pull-through turnout to south.

DC 727.9 (1209.5 km) **DJ 662.1** (1065.5 km) Logjam Creek.

DC 735.8 (1222.5 km) **DJ 654.2** (1052.8 km) Smart River bridge. The Smart River flows south into the Cassiar Mountains in British Columbia. The river was originally called Smarch, after the Indian family of that name who lived and trapped in this area. The Smarch family currently includes well-known artists Keith and Jack Smarch.

DC 741.4 (1231.7 km) **DJ 648.6** (1043.8 km) Microwave tower access road to north.

DC 744.1 (1236 km) **DJ 645.9** (1039.4 km) Upper Hazel Creek.

DC 745.2 (1238 km) **DJ 644.8** (1037.7 km) Lower Hazel Creek.

DC 746.9 (1240.7 km) **DJ 643.1** (1034.9 km) Turnouts both sides of highway; litter barrel at south turnout.

DC 749 (1245 km) **DJ 641** (1031.5 km) Andrew Creek.

DC 751.5 (1249.2 km) **DJ 638.5** (1027.5 km) Morley Lake to north. The Alaska Highway re-enters the Yukon Territory northbound. This is the last of 7 crossings of the YT–BC border.

DC 752 (1250 km) **DJ 638** (1026.7 km) Sharp turnoff to north for **Morley River** Yukon government day-use area; large gravel parking area, picnic tables, kitchen shelter, water, litter barrels and outhouses.

Fishing.

DC 752.3 (1251 km) **DJ 637.7** (1026.2 km) Morley River bridge; turnout with litter barrel to north at east end of bridge. Morley River flows into the southeast corner of Teslin Lake. The river, lake and Morley Bay (on Teslin Lake) were named for W. Morley Ogilvie, assistant to Arthur St. Cyr on the 1897 survey of the Telegraph Creek–Teslin Lake route.

Morley Bay and **River,** good fishing near mouth of river for northern pike 6 to 8 lbs., best June to August, use small Red Devils;

grayling 3 to 5 lbs., in May and August, use small spinner; lake trout 6 to 8 lbs., June to August, use large spoon.

DC 752.9 (1252 km) **DJ 637.1** (1025.3 km) **Historic Milepost 777.7.** Morley River Lodge, food, gas, diesel, towing, tires, camping and lodging. Open year-round. ▲

Morley River Lodge. See display ad this section. ▲

DC 754.8 (1256 km) **DJ 635.2** (1022.2 km) *CAUTION: Watch for livestock on highway.*

DC 757.9 (1261 km) **DJ 632.1** (1017.2

km) Small marker to south (no turnout) reads: "In memory of Max Richardson 39163467, Corporal Co. F 340th Eng. Army of the United States; born Oct. 10, 1918, died Oct. 17, 1942. Faith is the victory."

DC 761.5 (1267.9 km) **DJ 628.5** (1011.4 km) Strawberry Creek.

DC 764.1 (1273.7 km) **DJ 625.9** (1007.3 km) Hayes Creek.

DC 769.6 (1282.5 km) **DJ 620.4** (998.4 km) **Historical Mile 797.** Food, lodging and camping. ▲

Dawson Peaks Resort & RV Park. Slow down folks! No need to drive any farther. Fishing's good, coffee's on, camping is easy and the rhubarb pie can't be beat. Couple that with our renowned Yukon hospitality and you'll have one of the best experiences on your trip. We're looking forward to seeing you this summer. [ADVERTISEMENT] ▲

DC 769.9 (1283 km) **DJ 620.1** (997.9 km) Food, gas and bar.

DC 776 (1292 km) **DJ 614** (988.1 km) **Nisutlin Bay Bridge,** longest water span on the Alaska Highway at 1,917 feet/584m. The Nisutlin River forms the "bay" as it flows into Teslin Lake here.

Good view northbound of the village of Teslin and Teslin Lake. Teslin Lake straddles the BC–YT border; it is 86 miles/138 km long, averages 2 miles/3.2 km across, and has an average depth of 194 feet/59m. The name is taken from the Indian name for the lake—Teslintoo ("long, narrow water").

Turnout with litter barrel and point of interest sign at south end of bridge, east side of highway.

Historic Milepost 804 at the north end of the bridge, west side of the highway; historic sign and interpretive panel, parking area, marina and day-use area with picnic tables and boat ramp. Turn west on side road here for access to Teslin village (description follows).

DC 776.3 (1294 km) **DJ 613.7** (987.6 km) Entering Teslin **(Historic Milepost 804)** at north end of bridge. Gas, food, camping and lodging along highway.

Yukon Motel Lakeshore Resort, just right (northbound) on the north side of Nisutlin Bridge. An excellent stop for a fresh lake trout dinner (or full menu), accompanied by good and friendly service topped off with a piece of fantastic rhubarb and strawberry pie (lots of fresh baking). Ice cream. New in 1998 ... visit our Yukon wildlife display. Five satellite TV channels. Open year-round, summer hours 6 A.M.–11 P.M. New lakeshore RV park (mosquito control area), 70 sites, full and partial hookups, 40 pull-throughs. "Good Sam Park"—washhouse rated TL 9.5. A real home away from home on the shore of beautiful Nisutlin Bay. Phone (867) 390-2575. [ADVERTISEMENT] ▲

Teslin

Located at **Historic Milepost 804,** 111 miles/179 km southeast of Whitehorse, 163 miles/263 km northwest of Watson Lake. **Population:** 482. **Emergency Services: RCMP,** phone (867) 390-5555 (if no answer call 867/667-5555). **Fire Department,** phone (867) 390-2222. **Nurse,** phone (867) 390-4444.

Elevation: 2,239 feet/682.4m. **Climate:** Average temperature in January, -7°F/-22°C, in July 57°F/14°C. Annual snowfall 66.2 inches/168.2 cm. Driest month April, wettest month July. Average date of last spring frost is June 19; first fall frost Aug. 19. **Radio:** CBC 940; CHONFM 90.5; CKRW 98.7. **Television:** Channel 13.

The village of Teslin, situated on a point of land at the confluence of the Nisutlin River and Teslin Lake, began as a trading post in 1903. Today the community consists of a trading post, Catholic church, health centre and post office. There is a 3-sheet regulation curling rink and a skating rink. A Native heritage centre is under development.

Teslin has one of the largest Native populations in Yukon Territory and much of the community's livelihood revolves around tra-

---

TESLIN ADVERTISERS

George Johnston
   Museum ....Ph. (867) 390-2550
Nisutlin Trading Post ....Ph. (867) 390-2521
Yukon Motel Lakeshore
   Resort ....N. end of the bridge

ditional hunting, trapping and fishing. In addition, some Tlingit residents are involved in the development of Native woodworking crafts (canoes, snowshoes and sleds); traditional sewn art and craft items (moccasins, mitts, moose hair tufting, gun cases); and the tanning of moose hides.

George Johnston Museum is located on the left side of the highway heading north. The museum, operated by the Teslin Historical Museum Society (phone 867/390-2550), is open daily, 9 A.M. to 7 P.M. in summer; minimal admission fee, wheelchair accessi-

ble. Get your Yukon Explorer's Passport stamped here. The museum displays items from gold rush days and the pioneer mode of living, Indian artifacts and many items of Tlingit culture. Website: www/yukon web.com/community/teslin/museum.

A Tlingit Indian, George Johnston (1884–1972) was an innovative individual, known for his trapping as well as his photography. With his camera he captured the life of the inland Tlingit people of Teslin and Atlin between 1910 and 1940. Johnston also brought the first car to Teslin, a 1928 Chevrolet. Since the Alaska Highway had not been built yet, George built a 3-mile road for his "Teslin taxi." In winter, he put chains on the car and drove it on frozen Teslin Lake. The '28 Chevy has been restored and is now on permanent display at the museum.

The Yukon Motel has an impressive display of Yukon wildlife.

Teslin is located west of the Alaska Highway, accessible via a short side road from the north end of Nisutlin Bay bridge. Nisutlin Trading Post in the village has groceries and

general merchandise. Gas, diesel and propane, car repair, gift shop, restaurants and motels are found along the Alaska Highway. The Teslin area has an air charter service, boat rentals and houseboat tours.

Nisutlin Trading Post, on short loop road, left northbound in Teslin Village. A pioneer store established in 1928, and located on the shore of Nisutlin Bay, an "arm" of Teslin Lake. This store handles a complete line of groceries, general merchandise including clothing, hardware, fishing tackle and licenses. Lottery tickets. Open all year 9 A.M. to 5:30 P.M. Closed Sunday. Founded by the late R. McCleery, Teslin pioneer, the trading post is now operated by Mr. and Mrs. Bob Hassard. Phone (867) 390-2521, fax 390-2103. [ADVERTISEMENT]

AREA FISHING: Guides and boats are available at Nisutlin Bay Marina. **Teslin Lake's Nisutlin Bay** (at the confluence of the Nisutlin River and Teslin Lake), troll the mud line in May and June for lake trout up to 25 lbs.; **Eagle Bay**, casting close to shore for northern pike to 15 lbs.; **Morley Bay**, excellent fishing for lake trout at south end of the bay's mouth, good fishing at the bay's shallow east side for northern pike to 10 lbs. **Morley River**, excellent fly fishing for grayling to 4 lbs. near river mouth and upriver several miles (by boat), fish deep water. ◂

Alaska Highway Log

(continued)

Distance* from Dawson Creek (DC) is followed by distance from Delta Junction (DJ). Original mileposts are indicated in the text as Historical Mile.

*In Canada, mileages from Dawson Creek are based on actual driving distance, not historical mileposts, and kilometres are based on physical kilometreposts. Mileages from Delta Junction are also based on actual driving distance, not historical mileposts, but are followed by the metric conversion to kilo-metres.

DC 777 (1295 km) **DJ 613** (986.5 km) **Historical Milepost 805. Private Aircraft:** Teslin airstrip to east; elev. 2,313 feet/705m; length 5,500 feet/1,676m; gravel; fuel 100, jet. Runway may be unusable during spring breakup.

DC 779.5 (1299 km) **DJ 610.5** (982.5 km) Fox Creek.

DC 784.3 (1306.7 km) **DJ 605.7** (974.7 km) **Historical Mile 812.** Mukluk Annie's; food, lodging and camping. ▲

Mukluk Annie's Salmon Bake. See display ad this section. ▲

DC 785.2 (1308 km) **DJ 604.8** (973.3 km) **Historical Mile 813.** Teslin Lake Yukon government campground to west; 27 sites (some level) in trees on **Teslin Lake**, water pump, litter barrels, kitchen shelter, firewood,

firepits, picnic tables. Camping fee $8. Fishing. Boat launch 0.3 mile/0.5 km north of campground. ◂▲

DC 785.3 (1308.2 km) **DJ 604.7** (973.1 km) Tenmile Creek.

DC 788.9 (1314 km) **DJ 601.1** (967.3 km) Lone Tree Creek.

DC 794.6 (1323 km) **DJ 595.4** (958.2 km) Deadman's Creek.

DC 800.8 (1333.3 km) **DJ 589.2** (948.2 km) Robertson Creek.

DC 801.6 (1334.4 km) **DJ 588.4** (946.9 km) **Historic Milepost 829.** Brooks' Brook. According to R.C. Coutts in *Yukon: Places & Names*, this stream was named by black Army engineers, who completed this section of road in 1942, for their company officer, Lieutenant Brooks.

DC 808.2 (1345 km) **DJ 581.8** (936.3 km)

Junction with the Canol Road (Yukon Highway 6) which leads northeast to the Campbell Highway. See the CANOL ROAD section for details.

Historic sign and interpretive panel about the Canol Project at junction. The Canol (Canadian Oil) Road was built in 1942–44 to provide access to oil fields at Norman Wells, NWT. Conceived by the U.S. War Dept., the $134 million project was abandoned soon after the war ended in 1945. Canol truck "graveyard" nearby.

DC 808.6 (1345.6 km) **DJ 581.4** (935.6 km) **Teslin River Bridge**, third longest water span on the highway (1,770 feet/539m), was constructed with a very high clearance above the river to permit steamers of the British Yukon Navigation Co. to pass under it en route from Whitehorse to Teslin. River steamers ceased operation on the Teslin River in 1942. Before the construction of the Alaska Highway, all freight and supplies for Teslin traveled this water route from Whitehorse.

DC 808.9 (1346 km) **DJ 581.11** (935.2 km) **Historic Milepost 836. JOHNSON'S**

CROSSING to east at north end of bridge; store, food, lodging and camping. One of the original lodges on the Alaska Highway, the history of Johnson's Crossing is related in Ellen Davignon's *The Cinnamon Mine*. Access to Teslin River; boat launch, no camping on riverbank. ▲

Johnson's Crossing Campground Services. Located across the Teslin River bridge, home of the "world famous cinnamon buns," including a small store with a full array of mouth-watering baked goods, souvenirs and groceries. Full-service RV campground facilities include treed pull-throughs, complete laundry and washhouse facilities, Shell gasoline products, cold beer and ice, and great fishing. Great view from our new facilities and motel units. Treat yourselves to the historically scenic Km 1346 (Mile 836) Alaska Highway, YT Y1A 9Z0. Phone (867) 390-2607. [ADVERTISEMENT] ▲

Teslin River, excellent grayling fishing from spring to late fall, 10 to 15 inches, use spinner or red-and-white spoons for spinning or black gnat for fly-fishing. King salmon in August. ⬤

Canoeists report that the Teslin River is wide and slow, but with gravel, rocks and weeds. Adequate camping sites on numerous sand bars; boil drinking water. Abundant wildlife—muskrat, porcupine, moose, eagles and wolves—also bugs and rain. Watch for bear. The Teslin enters the Yukon River at Hootalinqua, an old steamboat landing and supply point (under restoration). Roaring Bull rapids: choppy water. Pull out at Carmacks. Inquire locally about river conditions before setting out.

DC 809.1 (1346.5 km) **DJ 580.9** (934.8 km) Access road east to the Teslin River. The Big Salmon Range, also to the east, parallels the Teslin. For Alaska-bound travelers, the highway now swings west.

DC 812.8 (1352.5 km) **DJ 577.2** (928.9 km) Little Teslin Lake on south side of highway.

DC 819.8 (1364 km) **DJ 570.2** (917.6 km) In mid-June, the roadside is a profusion of purple Jacob's ladder and yellow dandelions.

DC 820.3 (1364.8 km) **DJ 569.7** (916.8 km) Seaforth Creek bridge.

DC 820.4 (1365 km) **DJ 569.6** (916.6 km) Large turnout to south; picnic area.

DC 820.6 (1365.3 km) **DJ 569.4** (916.3 km) Squanga Lake to northwest. Named Squanga by Indians for a type of whitefish of the same name found in the lake. Watch for **Historic Milepost 843**, with historic sign about Squanga Lake flightstrip. Look for the eagle's nest in the old observation tower.

Private Aircraft: Squanga Lake airstrip, 1 N; elev. 2,630 feet/802m; length 6,000 feet/965m; gravel, summer only, current status unknown; no services.

DC 821 (1366 km) **DJ 569** (915.7 km) Turnoff to northwest to **Squanga Lake** Yukon government campground: 13 sites, kitchen shelter, drinking water. Small boat launch. Fishing for northern pike, grayling, whitefish, rainbow and burbot. ⬤▲

DC 827.5 (1376.8 km) **DJ 562.5** (905.2 km) White Mountain, to the southeast, was named by William Ogilvie during his 1887 survey, for Thomas White, then Minister of the Interior. The Yukon government introduced mountain goats to this area in 1981.

DC 836.8 (1392.5 km) **F 651.2** (1048 km) **Historic Milepost 866. Junction,** commonly known as **JAKE'S CORNER;** gas, food and lodging. There's also a large collection on the premises of artifacts from the Canol Project, Alaska Highway construction, and the gold rush and other antiques.

Jake's Corner Inc. See display ad this section.

> **Junction** with Yukon Highway 7 south to Atlin, a very scenic spot that is well worth a side trip (see ATLIN ROAD section). This turnoff also provides access to Yukon Highway 8 to Carcross and Klondike Highway 2 to Skagway, AK (see TAGISH ROAD and KLONDIKE HIGHWAY 2 sections for details).

There are 2 versions of how Jake's Corner got its name. In 1942, the U.S. Army Corps of Engineers set up a construction camp here to build this section of the Alcan Highway and the Tagish Road cutoff to Carcross for the Canol pipeline. (The highway south to Atlin, BC, was not constructed until 1949–50.) The camp was under the command of Captain Jacobson, thus Jake's Corner. However, another version that predates the Alcan construction is that Jake's Corner was named for Jake Jackson, a Teslin Indian who camped in this area on his way to Carcross. Roman "Jake" Chaykowsky (1900–1995) operated Jake's Corner Service here for many years. It was known locally as The Crystal Palace, after the first lodge Chaykowsky had owned at Judas Creek, just up the road.

DC 843.2 (1402.7 km) **DJ 546.8** (880 km) Judas Creek bridge.

DC 850 (1413.5 km) **DJ 540** (869 km) Turnoff for **Marsh Lake** resort; boating and excellent fishing for grayling and northern pike. ⬤

DC 851.6 (1416 km) **DJ 538.4** (866.4 km) Several access roads along here which lead to summer cottages. Marsh Lake is a popular recreation area for Whitehorse residents.

DC 852.7 (1417.8 km) **DJ 537.3** (864.7 km) Good view of Marsh Lake to west. The highway parallels this beautiful lake for several miles. Marsh Lake (elev. 2,152 feet/656m) is part of the Yukon River system. It is approximately 20 miles/32 km long and was named in 1883 by Lt. Frederick Schwatka, U.S. Army, for Yale professor Othniel Charles Marsh.

DC 854.4 (1421 km) **DJ 535.6** (861.9 km) **Historic Milepost 883,** Marsh Lake Camp historic sign. Boat ramp turnoff to west.

DC 854.8 (1421.2 km) **DJ 535.2** (861.3 km) Caribou Road leads northwest to Airplane Lake; hiking trail, good skiing and snowmachining in winter. This road was bulldozed out to get men and equipment

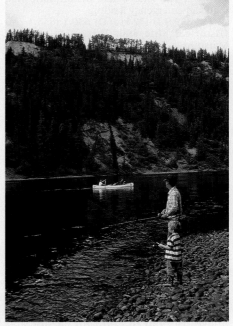

Fishing along the Teslin River, which flows into the Yukon River. The river offers excellent grayling fishing.
(© Earl L. Brown, staff)

into a small lake where an airplane had made an emergency landing.

DC 859.9 (1432 km) DJ 530.1 (853.1 km) **Historical Mile 890.** Turnoff to west for Marsh Lake Yukon government campground via 0.4-mile/0.6-km gravel loop road: 47 sites, most level, some pull-through; outhouses, firewood, firepits, litter barrels, picnic tables, kitchen shelter, water pump. Camping fee $8. ▲

For group camping and day-use area, follow signs near campground entrance. Day-use area includes sandy beach, change house, picnic area, playground, kitchen shelter and boat launch.

DC 861.1 (1433.9 km) DJ 528.9 (851.2 km) M'Clintock River, named by Lieutenant Schwatka for Arctic explorer Sir Francis M'Clintock. This river flows into the north end of Marsh Lake. Boat ramp turnoff to west at north end of bridge. M'Clintock River is narrow, winding and silty with thick brush along shoreline. However, it is a good river for boat trips, especially in late fall.

DC 864.3 (1437 km) DJ 525.7 (846 km) Bridge over Kettley's Canyon.

DC 867.3 (1441.8 km) DJ 522.7 (841.2 km) **Historic Milepost 897.** Yukon River bridge. Turnout to north for day-use area and boat launch on **Yukon River** at Marsh Lake bridge near Northern Canada Power

Commission (NCPC) control gate. Point of interest sign and litter barrels. From here (elev. 2,150 feet/645m) the Yukon River flows 1,980 miles/3,186 km to the Bering Sea. Good fishing for grayling, jackfish and some trout. ◄

DC 873.5 (1453.3 km) DJ 516.5 (831.2 km) **Historical Mile 904. Sourdough Country Campsite RV Park**, just 15 minutes from downtown Whitehorse. Good Sam. If you're looking for privacy and relaxation, then this is your destination! Many treed sites, marked walking trails—pets welcome. Our spacious pull-through sites have water, 15/30 amp power and cable TV. Laundromat, car wash and dump station. *Clean private washrooms.* From our guests: "After over a month on the road, the best showers/washrooms we encountered were at Sourdough Country Campsite. We'll be back!" (A. and A. Brown). We invite you to see for yourself! Phone (867) 668-2961. [ADVERTISEMENT] ▲

DC 874.4 (1455 km) DJ 515.6 (829.7 km) **Historical Mile 905.** Restaurant, convenience store, gas, diesel, propane, car repair and rock shop here.

Carcross Corner Services. See display ad this section.

Yukon Rock Shop. See display ad this section.

Junction with Klondike Highway 2 (Carcross Road) which leads south to Carcross and Skagway. See KLONDIKE HIGHWAY 2 section.

DC 874.6 (1455.3 km) DJ 515.4 (829.4

km) Whitehorse city limits. Incorporated June 1, 1950, Whitehorse expanded in 1974 from its original 2.7 square miles/6.9 square kilometres to 162 square miles/421 square kilometres.

DC 875.6 (1456.9 km) DJ 514.4 (827.8 km) Kara Speedway to west.

DC 875.9 (1457.4 km) DJ 514.1 (827.3 km) Cowley Creek.

DC 876.8 (1459 km) DJ 513.2 (825.9 km) **Historical Mile 906. Wolf Creek** Yukon government campground to east. An 0.8-mile/ 1.3-km gravel loop road leads through this campground: 49 sites, most level, some pull-through; kitchen shelters, water pumps, picnic tables, firepits, firewood, outhouses, litter barrels, playground. Wolf Creek self-guiding trail; varied and abundant plant life, views of and access to Yukon River. Camping fee $8. Fishing in Wolf Creek for grayling. ◄▲

DC 878 (1461 km) DJ 512 (824 km) Meadow Lakes Golf and Country Club, 9-hole, par 36 course; cart rentals, club rentals, licensed clubhouse.

DC 879.4 (1463 km) DJ 510.6 (821.7 km) Highway crosses abandoned railroad tracks of the White Pass & Yukon Route (WP&YR) narrow-gauge railroad. Construction of the WP&YR began in May 1898 at the height of the Klondike Gold Rush. Completion of the railway in 1900 linked the port of Skagway, AK, with Whitehorse, YT, providing passenger and freight service for thousands of gold seekers. The WP&YR ceased operation in 1982, but started limited service again in 1988 between Skagway and Fraser. (See Railroads in the TRAVEL PLANNING section for current schedule.)

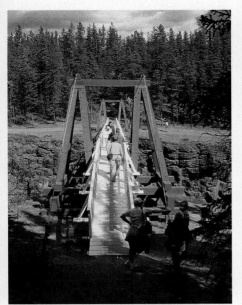

Footbridge across Miles Canyon provides good photo opportunities.

(© Earl L. Brown, staff)

DC 879.6 (1463.3 km) **DJ 510.4** (821.4 km) Point of interest sign about 135th meridian to east; small turnout. Gas station.

DC 879.8 (1463.7 km) **DJ 510.2** (821.1 km) **Historic Milepost 910.** Historic sign reads: "McCrae originated in 1900 as a flag stop on the newly-constructed White Pass & Yukon Railway. During WWII, this area served as a major service and supply depot, a major construction camp and a recreation centre." McCrae truck stop to east.

DC 880 (1464 km) **DJ 510** (820.7 km) **Historical Mile 910.5. Fireweed R.V. Services.** See display ad this section.

DC 880.4 (1464.5 km) **DJ 509.6** (820.1 km) Turnoff to west for Whitehorse Copper Mines (closed). Road to east leads to Yukon River.

DC 881 (1465.5 km) **DJ 509** (819.1 km) **Historic Milepost 911.** Site of Utah Construction Co. Camp. Campground to east.

Pioneer R.V. Park. See display ad this section. ▲

DC 881.3 (1466 km) **DJ 508.7** (818.6 km) White Pass & Yukon Route's Utah siding to east. This was also the site of an Army camp where thousands of soldiers were stationed during construction of the Alaska Highway.

DC 881.7 (1466.6 km) **DJ 508.3** (818 km) Sharp turnoff to east (watch for camera viewpoint sign) to see **Miles Canyon.** Drive down side road 0.3 mile/0.5 km to fork. The right fork leads to Miles Canyon parking lot. From the parking area it is a short walk to the Miles Canyon bridge; good photo spot. Cross bridge for easy hiking trails overlooking Yukon River.

A 1.1-mile/1.7-km hiking trail from the bridge leads to the historic site of **Canyon City**, a gold rush settlement that existed from 1897 to 1900 as a portage point around Miles Canyon and Whitehorse Rapids. Two tramways, each several miles long, transported goods along the east and west sides of the river. Completion of the White Pass & Yukon Route in 1900 made the trams obsolete, and the settlement was abandoned. Canyon City is currently undergoing archae-

ological excavation. Interpreter on site weekdays in July and part of August. No restrooms or litter barrels available at site; plan accordingly.

The left fork on this side road leads to Schwatka Lake Road, which follows the lake and intersects the South Access Road into Whitehorse. Turnouts along road overlook Miles Canyon.

DC 881.9 (1466.9 km) **DJ 508.1** (817.7 km) Riding stable with daily trail rides in summer.

DC 882.6 (1468 km) **DJ 507.4** (816.5 km) **Historical Mile 912. Philmar RV Service and Supply.** See display ad this section.

DC 882.9 (1468.5 km) **DJ 507.1** (816.1 km) **Mountain Ridge Motel & RV Park.** See display ad this section. ▲

DC 883.2 (1468.9 km) **DJ 506.8** (815.6 km) **Historical Mile 913. Whitehorse Shell.** See display ad this section.

DC 883.7 (1469.7 km) **DJ 506.3** (814.8 km) Turnout to east with litter barrel, outhouses and information sign.

DC 884 (1470.2 km) **DJ 506** (814.3 km) **Hi-Country R.V. Park.** Good Sam. New facilities to serve the traveler. Large wooded

sites, full hookups, 30-amp power, cable TV, dump station, hot clean showers, some serviced sites. Picnic tables and firepits, gift shop with wildlife display. Conveniently located on the highway at the south access to Whitehorse. Just 2 minutes by vehicle to Miles Canyon, the Beringia Centre and the Transportation Museum. Mile 913.4 Alaska Highway. P.O. Box 6081, Whitehorse, YT Y1A 5L7; phone (867) 667-7445, fax (867) 668-6342. Toll-free reservations 1-877-458-3806. See display ad this section. ▲

[ADVERTISEMENT]

DC 884 (1470.2 km) **DJ 506** (814.3 km). First exit northbound for Whitehorse. Exit

east for Robert Service Way (also known as South Access Road) to Whitehorse via 4th Avenue and 2nd Avenue. At Mile 1.4/2.3 km on this access road is the side road to Miles Canyon and Schwatka Lake; at Mile 1.6/2.6 km is Robert Service Campground (tent camping only) with a picnic area for day use; at Mile 2.6/4.2 km is the SS *Klondike* National Historic Site, turn left for downtown Whitehorse. ▲

DC 884.5 (1471.1 km) **DJ 505.5** (813.5 km) Government weigh scale and vehicle inspection station to west.

DC 885.3 (1472.3 km) **DJ 504.7** (812.2 km) New (1998) entrance to Yukon Beringian Centre (see description next milepost).

DC 885.7 (1472.9 km) **DJ 504.3** (811.6 km) **Yukon Beringia Interpretive Centre** traces the Ice Age in Yukon, which unlike

Whitehorse Vicinity

N W E S

To Dawson City

To Fairbanks 2

MacPherson

Alaska Highway 1

Crestview

Yukon River

Porter Creek Mall

Wann Rd.

Porter Creek

Mountain View Golf Course

Fish Lake Road

Range Road

Kopper King

Takhini

Yukon College, Yukon Archives, Yukon Arts Centre

Marwell

Long Lake Road

Valleyview

McIntyre

Two Mile Hill

Granger

Hillcrest

Downtown (See detailed map this section)

Transportation Museum

Yukon Beringia Interpretive Centre

Grey Mountain Nature Trail

Riverdale

Airport

Dam and Fish Ladder

Schwatka Lake

Yukon Gardens

South Access Road

Chadburn Lake Road

Alaska Highway

Miles Canyon

White Pass & Yukon Route

Yukon River

1

To Dawson Creek

MacRae

the rest of Canada, was ice-free. The Blue Fish Caves near Old Crow reputedly hold the earliest evidence of humans in the New World. Displays at the centre trace the science and myth of an Ice Age subcontinent inhabited by great woolly mammoths, giant short-faced bears, lions, scimitar cats, camels and Jefferson's Ground Sloth. Ice Age artifacts include a cast of the largest woolly mammoth skeleton ever recovered. Open daily late May to mid-September. Theatre, gift shop and cafe. Phone (867) 667-8895, fax (867) 667-8844.

DC 885.8 (1473.1 km) DJ 504.2 (811.4 km) Yukon Transportation Museum features exhibits on all forms of transportation in the North (see Attractions in description of Whitehorse following for more details). A mural on the front of the museum depicts the methods of transportation used in construction of the Alaska Highway in 1942. The 16-by-60-foot/5-by-8-m mural was painted by members of the Yukon Art Society. Open mid-May to mid-September. Admission fee.

Cairns in front of the museum commemorate 18 years of service on the Alaska Highway (1946–64) by the Corps of Royal Canadian Engineers. Near this site, the U.S. Army officially handed over the Alaska Highway to the Canadian Army on April 1, 1946.

Yukon Transportation Museum. See display ad this section.

DC 886.2 (1473.8 km) DJ 503.8 (810.7 km) Turnoff to east for Whitehorse International Airport. Built for and used by both U.S. and Canadian forces during WWII. Watch for the DC–3 weathervane (see Attractions in description of Whitehorse following for more details).

DC 887.4 (1475.6 km) DJ 502.6 (808.8

RCMP in red serge poses for photo in front of SS Klondike. (© Earl L. Brown, staff)

km) Second (and last) exit northbound for Whitehorse. North access road to Whitehorse (exit east) is via Two-Mile Hill and 4th Avenue. Access to private RV park. At Mile 1.2/1.9 km on this access road is Qwanlin Mall.

Alaska Highway log continues on page 156. Description of Whitehorse follows.

Whitehorse

Historic Milepost 918. Located on the upper reaches of the Yukon River in Canada's subarctic at latitude 61°N. Whitehorse is 100 miles/160 km from Haines Junction; 109 miles/175 km from Skagway, AK; 250 miles/241 km from Haines, AK; and 396 miles/637 km from Tok, AK. **Population: 23,474. Emergency Services: RCMP, Fire Department, Ambulance, Hospital,** phone 911.

Visitor Information: Tourism Yukon's Visitor Reception Centre is located next to

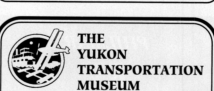

the Yukon Territorial Government Building on 2nd Avenue. Visitor guides and touch-screen terminals are available; 15-minute film on the Yukon; daily updated information on accommodations, weather and road conditions; printout information on attractions, restaurants or events in Whitehorse. The centre is open mid-May to mid-September daily 8 A.M. to 8 P.M.; phone (867) 667-2915. Or contact Tourism Yukon, Box 2703, Whitehorse, YT Y1A 2C6; phone (867) 667-5340; fax (867) 667-3546; Internet www.touryukon.com.

The city of Whitehorse offers year-round visitor information through their Tourism Coordinator; phone (867) 668-8687. Through the year 2000, Whitehorse is celebrating many gold rush anniversaries; their Anniversary Coordinator can be reached at (867) 668-8665. Phone either of these numbers for information or write: Tourism Coordinator, City of Whitehorse, 2121 Second Avenue, Whitehorse, YT Y1A 1C2. Access up-to-date information on events, accommodations and attractions on the City of Whitehorse Internet web page at www.city.whitehorse.yk.ca.

SS *Klondike* greets the visitor arriving in Whitehorse from the South. This site, operated by Parks Canada, has a visitor centre with helpful information for tourists.

Elevation: 2,305 feet/703m. **Climate:** Wide variations are the theme here with no two winters alike. The lowest recorded temperature is -62°F/-52°C and the warmest 94°F/35°C. Mean temperature for month of January is -6°F/-21°C and for July 57°F/14°C.

Whitehorse

In Yukon, phone toll-free 1-877-456-ROAD(7623) for road conditions.

Annual precipitation is 10.3 inches, equal parts snow and rain. On June 21 Whitehorse enjoys 19 hours, 11 minutes of daylight and on Dec. 21 only 5 hours, 37 minutes. **Radio:** CFWH 570, CBC network with repeaters throughout territory; CBC Montreal; CKRW 610, local; CHON-FM 98.1. **Television:** CBC–TV live, colour via ANIK satellite, Canadian network; WHTV, NADR (First Nation issues), local cable; CanCom stations via satellite, many channels. **Newspapers:** *Whitehorse Star* (weekdays); *Yukon News* (twice-weekly).

Private Aircraft: Whitehorse International Airport, 3 runways; has approach over

city and an abrupt escarpment; elev. 2,305 feet/703m; main runway length 7,200 feet/2,195m; surfaced; fuel 80, 100, jet fuel available. Customs clearance available.

Floatplane base on Schwatka Lake above Whitehorse Dam (take the South Access Road from Alaska Highway and turn on road by the railroad tracks).

DESCRIPTION

Whitehorse has been the capital of Yukon Territory since 1953, and serves as the centre for transportation, communications and supplies for Yukon Territory and the Northwest Territories.

The downtown business section of Whitehorse lies on the west bank of the

---

WHITEHORSE ADVERTISERS

A Taste of '98 Yukon River
Tours ....Ph. (867) 633-4767
Best Western
Gold Rush Inn ....411 Main St.
Bonanza Inn ....Ph. (867) 668-4545
Broke BookWorms, The ....4230 4th Ave.
Canadian Heritage ....Ph. (800) 661-0486
Casey's Bed & Breakfast...Ph. (867) 668-7481
Chilkoot Brewing Co. .....Ph. (867) 668-4183
City of Whitehorse...........Ph. (867) 668-8687
Coffee • Tea & Spice ....Qwanlin Mall
Dairy Queen.........................2nd Ave. at Elliott
Delta Western/
Totem Oil....................See ad for locations
Edgewater Hotel, The .....Ph. (867) 667-2572
Four Seasons
Bed & Breakfast ....Ph. (867) 667-2161
Frantic Follies ......Westmark Whitehorse Hotel
Go Wild Tours &
T-Shirts....................Ph. (867) 668-2411
Happy Daze R.V. Center...Ph. (867) 667-7069
Hawkins House Bed &
Breakfast ....Ph. (867) 668-7638
Hi-Country R.V. Park......Mile 913.4 Alaska Hwy.
High Country Inn ....Ph. (800) 554-4471
Historical House
Bed & Breakfast ....Ph. (867) 668-3907
Klondike Recreational
Rentals Ltd. ....Ph. (867) 668-2200
Klondike Rib &
Salmon BBQ ....Ph. (867) 667-7554
Kluane National Park and
Reserve ....Ph. (867) 634-7250
Learning to Fly World Class
Fly Shop......................Ph. (867) 633-5570
MacBride Museum ....Ph. (867) 667-2709
MacKenzie's RV Park......Km 1484 Alaska Hwy.
Mac's Fireweed Books................203 Main St.
Main Man, The ....Ph. (867) 633-6139
Meadows Bed and
Breakfast.......................Ph. (867) 668-5713
Midnight Sun Gallery & Gifts.....205C Main St.
Murdoch's ....207 Main St.
M.V. Schwatka Yukon
River Cruise ....Ph. (867) 668-4716

Norcan Sales, Rentals,
Leasing ....Ph. (867) 668-2137
North West Company
Trading Post, The.........Next to bus depot
Pioneer RV Park...............Ph. (867) 668-5944
Pizza Hut ....Ph. (867) 667-6766
Pot O' Gold ....4th Ave. & Wood
Qwanlin Mall, The.............4th Ave. & Ogilvie
River View Hotel..............Ph. (867) 677-7801
Rocky Mountain
Voyageurs ....Ph. (867) 633-4836
Sandor's............................Ph. (867) 667-6171
Select Reservations ....Ph. (867) 667-2161
Special Discoveries..........Ph. (867) 667-6765
Spring Shop, The ....Mile 922 Alaska Hwy.
S.S. *Klondike* National Historical
Site ....Ph. (867) 634-7250
Stop In Family Hotel........Ph. (867) 668-5558
Stratford Motel ....Ph. (867) 667-4243
Sourdough Country
Campsite ....Ph. (867) 668-2961
Spirit Bear Retreat...............Ph. (867) 667-2288
Takhini Hot Springs.......Takhini Hot Springs Rd.
Three Beans Natural Foods......Ph. (867) 668-4908
Town & Mountain
Hotel, The ....Ph. (867) 668-7644
Trail of '98 RV Park..........Ph. (867) 668-3768
Trails North Car & Truck
Stop Ltd. ....Mile 922 Alaska Hwy.
Up North Bed & Breakfast, Boat &
Canoe Rentals ....Ph. (867) 667-7905
Wharf On Fourth, The ....Ph. (867) 667-7473
Westmark Klondike Inn......Ph. (800) 544-0970
Westmark Whitehorse ....Ph. (800) 544-0970
Whitehorse Performance
Centre ....4th Ave. at Jarvis
Whitehorse Shell ....Mile 913 Alaska Hwy.
White Pass & Yukon
Route ....Ph. (867) 668-RAIL
Yukon Inn, The.........................4220 4th Ave.
Yukon Mining Co. ....4051 4th Ave.
Yukon Radiator...................108 Industrial Rd.
Yukon Tire Centre Ltd. ......107 Industrial Rd.
Yukon Transportation
Museum ....Ph. (867) 668-4792

Yukon River. The Riverdale subdivision is on the east side. The low mountains rising behind Riverdale are dominated by Canyon Mountain, known locally as Grey Mountain. Wolf Creek, Hillcrest and Granger subdivisions lie south of the city; McIntyre subdivision is to the west; and Porter Creek, Takhini and Crestview subdivisions are north of the city. The Takhini area is the location of the Yukon College campus.

Downtown Whitehorse is flat and marked at its western limit by a rising escarpment dominated by the Whitehorse International Airport. Originally a woodcutter's lot, the airstrip was first cleared in 1920 to accommodate 4 U.S. Army planes on a test flight from New York to Nome. Access to the city is by Two-Mile Hill from the north and by Robert Service Way (South Access Road) from the south; both connect with the Alaska Highway.

In 1974, the city limits of Whitehorse were expanded from the original 2.7 square miles/6.9 square kilometres to 162 square miles/421 square kilometres, making Whitehorse at one time the largest metropolitan area in Canada. More than two-thirds of the

View down Main Street, one of the shopping districts in Whitehorse. (© Earl L. Brown, staff)

Whitehorse
Welcomes you!

Summer Events

This is your year to visit the Yukon!

June to August
"Summer Arts in the Park"
LePage Park

April 30-May 2
Yukon Trade Show

June
Yukon International Storytelling Festival

June 21
Summer Solstice

June 21
Commissioners Potlatch

July 1
Canada Day. Event of the summer! Parade, all day and evening entertainment. Too much fun! All welcome.

July 1
Great Canadian Rubber Ducky Race

July 3
Peter Gzwoski Invitational Golf Tournament

July 9-11
Yukon Rodeo

July 9-11
Annual Dustball Tournament

July 17
Go for Gold Sister Cities Golf Tournament

August 13-16
Sourdough Yukon Bathtub Race

August
Klondike Harvest Fair Rotary Peace Park 668-6864

September 10-11
Klondike Road Relay - Skagway to Whitehorse. Huge event with teams from Canada and U.S.

October 18-22
Francophile Festival 668-2663

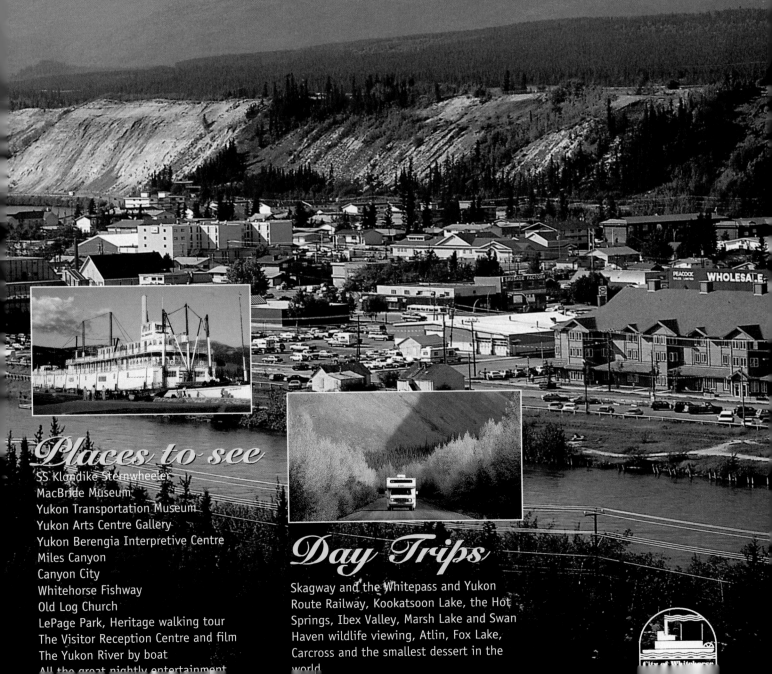

Whitehorse welcomes visitors travelling the Alaska Highway. Take time to stay in the Capital of Yukon and enjoy some of our warm Yukon hospitality. There is lots to see and do in Whitehorse and the surrounding areas: great Fishing, beautiful Hotsprings, trips on the historic Yukon River, a walking tour of our downtown, great shopping, exciting entertainment from Vaudeville to Bach, an interpreted River Walk, Golf under the midnight sun, wildlife viewing, restaurants both casual and chic, tons of summer events and a gorgeous new Visitor Reception Centre with easy access RV Parking.

Whitehorse provides RV Parking, at the waterfront and throughout the city core. We have some of the best RV Campgrounds surrounding us, with the nicest hosts you would wish to meet. Please take your time to enjoy us for a few days. Stop in at the City Hall for more information, sign our guest book and collect your city pin.
Call or write ahead to

Tourism,
City of Whitehorse,
2121, 2nd Avenue
Whitehorse, Yukon
(867) 668-8687
F(867)668-8384

www.city.whitehorse.yk.ca

Places to see

SS Klondike Sternwheeler
MacBride Museum
Yukon Transportation Museum
Yukon Arts Centre Gallery
Yukon Berengia Interpretive Centre
Miles Canyon
Canyon City
Whitehorse Fishway
Old Log Church
LePage Park, Heritage walking tour
The Visitor Reception Centre and film
The Yukon River by boat
All the great nightly entertainment

Day Trips

Skagway and the Whitepass and Yukon Route Railway, Kookatsoon Lake, the Hot Springs, Ibex Valley, Marsh Lake and Swan Haven wildlife viewing, Atlin, Fox Lake, Carcross and the smallest dessert in the world population of Yukon Territory live in the city. Whitehorse is the hub of a network of about 2,664 miles/4,287 km of all-weather roads serving Yukon Territory.

HISTORY, ECONOMY

When the White Pass & Yukon Route railway was completed in July 1900, connecting Skagway with the Yukon River, Whitehorse came into being as the northern terminus. Here the famed river steamers connected the railhead to Dawson City, and some of these boats made the trip all the way to St. Michael, a small outfitting point on Alaska's Bering Sea coast.

Klondike stampeders landed at Whitehorse to dry out and repack their supplies after running the famous Whitehorse Rapids. (The name Whitehorse was in common use by the late 1800s; it is believed that the first miners in the area thought that the foaming rapids resembled white horses' manes and so named the river rapids.) The rapids are no longer visible since construction of the Yukon Energy Corporation's hydroelectric dam on the river. This dam created man-made Schwatka Lake, named in honour of U.S. Army Lt. Frederick Schwatka, who named many of the points along the Yukon River during his 1883 exploration of the region.

The gold rush brought stampeders and the railroad. The community grew as a transportation centre and trans-shipment point for freight from the Skagway–Whitehorse railroad and the stern-wheelers plying the Yukon River to Dawson City. The river was the only highway until WWII, when military expediency built the Alaska Highway in 1942.

Whitehorse was headquarters for the western sector during construction of the Alaska Highway. Fort St. John was headquarters for the eastern sector. Both were the largest construction camps on the highway.

The first survey parties of U.S. Army engineers reached Whitehorse in April of 1942. By the end of August, they had constructed a pioneer road from Whitehorse west to White River, largely by following an existing winter trail between Whitehorse and Kluane Lake. November brought the final breakthrough on the western end of the highway, marking completion of the pioneer road.

During the height of the construction of the Alaska Highway, thousands of American military and civilian workers were employed in the Canadian North. It was the second boom period for Whitehorse.

There was an economic lull following the war, but the new highway was then opened to civilian travel, encouraging new development. Mineral exploration and the development of new mines had a profound effect on the economy of the region, as did the steady growth of tourism. The Whitehorse Copper Mine, located a few miles south of the city in the historic Whitehorse copper belt, is now closed. The Grum Mine site north of Faro produced lead, silver and zinc concentrates for Cyprus–Anvil (1969– 1982), Curragh Resources (1986–1992) and Anvil Range Mining Corp. (1994–present). Stop by the Yukon Chamber of Mines office on Main Street for information on mining and rockhounding in Yukon Territory. The Chamber of Mines log building also houses a mineral display.

Because of its accessibility, Whitehorse became capital of the Yukon Territory (replacing Dawson City in that role) on March 31, 1953.

Bridges built along the highway to Dawson City, after Whitehorse became capital of the territory, were too low to accommodate the old river steamers, and by 1955 all steamers had been beached. After her last run in 1960, the SS *Keno* was berthed on the riverbank in Dawson City where she became a national historic site in 1962. The SS *Klondike* was moved through the streets of Whitehorse in 1966 to its final resting place as a riverboat museum beside the Robert Campbell bridge.

ACCOMMODATIONS/VISITOR SERVICES

Whitehorse offers 22 hotels and motels for a total of 840 rooms. Several hotels include conference facilities; most have cocktail lounges, licensed dining rooms and taverns. Rates range from $60 to $150 for a double room with bath. Bed-and-breakfast accommodations are also available.

The city has 31 restaurants downtown and in surrounding residential subdivisions that serve meals ranging from French cuisine to fast food; 14 have liquor licenses.

Whitehorse has a downtown shopping district stretching along Main Street. The Qwanlin Mall at 4th Avenue and Ogilvie has a supermarket and a variety of shops. The Yukon Centre Mall on 2nd Avenue has a liquor store. The Riverdale Mall is located on the east side of the river in the Riverdale subdivision. Another shopping mall is located in the Porter Creek subdivision north of the city on the Alaska Highway.

In addition to numerous supermarkets, garages and service stations, there are churches, movie houses, beauty salons and a covered swimming pool. Whitehorse also has several banks with ATMs. (Many businesses in Whitehorse participate in the Fair Exchange Program, which guarantees an exchange rate within 4 percent of the bank rate set once a week on Mondays. Participating businesses display the Fair Exchange logo.)

NOTE: *There is no central post office in Whitehorse.* Postal services are available in Qwanlin Mall at Coffee • Tea & Spice; The Hougen Centre on Main Street (lower floor below Shoppers Drugs); and in Riverdale and Porter Creek subdivisions. Stamps are available at several locations. General delivery pickup at corner of 3rd Avenue and Wood Street.

Specialty stores include gold nugget and ivory shops where distinctive jewelry is manufactured, and Indian craft shops specializing in moose hide jackets, parkas, vests, moccasins, slippers, mukluks and gauntlets. Inuit and Indian handicrafts from Canada's Arctic regions are featured in some stores. Whitehorse area maps are available at JMac's Fireweed Bookstore at 203 Main Street; phone (867) 668-2434.

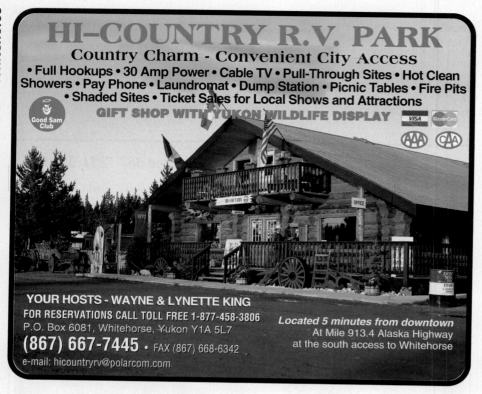

HI-COUNTRY R.V. PARK

Country Charm - Convenient City Access

• Full Hookups • 30 Amp Power • Cable TV • Pull-Through Sites • Hot Clean Showers • Pay Phone • Laundromat • Dump Station • Picnic Tables • Fire Pits • Shaded Sites • Ticket Sales for Local Shows and Attractions

GIFT SHOP WITH YUKON WILDLIFE DISPLAY

VISA MasterCard AAA CAA

YOUR HOSTS - WAYNE & LYNETTE KING

FOR RESERVATIONS CALL TOLL FREE **1-877-458-3806**

P.O. Box 6081, Whitehorse, Yukon Y1A 5L7

(867) 667-7445 • FAX (867) 668-6342

e-mail: hicountryrv@polarcom.com

Located 5 minutes from downtown
At Mile 913.4 Alaska Highway
at the south access to Whitehorse

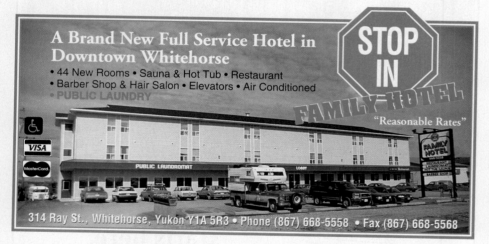

A Brand New Full Service Hotel in Downtown Whitehorse

• 44 New Rooms • Sauna & Hot Tub • Restaurant
• Barber Shop & Hair Salon • Elevators • Air Conditioned
• PUBLIC LAUNDRY

STOP IN

FAMILY HOTEL

"Reasonable Rates"

VISA MasterCard

314 Ray St., Whitehorse, Yukon Y1A 5R3 • Phone (867) 668-5558 • Fax (867) 668-5568

Pick up a Yukon memory... pick up a book from Mac's

Long after the vacation is over, the North will live on in your bookshelves. The finest selection of Northern books, magazines & newspapers in the North.

MAC's fireweed BOOKS

Open Daily from 8:00 am - 9:00 pm Mail Orders Welcome • E-mail: macsbook@yknet.yk.ca
203 Main Street, Whitehorse Y1A 2B2 Phone (867) 668-2434

The majority of Yukon Territory's First Nation people belong to either the Athapaskan or Tlingit language families.

Hawkins House Bed & Breakfast. Enjoy the Yukon's most luxurious accommodations in our Victorian home in downtown Whitehorse. Turn-of-the-century charm includes a grand foyer, guest parlor, high ceilings, balconies, hardwood floors, and historical and cultural themes. 5 star rating Canada Select. Rates $100–$130. Phone (867) 668-7638, fax (867) 668-7632, or write 303 Hawkins St., Whitehorse, YT, Canada Y1A 1X5. www.hawkinshouse.yk.ca. [ADVERTISEMENT]

High Country Inn. During your stay in Whitehorse, relax and enjoy "Country Inn" atmosphere and great Northern hospitality. We offer 100 rooms from executive and Jacuzzi suites to deluxe double rooms. Located downtown, great views, elevators, guest laundry, exercise room, colour TV, coffee maker, etc. AAA approved (3 stars, reservations recommended). Phone (800) 554-4471 or (403) 667-4471, fax (403) 667-6457. See our display advertisement. [ADVERTISEMENT]

Historical House Bed and Breakfast. Sleep in Sam McGee's house! Built for the real "Sam McGee" in 1907 by the "Cyr" brothers, Historical House offers our guests comfort and friendliness in authentic heritage surroundings. Convenient downtown location. Complimentary fax, phone and e-mail. Continental breakfast. VISA/MasterCard. 5128 Fifth Ave., Whitehorse, YT Y1A 1L6. Phone/fax (867) 668-3907. E-mail pam.phillips@yt.sympatico.ca. www.yukon-web.com/tourism/historicbb. [ADVERTISEMENT]

Klondike Rib & Salmon BBQ. Located in 2 of the oldest buildings in Whitehorse at Second and Steele, across from the Frantic Follies and Westmark Hotel. Delicious fresh Alaskan halibut and salmon BBQ, Texas BBQ ribs, English-style fish and chips, and specialty northern food like caribou, musk-ox, arctic char and fresh bannock. Just some of the mouthwatering fare served in a unique historic Klondike Airways building with historical exhibits as part of the fascinating decor. Indoor and outdoor seating. Beer and wine licensed. Free parking after 5 P.M. across the street. Phone (867) 667-7554. [ADVERTISEMENT]

Meadows Bed and Breakfast. Located just 10 minutes from the centre of Whitehorse, our modern home is located on quiet and private acreage. We offer courtesy, com-

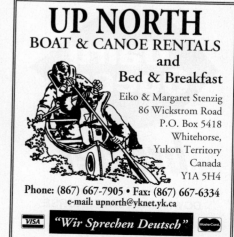

UP NORTH

BOAT & CANOE RENTALS

and

Bed & Breakfast

Eiko & Margaret Stenzig
86 Wickstrom Road
P.O. Box 5418
Whitehorse,
Yukon Territory
Canada
Y1A 5H4

Phone: (867) 667-7905 • Fax: (867) 667-6334
e-mail: upnorth@yknet.yk.ca

VISA *"Wir Sprechen Deutsch"* MasterCard

Located on the Yukon River opposite the McBride Museum. For information and friendly service about Canoe Rentals and Bed & Breakfast, please contact us.

Old Log Church Museum, a territorial historic site, was built in 1900.

(© Earl L. Brown, staff)

Tent camping only is available at Robert Service Park on Robert Service Way (South Access Road). There are 4 private campgrounds south of downtown Whitehorse on the Alaska Highway (see **Mileposts DC 873.5, 881, 882.9** and **883.7** in the highway log), and 1 private campground 6 miles/9.6 km north of the city on the highway (see **Milepost DC 891.9**). Wolf Creek Yukon government campground is 7 miles/11 km south of Whitehorse on the Alaska Highway. A private campground and Yukon government campground are located at Marsh Lake. Takhini Hot Springs on the Klondike Loop is also a popular camping spot (1/2-hour drive from Whitehorse).

IMPORTANT: RV caravans should contact private campground operators well in advance of arrival regarding camping arrangements. At our press time, there was no designated RV parking in downtown Whitehorse.

TRANSPORTATION

Air: Service by Canadian Airlines International and Alkan Air daily to major cities and Yukon communities. Air North to Dawson City, Old Crow, Juneau and Fairbanks, AK. (Air North offers a 21-day Klondike Explorer's Pass between Juneau, Old Crow, Fairbanks, Whitehorse and Dawson City). Royal Airlines and N.W.T. Air offer summer service with connections to major Canadian and U.S. cities. Whitehorse International Airport is reached from the Alaska Highway.

Seaplane dock on Schwatka Lake just above the Whitehorse Dam (take Robert Service Way from Alaska Highway and turn right on road by the railroad tracks to reach the base). Flightseeing tours available.

Trans North Air offers helicopter sightseeing tours from the airport.

Bus: Whitehorse Transit offers downtown and rural service. See also Bus Lines in the TRAVEL PLANNING section.

Railroad: Arrangements for White Pass & Yukon Route rail trips may be made by phoning WP&YR in Whitehorse at (867) 668-RAIL, or contacting local travel agencies.

View of Upper Yukon River Valley from Grey Mountain near Whitehorse.
(© George Wuerthner)

Taxi: 5 taxi companies operate in Whitehorse.

Car, Truck, Motorhome and Camper Rentals: Several local and national agencies are located in Whitehorse.

ATTRACTIONS

The **SS Klondike** National Historic Site is hard to miss. This grand old stern-wheeler sits beside the Yukon River near the Robert Campbell bridge. After carrying cargo and passengers between Whitehorse and Dawson City from 1937 until the 1950s, the SS Klondike went into permanent retirement on the bank of the Yukon River, donated to the people of Canada by the White Pass & Yukon Route. Refurbished by Parks Canada, the stern-wheeler is open to the public. Built by British Yukon Navigation Co., the SS Klondike is 210 feet/64m long and 41.9 feet/12.5m wide. Visitor information centre, gift shop and public parking at the site. A film on the history of riverboats is shown continuously in a tent theatre adjacent the boat. Tours of the stern-wheeler leave on the half hour. The 20-minute film is shown prior to each tour. Admission fee charged. Large groups are advised to book tours in advance. Contact Canadian Heritage, 300 Main St., Room 205, Whitehorse, YT Y1A 2B5; phone (867) 667-3970, fax (867) 398-6701. The SS *Klondike* visitor centre and stern-wheeler are open from mid-May to mid-September.

Live Shows. Frantic Follies, a very popular vaudeville stage show, is held nightly mid-May through mid-September at the Westmark Whitehorse Hotel. 1999 marks the 30th season for this 1½-hour show which features a chorus line, rousing music and hilarious skits from Robert W. Service ballads. Visitors are advised to get tickets in advance; available at the box office in the Westmark or phone (867) 668-2042. Tickets are also available at most area RV parks.

Special Events. The Yukon International Storytelling Festival, held June 4–6, 1999, features storytellers, musicians and theatre groups from around the world. July 1st is Canada Day, commemorating Canada's 132nd birthday in 1999, and it's celebrated with events and entertainment for the whole family. The 8th Annual Sourdough Yukon Bathtub Race, scheduled for Aug. 13-16, 1999, is the longest and toughest bath-tub race in the world; it runs on the Yukon River from Whitehorse to Dawson City. The Klondike Trail of '98 International Road Relay, Sept. 10–11, 1999, is the 17th annual running of the road relay from Skagway, AK, to Whitehorse, YK; it attracted more than 1,300 runners last year. See Summer Events calendar on pages 142-143.

Take a hike. Grey Mountain Nature Trail, east of downtown and the Riverdale subdivision, offers views of the Upper Yukon River valley. The Yukon Conservation Society (YCS) offers free guided nature walks, ranging in difficulty from easy to strenuous, from July to late August. Trips are 1 to 6 hours in length and informative guides explain the local flora, fauna, geology and history along the trails. The YCS conducts interpretive walks at Canyon City (see **Milepost DC 881.7**) during the summer on a regular basis, including evenings and weekends. For a schedule of hikes, contact the Yukon Conservation Society, at 302 Hawkins St.; phone (867) 668-5678.

World's largest weathervane. Located in front of the Whitehorse International Airport is the world's largest weathervane—a Douglas DC–3. This vintage plane (registration number CF–CPY) flew for several Yukon airlines from 1946 until 1970, when it blew an engine during takeoff. The plane was restored by Joe Muff with the help of the Yukon Flying Club and the Whitehorse community. It is now owned and managed by the Yukon Transportation Museum. The restored plane was mounted on a rotating pedestal in 1981 and now acts as a weather-vane, pointing its nose into the wind.

The Yukon Transportation Museum, located on the Alaska Highway adjacent to the Whitehorse Airport (see **Milepost DC 885.8**), features exhibits on all forms of transportation in the North. Displays inside include the full-size replica of the *Queen of the Yukon* Ryan monoplane, sister ship to Lindbergh's *Spirit of St. Louis;* railway rolling stock; Alaska Highway vintage vehicles, dogsleds and stagecoaches. Also featured are the Chilkoot Trail, the Canol Highway and bush pilots of the North. The museum includes video theatres and a gift shop. Plenty of parking. Admission charged. Open daily, 9 A.M. to 6 P.M., mid-May to mid-September. Write P.O. Box 5867, Whitehorse, YT Y1A 5L6 or phone (867) 668-4792, fax 633-5547.

Historical walking tours of Whitehorse are conducted by the Yukon Historical & Museums Association. Tour guides wear period costumes for these walks that take in the city's heritage buildings. Meet at the Donnenworth House, 3126 3rd Ave.; phone 667-4704. Fee charged. There are tours Monday through Saturday from June to the end of August. For self-guided tours, *A Walking Tour of Yukon's Capital* or *Exploring Old Whitehorse* are available from local stores or from the Yukon Historical & Museums Assoc., Box 4357, Whitehorse, YT Y1A 3T5.

MacBride Museum, on 1st Avenue between Steele and Wood streets, showcases Yukon's cultural and natural history in 4 indoor galleries featuring gold rush exhibits and outdoor displays featuring Sam McGee's cabin. The Museum Shop features books, local arts and crafts and northern souvenirs. Admission charged. Open daily, 10 A.M. to 6 P.M., June, July and August; phone for seasonal hours, (867) 667-2709, fax 633-6607 or write Box 4037, Whitehorse, YT Y1A 3S9. Phone for winter hours.

Old Log Church Museum, 1 block off Main on Elliott at 3rd. Built in 1900 by Rev. R.J. Bowen for the Church of England, this recently restored log church and rectory have been declared the first territorial historic sites in the Yukon. The museum, located in the log church, displays relics of

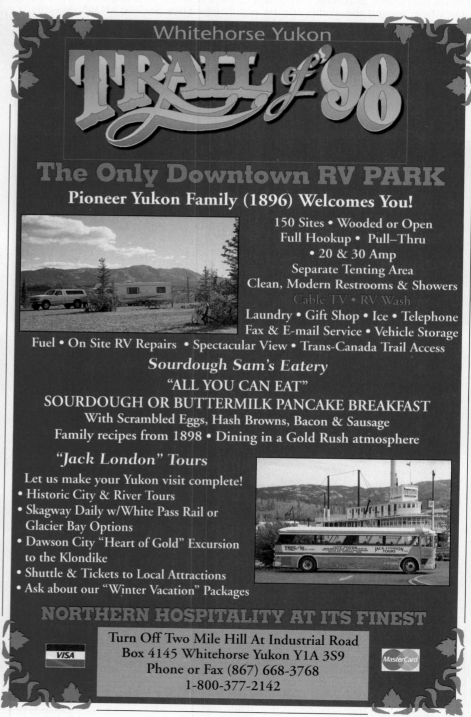

Welcome to the North!

Northern residents depend on Totem Oil every day for the finest fuel, diesel, automobile repair and convenience store items. Visitors will discover the same level of service and quality throughout the north. Our 21 Totem Oil service stations will help energize your northern adventure.

Call 1-800-661-0550

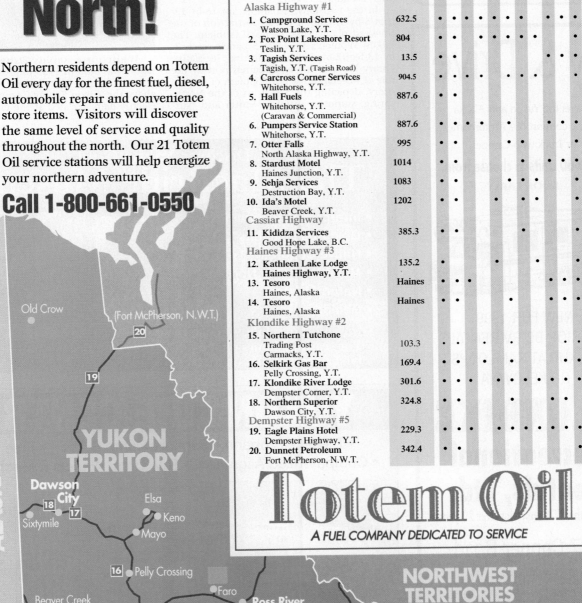

WPI Delta Western — Totem Oil

CITGO

	MILE POST	GAS	DIESEL	PROPANE	GROCERIES	LODGING	SANI DUMP	RV PARK	RESTAURANT	MECHANICAL	TIRES	CONV STORE
Alaska Highway #1												
1. Campground Services — Watson Lake, Y.T.	632.5	•	•	•				•			•	•
2. Fox Point Lakeshore Resort — Teslin, Y.T.	804	•	•			•	•	•	•			•
3. Tagish Services — Tagish, Y.T. (Tagish Road)	13.5	•	•									•
4. Carcross Corner Services — Whitehorse, Y.T.	904.5	•	•	•	•			•				•
5. Hall Fuels — Whitehorse, Y.T. (Caravan & Commercial)	887.6	•	•									
6. Pumpers Service Station — Whitehorse, Y.T.	887.6	•	•									•
7. Otter Falls — North Alaska Highway, Y.T.	995	•	•									•
8. Stardust Motel — Haines Junction, Y.T.	1014	•	•			•					•	•
9. Sehja Services — Destruction Bay, Y.T.	1083	•	•									•
10. Ida's Motel — Beaver Creek, Y.T.	1202	•	•			•			•			
Cassiar Highway												
11. Kididza Services — Good Hope Lake, B.C.	385.3	•	•									•
Haines Highway #3												
12. Kathleen Lake Lodge — Haines Highway, Y.T.	135.2	•				•			•			•
13. Tesoro — Haines, Alaska	Haines	•	•	•						•	•	•
14. Tesoro — Haines, Alaska	Haines	•	•				•				•	•
Klondike Highway #2												
15. Northern Tutchone Trading Post — Carmacks, Y.T.	103.3	•	•		•			•			•	•
16. Selkirk Gas Bar — Pelly Crossing, Y.T.	169.4	•	•		•				•		•	•
17. Klondike River Lodge — Dempster Corner, Y.T.	301.6	•	•	•		•		•	•	•		•
18. Northern Superior — Dawson City, Y.T.	324.8	•	•					•				•
Dempster Highway #5												
19. Eagle Plains Hotel — Dempster Highway, Y.T.	229.3	•	•	•		•			•	•	•	•
20. Dunnett Petroleum — Fort McPherson, N.W.T.	342.4	•	•	•								•

Totem Oil
A FUEL COMPANY DEDICATED TO SERVICE

Old Crow
(Fort McPherson, N.W.T.) 20
19
YUKON TERRITORY
ALASKA
Dawson City 18 17
Sixtymile
Elsa
Keno
Mayo
16 Pelly Crossing
Faro
Ross River
NORTHWEST TERRITORIES
Beaver Creek 10
15 Carmacks
Burwash Landing
Aishihik
9 7 Champagne
Whitehorse 4-6 Johnson's Crossing
Destruction Bay
Haines Junction 8 Tagish 3 2 Teslin
Klukshu
Carcross 12 Jake's Corner
Dalton Post
13-14 (Haines, Alaska)
Good Hope Lake 11
Upper Liard Village
Watson Lake 1
BRITISH COLUMBIA

pioneer northern missions. Open to the public June to September; admission fee.

Yukon Government Building, 2nd Avenue and Hawkins, open 9 A.M. to 5 P.M. Administrative and Legislative headquarters of Yukon Territory, the building contains some notable artworks. On the main floor mall is an acrylic resin mural, 120 feet/37m long, which portrays the historical evolution of the Yukon. The 24 panels, each measuring 4 by 5 feet/1.2 by 1.5m, highlight events such as the arrival of Sir John Franklin at Herschel Island in 1825, the Klondike Gold Rush, and the coming of the automobile. The mural was created by Vancouver, BC, artist David MacLagen.

In the Legislative Chamber, an 18-by-12-foot/5-by-4m tapestry is an abstraction of the fireweed plant, Yukon's floral emblem. The Yukon Women's Tapestry, 5 panels each 7-by-13-feet/2-by-4m, hangs in the legislative library lounge. The wool panels portray the role of women in the development of the territory, depicting the 5 seasons of the North; spring, summer, autumn, winter and "sur-

vival," the cold gray season between winter and spring and fall and winter. Begun by the Whitehorse Branch of the Canadian Federation of Business and Professional Women in 1976 to mark International Women's Year, the wall hangings were stitched by some 2,500 Yukoners.

Whitehorse Rapids Fishway. The fish ladder was built in 1959 to provide access for chinook (king) salmon and other species above the Yukon Energy Corporation hydroelectric dam. Located at the end of Nisutlin

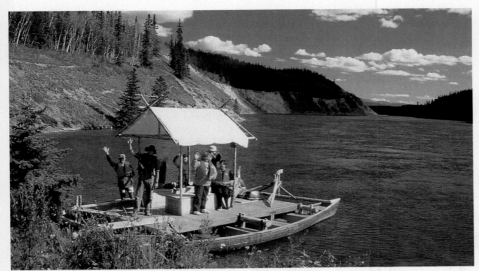

Visitors can experience the Yukon River via a variety of water craft that tour Schwatka Lake. *(© Earl L. Brown, staff)*

for hours, or write Box 2703, Whitehorse, YT Y1A 2C6, for more information.

A Taste of '98 Yukon River Tours. The best 3-hour river tour in the Yukon. Experience gold rush history first hand, and discover the abundant wildlife of the Whitehorse area on motorized steel pontoon river craft. Tours, as well as the unique craft, were designed to enhance your Yukon experience and the thrill of discovery. Just $39 per person (group rates available). Daily at 12 noon and 3:30 P.M. Ask about our aboriginal river tour. Phone (867) 633-4767. [ADVERTISEMENT]

Boat Tours. Yukon River tours are offered

Drive in the Riverdale suburb. Open daily, 9 A.M. to 5 P.M. from May 25 to July 1, 8 A.M. to 10 P.M. from July to September. Interpretive displays and viewing decks.

Play Golf. Mountain View Public Golf Course is accessible via the Porter Creek exit off the Alaska Highway or from Range Road; 18 holes, grass greens; green fees. Meadow Lakes Golf and Country Club, 5 minutes south of Whitehorse at **Milepost DC 878,** has a 9-hole par 36 course, clubhouse, cart and club rentals; phone (867) 668-4653.

Picnic in a Park. Lepage Park, located across from the Yukon Theatre, is open to everyone for daily lunches, Monday to Friday, in summer. Picnic facilities are also available at Robert Service Campground, located on Robert Service Way into Whitehorse. Rotary Peace Park is central to downtown and a popular picnic spot.

Whitehorse Public Library, part of the Yukon Government Building on 2nd Avenue, has a room with art displays and books about the Yukon and the gold rush. It features a large stone and copper double fireplace, comfortable chairs, tables and helpful staff. Open noon to 9 P.M. weekdays, 10 A.M. to 6 P.M. Saturday, 1 to 9 P.M. Sunday and closed holidays. Phone (867) 667-5239.

Yukon Archives is located adjacent Yukon College at Yukon Place. The archives was established in 1972 to acquire, preserve and make available the documented history of the Yukon. The holdings, dating from 1845, include government records, private manuscripts, corporate records, photographs, maps, newspapers (most are on microfilm), sound recordings, university theses, books, pamphlets and periodicals. Visitors are welcome. Phone (867) 667-5321 by A Taste of '98 Yukon River Tours. The 3-hour tours depart from near the old WP&YR train depot in downtown Whitehorse. Boat tours of scenic Miles Canyon, aboard the MV *Schwatka*, depart from the dock on Schwatka Lake. Gold Rush raft float trous of Miles Canyuon are offered by Rocky Mountain Voyageurs and Go Wild Tours. Miles Canyon is accessible by road: take Schwatka Lake Road off Robert Service Way (South Access Road) into Whitehorse, or turn off the Alaska Highway (see **Milepost DC 881.7**); follow signs.

Day trips from Whitehorse. Marsh Lake, 24 miles/39 km south of Whitehorse on the Alaska Highway, and Takhini Hot Springs, 17 miles/27 km north of town via the Alaska and Klondike highways, are within easy driving distance of Whitehorse. Drive south on the Alaska Highway to turnoff for Marsh Lake Yukon Government Recreation Site, a scenic 30-minute drive from Whitehorse city centre. The recreation area offers an excellent day-use area and campground at Army Beach on Marsh Lake. In the winter, trails originating from this recreation site are used for cross-country skiing and snowmobiling. In spring, this is a popular swan migration viewing area. "Swan Haven" viewing site is equipped with binoculars.

Go north on the Alaska Highway to **Milepost DC 894.8** and turn off onto Klondike Highway 2 (the road to Dawson City) and drive just 3.8 miles/6.1 km from the junction to reach Takhini Hot Springs. The resort offers swimming, horseback riding and camping. See Milepost J3.8 in the KLONDIKE LOOP section for more information on Hot Springs and other attractions on the North Klondike Highway.

Longer trips (which you may want to extend to an overnight) are to Atlin, about 2½ hours by car, and Skagway, 3 hours by car. Skagway is an old gold rush town and port of call for both the Alaska state ferries and cruise ships. Skagway is also home to the famed White Pass & Yukon Route Railway, said to be the most scenic railway in the world as it climbs through beautiful mountain terrain to White Pass summit. Book ahead for the trip. Complete your Skagway visit with a trip to Dyea, a short drive from downtown, to see the start of the Chilkoot Trail and a gold rush graveyard. Atlin, which also dates from 1898, is known for its spectacular scenery. Visitors heading for Skagway should call ahead for accommodations if they expect to overnight. You may make a circle tour, driving down to Skagway then turning off onto the Tagish Road on your way back and continuing on to Atlin via the Atlin Road.

Rockhounding and Mining. A wide variety of minerals can be found in the Whitehorse area. Sources of information for rock hounds and gold panners include the Yukon Rock Shop, at the junction of the Alaska Highway and Klondike Highway 2 (Carcross Road), which has mineral samples, gold pans and nuggets, and Murdoch's gem shop on Main Street, which displays gold nugget jewellery and gold rush artifacts and photos.

The following rockhounding location is suggested by Fred Dorward of the Whitehorse Gem & Mineral Club (26 Sunset Dr. N., Whitehorse, YT Y1A 4M8). Drive north on the Alaska Highway to the Fish Lake Road turnoff (**Milepost DC 889.4**), located 2 miles/3.2 km from the north entrance to Whitehorse. About 0.5 mile/0.8 km in on Fish Lake Road, park and walk across McIntyre Creek to the old Copper King mine workings. Excellent but small specimens of brown garnet, also serpentine. *IMPORTANT: Rock hounds should exercise extreme caution when exploring. Do not enter old mine workings. Please respect No Trespassing signs.*

Canoe, Raft or Boat to Dawson City. Canoe rentals by the day, week or month, and guide services are available in Whitehorse. From the Yukon River's outlet at Marsh Lake south of Whitehorse to the Alaska border it is 530 river miles/853 km; from Whitehorse to Dawson City it is 410 river miles/660 km. There is a boat launch at Rotary Peace Park, behind the Yukon Government Bldg. You may also launch at Deep Creek Campground on Lake Laberge. Contact Up North Canoe Rentals, phone (867) 667-7905.

NOTE: Before leaving on any river or other wilderness trip, for your own protection, report your plans and itinerary to the RCMP. Be guided by the advice in government publications regarding travel on the Yukon's rivers and lakes. Do not attempt the Five Finger Rapids on the Yukon River without qualified advice.

For more information on wilderness travel, contact Tourism Yukon office, located between 2nd and 3rd on Hawkins; phone (867) 667-5340. Maps are available at Mac's

Fireweed Bookstore at 203 Main Street.

Hikers planning to do the Chilkoot Trail should check with Parks Canada, in the Federal Building at 4th and Main; phone (867) 667-3910 or 1-800-661-0486. The Chilkoot Trail fee is $35 for adults ($17.50 for children under 14).

Mount McIntyre Recreation Centre, 0.9 mile/1.5 km west of the Alaska Highway (see **Milepost DC 887.6),** has 70 kilometres of groomed cross-country ski trails (open for hiking, running and mountain biking in summer). Contact Whitehorse Cross-Country Ski Club, P.O. Box 4639, Whitehorse, YT Y1A 3Y7.

Sportsmen can obtain complete information on fishing and hunting in the Whitehorse area by writing Tourism Yukon, Box 2703, Whitehorse, YT Y1A 2C6. They will provide lists of guides and advise what licenses are required.

AREA FISHING: Fish for rainbow and coho salmon in the following lakes: **Hidden, Scout, Long, Jackson** and **McLean.** Inquire locally for directions. Nearby fly-in fishing lakes are accessible by charter plane; see advertisements in this section. **Yukon River,** fish for grayling below the dam and bridge. Fishing below the dam prohibited in August during the salmon run.

Alaska Highway Log
(continued from page 138)
Distance* from Dawson Creek (DC) is followed by distance from Delta Junction (DJ). Original mileposts are indicated in the text as Historical Mile.
**In Canada, mileages from Dawson Creek are based on actual driving distance, not historical mileposts, and kilometres are based on physical kilometreposts *as they occured in summer 1998.* Mileages from Delta Junction

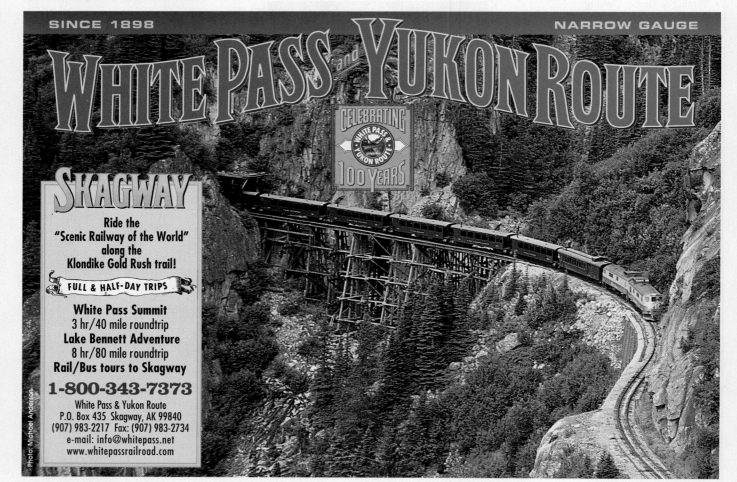

are also based on actual driving distance, not historical mileposts, but are followed by the metric conversion to kilometres.

DC 887.4 (1475.6 km) DJ 502.6 (808.8 km) First exit southbound for Whitehorse. North access road to Whitehorse (exit east) is via Two-Mile Hill and 4th Avenue.

DC 887.6 (1476 km) DJ 502.4 (808.5 km) Turnoff to west on Hamilton Boulevard for Mount McIntyre Recreation Centre (0.9 mile/1.5 km); 70 kilometres of cross-country ski trails (summer hiking and biking), chalet for indoor waxing, curling and bonspiels.

DC 888.6 (1477.5 km) DJ 501.4 (806.9 km) Historical Mile 918.3. Gas, store, food.

DC 889.3 (1478.6 km) DJ 500.7 (805.8 km) McIntyre Creek.

DC 889.4 (1478.8 km) DJ 500.6 (805.6 km) Fish Lake Road to west. Located only 9.3 miles/15 km from Whitehorse, Fish Lake and adjacent Bonneville Lakes were the site of a Kwanlin Dun First Nations archaeology project documenting the long history of habitation in this area.

DC 890.1 (1479.9 km) DJ 499.9 (804.5 km) Rabbit's Foot Canyon.

DC 890.5 (1480.6 km) DJ 499.5 (803.8 km) Turnoff to Porter Creek to east.

DC 891 (1481.4 km) DJ 499 (803 km) Porter Creek grocery.

DC 891.3 (1482 km) DJ 498.7 (802.6 km) Historical Mile 921, laundromat, gas and other businesses.

DC 891.5 (1482.3 km) DJ 498.5 (802.2 km) Clyde Wann Road and Porter Creek subdivision, a residential suburb of Whitehorse. Access to Range Road and Mountain View Golf Course (18 holes).

DC 891.6 (1482.4 km) DJ 498.4 (802 km) Historical Mile 922. Trails North Car & Truck Stop, and Tamarack Welding and Spring Shop are located here.

DC 891.8 (1482.5 km) DJ 498.2 (801.7 km) MacDonald Road to north.

DC 891.9 (1484 km) DJ 498.1 (801.6 km) Historical Mile 922.5. Azure Road. Access to MacKenzie's RV Park. ▲

DC 894.3 (1486.4 km) DJ 495.7 (797.7 km) Turnoff east to Cousins dirt airstrip.

DC 894.5 (1486.7 km) DJ 495.5 (797.4 km) Rest area to west with litter barrels, outhouses, information sign and pay phone.

DC 894.8 (1487.2 km) DJ 495.2 (796.9 km) For Alaska-bound travelers, the highway now swings west. Turn off to north on Klondike Highway 2 for Takhini Hot Springs (swimming, camping), 3.8 miles/6.1 km north. ▲

Junction with Klondike Highway 2 to Dawson City. See KLONDIKE LOOP section for log of that route.

STOP FOR DAWSON CITY

1999

TAKE THE KLONDIKE HIGHWAY JUST NORTH OF WHITEHORSE

DC 895.5 (1488.3 km) DJ 494.5 (795.8 km) Turnoff to south for Haeckel Hill. Not recommended for hiking as this area is used for target practice.

DC 899.1 (1495.4 km) DJ 490.9 (790 km) Turnoff for 3-mile/4.8-km loop drive on old section of Alaska Highway. Access to stocked lake. ✦

DC 901.6 (1499.3 km) DJ 488.4 (786 km) Turnoff to north to sled dog track.

DC 905.4 (1507.1 km) DJ 484.6 (779.9 km) Historic Milepost 937. Camera viewpoint turnout to north with point of interest sign about the old Dawson Trail. There were at least 50 stopping places along the old Dawson Trail winter stagecoach route between Whitehorse and Dawson City, and from 1 to 3 roadhouses at each stop. At this point, the stagecoach route crossed the Takhini River. This route was discontinued in 1950 when the Mayo–Dawson Road (now Klondike Highway 2) was constructed.

DC 908.7 (1512.4 km) DJ 481.3 (774.5 km) Private farm and windmill; good example of Yukon agriculture. Facilities for overnighting large livestock.

DC 914.7 (1525 km) DJ 475.3 (764.9 km) Takhini River bridge. According to R. Coutts in *Yukon: Places & Names,* the name Takhini derives from the Tagish Indian *tahk,* meaning mosquito, and *heena,* meaning river.

DC 922.7 (1535 km) DJ 467.3 (752 km) Watch for horses and other livestock grazing on open range near highway.

DC 924.5 (1538.4 km) DJ 465.5 (749.1 km) Stoney Creek.

DC 924.7 (1538.7 km) DJ 465.3 (748.8 km) View of Mount Bratnober, elev. 6,313 feet/1,924m. According to R. Coutts in *Yukon: Places & Names,* the mountain was named in 1897 by J.J. McArthur, Canadian government surveyor, for Henry Bratnober, who along with Jack Dalton was assisting in a cursory survey of the Dalton Trail.

DC 926 (1540.8 km) DJ 464 (746.7 km) Turnout to south with litter barrels and information panels on Takhini River valley, Kusawa Lake, and the changing landscape and wildlife of the area. Point of interest sign about 1958 burns; more than 1.5 million acres/629,058 hectares of Yukon forest lands were burned in 1958. Campfires were responsible for most of these fires.

DC 927.3 (1542.9 km) DJ 462.7 (744.6 km) Turnoff to south for viewpoint (1.9 miles/3 km) and **Kusawa Lake** Yukon government campground (15 miles/24 km). Access road to campground is a narrow, winding gravel road, very slippery when wet; not recommended for long trailers or heavily loaded vehicles. ▲

Day-use area with sandy beach, boat dock, kitchen shelter and drinking water; boat launch 0.6 mile/1 km south. Campground at north end of lake has 48 sites, kitchen shelter, firepits and drinking water. Camping fee $8. Fishing for lake trout to 20 lbs., good to excellent; also grayling and pike.

Kusawa Lake (formerly Arkell Lake), located in the Coast Mountains, is 45 miles/72 km long and averages 2 miles/3.2 km wide, with a shoreline perimeter of 125 miles/200 km. An access road to the lake was first constructed by the U.S. Army in 1945 to obtain bridge timbers for Alaska Highway construction.

DC 936.8 (1558 km) DJ 453.2 (729.3 km) Mendenhall River bridge. A tributary of the Takhini River, the Mendenhall River—like the Mendenhall Glacier outside Juneau,

AK—was named for Thomas Corwin Mendenhall (1841–1924), superintendent of the U.S. Coast & Geodetic Survey.

DC 939.5 (1562.3 km) DJ 450.5 (725 km) View of 3 prominent mountains northbound (from left to right): Mount Kelvin; center mountain unnamed; and Mount Bratnober.

DC 942.2 (1565.5 km) DJ 447.8 (720.6 km) Native traditional camp, **Kwaday Dan Kenji,** featuring Native crafts in a replica traditional First Nation camp interpretive site.

Fee charged, open daily 9 A.M. to 7:30 P.M. May to October. Dry camping available. Phone (867) 667-6375. ▲

DC 942.8 (1567.6 km) DJ 447.2 (719.7 km) NorthwesTel microwave tower to south.

DC 943.5 (1568.5 km) DJ 446.5 (718.5 km) Historic Milepost 974. Historic sign and interpretive panel about CHAMPAGNE; snack bar.

Originally a camping spot on the Dalton Trail to Dawson City, established by Jack Dalton in the late 1800s. In 1902, Harlow "Shorty" Chambers built a roadhouse and trading post here, and it became a supply centre for first the Bullion Creek rush and later the Burwash Creek gold rush in 1904. The origin of the name is uncertain, although one account is that Dalton's men—after successfully negotiating a herd of cattle through the first part of the trail—celebrated here with a bottle of French champagne. Today, it is home to members of the Champagne–Aishihik Indian Band. There is an Indian cemetery on right westbound, just past the log cabin homes; a sign there reads: "This cemetery is not a tourist attraction. Please respect our privacy as we respect yours."

For northbound travelers, the Alaska Highway parallels the Dezadeash River (out of view to the south) from here west to Haines Junction. The Dezadeash Range is to the south and the Ruby Range to the north.

DC 944.4 (1570 km) DJ 445.6 (717.1 km) Gravel turnout with litter barrel.

DC 955.8 (1588 km) DJ 434.2 (698.7 km) First glimpse northbound of Kluane Range.

DC 957 (1590 km) DJ 433 (696.8 km) Historic Milepost 987. Cracker Creek. Former roadhouse site on old stagecoach trail. Watch for "Old Man Mountain" on right northbound (the rocky crags look like a face, particularly in evening light).

Otter Falls on Aishihik Road once appeared on the back of a $5 bill. (© Harry M. Walker)

DC 964.6 (1602.2 km) **DJ 425.4** (684.6 km) **Historical Mile 995.** Otter Falls Cutoff, **junction** with Aishihik Road. Gas station, store and camping to south, Aishihik Road turnoff to north. Bird-watching trails. ▲

Otter Falls Cutoff. See display ad this section. ▲

Aishihik Road leads 84 miles/135 km north to the old Indian village of **Aishihik** (AYSH-ee-ak, means high place). Northern Canada Power Commission built a 32-megawatt dam at the foot of Aishihik Lake in 1976 to supply power principally to the mining industry. Flow hours for the Otter Falls hydro project are given at the start of Aishihik Road. This is a narrow, gravel road, maintained for summer travel only to the government campground. Aishihik Road is not recommended for large RVs and trailers.

There is a day-use recreation site at Otter Falls, 18.6 miles/30 km distance; picnic shelter, tables, outhouses and boat ramp.

The Yukon government Aishihik Lake Campground is located at the south end of Aishihik Lake, approximately 26 miles/41.8 km distance; 13 sites, drinking water, picnic tables, firepits, kitchen shelter, boat launch and playground. Camping fee $8. ▲

Aishihik Lake, fishing for lake trout and grayling. As with most large Yukon lakes, ice is not out until late June. Low water levels may make boat launching difficult. *WARNING: Winds can come up suddenly on this lake.* **Pole Cat Lake**, just before the Aishihik weather station; fishing for pike. ⌐●

CAUTION: Bears in area. Other wildlife includes eagles, moose and caribou.

DC 965.6 (1603.8 km) **DJ 424.4** (683 km) **Historic Milepost 996.** Turnoff to north at east end of Aishihik River bridge (watch for camera viewpoint sign) to see **Canyon Creek Bridge**. The original bridge was built about 1920 by the Jacquot brothers to move freight and passengers across the Aishihik River to Silver City on Kluane Lake, and from there by boat to Burwash Landing. The bridge was reconstructed in 1942 by Army Corps of Engineers during construction of the Alaska Highway. It was rebuilt again in 1987.

DC 965.7 (1604 km) **DJ 424.3** (682.8 km) Aishihik River bridge.

DC 966.3 (1605 km) **DJ 423.7** (618.9 km) View of impressive Kluane Range ice fields straight ahead northbound between Kilometreposts 1604 and 1616.

DC 974.9 (1619 km) **DJ 415.1** (668 km) Turnout to south on Marshall Creek.

DC 977.1 (1622.4 km) **DJ 421.9** (664.5 km) The rugged snowcapped peaks of the Kluane Icefield Ranges and the outer portion of the St. Elias Mountains are visible to the west, straight ahead northbound.

The Kluane National Park Icefield Ranges are Canada's highest and the world's largest nonpolar alpine ice field, forming the interior wilderness of the park. In clear weather, Mount Kennedy and Mount Hubbard, 2 peaks that are twice as high as the front ranges seen before you, are visible from here.

DC 979.3 (1626 km) **DJ 410.7** (660.9 km) Between Kilometreposts 1626 and 1628, look for the NorthwesTel microwave repeater station on top of Paint Mountain. The station was installed with the aid of helicopters and supplied by the tramline carried by high towers, which is also visible from here.

DC 980.8 (1628.4 km) **DJ 409.2** (658.5 km) Turnoff to north for Yukon government **Pine Lake Recreation Park.** Day-use area with sandy beach, boat launch and dock, group firepits, drinking water and 7 tent sites near beach. The campground, adjacent Pine Lake with a view of the St. Elias Mountains, has 33 sites, outhouses, firewood, litter barrels, kitchen shelter, playground and drinking water. Camping fee $8. Fishing is good for lake trout, northern pike and grayling. ⌐●▲

There is a half-mile nature trail between the beach area and the floatplane dock. The Lakeside Interpretive Trail has 9 panels describing the Pine Lake environment, including the effect of marl buildup on lake color. The white sediment is a form of calcium carbonate, and the marl beds intensify the blue and green reflections of the lake on a sunny day.

A 3.5-mile/6-km walking and biking trail begins at the campground entrance and ends at Haines Junction.

DC 980.9 (1628.5 km) **DJ 409.1** (658.4 km) Access road to floatplane dock.

DC 982.2 (1630.8 km) **DJ 407.8** (656.3 km) Turnoff to north for Haines Junction airport. Flightseeing tours of glaciers, fly-in fishing and air charters available; fixed-wing aircraft or helicopters.

Private Aircraft: Haines Junction airstrip; elev. 2,150 feet/655m; length 5,500 feet/1,676m; gravel. Fuel sales (100L) from Sifton Air.

Highway swings to south for last few miles into Haines Junction, offering a panoramic, close-up view of the Auriol Range straight ahead.

DC 984.8 (1635 km) **DJ 405.2** (652.1 km) Northbound travelers turn right (southbound travelers turn left) on Kluane Street for Kluane National Park Visitor Centre.

DC 985 (1635.3 km) **DJ 405** (651.8 km)

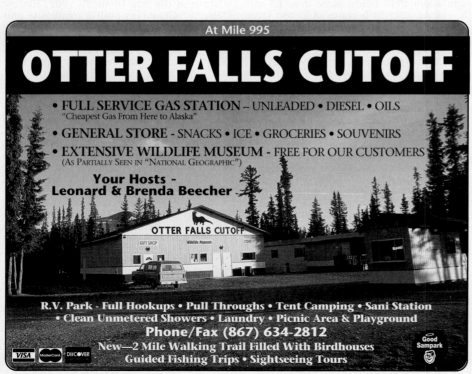

Historic Milepost 1016. *IMPORTANT: THIS JUNCTION CAN BE CONFUSING; CHOOSE YOUR ROUTE CAREFULLY! Fairbanks- and Anchorage-bound travelers TURN NORTH at this junction for continuation of Alaska Highway (Yukon Highway 1). Alaska Highway log continues on page 159.* (Haines-bound motorists note: It is a good idea to fill up with gas in Haines Junction.)

Junction of Alaska Highway and Haines Highway (Haines Road). Head west on the Haines Highway (Yukon Highway 3) for port of Haines, AK. See HAINES HIGHWAY section.

Haines Junction

DC 985 (1635.3 km) DJ 405 (651.8 km) **Historic Milepost 1016,** at the **junction** of the Alaska Highway (Yukon Highway 1) and the Haines Highway (Yukon Highway 3, also known as the Haines Road). Driving distance to Whitehorse, 100 miles/161 km; YT–AK border, 205 miles/330 km; Tok, 296 miles/476 km; and Haines, 150.5 miles/242 km. **Population:** 811. **Elevation:** 1,956 feet/596m. **Emergency Services: RCMP,** phone (867) 634-5555 or (867) 667-5555 **Fire Department,** phone (867) 634-2222. **Nursing Centre,** phone (867) 634-4444.

Visitor Information: At the Yukon Government and **Kluane National Park Visitor Information Centre,** 0.2 mile/0.3 km east of the junction just off the Alaska Highway.

Phone (867) 634-2345. Interpretive exhibits, displays and a multi-image slide presentation on Yukon national parks and historic sites (fee charged). The centre is open 8 A.M. to 8 P.M. daily from May to September; 9 A.M. to 5 P.M., Monday through Friday, the rest of the year.

Private Aircraft: Haines Junction airstrip, 2 NW; see description at **Milepost DC 982.2. Radio:** 106.1 FM, 103.5 FM, CKRW 98.7 FM, CHON 90.5 FM.

Haines Junction was established in 1942 during construction of the Alaska Highway. The first buildings here were Army barracks for the U.S. Army Corps of Engineers. The engineers were to build a new branch road connecting the Alaska Highway with the port of Haines on Lynn Canal. The branch road—today's Haines Highway—was completed in 1943.

Haines Junction is still an important stop for travelers on the Alaska and Haines highways. Services are located along both highways, and clustered around Village Square at the junction, where the 24-foot **Village Monument** depicts area wildlife.

Haines Junction offers an excellent range of accommodations. Visitor services include motels, 4 bed and breakfasts, restaurants, gas stations, garage services, groceries, souvenirs and a bakery. Gourmet dining at The Raven. There is a full-facility indoor heated swimming pool with showers available; open daily from May to late-August, fee charged. Also here are a RCMP office, Lands and

HAINES JUNCTION ADVERTISERS

Bed & Breakfast ....Ph. (867) 634-2850
Cozy Corner Motel &
    Restaurant ....Ph. (867) 634-2511
Fish Hook, The ....At the Village Bakery
Frosty Freeze....................Ph. (867) 634-2674
Gateway Motel and
    Lounge ....Ph. (867) 634-2371
Kluane Park Adventure
    Center........................Ph. (867) 634-2313
Kluane Park Inn Ltd. ....Ph. (867) 634-2261
Kluane R.V.
    Kampground ....Ph. (867) 634-2709
Madley's General Store ....Ph. (867) 634-2200
Mountain View
    Motor Inn ....Ph. (867) 634-2646
North Country R.V. Park...Ph. (867) 634-2505
Raven, The ....Ph. (867) 634-2500
Sifton Air..........................Ph. (867) 634-2916
Source Motors Ltd. ....Ph. (867) 634-2268
Stardust Motel ....Ph. (867) 634-2591
Trans North Helicopters............At the airport
Triple S Service Station.....Ph. (867) 634-2915
Village Bakery ....Next to visitor centre
Village of Haines
    Junction ....Ph. (867) 634-7103

Forest District Office and health centre. The post office and bank are located in Madley's General Store. (Banking service weekday afternoons; extended hours on Fridays.) The

Rafting trips down the Tatshenshini River are available in Haines Junction.
(© Alisha A. Brown)

Commissioner James Smith Administration Building, at Kilometre 255.6 Haines Road, 0.2 mile/0.3 km south from the Alaska Highway junction, contains the government liquor store and public library. The airport is located on the Alaska Highway just east of town (see **Milepost DC 982.2**).

Haines Junction is on the eastern boundary of **Kluane National Park Reserve**. Administration offices and the visitor centre for the park are located north of town along with the park warden and general works station. Kluane (pronounced kloo-WA-nee) National Park Reserve encompasses extensive ice fields, mountains and wilderness. There is one campground, Kathleen Lake, located 16 miles/27 km south of town on the Haines Highway. There are numerous hiking trails of varying degrees of difficulty; check with the park visitor centre or see Vivien Lougheed's *Kluane Park Hiking Guide*. Flightseeing the park by fixed-wing aircraft or helicopter from Haines Junction is a popular way to see Kluane's scenery; check with charter services at the airport.

The park was first suggested in 1942, and in 1943 land was set aside and designated the Kluane Game Sanctuary. A formal park region was established in 1972 and the national park boundaries were official in 1976. In 1980, Kluane National Park Reserve, along with Wrangell–St. Elias National Park in Alaska, became a joint UNESCO World Heritage Site. Kluane has become a world-class wilderness destination among outdoor recreation enthusiasts. Hikers note: There is mandatory registration for overnight trips into the park. Nightly or annual wilderness permits may be purchased. Bear resistant food canisters are mandatory on some overnight hikes ($150 deposit required).

For more information on Kluane National Park Reserve, stop by the excellent visitor centre and see the exhibits and the slide presentation; shown on the hour and half hour, fee charged. Also check at the visitor centre for a schedule of guided hikes, walks and campfire talks. These interpretive programs are available daily from the third week in June through August; fee charged. Contact Kluane National Park at Box 5495, Haines Junction, YT Y0B 1L0, or phone (867) 634-7209, fax (867) 634-7208.

Haines Junction is also headquarters for the new **Tatshenshini–Alsek Wilderness**

Park. Created in 1993, the park protects the magnificent Tatshenshini and Alsek rivers area in Canada, where the 2 rivers join and flow (as the Alsek) to the Gulf of Alaska at Dry Bay. Known to river runners as "the Tat," the Tatshenshini is famous for its whitewater rafting, stunning scenery and wildlife. Due to a dramatic increase in river traffic in recent years, permits are required from the park agencies (the National Park Service in Alaska and B.C. Parks in Canada). Locally, Kluane Park Adventure Center (867/634-2313) offers rafting trips to the Tatshenshini. For more information about the park, contact BC Parks, Tatshenshini Office,

Box 5544, Haines Junction, YT Y0B 1L0; phone (867) 634-7043, fax (867) 634-7208.

The Dezadeash River offers a more relaxed rafting experience. Guided 2- to 3-hour float trips are available from Kluane Park Adventure Center. Picnicking available at the day-use area on the Dezadeash River, located at the west edge of town on the Haines Highway, which also has a trail.

Other outdoor recreation available locally includes guided fishing and boating (canoe and boat rentals available).

RV camping available at several campgrounds in and near town; see advertisements this section. Dump stations and water are also available at local service station and campgrounds. Yukon government campground located 4.2 miles/6.7 km east of junction on the Alaska Highway at Pine Lake. ▲

A local landmark and visitor attraction is the picturesque **Our Lady of the Way**

Alaska Highway heads north from Haines Junction. The Haines Highway heads southwest to Haines. *(© Earl L. Brown, staff)*

Haines Junction, Yukon

"Gateway to Kluane"

Haines Junction is the ideal base for adventure travel in Kluane National Park & Tatshenshini-Alsek Park. You can go flightseeing, river rafting, mountain biking, horseback riding, llama trekking, hiking, fishing and hunting! Or bring your business and social gatherings to the new St. Elias Tourism & Convention Centre, overlooking spectacular mountains and glaciers. There is something for everyone in Haines Junction. Join us for these special events in 1999:

May 29   Trail of '42 Road Relay
Ride, walk or run a section of the Old Alaska Highway.   634-2561

June 11-13   Alsek Music Festival
A showcase of Northern Talent, Under the St. Elias Mountains.   634-2520

Saturday, June 19 Kluane to Chilkat International Bike Relay
On a team of eight, four, or two cycle one of the most scenic mountain passes in the world. In 1998 over 1000 riders participated!   633-2579

Late June - August   Kluane National Park Interpretive Programs Begin
Join the experienced park staff for campfire talks and guided hikes.   634-7207

Thursday, July 1   Canada Day
Celebrate Canada's 132nd Birthday Haines Junction Style   634-7100

For more information about **Haines Junction** *contact: Village of Haines Junction, Box 5339, Haines Junction, YT Y0B 1L0*
867-634-7100 or Fax 867-634-2008
Email: vhj@yknet.yk.ca
www.yukonweb.com/community/kluane

Catholic Mission. It was built in 1954, using parts from an old Army hut left from highway construction days.

Special events in Haines Junction include the Alsek Music Festival held June 11–13, 1999, and Canada Day (the anniversary of Canada's confederation), celebrated on July 1st with parades, barbecue and flags.

Bicycling offers several events, including the Trail of '42 Road Race (May 29, 1999) and the Kluane to Chilkat International Bike Relay (June 19, 1999). *IMPORTANT: Watch for cyclists on the Alaska and Haines highways during these events.*

Alaska Highway Log

(continued)

Distance* from Dawson Creek (DC) is followed by distance from Delta Junction (DJ). Original mileposts are indicated in the text as Historical Mile.

**In Canada, mileages from Dawson Creek are based on actual driving distance, not historical mileposts, and kilometres are based on physical kilometreposts *as they occurred in summer 1998.* Mileages from Delta Junction are also based on actual driving distance, not historical mileposts, but are followed by the metric conversion to kilometres.

DC 985 (1635.3 km) **F 503** (809.5 km) **Junction** of the Alaska Highway (Yukon Highway 1) and the Haines Highway (Yukon Highway 3).

NOTE: This junction can be confusing; choose your route carefully! Whitehorse-bound travelers turn east at junction for continuation of Alaska Highway (Yukon Highway 1). Turn west for the Haines Highway (Yukon Highway 3) to the port of Haines, AK, 152 miles/246 km from here.

See the HAINES HIGHWAY section for log of that route. (Haines-bound motorists note: It is a good idea to fill up with gas in Haines Junction.)

Northbound: Markers indicate distance to Destruction Bay 67 miles/108 km, Beaver Creek 186 miles/299 km. From Haines Junc-

tion to the YT–AK border, the Alaska Highway is in fair to good condition but narrow, often without shoulders. Watch for frost heaves north from Destruction Bay to Beaver Creek.

Southbound: Good paved highway with wide shoulders next 380 miles/611.5 km (from here to Watson Lake) with the exception of some short sections of narrow road and occasional gravel breaks.

DC 985.3 (1635.9 km) **DJ 404.7** (651.3 km) Kluane RV Kampground; RV and tent camping, gas, diesel, dump station, pay phone.

DC 985.8 (1636.5 km) **DJ 404.2** (650.2 km) **Historical Mile 1017.** Source Motors; gas, diesel, propane, auto repair, towing, snowmachine, ATV and watercraft rentals and repairs. Open daily, year-round.

DC 985.9 (1636.7 km) **DJ 404.1** (650.3 km) Stardust Motel and Triple S Service Station.

DC 986.6 (1637.8 km) **DJ 403.4** (649.2 km) Highway follows the Kluane Ranges which are to the west.

DC 987.8 (1639.8 km) **DJ 402.2** (647.3 km) **Historical Mile 1019.** Kluane National Park warden headquarters. (Visitor information in Haines Junction at the visitor centre.)

DC 988.3 (1640.6 km) **DJ 401.7** (646.4 km) Rest area to west with pit toilets.

DC 991.4 (1645.6 km) **DJ 398.6** (641.5 km) Highway climbs next 9 miles/14.5 km northbound to Bear Creek Summit.

DC 991.6 (1646 km) **DJ 398.4** (641.1 km) **Historic Milepost 1022,** Mackintosh Trading Post historic sign. Bear Creek Lodge to east; food, gas, lodging and camping. Corral for overnighting horses. Trailhead to west for Alsek Pass trail; 18 miles/29 km long, suitable for shorter day hikes, mountain bikes permitted. ▲

Bear Creek Lodge offers something for everyone, from delicious homemade meals to warm rooms. A favorite stopping spot for Alaskan travelers. Across from the lodge, the Alsek Trail leads to Kluane National Park, a world heritage site. [ADVERTISEMENT]

DC 999 (1653.2 km) **DJ 391** (629.2 km) Turnout with 0.8-mile/1.3-km loop interpretive trail on the spruce bark beetle.

DC 1000.1 (1660 km) **DJ 389.9** (627.5 km) **Bear Creek Summit** (elev. 3,294 feet/1,004m), highest point on the Alaska Highway between Whitehorse and Fairbanks.

Glimpse of Kloo Lake to north of highway between Kilometreposts 1660 and 1662.

DC 1003.5 (1665.4 km) **DJ 386.5** (622 km) Jarvis River.

DC 1003.6 (1665.6 km) **DJ 386.4** (621.8 km) **Historic Milepost 1035.** Turnout to west just north of crossing Jarvis River. Pretty spot for a picnic. Poor to fair fishing for grayling 8 to 16 inches all summer; Dolly Varden 8 to 10 inches, early summer.

DC 1013.6 (1682 km) **DJ 376.4** (605.7 km) Beautiful view to west of the snow-covered **Kluane Ranges.** For northbound travelers, the Alaska Highway parallels the Kluane Ranges from Haines Junction to Koidern, presenting a nearly unbroken chain of 7,000- to 8,000-foot/2,134- to 2,438-m summits interrupted only by a few large valleys cut by glacier-fed rivers and streams. West of the Kluane Ranges is the Duke Depression (not visible from the highway), a narrow trough separating the Kluane Ranges from the St. Elias Mountains. Major peaks in the St. Elias (not visible from the highway) are: Mount Logan, Canada's highest peak, at 19,545 feet/5,959m (recalculated in 1992 from 19,520 feet by a scientific expedition); Mount St. Elias, 18,008 feet/5,489m; Mount Lucania, 17,147 feet/5,226m; King Peak, 16,971 feet/5,173m; Mount Wood, Mount Vancouver, Mount Hubbard and Mount Steele, all over 15,000 feet/4,572m. Mount Steele (16,664 feet/5,079m) was named for Superintendent Sam Steele of the North West Mounted Police. As commanding officer of the NWMP in the Yukon in 1898, Steele established permanent detachments at the summits of the White and Chilkoot passes to ensure not only that gold stampeders obeyed Canadian laws, but also had sufficient supplies to carry them through to the gold fields.

DC 1016.5 (1686.7 km) **DJ 373.5** (601.1 km) Large gravel turnout to west with view of Kluane Ranges.

DC 1017.2 (1687.8 km) **DJ 372.8** (599.9 km) Christmas Creek.

DC 1019 (1689 km) **DJ 371** (597 km) Highway climbs northbound.

DC 1019.8 (1692 km) **DJ 370.2** (595.7 km) First glimpse of Kluane Lake for northbound travelers at **Boutillier Summit** (elev. 3,293 feet/1,003m), second highest point on the highway between Whitehorse and Fairbanks.

DC 1020 (1692.5 km) **DJ 370** (595.4 km) Double-ended photo viewpoint to east with information plaques on area history and geography.

DC 1020.3 (1693 km) **DJ 369.7** (595km) **Historic Milepost 1053.** Historic sign and interpretive panel at turnoff for **Silver**

View of Mount Logan, Canada's highest peak, on a flightseeing tour.
(© Earl L. Brown, staff)

City. Access to a bed and breakfast. Follow dirt and gravel road east 3.1 miles/5 km to ruins of Silver City. This old trading post, with roadhouse and North West Mounted Police barracks, was on the wagon road from Whitehorse to the placer goldfields of Kluane Lake (1904–24). Good photo opportunities.

Kluane Bed and Breakfast. Just 3 miles off the highway at historical Silver City on the shore of Kluane Lake. Private, heated, A-frame cabins on lakeshore with mountain view, cooking and shower facilities, full family-style breakfast. Your hosts—The Sias Family, a sixth generation Yukon family. Contact mobile operator, Destruction Bay channel 2M 3924. Reservations recommended. Mailing address: c/o Box 5459, Haines Junction, YT Y0B 1L0. [ADVERTISEMENT]

DC 1020.9 (1694 km) **DJ 369.1** (594 km)

A trail at Milepost DC 1030.7 leads up to Soldier's Summit cairn.

(© Earl L. Brown, staff)

Silver Creek.

DC 1022.5 (1696.5 km) **DJ 367.5** (591.4 km) Turnoff to east for Kluane Lake Research Station; station and airstrip are 0.9 mile/1.4 km via a straight gravel road. This research station is sponsored by the Arctic Institute of North America, University of Calgary.

Private Aircraft: Silver City airstrip; elev. 2,570 feet/783m; length 3,000 feet/914m; gravel; no services.

Highway follows west shore of Kluane Lake next 39 miles/63 km northbound to Burwash Landing.

DC 1023.7 (1698.5 km) **DJ 366.3** (589.5 km) **Historical Mile 1056** (**Historical milepost 1055**). Kluane Camp commemorative plaque. Kluane Lake Lodge (closed). Trans North helicopter base operates here, offering flightseeing trips in summer. These highly recommended flightseeing trips offer spectacular views of the Slims River Valley and Kaskawulsh Glacier.

Trans North Helicopters. See display ad this section.

DC 1024.6 (1700 km) **DJ 365.4** (588 km) Informal gravel turnout on Kluane Lake; access to beach.

DC 1026.8 (1703.4 km) **DJ 363.2** (584.5 km) Slim's River East trail turnoff (2-mile/3.3-km access road, not recommended for motorhomes); parking at trailhead. This 12.4-mile/20-km trail is rated "easy" by the *Kluane Hiking Guide*. NOTE: Hikers must register for overnight hikes in Kluane National

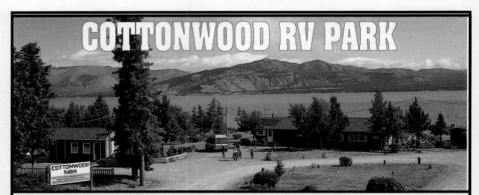

Park at either the Sheep Mountain or Haines Junction visitor centres.

DC 1027.8 (1705 km) **DJ 362.2** (582.9 km) Slim's River bridge (clearance 17.7 feet/5.4m). Slim's River, which flows into Kluane Lake, was named for a packhorse that drowned here during the 1903 Kluane gold rush. Sheep Mountain is directly ahead for northbound travelers. The highway winds along Kluane Lake: Drive carefully!

DC 1028.8 (1706.6 km) **DJ 361.2** (581.3 km) **Sheep Mountain Visitor Information Centre**. Excellent interpretive programs, laser disc information videos, parking and outhouses are available. Open mid-May to mid-September. Hours are 9 A.M. to 5 P.M. June through August, 9:30 A.M. to 5 P.M. in May and September. Stop here for information on Kluane National Park's flora and fauna. A viewing telescope is set up to look for sheep on Sheep Mountain. This is the sheep's winter range; best chance to see them is late August and September, good chance in late May to early June. Register at the Sheep Mountain Centre for hiking in the park. NOTE: The face of Sheep Mountain has been designated a special preservation zone. Check with the centre for designated hiking areas.

DC 1029 (1706.9 km) **DJ 361** (581 km) Slim's River West trail; trailhead adjacent visitor information centre.

The small white cross on the side of Sheep Mountain marks the grave of Alexander Clark Fisher, a prospector who came into this area about 1906.

DC 1030.7 (1709.5 km) **DJ 359.3** (578.2 km) **Historic Milepost 1061**. Large gravel turnouts both sides of highway at **Soldier's Summit**. The Alaska Canada Military Highway was officially opened with a ribbon-cutting ceremony here on blizzardy Nov. 20, 1942. A rededication ceremony was held Nov. 20, 1992, commemorating the 50th anniversary of the highway. A trail leads up to the original dedication site from the parking area.

Several turnouts overlooking **Kluane Lake** next mile northbound. This beautiful lake is the largest in Yukon Territory, covering approximately 154 square miles/400 square km. The Ruby Range lies on the east side of the lake. Boat rentals are available at Destruction Bay and Burwash Landing. Excellent fishing for lake trout, northern pike and grayling. ◀━

DC 1034.5 (1715.8 km) **DJ 355.5** (572.1 km) Williscroft Creek. Named for Walt Williscroft, Superintendent of Highway maintenance for the southern part of the Alaska Highway from 1950 to 1970.

DC 1034.9 (1717 km) **DJ 355.1** (571.5 km) **Historical Mile 1067. Cottonwood RV Park and Campground**. See display ad this section. ▲

DC 1039.9 (1725 km) **DJ 350.1** (563.4 km) **Historical Mile 1072**. Turnoff to east for Congdon Creek Yukon government campground on Kluane Lake. Drive in 0.4 mile/0.6 km via gravel loop road; tenting area, 77 level sites (some pull-through), outhouses, kitchen shelters, water pump, firewood, firepits, picnic tables, sandy beach, interpretive talks, playground, boat launch. Camping fee $8. ▲

DC 1040.4 (1725.6 km) **DJ 349.6** (562.6 km) Congdon Creek. According to R. Coutts, *Yukon: Places & Names*, Congdon Creek is believed to have been named by a miner after Frederick Tennyson Congdon. A lawyer from Nova Scotia, Congdon came to the

Yukon in 1898 and held various political posts until 1911.

DC 1040.6 (1726 km) **DJ 349.4** (562.3 km) Hills next 1.2 miles/2 km northbound; winding 2-lane road, no shoulders, informal gravel turnouts.

DC 1046.9 (1735.3 km) **DJ 343.1** (552.1 km) Nines Creek. Turnout to east.

DC 1047.3 (1736.2 km) **DJ 342.7** (551.5 km) Mines Creek.

DC 1048.9 (1739 km) **DJ 341.1** (548.9 km) Bock's Brook.

DC 1051.5 (1743 km) **DJ 338.5** (544.7 km) **Historic Milepost 1083. DESTRUCTION BAY** (pop. less than 100). **Emergency Services: Health clinic**, phone (867) 841-4444; **Ambulance**, phone (867) 841-3333; **Fire Department**, phone (867) 841-2221.

Located on the shore of Kluane Lake, Destruction Bay is one of several towns that grew out of the building of the Alaska Highway. It earned its name when a storm destroyed buildings and materials here. Destruction Bay was one of the many relay stations spaced at 100-mile intervals to give truck drivers a break and a chance to repair their vehicles. Historic sign adjacent historic milepost. A highway maintenance camp is located here. Destruction Bay has camping, boat launch, boat rentals and guided fishing tours. A fishing derby is held first weekend in July. Food, gas, camping and lodging available at the Talbot Arm (open year-round). ◀▲

Talbot Arm Motel. See display ad this section

Burls, a deformity found in spruce trees, are turned into a variety of objects.
(© Earl L. Brown, staff)

DC 1051.7 (1743.3 km) DJ 338.3 (544.4 km) Gas, meals, lodging and camping. ▲

Destruction Bay Lodge. See display ad this section.

DC 1051.9 (1743.6 km) DJ 338.1 (544.1 km) Rest area with litter barrels and toilet.

DC 1055.1 (1748.8 km) DJ 334.9 (539 km) Lewes Creek.

DC 1058.3 (1753.9 km) DJ 331.7 (533.8 km) Halfbreed (Copper Joe) Creek trailhead.

DC 1061.3 (1758.7 km) DJ 328.7 (529 km) Store, RV park and snack bar.

Duke River Trading Co. See display ad this section. ▲

DC 1061.5 (1759 km) DJ 328.5 (528.6 km) **Historic Milepost 1093.** Kluane Museum and turnoff to east for **BURWASH LANDING,** (pop. 84) a village with post office, community hall, church and gas, food, camping and lodging on Kluane Lake. Boat rentals and Kluane Lake fishing trips available. Flightseeing trips of Kluane National Park are also available out of Burwash Landing. ◄▲

Burwash Landing is known for its black spruce burl bowls. Burls start as an irritation in the spruce. The tree sends extra sap as healant, which creates a growth or burl. Burls are either "green," harvested from live trees in the spring, or they are "dry burls," taken from dead burl trees. Burls are peeled of their bark and used in their natural form as fenceposts, for example, or they may be shaped and finished into a variety of objects, such as bowls. Check out Burlbilly Hill at **Milepost DC 1061.6.**

The highly recommended **Kluane Museum of Natural History** is located on the east side of the highway at the turnoff; open 9 A.M. to 9 P.M. in summer; phone (867) 841-5561. The museum features displays of wildlife in natural habitats; Native (First Nations) clothing and artifacts, including a moose skin boat; minerals exhibit; and videos. Modest admission is charged. Get your Yukon Explorer's Passport stamped here. Next to the museum is the world's largest gold pan, measuring 28 feet/ 8m high.

Burwash Landing was settled in 1904 by the Jacquot brothers, Louis and Eugene, as a supply centre for local miners. The log **Our Lady of the Holy Rosary Mission,** was built in 1944. Sign reads: "This was the first church northwest of Whitehorse on the new Alcan Highway. Father Morrisset, then auxiliary chaplain to the U.S. Army at the road construction camps, was asked by the local residents to start a mission and day school.

Land was donated by Eugene Jacquot, trading post owner. Building materials came from the Duke River camp site and included an unfinished U.S. Army mess hall and a log cabin, which form the 2 arms of the complex. The day school closed in 1952. The church opened with Christmas eve mass in

1944 and is still in use today."

Burwash Landing Resort & RV Park. See display ad this section. ▲

Destruction Bay Fishing Charters. See dipslay ad this section.

Kluane Museum of Natural History. See display ad this section.

DC 1061.6 (1759.2 km) **DJ 328.4** (528.5 km) **Burlbilly Hill**. The most unique stop at Mile 1093 is "Burlbilly Hill," 200 feet north of the museum. The visitor will see rows of "burly logs" on the hill. Another surprise is a small woodshop with its variety of finely finished burl products, "burl bowls" and "diamond willow canes." Come and watch Obie and Karin at work. Wir sprechen deutsch! Phone (867) 841-4607. [ADVERTISEMENT]

DC 1062 (1759.8 km) **DJ 328** (527.8 km) Campground to north. ▲

DC 1062.7 (1761 km) **DJ 327.3** (526.7 km) **Historic Milepost 1094. Private Aircraft:** Burwash Yukon government airstrip to north; elev. 2,643 feet/806m; length 6,000 feet/1,829m; gravel, no fuel.

DC 1067 (1768.8 km) **DJ 323** (519.8 km) Duke River bridge (clearance 17.7 feet/5.4m). The Duke River flows into Kluane Lake; named for George Duke, an early prospector.

DC 1071.9 (1776.5 km) **DJ 318.1** (511.9 km) Turnout to north. Burwash Creek, named for Lachlin Taylor Burwash, a mining recorder at Silver City in 1903.

DC 1076.7 (1784.1 km) **DJ 313.3** (504.2 km) Sakiw Creek.

DC 1077.3 (1785.1 km) **DJ 312.7** (503.2 km) Rest area with information panels and observation platform overlooking Kluane River.

DC 1078.5 (1787 km) **DJ 311.5** (501.3

km) Buildings to west belong to Hudson Bay Mining and Smelting Co.'s Wellgreen Nickel Mines, named for Wellington Bridgeman Green, the prospector who discovered the mineral showing in 1952. During the mine's operation, from May 1972 to July 1973, three shiploads of concentrates (averaging 13,000 tons each) were trucked to Haines, AK. The material proved to be too insufficient to be economical. No facilities or services.

NOTE: Watch for road construction between Kilomeptreposts 1787 and 1800 in summer of 1999.

DC 1079.4 (1788.5 km) **DJ 310.6** (499.8 km) Quill Creek.

DC 1080.9 (1791 km) **DJ 309.1** (497.4 km) Glacier Creek. Kluane River to east of highway.

DC 1083.5 (1795.5 km) **DJ 306.5** (493.2 km) **Historic Milepost 1117.** Photo viewpoint turnout. Sign commemorates 1st Lt. Roland Small, of the 18th Engineers Regiment, who died in a jeep accident near this site during construction of the Alaska Highway in 1942. Short road to Kluane River; no turnaround.

DC 1084.6 (1797.2 km) DJ 305.4 (491.5 km) **Historical Mile 1118, Kluane Wilderness Village** (unincorporated). Lodge complex with gas, restaurant, bar; camping and lodging. Open year-round. Scully, "Burl King of the North," resides here. His work can be seen across the highway from Kluane Wilderness Village, as well as in the saloon (which has a burl bar). Viewing platform of Mount Kennedy, Mount Logan and Mount Lucania. Halfway mark between Whitehorse and Tok. ▲

Kluane Wilderness Village offers all amenities to modern day travelers. 24-hour service station. Full-menu restaurant, "Scully's Saloon" and comfortable accommodation. Our Good Sam R.V. Park (with direct Satellite TV) is the ideal resting location halfway between Whitehorse and Tok, nestled in the beautiful Kluane Mountains. See our display ad this page for more. Phone/fax (867) 841-4141. [ADVERTISEMENT] ▲

DC 1086.6 (1799.5 km) DJ 303.4 (488.3 km) Swede Johnson Creek. Turnout to east.

DC 1091.3 (1808 km) DJ 298.7 (480.7 km) Buildings to east are a dormant pump station once used to pressure up fuel being transferred from Haines to Fairbanks.

DC 1095 (1814 km) DJ 295 (474.7 km) NorthwesTel microwave tower visible ahead northbound.

DC 1095.4 (1814.6 km) DJ 294.6 (474.1 km) Abandoned Mountain View Lodge. View of Donjek River Valley.

Alaska Highway workers faced one of their toughest construction jobs during completion of the Alaska Highway in 1943 from the Donjek River to the Alaska border. Swampy ground underlain by permafrost, numerous creeks, lakes and rivers, plus a thick insulating ground cover made this section particularly difficult for road builders.

In recent years, this same section of highway has been the object of a massive, ongoing reconstruction known as the Shakwak Highway project.

DC 1096.3 (1816 km) DJ 293.7 (472.6 km) Turnout to west with view of Donjek River Valley and the Icefield Ranges of the St. Elias Mountains. Interpretive display.

DC 1099.7 (1819.5 km) DJ 290.3 (467.2 km) **Historic Milepost 1130.** Turnout with interpretive panel on the Donjek River bridge. Sign reads: "Glacial rivers, like the Donjek, posed a unique problem for the builders of the Alaska Highway. These braided mountain streams would flood after a heavy rainfall or rapid glacial melt, altering the waters' course and often leaving bridges crossing dry ground."

DC 1100 (1820 km) DJ 290 (466.7 km) *NOTE: Watch for road construction between Kilometreposts 1820 and 1830 in summer 1999.*

Donjek River bridge (clearance 17.4 feet/5.3m). Access to river at north end of bridge on west side of highway. This wide silty river is a major tributary of the White River. According to R. Coutts, *Yukon: Places & Names*, the Donjek is believed to have been named by Charles Willard Hayes in 1891 from the Indian word for a peavine that grows in the area.

DC 1008.7 (1834 km) DJ 381.3 (613.6 km) *CAUTION: Loose gravel next 5 miles/8 km northbound; narrow, winding road, no shoul-*

Bicyclists on the Alaska Highway south of Beaver Creek. (© Ruth von Spalding)

ders. Road conditions alternate between excellent surface and wide road with gravel shoulders, to narrow road with loose gravel and no shoulders, northbound to Beaver Creek. Good highway begins northbound at Beaver Creek Highway Maintenance section and continues to the border.

Yukon Highway Dept. was to begin replacing moved and missing kilometreposts in late 1998. Post locations may differ from The MILEPOST® *log.*

DC 1113.5 (1844.4 km) DJ 276.5 (445 km) **Edith Creek** bridge, turnout to west. Try your hand at gold panning here; "colours" have been found. Grayling fishing, June through September. ⊶

DC 1113.8 (1844.8 km) DJ 276.2 (444.5 km) **Historical Mile 1147. Pine Valley Motel and Cafe.** Hi! Thanks to all our customers for your patronage from your host Carmen and our staff. Open 24 hours. We have unleaded and diesel available (seniors gas discount). Minor repairs. RV park and campground, pull-throughs, power, picnic tables, free showers included. Free coffee included with any overnight stay. Good fishing stream nearby. Rooms, cabins with TV, bath, showers. Lounge and cafe with full menu bakery featuring hearty soups, homemade breads, pies, pastries—all made here. Enjoy a scenic view while our friendly morning cook prepares you up a mean breakfast, or sink your teeth into Carmen's wonderful sweet rolls. We have cold beer and spirits for take-out, or sit and relax in our lounge. Pay phone, cubed ice, fishing license and tackle, souvenirs. Book exchange. Harleys welcome. Corral for overnighting horses. MasterCard and VISA. Interac direct payment. Enjoy your drive through Kluane National Park and keep it clean and green. Thanks! Phone/fax (867) 862-7407. [ADVERTISEMENT] ▲

DC 1118.3 (1852.2 km) DJ 271.7 (437.2 km) Koidern River bridge No. 1.

DC 1118.8 (1853 km) DJ 271.2 (436.4 km) **Historical Mile 1152.** Lake Creek Yukon government campground just west of highway; 30 large level sites (6 pull-through), water pump, litter barrels, firewood, firepits, picnic tables, kitchen shelter and outhouses. Camping fee $8. ▲

DC 1122.7 (1859.5 km) DJ 267.3 (430.2 km) **Historical Mile 1156.** Longs Creek.

NOTE: Watch for road construction between

Kilometreposts 1862 and 1868 in summer 1999.

DC 1125 (1863.5 km) DJ 265 (426.5 km) Turnout to east with litter barrel.

DC 1125.7 (1864.7 km) DJ 264.3 (425.3 km) **Pickhandle Lake** to west; interpretive panels on Native trading routes, pond life and muskrats. Good fishing from boat for northern pike all summer; also grayling, whitefish and lingcod. ⊶

DC 1128 (1868.4 km) DJ 262 (421.6 km) Aptly named Reflection Lake to west mirrors the Kluane Range. The highway parallels this range between Koidern and Haines Junction.

DC 1130.6 (1872.6 km) DJ 259.4 (417.4 km) **Historical Mile 1164.** Lodge.

DC 1130.7 (1872.8 km) DJ 259.3 (417.3 km) Koidern River bridge No. 2.

DC 1133.7 (1877.6 km) DJ 256.3 (412.5 km) **Historic Milepost 1167.** Bear Flats Lodge (closed in 1998, current status unknown).

DC 1135 (1880 km) DJ 255 (410.4 km) **Historical Mile 1169,** Food, gas, diesel, dump station and camping. ▲

White River RV Park. See display ad this section. ▲

DC 1135.6 (1881 km) DJ 254.4 (409.4

km) **White River** bridge (new bridge 1998). The White River, a major tributary of the Yukon River, was named by Hudson's Bay Co. explorer Robert Campbell for its white colour, caused by the volcanic ash in the water. *This river is considered very dangerous; not recommended for boating.*

DC 1141.5 (1890.5 km) DJ 248.5 (399.9 km) **Moose Lake** to west, grayling to 18 inches, use dry flies and small spinners, midsummer. Boat needed for lake. ⊶

DC 1144.3 (1895 km) DJ 245.7 (395.4 km) Sanpete Creek, named by an early prospector after Sanpete County in Utah.

DC 1147.5 (1900.3 km) DJ 242.5 (390.2 km) Dry Creek No. 1. Turnout to east.

DC 1150.3 (1904.5 km) DJ 239.7 (385.7 km) **Historical Mile 1184.** Dry Creek No. 2. Historical marker to west about the Chrisna gold rush.

DC 1155 (1911.8 km) DJ 235 (378.2 km) Small Lake to east.

DC 1155.2 (1913 km) 234.8 (377.9 km) **Historical Mile 1188.** Turnoff for Snag Junction Yukon government campground, 0.4 mile/0.6 km in on gravel loop road. There are 15 tent and vehicle sites (some level), a kitchen shelter, outhouses, picnic tables, firewood, firepits and litter barrels. Camping fee $8. Small-boat launch. Swimming in Small Lake. A dirt road (status unknown) connects the Alaska Highway here with the abandoned airfield and Indian village at

Interpretive signs at Beaver Creek, Historical Mile 1202. (© Harry M. Walker)

Snag to the northeast. Snag's claim to fame is the lowest recorded temperature in Canada: -81°F/-63°C on Feb. 3, 1947. ▲

DC 1162.1 (1924.5 km) **DJ 227.9** (366.7 km) Inger Creek.

DC 1165.7 (1930 km) **DJ 224.3** (361 km) View of Nutzotin Mountains to northwest, Kluane Ranges to southwest. On a clear day you should be able to see the snow-clad Wrangell Mountains in the distance to the west.

DC 1167.2 (1932.4 km) **DJ 222.8** (358.5 km) Beaver Creek plank bridge, clearance 17.1 feet/5.2m.

Beaver Creek

DC 1168.5 (1934.5 km) **DJ 221.5** (356.4 km) **Historic Milepost 1202.** Driving distance to Haines Junction, 184 miles/295 km; to Tok, 113 miles/182 km; to Haines, 334 miles/537.5 km. **Population:** 140. **Emergency Services:** RCMP, phone (867) 862-5555. Ambulance, phone (867) 862-3333. **Nursing Station:** (867) 862-4444.

Visitor Information: Yukon government visitor information centre, open daily late May through mid-September. Phone (867) 862-7321. The visitor centre has a book of dried Yukon wildflowers for those interested in the flora of the territory.

Private Aircraft: Beaver Creek Yukon government airstrip 1 NW; see description at **Milepost DC 1170.3.**

Site of the old Canadian customs station. Local residents were pleased to see customs relocated north of town in 1983, having long endured the flashing lights and screaming sirens set off whenever a tourist forgot to stop.

Beaver Creek is 1 of 2 sites where Alaska Highway construction crews working from opposite directions connected the highway. In October 1942, Alaska Highway construction operations were being rushed to conclusion as winter set in. Eastern and western

BEAVER CREEK ADVERTISERS

Beaver Creek
  Motor Inn ....Ph. (867) 862-7600
Ida's Motel &
  Restaurant ....Ph. (867) 862-7223
Westmark
  Beaver Creek................Ph. (800) 544-0970

sector construction crews (the 97th and 18th Engineers) pushed through to meet at a junction on Beaver Creek on Oct. 28., thus making it possible for the first time for vehicles to travel the entire length of the highway. East–west crews had connected at Contact Creek on Sept. 24, 1942.

Motels, gas stations with repair service, a post office and licensed restaurants are located here. Beaver Creek is also an overnight stop for bus travelers. A hostel operated here in 1998; inquire locally. Private RV park with hookups, hot showers, store, laundry and dump station. Informational panels on the Yukon Centennial are located throughout the city. ▲

The interesting looking church here is Our Lady of Grace mission. Built in 1961, it is 1 of 3 Catholic missions on the north Alaska Highway (the others are in Burwash Landing and Haines Junction). Services from the last Sunday of May to first Sunday of September. There is a public swimming pool beside the community club. Check with the information centre about the live stage show at the Westmark Inn, evenings in summer; admission charged. The Westmark also has a wildlife display.

Alaska Highway Log
(continued)

Distance* from Dawson Creek (DC) is followed by distance from Delta Junction (DJ). Original mileposts are indicated in the text as Historical Mile.

**In Canada, mileages from Dawson Creek are based on actual driving distance, not historical mileposts, and kilometres are based on physical kilometreposts *as they occurred in summer 1998.* Mileages from Delta Junction are also based on actual driving distance, not historical mileposts, but are followed by the metric conversion to kilometres.

DC 1169.7 (1936.3 km) DJ 220.3 (354.5 km) Rest area to west with litter barrels, picnic tables and outhouses.

DC 1170.3 (1937.3 km) DJ 219.7 (353.6km) **Private Aircraft:** Beaver Creek Yukon government airstrip; elev. 2,129 feet/ 649m; length 3,740 feet/1,140m; gravel; no fuel. Airport of entry for Canada customs.

DC 1170.5 (1937.6 km) DJ 219.5 (353.2 km) Beaver Creek Canada customs station; phone (403) 862-7230. Open 24 hours a day year-round. All traffic entering Canada must stop here for clearance.

DC 1175.4 (1945.5 km) DJ 214.8 (345.7 km) Snag Creek plank bridge.

DC 1176.3 (1946.9 km) DJ 213.7 (343.9 km) Mirror Creek.

DC 1178.3 (1952 km) DJ 211.7 (340.7 km) Lake to east, turnout to west.

DC 1186 (1963 km) DJ 204 (328.3 km) Little Scottie Creek.

DC 1189.5 (1967.5 km) DJ 200.5 (322.7 km) **Historic Milepost 1221.** Turnout with plaque and other markers at **Canada–U.S. International Border.** Litter barrels. From the viewing decks, note the narrow clearing marking the border. This is part of the 20-foot-/6-m-wide swath cut by surveyors from 1904 to 1920 along the 141st meridian (from Demarcation Point on the Arctic Ocean south 600 miles/966 km to Mount St. Elias in the Wrangell Mountains) to mark the Alaska–Canada border. This swath continues south to mark the boundary between southeastern Alaska and Canada. Portions of the swath are cleared periodically by the International Boundary Commission.

TIME ZONE CHANGE: Alaska observes Alaska time; Yukon Territory observes Pacific time. Alaska Time is 1 hour earlier than Pacific Time.

DC 1189.8 (1968 km) DJ 200.2 (322.2 km) **Historical Mile 1221.8.** U.S. customs border station.

IMPORTANT: The MILEPOST® log now switches to physical mileposts for northbound travelers. For southbound travelers, the log is based on actual driving distance. The Alaska Highway is approximately 32 miles/51 km shorter than the traditional figure of 1,221.8 miles between Dawson Creek and the YT–AK border. Please read the information on Mileposts and Kilometre posts in the introduction to the Alaska Highway.

Northbound: Fair to good pavement to Fairbanks. Watch for frost heaves, potholes and pavement breaks next 40 miles/64 km.

Southbound: Narrow, winding road to Haines Junction. Improved highway to Beaver Creek, fair to good pavement to Haines Junction. Watch for rough spots, gravel breaks and road construction.

ALASKA ROUTE 2
Distance* from Dawson Creek (DC) is followed by distance from Delta Junction (DJ).
*Mileages from Dawson Creek and Fairbanks are based on physical mileposts in Alaska. Kilometres given are the metric equivalents of these mileages.

Barrow's Goldeneye (male). These ducks are common in Central Alaska lakes and ponds. (© Chris Sharp)

DC 1221.8 (1966.3 km) **DJ 200.2** (322.2 km) **Port Alcan** U.S. Customs and Immigration Service border station, open 24 hours a day year-round; pay phone (credit card and collect calls only) and restrooms. All traffic entering Alaska must stop for clearance. Phone (907) 774-2242; emergencies, (907) 774-2252.

Border Branch U.S. post office is located here (ZIP 99764); ask for directions at the customs office.

DC 1222.5 (1967.4 km) **DJ 199.5** (321.1 km) **Tetlin National Wildlife Refuge** boundary sign to west. Established in 1980, the 730,000-acre refuge stretches south from the Alaska Highway and west from the Canadian border. The major physical features include rolling hills, hundreds of small lakes and 2 glacial rivers (the Nabesna and Chisana) which combine to form the Tanana River. The refuge has a very high density of nesting waterfowl. Annual duck production in favorable years exceeds 50,000. Among the larger birds using the refuge are trumpeter swans, sandhill cranes, Pacific and common loons, osprey, bald eagles and ptarmigan. Other wildlife includes moose, black and grizzly bear, wolf, coyote, beaver, red fox, lynx and caribou. Activities allowed on the refuge include wildlife observation, hunting, fishing, camping, hiking and trapping. Check with refuge personnel at the USF&WS office in Tok prior to your visit for more detailed information. Write Refuge Manager, Tetlin National Wildlife Refuge, Box 779, Tok, AK 99780; or phone (907) 883-5312. Information on the refuge is also available at the USF&WS visitor center at **Milepost DC 1229** on the Alaska Highway.

DC 1223.4 (1968.9 km) **DJ 198.6** (319.6 km) Scotty Creek bridge.

DC 1224.6 (1970.7 km) **DJ 197.4** (317.7 km) Double-ended gravel turnout to southwest at Highway Lake with USF&WS interpretive sign on wetlands. Beaver lodges southwest side of highway.

DC 1225.4 (1972 km) **DJ 196.6** (316.4 km) USF&WS Desper Creek parking area and canoe launch.

DC 1225.5 (1972.2 km) **DJ 196.5** (316.2 km) **Border City Motel & RV Park.** See display ad this section. ▲

DC 1226 (1973 km) **DJ 196** (315.4 km) **Scottie Creek Services.** See display ad on page 173.

DC 1227.8 (1975.9 km) **DJ 194.2** (312.5 km) Large double-ended paved parking area to southwest with USF&WS interpretive sign on migratory birds and area geography. View to south of lakes in Chisana (SHOE-sanna) River valley along Scotty Creek and west to the Nutzotin Mountains. The Chisana gold rush took place in 1913. A mining camp was established on Cross Creek near the Chisana River, 38 miles southeast of Nabesna in the Wrangell Mountains. The settlement's population peaked at 148 in 1920.

DC 1229 (1977.8 km) **DJ 193** (310.6 km) **USF&WS Log Cabin Visitor Center** to south. Viewing deck and outdoor displays on wildlife and other subjects. Indoor

wildlife displays and mounts. Deckside nature talks given daily. Restrooms (wheelchair accessible). Open 7 A.M. to 7 P.M. Memorial Day to Labor Day. Current highway conditions and fishing information posted on bulletin board. ♿

DC 1230.9 (1980.9 km) **DJ 200.1** (322 km) View of Island Lake.

DC 1233.3 (1984.7 km) **DJ 188.7** (303.7 km) Large paved double-ended parking area to northeast on old alignment. Watch for bears and frost heaves.

DC 1237 (1990.7 km) **DJ 185** (297.7 km) Trail to **Hidden Lake** (1 mile/1.6 km); rainbow fishing. USF&WS interpretive signs on rainbow trout and permafrost.

DC 1240 (1995.5 km) **DJ 182** (292.9 km) Turnout to west; no easy turnaround. Walk-in access to **Willow Lake** for fishing (stocked with trout every other year). 🐟

DC 1240.3 (1996 km) **DJ 181.7** (292.4 km) Vertical culverts on either side of highway are an experiment to keep ground from thawing and thus prevent frost heaves.

DC 1243.6 (2001.3 km) **DJ 178.4** (287.1 km) Paved turnout. Scenic viewpoint to south on loop road has USF&WS interpretive signs on fire management and the effects of forest fires on the natural history of area. Sand dunes.

DC 1246.6 (2006.1 km) **DJ 175.4** (282.3 km) **Historic Milepost 1248. Gardiner Creek** bridge; parking to west at south end of bridge. Grayling fishing. 🐟

DC 1247.6 (2007.8 km) **DJ 174.4** (280.7 km) Paved double-ended viewpoint to east.

DC 1249.3 (2010.5 km) **DJ 172.7** (277.9 km) **Historic Milepost 1254. Deadman Lake** USF&WS campground, 1.2 miles/1.9 km in on dirt road. Turnout at highway junction with campground access road. The campground has 18 sites on long loop road, firepits, toilets, picnic tables, no drinking water, boat ramp, interpretive signs, information board and self-guided nature trail. Occasional evening programs offered. Wheelchair accessible. Scenic spot. Swimming and fishing. Northern pike average 2 feet, but skinny (local residents call them "snakes"); use wobbling lures or spinners. ♿🐟⛺

DC 1250.1 (2011.8 km) **DJ 171.9** (276.6 km) Rest area to west. Double-ended paved parking area, 4 picnic tables, concrete fireplaces, no water or toilets.

DC 1252.2 (2015.2 km) **169.8** (273.2 km)

Double-ended gravel turnout to southwest with USF&WS interpretive sign on solar basins (warm ponds and shallow marshes) and scenic viewpoint.

DC 1253 (2016.5 km) **DJ 169** (272 km) Views of lakes and muskeg in Chisana River valley.

DC 1253.6 (2017.4 km) **DJ 168.4** (271 km) **Frontier Surplus.** Military surplus goods. Clothing, sleeping bags, extreme cold weather "bunny boots," military tents, ammunition, tanned furs. Alaska T-shirts and caps. Local crafts, shed moose and caribou antlers. Antler products, belt buckles,

boloties, hat racks, handmade ulus. "Moosquitoes," diamond willow lamps and canes, finished or unfinished. Used Alaska license plates, cold pop. Open late every day. Motorhome and RV loop. Phone (907) 778-

Northway

Northway

Located 7 miles/11.3 km south of the Alaska Highway via a side road. **Population:** 364 (area). **Emergency Services: Alaska State Troopers,** phone (907) 778-2245. **EMS,** phone (907) 778-2211. **Fire Department,** emergency phone, (907) 778-2211. **Clinic,** phone (907) 778-2283.

Elevation: 1,710 feet/521m. **Climate:** Mean monthly temperature in July, 58.5°F/15°C. In January, -21°F/-30°C. Record high 91°F/33°C in June 1969; record low -72°F/-58°C in January 1952.

Private Aircraft: Northway airport, adjacent south; elev. 1,716 feet/523m; length 5,130 feet/1,564m; asphalt; fuel 100LL, Jet, MOGAS; customs available. Floatplanes use Yarger Lake 8 nm E.

Northway has a community hall, post office, modern school. FAA station and customs office. Visitor services include motels, liquor store, propane, gas and air taxi service at the airport. Northway is the aviation entry point into Alaska for most private planes.

Northway's airport was built in the 1940s as part of the Northwest Staging Route. This cooperative project of the United States and Canada was a chain of air bases from Edmonton, AB, through Whitehorse, YT, to Fairbanks. This chain of air bases helped build up and supply Alaska defense during WWII and also was used during construction of the Alcan and the Canol project. Lend-lease aircraft bound for Russia were flown up this route to Ladd Field (now Fort Wainwright) in Fairbanks.

Historically occupied by Athabascan Indians, Northway was named to honor the village chief who adopted the name of a river-boat captain in the early 1900s. (Chief Walter Northway died in 1993. He was thought to be 117 years old.) The rich Athabascan traditions of dancing, crafts, and hunting and trapping continue today in Northway Village. Local Athabascan handicrafts available for purchase include birch-bark baskets, beadwork accessories, and moose hide and fur items such as moccasins, mukluks, mittens and hats.

Confluence of Moose Creek and Chisana River, about 0.8 mile/1.3 km downstream from Chisana River bridge on Northway Road, south side of river, northern pike to 15 lbs., use red-and-white spoon, spring or fall. **Chisana River,** downstream from bridge, lingcod (burbot) to 8 lbs., use chunks of liver or meat, spring. **Nabesna Slough,** south end of runway, grayling to 3 lbs., use spinner or gold flies, late May. 🐟

Northway Airport Lodge & Motel. See display ad this section.

2274. [ADVERTISEMENT]
DC 1256.3 (2021.7 km) **DJ 165.7** (266.7 km) Northway state highway maintenance camp; no services.

DC 1256.7 (2022.5 km) **DJ 165.3** (266 km) Lakeview USF&WS campground on beautiful Yarger Lake; 8 sites, tables, toilets, firepits, firewood, no drinking water, occasional evening programs offered. Wheelchair accessible. Interpretive signs. *NOTE: No turnaround space. Not recommended for trailers, 5th wheels or RVs over 30 feet. (Large vehicles use Deadman Lake Campground at **Milepost DC 1249.3**.)* ♿▲

This is a good place to view ducks and loons. Look for the Nutzotin Mountains to the south and Mentasta Mountains to the west.

Roadside wildflowers include sweet pea, pale yellow Indian paintbrush, yarrow and Labrador tea.

DC 1260.2 (2028 km) **DJ 161.8** (260.4 km) 1260 Inn roadhouse (closed in 1998, current status unknown).

DC 1263 (2032.5 km) **DJ 159** (255.9 km) Truck stop with gas and diesel; lodging.

DC 1263.5 (2033.4 km) **DJ 158.5** (255.1 km) Chisana River parallels the highway to the southwest. This is the land of a thousand ponds, most unnamed. Good trapping country. In early June, travelers may note numerous cottony white seeds blowing in the wind; these seeds are from willow and poplars.

DC 1264 (2034.2 km) **DJ 158** (254.3 km) **Northway Junction.** Campground, gas, laundromat, store, and Native arts and crafts shop located at junction. An Alaska State Trooper office is located on the east side of the highway. ▲

Naabia Niign Campground & Athabascan Indian Crafts. See display ad on page 175. ▲

Junction with 7-mile/11.3-km side road (hard-packed dirt and gravel) which leads south across the Chisana River bridge to the community of Northway (see description this page).

DC 1267.4 (2039.6 km) **DJ 154.6** (248.8 km) Wonderful view of the Tanana River at Beaver Slide. Northbound, the highway cuts through several sand dunes stabilized by aspen and spruce trees.

CAUTION: Watch for and slow down for sections of rough road, loose gravel, frost heaves and pavement cracks northbound to Tok.

DC 1268.1 (2040.8 km) **DJ 153.9** (247.7 km) Beaver Creek bridge. The tea-colored water flowing in the creek is the result of tannins absorbed by the water as it flows through muskeg. This phenomenon may be observed in other Northern creeks.

DC 1269 (2042.2 km) **DJ 153** (246.2 km) **Historic Milepost 1271.** Scenic viewpoint. Double-ended gravel turnout to west has a litter barrel and USF&WS interpretive sign (missing in 1998) about the Tanana River, largest tributary of the Yukon River.

DC 1272.7 (2048.2 km) **DJ 149.3** (240.3 km) Scenic viewpoint. Double-ended paved turnout to west with USF&WS interpretive sign (missing in 1998) on pond ecology and mosquitoes.

To the northwest the Tanana River flows near the highway; beyond, the Kalukna River snakes its way through plain and marshland. Mentasta Mountains are visible to the southwest.

DC 1273.9 (2050.1 km) **DJ 148.1** (238.3

km) Paved parking area to west by Tanana River.

In June, wild sweet peas create thick borders along the highway. This is rolling country, with aspen, birch, cottonwood, willow and white spruce.

DC 1275.5 (2052.7 km) **DJ 146.5** (235.8 km) Slide area next 0.3 mile/0.5 km northbound.

DC 1284 (2066.3 km) **DJ 138** (222.1 km) Distance marker shows Tok 30 miles, Fairbanks 235 miles, Anchorage 365 miles.

DC 1284.6 (2067.3 km) **DJ 137.4** (221.1 km) Large double-ended turnout to east.

DC 1285.7 (2069.1 km) **DJ 136.3** (219.3 km) Granite intrusion in older metamorphosed rock is exposed by road cut.

DC 1289 (2074.4 km) **DJ 133** (214 km) First view northbound of 3.4-mile-/5.5-km-long Midway Lake.

DC 1289.4 (2075 km) **DJ 132.6** (213.4 km) **Historic Milepost 1292.** Turnout uphill on east side of highway. *NOTE: Difficult access for large vehicles and trailers, easier access from southbound lane.* View of Midway Lake and the Wrangell Mountains. USF&WS interpretive signs on Wrangell–St. Elias National Park and Native peoples.

DC 1290 (2076 km) **DJ 132** (212.4 km) Beautiful view of Midway Lake southbound.

DC 1292.4 (2079.8 km) **DJ 129.6** (208.5 km) Paved turnout west side.

DC 1293.7 (2081.9 km) **DJ 128.3** (206.5 km) Paved turnout west side.

DC 1294.3 (2082.9 km) **DJ 127.7** (205.5 km) Distance marker shows Tok 20 miles, Fairbanks 225 miles, Anchorage 355 miles.

DC 1301.7 (2094.8 km) **DJ 120.3** (193.6 km) **Historic Milepost 1306 Tetlin Junction.** 40 Mile Roadhouse; status of services unknown.

> **Junction** of the Alaska Highway (Alaska Route 2) and Taylor Highway (Alaska Route 5). The Taylor Highway (gravel, open summer only) heads northeast via Jack Wade Junction to Eagle (see TAYLOR HIGHWAY section) and to Yukon Highway 9 (Top of the World Highway) to Dawson City.

See KLONDIKE LOOP section for log of Yukon Highway 9 (Top of the World Highway) and description of Dawson City. *NOTE: If you are traveling to Dawson City, keep in mind that both the Canada and U.S. customs stations are closed at night; you CANNOT cross the border unless customs stations are open. Customs hours in summer have been 8 A.M. to 8 P.M. Alaska time, 9 A.M. to 9 P.M. Pacific time on the Canadian side. Travelers are advised to check for current information at Alaska Public Lands Information Center, (907) 883-5667.*

DC 1302.7 (2096.4 km) **DJ 119.3** (192 km) Scenic viewpoint at paved turnout to southwest. Distance marker shows Tok 12 miles, Fairbanks 217 miles, Anchorage 347 miles.

DC 1303.4 (2097.5 km) **DJ 118.6** (190.9 km) Tanana River bridge. Informal parking area and boat launch to east at north end of bridge. Tanana (TAN-uh-naw), an Indian name, was first reported by the Western Union Telegraph Expedition of 1886. According to William Henry Dall, chief scientist of the expedition, the name means "mountain river." The Tanana is the largest tributary of the Yukon River in Alaska. From here the highway parallels the Tanana to Fairbanks. The Alaska Range looms in the distance.

DC 1304.6 (2099.5 km) **DJ 117.4** (188.9 km) Evidence of burn from here north to Tok. The Tok River fire occurred in July of 1990 and burned 97,352 acres. The fire closed the Alaska and Glenn highways at times and threatened the town of Tok.

DC 1306.6 (2102.7 km) **DJ 115.4** (185.7 km) Road east to lake.

DC 1308.5 (2105.7 km) **DJ 113.5** (182.6 km) Weigh station; phone. Turnoff to U.S. Coast Guard loran-C station and signal towers.

This loran (long range navigation) station is 1 of 7 in Alaska. A series of four 700-foot/213-m towers suspends a multi-element wire antenna used to transmit navigation signals. These signals may be used by air, land and sea navigators as an aid in determining their position. This station is located here as necessary for good geometry with 2 Gulf of Alaska loran transmitting stations.

DC 1308.8 (2106.3 km) **DJ 113.2** (182.2 km) Paved turnout to west.

DC 1309.2 (2106.9 km) **DJ 112.8** (181.5 km) **Tok River State Recreation Site;** 25 campsites, overflow parking, tables, firepits, toilets (wheelchair accessible), litter barrels, nature trail, boat launch and pay phone. Check bulletin board for schedule of interpretive programs. Camping fee $10/night or annual pass. *CAUTION: Swift water.* ♿▲

Annual passes good for unlimited camping at all Alaska state parks within a calendar year are available for $75 for Alaska residents and $200 for nonresidents. Annual daily parking pass is $25, annual boat launch pass is $50. Super Pass (camping, boat launch and parking) is available to Alaska residents only for $135. Passes may be purchased at the Alaska Public Lands Information Center in Tok.

DC 1309.4 (2107.2 km) **DJ 112.6** (181.2 km) Tok River bridge.

DC 1312.7 (2112.5 km) **DJ 109.3** (175.9 km) Tok community limits. Mountain views ahead northbound.

DC 1312.8 (2112.7 km) **DJ 109.2** (175.7 km) Tok Dog Mushers Assoc. track and buildings. Paved bike trail from Tok ends here.

DC 1312.9 (2112.8 km) **DJ 109.1** (175.6 km) **Rod's Automotive.** All automotive work. RVs, light trucks and towing. Estimates given first. Come in and have some coffee with us. Open Monday–Saturday 9 A.M.– 6 P.M. Phone (907) 883-2886. [ADVERTISEMENT]

DC 1313 (2113 km) **DJ 109** (175.4 km) Tok Junction airstrip. See Private Aircraft information in Tok section. Entering Tok (northbound), description follows.

Southbound travelers: Driving distance from Tok to Beaver Creek is 113 miles/182 km; Haines Junction 296 miles/476 km;

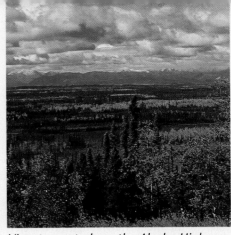

View to west along the Alaska Highway between Tetlin Junction and Tok.

(© Ruth von Spalding)

Haines (departure point for Alaska state ferries) 446.5 miles/718.5 km; and Whitehorse 396 miles/637 km.

CAUTION: Watch for and slow down for sections of rough road with lose gravel, frost heaves and pavement cracks southbound to border.

DC 1313.1 (2113.1 km) **DJ 108.9** (175.3 km) **Tok Gateway Salmon Bake and RV Park.** Rated, *Alaska's Best Places*, Tok's Gateway Salmon Bake, features outdoor flame-

grilled Alaska king salmon, halibut, ribs and reindeer sausage. Buffalo burgers. Chowder. Good food, friendly people; casual dining at its best. Open 11 A.M. to 9 P.M., except Sunday 4 P.M. to 9 P.M. Free shuttle bus service from local hotels and RV parks. Wooded RV and tent sites with tables, clean restrooms, dump station and water. Showers available. Free dry camping with dinner. Phone/fax (907) 883-5555. Internet www.tokalaska.com/tok samon.shtml. [ADVERTISEMENT] ▲

DC 1313.2 (2113.3 km) DJ 108.8 (175.1 km) **Willard's Full Service Repair.** See display ad this section.

DC 1313.3 (2113.5 km) DJ 108.7 (174.9 km) **Village Texaco Foodmart.** Filtered unleaded and premium gas and diesel. Lubricants and propane. Automatic teller machine, laundromat, phone cards, pay phones and clean restrooms. Deli chicken, burritos, mojos, snacks, pop, ice, milk shakes, ice cream and espresso. RV supplies. Alaskan souvenirs. Across highway from Tok RV Village. See display ad this section. [ADVERTISEMENT]

DC 1313.3 (2113.5 km) DJ 108.7 (174.9 km) **Young's Motel and Fast Eddy's Restaurant.** A touch of Alaskana in a modern setting. Affordable, clean and spacious. We cater to the independent highwaytraveler. Open year-round with all the amenities: telephones, private baths, satellite TV, ample parking. Nonsmoking rooms available. Check in at Fast Eddy's full-service restau-

rant, open 6 A.M. to midnight. Reserve early! P.O. Box 482, Tok, AK 99780. (907) 883-4411; fax (907) 883-5023. [ADVERTISEMENT] MP

DC 1313.3 (2113.5 km) DJ 108.7 (174.9 km) **The Bull Shooter Sporting Goods & RV Park.** Fishing and hunting licenses and supplies. Stay at the Bull Shooter's RV park. 30 spaces, 24 pull-throughs. Full or partial hookups, 30-amp electric, dump station.

Non-metered showers, ice, phone. VISA, MasterCard. On the left coming into Tok. P.O. Box 553, Tok, AK 99780. Reservations: (907) 883-5625. See display ad in Tok section. [ADVERTISEMENT] ▲

DC 1313.3 (2113.5 km) DJ 108.7 (174.9 km) **Shamrock Hardware.** See display ad this section.

DC 1313.4 (2113.6 km) DJ 108.6 (174.8 km) **Tok RV Village.** Alaska's finest. Good Sam or KOA cards honored. Convenient pull-through spaces with 20-30-50 amp. Full and partial hookups, clean restrooms and showers, dump station, laundry, vehicle wash, picnic tables, public phones, e-mail terminals. Gift shop. RV supplies, ice. MasterCard, VISA and Discover. Located across highway from Village Texaco Foodmart. Restaurants, liquor store, night club, hardware store, oil change and lube service nearby. See display ad this section. [ADVERTISEMENT] ▲

DC 1313.9 (2114.5 km) DJ 108.1 (174 km) **Tok Machine & Welding/Tok Northern Exposures 1-Hour Photo.** Your one stop in Tok for RV repair needs. Machine shop and certified welder; oil change; lubrication; (907) 883-5670. Get your film developed next door and have your "olde tyme" portrait taken. Film, batteries, albums, frames, gifts; (907) 883-5424. On your left northbound. See display ad. [ADVERTISEMENT]

DC 1314.1 (2114.8 km) DJ 107.9 (173.6 km) U.S. Fish and Wildlife Office to west; State Troopers to east.

DC 1314.2 (2115 km) DJ 107.8 (173.5 km) Tok Mainstreet Visitor Center and Tok Memorial Park (picnicking) to east at intersection with Alaska Route 1. See description of Tok following.

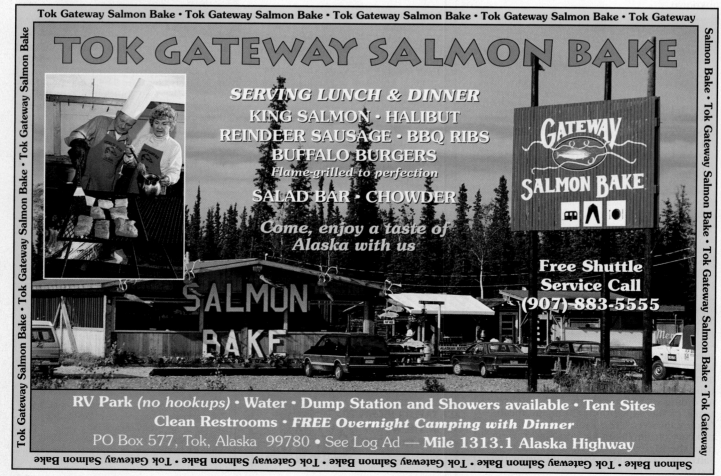

Junction of the Alaska Highway (Alaska Route 2) and the Tok Cutoff/Glenn Highway (Alaska Route 1), which leads 328 miles to Anchorage. Turn to the GLENN HIGHWAY section for log of that route.

Tok

Milepost 1314.2 Alaska Highway, at the junction with the Tok Cutoff (Glenn Highway). **Population:** 1,405. **Emergency Services:** Phone 911 for emergency services. **Alaska State Troopers,** phone (907) 883-5111. **Fire Department,** phone (907) 883-2333. **Ambulance,** phone (907) 883-5855. EMT squad

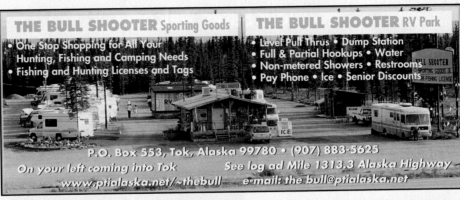

To Fairbanks ◄ Alaska Highway ②

Tok Memorial Park

Fish & Game Headquarters

Mainstreet Visitor Center, Alaska Public Lands Information Center

State Troopers, Public Health Clinic

② Alaska Highway ► To Canada

Post Office · Center St. · USF&W Office

Tok Cutoff (Glenn Highway)

① ▼ **To Anchorage**

Tok

and air medivac available. **Community Clinic,** across from the fire hall on the Tok Cutoff, phone (907) 883-5855 during business hours. **Public Health Clinic,** next to the Alaska State Troopers at **Milepost 1314.1,** phone (907) 883-4101.

Visitor Information: Tok Mainstreet

(Continues on page 183)

TOK ADVERTISERS

Tok Chamber of Commerce Welcomes You To Alaska

Partial
Membership
Sponsors

Photo: Donna Blasor-Bernhardt

MAINSTREET VISITOR CENTER
Trip planning, travel information. Wildlife displays, gifts. 8 a.m.-8 p.m. daily.
http://www.TokAlaskaInfo.com
e-mail: info@TokAlaskaInfo.com
(907) 883-5775

Cleft of the Rock
BED & BREAKFAST
cabins, rooms, complete breakfast
1-800-478-5646 *or* Fax 907-883-5963
http:tokalaska.com/cleftroc.shtml

NORTHERN ENERGY
One-Stop TLC for your RV
Discounts • Gas • Diesel • Tires
Propane • Free use of car wash
& dump with fill-up • Mi 1315 AK Hwy
(907) 883-4251

JACK WADE GOLD CO.
Mining Museum-Antique display. Alaska gold nugget jewelry made in-store. Year-round, 7am-9pm.
(907) 883-5887
1 block south on Tok Cutoff.

RITA'S CAMPGROUND/RV PARK
Cheryl's Old Fashion B&B. Alaska Pioneers
Mi. 1315.7, Alaska Hwy.
(907) 883-4342
"A relaxing Alaska atmosphere"

40-MILE AIR FLIGHTSEEING AND FISHING CHARTERS
Scenic/photo., glaciers, wildlife, mountains, historic Native village.
(907) 883-5191

TOK LODGE
Historical lodge w/10 rooms & 38 new motel units. Gift shop, cocktail lounge w/ patio dining. Cafe specializes in home cooking featuring prime rib, salmon, halibut & daily lunch specials, sourdough breakfasts. Open year-round.

Reservations
1-800-883-3007
P.O. Box 135 CM, Tok, AK 99780

TOK LIQUOR MINI-MART
Full line of beverages, ice, snacks, grocery items. 2 blocks south on Tok Cutoff.

A WINTER CABIN B&B
New log cabins w/GREAT BEDS, carpeted, microwaves, breakfast-stocked refrigerators. Quiet. Modern, separate bath house.
(907) 883-5655
http://www.ptialaska.net/~wntrcabn/donna.html

SOURDOUGH CAMPGROUND
Full hook-ups, wooded sites, Sourdough breakfast daily 7am-11am. June 1-August 31.
(907) 883-5543
FAX (907) 883-3332
1 1/2 Mi. South on Tok Cutoff

ALL ALASKA GIFTS & CRAFTS
Quality T-shirts, jewelry, Native crafts, Eskimo dolls, Jorgensen Bros. Wildlife displays. You'll like our prices.
At main intersection in Tok.

BURNT PAW
Free dog team show, 7:30pm, except Sun., next to Post Office. Log gift shop w/ sod roof. Box 7, Tok.
(907) 883-4121

CABINS OUTBACK B&B
@ Burnt Paw, nightly rentals log cabins; rustic outside, all conveniences inside. Summer. Box 7, Tok.
(907) 883-4121
(907) 456-7117 (winter)

GRIZZLY AUTO SERVICE
RV and Trailer Parts and Repairs
All Autos and Light Trucks Full-service Center. NAPA Auto Care. Good Sam Welcome.
(907) 883-5514/1-800-478-5514

MINERAL LAKES B&B
Cabin on lake, fishing, boating, RV parking, open year round.
(907) 883-5498
HC72, Box 830, Tok, AK 99780

TOKLAT AUTO PARTS
For All Your Automotive Needs
Mail Orders Welcome•RV Supplies
(907) 883-5858/1-800-906-5858
Mile 1314 Alaska Highway, Tok

SNOWSHOE GIFTS
Souvenirs, fine art, carvings, prints, jewelry, Alaska made gifts. Adjacent to Snowshoe Motel.
(907) 883-4181

SNOWSHOE MOTEL
24 Modern units w/satellite color TV, phones. Year-round. Summer: Continental breakfast, new picnic area.
Reservations:
(907) 883-4511
AK/YT: 1-800-478-4511
FAX: (907) 883-4512
P.O. Box 559, Tok, AK 99780
Hosts: Geneva Smith
Candy & Dannie Troupe

YOUNG'S CHEVRON
Volume Discounts, food mart, gas, diesel, propane, fast lube, full auto service center. Tire sales/service & RV wash. Alcan Espresso. At the Junction.
(907) 883-5835

YOUNG'S CAFE
Dinners-Beer-Wine-Full Menu
Daily Lunch Specials
Homemade Pies - Giant Cookies
Megamuffins - At the Junction
(907) 883-2233

TUNDRA LODGE & RV PARK
78 Large shaded sites, 30-50 Amp. service, tent sites, RV wash, laundromat, modem hookup, cocktail lounge.
(907) 883-7875
e-mail: tundrarv@ptialaska.net

TOK ALASKA

Good Sampark

Village TEXACO

Mile 1313.3 Alaska Highway
P.O. Box 739
Tok, Alaska 99780
Phone (907) 883-4660

Foodmart
Laundromat
Deli
Alaskan Souvenirs
Clean Restrooms
Gas • Diesel • Propane
ATM Machine • Phone Cards

TOK RV VILLAGE

Good Sampark

Mile 1313.4 Alaska Highway
P.O. Box 739 • Tok, Alaska 99780
(907) 883-5877 • Fax (907) 883-5878
1-800-478-5878

95 Sites • Full & Partial Hookups
Pull Thrus • Tent Sites
20/30/50 Amp Available
Dump Station • Vehicle Wash Facility
Gift Shop • Hunting & Fishing Licenses
Clean Restrooms & Showers • Laundry
RV Supplies • Good Sam Discounts
• E-mail Terminals

Come visit the

TOK RV VILLAGE GIFT SHOP

A small gift shop full of surprises

T-shirts • Sweatshirts
Hats • Videos
Postcards • Jewelry
Alaskan Made Crafts

Quality Gifts
at Reasonable Prices

Tourist Information Center ■ ● TOK RV VILLAGE
← FAIRBANKS   ALASKA HIGHWAY
N
ANCHORAGE
Village TEXACO
Tok Airport

We thank all of you wonderful customers who help to make our business such a great success.

The Jernigan Family

Tetlin National Wildlife Refuge. Office hours are 8 A.M. to noon and 1 P.M. to 4:30 P.M., weekdays. Write Box 155, Tok, AK 99780, or phone (907) 883-5312.

Elevation: 1,635 feet/498m. **Climate:** Mean monthly temperature in January, -19° F/-29°C; in July 59°F/14°C. Record low was -71°F/-57°C in January 1965; record high,

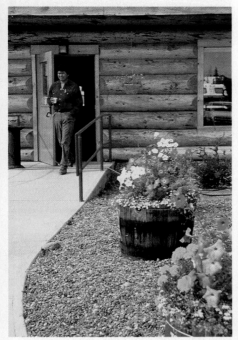

Entrance to Mainstreet Visitors Center, a must-stop for highway travelers.

(© Kris Graef, staff)

(Continued from page 179)
Visitior Center, is located at the junction of the Alaska Highway and Tok Cutoff. This huge log building is a center for local and state information, trip planning, art exhibits and shows. Alaska State Parks annual passes and Alaska Marine Highway reservations available; phone (907) 883-3259. The center offers free coffee, public telephones, restrooms and a message board. It is open daily 8 A.M. to 8 P.M. Memorial Day to Labor Day. Write P.O. Box 359, Tok, Alaska 99780; phone (907) 883-5775. http://www. TokAlaskaInfo.com. E-mail: info@TokAlaska Info.com.

The U.S. Fish & Wildlife Service office is located at **Milepost DC 1314.1** next to the grocery store, directly across the highway from the State Troopers. Visitors are welcome. Stop in for information regarding

96°F/36°C in June 1969. **Radio:** FM stations are 90.5, 91.1 (KUAC-FM, University of Alaska–Fairbanks) and 101.5. **Television:** Satellite channel 13. **Newspaper:** *Mukluk News* (twice monthly).

Private Aircraft: Tok Junction, 1 E; elev. 1,630 feet/497m; length 2,510 feet/765m; asphalt; fuel 100LL; unattended. Tok airstrip, on Tok Cutoff, 2 S; elev. 1,670 feet/509m; length 1,690 feet/515m; gravel; no fuel, unattended.

Tok had its beginnings as a construction camp on the Alcan Highway in 1942. Highway engineer C.G. Polk was sent to Fairbanks in May of 1942 to take charge of Alaskan construction and start work on the road between Tok Junction and Big Delta. Work was also under way on the Gulkana–Slana–Tok Junction road (now the Tok Cutoff on the Glenn Highway to Anchorage). But on June 7, 1942, a Japanese task force invaded Attu and Kiska islands in the Aleutians, and the Alcan took priority over the Slana cutoff.

The name Tok (rhymes with poke) was long believed to be derived from Tokyo Camp, patriotically shortened during WWII to Tok. There exist at least three other versions of how Tok got its name. According to local author Donna Blasor–Bernhardt in *Tok, the Real Story* (1996), Tok was named for a young husky pup during construction of the Alaska Highway in 1942.

Because Tok is the major overland point of entry to Alaska, it is primarily a trade and service center for all types of transportation, especially for summer travelers coming up the Alaska Highway. A stopover here is a

Young visitor holds a puppy from Burnt Paw gift shop's kennels. (© Kris Graef, staff)

good opportunity to meet other travelers and swap experiences. Tok is the only town in Alaska that the highway traveler must pass through twice—once when arriving in the state and again on leaving the state. The governor proclaimed Tok "Mainstreet Alaska" in 1991. Townspeople are proud of this designation and work hard to make visitors happy.

Tok's central business district is at the junction of the Alaska Highway and Tok Cutoff (Glenn Highway). From the junction, homes and businesses spread out along both highways on flat terrain dotted with densely timbered stands of black spruce.

Tok has 13 churches, a public library, an elementary school, a 4-year accredited high school and a University of Alaska extension program. Local clubs include the Lions, Disabled American Veterans, Veterans of Foreign Wars and Chamber of Commerce.

ACCOMMODATIONS/VISITOR SERVICES

There are 8 hotels/motels, a variety of restaurants and several gas stations, as well as bed and breakfasts in Tok, just north of Tok Junction along the Alaska Highway and south on the Glenn Highway (Tok Cutoff). U.S. Post Office is located between the Westmark and Burnt Paw gift shop on the west side of the Alaska Highway. Grocery, hardware and sporting goods stores, bakery, beauty shop, gift shops, liquor stores, auto repair and auto parts stores, wrecker service and laundromats are available. The bank is located across the highway from the Public Lands Information Center. There is an ATM at Village Texaco.

Tok Memorial Park, at the Alaska Highway and Tok Cutoff intersection (across from Tok Mainstreet Visitors Center), has day parking and picnicking.

Tok AYH youth hostel is located on Pringle Road, 0.8 mile/1.3 km south of **Milepost DC 1322.6**; phone (907) 883-3745.

There are several private RV parks in Tok. Nearby state campgrounds include: Tok River State Recreation Site at **Milepost DC 1309.2** and Moon Lake State Recreation Site at Milepost DC 1331.9 Alaska Highway; and Eagle Trail State Recreation Site at **Milepost GJ 109.3** Tok Cutoff (Glenn Highway) 16 miles/25 km west. ▲

A WinterCabin Bed & Breakfast. New, individual log cabins each with peaceful surroundings, sun porch, picnic table, barbecue, microwave, breakfast-stocked refrigerator, excellent beds, fully carpeted. Special feature: Alaskan-size tub/shower in modern, separate, shared bath house. No pets. Non-smoking. Reservations advised. Built on original site of the "Tent In Tok." Reservations/brochure—P.O. Box 61, Tok, AK 99780. Phone (907) 883-5655. Internet: http://www.ptialaska.net/~wntrcabn/cabin.html. E-mail: wntrcabn@ptialaska.net. [ADVERTISEMENT]

Golden Bear Motel. Quiet location, 62 deluxe units, RV park with wooded pull-through sites, heated bathhouse, laundry; fine restaurant. Open 6 A.M. to 11 P.M. Our gift shop carries an extensive selection of Alaskana, jewelry, T-shirts and souvenirs. The friendly atmosphere you came to Alaska to find! Phone (888) 252-2123. Inter-

Flowers brighten Tok's parking lots, sidewalks and yards in summer. (© Kris Graef, staff)

net: www.tokalaska.com/gol. See display ad this section. [ADVERTISEMENT] MP▲

Sourdough Campground's Pancake Breakfast, served 7–11 A.M. (June, July, August). Genuine "Sourdough!" Full and partial RV hookups. Dry campsites. Showers included. Guaranteed clean restrooms. High-

pressure car wash. Open-air museum with gold rush memorabilia. Free evening video program. Located 1.7 miles from the junction toward Anchorage on Tok Cutoff (Glenn Highway). See display ad this section. [ADVERTISEMENT] MP▲

Snowshoe Motel. 24 units with private

baths. Excellent accommodations for families or 2 couples traveling together. In-room phones, satellite TV. Free continental breakfast served summers only. Our guests are invited to enjoy panoramic mountain views and sunsets from our upstairs porch. (800) 478-4511 or (907) 883-4511. [ADVERTISEMENT]

Tok Lodge, located on Glenn Highway, 1 block from junction. Alcan Room serves buses, leaving full-service restaurant open for car traffic. 36 new motel rooms. Common comments are "nicest rooms on the highway" and "best meal since leaving home." Locally owned by Pam and Bud Johnson for 22 years. Mini-Mart and liquor store located on premises. Internet: www.alaskan.com/toklodge. E-mail: toklodge@polarnet.com. See display ad this section. [ADVERTISEMENT] MP

Tundra Lodge & RV Park. Spacious, tree-shaded camping sites. Full and partial hookups; 20-, 30-, 50-amp power. Tent sites. Pull-throughs. Clean restrooms and showers included in price. Picnic tables, fire rings and wood. Dump station. Laundromat. Vehicle wash. Pay phone. Ice. Cocktail lounge and meeting room. E-mail access: tundrarv@pti.net. See display ad **Milepost**

TRANSPORTATION

Air: Charter air service available; inquire at Tok state airstrip (**Milepost DC 1313**). Charter flightseeing and fly-in fishing trips available. Scheduled passenger and freight service between Tok, Delta Junction and Fairbanks 4 days a week via 40-Mile Air.

ATTRACTIONS

Tok Mainstreet Visitors Center. Located at the junction of the Tok Cutoff and the Alaska Highway, this 7,000-square-foot building houses the Tok Mainstreet Visitor

Center, the Alaska Public Lands Information Center and the Tok Community Library. Huge natural spruce logs support an open-beamed, cathedral ceiling. Large picture windows frame the Alaska Range. Displays include: the gold rush; rock, gems and fossils; Alaskan wildlife; waterfowl; and Alaska Highway memorabilia. The Alaska Public Lands Information Center offers videos on Alaska destinations and trip-planning services. Alaska Marine Highway reservations may be booked here. Restrooms, pay phone and message board.

Local Events: There is a variety of things to do in Tok, thanks to local individuals, businesses and clubs. Local campgrounds offer slide shows, movies, gold panning, a salmon bake, miniature golf and sourdough pancake breakfasts. Sled dog demonstrations are given at Burnt Paw gift shop and at the Westmark.

Other local events include bingo games and softball games at the local field. Visitors are welcome at the senior citizens center. The Tok Triathlon (12 miles of biking, 10 of canoeing and 5 of jogging) and Tok Trot are both held annually. Tok's Fourth of July celebration is a major event, complete with a parade, picnic and games. Check at the Mainstreet Visitor Center for more information on these local events.

Bike Trail: A wide paved bike trail extends southeast from Tok on the Alaska Highway as far east as the Dog Mushers Assoc. track, and as far west as Tanacross Junction; approximate length is 13.2 miles/21.2 km. You may also bike out the Tok Cutoff past Sourdough Campground. Travelers may park their vehicles in and around Tok and find a bike trail nearby leading into or out of Tok.

Native Crafts: Tok is a trade center for the Athabascan Native villages of Tanacross, Northway, Tetlin, Mentasta, Dot Lake and Eagle. Several of the Native women make birch baskets, beaded moccasins, boots and beaded necklaces. Examples of Native work may be seen at the Native-operated gift shop at Northway junction and at several gift shops and other outlets in Tok.

The state of Alaska has a crafts identification program which identifies authentic Native and Alaskan handicrafts. This symbol is of a polar bear.

Birch baskets were once used in the Native camps and villages. Traditionally they had folded corners, which held water, and were even used for cooking by dropping heated stones into the liquid in the baskets. The baskets are made by peeling the bark from the birch trees, usually in the early summer months. The bark is easiest to work

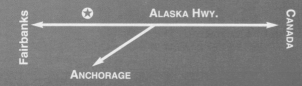

with when moist and pliable. It is cut into shape and sewn together with strips of spruce root dug out of the ground and split. If the root is too dry it is soaked until it is manageable. Holes are put in the birch bark with a punch or screwdriver, and the spruce root is laced in and out. Native women dye the spruce root with food coloring, watercolors or berry juice. A few Natives also make birch canoes and birch baby carriers.

Many of the moccasins and mukluks for sale in Tok are made with moose hide that has the "Native tan." This means moose hide tanned by the Native. First the excess fat and meat is scraped off the hide, then it is soaked in a soap solution (some use a mixture of brains and ashes). After soaking, all the moisture is taken out by constant scraping with a dull knife or scraper. The hide is then scraped again and rubbed together to soften it. Next it is often smoke-cured in rotted spruce wood smoke. The tanning process takes from a few days to a week.

Beading can be a slow and tedious process. Most women say if they work steadily all day they can put the beading on one moccasin, but usually they do their beadwork over a period of several days, alternating it with other activities.

Snowshoe Fine Arts and Gifts invites you to come browse and shop in our gift store. See our gallery of art prints, figurines,

Alaska Native-made carvings, masks, dolls, birch and grass baskets, and beadwork. Jewelry made of natural Alaska gemstones, ivory and gold nugget. Lots of caps, T-shirts and sweatshirts. Souvenir items and Alaska-made products. Phone (907) 883-4181. [ADVERTISEMENT]

Sled Dog Breeding and Training: Dog mushing is Alaska's official state sport, and Tok has become known as the "Sled Dog Capital of Alaska," with at least 1 out of every 3 people in town involved in some way with raising dogs. Kennels range in size from 100 dogs to a single family pet. Visitors who come to Tok seeking either a pet or a racing sled dog will probably find what they are looking for here.

The Siberian husky is the most popular sled dog and oftentimes has distinctive blue eyes. The Alaskan malamute is much larger than the Siberian and is used for hauling heavy loads at a slower pace. Both breeds are AKC recognized. The Alaskan husky (or husky) is a catchall term for any of the arctic breeds or northern types of dogs and is usually a cross. Sled dogs may be any registered breed or crossbreed, since mushers look for conformation, attitude and speed when putting together a working team rather than pedigrees. Common strains in racing dogs have included Irish setter, Labrador and wolf, among others.

Sled Dog Trails and Races: Tok boasts a well-known and long-established dog mushing trail, which draws many world-class and recreational mushers. The 20.5-mile/33-km trail begins at the rustic log Tok Dog Mushers Assoc. building at **Milepost DC 1312.8** on the Alaska Highway. The trail is a favorite with spectators because it affords many miles of viewing from along the Alaska

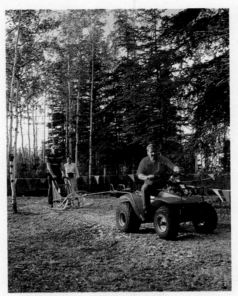

Mukluk Land at Milepost DC 1317 offers dog sled rides. (© Earl L. Brown)

Highway.

Racing begins in late November and extends through the end of March. Junior mushers include 1-, 2-, 3- and 5-dog classes; junior adult mushers include 5- and 8-dog classes. Open (unlimited) classes can run as many as 16 dogs.

The biggest race of the season in Tok is the Race of Champions, held in late March, which also has the largest entry of any sprint race in Alaska. Begun in 1954 as a bet between 2 roadhouse proprietors, today the Race of Champions includes over 100 teams in 3 classes competing for prize money and

trophies. It is considered to be the third leg of sled dog racing's "triple crown," following the Fur Rendezvous in Anchorage and the Fairbanks North American Championship. Visitors are also welcome to attend the Tok Native Assoc.'s potlatch, held the same weekend as the race, in the Tok school gym.

AREA FISHING: Fly-in fishing to area lakes for northern pike, grayling and lake trout; inquire at Tok state airstrip. There are 43 lakes in the Delta–Tok area that are stocked by the Alaska Dept. of Fish and Game. Lakes are stocked primarily with rainbow trout; other stocked species include arctic grayling, lake trout, arctic char and king salmon. Most of these lakes are located close to the road system, but there are walk-in lakes available as well. Most easily accessible are **North Twin, South Twin** and **Mark** lakes. There is a trailhead 0.5 mile/0.8 km east of the Gerstle River bridge for **Big Donna Lake** (3.5-mile/5.6-km hike) and **Little Donna Lake** (4.5 miles/7.2 km). **Quartz Lake,** north of Delta Junction, is a popular spot for rainbow trout and silver salmon. Consult ADF&G offices in Tok or Delta Junction for other locations. ⌐≈

Alaska Highway Log
(continued)

DC 1314.8 (2115.9 km) **DJ 107.2** (172.5 km) Gas, diesel, tire repair and car wash.

Northern Energy Corp. See display ad this section.

DC 1315 (2116.2 km) **DJ 107** (172.2 km) **Tundra Lodge and RV Park.** See display ad this section. ▲

DC 1315.7 (2117.3 km) **DJ 106.3** (171 km) **Rita's Campground RV Park & Cheryl's Old Fashion Bed & Breakfast Cabin.** See display ad this section. ▲

DC 1316.6 (2118.8 km) **DJ 105.4** (169.6 km) Scoby Road, Sundog Trail. Access to bed and breakfasts.

DC 1317 (2119.4 km) DJ 105 (169 km) **Mukluk Land.** See display ad this section.

DC 1318.5 (2121.8 km) DJ 103.5 (166.6 km) **Off The Road House.** See display ad this section.

DC 1322.6 (2128.5 km) DJ 99.4 (160 km) Pringle Road. Tok youth hostel, housed in a wall tent, is located 0.8 mile/1.3 km south; 10 beds, tent space available.

DC 1324.6 (2131.7 km) DJ 97.4 (156.7 km) Dept. of Natural Resources Tanacross Air Tanker Base. Gravel access road leads 1.6 miles/2.6 km northeast to Tanacross airstrip.

Private Aircraft: Tanacross airstrip; elev. 1,549 feet/472m; 2 runways, length 5,000 feet/1,524m and 5,100 feet/1,554m; asphalt; unattended.

DC 1325.6 (2133.3 km) DJ 96.4 (155.1 km) End of paved bike trail from Tok and access road northeast to Tanacross. Drive in 1.2 miles/1.9 km on gravel road to 'Y' inter-section; turn right for airstrip (see **Milepost DC 1324.6**); turn left for loop road through residential community of **TANACROSS** (pop. 106), home of the once numerous branch of the Tanah, or Tinneh, Indians. No visitor services.

DC 1325.7 (2133.4 km) DJ 96.3 (155 km) **Historic Milepost 1328.**

DC 1327.4 (2136.2 km) DJ 94.6 (152.2 km) Parking area at lake to north.

DC 1330.1 (2140.5 km) DJ 91.9 (147.9 km) Paved parking area to east. View of Alaska Range to the west.

DC 1331.9 (2143.5 km) DJ 90.1 (145 km) **Moon Lake State Recreation Site,** 0.2 mile/0.3 km north off highway; 15 camp-sites, toilets, tables, water, firepits, swim-ming (watch for floatplanes). Camping fee $10/night or annual pass. ▲

DC 1333.6 (2146.2 km) DJ 88.4 (142.3 km) **Historic Milepost 1339.** Yerrick Creek bridge.

DC 1338.2 (2153.5 km) DJ 83.8 (134.8 km) Highway crosses Cathedral Creeks 3 times between here and **Milepost DC 1339.**

DC 1342.2 (2160 km) DJ 79.8 (128.4 km) Sheep Creek culvert.

DC 1344.5 (2163.8 km) DJ 77.5 (124.7 km) **Historic Milepost 1352.** Paved parking area to east. Interpretive panel on the "father of the international highway," Donald MacDonald. Alaska Range to the south. Good photo stop.

DC 1347.2 (2168 km) DJ 74.8 (120.4 km) **Forest Lake** trailhead (not signed in 1998); 6 mile/9.6 km ATV trail (not easy access) to lake stocked with rainbow trout. ⊶

DC 1347.3 (2168.2 km) DJ 74.7 (120.2 km) Entering Game Management Unit 20D northbound, Unit 12 southbound.

DC 1347.5 (2168.5 km) DJ 74.5 (119.9 km) Robertson River bridge. The river was named by Lt. Henry T. Allen for a member of his 1885 expedition. The Robertson River heads at the terminus of Robertson Glacier in the Alaska Range and flows 33 miles northeast to the Tanana River.

DC 1348 (2169.3 km) DJ 74 (119.1 km)
CAUTION: Watch for loose gravel northbound.

DC 1348.1 (2169.5 km) DJ 73.9 (118.9 km) Side road west to public fishing access; parking. Hike in 0.3 mile/0.5 km for **Robertson No. 2 Lake**; rainbow fishing (stocked by ADF&G). ◄

DC 1350.5 (2173.3 km) DJ 71.5 (115.1 km) Double-ended paved turnout to west. Rough road next mile northbound.

DC 1353.6 (2178.3 km) DJ 68.3 (109.9 km) Jan Lake Road. Drive in 0.5 mile/0.8 km to parking area with boat launch and toilets. No overnight camping, carry out garbage. **Jan Lake** is stocked by ADF&G with rainbow; use spinners, flies, or salmon eggs with bobber. Dot Lake Native Corp. land, limited public access.

DC 1357.3 (2184.4 km) DJ 64.7 (104.1 km) Bear Creek bridge. Paved parking area to west at north end of bridge.

DC 1358.7 (2186.6 km) DJ 63.3 (101.9 km) Chief Creek bridge. Paved parking area to west at north end of bridge.

DC 1361 (2190.2 km) DJ 60.4 (97.2 km) Dot Lake School.

DC 1361.3 (2190.7 km) DJ 60.7 (97.7 km) DOT LAKE (pop. 70). Lodge with gas, groceries, restaurant, car wash, motel, camping and post office. Headquarters for the Dot Lake (Athabascan) Indian Corp. Homesteaded in the 1940s, a school was established here in 1952. Dot Lake's historic chapel was built in 1949. ▲

Dot Lake Lodge. See display ad this section.

DC 1361.6 (2191 km) DJ 60.4 (97.2 km) Historic Milepost 1368. *CAUTION: Rough road northbound; watch for gravel breaks.*

DC 1370.2 (2205.1 km) DJ 51.8 (83.4 km) Double-ended paved scenic viewpoint to east.

DC 1370.8 (2206 km) DJ 57.8 (83.4 km) Entering Tanana Valley State Forest northbound.

DC 1371.5 (2207.2 km) DJ 50.5 (81.3 km) Berry Creek bridge. Parking area to west.

DC 1374.2 (2211.5 km) DJ 47.8 (76.9 km) Sears Creek bridge. Parking area to west at north end of bridge.

DC 1378 (2217.6 km) DJ 44 (70.8 km) Bridge over Dry Creek. Evidence of forest fire next mile northbound.

DC 1379 (2219.2 km) DJ 43 (69.2 km) Double-ended paved turnout with mountain views to west. Pay phone.

DC 1380.5 (2221.6 km) DJ 41.5 (66.8 km) Johnson River bridge (clearance 15′ 6″). A tributary of the Tanana River, the Johnson River was named by Lt. Henry T. Allen in 1887 for Peder Johnson, a Swedish miner and member of his party.

Moose hunters: Antler restriction area.

NOTE: $1,000 fine for littering.

DC 1381.1 (2222.6 km) DJ 40.9 (65.8 km) Paved turnout to west. Hiking trail to **Lisa Lake** (stocked). ◄

DC 1383.8 (2226.9 km) DJ 38.2 (61.5 km) Craig Lake access west side of highway via 0.5-mile/0.8-km trail; rainbow trout fishing. ◄

DC 1385 (2228.9 km) DJ 37 (59.5 km) Paved parking area to east with access to Tanana River.

DC 1386 (2230.5 km) DJ 36 (57.9 km) Road narrows northbound.

CAUTION: Watch for major road construction between **Mileposts DC 1386** *and* **1398** *in 1999.*

DC 1388.4 (2234.4 km) DJ 33.6 (54.7 km) Little Gerstle River bridge (to be replaced in 1999).

DC 1391.9 (2240 km) DJ 30.1 (48.4 km) Trailhead to **Big Donna Lake**, 3.5 miles/5.6 km, and **Little Donna Lake**, 4.5 miles/7.2 km; stocked with rainbow. ◄

DC 1392.7 (2241.3 km) DJ 29.3 (47.2 km) Gerstle River Black Veterans Recognition bridge. The river was named for Lewis Gerstle, president of the Alaska Commercial Co., by Lt. Henry T. Allen, whose 1885 expedition explored the Copper, Tanana and Koyukuk river regions for the U.S. Army Dept. of the Columbia.

Rest area on north side of bridge, overnight RV parking and camping permitted; toilets, tables and firepits. ▲

DC 1400.9 (2254.5 km) DJ 21.1 (33.9 km) Double-ended paved parking area to northeast.

DC 1403.3 (2258.3 km) DJ 18.7 (30.1 km) Sawmill Creek Road to northeast. This rough gravel road goes through the heart of the Delta barley fields. A sign just off the highway explains the barley project. Visiting farmers are welcome to talk with local farmers along the road, except during planting (May) and harvesting (August or September) when they are too busy. Commercial farm tours available.

Farm Tours. See display ad this section.

DC 1403.6 (2258.8 km) DJ 18.4 (29.6 km) Sawmill Creek.

DC 1403.8 (2259.1 km) DJ 18.2 (29.3 km) Silver Fox Lodge.

DC 1404.3 (2259.9 km) DJ 17.7 (28.5 km) Watch for buffalo sign. On the southwest side of the Alaska Highway approaching Delta Junction is the Bison Sanctuary. This range provides the bison herd with autumn and winter grazing on over 3,000 acres of grassland. It was developed to reduce agricultural crop depredation by bison.

DC 1408 (2265.9 km) DJ 14 (22.5 km) Access to University of Alaska Agricultural and Forestry Experiment Station. Major research at this facility concentrates on agricultural cropping, fertilization and tillage management.

DC 1410 (2269.1 km) DJ 12 (19.3 km) Spruce Road. Access road north to Delta barley project.

DC 1411.7 (2271.8 km) DJ 10.3 (16.6 km) Paved loop road to west scenic viewpoint of Alaska Range to south.

DC 1412.5 (2273.1 km) DJ 9.5 (15.3 km) Cherokee Lodge and RV Park. See display ad this section. ▲

DC 1413.3 (2274.4 km) DJ 8.7 (14 km) Grain storage facility.

DC 1413.4 (2274.6 km) DJ 8.6 (13.8 km) Sausage factory.

DC 1414.8 (2276.8 km) DJ 7.2 (11.6 km) Clearwater Road leads north past farmlands to Clearwater State Recreation Site campground and junctions with Remington Road. Stay on pavement leading to Jack Warren Road, which goes west to the Richardson Highway at **Milepost V 268.3**. Good opportunity to see area agriculture; see Delta Vicinity map this page.

To reach the state campground, follow Clearwater Road 5.2 miles/8.4 km north to junction with Remington Road; turn right and drive 2.8 miles/4.5 km east for Clearwater state campground, situated on the bank of Clearwater Creek. There are 15 campsites, toilets, tables, firepits, water and boat ramp. Camping fee $8/night or annual pass. ▲

Delta–Clearwater River (local reference; stream is actually Clearwater Creek, which flows northwest to the Tanana River), boat needed for best fishing; beautiful spring-fed stream; grayling and whitefish; silver salmon spawn here in October. **Goodpaster River,** accessible by boat via Delta–Clearwater and Tanana rivers; excellent grayling fishing. ◄

DC 1415.4 (2277.8 km) DJ 6.6 (10.6 km) Dorshorst Road; access to homestead farm and private museum, open to public June 1 to Sept. 15, admission charged. Guided tours of an authentic Alaska homestead farm. There's also a large collection of historical farming equipment. Open daily 10 A.M. to 7 P.M.

DC 1420.7 (2286.3 km) DJ 1.3 (2.1 km) Alaska State Troopers. Veterinarian.

DC 1420.9 (2286.7 km) DJ 1.1 (1.8 km) Bergstad's Travel and Trailer Court. See display ad this section. ▲

DC 1422 (2288.4 km) DJ 0 V 266 (428.1 km) End of the Alaska highway at Delta Junction (description follows); visitor center.

Junction of the Alaska Highway (Alaska Route 2) and the Richardson Highway (Alaska Route 4). Turn to **Milepost V 266** in the RICHARDSON HIGHWAY section for log of the highway north to Fairbanks (98 miles/158 km), and south to Paxson (81 miles/130 km) and Valdez (266 miles/428 km).

To Fairbanks

Tanana Loop Extension

Tanana Loop Road

Richardson Highway

(2)

Jack Warren Road

Tanana River

Clearwater Lake

Triple H Road

Goodpaster River

Delta - Clearwater River

MILE 13   **MILE 10.2**

Mill-Tan Road

MILE 5.2

Remington Road

Delta River

?   Delta Junction

Nistler Road

Keaster Road

Clearwater Road

(4)

Jarvis Creek

Alaska Highway (2)

Richardson Highway

MILE 0

Delta Junction Vicinity

N
W   E
S

To Valdez   **To Tok**

Two Alaska Highway travelers have their picture taken at the End of the Alaska Highway monument in Delta Junction. (© Earl L. Brown, staff)

Delta Junction

Milepost 1422 Alaska Highway, at the junction of the Alaska and Richardson highways. **Population:** 657. **Emergency Services:** Emergencies only phone 911. **Alaska State Troopers**, in the Jarvis Office Center at **Milepost DC 1420.7**, phone (907) 895-4800. **Fire Department** and **Ambulance Service**, emergency only phone 911. **Clinics**, Two doctors and 2 dentists in private practice at Family Medical Center.

Visitor Information: Visitor Center junction of Alaska and Richardson highways, open daily 8 A.M. to 7:30 P.M., May to mid-September; phone (907) 895-5068, fax (907) 895-4628. The visitor center has historical and wildflower displays and a pay phone. Highway information, phone (907) 451-2207. Dept. of Fish and Game at north edge of town; phone (907) 895-4632.

City Hall and the Delta Junction Library, located at **Milepost V 266.5**, are also good sources of information. City Hall, open 2 P.M. to 5 P.M. weekdays, has a pay phone, public restrooms and can give local directions. The library has a free paperback book and magazine exchange, Anchorage newspaper, public fax and copier service. The library, open Wednesdays and Saturdays, also offers free Alaska video programs to any traveler waiting for vehicle repairs in Delta (ask at the circulation desk).

Elevation: 1,180 feet/360m. **Climate:** Mean monthly temperature in January, -15° F/-26°C; in July 58°F/14°C. Record low was -66°F/-54°C in January 1989; record high was 88°F/31°C in August 1990. Mean monthly precipitation in July, 2.57 inches/6.5cm. **Radio:** KUAC-FM 91.7 broadcasts

from University of Alaska, Fairbanks; Fort Greely broadcasts on 90.5 FM and 93.5 FM. **Television:** Three channels from Fairbanks.

Private Aircraft: Delta Junction (former BLM) airstrip, 1 mile/1.6 km north; elev. 1,150 feet/350m; length 2,400 feet/731m, gravel; length 1,600 feet/488m, dirt; no fuel; unattended.

Delta Junction is the end of the Alaska Highway. From here, the Richardson Highway leads to Fairbanks. The Richardson Highway, connecting Valdez at tidewater with Fairbanks in the Interior, predates the Alaska Highway by 20 years. The Richardson was already a wagon road in 1910, and was updated to automobile standards in the 1920s by the Alaska Road Commission (ARC).

Named after the nearby Delta River, Delta Junction began as a construction camp on the Richardson Highway in 1919. (It was first known as Buffalo Center because of the American bison that were transplanted here in the 1920s.)

Since the late 1970s, the state has encouraged development of the agricultural industry in the Delta area. They have conducted local land disposal programs involving more than 112,000 acres. These programs generated 37 farms averaging 2,310 acres and 169 small farms averaging 161 acres.

In 1996, nearly 40,000 acres were in some form of agricultural use (including production of barley, oats, wheat, forage, pasture, grass seed, canola, potatoes, field peas, forage brassicas) and conservation use. Barley is the major feed grain grown in Delta. It is an excellent energy feed for cattle, hogs and sheep. Production acreages are determined by the anticipated in-state demand for barley.

Delta barley is stored on farms or in a *(Continues on page 199)*

Alaska's Friendly Frontier
Delta Junction, Alaska

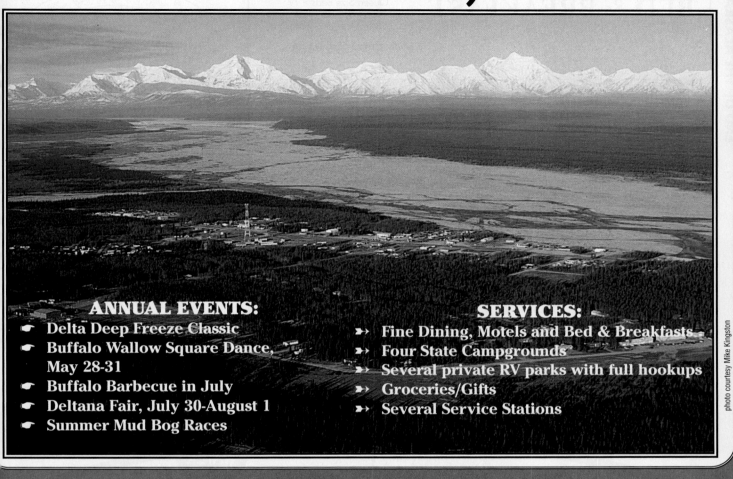

ANNUAL EVENTS:
- Delta Deep Freeze Classic
- Buffalo Wallow Square Dance, May 28-31
- Buffalo Barbecue in July
- Deltana Fair, July 30-August 1
- Summer Mud Bog Races

SERVICES:
- Fine Dining, Motels and Bed & Breakfasts
- Four State Campgrounds
- Several private RV parks with full hookups
- Groceries/Gifts
- Several Service Stations

ACTIVITIES:

- Spectacular Mountain Views
- Agricultural, Scenic and Wildlife Tours
- Great Fishing & Hunting, guided or independent
- Pipeline Pump Station Tours
- Historical Sites, Roadhouses, Museums

For further information contact:

Delta Chamber of Commerce
PO Box 987MP
Delta Junction, AK 99737

(907) 895-5068 (year 'round)
(907) 895-5069 (summer only)
(907) 895-5141 (Fax)
e-mail: deltacc@knix.net

Delta Junction, Alaska
Accommodations, Restaurants & Services

When you enter Alaska, avoid the rush & crowds.
Stay with Us!

Official End of the
Alaska Highway

(Continued from page 192)

local co-op elevator, sold on the open market or used to feed livestock. Small-scale farming of vegetables, 3 commercial potato farms, 5 active dairies, a dairy processing center, 6 beef producers, 2 beef feedlots, 3 swine producers, 3 bison ranches, 1 red-meat processing plant and 4 commercial greenhouses all contribute to Delta Junction's agriculture.

ACCOMMODATIONS/VISITOR SERVICES

Delta Junction has 3 motels, several bed and breakfasts, restaurants, gas stations, a coin-operated car wash, a shopping center, post office, gift shops, RV parks, bank with ATM and other businesses. There are several churches. Delta Community Park, on Kimball Street one block off the highway, has softball and soccer fields and playground.

There are private RV parks just south and just north of town. Three public campgrounds are located nearby: Delta state campground at **Milepost V 267.1**, and Clearwater state campground on Remington Road (see **Milepost DC 1414.9** and **V 268.3**) and Quartz Lake campground. ▲

TRANSPORTATION

Air: Scheduled service via 40-Mile Air from Tok to Fairbanks; Delta stop on request. Local air service available.

ATTRACTIONS

Delta Junction Visitor Center. Have your picture taken with the monument in front of the visitor center that marks the highway's end. The chamber of commerce visitor center also has free brochures describing area businesses and attractions, and displays of Alaska wildflowers, mounted animals and furs to touch. Travelers may also purchase certificates here, certifying that they have reached the end of the Alaska Highway. There is also an interesting display of pipe used in 3 Alaska pipeline projects outside the visitor center.

Visit Pump Station No. 9. Located 7.7 miles/12.4 km south of Delta Junction at **Milepost V 258.3** Richardson Highway, the pump station has 1-hour tours daily (except Sunday) from June to August. Tours limited to 10 people; children must be at least 9 years old. Reservations recommended. (Tours were scheduled for 9, 10, and 11 A.M. and 1:30, 2:30 and 3:30 P.M. in summer 1998.) Stop by or phone (907) 869-3270.

See the Pipeline Crossing. Delta Junction is the first view of the trans-Alaska pipeline for travelers coming up the Alaska Highway from Canada. A good spot to see and photograph the pipeline is at **Milepost V 275.4**, 9.5 miles/15.3 km north of town, where the pipeline crosses the Tanana River.

Buffalo Herd. American bison were transplanted into the Delta Junction area

in the 1920s. Because the bison have become costly pests to many farmers in the Delta area, the 90,000-acre Delta Bison Sanctuary was created south of the Alaska Highway in 1980. However, keeping the bison on their refuge and out of the barley fields is a continuing problem. Summer visitors who wish to look at the bison are advised to visit the viewpoint at **Milepost V 241.3** on the Richardson Highway; use binoculars. The herd contained 482 bison in 1992 when the last census was taken by the ADF&G.

Rika's Roadhouse. Located north of town about 8 miles/12.9 km at **Milepost V 275** Richardson Highway at Big Delta State Historical Park, this restored roadhouse was built in 1910. Open daily in summer. There are a number of other historic outbuildings, a gift shop and restaurant.

Special Events: Delta Junction celebrates a traditional Fourth of July with a Buffalo Barbecue. Buffalo Wallow, a 4-day square dance festival hosted by Buffalo Squares, is held every Memorial Day weekend. The Buffalo Squares also sponsors a campout and dance at Delta state campground the second Saturday in July.

The Deltana Fair is held in late July. The fair includes a barbecue, Lions' pancake breakfast, local handicrafts, horse show, livestock display and show, games, concessions, contests and a parade. A highlight of the fair is the Great Alaska Outhouse Race, held on Sunday, in which 4 pushers and 1 sitter compete for the coveted "Golden Throne" award.

A Festival of Lights is held each February in Delta Junction. This special event, designed to break up the monotony of long winter nights, features a parade of lights where the local citizenry builds and decorates floats with lights. There are also dog races, fireworks, square dancing, ice sculpting and more.

Winter is also celebrated in Delta with

the Deep Freeze Classic, a lottery based on guessing the exact time when the thermometer will hit its lowest point for the winter. Results aren't final until early spring. Winning times were 6:12 P.M. Jan. 4, 1998, with a low of -51.6°F/-46.4°C, and 10:09 A.M. Jan. 7, 1997, with a low of -55.6°F/-48.6°C.

Sullivan Roadhouse, relocated across from the visitor center, was originally built in 1906. It is one of the last remaining roadhouses from Valdez to Fairbanks. Open daily in summer as a walk-through museum.

Tour the agriculture of the area by driving Sawmill Creek Road (turn off at **Milepost DC 1403.6** Alaska Highway) and Clearwater Road (see **Milepost DC 1414.9**). Sawmill Creek Road goes through the heart of the grain-producing Delta Ag Project. Along Clearwater and Remington roads you may view the older farms, which produce forage crops and livestock. Tanana Loop Road (**Milepost V 271.7**), Tanana Loop Extension and Mill–Tan Road also go past many farms. The visitor information center in downtown Delta Junction can answer many questions on local agriculture and has information about local tours.

Delta's barley fields are a popular migration stop for 150,000 to 200,000 sandhill cranes in the fall. In 1998, a common crane was sighted among a flock of lesser sandhill cranes. It was only the sixth sighting of a common crane—classified as a Eurasian species—in North America.

AREA FISHING: Delta–Clearwater River, grayling and whitefish; silver salmon spawn here in October. Access via Clearwater Road or Jack Warren Road (see Delta Vicinity map). (Although USGS topographic maps show this tributary of the Tanana River as Clearwater Creek, local residents refer to the stream as the Delta–Clearwater River.) **Goodpaster River**, accessible by boat via Delta–Clearwater and Tanana rivers; excellent grayling fishing.

There are 43 lakes in the Delta–Tok area that are stocked by the Alaska Dept. of Fish and Game. Lakes are stocked primarily with rainbow trout, and also with arctic grayling, lake trout, arctic char and king salmon. Most of these lakes are located close to the road system, but there are walk-in lakes available as well. **Quartz Lake**, at **Milepost V 277.7** north of Delta Junction, one of the most popular fishing lakes in the Delta area, is also the largest and most easily accessed of area lakes; angler success is excellent. Consult ADF&G offices in Delta or Tok for other locations. ⌐⊷

LIARD HIGHWAY

Connects: Alaska Hwy. to Mackenzie Hwy.   **Length:** 244 miles
Road Surface: Gravel   **Season:** Open all year
Steepest Grade: 10 percent
Major Attraction: Nahanni National Park

	Fort Liard	Fort Nelson	Fort Simpson
Fort Liard		126	176
Fort Nelson	126		302
Fort Simpson	176	302	

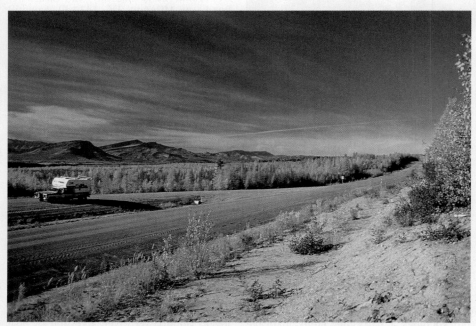

Fall colors along the Liard Highway between Fort Liard and Blackstone Park.
(© Earl L. Brown, staff)

The Liard Highway, also called the Liard Trail or "Moose Highway" (after the road sign logo), is named for the Liard River Valley through which it runs for most of its length. The Liard Highway begins about 17 miles/27 km north of Fort Nelson on the Alaska Highway and leads northeast through British Columbia and Northwest Territories for 244.4 miles/393.4 km to junction with the Mackenzie Highway (NWT Highway 1).

The Liard is a relatively straight 2-lane gravel road through boreal forest and muskeg. In French, Liard means "black poplar," and this wilderness highway (officially opened in June 1984) is a corridor through a forest of white and black spruce, trembling aspen and balsam poplar.

The road can be dusty when dry and very muddy when wet. Poor road conditions (potholes, lack of grading) were reported on the BC portion of the Liard Highway in 1998. The NWT portion of the highway is well-maintained. Travelers may check current road conditions on the BC section of the highway (first 85 miles/136.8 km of road) by inquiring at the Visitor Infocentre in Fort Nelson, BC. Travel information for the Northwest Territories is available from Northwest Territories Tourism; phone toll free weekdays (800) 661-0788. Food, gas and lodging are available at Fort Liard. Gas and accommodations are also available at the Mackenzie Highway junction. It is a good idea to fill up in Fort Nelson.

Although the Northwest Territories portion of the Liard Highway parallels the Liard River, there is little access to the river. Travelers may enhance their trip by visiting Blackstone Territorial Park and exploring Nahanni National Park by air charter out of Fort Liard, Fort Simpson or Fort Nelson. Blackstone Territorial Park is accessible by road.

Fishing the highway streams is only fair, but watch for wildlife such as moose, black bear, wood bison and grouse. Remember to bring along lots of insect repellent!

Liard Highway Log

Distance from the junction with the Alaska Highway (A) is followed by distance from the Mackenzie Highway junction (M).
    NOTE: Physical kilometreposts are up on the British Columbia portion of the highway about every 5 kilometres, starting here with Km 0 at the Alaska Highway junction and ending at the BC–NWT border.

BC HIGHWAY 77

A 0 M 244.4 (393.4 km) **Junction** with the Alaska Highway.

A 6.2 (10.1 km) **M 238.2** (383.3 km) Beaver Creek.

A 6.4 (10.3 km) **M 238** (383.1 km) Short side road east to Beaver Lake recreation site; 2 picnic tables, litter barrels, pit toilets, firewood, turnaround space. Short hike downhill through brush to floating dock; limited lake access.

A 14.3 (23.1 km) **M 230.1** (370.3 km) Stanolind Creek. Beaver dams to west.

A 17.5 (28.2 km) **M 226.9** (365.2 km) Pond to west and cut line through trees shows Cat access in summer, ice road in winter.

A 21.1 (34 km) **M 223.3** (359.4 km) Westcoast Transmission Pipeline crossing. Pipeline transports natural gas from Pointed Mountain near Fort Liard to the company's gas plant on the Alaska Highway just south of Fort Nelson.

A 24.2 (38.9 km) **M 220.2** (354.5 km) Road begins descent northbound to Fort Nelson River.

A 26.4 (42.5 km) **M 218** (350.9 km) **Fort Nelson River bridge** (elev. 978 feet/298m), single lane, reduce speed. The Nelson bridge is the longest Acrow bridge in the world at 1,410 feet/430m. It is 14 feet/4m wide, with a span of 230 feet/70m from pier to pier. The Acrow bridge, formerly called the Bailey bridge after its designer Sir Donald Bailey, is designed of interchangeable steel panels coupled with pins for rapid construction.

A 26.6 (42.9 km) **M 217.8** (350.5 km) Turnout at north end of bridge with pit toilet, table and garbage container.

A 39.7 (63.9 km) **M 204.7** (329.5 km) **Tsinhia Creek,** grayling run for about 2 weeks in spring.   ◄

A 43.4 (69.8 km) **M 201** (323.5 km) Trapper's cabin to east.

A 51.8 (83.3 km) **M 192.6** (310.1 km) Side road leads west 1.9 miles/3 km to Tsinhia Lake and dead-ends in soft sandy track. A recreation site is planned at Tsinhia Lake.

A 59.2 (95.3 km) **M 185.2** (298.1 km) There are several winter roads in this area used by the forest, oil and gas industries. To most summer travelers these roads look like long cut lines or corridors through the Bush.

The Liard Highway replaced the old Fort Simpson winter road that joined Fort Nelson and Fort Simpson. The original Simpson Trail was first blazed in November 1942 by Alaska Highway engineers, including the 648th, Company A detachment.

A 69.4 (111.7 km) **M 175** (281.7 km) Bridge over d'Easum Creek (elev. 1,608 feet/490m). Good bird-watching area.

A 71.4 (115 km) **M 173** (278.4 km) Access to Maxhamish Lake via 8-mile/13-km winter road accessible in summer by all-terrain vehicles only. A recreation site is planned for Maxhamish Lake.

A 74 (119.1 km) **M 170.4** (274.3 km) Wide unnamed creek flows into Emile Creek to east. Good bird-watching area, beaver pond.

A 75.4 (121.4 km) **M 169** (272 km) Highway emerges from trees northbound; view west of Mount Martin (elev. 4,460 feet/1,360m) and the Kotaneelee Range.

A 80.6 (129.7 km) **M 163.8** (263.7 km) View northwest of mountain ranges in Northwest Territories.

A 81.2 (130.7 km) **M 163.2** (262.6 km) *Highway begins 7 percent downgrade northbound to Petitot River.*

A 82.8 (133.2 km) **M 161.6** (260.2 km) Petitot River bridge. The **Petitot River** is reputed to have the warmest swimming water in British Columbia (70°F/21°C). A 9-hour canoe trip to Fort Liard is possible from here (some sheer rock canyons and rapids en route). Good bird-watching area. Also freshwater clams, pike and pickerel; short grayling run in spring.

The Petitot River was named for Father Petitot, an Oblate missionary who came to this area from France in the 1860s.

The Petitot River bridge was the site of the official opening of the Liard Highway on June 23, 1984. The ceremony was marked by an unusual ribbon-cutting: A 1926 Model T Ford, carrying dignitaries, was driven through the ribbon (which stretched for about 20 feet before snapping) while a guard of kilted pipers from Yellowknife played. The Model T, driven by Marl Brown of Fort Nelson, had been across this route in March 1975 just weeks after the bush road had been punched through by Cats and seismic equipment. This earlier trip, in which Mr. Brown was accompanied by Mickey Hempler, took 44 hours from Fort Nelson to Fort Simpson.

A 84.1 (135.4 km) **M 160.3** (258 km) Crest of Petitot River hill. *Highway begins 10 percent downgrade northbound.*

NWT HIGHWAY 7

A 85 (136.8 km) **M 159.4** (256.6 km) **BC–NWT border.** TIME ZONE CHANGE: British Columbia observes Pacific time, Northwest Territories observes Mountain

LIARD HIGHWAY

Alaska Highway Junction to Mackenzie Route Junction

© 1999 The MILEPOST®

Principal Route
Paved — Unpaved
Other Roads
Paved — Unpaved
Ferry Routes — **Hiking Trails**

Refer to Log for Visitor Facilities

Scale
0 — 10 Miles
0 — 10 Kilometres

Key to Advertiser Services
C -Camping
D -Dump Station
d -Diesel
G -Gas (reg., unld.)
I -Ice
L -Lodging
M -Meals
P -Propane
R -Car Repair (major)
r -Car Repair (minor)
S -Store (grocery)
T -Telephone (pay)

Fort Simpson
Ferry Crossing
Mackenzie River
A-244/393km
M-0
FS-40/64km
Y-352/567km
N61°26' W121°14'
To Yellowknife (see MACKENZIE ROUTE section, page 204)

Liard River

A-179/288km
M-65/105km
N61°05' W122°51'

Poplar River

Nahanni National Park

Nahanni Butte 4,579 ft./1,396m
Nahanni Butte

Blackstone River

Carmack Lake

Mt. Sawmill 3,925 ft./1,200m

Mt. Flett 3,775 ft./1,150m

Nahla River

Trout Lake

Trout Lake

A-109/175km
M-136/219km

Pointed Mountain

Muskeg River

N60°14' W123°28'
Fort Liard
N60°13' W123°22'

Petitot River

N60°00' W122°56'

NORTHWEST TERRITORIES
BRITISH COLUMBIA

Maxhamish Lake

Liard River

A-85/137km
M-159/257km

d'Easum Creek

77

Fort Nelson River

A-0
M-244/393km
FN-17/27km
DC-283/454km
N58°54' W123°07'

Kotcho Lake

Key to mileage boxes
miles/kilometres
miles/kilometres from:
A- Alaska Highway Junction
M- Mackenzie Highway Junction
DC- Dawson Creek
FN- Fort Nelson
FS- Fort Simpson
Y- Yellowknife

Map Location

Fort Nelson

97

Muskwa River
Prophet River

To Watson Lake (see ALASKA HIGHWAY section, page 83)

To Fort St. John

Fort Liard is known for its birch-bark baskets and porcupine quill workmanship.

(© Lyn Hancock)

time. Northwest Territories restricts liquor importation as follows: 1 40-oz. hard liquor, 1 40-oz. wine or 1 dozen bottles of beer per person.

NOTE: Kilometreposts are up about every 2 kilometres on the Northwest Territories portion of the highway, starting here with Km 0 at the BC–NWT border and ending at the junction with the Mackenzie Highway.

A 85.2 (137.1 km) **M 159.2** (256.2 km) Turnout to east with litter barrels.

A 107 (172.2 km) **M 137.4** (221.1 km) Vehicle inspection station and weigh scales to east.

A 108.6 (174.8 km) **M 135.8** (218.5 km) **Junction** with side road that leads 4 miles/6.4 km to Fort Liard (description follows). Gas and diesel available in Fort Liard. Tourist information is available at the Acho Craft Shop; phone (867) 770-4161; fax (867) 770-4160.

Views from road into Fort Liard across the Liard River of Mount Coty (elev. 2,715 feet/830m) and Pointed Mountain (elev. 4,610 feet/1,405m) at the southern tip of the Liard Range.

Fort Liard

Located on the south bank of the Liard River near its confluence with the Petitot River (known locally as Black River because of its colour), about 50 miles/80 km south of Nahanni Butte. **Population:** 500. **Emergency Services:** RCMP, phone (867) 770-4221. **Fire Department,** phone (867) 770-2222. **Health Centre,** phone (867) 770-4301.

Visitor Information: Hamlet of Fort Liard, phone (867) 770-4104 or contact Acho Dene Native Crafts, phone (867) 770-4161; e-mail achoart@internet.com.

Elevation: 686 feet/209m. **Climate:** There is no permafrost here. Good soil and water, a long summer season with long hours of daylight, and comparatively mild climate considering Fort Liard's geographical location. Several luxuriant local gardens. The Liard River here is approximately 1,500 feet/450m wide, fairly swift and subject to occasional flooding. **Radio** and **Television:** CBC radio (microwave), a Native language station from Yellowknife and a community radio station; 4 channels plus CBC Television (Anik), TVNC and private satellite receivers. Canadian Aerodrome Radio Station (CARS) operates Monday through Friday 8 A.M. to 7 P.M.

Private Aircraft: Fort Liard airstrip; elev. 700 feet/213m; length 2,950 feet/899m; gravel; fuel 100/130 (obtain from Deh Cho Air Ltd.).

Transportation: Air—Charter service year-round via Deh Cho Air. **Barge**—Non-scheduled barge service in summer. Scheduled and charter taxi service available.

This small, well-laid-out settlement of traditional log homes and new modern housing is located among tall poplar, spruce and birch trees on the south bank of the Liard River. The residents live a comparatively traditional life of hunting, trapping, fishing and making handicrafts, although

FORT LIARD ADVERTISERS

there are more people taking jobs in construction and highway maintenance. Fort Liard residents are well known for the high quality of their birch-bark baskets and porcupine quill workmanship. Local arts and crafts are featured at Acho Dene Native Crafts shop.

Recreation and sightseeing in the area include fishing (for pike, pickerel, goldeye and spring grayling) at the confluence of the Liard and Petitot rivers and Liard River interpretive boat tours (Hope's Adventures). Air charters and self-guided canoe trips to Trout Lake, Virginia Falls in Nahanni National Park, Nahanni Butte and other destinations are available from Deh Cho Air Ltd. The traditional Dene settlement of **TROUT LAKE** (pop. less than 100) is also accessible by air from Fort Liard.

The North West Co. established a trading post near here at the confluence of the Liard and Petitot rivers called Riviere aux Liards in 1805. The post was abandoned after the massacre of more than a dozen residents by Indians. It was re-established in 1820, then taken over by the Hudson's Bay Co. in 1821 when the 2 companies merged. The well-known geologist Charles Camsell was born at Fort Liard in 1876.

Food and lodging are available at Liard Valley General Store and Motel. Gas, diesel and propane fuel available. Food and general merchandise at the Northern Store, which also houses the Canada Post outlet. There are also a cafe/take-out, the modern Acho Dene School and a Roman Catholic mission. There is no bank in Fort Liard.

Community-run Hay Lake Campground located just off the access road into Fort Liard; campsites, picnic tables, toilets and floating dock. *Bring insect repellent.* Campground road may be slippery when wet. ▲

Liard Highway Log
(continued)

A 113.3 (182.4 km) **M 131.1** (211 km) **Muskeg River** bridge (elev. 814 feet/248m); turnout at north end. Gravel bars on the river make a good rest area. Trapper's cabin on left. Fishing for pike, pickerel and freshwater clams. The Muskeg River is the local swimming hole for Fort Liard residents.

A 124.9 (201 km) **M 119.5** (192.4 km) Rabbit (Big Island) Creek bridge (elev. 827 feet/252m). Highway now runs close to the Liard River with good views of Liard Range to the west and northwest for the next 13 miles/21 km northbound.

A 128 (206 km) **M 116.4** (187.4 km) Kilometrepost 70.

A 131.1 (211 km) **M 113.3** (182.4 km) Good view of Mount Flett (elev. 3,775 feet/1,150m) ahead northbound.

A 136.7 (220 km) **M 107.7** (173.4 km) Access to Liard River (15-minute hike) via Paramount Mine winter road, an abandoned exploration road across the Liard River into the Liard Range.

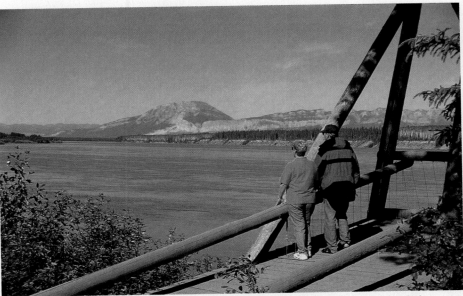
View of Nahanni Butte from Blackstone Territorial Park at Milepost A 179.1.
(© Leslie Leong)

A 146.9 (236.4 km) **M 97.5** (157 km) Short road west to locally named Whissel Landing on the Liard River, where road construction materials were brought in by barge during construction of the Liard Highway.

A 147.3 (237 km) **M 97.1** (156.4 km) Road widens for an emergency airstrip; elev. 981 feet/299m.

A 157.8 (253.9 km) **M 86.6** (139.5 km) Netla River bridge. The Netla River Delta is an important waterfowl breeding habitat, and Indian fishing and hunting area.

A 163.7 (263.4 km) **M 80.7** (130 km) Road widens for an emergency airstrip; elev. 512 feet/156m.

A 165.9 (267 km) **M 78.5** (126.4 km) Turnoff to west for winter ice road that leads 13.8 miles/22.3 km to the Dene settlement of **NAHANNI BUTTE** (pop. 87), at the confluence of the South Nahanni and Liard rivers. Summer access by boat or floatplane.

A 171.8 (276.5 km) **M 72.6** (116.8 km) Creek Bridge, once called Scotty's Creek after an old trapper who had a cabin upstream. There are many such cabins in this area that once belonged (and still belong) to prospectors and trappers, but they are not visible to the motorist. Stands of white spruce, white birch and balsam poplar along highway.

A 176.3 (283.7 km) **M 68.1** (109.7 km) Bridge over Upper Blackstone River (elev. 666 feet/203m). Picnic day-use area on riverbank with tables, firewood, firepits and garbage containers.

A 176.6 (284.2 km) **M 67.8** (109.2 km) Blackstone River bridge.

A 179.1 (288.3 km) **M 65.3** (105.1 km) Entrance to **Blackstone Territorial Park**; 19 campsites with tables and firepits; firewood, water and garbage containers, boat dock and state-of-the-art restroom. The boat launch is usable only in high water early in the season; use boat launch at Cadillac Landing, Milepost **A 182.9**, during low water. The visitor information building, built with local logs, is located on the bank of the Liard River with superb views of Nahanni Butte (elev. 4,579 feet/1,396m). The centre is open mid-May to mid-September. ▲

A 180.9 (291.2 km) **M 63.5** (102.2 km)

Entrance to Lindberg Landing, the homestead of Liard River pioneers Edwin and Sue Lindberg. The Lindbergs offer a bed and breakfast; rustic accommodations, bring your own sleeping bag. By appointment only. Contact Mobile Telephone JR36644 Arrowhead Channel, or write Sue and Edwin Lindberg, Box 28, Fort Simpson, NWT XOE ONO.

A 182.9 (294.3 km) **M 61.5** (99.1 km) Barge landing once used to service Cadillac Mine and bring in construction materials. Access to river via 0.6-mile/0.9-km road (muddy when wet).

A 192.8 (310.3 km) **M 51.6** (83.1 km) Road widens for emergency airstrip.

A 197.8 (318.4 km) **M 46.6** (75 km) Kilometrepost 180.

A 211.3 (340.1 km) **M 33.1** (53.3 km) Bridge over Birch River (elev. 840 feet/256m).

A 216.7 (348.8 km) **M 27.7** (44.6 km) Kilometrepost 210.

A 222.8 (358.5 km) **M 21.6** (34.9 km) Good grayling and pike fishing in **Poplar River** culverts.

A 223 (358.8 km) **M 21.4** (34.6 km) Dirt road on left northbound leads 4 miles/6.4 km to Liard River; 4-wheel drive recommended. Wide beach, good spot for viewing wildlife.

A 228.1 (367.1 km) **M 16.3** (26.3 km) Microwave tower to east. Vegetation changes northbound to muskeg with black spruce, tamarack and jackpine.

A 235.6 (379.2 km) **M 8.8** (14.2 km) Kilometrepost 240.

A 244.2 (393 km) **M 0.2** (0.4 km) Road maintenance camp.

A 244.4 (393.4 km) **M 0** "Checkpoint": gas, diesel, propane; licensed restaurant and 4-room motel. Phone (867) 695-2953. Turn right (south) for Hay River and Yellowknife; turn left (north) for Fort Simpson.

Junction with the Mackenzie Highway (NWT 1). Turn to **Milepost G 551** in the MACKENZIE ROUTE section following for log.

Connects: Grimshaw, AB to Western NWT **Length:** 1,231 miles
Road Surface: 47% paved, 53% gravel **Season:** Open all year
Major Attractions: Nahanni National Park; Wood Buffalo National Park

(See maps, pages 205–206)

	Ft. Resolution	Ft. Simpson	Ft. Smith	Valleyview	Yellowknife
Ft. Resolution		358	185	560	391
Ft. Simpson	358		431	692	393
Ft. Smith	185	431		633	464
Valleyview	560	692	633		725
Yellowknife	391	393	464	725	

Mackenzie Highway extension to Wrigley is the newest road in Northwest Territories. (© Leslie Leong)

Named for explorer Alexander Mackenzie, who in 1779 navigated Great Slave Lake and sailed to the mouth of the Mackenzie River seeking a trade route for the Hudson's Bay Co., the Mackenzie Route is an adventure for modern explorers. It is not a trip for the impulsive. While there are accommodations, gas stations and other services in cities and settlements along the highways, long distances require that motorists plan in advance.

The Mackenzie Route covers the following highways: Alberta Highway 35 and NWT Highway 1 to Fort Simpson (Mackenzie Highway) and the extension to Wrigley; Highway 2 to Hay River; Highway 3 to Yellowknife; Highway 4 (Ingraham Trail); Highway 5 to Fort Smith; and Highway 6 to Fort Resolution. NWT Highway 7, the Liard Highway, connecting the Mackenzie Highway with the Alaska Highway north of Fort Nelson, is covered in the LIARD HIGHWAY section. The Dempster Highway (NWT Highway 8) to Inuvik is covered in the DEMPSTER HIGHWAY section.

Allow at least 2 weeks to travel the entire route. For general information on travel in the Northwest Territories, phone Northwest Territories Tourism toll free at (800) 661-0788 during business hours on weekdays.

Northwest Territories highways are both paved and gravel. Asphalt chip seal surfacing is under way on the remaining gravel portions of Highways 1 (Mackenzie Highway) and 3 (Yellowknife Highway). Gravel road is treated with calcium chloride to control the dust; wash your vehicle when possible. For road conditions, phone (800) 661-0750.

In summer, the Northwest Territories government provides free ferry service for cars and passengers across the Mackenzie River to Fort Providence, across the Liard River to Fort Simpson and across the Mackenzie River to Wrigley. In winter, traffic crosses on the ice. For current ferry information call (800) 661-0751.

The Mackenzie Highway begins at Grimshaw, AB. There are several routes to Grimshaw to choose from (see map). *The MILEPOST®* logs the Valleyview–Peace River route to the Mackenzie Highway via Highways 49 and 2.

Log of the Valleyview–Peace River Route to the Mackenzie Highway

Distance from Valleyview (V) is followed by distance from Mackenzie Highway (MH).

ALBERTA HIGHWAY 49

V 0 MH 101.1 (162.7 km) **Junction** of Highways 43 and 49. Follow Highway 49 north.

V 0.6 (1 km) **MH 100.5** (161.6 km) Turnoff to west for downtown Valleyview (see description of Valleyview in the EAST ACCESS ROUTE section).

V 2.2 (3.5 km) **MH 98.9** (159.3 km) **Junction** with Secondary Road 669 which leads

MACKENZIE ROUTE

Valleyview, AB, to Steen River, AB

© 1999 The MILEPOST®

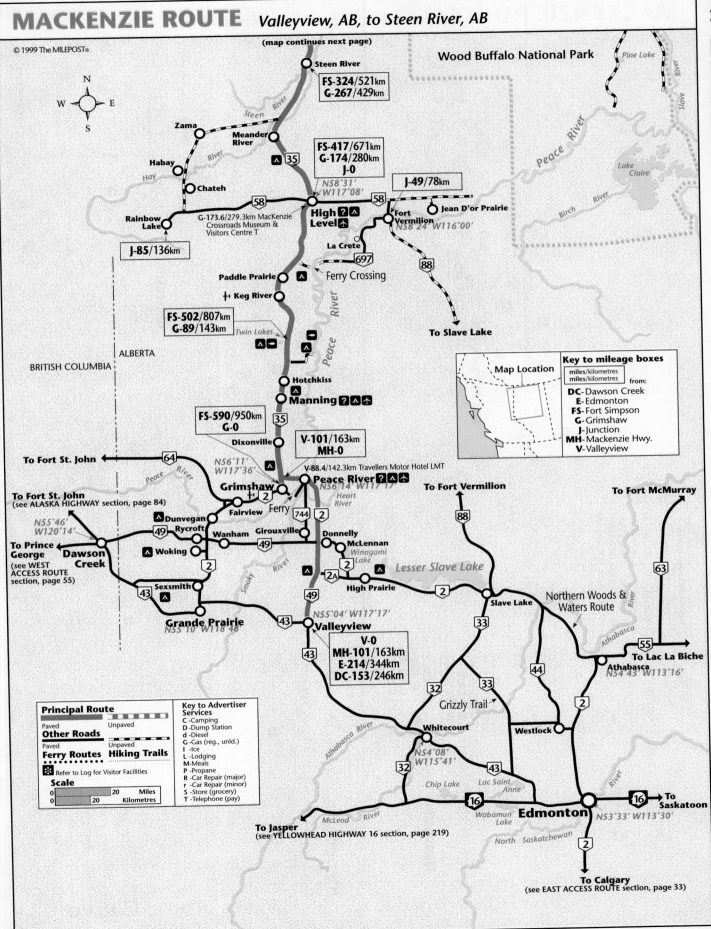

Wood Buffalo National Park

Steen River

FS-324/521km
G-267/429km

Zama

Meander River

35

FS-417/671km
G-174/280km
J-0

N58°31'
W117°08'

J-49/78km

Habay

58   58

Chateh

Jean D'or Prairie

N58°24' W116°00'

Rainbow Lake

G-173.6/279.3km MacKenzie
Crossroads Museum &
Visitors Centre T

High Level

Fort Vermilion

La Crete

697

88

J-85/136km

Paddle Prairie

Ferry Crossing

Keg River

FS-502/807km
G-89/143km

Twin Lakes

To Slave Lake

BRITISH COLUMBIA

ALBERTA

Hotchkiss

Manning

FS-590/950km
G-0

35

Key to mileage boxes

Map Location

miles/kilometres
miles/kilometres   from:

DC- Dawson Creek
E- Edmonton
FS- Fort Simpson
G- Grimshaw
J- Junction
MH- Mackenzie Hwy.
V- Valleyview

Dixonville

V-101/163km
MH-0

To Fort St. John

64

N56°11'
W117°36'

V-88.4/142.3km Travellers Motor Hotel LMT

Grimshaw

Peace River

Fairview   Ferry

744

N56°14' W117°17'

Heart River

To Fort Vermilion

To Fort St. John
(see ALASKA HIGHWAY section, page 84)

N55°46'
W120°14'

Dunvegan

Rycroft

49

Wanham

Girouxville

Donnelly

McLennan

88

Winagami Lake

To Fort McMurray

To Prince George
(see WEST ACCESS ROUTE
section, page 55)

Dawson Creek

Woking

2

49

2

Lesser Slave Lake

Northern Woods &
Waters Route

63

43

Sexsmith

High Prairie

2

Slave Lake

Grande Prairie

N53°10' W118°48'

43

Valleyview

N55°04' W117°17'

33

44

2

Athabasca

N54°43' W113°16'

To Lac La Biche

55

49

V-0
MH-101/163km
E-214/344km
DC-153/246km

43

32

33

Grizzly Trail

Principal Route

Paved   Unpaved

Other Roads

Paved   Unpaved

Ferry Routes   **Hiking Trails**

Refer to Log for Visitor Facilities

Scale

0   20 Miles
0   20 Kilometres

Key to Advertiser Services

C - Camping
D - Dump Station
d - Diesel
G - Gas (reg., unld.)
I - Ice
L - Lodging
M - Meals
P - Propane
R - Car Repair (major)
r - Car Repair (minor)
S - Store (grocery)
T - Telephone (pay)

Whitecourt

N54°08'
W115°41'

Westlock

32

43

Chip Lake

Lac Saint Anne

16

Edmonton

N53°33' W113°30'

16   To Saskatoon

Wabamun Lake

To Jasper
(see YELLOWHEAD HIGHWAY 16 section, page 219)

McLeod River

North Saskatchewan

2

To Calgary
(see EAST ACCESS ROUTE section, page 33)

MACKENZIE ROUTE Steen River, AB, to Yellowknife, NWT

© 1999 The MILEPOST®

SASKATCHEWAN

Fort Chipewyan

Lake Athabasca

Winter Road

Slave River

Fort Fitzgerald

Fort Smith
N60°00' W111°53'

J-166/267km
FT-0

Salt River
N60°10' W113°41'

Pine Lake

Peace Point

Lake Claire

Peace River

Wood Buffalo National Park

FR-56/90km
J-0

5

Fort Resolution
N61°10' W113°41'

FR-0
J-56/90km

6

Pine Point

5

2

Hay River
N60°48' W115°47'

H-0
E-24/38km

FT-166/267km
J-0

E:8.7/14km Paradise Garden Campground CDT

Enterprise
N60°33' W116°08'

1

Buffalo Lake

Hay River

FS-297/478km
G-294/473km
B-0

FS-324/521km
G-267/429km

Meander River

35

Indian Cabins

Steen River

Y-43/69km

Prelude L.
Cameron R.
Tibbett L.
Reid L.

Y-0
J-213/342km

4

The Yellowknife Bookcellar

Prosperous Lake

Yellowknife River

J-212.5/342km

Yellowknife
N62°27' W114°21'

3

Rae

Edzo

Russell Lake

Slemmon Lake

Marion Lake

Y-64/103km
J-149/239km

3

Great Slave Lake

Chan Lake

J-0
Y-213/342km
FS-180/289km
G-411/661km
B-117/189km

1

FS-245/394km
G-346/557km
B-52/84km
E-0
H-24/38km

Tathlina Lake

Kakisa Lake

Dogface Lake

Kakisa River

NORTHWEST TERRITORIES
ALBERTA

Bistcho Lake

J-19.6/31.6km Big River Service Centre dGLMPr

N61°04' W117°30'

Mills Lake

Fort Providence
N61°22' W117°39'
Free Ferry

Bouvier R.

River

1

Trout Lake

Trout River

FL-136/219km
FS-40/64km
G-551/886km
B-257/413km

Jean Marie R.

7

Poplar River

FS-0
G-590/950km
B-297/478km
W-137/221km

Fort Simpson
N61°51' W121°20'
Free Ferry

Mackenzie

Free Ferry

Liard

To Fort Liard
(see LIARD HIGHWAY section, page 200)

FS-137/221km
W-0

Wrigley
N63°16' W123°36'

1

(map continues previous page)

BRITISH COLUMBIA

Key to mileage boxes

miles/kilometres		miles/kilometres	
B- Border		G- Grimshaw	
E- Enterprise		H- Hay River	
FL- Fort Liard		J- Junction	
FR- Fort Resolution		W- Wrigley	
FS- Fort Simpson		Y- Yellowknife	
FT- Fort Smith			

Map Location

Key to Advertiser Services

C - Camping
D - Dump Station
d - Diesel
G - Gas (reg., unld.)
I - Ice
L - Lodging
M - Meals
P - Propane
R - Car Repair (major)
r - Car Repair (minor)
S - Store (grocery)
T - Telephone (pay)

Principal Route

Paved
Unpaved

Other Roads
Paved
Unpaved

Ferry Routes   **Hiking Trails**

Refer to Log for Visitor Facilities

Scale
Miles
Kilometres
0   20
0   20

east 20 miles/32 km to Sunset House Community Campground on Snipe Lake; 20 sites, firewood, playground, boat launch, camping fee. ▲

V 4 (6.4 km) **MH 97.1** (156.3 km) Sturgeon Creek.

V 18 (29 km) **MH 83.1** (133.7 km) East Dollar Lake to west.

V 23.1 (37.2 km) **MH 78** (125.6 km) Entering Midnight Twilight Tourist Zone northbound, entering Game Country Tourist Zone southbound.

V 25.1 (40.4 km) **MH 76** (122.3 km) **Junction** with Secondary Road 676 to Whitemud Creek, 14 miles/22 km west.

V 28.3 (45.6 km) **MH 72.8** (117.3 km) Entering Grande Prairie Forest southbound.

V 29.1 (46.8 km) **MH 72** (115.8 km) Little Smokey River bridge. Little Smokey River provincial recreation area to west on south bank of river; 12 sites, shelters, picnic tables, camping fee. ▲

V 30.3 (48.8 km) **MH 70.8** (114 km) **Junction** with Highway 2A east, a spur road which leads 17 miles/27 km to junction with Highway 2.

V 31.3 (50.4 km) **MH 69.8** (112.3 km) Turnout with litter barrels to east.

V 32.4 (52.1 km) **MH 68.7** (110.6 km) Entering Peace River Forest northbound.

V 36.4 (58.6 km) **MH 64.7** (104.2 km) Community of GUY (pop. 57) to east; pay phone. Access road leads west 7 miles/11 km to Five Star Golf Course; 9 holes, grass greens, pro shop.

V 40.5 (65.2 km) **MH 60.6** (97.5 km) **Junction** with Secondary Road 679 to Highway 2 and Winigami Lake Provincial Park (19 miles/30.5 km east).

V 48.7 (78.4 km) **MH 52.4** (84.4 km) **Donnelly Corners, junction** of Highways 2 and 49. DONNELLY (pop. 450) has a hotel, restaurants, stores, service stations with repair facilities and a library. Historic site 3 miles/5 km south of town features a fully operational 1904 Case Steam Engine. Highway 49 ends northbound. Continue on Highway 2 North.

ALBERTA HIGHWAY 2

V 61 (98.1 km) **MH 40.1** (64.5 km) Access leads west 7 miles/11 km to JEAN COTE (pop. 65), and 18 miles/28 km to Rainbow Trout Park and Campground; 55 sites, hookups, picnic tables, shelter, firewood, playground, rental cabins, mini-golf, horseshoe pits. Camping fee $9. ▲

V 66.1 (106.5 km) **MH 35** (56.3 km) Entering Land of the Mighty Peace Tourist Zone northbound, Midnight Twilight Tourist Zone southbound.

V 67.2 (108.1 km) **MH 33.9** (54.6 km) Access road leads east 5.5 miles/9 km to Reno.

V 70.7 (113.8 km) **MH 30.4** (49 km) Nampa visitor centre and museum to west. NAMPA (pop. 500) was founded in 1917 when the East Dunvegan and BC Railway Company built a line through the area. Visitor facilities include a hotel, motel, restaurants, grocery and retail stores, service stations with repair facilities and a library. Recreational facilities include a curling rink, ball diamonds and tennis courts. Heart River Golf Club, 5 miles/8 km northeast, has 9 holes. Camping at Mill Brown Memorial Park. ▲

V 71.3 (114.7 km) **MH 29.8** (48 km) **Junction** with Secondary Road 683 which leads west 6 miles/10 km to Secondary Road 744 to Marie Reine.

V 72.1 (116 km) **MH 29** (46.6 km) Heart River bridge.

V 73.4 (118.1 km) **MH 27.7** (44.6 km) South Harmon Road east to Harmon Valley Fairgrounds (14 miles/23 km).

V 73.5 (118.3 km) **MH 27.6** (44.4 km) Access road leads east 3 miles/5 km to Harmon Valley Golf Course.

V 75.3 (121.2 km) **MH 25.8** (41.6 km) Grain storage equipment on both sides of highway.

V 79.6 (128.1 km) **MH 21.5** (34.6 km) North Harmon Valley Road east to Harmon Valley Fairgrounds (12 miles/20 km).

V 84.3 (135.7 km) **MH 16.8** (27 km) **Junction** with Secondary Road 688 (Three Creeks Road) which leads east 5 miles/8 km to **ST. ISIDORE** (pop. 180); gas station, pay phone and library.

V 85 (136.8 km) **MH 16.1** (25.9 km) Highway begins descent northbound into Peace River Valley.

V 87.6 (141 km) **MH 13.5** (21.7 km) Turnout to east with information sign about Peace River.

Peace River

V 88.4 (142.3 km) **MH 12.7** (20.5 km). Located on the banks of the Peace River, 15 miles/24 km northeast of Grimshaw (Mile 0 of the Mackenzie Highway). **Population:** 6,700. **Emergency Services: RCMP,** phone (780) 624-6611. **Hospital,** phone (780) 624-7500. **Ambulance** and **Fire Department,** phone (780) 624-3911.

Visitor Information: Tourist Information located in the NAR station at the first right after the railway trestle at the east entrance to downtown; phone (780) 624-2044. Open mid-May to mid-September, 9 A.M. to 9 P.M. The Mighty Peace Tourist Association, at the north end of Main Street in the restored railway station, also has information on northern Alberta destinations; phone (780) 624-4042. **Elevation:** 1,066 feet/325m.

Private Aircraft: Peace River airport, 7 miles/11.2 km west; elev. 1,873 feet/571m; length 5,000 feet/1,524m; asphalt; fuel 80, 100, Jet B.

An important transportation centre on the Peace River, the town of Peace River was incorporated in 1919, 3 years after the railroad reached Peace River Crossing. Today, Peace River is a centre for government services in the region. Area industry includes Peace River Pulp, Shell Canada and farming.

Visitor facilities include 3 hotels, a motel and many restaurants. Camping at Lions Club Campground on the west side of the river; 85 sites, hookups, restrooms, dump station and laundry. ▲

There are 9 campgrounds along the Peace River. For details, contact the Peace Valley

Conservation, Recreation and Tourism Society, phone (867) 835-2616 or fax 835-3131.

The **Centennial Museum** (on the south side of town along the river) houses archives and exhibits on Sir Alexander Mackenzie, the fur trade and local history. Historical re-enactments in summer. Open 9 A.M. to 5 P.M. Monday to Wednesday, noon to 8 P.M. Thursday to Saturday (May 1 to Aug. 31); 9 A.M. to 5 P.M. weekdays Sept. 1 to April 31. Rail transportation exhibit at restored NAR railway station. Phone (780) 624-4261.

Visitors can take the Historic Mackenzie Moose Walking Trail by following the moose tracks from the Centennial Museum to various points of interest around town. The tour includes the statue of Twelve-Foot Davis, a gold miner who struck it rich on a 12-foot strip of land between 2 larger claims in the Cariboo gold fields. He invested his $15,000 in gold in a string of trading posts along the Peace. He is buried on Grouard Hill overlooking the Peace River Valley; a stone memorial marks the spot.

Travellers Motor Hotel. 144 units, air conditioned, colour TV satellite service, courtesy in-room coffee, plug-ins, complimentary passes to golf course, indoor swimming pool, fitness centre. Courtesy airport limo, restaurant, dining room, pub, banquet and meeting room facilities. All major credit cards accepted. Senior citizen discount, commercial rates. 9510–100 St., Box 7290, Peace River, AB T8S 1S9. (800) 661-3227. Phone (780) 624-3621, fax (780) 624-4855. [ADVERTISEMENT]

Log of Valleyview–Peace River Route
(continued)

V 89.2 (143.5 km) **MH 11.9** (19.1 km) Peace River bridge.

V 90 (144.8 km) **MH 11.1** (17.9 km) **Junction** with Secondary Road 684 which leads southwest 15 miles/24 km to Secondary Road 740 and the Shaftsbury Ferry Crossing of the Peace River.

V 90.8 (146.1 km) **MH 10.3** (16.5 km) **Junction** with Secondary Road 743 which leads north 10 miles/16 km to Secondary Road 686 to the Mackenzie Highway. Access to Peace View golf course, 2.5 miles/4 km north; 9 holes, sand greens, pro shop.

V 91.6 (147.4 km) **MH 9.5** (15.3 km) Turnout to south with information sign about Peace River.

V 94.7 (152.4 km) **MH 6.4** (10.3 km) Peace River airport to south.

V 96 (154.5 km) **MH 5.1** (8.2 km) **Roma Junction** with Highway 2A to Grimshaw (7 miles/12 km southwest).

V 97.1 (156.3 km) **MH 4** (6.5 km) Access road leads 1.2 miles/2 km to Mighty Peace golf course; 18 holes, licensed dining room, pro shop, camping.

V 99.1 (159.5 km) **MH 2** (3.2 km) Access road leads south 0.6 mile/1 km to Wilderness Park; picnic tables, outhouses, hiking trails.

V 101.1 (162.7 km) MH 0 Junction with Highway 35 (Mackenzie Highway).

Mackenzie Highway Log

Distance from Grimshaw (G) is followed by distance from Fort Simpson (FS).

ALBERTA HIGHWAY 35

Grimshaw

G 0 FS 590.4 (950.2 km) Mile 0 of the Mackenzie Highway. **Population:** 2,812. **Emergency Services:** RCMP, phone (780) 332-4666. **Hospital** and **Ambulance**, phone (780) 332-1155. **Fire Department**, phone (870) 332-4430. **Visitor Information:** In the NAR railway car located adjacent the centennial monument marking Mile 0 of the Mackenzie Highway.

Named for pioneer doctor M.E. Grimshaw, who established a practice at Peace River Crossing in 1914, Grimshaw developed as a community centre for area farmers and as a shipping point with the arrival of the railroad in 1921. Scheduled air service from Edmonton and High Level to Peace River airport, 8 miles/12.8 km east.

Grimshaw became a town in February 1953. Local resources are wheat and grains, livestock, gravel, lumber, gas and oil.

Grimshaw has a motel with restaurant (Mile 0 Motor Inn), 2 hotels, 6 service stations, 2 car washes, a laundromat and all other visitor facilities. RV dump station and drinking water located south of the Mile 0 marker and 2 blocks east. Camping just north of town (see **Milepost G 1.9**). There are also an outdoor swimming pool, tennis courts, golf course and seasonal market garden located here.

Mackenzie Highway Log

(continued)

G 0.2 (0.4 km) FS 590.2 (949.8 km) **Private Aircraft:** Airstrip to west; elev. 2,050 feet/625m; length, 3,000 feet/914m; turf; fuel 80, 100.

G 1.9 (3 km) FS 588.5 (947.2 km) Grimshaw provincial campsite and **Queen Elizabeth Provincial Park** to west. Grimshaw campsite has 20 sites, picnic shelter, firepits, firewood, tables, outhouses, water pump and no camping fee. Queen Elizabeth park (located 3 miles/5 km west) on Lac Cardinal has 56 campsites, picnic shelter, firewood, firepits, toilets, playground and swimming. ▲

G 2.8 (4.6 km) FS 587.6 (945.6 km) Junction of Highways 35 and 2 East.

G 3.4 (5.5 km) FS 587 (944.7 km) Signs about construction of the Mackenzie Highway and historic Pine Bluff post office.

G 4.1 (6.6 km) FS 586.3 (943.6 km) Turnout to east with litter barrels.

G 5 (8 km) FS 585.4 (942.1 km) **Junction** with Chinook Valley Road to east.

G 6.9 (11.1 km) FS 583.5 (939.1 km) Truck scales to west.

G 7.8 (12.5 km) FS 582.6 (937.6 km) Bear Creek Drive and Bear Creek golf course to west; 9 holes, sand greens, clubhouse.

Campground.

G 8.6 (13.8 km) FS 581.8 (936.3 km) Junction with Secondary Road 737 (Warrensville) to west.

G 12.3 (19.8 km) FS 578.1 (930.3 km) Road widens to 4 lanes northbound.

G 12.6 (20.3 km) FS 577.8 (929.8 km) **Junction** with Secondary Road 986 to east.

G 13 (20.9 km) FS 577.4 (929.2 km) Road narrows to 2 lanes northbound.

G 19 (30.6 km) FS 571.4 (919.5 km) Entering Manning Ranger District northbound.

G 20.8 (33.5 km) FS 569.6 (916.7 km) Chinook Valley to east; cafe and gas station (current status unknown).

G 21 (33.8 km) FS 569.4 (916.3 km) Chinook Valley Road to east.

G 23 (37 km) FS 567.4 (913.1 km) Whitemud River.

G 25.1 (40.4 km) FS 565.3 (909.8 km) DIXONVILLE (pop. 200) has a post office, gas station, souvenir shop, museum, store and cafe. Sulphur Lake provincial campground is located 34 miles/55 km west via Highway 689 (the first 14 miles/22.5 km are paved, the remainder is gravel to the campground).

G 26.9 (43.3 km) FS 563.5 (906.8 km) Sulphur Lake Road leads west to junction with Highway 689 from Dixonville.

G 38.4 (61.8 km) FS 552 (888.4 km) Junction with Secondary Road 690 east to Deadwood (6.8 miles/11 km). There is a private exotic bird farm located 2 miles/3.2 km east then 1 mile/1.6 km south. The Bradshaws have geese, peacocks, turkeys, pheasants and other birds; visitors welcome.

G 44.4 (71.5 km) FS 546 (878.7 km) Buchanan Creek.

G 46.8 (75.4 km) FS 543.6 (874.8 km) Community of **NORTH STAR** (pop. 52) to east.

Manning

G 50.6 (81.4 km) FS 539.8 (868.8 km) Located on the Notikewin River at the junction of Highways 35 and 691. **Population:** 1,260. **Emergency Services:** RCMP, phone (780) 836-3007. **Hospital** and **Ambulance**, phone (780) 836-3391. **Fire Department**, phone (780) 836-3000.

Visitor Information: In the information centre. There is a playground adjacent the centre and a dump station across the street.

Named for an Alberta premier, Manning was established in 1947. The railway from Roma, AB, to Pine Point, NWT, reached Manning in September 1962. Today, Manning is a service centre and jumping-off point for hunters and fishers.

Manning has 5 restaurants, 3 hotel/motels, a pharmacy, food market, golf

course, swimming pool and ice rink. Attractions here include the Battle River Pioneer Museum, located on the grounds of the Battle River Agricultural Society, 0.6 mile/1 km east via Highway 691. The museum, which features tools and machinery from the pioneer days, is open daily 1–5 P.M., from June 1 to mid-September. A small ski hill is located 12.5 miles/20 km northeast of town via Highways 691 and 741; 1 T-lift and 3 runs.

Turn east at the information centre for Manning municipal campground; 19 sites on the banks of the Notikewin River, fireplaces, tables, water and flush toilets. ▲

NOTE: Last sizable community with all facilities for the next 123 miles/198 km northbound.

Mackenzie Highway Log

(continued)

G 50.7 (81.6 km) FS 539.7 (868.5 km) Downtown Manning; bridge over the Notikewin River.

G 52.9 (85.1 km) FS 537.5 (865.1 km) **Private Aircraft:** Manning airstrip to west; elev. 1,611 feet/491m; length 5,577 feet/1,700m; asphalt; fuel 100/130, Jet B.

G 53.2 (85.6 km) FS 537.2 (864.5 km) Truck stop with 24-hour food and gas; lodging.

G 54.6 (87.8 km) FS 535.8 (862.4 km) Community of Notikewin to west.

G 60.6 (97.6 km) FS 529.8 (852.6 km) Hotchkiss River bridge.

G 60.8 (97.8 km) FS 529.6 (852.4 km) Hotchkiss Provincial Park to east; 10 sites, no fee, picnic shelter, tables, firepits, fishing, outhouses and water pump. ◆▲

G 61.3 (98.6 km) FS 529.1 (851.6 km) Community of **HOTCHKISS** to east, golf course to west. Hotchkiss has a post office, service station, pay phone, coffee bar, grocery, and fuel and propane available. Condy Meadow golf course; 9 holes, grass greens, pro shop.

G 63.3 (101.8 km) FS 527.1 (848.3 km) Large lumber plant to west.

G 66.9 (107.6 km) FS 523.5 (842.6 km) Meikle River bridge.

G 71.2 (114.6 km) FS 519.2 (835.5 km) Turnout with litter barrel to west.

G 74.3 (119.5 km) FS 516.1 (830.7 km) Junction with Highway 692 and access to **Notikewin Provincial Park** (18.6 miles/30 km) on the Notikewin and Peace rivers. Highway 692 is fairly straight with pavement for the first 8 miles/13 km followed by good gravel surface to the park, although the road narrows and the surfacing may be muddy in wet weather as you approach the park. Just past the entrance to the park is the Top of Hill trailer drop-off site; 10 campsites with tables, toilets, water pump and garbage container. The park road then winds down the hill for 1.4 miles/2.2 km (not recommended for trailers, slippery when wet) to the riverside campground and day-use area; 19 campsites on the **Notikewin** River and 6 picnic sites on the **Peace River**; facilities include tables, water pump, pit toilets, garbage containers, firepits, boat launch and fishing. *CAUTION: Bears in area.* ◆▲

G 88.4 (142.3 km) FS 502 (807.9 km) Twin Lakes Lodge to east; gas, food, lodging, pay phone and fishing supplies.

G 88.9 (143 km) FS 501.5 (807.2 km) Twin Lakes Campground to west; 48 shaded sites, picnic shelter, fireplaces, firewood, tables, outhouses, water; beach, boat launch (no gas motors). Camping fee $9. **Twin Lakes** is stocked with rainbow; good fishing June to September. ◄▲

G 95.8 (154.1 km) **FS 494.6** (796.1 km) Turnout to west.

G 102.9 (165.6 km) **FS 487.5** (784.6 km) Kemp Creek.

G 111.2 (179 km) **FS 479.2** (771.2 km) **Junction** with Highway 695 East which leads 24 miles/38 km to community of CARCAJOU (pop. 50). Access to Keg River airstrip 0.4 mile/0.6 km east. **Private Aircraft**: Keg River airstrip; elev. 1,350 feet/410m; approximate length 2,700 feet/ 832m; turf; emergency only.

G 112.3 (180.8 km) **FS 478.1** (769.4 km) Keg River bridge. The community of **KEG RIVER** (area pop. 400) just north of the bridge has a gas station, post office, grocery, cafe, motel, pay phone and airstrip.

G 115.6 (186 km) **FS 474.8** (764 km) **Junction** with Secondary Road 695 West. This paved road leads 9 miles/14.5 km to Keg River Post.

G 124 (199.6 km) **FS 466.4** (750.6 km) Boyer River bridge.

G 129.5 (208.4 km) **FS 460.9** (741.8 km) **PADDLE PRAIRIE** (pop. 164) has a gas station, grocery store and cafe. Paddle Prairie is a Metis settlement. The Metis culture, a combination of French and Amerindian, played a key role in the fur trade and development of northwestern Canada.

G 134.2 (216 km) **FS 456.2** (734.2 km) Turnout to west with litter barrels.

G 136.2 (219.2 km) **FS 454.2** (731 km) **Junction** with Secondary Road 697, which leads northeast 75 miles/121 km to junction with Highway 88 near Fort Vermilion. This is a 2-lane, mostly paved road with a ferry crossing of the Peace River at Tompkin's Landing, 11 miles/18 km east from here. The ferry operates 24 hours a day, except in heavy fog, and carries 6 cars or 4 trucks.

Highway 697 provides access to **BUFFALO HEAD PRAIRIE** (pop. 453), 43.6 miles/70.2 km east, which has a small store and gas. Highway 697 also accesses **LA CRETE** (pop. 902), 53.8 miles/86.6 km east and north, Canada's most northerly agricultural community. La Crete has a motel, 3 restaurants, service stations with repair facilities, car wash, grocery, hardware and retail stores, a laundromat and bank. Recreation facilities include a golf course and a sports complex with hockey, curling and bowling.

G 141 (226.9 km) **FS 449.4** (723.2 km) Entering High Level Ranger District northbound.

G 146.3 (235.4 km) **FS 444.1** (714.7 km) Chuckegg Creek.

G 153.5 (247 km) **FS 436.9** (703.2 km) Turnout with litter barrel to west. Watch for waterfowl in small lakes along highway.

G 161.2 (259.4 km) **FS 429.2** (690.7 km) Bede Creek.

G 161.9 (260.5 km) **FS 428.5** (689.6 km) Parma Creek.

G 165.5 (266.3 km) **FS 424.9** (683.9 km) Melito Creek.

G 170.6 (274.6 km) **FS 419.8** (675.6 km) Turnout with litter barrel to west.

G 171.9 (276.7 km) **FS 418.5** (673.5 km) Private campground with hot showers and electrical hookups. ▲

G 173.3 (278.9 km) **FS 417.1** (671.3 km) **Junction** with Highway 58 West, which leads 84.5 miles/136 km to **RAINBOW LAKE** (pop. 1,146), a service community for oil and natural gas development in the region. Food, gas and lodging available.

High Level

G 173.6 (279.3 km) **FS 416.8** (670.9 km) Located at the junction of Highways 35 and 58. **Population**: 3,093. **Emergency Services**: RCMP, phone (780) 926-2226. **Hospital**, 25 beds, 6 doctors, phone (780) 926-3791. **Ambulance**, phone (780) 926-2545. **Fire Department**, phone (780) 926-3141.

Visitor Information: The visitors centre and Mackenzie Crossroads Museum are located at the south end of town; displays, souvenirs and rest area. Open year-round; 9 A.M. to 9 P.M. daily in summer. Internet address is www.town.highlevel.ab.ca. **Radio**: 530 AM, 89.9, 104.1-FM.

Begun as a small settlement on the Mackenzie Highway after WWII, High Level grew with the oil boom of the 1960s and completion of the railroad to Pine Point. High Level has a strong agricultural economy and boasts the most northerly grain elevators in Canada. The community is also supported by a sawmill complex and serves as a transportation centre for the northwestern Peace River region. There is scheduled air service to Edmonton daily.

Visitor facilities include 7 motels, restaurants and service stations with major repair. RV dump located at the Shell station. There are also an ice arena and curling rink, golf course, swimming pool, playgrounds, banks, schools and churches. Recreation includes hunting (moose, caribou, deer) and fishing for northern pike, perch, walleye, whitefish, goldeye and grayling.

There is a private campground at the south edge of town. A campground operated by the local Lions Club is located just east of town on Highway 58. ▲

Mackenzie Crossroads Museum and Visitors Centre. See display ad this section.

Mackenzie Highway Log
(continued)

G 173.6 (279.3 km) **FS 416.8** (670.9 km) Downtown High Level.

G 174 (280 km) **FS 416.4** (670.2 km) **Junction** with Highway 58 East to Jean D'Or Prairie and **junction** with Highway 88 (77.4 miles/124.5 km, gravel). Highway 88 (the Bicenntennial Highway) leads 48.5 miles/78 km (paved) to **FORT VERMILION** (pop. 850) on the Peace River, established as a trading post by the North West Co. in 1786. Visitor services in Fort Vermilion include food, gas and lodging. Highway 88 continues 255 imles/410 km to Slave Lake; no services on highway south of Fort Vermilion.

G 176.2 (283.5 km) **FS 414.2** (666.7 km) High Level golf and country club to east. Open daily, May 1 to first snow, until midnight. Clubhouse, grass greens and 9 holes.

G 181.1 (291.5 km) **FS 409.3** (658.7 km) **Private Aircraft**: High Level airport; elev. 1,110 feet/338m; length 5,000 feet/1,524m; asphalt; fuel 80, 100, Jet B. Floatplane base at Footner Lake, 0.6 mile/1 km west.

G 193.4 (311.2 km) **FS 397** (639 km) Turnoff to west for **Hutch Lake Recreation Area**; parking, 8 picnic sites with tables and firepits, toilets. Short path leads down to lake. Bring mosquito repellent.

G 196 (315.5 km) **FS 394.4** (634.7 km) Hutch Lake provincial campground, 2.9 miles/4.6 km west; 12 sites, firepits, firewood, tables, toilets. Beach and boat launch on Hutch Lake. Hiking trails. Good spot for bird watchers. Camping fee $7.50. ▲

G 196.8 (316.7 km) **FS 393.6** (633.5 km) Turnouts with litter barrels both sides of highway.

Scenic trail at Twin Falls Park, Milepost G 338.8, leads to Louise Falls. (© Leslie Leong)

G 207.3 (333.6 km) **FS 383.1** (616.6 km) Wooden railway bridge to east.

G 219.3 (352.9 km) **FS 371.1** (597.3 km) **MEANDER RIVER** (pop. 340) has a post office, gas, grocery store and confectionary with pay phone. *NOTE: Last gas northbound until Enterprise at **Milepost G 345.8**, 126.5 miles/203.6 km from here.*

G 221.5 (356.4 km) **FS 368.9** (593.7 km) Mission Creek.

G 223.8 (360.1 km) **FS 366.6** (590.1 km) The Mackenzie Highway crosses the Hay River here and follows it north into Northwest Territories.

G 227.5 (366.2 km) **FS 362.9** (584 km) Railway bridge over Hay River to east. Construction of the Great Slave Lake Railway (now part of Canadian National Railway's Peace River Division) was one of the largest railway construction projects since the boom of the first transcontinental railway lines in the late 1800s and early 1900s in Canada. The line extends 377 miles/607 km from Roma Junction near Peace River, AB, to Hay River, NWT, on the shore of Great Slave Lake. (A 54-mile/87-km branch line extended the line to the now-defunct lead–zinc mine at Pine Point, NWT.) Opened for traffic in 1964, the line carries mining shipments south and supplies north to Hay River.

G 228.1 (367.1 km) **FS 362.3** (583.1 km) Gravel road leads west 39 miles/63 km to **ZAMA** (pop. 200), an oil field community. Drilling and related operations take place at Zama in winter. Zama is the southern terminal of the interprovincial pipeline, carrying Norman Wells crude to Edmonton refineries.

G 231.5 (372.5 km) **FS 358.9** (577.6 km) Slavey Creek.

G 243.5 (391.9 km) **FS 346.9** (558.3 km) Paved turnout with litter barrels to west.

G 250.2 (402.6 km) **FS 340.2** (547.5 km) Lutose Creek.

G 263.3 (423.7 km) **FS 327.1** (526.5 km) Steen River bridge.

G 266.7 (429.2 km) **FS 323.7** (521 km) **STEEN RIVER** (pop. 25) to east; no services.

G 266.9 (429.5 km) **FS 323.5** (520.7 km) Steen River Forestry Tanker Base to west. Grass airstrip.

G 268.1 (431.5 km) **FS 322.5** (518.7 km) Sam's Creek.

G 270.1 (434.7 km) **FS 320.3** (515.4 km) Jackpot Creek.

G 276.2 (444.5 km) **FS 314.2** (505.6 km) Bannock Creek.

G 283.3 (455.9 km) **FS 307.1** (494.2 km) Indian Cabins Creek.

G 284 (457 km) **FS 306.4** (493.2 km) **INDIAN CABINS** (pop. 10); no services, historic log church. The old Indian cabins that gave this settlement its name are gone, but nearby is an Indian cemetery with spirit houses.

G 285.3 (459.1 km) **FS 305.1** (491 km) Delphin Creek.

G 293.7 (472.7 km) **FS 296.7** (477.5 km) 60th parallel. Border between Alberta and Northwest Territories. The Mackenzie Highway now changes from Alberta Highway 35 to NWT Highway 1.

Distance from Grimshaw (G) is followed by distance from Fort Simpson (FS) and distance from the AB–NWT border (B). Highway 1 begins its own series of kilometre markers, starting with Kilometre 0 at the border, which appear about every 2 kilometres.

NWT HIGHWAY 1

G 293.7 (472.7 km) **FS 296.7** (477.5 km) **B 0** AB–NWT border, 60th Parallel. A government visitor information centre here has brochures, maps, fishing licenses, camping permits, a dump station and emergency radiophone. Dene (Indian) arts and crafts are on display. Also check here on road and ferry conditions before proceeding. The visitor centre is open May 15 to Sept. 15 from 8 A.M. to 10 P.M.

60th Parallel Campground and picnic area adjacent visitor centre. Facilities include 12 campsites, 5 picnic sites, kitchen shelter and drinking water. The park overlooks the Hay River and canoeists may launch here. Information on canoeing the river can be obtained at the visitor centre. ▲

Driving distances from the border to destinations in Northwest Territories are as follows (see individual highway logs this section for details): Hay River 76 miles/122 km; Fort Simpson 297 miles/478 km; Wrigley 430 miles/694 km; Fort Providence 140

miles/225 km; Yellowknife 330 miles/531 km; Fort Smith 238 miles/383 km.

G 295.5 (475.6 km) **FS 294.9** (474.6 km) **B 1.8** (2.9 km) Reindeer Creek.

G 318.5 (512.6 km) **FS 271.9** (437.6 km) **B 24.8** (39.9 km) Grumbler Rapids, just off highway, is audible during low water periods in late summer.

G 319.1 (513.5 km) **FS 271.3** (436.6 km) **B 25.4** (40.8 km) Swede Creek.

G 319.8 (514.6 km) **FS 270.6** (435.5 km) **B 26.1** (42 km) Large turnout and gravel stockpile to west.

G 334.2 (537.8 km) **FS 256.2** (412.4 km) **B 40.5** (65.1 km) Mink Creek.

G 335.5 (539.9 km) **FS 254.9** (410.2 km) **B 41.8** (67.3 km) Large turnout and gravel stockpile to west.

G 338.8 (545.3 km) **FS 251.6** (404.9 km) **B 45.1** (72.6 km) **Twin Falls Gorge Territorial Park**; Alexandra Falls picnic area to east. Paved parking area and gravel walkway to falls viewpoint, overlooking the Hay River, which plunges 109 feet/33m to form **Alexandra Falls**. Excellent photo opportunities; easy hike down to top of falls. A walking trail connects with Louise Falls.

G 340.3 (547.6 km) **FS 250.1** (402.6 km) **B 46.6** (74.9 km) Turnoff to east for Louise Falls picnic area and campground, now part of Twin Falls Gorge Territorial Park; 18 campsites, 6 picnic sites, kitchen shelters, tables, toilets, firepits, firewood, water. Hiking trails to viewpoint overlooking 3-tiered **Louise Falls**, which drops 50 feet/15m. (It is not advisable to walk down to the water.) Hike along bluff 3 miles/5 km for Alexandra Falls. ▲

G 341.9 (550.2 km) **FS 248.5** (400 km) **B 48.2** (77.5 km) **Escarpment Creek** picnic area; tables, shelter, toilets, firepits, garbage container, water pump. Spectacular series of waterfalls downstream.

G 342.1 (550.5 km) **FS 248.3** (399.7 km) **B 48.4** (77.8 km) Highway crosses Escarpment Creek.

G 345.4 (555.9 km) **FS 245** (394.3 km) **B 51.7** (83.2 km) Truck weigh scales to east, service station to west. Entering Enterprise northbound.

G 345.5 (556 km) **FS 245** (394.2 km) **B 51.8** (83.3 km) **Junction** of Highway 1 and Highway 2. Weigh station. Highway 2 leads 23.6 miles/38 km from here to **HAY RIVER** (pop. 2,891), the hub for transportation on Great Slave Lake and a major service centre with all visitor facilities (see HAY RIVER HIGHWAY log this section for details on Hay River). Continue on Highway 1 for Enterprise (description follows) and Fort Simpson.

ENTERPRISE (pop. 56), a highway community with food, grocery store, gas, diesel and lodging. Pay phone. It is a good idea to fill up gas tanks here. View of Hay River Gorge just east of the highway.

*NOTE: Last gas southbound until Meander River at **Milepost G 219.3**, 126.5 miles/203.6 km from here.*

G 368.2 (592.5 km) **FS 222.2** (357.6 km) **B 74.5** (120 km) Turnout with outhouse to north with view of McNally Creek Falls.

Highway crosses McNally Creek northbound.

G 370.5 (596.2 km) **FS 219.9** (353.9 km) **B 76.8** (123.6 km) Large paved turnout to north with litter barrels and scenic view.

G 374.7 (603 km) **FS 215.7** (347.2 km) **B 81** (130.3 km) Easy-to-miss **Hart Lake Fire Tower** access road turnoff leads 0.5 mile/0.8 km to picnic area and forest fire lookout tower. Panoramic view over more than 100 square miles/259 square km of forest to Great Slave Lake and Mackenzie River. Path to ancient coral reef. *CAUTION: Keep the fly repellent handy and stay away from the edge of escarpment.*

G 378.2 (608.6 km) **FS 212.2** (341.5 km) **B 84.5** (136 km) Crooked Creek.

G 378.7 (609.4 km) **FS 211.7** (340.7 km) **B 85** (136.8 km) Trapper's cabin to north.

G 385.5 (620.4 km) **FS 204.9** (329.7 km) **B 92** (148.1 km) Side road to highway maintenance camp.

G 398.2 (640.8 km) **FS 192.2** (309.3 km) **B 104.5** (168.2 km) Highway maintenance camp and stockpiles to north.

G 398.7 (641.7 km) **FS 191.7** (308.5 km) **B 105** (169 km) Access road leads south 4.5 miles/7.2 km to **Lady Evelyn Falls** where the Kakisa River drops 49 feet/15m over an escarpment. Staircase down to viewing platform. Hiking trail to base of falls; swimming and wading. Ample parking, interpretive display, territorial campground with 10 tent sites, 18 RV sites and 5 picnic sites; tables, firepits, firewood, garbage containers, water pump, kitchen shelters. At end of road, 4 miles/6.4 km past campground, is Slavey Indian village and **Kakisa Lake**; fair fishing for walleye, pike and grayling.

G 399.6 (643.1 km) **FS 190.8** (307.1 km) **B 105.9** (170.4 km) Kakisa River bridge.

G 399.8 (643.4 km) **FS 190.6** (306.8 km) **B 106.1** (170.7 km) Kakisa River bridge picnic area with 10 sites, tables, fireplaces and firewood. Hiking trails along river lead upstream to Lady Evelyn Falls. Fair fishing in **Kakisa River** for grayling.

G 410.5 (660.6 km) **FS 179.9** (289.5 km) **B 116.8** (187.9 km) Turnout with litter barrels, log cabin, outhouse, picnic tables and map display on Highways 1 and 3.

G 410.9 (661.2 km) **FS 179.5** (289 km) **B 117.2** (188.5 km) **Junction** of Highway 1 and Highway 3. Highway 3 (paved and gravel) leads 212.5 miles/342 km north to Yellowknife, capital of Northwest Territories (see YELLOWKNIFE HIGHWAY log this section).

G 438.4 (705.5 km) **FS 152** (244.7 km) **B 144.7** (232.8 km) Emergency survival cabin and turnout with litter barrels and outhouse to south.

G 450.5 (725 km) **FS 139.9** (225.1 km) **B 158.6** (255.3 km) Turnout to north with parking and scenic view.

G 466.2 (750.3 km) **FS 124.2** (199.9 km) **B 172.5** (277.6 km) Bouvier River.

G 467 (751.6 km) **FS 123.4** (198.6 km) **B 173.3** (278.9 km) Emergency survival cabin and turnout with litter barrels to south.

G 471.9 (759.5 km) **FS 118.5** (190.7 km) **B 180.1** (289.8 km) Turnout to north.

G 473.6 (762.1 km) **FS 116.9** (188.1 km) **B 179.9** (289.5 km) Wallace Creek. Scenic canyon to north.

G 477 (767.6 km) **FS 113.4** (182.6 km) **B 183.3** (294.9 km) Highway maintenance camp to south.

G 477.6 (768.6 km) **FS 112.8** (181.6 km) **B 183.9** (295.9 km) Redknife River.

G 488.7 (786.4 km) **FS 101.7** (163.8 km) **B 195** (313.7 km) Morrissey Creek.

G 491.7 (791.8 km) **FS 98.7** (158.8 km) **B 199.8** (321.6 km) Winter ice road leads south 78 miles/126 km to **TROUT LAKE** (pop. 66), a Dene settlement.

G 493.3 (793.9 km) **FS 97.1** (156.3 km) **B 201.3** (324 km) Trout River bridge just east of turnoff to **Whittaker Falls (Sambaa Deh) Territorial Park**; 3 picnic sites, 8 campsites, tables, litter barrels, showers, kitchen shelter, firepits and firewood.

The park overlooks the **Trout River Canyon** *(CAUTION: Stay away from edge)*. Walk along the river to view large deposits of shale and limestone. Grayling fishing, use dry flies in deep pools. Hike to Coral Falls.

G 498.1 (801.6 km) **FS 92.3** (148.5 km) **B 206.1** (331.7 km) Emergency survival cabin and turnout with litter barrels to north.

G 523.7 (842.8 km) **FS 66.7** (107.3 km) **B 229.9** (370 km) **Ekali Lake** access; pike and pickerel fishing.

G 527.4 (848.7 km) **FS 63** (101.4 km) **B 233.6** (376 km) All-weather road leads 17 miles/27 km to **JEAN MARIE RIVER** (pop. 67), a traditional Slavey community known for its hand-crafted moose hide clothing decorated with moose tufting, porcupine quilling and embroidery. Also accessible by boat from Fort Simpson.

G 529.2 (851.7 km) **FS 61.2** (98.5 km) **B 235.5** (379 km) Emergency survival cabin and turnout to north with outhouse and litter barrels.

G 534.8 (860.7 km) **FS 55.6** (89.5 km) **B 241.1** (388 km) I.P.L. pipeline camp and pump station to north. Highway crosses pipeline.

G 536.3 (863 km) **FS 54.1** (87 km) **B 242.6** (390.4 km) Microwave tower to south.

G 550.4 (885.8 km) **FS 40** (64.4 km) **B 256.7** (413.1 km) Jean Marie Creek bridge.

G 550.5 (885.9 km) **FS 39.9** (64.3 km) **B 256.8** (413.2 km) "Checkpoint"; 24-hour gas, diesel, propane, licensed restaurant and accommodations. Phone (403) 695-2953. Open year-round.

G 551 (886.7 km) **FS 39.5** (63.5 km) **B 257.3** (414 km) **Liard Highway leads south to Fort Liard and junctions with the**

Alaska Highway near Fort Nelson.

Junction with the Liard Highway (NWT Highway 7). See the LIARD HIGHWAY section for details.

G 552 (888.4 km) **FS 38.4** (61.8 km) **B 258.3** (415.7 km) Turnout to east.

G 563.7 (907.1 km) **FS 26.7** (43.1 km) **B 270** (434.4 km) Emergency survival cabin and turnout with litter barrels and outhouse to west.

G 577.8 (929.8 km) **FS 12.6** (20.4 km) **B 284.1** (457.1 km) Highway crests hill; view of Liard River ahead. Ferry landing 3,280 feet/1,000m.

G 578.2 (930.5 km) **FS 12.2** (19.7 km) **B 284.5** (457.8 km) Liard River Campground to accommodate travelers who miss the last ferry at night, has 5 sites, tables, firepits, water, outhouse and garbage container.

G 578.5 (930.9 km) **FS 11.9** (19.3 km) **B 284.8** (458.2 km) Free government-operated Liard River (South Mackenzie) ferry service operates daily late May through October from 8 A.M. to 11:45 P.M., 7 days a week. Crossing time is 6 minutes. Capacity is 8 cars or 2 trucks, with a maximum total weight of 130,000 lbs./59,090 kg. An ice bridge opens for light vehicles in late November and heavier vehicles as ice thickens. *NOTE: This crossing is subject to extreme high and low water level fluctuations which may cause delays. No crossing possible during breakup (about mid-April to mid-May) and freezeup (mid-October to mid-November).* For ferry information phone (867) 695-2018 or (800) 661-0751.

G 580.7 (934.6 km) **FS 9.7** (15.6 km) **B 287** (461.9 km) Fort Simpson airport. See Private Aircraft information in Fort Simpson.

G 588.1 (946.4 km) **FS 2.3** (3.8 km) **B 294.4** (473.7 km) **Junction** with Fort Simpson access road which leads 2.3 miles/3.8 km to Fort Simpson (description follows). The extension of NWT Highway 1 to Wrigley was completed in 1994; see WRIGLEY EXTENSION log this section.

G 589.7 (949 km) **FS 0.7** (1.2 km) **B 296** (476.3 km) Causeway to Fort Simpson Island.

G 590.1 (949.6 km) **FS 0.3** (0.6 km) **B 296.4** (476.9 km) Turnoff for village campground; 30 campsites, 4 picnic sites, kitchen shelter; shower planned.

Visitors take in spectacular Sambaa Deh Falls along the Trout River. (© Leslie Leong)

Fort Simpson

G 590.4 (950.2 km) FS 0 B 296.7 (477.5 km) Located on an island at the confluence of the Mackenzie and Liard rivers. **Population:** 1,450. **Emergency Services:** RCMP, phone (403) 695-3111. **Hospital** (12 beds), for medical emergency phone (403) 695-2291. **Fire Department** (volunteer), phone (403) 695-2222.

Visitor Information: Village office operates a visitor booth June through August and has a photo exhibit and films. The visitor information centre is open until 8 P.M., 7 days a week in summer; closed Sundays in winter. Nahanni National Park information centre is open 8:30 A.M. to 5 P.M., 7 days a week in July and August, weekdays the rest of the year.

Television: Channels 2, 4, 6, 7, 9, 11.

Transportation: Scheduled service to Yellowknife and Whitehorse, YT via First Air. Fixed wing and helicopter charters available.

Dene doll from Nats'enelu. Fort Simpson is a center for crafts and aboriginal fashion. (© Lyn Hancock)

Rental cars—Available. **Taxi service**—Available.

Private Aircraft: Fort Simpson airport; elev. 554 feet/169m; length 6,000 feet/1,829m; asphalt; fuel 100, Jet B. Fort Simpson Island; elev. 405 feet/123m; length 3,000 feet/914m; gravel; fuel 100, Jet B.

Fort Simpson is a full-service community. There is a motel with kitchenettes and a hotel with licensed dining; a gas station with repair service (unleaded, diesel and propane available); 2 grocery stores, department store, hardware store, a bank, laundromat, post office, crafts shop and sports shop. Small engine repair shop and mechanics available. Fort Simpson has grade schools, churches (Anglican, Catholic and Pentecostal), the Stanley Isaiah Senior Citizen's Centre, and various territorial and federal offices. Recreational facilities include an arena, curling rink, gym, ball diamond, tennis, small indoor pool, golf course and a boat launch at government wharf. A number of community activities are held at the Papal Site, a large field with a cross, log tepee and stone monument commemorating Pope John Paul II's visit here in 1987.

Public campground at edge of town in wooded area has 30 campsites and 4 picnic sites.

Fort Simpson is the oldest continuously occupied site on the Mackenzie River, dating from 1804 when the North West Co. established its Fort of the Forks. There is a histori-

FORT SIMPSON ADVERTISERS

cal marker on the bank of the Mackenzie. The Hudson's Bay Co. began its post here in 1821. At that time the fort was renamed after Sir George Simpson, one of the first governors of the combined North West Co. and Hudson's Bay Co. Fort Simpson served as the Mackenzie District headquarters for the Hudson's Bay Co. fur-trading operation. Its key location on the Mackenzie River also made Fort Simpson an important transportation centre. Anglican and Catholic missions were established here in 1858 and 1894.

Fort Simpson continues to be an important centre for the Northwest Territories water transport system. Visitors may walk along the high banks of the Mackenzie River and watch the boat traffic and floatplanes.

One of the easiest places to get down to the water is by Alfred Faille's cabin on Mackenzie Drive. Faille was a well-known Fort Simpson pioneer and prospector.

For visitors, Fort Simpson has Slavey crafts, such as birch-bark baskets and beadwork. Aboriginal Dene fashion designer Darcy Moses teaches at the Nats'enelu outlet in Fort Simpson. Nats'enelu is also an outlet for Dene dolls.

Fort Simpson is also the jumping-off point for jet boat trips on the North Nahanni River; Mackenzie River traffic; and fly-in trips to Nahanni National Park.

The 4,766-square-km **NAHANNI NATIONAL PARK**, listed as a unique geological area on the UNESCO world heritage site list, is accessible only by nonpowered boat or aircraft. Located southwest of Fort Simpson near the Yukon border, the park has day-trip flightseeing tours that may be arranged in Fort Simpson, Fort Liard and Yellowknife, and from Fort Nelson, BC, and Watson Lake, YT. Highlights include the spectacular

Virginia Falls (300 feet/90m, twice as high as Niagara Falls). One of the most popular attractions in the park is running the South Nahanni River or its tributary, the Flat River. The South Nahanni River route stretches

about 186 miles/300 km from Rabbitkettle Lake to the eastern park boundary. Rabbitkettle Hot Springs, a major feature on the upper section of the river, is reached by trail (restricted access, hikers must be guided by park staff). Near the east park boundary is Kraus Hot Springs, on the remains of the old Kraus homestead. The Flat River route stretches 80 miles/128 km from Seaplane Lake to the confluence with the South Nahanni. Charter air service for canoe drop-offs is available in Fort Simpson.

In order to evenly distribute visitor use and maintain ecological integrity within Nahanni National Park Reserve, the park has implemented a mandatory reservation system for overnight use. Twelve guided and 12 non-guided visitors are allowed to camp at Virginia Falls each day. The maximum length of stay at Virginia Falls is 2 nights. Reservations may be made by telephone or fax. User fees are charged. The seasonal overnight-use fee is $100, payable by VISA or MasterCard at the time a reservation is made. (Seasonal user fees are transferable to any national park in Northwest Territories.) A day-use fee of $10 per person is charged to those visitors flying into Virginia Falls for a day trip. Reservations are not required for day trips. Contact Nahanni National Park Reserve, Box 348, Fort Simpson, NT X0E 0N0; phone (867) 695-3151, fax 695-2446.

AREA FISHING: Willow, Dogface and **Trout lakes** accessible by air. Good fishing for trout and grayling. Inquire locally. ✒

Mackenzie Highway Log

(continued)

Distance from Fort Simpson (FS) is followed by distance from Wrigley (W).

Improved to all-weather road standards, this former trail to Wrigley officially opened in 1994 as part of Highway 1 (although it's still referred to locally as the "road to Wrigley"). Slippery when wet. Use caution approaching all bridges. Driving time is approximately 3 hours between Fort Simpson and Wrigley. Allow at least 2 hours from Wrigley to the Camsell ferry crossing.

WRIGLEY EXTENSION

FS 0 W 137 (220.5 km) **Junction** with Fort Simpson access road.

FS 9.5 (15.3 km) **W 127.5** (205.2 km) Single-lane bridge over Martin River. *CAUTION: Slow down for steep descent to bridge.*

FS 17.9 (28.8 km) **W 119.1** (191.7 km) Creek crossing. *CAUTION: Slow down, steep drop-offs and no guardrails.*

FS 33.4 (53.7 km) **W 103.6** (166.7 km) Single-lane bridge over Shale Creek.

FS 34 (54.7 km) **W 103** (165.8 km) Turnout to east.

FS 46.6 (75 km) **W 90.4** (145.5 km) Ferry crossing of the Mackenzie River at Camsell Bend (Ndulee Crossing). Ferry operates daily, late May through October, 9 to 11 A.M. and 2 to 8 P.M.. Capacity is 6 cars or 4 trucks. *NOTE: There are no overnight facilities for anyone missing the ferry. Ferry does not operate in fog. Be prepared to wait.*

FS 71 (114.3 km) **W 66** (106.2 km) Mackenzie Mountains come into view to the west, northbound.

FS 73.5 (118.3 km) **W 63.5** (102.2 km) Highway maintenance camp to east.

FS 94.2 (151.6 km) **W 42.8** (68.9 km) Willowlake River bridge, longest bridge in the Northwest Territories.

FS 95.2 (153.2 km) **W 41.8** (67.3 km) Highway climbs steep hill northbound.

FS 97.7 (157.2 km) **W 39.3** (63.2 km) Turnout to west at top of hill with litter barrels and scenic view of the Mackenzie River.

FS 110.9 (178.5 km) **W 26.1** (42 km) Single-lane wooden bridge over the "River Between Two Mountains."

FS 112.6 (181.2 km) **W 24.4** (39.3 km) Scenic view of the Mackenzie River to west.

FS 121.5 (195.5 km) **W 15.5** (25.1 km) Wrigley interprovincial pipeline pump station and radio tower to east.

FS 128.9 (207.4 km) **W 8.1** (13 km) Single-lane bridge over Smith's Creek.

FS 131.1 (211 km) **W 5.9** (9.5 km) Highway maintenance camp to west.

FS 132.2 (212.7 km) **W 4.8** (7.7 km) **Junction** with winter ice road to east which leads north to Fort Norman, Norman Wells, Fort Franklin and Fort Good Hope. Winter road mileages are as follows: Wrigley to Fort Norman, 148 miles/238 km; Fort Norman to Norman Wells, 50 miles/80 km; Norman Wells to Fort Good Hope, 91 miles/147 km; Norman Wells to Franklin, 68 miles/110 km.

FS 132.9 (213.9 km) **W 4.1** (6.6 km) Turnoff to west for Wrigley airport. **Private Aircraft:** Wrigley airport, 4 miles/7 km south of town; elev. 493 feet/142m; length 3,500 feet/1,148m; gravel; fuel 80.

FS 136.8 (220.1 km) **W 0.2** (0.4 km) Airport Lake, Wrigley community campground; 12 sites, firepits and washrooms. Suitable for RVs; located on high, dry ground in mostly birch and white spruce trees. ▲

FS 137 (220.5 km) **W 0** WRIGLEY (pop. 200; 90 percent Dene ancestry). **Emergency Services:** RCMP, station manned intermittently. **Nursing Station,** with full-time nurse, phone (867) 587-3441.

Visitor Information: Visitor Information Centre manned by knowledgeable young people, open daily in summer; local crafts.

The Hudson's Bay Co. built a trading post here in 1870 called Fort Wrigley. The fort was abandoned in 1910 due to disease and famine, and the inhabitants moved down river. Although a church and school were built at that site in 1957, the community decided to move to higher ground in 1965. 15 homes were built at the "new" townsite of present-day Wrigley. The church, school and other buildings were moved from the old townsite by boat. Wrigley is the home of the Pehdzeh Ki First Nation.

Visitor facilities here include the Petanea Hotel and restaurant; co-op store and craft shop; Ed's Mobile Mechanical Service; a convenience store; and a government gas station operating 9 A.M. to 6 P.M. weekdays and 1 to 6 P.M. weekends. There is also a community-built, walk-in campground with washrooms and fireplaces along the bank of the Mackenzie River, with picturesque, bug-free views of the Mackenzie Mountains. ▲

Hay River Highway Log

Distance from Enterprise (E) is followed by distance from Hay River (H).
Highway 2 is paved from Enterprise to Hay River. Kilometreposts along the highway reflect distance from Enterprise.

NWT HIGHWAY 2

E 0 H 23.6 (38 km) **Junction** of Highways 1 and 2.

E 8.7 (14 km) **H 14.9** (24 km) Private campground, 0.7 mile/1.1 km east, with large organic gardens. ▲

Paradise Garden Campground. See display ad this section.

E 11.6 (18.6 km) **H 12** (19.4 km) Sawmill Road to east.

E 16 (25.7 km) **H 7.6** (12.3 km) Gravel road leads east 0.6 mile/1 km to Hay River golf course; large log clubhouse, driving range, 9 holes (par 36), artificial greens. Site of the NWT Open every second year in late August.

E 20 (32.3 km) **H 3.6** (5.7 km) **Junction** with Highway 5 to Fort Smith (see FORT SMITH HIGHWAY Log this section).

Motel and restaurant north of junction.

E 22.4 (36 km) **H 1.2** (2 km) Chamber of Commerce Welcome to Hay River sign. Parking area to east.

E 23.4 (37.6 km) **H 0.2** (0.3 km) Chamber of Commerce tourist information sign.

Hay River

E 23.6 (38 km) **H 0** Located on the south shore of Great Slave Lake at the mouth of the Hay River, on both the mainland and Vale Island. **Population:** 3,800 **Emergency Services: RCMP,** phone (867) 874-6555. **Fire Department,** phone (867) 874-2222. **Ambulance,** phone (867) 874-9333. **Hospital,** phone (867) 874-6512.

Visitor Information: Visitor information centre, just east of the highway, is housed in a 2-story brown structure; phone (867) 874-3180. The centre is open daily, late May to early September; 9 A.M. to 9 P.M. There is a dump station located here. Write the Chamber of Commerce at 10K Gagnler St., Hay River, NWT X0E 1G1; phone (867) 874-2565, fax (867) 874-3255.

Radio: CKHR-FM 107.3, 93.7, 100.1-FM. **Television:** Channels 2 through 13 via satellite. **Newspaper:** *The Hub* (weekly). **Transportation: Air**—Canadian Regional Airline, First Air, Landa Aviation, Carter Air and Buffalo Airways. **Bus**—Coachways. **Rental cars**—Available.

Private Aircraft: Hay River airport; elev. 543 feet/165m; length 6,000 feet/1,830m, paved; 4,000 feet/1,219m, gravel; fuel 100, Jet B.

Hay River was established in 1868 with the building of a Hudson's Bay Co. post. Today's economy combines transportation, communications, commercial fishing and service industries.

The community is the transfer point from highway and rail to barges on Great Slave Lake bound for arctic and subarctic communities. Hay River harbour is also home port of the Mackenzie River barge fleet that plies the river in summer.

The airstrip was built in 1942 on Vale Island by the U.S. Army Corps of Engineers. Vale Island was the townsite until floods in 1951 and 1963 forced evacuation of the population to the mainland townsite, where most of the community is now concentrated. Vale Island, referred to as "Old Town," is bounded by Great Slave Lake and the west and east channels of the Hay River.

The town boasts the tallest building in the Northwest Territories—a 17-story apartment high-rise that can be seen for miles around— and a purple high school designed by Douglas Cardinal. Hay River also has Par-

adise Gardens, the largest market-gardening operation in Northwest Territories, and Perron's Funny Farm, one of the few livestock producers in the territories.

There are several places to eat, ranging from fine dining to fast food outlets. There are 3 hotels and 3 motels (reservations recommended); gas stations with unleaded gas, propane and repair service, and grocery stores. There is also a bed and breakfast. Other facilities include 2 banks, supermarkets, a laundromat, and a variety of gift and arts and crafts shops.

Hay River has schools, churches, a civic centre with a swimming pool (1 of only 2 year-round swimming pools in Northwest Territories), bowling alley, Hay River Golf Club (9-hole), curling sheets, hockey arena and dance hall. The Hay River Speedway has car racing. Northwest Territories Centennial Library headquarters is located here. There is a public boat launch at Porritt Landing on Vale Island.

Hay River Territorial Campground and Park, on Vale Island on Great Slave Lake (follow the signs; it is about 6 miles/10 km past the information centre), has 22 sites, some pull-throughs, hookups, laundry, showers, firewood and firepits, picnic area, playground and horseshoe pit. Camping fee is $15 per night. Open mid-May to mid-September. Paradise Garden Campground, 14.9 miles/24 km south of Hay River on Highway 2, is a private campground on the Hay River; dry campsites, hookups (electrical and water), dump station, playground and organic gardens. ▲

Great sportfishing area with fly-in fishing camps (check with the chamber of commerce). Boat rentals on nearby **Great Slave Lake,** where northern pike up to 40 lbs. are not unusual. Inconnu (sheefish), pickerel and grayling also found here. ◄

Yellowknife Highway Log

Distance from the junction of Highways 1 and 3 (J) is followed by distance from Yellowknife (Y).

NWT HIGHWAY 3

J 0 Y 212.5 (342 km) **Junction** of Highways 1 and 3. Turn right northbound for Fort Providence, Rae–Edzo and Yellowknife.

The first 152.3 miles/245.1 km of Highway 3 are paved. There is one remaining stretch of gravel— 56.2 miles/90.4 km— between Edzo and Yellowknife. Plans call for continued paving of this highway over the next several years.

J 4.8 (7.7 km) **Y 207.7** (334.3 km) Chiklee Creek.

J 4.9 (7.9 km) **Y 207.6** (334.1 km) Wolf Skull Creek.

J 9.1 (14.7 km) Y 203.4 (327.3 km) Dory Point maintenance camp to west.

J 10.6 (17 km) Y 201.9 (324.9 km) Turn-off for winter ice crossing to east.

J 13.2 (21.2 km) Y 199.3 (320.8 km) Dory Point picnic area to east with 5 sites and kitchen shelter, no drinking water; overlooking Mackenzie River with view of passing riverboats.

J 13.9 (22.4 km) Y 198.6 (319.6 km) Campground with hookups, service station with regular, unleaded and diesel, and restaurant. ▲

J 14.5 (23.3 km) Y 198 (318.6 km) Dory Point marine access camp to west.

J 15.1 (24.3 km) Y 197.4 (317.7 km) Free government-operated Mackenzie River ferry operates daily 6 A.M. to midnight, from mid- or late May through October or until ice conditions prevent operation. Crossing time is 8 minutes. Capacity is 10 cars or 4 trucks, with a maximum total weight of 220,000 lbs./100,000 kg. Ferry information phone (800) 661-00751. An ice bridge opens for light vehicles in December and heavier vehicles as ice thickens. *NOTE: No crossing possible during breakup (about April to mid-May).* Ice-breaking procedures now keep the channel open for the ferry during freezeup while an ice bridge is being constructed.

J 15.9 (25.6 km) Y 196.6 (316.4 km) Sign indicates Mackenzie Wood Bison Sanctuary. *NOTE: Use EXTREME CAUTION driving in this area; slow down and watch for bison on highway!*

J 19.4 (31.2 km) Y 193.1 (310.8 km) Motel, restaurant and service station with unleaded, diesel and propane. Pay phone.

J 19.6 (31.6 km) Y 192.9 (310.4 km) Motel, restaurant, lounge; Native crafts; gas station with unleaded, diesel, propane and tire repair.

Big River Service Centre. See display ad this section.

Junction with access road which leads 2.8 miles/4.5 km west to Fort Providence (description follows). There is an airstrip located 0.4 mile/0.6 km west on the access road. *NOTE: It is a good idea to fill gas tanks here if you are bound for Yellowknife. Next gas available is in Rae–Edzo.*

Fort Providence territorial campground is located 1.3 miles/2 km west of the highway on the access road; 30 sites, tables, firewood, kitchen shelter, garbage container, pump water and dump station. Situated on the banks of the Mackenzie River. Rental boats, boat launch and fishing nearby. ▲

Fort Providence

Located on the Mackenzie River, 2.8 miles/4.5 km northwest of Highway 3. **Population:** 688. **Emergency Services: Police,** phone (867) 699-3291. **Fire Department,** phone (867) 699-4222. **Nursing station,** phone (867) 699-4311. **Elevation:** 627 feet/191m. **Radio:** 1230. **Television:** Channels 6 and 13 (CBC). **Transportation: Air**—Air Providence and charter service. **Bus**—Coachways.

Private Aircraft: Fort Providence airstrip; elev. 530 feet/162m; length 3,000 feet/915m; gravel; fuel emergency only.

Facilities include 2 motels, 2 restaurants, gas stations, grocery and general stores. Car repair available at C&A Holdings and Snow-star Mechanical Ltd.

A Roman Catholic mission was estab-lished here in 1861. Although noted for its early agricultural endeavors, Fort Providence is traditionally a trapping community. Three historical markers in the community commemorate the roles of the church and explorer Alexander Mackenzie in settling the area.

Unique and popular with northern collectors is the moose hair embroidery found in local gift shops. Local craftswomen are also noted for their porcupine quill work. Along with seeing the crafts, visitors may cruise the Mackenzie River. Spectacular photo opportunities here for sunsets on the Mackenzie.

Good to excellent fishing in **Mackenzie River**; guides and cabins available, also boats and air charter trips. Northern pike to 30 lbs., May 30 to September, use large Red Devils; grayling and pickerel from 1 to 6 lbs., June to September, use anything (small Red Devils will do). ◂

Yellowknife Highway Log
(continued)

J 26.4 (42.5 km) Y 186.1 (299.5 km) Side road west to highway maintenance camp and stockpiles.

J 27.5 (44.3 km) Y 185 (297.7 km) Blue-fish Creek.

J 37 (59.5 km) Y 175.5 (282.4 km) Large turnout to east at sand and gravel stockpiles.

J 38.7 (62.3 km) Y 173.8 (279.7 km) Small gravel turnout to east.

J 42.3 (68.1 km) Y 170.2 (273.9 km) Turnout to east with litter barrels.

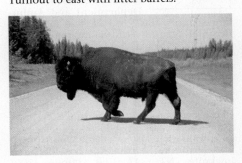

NOTE: Use EXTREME CAUTION driving in this area; slow down and watch for bison on highway!

J 51.7 (83.2 km) Y 160.8 (258.8 km) Turnout to west.

J 59.2 (95.3 km) Y 153.3 (246.7 km) Telecommunications building to east.

J 75.6 (121.6 km) Y 136.9 (220.4 km) Chan Lake picnic area to east with kitchen shelter, tables, firepits and firewood. No drinking water. Watch for waterfowl.

J 76.1 (122.5 km) Y 136.4 (219.5 km) Turnout with litter barrels to east.

100 (160.9 km) Y 112.5 (181.1 km)

Turnout with litter barrels, outhouse and highway map sign to east. Watch for buffalo.

J 104.4 (168 km) Y 108.1 (174 km) Telecommunications building to east.

J 124.7 (200.7 km) Y 87.8 (141.3 km) Entering Yellowknife District northbound.

J 129.7 (208.8 km) Y 82.8 (133.2 km) Turnout with litter barrels to east. Northbound travelers may notice the trees are getting shorter as you move farther north.

J 140.2 (225.7 km) Y 72.3 (116.3 km) Turnout to east. Highway descends north-bound to Mosquito Creek.

J 141.2 (227.3 km) Y 71.3 (114.7 km) Highway crosses **Mosquito Creek**. Fishing for pickerel and whitefish, May and June. ◂

J 144.2 (232 km) Y 68.3 (110 km) North Arm Territorial Park on the shores of Great Slave Lake. Picnic area with kitchen shelter, tables, toilets, firewood and firepits. Low-bush cranberries and other berries in area. *Beware of bears.*

J 148.3 (238.6 km) Y 64.2 (103.3 km) **Junction** with winter ice road north to communities of Lac La Marte and Rae Lakes.

J 148.5 (239 km) Y 64 (103 km) **Junction** with access road west to community of Edzo (see description at **Milepost J 152.2**).

J 148.8 (239.5 km) Y 63.7 (102.5 km) Picnic area to west. Pickerel fishing in **West Channel** in spring. ◂

J 149.3 (240.2 km) Y 63.2 (101.8 km) West Channel.

J 151.5 (243.8 km) Y 61 (98.2 km) Bridge over **Frank Channel**, which extends from the head of the North Arm of Great Slave Lake to the Indian village of Rae. Watch for turnoff to Rabesca's Bear Healing Rock; lodging, mud baths, boating and fishing for whitefish. ◂

J 152.2 (245 km) Y 60.3 (97 km) **Junction** with road which leads west 7 miles/11.2 km to community of Rae (description follows).

RAE–EDZO (pop. about 2,000). **Emergency Services: RCMP,** in Rae, phone 392-6181. **Nursing station** in Edzo, phone 371-3551. **Radio:** 105.9-FM. The 2 hamlets of Rae and Edzo contain the territories' largest Dene (Indian) community. The Rae area, where most of the community resides, is an old Indian hunting spot and was the site of 2 early trading posts. The Edzo site was developed in 1965 by the government to provide schools and an adequate sanitation system. Rae has grocery stores, a post office, Native crafts shop, 2 hotels, food service and gas stations with regular, unleaded and diesel. Pay phones are located at the community sports centre and at the cafe.

J 152.3 (245.1 km) Y 60.2 (96.9 km) Pavement ends, gravel begins, eastbound. Watch for road construction.

J 159.8 (257.2 km) Y 52.7 (84.8 km) Stagg River bridge. After crossing the North Arm of Great Slave Lake, the highway swings southeast toward Yellowknife. Winding road to Yellowknife, good opportunities to see waterfowl in the many small lakes.

J 160.4 (258.1 km) Y 52.1 (83.9 km) Turnout with litter barrels to south.

J 189.2 (304.5 km) Y 23.3 (37.5 km) Turnout with litter barrels to north.

J 189.5 (304.9 km) Y 23 (37.1 km) Boundary Creek.

J 203.8 (328 km) Y 8.7 (14 km) Yellowknife city limits.

J 208.5 (335.5 km) Y 4 (6.5 km) Gravel ends, pavement begins, eastbound.

J 208.7 (335.8 km) Y 3.8 (6.2 km)

Yellowknife

Yellowknife Golf Club to north; 9 holes, sand greens, pro shop, licensed clubhouse. Built on the Canadian Shield, the course is mostly sand and bedrock. Each player gets a small piece of carpet to take along on the round as their own portable turf. Site of the June 21 Midnight Tournament. Some modified rules have been adopted by this Far North golf course, among them: "No penalty assessed when ball carried off by raven."

J 209.8 (337.7 km) **Y 2.7** (4.3 km) Yellowknife airport to south.

J 210 (338 km) **Y 2.5** (4 km) **Fred Henne Territorial Park** on Long Lake. Attractive public campground with 82 sites, water, firewood, firepits, picnic area, boat launch, snack bar, showers and pay phone. Daily and seasonal rates available; open from mid-May to mid-September. Sandy beach and swimming in Long Lake. Interpretive trail. ▲

J 210.5 (338.7 km) **Y 2** (3.3 km) Old Airport Road access to Yellowknife. Just past the turnoff is the Welcome to Yellowknife sign and the hard-to-miss Wardair Bristol freighter to the south. A historical plaque commemorates the Bristol freighter, which was the first wheel-equipped aircraft to land at the North Pole. Picnic sites nearby.

J 211.4 (340.2 km) **Y 1.1** (1.8 km) Stock Lake to south.

J 211.7 (340.7 km) **Y 0.8** (1.3 km) **Junction** of Highway 3 and Highway 4 (Ingraham Trail); see INGRAHAM TRAIL log this section.

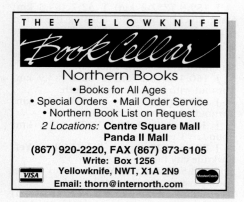
Yellowknife

J 212.5 (342 km) **Y 0** On the north shore of Great Slave Lake, approximately 940 miles/1,513 km from Edmonton, AB. **Population:** 17,500. **Emergency Services: RCMP,** phone (867) 920-8311. **Fire Department** and **Ambulance,** phone (867) 873-3434 or 873-2222. **Hospital,** Stanton Yellowknife, phone (867) 920-4111.

Visitor Information: Northern Frontier Regional Visitors Centre, showcasing the culture and crafts of the area, is located at 4807 49th St. Reservation desk for booking tours. Very helpful staff. Open daily year-round; summer hours 8 A.M. to 6 P.M. Phone (867) 873-4262, fax 873-3654.

Information also available from Northwest Territories Tourism, P.O. Box 1320, Yellowknife, NT X1A 2L9. Phone (800) 661-0788 or (867) 873-7200. Or write the Chamber of Commerce, No. 6, 4807 49th St. (MP), Yellowknife, NWT X1A 3T5; phone (867) 920-4944.

Radio: 1240, 1340, 101.1-FM. **Television:** Channel 8; 15 cable channels. **Newspapers:** *News/North* (weekly); *Yellowknifer* (twice weekly).

Private Aircraft: Yellowknife airport; elev. 674 feet/205m; length 7,500 feet/2,286m; asphalt; fuel 100/130, Jet B. Floatplane bases located at East Bay and West Bay of Latham Island.

Transportation: Air—Scheduled air service to Edmonton via NWT Airways and Canadian Airlines International; Winnipeg via NWT Airways. Carriers serving Yellowknife and Arctic communities are NWT Airways, Canadian Airlines International, Ptarmigan Airways, Simpson Air, Air Providence and First Air. Charter service available. **Bus**—Greyhound from Edmonton with connections at Enterprise. **Rentals**—Several major car rental agencies; boat, canoe and houseboat rentals.

Yellowknife, capital of Northwest Territories and considered the only "city" in Northwest Territories, is a relatively new community. White settlers arrived in the 1930s with the discovery of gold in the area and radium at Great Bear Lake.

Cominco poured its first gold brick in 1938. WWII intervened and gold mining was halted until Giant Yellowknife Mines began milling on May 12, 1948. It was not until 1960 that the road connecting the city with the provinces was completed. Yellowknife became capital of the Northwest Territories in 1967.

The most recent mining boom in Yellowknife was the discovery of diamonds north of Yellowknife at Lac de Gras in 1992. The find set off a rush of claim stakers. An estimated 150 companies have staked claims in an area stretching from north of Yellowknife to the Arctic coast, and east from the North Arm of Great Slave Lake to Hudson Bay. In winter, the Ingraham Trail (NWT Highway 4) is used as part of the 380-mile/612-km ice road to Lupin gold mine. The winter road also serves Lac de Gras, heart of the diamond rush.

For 2 to 6 weeks each spring, vehicle traffic to Yellowknife is cut off during breakup on the Mackenzie River crossing near Fort Providence. All fresh meat, produce and urgent supplies must be airlifted during this period, resulting in higher prices.

Yellowknife has continued to develop as a mining, transportation and government administrative centre for the territories.

Accommodations at 3 hotels, 3 motels, 14 bed and breakfasts, and the YWCA (co-ed). There are 47 restaurants, 7 dining lounges (no minors), 18 cocktail lounges and several shopping malls. Northern handicraft shops for fur parkas and other Native crafts are a specialty here, and there are shops specializing in Northern art.

Attractions include the **Prince of Wales Northern Heritage Centre,** built to collect, preserve, document, exhibit, study and interpret the North's natural and cultural history. There are many a variety of temporary exhibits ranging from Inuit stone sculpture to historical photographs, and permanent exhibits in the galleries. The orientation gallery gives general background on the Northwest Territories; the south gallery tells the story of the land and the Dene and Inuit people; the north gallery shows the arrival of the Euro–Canadians. The centre is located on Frame Lake, accessible via 48th Street or by way of a pedestrian causeway behind City Hall.

A variety of local tours is offered. At the visitors centre, pick up a free copy of *Historical Walking Tours of Yellowknife* from the City of Yellowknife Heritage Committee, for 4 do-it-yourself tours. Each short walk focuses on a district of Yellowknife. Willow Flats/The Woodyard, which includes Ragged Ass Road, and Peace River Flats have some of Yellowknife's earliest buildings. **The Rock,** where the original town sprang up on Yellowknife Bay and where there are now barges, fishing boats and a large floatplane base, is included. Climb the steps to the cairn on top of the Rock, a tribute to early-day bush pilots who opened up this country in the 1930s and 1940s. The log **Wildcat Cafe**

at the bottom of the rock is open May to September. Walk through Old Town on **Latham Island** to see structures dating back to the 1930s and to see some of the creative solutions modern builders have found to the problem of building on solid rock.

Public tours of **The Northwest Territories Legislative Assembly** building on the shore of Frame Lake are available by calling the Coordinator of Public Information at (867) 669-2230. Visitors may take a 2- or 3-hour tour of the city or a 2-hour cruise on Great Slave Lake. Local tour operators also offer tours out to Ingraham Trail (NWT Highway 4) and to a traditional Dene Camp in Ndilo's Rainbow Valley.

Walk along the popular Frame Lake Trail with its views of Yellowknife's skyline, including the Armed Forces Northern Headquarters and Legislative Assembly buildings. The trail is a favorite with dog walkers, bicyclists, bird-watchers and commuters. Niven Lake Trail is excellent for bird-watching.

The Yellowknife Bookcellar. See display ad this section.

Ingraham Trail Log

Distance from Yellowknife (Y) is shown. *NWT Highway 4 begins in Yellowknife and extends 43 miles/69 km along an almost continuous chain of lakes and streams, ending at Tibbett Lake. A day-use pass is required for all parking areas.*

NWT HIGHWAY 4

Y 0 Junction of Highways 3 and 4.

Y 1.9 (3.1 km) Giant Yellowknife Mines main office. The mine has been operating

since 1947.

Y 3.1 (5 km) Side road leads north 3 miles/5 km to Vee Lake.

Y 4.7 (7.5 km) Single-lane bridge across the **Yellowknife River.** Historical sign at north end of bridge about the Ingraham Trail. Picnic area with tables and boat launch. Good fishing for northern pike, lake trout and grayling. ⚓

Y 6.1 (9.8 km) Turnoff to south by 2 transmission towers for 7-mile/11-km road to Detah Indian village; no services.

Y 11.9 (19.2 km) **Prosperous Lake** picnic area and boat launch to north. Fishing for northern pike, whitefish and lake trout. ⚓

Y 14.9 (24 km) **Madeline Lake.** Boat launch to north. Fishing for northern pike, whitefish, cisco and yellow perch. ⚓

Y 16.4 (26.4 km) **Pontoon Lake** picnic area and boat launch to south. Fishing for northern pike, whitefish, cisco and suckers. ⚓

Y 17.5 (28.2 km) Side road leads north 1 mile/1.6 km to Prelude Lake territorial campground with 45 campsites, 20 picnic sites, boat launch and swimming. Prelude Wildlife Trail is a 1¹⁄₂- hour walk. The trail has 15 interpretive stations showing the adaptations and relationships of wildlife in the North. Boat rentals, cabins and a restaurant located here. ▲

Fishing in **Prelude Lake** for lake trout, grayling, whitefish, cisco, burbot, suckers and northern pike. ⚓

Good views of Prelude Lake from the highway next 10 miles/16 km eastbound.

Y 27.3 (44 km) Powder Point on Prelude Lake to north; parking area. Boat launch for canoeists doing the route into Hidden Lake Territorial Park, Lower Cameron River, or 4-day trip to Yellowknife River bridge.

Y 28.8 (46.4 km) Cameron River Falls trailhead to north; parking. This 0.6-mile/1-km trail leads to cliffs overlooking Cameron River Falls.

Y 34.2 (55 km) Bailey bridge across Cameron River; parking area, picnicking, canoeing, hiking and swimming.

Y 36.7 (59 km) Reid Lake territorial campground with 50 campsites, 10 picnic sites, kitchen shelter, swimming, hiking trail, boat launch and fishing. Canoe launch point for Upper Cameron River and Jennejohn Lake routes. *CAUTION: Watch for bears.* ⚓▲

Y 42.8 (68.9 km)Tibbett Lake. End of road. Launch point for Pensive Lakes canoe route (advanced canoeists only).

Fort Smith Highway Log

Distance from Highway 2 junction (J) followed by distance from Fort Smith (FT).

NWT HIGHWAY 5

J 0 FT 166 (267.2 km) Highway 5 begins its own series of markers giving distances in kilometres.

J 1.3 (2.2 km) **FT 164.7** (265 km) Railroad and auto bridge crosses Hay River.

J 1.5 (2.5 km) **FT 164.5** (264.7 km) Access road leads north 3.7 miles/5.9 km to Hay River reserve.

The first 37.7 miles/60.8 km of Highway 5 are paved. Watch for construction and rough spots in surfacing. There are no services or gas available until Fort Smith.

J 5.4 (8.8 km) **FT 160.6** (258.4 km) High-

way crosses Sandy Creek.

J 11 (17.7 km) **FT 155** (249.5 km) Highway maintenance yard to south.

J 17.3 (27.9 km) **FT 148.7** (239.3 km) Birch Creek bridge.

J 23.7 (38.2 km) **FT 142.3** (229 km) Highway crosses Twin Creek.

J 30.3 (48.8 km) **FT 135.7** (218.4 km) Good gravel road leads 1 mile/1.6 km north to **Polar Lake.** Lake is stocked with rainbow; no motorboats allowed. Good bird watching. ⚓

J 33.8 (54.4 km) **FT 132.2** (212.7 km) Buffalo River bridge.

J 34.1 (55 km) **FT 131.9** (212.2 km) Turnout to north with litter barrel and map.

J 37.3 (60 km) **FT 128.7** (207.1 km) **Junction** with Highway 6 east to Pine Point and Fort Resolution (see FORT RESOLUTION HIGHWAY log this section). Highway 5 turns south for Fort Smith (continue with this log). Highway maintenance camp.

J 54 (87 km) **FT 112** (180.2 km) Turnoff for **Sandy Lake,** 8 miles/13 km south; swimming, sandy beach, fishing for northern pike. ⚓

J 54.2 (87.2 km) **FT 111.8** (180 km) Pavement ends, gravel begins, southbound.

J 59.6 (96 km) **FT 106.4** (171.2 km) Entrance to Wood Buffalo National Park. Established in 1922 to protect Canada's only remaining herd of wood bison, **WOOD BUFFALO NATIONAL PARK** (a UNESCO world heritage site) is a vast wilderness area of 44,800 square kilometres with the greater portion located in the northeast corner of Alberta. Park headquarters and Visitor Reception Centre are located in Fort Smith and Fort Chipewyan; excellent audio-video presentations, exhibits and visitor information are available. Or write Wood Buffalo National Park, Box 750, Fort Smith, NT X0E 0P0; or phone (867) 872-7900 Fort Smith or (867) 697-3662 Fort Chipewyan.

The wood bison, a slightly larger and darker northern relative of the Plains bison, numbered about 1,500 in the area at the time the park was established, representing the largest free-roaming herd in Canada. Soon after this, more than 6,600 Plains bison were moved from southern Alberta to the park. Today's herd of about 3,500 bison is considered to be mostly hybrids.

Also found within the park are many species of waterfowl and the world's only remaining natural nesting grounds of the endangered whooping crane.

The park is open year-round. Check the schedule of events at the park office.

J 63.8 (102.7 km) **FT 102.2** (164.4 km) Paralleling most of the highway to Fort Smith are hydro transmission power lines carrying power that is generated at the Taltson Dam in the Canadian Shield north of the Slave River to Fort Smith, Pine Point and Fort Resolution .

J 66 (106.2 km) **FT 100** (160.9 km) Picnic area with tables to north at Angus Fire Tower. The sinkhole seen here is an example of karst topography. Sinkholes are formed when the roofs of caves (formed by underground water dissolving bedrock) collapse.

Buffalo wallow beside highway from here to approximately **Milepost J 98.9.**

J 74 (119.2 km) **FT 92** (148 km) Highway crosses Nyarling River, which runs underground beneath the dry creekbed.

J 74.2 (119.4 km) **FT 91.8** (147.7 km) Turnout to south with litter barrel.

J 98.9 (159.2 km) **FT 67.1** (108 km) Highway maintenance building to north.

J 110.8 (178.4 km) **FT 55.2** (88.8 km) Highway crosses Sass River. Shallow lakes from here south to Preble Creek provide nesting areas for whooping cranes.

J 116.2 (187 km) **FT 49.8** (80.1 km) Highway crosses Preble Creek.

J 121.2 (195 km) **FT 44.8** (72.1 km) Wetlands pull off with litter barrel and interpretive signs.

J 130.5 (210 km) **FT 35.5** (57.1 km) The highway leaves and reenters Wood Buffalo National Park several times southbound.

J 131 (211 km) **FT 34.9** (56.1 km) Little Buffalo River bridge. Day-use picnic area with picturesque waterfall.

J 142.5 (229.4 km) **FT 23.5** (37.8 km) Turnoff for Parsons Lake Road (narrow gravel) which leads south 8 miles/13 km to **Salt Plains Overlook**. Interpretive exhibit and viewing telescope. Springs at the edge of a high escarpment bring salt to the surface and spread it across the huge flat plain; only plants adapted to high salinity can grow here. Fine view of a unique environment. Gravel parking area with tables, firepits and toilets at overlook; hiking trail down to Salt Plains (bring boots). *CAUTION: Parsons Lake Road beyond the overlook may be impassable in wet weather.*

J 144.7 (232.8 km) **FT 21.4** (34.4 km) Turnout to south and gravel stockpile.

J 147.3 (237 km) **FT 18.7** (30.1 km) Pavement begins eastbound into Fort Smith.

J 147.9 (238 km) **FT 18.1** (29.1 km) Salt River bridge.

J 151.6 (244 km) **FT 14.4** (23.2 km) Thebacha (Salt River) private campground and picnic area 10 miles/16 km north via good gravel road. Located on the **Salt River**; 8 sites, toilets, parking, small-boat launch (cruise down to Slave River), and fishing for pike, walleye, inconnu and goldeye. ◢▲

J 163.4 (263 km) **FT 2.6** (4.2 km) Turnoff to north for Fort Smith airport and Queen Elizabeth Park campground with 19 campsites, 15 picnic sites, water, kitchen shelter, showers and dump station. Short hike from campground to bluff overlooking Rapids of the Drowned on the Slave River; look for pelicans feeding here. ▲

Fort Smith

J 166 (267.2 km) **FT 0** **Population:** 2,420. **Emergency Services: RCMP,** phone (867) 872-2107. **Fire Department,** phone (867) 872-6111. **Health Centre,** phone (867) 872-2713. **Visitor Information:** Visitor Information Centre in Conibear Park, open June to September, phone (867) 872-2515. Pick up *A Walking Tour Guide to Historic Trails* brochure here. Or contact the Town of Fort Smith, P.O. Box 147, Fort Smith, NT X0E 0P0; phone (867) 872-5758.

Climate: Mean high temperature in July 75°F/24°C; mean low 48°F/9°C. **Radio:** 860, 101.9-FM. **Television:** Channels 12 (local) and 5 (CBC) plus 15 cable channels. **Newspaper:** *Slave River Journal.*

Transportation: Air—Canadian Regional Airlines and Northwestern Air Lease provide scheduled service; there are also 3 charter air services here. **Bus**—Available. **Rental cars**—Available.

Private Aircraft: Fort Smith airport; elev. 666 feet/203m; length, 6,000 feet/1,829m; asphalt; fuel 80, 100.

Fort Smith began as a trading post at a

Exploring a salt mound at Salt Plains on Highway 5. (© Leslie Leong)

favorite campsite of the portagers traveling the 1,600-mile/2575-km water passage from Fort McMurray to the Arctic Ocean. The 4 sets of rapids, named (south to north) Cassette, Pelican, Mountain and the Rapids of the Drowned, separate the Northwest Territories from Alberta. In 1874 Hudson's Bay Co. established a permanent post, and the Roman Catholic mission was transferred here in 1876. By 1911 the settlement had become a major trading post for the area.

There are a 2 hotels, a motel, several bed and breakfast establishments, 2 groceries, a takeout outlet, 4 restaurants, 3 bars, 2 convenience stores, and gas stations with unleaded gas and repair service. Recreation includes a swimming pool, ice arena (open in summer for rollerblading), curling rink and cross-country ski and walking trails.

Wood Buffalo National Park headquarters is located in the Federal Building on McDougal Road, which also houses the post office. The multi-image presentation here is highly recommended. Exhibit area and trip planning assistance available at the visitor reception area. You can drive from Fort Smith to Peace Point via an all-weather gravel road. There are several hiking trails off the road, a picnic area at the Salt River, and a 36-site campground at Pine Lake, 38 miles/61 km south of Fort Smith. There is also a good opportunity for seeing bison on the road between Pine Lake and Peace Point. Contact the park office, phone (867) 872-7900.

Other attractions in Fort Smith include **The Northern Life Museum**, which features a comprehensive view of the area's Native culture and life of the white settlers since the mid-19th century. Open 1-5 P.M. daily and Tuesday and Thursday evenings in summer.

Fort Resolution Highway Log

Distance from junction with Highway 5 (J) is followed by distance from Fort Resolution (FR).

NWT HIGHWAY 6

J 0 FR 55.9 (90 km) **Junction** of Highways 5 and 6. The first 14.7 miles/23.7 km of the highway is paved; the rest is gravel to Fort Resolution. Narrow shoulders.

J 13.2 (21.3 km) **FR 42.7** (68.7 km) Main access road north to **PINE POINT**; no ser-

vices. A mining town, Pine Point was built in the 1960s by Cominco Ltd. The open-pit lead–zinc mine shut down in 1987. The town was once a community of almost 2,000 residents, but most people moved out in 1988, and houses and structures have been moved or destroyed. The Great Slave Lake Railway (now CNR) was constructed in 1961 from Roma, AB, to Pine Point to transport the lead–zinc ore to market.

J 14.6 (23.6 km) **FR 41.3** (66.4 km) Secondary access road to Pine Point.

J 14.7 (23.7 km) **FR 41.2** (66.3 km) Pavement ends, gravel begins, eastbound. Dust-free zone to Fort Resolution.

J 15.8 (25.5 km) **FR 40.1** (64.5 km) Pine Point airport to north, microwave and satellite dish to south.

J 24.6 (39.6 km) **FR 31.3** (50.3 km) Tailing piles from open-pit mining to south.

J 32.3 (52 km) **FR 23.6** (38 km) Turnoff to north for Dawson Landing viewpoint on Great Slave Lake, accessible via a 25-mile/40-km bush road (not recommended in wet weather).

J 36.5 (58.8 km) **FR 19.4** (31.2 km) Turnout to north with litter barrel.

J 37.8 (60.8 km) **FR 18.1** (29.1 km) Glimpse of Great Slave Lake to north.

J 41.4 (66.7 km) **FR 14.5** (23.3 km) Bridge over **Little Buffalo River.** Good fishing for northern pike and walleye. ◤

J 42.4 (68.3 km) **FR 13.5** (21.7 km) Access road to Little Buffalo River Indian village.

J 54.5 (87.7 km) **FR 1.4** (2.2 km) Campground to west; 5 gravel sites, outhouses, tables and firepits. ▲

J 55.9 (90 km) **FR 0 FORT RESOLUTION** (pop. 447), located on the south shore of Great Slave Lake on Resolution Bay. **Emergency Services: RCMP,** phone (867) 394-4111. This historic community grew up around a Hudson's Bay Co. post established in 1786, and was named Fort Resolution in 1821 when the Hudson's Bay Co. and North West Co. united. Missionaries settled in the area in 1852, establishing a school and hospital to serve the largely Chipewyan population. Walking tours through the village may be arranged. The road connecting Fort Resolution with Pine Point was built in the 1960s.

Today's economy is based on trapping, and a logging and sawmill operation. There are a small motel, 2 general stores, a gas station and cafe. Meals are also available at the community hall. Canada Post outlet located in Northern Store.

YELLOWHEAD HIGHWAY 16

Connects: Edmonton, AB, to Prince Rupert, BC **Length:** 898 miles
Road Surface: Paved **Season:** Open all year
Highest Summit: Obed Summit, 3,819 feet
Major Attractions: Jasper National Park, Mt. Robson, Fort St. James
National Historic Site

(See maps, pages 220–222)

	Edmonton	Jasper	Prince George	Prince Rupert	Terrace
Edmonton		216	450	898	807
Jasper	216		234	682	591
Prince George	450	234		448	357
Prince Rupert	898	682	448		91
Terrace	807	591	357	91	

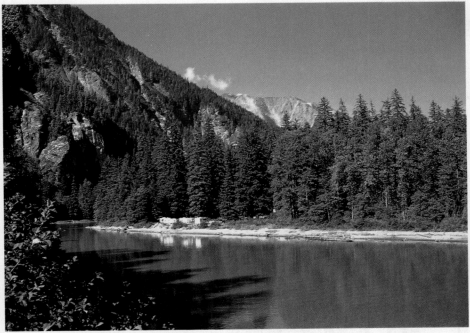

Scenic Exchamsiks River Provincial Park at Milepost PG 389.6 Yellowhead Highway, about an hour's drive east of Prince Rupert. *(© Judy Parkin)*

Yellowhead Highway 16 is a paved trans-Canada highway extending from Winnipeg, MB, through Saskatchewan, Alberta, and British Columbia to the coastal city of Prince Rupert. (The highway connecting Masset and Queen Charlotte on Graham Island has also been designated as part of Yellowhead Highway 16.) *The MILEPOST®* logs Yellowhead Highway 16 from Edmonton, AB, to Prince Rupert, BC, a distance of 898 miles/1,444 km.

Yellowhead Highway 16 terminates at Prince Rupert, BC, where you may connect with the Alaska Marine Highway System to southeastern Alaska cities, and the British Columbia ferry system to Port Hardy on Vancouver Island and Skidegate in the Queen Charlotte Islands.

This is a major east–west route, providing access to a number of attractions in Alberta and British Columbia. Yellowhead Highway 16 is also a very scenic highway, passing through mountains, forest and farmland. Visitor services are readily available in towns along the way, and campsites may be found in towns and along the highway at both private and provincial park campgrounds. (It is unsafe and illegal to overnight in rest areas.)

www.themilepost.com

Yellowhead Highway 16 Log

This section of the log shows distance from Edmonton (E) followed by distance from Prince George (PG).
The Yellowhead Highway log is divided into 2 sections: Edmonton to Prince George, and Prince George to Prince Rupert.
Kilometreposts on Yellowhead reflect distances within highway maintenance districts; The MILEPOST® periodically notes these physical posts as reference points.

HIGHWAY 16

E 0 PG 450 (724.2 km) **EDMONTON** city limit. See page 43 in the EAST ACCESS ROUTE section for description of city.

E 4 (6.4 km) **PG 446** (717.8 km) **Junction** of Highways 16 West and 60 (Devon Overpass); access to Glowing Embers Travel Centre campground with 273 sites. ▲

E 12 (19.3 km) **PG 438** (704.9 km) **SPRUCE GROVE** (pop. 13,076). All visitor facilities including motels, restaurants, gas and service stations, grocery stores, farmer's

market, shopping malls and all emergency services. Recreational facilities include a golf course, swimming pool, 2 ice skating rinks, a curling rink, and extensive walking and cycling trails. The chamber of commerce tourist information booth, located on Highway 16, is open year-round; phone (780) 962-2561.

E 18.1 (29.1 km) **PG 431.9** (695.1 km) **STONY PLAIN** (pop. 7,800). All visitor facilities including hotels, restaurants, supermarkets, shopping mall and gas stations with major repair service; RCMP and hospital; outdoor swimming pool and 18-hole golf course. The Multicultural Heritage Centre has historical archives, a craft shop and home-cooked meals. Other attractions include 16 outdoor murals; a teahouse; Oppertshauser Art Gallery; the Andrew Wolf Winery (visitors welcome); and the Pioneer Museum at Exhibition Park. Visitor information centres at Rotary Park and rest area. Camping at Lions RV Park and Campground; 26 sites. ▲

Bears & Bedtime. See display ad this section.

YELLOWHEAD HIGHWAY 16 *Edmonton, AB, to Prince George, BC*

© 1999 The MILEPOST®

E-0
PG-450/724km
DC-367/591km
C-181/292km

2 ⚠ ⛽ †

To Saskatoon

N53°33'
W113°30'

Edmonton

To Calgary
(see EAST ACCESS ROUTE section, page 33)

2

Spruce Grove

Stony Plain

E-18.1/29.1km
Bears & Bedtime Mfg.
The Multicultural Heritage Centre M
Stony Plain Highway Inn LM

Fallis

Lac Saint Anne

Athabasca River

33

To Slave Lake

Grizzly Trail

43

Whitecourt

Wabamun Lake

Isle Lakes

Entwistle

Carvel

Wildwood

Chip L.

Mackay

Nojack

Niton Junction

Carrot Creek

16

Edson

Marlboro

Sundance Cr.

McLeod River

Obed

Hinton

Bighorn Highway

Pocahontas

Talbot Lake

E-217/349km
PG-233/376km
LL-142/228km

Icefields Parkway

To Lake Louise

Banff National Park

Yoho National Park

Kootenay National Park

Columbia River

ALBERTA

BRITISH COLUMBIA

93

Athabasca R.

Columbia Icefield

Glaciated Area

N52°53' W118°05'

Jasper

Jasper National Park

E-172/277km
PG-278/447km
GP-207/333km

Mount Robson
12,972 ft./3,954m Jasper L.

Lucerne L.

Yellowhead L.

Yellowhead Pass
3,760 ft./1,146m

Mount Robson Provincial Park

Kinbasket Lake

Glaciated Area

Columbia River

To Grande Prairie
(see EAST ACCESS ROUTE section, page 33)

40

Grande Cache

Willmore Wilderness Park

ALBERTA

BRITISH COLUMBIA

E-279/449km
PG-171/275km
K-208/335km

N52°59' W119°31'

Tete Jaune Cache

J-11.5/18.5km
Irvin's Park & Campground C

Valemount

5

Glaciated Area

Wells Gray Provincial Park

North Thompson River

To Kamloops

ROCKY MOUNTAINS

COLUMBIA MOUNTAINS

Goat R.

Slim Cr.

Fraser River

McBride

E-318.8/513.1km McBride Chevron GD
North Country Lodge L
E-317.4/510.8km Beaverview Campsite CDiT

McBride Chevron GD

MOUNTAINS

E-409.5/659.1km
Purden Lake and Ski Resort CdGLMPT

Purden Lake

16

Tabor Lake

CARIBOO

Bowron River

PR-448/720km
E-450/724km
PG-0
DC-250/402km
CC-277/446km

N53°55' W122°46'

2 ⚠ ⛽ †

Prince George

To Dawson Creek
(see WEST ACCESS ROUTE section, page 55)

97

(map continues next page)

97

To Cache Creek
(see WEST ACCESS ROUTE section, page 55)

Key to mileage boxes

miles/kilometres
miles/kilometres from:

E-Edmonton
DC-Dawson Creek
GP-Grande Prairie
CC-Cache Creek
C-Calgary
K-Kamloops
LL-Lake Louise
PG-Prince George
PR-Prince Rupert

J-Junction

Key to Advertiser Services

C -Camping
D -Dump Station
d -Diesel
G -Gas (reg., unld.)
I -Ice
L -Lodging
M-Meals
P -Propane
R -Car Repair (major)
r -Car Repair (minor)
S -Store (grocery)
T -Telephone (pay)

⚠ Refer to Log for Visitor Facilities

Map Location

Principal Route
Paved
Unpaved
Other Roads
Paved
Unpaved
Hiking Trails
Ferry Routes

⚠ Refer to Log for Visitor Facilities

Scale
0   20   Miles
0   20   Kilometres

YELLOWHEAD HIGHWAY 16 *Prince George, BC, to Topley, BC*

© 1999 The MILEPOST®

Key to mileage boxes

	miles/kilometres
	miles/kilometres

from:
E-Edmonton
CC-Cache Creek
DC-Dawson Creek
PG-Prince George
PR-Prince Rupert
J-Junction

Key to Advertiser Services
C-Camping
D-Dump Station
d-Diesel
G-Gas (reg., unld.)
I-Ice
L-Lodging
M-Meals
P-Propane
R-Car Repair (major)
r-Car Repair (minor)
S-Store (grocery)
T-Telephone (pay)

Map Location

Principal Route
Paved
Unpaved

Other Roads
Paved
Unpaved

Ferry Routes **Hiking Trails**

⊞ Refer to Log for Visitor Facilities

Scale
Miles
Kilometres
0   10
0   10

CARIBOO MOUNTAINS

Purden Lake

(map continues previous page)

16

PG-0
PR-448/720km
E-450/724km
DC-250/402km
CC-277/446km

To Dawson Creek
(see WEST ACCESS ROUTE section, page 55)

97

97

To Cache Creek
(see WEST ACCESS ROUTE section, page 55)

Fraser River

Tabor Lake

Bowron River

Prince George
N53°55′ W122°46′

PG-14.2/22.8km North Country Arts & Crafts

INTERIOR PLATEAU

OMINECA MOUNTAINS

To Manson Creek

Fort St. James
J-37/59.5km Fort St. James National Historic Park
Stuart River Campgrounds CT

Tezzeron Lake

Pinchi Lake

Tachie
Tachie River

Stuart Lake

Nicoslie River

Stuart River

PG-39.5/63.6km
Lakeside Resort C

PG-57.3/92.3km Dave's
RV Park CDlST

PG-58.7/94.5km
Riverside Campsite CD
Siesta Motel L

PG-38/61.2km Brookside
Resort CDGILMPST

Cluculz Lake

Bednesti Lake

Nulki Lake

Tachick Lake

PG-59/95km
PR-389/625km

Vanderhoof
N54°01′ W124°01′ Nechako River

27

J-37/60km

N

W   E

S

Fort Fraser
N54°03′ W124°32′

PG-86.3/138.9km
Piper's Glen RV
Resort CDlT

Kenney Dam Road

Nechako River

Knewstubb Lake

PG-95/152km
PR-353/567km

Fraser Lake
N54°03′
W124°47′

Fraser L.

Endako

Stellako R.

16

Kenney Dam

Cheslatta Lake

Natalkuz Lake

Trembleur Lake

Taltapin Lake

Pinkut Lake

J-29.8/48km Babine Lake Resort CDlLST

PG-140/225km
PR-308/496km

PG-133.8/215.4km Burns
Lake KOA CDlLST

35

Burns Lake

Tchesinkut Lake

Ferry

Francois Lake

Takysie Lake

Uncha Lake

Francois Lake Road

Oosta Lake

Tweedsmuir Provincial Park

Babine Lake

Rose Lake

Decker Lake

Burns Lake
N54°13′ W125°46′

N54°03′/221.3km Sandy's RV and
Camping Resort
CDlLST

PG-137.5/221.3km Sandy's RV and
Camping Resort CDlLST

PG-171/275km
PR-277/446km

Topley
N54°31′ W126°18′

J-31/51km
Granisle

Topley Landing

J-24/39km

Takysie Lake Resort & Motel CDlLT

(map continues next page)

www.themilepost.com

YELLOWHEAD HIGHWAY • Map

YELLOWHEAD HIGHWAY 16 *Topley, BC, to Prince Rupert, BC*

© 1999 The MILEPOST®

Tweedsmuir Provincial Park

Francois Lake Road

J-31/51km

PG-171/275km
PR-277/446km

Topley (map continues previous page)

J-24/39km

PG-188.8/303.9km Shady Rest RV Park CDIT
PG-190.1/305.9km Houston Motor Inn L
Moose Meadows Resort CL

N54°31′ W126°18′

16

Houston

N54°24′ W126°39′

PG-190/306km
PR-258/416km

Smithers Landing

Granisle

Topley Landing

Babine Lake

Bulkley River

Bulkley

PG-229/369km
PR-219/353km

PG-220.3/354.5km Douglas Motel ILT
PG-219.8/353.7km Ft. Telkwa RV Park CDILT

Tyhee Lake

Telkwa

N54°46′ W127°10′

Smithers

PG-234.9/378km Glacier View RV Park C
Hudson Bay Mountain
8,450 ft./2,576m

PG-235.4/378.8km Adams Igloo Wildlife Museum

Babine River

Suskwa River

Kispiox River

N55°15′ W127°35′

PG-271/436km
PR-177/284km

Hazelton-'Ksan
New Hazelton
South Hazelton

Buckley River

Moricetown

McDonell Lake

Copper River

Kispiox

Skeena River

Skeena Crossing

Kitseguecla

PG-298/479km
PR-150/241km
SH-137/220km

37

Kitwanga
Kitwancool

Kitwanga Lake

Cedarvale

PG-299/481.2km Gitksan Paintbrush Native Arts & Crafts
PG-300.8/484.1km Seven Sisters RV Park CD

Skeena R.

PG-357/574km
PR-91/148km

Ferry
Usk

Kleanza Creek

Khyex River

Morice River Access Road

Owen Lake

Nechako Reservoir

Morice River

Morice Lake

N E
W S

Key to Advertiser Services
C –Camping
D –Dump Station
d –Diesel
G –Gas (reg., unld.)
I –Ice
L –Lodging
M –Meals
P –Propane
R –Car Repair (major)
r –Car Repair (minor)
S –Store (grocery)
T –Telephone (pay)

Principal Route
Paved / Unpaved
Other Roads
Paved / Unpaved
Ferry Routes ••••• **Hiking Trails**
Refer to Log for Visitor Facilities

Scale
Miles
Kilometres
0 — 10
0 — 10

Key to mileage boxes
miles/kilometres from:
PG –Prince George
PR –Prince Rupert
J –Junction
SH –Stewart/Hyder

Map Location

To Stewart/Hyder
(see CASSIAR HIGHWAY section, page 245)

Nass Forest Service Road

J-60/97km

New Aiyansh

Nisga'a Highway

Kitwanga Lake

Lava Lake

Kitsumkalum River

Kitsumkalum Lake

West Kalum Forest Service Road

Nisga'a Highway

Lakelse Lake

Terrace

N54°30′ W128°35′

37

Kitimat River

PG-37.6/60.5km Alcan Smelters and Chemical Ltd. Kitimat Chamber of Commerce

Hirsch Creek

J-38/61km

Kitimat

N54°00′ W128°42′

Kitsumkalum

16

Skeena River

Exchamsiks R.

COAST

MOUNTAINS

Glaciated Area

Under Construction

Greenville

Kincolith

Mill Bay

Nass River

ALASKA
BRITISH COLUMBIA

UNITED STATES
CANADA

Observatory Inlet

Portland Canal

Portland Inlet

Prudhomme Lake

Rainbow Lake

PG-448/720km
PR-0

Prince Rupert

N54°19′ W130°20′

Port Edward

Chatham Sound

Alaska State Ferry

Stony Plain Highway Inn. See display ad this section.

The Multicultural Heritage Centre. Features a regional museum, unique restaurant, a public art gallery featuring Canadian artists, as well as both local and imported craft shops. Award-winning grounds and historically significant buildings complete this rewarding experience. Open Monday to Saturday 10 A.M. to 4 P.M., Sunday 10 A.M. to 6:30 P.M. Phone (780) 963-2777. Address: 5411–51 St. [ADVERTISEMENT]

E 19.6 (31.5 km) **PG 430.4** (692.7 km) Turnoff to south for Edmonton Beach and campground. ▲

E 20.1 (32.3 km) **PG 429.9** (691.9 km) Hubbles Lake turnoff to north.

E 21.2 (34.1 km) **PG 428.8** (690.1 km) Restaurant, gas station and store to north.

E 25 (40.2 km) **PG 425** (684 km) **Junction** with Highway 43 to Dawson Creek, BC (337 miles/543 km). Continue west for Prince George.

Turn to **Milepost E 29.8** in the EAST ACCESS ROUTE section for log of Highway 43, which also accesses the Mackenzie Highway to Northwest Territories.

E 25.5 (41 km) **PG 424.5** (683.2 km) Hubbles Lake to north.

E 30.3 (48.8 km) **PG 419.7** (675.4 km) Gas and groceries south side of road at junction.

E 33 (53.1 km) **PG 417** (671.1 km) **Wabamun Lake Provincial Park**, 1 mile/1.6 km south on access road; 288 campsites, fishing, boating and swimming. ◄▲

E 34.7 (55.9 km) **PG 415.3** (668.3 km) Village of **WABAMUN** with gas, convenience store, car wash, laundromat, dump station, hotel and post office. Park with shelter, tables, litter barrels, washroom and flush toilets. Also located here is Trans Alta Utilities generating station, which generates electricity from coal.

E 38.5 (61.9 km) **PG 411.5** (662.3 km) Emergency phone to south. Propane, fuel and groceries.

E 42.5 (68.4 km) **PG 407.5** (655.8 km) **FALLIS** (pop. 190); no services. Strip mining of coal on north side of highway.

E 46.2 (74.4 km) **PG 403.8** (649.8 km) Private campground/RV park, open year-round. ▲

E 48.7 (78.3 km) **PG 401.3** (645.9 km) **GAINFORD** (pop. 205). Cafe, hotel and post office. Free public campground at west end of town with 8 sites, firewood, tables, pit toilets and water. ▲

E 56.6 (91.1 km) **PG 393.4** (633.1 km) **ENTWISTLE** (pop. 477). Restaurants, gas station, 2 motels, post office, swimming pool and grocery store. **Pembina River Provincial Park**, 1.9 miles/3.1 km north; 132 campsites, tables, showers, flush toilets, water and dump station. Open all year; camping fee $11 to $16. Fishing, swimming, playground and phone. ◄▲

E 66.2 (106.5 km) **PG 383.8** (617.7 km) **WILDWOOD** (pop. 375), the "Bingo Capital of Canada." Post office, hotel, gas station, restaurants and shops. Campground at **Chip Lake** with 14 sites, tables, firewood, pit toilets, water, fishing, swimming and boat launch. ◄▲

E 68.7 (110.6 km) **PG 381.3** (613.6 km) View of Chip Lake to north.

E 81.5 (131.1 km) **PG 368.5** (593.1 km) **NOJACK** and **MACKAY** (pop. 250). Grocery, post office, restaurant and gas station with towing, diesel and major repair service. Mackay is 1.9 miles/3.1 km north of Nojack on a gravel road. Campgrounds 1 mile/1.6 km and 3 miles/4.8 km west of town on Highway 16. ▲

E 81.6 (131.4 km) **PG 368.4** (592.8 km) Emergency phone.

E 84.6 (136.1 km) **PG 365.4** (588.1 km) Private campground to north. ▲

E 89.5 (144 km) **PG 360.5** (580.2 km) **NITON JUNCTION.** Hamlet has 2 gas stations with tires and parts, diesel, propane, car wash, pay phone, groceries, post office, 2 restaurants, lounge, motel. Private campground with full hookups. ▲

E 93.7 (150.8 km) **PG 356.3** (573.4 km) **CARROT CREEK.** Post office, grocery store, gas station, car wash and phone.

E 97.5 (157 km) **PG 352.5** (567.2 km) **Junction** with Highway 32 which leads to Whitecourt and Highway 43, 42 miles/67.6 km north on paved road. (See **Milepost E 112.7** in the EAST ACCESS ROUTE section for log of Highway 43.)

E 102.1 (164.4 km) **PG 347.9** (559.8 km) Wolf Lake public campground, 33 miles/53 km south on gravel road; 14 sites, pit toilets, tables, litter barrels. ▲

E 105 (169 km) **PG 345** (555.2 km) Edson rest area to south with flush toilets, water, tables, shelter, phone and sani-dump.

E 106 (170.6 km) **PG 344** (553.6 km) Rosevear Road; eastbound access to Edson rest area.

E 110 (177.1 km) **PG 340** (547.1 km) Private campground with full hookups to south, open May to Oct. ▲

E 113.1 (182 km) **PG 336.9** (542.2 km) McLeod River bridge.

E 114.9 (185 km) **PG 335.1** (539.2 km) **EDSON** (pop. 7,400). **Emergency Services: Hospital** and RCMP post **Visitor Information:** South on 55th Street. Edson's economy is based on coal mining, forestry, oil, natural gas and manufacturing. Edson is a large highway community with 16 motels, many restaurants and gas stations; 18-hole golf course and driving range; and an indoor pool. Camping at Lions Club Campground east of town (42 sites), and at Willmore Recreation Park, 3.7 miles/6 km south of town on the McLeod River. ▲

E 123.2 (198.3 km) **PG 326.8** (525.9 km) Food, gas, lodging and phone.

E 128 (206 km) **PG 322** (518.2 km) Government campground to north adjacent to highway. ▲

E 133 (214 km) **PG 317** (510.2 km) Small community of Marlboro to north. First view of Canadian Rockies westbound.

E 140.8 (226.6 km) **PG 309.2** (497.6 km) Westbound-only turnout with picnic tables, pit toilets and litter barrels; generous, paved parking area.

E 142.7 (229.6 km) **PG 307.3** (494.6 km) Eastbound-only turnout with litter barrels.

E 148.1 (238.3 km) **PG 301.9** (485.9 km) Obed Lake public campground to north; 13 sites, firewood, tables, pit toilets, water. ▲

E 150.3 (241.9 km) **PG 299.7** (482.3 km) **OBED.** Phone, gas and groceries.

E 156.4 (251.8 km) **PG 293.6** (472.4 km) **Obed Summit,** highest elevation on the Yellowhead Highway at 3,819 feet/1,164m. Paved turnout with picnic tables, toilets and litter barrels; good view of the Rockies, weather permitting.

E 157.7 (253.9 km) **PG 292.3** (470.3 km) Treed roadside turnout; generous parking area, picnic tables, toilets and litter barrels.

E 160.8 (258.8 km) **PG 289.2** (465.4 km) Motel to south.

E 166.7 (268.3 km) **PG 283.3** (455.9 km)

Yellowhead Highway 16 passes through elk territory. Elk can be dangerous during calving (May–June) and mating (Aug.–Oct.) seasons. (© Rick Driskell)

HINTON (pop. 10,000). All visitor facilities including hotels and motels, golf course, hospital, dentist, RCMP and recreation complex with indoor pool. Campground with 50 sites, hookups and dump station. Site of Weldwood of Canada Ltd. pulp mill; tours of mill complex may be arranged. ▲

E 171 (275.3 km) **PG 279** (448.9 km) South **junction** with Highway 40.

E 172.2 (277.1 km) **PG 277.8** (447.1 km) **William A. Switzer Provincial Park** 16.8 miles/27 km north on Big Horn Highway 40; camping, picnicking, fishing. ▲

Junction with Bighorn Highway 40 (paved), which leads north 88 miles/142 km to Grande Cache then another 117 miles/188 km to Grande Prairie. See BIG HORN HIGHWAY log on page 52.

E 176.8 (284.5 km) **PG 273.2** (439.7 km) Maskuta Creek picnic area with tables, shelter, toilets and litter barrels.

E 177.8 (286.2 km) **PG 272.2** (438 km) Weigh scales and pay phone.

E 179 (288.1 km) **PG 271** (436.1 km) Public campground 3.1 miles/5 km north. ▲

E 181.5 (292.2 km) **PG 268.5** (432 km) Private campground, pay phone. ▲

E 182.4 (293.6 km) **PG 267.6** (430.6 km) Turnout to north with litter barrels and point of interest sign about Athabasca River.

E 182.9 (294.4 km) **PG 267.1** (429.8 km) Resort with lodging to north.

E 184.2 (296.5 km) **PG 265.8** (427.7 km) **Jasper National Park, East Entrance.** Park fees are charged on a per-person basis and must be paid by all visitors using facilities in Rocky Mountain national parks. Public phones.

Alberta's Jasper National Park is the largest of Canada's Rocky Mountain parks, covering 4,200 square miles/20,878 square kms. It adjoins Banff National Park to the south. Most visitors sightsee Jasper's (and Banff's) spectacular mountain scenery from Highway 93 (Icefields Parkway).

E 185.6 (298.8 km) **PG 264.4** (425.4 km) Fiddle River bridge.

E 189 (304.2 km) **PG 261** (420 km) POCAHONTAS, a popular overnight stop to avoid crowds in Jasper townsite, has a motel with cabins, swimming pool and restaurant; grocery; and gas station with minor-repair service.

Junction with Miette Hot Springs Road, which leads 0.6 mile/1 km south to Park Service campground (140 sites) and 11 miles/17.7 km south to **Miette Hot Springs** and resort. There are 2 thermal pools; towels and bathing suits for rent; admission fee. Beautiful setting, look for mountain goats. ▲

E 192 (309 km) **PG 258** (415.2 km) Turnout with cairn to south. Mineral lick here is frequented by goats and sheep. Watch for wildlife, especially at dawn and dusk.

Highway 16 has restricted speed zones where wildlife sightings are frequent. Drive carefully and watch out for moose, elk, white-tailed and mule deer, mountain goats, bighorn sheep, and black and grizzly bears. *NOTE: It is illegal to feed, touch, disturb or hunt wildlife in the national park. All plants and natural objects are also protected and may not be removed or destroyed.*

Many turnouts next 25 miles/40 km westbound.

E 193 (310.6 km) **PG 257** (413.6 km) First Rocky River bridge westbound.

E 194.3 (312.7 km) **PG 255.7** (411.5 km)

Second Rocky River bridge westbound.

E 203 (326.7 km) **PG 247** (397.5 km) Two bridges spanning the Athabasca River. Raft trips down the Athabasca may be arranged in Jasper. Watch for elk and stone sheep.

E 205.1 (330.1 km) **PG 244.9** (394.1 km) Snaring River bridge.

E 206.7 (332.7 km) **PG 243.3** (391.5 km) Jasper airfield to south.

E 208.1 (335 km) **PG 241.9** (389.2 km) Snaring overflow camping south. ▲

E 208.4 (335.4 km) **PG 241.6** (388.8 km) Snaring rest area to south.

E 208.8 (336 km) **PG 241.2** (388.2 km) Palisades picnic area.

E 212.9 (342.6 km) **PG 237.1** (381.6 km) Access road to Jasper Park Lodge (lodging, restaurant, golf, etc.) and **Maligne Lake.** Glacier-fed Maligne Lake (35 miles/56 km south) is one of Jasper's premier attractions; scheduled boat tours.

E 215.8 (347.3 km) **PG 234.2** (376.9 km) **Junction** with Highway 93A. Lodging and restaurant to south.

E 216.6 (348.6 km) **PG 233.4** (375.6 km) Access to **JASPER** (pop. 3,500), townsite and park headquarters for Jasper National Park. All visitor services available. Many residents in this area maintain hummingbird feeders. The 2 species of hummingbirds found in the Canadian Rockies are the Rufous and the Calliope.

Junction with Highway 93, the scenic Icefields Parkway, south to junction with Trans-Canada Highway 1 (140 miles/225 km), providing access to Columbia Icefield, Lake Louise and Banff.

NOTE: No fuel next 62.5 miles/100.6 km westbound.

E 217.1 (349.5 km) **PG 232.9** (374.7 km) Miette River.

E 222.2 (357.6 km) **PG 227.8** (366.6 km) Paved turnout to north with outhouses, litter barrels and interpretive sign about Yellowhead Pass. Many turnouts next 25 miles/40 km eastbound.

E 223.2 (359.3 km) **PG 226.8** (364.9 km) Meadow Creek.

E 223.4 (359.5 km) **PG 226.6** (364.7 km) Trailhead for Virl Lake, Dorothy Lake and Christine Lake.

E 226.1 (363.9 km) **PG 223.9** (360.3 km) Clairvaux Creek.

E 229.4 (369.3 km) **PG 220.6** (354.9 km) **Jasper National Park, West Entrance.** Park fee must be paid by all visitors using facilities in Rocky Mountain national parks.

E 231.6 (372.7 km) **PG 218.4** (351.5 km) **Yellowhead Pass** (elev. 3,760 feet/1,146m), Alberta–British Columbia border. Named for an Iroquois trapper and guide who worked for the Hudson's Bay Co. in the early 1800s. His light-colored hair earned him the name Tete Jaune ("yellow head") from the French voyageurs.

Mount Robson Provincial Park, East Entrance. Portal Lake picnic area with tables, toilets, information board and hiking trail.

TIME ZONE CHANGE: Alberta observes Mountain standard time. Most of British Columbia observes Pacific standard time. Both observe daylight saving time.

E 232.8 (374.7 km) **PG 217.2** (349.5 km) Kilometrepost 75. Kilometreposts on Yellowhead Highway 16 reflect distances within highway maintenance districts; *The MILEPOST*® periodically notes these physical posts as reference points.

E 235.8 (379.6 km) **PG 214.2** (344.6 km) Rockingham Creek.

E 236.2 (380.1 km) **PG 213.8** (344.1 km) **Yellowhead Lake;** picnic tables, viewpoint, boat launch and fishing. ◣

E 238 (383 km) **PG 212** (341.2 km) Lucerne Campground; 32 sites, picnic tables, drinking water, firewood and swimming; camping fee charged. ▲

E 239.3 (385.2 km) **PG 210.7** (339 km) Fraser Crossing rest area to south; litter barrels and toilets.

E 239.4 (385.3 km) **PG 210.6** (338.9 km) Fraser River bridge No. 1.

E 242.4 (390.1 km) **PG 207.6** (334.1 km) Fraser River bridge No. 2.

E 245.2 (394.6 km) **PG 204.8** (329.6 km) Kilometrepost 55.

E 246.2 (396.2 km) **PG 203.8** (328 km) Grant Brook Creek.

E 249 (400.8 km) **PG 201** (323.4 km) Moose Creek bridge.

E 251.1 (404.2 km) **PG 198.9** (320 km) Turnout at east end of Moose Lake; information kiosk, tables, litter barrels, toilet and boat launch.

E 255.5 (411.2 km) **PG 194.5** (313 km) Turnout with litter barrels.

E 257.5 (414.4 km) **PG 192.5** (309.8 km) Kilometrepost 35.

E 263.7 (424.4 km) **PG 186.3** (299.8 km) Paved turnout with litter barrels.

E 268 (431.3 km) **PG 182** (292.9 km) **Overlander Falls** rest area to south; pit toilets and litter barrels. Hiking trail to Overlander Falls, about 30 minutes round-trip.

E 268.8 (432.7 km) **PG 181.2** (291.4 km) Viewpoint of **Mount Robson** (elev. 12,972 feet/3,954m), highest peak in the Canadian Rockies, and Visitor Infocentre. Parking, picnic tables, restrooms, litter barrels, gas and restaurant. Berg Lake trailhead; hike-in campgrounds. Private campground north of highway. Robson Meadows government campground south of highway with 125 sites, dump station, showers, pay phone, interpretive programs, tables, firewood, flush toilets, water and horseshoe pits; group camping; camping fee charged. ▲

E 269.4 (433.6 km) **PG 180.6** (290.6 km) Robson River government campground to north with 19 sites (some wheelchair-accessible), tables, firewood, pit toilets, showers, water and horseshoe pits; camping fee charged. ♿▲

E 269.8 (434.3 km) **PG 180.2** (289.9 km) Kilometrepost 15.

E 269.9 (434.4 km) **PG 180.1** (289.8 km) Robson River bridge. Look for Indian paintbrush June through August. The bracts are orange-red while the petals are green.

E 270.3 (435.1 km) **PG 179.7** (289.1 km) West entrance to Mount Robson Provincial Park. Turnout with litter barrels and statue.

E 270.5 (435.3 km) **PG 179.5** (288.9 km) Gravel turnout to south.

E 271.4 (436.8 km) **PG 178.6** (287.4 km) Swift Current Creek.

E 274.4 (441.7 km) **PG 175.6** (282.5 km) **Mount Terry Fox Provincial Park** picnic area with tables, restrooms and viewing telescope. The information board here points out the location of Mount Terry Fox in the Selwyn Range of the Rocky Mountains. The peak was named in 1981 to honour cancer victim Terry Fox, who, before his death from the disease, raised some $25 million for cancer research during his attempt to run across Canada.

E 276.3 (444.7 km) PG 173.7 (280.5 km) Gravel turnout to north with Yellowhead Highway information sign.

E 276.4 (444.9 km) PG 173.6 (280.3 km) **Rearguard Falls Provincial Park** picnic area. Easy half-hour round-trip to falls viewpoint. Upper limit of 800-mile/1,300-km migration of Pacific salmon; look for chinook in late summer.

E 277.8 (447.1 km) PG 172.2 (277.1 km) Gravel turnout to south overlooking Fraser River.

E 278.2 (447.8 km) PG 171.8 (276.4 km) Weigh scales.

E 278.7 (448.6 km) PG 171.3 (275.6 km) Tete Jaune Cache rest area with tables, litter barrels and toilets.

E 279 (449.1 km) PG 171 (275.1 km) **Junction** with Yellowhead Highway 5 south to the small community of **TETE JAUNE CACHE**, 1/2 mile (store and gas), and to **VALEMOUNT** (pop. 1,200), 12 miles/20 km;. tourist information office and all visitor facilities. Yellowhead Highway 5 junctions with Trans Canada Highway 1 at Kamloops, 208 miles/335 km from here.

Irvin's Park & Campground. See display ad this section. ▲

E 279.1 (449.2 km) PG 170.9 (275 km) Turnoff for gas, general store and deli, camping and lodging.

NOTE: No fuel eastbound next 62.5 miles/100.6 km.

E 279.6 (450.1 km) PG 170.4 (274.1 km) Private lodging, restaurants.

E 283.1 (455.7 km) PG 166.9 (268.5 km) Spittal Creek Interpretive Forest; hiking trails, tables, litter barrels and toilets. Kilometrepost 140.

E 288.2 (463.8 km) PG 161.8 (260.4 km) Private resort. Lodging, restaurant.

E 289.1 (465.3 km) PG 160.9 (258.9 km) Small River rest area by stream with tables, toilets and litter barrels.

E 293.6 (472.5 km) PG 156.4 (251.7 km) Horsey Creek.

E 295.4 (475.5 km) PG 154.6 (248.7 km) Kilometrepost 120.

E 300 (482.9 km) PG 150 (241.3 km) Turnoff to south for settlement of Dunster; gas and general store.

E 303.8 (489 km) PG 146.2 (235.2 km) Holiday Creek rest area with toilets, picnic tables, litter barrel and hiking trails.

E 304.3 (489.7 km) PG 145.7 (234.5 km) Baker Creek rest area with tables, litter barrels and toilets.

E 308.5 (496.6 km) PG 141.5 (227.6 km) Kilometrepost 100.

E 308.9 (497.2 km) PG 141.1 (227 km) Nevin Creek.

E 312 (502.1 km) PG 138 (222.1 km) Turnouts at both ends of Holmes River bridge.

E 317.4 (510.8 km) PG 132.6 (213.4 km) **Beaverview Campsite.** See display ad this section. ▲

E 317.9 (511.6 km) PG 132.1 (212.6 km) Fraser River bridge.

E 318.2 (512.1 km) PG 131.8 (212.1 km) Turnout to north with litter barrels.

E 318.8 (513.1 km) PG 131.2 (211.1 km) **McBRIDE** (pop. 700; elev. 2,369 feet/722.1m), located in the Robson Valley by the Fraser River. The Park Ranges of the Rocky Mountains are to the northeast and the Cariboo Mountains are to the southeast. A road leads to Teare Mountain lookout for a spectacular view of countryside. The village of McBride was established in 1913 as a divisional point on the railroad and was named for Richard McBride, then premier of British Columbia. Forest products are a major industry here today.

Visitor Information: Visitor Infocentre located in railcar on south side of Highway 16. Look for the carved grizzly bear family in front. When the Infocentre isn't open, try the McBride Village Office. Located beside the railcar in the same parking lot, it is open 9 A.M. to 5 P.M.

McBride has all visitor facilities, including 5 hotels/motels, 2 bed and breakfasts, 2 supermarkets, 2 convenience/video stores, clothing stores, restaurants, pharmacy, hospital and gas stations. A library, museum and neighborhood pub are 1.9 miles/3 km from town. There is a private campground just east of town. Dump station located at the gas station. ▲

While in McBride, watch wood ducks, scoters, teals and more at the Horseshoe Lake Bird Watch. In late summer, see the salmon run in the Holmes River. In winter, go cross-country skiing on developed trails and snowmobiling in the backcountry. Helicopter service available for fly-in skiing and hiking.

McBride Chevron. See display ad this section.

North Country Lodge. See display ad this section.

NOTE: Next gas westbound is 90.7 miles/146 km from here (Purden Lake).

E 321.9 (518.1 km) PG 128.1 (206.1 km) Dore River bridge.

E 326.7 (525.8 km) PG 123.3 (198.4 km) Macintosh Creek.

E 328.8 (529.2 km) PG 121.2 (195 km) Clyde Creek.

E 333.1 (536.2 km) PG 116.9 (188 km) Kilometrepost 60.

E 336.9 (542.3 km) PG 113.1 (181.9 km) West Twin Creek bridge.

E 343.6 (553.1 km) PG 106.4 (171.1 km) Goat River bridge. Paved rest area to north with tables, toilets and litter barrels.

E 346.7 (558 km) PG 103.3 (166.2 km) Little LaSalle Recreation Area and BC Forest Service site. Small lake, small wharf, toilet.

E 351.2 (565.2 km) PG 98.8 (159 km) Snowshoe Creek.

E 351.8 (566.2 km) PG 98.2 (158 km) Kilometrepost 30.

E 354.9 (571.2 km) PG 95.1 (153 km) Catfish Creek.

E 360.7 (580.6 km) PG 89.3 (143.6 km) Ptarmigan Creek bridge.

E 363.8 (585.6 km) PG 86.2 (138.6 km) Turnout with litter barrels to north.

E 369.2 (594.1 km) PG 80.8 (130.1 km) Dome Creek.

E 371.5 (597.9 km) PG 78.5 (126.3 km) Food, phone.

E 373.3 (600.8 km) PG 76.7 (123.4 km) Slim Creek paved rest area to south with information kiosk, tables, playground, litter barrels and wheelchair-accessible toilets. Watch for bears. ♿

E 373.4 (601 km) PG 76.6 (123.2 km) Ministry of Highways camp.

E 374.1 (602.1 km) PG 75.9 (122.1 km) Slim Creek bridge.

E 382.5 (615.6 km) **PG 67.5** (108.6 km) Kilometrepost 100.

E 385.6 (620.7 km) **PG 64.4** (103.5 km) Driscol Creek.

E 386.4 (621.9 km) **PG 63.6** (102.3 km) Forests in this area have been destroyed by the hemlock looper, an insect which has killed or damaged over 45.9 million cubic feet/1.3 million cubic metres of wood in British Columbia.

E 387.6 (623.9 km) **PG 62.4** (100.3 km) Gravel turnout with litter barrel to north.

E 388.9 (626 km) **PG 61.1** (98.2 km) Lunate Creek.

E 391.8 (630.6 km) **PG 58.2** (93.6 km) Grizzly hiking trail to south.

E 392 (630.9 km) **PG 58** (93.3 km) Hungary Creek. Watch for Ministry of Forests signs indicating the year in which a logged area was replanted. Wildflowers include fireweed, mid-July through August.

E 394.8 (635.4 km) **PG 55.2** (88.8 km) Kilometrepost 80.

E 395.8 (637 km) **PG 54.2** (87.2 km) Sugarbowl Creek.

E 400.5 (644.6 km) **PG 49.5** (79.6 km) Paved turnout with litter barrel to north.

E 407 (655.1 km) **PG 43** (69.1 km) Kilometrepost 60.

E 408.2 (657 km) **PG 41.8** (67.2 km) Kenneth Creek.

E 408.4 (657.4 km) **PG 41.6** (66.8 km) Purden Mountain ski resort.

E 409.1 (659.1 km) **PG 40.5** (65.1 km) Purden Lake resort with gas, phone, lodging and camping. ▲

Purden Lake and Ski Resorts. Campground with lakefront camping; hookups. Cabin rentals, boat rentals, boat launch. Good rainbow trout fishing. Cafe, gas station (propane, diesel, unleaded). Cafe and gas open 7 A.M. to 8 P.M. Ski area with 23 runs, 2 double chairs, T-bar, day lodge, ski rentals, ski school, cafeteria. P.O. Box 1239, Prince George, BC V2L 4V3. (250) 565-7777. [ADVERTISEMENT] ▲

NOTE: Next gas eastbound is 90.7 miles/146 km from here (McBride).

E 411.2 (661.9 km) **PG 38.8** (62.3 km) **Purden Lake Provincial Park**, 1.9 miles/3 km from highway; 78 campsites, 48 picnic tables, water, dump station, firewood, playground and horseshoe pits. This recreation area offers a sandy beach, change houses, swimming, walking trails, waterskiing and boat launch. Good rainbow fishing to 4 lbs. Camping fee charged. ⊶▲

E 412.6 (664.1 km) **PG 37.4** (60.1 km) Bowron River bridge. Paved rest area to north beside river, on west side of bridge; toilets, tables and litter barrels. Entrance on curve; use care.

E 420.7 (677.1 km) **PG 29.3** (47.1 km)

Kilometrepost 40.

E 421 (677.6 km) **PG 29** (46.6 km) Vama Vama Creek.

E 424 (682.4 km) **PG 26** (41.8 km) Wansa Creek.

E 427.1 (687.4 km) **PG 22.9** (36.8 km) Willow River bridge. Rest area at west end of bridge beside river; tables, litter barrels, toilets and nature trail. The 1.2-mile-/1.9-km-long Willow River Forest Interpretation Trail is an easy 45-minute walk.

E 429.5 (691.3 km) **PG 20.5** (32.9 km) Bowes Creek.

E 429.7 (691.6 km) **PG 20.3** (32.6 km) Turnout to north with litter barrels and information board on 1961 forest fire and moose habitat. Circle trail to moose observation site.

E 433 (697 km) **PG 17** (27.2 km) Kilometrepost 20.

E 435.2 (700.5 km) **PG 14.8** (23.7 km) Tabor Mountain ski hill.

E 435.4 (700.8 km) **PG 14.6** (23.4 km) Gravel turnout to north with litter barrels.

E 437.6 (704.3 km) **PG 12.4** (19.9 km) Access to **Tabor Lake**; good fishing for rainbow in spring. ⊶▲

E 444.8 (715.9 km) **PG 5.2** (8.3 km) **Junction** of Highway 16B with Highway 97 south bypass. Turn to page 70 in the WEST ACCESS ROUTE section for log of Highway 97 South to Cache Creek.

E 450 (724.2 km) **PG 0 PRINCE GEORGE** (see description on pages 70–74). Continue west on Yellowhead Highway 16 for Prince Rupert (log follows).

> **Junction** with Highway 97 north to Dawson Creek and the beginning of the Alaska Highway. Turn to page 74 in the WEST ACCESS ROUTE section for the log of Highway 97 North.

This section of the log shows distance from Prince George (PG) followed by distance from Prince Rupert (PR).

NOTE: Physical kilometreposts west from here are up along Highway 16 about every 5 km and reflect distance from Prince Rupert. Because the posts do not always accurately reflect driving distance, mileages from Prince Rupert are based on actual driving distance while the kilometre conversion is based on physical kilometreposts as they occurred in summer 1998.

PG 0 PR 447.7 (720 km) **Junction** of Highways 16 and 97 (Central Avenue/Cariboo Highway) in Prince George. From Prince George to Prince Rupert, Highway 16 is a 2-lane highway with 3-lane passing stretches. Fairly straight, with no high summits, the highway follows the valleys of the Nechako, Bulkley and Skeena rivers, paralleling the Canadian National Railway route. There are

few services between towns.

PG 0.2 (0.4 km) **PR 447.5** (719.6 km) Prince George Golf and Curling Club.

PG 0.6 (1 km) **PR 447.1** (719 km) Ferry Avenue.

PG 1.2 (1.9 km) **PR 446.5** (718.1 km) **Junction** with Vince–Cowart/Domano Blvd.; access to the University of Northern B.C.

PG 2.1 (3.4 km) **PR 445.6** (717.1 km) Tyner Blvd.

PG 3.8 (6.2 km) **PR 443.9** (714.4 km) Blue Spruce RV Park and Campground to north. ▲

PG 5.7 (9.2 km) **PR 442** (711.3 km) **West Lake** Provincial Park 8 miles/12.9 km south; day-use area with picnic shelter, swimming, fishing and boat launch. ⊶

PG 7.3 (11.8 km) **PR 440.4** (708.7 km) Western Road.

PG 12.5 (20.2 km) **PR 435.2** (700.4 km) Chilko Road.

PG 15.2 (24.5 km) **PR 432.5** (696 km) **North Country Arts & Crafts.** See display ad this section.

PG 28.2 (45.4 km) **PR 419.5** (675.1 km) Tamarac Lake to south.

PG 37.6 (60.5 km) **PR 410.1** (660 km) Access to lakeside resort and fishing at **Cluculz Lake** (not visible from highway). Rainbow to 3³/4 lbs. by trolling, use snell hook and worms; kokanee to 1¹/2 lbs., troll with snell hook and worms in spring; char to 57 lbs., use large flatfish, spoons, plugs and weights, early spring and late fall; whitefish to 5 lbs., year-round. Very good fishing in spring; ice goes out about the first week of May. Good ice fishing December to March. In September kokanee are at their peak. *Lake gets rough when windy.* ⊶▲

PG 38.7 (62.4 km) **PR 409** (658.2 km) Cluculz rest area to south with flush toilets (summer only), picnic tables and litter barrels.

PG 39.2 (63.1 km) **PR 408.5** (657.4 km) **Brookside Resort.** Stay in a quiet pine forest next to Cluculz Creek. Serviced and unserviced sites. 30-amp spacious, shaded, level pull-throughs. Tent and camper sites with tables. Clean washrooms. Free hot showers

for registered guests. Sani-dump, laundromat, convenience store, restaurant, driving range, gift shops. Ice, propane, gasoline and boat gas. Phone. VISA and MasterCard. R.R. #1, Site 16, Comp 78, Vanderhoof, BC V0J 3A0. (888) 441-0035. [ADVERTISEMENT] ▲

PG 39.5 (63.6 km) **PR 408.2** (656.9 km) **Lakeside Resort**. See display ad this section. ▲

PG 41.4 (66.7 km) **PR 406.3** (653.9 km) Cluculz Lake campground to south.

PG 58.6 (94.4 km) **PR 389.1** (626.2 km) **Dave's R.V. Park**. 2 miles east of downtown Vanderhoof, ¹/2 mile down paved Derksen Road. Quiet, clean, rural setting. Washrooms, free hot showers for guests. Laundry. Cable TV available. Public telephone. Full and partial hookups. Level landscaped graveled pads, each with grass site. 56 sites, 30–65 feet. Full hookup pull-throughs. Cable available on some (extra). Partial and no hookup regular sites. Grass or sand tent sites. Sani-dump. Limited groceries and RV supplies. Member of FMCA, BCMRCA. Pets on leash. VISA, MasterCard. Box 1512, Vander-

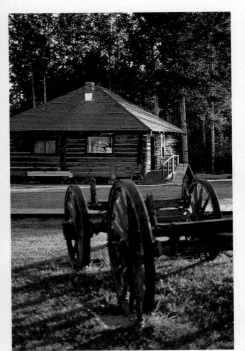

Pioneer buildings and artifacts at Vanderhoof's Heritage Village (© Judy Parkin)

hoof, BC V0J 3A0; phone (250) 567-3161. [ADVERTISEMENT] ▲

Vanderhoof

PG 58.7 (94.5 km) **PR 389** (624.8 km). Stoplight at junction with Highway 27; turnoff to downtown Vanderhoof. **Population:** 4,400; area 12,000. **Emergency Services: Police,** phone (250) 567-2222. **Fire Department,** phone (250) 567-2345. **Ambulance,** phone (800) 461-9911. **Hospital,** St. John's, Northside District, phone (250) 567-2211.

Visitor Information: Visitor Infocentre downtown on Burrard Avenue, 1 block off Highway 16. Write Vanderhoof & District Chamber of Commerce, Box 126-MP, Vanderhoof, BC V0J 3A0; phone (250) 567-2124.

Elevation: 2,225 feet/667.5m. **Radio:** CJCI 620, CFPR-FM 96.7, CKPG 550, CIVH 1340, CIRX-FM 95.9. **Television:** Channels 2, 4, 5, 6, 8. **Newspapers:** *Omineca Express–Bugle* (weekly). **Transportation: Air**—Vanderhoof airport, 2 miles/3.2 km from intersection of Highways 16 and 27; 5,000-foot/1,524-m paved runway. Seaplane landings on Nechako River at corner of View Street and Boundary Avenue. **Railroad**—VIA Rail, station at 2222 Church Ave. **Bus**—Greyhound.

Vanderhoof is the geographical centre of British Columbia. The city was named for Chicago publisher Herbert Vanderhoof, who founded the village in 1914 when he was associated with the Grand Trunk Development Co. Today, Vanderhoof is the supply and distribution centre for a large agricultural, lumbering and mining area.

The community's history is preserved at **Vanderhoof Heritage Village Museum,** just off Highway 16. Relocated pioneer structures furnished with period artifacts recall the early days of the Nechako Valley.

Located on the Nechako River, Vander-

hoof is a stopping place in April and September for thousands of migrating waterfowl. The river flats upstream of the bridge are a bird sanctuary. Pelicans have been spotted feeding at Tachick Lake south of town.

There are 7 hotels and motels and 17 restaurants in the town. All shopping facilities and several gas stations. An 18-hole golf course is located 1.9 miles/3.1 km north of town. Dump station at Dave's R.V. Park at Milepost PG 58.6 and at Riverside Campsite (municipal campground) on Burrard Avenue.. ▲

Riverside Campsite. Overlooking Nechako River with bird-watching tower and groomed walking trails. Private sites, some with 30-/50-amp service; some with hook-ups. Firepits and firewood. Flush toilets and free hot showers for guests. Public phone. Sani-dump. Pets welcome. Attendant on duty 24 hours. Gates open 7 A.M. to 10 P.M. 3100 Burrard Avenue, P.O. Box 380, Vanderhoof, BC V0J 3A0. Phone (250) 567-4710. [ADVERTISEMENT] ▲

Yellowhead Highway 16 Log
(continued)
PG 58.7 (94.5 km) **PR 389** (624.8 km)

> **Junction** with Highway 27 north 37 miles/60 km to Fort St. James. Ssee description of Fort St. James National Historic Site this section.

PG 59.2 (95.2 km) **PR 388.5** (624.1 km) Vanderhoof Heritage Museum to south.

PG 63.2 (101.7 km) **PR 384.5** (617.6 km) Second **junction** westbound with Highway 27 (see description at Milepost PG 58.7). This route skirts Vanderhoof. Truck weigh scales to north.

PG 72.3 (116.3 km) **PR 375.4** (602.9 km) Plateau Division Sawmill to south.

PG 81.5 (131.1 km) **PR 366.2** (588 km) Turnout to south with view of Nechako River. The Grand Trunk Pacific Railway was completed near this site in 1914. The railroad (later the Canadian National) linked Prince Rupert, a deep-water port, with interior British Columbia. Entering Lakes District. This high country has over 300 freshwater lakes.

PG 81.8 (131.6 km) **PR 365.9** (587.5 km) **FORT FRASER** (pop. 600). **Radio:** CBC-FM 102.9. Small community with food, gas, propane, lodging and first-aid station. Gas station with hot showers, convenience store and restaurant. Named for Simon Fraser, who established a trading post here in 1806. Now a supply centre for surrounding farms and sawmills. The last spike of the Grand Trunk Railway was driven here on April 7, 1914.

PG 82.6 (133 km) **PR 365.1** (586.1 km) Nechako River bridge. Turnout to south with parking, litter barrels and access to **Nechako River;** fishing for rainbow and Dolly Varden, June to fall. At the east end of Fraser Lake, the Nautley River—less than a mile long—drains into the Nechako River. ◄

PG 84.1 (135.4 km) **PR 363.6** (583.7 km)

Nautley Road. **Beaumont Provincial Park,** on beautiful **Fraser Lake,** north side of highway; site of original Fort Fraser. Boat launch, swimming, hiking, fishing, 49 campsites, picnic tables, firewood, flush toilets, water, playground, horseshoe pits, dump station. Fishing for rainbow and lake trout, burbot, sturgeon and Dolly Varden. ◄▲

PG 85.9 (138.3 km) **PR 361.8** (580.8 km) View of Fraser Lake to north.

PG 86.3 (138.9 km) **PR 361.7** (580.5 km) Access to private campground on Fraser Lake; chainsaw sculpture.

Pipers Glen RV Resort. See display ad this section. ▲

PG 87.9 (141.4 km) **PR 359.8** (578 km) Dry William Lake rest area to south with picnic tables, toilets and litter barrels.

PG 89.7 (144.4 km) **PR 358** (575 km) View of Mouse Mountain to northwest.

PG 90.9 (146.3 km) **PR 356.8** (573 km) Fraser Lake sawmill to north.

PG 91.3 (147 km) **PR 356.4** (572.3 km) Gas and diesel.

PG 94.5 (152.1 km) **PR 353.2** (567.2 km) **FRASER LAKE** (pop. 1,400; elev. 2,580 feet/786m). **Visitor Information:** Fraser Lake Museum and Visitor Infocentre in log building. **Radio:** CJCI 1450. Small community with all facilities. Created by Endako Mines Ltd. in 1964 on an older townsite; named after the explorer Simon Fraser. Endako Mines Ltd. began operating in 1965 and was Canada's largest molybdenum mine until production slowed in 1982. Mining resumed in 1986. Mine tours are available on Wednesdays; check with the Visitor Infocentre for reservations. Also located here is Fraser Lake Sawmills, the town's largest employer.

PG 96.9 (156 km) PR 350.8 (563.3 km) **Junction** with main access road south to scenic Francois Lake; also accessible via roads from Burns Lake to Houston. Francois Lake Road (chip seal surfacing) leads south 7 miles/11 km to the east end of Francois Lake (where the Stellako River flows from the lake) and back to Highway 16 at Endako. (It does *not* link up to the Francois Lake Ferry, south of Burns Lake.) Golf course and several resorts with camping, cabins and boats are located on this scenic rural road along the lake through the Glenannan area.

Francois Lake, good fishing for rainbow to 5 lbs., May to October; kokanee to ³/₄ lb., use flashers, willow leaf, flashers with worms, flatfish or spinners, August and September; char to 30 lbs., use large flatfish or spoon, June and July. **Stellako River** is considered one of British Columbia's better fly-fishing streams with rainbow over 2 lbs., all summer; whitefish averaging 1 lb., year-round. ⊷

PG 97.6 (157.1 km) PR 350.1 (562.2 km)

Bridge over Stellako River. Highway passes through the Stellako Indian Reserve. Slenyah Indian village to north.

PG 102.5 (164.9 km) PR 345.2 (554.3 km) Endako Mine (molybdenum) Road and Four Mile Creek.

PG 103 (165.8 km) PR 344.7 (553.4 km) **ENDAKO**, a small highway community. A log home construction company is located here. Several private campgrounds are located along Francois Lake Road to the south in the Glenannan area. ▲

Fort St. James

Fort St. James

Located 37 miles/59.5 km north of Vanderhoof on Highway 27. **Population:** 2,146. **Emergency Services: Police**, phone (250) 996-8269. **Ambulance:** phone 1-562-7241. **Elevation:** 2,208 feet/ 673m. **Radio:** CKPG 550, CJCI 1480; CBC-FM 107.0.

Fort St. James is the home of **FORT ST. JAMES NATIONAL HISTORIC SITE**. Established in 1806 by Simon Fraser as a fur trading post for the Northwest Co., Fort St. James served throughout the 19th century as headquarters for the Hudson's Bay Co.'s New Caledonia fur trade district. The fur warehouse, fish cache, men's house, officers' dwelling and trade store have been restored in 1896-style and are open to the public. Check with the Visitor Infocentre regarding program information.

From mid-May through September, visitors may experience "living history." Staff members, dressed in period costumes, play out historic scenarios, demonstrate old-time skills and provide interesting facts about fur trade history. Hours are 9 A.M. to 5 P.M. daily. For the remainder of the year, the site is closed. Admission charged.

The historic site and village are located on Stuart Lake. Named for John Stuart, the man who succeeded Simon Fraser as head of the New Caledonia district, the 59-mile-/95-km-long lake is the southernmost in a 3-lake chain which provides hundreds of miles of boating and fishing. Fort St. James also boasts the Nation Lakes, a chain of 4 lakes (Tsayta, Indata, Tchentlo and Chuchi) connected by the Nation River.

Attractions include the Our Lady of Good Hope Catholic Church and the Chief Kwah burial site. The recently renovated church is one of the oldest in British Columbia. Open for summer evening services only, check schedule. Chief Kwah was one of the first Carrier Indian chiefs to confront early white explorers. His burial site is located on the Nak'azdli Indian Reserve at the mouth of the Stuart River. At Cottonwood Park on the shore of Lake Stuart, look for a model of a Junkers airplane, which depicts the Fort's major role in early bush flying in Northern British Columbia.

Fort St. James has a hotel, 2 lodges, resort, 4 motels, 3 private campgrounds and a number of surrounding lodges and settlements, such as Tachie, Manson Creek and Germansen Landing in the Omineca Mountains. Other services in Fort St. James include 3 gas stations, 4 dump stations, a government marina, 2 private marinas and several restaurants. The district also has a theatre and 2 shopping centres. Picnicking and swimming at Cottonwood Park on Stuart Lake. A 9-hole golf course overlooks Stuart Lake; rentals available. Murray Ridge ski area, a 20-minute drive from town, has 21 downhill ski runs and 18.5 miles/30 km of cross-country ski trails. ▲

Fort St. James National Historic Park. See display ad this section.

Stuart River Campgrounds. Treed sites, tenting to full hookups, showers and laundry, firepits and firewood, pay phone. Playgrounds, horseshoe pits; marina with launching ramp and moorage space. Great fishing! River and lake charters, fishing licenses and tackle. Your hosts, George and Heather Malbeuf, Box 306, Fort St. James, BC V0J 1P0. (250) 996-8690. [ADVERTISEMENT] ▲

Camping is also available at **Paarens Beach Provincial Park**, located 6.8 miles/10.9 km off Highway 27 on Sowchea Bay Road; 36 campsites, picnic shelter, picnic tables, toilets, water, firepits, firewood, boat launch and swimming; camping fee. **Sowchea Bay Provincial Park**, located 10.6 miles/17.1 km off Highway 27 on Sowchea Bay Road, has 30 campsites, camping fee, picnic tables, toilets, water, firepits, firewood, boat launch and swimming. ▲

Good fishing in **Stuart Lake** for rainbow and char (to trophy size), kokanee and Dolly Varden. ⊷

Return to Milepost PG 58.7 or PG 63.2
Yellowhead Highway 16

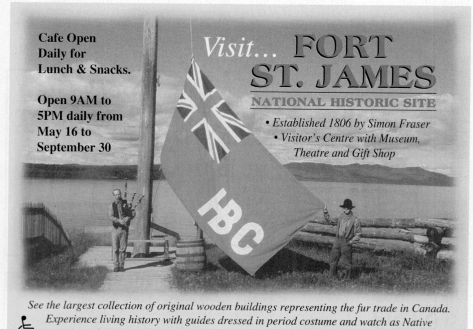

PG 103.8 (167.1 km) PR 343.9 (552 km) CNR Bunkhouse.

Watch for moose next 10 miles/16 km westbound.

PG 105.5 (169.8 km) PR 342.2 (549.3 km) Endako River bridge.

PG 109.1 (175.6 km) PR 338.6 (543.5 km) Savory rest area to north beside Watskin Creek.

PG 109.8 (176.8 km) PR 337.9 (542.3 km) Restaurant to north.

PG 112 (180.3 km) PR 335.7 (538.8 km) Ross Creek.

PG 112.9 (181.7 km) PR 334.8 (537.4 km) Tschinkut Creek and moose flats.

PG 120.4 (193.8 km) PR 327.3 (525.2 km) Moose meadow to south.

PG 121 (194.7 km) PR 326.6 (524.3 km) Paved turnout to south with litter barrel.

PG 125 (201.1 km) PR 322.7 (517.8 km) Babine Forest Products sawmill to south.

PG 128.3 (206.4 km) PR 319.4 (512.5 km) View of Burns Lake to south.

PG 130.1 (209.4 km) PR 317.6 (509.5 km) Tintagel Creek.

PG 130.2 (209.6 km) PR 317.5 (509.3 km) Rest area to south with toilet, tables, litter barrels and Tintagel Cairn point of interest.

PG 133.8 (215.4 km) PR 313.8 (503.4 km) **Burns Lake K.O.A.**, a day's drive from Prince Rupert ferry. Cabins, tenting to full hookups, store, heated showers, laundromat, game room, playground. Lake swimming. Open May 1 to Sept. 30. Pay phone. Your host, Ed Brown, Box 491, Burns Lake, BC V0J 1E0. Phone (250) 692-3105, (800) 562-0905. [ADVERTISEMENT] ▲

PG 136.7 (220 km) PR 311 (498.9 km) Motel.

PG 137.5 (221.3 km) PR 310.2 (497.5 km) Welcome to Burns Lake sign.

Junction with scenic Highway 35 (paved) south 18 miles/29 km past **Tchesinkut Lake** to **Francois Lake Ferry** landing. A free 36-car ferry departs from the south shore on the

hour, from the north shore on the half-hour. From the south shore of Francois Lake, Highway 35 continues to **Takysie Lake** and **Ootsa Lake**, with access to a number of other fishing lakes. Another of the Yellowhead's popular fishing areas with a variety of family-owned camping and cabin resorts. Gas stations, stores and food service are also available. ◄▲

Sandy's RV and Camping Resort. Over 50 full-service, easy-access sites along the shores of Francois Lake. Hot showers, laundromat, boat rentals, launch, marina, cabins and more. Enjoy northern hospitality; only 18 paved miles south of Burns Lake on Highway 35; located on a true fishing lake. Rainbow, kokanee and lake trout. Pets welcome. VISA, MasterCard. May 15–Oct. 1. Phone/fax (250) 695-6321. Box 42, Burns Lake, BC V0J 1E0. [ADVERTISEMENT] ▲

Takysie Lake Resort & Motel. See display ad this section.

Burns Lake

PG 139.9 (225.1 km) PR 307.8 (496.3 km) **Junction** with road to Babine Lake. **Population:** 2,500; area 10,000. **Visitor Information:** On Highway 16 in the **Burns Lake Heritage Centre.** The former Old Forestry Home, built in 1919, the Heritage Centre also houses the Lakes District Museum.. Or contact the Chamber of Commerce, Box 339, Burns Lake, BC V0J 1E0; phone (250) 692-3773; fax (250) 692-3493.

Elevation: 2,320 feet/707m. **Radio:** CFLD 730, CJFW-FM 92.9, CBC-FM 99.1. **Transportation:** Greyhound Bus, VIA Rail.

The village of Burns Lake had its modest beginnings in 1911, as the site of railway construction. Forestry is the mainstay of the economy, along with ranching and tourism.

Burns Lake has 5 motels, 7 bed and breakfasts, 14 restaurants, 3 shopping centres and a golf course. Overnight camping is available at the municipal campground at Radley Beach; washrooms, playground, picnic tables and swimming area. Winter recreation includes snowmobiling, curling, hockey, figure skating, ringette, broomball and cross-country skiing. ▲

Area attractions include Cheslatta Falls, Pinkut Creek spawning area, Skins Lake Dam, Nourse Creek Falls and a llama ranch. Rockhounds can visit the Eagle Creek Agate and Opal Beds, a short drive south of Burns Lake. Two trails lead into the beds: the opal trail is a challenging 45-minute hike, and the Agate trail is recommended for experienced hikers only. Burns Lake is also the gateway to Tweedsmuir Provincial Park, British Columbia's largest park. This pristine wilderness area is accessible by boat or air.

Burns Lake is situated in the heart of the Lakes District, which boasts "3000 miles of fishing." Species include kokanee, rainbow trout, char and salmon. Small family-owned campgrounds and fishing resorts, offering lodging, camping and boat rentals, are tucked along these lakes.

From Burns Lake, a side road leads north to **Babine Lake**, the longest natural lake in the province. One of British Columbia's most important salmon producing lakes, Babine Lake drains into the Skeena River. Excellent fishing for char and trout in summer. At Mile 15/Km 24.1 on this road is **Ethel F. Wilson Provincial Park** on **Pinkut Lake**; 10 campsites, fishing, swimming, drinking water, toilets, firewood, picnic tables, boat launch. Tours of nearby Pinkut Fish Hatchery available. Look for pictographs on cliffs across from hatchery. **Pendleton Bay Provincial Park** on Babine Lake, open May to October, offers 20 camp-

sites, picnic tables, fishing, swimming and boat launch. Resorts with cabins and camping on Babine Lake. ◄▲

Babine Lake Resort, 29.8 miles/48 km from Burns Lake. British Columbia's largest natural body of water. Good fishing. Photographer's dream. Self-contained cabins, power, water hookups, showers, tenting, boats, smokehouses, store, licensed dining by reservation only. Ausserdem sprechen wir deutsch. Accepting VISA. Bill and Traude Hoff welcome you. Box 528, Burns Lake. (250) 964-4692 or Burns Lake channel N696674. [ADVERTISEMENT] ▲

Yellowhead Highway 16 Log
(continued)

PG 143.9 (231.5 km) PR 303.8 (489.9 km) Small community of DECKER LAKE.

Decker Lake, good char and trout fishing; fly-fishing in **Endako River,** which joins Decker and Burns lakes. ◄

PG 149.3 (240.3 km) PR 298.4 (481.2 km) Golf course.

PG 150.9 (242.8 km) PR 296.8 (478.7 km) Palling rest area with picnic tables, toilets and litter barrels.

PG 153.2 (246.5 km) PR 294.5 (475 km) Baker Lake airstrip to south is used by firefighting tankers. Weather station. Emergency telephone.

PG 158 (254.2 km) PR 289.7 (467.3 km) Rose Lake to south.

PG 161.7 (260.3 km) PR 286 (461.2 km) **Broman Lake,** rainbow and char to 4 lbs., use white-winged flies, spring and summer. Dyncan Lake Indian band. Broman Lake Fuel. ◄

PG 164.7 (265.1 km) PR 283 (456.4 km) Six Mile Summit (elev. 4,669 feet/1,423m) to west. China Nose Mountain, with steep west-facing cliff, is visible to the south.

PG 165 (265.5 km) PR 282.7 (456 km) Turnout with litter barrel to south.

PG 166.3 (267.7 km) PR 281.4 (453.7 km) Turnout to south.

PG 171 (275.3 km) PR 276.7 (446.1 km) TOPLEY (pop. 300). Grocery, post office, cafe, motel and gas station. Turn north here for **Babine Lake Recreation Area.** This paved side road leads north to Topley Landing and Granisle on Babine Lake (descriptions follow). From its junction with the highway at Topley, mileages are as follows: Mile 23.6/38 km, private lodge; Mile 24.4/39.3 km, turnoff to village of Topley Landing; Mile 28.8/46.3 km, Fulton River spawning channel; Mile 28/45.1 km, **Red Bluff Provincial Park** with 43 campsites, picnicking and day-use facilities, boat launch, drinking water, toilets, firewood, swimming, fishing and hiking; Mile 30.6/49 km, Lions Beach Park with 16 campsites, picnicking and day-use facilities, boat launch, dock, toilets, firewood, swimming and fishing; Mile 31.4/50.5 km, Granisle; Mile 33.4/53.8 km, begin 16-mile/25.7-km gravel road to Smithers Landing Road, which connects Smithers Landing and Smithers. *CAUTION: Watch for moose along road.* ◄▲

TOPLEY LANDING has several resorts and an unmaintained provincial park. It is also the home of the restored, historic Church of Angels; open June through September. This rustic log church has a collage of angels, a museum and gift shop.

The government-operated **Fulton River spawning channel** has 2 major spawning channels on the river that connect Fulton Lake and Babine Lake. Babine Lake, which flows into the Skeena River, is one of the largest freshwater habitats for sockeye

salmon. The salmon enhancement project at Fulton River produces about 95 million sockeye fry annually. The sockeye run takes place in August and September. Tours may be available at hatchery office.

GRANISLE (pop. 400) was established in 1965 as a company town for the Granisle Copper Mine. In 1972, Noranda Bell Mines Copper Division went into operation. Granisle Copper was closed in 1982 and the Noranda mine was closed in 1992. During mining excavations, a mammoth skeleton was unearthed. The fossilized remains were donated to the Museum of Civilization in Ottawa–Hull. Granisle has become a retirement community and remains a resort area for fishing, boating, waterskiing and camping on Babine Lake. Facilities at Granisle include a convenience store, liquor outlet, hotel with licensed restaurant, resort condominiums, post office, museum, boat rentals, marina and tackle shop. Dump station, showers, laundromat and fresh water available at the Visitor Infocentre. ▲

Babine Lake, rainbow 6 to 8 lbs.; lake trout to 40 lbs., use spoons, flashers and red-and-white spoons, May through November. When fishing early in the year, use a short troll. ◄►

PG 172.3 (277.3 km) **PR 275.4** (444 km) Rest area to south with view of mountains.

PG 176.9 (284.7 km) **PR 270.8** (437.8 km) Byman Creek.

PG 178.7 (287.6 km) **PR 269** (434.9 km) Motel, laundromat and restaurant.

PG 180.1 (289.9 km) **PR 267.6** (432.5

km) Turnout to north.

PG 186.5 (300.1 km) **PR 261.2** (422.2 km) Golf course to south.

PG 188.8 (303.9 km) **PR 258.9** (418.4 km) **Shady Rest RV Park**. See display ad this section. ▲

Houston

PG 190.1 (305.9 km) **PR 257.6** (416.4 km) Houston Infocentre. **Population:** 3,960. **Emergency Services: Police,** phone (250) 845-2204. **Ambulance,** phone 112-562-7241. **Visitor Information:** Visitor Infocentre in log building

on Highway 16 across from the mall and next to Steelhead Park (look for the fish fountain); open year-round. Write Houston Visitor Infocentre, Box 396, Houston, BC V0J 1Z0, or phone (250) 845-7640.

Elevation: 1,949 feet/594m. **Radio:** CFBV 1450, CFPR-FM 102.1, CJFW-FM 105.5. **Transportation:** Greyhound bus, VIA Rail.

Established in the early 1900s, Houston was a tie-cutting centre during construction of the Grand Trunk Pacific Railway in 1912. It was named for Prince Rupert newspaperman John Houston, the former mayor of Nelson, BC. Logging continued to support the local economy with the rapid growth of mills and planer mills in the 1940s and 1950s. Houston was incorporated as a village in 1957.

The Equity Silver Mine began production in 1980. Production ceased in January 1994 and equipment was dismantled.

Today, the main industry in Houston is forest products. The 2 large sawmills here, Houston Forest Products and Northwood Pulp and Timber, offer forestry-awareness tours. The Chamber of Commerce and Visitor Infocentre arrange tours of the sawmills and also offer a day-long tour through the area's forests to provide a first-hand look at the forest industry.

Hunting, canoeing, cross-country skiing and especially sportfishing are major attractions here with the Bulkley River, nearby Morice River and several lakes. Look for the World's Largest Fly Fishing Rod on display at the Visitor Infocentre. The 60-foot-long anodized aluminum fly rod was designed by a local avid fly fisherman and built by local volunteers. (The 21-inch fly is a fluorescent "Skykomish Sunrise.")

Houston has all visitor facilities, including motels, campgrounds, restaurants, gas stations, a shopping centre and golf courses. ▲

Houston Motor Inn. See display ad this section.

Yellowhead Highway 16 Log
(continued)

PG 192.6 (310 km) **PR 255.1** (412.2 km) **Junction** with the Morice River access road

which extends 52 miles/84 km south to Morice Lake. Approximately 20 miles/32 km along the Morice River Road you can turn east on a gravel road which leads past Owen Lake and Nadina River Road to Francois Lake. From Francois Lake ferry landing Highway 35 leads north to Burns Lake.

The 2 famous salmon and steelhead streams, **Morice** and **Bulkley**, unite near Houston, and it is possible to fish scores of pools all along the Morice River. *NOTE: Special requirements apply to fishing these streams; check with Fish and Game office.* ◄►

PG 193 (310.7 km) **PR 254.7** (411.5 km) Bulkley River bridge and rest area; tables, litter barrel and toilets.

PG 196.7 (316.5 km) **PR 251** (405.7 km) Barrett Station Airport. View of Barrett's Hat northbound.

PG 200.5 (322.6 km) **PR 247.2** (399.6 km) **Hungry Hill Summit** (elev. 2,769 feet/844m). To the north are the snow-capped peaks of the Babine Mountains, to the west is the Hudson Bay Range.

PG 203.3 (327.2 km) **PR 244.4** (394.9 km) Bulkley View paved rest area with picnic tables, toilets and litter barrels.

PG 208.1 (334.9 km) **PR 239.6** (387 km) Deep Creek.

PG 210.4 (338.7 km) **PR 237.2** (383.2 km) Quick Road East. Original telegraph cabin.

PG 211.4 (340.2 km) **PR 236.3** (381.7 km) Garage.

PG 213.3 (343.3 km) **PR 234.4** (378.6 km) Quick Road West.

PG 216.8 (348.9 km) **PR 230.9** (373 km) Bulkley field and river.

PG 217.1 (349.4 km) **PR 230.6** (372.5 km) Rest area to west overlooking the Bulkley River.

PG 219.8 (353.7 km) **PR 227.9** (368.1 km) **Ft. Telkwa R.V. Park.** See display ad this section. ▲

PG 220.3 (354.5 km) **PR 227.4** (367.3 km) **TELKWA** (pop. 959). A pleasant village at the confluence of the Telkwa and Bulkley rivers (you can fish from Riverside Street or the riverbanks). Visitor Infocentre at the village office and museum. Facilities include a grocery, post office and a gas station with auto repair. Lodging at Douglas Motel, dining at 3 restaurants.

A unique shop found here is **Horsfield Leather**, which specializes in handmade fishing rod cases, leather water bottles and other leather goods. Fishing and hunting information, licenses and supplies available at the general store. Kinsmen Barbecue is held over Labour Day weekend; games, contests and demolition derby. Eddy Park, on the western edge of town beside the Bulkley River, is a good spot for picnicking (look for the wishing well). St. Stephen's Anglican Church was built in 1911 and the bell and English gate added in 1921. Other Heritage buildings date back to 1908.

Douglas Motel beside beautiful Bulkley River. Riverview units, suites, log cabins with fireplace in relaxing resort atmosphere. Hot pool, sauna complex, kitchens, cablevision, queen beds, electric heat, summer ceiling fans, picnic area, firepit, barbecues, horseshoe pitch, summer outdoor sports equipment. Salmon and steelhead fishing. Walking distance to stores, restaurants and lake. VISA and MasterCard. Douglas Family, (250) 846-5679. [ADVERTISEMENT]

PG 220.7 (355.3 km) **PR 227** (366.5 km) Turnoff to north for **Tyhee Lake Provincial Park;** 55 campsites, 20 picnic tables, dump station, hiking trails, fishing, swimming, boat launch. Seaplane base at lake; charter fly-in fishing.

Also turnoff here on the Telkwa High Road, which intersects with Babine Lake access road (gravel), which leads 46 miles/74 km north to Smithers Landing on Babine Lake and 56 miles/90 km to Granisle.

Tyhee Lake, rainbow and lake trout to 2 lbs., June through August; Kamloops trout to 2 lbs. **Babine River,** steelhead to 40 lbs., late fall. **Telkwa River,** spring and coho salmon to 24 lbs., summer to fall.

PG 221.1 (355.9 km) **PR 226.6** (365.9 km) Gas station.

PG 225.5 (362.9 km) **PR 222.2** (358.8 km) Second turnoff westbound for Babine Lake.

PG 227.2 (365.7 km) **PR 220.5** (356 km) Riverside Recreation Centre; golf, restaurant and campground. ▲

PG 227.5 (366.1 km) **PR 220.2** (355.7 km) Turnoff to north on gravel road for **Driftwood Canyon Provincial Park;** picnic area and toilets. Fossil beds in shale outcroppings along creekbank. This gravel side road continues north to Smithers Landing.

PG 227.7 (366.4 km) **PR 220** (355.3 km) Bridge over Bulkley River.

Smithers

PG 229.2 (368.8 km) **PR 218.5** (352.6 km). Smithers infocentre. **Population:** 6,000; area 30,000. **Emergency Services:** Police, phone (250)847-3233. **Hospital and Poison Centre,** 3950 8th Ave., phone (250) 847-2611. **Ambulance,** phone 1-562-7241.

Visitor Information: Visitor Infocentre and Chamber of Commerce are located adjacent to the Central Park Bldg., which houses the museum and art gallery; open year-round, phone (800) 542-6673.

Elevation: 1,621 feet/494m. **Climate:** Relatively warmer and drier than mountainous areas to the west; average temperature in July is 58°F/14°C, in January 14°F/-10°C; annual precipitation, 13 inches. **Radio:**

Swiss influence is seen in Smithers' storefronts and the Alpenhorn player downtown. (© Judy Parkin)

CFBV 1230, CFPR-FM 97.5. **Television:** Channels 5, 13 and cable. **Newspaper:** *Interior News* (weekly).

Transportation: Air—Scheduled service to Vancouver and Terrace via Canadian Airlines International. Daily flights to Prince George and Terrace via Central Mountain Air. **Railroad**—VIA Rail. **Bus**—Greyhound. **Car Rentals**—Available.

Sitting amidst rugged mountains, the town has been enhanced by Swiss-style storefronts that have been added to many of the buildings. Reconstructed in 1979, Main Street offers many shops and restaurants. Incorporated as a village in 1921, Smithers officially became a town in Canada's centennial year, 1967. The original site was chosen in 1913 by construction crews working on

---

the Grand Trunk Pacific Railway (the town was named for one-time chairman of the railway A.W. Smithers). Today it is a distribution and supply centre for farms, mills and mines in the area.

Smithers is the largest town in the Bulkley Valley and the site of Hudson Bay Mountain, a popular ski area (skiing from November to mid-April).

Smithers has several motels, gas stations, restaurants, laundromat/car wash and good shopping. Government liquor store located on Queen Street at Broadway Avenue. There are 2 18-hole golf courses, both with rentals and clubhouses.

There is a municipal campground with security and firewood (no hookups) at Riverside Park on the Bulkley River; turn north at the museum across from Main Street and drive up the hill about a mile and watch for sign. There are private campgrounds located east and west of town; see highway log. ▲

Special events include the Bulkley Valley Fall Fair, held on the last weekend in August each year, one of the largest agricultural exhibitions in the province. The Midsummer Music Festival in June features local, regional and national artists.

Smithers offers a number of scenic drives. Hudson Bay Mountain (elev. 8,700 feet/2,652m) is a 14-mile/23-km drive from Highway 16; the plateau above timberline at the ski area is a good spot for summer hikes. In the winter months, Smithers boasts one of the largest ski hills in northern British Columbia. A 6,000-foot/1,829-m triple chair and 2 T-bars climb the 1,750-foot/533-m

vertical, offering skiers 18 different runs.

Fossil enthusiasts should drive to Driftwood Canyon Provincial Park; turn off Highway 16 just east of the Bulkley River bridge (travelers are advised to stop first at the Visitor Infocentre in town for a map and directions). A display at the park illustrates the fossils, such as metasequoia, a type of redwood which occurs in the shale formation.

Adams Igloo Wildlife Museum, just west of town on Highway 16, has an excellent display of mammals found in British Columbia.

A beautiful spot not to be missed is Twin Falls and Glacier Gulch. Take the 4-mile-/6.4-km-long gravel road (steep in places) from Highway 16 on the western edge of town.

A 2.2-mile-/3.5-km-long interpretive nature trail with native wildlife and plant species is 10 miles/16 km west of Smithers on the Hudson Bay Mountain Ski Hill road in Smithers Community Forest. This trail can also be used in winter for cross-country skiing, and connects to other cross-country ski trails. Detailed maps of the area showing all hiking trails are available at the infocentre.

An extensive list of lake and river fishing spots in the area, with information on boat launches and boat rentals, is available from the Smithers District Chamber of Commerce, Box 2379, Smithers, BC V0J 2N0; phone (250) 847-9854; or ask at the Visitor Infocentre. ◄►

Moose, mule deer, grizzly and black bears, mountain goats and caribou are found in the area, and guides and outfitters are available locally. All species of grouse can be hunted in the Bulkley Valley during the fall. Information is available from the Fish and Wildlife Branch office in Smithers.

Yellowhead Highway 16 Log
(continued)

PG 230.6 (371.1 km) **PR 217.1** (350.1 km) Smithers golf club.

PG 231.7 (372.8 km) **PR 216** (348.4 km) Paved access road to Lake Kathlyn. There is a municipal park with small beach and boat launch located here. Powerboats not permitted. Closed to waterfowl hunting. Side road continues 4 miles/6.4 km (gravel) to Twin

Falls and Glacier Gulch.

PG 232.7 (374.5 km) **PR 215** (346.7 km) Road to north leads to Smithers airport.

PG 234 (376.6 km) **PR 213.7** (344.6 km) Lake Kathlyn Road to west.

PG 234.9 (378 km) **PR 212.8** (343.6 km) **Glacier View RV Park.** Wake up to a panoramic view of the Hudson Bay Glacier. Eight level gravel sites with 15-/30-amp service and water hookups. Dry pull-throughs up to 55 feet. Pit toilets. Walking distance to Wildlife Museum. Easy access. Reservations: RR 1, S 9 C 31, Smithers, BC V0J 2N0, (250) 847-3961. [ADVERTISEMENT] ▲

PG 235.1 (378.3 km) **PR 212.6** (342.9 km) Hudson Bay rest area to west with picnic tables, toilets and litter barrels. Beautiful view of Hudson Bay Mountain.

PG 235.4 (378.8 km) **PR 212.3** (342.4 km) **Adams Igloo Wildlife Museum.** The finest collection of big game animals, furbearers and birds native to British Columbia, mounted life-size and displayed in their natural habitat. The inside mural, painted by leading wildlife artist Tom Sander, gives a 3-dimensional impression for realism. Stop at the White Dome, 6 miles west of Smithers beside one of the highway's most beautiful viewpoints. Fur rugs and souvenirs for sale. Ted Moon, Curator. [ADVERTISEMENT]

PG 238.4 (383.6 km) **PR 209.3** (337.6 km) Toboggan Creek Fish Hatchery.

PG 243.1 (391.3 km) **PR 204.6** (329.8 km) Trout Creek bridge. Store with groceries, post office and phone; fishing licenses available.

PG 248.7 (400.3 km) **PR 199** (320.7 km) Turnout to north with picnic tables and view of Bulkley River and Moricetown Canyon; good photo stop.

PG 248.9 (400.6 km) **PR 198.8** (320.4 km) Telkwa High Road is a short side road on the north side of the highway leading to **Moricetown Canyon and Falls** on the Bulkley River and Moricetown campground. For centuries a famous First Nation's fishing spot, Aboriginal people may still be seen here gaffing, jigging and netting salmon in July and August. A worthwhile stop. ▲

PG 249.2 (401.1 km) **PR 198.5** (319.9 km) **MORICETOWN** (pop. 680; elev. 1,341 feet/409m). **Radio:** CBC-FM 96.5. Moricetown has a gas station with minor repair service and diesel fuel. There is a handicraft store. A campground is located in Moricetown Canyon (turnoff at **Milepost PG 255.7**). Moricetown is a First Nations reserve and village, the oldest settlement in the Bulkley Valley. Traditionally, the Native people (Wet'su-wet'en) took advantage of the narrow canyon to trap salmon. The centuries-old settlement ('Kyah Wiget) is now named after Father A.G. Morice, a Roman Catholic missionary. Born in France, Father Morice came to British Columbia in 1880 and worked with the Aboriginals of northern British Columbia from 1885 to 1904. He achieved world recognition for his writings in anthropology, ethnology and history.

PG 253.8 (408.5 km) **PR 193.9** (312.4 km) Chicken Creek.

PG 255.9 (411.9 km) **PR 191.8** (306.6 km) East Boulder Creek.

PG 258.9 (416.6 km) **PR 188.8** (304.3 km) Paved turnout.

PG 260.7 (419.5 km) **PR 187** (301.4 km) Paved turnout with picnic tables and litter barrels.

PG 260.9 (419.9 km) **PR 186.8** (300.9 km) View of Bulkley River.

PG 261.5 (420.9 km) PR 186.2 (299.9 km) Paved turnout.

PG 263.9 (424.8 km) PR 183.8 (296 km) Turnoff to north for Forest Service campsite (7.5 miles/12.1 km) with pit toilets, tables and litter barrels. Fishing in **Suskwa River**; coho salmon to 10 lbs., use tee-spinners in July; steelhead to 20 lbs., use Kitamat #32 and soft bobbers in late fall. ◄◄▲

PG 269.1 (433.1 km) PR 178.6 (287.6 km) Turnoff to north for **Ross Lake Provincial Park**; 25 picnic sites, boat launch (no powerboats), swimming. Fishing for rainbow to 4 lbs. ◄►

PG 270.5 (435.3 km) PR 177.2 (285.4 km) Entering New Hazelton, the first of 3 communities westbound sharing the name Hazelton (the others are Hazelton and South Hazelton), known collectively as The Hazeltons; description follows.

New Hazelton

PG 271.1 (436.3 km) PR 176.6 (284.4 km) **Junction** of Highway 16 with Highway 62 to Hazelton, 'Ksan and Kispiox (descriptions follow). The turnoff for Highway 62 is located just west of the railway overpass in New Hazelton. The easy-to-miss turn is on the north side (right for westbound travelers) of Highway 16 between the overpass and the Visitor Infocentre at the base of the hill. **Population:** area 1,300. **Emergency Services:** Police, phone (250) 842-5244.

Visitor Information: Visitor Infocentre in 2-story log building at the junction. Look for the 3 statues representing the gold rush packer Cataline, the Northwest miner, and the Upper Skeena logger. Museum located in

www.themilepost.com

Hazelton/Kitwanga Area

Infocentre.

Elevation: 1,150 feet/351m. **Radio:** CBC 1170. **Transportation:** VIA Rail. Greyhound bus.

This small highway community has gas stations, major auto repair, restaurants, cafes, post office, general store, a hotel and a motel. Laundromat, propane, sporting goods, and hunting and fishing licenses available in town. An ATM is located at the Chevron station in New Hazelton and at the mall on the highway.

Attractions here include historic Hazelton, the Indian village of 'Ksan and sportfishing the Bulkley and Kispiox rivers (descriptions follow). Mount Rocher Deboule, elev. 8,000 feet/2,438m, towers behind the town.

HAZELTON. Situated at the confluence of the Skeena and Bulkley rivers, Hazelton grew up at "The Forks" as a trans-shipping point at the head of navigation on the Skeena and a wintering place for miners and prospectors from the rigorous Interior. Thomas Hankin established a Hudson's Bay Co. trading post here in 1868. The name Hazelton comes from the numerous hazel-nut bushes growing on the flats.

Cataline, famous pioneer packer and traveler, is buried near here in an unmarked grave at Pioneer Cemetery. Jean Caux (his real name) was a Basque who, from 1852 to 1912, with loaded mules plodding 12 miles/19 km a day, supplied mining and construction camps from Yale and Ashcroft northward through Hazelton, where he often wintered. His mule trails became roads; his exploits are legends.

For some years, before the arrival of the railroad and highways, supplies for trading posts at Bear and Babine lakes and the Omineca goldfields moved by riverboat from the coast to Hazelton and from there over trails to the backcountry. Some of the Yukon gold rushers passed through Hazelton on their way to the Klondike, pack trains having made the trip from Hazelton to Tele-graph Creek over the old Telegraph Trail as early as 1874.

This community has reconstructed much of what the town was like in the 1890s. Look for the antique machinery downtown. The history of the Hazelton area can be traced by car on the Hand of History tour. Pick up a brochure from the Visitor Infocentre show-ing the location of the 19 historic sites on the driving tour.

'KSAN HISTORICAL VILLAGE and Museum, a replica Gitksan Indian village, is 4.5 miles/7.2 km from Highway 16. It is a

reconstruction of the traditional Gitksan Vil-lage, which has stood at this site for cen-turies. It is located at the confluence of the Bulkley and Skeena rivers by the 'Ksan Assoc. There are 7 communal houses, totem poles and dugout canoes. At the carving

shed, carvers produce First Nation's arts and crafts which can be purchased. Food service is available on site.

For a nominal charge from May to September, you can join a guided tour of the communal houses. Performances of tradi-tional song and dance are presented every Friday evening during July and August in the Wolf House. Admission to grounds is $2, children under 6 are free. Guided tours of the grounds run $7 for adults, $6 for stu-dents. The site is open year-round, hours vary. Open daily April 15–Oct. 15. Tours are available mid-April to late September. Phone (250) 842-5544.

A well-maintained full-service trailer park and campground on the banks of the Skeena and Bulkley rivers is operated by the Gitan-maax Indian Band from the Gitanmaax Reserve. ▲

KISPIOX (pop. 825) Indian village and 3 fishing resorts are 20 miles/32 km north on a good paved road at the confluence of the Skeena and Kispiox rivers. Kispiox is noted for its stand of totems close to the river. There is a market garden (fresh vegetables) located approximately 7 miles/11 km north on the Kispiox Road (about 2 miles/ 3.2 km before the Kispiox totem poles). Camping, cabins and fishing at lodges and camp-grounds in the valley. Valley residents host the Kispiox Rodeo the first weekend of June. This excellent event has run annually since 1952. ◄▲

Bulkley River, Dolly Varden to 5 lbs.; spring salmon, mid-July to mid-August; coho salmon 4 to 12 lbs., Aug. 15 through Septem-ber, flies, spoons and spinners; steelhead to 20 lbs., July through November, flies, Kita-mats, weighted spoons and soft bobbers. **Kispiox River** is famous for its trophy-sized steelhead. Check on regulations and obtain a fishing license before your arrival. Fishing is done with single-hook only, with catch-release for steelhead between Aug. 15 and Sept. 30. Season is July 1 to Nov. 30 for salmon, trout and steelhead. Excellent fly-fishing waters: spring salmon, July to early August; coho salmon, late August to early September; steelhead from September until freezeup. Sizable Dolly Vardens and cut-throat. Steelhead average 20 lbs., with some catches over 30 lbs. ◄

Yellowhead Highway 16 Log

(continued)

PG 273.3 (439.9 km) **PR 174.4** (280.8 km) Turnoff to north for 2-mile/3.2-km loop road through small community of **SOUTH HAZELTON**; restaurant, general store, gas station with minor repair, lodging.

PG 277.1 (445.9 km) **PR 170.6** (274.8 km) **Seeley Lake Provincial Park**; 20 camp-sites, drinking water, pit toilets, firewood, sani-dump, day-use area with picnic tables, swimming, fishing. ◄▲

PG 278.8 (448.8 km) **PR 168.8** (271.8 km) Restaurant.

PG 282.4 (454.5 km) **PR 165.3** (266.1 km) Carnaby Sawmill.

PG 286.6 (461.2 km) **PR 161.1** (259.3 km) Skeena Crossing. Historic Canadian National Railways bridge (see plaque at Kit-seguecla).

PG 287.4 (462.5 km) **PR 160.3** (258 km) KITSEGUECLA, First Nation's village. Totem poles throughout village are classic exam-ples, still in original locations. Historical plaque about Skeena Crossing.

PG 287.7 (463 km) **PR 160** (257.6 km) Sheep's Rapids.

Many classic examples of totems are found in the Kitseguecla, Kitwanga and Kitwancool areas. (© Judy Parkin)

PG 292.5 (470.7 km) **PR 155.2** (250 km) Road winds along edge of river.

CAUTION: Watch for falling rock next 32 miles/51.5 km.

PG 297.7 (479.1 km) **PR 150** (241.4 km) Gas station and cafe at Cassiar Highway turnoff. Kitwancool, 13 miles/21 km north on the Cassiar, has many fine old totems.

Junction with Cassiar Highway (BC Highway 37). Bridge across Skeena River to Kitwanga and Cassiar Highway to Stewart, Hyder, AK, and Alaska High-way. See CASSIAR HIGHWAY section.

Westbound, the Yellowhead Highway passes Seven Sisters peaks; the highest is 9,140 feet/2,786m.

PG 299 (481.2 km) **PR 148.7** (239.4 km) **Gitksan Paintbrush Native Arts & Crafts.** Silver and gold jewelry: rings, earrings, bracelets. BC jade. Limited edition prints and originals. Smoked moosehide moc-casins, beaded leatherwork. Wood carvings, cedar baskets. Clothing and souvenirs. Qual-ity merchandise, most from local artists. Excellent prices. Easy access. Summer hours 9 A.M.–7 P.M. P.O. Box 97, Kitwanga, BC V0J 2A0. Phone or fax (250) 849-5085. [ADVERTISEMENT]

PG 300.8 (484.1 km) **PR 146.9** (236.5 km) **Seven Sisters RV Park and Camp-ground.** Outstanding value. Beautiful park-like setting. Many treed sites. Fresh water, sani-dump, picnic tables at every site, flush toilets, shower, firepits with free firewood, all for $9. Excellent salmon fishing close by. Tenters and cyclists welcome. (250) 849-5489 for reservations. Box 338, Kitwanga, BC V0J 2A0. [ADVERTISEMENT] ▲

PG 303.4 (488.2 km) **PR 144.3** (232.4 km) Boulder Creek rest area; parking for large vehicles; toilets, litter barrels and picnic tables.

PG 306.6 (493.4 km) **PR 141.1** (227.3 km) Whiskey Creek.

PG 307.6 (495 km) **PR 140.1** (225.8 km)

Gravel turnout to north with litter barrel.

PG 308 (495.6 km) **PR 139.7** (225.2 km) Gull Creek.

PG 309.1 (497.4 km) **PR 138.6** (223.4 km) CEDARVALE, cafe. Loop road through rural setting. Historical plaque about Holy City.

PG 309.2 (497.6 km) **PR 138.5** (223.2 km) Hand of History sign about "Holy City."

Watch for bears fishing the river for salmon in late July and early August.

PG 312.5 (502.9 km) **PR 135.2** (218 km) Gravel turnout to north with litter barrel.

PG 313.6 (504.6 km) **PR 134.1** (216.4 km) Watch for fallen rock on this stretch of highway.

PG 315.3 (507.4 km) **PR 132.4** (213.6 km) Flint Creek.

PG 318.5 (512.6 km) **PR 129.2** (208.5 km) Turnout with historical plaque about Skeena River Boats: "From 1889, sternwheelers and smaller craft fought their way through the Coast Mountains, churning past such awesome places as 'The Devil's Elbow' and 'The Hornet's Nest.' Men and supplies were freighted upstream, furs and gold downstream. A quarter century of colour and excitement began to fade in 1912, as the Grand Trunk Pacific neared completion."

PG 322.4 (518.8 km) **PR 125.2** (202.4 km) Gravel turnout to north.

PG 323.2 (520.1 km) **PR 124.5** (201.1 km) Gravel turnout to south with litter barrel.

PG 332 (534.3 km) **PR 115.7** (187.3 km) Legate Creek.

PG 335.7 (540.2 km) **PR 112** (181.5 km) Rest area on river with water pump, picnic tables, toilets and litter barrels.

PG 336 (540.7 km) **PR 111.7** (181 km) Skeena Cellulose bridge (private) crosses Skeena River to access tree farms on north side.

PG 336.9 (542.1 km) **PR 110.8** (179.6 km) St. Croix Creek.

PG 340.3 (547.7 km) **PR 107.4** (173.9 km) Chindemash Creek.

PG 342.8 (551.6 km) **PR 104.9** (170 km) Tiny chapel to south serves small community of USK; the village is reached via the reaction ferry seen to north. The nondenominational chapel is a replica of the pioneer church that stood in Usk until 1936, when the Skeena River flooded, sweeping away the village and the church. The only item from the church to survive was the Bible, which was found floating atop a small pine table.

PG 345 (555.2 km) **PR 102.7** (166.4 km) Entrance to Kitselas Canyon (1 mile/1.6 km).

PG 345.2 (555.6 km) **PR 102.4** (166 km) Side road leads 0.5 mile/0.8 km south to **Kleanza Creek Provincial Park**; 21 campsites, 25 picnic sites, fishing, drinking water, toilets, firewood, wheelchair access. Short trail to remains from Cassiar Hydraulic Mining Co. gold-sluicing operations here (1911–14). ♿ 🏕

PG 345.4 (555.9 km) **PR 102.3** (165.7 km) Kleanza Bridge.

PG 346.9 (558.3 km) **PR 100.8** (163.3 km) Gravel turnout to north.

PG 349.7 (562.8 km) **PR 98** (158.7 km) Fishing lodge.

PG 350.5 (564.1 km) **PR 97.2** (157.4 km) Gas and lodging. **Copper (Zymoetz) River,** can be fished from Highway 16 or follow local maps. Coho salmon to 10 lbs., use tee-spinners in July; steelhead to 20 lbs., check locally for season and restrictions. 🐟

PG 352 (566.5 km) **PR 95.7** (155 km) Turnout to north with tourist information

Highway 37 South Log

Distance is measured from the junction with Yellowhead Highway 16 (J).

J 0 Junction with Yellowhead Highway 16 at **Milepost PG 354.7** (east exit to Terrace).

J 0.9 (1.4 km) Krumm Road. Turn east for golf course.

J 3.1 (5 km) Terrace–Kitimat airport access road.

J 7.9 (12.7 km) Lakelse Lake Provincial Park parking area and trail to Gruchy's Beach.

J 8.7 (14 km) Lakelse Lake Provincial Park parking areas and picnic area; tables, toilets, showers, changehouses and beach. Park headquarters located here.

J 10.6 (17.1 km) Waterlily Bay; food, lodging, boat launch.

J 11.4 (18.3 km) **Lakelse Lake Provincial Park** Furlong Bay campground and picnic area; 156 vehicle and tent campsites, nature trails, swimming, sandy beach, flush toilets, showers, dump station, boat launch, drinking water, wheelchair access, firewood and interpretive programs. ♿🏕

J 13.8 (22.2 km) Onion Lake hiking and ski trails to west.

J 20.6 (33.2 km) Access to Kitimat River.

J 27.4 (44.1 km) Kitimat Airpark landing strip for small planes.

J 34.8 (56 km) Hirsch Creek Park to west; picnic area, camping, fishing and hiking. 🐟🏕

J 35 (56.3 km) Hirsch Creek bridge.

J 35.8 (57.6 km) Kitimat Travel Info-centre to east.

J 36.2 (58.3 km) Minette Bay Road leads east to MK Bay Marina.

J 36.6 (58.9 km) Viewpoint of Douglas Channel and city map. Picnic tables, garden.

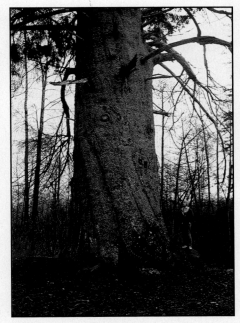

Radley Park is the site of a 500-year-old Sitka spruce. (© Tom W. Parkin)

Kitimat

J 37.6 (60.5 km) Located at the head of Douglas Channel. **Population:** 12,000. **Emergency Services: RCMP,** phone (250) 632-7111. **Fire Department,** phone (250) 639-9111. **Ambulance,**

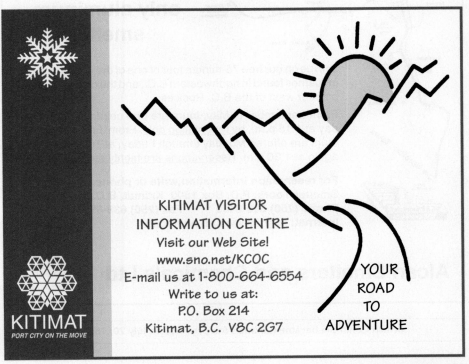

Highway 37 South Log (cont'd)

phone (250) 632-5433. **Hospital**, phone (250) 632-2121. **Radio:** CKTK 1230; CBC-FM 101.1, CJFW-FM 103.1. **Newspaper:** *The News Advertiser* (weekly); *Northern Sentinel* (weekly).

This community was planned and built in the early 1950s when the B.C. government attracted Alcan (Aluminum Co. of Canada) to establish a smelter here. Today, Kitimat is a major port and home to several industries. Free tours are available (primarily in summer, reservations recommended) at Alcan, (250) 639-8259; Eurocan Pulp and Paper, (250) 639-3597; Methanex Corp., (250) 639-9292; and Kitimat fish hatchery, (250) 639-9616. Tour Mike's Wildlife Museum to see over 100 mounts; admission fee; (250) 632-7083.

Kitimat's location at the head of Douglas Channel makes it a popular boating, fishing and scuba diving destination. There are several charter operators.

Kitimat has all visitor facilities, including a modern shopping mall,

restaurants and motels; library, theatre, swimming pool and gym; and an 18-hole golf course. Many scenic hiking trails are available. A free guide to area day hikes is available at the Visitor Infocentre. The Centennial Museum is located at city centre. Information on local Native art, canoe trips and heli-adventures available at the Chamber of Commerce, Box 214 (M), Kitimat, BC V8C 2G7; phone (800 664-6554 or (250) 632-6294; fax (250) 632-4685; e-mail gguise@kitimat.sno.net.

There is camping at Radley Park in town; electrical hookups, showers, fishing, toilets, playground and dump station. (Radley Park—on the other side of the river—is also the site of a 500-year-old, 165-foot/50-m Sitka spruce, one of the largest of its kind in the province.) There is also camping at Hirsch Creek Park on the edge of town and private campgrounds. ◄▲

Local fishermen line the banks of the **Kitimat River** in May for the steelhead run. Chinook salmon run in June and July. Coho run from August into September. 🐟

Kitimat also offers many winter activities, including cross-country skiing and indoor ice rinks. Downhill skiing at nearby Terrace and Smithers.

Alcan Smelters and Chemical Ltd. See display ad this section.

Kitimat Chamber of Commerce. See display ad this section.

Return to Milepost PG 354.7
Yellowhead Highway 16

sign and area map.

PG 352.2 (566.8 km) **PR 95.5** (154.7 km) Motel and gas.

PG 352.9 (568 km) **PR 94.8** (153.5 km) Motel.

PG 354.3 (570.2 km) **PR 93.4** (151.3 km) Old Lakelse Lake Road.

PG 354.7 (570.8 km) **PR 93** (150.7 km) Four-way stop. For access to downtown Terrace, turn north here and continue over 1-lane bridge. For west access to Terrace and continuation of Yellowhead Highway 16 westbound, go straight at intersection. Turn off for Kitimat, 37 miles/60 km south via Highway 37. Kitimat is a major port and home to several industries.

> **Junction** with Highway 37 South to Kitimat. Log of HIGHWAY 37 SOUTH begins on page 235.

PG 354.9 (571.1 km) **PR 92.8** (150.4 km) First bridge westbound over **Skeena River**. "Skeen" means "River of the mist" in First Nation's language.

PG 355.2 (571.7 km) **PR 92.5** (149.8 km) Ferry Island municipal campground; 68 sites, some electrical hookups. Covered picnic shelters, barbecues, walking trails and a fishing bar are also available. ◄▲

PG 355.3 (571.8 km) **PR 92.4** (149.7 km) Second westbound Skeena River Bridge.

PG 355.7 (572.4 km) **PR 92** (149.1 km) Terrace Chamber of Commerce Visitor Infocentre.

PG 356.6 (573.8 km) **PR 91.1** (147.7 km) Stoplight; west access to Terrace. Turn north at intersection for downtown.

Continue through intersection on Highway 16 westbound for Prince Rupert, eastbound for Prince George.

CAUTION: No gas or services available between Terrace and Prince Rupert.

Terrace

Located on the Skeena River. City centre is located north of Highway 16: Exit at PG 356.6 or at Highway 37 junction (PG 354.7). **Population:** 13,000; area 21,500. **Emergency Services:** Police, fire and ambulance located at intersection of Eby Street and Highway 16. **Police**, phone (250) 635-4911. **Fire Department**, phone (250) 638-8121. **Ambulance**, phone (250) 638-1102. **Hospital**, phone (250) 635-2211.

Visitor Information: Visitor Infocentre located in the chamber of commerce log building at **Milepost PG 355.7** Open daily in summer, 9 A.M. to 8 P.M.; weekdays in winter, 8 A.M. to 4:30 P.M. Write 4511 Keith Ave, Terrace, BC V8G 1K1; phone (250) 635-2063. Information also available from Municipal Hall, #5-3215 Eby St.; open weekdays, phone (250) 635-6311.

Elevation: 220 feet/67m. **Climate:** Aver-

British Columbia became Canada's 6th province on July 20, 1871.

TERRACE ADVERTISERS

age summer temperature is 69°F/21°C; average annual rainfall 44 inches/112 cm, snowfall 129 inches/327 cm. **Radio:** CFTK 590; CFPR-FM 95.3, CFNR 92.1. **Television:** 13 channels (cable). **Newspapers:** *Terrace Standard* (weekly) *Terrace Times* (weekly).

Transportation: Air—Canadian Airlines International, Air BC and Central Mountain Air from Terrace-Kitimat airport on Highway 37 South. **Railroad**—VIA Rail, 4531 Railway Ave. **Bus**—Farwest Bus Lines, Greyhound and Seaport Limousine with connection between Terrace and Stewart/Hyder. **Car Rentals**—Available.

Terrace was once a port of call for Skeena River stern-wheelers. The first farmer in the area, George Little, gave land to the community that became a port of call and post office in 1905. Originally it was known as Little Town, and later was named Terrace because of the natural terraces cut by the river. The village site was laid out in 1910 and the Grand Trunk Pacific Railway reached Terrace in 1914. The municipality was incorporated in 1927.

There are 17 motels/hotels, 35 restaurants and 2 shopping centres. The government liquor store is at 3250 Eby St. There are 5 laundromats. The community has a library and art gallery, indoor swimming pool, tennis courts, a golf course, bingo parlor, bowling alley, theatre and billiards.

Terrace has private campgrounds (see advertisements this section) and a public campground located at Ferry Island (see **Milepost PG 355.2**). Lakelse Lake Provincial Park at Furlong Bay, 11.4 miles/18.3 km south of Highway 16 on Highway 37, offers campsites and day-use facilities, restrooms, changing rooms, showers, boat launch, sandy beaches, swimming, nature trails and interpretive forestry programs. ▲

Major attractions in Terrace include **Heritage Park**, a collection of original log buildings from this region. Chosen to represent both the different aspects of pioneer life as well as different log building techniques, the structures include a trapper's cabin, miner's cabin and lineman's cabin. The 9 structures also house artifacts from the period. Managed by the Terrace Regional Museum Society; guided tours available in

summer, admission charged.

Recreation includes hiking, biking, rock-climbing, canoeing, kayaking and snowmobiling. Hiking trails in the Terrace area range from easy to moderate. Terrace Mountain Nature Trail is a 3.2-mile/5.1-km uphill hike which offers good views of the area; it begins at Halliwell and Anderson streets. Check with the Visitor Infocentre for details on other area trails.

Special events in Terrace include the Skeena Valley Fall Fair, Labour Day weekend; River Boat Days, B.C. Day weekend; and the

Nisga'a Highway/Nass Road Log

The Nisga'a Highway/Nass Forest Service Road junctions with Yellowhead Highway 16 west of Terrace at **Milepost PG 357.5** and travels north to join the Cassiar Highway at **Milepost J 44.9**. Total driving distance is 98.6 miles/158.7 km and the first 39.3 miles/63.2 km are paved; the remainder is gravel. Services along this route are limited.

Distance is measured from junction (J) with Yellowhead Highway 16.

J 0 Junction with Yellowhead Highway 16 at **Milepost PG 357.5.**

J 7 (11.2 km) Finlay Lake to west.

J 13.7 (22 km) Kitsumkalum River to west.

J 17.4 (28 km) View of Kitsumkalum Lake to west.

J 19.8 (31.9 km) Paved turnout to west overlooking Kitsumkalum Lake.

J 23 (37 km) Rosswood settlement at the head of the lake, named for Annie Ross, who homesteaded here with her 4 children at the turn of the century.

J 25.8 (41.5 km) Rosswood General Store; groceries, fishing tackle (open year-round).

J 30.4 (48.9 km) Entering Skeena Cellulose Tree Farm License #1. Twenty-five year tree farm licenses are issued by the Crown and define the terms of timber harvest, including taxation, reforestation and long-term planning requirements.

J 31.4 (50.5 km) One-lane bridge crosses Cedar River.

J 37 (59.6 km) Sand Lake, marshy area to south. Watch for wildlife.

J 39.3 (63.2 km) Pavement ends, gravel begins, northbound. **Junction** with West Kalum Road.

J 39.5 (63.6 km) Gainor Lake west.

J 42.2 (67.9 km) Southern park boundary for **Nisga'a Memorial Lava Bed Park.** Lava Lake to west. Narrow winding road next 6.2 miles/10 km northbound. *Note: Removal of lava prohibited; stay on designated trails and roads.*

The flow is thought to be the most recent volcanic eruption in Canada (approximately 300 years ago). It covers an area approximately 6.3 miles/10 km long and 1.8 miles/3 km wide and was created by a volcano less than 361 feet/100m high. The eruption produced little ash or cinder, but large quantities of basalt. The eruption destroyed 2 villages and killed more than 2,000 people.

The flow entered the Tseax Valley, filling it to depths of more than 98 feet/30m, and blocking the upper section of the valley. Waters from the surrounding drainage filled the valley to form the 180 foot-/55m-deep Lava Lake, which in turn drains into the permeable lava flow and reappears approximately 1.2 miles/2 km downstream as the Tseax River and Vetter Creek.

J 46 (74.1 km) Access to Lava Lake on west side of road.

J 48.3 (77.8 km) North end of Lava Lake. Sil Tax picnic site; toilets, litter barrels, tables, park information. No overnight camping.

J 48.7 (78.4 km) Lava flow to east. Interpretive sign, trail (0.6 mile/1 km) and photo viewpoint.

J 50.1 (80.6 km) One-lane wooden bridge.

J 54.7 (88 km) Beaupre Falls trail (10 minutes round trip).

J 56.2 (90.5 km) Vetter Falls viewpoint and "phantom fish." Near Vetter Falls the Tseax River divides; the western channel flows into the Nass River. The eastern channel flows over Vetter Falls to join Vetter Creek. Just east of the Vetter Falls campsite, the runoff sinks into channels below the lava. Often, steelhead spawning in the Tseax River return to the ocean; occasionally the fish take the eastern channel and go over the falls, becoming trapped in this section of the river. They starve and become "snake-like" in appearance. Locals refer to them as "phantom fish."

J 58.5 (94.1 km) **Junction** with road to Gitwinksihlkw (Canyon City) and Greenville. Information sign. Turn east (right). Road presently ends at Greenville. Vetter Falls campsite to northwest; tables, fire rings, and toilets. Water from creek; recommend boiling. ▲

Nisga'a Enterprises operates a fishing lodge at Nass Harbour with good fishing and ocean kayaking. ◀

J 59.6 (95.9 km) Northern boundary for Nisga'a Memorial Lava Bed Park; information, toilets, viewpoint. Turnout by creek to south. One-lane bridge.

J 60.1 (96.7 km) RCMP station to north.

J 60.2 (96.9 km) Village of **NEW AIYANSH** to south is the major settlement on the Nisga'a Highway. Repairs, gas, grocery and convenience stores, community hall with Native design, a school, post office, first aid, fire and police stations, post office and gift shop are available. Area bed and breakfast and lodge operators offer meals and accommodation. Limited campsites are available. ▲

J 67.7 (109 km) Northbound: Highway becomes Nass Forest Service Road at Y-intersection. Keep left for Nass Camp/Bill-Nor Tillicum Lodge (all visitor services), keep right for Cassiar Highway.

J 71.3 (114.7 km) BC Forest Recreation Site on Dragon Lake. A medium, semi-open, user-maintained site with good water and broad access; mixed forest; boat launch. ▲

J 73.7 (118.6 km) Y-intersection: Keep to right for Cassiar Highway, left for Alice Arm/Kitsault. Follow hydro lines.

J 80.5 (129.5 km) One-lane wooden bridge with turnouts at each end. Leaving Skeena Tree Fall License #1 northbound.

J 94.8 (152.5 km) Y-intersection: Follow yellow kilometreposts on right side of road for Cassiar Highway.

J 98.6 (158.7 km) **Junction** with Cassiar Highway 37 (see Cassiar Highway section).

Return to Milepost PG 357.5
Yellowhead Highway or
J 46.8 Cassiar Highway

Nisga'a Memorial Lava Bed Park is north of Terrace. (© Lyn Hancock)

Terrace Trade Show in late April.

Nisga'a Lava Memorial Park lava beds are 42 miles/67 km north of Terrace via the Nisga'a Highway (see NISGA'A HIGHWAY/NASS ROAD log this section). Limited picnic spots; limited camping; interesting hikes. Canada's youngest volcano last erupted approximately 250 years ago, burying 2 Indian villages. Guided hikes into the cones are available; phone (250) 798-2277.

Terrace is ideally situated for sportfishing, with easy access to the **Skeena, Copper, Kalum, Kitimat** and **Lakelse rivers.** Cutthroat, Dolly Varden and rainbow are found in all lakes and streams; salmon (king and coho) from May to late autumn. Kings average 40 to 70 lbs.; coho 14 to 20 lbs. Check locally for season and restrictions on steelhead. Information and fishing licenses are available from B.C. Government Access Centre, 3220 Eby St., Terrace (phone 250/638-6515), and at most sporting goods stores. ◀

Yellowhead Highway 16 Log
(continued)

PG 356.6 (573.8 km) **PR 91.1** (147.7 km) Stoplight; west access to Terrace. Turn north at intersection for downtown. Continue through intersection eastbound for Prince George, westbound for Prince Rupert.

PG 357.5 (575.4 km) **PR 90.2** (146.1 km)

Junction with Nisga'a Highway (Kalum Lake Road) to New Aiyansh. Beyond the Nass Road junction, the Nisga'a Highway is a narrow gravel and pavement road used by logging trucks. See NISGA'A HIGHWAY/NASS ROAD log this page.

The Nisga'a Highway junctions with the Cassiar Highway. The Cassiar Highway junctions with the Yellowhead Highway at Kitwanga; see **Milepost PG 306.6.**

PG 357.9 (576 km) **PR 89.8** (145.5 km) West Fraser Sawmill.

PG 359 (377.8 km) **PR 88.7** (143.7 km) Kalum Bridge.

PG 359.2 (578 km) **PR 88.5** (143.5 km) Access road to boat launch (fee charged) on the Kitsumkalum River downstream from Highway 16 bridge; RV parking.

Leaving Terrace, Highway 16 is in good condition westbound although the few straightaways are interrupted by some amazing 70-degree zigzags as the highway crosses the railroad tracks. The highway along the Skeena River is spectacular, with waterfalls cascading down the steep rock faces.

PG 359.3 (578.2 km) **PR 88.4** (143.3 km) KITSUMKALUM. Grocery store and Native craft centre. House of Sim-oi-Ghets handles only authentic arts and crafts such as totem poles, leather goods and local carvings.

This is also the **junction** with West Kalum Forest Service Road, which leads north to **Kitsumkalum Provincial Park** (15 miles/24 km), with 20 campsites, and to Red Sand Demonstration Forest, with 14 campsites. West Kalum Road junctions with the Nisga'a Highway.   ▲

PG 359.7 (578.8 km) **PR 88** (142.7 km) Turnout to south.

PG 360 (579.4 km) **PR 87.7** (142.1 km) Paved turnout to south.

PG 363.1 (584.4 km) **PR 84.6** (137 km) Zimacord Bridge.

PG 366.1 (589.2 km) **PR 81.6** (132.1 km) Turnout to south.

PG 368.7 (589.2 km) **PR 79** (127.9 km) Delta Creek.

PG 371.3 (597.5 km) **PR 76.4** (123.7 km) Shames River.

PG 371.4 (597.7 km) **PR 76.3** (123.5 km) Shames Mountain Ski Area.

PG 377.2 (607.1 km) **PR 70.5** (113.8 km) Rest area on left westbound with picnic tables, toilets and water pump.

PG 378.2 (608.7 km) **PR 69.5** (112.4 km) Exstew River.

PG 383 (616.4 km) **PR 64.7** (104.9 km) CAUTION! Highway turns sharply across railroad tracks.

PG 385.3 (620.1 km) **PR 62.4** (100.9 km) CAUTION: Carwash Rock overhangs highway. Water cascades down mountain and onto highway during heavy rains.

PG 385.8 (620.8 km) **PR 61.9** (100.2 km) Sharp curves and falling rocks approximately next mile westbound. CAUTION: Slow down for sharp curve and steep grade.

PG 389.6 (627 km) **PR 58.1** (94 km) **Exchamsiks River Provincial Park**; 20 campsites and 20 picnic sites among old-growth Sitka spruce. Open May to October, camping fee, water and pit toilets. Good salmon fishing in Exchamsiks River. Access to Gitnadoix River canoeing area across Skeena River.   ◄▲

PG 389.8 (627.3 km) **PR 57.9** (93.7 km) Very pleasant rest area north side of road at west end of Exchamsiks bridge; boat launch on Exchamsiks River. Toilets, tables and litter barrels.

PG 390 (627.7 km) **PR 57.7** (93.3 km) Boat launch.

PG 390.2 (628 km) **PR 57.5** (93 km) CAUTION: Very narrow road next to railway.

PG 391.3 (629.7 km) **PR 56.4** (91.3 km) Conspicuous example of Sitka spruce on north side of highway. Aboriginal people ate

Pictograph on rock face is visible to eastbound traffic at Milepost PG 422.5.
(© Judy Parkin)

its inner bark fresh or dried in cakes, served with berries. As you travel west, the vegetation becomes increasingly influenced by the maritime climate.

PG 394.1 (634.2 km) **PR 53.6** (86.8 km) Kasiks River and view of mountains.

PG 394.8 (635.3 km) **PR 52.9** (85.7 km) Kasiks River; boat launch.

PG 394.9 (635.5 km) **PR 52.8** (85.5 km) River access at the west end of bridge.

PG 396 (637.3 km) **PR 51.7** (83.7 km) Bridal Falls.

PG 399.9 (643.5 km) **PR 47.8** (77.4 km) Boat launch.

PG 401.1 (645.6 km) **PR 46.6** (75.3 km) Hanging Valley and Blackwater Creek.

PG 404.8 (651.4 km) **PR 42.9** (69.5 km) Kwinitsa River bridge and boat launch. No public moorage.

PG 409.3 (658.7 km) **PR 38.4** (62.1 km) Telegraph Point rest area to south on bank of Skeena River; paved turnout with outhouses, picnic tables, litter barrels and water pump. Watch for seals and sea lions in spring and during salmon season.

PG 413.3 (665.1 km) **PR 34.4** (55.7 km) Paved turnout with litter barrel.

PG 415.5 (668.7 km) **PR 32.2** (52.1 km) Basalt Creek rest area to south with picnic tables.

PG 416.3 (669.9 km) **PR 31.4** (50.8 km) Khyex River bridge. Remains of old sawmill visible at west end of bridge to south.

PG 420.2 (676.2 km) **PR 27.5** (44.5 km) Turnout to south.

PG 422.5 (680 km) **PR 25.2** (39.8 km) Watch for pictograph, visible from the road for eastbound traffic only, possibly a boundary marker for Chief Legaic over 150 years ago. It was rediscovered in the early 1950s by Dan Lippett of Prince Rupert.

PG 423.7 (681.8 km) **PR 24** (38 km) Scenic viewpoint to south with litter barrels and historical plaque about Skeena River. Highway leaves Skeena River westbound. Abandoned townsite of Port Essington visible on opposite side of river.

PG 424.6 (683.3 km) **PR 23.1** (37.4 km) Green River Forest Service road.

PG 427.5 (688 km) **PR 20.2** (32.7 km) **Rainbow Summit**, elev. 528 feet/161m.

PG 430 (692 km) **PR 17.7** (28.7 km) Side road south to Rainbow Lake Reservoir; boat launch. The reservoir water is used by the pulp mill on Watson Island.

PG 432.3 (695.9 km) **PR 15.2** (24.7 km) **Prudhomme Lake Provincial Park**; 24

campsites, well water, toilets, firewood, fishing, camping fee.   ◄▲

PG 432.9 (696.6 km) **PR 14.8** (24 km) Turnout to north with litter barrel.

PG 433.4 (697.5 km) **PR 14.3** (23.1 km) Turnoff for **Diana Lake Provincial Park**, 1.5 miles/2.4 km south via single-lane gravel road (use turnouts). Day-use facility. Very pleasant grassy picnic area on lakeshore with 50 picnic tables, kitchen shelter, firewood, grills, wheelchair access, outhouses, water pump and garbage cans. Parking for 229 vehicles. The only freshwater swimming beach in the Prince Rupert area. Fish viewing at Diana Creek on the way into the lake; 2 hiking trails.   ♿

PG 438 (704.9 km) **PR 9.7** (15.6 km) **Junction.** Turnoff for **PORT EDWARD**, pulp mill and historic cannery. The **North Pacific Historic Fishing Village** at Port Edward is open daily in summer. Built in 1889, this is the oldest cannery village on the north coast. Phone (250) 628-3538 for more information.

PG 438.3 (705.3 km) **PR 9.4** (15.2 km) Galloway Rapids rest area to south with litter barrels, picnic tables and visitor information sign. View of Watson Island pulp mill.

PG 439.1 (706.6 km) **PR 8.6** (13.9 km) Miller Bay Hill campground.   ▲

PG 439.5 (707.3 km) **PR 8.2** (13.2 km) Ridley Island access road. Ridley Island is the site of terminals used for the transfer of coal and grain—from, respectively, the North East Coal resource near Dawson Creek and Canada's prairies—to ships

PG 440.2 (708.5 km) **PR 7.5** (12 km) Oliver Lake rest area to south just off highway; picnic tables, grills, firewood. Point of interest sign about bogs.

PG 441.2 (710 km) **PR 6.5** (10.5 km) Shoe Tree or Tree of Lost Soles to east. Tongue-in-cheek local attraction which has grown over years. Worn-out footwear is hung from trees in this local shrine to shoes.

PG 442.3 (711.8 km) **PR 5.4** (8.7 km) Butze Rapids viewpoint.

PG 442.7 (712.4 km) **PR 5** (8.1 km) Prince Rupert industrial park on the outskirts of Prince Rupert. Yellowhead Highway 16 becomes McBride Street as you enter the city centre.

PG 443.4 (713.7 km) **PR 4.2** (6.8 km) Frederick Street junction.

PG 447 (719.3 km) **PR 0.7** (1.2 km) Park Avenue campground.

PG 447.7 (720 km) **PR 0** Ferry terminal

Prince Rupert

for B.C. Ferries and Alaska state ferries. Airport ferry terminal. End of Highway 16.

CAUTION: No gas or services available eastbound between Prince Rupert and Terrace.

Prince Rupert

Located on Kaien Island near the mouth of the Skeena River, 90 miles/ 145 km by air or water (6-hour ferry ride) south of Ketchikan, AK. **Population:** 17,500; area 25,000. **Emergency Services:** Phone 911 for **Police, Ambulance** and **Fire Department.** RCMP, 6th Avenue and McBride Street, non-emergency phone (250) 627-0700. **Hospital,** Prince Rupert Regional, phone (250) 624-2171.

Visitor Information: Visitor Infocentre at 1st Avenue and McBride Street. Open daily in summer, 9 A.M. to 9 P.M. Travel information is also available at the Park Avenue Campground; open daily in summer, 9 A.M. to 8 P.M., and until midnight for B.C. Ferry arrivals. Write Box 669-MP, Prince Rupert, BC V8J 3S1, phone (800) 667-1994 and (250) 624-5637, fax (250) 627-8009.

Elevation: Sea level. **Climate:** Temperate with mild winters. Annual precipitation 95.4 inches. **Radio:** CHTK 560, CBC 860; CJFW-FM 101.9. **Television:** 31 channels, cable. **Newspaper:** *The Prince Rupert Daily News, Prince Rupert This Week* (weekly).

Prince Rupert, "Gateway to Alaska," was surveyed prior to 1905 by the Grand Trunk Pacific Railway (later Canadian National Railways) as the terminus for Canada's second transcontinental railroad.

Twelve thousand miles/19,300 km of survey lines were studied before a final route along the Skeena River was chosen. Some 833 miles/1,340 km had to be blasted from solid rock, 50 men drowned and costs rose to $105,000 a mile (the final cost of $300 million was comparable to Panama Canal construction) before the last spike was driven near Fraser Lake on April 7, 1914. Financial problems continued to plague the company, forcing it to amalgamate to become part of the Canadian National Railways system in 1923.

Charles M. Hays, president of the company, was an enthusiastic promoter of the new terminus, which was named by competition from 12,000 entries. While "Port Rupert" had been submitted by two contestants, "Prince Rupert" (from Miss Eleanor M. Macdonald of Winnipeg) called to mind the dashing soldier–explorer, cousin to Charles II of England and first governor of the Hudson's Bay Co., who had traded on the coast rivers for years. Three first prizes of $250 were awarded and Prince Rupert was officially named in 1906.

Prince Rupert's proposed port and adjacent waters were surveyed by G. Blanchard Dodge of the Hydrographic branch of the Marine Dept. in 1906, and in May the little steamer *Constance* carried settlers from the village of Metlakatla to clear the first ground on Kaien Island. Its post office opened Nov. 23, 1906, and Prince Rupert, with a tent-town population of 200, began an association with communities on the Queen Charlotte Islands, with Stewart served by Union steamships and Canadian Pacific Railways boats, and with Hazelton 200 miles/322 km up the Skeena River on which the stern-wheelers of the Grand Trunk Pacific and the Hudson's Bay Co. traveled.

Incorporated as a city March 10, 1910, Prince Rupert attracted settlers responding to the enthusiasm of Hays, with his dreams of a population of 50,000 and world markets supplied by his railroad. Both the city and the railway suffered a great loss with the death of Charles M. Hays when the *Titanic* went down in April 1912. Even so, work went ahead on the Grand Trunk Pacific. Two years later the first train arrived at Prince Rupert, linking the western port with the rest of Canada. Since then, the city has progressed through 2 world wars and economic ups and downs to its present period of growth and expansion, not only as a busy port but as a visitor centre.

During WWII, more than a million tons of freight and 73,000 people, both military and civilian, passed through Prince Rupert on their way to military operations in Alaska and the South Pacific.

Construction of the pulp operations on Watson Island in 1951 greatly increased the economic and industrial potential of the area. The operations include a pulp mill and a kraft mill.

With the start of the Alaska State Ferry System in 1963, and the British Columbia Ferry System in 1966, Prince Rupert's place as an important visitor centre and terminal

PRINCE RUPERT ADVERTISERS

Aleeda Motel ....Ph. (250) 627-1367
Anchor Inn ....Ph. (888) 627-8522
Boulet's Seafood House....Ph. (250) 624-9309
Coast Prince Rupert
   Hotel, The ....Ph. (800) 663-1144
Cow Bay Bed & Breakfast .Ph. (250) 627-1804
Cow Bay Cafe....................Ph. (250) 627-1212
Cow Bay Gift Galley..........Ph. (250) 627-1808
Crest Motor Hotel ....Ph. (800) 663-8150
Eagle Bluff
   Bed & Breakfast...........Ph. (800) 833-1550
Harbour Air Ltd. ....Ph. (250) 627-1341
Highliner Inn....................Ph. (250) 624-9060
Inn on the Harbour...........Ph. (800) 663-8155
Moby Dick Inn ....Ph. (800) 663-0822
Museum of Northern British
   Columbia, The ....Ph. (250) 624-3207
North Pacific Historic Fishing
   Village ....Ph. (250) 628-3538
Pacific Inn ....Ph. (888) 663-1999
Park Avenue
   Campground ....Ph. (250) 624-5861
Pike Island Guided Tours
   (Laxpa'aws) ....Ph. (250) 628-3201
Prince Rupert
   Visitor Services ....Ph. (800) 667-1994
Rose's Bed & Breakfast .....Ph. (250) 624-5539
Totem Lodge ....Ph. (800) 550-0178

Statue of Charles M. Hays, president of the Grand Trunk Pacific Railway and an enthusiastic promoter of Prince Rupert. Hays went down on the Titanic *in 1912. (© Blake Hanna, staff)*

point for highway, rail and marine transportation was assured.

Prince Rupert is the second major deep-sea port on Canada's west coast, exporting grain, pulp, lumber and other resources to Europe and Asia. Prince Rupert has also become a major coal and grain port with facilities on Ridley Island. Other industries include fishing and fish processing, and the manufacture of forest products.

Prince Rupert is underlaid by muskeg (a deep bog common to Northwest Canada and Alaska) over solid rock, which makes for a difficult foundation to build on. Many sites are economically unfeasible for development as they would require pilings 70 feet/21m or more into the muskeg to provide a firm foundation. Some of the older buildings have sagged slightly as a result of unstable foundations.

ACCOMMODATIONS/VISITOR SERVICES

More than a dozen hotels and motels accommodate the influx of ferry passengers each summer. Many restaurants feature fresh local seafood in season.

Modern supermarkets, shopping centres and a hospital are available. Government liquor store is at the corner of 2nd Avenue and Highway 16. There are 5 main banks, 2 laundromats, the Civic Centre Recreation Complex, 18-hole golf course, racquet centre, bowling alley, a swimming pool and tennis courts.

Park Avenue Campground on Highway 16 in the city has 87 campsites with hookups, unserviced sites, restrooms with hot showers, coin-operated laundry facilities, children's play area and picnic shelters. There are 24 campsites at Prudhomme Lake Provincial Park, 12.5 miles/20.1 km east on Highway 16. A private RV park on McBride

Street offers camper and trailer parking. ▲

TRANSPORTATION

Air: Harbour Air and Inland Air Charter to outlying villages and Queen Charlotte Islands; Canadian Airlines International and Air BC offer daily jet service to Terrace and Vancouver; Taquan Air daily floatplane service in summer to Ketchikan, AK (weekly air services in winter).

Prince Rupert airport is located on Digby Island, which is connected by city-operated ferry to Prince Rupert. There is a small terminal at the airport. The airport ferry leaves from the Fairview dock, next to the Alaska state ferry dock; fare is charged for the 20-minute ride. Check with the Canadian Airlines International office at the downtown Rupert Mall (office is open for passenger check-in only when planes are arriving or departing). Air BC check-in at corner of 6th Street and 1st Avenue West. Bus service to airport from airline check-in areas.

There is a seaplane base at Seal Cove with airline and helicopter charter services.

Ferries: British Columbia Ferry System, Fairview dock, phone (250) 624-9627, provides automobile and passenger service from Prince Rupert to Port Hardy, and between Prince Rupert and Skidegate in the Queen Charlotte Islands.

Alaska Marine Highway System, Fairview dock, phone (250) 627-1744 or (800) 642-0066, provides automobile and passenger service to southeastern Alaska.

NOTE: Vehicle storage is available; inquire at the Information Centre.

Car Rentals: Tilden, phone (250) 624-5318, and Budget, phone (250) 627-7400.

Taxi: Available. Prince Rupert taxi cabs are powered by LNG (liquefied natural gas); phone (250) 624-2185.

Railroad: VIA Rail, in British Columbia, phone (800) 561-8630 (from Manitoba west to British Columbia) or (800) 561-3949 (from the United States).

Bus: PR Transit System, phone (250) 624-3343. Greyhound, phone (250) 624-5090. Farwest Bus Lines, phone (250) 624-6400. Charter sightseeing tours available.

ATTRACTIONS

Take a City Tour. Tour the city's historic and scenic points of interest. Maps are available at the Visitor Infocentre. Scattered throughout the city are 18 large cedar totem poles, each with its own story. Most are reproductions by Native craftsmen of the original Tsimshian (SHIM shian) poles from the mainland and the Haida (HI duh) carvings from the Queen Charlotte Islands. The originals are now in the British Columbia

Provincial Museum in Victoria. Several totem poles may be seen at Service Park, near 3rd Avenue W. and Fulton.

New Museum of Northern British Columbia/Art Gallery, situated in an award-winning Chatham Village Longhouse, displays an outstanding collection of artifacts depicting the settlement history of British Columbia's north coast. Traveling art collections are displayed in the gallery, and works by local artists are available for purchase. Centrally located at 1st Avenue and McBride Street, marked by several tall totem poles. Summer hours 9 A.M. to 8 P.M. Monday through Saturday; 9 A.M. to 5 P.M. Sunday. Winter hours 10 A.M. to 5 P.M. Monday through Saturday. Phone (250) 624-3207. Admission charged.

Pike Island Guided Tours. Knowledge-

able First Nations' guides conduct excursions of Pike Island, site of 3 ancient Tsimshian village sites. Pike Island is accessible by 40-minute water taxi from Prince Rupert Harbour. The walking tour also explores the natural history of this tiny island. Tour tickets may be purchased at the museum, which is also the departure point for the tours. Daily departures at 11 A.M.. in summer. The 5-hour tour includes transportation, lunch and guide services.

Kwinitsa Station Railway Museum. Built in 1911, Kwinitsa Station was one of nearly 400 identical stations along the Grand Trunk Pacific Railway line. In 1985 the station was moved to the Prince Rupert waterfront park. Restored rooms, exhibits and videos tell the story of early Prince Rupert and the role the railroad played in the city's development. Open daily in summer; contact the Museum of British Columbia for more information.

Performing Arts Centre offers both professional and amateur theatre, with productions for children, and classical and contemporary plays presented. The 700-seat facility may be toured in summer; phone (250) 627-8888.

Special Events. Seafest is a 4-day celebration, held the second weekend in June, which includes a parade and water-jousting competition. Indian Culture Days, a 2-day event held during Seafest, features Native food, traditional dance, and arts and crafts. The All Native Basketball Tournament, held in February, is the largest event of its kind in Canada.

The Civic Centre Recreation Complex located on McBride Street (Highway 16) welcomes visitors. Activities include fitness gym, squash, basketball and volleyball. Supervised children's activities during summer. Ice skating and roller skating rinks also located at the centre. Phone (250) 624-6707 for more information.

Swim at Diana Lake. This provincial park, about 13 miles/21 km from downtown on Highway 16, offers the only freshwater swimming in the Prince Rupert area. Picnic tables, kitchen shelter, parking and beach.

Swim at Earl Mah Aquatic Centre, located next to the Civic Centre Recreation Complex. There is an indoor swimming pool, tot pool, weight room, saunas, showers, whirlpool, slides and diving boards. Access for persons with disabilities. Phone (250) 627-7946. Admission charged.

Golf Course includes 18-hole course, resident pro, equipment rental, clubhouse and restaurant. Entrance on 9th Avenue W.

Cannery Tour. North Pacific Historic Fishing Village at Port Edward (turn off Highway 16 at **Milepost PG 438**). Built in 1889, this restored heritage site has dozens of displays on this once-major regional industry. A live performance highlights the history of the cannery. Open daily in summer, closed Mondays and Tuesdays October through April; admission charged. Phone (250) 628-3538.

Watch the Seaplanes. From McBride Street, head north on 6th Avenue E. (watch for signs to seaplane base); drive a few miles to Solly's Pub, then turn right to Seal Cove seaplane base. Visitors can spend a fascinating hour here watching seaplanes loading, taking off and landing. Helicopter and seaplane tours of the area are available at Seal Cove.

Visit the Queen Charlotte Islands. Ferry service is available between Prince Rupert and Skidegate on Graham Island, largest of the 150 islands and islets that form the Queen Charlotte Islands. Located west of Prince Rupert—a 6- to 8-hour ferry ride—Graham Island's paved road system connects Skidegate with Masset, the largest town in the Queen Charlottes. Scheduled flights from Prince Rupert to Sandspit and Masset are available. Island attractions include wild beaches, Haida culture, flora and fauna. For more information, contact the Visitor Infocentre in Queen Charlotte; phone (250) 559-8316.

Go Fishing. Numerous freshwater fishing areas are available near Prince Rupert. For information on bait, locations, regulations and licensing, contact local sporting goods stores or the Visitor Infocentre. This area abounds in all species of salmon, steelhead, crab and shrimp. Public boat launch facility is located at Rushbrook Public Floats at the north end of the waterfront. Public floats are also available at Fairview, past the Alaska state ferry terminal near the breakwater.

Harbour Tours and Fishing Charters are available. For information, contact the Prince Rupert Infocentre at (800) 667-1994.

CASSIAR HIGHWAY ㊲

Connects: Yellowhead Hwy. 16 to Alaska Hwy.   **Length:** 446 miles
Road Surface: 75% paved, 25% gravel   **Season:** Open all year
Highest Summit: Gnat Pass 4,072 feet
Major Attractions: Bear and Salmon glaciers, Stikine River

(See map, page 246)

	Alaska Hwy.	Dease Lake	Iskut	Stewart/Hyder	Yellowhead Hwy.	Watson Lake
Alaska Hwy.		145	196	390	446	14
Dease Lake	145		51	245	301	159
Iskut	196	51		194	250	210
Stewart/Hyder	390	245	194		136	404
Yellowhead Hwy.	446	301	250	136		460
Watson Lake	14	159	210	404	460	

Spectacular Salmon Glacier is located about 17 miles/28 km from Hyder/Stewart on the Salmon Glacier (Granduc) Road. (© Rick Driskell)

The Cassiar Highway junctions with Yellowhead Highway 16 at the Skeena River bridge (**Milepost PG 297.7** in the YELLOWHEAD HIGHWAY 16 section) and travels north to the Stewart, BC–Hyder, AK, access road, Telegraph Creek access road and Dease Lake, ending at the Alaska Highway 13.3 miles/21.4 km west of Watson Lake, YT. Total driving distance is 446.1 miles/718 km.

Travelers driving between Prince George and the junction of the Alaska and Cassiar highways will save 132.4 miles/213 km by taking the Cassiar Highway. (Yellowhead–Cassiar route is 743.8 miles/1,197 km; Alaska Highway route is 876.2 miles/1,410.1 km.) The Cassiar Highway, which was completed in 1972, is a rougher road and has fewer facilities than the Alaska Highway, but it does offer outstanding scenery.

In summer 1998, the highway was paved from **Milepost J 0** to **J 136.1** (Deltaic Creek). From Deltaic Creek to Iskut, there were 31 miles/50 km of gravel and 84 miles/135 km of seal coat. From Iskut north to the Alaska Highway, there were 2 short sections of gravel.

Current road conditions are available by phoning the Highways Maintenance Contractor at (250) 771-3000 (if no answer, contact the District Highways office at 250/771-4511). If north of 60° only call (900) 565-4997 within Canada; (900) 288-4997 in USA; or on the Internet http://www.th.gov.bc.ca/bchighways/.

In 1999, travelers are advised to watch for road construction between Deltaic Creek and Hodder Lake. There will be some gravel work between Dease Lake and Jade City, and seal coating is planned in the Good Hope Lake area in early spring.

On gravel stretches of highway watch for washboard and potholes. Gravel road may be dusty in dry weather and muddy in wet weather. The calcium chloride, which is used for dust control and to stabilize the road base, results in the road surface becoming muddy and rough in wet weather. (Wash calcium chloride off your vehicle as soon as possible.) Seal coat is subject to deterioration from weather and traffic. A few bridges are still single lane. Watch for potholes at bridge ends and slippery bridge decks. There are several 8 percent grades. Drive with your headlights on at all times.

Watch for logging and freight trucks on the highway. *WARNING: Exercise extreme caution when passing or being passed by these trucks; reduce speed and allow trucks adequate clearance.*

The Cassiar also provides access to Hyder and Stewart. These communities are described in detail in this section beginning on page 271. Watch for bears with cubs along the highway (especially in spring); cariboo at Gnat Pass (spring and fall); and Dall sheep south of Good Hope.

Food, gas and lodging are available along the Cassiar Highway, but check the highway log for distances between services. Be sure your vehicle is mechanically sound with good tires. It is a good idea to carry a spare tire and extra fuel, especially in the off-season. In case of emergency, motorists are advised to flag down trucks to radio for help. *NOTE: It is unlawful to camp overnight in turnouts and rest areas unless otherwise posted.* Camp at private campgrounds or in provincial park campgrounds.

According to the Ministry of Highways, litter barrels on the Cassiar Highway are often moved to areas which are being used more frequently. Litter barrels may not be in the same location from season to season. *The MILEPOST*® log indicates their location as of summer 1997.

Cassiar Highway Log

Distance from junction with the Yellowhead Highway (J) is followed by distance from Alaska Highway (AH). Kilometreposts are along the Cassiar Highway every 5 km. Because the posts do not always accurately reflect driving distance, mileages from the Yellowhead Highway 16 junction are based on actual driving distance while the kilometre conversion is based on physical kilometreposts as they occurred in summer 1998.

BC HIGHWAY 37
J 0 AH 446.1 (718 km) Gas station. Bridge across Skeena River from Yellowhead Highway 16 to start of Cassiar Highway.

Junction with Yellowhead Highway 16 (see **Milepost PG 297.7** in the YELLOWHEAD HIGHWAY 16 section).

J 0.2 (0.4 km) **AH 445.9** (717.6 km) Turn east on side road to view totem poles of **GITWANGAK**. The Native reserve of Gitwangak was renamed after sharing the name Kitwanga with the adjacent white settlement. Gitwangak has some of the finest authentic totem poles in the area. Also here is St. Paul's Anglican Church (the original old bell tower standing beside the church dates back to 1893) and one of the last existing Grand Trunk Pacific railway stations.

J 2.5 (4 km) **AH 443.6** (714 km) Kitwanga post office, a private RV park, and a bed and breakfast.

CASSIAR HIGHWAY
Yellowhead Highway Junction to Alaska Highway Junction

© 1999 The MILEPOST®

Map Location

Key to mileage boxes

miles/kilometres
miles/kilometres

from:
J-Yellowhead Hwy. Jct.
AH-Alaska Highway Jct.
M-Meziadin Lake Junction
D-Dease Lake Junction
PG-Prince George
PR-Prince Rupert
WL-Watson Lake
T-Teslin

To Teslin
(see ALASKA
HIGHWAY
section,
page 83)

To Ross River
(see CAMPBELL HIGHWAY section)

Watson Lake
N60°07' W128°48'

YUKON TERRITORY
BRITISH COLUMBIA

To Fort Nelson
(see ALASKA HIGHWAY section, page 83)

J-446.1/723.7km Junction 37
Services CDdGILMPrST

AH-0
J-446/718km
WL-13/21km
T-150/241km

AH-74/118km
J-372/600km

Watson Lake

Baking Powder Creek
Boya Lake

Centreville
Cassiar
Good Hope Lake
Good Hope Lake
McDame Post

J-371.3/602.2km Jade Store & Gift Shop

Vines L.
Cotton Lake

Cottonwood R.
Pine Tree Lake

J-352.8/572.4km Moose Meadows Resort CL

Joe Irwin Lake
Beady Creek

AH-145/234km
D-0
J-301/484km

Dease
Lake

Tasto Creek

CASSIAR

MOUNTAINS

J-292.5/479.1km Dease Lake Lions Tanzilla River Campground C

Dease Lake
N58°27' W130°02'

J-257.7/418.1km Forty Mile Flats CDdGLMr
J-256/415.4km Trappers Souvenirs
J-255.2/410.7km Bear Paw Resort
J-251.8/408.3km Mountain Shadow RV Park & Campground CDLT

Tuya River
Tanzilla River
Stikine River

D-70/113km

Telegraph Creek
N57°54' W131°09'

Morchuea L.
N57°36'
W130°07'

Iskut

AH-196/315km
J-250/403km

D-70.1/112.8km Stikine RiverSong Cafe, Lodge and
General Store GLMST
Stikine RiverSong Boat Tours

Tahltan R.

Glenora

Kluachon L.
Eddontenajon
Lake

J-250.2/405.7km Kluachon Centre GST
J-248.3/402.5km Tenajon Motel & Cafe LMT
J-248.2/402.3km Red Goat Lodge CLT
J-240.7/390.2km Harbour Air Ltd.
Tatogga Lake Resort CDdGrT

Mount Edziza ▲
9,143 ft./2,787m

Tatogga L.

Kinaskan L.

Natadesleen
Lake

J-217.8/353.1km Willow Ridge Resort CDILMr

**Mount Edziza
Provincial Park**

SKEENA MOUNTAINS

**Spatsizi
Wilderness
Provincial
Park**

COAST

Bob
Quinn L.

Ningunsaw R.

Thomas Creek
Devil Creek

Nass River

MOUNTAINS

Iskut River

Snowbank
Creek

Bell II

Principal Route

Paved
Gravel & intermittent
seal coat
Other Roads
Paved
Unpaved
Ferry Routes **Hiking Trails**

Refer to Log for Visitor Facilities

Scale
0   20   Miles
0   20   Kilometres

**Key to Advertiser
Services**
C -Camping
D -Dump Station
d -Diesel
G -Gas (reg., unld.)
I -Ice
L -Lodging
M -Meals
P -Propane
R -Car Repair (major)
r -Car Repair (minor)
S -Store (grocery)
T -Telephone (pay)

Wrangell
N56°05' W132°04'

Alaska State Ferry

ALASKA
BRITISH COLUMBIA

Bell I

AH-336/541km
J-110/179km

Bell-Irving R.

Bowser
Lake

Mount Bell-Irving
5,148 ft./1,569m

J-96.2/156.4km Meziadin Junction

AH-350/563km
M-0
J-96/155km

M-2.8/4.69km Nothing
Fancy CIM

M-40.1/64.4km Bear
Country Gifts

Premier

Salmon River

Meziadin L.

J-85.7/138.9km Meziadin Lake General Store dGIPST

M-36.1/58.1km
Bear River
Trailer Court Ltd. CT

Meziadin
R.

**Prince of
Wales
Island**

N55°04' W131°06'

Ketchikan

Hyder
N55°09' W130°00'

Stewart

M-41/66km
N55°56'
W130°00'

AH-399/643km
J-47/75km

37

Nass Forest
Service Road

Alice Arm

New Aiyansh

**Nisga'a
Highway**

J-2.6/4.2km Kitwanga Auto Service dGPr
J-2.5/4km Cassiar RV Park CT

Kitwancool
N55°06'
W128°04'

Kitwanga

Kitseguecla

Hazelton
New Hazelton
South Hazelton

16

To Prince George
(see YELLOWHEAD
HIGHWAY 16 section, page 219)

Portland Canal

Observatory Inlet

Dragon
L.

Nass

Lava Lake

Kitsumkalum Lake

Skeena River

AH-446/718km
J-0
PG-150/241km
PR-298/479km

UNITED STATES
CANADA

West Kalum
Forest Service
Road

16

Terrace

Dixon Entrance

Prince Rupert

Skeena

To Kitimat
(see YELLOWHEAD HIGHWAY 16 section, page 219)

Visitors can enjoy the artistry of the Kitwancool totem poles. *(© Gladys Blyth)*

Cassiar RV Park. See display ad this section. ▲

J 2.6 (4.2 km) **AH 443.5** (713.8 km) South end of 1.6-mile/2.5-km loop access road which leads to **KITWANGA** (pop. 1,200). **Radio:** CBC 630 AM. **Emergency Services:** Ambulance. Gas station, towing, car wash, a general store and small restaurant. There is a free public campground across from the gas station. (Donations for campground upkeep gratefully accepted at the Kitwanga Tempo service station.) ▲

Kitwanga is at the crossroads of the old upper Skeena "grease trail" trade. The "grease" was eulachon (candlefish) oil, which was a trading staple among tribes of the Coast and Interior. The grease trails are believed to have extended north to the Bering Sea.

A paved turnout with litter barrel and

sign on the Kitwanga access road mark **Kitwanga Fort National Historic Site**, where a wooden fortress and palisade once crowned the large rounded hill here. Seven interpretive panels along the trail up Battle Hill explain the history of the site. Kitwanga Fort was the first major western Canadian Native site commemorated by Parks Canada.

Kitwanga Auto Service. See display ad this section.

J 4 (6.5 km) **AH 442.1** (711.5 km) North end of 1.6-mile/2.6-km loop access road (Kitwanga North Road) to Kitwanga; see description preceding milepost.

J 4.1 (6.6 km) **AH 442** (711.4 km) **Junction** with alternate access route (signed Hazelton–Kitwanga Road) from Hazelton to the Cassiar Highway via the north side of the Skeena River.

J 5 (8 km) **AH 441.1** (710 km) The mountain chain of Seven Sisters is visible to southwest (weather permitting) next 4 miles/6.4 km northbound.

J 12.5 (20.2 km) **AH 433.6** (697.9 km) Turnout with litter barrels to west.

J 12.6 (20.3 km) **AH 433.5** (697.7 km) Highway follows Kitwanga River and former grease trail route.

J 13 (21 km) **AH 433.1** (697.1 km) South

access to **KITWANCOOL** (2 miles/3.3 km from highway) is a small Indian village with many fine old totems, some recently restored. Guided tours of the totem poles may be available; inquire at the Visitor Info-centre. A Native craft shop in the village sells local art. The village of Kitwancool was originally called Gitanyow, meaning place of many people, but was renamed Kitwancool, meaning place of reduced number, after many of its inhabitants were killed in raids.

J 16.1 (26.1 km) **AH 430** (692.1 km) North access to Kitwancool.

J 18.8 (30.4 km) **AH 427.3** (687.8 km) Bridge over Moonlit Creek.

J 18.9 (30.7 km) **AH 427.2** (687.5 km) Rest area north of creek, east of road, with tables, toilets and litter barrels. Road west is the old highway and access to **Kitwanga Lake**. Fishing, camping and boat launch spots on lake. Old highway may be in poor condition; drive carefully. It rejoins the main highway at Mile 24.1. Access to the lake is strictly from the old highway. ⚓▲

J 19.9 (32.2 km) **AH 426.2** (686 km) Access to Kitwanga Lake.

J 21.3 (34.5 km) **AH 424.8** (683.7 km) Good views of Kitwanga Lake to west; old highway visible, below west, winding along lakeshore.

J 26.1 (42.2 km) **AH 420** (676 km) Kit-wancool Forest Road to west.

J 38.8 (62.9 km) **AH 407.3** (655.5 km) **Cranberry River** bridge No. 1. A favorite salmon stream in summer; consult fishing regulations. 🐟

J 46.5 (75.3 km) **AH 399.6** (643.2 km) Paved turnout to west.

J 46.8 (75.9 km) **AH 399.3** (642.6 km)

Junction with the Nass Forest Service Road to New Aiyansh (38.4 miles/61.8 km) and Terrace. *NOTE: This intersection is easy to miss.* See Nisga'a Highway/Nass Road log in the YELLOWHEAD HIGHWAY section.

J 47.1 (76.3 km) **AH 399** (642.2 km) Cranberry River bridge No. 2. Turnout with toilets, tables and litter barrels.

J 53.1 (86 km) **AH 393** (632.6 km) BC Hydro power line crosses and parallels highway. Completed in 1990, this line links Stewart to the BC Hydro power grid. Previously, Stewart's power was generated by diesel fuel.

Entering Kalum Forest District northbound. Watch for signs telling dates of logging activity, and observe patterns of regrowth.

J 58.6 (94.9 km) **AH 387.5** (623.7 km) Kelly Lake rest area at north end of lake on west side of highway, with tables, toilet and litter barrels. First view northbound of Nass River.

J 64.1 (103.8 km) **AH 382** (614.9 km) Paved turnout.

J 65.6 (106.4 km) **AH 380.5** (612.4 km) View of Nass River to west. The Nass River is one of the province's prime producers of sockeye salmon.

J 66.4 (107.7 km) **AH 379.7** (611.1 km) Views northbound (weather permitting) of the Coast Mountains to the west. Cambrian ice field to west.

J 70.1 (113.6 km) **AH 376** (605.2 km) Paved turnout with litter barrel to west.

J 78.7 (127.4 km) **AH 367.4** (591.3 km) Paved turnout with litter barrel.

J 85 (137.8 km) **AH 361.1** (581.2 km) Paved turnout with litter barrels to west.

J 85.7 (138.9 km) **AH 360.4** (580.1 km) Elsworth logging camp and Meziadin Lake General Store (VanDyke Camp Services), open to public; fuel, groceries, dump station, hunting and fishing licenses, emergency phone. Private airstrip.

Meziadin Lake General Store. See display ad this section.

J 87.9 (142.4 km) **AH 358.2** (576.6 km) *CAUTION: 1-lane bridge over Nass River.* Paved rest area with picnic tables, toilets and litter barrel to east at south end of bridge. A plaque at the north end commemorates bridge opening in 1972 that joined roads to form Highway 37. The gorge is almost 400 feet/122m wide; main span of bridge is 1feet/57m. Bridge decking is 130 feet/40m above the riverbed.

J 89.4 (145 km) **AH 356.7** (574.1 km) Tintina Logging Road.

J 93.1 (151 km) **AH 353** (568.1 km) Tintina Creek. Along with Hanna Creek, this stream produces 40 percent of the sockeye salmon spawning in the Meziadin Lake watershed.

J 94.3 (152.8 km) **AH 351.8** (566.3 km) Large gravel turnout to west with litter barrels.

J 94.4 (153 km) **AH 351.7** (566 km) Bridge over Hanna Creek South. Sockeye salmon spawn here in autumn and can be observed from creek banks and bridge deck. It is illegal to fish for or harass these fish. *CAUTION: Watch for bears.*

J 95.6 (155.3 km) **AH 350.5** (564.2 km) **Meziadin** (Mezy-AD-in) **Lake Provincial Park**; 46 campsites (many on lake), drinking water, toilets, wheelchair access, swimming, firewood, bear-proof garbage containers, boat launch. The lake has a significant fish population, including rainbow trout, mountain whitefish and Dolly Varden Fishing is especially good at the mouths of small streams draining into Meziadin Lake. ♿⚓▲

Four species of salmon spawn in the lake. This is one of only 3 areas in the province where salmon spawn in the bays and inlets of a lake. *CAUTION: Watch for bears. The hills around the lake are prime bear habitat.*

J 96.2 (156.4 km) **AH 349.9** (563.1 km) **Meziadin Junction.** Fuel, minor car repair, food, laundry, RV parking and dump station at turnoff for Stewart/Hyder. *NOTE: This junction can be confusing. Choose your route carefully.*

Meziadin Junction. See display ad this section.

HIGHWAY 37A
Distance is measured from Meziadin Lake Junction (M).

M 0 Junction with Cassiar Highway at Milepost J 96.2. Visitor information cabin, status unconfirmed at press time.

M 2.8 (4.6 km) **Nothing Fancy.** RV, camping, lodging and cafe in beautiful lake setting. Extra-long, level, lakeside sites with fantastic view of mountains and lake. Full service with 30-amp electrical. Tenting area. Showers available. Cafe with tasty home cooking. Summer hours 7 A.M.–7 P.M. Open year-round. (250) 636-9171. P.O. Box 42, Stewart, BC V0T 1W0. ▲
[ADVERTISEMENT]

M 7.7 (12.4 km) Surprise Creek bridge.

M 10.1 (16.3 km) Turnout to north with view of hanging glaciers.

M 10.4 (16.7 km) Turnout to south with view of hanging glaciers.

M 11.5 (18.5 km) Windy Point bridge.

M 12.5 (20.1 km) Cornice Creek bridge.

M 13.5 (21.7 km) Strohn Creek bridge.

M 14.4 (23.2 km) Rest area with litter barrels, view of Bear Glacier.

M 15.4 (24.8 km) Turnouts along lake into which **Bear Glacier** calves its icebergs. Watch for falling rock from slopes

above road in spring. Morning light is best for photographing spectacular Bear Glacier. At one time the glacier reached this side of the valley; the old highway can be seen hundreds of feet above the present road.

M 17.5 (28.8 km) Cullen River bridge.

M 19.8 (31.9 km) Huge delta of accumulated avalanche snow. Little shoulder; no stopping.

M 21 (33.8 km) Argyle Creek.

M 22.4 (36.1 km) Narrow, steep-walled Bear River canyon. Watch for rocks on road.

M 23.9 (38.5 km) Turnout with litter barrel to north.

M 28.9 (46.5 km) Turnout with litter barrel to south.

M 29.4 (47.4 km) Bitter Creek bridge.

M 31.8 (51.2 km) Wards Pass cemetery. The straight stretch of road along here is the former railbed from Stewart.

M 36.1 (58.1 km) Bear River bridge and welcome portal to Stewart.

Bear River Trailer Court Ltd. See display ad this section. ▲

M 37.8 (60.8 km) Highway joins main street of Stewart (description follows).

M 40.1 (64.4 km) **U.S.–Canada Border.** Hyder (description follows). *TIME ZONE CHANGE: Stewart observes Pacific*

time, Hyder observes Alaska time.

Bear Country Gifts. See display ad this section.

Stewart, BC–Hyder, AK

Stewart is at the head of Portland Canal on the AK–BC border. **Hyder** is 2.3 miles/3.7 km beyond Stewart. **Population: Stewart** about 1,000; **Hyder** 102. **Emergency Services:** In Stewart, RCMP, phone (250) 636-2233. EMS personnel and Medivac helicopter in Hyder. **Fire Department,** phone (250) 636-2345. **Hospital** and **Ambulance,** Stewart Health Care Facility (3 beds), phone (250) 636-2221.

Visitor Information: Stewart Visitor Infocentre (Box 306, Stewart, BC V0T 1W0), located in Chamber of Commerce/Infocentre Building on 5th Avenue; phone (250) 636-9224 or fax (250) 636-2199. Limited off-season hours. Hyder Information Center and Museum is located in the Hyder Community Association Bldg.

Elevation: Sea level. **Climate:** Maritime, with warm winters and cool rainy summers. Summer temperatures range from 50°F/11°C to 68°F/20°C; winter temperatures range from 25°F/-4°C to

43°F/6°C. Average temperature in January is 27°F/-3°C; in July, 67°F/19°C. Reported record high 89°F/32°C, record low -18°F/-28°C. Slightly less summer rain than other Northwest communities, but heavy snowfall in winter. **Radio:** CFPR 1450, CJFW-FM 92.9, CFMI-FM 101. **Television:** Cable, 15 channels.

Private Aircraft: Stewart airport, on 5th Street; elev. 10 feet/3m; length 3,900 feet/1,189m; asphalt; fuel 80, 100.

Stewart and Hyder are on a spur of the Cassiar Highway, at the head of Portland Canal, a narrow saltwater fjord approximately 90 miles/145 km long. The fjord forms a natural boundary between Alaska and Canada. Stewart has a deep harbour and boasts of being Canada's most northerly ice-free port.

STEWART ADVERTISERS

Bitter Creek Cafe and
  Marmot Bay Trading ....5th Ave.
King Edward Motel/
  Hotel ....5th & Columbia
Rainey Creek Municipal Campground
  & RV Park ....Ph. (250) 636-2537

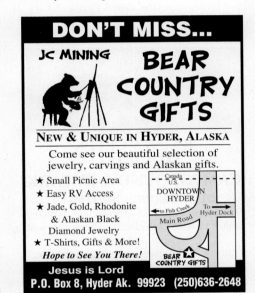

Stewart, BC–Hyder, AK, Access Road Log

Prior to the coming of the white man, Nass River Indians knew the head of Portland Canal as *Skam-A-Kounst,* meaning safe place, probably referring to the place as a retreat from the harassment of the coastal Haidas. The Nass came here annually to hunt birds and pick berries. Little evidence of their presence remains.

In 1896, Captain D.D. Gaillard (after whom the Gaillard Cut in the Panama Canal was later named) explored Portland Canal for the U.S. Army Corps of Engineers. Two years after Gaillard's visit, the first prospectors and settlers arrived. Among them was D.J. Raine, for whom a creek and mountain in the area were named. The Stewart brothers arrived in 1902 and in 1905 Robert M. Stewart, the first postmaster, named the town Stewart. Hyder was first called Portland City. It

was then renamed Hyder, after Canadian mining engineer Frederick B. Hyder, when the U.S. Postal Authority told residents there were already too many cities named Portland.

Gold and silver mining dominated the early economy. Hyder boomed with the discovery of rich silver veins in the upper Salmon River basin in 1917–18. Hundreds of pilings, which supported structures during this boom period, are visible on the tidal flats at Hyder.

Hyder became an access and supply point for the mines, while Stewart served as the centre for Canadian mining activity. Mining ceased in 1956, with the exception of the Granduc copper mine, which operated until 1984. Today the economy is driven by forestry, mining and tourism.

ACCOMMODATIONS/VISITOR SERVICES

Stewart: 3 hotels/motels, 3 restaurants, 1 grocery store, 4 churches, service stations, laundromat, pharmacy, post office, a bank (open Monday, Wednesday and Friday), ATM, liquor store and other shops. Camping at 2 campgrounds/RV parks with washrooms, showers and hookups. ▲

Hyder: 2 groceries, 4 gift shops, a post office, 3 cafes, a Baptist church, 2 motels and 2 bars. Boat launch at salt water, tenting area and RV park with TV reception. Visitor infocentre and museum. Laundromat, public restroom and showers. There is no bank in Hyder. There is an ATM in Stewart. ▲

TRANSPORTATION

Air: Taquan Air; scheduled service from Hyder to Ketchikan. **Bus:** Limousine service to Terrace with connections to Greyhound and airlines. **Ferry:** Service between Ketchikan and Hyder.

IMPORTANT: Check ferry departure times carefully!

ATTRACTIONS

Historic Buildings: In Stewart, the former fire hall at 6th and Columbia streets built in 1910, which now houses the Historical Society Museum; the Empress Hotel (now occupied by a hardware store) on 4th Street; and St. Mark's Church (built in 1910) on 9th Street at Columbia. On the border at Eagle Point is the stone storehouse built by Captain D.D. Gaillard of the U.S. Army Corps of Engineers in 1896. This is the oldest masonry building in Alaska. Originally 4 of these buildings were built to hold exploration supplies. This one was subsequently used as a cobbler shop and jail. Storehouses Nos. 3 and 4 are included on the (U.S.) National Register of Historic Places.

Stewart Historical Society Museum, in the fire hall, has a wildlife exhibit on the main floor and an exhibit of historical items on the top floor. Included is a display on movies filmed here: "Bear Island" (1978), John Carpenter's "The Thing" (1981), and "The Ice Man" (1982).

Hyder's night life is well-known, and has helped Hyder earn the reputation and town motto of "The Friendliest Little Ghost Town in Alaska."

Recreation in Stewart includes winter sports at the indoor skating rink; an outdoor tennis court; ball parks; hiking trails; and a self-guided historical walking tour.

Granduc (Salmon Glacier) Road. Guided sightseeing tours are available or check with the Stewart Info Centre for self-guided auto tours out the Granduc Road. This narrow winding road connected Stewart with mining interests to the north. Extended from Premier Mine to Grand Duc in 1965, the road now offers visitors the opportunity to take in active and abandoned mine sites, such as Granduc, and glaciers, including the spectacular **Salmon Glacier;** the toe of Salmon Glacier is seen at Mile 17.2/27.7 km on the self-guided auto tour from Stewart. Summit Viewpoint at Mile 22.9/37 km provides a spectacular view of the glacier.

Other sights include nearby **Fish Creek Wildlife Viewing Area** at Mile 6/9.6 km. Chum and pink salmon are seen in their spawning colors in Fish Creek from July to September; they ascend the streams and rivers in great numbers to spawn. Visitors may also photograph feeding bald eagles and black bears which are drawn to the streams by the salmon.

International Days. Fourth of July begins July 1 as Stewart and Hyder celebrate Canada Day and Independence Day. Parade and fireworks.

International Rodeo. The Stewart–Hyder International Rodeo is held the second weekend in June.

Charter trips by small boat on Portland Canal and vicinity available for sightseeing and fishing. Flightseeing air tours available.

AREA FISHING: Portland Canal, salmon to 50 lbs., use herring, spring and late fall; coho to 12 lbs. in fall, fly-fishing. *(NOTE: Alaska or British Columbia fishing license required, depending on whether you fish U.S. or Canadian waters in Portland Canal.)* Excellent fishing for salmon and Dolly Varden at mouth of **Salmon River.** Up the Salmon River road from Hyder,

Fish Creek has Dolly Varden 2 to 3 lbs., use salmon eggs and lures, best in summer. Fish Creek is a spawning ground for some of the world's largest chum salmon, mid-summer to fall; it is illegal to kill chum in fresh water in British Columbia. It is legal to harvest chum from both salt and fresh water in Alaska.

Return to Milepost J 96.2 on the Cassiar Highway

Black bears are not uncommon along the Cassiar Highway. (© Lyn Hancock)

Junction with the access road to Stewart, BC, and Hyder, AK. See the STEWART, BC–HYDER, AK, ACCESS ROAD this section.

J 97.5 (158.5 km) **AH 348.6** (561.1 km) Travelers will notice large areas of clear-cut along the southern half of the Cassiar Highway. Bark beetle infestation necessitated the harvest of timber along this particular stretch of highway. After logging, it was reforested.

J 100.8 (164.8 km) **AH 345.3** (555.8 km) Hanna Creek North river and bridge. Gravel turnout at north end of bridge on west side of road with litter barrel.

J 104.1 (169.2km) **AH 342** (550.5 km) Large paved turnout to west with litter barrels.

J 116 (189.2 km) **AH 330.1** (531.3 km) **Bell I Crossing** of Bell-Irving River. Rest area at north end of Bell–Irving bridge with picnic tables, pit toilets and litter barrels.

J 118.2 (192.2 km) **AH 327.9** (527.7 km) Spruce Creek bridge.

J 122.8 (198.9 km) **AH 323.3** (520.3 km) Bell–Irving River parallels highway.

J 125.1 (202.5 km) **AH 321** (516.7 km) Cousins Creek.

J 126.7 (205.2 km) **AH 319.4** (514.1 km) Ritchie Creek bridge, wooden-decked, slippery when wet.

J 130.4 (211.2 km) **AH 315.7** (508.1 km) Taft Creek bridge, wooden-decked, slippery when wet.

J 136.1 (220.4 km) **AH 310** (499 km) **Deltaic Creek**. Pavement ends, gravel begins, northbound. *NOTE: Watch for road construction north to Hodder Lake in summer 1999.*

J 141.5 (229.2 km) **AH 304.6** (490.3 km) Glacier Creek.

J 142 (230 km) **AH 304.1** (489.5 km) Seal coat begins, gravel ends northbound.

J 143.6 (232.7 km) **AH 302.5** (486.8 km) Skowill Creek Bridge.

J 145.1 (235 km) **AH 301** (484.5 km) Large gravel turnout with litter barrels.

J 148.1 (239.8 km) **AH 298** (479.7 km) Oweegee Creek.

J 152.1 (246.2 km) **AH 294** (473.2 km) Provincial rest area by **Hodder Lake**; information kiosk, tables, litter barrels, pit toilets, cartop boat launch. Fly or troll for small rainbows.

J 153.6 (248.8 km) **AH 292.5** (470.7 km) **Bell II Crossing**; food, gas, diesel, propane, pay phone and lodging just south of second crossing (northbound) of Bell-Irving River.

J 153.8 (249.3 km) **AH 292.3** (470.5 km) Bridge crosses Bell–Irving River.

J 156.8 (254.2 km) **AH 289.3** (465.6 km) Large gravel turnout with litter barrel.

J 159.2 (258.1 km) **AH 286.9** (461.7 km) Snowbank Creek.

J 161.2 (261.1 km) **AH 284.9** (458.6 km) Avalanche area: No stopping in winter or spring. Avalanche chutes are visible on slopes to west in summer. Highway serves as emergency airstrip. Watch for aircraft landing or taking off; keep to side of road!

J 161.6 (261.8 km) **AH 284.5** (457.9 km) Redflat Creek.

J 164.1 (266 km) **AH 282** (453.8 km) Revision Creek.

J 165.1 (267.6 km) **AH 281** (452.2 km) Fan Creek.

J 167.3 (271 km) **AH 278.8** (448.7 km) Avalanche area. No stopping.

J 168.7 (273.2 km) **AH 277.4** (446.5 km) Turnout with litter barrels to east overlooking large moose pasture, beaver lodge.

J 169.6 (274.9 km) **AH 276.5** (445 km) **Ningunsaw Pass** (elev. 1,530 feet/466m). Nass–Stikine water divide; turnout with litter

barrels to west beside **Ningunsaw River**. Mountain whitefish and Dolly Varden. The highway parallels the Ningunsaw northbound. Watch for fallen rock on road through the canyon. The Ningunsaw is a tributary of the Stikine watershed.

J 169.9 (275.4 km) **AH 276.2** (444.5 km) Beaverpond Creek Bridge.

J 170.3 (276 km) **AH 275.8** (443.9 km) Liz Creek Bridge.

J 172.7 (279.9 km) **AH 273.4** (440 km) Alger Creek. The massive piles of logs and debris in this creek are from a 1989 avalanche. Avalanche chutes visible to west.

J 173 (280.3 km) **AH 273.1** (439.5 km) Large gravel turnout to east with litter barrel.

J 174.8 (283.2 km) **AH 271.3** (436.7 km) Bend Creek.

J 175.6 (284.5 km) **AH 270.5** (435.4 km) Gamma Creek.

J 176.9 (286.9 km) **AH 269.2** (433.2 km) Ogilvie Creek.

J 177.8 (288.2 km) **AH 268.3** (431.9 km) Point of interest sign about Yukon Telegraph line. The 1,900-mile/3,057-km Dominion Telegraph line linked Dawson City with Vancouver. Built from 1899–1901, the line was a route for prospectors and trappers headed to Atlin, BC; it was replaced by radio in the 1930s.

J 178 (288.6 km) **AH 268.1** (431.5 km) Echo Lake. Flooded telegraph cabins are visible in the lake below. Good view of Coast Mountains to west. Spectacular cliffs seen to the east are part of the Skeena Mountains (Bowser Basin).

J 181 (293.7 km) **AH 265.1** (426.6 km) Bob Quinn Forest Service Road, under construction as the Iskut Mining Road, will provide year-round access to goldfields west of the Ningunsaw River. The road will follow the Iskut River Valley toward the Stikine River, with a side branch to Eskay Creek gold deposit. *CAUTION: Watch for turning trucks.*

J 181.5 (294.4 km) **AH 264.6** (425.9 km) **Little Bob Quinn Lake**, rainbow and Dolly Varden, summer and fall. Access to Bob Quinn Lake at **Milepost J 183.3**.

J 182.2 (295.3 km) **AH 263.9** (424.7 km) Bob Quinn flight airstrip. This is a staging site for supplies headed for the Stikine/Iskut goldfields. Paved rest area with litter barrels, picnic tables and toilet.

J 183.3 (297 km) **AH 262.8** (423 km) Bob Quinn highway maintenance camp; helicopter base. Emergency assistance. Access to Bob Quinn Lake; toilet, picnic table, cartop boat launch.

J 187 (303.1 km) **AH 259.1** (417 km) Gravel turnout with litter barrels on both sides of road.

J 188.3 (305.2 km) **AH 257.8** (415 km) Old kilometrepost 150, which reflects distance from Meziadin Junction.

J 190.2 (308.4 km) **AH 255.9** (411.8 km) Devil Creek Canyon bridge.

J 191.1 (309.7 km) **AH 255** (410.5 km) Gravel turnout with litter barrel to west.

J 191.6 (310.7 km) **AH 254.5** (409.6 km) Devil Creek Forest Service Road.

J 193.6 (313.9 km) **AH 252.5** (406.4 km) Thomas Creek and Thomas Creek Forest Service Road.

Highway passes through Iskut burn, where fire destroyed 78,000 acres in 1958. This is also British Columbia's largest huckleberry patch.

Northbound, the vegetation begins to change to northern boreal white and black spruce. This zone has cold, long winters and low forest productivity. Look for trembling aspen and lodgepole pine.

Southbound, the vegetation changes to become part of the interior cedar–hemlock zone. Cool wet winters and long dry summers produce a variety of tree species including western hemlock and red cedar, hybrid white spruce and subalpine fir.

CAUTION: Watch for turning trucks.

J 196.3 (318.1 km) **AH 249.8** (402 km) Large gravel turnout with litter barrel to west.

J 197.3 (319.6 km) **AH 248.8** (400.5 km) Slate Creek.

J 198.4 (321.5 km) **AH 247.7** (398.6 km) Gravel turnout with litter barrels to east.

J 199 (322.6 km) **AH 247.1** (397.7 km) Brake-check pullout.

J 199.7 (323.7 km) **AH 246.4** (396.6 km) Durham Creek.

J 203.7 (330.2 km) **AH 242.4** (390.1 km) Gravel begins, seal coat ends northbound.

J 204 (330.6 km) **AH 242.1** (389.7 km) Gravel turnout with litter barrels to west.

J 205.1 (332.4 km) **AH 241** (387.9 km) Single-lane bridge crosses Burrage River, northbound traffic yields. Note the rock pinnacle upstream to east.

J 205.5 (333 km) **AH 240.6** (387.2 km) Iskut River to west.

J 206.8 (335 km) **AH 239.3** (385.2 km) Gravel turnout to west.

J 207.8 (336.6 km) **AH 238.3** (383.6 km) Emergency airstrip crosses road; no stopping, watch for aircraft.

J 213 (345.4 km) **AH 233.1** (375.1 km) Rest area by Eastman Creek; picnic tables, outhouses, litter barrels, and information sign with map and list of services in Iskut Lakes Recreation Area. The creek was named for George Eastman (of Eastman Kodak fame), who hunted big game in this area before the highway was built.

J 216 (350.2 km) **AH 230.1** (370.3 km) Slow down for 1-lane bridge across **Rescue Creek**, northbound traffic yields. *NOTE: New 2-lane bridge planned for spring 1999.*

J 217.8 (353.1 km) **AH 228.3** (367.4 km) **Willow Ridge Resort**. See display ad this section. ▲

J 217.9 (353.2 km) **AH 228.2** (367.2 km) New (1998) 2-lane bridge over Willow Creek.

J 218.3 (353.9 km) **AH 227.8** (366.6 km) Willow Creek Forest Service Road. *CAUTION: Watch for turning trucks.*

J 219.9 (356.6 km) **AH 226.2** (364 km) Gravel turnout with litter barrels to east.

J 220.6 (357.7 km) **AH 225.5** (362.9 km) Natadesleen Lake trailhead to west; toilets and litter barrel. Hike 0.6 mile/1 km west to lake.

J 222.6 (360.9 km) **AH 223.5** (359.7 km) Gravel turnout to west.

J 223.9 (362.9 km) **AH 222.2** (357.7 km) Snapper Creek.

J 225.1 (365 km) **AH 221** (355.7 km) Entrance to Kinaskan campground with 50 sites, outhouses, firewood, picnic and day-use area, wheelchair access, swimming, 2 hiking trails, drinking water and boat launch on **Kinaskan Lake**; rainbow fishing, July and August. Start of 15-mile/24.1-km hiking trail to Mowdade Lake in Mount Edziza Provincial Park. ৬ ▸▲

J 230.1 (373.1 km) **AH 216** (347.6 km) Turnout with litter barrel and view of Kinaskan Lake to west.

J 231.1 (374.6 km) **AH 215** (346.1 km) Small lake to east.

J 233.1 (377.9 km) **AH 213** (342.8 km) Gravel turnout with litter barrels to east.

J 233.4 (378.4 km) **AH 212.7** (342.3 km)

Todagin Creek 1-lane bridge, northbound traffic yields. *NOTE: New 2-lane bridge proposed for 1999.*

J 239.4 (388.1 km) **AH 206.7** (332.7 km) Gravel turnout to west.

J 240.7 (390.2 km) **AH 205.4** (330.6 km) Resort with gas, diesel, food, lodging, camping and air charter service.

Harbour Air Ltd. See display ad this section.

Tatogga Lake Resort. See display ad this section.

J 241.3 (391.1 km) **AH 204.8** (329.7 km) Coyote Creek.

J 241.9 (392.1 km) **AH 204.2** (328.7 km) **Ealue Lake** (EE-lu-eh) turnoff. Small B.C. Forest Service recreation area, 7.5 miles/12 km off highway on gravel access road. Rustic sites, picnic tables, rock fire rings (bring own firewood), user-maintained, no fee. ▲

J 244.5 (396.4 km) **AH 201.6** (324.5 km) Turnout with litter barrel.

J 244.6 (396.6 km) **AH 201.5** (324.3 km) Spatsizi trailhead to east. Turnout with litter barrel beside **Eddontenajon Lake** (Ed-don-TEN-ajon). It is unlawful to camp overnight at turnouts. People drink from the lake; be careful not to contaminate it. Use dump stations. Breakup in late May; freezeup early Nov. Rainbow fishing July and August. 🐟

J 248.2 (402.3 km) **AH 197.9** (318.6 km) **Red Goat Lodge**. Lovely treed lakeshore setting with power and water hookups for RVs.

Bed and Breakfast with unparalleled reputation. Coin showers, laundry, phone. Canoe and rowboat rentals. Fishing is excellent from shore. Choose Red Goat for a special vacation experience. AAA approved and undoubtedly one of the finest facilities on Highway 37. Open year-round. Your hosts, Jacquie and Mitch. Phone/fax (250) 234-3261. [ADVERTISEMENT] ▲

J 248.3 (402.5 km) AH 197.8 (318.4 km)

Tenajon Motel & Cafe. See display ad this section.

J 250 (405.4 km) AH 196.1 (315.6 km) Zetu Creek. B.C. Hydro generating plant, supplies power for Iskut area.

J 250.2 (405.7 km) AH 195.9 (315.3 km) ISKUT (pop. 300). Clinic: Phone (250) 234-3511. Small Tahltan Native community with post office in the Kluachon Centre on the highway, grocery store, public phone, motel and gas station. Quality leather goods available locally. Camping and cabins available at local lodges and guest ranches. Horse trips, canoe rentals and river rafting may be available; inquire at local lodges and resorts. ▲

Kluachon Centre. See display ad this section.

Private Aircraft: Eddontenajon airstrip, 0.6 mile/1 km north of Iskut; elev. 3,100 feet/945m; length 3,000 feet/914m; gravel; fuel available at Trans-Provincial Airlines base south on Eddontenajon Lake.

J 251.8 (408.3 km) AH 194.3 (312.7 km) **Mountain Shadow RV Park & Campground.** Quiet, secluded, park-like setting with spectacular mountain vistas and lake views. Away from highway noise for a restful stopover or extended stay. Short nature walk

to Kluachon Lake with excellent fishing. Wilderness trails, bird and wildlife viewing. A unique and breathtaking wilderness setting. [ADVERTISEMENT] ▲

J 255.2 (410.7 km) AH 190.9 (307.2 km) **Bear Paw Resort.** See display ad this section.

J 256 (415.4 km) AH 190.1 (306 km) **Trapper's Souvenirs.** See display ad this section.

J 257.6 (418 km) AH 188.5 (303.4 km) Tsaybahe Creek. Watch for beaver lodges which are visible from the highway.

J 257.7 (418.1 km) AH 188.4 (303.3 km) **Forty Mile Flats.** See display ad this section. ▲

J 260.6 (423 km) AH 185.5 (298.5 km) Turnout with litter barrels to west. From here the dormant volcano of **Mount Edziza** (elev. 9,143 feet/2,787m) and its adjunct cinder cone can be seen to the southwest. The park, not accessible by road, is a rugged wilderness with a glacier, cinder cones, craters and lava flows. Panoramic view of Skeena and Cassiar mountains for next several miles northbound. Information signs.

J 261.8 (424.9 km) AH 184.3 (296.6 km) Turnoff to Morchuea Lake B.C. Forest Service campsite. Rustic, some tables, rock fire rings (bring firewood), no fee. ▲

J 264 (428.4 km) AH 182.1 (293.1 km) Entering Stikine River Recreation Area.

J 266.3 (432.1 km) AH 179.8 (289.4 km) Steep grade. Winding road next 1.2 miles/2 km northbound.

J 267.2 (433.6 km) AH 178.9 (287.9 km) Hairpin turn: Keep to right. Highway descends to Stikine River in switchbacks.

J 269 (436.6 km) AH 177.1 (285 km) Turnout with litter barrels and toilets to south. Tourist map and services directory for area located here.

J 269.5 (437.3 km) AH 176.6 (284.3 km) Stikine River bridge. Turnout at north end of bridge.

J 271.3 (440.2 km) AH 174.8 (281.4 km) Turnout to east with litter barrel.

J 273.4 (443.6 km) AH 172.7 (278 km) Leaving Stikine River Recreation Area northbound.

J 277.3 (450 km) AH 168.8 (271.6 km) Turnout on **Upper Gnat Lake**; tables, toilets, litter barrels. Long scar across Gnat Pass valley to east is grading preparation for B.C. Railway's proposed Dease Lake extension from Prince George. Construction was halted in 1977. Grade is visible for several miles northbound.

J 279 (452.7 km) AH 167.1 (268.9 km) Large gravel turnout with litter barrel to east at Tees Creek.

J 282 (457.6 km) AH 164.1 (264.1 km) Gravel turnout with litter barrel to east.

J 283.9 (460.7 km) AH 162.2 (261.1 km) Gravel turnout to east.

J 284.2 (461.3 km) AH 161.9 (260.5 km) Upper Gnat Rest Area.

J 284.5 (461.7 km) AH 161.6 (260.1 km) Wilderness trail rides.

J 285.8 (463.8 km) AH 160.3 (258 km) Turnout overlooking **Lower Gnat Lake**, abundant rainbow. ⇤

J 287.9 (467.1 km) AH 158.2 (254.7 km) Turnout with litter barrel.

J 290.6 (467.7 km) AH 155.5 (250.2 km) **Gnat Pass Summit**, elev. 4,072 feet/1,241m. Watch for cariboo in spring.

J 291.7 (473.3 km) AH 154.4 (248.5 km) Steep grade, 8 percent downhill.

J 295.2 (479.1 km) AH 150.9 (242.8 km) **Tanzilla River** bridge. Pleasant rest area with picnic tables and outhouses at north end of bridge beside river. Fishing for grayling to 16 inches, June and July; use flies.

Dease Lake Lions Tanzilla River Campground. 16 natural wooded RV sites plus tenting on Tanzilla River, adjacent to Highway 37. Facilities: Picnic tables, firepits, overnight or day-use, no hookups, non-flush toilets. Fees: $7 per night, $3 per bundle for firewood. Voluntary donation for day-use. ▲

J 296.5 (481.2 km) AH 149.6 (240.7 km) Dalby Creek.

J 298.4 (484.1 km) AH 147.7 (237.8 km) Turnout with litter barrel to west.

J 300.2 (487.1 km) AH 145.9 (234.9 km) Divide (elev. 2,690 feet/820m) between Pacific and Arctic ocean watersheds.

J 300.9 (488.3 km) AH 145.2 (233.7 km) **Dease Lake Junction.** Access west to Dease Lake (description follows) and Telegraph Creek.

Junction with Telegraph Creek Road. See TELEGRAPH CREEK ROAD on page 256.

Stikine River bridge at Milepost J 269.5 Cassiar Highway. (© Rick Driskell)

Dease Lake

Located just west of the Cassiar Highway. **Emergency Services: RCMP** detachment. **Private Aircraft:** Dease Lake airstrip, 1.5 miles/2.4 km south; elev. 2,600 feet/792m; length 6,000 feet/1,829m; asphalt; fuel JP4, 100. **Visitor Information:** Write Dease Lake and Tahltan District Chamber of Commerce, Box 338, Dease Lake, BC V0C 1L0; phone (250) 771-3900.

Dease Lake has motels, gas stations (with regular, unleaded, diesel, propane and minor repairs), food stores, restaurant, a post office, hardware/sporting goods, highway maintenance centre and government offices. Charter flights and regular air service to Terrace and Smithers with interprovincial connections. Information kiosks at south entrance to town. ▲

A Hudson's Bay Co. post was established by Robert Campbell at Dease Lake in 1838, but abandoned a year later. The lake was named in 1834 by John McLeod of the Hudson's Bay Co. for Chief Factor Peter Warren Dease. Laketon, on the west side of the lake (see **Milepost J 327.7**), was a centre for boat building during the Cassiar gold rush of 1872–80. In 1874, William Moore, following an old Indian trail, cut a trail from Telegraph Creek on the Stikine River to the gold rush settlement on Dease Lake. This trail became Telegraph Creek Road, which was used in 1941 to haul supplies for Alaska Highway construction and Watson Lake Airport to Dease Lake. The supplies were then ferried down the Dease River.

Today, Dease Lake is a government centre and supply point for the district. The

community has dubbed itself the "jade capital of the world." Jade is available locally. It is a popular point from which to fly-in, hike-in, or pack-in by horse to Mount Edziza and Spatsizi wilderness parks.

Trapper's Den Gift Shoppe. Quality Canadian and British Columbian gift items ranging from local jade to Native moccasins

and cottage crafts. Come visit the "Trapper" in his "den." Very reasonable jade prices. VISA/MasterCard accepted. Located around the corner from the grocery store, just 200 feet off Highway 37. Box 70, Dease Lake, BC V0C 1L0. (250) 771-3224. [ADVERTISEMENT]

Cassiar Highway Log
(continued)

J 300.9 (488.3 km) AH 145.2 (233.7 km) **Dease Lake Junction.** Access west to Dease Lake and Telegraph Creek.

Junction with Telegraph Creek Road. See TELEGRAPH CREEK ROAD on page 256.

Telegraph Creek Road Log

Built in 1922, this was the first road in the Cassiar area of northern British Columbia. The scenery is remarkable and the town of Telegraph Creek is a picture from the turn of the century. Many of the original buildings remain from the gold rush days.

CAUTION: Telegraph Creek Road has some steep narrow sections and several sets of steep switchbacks; it is not recommended for trailers or large RVs. Car and camper drivers who are familiar with mountain driving should have no difficulty, although some motorists consider it a challenging drive even for the experienced. DRIVE CAREFULLY! Use caution when road is wet or icy. Watch for rocks and mud. There are no visitor facilities en route. Allow a minimum of 2 hours driving time with good conditions. Check road conditions at highway maintenance camp or RCMP office in Dease Lake before starting the 70.1 miles/112.8 km to Telegraph Creek. Phone the Stikine RiverSong Cafe (250) 235-3196 for weather and road conditions.

Distance from Dease Lake junction (D) on the Cassiar Highway is shown.

Historic Telegraph Creek, former head of navigation on the Stikine River.

(© Kathleen Marie Menke, Crystal Images)

D 0 Dease Lake junction, Milepost J 300.9 Cassiar Highway.

D 0.9 (1.4 km) **Junction** with road to Dease Lake. Turn left for Telegraph Creek.

D 1.4 (2.3 km) Entrance to airport.

D 3.1 (5 km) Pavement ends, gravel begins westbound.

D 5 (8 km) Entering Tanzilla Plateau.

D 7.2 (11.6 km) Tatsho Creek (Eightmile).

D 15.9 (25.6 km) 16 Mile Creek.

D 17.1 (27.5 km) Augustchilde Creek, 1-lane bridge.

D 18.8 (30.3 km) 19 Mile Creek.

D 20.2 (32.5 km) 22 Mile Creek. Turnout with litter barrels south.

D 22.4 (36 km) Tanzilla River to south.

D 35.7 (57.5 km) Cariboo Meadows. Entering old burn area for 12 miles/19.3 km.

D 36.7 (59.1 km) Entering **Stikine River Recreation Area**. Tuya River valley viewpoint to north; turnout with litter barrels. Short walk uphill for good views and photographs.

D 37.7 (60.6 km) Approximate halfway point to Telegraph Creek from Dease Lake. Turnout with litter barrels to north. Excellent view of Mount Edziza on clear days.

D 45.5 (73.2 km) *CAUTTION: Begin 18 percent grade as road descends canyon; steep and narrow with switchbacks.*

D 46 (74.1 km) Turnout with litter barrels to south.

D 47.2 (76 km) Tuya River bridge.

D 47.7 (76.8 km) End of burn area.

D 49 (78.9 km) Road makes Y–intersection. Old road to left; keep right for newer section.

D 50.4 (81.1 km) Old road rejoins newly constructed section.

D 50.8 (81.7 km) Golden Bear Mine access road. Private.

D 51.1 (82.2 km) Twenty percent downhill grade for approximately 0.6 mile/1 km. Day's Ranch on left.

D 54.2 (87.3 km) Rest area with table, toilet and litter barrel; overlooks river gorge.

D 55.7 (89.7 km) Road runs through lava beds, on narrow promontory about 150 feet/51m wide, dropping 400 feet/122m on each side to Tahltan and Stikine rivers.

CAUTION: Sudden 180-degree right turn begins steep descent to Tahltan River and Indian fishing camps. Excellent views of the **Grand Canyon of the Stikine** and Tahltan Canyon can be seen by walking a short distance across lava beds to promontory point. Best views of the river canyon are by flightseeing trip. The Stikine River canyon is only 8 feet/2.4 m wide at its narrowest point.

D 56.1 (90.3 km) Sudden 180-degree turn begins 18 percent downhill grade to Tahltan River.

D 56.5 (90.9 km) **Tahltan River** bridge. Turnout with litter barrel south, on north side of bridge. Traditional communal Indian smokehouses adjacent to road at bridge. Smokehouse on north side of bridge is operated by a commercial fisherman; fresh and smoked salmon sold. There is a commercial inland fishery on the Stikine River, one of only a few such licensed operations in Canada.

D 57.5 (92.6 km) Start of very narrow road on ledge rising steeply up the wall of the Stikine Canyon for 3 miles/4.8 km, rising to 400 feet/122m above the river.

D 60 (96.6 km) Ninemile Creek.

D 60.1 (96.7 km) Old **Tahltan** Indian community above road. *Private property: No trespassing!* Former home of Tahltan bear dogs. The Tahltan bear dog, believed to be extinct, was only about a foot high and weighed about 15 pounds. Shorthaired, with oversize ears and shavingbrush tail, the breed was recognized by the Canadian Kennel Club. First seen by explorer Samuel Black in 1824, the dogs were used to hunt bears.

D 61.8 (99.5 km) Eightmile Creek bridge. Spectacular falls into canyon on left below. Opposite the gravel pit at the top of the hill there is a trailhead and parking on the west side of the creek.

D 63.1 (101.5 km) Turnout. Good photos of Stikine Canyon to east.

D 69.1 (111.2 km) Indian community.

Road follows steep winding descent into old town, crossing a deep narrow canyon via a short bridge. Excellent picture spot 0.2 mile/0.3 km from bridge.

Glenora Road junction; 12-mile/19.3-km road leads west to Glenora, site of attempted railroad route to the Yukon and limit of larger riverboat navigation. There are 2 primitive B.C. Forest Service campsites and a full-service private campground on the road to Glenora. Several spur roads lead to the Stikine River and to Native fish camps. ▲

D 70.1 (112.8 km) TELEGRAPH CREEK (pop. 300; elev. 1,100 feet/335m). Former head of navigation on the Stikine and once a telegraph communication terminal. During the gold rush, an estimated 5,000 stampeders set off from Telegraph Creek to attempt the Stikine–Teslin Trail to the goldfields in Atlin and the Klondike.

There are a cafe, lodge, general store, post office, and a public school and nursing station here. Gas, minor auto and tire repair are available. Stikine River trips and charter flights are available. Anglican church services held weekly; Roman Catholic services held every-other week.

Residents make their living fishing commercially for salmon, doing local construction work and guiding visitors on hunting, fishing and river trips. Telegraph Creek is becoming a jumping-off point for wilderness hikers headed for Mount Edziza Provincial Park.

The scenic view along the main street bordering the river has scarcely changed since gold rush days. The 1898 Hudson's Bay Co. post, which now houses the River-Song Cafe, is a recognized Heritage Building. Historic St. Aidan's Church (Anglican) and several other buildings pre-dating 1930 are also located here.

Stikine RiverSong Cafe, Lodge & General Store. Awaken to the fresh song of the Stikine River. Located on the banks of the great river, the RiverSong offers accommodation in a renovated, historic (1898) Hudson's Bay Post. Great food including fresh home-baked bread and pies, sockeye salmon, comfortable rooms plus gifts, groceries and gas. Rooms include shared bath, sitting room and kitchen. Continental Breakfasts available June 1 through Labour Day. Fresh frozen sockeye salmon available. Reservations recommended. Phone (250) 235-3196 or message/fax (250) 235-3194. [ADVERTISEMENT]

Stikine RiverSong Boat Tours. Tour the historic Stikine River route to the Klondike in the comfort of our enclosed riverboat. You are guaranteed to find the scenery spectacular as you motor/float down the great river. Pass through the Coast Mountains, glacier country and Stikine LaConte Wilderness Area on your way to the Pacific Ocean at Wrangell, Alaska. One hour, half day, day trips and overnight camping trips. Information and reservations: (250) 235-3196 or message/fax (250) 235-3194. [ADVERTISEMENT]

**Return to Milepost J 300.9
Cassiar Highway**

J 301.7 (489.6 km) AH 144.4 (232.4 km) Hotel Creek.

J 308.8 (501.3 km) AH 137.3 (220.9 km) Turnout with litter barrel to west.

J 309.6 (502.5 km) AH 136.5 (219.7 km) Serpentine Creek.

J 313.5 (508.7 km) AH 132.6 (213.5 km) Gravel turnout to west with litter barrel.

J 314.1 (509.8 km) AH 132 (212.4 km) Good views of Dease Lake, limited access to lake shore.

J 315.7 (512.3 km) AH 130.4 (209.9 km) Gravel turnout to west.

J 316.3 (513.3 km) AH 129.8 (208.9 km) Halfmoon Creek.

J 318.8 (517.4 km) AH 127.3 (204.9 km) Rabid Grizzly rest area with picnic tables, travel information signs, litter barrels and outhouses. View of Dease Lake.

J 322.1 (522.8 km) AH 124 (199.5 km) Gravel turnout to west.

J 324.2 (526.1 km) AH 121.9 (196.2 km) Black Creek.

J 326.3 (529.5 km) AH 119.8 (192.8 km) Sawmill Point Recreation Site to west; side road leads to **Dease Lake** for fishing. Lake trout to 30 lbs., use spoons, plugs, spinners, June to October, deep trolling in summer, spin casting in fall. ◂━▸

J 327.2 (531.2 km) AH 118.9 (191.4 km) Dorothy Creek.

J 327.7 (532 km) AH 118.4 (190.5 km) The site of the ghost town **Laketon** lies across the lake at the mouth of Dease Creek. Laketon was the administrative centre for the district during the Cassiar gold rush (1872–80). Boat building was a major activity along the lake during the gold rush years, with miners heading up various creeks and rivers off the lake in search of gold. Today's miners ford the lake when the water is low to reach claims on the northwest side.

J 330.2 (535.9 km) AH 115.9 (186.5 km) Beady Creek. Entering the Cassiar Mountains northbound.

J 333.5 (541.1 km) AH 112.6 (181.3 km) Turnout to west with litter barrels.

J 333.8 (541.7 km) AH 112.3 (180.7 km) Turnout with litter barrel to west. **Dease River** parallels the highway. Grayling to 17 inches; Dolly Varden and lake trout to 15 lbs.; northern pike 8 to 10 lbs., May through September. ◂━▸

Marshy areas to west; good moose pasture. Watch for wildlife, especially at dawn and dusk.

J 334.4 (542.7 km) AH 111.7 (179.7 km) Packer Tom Creek, named for a well-known Indian who lived in this area.

J 336.1 (545.4 km) AH 110 (177 km) Elbow Lake.

J 342 (554.7 km) AH 104.1 (167.5 km) Pyramid Creek.

J 342.4 (555.6 km) AH 103.7 (166.9 km) Dease River 2-lane concrete bridge.

J 343.9 (558 km) AH 102.2 (164.5 km) Beale Creek.

J 350.9 (563.4 km) AH 95.2 (153.2 km) Turnout beside **Pine Tree Lake**. Good grayling and lake char fishing. ◂━▸

J 351 (569.5 km) AH 95.1 (153.1 km) Burn area. An abandoned campfire started the fire in July 1982.

J 352.8 (572.4 km) AH 93.3 (150.2 km) **Moose Meadows**. Ideal for nature lovers. Tranquil setting on Cotton Lake and Dease River. Log cabins and many sites right on the lake. Enjoy the scenery and the evening cry of the loons. Potential wildlife may include beaver, moose, mountain goats and a variety of birds. Dry sites. Hot showers. Drinking

Elaborate cache at Moose Meadows.

(© Blake Hanna, staff)

water. Pit toilets. Extra-long level pull-throughs. Covered tenting sites. Group sites. RV wash. Boat launch. Fishing. Canoe Adventure packages available. Canoe rentals and shuttles. Trips from 6 to 180 miles. Emergency phone. Reasonable rates. Box 299, Dease Lake, BC V0C 1L0. Radio phone (250) N416219. Chicken Neck Channel. Voice call Whitehorse operator. [ADVERTISEMENT] ▲

J 353.7 (573.9 km) AH 92.4 (148.7 km) Gravel turnout with litter barrels to east. Views of **Needlenose Mountain** southbound.

J 357.9 (580.9 km) AH 88.2 (141.9 km) **Cottonwood River** bridge; rest area 0.4 mile/0.6 km west on old highway on south side of river. Fishing for grayling and whitefish. Early summer runs of Dolly Varden. ◂━▸

J 358.7 (582 km) AH 87.4 (140.7 km) Cottonwood River rest area No. 2 is 0.5 mile/0.8 km west on old highway on north side of river.

J 363.6 (589.8 km) AH 82.5 (132.8 km) Turnout to west beside **Simmons Lake**; information kiosk, picnic tables, picnic shelter, toilets, small beach and dock. Fishing for lake trout.

J 365.3 (592.7 km) AH 80.8 (130 km) Road runs on causeway between Twin Lakes.

J 365.8 (593.5 km) AH 80.3 (129.2 km) **Vines Lake**, named for bush pilot Lionel Vines; fishing for lake trout. ◂━▸

J 366.9 (595.3 km) AH 79.2 (127.4 km) Limestone Creek.

J 367.3 (595.9 km) AH 78.8 (126.8 km) Lang Lake and creek. Needlepoint Mountain visible straight ahead southbound.

J 369.8 (599.9 km) AH 76.3 (122.8 km) Cusak gold mine visible on slopes to east. Gold mined on the far side of the mountain is processed in the mill here.

J 370.1 (600.3 km) AH 76 (122.3 km) Side road east leads to McDame Lake.

J 370.9 (601.6 km) AH 75.2 (121 km) Trout Line Creek.

J 371.1 (601.9 km) **AH 75** (120.7 km) **JADE CITY** (pop. 12), named for the jade deposits found to the east of the highway community. The huge jade boulders that visitors can see being cut here are from the Princess Jade Mine, 82 miles/132 km east, one of the largest jade claims in the world.

J 371.3 (602.2 km) **AH 74.8** (120.4 km) **Jade Store & Gift Shop.** World famous jade capital. Extensive selection of raw jade, jade jewellery and carvings crafted from local Cassiar jade. Best jade and jewellery prices in the North. Rock hounds will appreciate the extensive selection of raw Canadian gemstones and jewellery. See display ad this section. Jesus is Lord. [ADVERTISEMENT]

J 372.5 (604.1 km) **AH 73.6** (118.5 km) **Cassiar junction.** Cassiar Road to west leads 9.7 miles/15.6 km to the former Cassiar townsite and Cassiar Asbestos Mine. Continue straight ahead for Alaska Highway.

CASSIAR (pop. 25) was the company town of Cassiar Mining Corp. Much of the world's high-grade chrysotile asbestos came from Cassiar. The mine closed in March 1992, and the site is closed to visitors. It is now the site of a B.C. Chrysotile Corp. reclamation project. No services available.

J 372.7 (604.4 km) **AH 73.4** (118.2 km) Snow Creek.

J 372.8 (605.6 km) **AH 73.3** (117.9 km) Gravel turnout with litter barrel to east.

J 373.5 (606.1 km) **AH 72.6** (116.8 km) Deep Creek.

J 377.4 (612.2 km) **AH 68.7** (110.6 km) No. 3 North Fork Creek.

J 378.4 (613.9 km) **AH 67.7** (108.9 km) No. 2 North Fork Creek. Small gold mining operations may be visible to east.

J 381 (618 km) **AH 65.1** (104.7 km) Historic plaque about Cassiar gold.

CENTREVILLE (pop. 2; elev. 2,600 feet/792m), a former gold rush town of 3,000. The only evidence of Centreville along the highway today is the town name painted on an old piece of mining equipment parked on the east side of the road. Centreville was founded and named by miners for its central location between Sylvester's Landing (later McDame Post) at the junction of McDame Creek with the Dease River, and Quartzrock Creek, the upstream limit of pay gravel on McDame Creek. A miner named Alfred Freeman washed out the biggest all-gold (no quartz) nugget ever found in British Columbia on a claim near Centreville in 1877; it weighed 72 ounces. Active mining in area.

J 381.1 (618.2 km) **AH 65** (104.6 km) No. 1 North Fork Creek.

J 383 (621.3 km) **AH 63.1** (101.5 km) Watch for Dall sheep in this area.

J 385.2 (625 km) **AH 60.9** (98 km) **GOOD HOPE LAKE** (pop. 100), Indian village with limited services; fuel may be available.

Turn east on Bush Road and drive 9 miles/14.5 km for **McDAME POST**, an early Hudson's Bay post, at the **confluence of Dease River and McDame Creek.** Good fishing and hunting here.

J 386.9 (627.7 km) **AH 59.2** (95.3 km) Turnout to east alongside Aeroplane Lake.

J 387.7 (629 km) **AH 58.4** (94 km) Dry Creek. Old cabin.

J 389.5 (631.9 km) **AH 56.6** (91.1 km) Mud Lake to east.

J 393.6 (638.5 km) **AH 52.5** (84.5 km) Turnout with litter barrels at entrance to **Boya Lake Provincial Park.** The park is 1.6 miles/2.6 km east of highway; 45 campsites, picnic area on lakeshore, boat launch, toilets, wheelchair access, walking trails, drinking water, firewood and swimming. Fishing for lake char, whitefish and burbot. Attendant on duty during summer.

J 393.7 (638.6 km) **AH 52.4** (84.4 km) Turnout. Horseranch Range may be seen on the eastern horizon northbound. These mountains date back to the Cambrian period, or earlier, and are the oldest in northern British Columbia. According to the Canadian Geological Survey, this area contains numerous permatites with crystals of tourmaline, garnet, feldspar, quartz and beryl. Road crosses Baking Powder Creek and then follows Dease River.

J 397.9 (645.4 km) **AH 48.2** (77.6 km) Camp Creek.

J 399.4 (648 km) **AH 46.7** (75.1 km) Beaver Dam Creek.

J 400.3 (649.4 km) **AH 45.8** (73.7 km) Beaver Dam rest area with visitor information sign to west.

J 400.6 (649.8 km) **AH 45.5** (73.3 km) Leaving Cassiar Mountains, entering Yukon Plateau, northbound.

J 402.5 (652.9 km) **AH 43.6** (70.2 km) Baking Powder Creek.

J 410.9 (666.5km) **AH 35.2** (56.7 km) Gravel access road to French Creek B.C.

Forest Service campsite 0.6 miles/1 km from highway. Rustic. Tables, rock fire ring (bring firewood), small boat launch into Dease River, no fee.

J 411.2 (667 km) **AH 34.9** (56.1 km) French Creek 2-lane concrete bridge.

J 417.5 (677.2 km) **AH 28.6** (46.1 km) Twentyeight Mile Creek. Cassiar Mountains rise to south.

J 420.2 (681.8 km) **AH 25.9** (41.6 km) Wheeler Lake to west.

J 422.9 (686.1 km) **AH 23.2** (37.3 km) Blue River Forest Service Road to east.

J 426.3 (691.5 km) **AH 19.8** (31.9 km) Blue River 2-lane concrete bridge.

J 429.7 (697.1 km) **AH 16.4** (26.4 km) Turnout at **Blue Lakes**; litter barrels, picnic tables and fishing for pike and grayling.

J 431.5 (700 km) **AH 14.6** (23.5 km) Mud Hill Creek.

J 436 707.4 km) **AH 10.1** (16.2 km) Old Faddy Forest Service Road.

J 440.1 (714 km) **AH 6** (9.6 km) Turnout with litter barrels beside Cormier Creek.

J 441.3 (718.5 km) **AH 4.8** (7.7 km) High Lake to east.

J 444 (720.3 km) **AH 2.1** (3.4 km) Turnout to west at **BC–YT Border**, 60th parallel. Information sign.

Yukon Territory's flag consists of 3 vertical panels of colour: blue, representing the rivers and lakes; green symbolizing forests; and white signifying snow. The Yukon coat of arms appears on the central panel, framed by 2 stems of fireweed, the territory's floral emblem. The flag was chosen from a design competition sponsored in 1967. Yukon Territory was made a district of Northwest Territories in 1895 and became a separate territory in June 1898, at the height of the Klondike Gold Rush.

NOTE: Drive with headlights on at all times in Yukon Territory.

J 445.3 (722.5 km) **AH 0.8** (1.2 km) **Albert Creek.** Good grayling fishing. Yukon Territory fishing license required.

J 446.1 (723.7 km) **AH 0 Junction** of Cassiar Highway with Alaska Highway. Gas, store, campground and RV park, cafe, souvenirs, laundromat, camp-style motel, saloon, propane, towing and car repair at junction. Turn left for Whitehorse, right for Watson Lake, 13.3 miles/21.4 km southeast. Watson Lake is the nearest major community.

Junction 37 Services. See display ad this section.

Turn to **Milepost DC 626.2** on page 128 in the ALASKA HIGHWAY section for log of Alaska Highway from this junction.

KLONDIKE LOOP

Connects: Alaska Hwy. to Taylor Hwy.   **Length:** 406 miles
Road Surface: Paved to Dawson City; seal coat and gravel to Taylor Highway junction
Season: Hwy. 2 open all year, Hwy. 9 closed in winter
Major Attraction: Dawson City

(See maps, pages 260–261)

	Alaska Hwy. Jct.	Carmacks	Dawson City	Taylor Hwy Jct.	Whitehorse
Alaska Hwy Jct.		103	327	406	10
Carmacks	103		225	303	113
Dawson City	327	225		79	337
Taylor Hwy Jct.	406	303	79		416
Whitehorse	10	113	337	416	

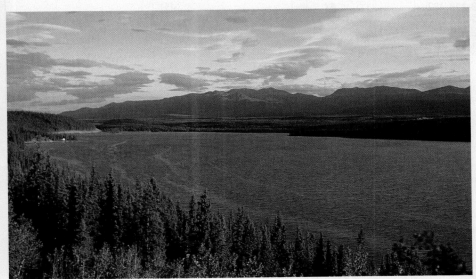

Sunset on Fox Lake. Good view of the lake from turnout at Milepost J 35.2.

(© George Wuerthner)

The "Klondike Loop" refers to the 327-mile/527-km-long stretch of Yukon Highway 2 (the North Klondike Highway, also sometimes called the "Mayo Road"), from its junction with the Alaska Highway north of Whitehorse to Dawson City; the 79-mile/127-km Top of the World Highway (Yukon Highway 9); and the 96 miles/154 kms of the Taylor Highway (Alaska Route 5) that connect with the Alaska Highway near Tok. The North Klondike Highway and Top of the World Highway are logged in this section. The Taylor Highway is logged in the TAYLOR HIGHWAY section following.

Alaska-bound motorists turn off the Alaska Highway north of Whitehorse (**Milepost DC 894.8**); follow the Klondike Highway to Dawson City; ferry from there across the Yukon River; drive west via the Top of the World Highway into Alaska; then take the Taylor Highway south back to the Alaska Highway near Tok (**Milepost DC 1301.7**). Total driving distance is 501 miles/806 km. (Driving distance from Whitehorse to Tok via the Alaska Highway is approximately 396 miles/637 km.)

All of the Klondike Highway between the Alaska Highway junction and Dawson City is asphalt-surfaced. The Top of the World Highway—a truly scenic route—is seal-coated on the Canadian portion with some hills. It is gravel on the U.S. side with some steep grades and winding sections that can be slippery in wet weather. Check with the Dawson City Visitor Centre for current road and weather conditions; phone (867) 993-5566.

The Taylor Highway is a narrow gravel road with some steep, winding sections and washboard (see the TAYLOR HIGHWAY section). Both the Taylor and Top of the World highways are not maintained from mid-October to April and the arrival of snow effectively closes the roads for winter. Yukon Highway 2 is open year-round. *Drive with your headlights on at all times.*

Travelers should be aware that the Top of the World Highway (reached by ferry from Dawson City) may not open until late spring. In heavy traffic, there may be a wait as long as 3 hours for the Yukon River ferry at Dawson City during peak hours. Customs stations are open in summer only, 12 hours a day: 9 A.M. to 9 P.M. (Pacific time), 8 A.M. to 8 P.M. (Alaska time). There are no restrooms, services or currency exchanges available at the border.

The highway between Skagway and the Alaska Highway, sometimes referred to as the South Klondike, is also designated Klondike Highway 2 (see KLONDIKE HIGHWAY 2 section for log of that road).

Kilometreposts along the highway to Dawson City reflect distance from Skagway. Our log's driving distances were measured in miles from the junction of the Alaska Highway to Dawson City by our field editor. These mileages were converted into kilometres with the exception of the kilometre distance following Skagway (**S**). That figure reflects the physical location of the kilometrepost and is not necessarily an accurate conversion of the mileage figure.

The route from Whitehorse to Dawson City began as a trail, used first by Natives, trappers and prospectors, and then by stampeders during the Klondike Gold Rush of 1897–98. Steamships also provided passenger service between Whitehorse and Dawson City. A road was built connecting the Alaska Highway with the United Keno Hill Mine at Mayo in 1950. By 1955, the Mayo Road had been upgraded for automobile traffic and extended to Dawson City. In 1960, the last of 3 steel bridges, crossing the Yukon, Pelly and Stewart rivers, was completed. The only ferry crossing remaining is the Yukon River crossing at Dawson City. Mayo Road (Yukon Highway 11) from Stewart Crossing to Mayo, Elsa and Keno was redesignated the Silver Trail in 1985 (see SILVER TRAIL section for road log).

Emergency Medical Services: On Yukon Highway 2 from **Milepost J 0** to **J 55.6** (Whitehorse to Braeburn Lodge), phone Whitehorse Ambulance toll free 1-667-3333 or RCMP 1-667-3333. From **Milepost J 55.6** to **J 169.4** (Braeburn Lodge to Pelly Crossing), phone Carmacks Medical Emergency (867) 863-4444 or RCMP (867) 863-5555. From **Milepost J 169.4** to **J 242.9** (Pelly Crossing to McQuesten River Lodge), phone Mayo Medical Emergency (867) 996-4444 or RCMP (867) 996-5555. From **Milepost J 242.9** to **J 327.2** and on Yukon Highway 9 from **Milepost D 0** to **D 66.1** (McQuesten River Lodge to Dawson City to Alaska border), phone Dawson City Medical Emergency (867) 993-4444 or RCMP (867) 993-5555. From **Milepost D 66.1** to **D 78.8** (Alaska border to Taylor Highway), phone Tok Area EMS at 911 or (907) 883-5111.

Klondike Loop Log

This section of the log shows distance from junction with the Alaska Highway (J) followed by distance from Dawson City (D) and distance from Skagway (S). Physical kilometreposts show distance from Skagway.

YUKON HIGHWAY 2
J 0 D 327.2 (526.6 km) **S 119.2** (191.8 km) **Junction** with the Alaska Highway

KLONDIKE LOOP
Milepost J 0 to Milepost J 296 (includes Silver Trail)

© 1999 The MILEPOST®
(map continues next page)

OGILVIE MOUNTAINS

Klondike River

Flat Creek

Clear Creek

McQuesten River

Moose Creek

N63°55'
W135°29'
K-69/111km

Elsa

Keno
N63°54' W135°18'
K-69.1/111.2km Keno City Snack Bar

Mt. Haldane
6,032 ft./1,839m
Halfway Lakes

Duncan Creek

Mayo River

Janet Lake

Mayo Lake

Minto Lake
Minto Cr.

K-32/51km

Mayo N63°36' W135°55'
Silver Trail

J-296/476km
D-31/50km
S-415/669km

(2)

J-229.1/368.7km
Moose Creek
Lodge LM

J-214/345km
D-113/182km
S-334/538km
K-0

(11)

Stewart R.

Ethel Lake

Stewart River

Stewart
Crossing

J-213.9/344.2km Stewart Crossing Chevron dGIrST
Whispering Willows RV Park and
Bed & Breakfast CDLMT

Crooked Creek

Stewart River

J-169/273km
D-158/254km
S-289/465km

Willow Creek

J-169.4/272.6km Penny's Place M
Selkirk Gas Bar & Grocery CDdGIPST

Pelly Crossing
N62°50' W136°35'
Von Wilczek
Lakes

Pelly River

Fort Selkirk
N62°46' W137°23'

Yukon
River

Tatlmain
Lake

DAWSON

Minto
N62°35' W136°50'

J-148/238.2km Big River Enterprises
Minto Resorts Ltd. RV Park CDI

RANGE

(2)

Tatchun Lake

Drury Lake

Tatchun River

To Ross River
(see CAMPBELL
HIGHWAY section,
page 287)

Frenchman
Lake

Little Salmon
Lake

Little Salmon River

Yukon
River

(4)

Carmacks
N62°06' W136°19'

J-103/165km
D-225/361km
S-222/357km
RR-241/388km

Twin Lakes

▲ Conglomerate Mountain
3,362 ft./1,025m

J-55.6/89.5km Braeburn Lodge Ltd. CdGLM

Braeburn
Lake

Key to mileage boxes
miles/kilometres
miles/kilometres   from:
J-Junction
D-Dawson City
S-Skagway
K-Klondike Highway
RR-Ross River
HJ-Haines Junction
W-Whitehorse

Map Location

Nordenskiold River

Little
Fox Lake

J-29.8/48km Cranberry Point Bed & Breakfast CL

Fox
Lake

Fox
Creek

Lake
Laberge

Teslin River

Principal Route
Paved   Unpaved
Other Roads
Paved   Unpaved
Ferry Routes   **Hiking Trails**

Refer to Log for Visitor Facilities

Scale
0   10   Miles
0   10   Kilometres

**Key to Advertiser
Services**
C -Camping
D -Dump Station
d -Diesel
G -Gas (reg., unld.)
I -Ice
L -Lodging
M -Meals
P -Propane
R -Car Repair (major)
r -Car Repair (minor)
S -Store (grocery)
T -Telephone (pay)

J-20.4/32.8km Mom's Bakery IMST

Takhini Hot Springs

Takhini River

Yukon
River

(2)

To Haines Junction
(see ALASKA HIGHWAY section, page 83)

(1)

(1)

J-0
D-327/527km
S-119/192km
HJ-90/145km
W-9/14km

To Jake's Corner
(see ALASKA HIGHWAY section, page 83)

Whitehorse

KLONDIKE LOOP
Milepost J 296 to Tetlin Junction, Alaska Highway (includes Taylor Highway)

© 1999 The MILEPOST®

Key to mileage boxes

miles/kilometres
miles/kilometres from:

J-Junction
D-Dawson City
E-Eagle
T-Taylor Hwy. Jct.
TJ-Tetlin Jct.
S-Skagway

Map Location

Key to Advertiser Services

C -Camping
D -Dump Station
d -Diesel
G -Gas (reg., unld.)
I -Ice
L -Lodging
M -Meals
P -Propane
R -Car Repair (major)
r -Car Repair (minor)
S -Store (grocery)
T -Telephone (pay)

Principal Route

Paved — Unpaved
Other Roads
Paved — Unpaved
Ferry Routes **Hiking Trails**

Refer to Log for Visitor Facilities

Scale

0 ___ 20 Miles
0 ___ 20 Kilometres

(Milepost DC 894.8).

J 0.6 (1 km) **D 326.6** (525.6 km) **S 119.8** (192.8 km) Road west leads to McPherson subdivision.

J 1 (1.6 km) **D 326.2** (525 km) **S 120.2** (193.4 km) Ranches, farms and livestock next 20 miles/32 km northbound.

J 2.3 (3.7 km) **D 324.9** (522.9 km) **S 121.5** (195.5 km) Takhini River bridge. The Takhini flows into the Yukon River. The name is Tagish Indian, *tahk* meaning mosquito and *heena* meaning river, according to R. Coutts in *Yukon: Places & Names*.

J 3.8 (6.1 km) **D 323.4** (520.4 km) **S 123** (197.9 km) Gas bar and convenience store at **junction** with Takhini Hot Springs Road. Drive west 6 miles/9.7 km via paved road for **Takhini Hot Springs**; bed and breakfasts,

camping, cafe, trail rides, ski trails in winter. The source of the springs maintains a constant 117°F/47°C temperature and flows at 86 gallons a minute. The hot springs pool averages 100°F/38°C year-round. The water contains no sulfur. The chief minerals present are calcium, magnesium and iron. ▲

Trappers and Indians used these springs around the turn of the century, arriving by way of the Takhini River or the old Dawson Trail. During construction of the Alaska Highway in the early 1940s, the U.S. Army maintained greenhouses in the area and reported remarkable growth regardless of the season.

J 6.7 (10.8 km) **D 320.5** (515.8 km) **S 125.9** (202.6 km) Start odometer test section next 5 km northbound.

J 7 (11.3 km) **D 320.2** (515.3 km) **S 126.2** (203.1 km) Whitehorse rodeo grounds to west. The Yukon Rodeo takes July 9–11, 1999.

J 9.4 (15.1 km) **D 317.8** (511.4 km) **S 128.6** (207 km) Sawmill to west.

J 10.7 (17.2 km) **D 316.5** (509.3 km) **S 129.9** (209 km) Shallow Bay Road.

J 12.7 (20.4 km) **D 314.5** (506.1 km) **S 131.9** (212.2 km) Horse Creek Road leads east to Lower Laberge Indian village and lakeshore cottages. **Horse Creek**; good grayling fishing from road.

J 15.1 (24.3 km) **D 312.1** (502.3 km) **S 134.3** (216.1 km) Access to bed and breakfast, 0.9 miles/1.5 km west.

J 15.8 (25.4 km) **D 311.4** (501.1 km) **S 135** (217.2 km) Microwave site near road.

J 16.8 (27 km) **D 310.4** (499.5 km) **S 136** (219.1 km) Large turnout to west.

J 17.4 (28 km) **D 309.8** (498.6 km) **S 136.6** (220 km) Lake Laberge to east. The Yukon River widens to form this 40-mile-/64-km-long lake. Lake Laberge was made famous by Robert W. Service with the lines: "The Northern Lights have seen queer sights. But the queerest they ever did see, was that night on the marge of Lake Lebarge I cremated Sam McGee," (from his poem "The Cremation of Sam McGee").

J 18.2 (29.3 km) **D 309** (497.3 km) **S 137.4** (221.1 km) Gravel pit turnout to east.

J 20.3 (32.7 km) **D 306.9** (493.9 km) **S 139.5** (224.5 km) Deep Creek.

J 20.4 (32.8 km) **D 306.8** (493.7 km) **S 139.6** (224.6 km) Turnoff for Lake Laberge Yukon government campground. Campground road leads past residential area with a small store, bakery, canoe rentals, emergency phone and message post. The campground is situated 1.8 miles/2.9 km east on Lake Laberge next to Deep Creek (see description following).

Lake Laberge Yukon government campground has 22 RV sites, $8 camping fee, resident campground host, group camping area, kitchen shelter, water, boat launch, and fishing for lake trout, grayling and northern pike. Interpretive panels located lakeside at the campground highlight the 30-mile Heritage River. *CAUTION: Storms can blow up quickly and without warning on Lake Laberge, as on other northern lakes. Canoes and small craft stay to the west side of the lake, where the shoreline offers safe refuges. The east side of the lake is lined with high rocky bluffs, and there are few places to pull out. Small craft should not navigate the middle of the lake.* ▶▲

J 20.9 (33.6 km) **D 306.3** (492.9 km) **S 140.1** (225.5 km) View of Lake Laberge for southbound travelers.

J 21.2 (34.1 km) **D 306** (492.4 km) **S 140.4** (225.9 km) Northbound the highway enters the Miners Range, plateau country of the Yukon, an immense wilderness of forested dome-shaped mountains and high ridges, dotted with lakes and traversed by tributaries of the Yukon River. To the west, Pilot Mountain in the Miners Range (elev. 6,739 feet/2,054m) is visible.

J 22.8 (36.7 km) **D 304.4** (489.9 km) **S 142** (228.5 km) **Fox Creek**; grayling, excellent in June and July. ✦

J 23.5 (37.8 km) **D 303.7** (488.7 km) **S 142.7** (229.8 km) Marker shows distance to Dawson City 486 km.

J 26.9 (43.3 km) **D 300.3** (483.3 km) **S 146.1** (235.1 km) Gravel pit turnout to east.

J 28.8 (46.3 km) **D 298.4** (480.2 km) **S 148** (238.2 km) Highway now follows the east shoreline of Fox Lake northbound.

J 29.4 (47.3 km) **D 297.8** (479.2 km) **S 148.6** (239.1 km) Turnout to west on Fox Lake. Sign reads: "In 1883, U.S. Army Lt. Frederick Schwatka completed a survey of the entire length of the Yukon River. One of many geographical features that he named was Fox Lake, which he called Richthofen Lake, after geographer Freiherr Von Richthofen. Known locally as Fox Lake, the name was adopted in 1957. The Miners Range to the west was named by geologist/explorer George Mercer Dawson in 1887 'for the miners met by us along the river.'"

J 29.8 (48 km) **D 297.4** (478.6 km) **S 149** (239.8 km) **Cranberry Point Bed & Breakfast.** Open year-round. Wonderful old-time northern wilderness experience on beautiful Fox Lake. Sauna, gravity showers, oil lamps

and sanitized outhouses with a view. Wood-stove cooking, full breakfast, other meals arranged. Double guest-room and cabins. Radio phone Whitehorse mobile operator, JJ3-9257 Fox Lake Channel. Km 240 Klondike Hwy., Site 15, #91, Whitehorse, YT Y1A 5W8. [ADVERTISEMENT]

J 34.8 (56 km) **D 292.4** (470.6 km) **S 154** (247.8 km) Turnoff west for **Fox Lake** Yukon government campground; 30 RV and 3 tent-only sites, $8 camping fee, kitchen shelter, drinking water and boat launch. Good fishing for lake trout and burbot from the shore at the campground; excellent grayling year-round. ✦▲

J 35.2 (56.6 km) **D 292** (469.9 km)

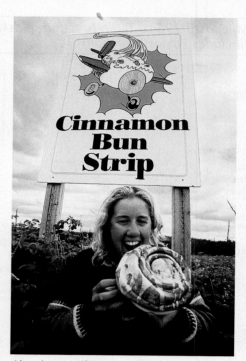

Airstrip at Milepost J 55.6 is named for Braeburn Lodge's cinnamon buns.

(© Lyn Hancock)

S 154.4 (248.5 km) Turnout with view of Fox Lake. Good photo spot.

J 39.8 (64.1 km) **D 287.4** (462.5 km) **S 159** (255.8 km) North end of Fox Lake.

There was a major forest fire in this area in summer 1998; burn areas on both sides of road should have some spectacular fireweed displays in the next couple of years.

J 42 (67.6 km) **D 285.2** (459 km) **S 161.2** (259.4 km) **Little Fox Lake** to west; lake trout 3 to 8 lbs., fish the islands. ✦

J 43.8 (70.5 km) **D 283.4** (456.1 km) **S 163** (262.1 km) Double-ended turnout with litter barrel to west beside Little Fox Lake. Small boat launch.

J 49.5 (79.7 km) **D 277.7** (446.9 km) **S 168.7** (271.5 km) Large turnout to west.

J 50.1 (80.6 km) **D 277.1** (445.9 km) **S 169.3** (272.4 km) First glimpse of Braeburn Lake for northbound travelers.

J 52.5 (84.5 km) **D 274.7** (442.1 km) **S 171.1** (276.3 km) Gravel pit turnout to east. *CAUTION: Watch for elk along highway.*

J 55.6 (89.5 km) **D 271.6** (437.1 km) **S 174.8** (281.5 km) Braeburn Lodge to west; food, gas, lodging and minor car repairs. One Braeburn Lodge cinnamon bun will feed 4 people. The lodge is also home of the 200-mile/320-km "Cinnamon Bun" Dog Sled Race, held the first weekend in February.

Braeburn Lodge. See display ad this section.

Private Aircraft: Braeburn airstrip to east, dubbed Cinnamon Bun Strip; elev. 2,350 feet/716m; length 3,000 feet/914m; dirt strip; wind sock.

J 55.8 (89.8 km) **D 271.4** (436.8 km) **S 175.1** (281.8 km) Side road to Braeburn Lake.

J 66.3 (106.7 km) **D 260.9** (419.9 km) **S 185.5** (298.5 km) Photo stop; pull-through turnout on east side of highway with information sign about **Conglomerate Mountain** (elev. 3,361 feet/1,024m). Sign reads: "The Laberge Series was formed at the leading edge of volcanic mud flows some 185 million years ago (Early Jurassic). These flows solidified into sheets several kilometres long and about 1 km wide and 100m thick. This particular series of sheets stretches from Atlin, BC, to north of Carmacks, a distance of about 350 km. Other conglomerates of this series form Five Finger Rapids."

Rock hounds can find pieces of conglomerate in almost any borrow pit along this stretch of highway.

J 71.6 (115.2 km) **D 255.6** (411.3 km) **S 190.8** (307 km) Turnouts on both sides of highway between Twin Lakes. These 2 small lakes, 1 on either side of the road, are known for their beauty and colour.

J 72.3 (116.4 km) **D 254.9** (410.2 km) **S 191.5** (308.2 km) Turnoff to west for **Twin Lakes** Yukon government campground; 8 sites, $8 camping fee, drinking water, boat launch. Lake is stocked. Large parking area with informational panels on the Nordenskiold River. Enjoyable fishing for lake trout, grayling and pike. Good swimming for the *hardy!* ✦▲

J 81.4 (131 km) **D 245.8** (395.6 km) **S 200.6** (323 km) Large turnout with litter barrel to east at remains of **Montague House**, a typical early-day roadhouse which offered lodging and meals on the stagecoach route between Whitehorse and Dawson City. A total of 52 stopping places along this route were listed in the Jan. 16, 1901, edition of the *Whitehorse Star* under "On the Winter Trail between White Horse and Dawson Good Accommodations for Travellers." Montague House was listed at Mile 99. Good photo stop.

J 87.4 (140.7 km) **D 239.8** (385.9 km) **S 206.6** (332.5 km) Small lake to west.

J 93.7 (150.8 km) **D 233.5** (375.8 km) **S 212.9** (343.9 km) Plume Trail Agate Road to east, information sign about agate deposits.

J 100.1 (161.1 km) **D 227.1** (365.5 km) **S 219.3** (352.9 km) Carmacks town limits.

J 101.3 (163 km) **D 225.9** (363.5 km) **S 220.5** (354.8 km) **Nordenskiold River** to west was named by Lt. Frederick Schwatka, U.S. Army, for Swedish arctic explorer Erik Nordenskiold. Good grayling and pike fishing all summer. This river, which parallels the highway for several miles, flows into the Yukon River at Carmacks. ✦

J 101.5 (163.3 km) **D 225.7** (363.2 km) **S 220.7** (355.2 km) Pull-through rest area to east with large mural of *Moment at Tantalus Butte.* Litter barrels and outhouses.

River travelers make their way down the Yukon. (© Lyn Hancock)

River; beautiful view of countryside and Tantalus Butte, gazebo and park at end of trail. Wheelchair accessible. ▲&

The Northern Tutchone First Nations Interpretive Centre features archaeological displays on Native life in a series of indoor and outdoor exhibits, and marked interpretive trails.

Carmacks is also an excellent area for rock hounds. There are 5 agate trails in the area, which can double as good, short hiking trails.

Check locally for boat tours to Five Finger and Rink rapids and Fort Selkirk. Fort Selkirk was an important trading post and subsequent RCMP post (see **Milepost J 148.6**). Helicopter service and local canoe and hiking tours available. Abundant fishing in area rivers and lakes: salmon, grayling, northern pike, lake and rainbow trout, whitefish and ling cod.

Mukluk Manor Bed & Breakfast. Peaceful country acreage on edge of town. Spectacular northern view. Fully equipped 1-bedroom suite. Private entrance. Also,

large cozy carriage suite, private deck. Smoke if you wish. Closed Saturdays. Reservations recommended. Mick and Laurie Larkin,

Carmacks

J **102.7** (165.3 km) **D 224.5** (361.3 km) **S 221.9** (357.1 km). Located on the banks of the Yukon River, Carmacks is the only highway crossing of the Yukon River between Whitehorse and Dawson City. **Population:** 489. **Emergency Services: RCMP**, phone (867) 863-5555. **Fire Department**, phone (867) 863-2222. **Nurse**, phone (867) 863-4444. **Ambulance**, phone (867) 863-4444. **Forest Fire Control**, (867) 863-5271.

Private Aircraft: Carmacks airstrip; elev. 1,770 feet/539m; length 5,200 feet/1,585m; gravel; no fuel.

Carmacks was once an important stop for Yukon River steamers traveling between Dawson City and Whitehorse, and it continues as a supply point today for modern river travelers. Carmacks has survived—while other river ports have not—as a service centre for highway traffic and mining interests. Carmacks was also a major stopping

CARMACKS ADVERTISERS

point on the old Whitehorse to Dawson Trail.

Carmacks was named for George Carmack, who established a trading post here in the 1890s. Carmack had come North in 1885, hoping to strike it rich. He spent the next 10 years prospecting without success. In 1896, when the trading post went bankrupt, Carmack moved his family to Fortymile, where he could fish to eat and cut timber to sell. That summer, Carmack's remarkable persistence paid off—he unearthed a 5-dollar pan of coarse gold, during a time when a 10-cent pan was considered a good find. That same winter, he extracted more than a ton of gold from the creek, which he renamed Bonanza Creek, and its tributary, Eldorado. When word of Carmack's discovery reached the outside world the following spring, it set off the Klondike Gold Rush.

Traveler facilities include a hotel, motel, bed and breakfast, the village-operated Tantalus Campground on the bank of the Yukon River; restaurant, gas bar, general store (with groceries, bakery and hardware) and laundromat at Hotel Carmacks; post office and bank (both with limited hours), general store, gas bar and dump station at Northern Tutchone Trading Post. The trading post also has some Native crafts for sale. There are also churches, a school, swimming pool, service centre, cafe and a community library. A 1.2-mile/2-km interpretive boardwalk makes it possible to enjoy a stroll along the Yukon

Guder Street, Boxo 104, Carmacks, Yukon Y0B 1C0. (867) 863-5232. [ADVERTISEMENT]

Klondike Loop Log
(continued)

J 103.2 (166.1 km) **D 224** (360.5 km) **S 222.4** (357.9 km) Yukon River bridge. Turnout and parking area at south end of bridge; 2.3-mile-/3.7-km-long trail to Coal Mine Lake.

J 103.3 (166.2 km) **D 223.9** (360.3 km) **S 222.5** (358.1 km) Northern Tutchone Trading Post with store, gas and diesel, vehicle repair and post office at north end of Yukon River bridge. Fishing tackle and licenses available. Interpretive centre.

J 104.4 (168 km) **D 222.8** (358.6 km) **S 223.6** (359.8 km) Turnoff to east for Campbell Highway, also known as Watson Lake–Carmacks Road, which leads south to Faro, Ross River and Watson Lake.

> **Junction** with Campbell Highway (Yukon Highway 4). See CAMPBELL HIGHWAY section.

J 105.1 (169.1 km) **D 222.1** (357.4 km) **S 224.3** (361 km) Side road east to Tantalus Butte Coal Mine; the coal was used in Cyprus Anvil Mine's mill near Faro for drying concentrates. The butte was named by Lt. Frederick Schwatka because it is seen many times before it is actually reached.

J 105.4 (169.6 km) **D 221.8** (356.9 km) **S 224.6** (361.4 km) Turnout to west with litter barrels, information sign, view of Yukon River Valley.

J 108 (173.8 km) **D 219.2** (352.8 km) **S 227.2** (365.3 km) Side road west to agate site for rock hounds.

J 110 (177 km) **D 217.2** (349.5 km) **S 229.2** (368.8 km) Small lake to west.

J 117.5 (189.1 km) **D 209.7** (337.5 km) **S 236.7** (378.5 km) Large double-ended rest area to west with toilets, litter barrels and viewing platform for **Five Finger Rapids**. Information sign here reads: "Five Finger Rapids named by early miners for the 5 channels, or fingers, formed by the rock pillars. They are a navigational hazard. The safest passage is through the nearest, or east, passage." Stairs (219 steps) and a trail lead down to a closer view of the rapids.

J 118.9 (191.3 km) **D 208.3** (335.2 km) **S 238.1** (380.6 km) Tatchun Creek. Side road

to Five Finger Rapids boat-tour operator.

J 119 (191.5 km) **D 208.2** (335.1 km) **S 238.2** (380.8 km) First turnoff (northbound) to east for **Tatchun Creek** Yukon government campground; 12 sites, $8 camping fee, kitchen shelter and drinking water. Good fishing for grayling, June through September; salmon, July through August.　　　　⊶▲

J 119.1 (191.7 km) **D 208.1** (334.9 km) **S 238.3** (380.9 km) Second turnoff (northbound) east for Tatchun Creek Yukon government campground.

J 119.6 (192.5 km) **D 207.6** (334.1 km) **S 238.8** (381.8 km) Side road leads east to **Tatchun Lake**. Follow side road 4.3 miles/6.9 km east to boat launch and pit toilets. Continue past boat launch 1.1 miles/1.8 km for Tatchun Lake Yukon government campground with 20 sites, $8 camping fee, pit toilets, firewood, litter barrels and picnic tables. Fishing for northern pike, best in spring or fall.　　　　⊶▲

This maintained side road continues east past Tatchun Lake to Frenchman Lake, then loops south to the Campbell Highway, approximately 25 miles/40 km distance. The main access to Frenchman Lake is from the Campbell Highway.

J 121.8 (196 km) **D 205.4** (330.6 km) **S 241** (388 km) Tatchun Hill.

J 126.6 (203.7 km) **D 200.6** (322.8 km) **S 245.8** (395.8 km) Large turnout overlooking Yukon River. Good photo stop.

J 126.9 (204.2 km) **D 200.3** (322.3 km) **S 246.1** (396.3 km) Highway descends hill, northbound. Watch for falling rocks.

J 132 (212.4 km) **D 195.2** (314.1 km) **S 251.2** (404.5 km) McGregor Creek.

J 135 (217.3 km) **D 192.2** (309.3 km) **S 254.2** (409.4 km) Northbound, first evidence of 1995 burn. The fire consumed 325,000 acres of forest. Dramatic fireweed displays here in July 1997 and 1998.

J 136.6 (219.8 km) **D 190.6** (306.7 km) **S 255.8** (411.9 km) Good representation of White River ash layer for approximately one mile northbound. About 1,250 years ago a layer of white volcanic ash coated a third of the southern Yukon, or some 125,000 square miles/323,725 square km, and it is easily visible along many roadcuts. This distinct line conveniently provides a division used by archaeologists for dating artifacts: Materials found below this major stratigraphic marker are considered to have been deposited before A.D. 700, while those found above the ash layer are postdated A.D. 700. The small amount of data available does not support volcanic activity in the White River area during the same period. One theory is that the ash could have spewn forth from a single violent volcanic eruption. The source

may be buried under the Klutlan Glacier in the St. Elias Mountains in eastern Alaska.

J 144 (231.7 km) **D 183.2** (294.8 km) **S 263.2** (423.8 km) McCabe Creek.

J 148 (238.2 km) **D 179.2** (288.4 km) **S 267.2** (430.4 km) Private RV park and boat tours. Trees along this portion of highway were burned in a 1995 forest fire. Amazingly, the businesses in the immediate surrounding area were spared.

Big River Enterprises. See display ad this section.

Minto Resorts Ltd. R.V. Park. 1,400-foot Yukon River frontage. Halfway between Whitehorse and Dawson City on the Old Stage Road, Minto was once a steamboat landing and trading post. 27 sites, wide easy access, picnic tables, firepits, souvenirs, fishing licenses, ice, snacks, pop. Coin-op showers and laundry, clean restrooms, dump station and water. Bus tour buffet, reservation only. Caravans welcome. Wildlife viewing opportunities. Try fishing the river. Owned and operated by Yukoners. Come and visit us! See display ad this section. [ADVERTISEMENT]　　　▲

J 148.6 (239.1 km) **D 178.6** (287.4 km) **S 267.8** (431.4 km) Minto Road, a short loop road, leads west to location of the former riverboat landing and trading post of **MINTO**. Check with Big River Enterprises about river tours to Sheep Mountain and Fort Selkirk leaving daily from Minto Resorts.

FORT SELKIRK, 25 river miles/40 km from here, was established by Robert Campbell in 1848 for the Hudson's Bay Co. In 1852, the fort was destroyed by Chilkat Indians, who had dominated the fur trade of central Yukon—trading here with the Northern Tutchone people (Selkirk First Nation), who used the area as a seasonal home and exchanged furs for the Chilkats' coastal goods—until the arrival of the Hudson's Bay Co. The site was occupied sporadically by traders, missionaries and the RCMP until the 1950s. About 40 buildings—dating from 1892 to 1940—still stand in good repair. A river trip to Fort Selkirk lets travelers see the fort virtually unchanged since the turn of the century. A highly recommended side trip, if time permits. Government preservation and interpretation staff are available on site.

Private Aircraft: Minto airstrip; elev. 1,550 feet/472m; length 5,000 feet/1,524m; gravel.

J 160.3 (258 km) **D 166.9** (268.6 km) **S 279.5** (450.5 km) Side road east to Von Wilczek Lakes.

J 162.8 (262 km) **D 164.4** (264.6 km) **S 282** (454.5 km) Northern limits of 1995 burn. Fireweed displays southbound in July.

J 163.4 (263 km) **D 163.8** (263.6 km) **S 282.6** (455.5 km) Rock Island Lake to east.

J 164.2 (264.2 km) **D 163** (262.3 km) **S 283.4** (456.8 km) Turnout. Small lake to west.

J 168.7 (271.5 km) **D 158.5** (255.1 km) **S 287.9** (464 km) Road west to garbage dump.

J 169.4 (272.6 km) **D 157.8** (253.9 km) **S 288.6** (465 km) Side road to **PELLY CROSSING** (pop. about 350). **Emergency Services:** RCMP, phone (867) 537-5555; Nurse, phone (867) 537-4444. Located on the banks of the Pelly River, traveler facilities include take-out food, grocery store, gas, minor vehicle repairs, campground, post office and a bank. There is a school, curling rink, baseball field, swimming pool and church. ▲

Private Aircraft: Pelly Airstrip, elev. 1,870 feet/570m; length 3,000 feet/914m; gravel; no services.

Pelly Crossing became a settlement when the Klondike Highway was put through in 1950. A ferry transported people and vehicles across the Pelly River, where the road eventually continued to Dawson City. Most inhabitants of Pelly Crossing came from historic Fort Selkirk. Today, the restored Fort Selkirk can be visited by boat from Pelly Crossing.

This Selkirk Indian community attracted residents from Minto when the highway to Dawson City was built. School, mission and sawmill located near the big bridge. The local economy is based on hunting, trapping, fishing and guiding. The Selkirk Indian Band has erected signs near the bridge on the history and culture of the Selkirk people.

The **Selkirk Heritage Centre**, located adjacent to the Selkirk Gas Bar, is a replica of the Big Jonathon House at Fort Selkirk. The centre will offer a self-guided tour of First Nation heritage.

Selkirk Gas Bar & Grocery. See display ad this section. ▲

Penny's Place. A unique and cozy oasis in the middle of Yukon's vast wilderness, a "must" visit on your travels North. Stop by for your favourite ice cream, a delicious burger, an espresso while enjoying this quaint spot. "Neat stuff" and unique gifts for the stylish shopper. Drop by and see for yourself. Phone (867) 537-3011. [ADVERTISEMENT]

J 169.7 (273.1 km) **D 157.5** (253.5 km) **S 288.9** (465.5 km) Pelly River bridge.

J 170.4 (274.2 km) **D 156.8** (252.3 km) **S 289.6** (467 km) Turnout with litter barrel to east. View of Pelly Crossing and river valley. A historical marker here honours the Canadian Centennial (1867–1967). The Pelly River was named in 1840 by explorer Robert Campbell for Sir John Henry Pelly, governor of the Hudson's Bay Co. The Pelly heads near the Northwest Territories border and flows approximately 375 miles/603 km to the Yukon River.

J 171.5 (276 km) **D 155.7** (250.6 km) **S 290.7** (468.6 km) **Private Aircraft:** Airstrip to east; elev. 1,870 feet/570m; length 3,000 feet/914m; gravel. No services.

J 179.6 (289 km) **D 147.6** (237.5 km) **S 298.8** (481.7 km) Pull-through turnout to east.

J 180.9 (291.1 km) **D 146.3** (235.4 km) **S 300.1** (483.8 km) Small lake to west.

J 183.8 (295.8 km) **D 143.4** (230.8 km) **S 303** (488.6 km) Large turnout to west. Bridge over Willow Creek.

J 185.5 (298.5 km) **D 141.7** (228 km) **S 304.7** (491.3 km) Side road west to Jackfish Lake.

J 195.6 (314.8 km) **D 131.6** (211.8 km) **S 314.8** (506.6 km) Access road west to **Wrong Lake** (stocked); fishing. ⊷

J 197.4 (317.7 km) **D 129.8** (208.9 km) **S 316.6** (511 km) Turnout with litter barrel to west. Winding descent begins for northbound traffic.

J 203.6 (327.7 km) **D 123.6** (198.9 km) **S 322.8** (521 km) Pull-through turnout to east.

J 205.9 (331.4 km) **D 121.3** (195.2 km) **S 325.1** (524.6 km) **Crooked Creek;** pike; grayling, use flies, summer best. ⊷

J 207.2 (333.4 km) **D 120** (193.1 km) **S 326.4** (526.7 km) Pull-through turnout with litter barrel to east at turnoff for **Ethel Lake** Yukon government campground. Drive in 16.6 miles/26.7 km on narrow and winding side road (not recommended for large RVs) for campground; 12 sites, boat launch, fishing. Camping fee $8. ⊷▲

J 213.8 (344.1 km) **D 113.4** (182.5 km) **S 333** (537.3 km) Stewart Crossing government maintenance camp to east.

J 213.9 (344.2 km) **D 113.3** (182.3 km) **S 333.1** (537.5 km) Stewart Crossing; private RV park and campground, and gas station with towing, tires and minor repair, east side of highway. Turnout with information sign west side of highway; Silver Trail information booth (unmanned) contains information on the Silver Trail, or listen to a 5-minute message on the radio at 93.3 FM. ▲

In 1886 **STEWART CROSSING** was the site of a trading post established by Arthur Harper, Alfred Mayo and Jack McQuesten to support gold mining in the area. Later a roadhouse was built here as part of the Whitehorse to Dawson overland stage route. Stewart Crossing also functioned as a fuel stop for the riverboats and during the 1930s was a transfer point for the silver ore barges from Mayo. Harper, Mayo and McQuesten are 3 prominent names in Yukon history. Harper, an Irish immigrant, was one of the first white men to prospect in the Yukon, although he never struck it rich. He died in 1898 in Arizona. (His son, Walter Harper, was on the first complete ascent of Mount McKinley in 1913. Walter died in 1918 in the SS *Princess Sophia* disaster off Juneau.)

Mayo, a native of Maine, explored, prospected and traded in the Yukon until his death in 1924.

McQuesten, like Harper, worked his way north from the California goldfields. Often referred to as the "Father of the Yukon" and a founding member of the Yukon order of Pioneers, Jack Leroy Napoleon McQuesten ended his trading and prospecting days in 1898 when he moved to California. He died in 1909 while in Seattle for the Alaska–Yukon–Pacific Exposition.

Stewart Crossing Chevron. See display ad this section.

Whispering Willows RV Park and Bed & Breakfast. Our tidy RV park along the Stewart River (just before the bridge) has power and water hookups, dump station, clean showers and washrooms, back-in and pull-through sites. A tasty menu includes fresh-made bread, homemade perogies and sausages, fresh ground and brewed coffee. Great area fishing; ask us where. Your new hosts, Jerald and Lorraine look forward to meeting you. Phone (867) 996-2284, fax (867) 996-2422. [ADVERTISEMENT]

J 214.3 (344.9 km) **D 112.9** (181.7 km) **S 333.5** (538 km) Stewart River bridge. The Stewart River flows into the Yukon River upstream from Dawson City.

J 214.4 (345 km) **D 112.8** (181.5 km) **S 333.6** (538.2 km) **Silver Trail (Stewart Crossing)**; turnoff for Mayo and Keno City at north end of Stewart River bridge. Marker shows distance to Dawson 182 km.

Silver Trail Tourism Association. See display ad this section.

Junction with the Silver Trail (Yukon Highway 11) which leads northeast to Mayo, Elsa and Keno; see SILVER TRAIL section.

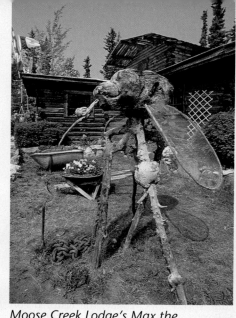

Moose Creek Lodge's Max the Mosquito is a popular photo subject.

(© Beth Davidow)

J 214.8 (345.7 km) **D 112.4** (180.9 km) **S 334** (538.8 km) View to west of Stewart River and mountains as highway climbs northbound.

J 220.8 (355.3 km) **D 106.4** (171.2 km) **S 340** (545.1 km) Dry Creek.

J 224.4 (361.1 km) **D 102.8** (165.4 km) **S 343.6** (556.2 km) Access to Stewart River to west. Historical information sign about Stewart River. A major tributary of the Yukon River, the Stewart River was named for James G. Stewart, who discovered it in 1849. Stewart was assistant to Robert Campbell of the Hudson's Bay Co.

J 229.1 (368.7 km) **D 98.1** (157.9 km) **S 348.3** (561.9 km) **Moose Creek Lodge.** A must for Yukon travelers! An authentic trapper's cabin and a large selection of Northern books, souvenirs and crafts. In our cozy cafe, enjoy a hearty breakfast, our scrumptious cinnamon buns and home-baked bread. We feature daily homemade soups, delicious belt-bustin' sandwiches and burgers, and mouth-watering home-baked pies. Meet Max the Mosquito and Murray the Moose! Cozy log cabins. For reservations, phone (867) 667-1324; fax (867) 393-1936 or write Bag 1, Mayo, YT Y0B 1M0. Moose Creek is also serving group tours in their beautiful open-air gazebo, reservations a must. VISA and MasterCard. Your hosts, Tonya and Neil Salvin. [ADVERTISEMENT]

J 229.2 (368.9 km) **D 98** (157.7 km) **S 348.4** (562 km) Moose Creek bridge.

J 229.5 (369.3 km) **D 97.7** (157.2 km) **S 348.7** (562.4 km) Turnout to west at turnoff for Moose Creek Yukon government campground adjacent to **Moose Creek** and Stewart River; good picnic spot. There are 30 RV sites, 6 tent-only sites, kitchen shelter, playground and playfield. Camping fee $8. Short trail to Stewart River. Good fishing for grayling, 1 to 1¼ lbs.

J 242.7 (390.6 km) **D 84.5** (136 km) **S 361.9** (583.7 km) McQuesten River, a tributary of the Stewart River, named for Jack (Leroy Napoleon) McQuesten.

J 242.9 (390.9 km) **D 84.3** (135.7 km) **S 362.1** (584 km) McQuesten, a lodge with cafe, cabins and RV sites. Site of Old McQuesten River Lodge to east.

J 247.5 (398.3 km) **D 79.7** (128.3 km) **S 366.7** (590.1 km) Partridge Creek Farm. Organic vegetables in season.

J 249.3 (401.2 km) **D 77.9** (125.4 km) **S 368.5** (594 km) **Private Aircraft:** McQuesten airstrip 1.2 miles/1.9 km west; elev. 1,500 feet/457m; length 5,000 feet/1,524m; gravel and turf. No services.

J 251.3 (404.4 km) **D 75.9** (122.1 km) **S 370.5** (596.5 km) Clear Creek, access via side road west.

J 260.4 (419.1 km) **D 66.8** (107.5 km) **S 379.6** (612 km) Barlow Lake, access via 0.6-mile-/1-km-long side road west.

J 263.7 (424.4 km) **D 63.5** (102.2 km) **S 382.9** (617.2 km) Beaver Dam Creek.

J 266 (428.1 km) **D 61.2** (98.5 km) **S 385.2** (621 km) Willow Creek.

J 268.5 (432.1 km) **D 58.7** (94.5 km) **S 387.7** (625 km) Flat Hill.

J 268.8 (432.6 km) **D 58.4** (94 km) **S 388** (625.5 km) Gravel Lake to east.

J 272.1 (437.9 km) **D 55.1** (88.7 km) **S 391.3** (630.8 km) Meadow Creek.

J 272.5 (438.5 km) **D 54.7** (88 km) **S 391.7** (631.4 km) Rest area with litter barrel to south.

J 276.5 (445 km) **D 50.7** (81.6 km) **S 395.7** (637.9 km) French Creek.

J 279.7 (450.1 km) **D 47.5** (76.4 km) **S 398.9** (643.1 km) Stone Boat Creek.

J 288.9 (464.9 km) **D 38.3** (61.6 km) **S 408.1** (657.9 km) Rest area.

J 289.3 (465.6 km) **D 37.9** (61 km) **S 408.5** (658.5 km) Large gravel turnout with geologic point of interest information sign, to east overlooking **Tintina Trench**. This geologic feature, which extends hundreds of miles across Yukon and Alaska, provides visible proof of plate tectonics.

J 295.1 (474.9 km) **D 32.1** (51.7 km) **S 414.3** (667.8 km) Flat Creek.

J 295.9 (476.2 km) **D 31.3** (50.4 km) **S 415.1** (669 km) Klondike River to east.

J 297.6 (478.9 km) **D 29.6** (47.6 km) **S 416.8** (671.9 km) Large turnout to east with historic sign about Klondike River and information sign on Dempster Highway.

J 298 (479.6 km) **D 29.2** (47 km) **S 417.2** (672.5 km) Watch for livestock.

J 301.6 (485.4 km) **D 25.6** (41.2 km) **S 420.8** (678.5 km) **Dempster Corner;** Klondike River Lodge east side of highway just north of the junction; open year-round, food, lodging, camping, gas, diesel and propane.

Klondike River Lodge. See display ad this section.

> **Junction** of Klondike Highway and the Dempster Highway (Yukon Highway 5), which leads northeast to Inuvik, NWT. See DEMPSTER HIGHWAY section for log of that road.

J 307.3 (494.5 km) **D 19.9** (32 km) **S 426.5** (687.4 km) Goring Creek.

J 308.4 (496.3 km) **D 18.8** (30.3 km) **S 427.6** (689.2 km) Turnout to north for Rock Creek subdivision and Klondike River access.

J 315.2 (507.3 km) **D 12** (19.3 km) **S 434.4** (700 km) Turnoff to north for Klondike River Yukon government campground, located on Rock Creek near the Klondike River; 38 sites, kitchen shelter, drinking water, playground. Camping fee $8.

J 315.7 (508.1 km) **D 11.5** (18.5 km) **S 434.9** (700.8 km) Dawson City airport to south. **Private Aircraft:** Runway 02-20; elev. 1,211 feet/369m; length 5,000 feet/1,524m; gravel; fuel 80 (in drums at Dawson City), 100, JP4. Flightseeing trips and air charters available.

J 317.1 (510.3 km) **D 10.1** (16.3 km) **S 436.3** (703.4 km) Hunker Creek Road to south. Hunker Creek Road (gravel) connects with Upper Bonanza Creek Road and loops back to the Klondike Highway via Bonanza Creek Road.

Access to Goldbottom Mining Tours, 9 miles/15 km south, a family-run placer mine offering tours and gold panning; fee charged.

Goldbottom Mining Tours and Gold Panning. See display ad this section.

J 318.4 (512.4 km) **D 8.8** (14.2 km) **S 437.6** (705.4 km) Turnout to south with point of interest sign about Hunker Creek. Albert Hunker staked the first claim on Hunker Creek Sept. 11, 1896. George Carmack made the big discovery on Bonanza Creek on Aug. 17, 1896. Hunker Creek is 16 miles/26 km long, of which 13 miles/21 km was dredged between 1906 and 1966.

J 318.9 (513.2 km) **D 8.3** (13.4 km) **S 438.1** (706.1 km) Bear Creek Road leads to subdivision.

J 319.6 (514.3 km) **D 7.6** (12.2 km) **S 438.8** (707.2 km) Turnout with historic sign about the Yukon Ditch and tailings to north. To the south is **Bear Creek Historical Site,** operated by Parks Canada. This 62-acre

compound of the Yukon Consolidated Gold Corp. features blacksmith and machinery shops and Gold Room. Open daily in summer, with tours twice daily from the end of May to early September. Admission: adults $5, youth $2.50, family $12.50, or Parks Pass.

J 323.3 (520.3 km) **D 3.9** (6.3 km) **S 442.5** (712 km) Callison industrial area; charter helicopter service, mini-storage, bulk fuel plant and heavy equipment repairs. Access to Ridge Road Heritage Trail lower trailhead (see Attractions in Dawson City).

J 324.5 (522.2 km) **D 2.7** (4.3 km) **S 443.7** (714 km) Commercial RV park and gold panning at **junction** with **Bonanza Creek Road;** access to Dredge No. 4 (7.8 miles/12.3 km) and Discovery Claim (9.3 milew/14.8 km). Bonanza Creek Road is maintained for 10 miles/16.1 km. It connects with Upper Bonanza Creek Road (gravel), which provides access to Ridge Road Heritage Trail and loops back to the Klondike Highway via Hunker Creek Road.

GuggieVille. Good Sam. This clean, attractive campground is built on dredge

tailings at the former site of the Guggenheim's mining camp. 72 RV sites with water and electricity, 28 unserviced sites, public showers ($2 each). Car wash, dump

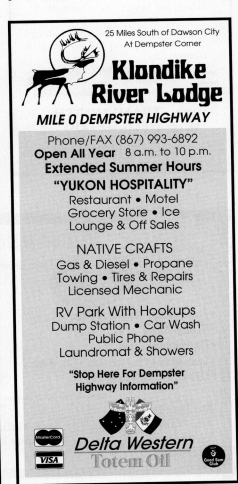

station and laundromat are available. A mining public display is open to the public free of charge. Gold panning discount for those staying at GuggieVille. Phone (867) 993-5008. Fax (867) 993-5006. Off-season phone/fax (867) 993-5319. [ADVERTISEMENT] ▲

Dredge No. 4 is the largest wooden hull dredge in North America. Interpretive centre at dredge site; scheduled tours and a 10-minute video on the restoration of this historic site are offered daily, end of May through August. Admission: $5 adults,

$2.50 youth, $12.50 family, or Parks Pass.

Marked by a plaque, **Discovery Claim** was the first gold claim on Bonanza Creek and the one that started the Klondike Stampede of 1898. Special presentations and gold panning offered in summer.

J 324.6 (522.4 km) **D 2.6** (4.2 km) **S 443.8** (714.2 km) **Bonanza Gold R.V. park & Motel**. See display ad this section. ▲

J 324.7 (522.5 km) **D 2.5** (4 km) **S 443.9** (715.3 km) Campground, gas station and store. ▲

Dawson City R.V. Park & Campground and **Bonanza Esso**. See display ad this section. ▲

J 324.8 (522.7 km) **D 2.4** (3.9 km) **S 444** (715.5 km) Klondike River bridge.

J 325.3 (523.5 km) **D 1.9** (3.1 km) **S 444.5** (716.4 km) Large turnout with information sign and map.

J 325.8 (524.3 km) **D 1.4** (2.3 km) **S 445** (717.2 km) Dome Road to north leads 4.5 miles/7.2 km to **Dome Mountain** (elev.

2,911 feet/887m), which offers views of Dawson City, the Yukon and Klondike rivers, Bonanza Creek and the Ogilvie Mountains.

J 325.9 (524.5 km) **D 1.3** (2.1 km) **S 445.1** (717.4 km) Trans North Helicopter base to south; Klondike goldfield tours. Rock face on right northbound is known locally as Crocus Bluff; short, interpretive foot trail leads to viewpoint overlooking Klondike River and Dawson City.

Trans North Helicopters. See display ad this section.

J 326.1 (524.8 km) **D 1.1** (1.8 km) **S 445.3** (717.7 km) Fifth Avenue. Turnout with sign about the Klondike River to south: "With headwaters in the Ogilvie Mountains, the Klondike River and its tributaries gave birth to the world's greatest gold rush—the Klondike Gold Rush of '98."

J 327.2 (526.6 km) **D 0 S 446.4** (719.5 km) Dawson City, ferry at Yukon River. *Description of Dawson City follows. Log of Klondike Loop continues on page 278.*

Dawson City

J 327.2 (526.6 km) **D 0 S 446.4** (719.5 km) Located 165 miles/266 km south of the Arctic Circle on the Yukon River at its junction with the Klondike River. **Population:** 2,019. **Emergency Services:** RCMP, 1st Avenue S., phone (867) 993-5555. **Fire Department,**
(Continues on page 274)

DAWSON CITY

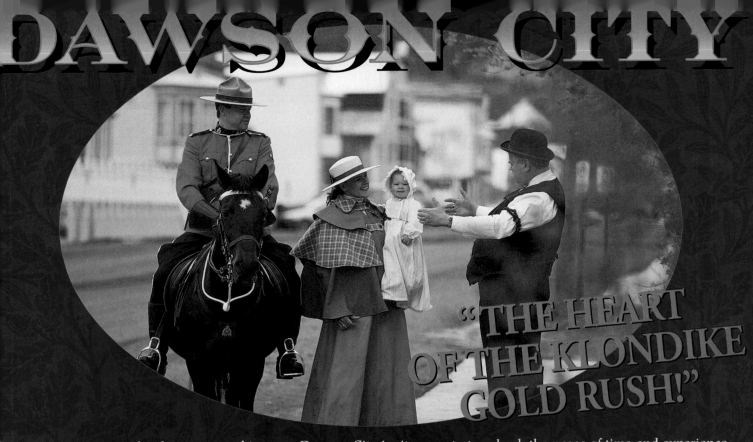

"THE HEART OF THE KLONDIKE GOLD RUSH!"

A modern community that has preserved its past, Dawson City invites you to turn back the pages of time and experience the rich living history of the Klondike Gold Rush. Meander the wooden boardwalks and visit national historic treasures. Join interpretive programs and amazing special events. Tour the Klondike Gold Fields and operating gold mines. Participate in unforgettable First Nations Tours. And of course, don't miss Diamond Tooth Gerties Casino, Canada's first, and most unique legalized gambling hall! Without a doubt ~ YOU WILL NEED A WEEK TO SEE IT ALL!

For more information contact:
THE KLONDIKE VISITORS ASSOCIATION

P.O.Box 389M, Dawson City, YT   Y0B 1G0
Tel: (867) 993-5575   Fax: (867) 993-6415
e mail: KVA@Dawson.net   www.DawsonCity.com

ACCOMMODATIONS

DOWNTOWN HOTEL

- Modern Comfortable Rooms
- Jacuzzi • Plug-ins
- Telephones • Cable TV
- Complimentary Airport Transfers
- Grace's Gift Shop
- Sterndeck BBQ
- Locally Owned & Operated by Yukoners

JACK LONDON GRILL • SOURDOUGH SALOON • BANQUET AND MEETING FACILITIES

PROUD SUPPORTER
KLONDIKE GOLD RUSH CENTENNIAL

Box 780, Dawson City, Yukon Canada Y0B 1G0 Ph: (867) 993-5346 Fax: (867) 993-5076

RESERVATIONS ONLY: 1-800-661-0514
Major Credit Cards Accepted

E-mail: downtown@yknet.yk.ca Homepage: www.yukonweb.com/tourism/downtown

---

THE ELDORADO HOTEL

• Owned & Operated year-round by Yukoners •

Sluice Box Lounge
Air Conditioned

Bonanza Dining Room
Featuring northern specialties
Pleasant surroundings, excellent service

We are northern hospitality!

Open Year-Round • All Modern Rooms • Suites • Kitchenettes
Phones • Color TV • Laundry • Winter Plug-Ins
All Major Credit Cards Accepted

3RD AVENUE & PRINCESS STREET P.O. BOX 338 DAWSON CITY, YUKON Y0B 1G0
FOR RESERVATIONS CALL (867) 993-5451• FAX 993-5256
NORTHERN B.C. & YUKON 1-800-661-0518 AK. 1-800-764-ELDO
e-mail: eldo@dawson.net • www.yukon.net/eldorado

DAWSON CITY
TRIPLE J HOTEL

- Hotel Rooms • Executive Suite
- Cabins with Kitchenettes/Full Baths
- Air-Conditioned Lounge & Restaurant
- Licensed Outdoor Patio
- Coin Laundry, Satellite TV
- Complimentary Airport Limo

Toll Free Reservations 1-800-764-3555 • E-mail: JJJ@dawson.net

5th AVE & QUEEN, BOX 359, DAWSON CITY, Y0B 1G0 • PH: (867) 993-5323 • FAX: (867) 993-5030

FAIRBANKS DAWSON CITY
TOK BEAVER CREEK
ANCHORAGE WHITEHORSE
VALDEZ SKAGWAY
JUNEAU
SITKA
KETCHIKAN

In Dawson City & Almost Everywhere Else.

Nobody knows the Yukon and Alaska like Westmark Hotels. We've got the locations like Dawson City, the quality you desire and the service you expect. Comfortable rooms and warm northern hospitality are yours at every Westmark Hotel. Call us today for information about locations, rates and room availability in the Yukon or anywhere in Alaska.

◆

- Full Service Locations •
- Free Parking •
- Convenient Locations •
- Restaurants & Lounges •
- Meeting Facilities •
- Alaska Airlines Miles •
- Canadian Plus Points •
- Guest Rewards Points •

◆

Ask About Our Summer Explorer Rates

Westmark
I N N
DAWSON CITY

Fifth & Harper Streets
P.O. Box 420
Dawson City, Yukon Territory Y0B1G0

403-993-5542

Central Reservations
1-800-544-0970
www.westmarkhotels.com

ACCOMMODATIONS

GOLD RUSH
CAMPGROUND RV PARK

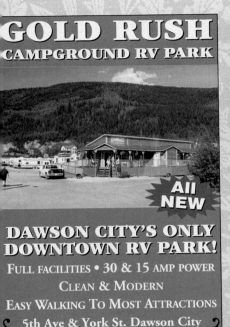

All NEW

DAWSON CITY'S ONLY DOWNTOWN RV PARK!
FULL FACILITIES • 30 & 15 AMP POWER
CLEAN & MODERN
EASY WALKING TO MOST ATTRACTIONS
5th Ave & York St. Dawson City
Phone: (867) 993-5247

For Accommodation
Information, Contact
The Visitors Reception Centre
(867) 993-5566

1899 1999

KLONDIKE KATE'S
RESTAURANT & CABINS
EST. 1990

Historic 3rd Ave. & King St.
- *Clean, Affordable Accommodation*
- *Open Daily 7 am - 11 pm*
- *$3.99 Breakfast Special*
- *Canadian & Ethnic Food*
- *Fully Licensed Dining*
- *Espresso Coffee*
- *Dine In or On Our Covered Outdoor Patio*

Box 417
Dawson City YT Y0B 1G0
ph. 867.993.6527
fx. 867.993.6044

BEAR CREEK
Bed & Bannock

First Nation Family Owned & Operated
- Elder & Family Discounts
- Cultural Displays
- Peaceful Country Setting
- 4 Bedrooms & Full Facilities Separate from Main Home
Box 679, Dawson City

ph: 993-6765 or 993-5605

E-mail: Kormendy@yukon.net

Midnight Sun Hotel

Great Rooms! Great Rates!
(867) **993-5495**

Third & Queen St., Dawson City

May-October
Box 840, Dawson City, Y.T. Y0B 1G0
Ph: (867) 993-5495 • Fax:(867) 993-6425

November-April
1645 Kensington Ave., Burnaby B.C. V5B 4C7
Ph: (604) 291-2652 • Fax: (604) 291-2652

GOLD GOLD GOLD GOLD GOLD GOLD GOLD GOLD GOLD GOLD GOLD

ENTERPRISES

CLEAN AND QUIET CAMPGROUND ON FAMOUS BONANZA CREEK

3 Minutes From City Centre on Bonanza Road

★ HOOKUPS
★ GOLD PANNING
★ GIFT SHOP

★ SHOWERS
★ CAR WASH
★ LAUNDROMAT

Box 311, Dawson City, Yukon Territory Y0B 1G0
(867) 993-5008 or Off-season Ph/Fax (867) 993-5319

GOLD GOLD GOLD GOLD GOLD GOLD GOLD GOLD GOLD GOLD

Dawson City, Yukon
White Ram Manor
Bed & Breakfast
Look for the PINK HOUSE at 7th & Harper

- Sun Decks
- Hot Tub
- BBQ
- Picnic Area
- Canoe Rentals

John & Gail Hendley
Ph: (867) 993-5772 • Fax: 993-6509
Box 302, Dawson City, Yukon Y0B 1G0
e-mail: accomodations@dawsoncity.net

BONANZA GOLD

MOTEL
• HANDICAP SUITE • QUEEN ROOMS & JACUZZI SUITES
• NON-SMOKING ROOMS
• FAX/MODEM ACCESS
• SATELLITE CABLE TV
E-mail: accomodations@dawsoncity.net
1 mile from city centre • Ph: 993-6789 Fax: 993-6777

BONANZA GOLD

RV PARK
• FULL HOOKUPS • SPACIOUS SITES • 30 AMP SERVICE •
DRY PARKING/TENTING
• LAUNDROMAT • CAR WASH
• ON SITE MANAGER
E-mail: accomodations@dawsoncity.net
1 mile from city centre • Ph: 993-6789 Fax: 993-6777

DAWSON CITY

ATTRACTIONS

GOLD CITY TOURS

Sightseeing Tours
Dawson City
Klondike Goldfields
Midnight Dome
(867) 993-5175

"Locally owned & operated"
Open year-round

Tickets & Reservations
All Airlines & Hotels
Alaska & B.C. Ferries
Cruises & Car Rentals
(867) 993-6424

GOLD CITY TRAVEL

DEMPSTER HIGHWAY VAN & BUS CHARTERS, CROSSING THE ARCTIC CIRCLE

P.O. Box 960, Dawson City, Yukon Y0B 1G0 • FAX 993-5261
Located on Front Street, Across from the Steamship "Keno"

Top of the World Golf Course

Across the Yukon River on the Top of the World Highway
5 miles from Dawson City

COME TEE OFF AT MIDNIGHT ON CANADA'S MOST NORTHERN
GOLF COURSE WITH GRASS GREENS

- Public 9 holes • Driving Range • Power Cart & Equipment Rentals
- Pro Shop • Licensed Lounge • Snack Bar
- Unserviced Overnight RV Parking for Golfers
- Shuttle Service Available

Located in the scenic Yukon River Valley with its strategically placed
bunkers & water hazards. It's challenging & enjoyable for all levels of golfers.

Box 189, Dawson City, YT Y0B 1G0   **Tel (867) 667-1472**

Experience Our Heritage
Découvrez notre patrimoine

For additional
Information Contact:
Parks Canada
205-300 Main Street,
Whitehorse, Yukon
Y1A 2B5
Phone: (867) 667-3910
Fax: (867) 393-6701
Toll free:
1-800-661-0486

Pour de plus amples
renseignements, vous
adresser à :
Parcs Canada
Bureau 205, 300, rue Main
Whitehorse, (Yukon)
Y1A 2B5
Tél. : (867) 667-3910
Téléc. : (867) 393-6701
Sans frais :
1-800-661-0486

Canadian Heritage   Patrimoine canadien

Canada

- Evening BBQs
- Day & Package Trips
- Experience First
Nations Traditional Way of Life
Tickets at The Trading Post

http://www.yukon.net/avwcamp
Box 679, Dawson City
Phone: 993-5605

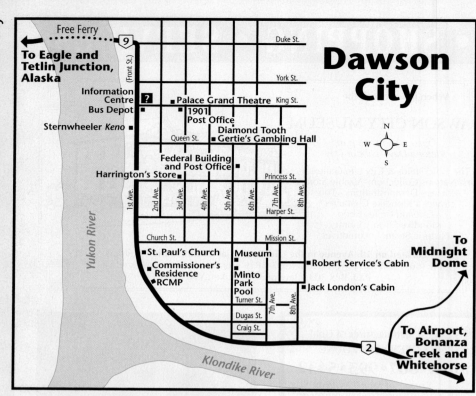

Dawson City

(Continued from page 268)

phone (867) 993-2222. **Nursing station,** phone (867) 993-4444. **Ambulance,** phone (867) 993-4444.

Visitor Information: Visitor Reception Centre, operated by Tourism Yukon and Parks Canada, at Front and King streets, is housed in a replica of the 1897 Alaska Commercial Co. store. Accommodation information, schedule of daily events and a Dawson City street map are available. Three continuous films/videos on Dawson history. Walking tours are part of the daily schedule (fee charged). Open daily, 8 A.M. to 8 P.M. mid-May to mid-September, phone (867) 993-5566, fax (867) 993-6449. Dawson City has lots to do and see. If you want to take it all in, plan for 3 days to cover most of the attractions. Ask about a Parks Pass, which entitles you to admission to 6 Parks Canada sites for half-price.

The Dempster Highway and Northwest

DAWSON CITY ADVERTISERS

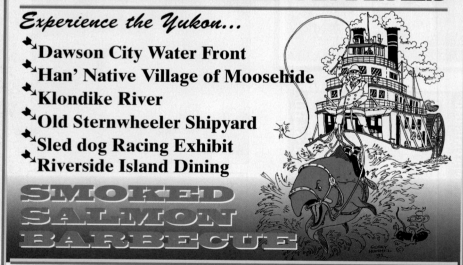

YUKON RIVER CRUISES
Experience the Yukon...
- **Dawson City Water Front**
- **Han' Native Village of Moosehide**
- **Klondike River**
- **Old Sternwheeler Shipyard**
- **Sled dog Racing Exhibit**
- **Riverside Island Dining**

SMOKED SALMON BARBECUE

PLEASURE ISLAND RESTAURANT

Luncheon Cruise
1 p.m. daily. Returns for Robert Service Readings
or
Dinner Cruises
Reservations required.
Returns for the Palace Grand Theatre

Northern hospitality at its finest. Soup and salad buffet luncheon or dine on an all-you-can-eat King Salmon dinner, caught fresh and delicately smoked, then barbequed to perfection. Condiments and garden fresh salad included. Steak or Chicken available on request.

For Information & Reservations

BIRCH CABIN GIFT SHOP ON FRONT STREET
P.O. Box 859, Dawson City, Yukon Territory Y0B 1G0

"FAIR EXCHANGE ON US CURRENCY"
(867) 993-5482 WTR PH: (907) 883-3292

Dawson City's buildings recall the frontier look of the Gold Rush days. (© Lee Foster)

bedroom, full facility bed and breakfast is separate from the main home. We offer a continental breakfast with fresh bannock. Elder and family discounts in a quiet, natural setting 10 minutes from downtown. Handicap accessible. Reservations recommended. (867) 993-6765 or fax (867) 993-6532. E-mail: kormendy@yukon.net. VISA/MasterCard. [ADVERTISEMENT]

Bonanza Gold Motel. Dawson City's newest accommodation. Queen rooms and Jacuzzi suites, non-smoking available, handicap suite. Satellite cable TV, direct dial phones. Fax and modem service. Hungry? Black Bird Bistro next door for great food. Just minutes from downtown; look for the gold entrance arch past Bonanza Road on your way into Dawson. Full RV facilities at Bonanza Gold RV Park. Phone (867) 993-6789. Fax (867) 993-6777. Bag 5000, Dawson City, Yukon Y0B 1G0l E-mail: accommodations@dawsoncity.net. [ADVERTISEMENT]

5th Avenue Bed and Breakfast. Located adjacent to the museum overlooking Victory Gardens. A modern home with a historic

finish, serving a hearty, healthy, all-you-can-eat breakfast. We guarantee comfort, cleanliness and courteous service along with the most convenient location in town. VISA, MasterCard. Call or write Larry and Pat Vezina, Box 722, Dawson City, YT Y0B 1G0. Phone/fax (867) 993-5941; e-mail: 5thave@dawson.net. [ADVERTISEMENT]

Klondike Kate's Cabins and Restaurant. We offer you charming, clean and affordable accommodations with private bath. Located near all major attractions. Enjoy the friendly atmosphere of our restaurant, set in a 1904 historic building. Dine inside or on our outdoor patio. Full-service, fully licensed restaurant with Canadian and ethnic foods. Espresso coffees. Special $3.99 breakfast. Box 417, Dawson City, YT Y0B 1G0. Phone (867) 993-6527. Fax (867) 993-6044. [ADVERTISEMENT]

White Ram Manor Bed & Breakfast. Look for the pink house at 7th and Harper. Centrally located. A clean, comfortable, friendly home-away-from-home. Full breakfast. Laundry. Guest kitchen. Barbecue/picnic sun deck area. Hot tub. Also, for Dawson's newest motel accommodation, consider our Bonanza Gold Motel & RV Park (see our display ad for more). Our guarantee: If there is a room in Dawson, we'll find it for

Territories Information Centre is located in the B.Y.N. (British Yukon Navigation) Building on Front Street, across from the Yukon visitor centre; open 9 A.M. to 8 P.M., June to September. Information on Northwest Territories and the Dempster Highway. Phone (867) 993-6167, fax 993-6334.

Elevation: 1,050 feet/320m. **Climate:** There are 20.9 hours of daylight June 21, 3.8 hours of daylight on Dec. 21. Mean high in July, 72°F/22.2°C. Mean low in January, -30.5°F/ -34.7°C. First fall frost end of August, last spring frost end of May. Annual snowfall 59.8 inches. **Radio:** CBC 560 AM and 104.9-FM. **Television:** Cable channels include 2 (ABC), 4 (ITV), 7 (CBC), 13 (BCTV), 28 (TBS), 31 (CNN) and others. **Newspaper:** *Klondike Sun* (semi-monthly) and *Dawson City Insider* (weekly).

Private Aircraft: Dawson City airport located 11.5 miles/18.5 km southeast (see **Milepost J 315.7**). Customs available.

Historically, Dawson City dates from the discovery of gold on a Klondike River tributary (Rabbit Creek, renamed Bonanza Creek) in 1896. Previously, the site had been a Native fish camp. There were several hundred prospectors in the Fortymile area before the big strike, and most of them swarmed over the Klondike creeks, staking claims long before stampeders began trickling into the country the following year.

Dawson City was Yukon's first capital, when the Yukon became a separate territory in 1898. But by 1953, Whitehorse—on the railway and the highway, and with a large airport—was so much the hub of activity that the federal government moved the capital from Dawson City, along with 800 civil servants, and years of tradition and pride. Some recompense was offered in the form of a road linking Whitehorse with the mining at Mayo and Dawson City. With its completion, White Pass trucks replaced White Pass river steamers.

New government buildings were built in Dawson, including a fire hall. In 1962 the federal government reconstructed the Palace Grand Theatre for a gold rush festival that featured the Broadway musical *Foxy,* with Bert Lahr. A museum was established in the Administration Building and tours and entertainments were begun.

Dawson City was declared a national his-

toric site in the early 1960s. Parks Canada is currently involved with 35 properties in Dawson City. Many buildings have been restored, some reconstructed and others stabilized. Parks Canada offers an interpretive program each summer for visitors to this historic city.

Dawson City is hosting a "Decade of Centennials" to 2002. For further information on events, contact the Klondike Centennial Society, Bag 1996, Dawson City, YT Y0B 1G0.

ACCOMMODATIONS/VISITOR SERVICES

Accustomed to a summer influx of visitors, Dawson has modern hotels and motels (rates average $75 and up) and several bed and breakfasts. The community has a bank, ATM (cash advances on MasterCard and VISA are also available at Diamond Tooth Gertie's Casino), restaurants, 4 laundromats (with showers), a grocery store with bakery, a deli/grocery store, general stores, souvenir shops, churches, art gallery, post office, government offices, government liquor store, nursing station and doctor services, information centre, hostel, swimming pool, tennis, basketball and plenty of entertainment. Many Dawson City merchants abide by the Fair Exchange Policy, offering travelers an exchange rate within 4 percent of the banks'. Dawson City's hotels and motels fill up early, especially at times of special events. Reservations are a must from June through August.

Bear Creek Bed & Bannock. First Nation family offers "a touch of culture." This 4 you. (Reservations recommended.) VISA, MasterCard. Box 302, Dawson City, YT Y0B 1G0. Phone (867) 993-5772. Fax (867) 993-6509. Internet: www.dawson.net/ white-ram. [ADVERTISEMENT]

There are 2 Yukon government (YTG) campgrounds in the Dawson area. Yukon River YTG campground is across the Yukon River (by ferry) from town, adjacent to the west-side ferry approach (see **Milepost D 0.2** on Top of the World Highway log, following Dawson City section). Klondike River YTG campground is southeast of town near the airport (see **Milepost J 315.2**). Private RV parks in the Dawson area include Gold Rush Campground, downtown at 5th and York; GuggieVille, east of town at **Milepost J 324.5**; Bonanza Gold RV Park at **Milepost J 324.6**; and Dawson City R.V. Park and Campground at **Milepost J 324.7**. ▲

TRANSPORTATION

Air: Dawson City airport is 11.5 miles/18.5 km southeast of the city. Air North connects Dawson City with Whitehorse (daily service in summer); with Inuvik, NWT, Old Crow and Juneau (3 times weekly in summer); and Fairbanks (4 times weekly in summer). Charter service available from Alkan Air. Charter and flightseeing tours available from South Arctic Air. Helicopter tours from Trans North Air.

Ferry: The Yukon government operates a free ferry, the *George Black,* across the Yukon River from about the third week in May to mid-October (depending upon breakup and freezeup). The ferry operates 24 hours a day (except for Wednesdays, 5–7 A.M. when it is shut down for servicing), and departs Dawson City on demand. The ferry carries vehicles and passengers across to the public campground and is the only connection to the Top of the World Highway (Yukon Highway 9). Be prepared to wait as long as 3 hours during peak traffic periods (7–11 A.M. and 4–7 P.M. daily). Shut off all propane appliances and follow directions from ferry personnel when loading and unloading. Tour bus traffic has priority 6–9 A.M. and 5–9 P.M.; fuel truck traffic has priority 7 P.M. to 6 A.M. Phone (867) 993-5441 or 993-5344 for more information.

Bus: Service between Whitehorse and Dawson City by Norline coaches; 3 times weekly June through September. Service between Inuvik, NWT, and Dawson City available by charter only, contact Gold City Tours. Service from Whitehorse via Dawson City to Tok, AK, by Alaska Direct Buslines; weekly. Phone (800) 770-6652.

Taxi: Airport taxi service available from downtown hotels and bed and breakfasts. Scheduled and charter limo service available from Gold City Tours.

Rental Car: Car and truck rentals at Norcan, located in the Northern Superior Bldg., and Budget Rent-A-Car, located on Craig Street.

Yukon Native heritage is demonstrated at Ancient Voices Wilderness Camp.

(© Earl L. Brown, staff)

ATTRACTIONS

Take a Walking Tour. Town-core tours leave the Visitor Reception Centre 2 times daily June to mid-August, once daily end of May to early June and late August to early September. The 1½ hour guided walk highlights the history and charters of Dawson City. Audio tapes also available. Fee is $5 adult, $2.50 youth, $12.50 family.

The Commissioner's Residence on Front Street was once the residence of Hon. George Black, M.P., Speaker of the House of Commons, and his famous wife, Martha Louise, who walked to Dawson City via the Trail of '98 and stayed to become the First Lady of the Yukon. A 1-hour tour, is given 2 times daily in summer. Admission is $5 adult, $2.50 youth, $12.50 family.

Take a Bus Tour. Motorcoach and van tours of Klondike creeks, goldfields and Dawson City are available; inquire at Gold City Tours (ask about step-on guide service, too). For a panoramic view of Dawson City, the Klondike River, Bonanza Creek and Yukon River, take the bus or drive the 5 miles/8 km to the top of Dome Mountain (elev. 2,911 feet/887m).

South Arctic Air provides air charter service to destinations within Alaska, Northwest Territories and the Yukon Take an adventure tour: Enjoy the relaxing hot mineral pools at Circle Hot Springs; dip your toes in the Arctic Ocean at Tuktoyaktuk; or soar over majestic mountain ranges to the Arctic Circle. Specialized tours offering unique Yukon flying experiences are available for budget travelers. Offices based in Dawson City at the airport or at the Whitehorse Motel (north end of Front Street). Phone (867) 993-6026, 1-800-376-4455. E-mail: flyer@southarcticair.yk.ca. Web site: http://www.southarcticair.yk.ca.[ADVERTISEMENT]

Take a River Tour: Yukon River Cruises offers tours aboard the miniature stern-wheeler launch *Yukon Lou,* leaving the dock behind Birch Cabin booking office near SS *Keno* at 1 P.M. daily in summer and traveling to Pleasure Island and the stern-wheeler

graveyard. Cruise takes 1½ hours. Fishwheel Charter offers guided 2-hour river tours 2 times a day; tickets at the Han Cultural Centre. Westours (Grayline Yukon) operates the *Yukon Queen II* on the Yukon River between Dawson City and Eagle, AK; check with the Grayline Yukon office about tickets. One-way and round-trip passage is sold on a space-available basis. The trip takes 4 hours downstream to Eagle, and 6 hours back to Dawson. Ancient Voices Wilderness Camp transports their guests via *River Dancer* boat to their camp on the Yukon River. Canoe rentals available from Dawson Trading Post and at the hostel across the river.

Ancient Voices Wilderness Camp. Let your adventurous spirit soar as you discover nature's splendor in an authentic First Nation's camp. Three northern Native cultures share their traditional way of life in a wilderness setting along the banks of the mighty Yukon River. Rustic cabins, wall tents, meals and cultural activities provided. Experience our highly acclaimed, personalized evening salmon barbecue feast. Day, overnight or package trips also available from Dawson City, transportation provided via our Ancient Voices "River Dancer" boats. Tickets sold locally at the Trading Post on 5th Ave. Canoe travelers from Whitehorse to Dawson have enthusiastically remarked, "We have discovered an oasis in the Yukon!" Group discounts. VISA, MasterCard accepted. Mailing address: Box 679, Dawson City, YK Y0B 1G0. Phone (867) 993-5605. Fax (867) 993-6532. Internet: www.yukon.net/avw-camp. [ADVERTISEMENT]

Cruise the Yukon River. Cruise from Dawson City down the famous Yukon River to Eagle, Alaska, aboard the MV *Yukon Queen II*. Retrace the old stern-wheeler route of this historic Gold Rush area as you cruise past abandoned settlements among the forested hills. A hearty prospector's meal is included. Daily departures. Roundtrip fare is $176 U.S. per person. Prices subject to change. Phone (867) 993-5599. [ADVERTISEMENT]

Pleasure Island Restaurant. Don't miss the riverboat cruise on the MV *Yukon Lou* (refurbished 1996). See the old stern-wheeler shipyard, historic Native village of Moose

hide and stop in at Pleasure Island for an all-you-can-eat smoked salmon barbecue. Dinner includes garden fresh salad and slow-baked potatoes, topped off by homemade chocolate cake. Steak or chicken available on request. Lunch cruises include a soup and salad buffet. This is a "must" when in Dawson City. For reservations phone (867) 993-5482 or (907) 883-3292 (September–May). Group rates. [ADVERTISEMENT]

Visit the Palace Grand Theatre. This magnificently reconstructed theatre, now a national historic site, is home to the "Gaslight Follies," a turn-of-the-century entertainment. Performances nightly except Tuesday, from mid-May to mid-September. Arizona Charlie Meadows opened the Palace

Grand in 1899, and today's visitors, sitting in the curtained boxes around the balcony, will succumb to the charm of this beautiful theatre. Tours of the building are conducted once daily by Parks Canada, from the end of May through early September. Films and presentations daily in summer. Admission $5 adult, $2.50 youth, $12.50 family, or Parks Pass.

Diamond Tooth Gertie's Casino, open daily 7 P.M. to 2 A.M. mid-May to mid-September, has Klondike gambling tables (specially licensed in Yukon), 56 "Vegas-style" slot machines, bar service and floor shows nightly. You may have a soft drink if you prefer, and still see the cancan girls present their floor show. Persons under 19 not admitted. Gertie's hosts Yukon Talent Night in August.

Dawson City Museum. Housed in the renovated Territorial Administration Building on 5th Avenue, the museum is open daily from 10 A.M. to 6 P.M., mid-May through early September; by appointment year-round. Admission fees: $4 adults, $3 senior or youth, $10 family.

Featured are the Kings of the Klondike and City Life Galleries, hourly audiovisual and dramatic presentations, and the museum's collection of narrow-gauge locomotives, including a Vauclain-type Baldwin engine, the last one in existence in Canada. Weekly lecture series during summer; check for schedule. The films "City of Gold" and "The Yukoner" are shown daily. A selection of silent film serials, news and documentary reels from 1903 to 1929 is shown in the gallery. Also take part in the "Meet a Klondike Character" show and explore the "Klondike Gold" CD Rom.

The museum has a gift shop, wheelchair ramp, resource library, genealogy service and an extensive photography collection. For more information write the museum at Box 303, Dawson City, YT Y0B 1G0; phone (867) 993-5291, fax 993-5839.

Art's Gallery offers limited edition and original works by Northern artists, and specializes in Yukon-made crafts; pottery, baskets, moosehair tuftings. Featuring soapstone carvings and unique creations from Canada's Arctic. Mastodon, antler, silver jewelry, and a wide selection of Klondike and illustrated children's books also offered, with post and art cards too! We ship everywhere! Third Ave. across from Old Post Office. (867) 993-6967. [ADVERTISEMENT]

Peabody's Photo Parlour. Capture summer memories with a unique Klondike photo in 1900s costumes. Same-day film processing (ask about our 1-hour service), film and camera supplies. Northern artwork, a great selection of postcards, Yukon souvenirs, topographical maps. VISA, MasterCard. Located on 2nd Avenue at Princess. Phone (867) 993-5209. [ADVERTISEMENT]

SS _Keno_ National Historic Site. The SS _Keno_ was the last steamer to run the Yukon River when she sailed from Whitehorse in 1960 to her present berth on the riverbank next to the bank. Under restoration in 1998. An interpretive display is set up beside the site.

Visit Robert Service's Cabin. Highly recommended. On the hillside on 8th Avenue, the author–bank clerk's cabin has been restored by Parks Canada. Stories and poetry recitals are offered daily in summer. Photographers are welcomed, but no videotaping. Visitors come from every part of the world to sign the guest book on the rickety desk

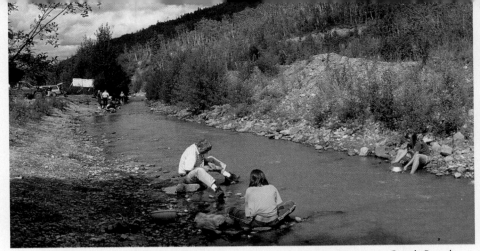

Visitors try their hand at gold panning at Claim No. 6 on Bonanza Creek Road.
(© Earl L. Brown, staff)

where Service wrote his famous poems, including "The Shooting of Dan McGrew" and "The Cremation of Sam McGee." Open daily. Admission: $6 adult, $3 youth.

Visit the Historic Post Office, where you may buy stamps; all first-class mail sent from here receives the old hand-cancellation stamp. Open daily.

Fire Fighters Museum, located at the fire hall at 5th Avenue and King Street, is open Monday to Saturday, 12:30 to 5:30 P.M. Admission: Donation.

Tr'ondek Hwech'in (Han) Cultural Centre, at Front and York streets overlooking the Yukon River, presents the culture and history of the Han First Nation people. The centre has a theatre, arts and crafts shop, art exhibit area and barbecue and picnic facilities.

Visit the Jack London Interpretive Centre: Along 8th Avenue and past Service's home is Jack London's cabin, built from half of the logs saved from the original cabin in the Bush where the writer stayed on his way to the Klondike. Also at the site are a cache for perishables and a museum with photos and memorabilia. Interpretation daily at noon and 2:15 P.M. mid-May to mid-September. Admission charged. Dick North, author of _Cabin Fever—the Story of Jack London in Alaska and Yukon_, is curator and consultant at the cabin.

Pierre Berton Residence, located on 8th Avenue, was once home of the famous Canadian author. Now used for a writer-in-residence program. View the grounds and interpretive signage placed by the Klondike Visitors Association.

Special Events. Dawson City hosts a number of unique celebrations during the year. In May, there's the Dawson City International Gold Show; phone (867) 993-6720 for dates. Gertie's International Dart Tournament is scheduled for May 28–30, 1999. The Commissioner's Ball is held June 5, 1999. This gala event, commemorating Yukon becoming a territory in 1898, features turn-of-the-century fashion. The Yukon Gold Panning Championship is held July 1 each year in Dawson City, along with a celebration of Canada Day. The Annual Dawson City Music Festival, July 23–25, 1999, features entertainers and artists from Canada and the United States, free workshops, dances and dinners. Tickets and information from the Music Festival Assoc., phone (867) 993-5584, fax (867) 993-5510.

If you are near Dawson Aug. 14–16, 1999, be sure to join the Discovery Days Festival fun when Yukon Order of Pioneers stages its annual parade. This event is a Yukon holiday commemorating the Klondike gold discovery of Aug. 17, 1896.

The Great Klondike International Outhouse Race, held the Sunday of Labour Day weekend (Sept. 5, 1999), is a race of decorated outhouses on wheels over a 1.9 mile/3-km course through the streets of Dawson City. The Mixed Slo-Pitch Tournament, Sept. 3–6, 1999, draws teams from the Yukon and Alaska. And at Yukon Talent Night, Sept. 24, 1999, local stars and visitors take to the stage at Diamond Tooth Gertie's Casino to perform songs, skits and comedy.

See the Midnight Sun: If you are in Dawson City on June 21, be sure to make it to the top of the Dome by midnight, when the sun barely dips behind the 6,000-foot/1,829-m Ogilvie Mountains to the north—the picture of a lifetime. There's quite a local celebration on the Dome on June 21, so for those who don't like crowds, a visit before or after summer solstice will also afford fine views and photos. Turnoff for Dome Mountain is at **Milepost J 325.8**; it's about a 5-mile/8-km drive.

Klondike Nugget & Ivory Shop features a unique display of gold nuggets from the Klondike creeks. Gold from each creek is very different and can be clearly seen in this

display. We also specialize in gold nuggets, locally produced gold nugget jewellery and mammoth ivory jewellery and carvings. Don't miss the 9-foot mammoth tusk also on exhibit! Located at the corner of Front and Queen streets. Phone (867) 993-5432. [ADVERTISEMENT]

Pan for Gold. The chief attraction for many visitors is panning for gold. There are several mining operations set up to permit you to actually pan for your own "colours" under friendly guidance. The Klondike Visitors Assoc. sponsors a public panning area at No. 6 above Discovery, 13 miles/21 km from Dawson City on Bonanza Creek Road. Check with the Visitor Reception Centre for more information.

Dredge No. 4. Built in 1912 for the Canadian Klondike Mining Co.'s claim on Bonanza Creek, this historic dredge is the largest wooden hull bucket-line dredge in North America. Scheduled 1-hour tours several times daily June through August. Admission: $5 adult, $2.50 youth, $12.50 family, or Parks Pass. To reach the dredge, take Bonanza Creek Road from **Milepost J 324.5** 7.8 miles/12.3 km up famous Bonanza Creek, to Dredge No. 4. Continue up Bonanza Creek Road for Discovery Claim and to see miles of gravel tailings worked over 2 and 3 times in the continuing search for gold.

Bear Creek Camp, (see **Milepost J 319.6** on the Klondike Highway), was operated by Yukon Consolidated Gold Corp. until 1966. Tours are conducted by Parks Canada interpreters; check with the Visitor Reception Centre for current tour schedule. The compound features the Gold Room, where the gold was melted and poured into bricks, complete blacksmith and machinery shops, and other well-preserved structures. Open 9:30 A.M. to 5 P.M. from mid-June to late August. Admission: $5 adults, $2.50 youth, $12.50 family, or Parks Pass.

Ridge Road Heritage Trail. Originally built in 1899 to move mining supplies along Bonanza Creek, the Ridge Road was abandoned by 1902. The road was reopened in 1996 as a 20-mile/32-km heritage trail. Travel time is 1¹/₂ to 2 days by foot (or 4–6 hours by mountain bike). Interpretive signs and building remnants are along the route, which winds along the high ground between Bonanza and Hunker creeks. Short walks possible from the Upper Trailhead (outhouses) on Upper Bonanza Road to Soda Station on the abandoned Klondike Mines Railway line, and from Jackson Gulch (Lower) Trailhead behind Callison subdivision to the Yukon Ditch (Trail Gulch diversion). There are 2 tent campgrounds on the trail: 11-Mile at Mile 7/11.3 km, and 15-Mile at Mile 12.2/19.2; outhouses, firepits and water pump.

Klondike Loop Log

(continued from page 268)

The **Top of the World Highway** (Yukon Highway 9) connects Dawson City with the Taylor Highway (Alaska Route 5). The Alaska Highway is 174.5 miles/280.8 km from here; Eagle, AK, is 143.4 miles/230.8 km from here. Yukon Highway 9 and the Taylor Highway (Alaska Route 5) in Alaska are not maintained from mid-October to April, and the arrival of snow effectively closes the roads for winter. *CAUTION: Allow plenty of time for this drive; average speed for this road is 25 to 40 mph/40 to 64 kmph. DRIVE WITH YOUR HEADLIGHTS ON! The Canadian portion of the highway is seal coated; the Alaska side is gravel. Check with the Dawson City Visitor Reception Centre for current road and weather conditions; phone (867) 993-5566.*

This section of the log shows distance from Dawson City (D) followed by distance from junction with the Taylor Highway (T) at Jack Wade Junction. Physical kilometreposts show distance from Dawson City.

YUKON HIGHWAY 9

D 0 T 78.8 (126.8 km) **DAWSON CITY.** A free ferry carries passengers and vehicles from Dawson City across the Yukon River to the beginning of the Top of the World High-

way in summer. *NOTE: The ferry wait in heavy traffic may be as long as 3 hours during peak times.*

D 0.2 (0.3 km) **T 78.6** (126.5 km) **Yukon River** government campground on riverbank opposite Dawson City; 74 RV sites, 24 tent-only sites, 2 kitchen shelters, playground and drinking water. Camping fee $8. Within walking distance of stern-wheeler graveyard. Put in and takeout spot for Yukon River travelers. ▲

D 2.7 (4.4 km) **T 76.1** (122.5 km) Access to 9-hole golf course via 3.2-mile/5.1-km gravel road; rentals.

D 2.9 (4.6 km) **T 75.9** (122.1 km) Turnout for viewpoint overlooking Dawson City and the Yukon and Klondike rivers.

D 3.2 (5 km) **T 75.6** (121.7 km) Turnout with good view of Yukon River and river valley farms.

D 9 (12.4 km) **T 69.8** (112.3 km) Large rest area with toilets, picnic tables, litter barrels. Interpretive displays about the Fortymile caribou herd and information sign about Top of the World Highway (also has ferry information for travelers to Dawson City).

D 11 (15.6 km) **T 67.8** (109.1 km) "Top of the world" view as highway climbs above tree line.

D 16.4 (26.2 km) **T 62.4** (100.4 km) Snow fence along highway next 8 miles/13 km westbound.

D 18.4 (29.4 km) **T 60.4** (97.2 km) Turnout to south.

D 29.2 (47 km) **T 49.6** (79.8 km) Evidence of 1989 burn.

D 32.1 (51.2 km) **T 46.7** (75.2 km) First outcropping (westbound) of Castle Rock. Turnout to south with panoramic view of countryside.

D 33.1 (52.8 km) **T 45.7** (73.5 km) Distance marker shows customs 52 km, Dawson City 53 km.

D 35.2 (56 km) **T 43.6** (70.2 km) Main outcropping of Castle Rock; lesser formations are also found along this stretch. Centuries of erosion have created these formations. Turnout to south.

D 37.4 (59 km) **T 41.4** (66.6 km) Unmaintained road leads 25 miles/40 km to the former settlement of Clinton Creek, which served the Cassiar Asbestos Mine from 1967–79. There are no facilities or services available there. Distance marker shows U.S. border 43 km.

The confluence of the Yukon and Fortymile rivers is 3 miles/4.8 km below the former townsite of Clinton Creek. Clinton Creek bridge is an access point on the Fortymile River National Wild and Scenic River system, managed by the Bureau of Land Management. The Fortymile River offers intermediate and advanced canoeists over 100 miles/160 km of challenging water.

Yukon River, near Clinton Creek, grayling to 3 lbs. in April; chum salmon to 12 lbs. in August; king salmon to 40 lbs., July and August. **Fortymile River,** near Clinton Creek, grayling to 3 lbs. during spring breakup and fall freezeup; inconnu (sheefish) to 10 lbs. in July and August. ◄

D 54 (85.6 km) **T 24.8** (39.9 km) Old sod-roofed cabin to north, originally a supply and stopping place for the McCormick Transportation Co.

D 54.3 (86.1 km) **T 24.5** (39.4 km) Road forks south to old mine workings at Sixtymile, which have been reactivated by Cogasa Mining Co. Keep to right for Alaska. The road winds above timberline for many miles. The lack of fuel for warmth and shel-

ter made this a perilous trip for the early sourdoughs.

D 64.1 (101.9 km) **T 14.7** (23.7 km) Large gravel turnout. Information sign about Top of the World Highway viewpoint.

D 65.2 (103.7 km) **T 13.6** (21.9 km) Pull-through rest area with toilet and litter barrels; good viewpoint. Just across the highway, short hike to cairn, excellent viewpoint. Highest point on Top of the World Highway (elev. 4,515 feet/1,376 m).

D 66.1 (105.1 km) **T 12.7** (20.4 km) **U.S.–Canada Border** (elev. 4,127 feet/1,258m). Customs only; no public facilities available. *IMPORTANT: U.S. and Canada customs are open from about May 15 to Sept. 15. In summer 1998, customs was open 7 days a week, 9 A.M. to 9 P.M. (Pacific time) on the Canadian side; 8 A.M. to 8 P.M. (Alaska time) on the U.S. side. Customs hours of operation subject to change. Check with the RCMP or Visitor Reception Centre in Dawson City to make certain the border crossing will be open. Serious fines are levied for crossing the border without clearing customs! There are no restrooms, services or currency exchanges available here.*

Canada Customs and Immigration Little Gold Creek. All traffic entering Canada must stop here.

The **U.S. Poker Creek Border Station** office, just west of the Canadian station. All traffic entering the United States must stop here. A short hike up the hill behind U.S. border station provides good viewpoint.

TIME ZONE CHANGE: Alaska observes Alaska time; Yukon Territory observes Pacific time.

D 67.1 (108 km) **T 11.7** (18.8 km) Large double-ended turnout to north with viewing platform, toilet, litter barrel. Welcome to Alaska and Fortymile River interpretive signs.

D 69.2 (111.4 km) **T 9.6** (15.4 km) **BOUNDARY.** Boundary Lodge was one of the first roadhouses in Alaska; food, gas, lodging, diesel, tire repair, emergency phone.

Watch your gas supply. Between here and Tetlin Junction on the Alaska Highway, gas is available again only at Chicken, **Milepost TJ 66.5.** From here to Eagle, gas may be available at O'Brien Creek Lodge, **Milepost TJ 125.4.** Gas is available in Eagle.

Private Aircraft: Boundary airstrip; elev. 2,940 feet/896m; length 2,100 feet/640m; earth and gravel; fuel 80; unattended.

D 78 (125.6 km) **T 0.8** (1.3 km) Viewpoint.

D 78.8 (126.9 km) **T 0 Jack Wade Junction.**

Junction with the Taylor Highway (Alaska Route 5), which leads north 64.6 miles/104 km to Eagle, AK, or south 95.7 miles/154 km to Tetlin Junction, just east of Tok, on the Alaska Highway. Turn to **Milepost TJ 95.7** in the TAYLOR HIGHWAY section.

SILVER TRAIL HIGHWAY ⑪

Connects: Klondike Hwy. to Keno City, YT **Length:** 69 miles
Road Surface: 50% paved, 50% gravel
Season: Open all year to Mayo and Keno City
Major Attraction: Keno City Mining Museum

(See map page 260)

	Keno City	Klondike Hwy. Jct.	Mayo
Keno City		69	37
Klondike Hwy. Jct.	69		32
Mayo	37	32	

Keno Mining Museum is well worth a stop to learn more about the mining history of the area. (© Earl L. Brown, staff)

The Silver Trail leads northeast from the Klondike Highway (see **Milepost J 214.4** in the KLONDIKE LOOP section) to Mayo, Elsa and Keno City. From its junction with the Klondike Highway (Yukon Highway 2), the Silver Trail (Yukon Highway 11) leads 31.9 miles/51.3 km to Mayo; 60.3 miles/97 km to Elsa; and 69.1 miles/111.2 km to Keno City. The Silver Trail also provides access to Duncan Creek Road, the original Silver Trail. It is approximately 140 miles/225 km round-trip to Keno City and an easy day trip for motorists. The road is asphalt-surfaced to Mayo, hard-packed gravel from Mayo to Keno. Watch for soft shoulders, especially in wet weather. The highway is open all year to Mayo; maintained winter road to Keno City. Gas is available only at Mayo and at Stewart Crossing.

There is an information kiosk on the Klondike Highway at the south end of Stewart River bridge. Stop at the kiosk for information on the Silver Trail, or visit Binet House in Mayo. Or write Silver Trail Tourism, Box 268, Mayo, YT Y0B 1M0; phone (in summer) (867) 996-2926, fax (867) 995-2409, winter phone (867) 996-2290.

If you have a Yukon Explorer's Passport, the Binet House and Keno Mining Museum are considered the 2 most exclusive passport stamps.

The Silver Trail to Mayo follows the Stewart River through what has been one of the richest silver mining regions in Canada. The Silver Trail region encompasses the tradi-tional lands of the Na Cho N'y'ak Dun First Nations.

Emergency medical services: In Mayo, phone (867) 996-4444; or phone the RCMP toll free, Yukon-wide, at (867) 667-5555.

Silver Trail Log

Distance is measured from the junction with the Klondike Highway (K).

K 0 Silver Trail (Stewart Crossing) . The Silver Trail leads northeast from **Milepost J 214.4** on the Klondike Highway.

Junction of Silver Trail (Yukon Highway 11) and Klondike Highway (Yukon Highway 2). Turn to **Milepost J 214.4** in the KLONDIKE LOOP section for log of Klondike Highway.

K 0.2 (0.3 km) Marker shows distance to Mayo 51 km, Elsa 97 km, Keno 110 km.
K 1.2 (2 km) Stewart River to the south.
K 3 (4.8 km) Bad curve. Turnout to south.
K 9.6 (15.4 km) Large gravel pit turnout to south.
K 12 (19.2 km) Large double-ended turnout with litter barrels overlooking the Stewart River.
K 27.4 (44.1 km) Pull-through rest area; outhouses, litter barrel, picnic tables.
K 30.7 (49.5 km) Winding descent for northeast-bound traffic; good view of valley.
K 31.2 (50.2 km) McIntyre Park picnic area to south on banks of the Mayo River; 9 picnic sites and a shelter.
K 31.3 (50.3 km) **Mayo River** bridge. Good fishing from bridge for grayling. 🐟
K 31.9 (51.3 km) **Junction** with access road to Mayo (description follows). Turn right (south) for Mayo, keep left (north) for road to Elsa and Keno City.

Mayo

Located on the bank of the Stewart River near its confluence with the Mayo River. **Population:** 500. **Emergency Services: RCMP**, phone (867) 996-5555. **Fire Dept.**, phone (867) 996-2222. **Nursing Station**, phone (867) 996-2345. **Ambulance**, phone (867) 996-4444.

Visitor Information: At **Binet House Interpretive Centre**, open 10 A.M. to 6 P.M. daily from late June through first week in September; phone (867) 996-2926. Exhibits include floral and mineral displays, silver and galena samples, and information panels on mining and geology. Get your Yukon Explorer's Passport stamped here.

Elevation: 1,650 feet/503m. **Climate:** Residents claim it's the coldest and hottest spot in Yukon. Record low, -80°F/-62.2°C (February 1947); record high, 97°F/36.1°C (June 1969). **Radio:** CBC 1230, CHON-FM 98.5, CKRN 98-FM. **Television:** CBC Anik, Channel 7, BCTV, TVNC, ITV, WDIV. **Transportation:** Charter floatplane and helicopter service available. Scheduled bus service.

Private Aircraft: Mayo airstrip, 4 miles/6.5 km north; elev. 1,653 feet/504m;

length 4,850 feet/1,478m; gravel; fuel 100, Jet B.

Mayo began as a river settlement and port in 1902–03 after gold was discovered in the area. It was also known as Mayo Landing. River traffic increased with silver ore shipments from Keno Hill silver mines to Whitehorse. A walking tour brochure of Mayo's historic sites is available.

Today, Mayo is a service centre for mineral exploration in the area. Yukon Electrical Co. Ltd. operates a hydroelectric project here. Canoeists can put in at Mayo on the Stewart River for a paddle to Stewart Crossing or Dawson City.

The Mayo Midnight Marathon is scheduled for June 18, 1999. The race includes a half marathon, half marathon walk and 10K races. Phone (867) 996-2368 or fax (867) 996-2378 for details.

Mayo has most traveler facilities including 2 motels and bed and breakfasts; food service at Bedrock Motel, Chinese restaurant and a cafe; laundromat; 2 gas station (diesel); fishing licenses and snack bar at Heartland Services–Mayo Chevron; hardware, grocery and variety stores (closed Sunday). Tire repair and minor vehicle repair are available. Post office, liquor store and library located in the Territorial Building. Bank service available 10 A.M. to 2 P.M., Tuesday, Thursday and Friday.

Bedrock Motel. Located 1 mile north of Mayo on the Silver Trail. New facility containing 12 spacious rooms and lounge. Full baths, continental breakfast, home-cooked

meals, laundry facilities, air conditioning, wheelchair-accessible suite. Major credit cards accepted. Rates from $75 up. Automotive and bottle propane available, dump station, shower, camping, grassed RV sites (power available). Darren and Joyce Ronaghan, Box 69, Mayo, YT Y0B 1M0. Phone (867) 996-2290, fax (867) 996-2728 or e-mail bedrock@yknet.yk.ca. [ADVERTISEMENT] ▲

Silver Trail Log
(continued)

K 32.8 (52.8 km) Mayo airport, built in 1928 by the Treadwell Mining Co.

K 34.9 (56.2 km) Side road to Mayo hydro dam, built in 1951 and completed in 1952.

K 35.8 (57.6 km) Turnoff to west for Five Mile Lake Yukon government campground; 20 sites, boat launch, picnic tables, firepits.

K 36.1 (58.1 km) Five Mile Lake day-use area. Pavement ends, gravel begins, northbound. ▲

K 37.6 (60.5 km) Wareham Lake to east, created by the Mayo River power project.

K 38.2 (61.4 km) Survival shelter to east.

K 42.9 (69 km) **Junction** of Yukon Highway 11 with Minto Lake Road and Duncan Creek Road. Turn west and drive 12 miles/19 km for **Minto Lake;** good fishing for lake trout and grayling. Also access to Highet Creek. ⚓

Turn east at junction for 25-mile/40-km **Duncan Creek Road,** which leads to Keno City. The original Silver Trail, Duncan Creek Road was used by Treadwell Yukon during the 1930s to haul silver ore from Keno into Mayo, where it was loaded onto riverboats.

The road is mostly good hard-packed gravel. Motorists note, however, that the last 10 miles/16 km into Keno City via Duncan Creek Road are narrow and winding, slippery when wet and not recommended for large vehicles or trailers. At Mile 14 Duncan Creek Road junctions with a 6-mile/10-km side road which leads to **Mayo Lake.** The lake was named for Alfred S. Mayo, a steamboat captain and a prospecting and trading post partner of Harper and McQuesten in the late 1800s. There is good fishing along the **Mayo River** to the dam at the west end of Mayo Lake. At Mile 14.2 there is a private gold mine (gold panning and guided placer mine tour). At Mile 25 Duncan Creek Road junctions with Highway 11 at Keno City. ⚓

K 47.1 (77 km) Watch for turnoff for Mount Haldane trail; follow gravel road 2 miles/3.2 km to trailhead. This 4-mile-/6.4-km-long walking trail leads to the summit of **Mount Haldane,** elev. 6,023 feet/1,836m, and offers sweeping views of the McQuesten River valley and the towns of Elsa and Mayo. A brochure on the trail suggests anyone in average physical condition can make the round-trip in 6 hours (including an hour for lunch at the top). But in 1998, *MILEPOST®* readers reported the trail was poorly marked and dangerous, a *strenuous* 6-hour (minimum) hike with slippery sections and a huge scree at the end.The switch-backed trail is visible on the south face of Mount Haldane. The trail was cut by a mining company in the 1970s. The Mount Haldane Climb is scheduled for June 1999; phone (876) 996-2600 or fax (876) 996-2907 for details.

K 48 (77.2 km) **Halfway Lakes;** fishing for northern pike. Silver Trail Inn; food and lodging in summer. ⚓

K 49 (78.8 km) Mount Haldane Lions survival shelter.

K 54.9 (88.3 km) South McQuesten River Road.

K 60.3 (97 km) **ELSA** (pop. 10) was a company town for United Keno Hill Mines, formerly one of the largest silver mines in North America and one of the Yukon's oldest continuously operating hardrock mines until its closure in 1989. The Elsa claim is a well-mineralized silver vein, located on Galena Hill and named for the sister of prospector Charlie Brefalt, who received $250,000 for Treadwell Yukon's richest mine. A plaque here commemorates American engineer Livingston Wernecke, who came to the Keno Hill area in 1919 to investigate the silver–lead ore discoveries for Treadwell–Yukon Mining Co.

K 63.8 (102.6 km) Side road leads north to Hanson Lakes and McQuesten Lake. Galena Mountains to east. An information sign marks the Wind River trail, a former winter road to oil and mining exploration sites, which leads 300 miles/483 km north to the Bell River. The twin towers are abandoned telephone relays.

Keno City

K 69.1 (111.2 km) End of the Silver Trail. **Population:** about 25. Originally called Sheep Hill by the early miners, Keno City was renamed Keno—a gambling game—after the Keno mining claim that was staked by Louis Bouvette in July 1919. This enormously rich discovery of silver and galena sparked the interest of 2 large mining companies, the Guggenheims and Treadwell Yukon, who set up camps in the area. During the 1920s, Keno City was a boom town.

Keno has the Keno City Hotel, with a unique bar (no food service available), and a snack bar. Washers, dryers and showers available for the public at the recreation hall. There is a city campground on Lightning Creek; 17 sites, water, firewood and firepits. ▲

Well worth a visit here is the Keno Mining Museum, phone (867) 995-2792, fax (867) 395-2730. Photographs and tools recall the mining history of the area. It is open 10 A.M. to 6 P.M. in summer. Get your Yukon Explorer's Passport stamped here.

There are a number of hiking trails in the Keno area; inquire at the museum. The Summit trail (can be driven) leads 6.5 miles/10.5 km to the milepost sign on top of **Keno Hill,** elev. 6,065 feet/1,849m. *NOTE: Before driving up to the summit, check at the Keno City Museum or the Keno City Snack Bar for current road conditions.*

Keno City Snack Bar. See display ad this section.

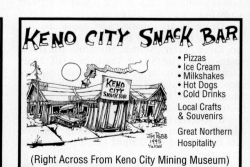

TAYLOR HIGHWAY ⑤

Connects: Alaska Hwy. (Tetlin Jct.) to Eagle, AK   **Length:** 160 miles
Road Surface: 85% gravel, 15% paved   **Season:** Closed in winter
Steepest Grade: 9 percent
Major Attraction: Fort Egbert

(See map, page 261)

	Chicken	Dawson City	Eagle	Tok
Chicken		109	94	78
Dawson City	109		144	187
Eagle	94	144		172
Tok	78	187	172	

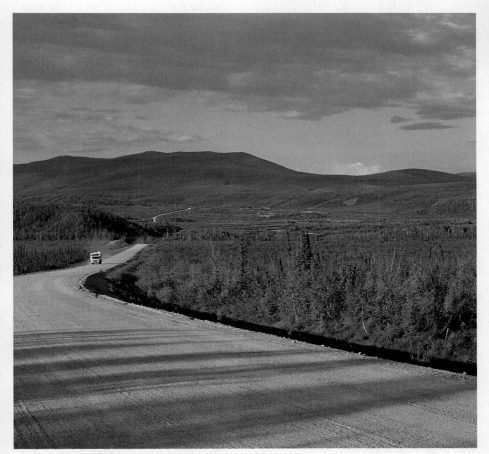

The Taylor Highway near Chicken, AK. (© Tom Culkin)

The 160.3-mile/258-km Taylor Highway (Alaska Route 5) begins at Tetlin Junction on the Alaska Highway and ends at the small town of Eagle on the Yukon River. This is a beautiful "top of the world" drive, and Eagle is well worth a visit. Construction of the Taylor Highway began in 1946, and was completed to Eagle in late 1953, providing access to the historic Fortymile Mining District.

The Taylor Highway is a narrow, winding, mountain road with many steep hills and some hairpin curves. Allow plenty of time to drive its length. The first 24 miles/38.6 km are seal coated, the rest is gravel with sporadic soft spots during breakup or after heavy rains. Road surface ranges from very poor to good depending on maintenance. Shoulders are narrow and may be unstable. Large RVs and trailers especially should use caution in driving this road. Watch for large tanker trucks, some with double trailers, hauling fuel between Tetlin Junction and Boundary. (Your best defense is to pull over

and stop, if possible.) The Taylor Highway is not maintained from mid-October to April, and the arrival of snow effectively closes the road for winter.

The Taylor is the shortest route to Dawson City, YT, from Alaska. Drive 95.7 miles/154 km north on the Taylor Highway to Jack Wade Junction, and turn east on the Top of the World Highway (Yukon Highway 9) for Dawson City. (See end of KLONDIKE LOOP section for log of Yukon Highway 9.)

Dawson City-bound travelers keep in mind that gas is available only at Chicken and at Boundary Lodge. Also, the U.S. and Canadian customs offices at the border are open from about mid-May to mid-September. Customs hours for summer 1998 were 8 A.M. to 8 P.M. Alaska time; 9 A.M. to 9 P.M. Pacific time on the Canadian side. Check for current information with Alaska Public Lands Information Center; (907) 883-5667. There are no restrooms, services or currency exchanges available at the border. *IMPORTANT: You cannot cross the border*

unless the customs office for the country you are entering is open. Severe fines are levied for crossing without clearing customs. Officials at Canadian customs are concerned about child abductions. If you are traveling with children, remember to bring identification for them.

NOTE: All gold-bearing ground in area is claimed. Do not pan in streams.

The highway also provides river runners with access to the Fortymile River National Wild and Scenic River system. A brochure on access points and float times is available from the Bureau of Land Management, 1150 University Ave., Fairbanks, AK 99709-3844; phone (907) 474-2350.

The Fortymile Mining District is home range for the Fortymile caribou herd. Once a massive herd of 500,000 animals, the herd is now stable at about 23,000 caribou. The herd moves east across the highway in late fall for the winter, and returns again in spring for calving. During the summer, small bands of caribou can sometimes be seen in the high country above timberline. The Fortymile Caribou Planning Team, a group of Alaskan and Yukon residents, was created to develop a strategy for restoring the caribou herd and other area wildlife. State, federal and territorial agencies sponsored the effort and provide logistical support.

Emergency medical services: Between Tetlin Junction and O'Brien Creek bridge at **Milepost TJ 113.2**, phone the Tok Area EMS at 911 or (907) 883-5111. Between O'Brien Creek bridge and Eagle, phone the Eagle EMS at (907) 547-2300 or (907) 547-2211. Use CB channel 21.

Taylor Highway Log

Distance from Tetlin Junction (TJ) is followed by distance from Eagle (E).

ALASKA ROUTE 5
TJ 0 E 160.3 (258 km) **Tetlin Junction.** 40 Mile Roadhouse; current status of services unknown.

Junction with the Alaska Highway. Turn to **Milepost DC 1301.7** in the ALASKA HIGHWAY section for log of that route.

Taylor Highway begins 9 miles/14.5 km of winding road northeast up out of the Tanana River valley. Highway traverses stabilized sand dunes first 5 miles/8 km. The first

Willow ptarmigan in late summer. (© Craig Brandt)

21.2 miles/34.1 km of the Taylor Highway are seal coated.

TJ 0.9 (1.4 km) **E 159.4** (256.5 km) Double-ended turnout to east.

TJ 2.7 (4.3 km) **E 157.6** (253.6 km) Large double-ended turnout to east.

TJ 4.5 (7.2 km) **E 155.8** (250.7 km) Large double-ended gravel turnout to east. A 0.7-mile/1.1-km trail leads to **Four Mile Lake;** rainbow trout and sheefish.   ➤

TJ 5.4 (8.7 km) **E 154.9** (249.3 km) Evidence of 1990 forest fire known as the Porcupine burn.

TJ 5.9 (9.5 km) **E 154.4** (248.5 km) Entering Tok Management Area, Tanana Valley State Forest, northbound.

TJ 6 (9.7 km) **E 154.3** (248.3 km) Double-ended turnout to east, easy for trailers.

Wildflowers along the highway include arnica, chiming bells, wild roses and Labrador tea. As the name suggests, Labrador tea leaves (and flowers) may be steeped in boiling water to make tea. However, according to Janice Scofield, author of *Discovering Wild Plants*, Labrador tea contains a narcotic toxin that can cause ill effects if used too frequently or in high concentrations.

TJ 9.4 (15.1 km) **E 150.9** (242.8 km) Entering Game Management Unit 20E northbound; entering GMU 12 southbound. Road begins gradual climb of Mount Fairplay for northbound travelers.

TJ 10 (16 km) **E 150.3** (240.5 km) Double-ended turnout to east.

TJ 12.1 (19.5 km) **E 148.2** (238.5 km) Entering Tok Management Area, Tanana State Forest, southbound.

TJ 14.6 (23.5 km) **E 145.7** (234.5 km) Small turnout to west. Blueberries in season.

TJ 16 (25.7 km) **E 144.3** (232.2 km) Parking at one of Mount Fairplay's several summits.

TJ 18.9 (30.2 km) **E 141.4** (226.2 km) Double-ended turnout to west.

TJ 21.2 (34.1 km) **E 139.1** (223.9 km) Long descent northbound from true summit of Mount Fairplay.

TJ 22.1 (35.4 km) **E 138.2** (221.1 km) Double-ended turnout to east. Information panels on Fortymile region and caribou herd.

TJ 22.4 (35.8 km) **E 137.9** (220.6 km) Double-ended turnout to east.

TJ 23 (37 km) **E 137.3** (219.4 km) Scenic views, Alaska Range to west.

TJ 24 (38.6 km) **E 136.3** (219.3 km) Pavement ends, gravel begins, northbound.

TJ 28.3 (45.5 km) **E 132** (212.4 km) Turnout with view to west.

TJ 32.8 (52.8 km) **E 127.5** (205.2 km) Turnout to west.

TJ 34.4 (55.4 km) **E 125.9** (202.6 km) Double-ended turnout with view to west.

TJ 35.1 (56.5 km) **E 125.2** (201.5 km) Entering **Fortymile Mining District** northbound. The second-oldest mining district in Alaska, it first yielded gold in 1886. Claims were filed in both Canada and Alaska due to boundary uncertainties.

Large double-ended turnout to east near summit of **Mount Fairplay** (elev. 5,541 feet/1,689m). Interpretive sign, viewing platform, litter barrels, aluminum recycling, toilet, wheelchair accessible.   ♿

NOTE: 9 percent downgrade northbound. Southbound, the road descends for the next 25 miles/40 km from Mount Fairplay's summit, winding through heavily forested terrain. Panoramic views of the Fortymile River forks' valleys. Views of the Alaska Range to the southwest.

TJ 39.1 (62.9 km) **E 121.2** (195 km) Large turnout to west, no easy turnaround.

TJ 43 (69.2 km) **E 117.3** (188.8 km) **Logging Cabin Creek** bridge (abrupt edge on bridge); small turnout to west at south end of bridge. Side road to creek. This is the south end of the Fortymile River National Wild and Scenic River system managed by BLM. Evidence of old forest fire.

TJ 49 (78.9 km) **E 111.3** (179.1 km) Loop roads through BLM West Fork Recreation Site; 25 sites (7 pull-through sites), tables, firepits, no water, covered tables, toilets, dumpsters. Access point of Fortymile River canoe trail. Improved campground. ▲

TJ 49.3 (79.3 km) **E 111** (178.6 km) Bridge over West Fork of the Dennison Fork of the Fortymile River. Access point for Fortymile River National Wild and Scenic River system.

TJ 50.5 (81.3 km) **E 109.8** (176.7 km) Taylor Creek bridge. Watch for potholes and rough road at bridge approaches (abrupt edge on bridge). All-terrain vehicle trail to Taylor and Kechumstuk mountains; heavily used in hunting season.

TJ 57 (91.7 km) **E 103.3** (166.2 km)

Scenic viewpoint turnout to east, no easy turnaround.

TJ 58.9 (94.8 km) **E 101.4** (163.2 km) Scenic viewpoint turnout to east.

TJ 62.5 (100.6 km) **E 97.8** (157.4 km) Turnout to west. Drive-in, no easy turnaround.

TJ 63.2 (101.7 km) **E 97.1** (156.3 km) View of Chicken.

TJ 63.3 (101.9 km) **E 97** (156.1 km) Turnout to west. Drive-in, no easy turnaround.

CAUTION: Steep descent northbound to Mosquito Fork.

TJ 64.1 (103.2 km) **E 96.2** (154.8 km) Well-traveled road leads to private buildings, not into Chicken.

TJ 64.3 (103.5 km) **E 96** (154.5 km) Bridge over Mosquito Fork of the Fortymile River; day-use area with table, toilet and litter barrel at north end of bridge. The Mosquito Fork is a favorite access point for the Fortymile National Wild and Scenic River system, according to the BLM.

TJ 66 (106.2 km) **E 94.3** (151.8 km) Entering **CHICKEN** (pop. 37), northbound. *(NOTE: Driving distance between Mileposts TJ 66 and 67 is 0.7 mile.)* This is the newer commercial settlement of Chicken. The original mining camp (abandoned, private property) is north of Chicken Creek (see **Milepost TJ 67**). Chicken is a common name in the North for ptarmigan. One story has it that the early miners wanted to name their camp ptarmigan, but were unable to spell it and settled for Chicken. Access point for the Fortymile River canoe trail is below Chicken airstrip.

Fuel is available in Chicken. Gas is also available at O'Brien Creek Lodge, en route to Eagle, **Milepost TJ 125.4**; in Boundary, en route to Canada (Top of the World Highway, **Milepost D 69.2**); or in Tok.

TJ 66.3 (106.7 km) **E 94** (151.3 km) Chicken post office (ZIP code 99732) located on hill beside the road. The late Ann Purdy lived in this area. The book *Tisha* is based on her experiences as a young schoolteacher in the Alaska Bush.

TJ 66.4 (106.9 km) **E 93.9** (151.1 km) Airport Road. Access to Chicken airstrip and "downtown" Chicken. Combination grocery store, restaurant, bar and gas station located here.

Private Aircraft: Chicken airstrip, adjacent southwest; elev. 1,640 feet/500m; length 2,500 feet/762m; gravel; maintained year-round.

The Chicken Creek Salmon Bake uses only wild Alaska–Yukon king salmon. Besides salmon, we also feature halibut, barbecue chicken, buffalo and halibut burgers, our famous potato salad and chowder. All are offered daily from 4 P.M. to 8 P.M. Another good reason to visit Beautiful Downtown Chicken, Alaska! [ADVERTISEMENT]

Downtown Chicken Mercantile Emporium, Chicken Creek Cafe, Saloon and Gas. Unfortunately, as too often happens, the main road bypasses the most interesting part of Chicken. If it's modern facilities you are looking for, original Chicken is not for you. The Chicken Creek Saloon and Cafe are some of the last remnants of the old frontier Alaska. It is a trading post where local miners (some straight out of Jack London and Robert Service) trade gold for supplies and drink. Tisha's schoolhouse and other historic buildings may be seen on the walking tour of old Chicken, meeting daily at

Beautiful Downtown Chicken Alaska

CHICKEN CREEK

CAFE

GREAT HOMEMADE FOOD!

Hamburgers - Pies
Pastries and Cinnamon Buns

Chicken Mercantile Emporium

World Famous Chicken T-Shirts
Chicken Souvenirs, Local Gold

Tisha Books

CHICKEN CREEK

SALMON BAKE

**Wild Yukon King Salmon
Halibut**

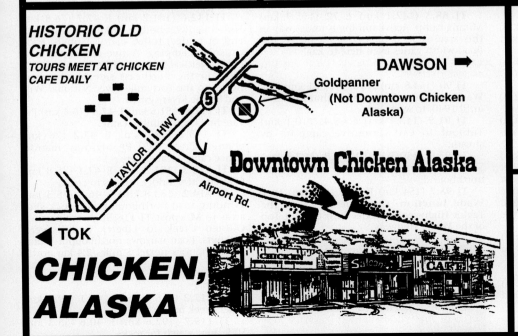

HISTORIC OLD CHICKEN
TOURS MEET AT CHICKEN CAFE DAILY

DAWSON ➡

Goldpanner
(Not Downtown Chicken Alaska)

TAYLOR HWY
5

Downtown Chicken Alaska

Airport Rd.

◀ TOK

CHICKEN, ALASKA

CHICKEN GAS

Always the Lowest Priced Gas, and Friendliest Service in CHICKEN

REMEMBER!

To find *REAL* Downtown Chicken Alaska you have to Turn Off the Taylor Hwy.

the Chicken Creek Cafe at 1 P.M. It's also possible to purchase an autographed copy of *Tisha* at the Chicken Mercantile Emporium. A wealth of gifts abound in the Chicken Mercantile Emporium, and the cafe is famous throughout Alaska for its excellent food, homemade pies, pastries and cinnamon buns. For a bird's-eye view of this spectacular country and fantastic photo opportunities, check out the local flightseeing service, Chicken Air. Chicken Creek Saloon, Cafe and Mercantile Emporium are a rare treat for those with the courage to stray just a few hundred yards from the beaten path. Major credit cards accepted. Note: The Goldpanner, located on the main road, is not the same as "Beautiful Downtown Chicken, Alaska." [ADVERTISEMENT]

TJ **66.6** (107.2 km) E **93.7** (150.8 km) Chicken Creek bridge.

The Goldpanner. Walking tours of Historic Chicken are given exclusively through The Goldpanner. These multilingual tours begin each day at 2 P.M. The tour includes Tisha's Schoolhouse and other historic buildings. The Goldpanner offers FREE RV parking and gold panning, souvenirs, gas, diesel, light mechanics and tire repair. Buses and caravans are welcome. [ADVERTISEMENT]

TJ **67** (107.8 km) E **93.3** (150.1 km) View of abandoned old townsite of Chicken. The road in is blocked off, and the dozen or so old buildings are owned by a mining company. Private property, do not trespass. Guided walking tours available only from The Goldpanner; inquire at **Milepost TJ 66.6.** Look upstream (northwest) on Chicken Creek to see the old gold dredge, which was shut down in the 1960s.

TJ **68.2** (109.8 km) E **92.1** (148.2 km) BLM Chicken field station; information and emergency communications. Trailhead for Mosquito Fork Dredge trail (3 miles/4.8 km round-trip). *NOTE: Watch for potholes and soft spots.*

TJ **68.9** (110.9 km) E **91.4** (147.1 km) Lost Chicken Creek. Site of Lost Chicken Hill Mine, established in 1895. Mining was under way in this area several years before the Klondike Gold Rush of 1897–98. The first major placer gold strike was in 1886 at Franklin Gulch, a tributary of the Fortymile. Hydraulic mining operations in the creek.

TJ **70** (112.7 km) E **90.3** (145.3 km) Turnouts at gravel pits on both sides of road. *CAUTION: Watch for hairpin turns.*

TJ **71.7** (115.4 km) E **88.6** (142.6 km) *NOTE: Slow for steep descent northbound as road switchbacks down to South Fork.*

TJ **74.4** (119.7 km) E **85.9** (138.2 km) South Fork River access road.

TJ **74.5** (119.9 km) E **85.8** (138.1 km) South Fork DOT/PF state highway maintenance station.

TJ **75.3** (121.2 km) E **85** (136.8 km) South Fork bridge. Day-use area with toilet and litter barrels at south end of bridge, west side of road. Access point for the Fortymile River National Wild and Scenic River system. The muddy, bumpy road leading into the brush is used by miners.

TJ **76.8** (123.6 km) E **83.5** (134.4 km) Turnout to west. View of oxbow lakes in South Fork valley. *CAUTION: Watch for rough road.*

TJ **78.5** (126.3 km) E **81.8** (131.6 km) Views of Fortymile River valley northbound to **Milepost TJ 82.**

TJ **78.8** (126.8 km) E **81.5** (131.2 km) Steep descent northbound.

TJ **81.9** (131.8 km) E **78.4** (126.2 km) Walker Fork bridge.

TJ **82.1** (132.1 km) E **78.2** (125.8 km) Walker Fork BLM campground; 16 campsites, picnic sites with covered tables, fee charged.

Top of the World Highway junctions with the Taylor Highway at Milepost TJ 95.7.
(© Earl L. Brown, staff)

TJ **86.1** (138.6 km) E **74.2** (119.4 km) Old **Jack Wade No. 1 dredge** in creek next to road. Turnout to east. This is actually the Butte Creek Dredge, installed in 1934 below the mouth of Butte Creek and eventually moved to Wade Creek. This was one of the first bucketline dredges used in the area, according to the BLM.

TJ **88.3** (142.1 km) E **72** (115.9 km) Mining camp. Active mining is under way in this area. *Do not trespass on mining claims.* Road width varies from here to Eagle. *NOTE: Large vehicles use turnouts when meeting oncoming vehicles.*

TJ **90** (144.8 km) E **70.3** (113.1 km) Jack Wade, an old mining camp that operated until 1940, to west.

TJ **91.9** (147.9 km) E **68.4** (110.1 km) Turnout to east. Primitive campsite by stream.

TJ **93.5** (150.5 km) E **66.8** (107.5 km) *Slow down for hairpin curve.* Road climbs northbound.

TJ **95.7** (154 km) E **64.6** (104 km) **Jack Wade Junction.** Continue north on the Taylor Highway for Eagle. Turn east for Top of the World Highway.

Junction with the Top of the World Highway (Yukon Highway 9) east to Boundary Lodge, the Alaska–Canada border and Dawson City, YT (78.8 miles/126.8 km). Turn to the end of the KLONDIKE LOOP section and read the Top of the World Highway log back to front.

TJ **96** (154.5 km) E **64.3** (103.5 km) Turnout. Lupine and chiming bells bloom in June. View to the north-northeast of Canada's Ogilvie Mountains in the distance.

TJ **99.5** (160.1 km) E **60.8** (97.8 km) Road winds around the summit of Steele Creek Dome (elev. 4,015 feet/1,224m) visible directly above the road to the east. *CAUTION: Road is slippery when wet.*

TJ **99.6** (160.3 km) E **60.7** (97.7 km) *CAUTION: Slow down for hairpin curve.*

TJ **105.5** (169.8 km) E **54.8** (88.2 km) Scenic viewpoint to east. The road descends next 7 miles/11.3 km northbound to the valley of the Fortymile River, so named because its mouth was 40 miles below Fort Reliance, an old trading post near the confluence of the Yukon and Klondike rivers. Along the road are abandoned cabins, tailings and dredges.

TJ **108.5** (174.6 km) E **51.8** (83.4 km) *CAUTION: Slow down for hairpin curve!*

TJ **109** (175.4 km) E **51.3** (82.6 km) *CAUTION: Steep, narrow, winding road northbound. Slow down!* Frequent small turnouts and breathtaking views to north and west. Watch for arctic poppies and lupine along the highway in June.

TJ **112.6** (181.2 km) E **47.7** (76.8 km) Fortymile River bridge; parking area at south end of bridge, toilet, canoe launch, trash cans. No camping. Active mining in area. Nearly vertical beds of white marble can be seen on the northeast side of the river. Access to the Fortymile River National Wild and Scenic River system.

TJ **112.8** (181.5 km) E **47.5** (76.4 km) Private home and mining camp.

TJ **113.1** (182 km) E **47.2** (76 km) O'Brien Creek DOT/PF highway maintenance camp located here.

TJ **113.2** (182.2 km) E **47.1** (75.8 km) O'Brien Creek bridge. Access to creek.

TJ **114.2** (183.8 km) E **46.8** (75.3 km) Winding road northbound with rock slide areas to **Milepost TJ 116;** highway parallels O'Brien Creek to Liberty Fork; several turnouts. Road narrows northbound: Watch for falling rock next 1.5 miles/2.4 km northbound. *CAUTION: Watch for small aircraft using road as runway.*

TJ **117.2** (188.6 km) E **43.1** (69.4 km) Alder Creek bridge.

TJ **119.7** (192.6 km) E **40.6** (65.3 km) Slide area, watch for rocks.

TJ **124.6** (200.5 km) E **35.7** (57.5 km)

Columbia Creek bridge.

TJ **125.4** (201.8 km) E **34.9** (56.2 km) O'Brien Creek Lodge; gas. Nearest gas stations in Eagle, Chicken and Boundary.

TJ **130.5** (208.8 km) E **29.8** (47.7 km) Turnout to east.

TJ **131.5** (211.6 km) E **28.8** (46.3 km) King Solomon Creek bridge. Highway follows King Solomon Creek next 0.5 mile/0.8 km northbound. (The creek has a tributary named Queen of Sheba.)

TJ **135.7** (218.4 km) E **24.6** (39.6 km) *CAUTION: Slow down for hairpin curve.*

TJ **135.8** (218.5 km) E **24.5** (39.4 km) North Fork Solomon Creek bridge.

TJ **141** (226.9 km) E **19.3** (31.1 km) Glacier Mountain management area; walk-in hunting only. Top of the world views to west.

TJ **143.2** (230.5 km) E **17.1** (27.5 km) Turnout on summit. Top of the world views. Road begins winding descent northbound to Yukon River.

TJ **148** (236.8 km) E **12.3** (19.7 km) Two small turnouts.

TJ **149.1** (239.9 km) E **11.2** (18 km) Bridge over Discovery Fork. Turnout to east by creek.

TJ **150.7** (242.5 km) E **9.6** (15.4 km) Old cabin by creek to west is a local landmark. Private property.

TJ **151.8** (244.3 km) E **8.5** (13.7 km) American Creek bridge No. 1. Outcroppings of asbestos, greenish or gray with white, and serpentine along creekbank. Doyon Ltd. claims ownership of surface and mineral estates on these lands; do not trespass.

TJ **152.5** (245.4 km) E **7.8** (12.6 km) Bridge No. 2 over American Creek.

TJ **153.2** (246.5 km) E **7.1** (11.4 km) Small turnout. Springwater piped to road.

TJ **153.6** (247.2 km) E **6.7** (10.8 km) Small turnout. Springwater piped to road.

TJ **159.3** (256.4 km) E **1** (1.6 km) Gas station.

TJ **159.7** (257 km) E **0.6** (1 km) Historical sign about the settlement of Eagle.

TJ **160.3** (258 km) E **0** Fourth Avenue, Eagle (description follows). Eagle school to east. Side road to west leads 1 mile/1.6 km to Fort Egbert mule barn, officers' quarters and parade ground. The U.S. Army established Fort Egbert in 1899, then abandoned it in 1911. From here a road leads 0.8 mile/1.3 km to Eagle BLM Campground; 13 sites, fee charged. ▲

Eagle

Population: 146. **Emergency Services:** Eagle EMS (907) 547-2300 or (907) 547-2211; use CB channel 21; Eagle health clinic. **Visitor Information:** Contact the Eagle Historical Society and Museums, Box 23, Eagle, AK 99738;

EAGLE ADVERTISERS

Eagle Canoe Rentals ....Ph. (907) 547-2203
Eagle Historical Society and
    Museums ....Chamberlain & 3rd.
Eagle Trading Co.
    Motel ....Ph. (907) 547-2220
Falcon Inn B&B ....Ph. (907) 547-2254
Sundog Gifts......................Behind Courthouse
Upper Yukon Enterprises..Ph. (907) 547-2254

Eagle

At summer solstice (June 21, 1999) in Eagle, sunrise is at 2:33 A.M., sunset is at 12:20 A.M. the following day. At winter solstice, (Dec. 21, 1999), sunrise is at 10:31 A.M., sunset is at 2:15 P.M.

View of Eagle from the Yukon River. (© Lee Foster)

Locals still practice traditional subsistence activities—fishing with nets, gathering berries, gardening and handcrafting necessities—and many of the town's original cabins, over 100 years old, are used today.

Eagle also boasts the largest museum system in the state. Walking tours, offered by the Eagle Historical Society and Museums, include the Wickersham Courthouse, Waterfront Customs House and the Mule Barn, Water Wagon Shed and NCO quarters at Fort Egbert. Tours are guided by long-time Eagle residents and begin at 9 A.M. daily (from the courtroom upstairs in the courthouse), Memorial Day through mid-September; cost is $5, members of Eagle Historical Society and Museums and children under 12 free (annual society membership: $10 individual, $15 family). Special tours may be arranged. Books, maps and gifts available at the museum store in the courthouse (10 percent discount for members). For more information, contact the Eagle Historical Society and Museums (Box 23, Eagle 99738; phone 907/547-2325; fax 907/547-2232).

Special events in Eagle include a Memorial Day Service; old-fashioned 4th of July celebration; and a Centennial Celebration for the Founding of Fort Egbert, July 30–Aug. 1, 1999.

Fort Egbert, renovated and restored by the Bureau of Land Management, has an interpretive exhibit and a photo display showing the stages of reconstruction. Videos of the Eagle area, art demonstrations, educational programs and readings by local authors are conducted every Monday at 7 P.M. in the public library (June 15 through Labor Day).

Historically an important riverboat landing, Eagle is still a popular jumping-off point for Yukon River travelers. Most popular is a summer float trip from Eagle downriver through the **YUKON–CHARLEY RIVERS NATIONAL PRESERVE** to Circle. Length of the Eagle–Circle trip is 154 river miles/248 km, with most trips averaging 5 to 10 days. Float trips may also be made from Dawson City, YT, to Circle (252 miles/406 km, 7 to 10 days) with a halfway stop at Eagle. Boaters also often float the Fortymile River to the Yukon River, then continue to the boat landing at Eagle to take out. Commercial boat trips are also available. The *Yukon Queen* makes round trips daily between Eagle and Dawson City, YT. Breakup on the Yukon is in May; freezeup in October. For details on weather, gear and precautions, contact the National Park Service, Box 167, Eagle 99738; phone (907) 547-2233.

Eagle Canoe Rentals. Canoe and raft rentals on the Yukon River between Dawson City, Yukon Territory; Eagle City, Alaska; and Circle City. Brochures available, or call for details. From April to October: Dawson City River Hostel, Dieter Reinmuth, Box 32, Dawson City, YT Y0B 1G0, (867) 993-6823; or Eagle Canoe Rentals, Mike Sager, Box 4, Eagle, AK 99738; phone/fax (907) 547-2203.

[ADVERTISEMENT]

phone 907/547-2325; fax 907/547-2232; e-mail ehsmuseums@aol.com.

The National Park Service office, headquarters for Yukon–Charley Rivers National Preserve, is located on the banks of the Yukon River at the base of Fort Egbert. Reference library available to the public. Office hours are 8 A.M. to 5 P.M. weekdays. The National Park Service Visitor Center offers maps and books for sale. Also a video on the preserve is shown on request. Informal talks and interpretive programs available. Visitor center hours are 8 A.M. to 5 P.M. daily in summer (Memorial Day weekend through Labor Day weekend). Check at the visitor center for information on the Yukon River, Yukon–Charley Rivers National Preserve and other parklands in Alaska. (Write them at Box 167, Eagle 99738, or phone 907/547-2233.)

Elevation: 820 feet/250m. **Climate:** Mean monthly temperature in July 59°F/15°C; in January -13°F/-25°C. Record low -71°F/-57°C in January 1952; record high 95°F/35°C in July 1925. July also has the greatest mean number of days (21) with temperatures above 70°F/21°C. Mean precipitation in July, 1.94 inches; in December, 10.1 inches. Record snow depth 42 inches in April 1948.

Transportation: By road via the Taylor Highway (closed by snow October to April); air taxi, scheduled air service; dog team and snow machine in winter. Eagle is also accessible via the Yukon River. U.S. customs available for persons entering Alaska via the Yukon River or by air.

Private Aircraft: Eagle airstrip, 2 miles/3.2 km east; elev. 880 feet/268m; length 3,500 feet/1,067m; gravel; unattended.

This small community was once the supply and transportation center for miners working the upper Yukon and its tributaries. Francois Mercier established his Belle Isle trading post here in 1874. Eagle City was founded in 1897 and became the commercial, military and judicial center for the Upper Yukon. Fort Egbert was established in 1899 adjacent to the city. By 1898, Eagle's population was 1,700. Gold strikes in Fairbanks and Nome lured away many, and by 1910, the population had dwindled to 178.

In the center of town stands a windmill and wellhouse (hand-dug in 1903); the well still provides water for over half the town's population. There are gas stations, restaurants, gift shops, museum store, post office, showers, laundromat, hardware store and mechanic shop with tire repair. Groceries and sundries are available. Fax service is available at both stores. Overnight accommodations at the motel, rental cabins and bed and breakfasts. RV parking with hookups is available or stay at Eagle BLM campground just outside town (turn left on 4th Avenue and left again along airstrip at Fort Egbert). Eagle Village, an Athabascan settlement, is 3 miles/4.8 km from Eagle. ▲

Eagle, perched on the south bank of the Yukon River below Eagle Bluff (elev. 1000 feet/305m), remains relatively untouched.

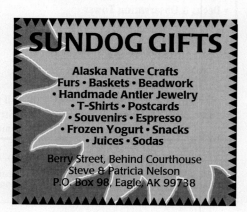

Connects: Watson Lake, YT, to Klondike Hwy. **Length:** 373 miles
Road Surface: 85% gravel, 15% paved **Season:** Open all year
Major Attraction: Pelly River, Wildlife

(See map, page 288)

	Carmacks	Dawson City	Faro	Ross River	Watson Lake
Carmacks		225	115	150	375
Dawson City	225		338	373	598
Faro	115	338		32	271
Ross River	150	373	32		239
Watson Lake	375	598	271	239	

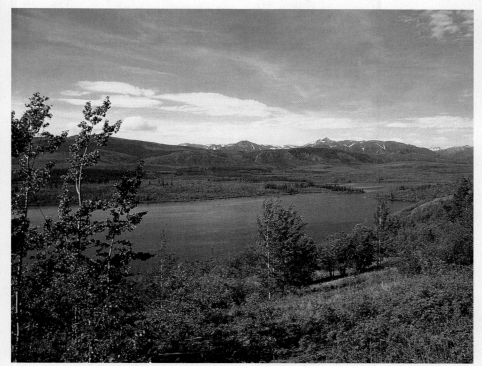

The Campbell Highway offers beautiful lake and mountain scenery. (© Rollo Pool)

Named for Robert Campbell, the first white man to penetrate what is now known as Yukon Territory, this all-weather, mostly gravel road leads 373 miles/600.2 km northwest from the Alaska Highway at Watson Lake, to junction with the Klondike Highway 2 miles/3.2 km north of Carmacks (see the KLONDIKE LOOP section). Gas is available at Watson Lake, Ross River, Faro and Carmacks.

The highway is gravel with the exception of stretches of pavement at Watson Lake, Ross River and the Klondike Highway junction (see map). *NOTE: Drive with your headlights on at all times.*

The Campbell Highway is an alternative route to Dawson City. It is about 20 miles/32 km shorter than driving the Alaska Highway through to Whitehorse, then driving up the Klondike Highway to Dawson City.

The Robert Campbell Highway was completed in 1968 and closely follows sections of the fur trade route established by Robert Campbell. Campbell was a Hudson's Bay Co. trader who was sent into the region in the 1840s to find a route west into the unexplored regions of central Yukon. Traveling from the southeast, he followed the Liard and Frances rivers, building a chain of posts along the way. His major discovery came in 1843, when he reached the Yukon River, which was to become the major transportation route within the Yukon.

Emergency medical services: Phone the RCMP or ambulance in Watson Lake, Ross River or Carmacks. Or phone toll free, Yukon-wide, the RCMP at (867) 667-5555, or the ambulance at (867) 667-3333.

Campbell Highway Log

Distance from Watson Lake (WL) is followed by distance from junction with the Klondike Highway just north of Carmacks (J).

Mileages reflect the location of physical kilometreposts; driving distance may vary from log.

YUKON HIGHWAY 4
WL 0 J 373 (600.2 km) **Watson Lake.**

Junction of the Campbell Highway with the Alaska Highway. Turn to description of Watson Lake on page 122 in the ALASKA HIGHWAY section.

The famous sign forest is located at this junction. In the parking area off the Campbell Highway (also called Airport Road) is a point of interest sign relating the highway's

history. Also located at this junction is the Alaska Highway Interpretive Centre and visitor information.

WL 0.6 (1 km) **J 372.4** (599.3 km) Hospital on right northbound.

WL 4.3 (6.9 km) **J 368.7** (593.3 km) Access road on right northbound to Mount Maichen ski hill.

WL 6.3 (10.1 km) **J 366.7** (590.1 km) Airport Road left to Watson Lake airport.

WL 6.7 (10.8 km) **J 366.3** (589.5 km) Watson Creek. The highway begins to climb to a heavily timbered plateau and then heads north following the east bank of the Frances River. Tamarack is rare in Yukon, but this northern type of larch can be seen along here. Although a member of the pine family, it sheds its needles in the fall.

WL 10.4 (16.7 km) **J 362.6** (583.5 km) MacDonald Creek.

WL 22.5 (36.2 km) **J 350.5** (564.1 km) Tom Creek, named after an Indian trapper whose cabin is at the mouth of the stream.

WL 27.3 (44 km) **J 345.7** (556.3 km) Sa Dena Hes Mine access.

WL 36.1 (58.1 km) **J 336.9** (542.2 km) **Frances River** bridge. Turnout at north end of bridge; picnic spot. The highway crosses to west bank and follows the river northward. Named by Robert Campbell for the wife of Sir George Simpson, governor of the Hudson's Bay Co. for 40 years, the Frances River is a tributary of the Liard River. Robert Campbell ascended the Liard River to the Frances River and then went on to Frances Lake and the Pelly River. The Frances River was part of Hudson's Bay Co.'s route into central Yukon for many years before being abandoned because of its dangerous rapids and canyons.

WL 47.2 (76 km) **J 325.8** (524.3 km) Lucky Creek.

WL 49.6 (79.8 km) **J 323.4** (520.4 km) Simpson Creek.

WL 51.8 (83.4 km) **J 321.2** (516.9 km) Access road leads west 1 mile/1.6 km to **Simpson Lake** Yukon government campground: 10 campsites, $8 fee, boat launch, dock, swimming beach, playground, kitchen shelter and drinking water (boil water). Excellent fishing for lake trout, arctic grayling and northern pike. ◄▲

WL 58.5 (94.2 km) **J 314.5** (506.1 km) Large turnout with litter barrels.

WL 58.7 (94.5 km) **J 314.3** (505.8 km) Access road west to Simpson Lake.

CAMPBELL HIGHWAY

**Watson Lake, YT, to Junction with Klondike Loop
(includes Nahanni Range Road)**

© 1999 The MILEPOST®

Key to mileage boxes

miles/kilometres
miles/kilometres
from:
WL-Watson Lake
J-Klondike Highway Junction
CJ-Campbell Highway Junction
D-Dawson City
FN-Fort Nelson
W-Whitehorse

Map Location

Key to Advertiser Services

C-Camping
D-Dump Station
d-Diesel
G-Gas (reg., unld.)
I-Ice
L-Lodging
M-Meals
P-Propane
R-Car Repair (major)
r-Car Repair (minor)
S-Store (grocery)
T-Telephone (pay)

Principal Route

Paved
Unpaved

Other Roads

Paved
Unpaved

Ferry Routes
.... Refer to Log for Visitor Facilities

Hiking Trails

Scale

Miles
Kilometres

WL 68.5 (110.2 km) J 304.5 (490 km) **Miner's Junction**, formerly known as Cantung Junction; no services.

Junction with Nahanni Range Road to Tungsten; see NAHANNI RANGE ROAD log this section.

WL 70.3 (113.2 km) J 302.7 (487.1 km) Yukon government Tuchitua River maintenance camp to east.

WL 70.5 (113.4 km) J 302.5 (486.8 km) One-lane bridge over Tuchitua River.

WL 91.7 (147.6 km) J 281.3 (452.7 km) Jules Creek.

WL 100 (160.9 km) J 273 (439.3 km) 99 Mile Creek.

WL 106.6 (171.6 km) J 266.4 (428.7 km) Caesar Creek.

WL 107.1 (172.4 km) J 265.9 (427.9 km) View of Frances Lake to east, Campbell Range of the Pelly Mountains to west.

WL 108.9 (175.3 km) J 264.1 (425 km) Access road east leads 0.6 mile/1 km to **Frances Lake** Yukon government campground: 24 campsites, $8 fee, boat launch, kitchen shelter, drinking water (boil water). The solitary peak between the 2 arms of Frances Lake is Simpson Tower (elev. 5,500 feet/1,676m). It was named by Robert Campbell for Hudson's Bay Co. Governor Sir George Simpson. Fishing for lake trout, grayling and northern pike. ⬥▲

WL 109.1 (175.5 km) J 263.9 (424.7 km) Money Creek, which flows into the west arm of Frances Lake, one of the Yukon's largest lakes. The creek was named for Anton Money, a mining engineer and prospector who found and mined placer gold in this area between 1929 and 1946. Money later operated "The Village" service station at Mile 442 on the Alaska Highway. He died in 1993, in Santa Barbara, CA.

WL 109.4 (176 km) J 263.6 (424.2 km) Gravel turnout. View southbound of Frances Lake.

WL 113.8 (183.2 km) J 259.2 (417.1 km) Dick Creek.

WL 123.8 (199.2 km) J 249.2 (401 km) Highway descends Finlayson River valley northbound, swinging west away from Frances Lake and following the Finlayson River that may be seen occasionally to the east for about the next 20 miles/32 km. Mountains to the west are part of the Campbell Range.

WL 126.4 (203.5 km) J 246.6 (396.9 km) Light Creek.

WL 129.1 (207.7 km) J 243.9 (392.5 km) Van Bibber Creek.

WL 134.1 (215.8 km) J 238.9 (384.5 km) Wolverine Creek.

WL 147.5 (237.4 km) J 225.5 (362.9 km) **Finlayson Creek**, which flows into the river of the same name, drains Finlayson Lake into Frances Lake. Named by Robert Campbell in 1840 for Chief Factor Duncan Finlayson, who later became director of the Hudson's Bay Co. Placer gold mined at the mouth of Finlayson River in 1875 is believed to be some of the first gold mined in the territory. Finlayson Lake (elev. 3,100 feet/945m), on the Continental Divide, separates watersheds of Mackenzie and Yukon rivers.

WL 148.1 (238.4 km) J 224.9 (361.9 km) Access road north to Finlayson Lake picnic area; litter barrels. To the southwest are the Pelly Mountains.

WL 149 (239.8 km) J 224 (360.5 km) Turnout with observation platform and information panel on Finlayson caribou

Nahanni Range Road Log

The Nahanni Range (Tungsten) Road branches off the Campbell Highway at **Milepost WL 68.5** and leads 125 miles/201.2 km northeast to the former mining town of Tungsten, NWT. The road is gravel surfaced with some washouts and soft steep shoulders. *CAUTION: The Yukon government does not recommend this road for tourist travel due to lack of services and maintenance.*

Construction of the Nahanni Range Road was begun in 1961 to provide access to the mining property. The road was completed in 1963 with the bridging of the Frances and Hyland rivers. *Distance from Campbell Highway junction (CJ) is shown.*

CJ 0 Junction with Campbell Highway.

CJ 5.1 (8.2 km) **Upper Frances River** bridge; good grayling fishing in stream on southeast side. ⬥

CJ 7.4 (11.9 km) Good grayling fishing at confluence of **Sequence Creek** and **Frances River.**

CJ 11.8 (19 km) Queen Creek.

CJ 13.1 (21.1 km) King Creek.

CJ 14.2 (22.8 km) Road passes between Mount Billings to the north (elev. 6,909 feet/2,106m) and Mount Murray to the south (elev. 7,093 feet/2,162m).

CJ 20.3 (32.7 km) Short access road to **Long Lake**, grayling fishing. ⬥

CJ 21.5 (34.6 km) Long Lake Creek. There are a few private log cabins along here.

CJ 24.1 (38.8 km) Dolly Varden Creek.

CJ 28.4 (45.7 km) French Creek.

CJ 28.9 (46.5 km) Road enters the narrow Hyland River valley through the Logan Mountains.

CJ 32.6 (52.4 km) South Bridge Creek.

CJ 33.2 (53.4 km) North Bridge Creek.

CJ 38.1 (61.3 km) Jackpine Creek.

CJ 40.6 (65.3 km) **Spruce Creek**, good glides and broken pools upstream for grayling fishing. ⬥

CJ 42.8 (68.9 km) Short access road to Hyland River.

CJ 45.8 (73.7 km) **Conglomerate Creek**, scenic spot to picnic. Good grayling fishing near small waterfall. ⬥

CJ 48 (77.2 km) Mining road to west.

CJ 52.1 (83.8 km) South Moose Creek.

CJ 52.2 (84 km) Yukon government campground (unmaintained); 10 sites, kitchen shelter, picnic tables. ▲

CJ 52.5 (84.5 km) North Moose Creek.

CJ 62.4 (100.4 km) **Flood Creek**, good grayling fishing. ⬥

CJ 68.4 (110.1 km) Hyland River bridge; turnout with litter barrel.

CJ 71 (114.2 km) Emergency airstrip to west.

CJ 75.9 (122.1 km) Ostensibility Creek.

CJ 82 (132 km) **Piggott Creek**, good grayling fishing. Outhouse. ⬥

CJ 116.8 (188 km) **YT–NWT Border**.

CJ 125 (201.2 km) **TUNGSTEN**, which was the company town for one of the richest mines in the world and Canada's only tungsten producer, was originally called Cantung (Canada Tungsten Mining Corp. Ltd.). Open-pit mining began here in the early 1960s with the discovery of scheelite in the Flat River area. Scheelite is an ore of tungsten, an oxide used for hardening steel and making white gold. The mine shut down in 1986, and the population of 500 moved out. Only a security staff remains. Hot springs in area.

Return to Milepost WL 68.5 Campbell Highway

herd.

WL 158.1 (254.5 km) J 214.9 (345.8 km) **Private Aircraft**: Finlayson Lake airstrip to south; elev. 3,300 feet/1,006m; length 2,100 feet/640m; gravel. No services.

WL 163.7 (263.5 km) J 209.3 (336.8 km) Nancy J. Creek.

WL 164.4 (264.5 km) J 208.6 (335.7 km) Little Campbell Creek. Robert Campbell followed this creek to the Pelly River in 1840.

WL 170.4 (274.2 km) J 202.6 (326 km) Bridge over Big Campbell Creek, which flows into Pelly River at Pelly Banks. Robert Campbell named the river and banks after Hudson's Bay Co. Governor Sir John Henry Pelly. Campbell built a trading post here in 1846; never successful, it burned down in 1849. Isaac Taylor and William S. Drury later operated a trading post at Pelly Banks, one of a string of successful posts established by their firm in remote spots throughout the Yukon from 1899 on.

The highway follows the Pelly River for the next 90 miles/145 km.

WL 179 (288.1 km) J 194 (312.2 km) Mink Creek culvert.

WL 193.9 (312 km) J 179.1 (288.2 km) Bridge over **Hoole Canyon**; turnout to

north. Confluence of the Hoole and Pelly rivers. Campbell named the Hoole River after his interpreter, Francis Hoole, a half-Iroquois and half-French Canadian employed by the Hudson's Bay Co. Dig out your gold pan—this river once yielded gold.

WL 199.8 (321.6 km) J 173.2 (278.7 km) Starr Creek culvert.

WL 206.5 (332.3 km) J 166.5 (267.9 km) Horton Creek.

WL 210.7 (339 km) J 162.3 (261.2 km) Bruce Lake to south.

WL 211.8 (340.8 km) J 161.2 (259.4 km) Bruce Creek.

WL 215.4 (346.6 km) J 157.6 (253.6 km) Private side road leads south 27.3 miles/44 km to Ketza River Project. The first gold bar was poured at Ketza River mine in 1988. The Ketza River hard-rock gold deposit was first discovered in 1947. No visitor facilities.

WL 217.9 (350.7 km) J 155.1 (249.6 km) Ketza River. St. Cyr Range to southwest.

WL 219.4 (353 km) J 153.6 (247.2 km) Ketza Creek.

WL 221.4 (356.3 km) J 151.6 (244 km) Beautiful Creek culvert.

WL 224.8 (361.8 km) J 148.2 (238.5 km) **Coffee Lake** to south; local swimming hole, picnic tables, trout fishing (stocked).

WL 227.3 (365.8 km) J 145.7 (234.5 km) Ross River Flying Service; floatplane base on **Jackfish Lake** here. Access to bed and breakfast.

Jackfish Lake Bed and Breakfast. See display ad this section.

Junction with South Canol Road, which leads south 129 miles/207 km to Johnson's Crossing and the Alaska Highway. See **Milepost J 136.8** in the CANOL ROAD section.

WL 227.5 (366.1 km) J 145.5 (234.1 km) Unmaintained side road on right westbound is continuation of Canol Road to Ross River. Use the main Ross River access road next milepost.

WL 232.3 (373.8 km) J 140.7 (226.4 km) Access road leads 7 miles/11.2 km to Ross River (description follows). Rest area with toilets on highway just north of this turnoff.

Ross River

Located on the southwest bank of the Pelly River. **Population:** about 352. **Emergency Services: RCMP,** phone (867) 969-5555. **Hospital,** phone (867) 969-2222. **Radio:** CBC 990, local FM station. **Transportation:** Scheduled air service via Trans North Air.

Private Aircraft: Ross River airstrip; elev. 2,408 feet/734m; length 5,500 feet/1,676m; gravel; fuel 40.

A point of interest sign on the way into Ross River relates that in 1843, Robert Campbell named Ross River for Chief Trader Donald Ross of the Hudson's Bay Co. From 1903, a trading post called Nahanni House (established by Tom Smith and later owned by the Whitehorse firm of Taylor and Drury) located at the confluence of the Ross and Pelly rivers supplied the Indians of the area for nearly 50 years. With the building of the Canol pipeline service road in WWII and the completion of the Robert Campbell Highway in 1968, the community was linked to the rest of the territory by road. Originally situated on the north side of the Pelly River, the town has been in its present location since 1964. Today, Ross River is a supply and communication base for prospectors testing and mining mineral bodies in this region.

Ross River has gas stations with diesel, mechanical and tire repair, grocery stores, 2 motels with dining, and a bed and breakfast. The nearest campground is Lapie Canyon (see **Milepost WL 233.5**). Self-contained RVs may overnight at the gravel parking lot at the end of the pedestrian suspension bridge on the Ross River side.

Ross River is also a jumping-off point for big game hunters and canoeists. There are 2 registered hunting outfitters here. Canoeists traveling the Pelly River can launch just downriver from the ferry crossing. Experienced canoeists recommend camping on the Pelly's many gravel bars and islets to avoid bears, bugs and the danger of accidentally setting tundra fires. The Pelly has many sweepers, sleepers and gravel shallows, some gravel shoals, and extensive channeling. There are 2 sets of rapids between Ross River and the mouth of the Pelly: Fish Hook and Granite Canyon. Water is potable (boil), firewood available and wildlife plentiful. Inquire locally about river conditions before setting out.

Rock hounds check Pelly River gravels for jaspers and the occasional agate.

The suspension footbridge at Ross River leads across the Pelly River to the site of an abandoned Indian village 1 mile/1.6 km upstream at the mouth of the Ross River.

A government ferry crosses the Pelly River daily in summer, from 8 A.M. to noon and 1–5 P.M. Across the river, the North Canol Road leads 144 miles/232 km to Macmillan Pass at the Northwest Territories border. See the CANOL ROAD section for details.

Ross River Service Centre Ltd. See display ad this section.

The Welcome Inn. See display ad this section.

Campbell Highway Log
(continued)

WL 232.3 (373.8 km) J 140.7 (226.4 km) Access road leads 7 miles/11.2 km to Ross River (see preceding description).

WL 232.5 (374.2 km) J 140.5 (226.1 km) Rest area with toilets.

WL 233.4 (375.6 km) J 139.6 (224.6 km) **Lapie River** bridge crosses deep gorge of Lapie River, which flows into the Pelly River from Lapie Lakes on the South Canol Road. Highway continues to follow the Pelly River and Pelly Mountains.

WL 233.5 (375.8 km) J 139.5 (224.5 km) Turnoff to left (south) to **Lapie Canyon** Yukon government campground adjacent Lapie River: short scenic trails, viewpoint, picturesque canyon; kitchen shelters, firewood, group firepit and picnic area; walk-in tent sites, 18 campsites, $8 fee, drinking water (boil water); boat launch. ▲

WL 236.3 (380.3 km) J 136.7 (220 km) Danger Creek. In 1905, naturalist Charles Sheldon named this creek after his horse, Danger.

WL 239.9 (386 km) J 133.1 (214.2 km) Panoramic view of the Pelly River valley just ahead westbound.

WL 243.6 (392 km) J 129.4 (208.2 km) *CAUTION: Hill and bad corner.*

WL 244.2 (393 km) J 128.8 (207.3 km) Highway narrows over Grew Creek, no guide rails. This creek was named for Hudson's Bay Co. trader Jim Grew, who trapped this area for many years before his death in 1906.

WL 251 (404 km) J 122 (196.3 km) Turnout to north.

WL 260.4 (419 km) J 112.6 (181.2 km) Buttle Creek, named for Roy Buttle, a trapper, prospector and trader who lived here in the early 1900s and at one time owned a trading post at Ross River.

WL 264.7 (426 km) J 108.3 (174.3 km) Across the wide Pelly River valley to the north is a view of the mining community of Faro.

WL 265.5 (427.3 km) J 107.5 (173 km) Access road on right westbound leads 5.6 miles/9 km to Faro. Point of interest sign about Faro at intersection. Rest area with toilets and litter barrels to south just west of this junction.

Faro

Located in east-central Yukon Territory, 220 road miles/354 km from Whitehorse. **Population:** 500.. **Emergency Services: RCMP,** phone (867) 994-5555. **Fire Department,** phone (867) 994-2222. **Hospital,** phone (867) 994-4444.

Visitor Information: Centre at the municipal-operated John Connelly RV Park, open June through August. For information on wildlife viewing, hiking, biking, horseback trails, town facilities and services, special events and individual businesses, phone (867) 994-2288 (seasonal). Or contact the Faro Town Office, phone (867) 994-2728, fax (867) 994-3154; web site faro.yk.net; e-mail townof@yknet.yk.ca. The Campbell Region

www.themilepost.com

Interpretive Tourist Information Centre, located directly across from John Connelly RV Park, has historical displays on the Yukon centennial; phone (867) 994-2728.

Climate: Temperatures range from -51°F/-46°C in winter to a summer maximum of 84°F/29°C. **Radio:** CBC-FM 105.1, CKRW-FM 98.7. **Television:** CBC and 7 cable channels. **Transportation:** Floatplane service from Horizons North.

Private Aircraft: Faro airstrip; 1.5 miles/2.4 km south; elev. 2,351 feet/717m; length 3,000 feet/914m; gravel; fuel 100.

The town of Faro lies on a series of benches or terraces on the northern escarpment of the Tintina Trench. Many places in town offer a commanding view of the Pelly River.

There are 2 restaurants in town: Redmond's (known locally as Cranky Frank's) and Sally's Road House. Both Redmond's and Sally's Road House offer motel accommodations. RV camping and dump station at municipal and private campgrounds. The service station has gas, diesel, propane and full garage services. The area offers excellent fly-in fishing. Other services in town include a large grocery, liquor store, video rental, post office, public library, movie theatre and recreation centre with indoor swimming pool, squash courts and outdoor tennis courts. Catholic and Protestant Sunday services are available.

Attractions include an all-season observation cabin and isolated photographer's blind for wildlife viewing. Viewing areas are accessible via a gravel road skirting the Fannin sheep grazing area and are within 4 miles/6.4 km of town. A public boat ramp and canoe rentals are available for exploring the Pelly River.

Discovery Store/The Case Place. See display ad this section.

Town of Faro. See display ad this section.

Campbell Highway Log
(continued)

WL 268.4 (432 km) **J 104.6** (168.3 km) **Johnson Lake** Yukon government campground; 15 sites (7 pull-throughs), $8 fee, toilets, water pump, firewood, picnic shelter, boat launch. ▲

Westbound, the Campbell Highway follows the Magundy River. There are several turnouts.

WL 285.8 (460 km) **J 87.2** (140.3 km) Magundy River airstrip to north; summer use only. Watch for livestock.

WL 288.1 (463.7 km) **J 84.9** (136.6 km) First glimpse of 22-mile-/35-km-long Little Salmon Lake westbound.

WL 299.3 (481.7 km) **J 73.7** (118.6 km) East end of **Little Salmon Lake.** Highway follows north shore. Lodge with meals, groceries, fishing licenses, guided fishing charters and boat rentals. Fishing for northern pike, grayling, lake trout. 🐟

WL 300.1 (483 km) **J 72.9** (117.3 km) Short access road south to Drury Creek Yukon government campground, situated on the creek at the east end of **Little Salmon Lake:** boat launch, fish filleting table, kitchen shelter, group firepit, 6 campsites, $8 fee, drinking water. Good fishing for northern pike, grayling, whitefish, lake trout 2 to 5 lbs., June 15 through July. 🐟▲

WL 300.4 (483.5 km) **J 72.6** (116.8 km) Turnout at east end Drury Creek bridge. Yukon government maintenance camp to north.

WL 308.2 (496 km) **J 64.8** (104.3 km) Turnout overlooking lake.

WL 311.3 (501 km) **J 61.7** (99.3 km) *CAUTION: Slow down for curves.* Highway follows lakeshore; no guide rails. Turnouts overlooking Little Salmon Lake next 8.5 miles/13.6 km westbound.

WL 316.9 (510 km) **J 56.1** (90.3 km) **Private Aircraft:** Little Salmon airstrip; elev. 2,200 feet/671m; length 1,800 feet/549m; sand and silt.

WL 321.4 (517.3 km) **J 51.6** (83 km) Steep, narrow, winding road south leads to Yukon government **Little Salmon Lake** campground; boat launch, fishing, 15 campsites, $8 fee, drinking water, picnic tables, outhouses, firepits and kitchen shelter. 🐟▲

WL 324.7 (522.6 km) **J 48.3** (77.7 km) **Bearfeed Creek,** a tributary of Little Salmon River, named because of the abundance of bears attracted to the berry patches in this area. Access to creek to north at west end of bridge.

Highway follows Little Salmon River (seen to south) for about 25 miles/40 km westbound.

WL 341 (548.7 km) **J 32** (51.5 km) *CAUTION: Slow down for hill.*

WL 343.8 (553.2 km) **J 29.2** (47 km) Picnic spot on Little Salmon River, which flows into the Yukon River.

WL 347.3 (559 km) **J 25.7** (41.4 km) Access road leads 4.9 miles/8 km north to **Frenchman Lake** Yukon government campground (10 sites), 5.6 miles/9 km to photo viewpoint of lake, and 9.3 miles/15 km to Nunatak Yukon government campground (10 sites, $8 fee). Access road narrows and surface deteriorates beyond Frenchman Lake Campground. South end of this 12-mile/19-km-long lake offers good fishing for trout, pike and grayling. 🐟▲

WL 349.5 (562.4 km) **J 23.5** (37.8 km) Turnoff to south for 0.9-mile/1.4-km gravel road to Little Salmon Indian village near confluence of Little Salmon River and Yukon River. There are some inhabited cabins in the area and some subsistence fishing. Private lands, no trespassing.

WL 356.2 (573.2 km) **J 16.8** (27 km) Turnout with point of interest sign overlooking **Eagles Nest Bluff** (formerly called Eagle Rock), well-known marker for river travelers. One of the worst steamboat disasters on the

Yukon River occurred near here when the paddle-wheeler *Columbian* blew up and burned after a crew member accidentally fired a shot into a cargo of gunpowder. The accident, in which 6 men died, took place Sept. 25, 1906.

WL 356.7 (574 km) **J 16.3** (26.2 km) View of the Yukon River. At this point Whitehorse is about 160 miles/258 km upstream and Dawson City is about 300 miles/483 km downriver.

WL 360.4 (580 km) **J 12.6** (20.3 km) Northern Canada Power Commission's transmission poles and lines can be seen along highway. Power is transmitted from Aishihik dam site via Whitehorse dam and on to Cyprus Anvil mine and Faro. Orange balls mark lines where they cross river as a hazard to aircraft.

WL 370 (595.4 km) **J 3** (4.8 km) **Private Aircraft:** Carmacks airstrip to south; elev. 1,770 feet/539m; length 5,200 feet/1,585m; gravel.

WL 370.7 (596.5 km) **J 2.3** (3.7 km) Tantalus Butte coal mine on hill to north overlooking junction of Campbell and Klondike highways. The butte was named by U.S. Army Lt. Frederick Schwatka in 1883 because of the tantalizing appearance of the formation around many bends of the river before it is reached.

WL 373 (600.2 km) **J 0** Turn south on the Klondike Highway for Carmacks (2 miles/3.2 km) and Whitehorse (115 miles/184 km); turn north for Dawson City (223 miles/357 km).

Junction with the Klondike Highway (Yukon Highway 2). Turn to **Milepost J 104.4** in the KLONDIKE LOOP section for highway log.

CANOL ROAD ⑥

Connects: Alaska Hwy. to NWT Border   **Length:** 286 miles
Road Surface: Gravel   **Season:** Closed in winter
Highest Summit: Macmillan Pass 4,480 feet
Major Attraction: Canol Heritage Trail

	Alaska Hwy. Jct.	Ross River	NWT Border
Alaska Hwy. Jct.		142	286
Ross River	142		144
NWT Border	286	144	

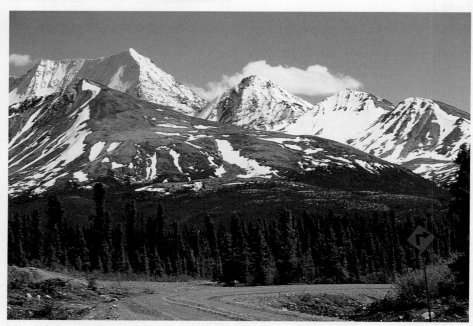

View of the Itsi Range at about Milepost R 113 North Canol Road. (© Rollo Pool)

The 513-mile-/825-km-long Canol Road (Yukon Highway 6) was built to provide access to oil fields at Norman Wells, NWT, on the Mackenzie River. Conceived by the U.S. War Dept. to help fuel Alaska and protect it from a Japanese invasion, the Canol (Canadian Oil) Road and a 4-inch-diameter pipeline were constructed from Norman Wells, NWT, through Macmillan Pass, past Ross River, to Johnson's Crossing on the Alaska Highway. From there the pipeline carried oil to a refinery at Whitehorse.

Begun in 1942 and completed in 1944, the Canol Project included the road, pipeline, a telephone line, the refinery, airfields, pumping stations, tank farms, wells and camps. Only about 1 million barrels of oil were pumped to Whitehorse before the war ended in 1945 and the $134 million Canol Project was abandoned. (Today, Norman Wells, pop. 757, is still a major supplier of oil with a pipeline to Zama, AB, built in 1985.) The Canol Road was declared a National Historic Site in 1990.

Since 1958, the Canol Road between Johnson's Crossing on the Alaska Highway and Ross River on the Campbell Highway (referred to as the South Canol Road) and between Ross River and the YT–NWT border (referred to as the North Canol Road) has been rebuilt and is open to summer traffic. It is maintained to minimum standards.

The 136.8-mile/220.2-km South Canol Road is a narrow winding road which crests the Big Salmon Range and threads its way above Lapie Canyon via a difficult but scenic stretch of road. Reconstruction on the South Canol has replaced many old bridges with culverts, but there are still a few 1-lane wooden bridges. Driving time is about 4 hours one way. Watch for steep hills and bad corners. There are no facilities along the South Canol Road, and it is definitely not recommended for large RVs or trailers. Not recommended for any size vehicle in wet weather. Inquiries on current road conditions should be made locally or with the Yukon Dept. of Highways in Whitehorse (867/667-8215) before driving this road.

The 144.2-mile/232-km North Canol Road is also a narrow, winding road which some motorists have compared to a roller coaster. All bridges on the North Canol are 1-lane, and the road surface can be very slippery when wet. Not recommended during wet weather and not recommended for large RVs or trailers. If mining is under way along the North Canol, watch for large transport trucks. *NOTE: Drive with headlights on at all times!*

Our log of the North Canol ends at the YT–NWT border, where vehicles may turn around. Road washouts prohibit travel beyond this point. From the border to Norman Wells it is 230 miles/372 km of unusable road that has been designated the Canol Heritage Trail by the NWT government. Northwest Territories Tourism recommends contacting the Norman Wells Historical Centre (phone 867/587-2415, fax 867/587-2469) for current description of trail conditions and recommended precautions.

WARNING: The only facilities on the Canol Road are at Ross River and at Johnson's Cross- ing on the Alaska Highway.

Emergency medical services: In Ross River, phone (867) 969-2222; or phone the RCMP, (867) 969-5555, or (867) 667-5555.

South Canol Road Log

Distance from the junction with the Alaska Highway (J) is followed by distance from the Campbell Highway junction (C). *Kilometre figures in the log from the Alaska Highway junction reflect the location of physical kilometreposts when they occur.*

YUKON HIGHWAY 6

J 0 C 136.8 (220.2 km) **Johnson's Crossing**, 0.7 mile/1.1 km from Canol Road turnoff, has food, gas and camping.

> **Junction** of the Canol Road (Yukon Highway 6) with the Alaska Highway (Yukon Highway 1). Turn to **Milepost DC 808.2** in the ALASKA HIGHWAY section for log.

J 0.2 (0.3 km) **C 136.6** (219.8 km) Information panel on the history and construction of Canol Road. Short, dirt road west to auto "boneyard" that includes several WWII Canol Project trucks (all have been significantly cannibalized). Limited turnaround area, not suitable for trailers. Not recommended for any vehicle in wet weather.

J 3.9 (6.2 km) **C 132.9** (213.8 km) Fourmile Creek. Road begins ascent across the Big Salmon Range to the summit (elev. about 4,000 feet/1,219m). Snow possible at summit early October to late spring.

J 13.9 (22.4 km) **C 122.9** (197.8 km) Moose Creek. Small gravel turnout with litter barrels.

J 27 (43.4 km) **C 109.8** (176.7 km) Evelyn Creek 1-lane wooden bridge.

J 28.7 (46.2 km) **C 108.1** (174 km) Sidney Creek 2-lane bridge.

J 30.6 (49.2 km) **C 106.2** (170.9 km) Access road east to **Sidney Lake**. Nice little lake and good place to camp.

From here northbound the South Canol follows the Nisutlin River, which is to the east and can be seen from the road the next 30 miles/48 km until the road crosses the Rose River beyond Quiet Lake.

J 30.9 (49.7 km) **C 105.9** (170.4 km) Turnout with litter barrel to east.

J 39.1 (62.9 km) **C 97.7** (157.2 km) Good view of Pelly Mountains ahead. Road crosses Cottonwood Creek.

CANOL ROAD
Alaska Highway Junction, YT, to NWT Border

© 1999 The MILEPOST®

SELWYN MOUNTAINS

BACKBONE

R-144/232km

Tsichu River

Keele River

Macmillan Pass

RANGES

ITSI RANGE

Macmillan River

North Macmillan River

South Macmillan River

Ross River

Mount Sheldon ▲
6,937 ft./2,114m

NORTHWEST TERRITORIES

YUKON TERRITORY

Sheldon Lake

Lewis Lake

Dragon Lake

Pup Cr.

Caribou Cr.

Tay Cr.

6

LOGAN MOUNTAINS

Pelly River

ANVIL RANGE

Beaver Creek

Orchie L.

Majorie L.

Pelly River

To Klondike Highway Junction
(see CAMPBELL HIGHWAY
section, page 287)

4

R-0

C-0
J-137/220km
K-141/227km
WL-232/374km

Tenas Cr.

Free Ferry

North Canol Road

Fox Creek

Ross River ✝
N61°59' W132°27'

4

To Watson Lake
(see CAMPBELL HIGHWAY section, page 287)

P E L L Y

Lapie River

Lapie Pass

Lapie Lakes

Pony Cr.

Ground Hog Creek

Caribou Mountain ▲
6,905 ft./2,105m

▲ Pass Peak
7,194 ft./2,193m

CAMPBELL RANGE

BIG SALMON RANGE

Upper Sheep Creek

M O U N T A I N S

Ross River

Mount St. Cyr ▲
6,725 ft./2,050m

Nisutlin River

Nisutlin Lake

Teslin River

Quiet Lake

Cottonwood Cr.

South Canol Road

Sidney Creek

Sidney Lake

Evelyn Cr.

Nisutlin River

C-137/220km
J-0
T-32/51km
W-78/126km

Murphy Cr.

6

▲ Johnson's Crossing

1

To Whitehorse
(see ALASKA HIGHWAY section, page 83)

1

Teslin Lake

To Teslin
(see ALASKA HIGHWAY section, page 83)

Key to mileage boxes

Map Location

miles/kilometres
miles/kilometres   from:

C -Campbell Highway Jct.
J -Alaska Highway Junction
R -Ross River
K -Klondike Highway Jct.
T -Teslin
W -Whitehorse
WL -Watson Lake

Principal Route
Paved   Unpaved
Other Roads
Paved   Unpaved
Ferry Routes   Hiking Trails

Refer to Log for Visitor Facilities

Scale
0   10   Miles
0   10   Kilometres

Key to Advertiser Services
C -Camping
D -Dump Station
d -Diesel
G -Gas (reg., unld.)
I -Ice
L -Lodging
M -Meals
P -Propane
R -Car Repair (major)
r -Car Repair (minor)
S -Store (grocery)
T -Telephone (pay)

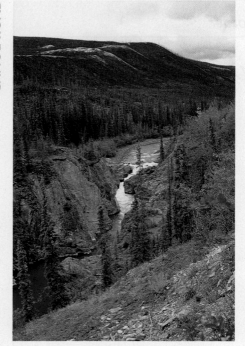

Lapie River Canyon at Milepost J 132.3.

(© Earl L. Brown, staff)

J 42 (67.6 km) **C 94.8** (152.5 km) Access road east 0.4 mile/0.6 km to **Nisutlin River**. Good place to camp with tables and outhouse. ▲

J 47.8 (76.9 km) **C 89** (143.2 km) Quiet Lake Yukon government campground; 20 sites, $8 fee, boat launch, picnic tables, kitchen shelter, firewood. Watch for steep hills northbound to Quiet Lake. ▲

J 54.7 (88 km) **C 82.1** (132.1 km) Lake Creek. Road now follows Quiet Lake to west; good fishing for lake trout, northern pike and arctic grayling. ➥

J 56 (90.1 km) **C 80.8** (130 km) Turnout with litter barrels and point of interest sign overlooking **Quiet Lake**. This is the largest of 3 lakes that form the headwaters of the Big Salmon River system. The 17-mile-/28-km-long lake was named in 1887 by John McCormack, 1 of 4 miners who prospected the Big Salmon River from its mouth on the Yukon River to its source. Although they did find some gold, the river and lakes have become better known for their good fishing and fine scenery. Until the completion of the South Canol Road in the 1940s, this area was reached mainly by boating and portaging hundreds of miles up the Teslin and Nisutlin rivers.

J 61.2 (98.5 km) **C 75.6** (121.6 km) Turnoff west for Quiet Lake, day-use area with picnic sites, water, boat launch and fishing. Entry point for canoeists on the Big Salmon River.

J 61.5 (99 km) **C 75.3** (121.2 km) Yukon government Quiet Lake maintenance camp on left northbound. A vintage Canol Project dump truck and pull grader is on display in front of the camp.

J 62.6 (100.7 km) **C 74.2** (119.4 km) Distance marker indicates Ross River 126 km.

J 63.7 (102 km) **C 73.1** (117.6 km) Steep hill and panoramic view of mountains and valley.

J 65.5 (105.4 km) **C 71.3** (114.7 km) One-lane Bailey bridge across **Rose River No. 1**.

The road now follows the valley of the Rose River into Lapie Pass northbound. According to R.C. Coutts in *Yukon Places and Names,"* Oliver Rose prospected extensively in this area in the early 1900s. He came to the Yukon from Quebec.

J 94.1 (151.4 km) **C 42.7** (68.7 km) Distance marker indicates Ross River 76 km.

J 95.1 (153 km) **C 41.7** (67.1 km) Upper Sheep Creek joins the Rose River here. To the east is **Pass Peak** (elev. 7,194 feet/2,193m).

J 96.4 (155.1 km) **C 40.4** (65 km) Rose River No. 6.

J 97.1 (156.2 km) **C 39.7** (63.9 km) Rose Lake to east.

J 97.5 (156.9 km) **C 39.3** (63.2 km) Pony Creek. **Caribou Mountain** (elev. 6,905 feet/2,105m) to west.

J 101.1 (162.7 km) **C 35.7** (57.4 km) Lakes to west are part of **Lapie Lakes** chain, headwaters of the Lapie River. These features were named by Dr. George M. Dawson of the Geological Survey of Canada in 1887 for Lapie, an Iroquois Indian companion and canoeman of Robert Campbell, who was the first to explore the Pelly River area in 1843 for the Hudson's Bay Co.

A short dirt road provides access to the lake shore. Watch for grazing moose. Unmaintained camping area and boat launch. ▲

J 102.5 (165 km) **C 34.3** (55.2 km) Access road west to Lapie Lakes. Good place to camp.

J 107.4 (172.8 km) **C 29.4** (47.3 km) Lapie River No. 1 culverts. Ponds reported good for grayling fishing. *NOTE: Watch for horses on the road.* ➥

J 107.5 (173 km) **C 29.3** (47.1 km) Ahead northbound is Barite Mountain (elev. about 6,500 feet/1,981m).

J 120.7 (194.2 km) **C 16.1** (25.9 km) The road follows the Lapie River Canyon for about the next 11 miles/18 km, climbing to an elevation of about 500 feet/152m above the river. *CAUTION: Narrow road, watch for rocks.*

J 123.3 (198.4 km) **C 13.5** (21.7 km) Kilometrepost 200. Distance marker indicates Ross River 26 km. Lapie River runs to east.

J 126.3 (203.2 km) **C 10.5** (16.9 km) Turnouts on right side of road northbound overlooking Lapie River Canyon.

J 132.3 (212.9 km) **C 4.5** (7.2 km) Narrow 1-lane bridge over **Lapie River No. 2**. Point of interest sign on north end of bridge about the **Lapie River Canyon**.

J 133 (214 km) **C 3.8** (6.1 km) Erosional features called hoodoos can be seen in the clay banks rising above the road.

J 133.3 (214.5 km) **C 3.5** (5.6 km) Ash layer can be seen in clay bank on right side of road.

J 135.6 (218.2 km) **C 1.2** (1.9 km) Jackfish Lake to west; floatplane dock.

J 136.8 (220 km) **C 0** Campbell Highway junction.

> **Junction** of South Canol Road with the Campbell Highway. Turn to **Milepost WL 227.3** in the CAMPBELL HIGHWAY section for log.

Approximately straight ahead northbound, across the Campbell Highway, a poorly maintained section of the Canol Road continues to Ross River. Motorists bound for Ross River or the North Canol Road are advised to turn left (west) on the

Campbell Highway from the South Canol and drive about 5 miles/8 km to the main Ross River access road (see map).

North Canol Road Log

The North Canol Road leads 144.2 miles/232 km to the NWT border. Physical kilometreposts along the North Canol Road reflect distance from the Alaska Highway junction. *WARNING: There are no services along this road.*

Distance from Ross River (R) is shown.

R 0 ROSS RIVER. Yukon government Ross River ferry (free) crosses the Pelly River. Ferry operates from 8 A.M. to noon and 1–5 P.M. daily from late May to mid-October. Those who miss the last ferry crossing of the day may leave their vehicles on the opposite side of the river and use the footbridge to walk into Ross River; vehicles can be brought over in the morning.

R 0.4 (0.6 km) Stockpile to west is barite from the Yukon Barite Mine.

R 0.6 (1 km) Road to east leads to original site of Ross River and Indian village.

R 0.9 (1.4 km) Second access road east to old Ross River and Indian village. Canol Road follows the Ross River.

R 2.1 (3.4 km) *CAUTION: Slide area, watch for falling rocks.*

R 4.7 (7.6 km) Raspberry patch. Good pickings.

R 6.8 (10.9 km) Tenas Creek 1-lane bridge.

R 20.9 (33.6 km) **Marjorie Creek.** Locals report good grayling fishing. ➥

R 21 (33.8 km) Access road to west leads to Marjorie Lake. Access road not recommended for large RVs.

R 28.1 (45.2 km) Boat launch on Orchie Lake to west.

R 29.8 (48 km) Distance marker indicates NWT border 195 km, Ross River 50 km.

R 31.9 (51.3 km) Gravel Creek 1-lane bridge. The next 15 miles/24 km are excellent moose country.

R 33.4 (53.7 km) Flat Creek 1-lane bridge.

R 37 (59.5 km) Beaver Creek 1-lane bridge.

R 41.8 (67.2 km) 180 Mile Creek 1-lane bridge.

R 43.9 (70.6 km) Tay Creek 1-lane bridge.

R 46.3 (74.5 km) Blue Creek 1-lane bridge.

R 48.1 (77.4 km) Kilometrepost 306. **R 57.6** (92.7 km) Clifford's Slough to the east.

R 58.6 (94.3 km) Steep hill to 1-lane bridge over Caribou Creek.

R 61.1 (98.3 km) Distance marker indicates NWT border 145 km, Ross River 100 km.

R 61.8 (99.4 km) **B 82.4** (132.6 km) Pup Creek 1-lane bridge.

R 64.8 (104.3 km) Turnout to west. Steep hill.

R 65.1 (104.7 km) Turnout to **Dragon Lake**; overnight parking, litter barrels. Locals report that early spring is an excellent time for pike and trout in the inlet. Rock hounds check roadsides and borrow pits for colorful chert, which can be worked into jewelry. ➥

R 65.4 (105.2 km) Kilometrepost 334. Large, level gravel turnout to west overlooking Dragon Lake; boat launch.

Abandoned Army vehicles from the Canol Project near Macmillan Pass. (© Rollo Pool)

R 69.6 (112 km) Wreckage of Twin Pioneer aircraft to west. WWII remnants can be found in this area.

R 69.9 (112.5 km) Road to Twin Creek.

R 70.8 (113.9 km) Airstrip.

R 71 (114.2 km) One-lane bridge over Twin Creek No. 1. Yukon government maintenance camp.

R 71.1 (114.4 km) One-lane bridge over Twin Creek No. 2. Good views of Mount Sheldon.

R 75.1 (120.8 km) Kilometrepost 350. **Mount Sheldon** (elev. 6,937 feet/2,114m) ahead northbound, located 3 miles/4.8 km north of Sheldon Lake; a very beautiful and distinguishable feature on the Canol Road. In 1900, Poole Field and Clement Lewis, who were fans of writer Rudyard Kipling, named this peak Kipling Mountain and the lake at its base Rudyard. In 1907, Joseph Keele of the Geological Survey of Canada renamed them after Charles Sheldon, a well-known sheep hunter and naturalist who came to the area to collect Stone sheep specimens for the Chicago Natural History Museum in 1905.

R 76.4 (123 km) Kilometrepost 352. Of the 3-lake chain, Sheldon Lake is farthest north, then Field Lake and Lewis Lake, which is just visible from here. Lewis Lake is closest to the confluence of the Ross and Prevost rivers.

Field Lake and Lewis Lake were named in 1907 by Joseph Keele of the Geological Survey of Canada after Poole Field and Clement Lewis. The 2 partners, who had prospected this country, ran a trading post called Nahanni House at the mouth of the Ross River in 1905.

R 77.6 (124.9 km) Kilometrepost 354. Riddell Creek 1-lane bridge. Tip of **Mount Riddell** (elev. 6,101 feet/1,859m) can be seen to the west.

R 78.8 (126.8 km) View of Sheldon Lake ahead, Field Lake to east.

R 79.8 (128.4 km) Access road east to Sheldon Lake.

R 82.7 (133.1 km) Sheldon Creek 1-lane bridge. Road climbs, leaving Ross River valley and entering Macmillan Valley northbound.

R 89.3 (143.7 km) Height of land before starting descent northbound into South Macmillan River system.

R 89.7 (144.3 km) *Steep hill*. Road may wash out during heavy rains. Deep ditches along roadside help channel water.

R 91.4 (147.1 km) Moose Creek 1-lane bridge.

R 91.6 (147.4 km) **B 52.6** (84.6 km) Milepost 230.

R 92.3 (148.5 km) Kilometrepost 378. Peaks of the Itsi Range ahead. Rugged, spectacular scenery northbound.

R 92.7 (149.1 km) Distance marker indicates NWT border 95 km, Ross River 150 km.

R 93.8 (151 km) First of several WWII vehicle dumps to west. To the east is a wannigan, or skid shack, used as living quarters by Canol Road workers during construction of the road. It was too far to return to base camp; these small buildings were strategically located along the route so the workers had a place to eat and sleep at night.

R 94 (151.3 km) To east are remains of a maintenance depot where heavy equipment was repaired. Concrete foundations to west. First glimpse of the South Macmillan River northbound.

R 94.7 (152.4 km) Kilometrepost 382. Another Canol project equipment dump to explore. Watch ditches for old pieces of pipeline.

R 97.8 (157.4 km) Boulder Creek 1-lane bridge.

R 98.5 (158.5 km) Access road west to **South Macmillan River** where boats can be launched. Locals advise launching boats here rather than from the bridge at **Milepost R 113.6**, which washes out periodically and leaves dangerous debris in the river.

R 100.8 (162.5 km) Kilometrepost 392. **Itsi Range** comes into view ahead northbound. Itsi is said to be an Indian word meaning "wind" and was first given as a name to Itsi Lakes, headwaters of the Ross River. The road dips down and crosses an unnamed creek.

R 104.5 (168.2 km) Kilometrepost 398. View of the South Macmillan River from here.

R 105.3 (169.4 km) View of **Selwyn Mountains**, named in 1901 by Joseph Keele of the Geological Survey of Canada for Dr. Alfred Richard Selwyn (1824–1902), a distin-

guished geologist in England. Dr. Selwyn later became director of the Geological Survey of Australia and then director of the Geological Survey of Canada from 1869 until his retirement in 1895.

R 111 (178.6 km) Itsi Creek 1-lane bridge.

R 112.2 (180.5 km) Wagon Creek 1-lane bridge.

R 113.6 (182.8 km) Turnout to east on South Macmillan River. Good place for a picnic but not recommended as a boat launch. One-lane Bailey bridge over South Macmillan River No. 1.

Robert Campbell, a Hudson's Bay Co. explorer on a journey down the Pelly River in 1843, named this major tributary of the Pelly after Chief Factor James McMillan, who had sponsored Campbell's employment with the company.

R 115.1 (185.2 km) Access road on left northbound leads about 7 miles/11 km to Yukon Barite Mine. Barite is a soft mineral that requires only crushing and bagging before being shipped over the Dempster Highway to the Beaufort Sea oil and gas wells, where it is used as a lubricant known as drilling mud.

R 118.9 (191.3 km) Jeff Creek 1-lane bridge.

R 121.2 (195 km) Hess Creek 1-lane bridge. Bears in area.

R 123.2 (198.3 km) Gravel turnout to west. Distance marker indicates NWT border 45 km, Ross River 200 km. One-lane bridge over Dewhurst Creek.

R 127.5 (205.2 km) Entering **Macmillan Pass**, "Mac Pass" (elev. 4,480 feet/1,366m).

R 129.4 (208.2 km) One-lane bridge over Macmillan River No. 2.

R 129.5 (208.4 km) Abandoned Army vehicles from the Canol Project to west and east.

R 133.6 (215 km) To the west is Cordilleran Engineering camp, managers of the mining development of Ogilvie Joint Venture's Jason Project. The Jason deposit is a zinc, lead, silver, barite property.

One-lane bridge over Sekie Creek No. 1.

R 136.4 (219.5 km) Access to Macmillan airstrip on left northbound. Access road east to Hudson Bay Mining & Smelting's Tom lead–zinc mineral claims.

R 137.7 (221.6 km) One-lane bridge over Macmillan River No. 3.

R 141.8 (228.2 km) One-lane bridge over Macmillan River No. 4.

R 142.9 (230 km) One-lane bridge over Macmillan River No. 5.

R 144.1 (231.9 km) One-lane bridge over Macmillan River No. 6.

R 144.2 (232 km) **YT–NWT Border**. Sign cautions motorists to proceed at their own risk. The road is not maintained and bridges are not safe beyond this point. Vehicles turn around here.

Ahead is the Tsichu River valley and the Selwyn Mountains. The abandoned North Canol Road continues another 230 miles/ 372 km from the YT–NWT border to Norman Wells, NWT. Designated the Canol Heritage Trail, and set aside as a territorial park reserve, the trail is currently under development. Some river crossings required; large stretches deemed dangerous and arduous. It passes through mountains, tundra and forest, and past many relics of the Canol Project. The Historical Centre museum in Norman Wells features the history of the Canol Project and has outdoor displays of Canol vehicles. Phone (867) 587-2415; fax (867) 587-2469.

Connects: Klondike Hwy. to Inuvik, NWT   **Length:** 456 miles
Road Surface: Gravel   **Season:** Open all year
Highest Summit: North Fork Pass 4,265 feet
Major Attractions: Lost Patrol Gravesite, Mackenzie River Delta

	Dawson City	Ft. McPherson	Inuvik	Klondike Hwy.
Dawson City		367	481	25
Ft. McPherson	367		114	342
Inuvik	481	114		456
Klondike Hwy.	25	342	456	

Two Moose Lake turnout at Milepost J 64.4 Dempster Highway. (© Earl L. Brown, staff)

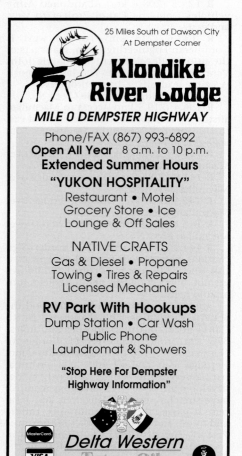

The Dempster Highway (Yukon Highway 5, NWT Highway 8) begins 25 miles/40.2 km east of Dawson City, YT, at its junction with Klondike Highway 2 and leads 456.3 miles/734.3 km northeast to Inuvik, NWT. The highway can be driven in 12 to 16 hours, but allow extra time to enjoy the wilderness. The Dempster offers hiking, camping, fishing and spectacular photo opportunities. It also has a reputation as a birder's paradise.

Construction of the Dempster Highway began in 1959, under the Road to Resources program, and was completed in 1978. A 5-year major reconstruction and surfacing program on the highway concluded in 1988, although freezing weather and heavy truck traffic may erode both road base and surfacing in areas. Calcium chloride is used in some areas to reduce dust and as a bonding agent; wash your vehicle as soon as practical.

The Dempster is a mostly gravel road. The first 5 miles/8 km were seal coated in 1998, and the last 6 miles/10 km are paved.) There are stretches of clay surface that can be slippery in wet weather. Summer driving conditions on the Dempster vary depending on weather and maintenance. Generally, road conditions range from fair to excellent, with highway speeds attainable on some sections. It is strongly recommended motorists carry at least 2 spare tires while traveling the Dempster. *Drive with your headlights on.*

Facilities are still few and far between on the Dempster. Full auto services are available at Klondike River Lodge at the Dempster Highway turnoff on Klondike Highway 2. Gas, propane, food and lodging, and car repair are also available at Eagle Plains Hotel, located at about the halfway point on the Dempster. Gas, food and lodging are also available in Fort McPherson. Gas up whenever possible.

The Dempster is open year-round, but summer travel gives visitors long hours of daylight for recreation. The highway is fairly well-traveled in summer: A driver may not see another car for an hour, and then pass 4 cars in a row. Locals say the highway is smoother and easier to drive in winter, but precautions should be taken against cold weather, high winds and poor visibility; check road conditions before proceeding in winter. Watch for herds of caribou mid-September to late October and in March and April.

There are 2 ferry crossings on the Dempster, at **Milepost J 334.9** (Peel River crossing) and **J 377.9** (Mackenzie River and Arctic Red River crossings). Free government ferry service is available 15 hours a day (9 A.M. to 12:45 A.M. Northwest Territories time) during summer(from about early June to late October. Cross by ice bridge in winter. For recorded messages on ferry service, road and weather conditions, phone (800) 661-0752.

General information on Northwest Territories is available by calling the Arctic Hotline at (800) 661-0788. If you are in Dawson City, we recommend visiting the Western Arctic Visitor Centre for information on Northwest Territories and the Dempster Highway. Located in the B.Y.N. Building on Front Street, across from the Yukon Visitor Centre, it is open 9 A.M. to 9 P.M., June to September; phone (867) 993-6167. Or write Western Arctic Trade & Tourism, Box 2600MP, Inuvik, NT X0E 0T0; phone (867) 777-4321, fax (867) 777-2434 for more information.

The MILEPOST® expresses its appreciation to the Yukon Dept. of Renewable Resources, Parks and Recreation for its assistance with information in this highway log.

Dempster Highway Log

Distance from junction with Klondike Highway 2 (J) is followed by distance from Inuvik (I).
Driving distance is measured in miles. The kilometre figure on the Yukon portion of the highway reflects the physical kilometreposts and is

DEMPSTER HIGHWAY Klondike Highway Junction to Inuvik, NWT

© 1999 The MILEPOST®

RICHARDSON MOUNTAINS

YUKON TERRITORY

NORTHWEST TERRITORIES

Mackenzie N68°21' W133°42'

Inuvik

I-0
J-456/734km

Delta

Noell Lake

Sitidgi Lake

Dolomite Lake

Campbell Lake

Caribou Lake

Caribou Creek

Bell River

Aklavik

Mackenzie River

Rengleng River

Old Crow

Porcupine River

I-115/184km
J-342/550km

N67°26' W134°52'

Fort McPherson

J-341.8/550km Fort McPherson Tent & Canvas

Free Ferry

Shiltee Rock

Frog Creek

Tsiigehtchic
(Arctic Red River)

Free Ferry

Arctic Red River

I-167/269km
J-289/465km

Rock River

Peel River

8

Eagle River

5

ARCTIC CIRCLE

I-204/329km
J-252/406km

YUKON TERRITORY   NORTHWEST TERRITORIES

Eagle Plains

J-229.3/369km Eagle Plains Hotel CDdGILMPrST

Peel River

Hart River

N
W   E
S

I-335/539km
J-122/194km

Engineer Creek

Ogilvie River

Blackstone River

OGILVIE

Chapman Lake

MOUNTAINS

West Fork

East Fork

5

Tombstone Mountain ▲

Bensen Creek

North Fork

I-456/734km
J-0
D-26/41km
C-199/320km

To Boundary, AK
(see KLONDIKE LOOP
HIGHWAY section,
page 259)

Free Ferry

2

Yukon River

Dawson City
N64°04'
W139°25'

J-0 Klondike River Lodge
CDdGILMPrST

2

Klondike River

To Carmacks
(see KLONDIKE LOOP HIGHWAY section, page 259)

Key to mileage boxes

miles/kilometres
miles/kilometres   from:

J-Junction
I-Inuvik
D-Dawson City
C-Carmacks

Map Location

Principal Route
Paved   Unpaved
Other Roads
Paved   Unpaved
Ferry Routes   Hiking Trails

❄ Refer to Log for Visitor Facilities

Scale
0   20   Miles
0   20   Kilometres

Key to Advertiser Services
C -Camping
D -Dump Station
d -Diesel
G -Gas (reg., unld.)
I -Ice
L -Lodging
M -Meals
P -Propane
R -Car Repair (major)
r -Car Repair (minor)
S -Store (grocery)
T -Telephone (pay)

not necessarily an accurate metric conversion of the mileage figure. Kilometreposts are green with white lettering and are located on the right-hand side of the highway, northbound.

YUKON HIGHWAY 5

J 0 I 456.3 (734.3 km) **Dempster Corner**, 25 miles/40.2 km east of Dawson City. Klondike River Lodge (open all year); food, gas, propane, lodging, camping, and tire repair and sales.   ▲

NOTE: Next available gas northbound is at Eagle Plains, 229 miles/369 km from here.

Klondike River Lodge. See display ad this section.

Junction of Klondike Highway (Yukon Highway 2) and Dempster Highway (Yukon Highway 5). Turn to **Milepost J 301.6** in the KLONDIKE LOOP section for log of Klondike Highway to Dawson City.

J 0.1 (0.2 km) **I 456.2** (734.2 km) Dempster Highway monument with information panels on history and culture, wildlife, ecology and driving tips.

J 0.2 (0.3 km) **I 456.1** (734 km) One-lane wood-planked bridge over Klondike River. The road follows the wooded (spruce and poplar) North Klondike River valley.

J 0.9 (1.4 km) **I 455.4** (732.9 km) Distance marker shows Eagle Plains 363 km (226 miles), Inuvik 735 km (457 miles).

J 3 (5 km) **I 453.3** (729.5 km) Burn area from 1991 fire that burned 5,189 acres/2,100 hectares.

J 4 (6.4 km) **I 452.3** (727.9 km) The North Fork Ditch channeled water from the North Klondike River to a power plant 15.5 miles/25 km farther west for nearly 60 years, until the 1960s, and it helped to provide electricity and water for huge gold-dredging operations farther down the valley. Watch for salmon migrating upstream from late July through August.

J 4.8 (7.7 km) **I 451.5** (726.6 km) Turnoff for Viceroy Brewery Creek Gold Mine (private road). Tours were offered here on Thursdays in summer 1998. Inquire locally or phone (867) 993-6057 about tours in 1999.

J 6.5 (10.5 km) **I 449.8** (723.9 km) Antimony Mountain (elev. 6,693 feet/2,040m) about 18.5 miles/30 km away, is one peak of the Ogilvie Mountains and part of the Snowy Range.

J 12.4 (20 km) **I 443.9** (714.4 km) North Klondike Range, Ogilvie Mountains to the west of the highway lead toward the rugged, interior Tombstone Range. These mountains were glaciated during the Ice Age.

J 15.4 (24.5 km) **I 440.9** (709.5 km) Glacier Creek.

J 16.6 (26.7 km) **I 439.7** (707.6 km) Pull-out to west.

J 18.1 (29 km) **I 438.2** (705.2 km) Bensen Creek.

J 25.6 (41 km) **I 430.7** (693.1 km) Pea Soup Creek.

J 29.8 (48 km) **I 426.5** (686.4 km) Scout Car Creek.

J 31.7 (51 km) **I 424.6** (683.3 km) Wolf Creek. Private cabin beside creek.

J 34.7 (55.8 km) **I 421.6** (678.5 km) Highway follows North Fork Klondike River.

J 36.6 (58.9 km) **I 419.7** (675.4 km) Grizzly Creek. Mount Robert Service to right northbound.

J 39.6 (63.7 km) **I 416.7** (670.6 km) Mike and Art Creek.

J 40.4 (65 km) **I 415.9** (669.3 km) Klondike Camp Yukon government highway maintenance station. No visitor services but may provide help in an emergency.

J 41.8 (67.3 km) **I 414.5** (667.1 km) First crossing of the **North Fork Klondike River**. The highway now moves above tree line and on to tundra northbound. At an elevation of approximately 4,003 feet/1,220m, you'll cross the watershed between the Yukon and Mackenzie basins.

J 43 (69.2 km) **I 413.3** (665.2 km) Spectacular first view of Tombstone Range northbound.

J 44.4 (71.5 km) **I 411.9** (662.9 km) Tombstone Mountain Yukon government campground (3,392 feet/1,034m above sea level) with 31 sites, $8 fee, shelter, fireplaces, water from the river, tables, pit toilets. Designated cyclist camping area. Stop in at the Dempster Interpretive Centre located at the campground; fossil displays, resource library, handouts with area information, campfire talks and nature walks. In summer 1998, the centre was open 9 A.M. to 9 P.M. Monday to Thursday and 10 A.M. to 10 P.M. Friday to Sunday, from mid-June to early September. Good hiking trail begins past the outhouses and leads toward the headwaters of the North Fork Klondike River. *CAUTION: Hikers should inquire about recent bear activity in the area before setting off.*   ▲

J 46 (74 km) **I 410.3** (660.3 km) Large double-ended viewpoint. Good views of North Fork Pass and river. To the southwest is the needle-like peak of **Tombstone Mountain** (7,195 feet/2,193m), which forms the centrepoint in a panorama of ragged ridges and lush green tundra slopes. To the north is the East Fork Blackstone River valley; on each side are the Ogilvie Mountains, which rise to elevations of 6,890 feet/2,100m. Watch for Dall sheep, grizzlies, hoary marmots and ptarmigan. The Tombstone, Cloudy and Blackstone mountain ranges are identified as a Special Management Area by the Yukon government and will eventually become a Yukon Territorial Park.

Day hikes up the North Klondike River valley and 4-day wilderness hikes to Tombstone Mountain are popular. Heli-hiking is also growing in popularity; inquire at Trans North Helicopters in Dawson City about fly-in/hike-out packages. There are no established trails. The staff at the Dempster Interpretive Centre at Tombstone Campground can provide maps and suggest itineraries. Hikers should be well prepared for rough terrain, drastic weather changes and potential wildlife encounters, as well as practicing "leave-no-trace" camping. For more information on the Tombstone region, call Yukon Dept. of Renewable Resources, Parks & Outdoor Recreation Branch at (867) 667-8299 or e-mail <jack.schick@gov.yk.ca>.

Outstanding aerial view of the mountain available through flightseeing trip out of Dawson City.

J 48.4 (77.9 km) **I 407.9** (656.4 km) Blackstone River culvert. Tundra in the region indicates permafrost.

J 51 (82 km) **I 405.3** (652.2 km) **North Fork Pass Summit**, elev. 4,265 feet/1,300m, is the highest point on the Dempster Highway. Wildflowers abundant late June–early July. Descent to the Blackstone River. Good bird-watching area. A hike up to the lower knoll to the right of the main mountain increases chances of seeing pika and marmots.

J 52.2 (84 km) **I 404.1** (650.3 km) Anglecomb Peak (also called Sheep Mountain) is a lambing and nursery habitat for Dall sheep during May and June. A 1994 census showed 250 sheep in the area. This is also a frequent nesting area for a pair of golden eagles.

J 54.2 (87.2 km) **I 402.1** (647.1 km) First crossing of East Fork Blackstone River.

J 54.6 (87.9 km) **I 401.7** (646.4 km) White fireweed in summer.

J 56.5 (91 km) **I 399.8** (643.4 km) Guide and outfitters camp to east. *CAUTION: Watch for horses on road.*

The Blackstone Uplands, stretching from North Fork Pass to Chapman Lake, are a rich area for birdlife (long-tailed jaegers, gyrfalcons, peregrine falcons, red-throated loons, whimbrels, upland sandpipers and oldsquaw ducks) and big game hunting for Dall sheep and grizzly bear.

J 63.4 (102 km) **I 392.9** (632.3 km) Distance marker shows Eagle Plains 261 km (162 miles), Inuvik 633 km (393 miles), Dawson 142 km (88 miles), Whitehorse 600 km (373 miles).

J 64.4 (103.6 km) **I 391.9** (630.7 km) **Two Moose Lake**; turnout with information panels and viewing platform.

J 66.9 (107.6 km) **I 389.4** (626.7 km) Large gravel pullout with dumpster. Access to Blackstone River.

J 71.5 (115 km) **I 384.8** (619.3 km) First crossing of **West Fork Blackstone River**. Watch for arctic terns. Good fishing for Dolly Varden and grayling a short distance downstream where the west and east forks of the Blackstone join to form the Blackstone River, which the road now follows. After the river crossing, 2 low, cone-shaped mounds called pingos are visible upriver about 5 miles/8 km.

J 72.1 (116 km) **I 384.2** (618.3 km) Turnout to west. View over **Chapman Lake**, one of the few lakes close to the highway that is large enough to permit floatplane operations. Common loons nest on island. Commemorative road sign about sled dog patrols of the Royal North West Mounted Police.

Porcupine caribou herd sometimes crosses the highway in this area in mid-October.

J 77.3 (124.4 km) **I 379** (609.9 km) **Private Aircraft:** Government airstrip (road is part of the strip); elev. 3,100 feet/945m; length 3,000 feet/914m.

J 96 (154.5 km) **I 360.3** (579.8 km) Northbound, highway passes through barren gray hills of Windy Pass. The mountain ridges are the breeding habitat for some species of butterflies and moths not known to exist anywhere else.

J 98.2 (158 km) **I 358.1** (576.3 km) Gyrfalcon nest on ledge on side of cliff.

J 106 (169.7 km) **I 350.3** (563.7 km) Creek culvert is red from iron oxide. Sulfurous smell is from nearby sulfur springs. Watch for interesting geological features in hills along road.

J 108.1 (173 km) **I 348.2** (560.4 km) Views of red-coloured **Engineer Creek**, and also erosion pillars and red rock of nearby hills between here and Kilometrepost 182.

J 121.7 (194 km) **I 334.6** (538.5 km) **Sapper Hill**, named in 1971 in honour of the 3rd Royal Canadian Engineers who built the Ogilvie River bridge. "Sapper" is a nickname for an army engineer. **Engineer Creek** Yukon government campground; 15 sites, $8 fee, fireplaces, water, tables, pit toilets. Grayling fishing.

J 122.9 (195.7 km) **I 333.4** (536.5 km) The 360-foot/110-m Jeckell Bridge spans the **Ogilvie River** here. Built by the Canadian Armed Forces Engineers as a training exercise, it is named in honour of Allan Jeckell, controller of the Yukon from 1932 to 1946. Fossil coral may be visible in limestone outcrops to the northeast of the bridge.

The Ogilvie River and Ogilvie Mountains were named in honour of William Ogilvie, a highly respected Dominion land surveyor and commissioner of the Yukon during the Klondike Gold Rush.

J 123 (195.8 km) **I 333.3** (536.4 km) Ogilvie grader station, Yukon government maintenance camp is on north side of the river.

For the next 25 miles/40 km, the highway follows the narrow valley of the Ogilvie River. For the first 12 miles/20 km, talus slopes edge the road, and game trails are evident along their precipitous sides.

J 124.3 (197.7 km) **I 332** (534.3 km) View of castlelike outcroppings of rock, known as **tors**, on mountaintops to north.

J 131.9 (209.5 km) **I 324.4** (522.1 km) Between here and Kilometrepost 216, watch for bird nests in the shale embankments along the highway and unusual rock outcroppings and erosion pillars in surrounding hills. Highway crosses rolling plateau country near Kilometrepost 218.

J 137.5 (221.2 km) **I 318.8** (513 km) Small turnout with litter barrels. Easy access to **Ogilvie River**. Good grayling fishing. Elephant Rock may be viewed from right side of road northbound. Fascinating mountain of broken rock and shale near Kilometrepost 224.

J 137.6 (221.5 km) **I 318.7** (512.9 km) Davies Creek.

J 149.1 (235.8 km) **I 307.2** (494.4 km) Ogilvie airstrip. The great gray owl, one of Canada's largest, is known to nest as far north as this area.

J 154.4 (244 km) **I 301.9** (485.8 km) Highway climbs away from the Ogilvie River, following a high ridge to the Eagle Plains plateau. One of the few unglaciated areas in Canada, this country is shaped by wind and water erosion rather than by ice. Views of Mount Cronkhite and Mount McCullum to the east.

Overgrown seismic lines next 62 miles/100 km are a reminder that this was the major area of oil and gas exploration activity for which the road was originally built. In season, fields of cotton grass and varieties of tundra plants make good photo subjects. The road continues to follow a high ridge (elev. 1,969 feet/600m) with broad sweeps and easy grades.

J 160.9 (259 km) **I 295.4** (475.4 km) Panoramic **Ogilvie Ridge** viewpoint is a large double-ended turnout with interpretive panels on the geology of the area; outhouse, litter barrels. Lowbush cranberries in August.

J 169.4 (272.6 km) **I 286.9** (461.7 km) Highway begins descent northbound and crosses fabulous high rolling country above tree line.

J 202 (325 km) **I 254.3** (409.2 km) Road widens to become part of an airstrip.

J 206.9 (325 km) **I 249.4** (401.3 km) Double-ended turnout with litter barrels.

J 215.6 (347 km) **I 240.7** (387.4 km) Richardson Mountains to the northeast. The thick blanket of rock and gravel that makes up the roadbed ahead is designed to prevent the underlying permafrost from melting. The roadbed conducts heat more than the surrounding vegetation does and must be extra thick to compensate. Much of the highway was built in winter.

J 229.3 (369 km) **I 227** (365.3 km) **Milepost 231. EAGLE PLAINS;** hotel, phone (867) 993-2453; food, gas, propane, aviation fuel, diesel, tire repair, lodging and camping. Open year-round. ▲

Built in 1978, just before completion of the Dempster Highway, the hotel here was an engineering challenge. Engineers considered the permafrost in the area and found a place where the bedrock was at the surface. The hotel was built on this natural pad, thus avoiding the costly process of building on pilings as was done at Inuvik.

Mile 231. Eagle Plains Hotel. Located midway on the Dempster, this year-round facility is an oasis in the wilderness. Modern hotel rooms, plus restaurant and lounge. Full camper services including electrical hookups, laundry, store, dump station, minor repairs, tires, propane and road and area information. Check out our historical photos. See display ad this section. ▲

[ADVERTISEMENT]

J 234.8 (377.8 km) **I 221.5** (356.5 km) Short side road to picnic site with information sign about Albert Johnson, "The Mad Trapper of Rat River." Something of a mystery man, Johnson killed one mounted policeman and wounded another in 2 separate incidents involving complaints that Johnson was tampering with Native trap lines. The ensuing manhunt became famous in the North, as Johnson eluded Mounties for 48 days during the winter of 1931–32. Johnson was killed in a shoot-out on Feb. 17, 1932. He was buried at Aklavik, a community located 36 miles/58 km west of Inuvik by air.

Dick North, author of 2 books on Johnson (and also author of *The Lost Patrol*), was quoted in the *New York Times* (June 3, 1990) as being 95 percent certain that Johnson, whose true identity has not been known, was a Norwegian–American bank robber named Johnny Johnson.

J 234.9 (378 km) **I 221.4** (356.3 km) **Eagle River** bridge. Like the Ogilvie bridge, it was built by the Dept. of National Defense as a training exercise. In contrast to the

Patch of "white" fireweed at Milepost J 54.6. (© Earl L. Brown, staff)

other rivers seen from the Dempster, the Eagle is a more sluggish, silt-laden stream with unstable banks. It is the main drainage channel for the western slopes of the Richardson Mountains. It and its tributaries provide good grayling fishing. Canoeists leave here bound for Alaska via the Porcupine and Yukon rivers. ◄•

J 239.4 (385.3 km) **I 216.9** (349.1 km) Views of the Richardson Mountains (elev. 3,937 feet/1,200m) ahead. Named for Sir John Richardson, surgeon and naturalist on both of Sir John Franklin's overland expeditions to the Arctic Ocean.

J 241.7 (389 km) **I 214.6** (345.4 km) **Private Aircraft:** Emergency airstrip; elev. 2,365 feet/721m; length 2,500 feet/762m; gravel. Used regularly by aircraft hauling freight to Old Crow, a Kutchin Indian settlement on the Porcupine River and Yukon's most northerly community.

J 252 (405.5 km) **I 204.3** (328.8 km) Large double-ended turnout at **Arctic Circle Crossing**, 66°33′N; picnic tables, litter barrels, outhouses. On June 21, the sun does not fall below the horizon for 24 hours at this latitude. Highway crosses arctic tundra on an elevated berm beside the Richardson Mountains; sweeping views.

J 269 (432.9 km) **I 187.3** (301.4 km) Rock River.

J 277 (445.8 km) **I 179.3** (288.5 km) **Cornwall River** Yukon government campground; 18 sites, $8 fee, tables, kitchen shelter, water, firepits, outhouses. Black flies prevalent; bring repellent. ▲

J 280.1 (450.8 km) **I 176.2** (283.6 km) Turnout. Northbound, the highway winds toward the Richardson Mountains, crossing them at George's Gap near the YT–NWT border. Good hiking area and excellent photo possibilities.

J 288 (463.5 km) **I 168.3** (270.8 km) Turnout; good overnight spot for self-contained vehicles.

J 288.5 (464.3 km) **I 167.8** (270 km) Plaque about Wright Pass, named for Al Wright, a highway engineer with Public Works Canada who was responsible for the routing of the Dempster Highway.

J 288.9 (465 km) **I 167.4** (269.4 km) **YT–NWT Border**. Historical marker. *TIME ZONE CHANGE: Yukon Territory observes Pacific standard time; Northwest Territories is on Mountain time.* Continental Divide in the Richardson Mountains: West of here, water flows to the Pacific Ocean. East of here, water flows to the Arctic Ocean. Good photo spot.

NWT HIGHWAY 8

IMPORTANT: Kilometreposts northbound (with white letters on a blue background) indicate distance from YT–NWT border and are indicated at intervals in our log. Highway descends, road narrows, northbound.

J 297.6 (479 km) **I 158.7** (255.4 km) Kilometrepost 14. **James Creek;** good grayling fishing. Highway maintenance camp. Good spot to park overnight. ⊸

J 299 (481.2 km) **I 157.3** (253.1 km) Sign advises no passing next 4.3 miles/7 km; climb to Wright Pass summit.

J 303.7 (488.7 km) **I 152.6** (245.6 km) **Wright Pass Summit.** From here northbound, the Dempster Highway descends 2,300 feet/853m to the Peel River crossing, 32 miles/51 km away.

J 316.3 (509 km) **I 140** (225.3 km) Kilometrepost 44. Side road leads down to **Midway Lake**.

J 319.4 (514 km) **I 136.9** (220.3 km) **Private Aircraft:** Highway widens to form Midway airstrip; length 3,000 feet/914m.

J 329.3 (530 km) **I 127** (204.4 km) View of Peel River Valley and Fort McPherson to north. Litter barrels.

J 332.4 (535 km) **I 123.9** (199.4 km) Kilometrepost 70. Highway begins descent northbound to Peel River.

J 334.9 (539 km) **I 121.4** (195.4 km) **Peel River Crossing**, locally called Eightmile because it is situated 8 miles/12.8 km south of Fort McPherson. Free government ferry (CF *Abraham Francis*) operates 15 hours a day during summer from early June to late October. Double-ended cable ferry: Drive on, drive off. Light vehicles cross by ice bridge in late November; heavier vehicles cross as ice thickens. *No crossing possible during freezeup or breakup.* Phone toll free (800) 661-0752 for information on ferry crossings, road conditions and weather.

The level of the Peel River changes rapidly in spring and summer in response to meltwater from the mountains and ice jams on the Mackenzie River. Extreme high and low water level fluctuations may cause delays in ferry service. The alluvial flood plain is covered by muskeg on the flats, and scrubby alder and stunted black spruce on the valley sides.

Indians from Fort McPherson have summer tent camps on the Peel River. The Indians net whitefish and sheefish (inconnu) then dry them on racks or in smokehouses for the winter.

About 4 miles/6.4 km south upstream is a trail leading to Shiltee Rock, which gives excellent views of the Peel River and the southern end of the Mackenzie.

J 335.9 (540.6 km) **I 120.4** (193.8 km) Nitainilaii territorial campground with 20 sites. (Campground name is from the Gwich'in term *Noo-til-ee,* meaning "fast flowing waters.") Information centre open daily June to September. Camping permits, potable water, firewood, pit toilets and kitchen shelter available. ▲

J 337.4 (543 km) **I 118.9** (191.3 km) Kilometrepost 78.

J 340.4 (547.8 km) **I 115.9** (186.5 km) Access road right to Fort McPherson airport.

J 341.8 (550 km) **I 114.5** (184.3 km) Side road on left to Fort McPherson (description follows).

Fort McPherson

Located on a flat-topped hill about 100 feet/30m above the Peel River, 24 miles/38 km from its junction with the Mackenzie River; 100 miles/160 km southwest of Aklavik by boat along Peel Channel, 31 miles/50 km directly east of the Richardson Mountains. **Population**: 632. **Emergency Services**: RCMP, phone (867) 952-2551. **Health Center**, phone (867) 952-2586.

Visitor Information: Located in a restored log house, the former home of elder Annie G. Robert; open daily, early June through mid-September, 9 A.M. to 9 P.M. **Radio:** CBC 680.

Transportation: Air—Aklak Air provides scheduled air service from Inuvik.

Private Aircraft: Fort McPherson airstrip; 67°24′N 134°51′W; elev. 142 feet/43m; length 3,500 feet/1,067m; gravel.

This Déné Indian settlement has a public phone, cafe, bed and breakfast, 2 general stores and 2 service stations (1 with tire repair). A co-op hotel here offers 8 rooms and a restaurant. Arts and crafts include beadwork and hide garments. Wildlife watching, adventure tours and canoe trips are popular along the Peel River.

Fort McPherson was named in 1848 for Murdoch McPherson, chief trader of the

Lost Patrol Gravesite in Fort McPherson.
(© Laurent Dick)

Hudson's Bay Co., which had established its first posts in the area 8 years before. Between 1849 and 1859 there were frequent feuds with neighboring Inuit, who later moved farther north to the Aklavik area, where they established a fur-trading post.

In addition to subsistence fishing and hunting, income is earned from trapping (mostly muskrat and mink), handicrafts, government employment, and commercial enterprises such as Fort McPherson Tent and Canvas factory, which specializes in travel

bags, tents and tepees. Tours during business hours, 9 A.M. to 5 P.M. weekdays; (867) 952-2179, fax (867) 952-2718.

Photos and artifacts depicting the history and way of life of the community are displayed in the Chief Julius School. Buried in the cemetery outside the Anglican church are Inspector Francis J. Fitzgerald and 3 men from the ill-fated North West Mounted Police patrol of 1910–1911 between Fort McPherson and Dawson.

Inspector Fitzgerald and the men had left Fort McPherson on Dec. 21, 1910, carrying mail and dispatches to Dawson City. By Feb. 20, 1911, the men had not yet arrived in Dawson, nearly a month overdue. A search party led by Corporal W.J.D. Dempster was sent to look for the missing patrol. On March 22, 1911, Dempster discovered their frozen bodies only 26 miles from where they had started. Lack of knowledge of the trail, coupled with too few rations, had doomed the 4-man patrol. One of the last entries in Fitzgerald's diary, quoted in Dick North's *The Lost Patrol*, an account of their journey, read: "We have now only 10 pounds of flour and 8 pounds of bacon and some dried fish. My last hope is gone. ... We have been a week looking for a river to take us over the divide, but there are dozens of rivers, and I am at a loss."

Fort McPherson Tent & Canvas. Be sure to visit our factory north of the Arctic Circle ... One of the most unique businesses in Canada. See our wide array of products, from tents to our renowned travel bags to custom work, crafted by dedicated all-aboriginal staff with individual attention to detail. Take home one of our high quality cordura nylon bags: backpacks, totebags, attaches and elite dufflebags with their lifetime guarantee of workmanship using only the best and toughest of materials. (Catalogue available.) You'll enjoy your factory tour, and we look forward to meeting you! P.O. Box 58, Fort McPherson, NWT X0E 0J0. Phone (867) 952-2179. Fax (867) 952-2718. [ADVERTISEMENT]

Dempster Highway Log
(continued)

J 342.4 (551 km) **I 113.9** (183.3 km) Kilometrepost 86.

J 365.1 (587.6 km) **I 91.2** (146.8 km) **Frog Creek.** Grayling and pike. Road on right northbound leads to picnic area. 🐟

J 377.1 (606.8 km) **I 79.2** (127.5 km) Mackenzie River wayside area.

J 377.9 (608.2 km) **I 78.4** (126.2 km) **Mackenzie River Crossing.** Free government ferry (MV *Louis Cardinal*) operates 15 hours a day during summer from early June to late October. Double-ended ferry: Drive on, drive off. Light vehicles may cross by ice bridge in late November; heavier vehicles can cross as ice thickens. *No crossing possible during freezeup and breakup.*

The ferry travels between landings on either side of the Mackenzie River and also provides access to **TSIIGEHTCHIC (formerly ARCTIC RED RIVER)**, a small Athapaskan community (pop. 140) located at the confluence of the Mackenzie and Arctic Red rivers. Tsiigehtchic has a community-owned grocery store and cafe. The Sunshine Inn provides accommodations for up to 8 people. Boat tours are available through the Band Store or local operators. For more information on lodging or tours call (867) 953-3003 or fax (867) 953-3906.

Tsiigehtchic, which means "mouth of iron river," is one of 4 communities in the Gwich'in Settlement Area. The residents speak a dialect of Gwich'in, one of the Athapaskan languages. They refer to themselves as the Gwichya Gwich'in or "People of the flat land." The Gwich'in Social & Cultural Institute here was formed at an annual assembly in Fort McPherson in 1992 in response to people's concern about the loss of their culture and language.

The Arctic Red River (Tsiigehnjik) was declared a Canadian Heritage River in 1993. Tsiigehnjik, the Gwich'in name for the river, winds it way out of the Mackenzie Mountains and flows into the Mackenzie River at Tsiigehtchic. The Gwichya Gwich'in have long used and traveled the river for fishing, hunting and trapping.

J 399.6 (643 km) **I 56.7** (91.2 km) **Rengling River,** grayling fishing. 🐟

J 404.4 (650.8 km) **I 51.9** (83.5 km) Beginning of 13-mile/21-km straight stretch.

J 409.7 (659.3 km) **I 46.6** (75 km) Distance marker shows Inuvik 75 km.

J 426.3 (686 km) **I 30** (48.3 km) Vadzaih Van Tshik picnic and camping area. ▲

J 431.4 (694.3 km) **I 24.9** (40.1 km) Campbell Lake and Campbell escarpment ahead northbound. Good place to glass for peregrine falcons.

J 440.6 (709 km) **I 15.7** (25.3 km) Ehjuu Njik picnic spot; pit toilets.

J 442.4 (712 km) **I 13.9** (22.4 km) Nihtak campground picnic area; pit toilets. Good fishing for pike and whitefish, some sheefish (inconnu). Creek leads a short distance to Campbell Lake. Boat launch. Bring mosquito repellent. 🐟

J 449.9 (724 km) **I 6.4** (10.3 km) Airport Road turnoff; pavement begins.

J 451.7 (727 km) **I 4.6** (7.4 km) Kilometrepost 262.

J 454 (730.6 km) **I 2.3** (3.7 km) Chuk Park territorial campground; 38 campsites, 20 pull-through, electric hookups, firewood, water, showers, $15 fee. Lookout tower. Interpretive information available. ▲

J 456.3 (734.3 km) **I 0** Turn left northbound for Inuvik town centre (description follows).

Inuvik

Situated on a flat wooded plateau on the east channel of the Mackenzie River, some 60 air miles/96 km south of the Beaufort Sea, 36 air miles/58 km and 70 water miles/113 km from Aklavik on the western edge of the delta. **Population:** 3,206, Déné, White and Inuvialuit.

Emergency Services: RCMP, phone (867) 777-2935. **Hospital,** Inuvik General, phone (867) 777-2955.

Visitor Information: Western Arctic Regional Visitors Centre is located on Mackenzie Road across from the hospital. The centre is open mid-May to mid-September and features interactive displays, excellent wildlife displays, clean restrooms and knowledgeable staff. A must visit in Inuvik. A green and white Cessna 170 is mounted as a weather vane at the centre and rotates to face into the wind. Phone (867) 777-4727. Or contact Western Arctic Trade & Tourism, Box 2600MP, Inuvik, NT X0E 0T0, phone (867) 777-4321, fax (867) 777-2434. Or on the internet: http://www.inuvik.net. Visitors are also welcome to stop by the Ingamo Hall

Inuvik's most recognizable landmark— the Igloo Church. (© Leslie Leong)

Friendship Centre.

Visitors are encouraged to stop by the town office (2 First St.) to sign the guest book and pick up an "Order of the Arctic" adventures certificate. Phone (867) 777-2607 for more information.

Elevation: 224 feet/68m. **Climate:** Weather information available by calling (867) 979-4381. May 24 marks 57 days of midnight sun. The sun begins to set on July 19; on Dec. 6, the sun sets and does not rise until Jan. 6. Average annual precipitation 4 inches rainfall, 69 inches snowfall. July mean high 67°F/19°C, mean low 45°F/7°C. January mean high -11°F/-24°C, mean low is -30°F/-35°C. **Radio** and **Television:** CBC and local. **Newspaper:** *The Drum* (weekly).

Private Aircraft: Inuvik airstrip; elev. 224 feet/68m; length 6,000 feet/1,829m; asphalt; fuel 80, 100. Townsite airstrip; elev. 10 feet/3m; length 1,800 feet/549m; gravel; fuel 80, 100, Jet B, F40. High pressure refueling.

Inuvik, meaning "The Place of Man," is the largest Canadian community north of

Entertainment at the Great Northern Arts Festival in July includes the traditional blanket toss.

(© Roger Pickenpaugh)

the Arctic Circle, and the major government, transportation and communication centre for Canada's western arctic. Construction of the town began in 1955 and was completed in 1961. It was the main supply base for the petrochemical exploration of the delta until Tuktoyaktuk took over that role as activity centered in the Beaufort Sea. In Inuvik some hunting, fishing and trapping is done, but most people earn wages in government and private enterprises, particularly in transportation and construction. As the delta is one of the richest muskrat areas in the world, Inuvik is the western centre for shipping furs south.

The town's official monument says, in part, that Inuvik was "the first community north of the Arctic Circle built to provide the normal facilities of a Canadian town."

TRANSPORTATION

Air: Aklak Air provides scheduled service between Inuvik and Tuktoyaktuk, Sachs Harbour, Fort McPherson and Paulatuk. Scheduled service to Whitehorse and Old Crow, YT, via Alkan Air. Scheduled service to Edmonton, AB, and to Yellowknife, NWT, via NWT Air and Canadian Airlines International. Scheduled service to Aklavik and Tuktoyaktuk via Arctic Wings. Several air charter services operate out of Inuvik, offering flights to delta communities and charter service for hunting, fishing and camping trips.

Highways: Dempster Highway from Dawson City. Winter roads (December into April) to Aklavik and Tuktoyaktuk.

Bus: Service from Dawson City to Inuvik by charter service via Arctic Tour Co., phone (867) 777-4100.

Taxi and **rental cars:** Available.

ACCOMMODATIONS/VISITOR SERVICES

Visitors will find most facilities available, although accommodations should be reserved in advance. Inuvik has 3 hotels, all with dining lounges, and bed and breakfasts. There are also a laundry, post office, territorial liquor store, banks and churches. There are 3 gas stations and a car wash; propane, auto repair and towing are available. Hardware, grocery and general stores, and gift shops are here.

Happy Valley territorial campground; 38 RV sites, electrical hookups, 10 tent pads, hot showers, firewood, water, dump station, fee. Chuk Park territorial campground; 36 sites, electrical hookups, firewood, water, showers, $10 fee. ▲

Arctic Chalet B&B. Lakeside country setting on edge of town. 7 rooms and private cabins with private or shared bath. Clean, comfortable, non-smoking rooms with single, double and queen beds. Laundry facility. Complimentary canoes. A hearty breakfast included in rates. $80–$100. VISA, MasterCard accepted. Phone (867) 777-3535; fax (867) 777-4443. [ADVERTISEMENT]

ATTRACTIONS

Igloo Church, painted white with lines to simulate snow blocks, is on Mackenzie Road as you drive into Inuvik. Inside the church is Inuit painter Mona Thrasher's interpretation of the Stations of the Cross. Visitors are welcome.

Ingamo Hall is a 2-story log community hall that serves the social and recreational needs of Native families. Visitors are welcome. The hall was built by Allan Crich over a 3-year period, using some 1,020 logs that were cut from white spruce trees in the southern part of the Mackenzie River valley and floated down the river to Inuvik.

Tour Western Arctic Communities: Air charter service is available to **AKLAVIK** (pop. 800), an important centre for muskrat harvesting; **TUKTOYAKTUK** (pop. 950), an Inuit village on the Arctic coast and site of oil development; **SACHS HARBOUR** (pop. 158) on Banks Island, an Inuit settlement supported by trapping and some big game outfitters; **PAULATUK** (pop. 255), an Inuit settlement supported by hunting, fishing, sealing and trapping; and **HOLMAN** (pop. 360), an Inuit community on the west coast of Victoria Island, famous for its printmaking. Scheduled air service is also available to **OLD CROW** (pop. 267), an Indian settlement on the Porcupine River in Yukon Territory.

The **Mackenzie River delta**, one of the largest deltas in North America and an important wildlife corridor to the Arctic, is 40 miles/64 km wide and 60 miles/97 km long. A maze of lakes, channels and islands, the delta supports a variety of bird life, fish and muskrats. Boat tours of the Mackenzie River are available.

Boreal Books carries a full range of northern books on history, Native studies, exploration and wildlife. Full selection of area postcards, northern posters and local music. Authorized agent for topo maps, marine charts and air charts. Heritage books. Catalogue available. Mail orders welcome. Open year-round. Phone (867) 777-3748, fax (867) 777-4429. [ADVERTISEMENT]

Special Events. The annual Northern Games are held in Inuvik or other western Arctic communities in summer. Visitors are welcome to watch participants compete in traditional Inuit and Déné sports; dances, and crafts are also part of the festival. For information, write Northern Games Assoc., Box 1184, Inuvik, NT X0E 0T0.

The 11th annual **Great Northern Arts Festival** is scheduled for July 16–25, 1999. Over 90 artists and 40 entertainers from across the North—Inuit, Inuvialuit, Gwich'in, Dene, Metis and non-Native—gather for 10 days every summer for a festival under the midnight sun. Soapstone carvers, print-makers, painters and sewers create works of art as visitors look on. Meet the artists, take art workshops or purchase works of art. Evenings are full of music, dance, story-telling and fashion shows showcasing the diverse cultures of the North. A remarkable cultural event. For more information contact the Arts Festival, Box 2921, Inuvik, NT X0E 0T0; phone (867) 777-3536, fax (867) 777-4445. Or check out their web site at www.greatart.nt.ca for current information on participating artists and a schedule of events.

Connects: Tok to Anchorage, AK   **Length:** 328 miles
Road Surface: Paved   **Season:** Open all year
Highest Summit: Eureka Summit 3,322 feet
Major Attractions: Matanuska Glacier, Palmer State Fair, Independence Mine State Historical Park

(See maps, pages 305-306)

	Anchorage	Glennallen	Palmer	Tok	Valdez
Anchorage		189	42	328	304
Glennallen	189		147	139	115
Palmer	42	147		286	262
Tok	328	139	286		254
Valdez	304	115	262	254	

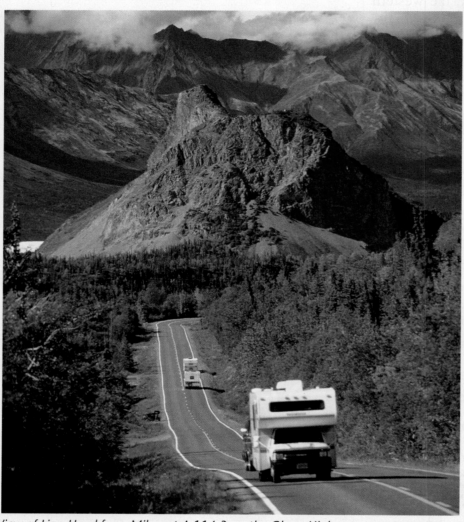

View of Lion Head from Milepost A 114.3 on the Glenn Highway. (© Susan Cole Kelly)

from the log.

Four side roads are logged in this section: the Nabesna Road to the old Nabesna Mine, which also provides access to Wrangell–St. Elias National Park and Preserve; Lake Louise Road to Lake Louise Recreation Area; the Hatcher Pass Road, connecting the Glenn and Parks highways to Independence Mine State Historical Park; and the Old Glenn Highway, an alternate route between Palmer and Anchorage.

Emergency medical services: Between Tok and Duffy's Roadhouse at **Milepost GJ 63**, phone the Alaska State Troopers at 911 or (907) 883-5111. Between Duffy's and Gakona Junction, phone the Copper River EMS at Glennallen at (907) 822-3203 or 911. From Gakona Junction to Anchorage phone 911. CB channel 9 between **Milepost A 30.8** and Anchorage.

Tok Cutoff Log

Distance from Gakona Junction (GJ) is followed by distance from Anchorage (A) and distance from Tok (T).
*Physical mileposts read from **Milepost 125** at Tok to **Milepost 0** at Gakona Junction, the north junction with the Richardson Highway.*

ALASKA ROUTE 1
GJ 125 (201.2 km) **A 328** (527.8 km) **T 0** TOK.

Junction of the Glenn Highway (Alaska Route 1) and the Alaska Highway (Alaska Route 2) at Tok. Turn to page 181 in the ALASKA HIGHWAY section for log of the Alaska Highway southeast to the Canadian border or northwest to Delta Junction.

GJ 124.2 (199.9 km) **A 327.2** (526.6 km) **T 0.8** (1.3 km) Tok Community Center.
GJ 124.1 (199.7 km) **A 327.1** (526.4 km) **T 0.9** (1.4 km) Tok Community Clinic, Tok Fire Station.
GJ 124 (199.6 km) **A 327** (526.2 km) **T 1** (1.6 km) Dept. of Natural Resources.
GJ 123.9 (199.4 km) **A 326.9** (526.1 km) **T 1.1** (1.8 km) Dept. of Transportation and Public Facilities, Tok Station.
GJ 123.7 (199.1 km) **A 326.7** (525.8 km) **T 1.3** (2.1 km) Borealis Avenue.

The Glenn Highway/Tok Cutoff (Alaska Route 1) is the principal access route from the Alaska Highway west to Anchorage, a distance of 328 miles/527.8 km. This route includes the 125-mile/201-km Tok Cutoff, between Tok and the Richardson Highway junction; a 14-mile/22.5-km link via the Richardson Highway; and the 189-mile/304-km Glenn Highway, between the Richardson Highway and Anchorage.

It is a full day's drive between Tok and Anchorage on this paved all-weather highway. There is some spectacular scenery along the Glenn Highway with mountain peaks to the north and south. Road conditions are generally good. The highway between Tok and Glennallen has some very narrow sections with no shoulders. There is also winding road without shoulders between Matanuska Glacier and Palmer. Watch for frost heaves and pavement breaks along the entire highway. Slow down at signs saying Bump—they mean it!

NOTE: There was a lot of road construction along the Glenn Highway in summer 1998. In areas of road construction, the locations of physical mileposts and posted signs, the status of parking areas and road surface, may vary

GLENN HIGHWAY

Tok Cutoff (GJ-125 to GJ-0) to Milepost A 160

© 1999 The MILEPOST®

To Chicken and Eagle
(see TAYLOR HIGHWAY section, page 281)

To Haines Junction
(see ALASKA HIGHWAY section, page 83)

Tetlin Junction

Tetlin Lake

T-0
GJ-125/201km
A-328/528km
DJ-108/174km
HJ-296/476km

Tok

Tanacross

To Delta Junction
(see ALASKA HIGHWAY section, Page 83)

GJ-122.8/197.6km
Sourdough Campground
and Sourdough Pancake
Breakfast CDMT

Tanana River

Tok River

Little Tok River

Tok Cutoff

ALASKA RANGE

Mineral Lakes

Mentasta Summit
2,434 ft./742m

Station Cr.

Bartell Cr.

MENTASTA MOUNTAINS

Slana R.

GJ-89.8/144.5km
Mineral Lakes Bed & Breakfast L

GJ-78.1/125.7km
Mentasta Lodge dGILMPST

Mentasta Lake

Mentasta Lake

Mount Kimball
10,300 ft./3,139m

Carlson Cr.

Porcupine Cr.

Ahtel Cr.

Chistochina Glacier

Slana

GJ-62.7/100.9km Duffy's Roadhouse GIMPRST
GJ-61/98.2km Midway Service GCPS
N62°43' W143°55'
0.7/1.1km Hart D Ranch CDLT

Park Boundary

Noyes Mountain
8,147 ft./2,483m

Nabesna

J-45/72km

Rufus Creek

Copper Creek

Lost Creek

Jack Creek

Twin Lakes

Long Lake

Jack Lake

Tanada Lake

Copper Lake

Caribou Creek

Nabesna Road

Wrangell-St. Elias National Park
and Preserve

WRANGELL MOUNTAINS

Tanada Peak
9,240 ft./2,816m

Mount Sanford
16,237 ft./4,949m

Copper Glacier

Mount Wrangell
14,163 ft./4,317m

Glaciated

T-65/105km
J-0
GJ-60/96km
A-263/423km

GJ-53.8/5.3km Grizzly Lake
Ranch Bed & Breakfast L

Grizzly Lake

Cobb Lakes

Indian River

Slana River

GJ-36.5/58.7km Chistochina B&B L

GJ-32.8/52.8km Chistochina Lodge &
Trading Post CGLMrT

Tok Cutoff

GJ-34.4/55.4km Chistochina
RV Park C

GJ-3.5/5.6km Chistochina
RV Park C

Chistochina

Chistochina River

Sinona Creek

Sinona Cr.

Tulsona Cr.

Copper River

Park Boundary

Sanford River

Mount Drum
12,010 ft./3,661m

GJ-4.2/6.8km Gakona, Alaska RV Park CDLT
GJ-3.5/5.6km The River Wranglers
GJ-3/4.8km Riverview Bed & Breakfast L

Gakona

Gakona Junction

Cakona River

To Delta Junction
(see RICHARDSON HIGHWAY section)

G-0 Gakona Junction Village GLMS
A-189.5/305km Glennallen Quick Stop Truck Stop dGIST
A-189/304.2km Greater Copper Valley Chamber of Commerce T
Rendezvous Cafe IMT
Hub of Alaska and Hub Maxi-Mart dGIPRST
Gakona Fish-Camp Bed & Breakfast L
Copper Valley Fish Guides

A-189.5/305km Northern Nights Campground & RV Park
A-188.7/303.7km The Hitchin' Post M
A-187.8/302.2km Moose Hom RV Park
A-187.7/302.1km Old Post Office Gallery
A-187.5/301.7km Brown Bear Rhodehouse CLMT
Tastee-Freez MT

Gulkana

Trans-Alaska Pipeline

GJ-0
V-129/207km
T-125/201km
A-203/327km
DJ-137/220km

Glennallen

N62°09' W145°27'

N62°01' W145°06'

V-115/185km
T-139/224km
A-189/304km

Ewan Lake

Moose Cr.

Dry Creek

A-173/278.4km

A-183.6/295.5km Copper River
Paper Shack Office Supply)

A-182.2/293.2km Basin Liquors,

To Valdez
(SEE RICHARDSON HIGHWAY section)

Copper River

Deep Lake

Crosswind Lake

Lake Louise Road

Tolsona Wilderness Campground
& RV Park CDIT

Tolsona Cr.

Lost Cabin L

Tazlina R.

Tazlina Lake

A-160/257km
T-168/271km

(map continues next page)

GLENN HIGHWAY Area

Glaciated Area

Nabesna River

Key to mileage boxes

miles/kilometres
miles/kilometres
from:
T-Tok
GJ-Gakona Junction
A-Anchorage
J-Junction
V-Valdez
HJ-Haines Junction
DJ-Delta Junction

Map Location

Key to Advertiser Services
C -Camping
D -Dump Station
d -Diesel
G -Gas (reg./unld.)
I -Ice
L -Lodging
M-Meals
P -Propane
R -Car Repair (major)
r -Car Repair (minor)
S -Store (grocery)
T -Telephone (pay)

Principal Route
Paved
Unpaved

Other Roads
Paved
Unpaved **Hiking Trails**

Ferry Routes ·········

⊞ Refer to Log for Visitor Facilities

Scale
0   10   Miles
0   10   Kilometres

GLENN HIGHWAY

Milepost A 160 to Anchorage, AK

© 1999 The MILEPOST®

Key to mileage boxes

miles/kilometres
miles/kilometres

from:

T- Tok
A- Anchorage
J- Junction
F- Fairbanks
S- Seward

Key to Advertiser Services

C- Camping
D- Dump Station
d- Diesel
G- Gas (reg., unld.)
I- Ice
L- Lodging
M- Meals
P- Propane
R- Car Repair (major)
r- Car Repair (minor)
S- Store (grocery)
T- Telephone (pay)

Refer to Log for Visitor Facilities

Principal Route

Paved
Other Roads
Paved
Unpaved
Ferry Routes   Hiking Trails

Scale

0   10   Miles
0   10   Kilometres

Map Location

CAUTION: Road narrows westbound.

GJ 123.3 (198.4 km) **A 326.3** (525.1 km) **T 1.7** (2.7 km) Trading post to northwest.

GJ 122.8 (197.6 km) **A 325.8** (524.3 km) **T 2.2** (3.5 km) Campground to northwest.

Sourdough Campground's Pancake Breakfast served 7–11 A.M. June, July, August. Genuine "Sourdoughs." Full and partial RV hookups. Dry campsites. Showers included. Guaranteed clean restrooms. High-pressure car wash. Free evening video program. Located 1.7 miles from the junction toward Anchorage on Tok Cutoff (Glenn Highway). See display ad in Tok in the ALASKA HIGHWAY section. [ADVERTISEMENT] ▲

GJ 122.6 (197.3 km) **A 325.6** (524 km) **T 2.4** (3.9 km) Paved bike trail from Tok ends here.

Private Aircraft: Tok airstrip to southeast; elev. 1,670 feet/509m; length 1,700 feet/518m; gravel; unattended. No services. private airfield across the highway.

GJ 118 (189.9 km) **A 321** (516.6 km) **T 7** (11.3 km) *CAUTION: Watch for gravel breaks (signed "loose gravel") in construction areas, patched pavement and frost heaves westbound.*

GJ 116.7 (187.8 km) **A 319.7** (514.5 km) **T 8.3** (13.4 km) Entering Tok Management Area, Tanana Valley State Forest, westbound.

GJ 110 (177 km) **A 313** (503.7 km) **T 15** (24.1 km) Flashing lights to north are from U.S. Coast Guard loran station at **Milepost DC 1308.5** on the Alaska Highway.

GJ 109.3 (175.9 km) **A 312.3** (502.6 km) **T 15.7** (25.3 km) **Eagle Trail State Recreation Site** to northwest; 40 campsites, 15-day limit, 4 picnic sites, water, toilets, firepits, pay phone, rain shelter, hiking trail, Clearwater Creek. Camping fee $10/night or annual pass. The access road is designed with several loops to aid larger vehicles. A 0.9-mile/1.4-km section of the pioneer trail to Eagle is signed for hikers; trailhead near covered picnic tables. Historic Tok–Slana Cutoff road goes through this campground. ▲

GJ 104.5 (168.2 km) **A 307.5** (494.9 km) **T 20.5** (33 km) Extra wide shoulders to north for pulling off highway. **Little Tok River** overflow runs under highway in culvert; fishing for grayling and Dolly Varden. ◄

GJ 104 (167.4 km) **A 307** (494 km) **T 21** (33.8 km) Bridge over **Tok River**, side road north to riverbank and boat launch. The Tok River heads at Tok Glacier in the Alaska Range and flows northeast 60 miles to the Tanana River. Tok-bound travelers are in the Tok River Valley, although the river is out of sight to the southeast most of the time.

GJ 103.5 (166.6 km) **A 306.5** (493.3 km) **T 21.5** (34.6 km) Paved turnout to north. **Little Tok River** overflow; fishing for grayling and Dolly Varden. ◄

GJ 102.4 (164.8 km) **A 305.4** (491.5 km) **T 22.6** (36.4 km) Entering Tok Management Area, Tanana Valley State Forest, eastbound.

GJ 99.3 (159.8 km) **A 302.3** (486.5 km) **T 25.7** (41.4 km) Rest area; paved double-ended turnout to north. Cranberries may be found in late summer.

GJ 98 (157.7 km) **A 301** (484.4 km) **T 27** (43.5 km) Bridge over **Little Tok River**, which parallels highway. Parking at end of bridge. The Little Tok River heads at a glacier terminus in the Mentasta Mountains and flows north 32 miles to the Tok River.

GJ 91 (146.4 km) **A 294** (473.1 km) **T 34** (54.7 km) Side road south to **Little Tok River** bridge (weight limit 20 tons); good fishing for grayling, 12 to 14 inches, use small spinner. ◄

GJ 90 (144.8 km) **A 293** (471.5 km) **T 35**

The relatively straight Tok Cutoff offers views of the Wrangell Mountains to the south. (© Ruth von Spalding)

(56.3 km) Paved turnout to south.

GJ 89.8 (144.5 km) **A 292.8** (471.2 km) **T 35.2** (56.6 km) **Mineral Lakes Bed & Breakfast.** Cabins on lake with sourdough breakfast. RV parking. Northern pike

fishing trips, boating, fishing licenses, tackle; gift shop. Come relax—an Alaskan rural getaway. Your hosts, Gary, Patty and Ashley Stender. HC72, Box 830, Tok, AK 99780-9410. Phone (907) 883-5498. Reservations welcome. [ADVERTISEMENT]

GJ 89.5 (144 km) **A 292.5** (470.7 km) **T 35.5** (57.1 km) **Mineral Lakes.** Watch for moose and birds in ponds to southeast between **Mileposts A 89.5** and **86.** These are sloughs of the Little Tok River and provide both moose habitat and a breeding place for

waterfowl. Good fishing for northern pike and grayling. ◄

GJ 85.7 (137.9 km) **A 288.7** (464.6 km) **T 39.3** (63.2 km) Turnout to north.

GJ 83.2 (133.9 km) **A 286.2** (460.6 km) **T 41.8** (67.3 km) Bridge over Bartell Creek. Just beyond is the divide between the drainage of the Tanana River, tributary of the Yukon River system flowing into the Bering Sea, and the Copper River system, emptying into the North Pacific near Cordova.

GJ 81 (130.4 km) **A 284** (457 km) **T 44** (70.8 km) Access road leads north 7 miles/11.3 km to **MENTASTA** (pop. 72), a Native village.

GJ 79.4 (127.8 km) **A 282.4** (454.5 km) **T 45.6** (73.4 km) **Mentasta Summit** (elev. 2,434 feet/742m). The Mentasta Mountains rise to about 6,000 feet on either side of the highway. The 40-mile-long, 25-mile-wide Mentasta Range is bounded on the north by the Alaska Range. Watch for Dall sheep on mountainsides.

Boundary between Game Management Units 12 and 13C and Sportfish Management Units 8 and 2.

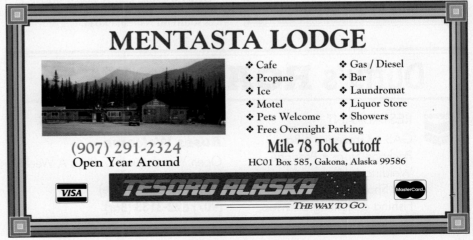

GJ 78.1 (125.7 km) A 281.1 (452.4 km) T 46.9 (75.5 km) Lodge with cafe, motel, gas, diesel, laundromat, showers, bar and liquor store.

Mentasta Lodge. See display on page 307.

GJ 78 (125.5 km) A 281 (452.2 km) T 47 (75.6 km) View for westbound traffic of snow-covered Mount Sanford (elev. 16,237 feet/4,949m).

GJ 77.9 (125.4 km) A 280.9 (452.1 km) T 47.1 (75.8 km) Paved turnout to north by Slana Slough; salmon spawning area in August. Watch for beavers.

GJ 76.3 (122.8 km) A 279.3 (449.5 km) T 48.7 (78.4 km) Bridge over Mabel Creek. Mastodon flowers (marsh fleabane) in late July; very large (to 4 feet) with showy seed heads.

GJ 76 (122.3 km) A 279 (449 km) T 49 (78.8 km) Bridge over Slana Slough.

GJ 75.6 (121.7 km) A 278.6 (448.3 km) T 49.4 (79.5 km) Bridge over **Slana River.** This river flows from its source glaciers some 55 miles/88.5 km to the Copper River. Parking area at west end of bridge (used for gravel stockpile in 1998).

GJ 74 (119.1 km) A 277 (445.8 km) T 51 (82.1 km) Scenic viewpoint to south over-looking Slana River.

GJ 68 (109.4 km) A 271 (436.1 km) T 57 (91.7 km) Carlson Creek bridge.

GJ 65.5 (105.4 km) A 268.5 (432.1 km) T 59.5 (95.8 km) Paved viewpoint to south. Magnificent views (weather permitting) of the Wrangell mountains. Highest peak is **Mount Sanford,** elev. 16,237 feet/4,949m.

GJ 64.2 (103.3 km) A 267.2 (430 km) T 60.8 (97.8 km) Bridge over Porcupine Creek. Turnoff to north at east end of bridge for **Porcupine Creek State Recreation Site** 0.2 mile/0.3 km from highway; 12 forested campsites on loop road, 15-day limit, $10 nightly fee (concessionaire-operated, annual state park pass not accepted), drinking water, firepits, toilets, picnic tables and fishing (wood and charcoal available from concessionaire at Hart D Ranch, Mile 0.7 Nabesna Road). Lowbush cranberries in fall. *CAUTION: Watch for bears.* ⬤▲

GJ 63 (101.4 km) A 266 (428 km) T 62 (99.8 km) Scenic viewpoint with view of Wrangell Mountains. The dominant peak to the southwest is Mount Sanford, a dormant volcano; the pinnacles of Capital Mountain can be seen against its lower slopes. Mount Jarvis (elev. 13,421 feet/4,091m) is visible to the south behind Mount Sanford; Tanada Peak (elev. 9,240 feet/2,816m) is more to the south. (Tanada Peak is sometimes mistaken for Noyes Mountain.)

Walk up the gravel hill to view Noyes Mountain (elev. 8,147 feet/2,483m), named for U.S. Army Brig. Gen. John Rutherford Noyes, a one-time commissioner of roads in the territory of Alaska. Appointed adjutant general of the Alaska National Guard in 1953, he died in 1956 from injuries and frostbite after his plane crashed near Nome.

GJ 62.7 (100.9 km) A 265.7 (427.6 km) T 62.3 (100.3 km) Roadhouse with food, gas, groceries, fishing and hunting licenses, bar, and car repair to southeast.

Duffy's Roadhouse. See display ad this section.

GJ 61 (98.2 km) A 264 (424.9 km) T 64 (103 km) Full-service grocery store with fishing and hunting licenses, showers, laundromat and campground to northwest.

Midway Service. See display ad this section. ▲

GJ 60.8 (97.8 km) A 263.8 (424.6 km) T 64.2 (103.3 km) Bridge over **Ahtell Creek;** grayling. Parking area to north at east end of bridge. This stream drains a mountain area of igneous rock, where several gold and silver-lead claims are located.

GJ 59.8 (96.2 km) A 262.8 (422.9 km) T 65.2 (104.9 km) Gas, post office and services south on Nabesna Road.

Distance marker westbound shows Glennallen 76 miles; Valdez 189 miles; Anchorage 263 miles.

GJ 59 (94.9 km) A 262 (421.6 km) T 66 (106.2 km) *SIGN: $1,000 fine for littering.*

GJ 58.6 (94.3 km) A 261.6 (421 km) T 66.4 (106.9 km) Ahtell Creek trailhead.
NOTE: Hill; 6 percent downgrade eastbound.

GJ 56.5 (90.9 km) A 259.5 (417.6 km) T 68.5 (110.2 km) Narrow double-ended turnout to south is a scenic viewpoint overlooking Cobb Lakes. View of Tanada Peak, Mount Sanford, Mount Blackburn and Mount Drum to the south and southwest. The Mentasta Mountains are to the east.

Gold Rush Centennial sign on Lieutenant Henry T. Allen, who led one of America's epic journeys of exploration in 1885. In 5 months, his expedition crossed 1,500 miles of largely unexplored territory including this valley. Ordered to investigate the unmapped Copper and Tanana river valleys, Allen started up the Copper River in March 1885 and passed this point 2 months later, reaching the headwaters of the Copper River and entering the Tanana Valley. Allen descended the Tanana River and trekked from the Yukon to the headwaters of the Koyukuk River.

GJ 55.2 (88.8 km) A 258.2 (415.5 km) T 69.8 (112.3 km) Tanada Peak viewpoint; gravel turnout to south.
CAUTION: Watch for horses on road.

GJ 53 (85.3 km) A 256 (412 km) T 72 (115.9 km) Grizzly Lake; lodging, camping, trail rides.

Grizzly Lake Ranch Bed & Breakfast. See display ad this section. ▲

GJ 47 (75.6 km) A 250 (402.3 km) T 78 (125.5 km) Indian Creek trailhead to north.

GJ 44.6 (71.8 km) A 247.6 (398.5 km) T 80.4 (129.4 km) Parking area to north. Eagle Trail access.

GJ 43.8 (70.5 km) A 246.8 (397.1 km) T 81.2 (130.6 km) Bridge over Indian River. This is a salmon spawning stream, usually late-June through July. Turnout to south at west end of bridge.

GJ 39 (62.8 km) A 242 (389.5 km) T 86 (138.4 km) Views of the Copper River valley and Wrangell Mountains. Looking south, peak on left is Mount Sanford and on right is Mount Drum (elev. 12,010 feet/3,661m).

GJ 38 (61.2 km) A 241 (387.8 km) T 87 (140 km) *CAUTION: Road narrows westbound. Eastbound, watch for gravel breaks (signed "loose gravel") in construction areas, patched pavement and frost heaves.*

GJ 36.5 (58.7 km) A 239.5 (385.4 km) T

Nabesna Road Log

The Nabesna Road leads 45 miles/72.4 km southeast from **Milepost GJ 59.8** Glenn Highway (Tok Cutoff) to the old mining community of Nabesna. This side trip can be enjoyable for campers; there are no formal public campgrounds but there are plenty of beautiful spots to camp and a private campground at Mile 0.7/1.1 km. The area also offers good fishing. Horses are permitted on all trails. Off-road vehicles must have permits from the National Park Service. The Nabesna Road provides access to the northwest corner of Wrangell–St. Elias National Park and Preserve. The National Park Service ranger station at Slana has information on current Nabesna Road conditions and on backcountry travel in the park. (The Wrangell–St. Elias National Park visitor center is near Copper Center on the old Richardson Highway.)

The first 4 miles/6.4 km of road is chip seal surface; the remainder is gravel. Beyond **Milepost J 28.6** the road becomes rough and crosses several creeks which may be difficult to ford. The state-maintained road ends at Mile 42; vehicles are not recommended beyond this point. **Distance is measured from the junction with the Glenn Highway (J).**

J 0.1 (0.2 km) Slana highway maintenance station.

J 0.2 (0.3 km) Slana NPS ranger station; information on road conditions and on Wrangell–St. Elias National Park and Preserve. Open 8 A.M. to 5 P.M. daily, June 1 through September. USGS maps and natural history books for sale. Phone (907) 882-5238. For more information contact: Superintendent, Wrangell–St. Elias National Park and Preserve, P.O. Box 439, Copper Center, AK 99573; phone (907) 822-5234.

J 0.7 (1.1 km) Slana post office and Hart D Ranch complex. The picturesque ranch is the home and studio of sculptor Mary Frances DeHart. The ranch offers RV and tent camping, an art gallery, bed and breakfast accommodations, pay phone and dog kennels (DeHart raises Affenpinscher dogs).

Hart D Ranch. See display ad this section. ♿▲

J 1 (1.6 km) **SLANA** (pop. 39), once an Indian village on the north bank of the Slana River, now refers to this general area. Besides the Indian settlement, Slana boasted a popular roadhouse, now a private home. Slana elementary school is located here.

J 1.5 (2.4 km) Slana River Bridge; undeveloped camping area. Boundary between Game Management Units 11 and 13C.

J 2 (3.2 km) BLM homestead area next 2 miles/3.2 km southbound. Blueberries in the fall; grouse are seen in this area.

J 3.9 (6.2 km) Entering Wrangell–St. Elias National Park and Preserve. The Glenn Highway follows the northern boundary of the preserve between Slana and Gakona Junction; Nabesna Road provides access to the northwest corner of the park.

Sunset over a pond near Slana.

(© Joe Prax)

J 4 (6.4 km) *Hard surface ends, gravel begins, southbound. There are numerous turnouts southbound.*

J 7 (11.3 km) Road crosses **Rufus Creek** culvert. Dolly Varden to 8 inches, June to October. Watch out for bears, especially during berry season.

J 11 (17.7 km) Suslota Lake trailhead No. 1 to north.

J 11.4 (18.3 km) Gravel pit, room to park or camp.

J 12.5 (20.1 km) Turnout to southeast; Copper Lake trailhead.

J 13.1 (21.1 km) Suslota Lake trailhead No. 2 to north.

J 15.4 (24.8 km) Beautiful views of Mount Sanford and Tanada Peak in the Wrangell Mountains, across the great plain of the Copper River.

J 18 (29 km) Pond to northeast. The highly mineralized Mentasta Mountains are visible to the north. This is sparsely timbered high country.

J 19.7 (31.7 km) Hiking trail to north.

J 22.3 (35.9 km) Rock Lake; turnouts both sides of road.

J 22.9 (36.8 km) **Long Lake**; grayling fishing. ◄━

J 23.4 (37.7 km) Turnout. Floatplane landing.

J 24.4 (39.3 km) Turnout to southwest with view of Wrangell Mountains. Tanada Lake trail.

J 25.2 (40.6 km) Boundary between Sportfish Areas C and K, and Game Management Areas 11 and 12.

J 25.5 (41 km) Lodge. Glimpse of Tanada Lake beneath Tanada Peak to the south.

J 25.9 (41.7 km) Little Jack Creek.

J 26.1 (42 km) Access road to private campground and floatplane service at **Jack Lake** (grayling fishing); no turnaround. ◄━▲

J 28.2 (45.4 km) Turnouts at Twin Lakes; primitive campsite, good place to observe waterfowl. Fishing for grayling 10 to 18 inches, mid-May to October, flies or small spinner; also burbot. Wildflowers in June include Lapland rosebay, lupine and 8-petaled mountain avens. ◄━

J 28.6 (46 km) Lodge.

J 28.6 (46 km) The road deteriorates beyond this point and you may have to ford several creeks. Inquire at lodge here or Slana Ranger Station about road con-

ditions.

J 29.6 (47.6 km) Trail Creek crosses road; no culvert but road has gravel base here. Easy to drive through creek, especially in fall. Overnight hikers may hike up Lost Creek and return via Trail Creek.

J 31.4 (50.5 km) Road crosses Lost Creek, a very wide expanse of water in spring, and may remain difficult to cross well into summer. Loose gravel makes it easy to get stuck in creek if you spin your wheels. Scout it out first. If you hesitate once in the creek, wheels may dig in. The road crosses several more creeks beyond here; these may also be difficult to ford.

J 31.6 (50.9 km) Boyden Creek (may have to ford after rain or during spring melt). Trailhead to north.

J 33 (53.1 km) Big Grayling Lake hiking trail. Horses allowed.

J 35 (56.3 km) Creek (must ford).

J 36 (57.9 km) Jack Creek Bridge.

J 36.1 (58.1 km) Informal campsites with picnic tables. The road crosses 5 creeks the next 4.3 miles/6.9 km southbound. Watch for loose gravel in creekbeds.

J 41 (66 km) A marked trail, approximately 5 miles/8 km long, leads to Nabesna River and old Reeves Field airstrip, once used to fly gold out of and supplies in to mining camps. Devil's Mountain is to the left of the trail. The trail on the river also leads to the old Indian village of Khiltat.

J 42 (67.6 km) Lodge (private property). State-maintained road ends. Hiking only recommended beyond this point. Bed and breakfast, trail rides, flightseeing and showers available.

J 45 (72.4 km) **NABESNA** (area pop. less than 25; elev. 3,000 feet/914m). No facilities. This region has copper reserves, as well as gold in the streams and rivers, silver, molybdenum and iron ore deposits. Tailings deposits here are currently closed to the public. Nabesna gold mine is located here. Area residents subsist on caribou, Dall sheep, moose, bear, fish and small game. Fire fighting and trapping also provide some income. Big game hunting is popular in this area; registered guides and several outfitters have headquarters along Nabesna Road.

Return to Milepost GJ 59.8 Glenn Highway (Tok Cutoff)

88.5 (142.4 km) Access to bed and breakfast.
Chistochina B&B. See display ad this section.

GJ 35.5 (57.1 km) **A 238.5** (383.8 km) **T 89.5** (144 km) Chistochina River Bridge No. 2. Mount Sanford is first large mountain to the southeast, then Mount Drum.

GJ 35.4 (57 km) **A 238.4** (383.7 km) **T 89.6** (144.2 km) **Chistochina River** Bridge No. 1; parking at west end. Chistochina River trailhead. This river heads in the Chistochina Glacier on Mount Kimball (elev. 10,300 feet/3,139m) in the Alaska Range and flows south 48 miles to the Copper River, which is just south of the highway here. The Tok Cutoff parallels the Copper River from here southeast to the Richardson Highway. Chistochina is thought to mean marmot creek.

GJ 34.7 (55.8 km) **A 237.7** (382.5 km) **T 90.3** (145.3 km) Sinona Creek Trading Post (closed in 1998; current status unknown).

GJ 34.6 (55.7 km) **A 237.6** (382.4 km)

View of Mount Sanford, elev. 16,237 feet/4,949m, from the Glenn Highway near Chistochina. (© Joe Prax)

T 90.4 (145.5 km) Bridge over Sinona Creek. Sinona is said to mean place of the many burls, and there are indeed many burls on area spruce trees.

GJ 34.4 (55.4 km) **A 237.4** (382 km) **T 90.6** (145.8 km) **Chistochina RV Park.** See display ad this section. ▲

GJ 34.1 (54.9 km) **A 237.1** (381.6 km) **T 90.9** (146.3 km) Chistochina ball fields.

GJ 32.9 (52.9 km) **A 235.9** (379.6 km) **T 92.1** (148.2 km) Chistochina school. Road access to Native village of **CHISTOCHINA** (pop. 56).

GJ 32.8 (52.8 km) **A 235.8** (379.5 km) **T 92.2** (148.4 km) Lodge to south with restaurant, lodging and RV park.

Chistochina Lodge. National Historic Site. Family restaurant specializing in sourdough pancakes, caribou sausage and steaks. Rooms, cabins and bunkhouse. RV hookups.

Hike the Eagle–Valdez trail. Learn of area gold mining. Fish, hunt or sightsee. Family-owned, operated and occupied. Summer and winter entertainment headquarters. "A place to feel at home." See display ad this section. ▲
[ADVERTISEMENT]

Private Aircraft: Chistochina airstrip, adjacent south; elev. 1,850 feet/564m; length 2,000 feet/ 610m; turf and gravel; autogas.

GJ 30.3 (48.4 km) **A 233.1** (375.1 km) **T 94.7** (152.4 km) *CAUTION: Road narrows eastbound; no shoulders. Watch for frost heaves. Westbound, major road construction was under way from here to Gakona Junction in 1998.*

GJ 28.1 (45.2 km) **A 231.1** (371.9 km) **T 96.9** (155.9 km) Double-ended paved parking area to south with a marker on the Alaska Road Commission. The ARC was established in 1905, the same year the first automobile arrived in Alaska at Skagway. The ARC operated for 51 years, building roads, airfields, trails and other transportation facilities. It was replaced by the Bureau of Public Roads (referred to by some Alaskans at the time as the Bureau of Parallel Ruts) in 1956. In 1960 the Bureau of Public Roads was replaced by the Dept. of Public Works.

GJ 24 (38.6 km) **A 227** (365.3 km) **T 101**

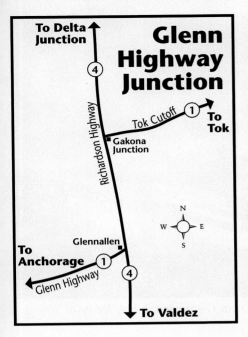

Glenn Highway Junction

To Delta Junction
4
Richardson Highway
Tok Cutoff
1
To Tok
Gakona Junction
N
W E
S
Glennallen
To Anchorage
1
4
Glenn Highway
To Valdez

(162.5 km) Large rest area to south with paved double-ended parking area, toilets, picnic tables and firepits. Gold Rush Centennial sign on Discovering Gold on the Chistochina. During the Klondike Gold Rush of 1898, a few stampeders heard of a gold discovery in the upper Copper River and actually found gold in the headwaters of the Chistochina River north of here.

Paths from parking area lead to the **Copper River.** The Copper River heads on the north side of the Wrangell Mountains and flows 250 miles to the Gulf of Alaska. The river parallels Nabesna Road then the Tok Cutoff and finally the Richardson Highway.

View of Mount Sanford is to the southeast, Mount Drum to the south.

GJ 17.8 (28.6 km) **A 220.8** (355.3 km) **T 107.2** (172.5 km) **Tulsona Creek** bridge. Good grayling fishing.

GJ 11.6 (18.7 km) **A 214.6** (345.4 km) **T 113.4** (182.5 km) Yellow pond lily *(Nuphar polysepalum)* in ponds north of highway.

GJ 11.3 (18.2 km) **A 214.3** (344.9 km) **T 113.7** (183 km) **HAARP** (High frequency Active Auroral Research Program) to north of highway. This is a major Dept. of Defense

Arctic facility for upper atmospheric and solar-terrestrial research. Principal elements include a high power, high frequency phased array radio transmitter—known as the Ionospheric Research Instrument (IRI)—and an ultra-high frequency incoherent scatter radar (IST). An annual open house is held in August. Approximate coordinates are N62º 23.5' W145º 8.8'.

GJ 9.4 (15.1 km) **A 212.4** (341.8 km) **T 115.6** (186 km) Fox Lake BLM trailhead.

GJ 8.8 (14.2 km) **A 211.8** (340.8 km) **T 116.2** (187 km) Paved turnout to north. BLM trailhead.

GJ 6 (9.7 km) **A 209** (336.3 km) **T 119** (191.5 km) View opens up westbound as highway descends to Gakona River.

GJ 4.2 (6.8 km) **A 207.2** (333.4 km) **T 120.8** (194.4 km) **Gakona, Alaska R.V. Park.** See display ad this section. ▲

GJ 3.5 (5.6 km) **A 206.5** (332.3 km) **T 121.5** (195.5 km) **The River Wrangellers.** See display ad this section.

GJ 3 (4.8 km) **A 206** (331.5 km) **T 122** (196.3 km) **Riverview Bed & Breakfast** to south. See display ad this section.

GJ 2.7 (4.3 km) **A 205.7** (331 km) **T 122.3** (196.8 km) **GAKONA** (pop. 24); post office. The village of Gakona lies between the Gakona and Copper rivers. (Gakona is Athabascan for rabbit.) Originally Gakona was a Native wood and fish camp, and fish wheels are still common.

GJ 2 (3.2 km) **A 205** (330 km) **T 123** (198 km) **Gakona Lodge**, entered on the National Register of Historic Places in 1977. Originally one of several roadhouses providing essential food and lodging for travelers, it opened in 1905 and was first called Doyle's Ranch. The original carriage house is now a restaurant.

GJ 1.8 (2.9 km) **A 204.8** (329.6 km) **T 123.2** (198.3 km) Bridge over **Gakona River**, which flows 64 miles south from Gakona Glacier in the Alaska Range to join the Copper River here. Fine view of the many channels where the Gakona and Copper rivers join.

Entering Game Management Unit 13B westbound and 13C eastbound.

GJ 1 (1.6 km) **A 204** (328.3 km) **T 124** (200 km) Paved viewpoint to south overlooks the valley of the Gakona and Copper rivers; picnic tables. View of Mount Drum and Mount Sanford. Good photo stop.

Gold Rush Centennial sign about Alaska's first telegraph, known as the Washington-Alaska Military Cable and Telegraph System (WAMCATS), built to assist communication between U.S. Army posts during the Gold Rush. Crews completed the 1,506-mile line in 1903. Although a military line, WAMCATS carried more civilian than military messages, as it assisted commerce and safe travel between gold camps and brought in

news of the outside world. By the late 1920s, radio technology made WAMCATS obsolete.

GJ 0 A 203 (326.7 km) **T 125** (201.2 km) **Gakona Junction**; food, gas, lodging, fishing guides. Stop sign westbound at **junction** of Tok Cutoff (Alaska Route 1) and Richardson Highway (Alaska Route 4). The 2 roads share a common alignment for the next 14 miles/22.5 km westbound. Turn north here for Delta Junction. Turn south for Anchorage or Valdez. *NOTE: This junction can be confusing. Choose your route carefully.*

Distance marker shows Paxson 56 miles, Delta Junction 137 miles; Fairbanks 235 miles.

Delta Junction-bound travelers turn to **Milepost V 128.6** in the RICHARDSON HIGHWAY section for log of that route.

Gakona Junction Village. See display ad this section.

Gakona Fish-Camp Bed and Breakfast. Clean, comfortable rooms for budge-minded travelers. Rooms from $59.95 (including breakfast), lowest in Copper Valley. Gakona Stop 'n Shop, Gakona Texaco and Gulkana Fish Guides, at the same location, provide one-stop shopping for highway visitors. Reservations: Phone (907) 822-3664, toll-free 1-800-462-3221; fax (907) 822-3696; e-mail:gakona@alaska.net. Internet connection: www.alaskaone.com/coppervalley. [ADVERTISEMENT]

Copper Valley Fish Guides operates from Gakona Junction Village. Fish for king salmon in Gulkana and Klutina Rivers. Half-day and full-day trips. All gear provided. We fillet, freeze and ship. Bed and breakfast, Texaco and groceries. Dress for the weather. We do the rest. Reservations phone (907) 822-3664, toll-free 1-800-462-3221; fax (907) 822-3696; e-mail gakona@alaska.net; Internet www.alaskaone.com/coppervalley. [ADVERTISEMENT]

Distance from Anchorage (A) is followed by distance from Tok (T) and distance from Valdez (V). *Physical mileposts for the next 14 miles/22.5 km southbound give distance from Valdez.*

Private planes parked at Gulkana airstrip near Glennallen, a hub for fly-in fishing in the Copper River basin. (© Bruce M. Herman)

ALASKA ROUTE 4

A 202.4 (325.7 km) **T 125.6** (202.1 km) **V 128** (206 km) Distance markers shows Tok 125 miles; Tetlin Junction 137 miles; Canadian border 210 miles.
CAUTION: Watch for horses.

A 201 (323.5 km) **T 127** (204.4 km) **V 126.9** (204.2 km) Access road to **GULKANA** (pop. 96) on the bank of the Gulkana River. Most of the Gulkana River frontage in this area is owned by Gulkana village and managed by Ahtna, Inc. Ahtna lands are closed to the public for hunting, fishing and trapping.

A 200.9 (323.3 km) **T 127.1** (204.5 km) **V 126.8** (204 km) **Gulkana River** bridge. Large gravel parking areas at both ends of bridge provide access to river. Camping permitted. Grayling fishing and good king and

sockeye salmon fishing (June and July). The Gulkana River flows 60 miles from the Gulkana Glacier in the Alaska Range to the Copper River. ◄◄

Entering Game Management Unit 13B eastbound, 13A westbound.

A 200.3 (322.3 km) **T 127.7** (205.5 km) **V 126.2** (203.1 km) Bear Creek Inn.

A 200.1 (322 km) **T 127.9** (205.8 km) **V 126** (202.8 km) Paved double-ended turnout.
CAUTION: Slow down for frost heaves.

A 197.3 (317.5 km) **T 130.7** (210.3 km) **V 123.2** (198.3 km) Large paved turnout.

A 192.1 (309.1 km) **T 135.9** (218.7 km) **V 118.1** (190 km) **Private Aircraft:** Gulkana airstrip; elev. 1,579 feet/481m; length 5,000 feet/1,524m; asphalt; fuel 100LL. Flying service located here.

A 192 (309 km) **T 136** (218.9 km) **V 118** (189.9 km) **Dry Creek State Recreation Site**; 58 campsites, 15-day limit, $10 nightly fee or annual pass, 4 picnic sites, toilets, picnic shelter. Bring mosquito repellent! ▲

A 189.5 (305 km) **T 138.5** (222.9 km) **V 115.5** (185.9 km) **Glennallen Quick Stop Truck Stop.** Stop for friendly family service, gas, diesel, convenience store with ice, pop, snacks, postcards, ice cream, specialty items, pay phone and free coffee. Truck, caravan, senior citizen discounts. Several interesting items on display, including an authentic Native Alaskan fish wheel. Full-service restaurant adjacent. See display ad this section. [ADVERTISEMENT]

A 189.5 (305 km) **T 138.5** (222.9 km) **V 115.5** (185.9 km) **Rendezvous Cafe.** Located at Mile 189.5, 1/2 mile north of the junction. We bake our own dinner breads and pies daily. Specialty desserts, pies and cheesecakes. Fresh ground whole bean Kona Coffee. Beer and wine, Alaskan beer on tap. Plenty of parking for RVs. Open daily year-round. Summer hours 7 A.M.–11 P.M. Phone (907) 822-5353. [ADVERTISEMENT]

A 189 (304.2 km) **T 139** (223.7 km) **V 115** (185.1 km) Greater Copper Valley Chamber of Commerce Visitor Center in log cabin; open 8 A.M. to 7 P.M. daily in summer. There's also a convenience grocery and a gas station (with diesel) at junction.

The Greater Copper Valley Chamber of Commerce. See display ad this section.

The Hub of Alaska and Hub Maxi-Mart. See display ad this section.

NOTE: *This junction can be confusing. Choose your route carefully.* Continue west on the Glenn Highway for Anchorage. Turn south here on the Richardson Highway for Valdez.

Junction of the Richardson Highway (Alaska Route 4) with the Glenn Highway (Alaska Route 1). Turn to **Milepost V 115** in the RICHARDSON HIGHWAY section for log of highway to Valdez.

Distance from Anchorage (A) is followed by distance from Tok (T).
Physical mileposts between Glennallen and Anchorage show distance from Anchorage.

ALASKA ROUTE 1

A 188.7 (303.7 km) **T 139.3** (224.2 km) **Northern Nights Campground RV Park.** See display ad this section. ▲

A 188.3 (303 km) **T 139.7** (224.8 km) Trans–Alaska pipeline passes under the highway.

A 187.8 (302.2 km) **T 140.2** (225.6 km) **The Hitchin' Post.** Serving breakfast, lunch and dinner. Open at 6 A.M. It's *THE* place for breakfast among locals, with a $2.99 special! Quaint dining room, drive-through window and clean outdoor tables. Hand-scooped gourmet ice creams, famous fries, Mexican fare, old-fashioned burgers. Look for the yellow place across from the car wash!
[ADVERTISEMENT]

A 187.7 (302.1 km) **T 140.3** (225.8 km) **Moose Horn RV Park.** See display ad this section. ▲

A 187.5 (301.7 km) **T 140.5** (226.1 km) **Tastee–Freez.** This popular spot features an excellent menu of fast food, including breakfast, with some of the lowest prices on the highway. We satisfy appetites of all sizes, from a quick taco to double cheeseburgers, cooked fresh and fast. Our comfortable dining room displays a selection of the finest original drawings and gifts. Plan to stop!
[ADVERTISEMENT]

Old Post Office Gallery. Owner and resident artist Jean René invites you to explore an appealing array of fine art and one-of-a-kind gifts. Here you will find original paintings, limited edition prints, Alaska Native crafts, photography, Alaskan books and more. Stop by for a memorable experience. See display ad this section.
[ADVERTISEMENT]

A 187.2 (301.3 km) **T 140.8** (226.6 km) National Bank of Alaska; ATM. Post office a block north of highway. Description of Glennallen follows.

Glennallen

A 187 (300.9 km) **T 141** (226.9 km) Near the south junction of Glenn and Richardson highways. **Population:** 488. **Emergency Services: Alaska State Troopers,** Milepost **A 189,** phone (907) 822-3263. **Fire Department,** phone 911. **Ambulance,** Copper River EMS, phone (907) 822-3203 or 911. **Clinic,** Milepost A 186.6, phone (907) 822-3203.

Visitor Information: The Greater Copper

Sod-roofed cabin located at Milepost A 189 serves as visitor center for Glennallen and the Copper River Valley. (© Barbara Willard)

in base for several guides and outfitters.

Four prominent peaks of the majestic Wrangell Mountains are to the east; from left they are Mounts Sanford, Drum, Wrangell and Blackburn. The best views are on crisp winter days at sunset. The rest of the countryside is relatively flat.

The main business district is 1.5 miles/2.4 km west of the south junction of the Glenn and Richardson highways. There are also

Valley Chamber of Commerce Visitor Center is located in the log cabin at the junction of the Glenn and Richardson highways. **Milepost A 189**; open 8 A.M. to 7 P.M. daily in summer, phone (907) 822-5555 or write Box 469MP, Glennallen, AK 99588. The Alaska Dept. of Fish and Game office is located at **Milepost A 186.3** on the Glenn Highway, open weekdays 8 A.M. to 5 P.M.; phone (907) 822-3309.

Elevation: 1,460 feet/445m. **Climate:** Mean monthly temperature in January, -10°F/-23°C; in July, 56°F/13°C. Record low was -61°F/-52°C in January 1975; record high, 90°F/32°C in June 1969. Mean precipitation in July, 1.53 inches/3.9cm. Mean precipitation (snow/sleet) in December, 11.4 inches/29cm. **Radio:** KCAM 790, KOOL 107.1, KUAC-FM 92.1. **Television:** KYUK (Bethel) and Wrangell Mountain TV Club via satellite; Public Broadcasting System.

Private Aircraft: Gulkana airstrip, northeast of Glennallen at **Milepost A 192.1**; elev. 1,579 feet/481m; length 5,000 feet/1,524m; asphalt; fuel 100LL. Parking with tie downs. Mechanic available.

The name Glennallen is derived from the combined last names of Capt. Edwin F.

Glenn and Lt. Henry T. Allen, both leaders in the early exploration of the Copper River region.

Glennallen lies at the western edge of the huge Wrangell–St. Elias National Park and Preserve. It is a gateway to the Wrangell Mountains and the service center for the Copper River basin. Glennallen is also a fly-

GLENNALLEN ADVERTISERS

Bishop's RV Park & Car Wash ....Downtown
Brown Bear
    Rhodehouse ....Mile 183.6 Glenn Hwy.
Caribou Cafe Family
    Restaurant.................................Downtown
Copper Valley Cellular ......Ph. (907) 835-8000
Glennallen Chevron..........Ph. (907) 822-3303
KCAM Radio.....................Ph. (907) 822-3434
Mechanix Warehouse
    Auto Parts.....................Ph. (907) 822-3444
Moose Horn RV Park ....Mile 187.7 Glenn Hwy
New Caribou Hotel, Gift Shop
    and Restaurant ....Ph. (907) 822-3302
Northern Nights Campground
    & RV Park.....................Ph. (907) 822-3199
Old Post Office Gallery ..Adjacent Tastee-Freez
Tastee-Freez ....Downtown
Tolsona Wilderness
    Campground ....Mile 173 Glenn Hwy.

several businesses located at the south junction. About two-thirds of the area's residents are employed by trade/service firms; the balance hold various government positions. Offices for the Bureau of Land Management, the Alaska State Troopers and Dept. of Fish and Game are located here. There are several small farms in the area. There is a substantial Native population in the area, and the Native-owned Ahtna Corp. has its headquarters in Glennallen at the junction of the Glenn and Richardson highways.

Also headquartered here is KCAM radio, which broadcasts on station 790. KCAM broadcasts area road condition reports daily and also airs the popular "Caribou Clatter," which will broadcast personal messages. Radio messages are still a popular form of communication in Alaska and a necessary one in the Bush. Similar radio programs throughout the state are KJNP's "Trapline Chatter"; KYAK's "Bush Pipeline"; KHAR's "Northwinds"; and KIAK's "Pipeline of the North."

ACCOMMODATIONS/VISITOR SERVICES

Because of its strategic location, most traveler services are available. During summer months reservations are advised for visitor accommodations. Glennallen has several lodges and motels and a variety of restaurants. Auto parts, groceries, gift shops, clothing, propane, sporting goods and other supplies are available at local stores. Services include a bank and ATM, a dentist, several churches, a chiropractic center, a laundromat, gas stations and major auto repair.

New Caribou Hotel, Gift Shop and Restaurant. The New Caribou Hotel in downtown Glennallen, on the edge of the largest national park in America, was completed fall of 1990. This 55-unit modern facility features custom-built furniture, state-of-the-art color coordinated Alaskan decor, 6 rooms with 2-person whirlpool baths, 2-bedroom, fully furnished suites with kitchens and cooking facilities. Alaskan art, handicap facilities, conference rooms, phones and fax lines, satellite TV. Large full menu restaurant with banquet room, unique Alaskan gift shop (a must stop in your travels). All major credit cards accepted. Tour buses welcome. Airport transportation. Ask us for travel and visitor information. Open year-round. Phone (907) 822-3302. Toll free in Alaska phone (800) 478-3302, fax (907) 822-3711. Web site: www.alaskan.com/caribouhotel/.
[ADVERTISEMENT]

There are private campgrounds west of town on the Glenn Highway (see **Milepost A 183.6, A 173** and **A 170.5**) and east of town at **Milepost A 188.7**. There are 2 private RV parks in Glennallen and at **Milepost V 110.5** Richardson Highway (4.5 m/7.2 km south of the junction). Northeast of Glennallen 5 miles/8 km is Dry Creek state campground (see **Milepost A 192**). ▲

TRANSPORTATION

Bus: Scheduled service between Anchorage and Whitehorse via Glennallen. Bus service between Glennallen and McCarthy via Copper Center and Chitina in summer.

ATTRACTIONS

Fourth of July weekend is a major event in Glennallen. Activities include the Ahtna Arts and Crafts Fair, a music festival, raft race, parade and salmon bake.

Recreational opportunities in the Glennallen area include hiking, flightseeing, hunting, river running, bird watching and fishing. According to the ADF&G, approximately 50 lakes in the Glennallen area are stocked with grayling, rainbow trout and coho salmon. A complete list of lakes, locations and species is available at the Copper River Valley Visitor Center at **Milepost A 189**, or from the ADF&G office at **Milepost A 186.3**. Locally, there is good grayling fishing in **Moose Creek**; **Tulsona Creek** to the east at **Milepost GJ 17.5**; west on the Glenn Highway at **Tolsona Creek**, Milepost A 173; and **Mendeltna Creek**, Milepost A 152.8. **Lake Louise**, approximately 27 miles/43 km west and 16 miles/25.7 km north from Glennallen, offers excellent grayling and lake trout fishing.

Many fly-in lakes are located in the Copper River basin and Chugach Mountains near Glennallen. **Crosswind Lake**, large lake trout, whitefish and grayling, early June to early July. **Deep Lake**, all summer for lake trout to 30 inches. **High Lake**, lake trout to 22 inches, June and early July with small spoons; some rainbow, fly-fishing; cabin, boat and motor rental. **Tebay Lakes**, excellent rainbow fishing, 12 to 15 inches, all summer, small spinners; cabin, boat and motor rental. **Jan Lake**, 12- to 14-inch silver salmon, June, spinners; also rainbow. **Hanagita Lake**, excellent grayling fishing all summer; also lake trout and steelhead in September. **Minnesota Lake**, lake trout to 30 inches, all summer; boat only, no cabins. ◄—►

Glenn Highway Log

(continued)

A 186.6 (300.3 km) **T 141.4** (227.6 km) Cross Road Medical Center clinic. Alaska Bible College, the state's only accredited resident 4-year Bible college, is located behind the clinic.

A 186.4 (300 km) **T 141.6** (227.9 km) Bureau of Land Management district office; phone (907) 822-3217.

A 186.3 (299.8 km) **T 141.7** (228 km) Alaska State Dept. of Fish and Game; phone (907) 822-3309.

A 186 (299.3 km) **T 142** (228.5 km) Copper Valley library.

Moose Creek culvert; good grayling fishing in spring. ◄—►

A 185 (297.7 km) **T 143** (230.1 km) *CAUTION: Slow down for severe frost heaves.*

A 183.6 (295.5 km) **T 144.4** (232.4 km) Lodge restaurant to north.

Brown Bear Rhodehouse. Because of the excellent food, reasonable prices and Alaskan hospitality, this famous old lodge is a favorite eating and gathering place for local people and travelers alike. If eating in the Glennallen area, we recommend stopping here, and if coming from south it is well worth the extra few minutes' wait. Superb steaks and seafood are the specialties, along with broasted chicken and the widest sandwich selection in the area. Your hosts, Doug and Cindy Rhodes, have managed to take one of the largest grizzly brown bear photograph collections anywhere. So, if not dining, you will enjoy just stopping and looking at the many photographs that cover the walls or listening to a few bear tales in the lounge. This is the only place in the area where you have a campground, camping cabins, motel, restaurant and bar at one stop. This is also the only place on the highway to get a bucket of golden brown broasted chicken to go. Phone (907) 822-3663. [ADVERTISEMENT] ▲

A 182.2 (293.2 km) **T 145.8** (234.6 km) Liquor and office supply store to south.

Basin Liquors, Paper Shack Office Supply. Liquor store opens 8 A.M., 7 days a

week, 365 days a year. Liquor, snacks, ice, cigarettes. We invite you to take a break; walk around in one of the most beautiful yards on the Glenn Highway and check out our book exchange. [ADVERTISEMENT]

A 176.6 (284.2 km) **T 151.4** (243.6 km) Paved historical viewpoint to south with interpretive sign about the Wrangell Mountains and view southeast across the Copper River valley to Mount Drum. Northeast of Mount Drum is Mount Sanford and southeast is Mount Wrangell (elev. 14,163 feet/ 4,317m), a semiactive volcano. Mount Wrangell last erupted in 1912 when lava flowed to its base and ash fell as far west as this point.

Wildflowers growing along the roadside include lupine, cinquefoil, oxytrope, Jacob's ladder and sweet pea.

A 174.5 (280.8 km) **T 153.5** (247 km) Double-ended paved turnout to south.
CAUTION: Slow down for frost heaves.

A 173 (278.4 km) **T 155** (249.4 km) Turnoff to north for RV park and campground with dump station and laundromat.

Tolsona Wilderness Campground & RV Park. AAA approved, Good Sam Park. This beautiful campground, located three-quarter mile north of the highway, is surrounded on 3 sides by untouched wilderness. All 80 campsites are situated beside sparkling Tolsona Creek and are complete with table, litter barrel and fireplace. It is a full-service campground with tent sites, restrooms,

dump station, hot showers, laundromat, water and electric hookups for RVs. Internet access available. Browse through the extensive turn-of-the-century antique display. Hiking trail and public phone. Open from May 20 through Sept. 10. $12 to $18 per night. Phone (907) 822-3865. E-mail:

twcg@alaska.net. See display ad in Glennallen section. [ADVERTISEMENT] ▲

A 172.9 (278.2 km) **T 155.1** (249.7 km) Ranch House Lodge.

A 172.8 (278.1 km) **T 155.2** (249.8 km) Bridge over **Tolsona Creek**, grayling to 16 inches, use mosquito flies in still, clear pools behind obstructions, June, July and August. Best fishing 1.5 miles/2.4 km upstream from highway. ◄—►

A 170.5 (274.4 km) **T 157.5** (253.5 km) Tolsona Lake Road to north. **Tolsona** and **Moose lakes**, rainbow trout, burbot, grayling to 16 inches, all summer; good ice fishing for burbot in winter. ◄—►

A 169.3 (272.3 km) **T 158.7** (255.4 km) Paved double-ended turnout to south. Long narrow **Mae West Lake**, fed by Little Woods Creek, is a little less than 1 mile/1.6 km away. Grayling fishing. ◄—►

A 168 (270.4 km) **T 160** (257.5 km) Soup Lake to north. Trumpeter swans can sometimes be seen in lakes and ponds along this section of highway. In June and July look for wildflowers such as sweet pea, fireweed, lupine, cinquefoil, oxytrope, Jacob's ladder and milk-vetch.

A 166.1 (267.3 km) **T 161.9** (260.5 km) **Atlasta House**, a local landmark, was named by the homesteader who was happy to have a real house at last.

A 166 (267.2 km) **T 162** (260.7 km) Paved double-ended turnout to south and 2-mile/3.2-km hiking trail to **Lost Cabin Lake**; grayling fishing. ◄—►

Tolsona Mountain (elev. 2,974 feet/906m), a prominent ridge just north of highway, is a landmark for miles in both directions. This area is popular with berry-pickers in late summer and early fall. Varieties of wild berries include blueberries, lowbush cranberries and raspberries.

A 164 (263.9 km) **T 164** (263.9 km) First glimpse westbound of Tazlina Glacier and lake to south. Half-way point between Tok and Anchorage.

A 162.3 (261.2 km) **T 165.7** (266.7 km) Paved turnout to south.

A 162 (260.7 km) **T 166** (267.1 km) Turnout to north; access to **Tex Smith Lake** to north; stocked with rainbow. ◄—►
NOTE: Watch for horses.

A 159.8 (257.2 km) **T 168.2** (270.7 km)

Junction with 19.3-mile/31-km Lake Louise Road (gravel) to Lake Louise Recreation Area. See LAKE LOUISE ROAD log on page 319.

View of 3 great peaks of the Wrangell Mountains (from left): Mount Sanford, Mount Drum and Mount Wrangell. *(© Alan D. Musy/ADM PhotoGraphics)*

A **159.6** (256.8 km) T **168.4** (271 km) **Little Junction Lake** fishing access, 0.3-mile/0.4-km hike south; grayling. ➤

A **157** (252.7 km) T **171** (275.2 km) Distance marker shows Palmer 109 miles, Anchorage 157 miles.

CAUTION: Slow down for severe frost heaves.

A **156.9** (252.5 km) T **171.1** (275.3 km) Trails to south to **DJ Lake** 0.5 mile/0.8 km (rainbow fishing) and **Sucker Lake** 4 miles/6.4 km (grayling and burbot). ➤

A **156.4** (251.7 km) T **171.6** (276.1 km) Good view (weather permitting) of **Tazlina Glacier** to the south. The glacier feeds into 20-mile/32-km-long **Tazlina Lake** at its foot.

A **156.3** (251.5 km) T **171.7** (276.3 km) **Buffalo Lake**; stocked with rainbow. ➤

A **156.2** (251.4 km) T **171.8** (276.5 km) Tazlina Glacier Lodge.

A **156** (251 km) T **172** (276.8 km) Tazlina airstrip; elev. 2,450 feet/747m; length 1,200 feet/366m; gravel. Not recommended for use.

A **155.8** (250.7 km) T **172.2** (277.2 km) **Arizona Lake** to south; fishing for grayling. ➤

A **155.6** (250.4 km) T **172.4** (277.4 km) Paved turnout to south.

A **155.2** (249.8 km) T **172.8** (278.1 km) **Gergie Lake** 1/4 mile to south; fishing for grayling and rainbow. ➤

CAUTION: Slow down for frost heaves.

A **154** (247.8 km) T **174** (280 km) **MENDELTNA** (pop. 59) sign.

A **153.7** (247.3 km) T **174.3** (280.5 km) Community chapel.

A **153** (246.2 km) T **175** (281.6 km) Lodge-type restaurant, bar, campground, liquor store, cabins and gas to south.

K.R.O.A. Kamping Resorts of Alaska on the Little Mendeltna, a natural spring-fed stream. Excellent fishing for grayling, whitefish and others. Many lakes nearby. Fishing, hunting guides available. Gateway to Tazlina Lake and Glacier. Skiing, hiking, snow machine trails. Modern hookups. Pull-throughs. Laundromat. Hot showers. Can handle any size caravan. Rustic cabins. Brick-oven fresh dough pizza. Homemade cinnamon rolls. Museum of Alaska's Drunken Forest, a collection of unusual and artistic natural designs of trees. Artifacts of Alaska's Drunken Forest. Gas, liquor store, bar. [ADVERTISEMENT] ▲

A **152.8** (245.9 km) T **175.2** (282 km) **Mendeltna Creek** bridge. Watch for spawning salmon in August. (The Mendeltna Creek drainage is closed to the taking of salmon.) Excellent fishing for grayling to 17 1/2 inches and whitefish to 16 inches, May to November, use spinners and flies. Walk or boat away from the bridge. Good fishing north to Old Man Lake; watch for bears. ➤

A **152.7** (245.7 km) T **175.3** (282.1 km) Paved double-ended rest area to north with picnic tables, dumpster and toilets.

A **150.4** (242 km) T **177.6** (285.8 km) **NELCHINA** (sign).

A **150** (241.4 km) T **178** (286.4 km) Distance marker shows Sutton 89 miles, Palmer 103 miles.

Eastbound view of Mount Sanford and Mount Drum straight ahead.

A **149.1** (239.9 km) T **178.9** (287.9 km) **Ryan Lake** public fishing access; grayling and rainbow. ➤

A **149** (239.8 km) T **179** (288.1 km) Food, lodging and towing to south.

Grizzly Country Enterprises. Our Log Cabin grocery store has a great selection with reasonable prices. Browse in our gift shop, find that special Alaskan gift and more. Home of the 50 cent soda. Novelty ice

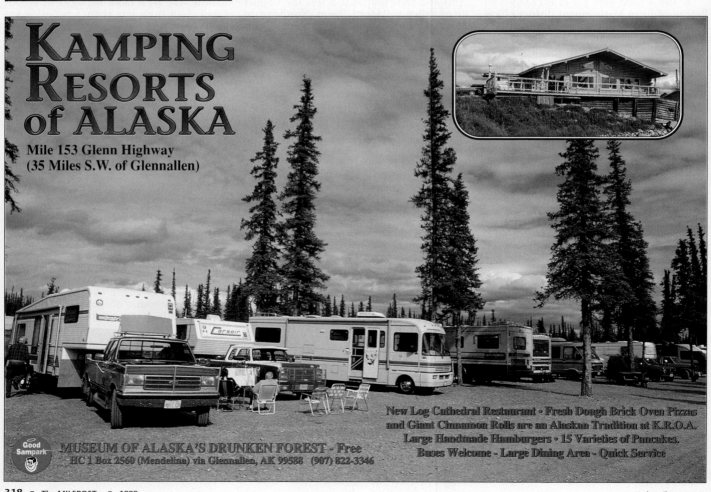

Lake Louise Road Log

This wide gravel road leads north 19.3 miles/31 km from **Milepost A 159.8** Glenn Highway to Lake Louise Recreation Area. The road is state-maintained and open year-round. Lake Louise is known for its lake trout and grayling fishing; lodges, dining, boat rentals and fishing charters at lake. Views of Tazlina Glacier and Lake; berry picking for wild strawberries and blueberries (July and August), and cranberries (September). Excellent cross-country skiing and snowmobiling in winter.

Distance is measured from the junction with the Glenn Highway (J).

J 0 Junction with Glenn Highway at **Milepost A 154.8.**

J 0.2 (0.3 km) **Junction Lake** to east; grayling fishing.

J 1.1 (1.8 km) Turnout.

J 1.2 (1.9 km) Double-ended turnout to west with view of Tazlina Glacier.

Just north is the road west to Little **Crater Lake**. There are a number of small lakes along the road with good fishing for grayling.

J 5.2 (8.4 km) **Old Road Lake and Round Lake** to east (1/4 mile); rainbow fishing.

J 6.7 (10.8 km) **Mendeltna Creek** to west 5 miles); grayling fishing.

J 7 (11.2 km) **Forgotten Lake** to east (0.1 mile/0.2 km); grayling fishing.

J 9.4 (15.1 km) Parking area to west with view of pothole lakes. First view of Lake Louise northbound.

J 10.5 (16.9 km) Hill; use low-gear. Good view on clear days of the Alaska Range and Susitna River valley.

J 11.5 (18.5 km) Road west to **Caribou Lake**; grayling fishing. Turnout to east by Elbow Lake.

J 14 (22.5 km) Boundary of Matanuska–Susitna Borough.

J 15.5 (24.9 km) Gas station.

J 15.9 (25.6 km) Parking rea to east.

J 16 (25.7 km) **North and South Jan's Lakes** to east (7 miles); fishing.

J 16.1 (25.9 km) Turnoff for Lake Louise Lodge (0.9 miles/1.4 km).

Lake Louise Lodge. See display ad this section.

J 16.5 (26.6 km) Turnoff for Evergreen Lodge (0.3 miles/0.5 km).

Evergreen Lodge at Lake Louise. See display ad this section.

J 16.8 (27 km) **Conner Lake**, rainbow and grayling fishing.

J 17.2 (27.7 km) Side road leads northeast to The Point Lodge (0.9 miles) and

Lake Louise State Recreation Area. Drive 0.4 miles to "T"; turn left for The Point Lodge (0.5 mile) and Lake Louise Campground (0.3 mile); turn right for Army Point Campground (0.7 mile). Army Point and Lake Louise campgrounds have 52 campsites on loop roads, firepits, water pumps, toilets (wheelchair

Lake Louise Road Log (continued)

Paved trail at Lake Louise Campground. (©Kris Graef, staff)

accessible), covered picnic tables, picnic shelter, walking trail and a boat launch.

Camping fee $10/night or annual pass. Swimming in Lake Louise. Winter ski trail access. ♿▲

J 18.8 (30.3 km) **Private Aircraft:** Lake Louise airstrip is closed. Seaplane landing and docking at all lodges. No avgas available.

J 19.3 (31 km) Road ends. Parking and boat launch to west on Dinty Lake. Side road east to Lake Louise rest area; picnic tables, fireplaces, toilets.

Lake Louise, grayling and lake trout fishing good year-round, best spring through July, then again in the fall; early season use herring or whitefish bait, cast from boat; later (warmer water) troll with #16 red-and-white spoon, silver Alaskan plug or large silver flatfish; for grayling, casting flies or small spinners, June, July and August; in winter jig for lake trout. Check ADF&G regulations for Lake Louise area. 🐟

Susitna Lake can be reached by boat across Lake Louise (narrow channel; watch for signs); burbot, lake trout and grayling fishing. *Both lakes can be rough; under-powered boats not recommended.* **Dinty Lake**, launch from public launch at Mile 19.3; grayling and lake trout fishing. 🐟

Return to Milepost A 159.8 Glenn Highway

cream year-round. We carry Interstate Batteries and provide new tire sales and service. Our tow company is known for excellent customer service. We proudly honor all motor clubs. RVs welcome. VISA and MasterCard. Open 8 A.M.–10 P.M. Towing and Recovery 24 hours. (907) 822-3700.
[ADVERTISEMENT]

A 146.5 (235.8 km) **T 181.5** (292.1 km) *CAUTION: Rough road. Slow down for frost heaves.*

A 144.9 (233.2 km) **T 183.1** (294.7 km) Lottie Sparks (Nelchina) Elementary School.

A 141.2 (227.2 km) **T 186.8** (300.6 km) Nelchina state highway maintenance station. Slide Mountain trailhead located behind station.

A 138.4 (222.7 km) **T 189.6** (305.1 km) NELCHINA (sign).

A 137.6 (221.4 km) **T 190.4** (306.4 km) **Little Nelchina State Recreation Site** 0.3 mile/0.5 km north from highway; 11 campsites, 15-day limit, no camping fee, no drinking water, tables, firepits, toilet, boat launch. Watch for moose and bear. ▲

A 137.5 (221.3 km) **T 190.5** (306.6 km) Little Nelchina River bridge.

NOTE: Eastbound, highway curves uphill from bridge. Westbound to summit it is good paved straightaway with passing lanes.

A 137 (220.5 km) **T 191** (307.4 km) Boundary of Matanuska–Susitna Borough. Good views to south of glaciers in the Chugach Mountains.

A 135.7 (218.4 km) **T 192.3** (309.5 km) Paved turnout to north.

Truck lane begins westbound.

A 135.3 (217.7 km) **T 192.7** (310.1 km) Store and cabins to south.

Nelchina Trail Store & Cabins. See display ad this section.

A 135 (217.3 km) **T 193** (310.6 km) *CAUTION: Watch for moose.*

A 134 (215.6 km) **T 194** (312.2 km) Gravel turnout to south.

A 133 (214 km) **T 195** (313.8 km) Paved turnout to north.

A 132.1 (212.6 km) **T 195.9** (315.2 km) Gravel turnout to north.

Great views to south of Nelchina Glacier. View of Mount Sanford eastbound.

A 130.5 (201 km) **T 197.5** (317.8 km) Large gravel parking area to north used by hunters and hikers. Old Man Creek trailhead. (Old Man Creek 2 miles/3 km; Crooked Creek 9 miles/14.5 km; Nelchina Town 14.5 miles/23 km.) Established trails west from here to Palmer are part of the Chickaloon–Knik–Nelchina trail system.

A 129.5 (208.4 km) **T 198.5** (319.4 km) **Eureka Summit** (elev. 3,322 feet/1,013m), highest point on the Glenn Highway. Turnout to south with unobstructed views of the Chugach Mountains. Snow poles along roadside guide snow plows in winter. Truck lane ends westbound.

Gold Rush Centennial sign about Captain Edwin F. Glenn, who passed near here on his way from Cook Inlet to the Tanana River in 1898. Glenn led one of 3 teams, the Cook Inlet Exploring Expedition. His orders were to locate the most practical route from Prince William Sound through Cook Inlet to the Tanana River. The Glenn Highway is named in his honor.

The Nelchina Glacier winds downward through a cleft in the mountains. To the northwest are the peaks of the Talkeetnas, and to the west the highway descends through river valleys which separate these 2 mountain ranges. This is the divide of 3 big river systems: Susitna, Matanuska and Copper.

A 128 (206 km) **T 200** (321.9 km) Food, gas, diesel, lodging, bar and liquor store at the first lodge on the Glenn Highway, the **Eureka Roadhouse.** It was opened in 1937 by Paul Waverly and has operated continuously ever since. The original log building is next to Eureka Lodge.

Eureka Lodge. See display ad this section.

Private Aircraft: Eureka (Skelton) airstrip, one of the highest in the state; elev. 3,289 feet/1,002m; length 2,400 feet/732m; gravel; fuel autogas; unattended. Runway narrows to 15 feet.

A 127 (204.4 km) **T 201** (323.4 km) Gravel turnout to south.

CAUTION: Watch for caribou. Caribou

crossing. The Nelchina caribou herd travels through here October through November.

A 126.4 (203.4 km) **T 201.6** (324.4 km) Watch for turnout to south to Belanger Creek–Nelchina River trailhead parking. (Eureka Creek 1.5 miles/2.4 km; Goober Lake 8 miles/13 km; Nelchina River 9 miles/14.5 km.)

A 125 (201.2 km) **T 203** (326.7 km) **Gunsight Mountain** (elev. 6,441 feet/1,963m) is visible to the west for the next few miles to those approaching from Glennallen.The notch or "gunsight" is plain if one looks closely. Eastbound views of snow-covered Mount Sanford (weather permitting), Mount Drum, Mount Wrangell and Mount Blackburn.

A 123.3 (198.4 km) **T 204.7** (329.4 km) Belanger Pass trailhead to north. (Belanger Pass 3 miles/5 km; Alfred Creek 6.5 miles/10.5 km; Albert Creek 8 miles/13 km.)

A 123.1 (198.1 km) **T 204.9** (329.8 km) Old Tahneta Inn to south (closed).

A 122.9 (197.8 km) **T 205.1** (330 km) Gunsight Mountain Lodge to north (closed in 1998; current status unknown).

A 122 (196.3 km) **T 206** (331.5 km) **Tahneta Pass** (elev. 3,000 feet/914m). Double-ended paved turnout to north.

Leila Lake trailhead (unsigned) on old alignment to north; grayling 8 to 14 inches abundant through summer, best fishing June and July. Burbot, success spotty for 12 to 18 inches in fall and winter.

A 121.4 (195.4 km) **T 206.6** (332.5 km) Trailhead to north; small parking area.

A 120.8 (194.4 km) **T 207.2** (333.4 km) Boundary of Sportfish Management Area 2 and Sheep Mountain Closed Area.

A 120.1 (193.3 km) **T 207.9** (334.6 km) Scenic viewpoint to south (double-ended paved turnout). The largest lake is Leila Lake; in the distance is Tahneta Lake.

A 120.2 (193.4 km) **T 207.8** (334.4 km) Turnout to south with beautiful view of Chugach Mountains and lakes (weather permitting).

A 118.1 (190 km) **T 209.9** (337.8 km) Truck lane ends eastbound and begins westbound.

A 117.8 (189.5 km) **T 210.2** (338.2 km) Turnout with viewpoint to south. Tip of Powell Glacier can be seen coming down the canyon of the South Fork Matanuska River. Knob Lake and the "knob" (elev. 3,000

feet/914m), topped by microwave tower, marks entrance to Chickaloon Pass for small planes.

A 117.6 (189.3 km) **T 210.4** (338.6 km) Large parking area to north at Squaw Creek trailhead. (Squaw Creek 3.5 miles/5.6 km; Caribou Creek 9.5 miles/15 km; Alfred Creek 13 miles/21 km; Sheep Creek 15 miles/24 km.)

A 117.4 (188.9 km) **T 210.6** (338.9 km) Paved turnout to south with view of Chugach Mountains.

A 117.3 (188.8 km) **T 210.7** (339.1 km) Bridge.

A 116.1 (186.8 km) **T 211.9** (341 km) Truck lane begins eastbound.

A 115.6 (186 km) **T 212.4** (341.8 km) Large paved turnout to south with view of Chugach Mountains.

A 115 (185 km) **T 213** (342.8 km) Turnout to north. Look for sheep on mineralized Sheep Mountain.

A 114.9 (184.9 km) **T 213.1** (342.9 km) Majestic Valley Lodge to south. Large construction gravel pit to north in 1998. (There was major road construction between Milepost **A 109** and **121** last summer.) Watch for sheep on mountainside.

Majestic Valley Lodge combines the rustic charm of a quaint mountain lodge with all modern conveniences. In the 3,000-for Tahneta Pass area, enjoy hiking treks, Dall sheep and other wildlife, blueberry picking, glacier walks, cross-country skiing and snowmobiling. Gourmet meals (advance reservation required). Sauna and the spectacular view top off a day in the mountains. Rooms include private baths and use of the

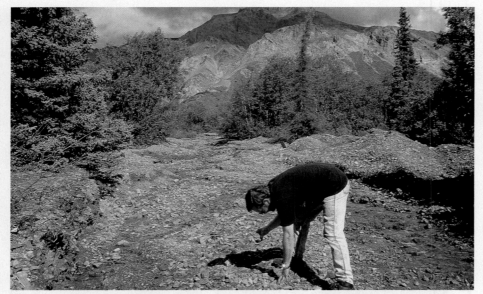

Rockhounding at Sheep Mountain near Milepost A 113 Glenn Highway.
(© Susan Cole Kelly)

large viewing lounge and Alaskan library. Phone (907) 746-2930; fax (907) 746-2931; e-mail: mvwl@mvwl.com. [ADVERTISEMENT]

A 114.6 (184.4 km) **T 213.4** (343.4 km) Truck lane ends eastbound.

For Anchorage-bound travelers a vista of incomparable beauty as the road descends in a long straightaway toward Glacier Point, also known as the **Lion Head**, an oddly formed rocky dome.

A 113.5 (182.7 km) **T 214.5** (345.2 km) Truck lane begins eastbound. Sheep Mountain Lodge on north side of highway.

Wonderful views to north of **Sheep Mountain** (elev. 6,300 feet/1,920m). Sheep are often seen high up these slopes. The area surrounding Sheep Mountain is closed to the taking of mountain sheep.

Sheep Mountain Lodge. Our charming log lodge, established in 1946, has been serving travelers for half a century. We're famous for our wholesome homemade food, fresh baked breads, pastries and desserts. Our comfortable guest cabins, all with private bathrooms, boast spectacular mountain views. We also have RV hookups, full bar, liquor store and Alaskan gifts. You can

watch Dall Sheep through our telescope and relax in the hot tub or sauna after a day of traveling or hiking. HC03 Box 8490, Palmer, AK 99645. Phone (907) 745-5121; fax (907) 745-5120. E-mail: sheepmtl@alaska.net. Internet: www.alaska.net/~sheepmtl. See display ad this section. [ADVERTISEMENT] ▲

Private Aircraft: Sheep Mountain airstrip; elev. 2,750 feet/838m; length 2,300 feet/701m; gravel/dirt; unattended.

A 113.5 (182.7 km) **T 214.5** (345.2 km) As the highway descends westbound into the valley of the Matanuska River, there is a view of the great glacier which is the main headwater source and gives the water its milky color.

A 113 (181.9 km) **T 215** (346 km) Gravel turnout to Sheep Mountain airstrip.

A 112.7 (181.4 km) **T 215.3** (346.5 km) Large paved turnout to south.

A 112.4 (180.9 km) **T 215.6** (347 km) Truck lane ends eastbound.

A 111.6 (179.6 km) **T 216.4** (348.2 km) Access to bed and breakfast to south. Truck lane begins eastbound.

A 110.9 (178.5 km) **T 217.1** (349.4 km) Truck lane ends eastbound.

A 110.5 (177.8 km) **T 217.5** (350 km) Truck lane begins eastbound.

A 109.7 (176.5 km) **T 218.3** (351.3 km) Log building to south. Good views westbound of Matanuska Glacier.

Grand View. See display ad this section.

A 109.5 (176.2 km) **T 218.5** (351.6 km) Paved turnout to south. Access to bed and breakfast.

Tundra Rose Bed & Breakfast. See display ad this section.

A 109.2 (175.7 km) **T 218.8** (352.1 km) *CAUTION: Narrow winding road westbound. Long stretches without shoulders. Watch for road construction between here and Palmer in 1999.*

A 107.8 (173.5 km) **T 220.2** (354.4 km) Slide area. Exceptional views of Glacier Point (Lion Head) and Matanuska Glacier.

A 107.1 (172.4 km) **T 220.9** (355.5 km) Large gravel turnouts to south, viewpoint.

A 106.8 (171.9 km) **T 221.2** (356 km) Caribou Creek Bridge. Caribou Creek trailhead parking to north at west end of bridge. Caribou Creek trail zigzags up the mountainside between the highway and the creek and leads back behind Sheep Mountain. A pleasant hike for good walkers. (Squaw Creek 9 miles/14.5 km; Alfred Creek 13 miles/21 km; Sheep Creek 15 miles/24 km; and Squaw Creek trailhead 18.5 miles/30 km.)

Fortress Ridge (elev. 5,000 feet/1,524m) above the highway to the north. Sheep Mountain reserve boundary.

NOTE: Highway makes a steep, winding descent (from both directions) down to Caribou Creek.

A 106 (170.6 km) **T 222** (357.3 km) Large gravel parking area for **Caribou Creek Recreational Gold Mining Area** (Dept. of Natural Resources); outhouse. Steep trail leads from parking area down to creek (pedestrians only, no ATVs). Recreational gold panning, mineral prospecting or mining using light portable field equipment (e.g. hand-operated pick, backpack power drill, etc.) allowed in designated recreational mining area on state lands without mining claims below the ordinary high water mark of Caribou Creek, its tributaries and the Matanuska River. Suction dredging requires a permit from the ADF&G. Contact Dept. of Natural Resources Public Information Center in Anchorage for more information; phone (907) 269-8400.

A 105.8 (170.3 km) **T 222.2** (357.6 km) Road (closed to public) to FAA station on flank of Glacier Point. Mountain sheep occasionally are seen on the upper slopes.

A 105.5 (169.8 km) **T 222.5** (358.1 km) Gravel turnout to south.

A 105.3 (169.4 km) **T 222.7** (358.4 km) Turnout to south. FAA station on Glacier Point.

Great views of Matanuska Glacier from the highway westbound.

A 104.1 (167.5 km) **T 223.9** (360.3 km) Access to Glacier View School, which overlooks Matanuska Glacier.

A 103.2 (166.1 km) **T 224.8** (361.8 km) **Majestic View RV Park.** New! 200 yards off the Glenn Highway. Quiet, secluded, and very scenic. Large, level pull-through sites overlooking the Matanuska Glacier and surrounding mountains. Fully self-contained RVs only. No facilities at this time. Wildlife, wildflowers and berries in season. Easy access south side of highway. [ADVERTISEMENT] ▲

A 102.8 (165.4 km) **T 225.2** (362.4 km) Paved turnout to south with view of Matanuska Glacier.

A 102.2 (164.5 km) **T 225.8** (363.4 km)

Long Rifle Lodge to south.

Long Rifle Lodge. Welcome to Alaska's most fabulous dining view of the Matanuska Glacier. We offer a complete breakfast, lunch and dinner menu, specializing in home-cooked meals. Twenty-five wildlife mounts make our lodge a "must see" for all ages. Numerous hiking, cross-country skiing and snowmobile trails surround the area. In addition, we have motel rooms, gasoline, 24-hour wrecker service, gift shop and a full-service lounge. Phone (800) 770-5151. Fax (907) 745-5153. E-mail: lrl@matnet.com. See display ad this section. [ADVERTISEMENT]

A 102 (164.2 km) **T 226** (363.7 km) Access to foot of Matanuska Glacier via Glacier Park Resort to south. Admission fee charged.

Wickersham Trading Post. See display ad this section.

Glacier Park. We invite you to experience the Matanuska Glacier through Glacier Park, a private park at the terminus of the Matanuska Glacier. Our location to the glacier allows us to offer you a most unique glacier tour. From our parking area it is about a 15-minute hike for the average person to the white ice. Offering half-hour, hour, half-day and full-day tours on the white ice, June 1–Sept. 7. Off-season reservations required. This is where the locals bring their guests for an Alaskan experience. Let us show you a reason people come to Alaska! The most common remark is "I never dreamed we could walk out on a glacier like this." Family, group and per person rates. Access at Milepost 102 Glenn Highway. HC03 Box 8449, Palmer, AK 99645. Phone (907) 745-2534. [ADVERTISEMENT] ▲

A 101.7 (163.7 km) **T 226.3** (364.2 km) Paved turnout with good view of **Matanuska Glacier**, which heads in the Chugach Mountains and trends northwest 27 miles/43.5 km. Some 18,000 years ago the glacier reached all the way to the Palmer area. The glacier's average width is 2 miles/3.2 km; at its terminus it is 4 miles/6.4 km wide. The glacier has remained fairly stable the past 400 years. At the glacier terminus meltwater drains into a stream which flows into the Matanuska River.

A 101 (162.5 km) **T 227** (365.3 km) Matanuska Glacier State Recreation Site; 12 campsites on loop drive, 15-day limit, $10, nightly fee or annual pass, wheelchair

Matanuska Glacier seen from the state recreation area at Milepost A 101 Glenn Highway. (© Mike Jones)

accessible, water and toilets. Excellent views of the glacier from hiking trails along the bluff. (Use caution when walking near edge of bluff.) Wildflowers here in late July include fireweed, yarrow and sweet peas.&▲

A 100.4 (161.6 km) **T 227.6** (366.3 km) Pinochle Hill.

A 99.7 (160.4 km) **T 228.3** (367.4 km) Paved turnout to north. Good view of Matanuska Glacier from highway.

A 99.1 (159.5 km) **T 228.9** (368.4 km) Truck lane begins westbound. Truck lane ends eastbound.

A 98.3 (158.2 km) **T 229.7** (369.6 km) Truck lane ends westbound.

A 97.5 (156.9 km) **T 230.5** (370.9 km) Truck lane begins eastbound.

A 96.6 (155.5 km) **T 231.4** (372.4 km) Private campground, lodge and store. Hicks Creek was named by Captain Glenn in 1898 for H.H. Hicks, the guide of his expedition. **Anthracite Ridge** to north offers good rock-hounding (jasper, rosy-banded agate, petrified wood and rock crystal); difficult to reach

Cottonwood in fall colors along the Matanuska River. (© Bruce M. Herman)

on foot.

Historical Hicks Creek Roadhouse. See display ad this section. ▲

A 96.5 (155.3 km) **T 231.5** (372.6 km) Bridge over Hicks Creek.

Winding road westbound as highway climbs above the Matanuska River.

A 95 (152.9 km) **T 233** (375 km) Beautiful views to south of Matanuska River and peaks and glaciers in the Chugach Range. The **Chugach Mountains** arc 250 miles from Bering Glacier on the Gulf of Alaska to the east to Turnagain Arm south of Anchorage. They are bounded on the north by the Matanuska, Copper and Chitina Rivers, and on the south by the gulf and Prince William Sound.

A 94.6 (152.2 km) **T 233.4** (375.6 km) Victory Road.

A 93.2 (150 km) **T 234.8** (377.9 km) Cascade state highway maintenance station.

A 90.8 (146.1 km) **T 237.2** (381.7 km) Gravel turnout to north; trailhead parking.

A 89 (143.2 km) **T 239** (384.6 km) Purinton Creek bridge; parking to north at west end of bridge for Purinton Creek trailhead. Good blueberry patches in season if you can beat the bears to them. The stream heads on Anthracite Ridge and flows into the Matanuska River.

Westbound, watch for moose.

A 88 (141.6 km) **T 240** (386.2 km) *CAUTION: Slide areas, winding road, westbound to* **Milepost A 84.** *Gravel turnouts on south side of highway to* **Milepost A 78.**

A 87.5 (140.8 km) **T 240.5** (387 km) **Weiner Lake** access; fishing for rainbow and grayling.

A 85.3 (137.3 km) **T 242.7** (390.6 km) **Long Lake**, in a narrow canyon below the highway, is a favorite fishing spot for Anchorage residents. Fair for grayling to 18 inches, spring through fall; fish deeper as the water warms in summer. Good ice fishing in winter for burbot, average 12 inches. **Long Lake State Recreation Site** has 9 campsites, 15-day limit, no camping fee, no water; tables, firepits and toilets. ◆▲

A 84 (135.2 km) **T 244** (392.7 km) *CAUTION: Slide areas, winding road, eastbound to* **Milepost A 88.**

Great views of Matanuska River and Chugach Mountains to south as highway descends eastbound.

A 83.2 (133.9 km) **T 244.8** (394 km) Narrow gravel road north to Ravine and Lower Bonnie lakes. Drive in 0.8 mile/1.3 km on side road to reach **Ravine Lake**; fishing from shore for rainbow. **Lower Bonnie Lake** is a 2-mile/3.2-km drive from the highway. **Bonnie Lake State Recreation Site** has 8 campsites, 15-day limit, no camping fee, no water, toilets and boat launch. Fishing for grayling and rainbow. *NOTE: Steep and winding road beyond Ravine Lake is signed as unsafe for large vehicles or trailers. All travel is at owner's risk. During rainy season this side road is not recommended for any vehicle.* ◆▲

A 82 (132 km) **T 246** (395.9 km) Distinctive pyramid shape of **King Mountain** (elev. 5,809 feet/1,770m).to the southeast.

A 80.8 (130 km) **T 247.2** (397.8 km) Eastern boundary of Matanuska Valley Moose Range

A 78.3 (126 km) **T 249.7** (401.8 km) Gravel turnout to south with view of King Mountain and Matanuska River.

NOTE: Highway climbs steeply eastbound to **Milepost A 84.** *Gravel turnouts to south of highway to* **Milepost A 88.**

A 77.7 (125 km) **T 250.3** (402.8 km) Chickaloon River bridge. Gravel turnout. Boundary between Game Management Units 13 and 14. The old Chickaloon Road winds upstream. Travelers have reported seeing no trespassing and private property signs a short distance up this road, indicating Native land claims along the road and river. Inquire locally about public access to the Chickaloon River via this side road before driving in.

A 77.5 (124.7 km) **T 250.5** (403.1 km) Gravel turnout to south. Highway closely parallels the **Matanuska River** westbound to Palmer. An outfitter in Chickaloon offers scenic floats and whitewater trips on the river. The Matanuska River is formed by its East and South Forks and flows southwest 75 miles to the Knik Arm of Cook Inlet.

NOTE: Slide areas, gravel turnouts to south, westbound to **Milepost A 68.**

A 76.2 (122.6 km) **T 251.8** (405.2 km) **CHICKALOON** (pop. 145); lodge, cafe, cabins, camping, general store, gas station and river rafting office. ▲

Nova River Runners. See display ad this section.

King Mountain Lodge, established 1947, oldest continuously operated lodge on the Glenn Highway, with its own resident ghost. Authentic Alaskan atmosphere in the plank-floor bar ("Chickaloon Performing Arts Center") dates from coal mining days. Stay in a real miner's cabin or camp free along the Matanuska River. All cooking from

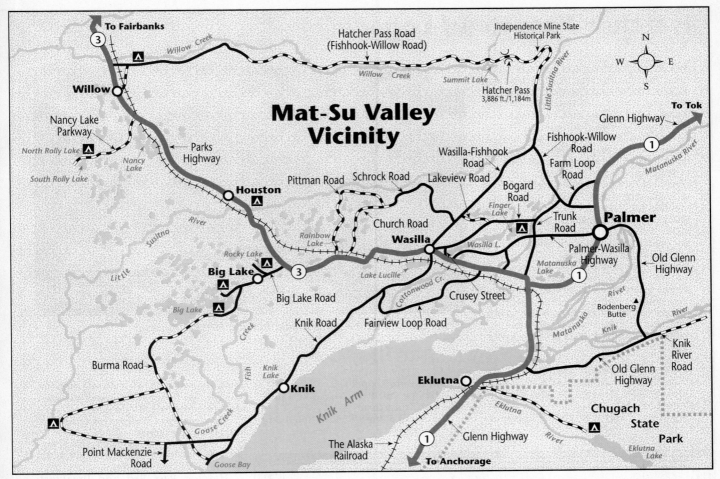

Mat-Su Valley Vicinity

scratch. Famous sausage gravy, musk ox or buffalo burgers. Home of the King Mountain Burger, the most bodacious burger of all. ▲

A 76.1 (122.5 km) **T 251.9** (405.4 km) **King Mountain State Recreation Site.** Pleasant campground on the banks of the Matanuska River with 22 campsites, 2 picnic sites, fireplaces, picnic tables, water, toilets. Camping fee $10/night or annual pass; 15-day limit. King Mountain to the southeast. ▲

A 73.7 (118.6 km) **T 254.3** (409.2 km) *"Hill"; winding descent eastbound.*

A 72.8 (117.2 km) **T 255.2** (410.7 km) Ida Lake.

A 70.6 (113.6 km) **T 257.4** (414.2 km) Access to Matanuska River to south.

A 69.7 (112.2 km) **T 258.3** (415.7 km) Chickaloon post office (ZIP code 99674). Private campground (closed in 1998, current status unknown).

A 68 (109.4 km) **T 260** (418.4 km) *Slide areas eastbound as highway winds along bank of the Matanuska River. Gravel turnouts to south.*

Pinnacle Mountain (elev. 4,541 feet/1,384m) rises directly southeast of the highway—easy to identify by its unusual top. Cottonwoods and aspen along the highway. Talkeetna Mountains to the north.

A 66.4 (106.8 km) **T 261.6** (421 km) **King River** bridge. Parking to north at east end of bridge. King River Trail (no sign in 1998); King River Crossing 5 miles/8 km. Fishing for trout, early summer best, use eggs. ◄►

A 65.9 (106.1 km) **T 262.1** (421.8 km) *CAUTION: Watch for moose.*

A 62.7 (100.9 km) **T 265.3** (426.9 km)

Large gravel turnout with interpretive sign to south along Matanuska River. Dwarf fireweed and sweet pea in June.

A 62.4 (100.4 km) **T 265.6** (427.4 km) **Granite Creek** bridge and access to River's Edge Recreation Park campground. Fishing for small Dolly Varden and trout, spring or early summer, use flies or single eggs. ◄►▲

River's Edge Recreation Park. Campground greeting, highway travelers! Camping in Alaska should include woods; wildflowers; clear, rushing streams; privacy; quiet; and wildlife. River's Edge Recreation Park offers that and more. As lifelong Alaskans, we value all the natural beauty in o u r 18-acre facility and try to maintain that natural splendor for our guests. Our campsites are perfect for tents and RVs. We have electrical hookups, 6 pull-through sites, dump station, drinking water, and very clean shower facilities. You'll find quality for your camp fee at River's Edge. Overnight and electrical fees include water and dump station. Showers are an extra charge and include towels, shampoo and soap in a private dressing room cleaned after each use. We have 27 sites. Looking for a wilderness setting for your camp tonight? Drive on in. Mid-May to mid-September. Phone (907) 745-2267. [ADVERTISEMENT] ♿▲

A 62.2 (100.1 km) **T 265.8** (427.7 km) Sutton post office. Sign in at their guest book.

A 61.6 (99.1 km) **T 266.4** (428.7 km) Alpine Historical Park, an open-air museum featuring the concrete ruins of the Sutton Coal Washery (1920–22). Access via Elementary School Road. The museum is still under

development. Donations accepted.

Alpine Historical Park. See display ad this section.

A 61 (98.2 km) **T 267** (429.7 km)
(Continues on page 327)

Hatcher Pass Road Log

The 49-mile-/79-km-long Hatcher Pass Road leads northwest from **Milepost A 49.5** on the Glenn Highway (as Palmer-Fishhook Road) over Hatcher Pass (elev. 3,886 feet/1,184m) and connects with the Parks Highway at **Milepost A 71.2** (as Fishhook-Willow Road). (See Mat-Su Valley Vicinity map on page 325.) If you don't have time to do the entire drive, do at least drive up to Independence Mine Historical Park (turnoff at Mile 17.3). This is a mostly gravel road, not recommended for large RVs or trailers beyond **Milepost J 14**, although road improvements are planned. The road usually does not open until late June or early July, and snow may close the pass in September. The road stays open to the historical park and to Hatcher Pass Lodge, a popular winter sports area for snowmobiling and cross-country skiing, in winter.

Distance from junction with the Glenn Highway (J) is followed by distance from junction with the Parks Highway (P).

Scenic Little Susitna River is a gold-bearing stream. (©Loren Taft)

J 0 P 49.1 (79 km) **Junction** with the Glenn Highway at **Milepost A 49.5**. Fishhook–Willow Road heads west through farm country.

J 1.4 (2.3 km) **P 47.7** (76.8 km) Junction with Farm Loop Road.

J 2.4 (3.9 km) **P 46.7** (75.2 km) **Junction** with Trunk Road.

J 6.5 (10.5 km) **P 42.5** (68.4 km)

Tesoro gas station with diesel, propane, grocery, ice, liquor store, laundromat and showers; overnight RV parking.

Hatcher Pass Gateway Center. See display ad this section.

J 6.8 (10.9 km) **P 42.3** (68.1 km) **Junction** with Wasilla–Fishhook Road. Access to bed and breakfast.

Hatcher Pass Bed and Breakfast. Experience our authentic Alaskan log cabins located at the base of beautiful Hatcher Pass, yet only minutes from Palmer and Wasilla. Cozy, comfortable, and private with all the modern amenities—come enjoy a peaceful getaway! Phone (907) 745-6788, fax (907) 745-6787. Web site www.AlaskaOutdoors.com/HPBB. [ADVERTISEMENT]

J 8.1 (13 km) **P 41** (66 km) Hatcher Pass Management Area boundary.

J 8.5 (13.7 km) **P 40.6** (65.3 km) **Little Susitna River** bridge. Large double-ended paved turnout at north end of bridge. Road parallels river. This scenic mountain stream heads at Mint Glacier in the Talkeetna Mountains and flows 110 miles to Cook Inlet. This is a gold-bearing stream.

J 8.7 (14 km) **P 40.4** (65 km) Pavement ends, gravel begins, northbound. Road parallels river; turnouts westbound.

J 9 (14.5 km) **P 40.1** (64.5 km) Gravel loop turnout and sign; entering Hatcher Pass public-use area westbound. No flower picking or plant removal without a permit.

J 9.3 (15 km) **P 39.8** (64.1 km) Graffiti Rock.

J 9.4 (15.1 km) **P 39.7** (63.9 km) Turnout; distance marker shows Independence Mine State Historical Park 10 miles.

J 9.7 (15.6 km) **P 39.4** (63.4 km) This area open to all recreational mining (sign).

J 10 (16 km) **P 39.1** (62.9 km) Turnout and sign on pass status.

J 11 (17.7 km) **P 38.1** (61.3 km) Long

loop turnout.

J 12.1 (19.4 km) **P 37** (59.5 km) Large turnout.

J 13.3 (21.4 km) **P 35.8** (57.6 km) Turnout.

J 13.8 (22.2 km) **P 35.3** (56.8 km) Motherlode Lodge; food and lodging.

J 13.9 (22.4 km) **P 35.2** (56.6 km) Large parking area with restrooms. Trailhead for Gold Mint and Arkose Ridge trails.

CAUTION: Westbound, Hatcher Pass Road makes a sharp turn and begins a very steep climb to Hatcher Pass via a series of switchbacks.

J 14.6 (23.5 km) **P 34.5** (55.5 km) Archangel Road (Fern Mine Road). Road crosses private property (do not trespass). Winter trails (snowmobiles prohibited east of Archangel Road). Reed Lakes Trail access.

J 16.4 (26.4 km) **P 32.7** (52.6 km) Parking lot to east. Summer trails up hill. Snowmobile trail to west.

J 17.5 (28.2 km) **P 31.6** (50.8 km) Gold Cord Road provides year-round access to Hatcher Pass Lodge (visible from road) and Independence Mine State Historical Park (1.2 miles/1.9 km). $5 per vehicle daily parking fee charged at park entrance.

Hatcher Pass Lodge. See display ad this section.

The 271-acre **INDEPENDENCE MINE STATE HISTORICAL PARK** includes several buildings and old mining machinery. Park visitor center is housed in what was originally the mine manager's home, built in 1939. The visitor center is open daily from June through Labor Day; weekends the rest of the year. One-hour guided tours were offered weekdays at 1:30 and 3:30 P.M. and weekends and holidays at 1:30, 3:30 and 4:30 P.M. in 1998; fee was $3 adults, $2 seniors; children under 10 years free; minimum of 3 people per tour. Phone the visitor center at (907) 745-2827 or phone Alasstka State Park's Mat-Su office at (907) 745-3975 for current information. Groups of 20 or more call ahead for tours. Office hours and tour times may vary, but visitors are always welcome to explore on their own.

Alaska Pacific Consolidated Mine Co., one of the largest gold producers in the Willow Creek mining district, operated here from 1938 through 1941. The Gold Cord Mine buildings (private property) are visible on the hill above and to the north of Independence Mine.

Snowmobiling is prohibited in the park.

CAUTION: Very steep and bumpy road westbound. Watch for rocks.

J 18.7 (30.1 km) **P 30.4** (48.9 km) Entering Summit Lake State Recreation Site westbound; no ground fires permitted. Watch for parasailers. many launch from a spot known as "Nixon's Nose."

J 19.2 (30.9 km) **P 29.8** (48 km) **Hatcher Pass Summit** (elev. 3,886 feet/1,184m); parking area, hiking trails.

J 19.4 (31.2 km) **P 29.7** (47.8 km) Parking area at Summit Lake, headwaters of Willow Creek. Summit Lake State

Independence Mine State Historical Park. (© Harry M. Walker)

Recreation Site under development.

Westbound, the road descends following Willow Creek from here to the Parks Highway.

J 20.4 (32.8 km) **P 28.6** (46 km) Upper Willow Creek Valley Road to mine (private).

J 23.8 (38.3 km) **P 25.3** (40.7 km) Craigie Creek Trail (very rough) leads to mine sites. Remains of historic Lucky Shot and War Baby mines on hillside are visible on hillside ahead westbound.

J 24.3 (39.1 km) **P 24.8** (39.9 km) Beaver lodges and dams.

J 25.6 (41.2 km) **P 23.5** (37.8 km) View of Beaver Ponds to west; mine site visible to south below road. Road begins descent westbound into Little Willow Creek valley; numerous turnouts.

J 30.3 (48.8 km) **P 18.7** (30.1 km) Leaving Hatcher Pass public-use area westbound.

J 33.1 (53.3 km) **P 16** (25.7 km) Last Chance Coffee House.

J 34.2 (55 km) **P 14.9** (24 km) Little Willow Creek bridge; large parking area.

J 38.1 (61.3 km) **P 11** (17.7 km) Gravel ends, pavement begins, westbound.

J 47.9 (77.1 km) **P 1.2** (1.9 km) **Willow Creek State Recreation Area** Deception Creek Campground; 7 campsites, 15-day limit, $10 nightly fee per vehicle or annual pass, covered picnic tables, water, toilets (wheelchair accessible). ♿▲

J 48 (77.2 km) **P 1.1** (1.8 km) Deception Creek Bridge.

J 49.1 (79 km) **P 0 Junction** with Parks Highway at **Milepost A 71.2.** (Turn to the PARKS HIGHWAY section.)

Return to Milepost A 49.5 Glenn Highway or Milepost A 71.2 Parks Highway

(Continues from page 325)
SUTTON (pop. 340) was established as a railroad siding in about 1918 for the once-flourishing coal industry and is now a small highway community. Sutton has a fire department, general store, post office and gas station. Fossilized shells and leaves can be found in this area 1.7 miles/2.7 km up the Jonesville Road. Inquire locally for directions.

Sutton General Store and Jonesville Cafe. Full line menu, good food, homemade pies, orders to go. We supply all your camping, fishing and cooking needs. Groceries,

snacks, ice cream, ice, general merchandise. Clean restrooms, shower, washers and dryers, phone and propane. Tour buses welcome. Stop by and see us! (907) 746-7461 and (907) 746-7561. (ADVERTISEMENT)

NOTE: Watch for major road construction westbound to Milepost A56 in summer 1999.

A 60.9 (98 km) **T 267.1** (429.8 km) Jonesville Road. Access to **Coyote Lake Recreation Area** (3 miles/4.8 km); Mat-Su Borough day-use area with pavilion, covered picnic tables, toilets, fireplaces, trails and swimming. Also access to Seventeenmile Lake (for recommended access see **Milepost A 57.9**). Drive north 1.7 miles/2.7 km to end of pavement; continue straight ahead for residential area and old Jonesville and Eska coal mines; turn left where pavement ends for Seventeenmile Lake (3.1 miles/5 km via a rough dirt road). 🐟

A 60.8 (97.8 km) **T 267.2** (430 km) **Eska Creek** bridge. Fishing for small Dolly Varden, spring; silver salmon, August or September. 🐟

A 60.7 (97.7 km) **T 267.3** (430.2 km) Paved double-ended turnout to south.

A 60 (96.6 km) **T 268** (431.3 km) *Long winding descent eastbound.*

A 59.5 (95.7 km) **T 268.5** (430.5 km) Tesoro gas station to south with diesel, groceries, snacks, showers and laundry.

Fisher's Hilltop Tesoro. See display ad this section.

A 58.6 (94.3 km) **T 269.4** (433.5 km) Gravel turnout to south. View of Matanuska River.

A 57.9 (93.2 km) **T 270.1** (434.7 km) Access to Palmer Correctional Center. 58 Mile Road north to **Seventeenmile Lake**; small grayling, early spring, use flies or spinners; trout, early spring, use eggs. Undeveloped camping on lakeshore. ◄━

A 57.3 (92.2 km) **T 270.7** (435.6 km) **Timberlings Bed and Breakfast.** A delight among B&Bs. Log house on 150 acres of

wooded hills with panoramic mountain view. Gracious artist hosts, exotic alpacas, friendly dog. Gourmet breakfast, in-room TV, VCR. One guestroom, shared bath. Call ahead: (907) 745-4445. Buz and Alma Blum, P.O. Box 732, Palmer, AK 99645. [ADVERTISEMENT]

A 56.7 (91.2 km) **T 271.3** (436.6 km) Western boundary of Matanuska Valley Moose Range. *NOTE: Watch for major road construction eastbound to **Milepost A 61** in summer 1999*

A 54.6 (87.9 km) **T 273.4** (440 km) Bridge over **Moose Creek**. Fishing for trout and Dolly Varden, summer, use eggs. ━►

A 54 (86.9 km) **T 274** (440.9 km) Truck lane starts westbound.

A 53.6 (86.3 km) **T 274.4** (441.6 km) Truck lane ends westbound.

A 53 (85.3 km) **T 275** (442.6 km) Buffalo Mine Road to north. Access to Wishbone Lake 4-wheel-drive trail.

A 52.3 (84.2 km) **T 275.7** (443.7 km) Soapstone Road.

A 51.2 (82.4 km) **T 276.8** (445.5 km) Fire station.

A 50.9 (81.9 km) **T 277.1** (445.9 km) Farm Loop Road, a 3-mile/4.8-km loop road connecting with Fishhook–Willow Road.

A 50.1 (80.6 km) **T 277.9** (447.2 km) Sharp turn north (watch for signs) for the Musk Ox Farm. Well worth a stop.

Palmer is Alaska's only community that developed primarily from an agricultural economy. (© Rich Reid)

Musk Ox Farm and Gift Shop. The world's only domestic musk-oxen farm. The animals are combed for the precious qiviut, which is then hand-knit by Eskimos in isolated villages, aiding the Arctic economy. During the farm tours in the summer, you can see these shaggy ice age survivors romping in beautiful pastures with Pioneer Peak as a backdrop. Open May to September. Phone (907) 745-4151. P.O. Box 587, Palmer, AK 99645. [ADVERTISEMENT]

A 50 (80.5 km) **T 278** (447.4 km) Matanuska River viewpoint to south is a double-ended turnout with a short pedestrian walkway up to a fenced viewing area.

A 49.5 (79.7 km) **T 278.5** (448.2 km)

Junction with Hatcher Pass (Fishhook–Willow) Road which leads west and north over Hatcher Pass to connect with the Parks Highway at **Milepost A 71.2** north of Willow. A great side trip! See HATCHER PASS ROAD log on page 326.

A 49 (78.9 km) **T 279** (449 km) Entering Palmer, which extends to **Milepost A 41**. Actual driving distance between **Milepost 49** and **42** is 1 mile/1.6 km. For westbound travelers, just beyond here the highway emerges on a hill overlooking the Matanuska Valley, a view of the farms and homes of one of Alaska's agricultural areas, and the business center of Palmer.

A 42.1 (67.8 km) **T 285.9** (460.1 km) West Arctic Avenue. Access to Palmer High School west at this junction. Turn east through Palmer for the **Old Glenn Highway**, a scenic alternate route to Anchorage that rejoins the Glenn Highway at **Milepost A 29.6**. Highlights along the old Glenn Highway include the original Matanuska Colony Farms, campgrounds and reindeer farm.

Turn to OLD GLENN HIGHWAY log on page 333 for log. (Anchorage-bound travelers read log back to front.)

Palmer

A 42 (67.6 km) T 286 (460.3 km) In the Matanuska Valley northeast of Anchorage. The city extends from about **Milepost A 49 to A 41**, an actual driving distance of 2.1 miles/3.4 km. **Population: 4,318. Emergency Services:** Phone 911. **Alaska State Troopers,** phone (907) 745-2131. **City Police,** phone (907) 745-4811. **Fire Department** and **Ambulance,** phone (907) 745-3271. **Valley Hospital,** Valley Hospital, 515 E. Dahlia, phone (907) 745-4813.

Visitor Information: Visitor center in log cabin across the railroad tracks on South Valley Way at East Fireweed Avenue. Pick up a brochure and map of downtown Palmer's historic buildings. Open daily 8 A.M. to 7 P.M. May to Sept. 15; weekdays 9 A.M. to 4 P.M. mid-September to May. Pay phone. Small museum in basement; Alaskan-made gifts may be for sale on main floor. Mailing address: Chamber of Commerce, P.O. Box 45, Palmer, AK 99645. Matanuska Valley Agricultural Showcase adjacent visitor center features flower and vegetable gardens.

Excellent local library, located at 655 S. Valley Way; open Monday through Saturday. Paperback and magazine exchange. Wheelchair accessible.

Elevation: 240 feet/74m. **Climate:** Temperatures range from 4° to 21°F/-16° to -6°C in January and December, with a mean monthly snowfall of 8 to 10 inches. Record low was -40°F/-40°C in January 1975. Temperatures range from 44° to 68°F/7° to 20°C

PALMER ADVERTISERS

City of Palmer	231 W. Evergreen Ave.
Colony Inn	325 Elmwood St.
Fairview Motel & Restaurant	Ph. (907) 745-1505
Farm Country Bed & Breakfast	Ph. (907) 745-1234
Gold Miner's Hotel	Ph. (800) 725-2752
Iditarod House Bed & Breakfast	Ph. (907) 745-4348
Motherlode Lodge	Ph. (907) 746-1464
Mountain View RV Park	Off Old Glenn Hwy.
Musk Ox Farm & Gift Shop	Mile 50.1 Glenn Hwy.
Pioneer Motel & Apt.	Ph. (907) 745-3425
Tara Dells Bed & Breakfast	Ph. (907) 745-0407
Treasures of the Attic	Ph. (907) 745-2588
Valley Hotel	Ph. (907) 745-3330
Wash Day Too	Ph. (907) 746-4141

Motorists stop on the Old Glenn Highway to photograph a bull moose. Watch for moose on the highway between Palmer and Anchorage. Don't get too close to them! (© Mike Jones)

in June and July, with a mean monthly precipitation of 2 inches. Record high was 89°F/32°C in June 1969. Mean annual rainfall is 15.5 inches, with 50.7 inches of snow. **Radio:** Anchorage stations; KMBQ (Wasilla). **Television:** Anchorage channels and cable. **Newspaper:** *The Frontiersman* (twice weekly).

Private Aircraft: Palmer Municipal Airport, 1 nm SE; elev. 232 feet/71m; length 6,000 feet/1,829m and 3,616 feet/1,102m; asphalt; fuel 100LL, Jet. FSS and full services.

Palmer is a commercial center for the Matanuska and Susitna valleys (collectively referred to as the Mat–Su valleys). The town

was established about 1916 as a railway station on the Matanuska branch of the Alaska Railroad.

In 1935, Palmer became the site of one of the most unusual experiments in American history: the Matanuska Valley Colony. The Federal Emergency Relief Administration, one of the many New Deal relief agencies created during Franklin Roosevelt's first year in office, planned an agricultural colony in Alaska to utilize the great agricultural potential in the Matanuska–Susitna valleys, and to get some American farm families—struck by first the dust bowl, then

the Great Depression—off the dole. Social workers picked 203 families, mostly from the northern counties of Michigan, Wisconsin and Minnesota, to join the colony, because it was thought that the many hardy farmers of Scandinavian descent in those 3 states would have a natural advantage over other ethnic groups. The colonists arrived in Palmer in the early summer of 1935, and though the failure rate was high, many of their descendants still live in the Matanuska Valley. Palmer gradually became the unofficial capital of the Matanuska Valley, acting as headquarters for a farmers cooperative marketing organization and as the business and social center for the state's most productive farming region.

Palmer is Alaska's only community that developed primarily from an agricultural economy. (Real estate now takes a close second to agriculture.) The growing season averages 80 to 110 days a year, with long hours of sunshine. Fresh vegetables from

Valley farms are popular with Anchorage residents, many of whom drive out to pick up "Valley peas" and other favorites in season. Local produce is available at roadside stands and is marketed in local stores.

The University of Alaska–Fairbanks has an Agricultural and Forestry Experiment Station Office and a district Cooperative Extension Service Office here. The university also operates its Matanuska Research Farm, located on Trunk Road off the Parks Highway, about a 7-mile/11.3-km drive from Palmer. The university farm conducts research in agronomy, horticulture, soil science and animal science.

The community has a hospital, the Mat–Su College (University of Alaska), a library, banks, the Mat–Su Borough offices, borough school district, and several other state and federal agency offices. Palmer has churches representing most denominations. The United Protestant Church in Palmer, the **Church of a Thousand Logs**, dates from Matanuska Colony days and is one of the oldest churches in Alaska still holding services. It is included in the National Register of Historic Places.

Painted hair and snow cones are favorites with youngsters at the Alaska State Fair. (© Kris Graef, staff)

ACCOMMODATIONS/VISITOR SERVICES

Palmer has all visitor facilities including 3 hotels, 2 motels, bed and breakfasts, gas stations, grocery stores, laundromat, auto repair and parts, and shopping. The Matanuska Valley region has several lake resorts offering boat rentals, golf, fly-in fishing, hunting and horseback riding.

There is a private RV park on Smith Road off the Old Glenn Highway. There are also private campgrounds on the Glenn Highway a few miles west of Palmer. The Mat–Su Borough operates **Matanuska River Park**, located 1.1 miles/1.8 km south of town at Mile 17.5 Old Glenn Highway; 80 campsites for tents or RVs, picnic area, water, dump station (fee charged), firewood for sale, flush toilets, hot showers, camping fee. **Finger Lake State Recreation Site** (see PALMER-WASILLA HIGHWAY log this section), has 69 campsites, 7-day limit, toilets, water, trails, boating and fishing; camping fee $10/night.

Mountain View RV Park offers breathtaking views of the Matanuska mountains. Watch wildlife from your door. Full hookups, hot showers included. New bathrooms and laundromat, dump station. Good Sam Park. Half-day scenic airboat tours on

Knik River. Call (907) 745-5747 for reservations. Mail forwarding. Write P.O. Box 2521, Palmer, AK 99745. From Mile A 42.1 Glenn Highway (Arctic), follow Old Glenn Highway 2.8 miles. Turn east on Smith Road,

drive 0.6 mile, turn right (0.3 mile). We're 3.7 miles from the Glenn Highway. See display ad this section. [ADVERTISEMENT]   &▲

TRANSPORTATION

Air: No scheduled service, but the local airport has a number of charter operators.

Bus: Charter service only.

ATTRACTIONS

Go Swimming: The 80 foot/25m swimming pool is open to the public weekdays (closed weekends)—$4 for adults, showers available. The pool is located at Palmer High School on West Arctic Avenue; phone (907) 745-5091.

Get Acquainted: Stop at the visitor information center, a log building just off the "main drag" (across the railroad tracks at the intersection of East Fireweed Avenue and South Valley Way). The center includes a museum, artifacts, a gift shop and agricultural showcase garden.

Visit the Musk Ox Farm. Located east of Palmer on the Glenn Highway at **Milepost 50.1**, the Musk Ox Farm is the only place in the world where these exotic animals are raised domestically. Hunted to near extinction in Alaska in 1865, the species was reintroduced in the 1930s. The farm is open May to September; admission is charged.

Visit a Reindeer Farm, located 8.1 miles/ 11.5 km south of Palmer via the Old Glenn Highway to Bodenburg Loop Road. This commercial reindeer farm is open daily in summer; admission is charged.

Play Golf in the spectacular Matanuska Valley. The Palmer Golf Course has 18 holes (par 72, USGA rated), rental carts and clubs, driving range, prop shop, practice green and snack bar. Phone (907) 745-4653.

Enjoy Water Sports. Fishing, boating, waterskiing and other water sports are popular in summer at Finger Lake west of Palmer. Kepler–Bradley Lakes State Recreation Area on Matanuska Lake has canoe rentals; turn off the Glenn Highway at **Milepost A 36.4**.

Special events include **Colony Days**

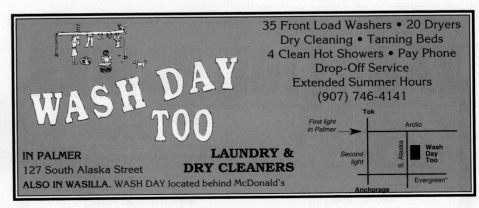
Alaska State Fair takes place Aug. 27–Sept. 6, 1999.

Palmer-Wasilla Highway Log

This 10.1 mile/16.3 km road connects the Glenn and Parks highways (Alaska Routes 1 and 3). It provides access to a number of Wasilla and Palmer businesses.

Distance from Palmer (P) is followed by distance from Wasilla (W).

P 0 W 10.1 (16.3 km) **Junction** with Glenn Highway at **Milepost A 41.8** in Palmer; Carr's Mall (24-hour supermarket) and fast-food outlet.

P 0.4 (0.6 km) **W 9.7** (15.6 km) Alaska Tsunami Warning Center; phone (907) 745-4212.

P 1.3 (2.1 km) **W 8.8** (14.2 km) Country store.

P 1.5 (2.4 km) **W 8.6** (13.8 km) Equestrian Acres subdivision.

P 1.9 (3.1 km) **W 8.2** (13.2 km) Loma Prieta Drive. Access to **Crevasse–Moraine Trail**; 0.7 mile/1.1 km south to trailhead parking. This loop trail system is used for cross-country skiing in winter and hiking, mountain biking and horseback riding in summer.

P 2.2 (3.5 km) **W 7.9** (12.7 km) Eagle View Car Wash. Animal Control to south.

P 2.9 (4.7 km) **W 7.2** (11.6 km) Moffit Road; access to 49th Street, Colony middle school, high school and refuse dump.

P 3.4 (5.5 km) **W 6.7** (10.8 km) Business Park; pizza.

P 4 (6.4 km) **W 6.1** (9.8 km) Tesoro gas station and grocery at **junction** with Trunk Road. Turn north for access to Bogard Road and **Finger Lake State Recreation Site**; go north on Trunk Road

1 mile/1.6 km to Bogard Road; turn west and drive 0.8 mile/1.3 km to park entrance; drive in 0.3 mile/0.5 km on gravel road. A scenic spot with 41 campsites, wheelchair-accessible toilets, picnic tables, water, hiking trails and boat launch, $10 camping fee, 7-day limit. Use the life jackets provided! Finger Lake is on the **7-Mile Canoe Trail**. Public access to the canoe trail is also from Wasilla Lake and Cottonwood Lake.

P 6.6 (10.6 km) **W 3.5** (5.6 km) **Cache Camper.** See display ad this section.

P 6.9 (11.1 km) **W 3.2** (5.1 km) Brentwood Plaza.

P 7.1 (11.4 km) **W 3** (4.8 km) Hatcher Business Park.

P 7.2 (11.6 km) **W 2.9** (4.7 km) Bed and breakfast.

Alaskan Agate Inn. See display ad this section.

P 8.2 (13.2 km) **W 1.9** (3.1 km) Fire station and gas station at **junction** with Seward Meridian Road, which connects to Parks Highway at **Milepost A 39.4.**

P 8.5 (13.7 km) **W 1.6** (2.6 km) Cottle Loop; Volunteer Park day-use area; bowling alley.

P 9 (14.5 km) **@ 1.1** (1.8 km) Country Lakes Bed and Breakfast.

P 9.4 (15.1 km) **W 0.7** (1.1 km) Cottonwood Creek; fish viewing platform; spawning salmon.

P 10.1 (16.3 km) **W 0 Junction** with Parks Highway at **Milepost A 41.1.** Access to drugstore, gas stations, auto body shops and other businesses.

**Return to Milepost
A 41.8 Glenn Highway or
A 41.1 Parks Highway**

(June 18-20, 1999), the **Palmer Pride Picnic** (July 23, 1999) and the **Alaska State Fair** (Aug. 27–Sept. 6, 1999). The 11-day state

fair, ending on Labor Day, has agricultural exhibits from farms throughout Alaska. There are also food booths, games, pony rides and midway rides. This is a very popular event, and fairgoers from Anchorage can tie up traffic. But it's worth the drive just to see the huge vegetables. Phone (907) 745-4827.

Visit Scenic Hatcher Pass: A 6- to 8-hour drive from **Milepost A 49.5** near Palmer that climbs through the beautiful Hatcher Pass Recreation Area and connects with the Parks Highway at **Milepost A 71.2.** Access to Independence Mine State Historical Park. See HATCHER PASS ROAD this section.

See the Matanuska Glacier: Drive 50 miles/80 km east on the Glenn Highway from Palmer to visit this spectacular 27-mile/43.5-km-long glacier, one of the few you can drive to and explore on foot. Access to the foot of the glacier is through a private campground at **Milepost A 102**; admission charged. If you're not interested in getting close, there are several vantage points along the highway and from trails at Matanuska Glacier Campground, **Milepost A 101.**

Glenn Highway Log
(continued)

A 41.8 (67.3 km) **T 286.2** (460.6 km) West Evergreen Avenue access to downtown Palmer. Gas station, fast food and Carrs Pioneer Square shopping mall (24-hour supermarket) north side of highway. A bronze sculpture by Jacques and Mary Regat dedicated to the Matanuska Valley pioneers is located at the mall.

Junction with Palmer–Wasilla Highway which leads northwest 10 miles/16 km to the Parks Highway at Wasilla. See the PALMER–WASILLA HIGHWAY LOG this section.

A 41.6 (66.9 km) **T 286.4** (460.9 km) Gas station and fast-food south side of highway.

A 41.2 (66.3 km) **T 286.8** (461.5 km) First access road to Palmer business district for eastbound travelers.

A 40.5 (65.2 km) **T 287.5** (462.7 km) Fairview Motel & Restaurant.

A 40.2 (64.7 km) **T 287.8** (463.2 km) Main entrance to fairgrounds (site of Alaska State Fair) and Herman Field (home of the Mat–Su Miners baseball team). Alaska State Fair will be held Aug. 27–Sept. 6, 1999 (heavy traffic during those dates; drive carefully!).

A 39.2 (63.1 km) **T 288.8** (464.8 km) Outer Springer Loop. Gift shop. Short, steep trail to **Meiers Lake**; grayling fishing.

A 37.4 (60.2 km) **T 290.6** (467.7 km) Kepler Drive; access to private campground and lake.

A 37.2 (59.9 km) **T 290.8** (468 km) **Echo**

Old Glenn Highway (Palmer Alternate) Log

This 18.6-mile/29.9-km paved road is a scenic alternate route between Palmer and Anchorage, exiting the Glenn Highway at **Milepost A 29.6** and rejoining the Glenn Highway at **Milepost A 42.1**. The Old Glenn Highway goes through the heart of the original Matanuska Colony agricultural lands.

Distance from south junction with the Glenn Highway (J) is followed by distance from Palmer (P).

J 0 P 18.6 (29.9 km) Exit from Glenn Highway at Milepost A 29.6.

J 4 (6.4 km) **P 14.6** (23.5 km) Eklutna Power Plant (Alaska Power Administration).

J 6 (9.6 km) **P 12.6** (20.3 km) Goat Creek Bridge.

J 6.6 (10.6 km) **P 12** (19.3 km) Alaska Raceway Park turnoff.

J 7.2 (11.6 km) **P 11.4** (18.3 km) View of Bodenburg Butte across Knik River.

J 8.7 (14 km) **P 9.9** (15.9 km) **Junction** with Knik River Road, a hard-packed dirt and gravel road that dead ends 11.2 miles/18 km east of here. Knik River Road is a mostly flat road that is bordered by private property (do not trespass). The only public access to the Knik River is at Mile 1.4. Of interest: Pioneer Falls (a waterfall) at Mile 1.2; Pioneer Ridge-Knik River trailhead at Mile 3.8; and a view of Knik Glacier at about Mile 7.

J 8.8 (14.2 km) **P 9.8** (15.8 km) Crossing Knik River bridge; pedestrian bridge adjacent highway bridge. Access to river at east end of bridge.

J 10 (16 km) **P 8.6** (13.8 km) Pioneer Peak dominates the skyline southbound.

J 11.5 (18.5 km) **P 7.1** (11.4 km) Gas station at **junction** of Bodenburg Loop Road and Plumley Road.

The 5.8-mile/9.3-km Bodenburg Butte Road rejoins the Old Glenn Highway opposite Dack Acres Road (**Milepost J 12.5**). From this junction it is ;0.6 mile to **Bodenburg Butte** trailhead and 0.7 mile to reindeer farm (visitors welcome, fee charged) and trail rides. The Bodenburg Butte area has original Matanuska Colony farms.

Reindeer Farm. Commercial reindeer farm and zoological park on Bodenburg Butte Loop Road 0.8 mile off Old Glenn Highway (turn at **Mile J 11.5** at the flashing light). View tame reindeer and famous Pioneer Peak. Hand feed reindeer, moose, black-tailed deer, elk. Guided horseback trail rides. Bring camera. Hours

10 A.M.–6 P.M. daily. Families with children welcome. Large parties please phone ahead. Fee charged. (907) 745-4000, e-mail: reindeer@corecom.net, Internet

Original homestead on Bodenburg Loop Road. (© Barbara Willard)

site: www.corecom.net/~reindeer/tours.
[ADVERTISEMENT]   MP

J 11.7 (18.8 km) **P 6.9** (11.1 km) **Butte** (pop. 2,654); fire and ambulance service station #21; emergency phone 911. Fire permits May 1 to Sept. 30. Area map.

J 12 (19.3 km) **P 6.6** (10.6 km) Store and post office. Marilyn Road.

J 12.5 (20.1 km) **P 6.1** (9.8 km) **Junction** with Dack Acres Road, north end of Bodenburg Butte Loop Road (see **Milepost J 11.5**).

J 14.6 (23.5 km) **P 4** (6.4 km) Maud Road. Access to **Mud Lake** (4 miles/6.4 km); fishing for Dolly Varden. ◄

J 15.5 (25 km) **P 3.1** (5 km) **Junction** with Smith Road. Access to private campground (0.8 mile/1.3 km). Turn east on Smith Road and drive 1.5 miles/2.4 km for Matanuska Peak trailhead.

Mountain View RV Park. See display ad this section. ▲

J 16.1 (25.9 km) **P 2.5** (4 km) Clark–Wolverine Road; access to Lazy Mountain Recreation Area hiking trails. Drive in 0.7 mile/1.1 km; turn right on Huntley Road at T; drive 1 mile/1.6 km on gravel road and take right fork to recreation area and overlook. Picnic tables, toilets, berry picking.

J 16.7 (26.9 km) **P 1.9** (3.1 km) paved loop road down to Matanuska River photo viewpoint.

J 17 (27.4 km) **P 1.6** (2.5 km) Matanuska River bridge. Photo viewpoint to east on old alignment; access to pedestrian bridge.

J 17.5 (28.2 km) **P 1.1** (1.8 km) Turnoff for **Matanuska River Park** (Mat-Su Borough Parks & Recreation) camping and day-use areas; 80 level tent/RV sites with picnic tables on gravel loop road. Day-use area has playground and picnic pavilions. Facilities include some pull-through sites, water, fireplaces, dump station, flush toilets, hot showers, softball fields and hiking trails. Camping, shower and dump station fees charged. Phone (907) 745-9631 for more information. ▲

J 17.7 (28.5 km) **P 0.9** (1.4 km) Palmer municipal airport. Pioneer cemetery.

J 18.6 (29.9 km) **P 0** Junction of Old Glenn Highway (West Arctic Avenue) at Palmer, **Milepost A 42.1** Glenn Highway.

Return to Milepost A 42.1 or A 29.6 Glenn Highway

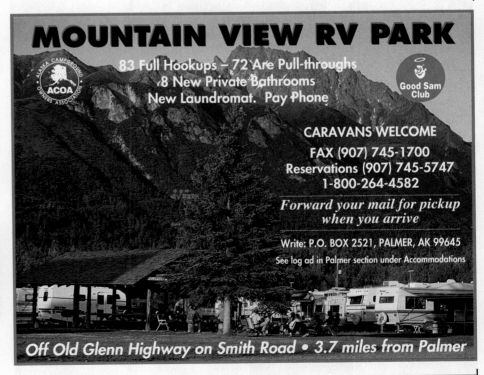

Lake turnout; parking and trail to lake. Fishing for landlocked salmon and rainbow. ◄

A 37 (59.5 km) T 291 (468.3 km) Echo Lake Road.

A 36.4 (58.6 km) T 291.6 (469.3 km) **Kepler–Bradley Lakes State Recreation Area** to north on Matanuska Lake; day-use area with water, toilets, parking, picnic tables, canoe rentals, hiking trails and fishing. ADF&G stocks lakes with rainbow trout, grayling and silver salmon. Wheelchair-accessible trail to lake. The lakes are Kepler, Bradley, Matanuska, Canoe, Irene, Long, Claire and Victor. &⚓

A 36.2 (58.3 km) T 291.8 (469.6 km) **The Homestead RV Park.** Beautiful, wooded setting overlooking the scenic Matanuska

Valley. Good Sam, AAA, 64 sites, pull-throughs to 70 feet, tent sites. Very clean restrooms and showers. Electric and water hookups; dump station; also on-site portable dumping. Laundry. Picnic tables, pay phone. Enclosed pavilion and Matanuska Amphitheatre, home of the musical narrative "Cream Puff Pioneers." Area tours, evening entertainment. Square dancing Thursday nights. Walking and jogging trails, trout fishing nearby. Handicap access. Commuting distance to Anchorage. Caravans welcome. Phone (907) 745-6005. Toll free in Alaska (800) 478-3570. See display ad this section. [ADVERTISEMENT]   &▲

A 35.3 (56.8 km) T 292.7 (471.1 km) Traffic signal at busy junction with Parks

Highway.

Junction of the Glenn Highway (Alaska Route 1) with the Parks Highway (Alaska Route 3) to Denali Park and Fairbanks. See the PARKS HIGHWAY section for log.

A 34.9 (56.2 km) T 293.1 (471.7 km) Highway crosses the Alaska Railroad tracks.

A 34 (54.7 km) T 294 (473.1 km) Paved double-ended turnout west side of highway. Rabbit Slough, a tributary of the Matanuska River.

A 32.4 (52.1 km) T 295.6 (475.7 km) **Palmer Hay Flats State Game Refuge.** According to the ADF&G, this is the most heavily utilized waterfowl hunting area in Alaska. Access to the refuge is via Fairview Loop Road off the Parks Highway. Moose winter in this area, and the cows and calves may be seen early in the morning and in the evening as late as early July.

CAUTION: Watch for moose.

A 31.5 (50.7 km) T 296.5 (477.2 km) Bridge over the Matanuska River, which is fed by the Matanuska Glacier.

A 30.8 (49.6 km) T 297.5 (478.8 km) There are 2 Knik River bridges. Exits to parking areas below highway between the bridges. The **Knik River** comes down from the Knik Glacier to the east and splits into several branches as it approaches Knik Arm. Knik Arm is a 3-mile-wide estuary that extends 40 miles southeast to Cook Inlet.

Game Management Unit 14C boundary. Also boundary of Matanuska–Susitna Borough.

A 29.6 (47.6 km) T 298.4 (480.2 km) Exit to the Old Glenn Highway (Palmer Alternate).

Junction with Old Glenn Highway. See OLD GLENN HIGHWAY log on page 333.

A 27.3 (43.9 km) T 300.7 (483.9 km) The highway crosses a swampy area known locally as Eklutna Flats. These flats are a protected wildflower area (picking flowers is strictly prohibited). Look for wild iris, shooting star, chocolate lily and wild rose in early June.

A 26.8 (43.1 km) T 301.2 (484.7 km) Highway crosses Alaska Railroad via overpass.

A 26.3 (42.3 km) T 301.7 (485.5 km) Eklutna overpass, exits both sides of highway. Access to Eklutna Road (description follows), the village of Eklutna and also access to Thunderbird Falls (see **Milepost A 25.3**) for Anchorage-bound travelers. West of the highway is the Indian village of **EKLUTNA** (pop. 25), site of Eklutna Historical Park, which preserves the heritage and traditions of the Athabascan Alaska Natives. Attractions include the Eklutna Heritage Museum, the historic St. Nicholas Russian Orthodox Church and a hand-built Siberian prayer chapel. Admission fee charged. Open daily mid-May to mid-September. The bright little grave houses or spirit houses in the cemetery are painted in the family's traditional colors.

Eklutna Historical Park. See display ad this section.

Eklutna Road leads east 10 miles/16.1 km to Eklutna Lake Recreation Area in Chugach State Park. General store at Mile 9. The recreation area has a campground, picnic area and hiking trails. The campground has 50

Guided hikes and nature programs are presented throughout the summer at Eagle River Nature Center. (© Mike Jones)

sites, drinking water, pit toilets and a 15-day limit. Camping fee $10/night or annual pass. The 32-unit picnic area is located at the trailhead parking lot, which will accommodate 80 cars and has a boat launch for hand-carried boats. Three trails branch off the trailhead: Twin Peaks, Lakeside and Bold Ridge. The Lakeside trail skirts Eklutna Lake and gives access to Eklutna Glacier (12.7 miles/20.4 km). **Eklutna Lake** is the largest lake in Chugach State Park, measuring approximately 7 miles long by a mile wide. Fed by Eklutna Glacier, it offers fair fishing for Dolly Varden. CAUTION: Afternoon winds can make the lake dangerous for boaters. Interpretive displays on wildlife and a telescope for viewing Dall sheep, eagles and other wildlife are located at the trailhead.

Rochelle's Ice Cream Stop and Cheely's General Store. Best milkshakes, old fashioned banana splits, espresso, fishing licenses, ice, groceries, picnic supplies, Eklutna Lake posters, and mountain bikes for rent. Cabins for rent—located within Chugach State Park wildlife viewing area. Shower and laundry available. Phone (907) 688-6201, fax (907) 688-6150. In Alaska (800) 764-6201. [ADVERTISEMENT]

A 25.7 (41.3 km) T 302.3 (486.5 km) Highway crosses Eklutna River.

A 25.3 (40.7 km) T 302.7 (487.1 km) Thunderbird Falls exit (northbound traffic only) and northbound access to Eklutna Road (see **Milepost A 26.3** for description). Drive about 0.3 mile/0.5 km to parking area. **Thunderbird Falls** is about 1 mile/1.6 km from the highway. The scenic trail to the falls winds through private property on a 25-foot right-of-way and follows a hillside down to Thunderbird Creek. The falls are just upstream. CAUTION: Do not climb the steep cliffs overhanging the falls!

A 24.5 (39.4 km) T 303.5 (488.4 km) Southbound exit to Edmonds Lake residential area and Mirror Lake picnic wayside. The shallow 73-acre **Mirror Lake** is located at the foot of Mount Eklutna; rainbow.

A 23.6 (38 km) T 304.4 (489.9 km) Access to Mirror Lake picnic wayside for northbound traffic only.

A 23 (37 km) T 305 (490.8 km) North Peters Creek overpass, exits both sides of highway.

A 21.5 (34.6 km) T 306.5 (493.3 km) South Peters Creek underpass, exits both sides of highway. Access to Peters Creek and portion of the Old Glenn Highway, which parallels the newer highway south to Eagle River and provides access to a number of local services. **PETERS CREEK** services include gas stations, grocery, car wash, body repair shop and restaurant.

Peters Creek Bed & Breakfast. Located on the north shore of Peters Creek only 0.8 mile from exit. Wheelchair accessible; open year-round. Rooms have private baths, cable TV, VCR, refrigerator; full Alaskan breakfast. Lovely new home, wooded setting, smoke-free environment, major credit cards accepted. Phone (888) 688-3465, (907) 688-3465, fax (907) 688-3466. [ADVERTISEMENT]

Peters Creek "Petite" RV Park. See display ad this section.

Peters Creek Trading Post. See display ad this section.

A 21.2 (34.1 km) T 306.8 (493.7 km) Peters Creek bridge.

A 20.9 (33.6 km) T 306.9 (493.9 km) North Birchwood Loop Road underpass, exits both sides of highway; turn east for community of **CHUGIAK** and for portion of Old Glenn Highway, which leads south to Eagle River and north to Peters Creek. There are many services and attractions in the Peters Creek–Chugiak–Eagle River area.

A 20.4 (32.8 km) T 307.6 (495 km) Exit for North Birchwood Loop Road, Chugiak post office, senior center and services.

A 17.2 (27.7 km) T 310.8 (500.2 km) South Birchwood Loop Road underpass, exits both sides of highway. Access to St. John Orthodox Cathedral, sled dog demonstrations, Chugiak High School and Old Glenn Highway.

Mush A Dog Team/Gold Rush Park. Ride Gold Tram pulled by Iditarod huskies. Outdoor pioneer museum. Gold panning on creek. Food, gift shop. Open daily (closed Sundays). Turn at South Birchwood exit. Drive west past the school 3/4 mile. Sign on left. Phone (907) 688-1391. [ADVERTISEMENT]

Saint John Orthodox Cathedral. Take a peaceful break from your travels. Visit this unique, geodesic-dome cathedral with birch ceiling and beautiful icons. Discover how this church connects to the early church and

how Christianity came to Alaska 200 years ago. Bookstore. Monastery Drive off Old Glenn. (907) 696-2002. [ADVERTISEMENT]

A 15.3 (24.6 km) T 312.7 (503.2 km) Exits for Fire Lake residential area, Old Glenn Highway and Eagle River.

A 13.4 (21.6 km) T 314.6 (506.3 km) Eagle River overpass. Exit east for community of Eagle River (all visitor services), the North Anchorage Visitor Information Center and Eagle River Road to Chugach State Park Eagle River Nature Center (a highly recommended stop); descriptions follow.

Eagle River

A 13.4 (21.6 km) T 314.6 (506.3 km) **Population:** Area 18,040. **Emergency Services:** Clinic, phone (907) 694-2807. **Visitor Information:** The North Anchorage Visitor Information Center is located in the Parkgate Building, along with the Southcentral Alaska Museum of Natural History, at 11723 Old Glenn Highway. Stop by for self-service information on Anchorage events, parking maps and brochures (closed Sundays). For information on Eagle River/Chugiak, contact the Chugiak–Eagle River Chamber of Commerce, P.O. Box 770353, Eagle River, AK 99577;

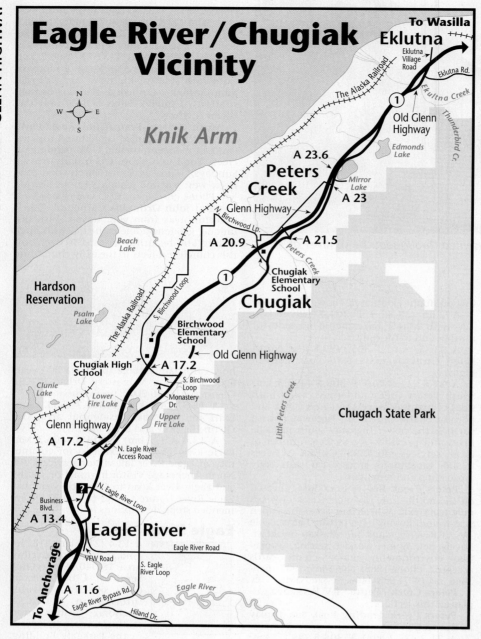

Eagle River/Chugiak Vicinity

To Wasilla
Eklutna

Knik Arm

Eklutna Village Road
Eklutna Rd.
The Alaska Railroad
Ekultna Creek
Thunderbird Cr.

Old Glenn Highway
A 23.6
Peters Creek
Edmonds Lake
A 23
Mirror Lake

Glenn Highway
N. Birchwood Lp.
A 20.9
A 21.5
Peters Creek

Beach Lake

Chugiak Elementary School

Hardson Reservation

Psalm Lake

The Alaska Railroad
S. Birchwood Loop

Chugiak

Little Peters Creek

Birchwood Elementary School
Old Glenn Highway

Chugiak High School
A 17.2

Clunie Lake

Lower Fire Lake
S. Birchwood Loop
Monastery Dr.
Upper Fire Lake

Chugach State Park

Glenn Highway
A 17.2
N. Eagle River Access Road

Business Blvd.
A 13.4

N. Eagle River Loop

Eagle River
Eagle River Road
VFW Road
S. Eagle River Loop
Eagle River

A 11.6
Eagle River Bypass Rd.
Hiland Dr.

To Anchorage

---

has churches, public schools, a library, movie theaters, bowling alley and recreation center.

Special events include fireworks and a parade (July 3–4) and the **Bear Paw Festival** and parade (July 8–11, 1999). Attractions in Eagle River include artist **Jon Van Zyle's** studio and the **Southcentral Alaska Museum of Natural History**. The museum features 20 exhibits on Cook Inlet, dioramas of local ecosystems, and a duck-billed dinosaur skeleton. Located across from McDonald's at the corner of Easy Street and Old Glenn Highway; phone (907) 694-0819 for hours. Boondock Sporting Goods store on Eagle River Loop Road has an antique gun display and also rents fishing tackle.

From downtown Eagle River, follow scenic Eagle River Road (paved) 12.7 miles/20.4 km to reach the Chugach State Park's **Eagle River Nature Center**. Beautiful views of the Chugach Mountains from the center's veranda; telescopes are set up for viewing Dall sheep and other wildlife. The center has a pay phone and restrooms, and is the trailhead for the Old Iditarod–Crow Pass trail. There are also short hiking trails from the center and guided hikes and naturalist programs. The center is staffed, but hours vary in summer and winter. Phone (907) 694-2108 for current information.

Kayaks, rafts and canoes can put in at Mile 7.5 Eagle River Road at the **North Fork Eagle River** access/day-use area with paved parking, toilets, fishing for rainbow trout, Dolly Varden and a limited king salmon fishery, along with cross-country skiing and snow machining in winter. The Eagle River offers class II, III and IV float trips. Check with rangers at Chugach State Park for information on river conditions.

Three Olde Ladies B&B. This cozy home, located 11 miles north of Anchorage off the Glenn Highway, offers a beautifully decorated suite with private bath, featherbed, sitting room with TV/VCR and a private hot tub room. Hearty continental breakfast delivered to your suite each morning. Open year-round. Reasonable rates. Military discount. All major credit cards accepted.

---

phone (907) 694-4702. You can also visit the Chamber office at 11401 Old Glenn Highway, #105, in the Eagle River Shopping Center.

The Chugiak–Eagle River area was homesteaded after WWII when the new Glenn Highway opened this rural area northeast of Anchorage. Today, the Eagle River community offers a full range of businesses, most located near or on Business Boulevard and the Old Glenn Highway east off the Glenn Highway. There are motels, restaurants, supermarkets, laundromat, post office, gas stations and shopping center. Eagle River

Hosts, military retired and antique shop owners, Alyce and Jon Cavanaugh. 18720 Danny Drive, Eagle, River, AK 99577. Phone (907) 696-7951. E-mail: threeoldeladies@servom.com. [ADVERTISEMENT]

Eagle River Car Wash and Duck Pond. Facilities available for washing cars, campers, trucks, boats and travel homes. Vacuums available. A duck pond on the premises is open to the public and features cedar viewing decks for observing some of the natural wild Alaskan waterfowl in their natural habitat. Mile 15.5 Old Glenn Highway. Turn off at North Eagle River access for car wash. See display ad this section. [ADVERTISEMENT]

Glenn Highway Log
(continued)

A 12.8 (20.6 km) **T 315.2** (507.3 km) Eagle River Bridge.

A 11.6 (18.7 km) **T 316.4** (509.2 km) Hiland Drive exit. Access to Alaska State Forest Nursery and Eagle River Campground in Chugach State Park. **Eagle River Campground**, 1.4 miles/2.3 km from the highway, has 58 campsites, walk-in tent camping, a 4-day camping limit, picnic shelter (may be reserved in advance), dump station, pay phones, flush toilets and drinking water. Camping fee $15/night. Day-use fee $3. Canoe/kayak staging area. This is one of the most popular campgrounds in the state. Phone the state park office at (907) 345-5014 for information. ▲

A 10.6 (17.1 km) **T 317.4** (510.8 km) Truck weigh stations on both sides of highway. Pay phones.

The last 9 miles/14.5 km of the Glenn Highway has been designated the Veterans' Memorial Parkway.

A 7.5 (12.1 km) **T 320.5** (515.8 km) Southbound exit to **FORT RICHARDSON** and Arctic Valley road.

CAUTION: Watch for moose.

A 6.1 (9.8 km) **T 321.9** (518 km) Northbound exit to Fort Richardson and Arctic Valley Road. Road to **Arctic Valley Ski Area** is steep and winding but offers spectacular views of Anchorage and Cook Inlet. It is

approximately 7.5 miles/12 km to the ski area. Alpine wildflowers in spring, good berry picking in late summer. Not recommended for large vehicles.

A 6 (9.7 km) **T 322** (518.2 km) Ship Creek.

A 4.4 (7.1 km) **T 323.6** (520.8 km) Muldoon Road overpass. Exit north for new **Alaska Native Heritage Center**, a 26-acre site featuring 5 traditional village sites along a walking path around a 2-acre lake. Cultural presentations, food and crafts in the dramatic Welcoming House. Admission fee charged. U.S. Air Force Hospital and Bartlett High School also to the north.

Exit south to connect with Seward Highway via Muldoon and Tudor roads bypass. Access to **Centennial Park** municipal campground. To reach the campground, go south on Muldoon to first left (Boundary); go about 100 yards then make a second left; continue about quarter-mile to campground entrance. ▲

There is a bicycle trail from Muldoon Road to Mirror Lake, **Milepost A 23.6**.

A 3 (4.8 km) **T 325** (523 km) Boniface Parkway; access to businesses. Russian Jack Springs city campground is located south of the Glenn Highway on Boniface Parkway just north of DeBarr. Turn north for Elmendorf AFB.

A 1.8 (2.9 km) **T 326.2** (525 km) Bragaw Street.

A 0.7 (1.1 km) **T 327.3** (526.7 km) Reeve Boulevard; access to **ELMENDORF AFB**.

A 0.3 (0.5 km) **T 327.7** (527.4 km) Concrete Street. Access to Elmendorf AFB.

A 0 T 328 (527.9 km) The Glenn Highway ends at Medfra Street. Continue straight ahead on 5th Avenue (one way westbound) to downtown Anchorage. Turn south at Gambell Street (one way southbound) for the Seward Highway and Kenai Peninsula (see SEWARD HIGHWAY section). See ANCHORAGE section following for description of city.

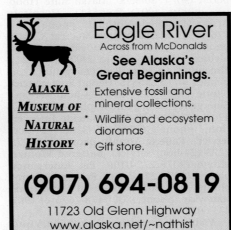

ANCHORAGE

(See maps, pages 339 and 344)

Enhanced view of a favorite landmark for Anchorage residents, "Sleeping Lady" (Mount Susitna), from Hillside area of Anchorage. *(© Barbara Willard)*

Anchorage, Alaska's largest city, is in the heart of the state's southcentral gulf coast. Located on the upper shores of Cook Inlet, at 61° north latitude and 150° west longitude, the Anchorage bowl is on a low-lying alluvial plain bordered by mountains, water and dense forests for spruce, birch and aspen. Cook Inlet's Turnagain Arm and Knik Arm define the broad peninsula that is the city's home, and the rugged Chugach Mountains form a striking backdrop. Of Alaska's 621,400 citizens, nearly half live in Anchorage and the Matanuska region. Anchorage is situated 358 miles/576 km south of Fairbanks via the Parks Highway; 304 miles/489 km from Valdez, southern terminus of the trans-Alaska pipeline, via the Glenn and Richardson highways; 2,459 driving miles/3,957 km via the West Access Route, Alaska Highway and Glenn Highway/Tok Cutoff; 1,644 nautical miles/2,646 km, and 3 hours flying time from Seattle. Prior to the opening of Russia's Far East to air traffic and refueling, Anchorage was considered the "Air Crossroads of the World," and today is still the major air logistics center and cargo carrier for Asia, Europe and North America. In terms of nonstop air mileages, Anchorage is the following distance from each of these cities: Amsterdam, 4,475/7,202 km; Chicago, 2,839/4,569 km; Copenhagen, 4,313/6,941

km; Hamburg, 4,430/7,129 km; Honolulu, 2,780/4,474 km; London, 4,487/7,221 km; Paris, 4,683/7,536 km; San Francisco, 2,015/3,243 km; Seattle, 1,445/2,325 km; Tokyo, 3,460/5,568 km.

Population: Anchorage Municipality, 258,782. **Emergency Services: Police, Fire Department, Ambulance** and **Search & Rescue,** phone 911, CB Channel 9. **Police,** phone (907) 786-8500. **Alaska State Troopers,** phone (907) 269-5511. **Hospitals:** Alaska Regional Hospital, phone (907) 276-1131; Alaska Native Medical Center, phone (907) 563-2662; Providence, Alaska Medical Center, phone (907) 562-2211; Elmendorf Air Force Base emergency room, phone (907) 552-5555. **Dental Emergencies,** phone (907) 279-9144 (24-hour service). **Emergency Management,** phone (907) 267-4904 or 1-800-478-8999. **Suicide Intervention,** phone (907) 563-3200 (24-hour service). **Rape & Assault,** phone (907) 276-7273 (24-hour service). **Battered Women,** phone (907) 272-0100. **Pet Emergency,** phone (907) 274-5636. **Poison Control,** phone (907) 261-3193. **Road Conditions,** statewide, phone (800) 478-7675 or (907) 273-6037.

Visitor Information: Log Cabin Visitor Information Center, operated by the Anchorage Convention and Visitors Bureau, is at 4th Avenue and F Street; open daily, year-round. Hours are 7:30 A.M. to 7 P.M. June through August; 8 A.M. to 6 P.M. in May and September; and 9 A.M. to 4 P.M. the remainder

of the year. The cabin offers a wide assortment of free brochures and maps. Write 524 W. 4th Ave., Anchorage 99501; phone (907) 274-3531; Internet, www.alaska.net/~acvb; e-mail at acvb@alaska.net. The bureau also operates a year-round visitor information phone with a recorded message of the day's special events and attractions, including films, plays, sports events and gallery openings, and it produces several publications including 2 visitor guides, a restaurant directory, a fall/winter discount book and a monthly calendar of events; phone (907) 276-3200. Additional visitor information centers are open daily at Anchorage International Airport, one on the lower level for passengers arriving on domestic flights; another in the customs-secured area of the international concourse; and a third in the lobby of the international terminal. The North Anchorage Visitor Information Center is located in the Parkgate Building, just off the Glenn Highway at 11723 Old Glenn Highway in Eagle River. The Anchorage Convention and Visitors Bureau offers information on community events, phone (907) 276-4118.

The Alaska Public Lands Information Center, 605 W. 4th, in the historic Old Federal Building, has extensive displays and information on outdoor recreation lands in Alaska; phone (907) 271-2737. (See detailed description under Attractions, this section.)

Elevation: 38 to 120 feet/16 to 37m. **Climate:** Anchorage has a climate resembling that of the Rocky Mountains area, tempered by proximity to the Pacific Ocean. Shielded from excess ocean moisture by the Kenai Mountains to the south, the city has an annual average of only 15.9 inches of precipitation. Winter snowfall averages about 70 inches per year, with snow on the ground typically from October to April. Anchorage is in a transition zone between the moderating influence of the Pacific and the extreme temperatures found in interior Alaska. The average temperature in January (coldest month) is 15°F/ -9°C; in July (warmest month), 58°F/14°C. A record 40 days of 70°F/21°C temperatures or higher was set in 1936, according to the National Weather Service. The record high was 85°F/29°C in June of 1969. The record low was -34°F/-37°C in January 1975. The growing season of 100 to 120 days typically extends from late May to early September. Anchorage has a daily maximum of 19 hours, 21 minutes of daylight in summer, and 5 hours, 28 minutes in winter. Prevailing wind direction is north.

Radio: AM stations: KTZN 550 (Sports Radio); KHAR 590 (Easy Listening); KENI 650 (News, Talk, Sports); KBYR 700 (News, Talk, Sports); KFQD 750 (News, Talk); KAXX 1020 (Sports Radio); KASH 1080 (Business/financial news, talk, BBC); FM stations: KRUA 88.1 (University of Alaska station); KATB

Anchorage

···· Major Bike Trails

Knik Arm

Turnagain Arm

Elmendorf Air Force Base

Loop Road

To **Fort Richardson and Palmer**

Alaska Native Heritage Center

Small-Boat Harbor

Ocean Dock Rd.

Hollywood Dr.

Post Road

Whitney Rd.

Oil Well Rd.

Centennial Park

Ship Creek

Glenn Highway

DOWNTOWN (see detailed map)

Resolution Park

Elderberry Park

Delaney Park Strip

Coastal Trail

Earthquake Park

Forest Park Dr.

Northern Lights Blvd.

Dempsey-Anderson Ice Arena

Westchester Lagoon

Hill Crest Dr.

Aurora Village

Northern Lights Center

Commercial Dr.

Peterkin Ave.

N. Price

N. Park

Pine St.

N. Pine

Bragaw St.

Klevin

S. Pine

Kevin

E. 2nd

E. 4th

E. 6th

E. 6th

Russian Jack Springs Park

DeBarr Road

Turpin St.

Oklahoma

Boundary Ave.

Northway Mall

Merrill Field

Alaska Regional Hospital

1st

3rd

5th

E. 9th

G

E

C

A

Cordova

Gambell

Medfra

E. 15th

Mulcahy Ball Park

Park for all People

Valley of the Moon Park

Chester Creek Greenbelt

Municipal Greenhouse

Golf Course

Cheney Lake

Chester Creek

Fairbanks

Goose Lake

Northern Lights Blvd.

Main Post Office

Postmark Dr.

Aircraft Drive

Wendy's Way

Lake Hood Airstrip

Lake Hood

Wisconsin Dr.

Tarnagan Blvd.

Spenard Road

Lake Spenard

Aurora Village

Benson Blvd.

C Street

Arctic Blvd.

A Street

Sears Mall

36th Ave.

Z.J. Loussac Library

Lake Otis

Lake Otis Parkway

University of Alaska

Alaska Pacific University

Boniface Mall

Baxter Rd.

Patterson St.

Muldoon Rd.

University Center Mall

Providence Hospital

Alaska Native Medical Center

Dale St.

Bragaw St.

Main Post Office

International

Frontage Rd.

Airport Terminal

Anchorage International Airport

Connors Lake

DeLong Lake

Raspberry Road

Cambridge Way

Newcastle Way

Potter Drive

Minnesota Dr.

Airport Road

A Street

Campbell Creek

YMCA

Tudor Rd.

Tudor Track

Bicentennial Park

Grummen St.

View Circle

Dowling Rd.

Dept. of Motor Vehicles

E. 64th Ave.

E. 68th Ave.

E. 72nd Ave.

Spruce St.

E. 76th Ave.

E. 80th Ave.

E. 84th Ave.

E. 88th Ave.

Abbott Road

Abbott Loop Road

Campbell Airstrip

Kincaid Park

Kincaid Rd.

Jodhpur St.

Sand Lake Rd.

Sand Lake

Sundi Lake

Jewel Lake

Jewel Lake Rd.

Dimond Blvd.

Minnesota Dr.

Campbell Creek Greenbelt

C Street

E. 72nd Ave.

Dimond Blvd.

Dimond Center Mall

Dimond-Jewel Lake Center

Campbell Lake

Victor Rd.

100th Ave.

Bayshore

Klatt Road

Seward Highway

Old Seward Highway

Elim St.

Hillside Park

Hilltop Ski Area

Anchorage Golf Course

O'Malley Road

Alaska Zoo

Lake Otis Parkway

Windward

Huffman Road

Birch Rd.

Hillside Dr.

Upper Huffman

Johns Road

Oceanview Dr.

The Alaska Railroad

DeArmoun Road

Rabbit Creek Road

Anchorage Coastal Wildlife Refuge (Potter Marsh)

To **Seward**

89.3 (Christian radio); KNBA 90.3 (Public Radio, Native-owned); KSKA 91.1 (National Public Radio); KQEZ 92.1 (Easy Favorites); KFAT 92.9 (Sports Radio); KEAG 97.3 (Oldies); KLEF 98.1 (Classical Music); KYMG 98.9 (Adult Contemporary); KBFX 100.5 (The Fox - Pure Rock); KGOT 101.3 (Top 40); KKRO 102.1 (Classic Rock); KMXS 103.1 (Hot Adult Contemporary); KBRJ 104.1 (Hot Country Favorites); KNIK 105.3 (The Breeze - Smooth Jazz); KWHL 106.5 (Modern Rock); KASH 107.5 (New Country). **Television:** KTUU (NBC), Channel 2; KTBY (Fox), Channel 4; KYES (Independent), Channel 5; KAKM (PBS), Channel 7; KTVA (CBS), Channel 11; KIMO (ABC), Channel 13; KCFT TV UHF 20 (Christian Family); KDMD TV UHF 33 (Home Shopping Network); other UHF channels and pay cable television are also available. **Newspapers:** *Anchorage Daily News* (daily); *Alaska Journal of Commerce, Anchorage Press* (weekly); *Chugiak-Eagle River Star* (semi-weekly).

Private Aircraft: Anchorage airports provide facilities and services to accommodate all types of aircraft. Consult the *Alaska Sup-* *plement,* the *Anchorage VFR Terminal Area Chart* and *Terminal Alaska Book* for the following airports: Anchorage International, Merrill Field, Campbell airstrip, and Lake Hood seaplane and strip.

HISTORY AND ECONOMY

In 1914 Congress authorized the building of a railroad linking an ocean port with the interior river shipping routes. The anchorage at the mouth of Ship Creek became the construction camp and headquarters for the Alaskan Engineering Commission. By the

ANCHORAGE ADVERTISERS

Town Square Park adjacent to the Performing Arts Center has great flower displays throughout the summer. (© Tom Bol)

summer of 1915 the population, housed mainly in tents, had grown to about 2,000.

Among the names suggested for the settlement were Ship Creek, Spenard, Woodrow and Knik Anchorage, and the name Anchorage was selected by the federal government when the first post office opened in May 1915. Later that year the bluff south of Ship Creek was cleared and surveyed, and 655 lots, on 347 acres, were auctioned off by the General Land Office for $148,000. The center of the business district was the 4th Avenue and C Street intersection. Anchorage prospered and was incorporated in 1920.

Anchorage's growth has been in spurts, spurred by: (1) construction of the Alaska Railroad and the transfer of its headquarters from Seward to Anchorage in 1917; (2) colonization of the Matanuska Valley, a farming region 45 miles/72 km to the north, in 1935; (3) construction of Fort Richardson and Elmendorf Field (now Elmendorf Air Force Base) in 1940; (4) discovery of oil in Cook Inlet between 1957 and 1961; and (5) the development of North Slope/Prudhoe Bay oil fields and the construction of the trans-Alaska pipeline—all since 1968.

The current population of 258,782 includes representation of diverse racial and cultural groups, with about 78 percent white, 8 percent Native Alaskan, and between 6 and 7 percent African-American, Asian-Pacific Islander and Hispanic groups. Government jobs, including the military, account for about one-quarter of the employment picture; service industries for another one-quarter. The oil, gas and mining industries employ roughly 3 percent. Other fields of work are similar to those in other American cities of this size (in the classified section of the Anchorage phone directory, 77 pages are devoted to attorneys and law firms).

The Good Friday earthquake of March 27, 1964, the most powerful quake (9.2 on the Richter scale) ever recorded in North America, caused more than $300 million in damage throughout southcentral Alaska. In Anchorage most losses resulted from landslides caused by changes in the composition of the clay underlying much of the city. Government Hill, dwntown neighborhoods and the Turnagain area now known as Earthquake Park suffered the most extensive damage, losing many homes and other buildings. Considering the severity of the disaster, the number of casualties (131) was miraculously low. Relief funds in the form of federal Small Business Administration loans helped many who chose to rebuild, and from the devastation a distinctly new Anchorage emerged.

In the 1970s and 1980s, Anchorage experienced a population and construction boom related to oil production. Major oil companies set up corporate headquarters, and Anchorage's first 20-story buildings punctuated the skyline. Declining oil prices in the 1980s and 1990s triggered a slowdown in the economic climate, but business prospects are upbeat today and the number of new building starts is high. The advent of several national retail chains during the past decade has resulted in the closure of many smaller, family-owned businesses. Mergers, malls and megastores are the order of the day here as in the Lower 48. With its strategic location and modern facilities, Anchorage's key role as the center of commerce and distribution for the rest of Alaska is assured

DESCRIPTION

Covering approximately 2,000 square miles/5,180 sq.km, Anchorage lies between the Chugach Mountains on the east and Knik Arm of Cook Inlet on the west. The surrounding mountain ranges--the Chugach, the Kenais, the Talkeetnas, the icy peaks of the Alaska Peninsula's mountains and volcanoes, and the dramatic peaks of the Alaska Range (with Mount McKinley visible on the northern horizon, weather permitting)--encompass the city in a setting of scenic splendor.

Perched on the edge of Alaska's vast, varied expanse of forests, mountains, rivers, taiga and tundra, Anchorage has sometimes been described as "half an hour from Alaska." Its similarities to other medium-sized American cities increase steadily, but,

although it is true that a half-hour trip in any direction from the city yields a wealth of wilderness experiences, this modern metropolis still possesses many features that mark it as uniquely Alaskan. Combining cosmopolitan amenities with the creative enthusiasm of a young, progressive state has made Anchorage a spirited city and an exciting destination.

Among the many buildings erected during Project 80s, the largest construction program in the city's history, funded by millions of dollars allocated by the legislature, is the **Alaska Center for the Performing Arts** on 5th Avenue and F Street. During its 10 years the center has hosted a wide range of productions, from Broadway shows, world-renowned performers and Anchorage's own symphony orchestra to local productions of choral, theatrical and dance groups. Visitors may wonder about the fences on the center's roof: these had to be added to prevent snow from sliding off the steep pitch of the roof onto unsuspecting pedestrians below. Other completed projects include the George M. Sullivan Sports Arena, William A. Egan Civic and Convention Center, Z.J. Loussac Public Library, and a major expansion and renovation of the Anchorage Museum of History and Art.

With its distinctive mixture of old frontier and jet age, Anchorage is a truly unique city. It is noted for the profusion of flowers and hanging baskets that decorate homes and businesses during summer months: parks, street medians and lamp posts are vibrant with the colors of millions of flowers. As shadows lengthen with winter's approach in October, residents are encouraged to follow the lead of municipal agencies in displaying strings of miniature white lights on homes, trees and office buildings, brightening the entire city "until the last Iditarod racer makes it to Nome" in March. The summertime City of Flowers becomes the wintertime City of Lights.

Anchorage is also the City of Moose, sharing its streets and yards with these largest members of the deer family, especially when winter's deep snows drive the moose toward easier browsing in settled areas where cultivated trees and shrubs abound. Recent frequent summertime sightings attest to the steady increase of the moose population.

CAUTION: Do not attempt to approach or intercept moose at any time, whether for purposes of photography or to satisfy curiosity. Unpredictable and aggressive, moose are huge wild animals that can be extremely dangerous. This applies also to bears that occasionally wander into the city.

In profile, Anchorage has:
• About 88 schools, including special education and alternative public programs, a number of privately operated schools, both secular and parochial; also the University of Alaska, Alaska Pacific University and Charter College, a computer-oriented, "career-building" technical school; also rehabilitation/training schools for the blind and the deaf.
• More than 200 churches and temples.
• Z.J. Loussac Public Library, plus 5 branch libraries, the National Bank of Alaska Heritage Library Museum, Dept. of the Interior's Alaska Resource Library, the Oil Spill Public Information Center, Alaska State Library Services for the Blind and the University of Alaska Library.
• Municipal bus service, 4 major taxi (Continues on page 346)

The extras aren't extra^{SM}

Great Alaskan Holidays has been providing unmatched value and service in motorhome rentals in Alaska for over a decade. Compare our packages with our competitors and discover why we say the "extras aren't extra" at Great Alaskan Holidays.

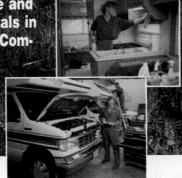

Great Alaskan Holidays Inc.™

3901 W. International Airport Rd.
Anchorage, Alaska 99502
(907) 248-7777 • Fax (907) 248-7878

Begin planning your Great Alaskan Holiday by calling for a free brochure at our new easy to remember Toll Free Number.

1-888-2-ALASKA
(1-888-225-2752)

Visit our home page at www.akholidays.com

Included in Rental

☑ Power generator, roof air & microwave.

☑ 1997 or newer motorhome, guaranteed!*

☑ Housekeeping and linen package.

☑ Cleaning of motorhome (you don't need to clean it to receive your deposit back).

☑ FREE camping at Alaska State Parks, a savings of up to $15 per night!

☑ Insurance coverage.

☑ No provisioning, dump or housekeeping fees.

☑ Located at Anchorage International Airport.

*1999 season

Downtown Anchorage

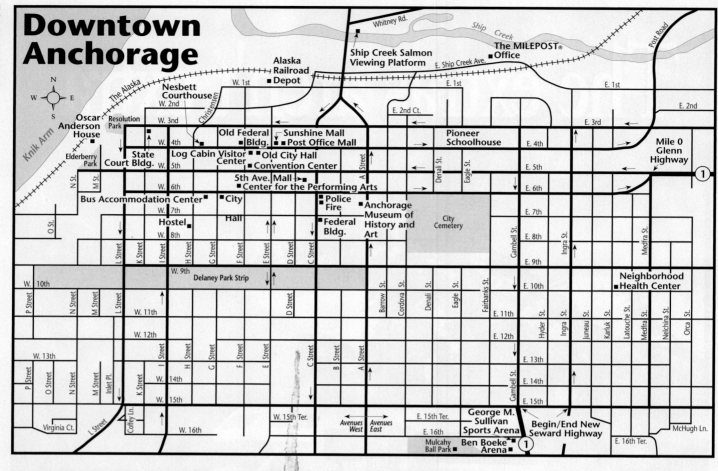

Whitney Rd.

Ship Creek

Post Road

Ship Creek Salmon Viewing Platform

The MILEPOST® Office

E. Ship Creek Ave.

Alaska Railroad Depot

The Alaska

W. 1st

E. 1st

E. 1st

E. 1st

E. 2nd

Nesbett Courthouse

W. 2nd

Christensen

E. 2nd Ct.

E. 3rd

Oscar Anderson House

Resolution Park

W. 3rd

Pioneer Schoolhouse

Mile 0 Glenn Highway

Knik Arm

Elderberry Park

Old Federal Bldg.

Sunshine Mall
Post Office Mall

E. 4th

1

W. 4th

State Court Bldg.

Log Cabin Visitor Center

Old City Hall
Convention Center

A Street

Denali St.

Eagle St.

E. 5th

W. 5th

5th Ave. Mall
Center for the Performing Arts

E. 6th

N St.

M St.

W. 6th

Police
Fire

Anchorage Museum of History and Art

City Cemetery

E. 7th

Bus Accommodation Center

City

Gambell St.

Ingra St.

Medfra St.

W. 7th

Hostel

Hall

Federal Bldg.

E. 8th

L Street

K Street

I Street

H Street

G Street

F Street

E Street

D Street

C Street

W. 8th

E. 9th

W. 9th

Delaney Park Strip

Neighborhood Health Center

W. 10th

Barrow St.

Cordova St.

Denali St.

Eagle St.

Fairbanks St.

E. 10th

P Street

N Street

M Street

L Street

Hyder St.

Ingra St.

Juneau St.

Karluk St.

Latouche St.

Medfra St.

Nelchina St.

Orca St.

W. 11th

E. 11th

W. 12th

E. 12th

W. 13th

P Street

O Street

N Street

M Street

Inlet Pl.

I Street

H Street

G Street

F Street

E Street

C Street

B Street

A Street

Gambell St.

E. 13th

K Street

W. 14th

E. 14th

W. 15th

E. 15th

Virginia Ct.

Coffey Ln.

L Street

George M. Sullivan Sports Arena

Begin/End New Seward Highway

W. 15th Ter.

W. 16th

W. 15th Ter.

Avenues West

Avenues East

E. 15th Ter.

E. 16th

McHugh Ln.

1

E. 16th Ter.

Mulcahy Ball Park

Ben Boeke Arena

RENT ALASKA'S LEADER

Rest Assured. Whether you are renting, or driving your own R.V. to Alaska, you can rely on Alaska Panorama in Anchorage. We've been renting motorhomes for perfect Alaskan vacations since 1981. Let us help make yours unforgettable! We offer late model, completely self-contained motorhomes of all sizes, free pickup from the airport or your hotel, and everything you need to know about motorhome travel in the Last Frontier.

Map:

N

Arctic Blvd.

C Street

Tudor Rd.

Int'l Airport Rd.

W. Potter Dr.

X

Call or write for our brochure!

ALASKA PANORAMA

712 W. Potter Drive, Anchorage, AK 99518
Toll Free 1-800-478-1401 Fax 907-561-8762
www.alaskan.com/alaskapanorama

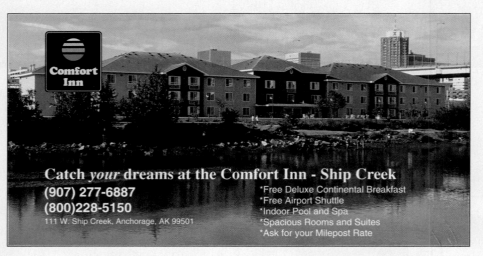

Catch *your* dreams at the Comfort Inn - Ship Creek

(907) 277-6887
(800)228-5150
111 W. Ship Creek, Anchorage, AK 99501

*Free Deluxe Continental Breakfast
*Free Airport Shuttle
*Indoor Pool and Spa
*Spacious Rooms and Suites
*Ask for your Milepost Rate

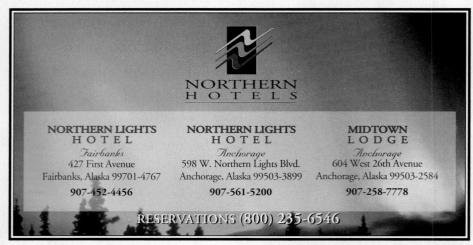

NORTHERN HOTELS

NORTHERN LIGHTS
H O T E L
Fairbanks
427 First Avenue
Fairbanks, Alaska 99701-4767

907-452-4456

NORTHERN LIGHTS
H O T E L
Anchorage
598 W. Northern Lights Blvd.
Anchorage, Alaska 99503-3899

907-561-5200

MIDTOWN
L O D G E
Anchorage
604 West 26th Avenue
Anchorage, Alaska 99503-2584

907-258-7778

RESERVATIONS (800) 235-6546

ARCTIC INN MOTEL

(907) 561-1328

Restaurant & Lounge • Fish Freezer
Cable T.V. • HBO • Kitchenettes
Phones • Microwaves • Refrigerators
Laundromat • Daily & Weekly Rates

842 W. INTERNATIONAL AIRPORT ROAD
ANCHORAGE, ALASKA 99518
Anchorage's Most Reasonable Rates
Located Corner of International & Arctic (2 Miles from Airport)

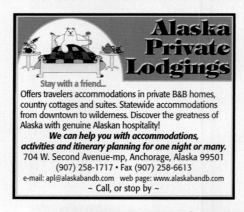

Alaska Private Lodgings

Stay with a friend...

Offers travelers accommodations in private B&B homes,
country cottages and suites. Statewide accommodations
from downtown to wilderness. Discover the greatness of
Alaska with genuine Alaskan hospitality!
*We can help you with accommodations,
activities and itinerary planning for one night or many.*
704 W. Second Avenue-mp, Anchorage, Alaska 99501
(907) 258-1717 • Fax (907) 258-6613
e-mail: apl@alaskabandb.com   web page: www.alaskabandb.com
~ Call, or stop by ~

*Free Continental Breakfast
*Free Airport Shuttle
*1.5 miles from Airport
*Laundry Facilities

Microtel Inn & Suites
(907) 245-5002 (888) 680-4500
5205 Northwood Drive, Anchorage, AK 99517

Ask for your Milepost Rate

(Continued from page 342)
companies and various shuttle bus services.

• In the arts—**Dance:** Alaska Center for the Performing Arts; Alaska Dance Theatre; Anchorage Concert Assoc.; Anchorage Opera; Ballet Alaska. **Music:** Alaska Airlines Autumn Classics; Anchorage Concert Chorus; Anchorage Community Concert Band; Anchorage Concert Assoc.; Anchorage Children's Choir; Anchorage Symphony Orchestra; Anchorage Festival of Music; Sweet Adelines (Cheechako and Sourdough chapters); University of Alaska Anchorage Singers; Young People's Concerts. **Theater:** Alaska Community Theatre; Alaska Festival Theatre; Alaska Junior Theater; Alaska Stage Company; Alaska Theatre of Youth; Cyrano's Off Center Playhouse; Out North Theater Company; UAA Theatre; Valley Performing Arts. **Art:** About 20 art galleries.

• A total of 259 miles of trails for hiking, biking, jogging, skiing and dog mushing, including 120 miles of paved trails and 105 miles of maintained ski trails.

ACCOMMODATIONS/VISITOR SERVICES

There are more than 70 motels and hotels in the Anchorage area with prices for a double room ranging from $50 to $70 and up. Reservations are a must. Bed-and-breakfast accommodations are also available in more than 100 private residences.

Hosteling International–Anchorage is located at 700 H St., 1 block from the People Mover Transit Center in downtown Anchorage. The hostel is open 7:30 A.M. to noon and 1 P.M. to 11 P.M. June through October; 8 A.M. to noon, 1 P.M. to 3 P.M. and 5 P.M. to 11 P.M., October through May. Common areas open all day. Cost for members is $16 per night, nonmembers $19. American Youth Hostel cards available at the hostel or by mail. The hostel has dormitory rooms with bunkbeds, kitchen facilities, common rooms, laundry room and TV room. For information or to make reservations no less than 1 day in advance with VISA or MasterCard, phone (907) 276-3635, or write for reservations (prepayment required): 700 H St., Anchorage 99501.

Spenard Hostel International is a nonaffiliated hostel located on the bus line at 2845 W. 42nd Place. Cost is $15 per night. For more information or to make reservations, phone (907) 248-5036; fax (907) 248-5063; e-mail: spenrdhstl@alaskalife.net; web site: http://www.alaskalife.net/spenrdhstl/hostel.html.

Restaurants number more than 600, with many major fast-food chains, formal dining rooms and specialty establishments including Italian, Japanese, Korean, Chinese (Cantonese and Mandarin), Mexican, Polynesian, Greek, German, Sicilian, Thai, soul food, seafood, smorgasbord and vegetarian.

Alaskan Frontier Gardens Bed and Breakfast. Elegant Alaska hillside estate on peaceful scenic 3 acres by Chugach State Park, 20 minutes from downtown. Spacious luxury suites with big Jacuzzi, sauna, king bed and fireplace. Getaway for honeymooners. Gourmet breakfast, museum-like environment with Alaskan hospitality and exceptional comfort. Truly Alaska's finest. Year-round service. Credit cards accepted. P.O. Box 241881, Anchorage, AK 99524-1881. (907) 345-6556. Fax (907) 562-2923.
[ADVERTISEMENT]

Anchorage Homestead Inn. (907) 561-3138; toll free: (888) 488-1800. E-mail:
(Continued on page 349)

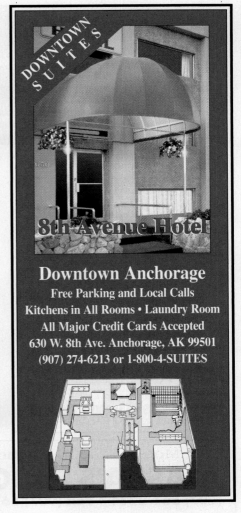
Seward's Day (the last Monday in March) is an Alaska state holiday commemorating the signing of the treaty by Secretary of State William Henry Seward that purchased Alaska from Russia for $7.2 million in 1867.

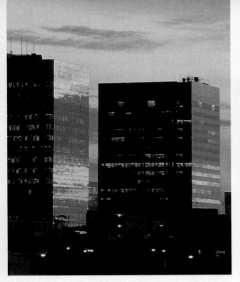

Downtown Anchorage office buildings at sunset. (© George Wuerthner)

homesteadinn@corecom.net. Clean, comfortable rooms conveniently located near airport and Lake Hood. Low rates. Open year-round. Free HBO, coffee, phone use. Kitchen, laundry and freezer facilities available. Walking distance from restaurants. 4215 Spenard Rd., Anchorage, AK 99517. [ADVERTISEMENT]

Arctic Fox Bed & Breakfast Inn. 326 E. 2nd Ct., Anchorage, AK 99501. Phone (907) 272-4818, fax 272-4819. Quiet downtown location with some inlet views. Tastefully decorated rooms and suites with moderate summer rates, low winter rates. Near downtown hotels, restaurants, museum, bike trail, train and Ship Creek. Laundry. Private baths, TV and phone in room. [ADVERTISEMENT]

The Aurora Winds. Anchorage's exceptional bed and breakfast resort is situated on 2 meticulously landscaped acres and features 5 suites, all with private bath, TV, VCR and phone. The "McKinley Suite" also has a fireplace, wide-screen TV, double Jacuzzi and a habitat-environment chamber. The atmosphere is one of quiet elegance: contemporary, with an Alaskan home-style atmosphere where breakfast is a gourmet delight, and the staff strives to satisfy your every need. Take advantage of the full gym, billiard room, sauna, theater room, 10-person outdoor hot tub, or one of the 4 fireplaces. "Our recommendation for Anchorage's best bed and breakfast, the Aurora Winds B & B Resort." For information, phone (800) 642-9640, (907) 347-2533, e-mail:awbnb@alaska.net or web page: www.aurorawinds.com. [ADVERTISEMENT]

Bed and Breakfast Association of Alaska. Stay where real Alaskans stay, in their homes! A new directory is available representing our members throughout Alaska. All types of accommodations, from homestays to inns, from luxurious B&B's to cabins, from cities to the bush. Licensed, insured and many inspected. BBAA, P.O. Box

202663, Anchorage, AK 99501; phone (907) 566-2627 or fax (907) 272-1899. [ADVERTISEMENT]

Caribou Inn. 501 L Street, Anchorage, AK 99501. Clean, comfortable rooms in an excellent downtown Anchorage location. Shared or private bath, some with kitchenettes. Major credit cards accepted. Free shuttle to airport and train station. (907) 272-0444 or fax (907) 274-4828. Toll free (800) 272-5878. E-mail: caribou@alaska.net. [ADVERTISEMENT]

Chugach Bed & Breakfast. Serene adult setting in a quiet neighborhood nestled at the foot of the beautiful Chugach Moun-

tains. Easy access to airport, city, wilderness. A full breakfast and other amenities too numerous to mention. Your hosts of 35 years plus. 3901 Laron Lane, Anchorage, AK 99504-4652; phone (907) 333-4615, fax (907) 337-6095. [ADVERTISEMENT]

"K" Street Bed & Breakfast. Downtown, 2 blocks to coastal trail, market, dining and bus line. Near airport, railroad and shopping. Healthy breakfast, gourmet coffee, teas. Private or shared bath with sitting areas. Secure area, ample parking, smoke-free. Hostess 23-year resident. Fully licensed. Phone/fax (907) 279-1443. 1443 "K" Street, Anchorage, AK 99501. E-mail: kstbb@alaska.net. Toll free (888) KST-BANB. [ADVERTISEMENT]

North Country Castle Bed & Breakfast. Luxuriate in our spacious, sunny, warm Victorian home! Relax on any of 4 decks with sparkling mountain and Cook Inlet views. Explore moose trails on our forested acreage or amble down our country road to nearby hiking paths. Only minutes from major Anchorage attractions and the wilds of Alaska. Bounteous breakfasts. Year-round. Credit cards accepted. P.O. Box 111876, Anchorage, AK 99511. (907) 345-7296. Online at customepu.com/ commercial/ nccbnb. [ADVERTISEMENT]

Puffin Inn. Experience comfortable, quality accommodations and exceptional service at reasonable rates. Our friendly Alaskan hospitality includes complimentary coffee, muffin and daily newspaper. Located near Lake Hood floatplane airport with courtesy airport shuttle, nonsmoking rooms, cable TV and freezer space for your hunting and fishing needs. Handicap accessible. 4400 Spenard Rd., Anchorage, AK 99517. Phone (907) 243-4044. Fax (907) 248-6853. (800) 4PU-FFIN. [ADVERTISEMENT]

Puffin Place Studios & Suites. Relax and enjoy 1 of our 38 attractively furnished studios and 1-bedroom suites featuring fully equipped kitchens with microwaves. Within walking distance of restaurants, shopping and Tony Knowles Coastal Trail. Our amenities include: courtesy airport shuttle, nonsmoking rooms, laundry facility, freezer space, cable TV. Weekly and monthly rates offered October–May. 1058 W. 27th, Anchorage, AK 99503, (907) 279-1058. Fax (907) 257-9595. (800) 71-PLACE. [ADVERTISEMENT]

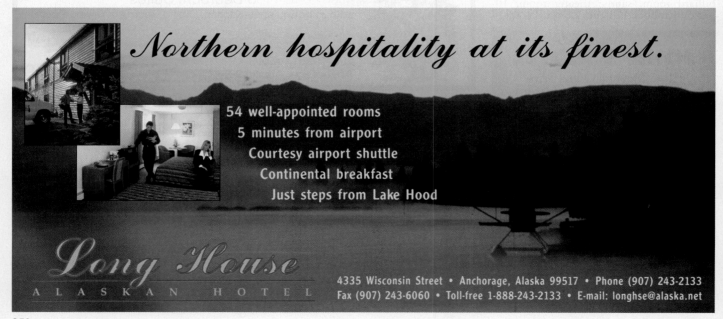

Susie's Lake View Bed & Breakfast. Enjoy the quiet setting overlooking scenic Campbell Lake. Unwind with a leisure tour of our quaint garden setting. The large deck areas offer comfortable privacy for an individual but are big enough for a family barbecue. Start or end your day with a steamy hot tub—available 24 hours a day and located where it should be … outside. Continental or traditional breakfast. Business travelers welcome. Located only 11 minutes from the airport. VISA and MasterCard accepted. 9256 Campbell Terrace, Anchorage, AK 99515. Phone (907) 243-4624. [ADVERTISEMENT]

The Teddy Bear House Bed & Breakfast. Experience a traditional home stay in our uniquely decorated home in a quiet south Anchorage neighborhood, 15 minutes from airport and downtown. Close to Anchorage Zoo and shopping. Twin or queen beds. Private and shared bath. Continental or traditional breakfast. Large deck for your relaxation. Open year-round. No smoking. P.O. Box 190265, Anchorage, AK 99519; (907) 344-3111, e-mail: tbearbb@alaska.net. [ADVERTISEMENT]

12th & L Bed and Breakfast. Downtown Anchorage. Private baths, cable TV. Free phone and laundry. Convenient, casual, comfortable, congenial and clean. Flexible check in/check out. Low winter rates. Informative brochure. (907) 276-1225. Fax (907) 276-1224. Web address http://www.goalaskan.com. [ADVERTISEMENT]

Anchorage has 2 public campgrounds: Centennial Park, open from May through September, and Lions Camper Park, open July and part of August on an as-needed basis. Fees are $13 for non-Alaskans and $11 for Alaska residents. To reach Centennial Park, take the Muldoon Road exit south off the Glenn Highway, take the first left onto Boundary, take the next left and follow the signs. Lions Camper Park is located at 5800 Boniface Parkway, half a mile south of the Glenn Highway. Centennial, recommended for large RVs, has 90 RV sites and 40 tent sites. Lions has 50 tent sites. Both feature barracks-type showers, flush toilets, water and dump stations and no hookups. Between May and September, phone (907) 333-9711 for details on either park. In the off-season, phone (907) 343-6397.

Chugach State Park has campgrounds located near Anchorage at Bird Creek (Seward Highway), and at Eagle River and Eklutna Lake (Glenn Highway). The Anchorage Ski Club rents space to RVs at its Alpenglow Lodge parking lot from June 15-September 1; mile 7 Arctic Valley Road;

Log cabin visitor center on Fourth Avenue. (© Barbara Willard)

phone (907) 346-4098. Anchorage also has several private campgrounds. ▲

Anchorage RV Park. Experience Alaska's premier RV park located in a quiet wooded setting just 10 minutes from downtown Anchorage. Fully equipped with all the essentials plus much more including: cable TV connections, laundry, showers, and work station with modem port in our comfortable main lodge. The park has 195 spaces with 78 pull-throughs and access to a network of bike trails. Open mid-May through mid-Sept. Enjoy Alaska's premier RV park. Call today for reservations 800-400-7275 or (907) 338-7275. GPS: N61° 13.81' W149° 44.46'. 7300 Oilwell Rd., Anchorage, AK 99506. [ADVERTISEMENT] ▲

The Anchorage Ski Club will rent space to RVs at its Alpenglow Lodge parking lot from June 15-September 1. Located at the 2,500' elevation in Chugach State Park, the area offers alpine hiking, wildlife viewing, berry picking and spectacular views. Moose Run Golf Course is conveniently located at the bottom of the hill! $10/day. No hook-ups. Dump station. Steep gravel road. Mile 7, Arctic Valley Road; phone (907) 346-4098. [ADVERTISEMENT] ▲

Electronic Solutions Midtown Camper Park and Superstore. 42 full hookup spaces. Free showers, clean restrooms. Across from Sears Mall, 1 block west of Seward Highway on East Northern Lights. Easy walk to Fred Meyers, bank, Wal★Mart, Carrs grocery across street. Great seafood restaurant, salon, children's store. Electronic Solutions Superstore on site. 2-way specialists, 12-volt supplies, musical instrument store, equipment rental. 2704 Fairbanks St., Anchorage, AK 99503. Reservations and brochure (907) 277-2407. [ADVERTISEMENT] ▲

TRANSPORTATION

Air: More than a dozen international and domestic air carriers and numerous intrastate airlines serve Anchorage International Airport, located 6.5 miles/10.5 km from downtown.

Note: Watch for road construction at inter-

section of Minnesota Drive and international Airport Road in summer 1999.

Ferry: The nearest ferry port to Anchorage is Whittier on Prince William Sound, served by Alaska state ferry from Cordova and Valdez. Whittier is accessible by train from either Anchorage or Portage on the Seward Highway.

Railroad: The Alaska Railroad offers daily passenger service in summer from Anchorage to Seward and to Fairbanks via Denali National Park. Reduced service in winter. Summer rail service is also available between Anchorage and Whittier, with optional connections to Prince William Sound cruises. In addition, a shuttle train for foot passengers and vehicles operates daily in summer between Portage and Whittier, connecting with the state ferry to Valdez and Cordova. Contact Passenger Services Dept., Box 107500, Anchorage 99510-7500; phone (800) 544-0552 or (907) 265-2494, fax 265-2323 or 265-2509.

The **Alaska Railroad Depot** is located on 1st Avenue, within easy walking distance of downtown.

Bus: Local service via People Mover, which serves most of the Anchorage bowl from Peters Creek to Oceanview. Fares are $1 for adults, 50¢ for youth 5 to 18, 25¢ for senior citizens and disabled citizens with transit identification. Monthly passes are sold at the Transit Center (6th Avenue and H Street), the Dimond Transit Center and municipal libraries. Day passes are also available for $2.50 at the Transit Center, Dimond Transit Center and 7–11 stores. For bus route information, phone the Rideline at (907) 343-6543.

Taxi: There are 4 major taxi companies, as well as various shuttle services. Consult the yellow pages under Taxicabs.

Car and Camper Rentals: There are dozens of car rental agencies located at the airport and downtown, as well as several RV rental agencies (see advertisements this section).

RV Parking: The Anchorage Parking Authority offers a lot with spaces for oversized vehicles (motorcoaches, campers, large trucks) at 3rd Avenue, north of the Holiday Inn, between A and C streets. Parking is $5 per space, per day. For more information, phone (907) 276-PARK or (800) 770-ACAR.

Highway: Anchorage can be reached via the Glenn Highway and the Seward Highway. See GLENN HIGHWAY and SEWARD HIGHWAY sections for details.

ATTRACTIONS

Get Acquainted: Stop by the Log Cabin Visitor Information Center at 4th Avenue and F Street, open 7:30 A.M. to 7 P.M. June through August; 8 A.M. to 6 P.M. in May and September; and 9 A.M. to 4 P.M. the remainder of the year; phone (907) 274-3531. Free visitor guidebooks.

Take a Historic Walking Tour: Start at

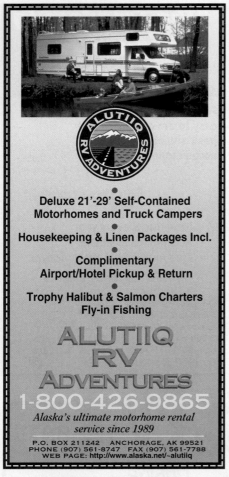

the Log Cabin Visitor Information Center at 4th Avenue and F Street. The Anchorage Convention and Visitors Bureau's *Anchorage Visitors Guide* suggests an excellent downtown walking tour.

Take a Tour: Several tour operators offer local and area sightseeing tours. These range from a 1-hour narrated trolley tour of Anchorage to full-day tours of area attractions such as Portage Glacier and Alyeska Resort. Two-day or longer excursions by motorcoach, rail, ferry and air to nearby attractions such as Prince William Sound or remote areas are also available. Inquire at

your hotel, see ads this section, or contact a travel agent.

Anchorage City Trolley Tours. It's fun. It's 1-hour. It's only $10. A lively, informative tour of Alaska's largest city. Located on

Fourth Avenue between F and G streets. Departs hourly. 9 A.M.–6 P.M. P.O. Box 102299, Anchorage, AK 99510. Phone (907) 276-5603. [ADVERTISEMENT]

The Alaska Public Lands Information Center, located in the historic Old Federal Building on 4th Avenue and F Street, offers a wide variety of exhibits, movies, special programs and information on all of Alaska's state and federal parks, forests and wildlife refuges. Natural history exhibits, cultural exhibits, a GIS computer and self-help trip-planning area provide an enjoyable way to obtain knowledge and information necessary for a safe and exhilarating Alaskan adventure whether you are a cruise passenger or an avid hiker. Expert staff provide additional assistance and supply maps, brochures and other aids. Federal passports (Golden Age, Eagle and Access) and state

park passes are available. Live animal demonstrations occur every Thursday and Saturday at 2 P.M. in the summer. Call for current schedule. Museum scavenger hunts are a popular activity enjoyed by young and old alike. The center is open year-round. Summer hours (Memorial Day to Labor Day) are 9 A.M. to 5:30 P.M. Monday through Friday; closed weekends and holidays. Phone (907) 271-2737, write the center at 605 W. 4th Ave., Suite 105, Anchorage 99501, or visit the web at www.nps.gov/aplic for more information.

The Anchorage Museum of History and Art, located at 121 W. 7th Ave., is a must stop. One of the most visited attractions in Anchorage, this world-class museum features permanent displays of Alaska's cultural heritage and artifacts from its history. The 15,000-square-foot/1,400-square-meter Alaska Gallery on the second floor is the museum's showcase, presenting Alaska Native cultures—Aleut, Eskimo and Indian—and displays about the Russians, New England whalers, as well as gold rush, WWII,

statehood and Alaska today. Displays include full-scale dwellings and detailed miniature dioramas. The gallery contains some 300 photographs, more than 1,000 artifacts, 33 maps, and specially made ship and aircraft models. The main floor of the museum consists of 6 connecting galleries displaying Alaska art, such as works by Sydney Laurence. Also on the 1st floor are a Children's Gallery and 3 temporary exhibition galleries. The museum has a reference library and archives, a free film series and public tours (daily in summer), the Museum Shop and a cafe in the atrium. Admission is $5 for adults, $4.50 for seniors, under 18 free. Open 9 A.M. to 6 P.M. daily, mid-May to mid-September; 10 A.M. to 6 P.M. Tuesday through Saturday, and 1–5 P.M. Sunday, in winter; (closed Monday and holidays). Phone (907) 343-6173 for recorded information about special shows, or (907) 343-4326 during business hours for more information.

Visit the Oscar Anderson House Museum, one of the city's first wood-frame houses. Built in 1915, it was home to Oscar Anderson, a Swedish immigrant and early Anchorage pioneer and businessman. Now on the National Register of Historic Places, it has been beautifully restored and is well worth a visit. Located in the north corner of Elderberry Park, at the west end of 5th Avenue, 420 M St. Open mid-May to mid-September for guided tours. Hours are 11 A.M. to 4 P.M., Tuesday through Saturday. Swedish Christmas tour, first 2 weekends in December. Adults, $3; seniors over 65, $2; children 5 to 12, $1. Group tours may be arranged year-round by appointment. Phone (907) 274-2336; fax (907) 274-3600.

The Knitting Frenzy Store. Best source for yarn, fiber, books, patterns, supplies for use in knitting, weaving, spinning, crochet and tatting. Largest Alaskan inventory. Choose a project for the road! Open Monday through Saturday 10–6. Day phone (907) 563-2717. In Alaska, (800) 478-8322. 4240 Old Seward Hwy. #18, corner of Old Seward and Tudor. Fax (907) 563-1081. E-mail: frenzy@alaska.net. [ADVERTISEMENT]

Laura Wright Alaskan Parkys. Known worldwide for beautiful Eskimo-style summer and winter parkas. Off the rack or custom-made. Started by Laura Wright in Fairbanks in 1947; continuing the tradition is granddaughter Sheila Ezelle. Purchase "Wearable Alaskan Art" for the whole family at 343 W. 5th Ave., Anchorage, AK 99501. Phone (907) 274-4215. Bank cards welcome. Mail and phone orders accepted. We airmail worldwide. [ADVERTISEMENT]

Oomingmak, Musk Ox Producers' Co-operative, is a Native-owned co-operative specializing in knitted masterpieces. Using Qiviut, the soft and rare fiber from the arctic Musk Oxen, our 250 Native Alaskan knitters create hats and scarves in a variety of traditional patterns from their culture. Since

1969, this co-operative organization has provided the opportunity for Native women to earn a supplementary income while still pursuing their subsistence lifestyle. For over 25 years, the exquisite items the co-op members make on their knitting needles have been worn with pride and enjoyment by satisfied customers from around the world. We invite you to visit us in downtown Anchorage at the little brown house with the Musk Ox mural on the corner of 6th and H streets. (907) 272-9225, 604 H Street, Anchorage, AK 99501. [ADVERTISEMENT]

Exercise Your Imagination: Visit the Imaginarium, 737 W. 5th Ave., Suite G (across from the Westmark Hotel), a hands-on science discovery center offering unique insights into the wonders of nature, science and technology. Open daily year-round Monday through Saturday 10 A.M. to 6 P.M., Sunday noon to 5 P.M., closed on major holidays. Adults, $5; seniors, $4; children 2 to 12, $4. Wheelchair accessible. Phone (907) 276-3179.

Tour a Campus: Two colleges are located in Anchorage: the University of Alaska Anchorage at 3211 Providence Dr. and

Alaska Pacific (formerly Alaska Methodist) University at 4101 University Dr.

Alaska Pacific University was dedicated June 29, 1959, the same year that Alaska became the 49th state, and is now the state's largest private 4-year university. APU's first students were enrolled in the fall of 1960. The university offers liberal arts-based educational programs for all ages, including an annual Elderhostel. The APU campus is located on 170 forested acres, featuring the 3-tiered Atwood Fountain, Waldron Carillon Bell Tower and the Jim Mahaffey Trail System for skiers, runners, hikers and mountain bikers. Phone (907) 564-8248 or (800) 252-7528 for tours or information about university programs, or access the university on the Internet at www.alaskapacific.edu.

The University of Alaska Anchorage is 1 of 3 regional institutions in the state's university system (the others are in Fairbanks and Southeast Alaska). For information on tours of the UA campus in Anchorage, phone (907) 786-1529.

Go to the Zoo: The Alaska Zoo is located on 25 acres of wooded land and displays more than 85 species of Arctic wildlife, including glacier bears, polar bears, brown (grizzly) and black bears, reindeer, moose, Dall sheep, otters, wolves, foxes, musk-oxen and wolverines, as well as non-Alaskan species such as Bactrian camels, Siberian tigers and an elephant.. Be sure to stop in at the gift shop, located on your right as you enter. The zoo is open 9 A.M. to 6 P.M. daily from May 1 to Oct. 1; 10 A.M. to 4:30 P.M. the remainder of the year. Drive south from the downtown area on the Seward Highway to **Milepost S 120.8.** Take O'Malley exit, turn left on O'Malley Road and proceed 2 miles/3.2 km to the zoo, which will be on your left. Admission $7 for adults, $6 for seniors, $5 for students 13 to 18, and $4 for children 3 to 12. Family passes $50. Free admission for children under 3. Handicap parking, wheelchair accessible. Phone (907) 346-3242 for details. &

Visit the Greenhouses: The municipality maintains extensive greenhouses at Russian Jack Park, 5200 DeBarr Road, where myriad plantings supply local parks and public gardens with summer's colorful flowers. Visitors enjoy the displays of tropical plants, the fish pond and the aviary where finches, cockatiels and tropical birds enliven an attractive area popular for small weddings and school tours. Open year-round, 8 A.M. to 3 P.M., the greenhouses are closed only on a few specific holidays. Phone (907) 343-4717 for additional information.

See Alaskan Wildlife: Fort Richardson Alaskan Fish and Wildlife Center, temporarily closed for renovations, will reopen in late
(Continues on page 364

Garrett's Tesoro
Open 24 Hours

2 LOCATIONS
Northern Lights & Seward Highway
(907) 277-6025

Arctic & International
(907) 561-2581

Credit Cards Accepted

GAS
DIESEL
(Volume Truck Rates)
PROPANE
WATER
AIR

TESORO ALASKA
— *THE WAY TO GO.*

Seattle — 2,440
Great Falls — 2,475

IF EVER THERE WAS A TIME

After driving the Highway, you'll want to make us your first stop in Anchorage. We'll do everything from changing your oil to topping off most vital fluids — all in a matter of minutes.

We service motor homes.

The Quality of Quaker State in an Oil Change®

360 W. Dimond Blvd.	3429 E. Tudor Rd.	1221 Bragaw St.
(directly in front of Costco)	(across from dog sled track)	(directly in front of Costco)
522-3800	562-0900	337-1248

SIX ROBBLEES' INC.

- Trailer Suspensions
- Custom Installation and Repair Shop
- Trailer Hitches
- Tires & Wheels
- Much More. . . .

201 East Dimond	3000 Commercial Drive
(Kings Row Mall)	907-276-5171
907-344-7497	1-800-478-5173

On June 21, 1999 (summer solstice) in Anchorage, sunrise is at 4:20 A.M. and sunset is at 11:42 P.M.

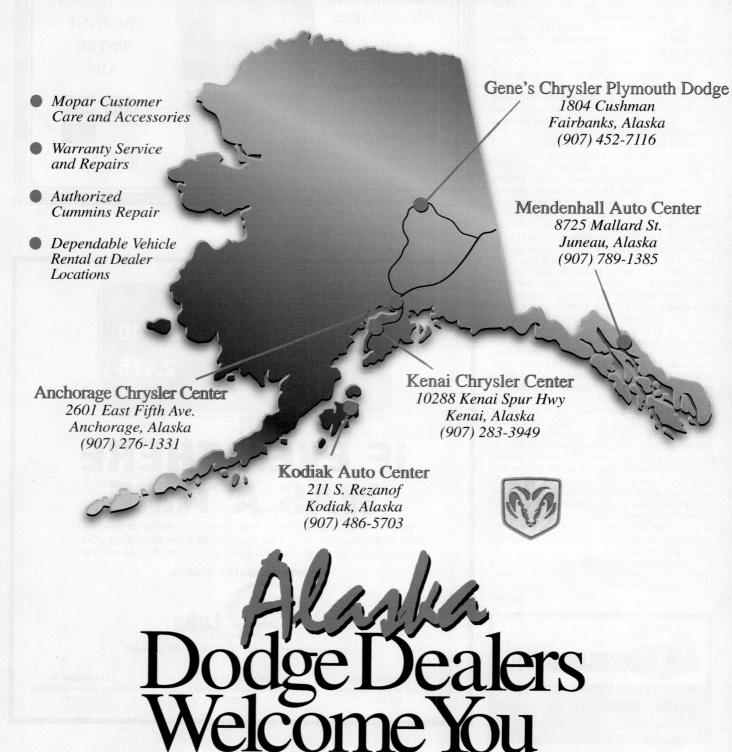

Dependable service as you travel the Last Frontier

- **Mopar Customer Care and Accessories**
- **Warranty Service and Repairs**
- **Authorized Cummins Repair**
- **Dependable Vehicle Rental at Dealer Locations**

Gene's Chrysler Plymouth Dodge
1804 Cushman
Fairbanks, Alaska
(907) 452-7116

Mendenhall Auto Center
8725 Mallard St.
Juneau, Alaska
(907) 789-1385

Anchorage Chrysler Center
2601 East Fifth Ave.
Anchorage, Alaska
(907) 276-1331

Kenai Chrysler Center
10288 Kenai Spur Hwy
Kenai, Alaska
(907) 283-3949

Kodiak Auto Center
211 S. Rezanof
Kodiak, Alaska
(907) 486-5703

Alaska
Dodge Dealers Welcome You

If horsepower were taxable, the IRS would be all over us.

If horsepower were taxable, our 8 liter Magnum® V-10 alone would be an auditor's dream. At 310 horsepower, we'd have to declare it the most powerful gasoline pickup engine available. A fitting title, indeed, for what was the very first 10-cylinder pickup engine the world had ever seen.

Dodge Ram's 5.9 liter Magnum V-8 is not easily overlooked, either. Put it down as a very substantial contribution of 245 horsepower. And while we're at it, we mustn't forget to account for the other Magnum V-8, the 5.2 liter. That adds another 230 horsepower to the Dodge Ram Magnum engine lineup.

File away another 175 horsepower for the standard 3.9 liter V-6, and we're totaling close to a thousand horsepower. Impressive.

Then there's the matter of the Ram Cummins Turbo Diesel. That's an additional 235 horsepower. For you torque-crunchers out there, the 24-valve, 5.9 liter Cummins tops out at 460 lb-ft.

It's a good thing power isn't taxable. Because with the Dodge Magnum engine lineup, we have, overall, the most powerful line of pickups on the planet.

We seem to have the power of endurance, too. Dodge Rams are the longest-lasting full-size pickups on the road.* And Dodge Ram has been ranked number one in its class, winning Strategic Vision's Total Quality Award™ for "Best Ownership Experience" for four consecutive years.†

You know, that's got to be pretty taxing for those other guys.

*Based on percentage of 7/88-7/97 new pickup registrations still registered on 7/1/97. Data source: The Polk Company. †Winner of Strategic Vision's 1995, 1996, 1997, and 1998 Total Quality Award™ for "Best Ownership Experience" in the Full-Size Pickup class. 1998 Vehicle Experience Study™ surveyed 32,191 Oct.-Nov. new vehicle buyers of 200+ models after the first 90 days of ownership. Always use seat belts. Remember a backseat is the safest place for children.

Ram ⬥ The New Dodge

1-800-4-A-DODGE or www.4adodge.com

1999. Located in Building 600 on Fort Richardson Military Reservation, the center features a display of approximately 250 mounts and trophies of Alaskan sport fish, birds and mammals, including a world-record Dall sheep. After November 1999, phone (907)384-0431 for hours. Elmendorf Air Force Base Wildlife Museum is open year-round Monday–Thursday 3 P.M.–4:45 P.M.; Friday noon–5 P.M.; Saturday 3 P.M.–4:45 P.M.; and closed on Sunday. Displays include more than 200 native Alaskan species, from big game to small birds and fish, displayed in groupings of forest, tundra, wetlands, mountains and coastal habitat. Wheelchair access but not to restroom. Enter the base from the intersection of Boniface Parkway and the Glenn Highway. Ask guards for directions to Building 4-803. Phone (907) 552-2282 for details.

Enter Your Dog in a Frisbee Contest: The Canine Frisbee Championship will take place Sunday, June 27, 1999, at the west end of the Delaney Park Strip, 10th and L streets; free registration at noon, competition at 1 P.M. All you need is a dog and a Frisbee!

See an Old Schoolhouse: The Pioneer Schoolhouse at 3rd Avenue and Eagle Street is a 2-story memorial to the late Ben Crawford, an Anchorage banker. This was the first school in Anchorage. The interior is not open to the public.

Visit the Library, City Hall, Federal Building, Post Office: The city hall offices are at 6th Avenue and G Street. The Federal

Golden Nugget
CAMPER PARK

ANCHORAGE • OPEN YEAR-ROUND • 215 SPACES • ALASKA

Map:
GLENN HIGHWAY · TO DOWNTOWN · SHOPPING CENTER · DEBARR RD. · RUSSIAN JACK PARK · BONIFACE PARKWAY · SHOPPING CENTER · S. BRAGAW ST. · NO. LIGHTS BLVD. · GOOSE LAKE PARK · N
CORNER OF DEBARR RD. & HOYT S.T

Back Packers Welcome

Picnic Tables At All Sites

Souvenir Shop

~ Friendly Service ~
~ Full Hookups ~
~ Free Hot Showers ~
~ Laundromat ~

Convenient to:
Shopping Centers • Restaurants
Service & Gas Stations
Beauty Salon • Propane
Churches • Price Costco

Ask For Reservation to:
Flightseeing
Cruise Tours
Guided Fishing Trips
Railroad Travel

215 Spaces

Clean Restrooms

You're Always Welcome at the Golden Nugget!

4100 DeBarr Road • Anchorage, Alaska • 907-333-5311 • 1-800-449-2012

Welcome

To the Best RV Parking Place in Anchorage

The only RV park in downtown Anchorage, Ship Creek Landings offers you 150 full-service spaces, and modern facilities, including laundry, showers, telephones, picnic tables, as well as electricity, water and sewer.

Drive right to us!

From the North/East – As you come into Anchorage, the Glenn Hwy. becomes 5th Ave. Turn right onto Ingra St. Stay in the center lane, cross 3rd Ave. and continue straight down the hill. Turn left onto First, and the RV Park is right in front of you. Welcome.

From the South – As you drive into Anchorage, the Seward Highway divides and you will be going north on Ingra St. Stay in the center lane, cross 3rd Ave. and continue down the hill. Turn left on First, and the RV Park is right in front of you. Welcome.

Shops, hotels, cafes, and a wealth of opportunities at the Anchorage Visitors' Center

Fishing in historic Ship Creek

Walk just a few blocks from the RV Park...

Excursions on the Alaska Railroad, Prince William Sound, and Resurrection Bay.

Shopping at the Saturday Market

Building, located at 7th Avenue and C Street, is one of the largest and most modern office buildings in Anchorage. The lobby features a multimedia collection of artwork, and the cafeteria is open to the public. In downtown Anchorage, the U.S. Post Office is located on the lower level of the Post Office Mall at 4th Avenue and D Street. The main post office, located near the airport, offers all services, 24 hours a day. Smaller postal stations are located throughout the city.

The modern **Z.J. Loussac Public Library**, located at 36th Avenue and Denali Street, is headquarters for the Anchorage library system.

Stroll through Alaska Botanical Garden. The 110-acre garden, located off Campbell Airstrip Road across from the Benny Benson School in East Anchorage, showcases perennials hardy to southcentral Alaska in several large display gardens, a pergola-enclosed herb garden and a rock garden. Interpretive signs guide visitors and identify plants. Paths provide easy walking through a native spruce and birch forest with wildflowers adding seasonal interest. A 1.2-mile/2-km nature trail offers views of Campbell Creek, the Chugach Mountains and a natural wetland. Many of the garden beds and trails are maintained by volunteers. Open year-round. Call for recorded information on hours, special events and guided tours; phone (907) 265-3165. Admission by donation.

"Whaling Wall": Stop by D Street between 5th and 6th avenues for a view of the 400-foot long, 5-story airbrushed mural of beluga whales, bowhead whales and seals by artist Wyland covering the west wall of the J.C. Penney store.

Visit Wolf Song of Alaska, at the corner of 6th Avenue and C Street in downtown Anchorage. Features over 4,000 square feet of educational exhibits and displays focusing on the wolf's natural history, its historical relation to humans, and its role as a major symbol in human folklore, art and religion. Also in the education center are wildlife dioramas, wolf photography and art, and a gift shop that includes educational books, tapes and videos. Open daily in summer; hours vary in winter. Parking is available on the street and at garages at 6th Avenue and E Street, or 5th Avenue and C Street. RV parking is available 3 blocks north of the center at 3rd Avenue and C Street. For more information about "experiencing the wolf," phone (907) 274-9653 or (907) 346-3073.; e-mail: wolfsong@alaska.net; web site: www.wolfsongalaska.org.

4th Avenue Theatre. Built in 1947 by Alaska millionaire "Cap" Lathrop, this Anchorage landmark has been refurbished and now includes a gift shop, city trolley tours, cafe, museum exhibit and special events center. Much of the original art-deco design has been preserved and the trademarks of the theater have been restored, including the bas-relief gold leaf murals and the ceiling lights marking the Big Dipper. There is no admission fee to the theater. The 4th Avenue Theatre is located a half block from the visitor center. Open year-round 8 A.M.–10 P.M. summers, 10 A.M.–6 P.M. Tues.-Sat. winters. For more information phone (907) 257-5635.

Visit the Alaska Native Heritage Center: Just 12 minutes north of downtown, the Alaska Native Heritage Center is Anchorage's newest attraction. Visitors have an opportunity to view, in one facility, all of Alaska's Native cultures. Located on a 26-acre parcel of wooded land at Heritage Center Drive at the intersection of Muldoon Road and the Glenn Highway, the center includes a 26,000-square-foot Welcome House, five traditional village settings, a 2-acre lake and walking trails. Programs and exhibits in the Welcome House demonstrate how Alaska Natives live their culture today. A 95-seat theater offers a film introduction, and Native performers and storytellers share through stories, song and dance at the Gathering Place. Artists and tradition bearers share their harmony with the land as visitors walk through the Hall of Cultures. The Village Store provides an outlet for authentic Native arts and crafts. In the summer months an outdoor walk offers a glimpse into rural Alaska as Native artisans use traditional techniques for fishing, hunting, building kayaks and constructing dwellings. Hours are from 9 A.M. to 9 P.M. daily. Adults, $20; Children (5-12), $15; group discounts and family rates are available. Phone (907) 263-5150.

Visit the Saturday Market. This popular market operates each Saturday between Memorial Day and Labor Day weekends

Anchorage residents take advantage of local parks on long summer days. This is Jewel Lake. (© Barbara Willard)

Anchorage lies at latitude 61°12'N,
longitude 149°52'W.

from 10 A.M. to 6 P.M. The festivities are held on 4th Avenue and in the parking lot at 3rd Avenue between C and E streets. There is no admission fee. Over 400 open-air booths sell a variety of Alaska-made and Alaska-grown products as well as antiques and imported home and novelty items of all types. Local entertainment and community groups add to the fun. For more information contact Saturday Market, phone (907) 272-5634.

Visit the Port of Anchorage: The Anchorage waterfront, with its huge cargo cranes off-loading supplies from container ships, makes an interesting stop, especially in winter when ice floes drift eerily past the dock on the fast-moving tide. Visitors may watch activity on the dock from a viewing platform on the 3rd floor of the port office building. To get there, drive north from the downtown area on A Street, take the Port off-ramp and follow Ocean Dock Road to the office about 1.5 miles/2.4 km from downtown. A good viewpoint of the port for downtown walkers is at the northeast corner of 3rd Avenue and Christensen Drive.

Alaska Statehood Monument. Located at the corner of 2nd Avenue and E Street (just a block down from the Hilton), a plaque and bronze bust of President Eisenhower commemorates the Alaska Statehood Act making Alaska the 49th state on January 3, 1959.

Heritage Library Museum, in the National Bank of Alaska, Northern Lights Boulevard and C Street, has an excellent collection of historical artifacts, Native tools, clothing and weapons, paintings by Alaskan artists and a research library. Free admission. Open weekdays noon to 5 P.M. between Memorial Day and Labor Day, noon to 4 P.M. at other times of the year. Phone (907) 265-2834.

Charter a Plane: Dozens of air taxi operators are based in Anchorage. Fixed-wheel (skis in winter) planes or floatplanes may be chartered for flightseeing trips to Mount McKinley and Prince William Sound, for fly-in hunting and fishing or just for transportation. Scheduled flightseeing trips by helicopter are also available. Consult the yellow pages of the Anchorage phone book.

Wildlife Quest in the Kenai Fjords National park. Enjoy the park's famous tidewater glaciers, sea lion rookeries, seabird colonies, whale watching waters and more. Our smooth-sailing, high-speed catamaran gets you to the park faster than any other vessel. That means you'll enjoy more sights— including more glaciers—in less time than other cruises. So call today and discover the most relaxing way to get wild. Also, ask about our relaxing Resurrection Bay Cruise, unique transportation packages and earning 500 Alaska Airlines Miles. Call Allen Marine Tours, 519 W. 4th Ave., Suite 200, Anchorage, AK 99501. 1-888-305-2515 or 1-(907) 276-5959. [ADVERTISEMENT]

Watch Small Planes: Drive out to Merrill Field, Lake Hood or Lake Spenard for an afternoon of plane watching. Lake Hood is the world's largest and busiest seaplane base, with more than 800 takeoffs and landings on a peak summer day. Easy access to lakes Hood and Spenard off International Airport Road (follow signs).

Merrill Field, named for early Alaska aviator, Russell Hyde Merriill, ranked 96th busiest light-plane airport in the nation in 1997, with 187,190 takeoffs and landings. Follow 15th Street East to light at Lake Otis Parkway and turn north on Merrill Field Drive. This route takes you under the approach to one of the runways. Merrill Field is also accessible off the Glenn Highway and from Airport Heights Drive (across from Northway Mall).

Alaska Aviation Heritage Museum, 4721 Aircraft Dr. on the south shore of Lake Hood, preserves the colorful history of

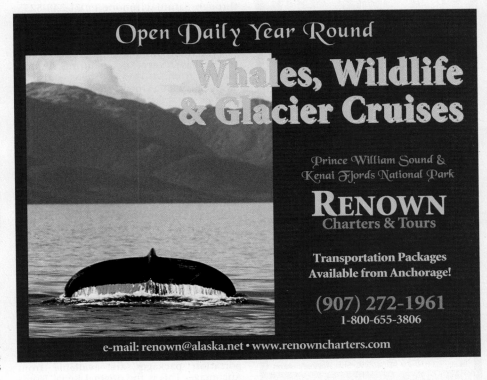

Open Daily Year Round

Whales, Wildlife & Glacier Cruises

Prince William Sound & Kenai Fjords National Park

RENOWN
Charters & Tours

Transportation Packages Available from Anchorage!

(907) 272-1961
1-800-655-3806

e-mail: renown@alaska.net • www.renowncharters.com

SOMETHING FOR EVERYONE

★ Racquetball ★ Aerobics ★
★ Weightroom ★ Dance ★ Ceramics ★
★ Badminton ★ Martial Arts ★ *Room Rentals* ★
★ Kitchen Facilities ★ Showers ★

& MUCH MUCH MORE!

We invite you to visit your 2 Community Recreation Centers or call to see which center offers the program for you.

• *Fairview Community Rec. Ctr.*
  1121 E. 10th Ave., 343-4130

• *Spenard Community Rec. Ctr.*
  2020 W. 48th, 343-4163

 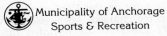
Municipality of Anchorage
Sports & Recreation

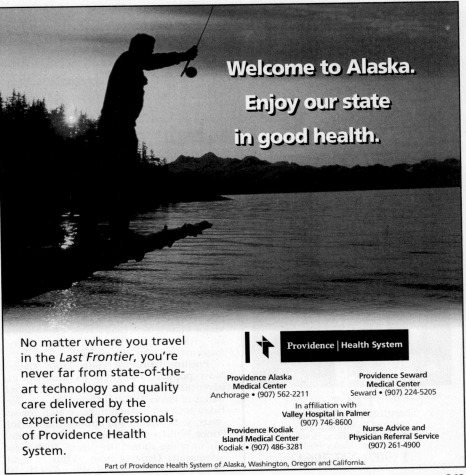

Welcome to Alaska. Enjoy our state in good health.

No matter where you travel in the *Last Frontier*, you're never far from state-of-the-art technology and quality care delivered by the experienced professionals of Providence Health System.

Providence | Health System

Providence Alaska Medical Center
Anchorage • (907) 562-2211

Providence Seward Medical Center
Seward • (907) 224-5205

In affiliation with
Valley Hospital in Palmer
(907) 746-8600

Providence Kodiak Island Medical Center
Kodiak • (907) 486-3281

Nurse Advice and Physician Referral Service
(907) 261-4900

Part of Providence Health System of Alaska, Washington, Oregon and California.

Alaska's pioneer bush pilots. Rare historical films and extensive photo exhibit. The museum features a collection of 28 Alaska bush planes. RV parkng. Open year-round, May 1 to Sept. 15, 9 A.M. to 6 P.M. daily; Oct. 1 to April 30, 10 A.M. to 4 P.M. Tuesday through Saturday; phone (907) 248-5235. Adults $5.75, seniors and active military, $4.50, children 7 to 12, $2.75, children 6 and under, free. Wheelchair accessible.

Elmendorf Air Force Base offers a tour of the base every Friday during summer months from 10-11 A.M. There is also an annual, day-long **Open House** on the base, a summer event featuring aerial shows, aircraft displays, ground demonstrations, booths and more. For more information, phone 3rd Wing Public Affairs (907) 552-8151.

Era Helicopters. Experience a panoramic view of the Anchorage area and the unspoiled wilderness and wildlife of the Chugach Mountains. Soar through picturesque mountains, valleys and glaciers, minutes away from Alaska's largest city. One- and 2-hour tours. Phone (800) 843-1947 or (907) 266-8351 locally. Tours also available in Juneau, Mount McKinley and Valdez. [ADVERTISEMENT]

Kenai Fjords Tours Ltd. Don't miss Kenai Fjords National Park with its abundant wildlife and glaciers. "Alaska's #1 Wildlife and Glacier Cruise" departs daily from Seward and has a convenient reservation office in downtown Anchorage. Located in the Hilton Hotel, Kenai Fjords Tours is at 536 W. 3rd Ave. Phone (970) 276-6249 or (800) 468-8068. Convenient one-day transportation packages are available from Anchorage. This is the original Kenai Fjords National Park cruise you've been looking for. [ADVERTISEMENT]

Major Marine Glacier Tours. At Major Marine Tours, we don't try to see every glacier in Prince William Sound...just the best glaciers. Our relaxing, 5-3/4-hour cruise takes you to see the many active tidewater glaciers in Blackstone Bay. We stop the boat, turn off the engines and drift in front of the glaciers, watching the wildlife and spectacular calving. Every passenger on board is assigned table seating in our comfortable heated cabin. Our outside viewing decks are perfect for spotting otters, eagles, seals and the large bird colonies on our route. A freshly prepared, all-you-can-eat salmon and roasted chicken buffet is available for only $10. The food is consistently rated as the best of any day-cruise company. Complete tours cost only $99 and depart daily from Whittier's boat harbor early May to mid-September. Convenient rail and bus packages are available from Anchorage. Why rush around Prince William Sound when you can relax and see the best of Alaska at a more leisurely pace? Major Marine Tours... always your best value in Prince William Sound. For reservations or a free brochure, phone: (800) 764-7300 or (907) 274-7300. Major Marine Tours, 411 West 4th, Anchorage, AK 99501. Internet address: www.majormarine.com. [ADVERTISEMENT]

Phillips' Cruises & Tours. Enjoy Alaska's most popular 1-day glacier and wildlife adventure through the calm and protected waters of Prince William Sound. It's a perfect 1-day tour from Anchorage. Watch for sea otters, seals, whales and bird life that inhabit Prince William Sound on this fully narrated 5-hour cruise aboard the deluxe, high-speed catamaran. Departs from Whittier, mid-May/mid-September. Sales office: 519 W. 4th

A plane approaches Anchorage International at sunset.
(©James D. Ronan, Jr.)

Avenue, Suite 100, Anchorage, AK 99501-2211. (907) 276-8023; 1-800-544-0529; Fax (907) 265-5890. [ADVERTISEMENT]

Portage Glacier Cruise. See Alaska's most popular attraction, up close from the deck of the MV *Ptarmigan*. This Gray Line of Alaska cruise takes you right to the face of imposing 10-story-high Portage Glacier. An incredible experience. Tours depart Anchorage twice daily or you may drive to Portage Glacier and board the MV *Ptarmigan* for the cruise-only portion. Tour price is $60 per person; cruise-only price is $25 per person. Prices subject to change. Phone (907) 277-5581. [ADVERTISEMENT]

Prince William Sound Cruise. Experience the spectacular beauty of Prince William Sound aboard the MV *Nunatak*. This Gray Line of Alaska tour cruises past Columbia Glacier, the largest glacier in Prince William Sound. Watch for abundant marine life as you travel to picturesque Valdez. Return to Anchorage via the scenic Matanuska Valley. Two days, 1 night from $285 ppdo. Prices subject to change. Tour departs Anchorage daily. Phone (907) 277-5581. [ADVERTISEMENT]

Train to Denali. Ride the luxurious private, domed railcars of the *McKinley Explorer* to Denali National Park from either Anchorage or Fairbanks. Overnight packages in Denali with roundtrip train service are available from $405 ppdo. for 3 days/2 nights. The overnight in either Anchorage or Fairbanks is included. Prices subject to change. Phone Gray Line of Alaska at (907) 277-5581 for train and package tour options. [ADVERTISEMENT]

Take in an Alaska Film: Alaska films can be seen at the Anchorage Museum of History and Art, 121 W. 7th Ave., at 3 P.M., daily during summer. Alaska Experience Center, located at 6th Avenue and G Street, offers "Alaska the Great Land," a 70mm film presented on a 180-degree domed screen, and a film and exhibit on the 1964 earthquake. Admission fee charged; open year-round. Call (907) 276-3730 for recorded information.

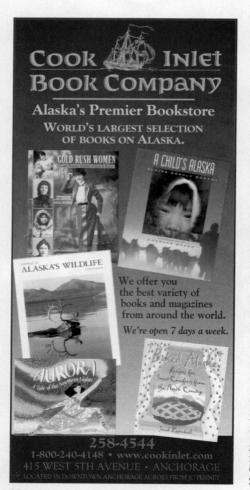
Watch the Tide Come In: With frequent tidal ranges of 30 feet/9m within 6 hours, and many approaching 40 feet/12m, one of Anchorage's best nature shows is the rise and fall of the tides in both the Knik and Turnagain arms of upper Cook Inlet. Among the better vantage points along Knik Arm are Earthquake Park, Elderberry Park (at the west end of 5th Avenue), Resolution Park (near the corner of 3rd Avenue and L Street) and the Anchorage small-boat harbor.

Turnagain Arm has the second highest tides in North America, rising to a maximum high of 42 feet, exceeded only by the Bay of Fundy in eastern Canada. A good overlook for Turnagain tides is Bird Creek State Recreation Site south of Anchorage at **Milepost S 101.2** on the Seward Highway. With good timing you might see a tidal bore, an interesting phenomenon rarely seen elsewhere. A bore tide is a foaming wall of tidal water, up to 6 feet/2m in height, formed by a flood tide surging into a constricted inlet such as Knik or Turnagain Arm.

CAUTION: In many places the mud flats of Knik and Turnagain arms are like quicksand. Don't go wading!

Play Golf: The Municipality of Anchorage maintains a 9-hole golf course at Russian Jack Springs Park, Debarr Road and Boniface Parkway, featuring artificial turf greens. It is open from mid-May through September; phone (907) 333-8338 or (907) 343-4474 off-season (October–April). Alyeska Resort maintains the Anchorage Golf Course, 3651 O'Malley Road, an all-grass, 18-hole course open from mid-May through mid-September; phone (907) 522-3363 for more information. Two military courses are open to civilians. Eagle Glen Golf Course, an 18-hole par-72 course, is located on Elmendorf Air Force Base, near the Post Road gate. Open mid-May through September. Phone (907) 552-2773 for tee times; rentals available. Fort Richardson's 18-hole Moose Run Golf Course is the oldest golf course in Alaska. The course is accessible from Arctic Valley Road (**Milepost A 6.1** on the Glenn Highway) and is open May through September. Rentals available. Phone (907) 428-0056 for tee times. All golf course hours depend on the amount of sunlight.

Play Tennis: The Municipality of Anchorage maintains more than 55 tennis courts, including those in Eagle River and Girdwood. In addition, private clubs offer year-round indoor courts.

Enjoy the Parks: Anchorage is rich in parks, and the parks are rich in the range of activities they offer. More than 190 designated parks have something for everyone's taste, from small "pocket parks" perfect for relaxing or picnicking to vast tracts set aside for skiing, hiking and bicycling; from Government Hill's appealing, 1.3-acre rest area renamed last year in memory of a noted local journalist to Kincaid Park's 1,516 acres of hills, forests and trails. Many parks are ideal for family picnics and outings. The **Chester Creek Greenbelt**, which stretches from Westchester Lagoon to Goose Lake, contains several parks, and a paved bike trail (also popular with joggers) runs the length of the greenbelt. The greenbelt is accessible from several streets: Spenard Road leads to Westchester Lagoon, and E Street leads to Valley of the Moon Park, with a large playground. Other attractive sites, with colorful, modern playground equipment, are David Green Park on 36th Avenue between the Seward Highway and Lake Otis Parkway and

Campbell Creek Park on Lake Otis Parkway near Tudor Road. **Delaney Park Strip** from A to P streets between 9th and 10th avenues near downtown, has ball fields, tennis courts and **Engine No. 556** at 9th and E Street, a real locomotive for children to explore. To make reservations to use picnic facilities, phone (907) 343-4474. The municipal division of Parks & Recreation publishes a complete listing of all parts and trails, $2. Municipality of Anchorage Web page: www.ci.anchorage.ak.us.

Elderberry Park, at the foot of 5th Avenue, faces Knik Arm. The highlight of nearby **Resolution Park** at 3rd Avenue and L Street is the statue of Capt. James Cook overlooking Knik Arm of the inlet which bears his name. The statue was dedicated in 1976 as a bicentennial project.

Tour Anchorage by Bicycle: The municipality has about 120 miles/193 km of paved bike trails (including trails in Eagle River and Girdwood) paralleling many major traffic arteries and also passing through some of the city's most beautiful greenbelt areas. Maps of the trail system are available at Anchorage Parks & Recreation, 120 South Bragaw St. Offering an especially unique experience is the 11-mile/17.7-km Tony Knowles Coastal Trail, which begins at 3rd Avenue and Christensen Drive, and follows the coast around Point Woronzof to Point Campbell and Kincaid Park. One of the most popular trails in the city, it is used by bicyclists, joggers and walkers who are treated to close-up views of Knik Arm (watch for beluga whales) and on clear days a beautiful view of the Alaska Range.

Another popular bike route for families is the Chester Creek Bike Trail from Westchester Lagoon, at 15th Avenue and U Street, to Russian Jack Springs Park. The 6.5-mile/10.5-km trail traverses the heart of Anchorage, following Chester Creek past Goose Lake, a favorite summer swimming beach.

Watch Birds: Excellent bird-watching opportunities are abundant within the city limits. Lakes Hood and Spenard, for example, are teeming with seaplanes but also, during the summer, are nesting areas for grebes and arctic loons. Also seen are widgeons, arctic terns, mew gulls, green-winged teals and sandpipers.

Huge flocks of Canada geese nest and raise their young during the summer. It is not unusual to see traffic at a standstill as a pair of geese, followed by a tandem procession of goslings, cross the city's busy highways.

Another great spot is the Potter Point State Game Refuge, south of downtown on the Seward Highway at **Milepost S 117.4.** Early July evenings are best, according to local bird watchers. Forests surrounding Anchorage also are good for warblers, juncos, robins, white-crowned sparrows, varied thrushes and other species.

At the Park for All People on W. 19th Avenue near Spenard Road in the Chester Creek Greenbelt, a nature trail winds through a bird-nesting area.

Go for a Hike. Hiking trails in the Anchorage area are found in Chugach State Park and in Municipality of Anchorage parks. Three popular hikes in Chugach State Park's Hillside Trail System, accessed from the Glen Alps trailhead, are Flattop Mountain, Powerline Trail and Williwaw Lakes. To reach the trailhead, take the Seward Highway south to the O'Malley exit and go east 4 miles/6.4 km to Hillside Drive; take a right on Hillside, go about 1.5 miles/2.4 km to the intersection of Hillside and Upper Huffman. Turn left on Upper Huffman and continue 4 miles/6.4 km to the Glen Alps trailhead and take a left turn to parking lot. The hike up Flattop Mountain begins here; elevation gain is 1,550 feet/472m in 3.5 miles/5.6 km, hiking time is 3 to 5 hours. Also accessible from Glen Alps is the Powerline trail; total length 11 miles/18 km, elevation gain 1,300 feet/396m. Williwaw Lakes trail branches off Powerline trail to several small alpine lakes; round-trip is 13 miles/21 km with a 742-foot/226-m elevation gain. For more information phone Chugach State Park at (907) 345-5014.

Hilltop Ski Area, 4 miles/6 km east of the Seward Highway at Dimond, is the trailhead for summer hiking, biking and horseback riding on trails in Bicentennial and Hillside municipal parks. The trails range in length from an easy mile walk to a strenuous 16-mile/26-km hike. For more information phone Hilltop Ski Area at (907) 346-1446.

Other Anchorage parks offering hiking, jogging or biking include Kincaid Park, Russian Jack Springs Park and Far North Bicentennial Park. For more information phone Anchorage Parks and Recreation at (907) 343-4474.

Run: Few summer days pass in Anchorage without at least one scheduled race for every cause, interest and level of ability imaginable. Parks & Recreation, (907) 343-4474, issues a complete schedule of these events, from 5k runs/walks to marathons and triathlons. Great fun for spectators and participants.

Summer Solstice. Alaskans celebrate the longest day of the year with a variety of special events. In Anchorage, there's the annual Mayor's Midnight Sun Marathon, a 26-mile/42-km, 385-yard run through the city. This event is usually scheduled on the Saturday nearest summer solstice (June 20 or 21).

See a Baseball Game: Some fine semi-pro baseball is played in Anchorage. Every summer some of the nation's top college players (among past notables are Tom Seaver and 1998 home-run king Mark McGwire) play for the Anchorage Glacier Pilots and Anchorage Bucs, the Peninsula Oilers, the Mat–Su Miners and the Fairbanks Goldpanners. Anchorage games are played at Mulcahy Ball Park, Cordova Street and E. 16th Avenue. Check local newspapers for schedules or call the Anchorage Bucs, (907) 561-2827, or the Glacier Pilots, (907) 344-5444.

Watch Salmon: King, coho, pink and a few chum salmon swim up Ship Creek and can be seen jumping a spillway in the dam just east of Ocean Dock Road. Watch for kings from early June until mid-July and for other species from mid-August until September. A fine wooden viewing platform

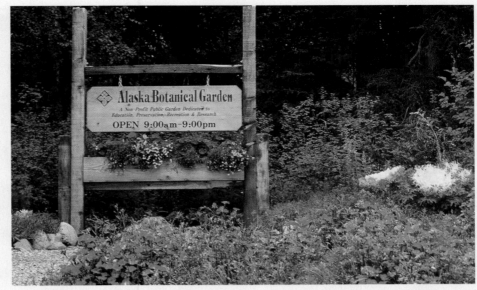

Entrance to 110-acre Alaska Botanical Garden, showcasing perennials hardy to southcentral. (Jill Shepherd)

Westchester Lagoon is on the Campbell Creek bike trail.

(© James D. Ronan, Jr.)

has been built to make salmon watching easy.

Watch an Equestrian Event. The William Clark Chamberlin Equestrian Center in 530-acre Ruth Arcand Park hosts a variety of equestrian events every weekend from late-May through August. This public facility is open from 11 A.M. to 9 P.M. Phone (907) 522-1552. The Eaton Equestrian Center at 5801 Moose Meadow on the Hillside offers riding lessons and special events. Phone (907) 346-3745 for more information.

Kayaking, Canoeing, Rafting: All are available in or near Anchorage. Guided tours from 1 to 14 days run on several rivers within 100 miles/160 km of Anchorage, including the Chulitna, Susitna, Little Susitna, Matanuska and Kenai rivers. Information on guided raft and canoe trips is available through travel agencies, local sporting goods stores and in the free *Visitors Guide* available from the Log Cabin Visitor Information Center.

Several flying services provide unguided float trips. The service flies customers to a remote river, then picks them up at a predetermined time and place downriver.

Several area streams offer excellent canoeing and kayaking. Information on the Swanson River and Swan Lake canoe trails on the Kenai Peninsula is available from the Kenai National Wildlife Refuge Manager, Box 2139, Soldotna, AK 99669-2139; phone (907) 262-7021. Nancy Lake State Recreation Area, 67 miles north of Anchorage, offers a popular canoe trail system. Contact the Alaska State Parks, Mat–Su/Valdez–Copper River Area, H.C. 32, Box 6706, Wasilla, AK 99654-9719; phone (907) 745-3975.

Sailing in the Anchorage area is limited to freshwater lakes and lagoons (usually ice free by May).

Mirror Lake, 24.5 miles/39.4 km north of Anchorage on the Glenn Highway, and Big Lake, 52.3 miles/84.2 km north of Anchorage on the Parks Highway, are also popular spots for small sailboats.

Motorboating: Big Lake and Lake Lucille along the Parks Highway offer motorboating. Several rivers, including the Susitna, offer riverboating, but the shallowness and silty, shifting beds of most Alaska rivers require jet-equipped, flat-bottomed boards for maximum safety.

Cruises on larger boats are available from Whittier into Prince William Sound, from Homer Spit into Kachemak Bay and Cook Inlet, and from Seward into Resurrection Bay and Kenai Fjords National Park. Venturing into those areas in small boats without a knowledgeable local guide is dangerous and should not be attempted..

Cook Inlet waters around Anchorage are only for the experienced because of powerful bore tides, unpredictable weather, dangerous mud flats and icy, silty waters. Turnagain Arm is strictly off-limits for any boat, and Knik Arm and most of the north end of Cook Inlet is the domain of large ships and experienced skiff and dory operators.

Swimming: Anchorage Parks & Recreation can answer questions about aquatics; phone (907) 343-4476.

Goose Lake is open daily, June through August, from 10:30 A.M. to 5:30 P.M.; lifeguards, bathhouse and picnic area. It is located 3 miles/4.8 km east from downtown Anchorage on UAA Drive.

Jewel Lake, 6.5 miles/10.4 km from downtown Anchorage on W. 88th Avenue off Jewel Lake Road, is open daily June through August, from 10:30 A.M. to 5:30 P.M.; lifeguards, restrooms and covered picnic area.

Spenard Lake is open daily, June through August, from 10:30 A.M. to 5:30 P.M.; lifeguards, restrooms, picnic area. Located 3 miles/4.8 km southwest of downtown Anchorage on Spenard Road, then west on Wisconsin Street to Lakeshore Drive.

CAUTION: Do not even consider swimming in Cook Inlet! Soft mud, swift tides and icy water make this extremely dangerous!

The YMCA, 5353 Lake Otis Parkway, offers discounts to outside members with YMCA identification. Phone (907) 563-3211 for pool schedule and more information.

The following pools are also open to the public: Service High School pool, 5577 Abbott Road, phone (907) 346-3040; Bartlett High School pool, 25-500 Muldoon Road, phone (907) 337-6375; West High School pool, 1700 Hillcrest Dr., phone (907) 274-5161; East High School pool, 4025 E. 24th Ave., phone (907) 278-9761; Dimond High School pool, 2909 W. 88th Ave., phone (907) 249-0355; Chugiak High School pool, South Birchwood Loop Road, off the Glenn Highway north of Anchorage, phone (907) 696-2010; and University of Alaska pool, Providence Drive, phone (907) 786-1233.

Charter Boats: Visitors must drive south to the Kenai Peninsula for charter boats. Sightseeing and fishing charters are available at Whittier, Seward and Homer.

Fishing: The Alaska Dept. of Fish and Game annually stocks about 28 lakes in the Anchorage area with rainbow trout, landlocked chinook (king) salmon, grayling and arctic char. Approximately 103,000 6- to 8-inch rainbow trout are released each year along with about 50,000 salmon. All lakes are open to the public. In addition, salmon-viewing areas and limited salmon fishing are available in the immediate Anchorage area. For specific information, check the Alaska fishing regulations book, call the agency at (907) 267-2218, or phone (907) 349-4687 for a recorded message. Urban salmon fisheries have been developed recently by the Alaska

Snow sculptures are on display during Fur Rendezvous in February. (© Tom Bol)

Dept. of Fish and Game in several Anchorage-area streams. King and coho salmon can be caught in **Ship Creek** in downtown Anchorage through July as well as in **Eagle River** just north of town. Coho salmon fisheries opened for the first time in 1993 in **Campbell Creek** in Anchorage and at **Bird Creek** just north of Girdwood on the Seward Highway. Natural-run pink salmon are also available in Bird Creek.

Several excellent fishing spots are within a day's drive of Anchorage. The Kenai Peninsula offers streams where king, red, silver, pink and chum salmon may be caught during the season. Dolly Varden and steelhead also run in peninsula streams. Several lakes contain trout and landlocked salmon. In-season saltwater fishing for halibut, rockfish and several species of salmon is excellent at many spots along the peninsula and out of Whittier, Homer and Seward. For specific fishing spots both north and south of Anchorage see the Seward, Sterling, Glenn and Parks highways sections. Because of the importance of fishing to Alaska both commercially and for sport, regulations are strictly enforced. Regulations are updated yearly by the state, often after *The MILEPOST* deadline, so it is wise to obtain a current regulations book. ●

WINTER ATTRACTIONS

Alyeska Resort. Located in the community of Girdwood, Alyeska Resort is a 45-mile/65-km drive south from Anchorage along scenic Turnagain Arm via the Seward Highway. Judged by *Conde Nast Traveler* as having the "best view" of any U.S. ski resort, Alyeska Resort is Alaska's largest ski resort, with snow from early November to the middle of April. Night skiing is available during holiday periods in December and on Fridays and Saturdays from January through March. Ski facilities include a high-speed detachable bubble quad, 2 fixed grip quads, 3 double chair lifts and 2 pony tows. In 1996, Alyeska Resort gained the North Face, the north-facing side of Mount Alyeska; this acquisition added 6 new runs and 104 acres of expert terrain. Chair 7, a fixed grip quad, added 20 acres of beginner and intermediate ski terrain to the resort's existing terrain. A 60-passenger aerial tram takes sightseers and skiers from the mountain's base at 250 feet/76m to a mountaintop facility at the 2,300-foot/701-m level. This facility, open year-round and accessible by wheelchair, features a large viewing deck, a cafeteria-style restaurant and a fine dining restaurant and lounge. Centerpiece for the resort is the 307-room, chateau-style Westin Alyeska Prince Hotel. The hotel features a fitness facility with indoor swimming pool and 16-person whirlpool, 4 restaurants and 2 lounges. For more information, phone (907) 754-1111 or (800) 880-3880.

Alpenglow at Arctic Valley: East of downtown Anchorage in the Chugach Mountains, Alpenglow Ski Area has a 4,500-foot/1,372-m double chair lift, a 2,200-foot/671-m double chair lift, a 2,800-foot/873-m T-bar platter lift combination and a 700-foot/213-m rope tow for beginners. Day lodge with full cafeteria and ski shop. Cross-country skiing is available, but trails are not maintained. The ski area operates from about late October until early May. Hours are 1–9 P.M. Wednesday and Thursday, 10 A.M. to 9 P.M. Friday, Saturday and all school holidays, and 10 A.M. to 6 P.M. Sunday. Drive northeast from downtown on the Glenn Highway. Just beyond Ship Creek, turn right on Arctic Valley Road and follow the main road 7.5 miles/12 km to the ski area. For more information, phone (907) 563-2524.

Hilltop Ski Area: Located 15 minutes from downtown Anchorage 4 miles/6.4 km east of the Seward Highway at Dimond, Hilltop has 2 miles/3.2 km of lighted slopes classified as beginner to intermediate. Ski facilities include a double chair lift; a beginner rope tow; 15m, 40m and 60m jumps; and certified snowboard half-pipe. Ski rentals (Alpine, Nordic and snowboards), ski school, gift shop and restaurant. Open daily with complete night lighting. Hours are 3–9 P.M. Monday through Friday, and 9 A.M. to 9 P.M. weekends. There are also 9 miles/15 km of cross-country ski trails in adjoining Hillside and Bicentennial parks, with 5 miles/8 km offering night lighting. For more information, phone (907) 346-1446.

Chugach State Park: Although the entire park is open to cross-country skiers, most

A floatplane lands at Lake Spenard. (© Terry Chick)

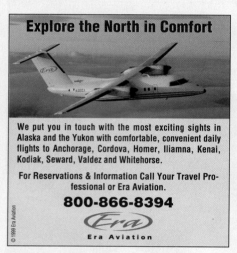

maintained ski trails are found in the Hillside Trail System/Campbell Creek area, accessible via Upper Huffman Road and Upper O'Malley Road. Skiers are encouraged to use established trails as most of Chugach State Park is prime avalanche country.

Five major areas in the park are open to snowmobiling when snow levels are deep enough: Eklutna Lake Valley, reached from the Glenn Highway via Eklutna Road; Eagle River valley, also accessible from the Glenn Highway; Bird Creek, **Milepost S 101.2** Seward Highway; Peters Creek Valley and Little Peters Creek, accessible from the Glenn Highway; and portions of the Hillside/Campbell Creek area, accessible from Upper Huffman Road. A 24–hour recorded message giving the status of all snowmobile areas is available at (907) 694-6391.

Ski trail maps and snowmobiling infor-

mation are available at the trailheads or from the park office, phone (907) 345-5014.

Russian Jack Springs: Located at DeBarr Road and Boniface Parkway. This ski area has a chalet, a ski rope tow and 8 miles/13 km of cross-country ski trails, 3 miles/5 km of which are lighted. The ski area is maintained by the Municipality of Anchorage. Ski trail maps are available at Anchorage Parks and Recreation, phone (907) 343-4474.

Far North Bicentennial/Hillside Parks: Best access to this 5,000-acre tract in the eastern portion of the Anchorage bowl is via Hilltop Ski Area on Abbott Road. There are 13.7 miles/22 km of groomed cross-country ski trails, 3.9 miles/6.3 km of which are lighted. There are also 6 miles/9.7 km of multi-use trails. Cross-country skiing is allowed anywhere in the area except on dogsled trails. For further information, phone Anchorage Parks and Recreation, (907) 343-4474.

Beach Lake Park: 10.5 miles/16.9 km of groomed cross-country ski trails with 3 miles/4.8 km lighted. There are approximately 20 miles/32 km of dog mushing trail. Wheelchair-accessible lodge and cabins available for a minimal user fee. Outstanding views of lake and wildlife from lodge deck and cabins. Contact Eagle River Parks and Recreation, phone (907) 694-2011.

Campbell Creek Green Belt: The municipality maintains approximately 3 miles/4.8 km of multi-use ski trails in south Anchorage.

Centennial Park: 3 miles/4.8 km of wooded cross-country ski trails over some hilly terrain, and located near Glenn Highway and Muldoon Road. Contact Anchorage Parks & Recreation (907) 333-8338 or (907) 343-4474 off season (October–April).

(Continues on page 382)

Chugach State Park

This 495,000-acre park, flanking Anchorage to the north, east and south, offers wilderness opportunities for all seasons: hiking, wildlife viewing, camping, berry picking, skiing and snowmobiling. Information about the park is available from Chugach State Park, H.C. 52, Box 8999, Indian, AK 99540; phone (907) 345-5014. The Chugach State Park office, located in Potter Section House on the Seward Highway, has maps showing access to the park's recreation areas.

Between June and September, park staff offer guided nature walks and more strenuous hikes on the weekends to various points of interest in the park. The nature walks, which last about 2 hours, focus on some aspect of natural history, such as wildflower identification or bird watching. The longer hikes last approximately 4 hours. Phone (907) 694-6391 for a recorded message.

There are several access points to Chugach State Park attractions from Anchorage. North from downtown on the Glenn Highway take the Eklutna Road exit (**Milepost A 26.3**) and drive in 10 miles/16 km to reach Eklutna Lake Recreation Area. Eklutna Lake is the largest lake in Chugach State Park. The

Hikers on the popular Flattop Mountain trail in Chugach State Park's Hillside trail system. (© Bill Sherwonit)

recreation area has a campground, picnic area and hiking trails. Cross-country skiing and snowmobiling in winter.

You may also reach Eagle River Nature Center for Chugach State Park by driving north on the Glenn Highway and taking the Eagle River exit (**Milepost A 13.4**). Follow Eagle River Road 12.7 miles/20.4 km to reach this beautifully situated visitor center with its views of the Chugach

Mountains. Excellent wildlife displays, a nature trail, Dall sheep viewing and other summer activities make this a worthwhile stop. Cross-country skiing and snowmobiling in winter. Phone (907) 694-2108 for more information.

Another park area easily accessible from downtown is Arctic Valley. Turn off the Glenn Highway at Arctic Valley Road, **Milepost A 6.1**, and drive in 7.5 miles/12 km. Spectacular views of Anchorage and Cook Inlet. Good berry picking and hiking in summer; downhill and cross-country skiing in winter.

The park's hillside trailheads may be reached by driving south from downtown to the O'Malley Road exit at **Milepost S 120.8** on the Seward Highway. Follow O'Malley Road east for 4 miles/6.4 km to Hillside Drive; turn right on Hillside and proceed about 1.5 miles/2.4 km to the intersection of Upper Huffman and Hillside Drive. Turn left on Upper Huffman and continue 4 miles/6.4 km to the Glen Alps trailhead and parking lot. Hiking in summer, cross-country skiing and snowmobiling in winter.

The Seward Highway south from Anchorage gives access to several

Cruise Alaska With a National Park Ranger

KENAI ★ STAR

Welcome aboard for Alaska's finest day cruises in the Kenai Fjords and Prince William Sound

Only Major Marine Tours offers:
- *National Park Ranger on every Kenai Fjords cruise*
- *Reserved table seating for every guest*
- *Freshly prepared, all-you-can-eat Alaskan salmon and chicken buffet*

Kenai Fjords National Park
- Half-day and full-day cruises
- Puffins, sea lions, otters, whales, bird colonies and more
- Spectacular alpine, piedmont and tidewater glaciers
- Educational Junior Ranger program for kids
- Departs daily from Seward at 11:30 am, 1:15 pm and 6:00 pm*
- Special Transportation/Cruise/SeaLife Center packages available

Starting at **$49**

*6:00 pm cruise commences mid-June.

Prince William Sound Glaciers

$99

- Relaxing 6-hour cruise in calm, protected waters
- Prince William Sound's best glacier viewing because we stop and drift in front of glaciers to see more calving than other cruises
- Abundant wildlife, towering waterfalls and more
- Departs Whittier at 11:45 am
- Whittier's best cruise value – compare and save!
- Rail/Cruise packages available from Anchorage and Portage

Famous $10 Salmon & Chicken Buffet

Our "cruising restaurant" service allows you to dine on an all-you-can-eat Alaskan salmon and chicken buffet (with dessert bar) while you sail past wildlife, glaciers and beautiful scenery.

Reservations/Information
274-7300
800-764-7300
www.majormarine.com

MAJOR MARINE TOURS

World-Class Wildlife and Glacier Cruises

411 West 4th • Anchorage
#2 Boardwalk • Seward
Railroad Station • Portage

Children 11 and under are half-price for both the cruise and the meal.

Vacation Cum Laude.

ARCTIC CIRCLE C L U B

THIS IS TO CERTIFY THAT

IS A FULLY ACCREDITED, LIFETIME MEMBER HAVING CROSSED THE ARCTIC CIRCLE IN THE STATE OF ALASKA ON

WITH ALASKA AIRLINES

JOHN F. KELLY
CHAIRMAN & CHIEF EXECUTIVE OFFICER

Alaska Airlines

•BARROW
•KOTZEBUE •FAIRBANKS
•NOME
•ANCHORAGE

Day Trips From Anchorage

View of Seward Highway along Turnagain Arm from McHugh Creek trail.
(© David Ranta, staff)

Several interesting and memorable sights may be taken in on a day's drive from Anchorage by heading either south of downtown on the Seward Highway or north on the Glenn or Parks highways. Following are some of the points of interest along these roads. Follow the mile-by-mile logs given in the related highway sections in *The MILEPOST*®. Keep in mind that several companies offer motorcoach tours to many of these same attractions and that you can see a great many attractions in a short amount of time by taking a flightseeing trip out of Anchorage; there's even a 1-day trip to Kotzebue from Anchorage.

South from Anchorage, the Seward Highway offers some spectacular views of Turnagain Arm less than 10 miles/16 km from downtown. Stop for photos at one of the scenic viewpoints, such as Beluga Point. Another stop close to Anchorage is Potter Marsh for bird watching.

Continue south to **Milepost S 90** (37 miles/59.5 km from Anchorage) for the Alyeska Highway Road turnoff. About 2 miles/3.2 km up this road, a gravel road forks to the left and leads 3.1 miles/5 km to **Crow Creek Mine**, a historic 1898 mining camp where visitors can tour the camp's old buildings and pan for gold. Returning from the mine to the main road, continue to the town of Girdwood. The **Girdwood Forest Fair** takes place on a weekend in early July. Drive up to the luxurious Alyeska Prince Hotel, Alaska's largest ski resort. The 60-passenger aerial tram carries skiers and sightseers from the base of the mountain to a viewing deck, a fine dining restaurant and lounge and a cafeteria-style restaurant at the 2,300-foot/701-m level. The tram ride offers an unsurpassed view of Turnagain Arm.

Back out on the Seward Highway, continue south 11 miles/17.7 km to **Milepost S 79.1** and the Portage Glacier Access Road. On the 5-mile/8-km drive to the glacier, watch for salmon spawning at

Williwaw Creek and look for the hanging Explorer Glacier. The Begich, Boggs Visitor Center at Portage Glacier has interpretive displays on glaciers, regular showings of films of interest and Forest Service naturalists available to answer your questions. You can stand on the shore of Portage Lake or take a tour boat for a close-up view of Portage Glacier.

Return to the Seward Highway. You may wish to head back up the highway to Anchorage, depending on your time. This would add up to about 114 miles/183 km total driving distance. Or extend your trip farther south to take in the old gold mining town of Hope.

North from Anchorage, the Glenn and Parks highways offer many attractions. Drive out on the Glenn Highway from downtown Anchorage to Palmer, 42 miles/67.6 km. Heart of the Matanuska-Susitna Valley, the Palmer–Wasilla area has the Alaska State Fair, Muskox Farm, Mushers' Hall of Fame and the Iditarod Trail Headquarters visitor center. Drive 59 miles/95 km east on the Glenn Highway from Palmer to see the spectacular **Matanuska Glacier**. Several lakes in the area offer picnicking and water sports. Largest is Big Lake, a year-round recreation area accessible from Big Lake Road off the Parks Highway, 52 miles/84 km from Anchorage. Kepler–Bradley State Recreation Area on Matanuska Lake, at **Milepost A 36.4** Glenn Highway, has canoe rentals.

You may wish to stop off at Eklutna Lake, the Chugach State Park Nature Center or the Alaska Museum of Natural History in Eagle River. Also, take the Eklutna Road exit for Eklutna Village Historical Park, which features 350 years of Athabascan culture. The park, which includes St. Nicholas Russian Orthodox Church and colorful spirit houses marking grave sites, is open daily, 9 A.M. to 9 P.M., from the end of May to mid-September; admission charged.

(Continued from page 378)

Chester Creek Green Belt: Located in the heart of Anchorage, the municipality maintains more than 6.2 miles/10 km of cross-country ski trails.

Connors Lake Park: A popular site to learn skijoring, run in conjunction with the local skijoring club. Over 4.8 miles/7.7 km of multi-use trails.

Kincaid Park: 31 miles/50 km of cross-country ski trails are marked and maintained for novice, intermediate and expert skiers by the municipality. There are 16.5 miles/26.5 km of lighted trails and a warm-up chalet. Access is from the west end of Raspberry Road. Ski trail maps are available at Anchorage Parks & Recreation, phone (907) 343-4474; or Kincaid Park, phone (907) 343-6397.

Turnagain Pass: On the Seward Highway, about 59 miles/95 km south of downtown Anchorage. Turnagain Pass (elev. 988 feet/301m) is a popular winter recreation area in the Chugach National Forest. The west side of the pass is open to snowmobiling as soon as snow cover permits; the east side is reserved for skiers. Snow depths in this pass often exceed 12 feet/4m.

Dog Mushing begins in December. Dog mushing organizations in the Montana Creek area, Knik, Chugiak, Palmer and Anchorage sponsor races every weekend. Anchorage races usually begin in January at the Tozier Track and continue through the end of February. In addition, some of the clubs offer instruction in the sport. Several of the races are considered preliminaries to the World Championship races held during the Anchorage Fur Rendezvous.

The annual Iditarod Trail Sled Dog Race, 1,049 miles/1688.2 km to Nome, takes place in March. The race begins on 4th Avenue in downtown Anchorage, and mushers on the trail can be seen along the Glenn Highway, in the Knik Bridge area about 30 miles/48 km north of Anchorage and at Knik on the west side of Knik Arm.

For race dates, times and locations, watch local newspapers for details.

Anchorage Fur Rendezvous: This is the major event of the winter season in Anchorage. Billed as the "Mardi Gras of the North," this elaborate winter festival, held in February, attracts thousands of celebrants annually.

The 10-day-long celebration dates from 1936 when it began primarily as a fur auction where trappers could bring their pelts to town and make a few extra dollars selling them to buyers from around the world. Trappers still bring their pelts, and the fur auction still attracts many buyers.

Alaskans shake off cabin fever during "Rondy" (the local term for the Fur Rendezvous). As spectators or participants, they enjoy arts and crafts exhibits, a parade, the Miners' and Trappers' Ball, a blanket toss, a carnival and pet shows. Some Rondy competitions are colorful: a beard-growing contest, a waiter and waitress race, an ice and snow sculpturing contest and a home-brew competition.

During the first weekend of the Fur Rendezvous, the Annual World Championship Dog Weight Pulling Contest attracts several thousand spectators at Mulcahy Park, located at E. 16th Avenue and Cordova Street.

The highlight of the Fur Rendezvous, however, is dog mushing. The World Championship Sled Dog Race, held during the final 3 days, attracts dozens of mushers from

$25

The movement of Portage Glacier is measured in inches per day. Our cruise is measured in gasps per hour.

Never before has something that moves so slow inspired reactions so large. Gray Line of Alaska's Portage Glacier cruise takes you aboard the mv Ptarmigan for a comfortable one–hour cruise to within 300 yards of this massive active glacier. Narrated by a representative from the US Forest Service, this tour gives you an up-close view of one of the most spectacular glaciers in all of Alaska.

Departures: Daily, May 13–Sept 19 at 10:30 am, 12:00 pm, 1:30 pm, 3:00 pm, and 4:30 pm.
Later departures may be available during the season.
Please contact Portage Glacier Cruises at (907) 783–2983.

GRAY LINE *Gray Line of Alaska*
A DIVISION OF HOLLAND AMERICA LINE-WESTOURS

Alaska, Canada and the Lower 48. Thousands of spectators line the 25-mile/40-km race course, which begins and ends on 4th Avenue in downtown Anchorage. *(CAUTION: Leave pets and flashbulbs home, as they'll distract the dog teams.)* The musher with the best total elapsed time in 3 heats over 3 days is declared the winner. The women's and junior world championship sled dog races are held at Tozier Track the first weekend of the Fur Rendezvous. For more information, phone (907) 277-8615.

Ice Skating: Three municipal facilities, Ben Boeke Ice Arena (334 E. 16th Ave., phone 907/274-2767), Dempsey-Anderson Ice Arena (1741 W. Northern Lights, phone 907/277-7571) and Harry J. McDonald Center (13701 Old Glenn Highway in Eagle River, phone 907/696-0051) offer a total of 4 indoor rinks for spectator as well as participatory uses; an additional indoor rink at Dempsey-Anderson is scheduled for completion in early 1999. The University of Alaska also has 1 indoor rink as does the Dimond Center shopping mall. Outdoor ice-skating areas include Cheney Lake, Chester Creek Sports Complex, Delaney Recreation Area, Goose Lake, Jewel Lake Park, Spenard Lake, Delong Lake, Tikishla Park and Westchester Lagoon.

Sledding: Popular sledding hills are at Balto Seppala Park, Centennial Park, Conifer Park, Kincaid Park, Nunaka Valley Park, Sitka Street Park, Sunset Park, Service High School and Alaska Pacific University.

Snowshoeing: Muldoon Park, Far North Bicentennial Park and Campbell Creek Green Belt are used for snowshoeing, as are backcountry areas of Chugach National Forest and Chugach State Park.

Winter Basketball. Anchorage hosts 2 major collegiate basketball events. The Great

Hikers on the popular Flattop Mountain trail in Chugach State Park's Hillside trail system. (© Bill Sherwonit)

Alaska Shootout, held every Thanksgiving weekend, features 8 major college basketball teams in this well-known invitational tournament. The Northern Lights Invitational showcases women's collegiate basketball with 8 teams in a 3-day playoff the last weekend in February.

Ice Fishing: Countless lakes in the Anchorage and the Matanuska–Susitna Valley areas offer excellent ice fishing. Ice fishing is especially good in the early winter in Southcentral. Some Anchorage lakes are stocked each year with landlocked king salmon or rainbow trout. Among them: **Beach Lake, Cheney Lake, Delong Lake, Jewel Lake, Little Campbell Lake** in Kincaid Park and **Sand Lake**. For more information contact the Alaska Dept. of Fish and Game at (907) 344-0541; for a recorded message on fishing and ice conditions, phone (907) 349-4687. ✇

PARKS HIGHWAY ① ③

Connects: Anchorage to Fairbanks, AK **Length:** 358 miles
Road Surface: Paved **Season:** Open all year
Highest Summit: Broad Pass 2,300 feet
Major Attraction: Denali National Park
(See maps, pages 386–387)

	Anchorage	Denali Park	Fairbanks	Talkeetna	Wasilla
Anchorage		237	358	113	42
Denali Park	237		121	153	195
Fairbanks	358	121		245	316
Talkeetna	113	153	245		71
Wasilla	42	195	316	71	

Sunrise on Mount McKinley above foggy Wonder Lake. *(© Beth Davidow)*

The Parks Highway was called the Anchorage–Fairbanks Highway after its completion in 1971, and renamed in July 1975, in honor of George A. Parks (1883–1984), the territorial governor from 1925 to 1933. The Parks Highway (Alaska Route 3) junctions with the Glenn Highway (Alaska Route 1) 35 miles/56.3 km from Anchorage and leads 323 miles/520 km north to Fairbanks. Together, these highways connect Alaska's largest population centers.

The entire route runs 358 miles/576 km through some of the grandest scenery that Alaska has to offer.

The Parks Highway is a good 2-lane paved road, but with few passing lanes. Several sections of moderate S-curves and heavy foliage reduce sight distance: Pass with care. *CAUTION: Drive with headlights on at all times. Watch for moose. Watch for local cross traffic.* Motorists who plan to drive the highway during the winter should check highway conditions before proceeding.

The Parks Highway provides the most direct highway access to Denali National Park and Preserve (formerly Mount McKinley National Park) from either Anchorage or Fairbanks. Driving distance to the park entrance is 237.3 miles/381.9 km from Anchorage and 120.7 miles/194.2 km from Fairbanks. Mount McKinley—also called Denali—(elev. 20,320 feet/6,194m) is visible from the highway, weather permitting, and there are several viewing turnouts. See DENALI NATIONAL PARK section for details on the park.

Emergency medical services: Between the Glenn Highway junction and **Milepost**

A 202.1, phone 911. Between **Milepost A 174** at Hurricane Gulch bridge and **Milepost A 224** at Carlo Creek bridge, phone the Cantwell ambulance at 768-2982 or the state troopers at 768-2202. Between **Milepost A 224** and Fairbanks, phone 911.

Parks Highway Log

Distance from Anchorage (A) is followed by distance from Fairbanks (F).
Mileposts along the Parks Highway indicate distance from Anchorage.

ALASKA ROUTE 1
A 0 F 358 (576.1 km) **ANCHORAGE.** Follow the Glenn Highway (Alaska Route 1) north 35 miles/56.3 km to junction with the Parks Highway. (Turn to the end of the GLENN HIGHWAY section on page 337 and read log back to front from Anchorage to junction with the Parks Highway.)

A 35.3 (56.8 km) F 322.7 (519.3 km) Traffic light at intersection of Glenn and

Parks highways; Fairbanks-bound travelers turn on Parks Highway.

> **Junction** of the Parks Highway (Alaska Route 3) and the Glenn Highway (Alaska Route 1). Turn to **Milepost A 35.3** in the GLENN HIGHWAY section for log of highway to Anchorage or Tok.

Fairbanks-bound travelers continue with this log. Begin truck lane northbound next 1.1 miles/1.8 km.

ALASKA ROUTE 3
A 35.4 (57 km) F 322.6 (519.2 km) Produce stand in summer on east side of highway just south of **junction** with Trunk Road. **Trunk Road** leads northeast 0.7 mile/1.1 km to University of Alaska Fairbanks' Matanuska agricultural research farm (no tours). Also access via Trunk Road to Mat-Su College (1.8 miles/2.9 km); Palmer-Wasilla Highway (3.1 miles/5 km); Bogard Road (4.2 miles/6.8 km); and Palmer-Fishhook Road (6.5 miles/10.5 km).

NOTE: In summer 1999, watch for road construction northbound next 2 miles/3.2 km as highway is widened to 4 lanes.

A 35.5 (57.1 km) F 322.5 (519 km) Turn uphill on Welcome Way for **Mat–Su Visitors Center** and Best View RV Park (0.6 mile/1 km on Best View Drive). The visitor center is

open May 15 to Sept. 15, 8 A.M. to 6 P.M. daily. This large center offers a wide variety of displays and information on the Mat–Su Valley; pay phone, gift shop. There is a veterans' memorial adjacent the visitor center. The visitor center operates a booking and

PARKS HIGHWAY
Anchorage, AK, to Milepost A 169

(map continues next page)

© 1999 The MILEPOST®

Denali National Park and Preserve

Glaciated Area

Mount McKinley
20,320 ft./6,193m

Mount Barrille
7,650 ft./2,332m
▲ The Mooses Tooth
10,335 ft./3,150m

Mount Hunter ▲
14,573 ft./4,442m
▲ Mount Huntington
12,240 ft./3,731m
▲ Mount Dickey
9,845 ft./3,001m

Buckskin Glacier

Tokositna Glacier

Ruth Glacier

Kahiltna Glacier

Eldridge Glacier

Denali

State

Park

TALKEETNA

East Fork

Honolulu Creek

F-189/305km
A-169/271km

Little Coal Creek

Susitna River

Spink Lake

A-147/236.6km Susitna Expeditions

Byers L.

Troublesome Cr.

A-134.5/216.5km Mary's McKinley View Lodge LM
A-134/215.6km ERA Helicopter
A-132.8/213.7km D&S Alaskan Trail Rides
Mt. McKinley Princess Lodge LM

The Alaska Railroad

Petersville

Petersville Road

F-243/391km
A-115/185km

J-18.7/30.1km Forks Roadhouse ILM
J-17.2/27.7km McKinley Foothills B&B/Cabins L
J-10.5/17.3km Gate Creek Cabins L
J-2.7/5km North Country Bed & Breakfast L
J-2/5.2km Denali View Chalets L
J-0.7/1.1km Trapper Creek Museum & Gifts
J-0.3/0.5km Trapper Creek B&B L

Trapper Creek

Talkeetna
N62°19' W150°06'

A-115.5/185.9km Trapper Creek Trading Post CDGILMPST
A-114.9/184.9km Trapper Creek's Old Historic Post Office

A-114.8/184.7km Trapper Creek Inn & General Store CDdGILMPST
A-101.8/163.8km Talkeetna Bluegrass Festival
A-99.5/160.1km H&H Lakeview Restaurant & Lodge CDdGILMPST
A-99/159.3km Denali Way Auto R
A-98.8/159km Sunshine One Stop dGIMPST
A-98.7/158.8km Moores' Mercantile
Mary Carey's Fiddlehead Fern Farm
Talkeetna/Denali Visitor Center
A-96.5/155.3km Montana Creek Campgrounds C
A-91.5/147.3km Susitna Dog Tours & Bed and Breakfast L
A-90.8/146.1km Mat-Su RV Park & Campground CDILPST
A-88.2/142km Sheep Creek Lodge CGILMPT
A-87.1/140.2km Camp Caswell CILPST

A-85.5/137.6km Willow Wildlife Art Gallery

J-14.3/23km Mountain Gift Shop & Visitor Info. Cabin

J-2.2/3.5km Gold Pan B&B L
J-1/1.6km Moose Dropping Inn Bed & Breakfast L

F-259/417km
A-99/159km

Caswell Cr.

Kashwitna River

Sheep Cr.

MOUNTAINS

Glaciated Area

A-88.1/141.8km Gigglewood Lakeside Inn LM

A-80/128.7km Lucky Husky

Kashwitna Lake

A-71.4/114.9km Pioneer Lodge CDILMPT
A-70/112.7km Willow Air Service Inc.
A-69.5/111.8km Willow Trading Post Lodge CDILMT
Ruth Lake Lodge
A-69.4/111.7km Townsite Texaco Foodmart
A-69/111km Willow True Value Hardware, Willow Creek Grocery, Willow Creek Service GIPrST
A-68.8/110.7km Newman's Hilltop Service dGIPST
A-68.1/109.6km Willow Winter Park
A-66.5/107km Alaskan Host B&B L
A-54.3/87.5km Alaska Explorers & Fishermen

A-71.5/115km Willow Island Resort CDLS
J-2/3.2km Alaska Creekside Bed & Breakfast L
A-64.5/103.8km Nancy Lake Resort CGILPST
A-57.8/93km Fisherman's Choice Charters
A-57.7/92.9km Riverside Camper Park CDIT
A-57.6/92.7km Miller's Place CILMST

Willow

Little Willow Cr.

Willow Cr.

Nancy L.

Hatcher Pass
3,886 ft./1,184m

To Glennallen
(see GLENN HIGHWAY section, page 304)

Mint Glacier

Hatcher Pass Road

A-49/78.9km Mile 49 Cafe
A-47/75.6km Museum of Alaska Transportation & Industry
A-45.5/73.2km Trading Post & Gifts
A-45/72.4km Wasilla Car Wash
A-42.7/68.7km The Rock Shop
A-42.5/68.4km The Deli Restaurant & Bakery M

Matanuska River

Mat-Su Valley Vicinity
(see detailed map on page 389)

A-51.3/82.6km Earth 'n Art Studio & Gift Shop

Houston

Wasilla

W-3.5/5.6km Cache Camper

Palmer

Big Lake

A-50.2/80.8km Iceworm RV Park & Country Store

Knik

Fish Creek

A-10.1/16.3km Knik Knack Mud Shack

Knik R.

A-41.1/66.1km Cottonwood Creek Mall MST
A-40.5/65.2km House of Tires, Inc. R
Pilgims Baptist Church
Valley Country Store & Motel LS
The Windbreak LM
A-40/64.4km Northern Recreation R

A-38.4/61.8km Alaska Jetboat Charters / Arctic Fox Taxidermy
A-35.5/57.1km Bestview RV Park CDIT
Matanuska-Susitna Convention & Visitors Bureau

J-29/46.6km Accord Guide Service Valley River Charters

J-13.9/22.4km Knik Museum Mushers' Hall Of Fame

F-323/519km
A-35/56km
G-152/245km

Little Susitna R.

Susitna R.

Knik Arm

Eklutna Lake

Knik Glacier

Chugach State Park

F-358/576km
A-0

Anchorage
N61°13' W149°52'

To Girdwood
(see SEWARD HIGHWAY section)

Cook Inlet

Glaciated Area

Key to mileage boxes
miles/kilometres
miles/kilometres from:
A-Anchorage
F-Fairbanks
J-Junction
W-Wasilla
G-Glennallen

Map Location

Principal Route
Paved / Unpaved
Other Roads
Paved / Unpaved
Ferry Routes / **Hiking Trails**

▓ Refer to Log for Visitor Facilities

Scale
0 ___ 10 Miles
0 ___ 10 Kilometres

Key to Advertiser Services
C-Camping
D-Dump Station
d-Diesel
G-Gas (reg., unld.)
I-Ice
L-Lodging
M-Meals
P-Propane
R-Car Repair (major)
r-Car Repair (minor)
S-Store (grocery)
T-Telephone (pay)

PARKS HIGHWAY   Milepost A 169 to Fairbanks, AK

© 1999 The MILEPOST®

Key to mileage boxes

miles/kilometres
miles/kilometres   from:

A- Anchorage
J- Junction
F- Fairbanks
P- Paxson

Map Location

Principal Route
Paved   Unpaved
Other Roads
Paved   Unpaved
Ferry Routes   **Hiking Trails**

Refer to Log for Visitor Facilities

Scale
0   10 Miles
0   10 Kilometres

Key to Advertiser Services
C -Camping
D -Dump Station
d -Diesel
G -Gas (reg., unld.)
I -Ice
L -Lodging
M -Meals
P -Propane
R -Car Repair (major)
r -Car Repair (minor)
S -Store (grocery)
T -Telephone (pay)

To Manley Hot Springs
(see ELLIOTT HIGHWAY section)

To Circle
(see STEESE HIGHWAY section)

Murphy Dome
2,930 ft./893m ▲

F-0
A-358/576km

A-352.5/567.3km Gold Hill dGI
Inua Wool Shoppe
Parks Highway Truck Stop dG

A-356.8/574.2km Justa Store

To Chena Hot Springs

N64°50' W148°01'   ●Ester

Fairbanks
N64°08' W147°08'

3

To Delta Junction
(see RICHARDSON HIGHWAY section)

The Alaska Railroad

A-328/527.8km Skinny Dick's Halfway Inn

N64°34' W149°05'   Nenana

F-53/86km
A-305/490km

A-304.5/490km A-Frame Service dGIPST

Teklanika River

Fish Creek

Anderson
Clear

Julius Creek

F-75/120km
A-284/456km

A-283.5/456.2km Anderson Riverside Park CDT
A-280.1/450.8km Rochester Lodge CLM
A-280/450.6km Clear Sky Lodge IMPT
A-276/444.2km Tatlanika Trading Co. CD

Rex Dome ▲
4,155 ft./1,266m

Jumbo Dome ▲
4,493 ft./1,369m

Walker Dome ▲
3,942 ft./1,202m

A-248.8/400.4km Denali North Star Inn L
Stampede Lodge & Bushmaster Grill LMT
A-248.7/400.2km Totem Inn LMT
A-248.5/399.8km Nenana Raft Adventures
A-248.4/399.8km McKinley RV & Campground CDIPST
A-248.3/399.6km Evans Industries, Inc. R
A-247/397.5km Black Diamond Golf Course
Homestead B&B L
Otto Lake B&B L
Otto Lake R.V. Park and Campground CD
A-245.1/394.4km Denali RV Park & Motel CLT

A-251.1/404.1km Earth Song Lodge L

N63°51' W148°58'

Healy

A-249.5/401.5km Motel Nord Haven L
A-249.2/401km Larry's Healy Tesoro dGIPST

Suntrana

Usibelli

Dora Peak ▲
5,572 ft./1,698m

Sugarloaf Mountain ▲
4,450 ft./1,356m

Healy Cr.

A-239.1/384.8km Alaska Raft Adventures
McKinley Chalet Resort LM
A-239/384.6km Northern Lights Theatre and Gift Shop IS
A-238.9/384.5km Denali Outdoor Center
A-238.8/384.3km Denali Sourdough Cabins L
A-238.7/384.1km Denali Windsong Lodge LT
A-238.5/383.8km Denali Princess Lodge
Denali Wilderness Lodge
A-238.4/383.6km Denali Bluffs Hotel LT
Denali River View Inn L
A-238.1/383.2km Denali Raft Adventures

Mount Healy ▲
5,716 ft./1,742m

Mount Fellow ▲
4,476 ft./1,364m

Yanert Fork

Park Road
(see DENALI NATIONAL PARK section, page 462)

Park Entrance

F-121/194km
A-237/382km

Denali National Park and Preserve

Pyramid Peak ▲
5,201 ft./1,585m

A-231.1/371.9km Denali Grizzly Bear Cabins & Campground CILPST
Denali River Cabins CDLT
McKinley Village Resort LM
A-224.1/360.6km Carlo Heights B&B
and Rick Swenson's Denali Sled Dog School L

A-229.2/368.8km
Denali Air
A-229/368.5km
Denali Backcountry Lodge L
Denali Cabins LM

Fang Mountain ▲
6,736 ft./2,053m

Kantishna

Carlo Cr.

A-224/360.5km The Perch LMT
McKinley Creekside L
A-223.9/360.3km Carlo Creek Lodge CDILPST

R A N G E

A-210.4/338.6km Cotter's Quality Services dGIPT
A-210.3/338.4km Cantwell Food Mart S
Parkway Gift Shop

Cantwell

Nenana River

A-209.7/337.4km Reindeer Mtn. Lodge L

A L A S K A

Broad Pass
2,300 ft./701m

West Fork

Middle Fork

F-148/238km
A-210/338km
P-136/218km

To Paxson
(see DENALI HIGHWAY section, page 481)

A-193/310.6km Sourdough Paul's Bed & Breakfast L

A-188.5/303.4km Igloo City Resort CdGPS

East Fork Chulitna R.

Mount McKinley ▲
20,320 ft./6,194m

Glaciated Area

Eldridge Glacier

Chulitna River

Honolulu Creek

Coal Cr.

3

Mount Huntington ▲
12,240 ft./3,731m

The Mooses Tooth ▲
10,335 ft./3,150m

Mount Barrille ▲
7,650 ft./2,332m

Mount Dickey ▲
9,845 ft./3,001m

Buckskin Glacier

F-189/305km
A-169/271km

(map continues previous page)

reservation service; phone (907) 746-5000.

Matanuska–Susitna Convention & Visitors Bureau. See display ad this section.

Best View RV Park. See display ad this section. ▲

A 36.2 (58.3 km) **F 321.8** (517.9 km) End truck lane northbound; highway narrows to 2 lanes.

A 36.7 (59.1 km) **F 321.3** (517.1 km) Pioneer Drive.

A 37.4 (60.2 km) **F 320.6** (515.9 km) Air Lane; access to airstrip.

A 37.8 (60.8 km) **F 320.2** (515.3 km) Hyer Road. Wasilla Creek bridge. Turnout.

A 38 (61.2 km) **F 320** (515 km) Gas station/foodmart at turnoff to Fairview Loop Road west to Knik Road (11 miles/17.7 km). Access to Palmer Hay Flats State Game Refuge.

A 38.3 (61.6 km) **F 319.7** (514.5 km) Pioneer Plaza.

A 38.4 (61.8 km) **F 319.6** (514.3 km) **Alaska Jetboat Charters, Arctic Fox Taxidermy.** (907) 376-4776. Fishing charters, guided big game hunts and taxidermy shop. Guided half- or full-day fishing trips for king salmon, May 25 to July 13; silver salmon, July 15 to August 15. Guided big game hunts for bear, caribou, Dall sheep, moose and mountain goat. Arctic Fox Taxidermy specializes in Alaska fish and big game mounts.
[ADVERTISEMENT]

A 39 (62.8 km) **F 319** (513.4 km) Dimond Way.

A 39.4 (63.4 km) **F 318.6** (512.7 km) Shopping center and RV park at **junction** with Seward Meridian Road, which junctions with the Palmer–Wasilla Highway. (See Mat-Su Vicinity map this section.)

A 39.5 (63.6 km) **F 318.5** (512.6 km)

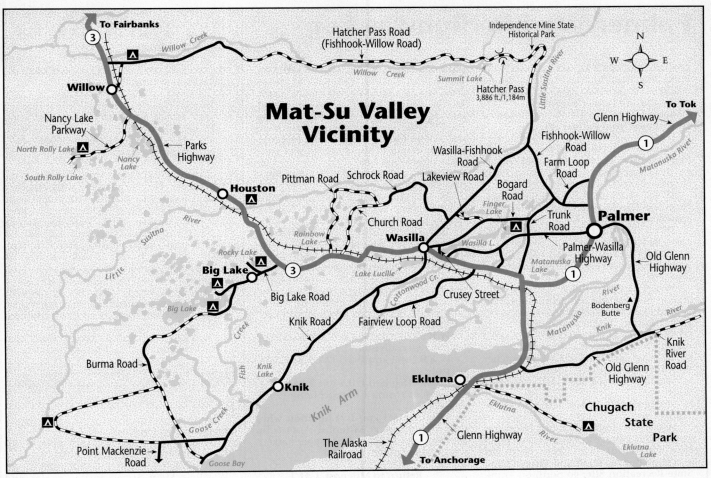

Mat-Su Valley
Vicinity

Wasilla city limits; medical clinic (376-1276). Wasilla shopping, services and attractions are located along the highway (from here north to **Milepost A 45**) and at Main Street in Wasilla city center.

A 40 (64.4 km) **F 318** (511.8 km) Herman Road. Gas station with diesel. Turnoff for RV service and supplies.

Northern Recreation. See display ad this section.

A 40.5 (65.2 km) **F 317.5** (511 km) Tire and auto repair, church, hotel, cafe and lounge.

House of Tires, Inc. See display ad this section.

Pilgrims Baptist Church. See display ad

this section.

Valley Country Store & Motel. See display ad this section.

Palmer-Wasilla Highway Log

This 10.1 mile/16.3 km road connects the Parks and Glenn highways (Alaska Routes 3 and 1). It provides access to a number of Wasilla and Palmer businesses.

Distance from Wasilla (W) is followed by distance from Palmer (P).

W 0 P 10.1 (16.3 km) **Junction** with Parks Highway at **Milepost A 41.1.** Access to drugstore, gas stations, auto body shops and other businesses.

W 0.7 (1.1 km) **P 9.4** (15.1 km) Cottonwood Creek; fish viewing platform; spawning salmon.

W 1.1 (1.8 km) **P 9** (14.5 km) Country Lakes Bed and Breakfast.

W 1.6 (2.6 km) **P 8.5** (13.7 km) Cottle Loop; Volunteer Park day-use area; bowling alley.

W 1.9 (3.1 km) **P 8.2** (13.2 km) Fire station and gas station at **junction** with Seward Meridian Road, which connects to Parks Highway at **Milepost A 39.4.**

W 2.9 (4.7 km) **P 7.2** (11.6 km) Alaskan Agate Inn bed and breakfast.

W 3 (4.8 km) **P 7.1** (11.4 km) Hatcher Business Park.

W 3.2 (5.1 km) **P 6.9** (11.1 km) Brentwood Plaza.

W 3.5 (5.6 km) **P 6.6** (10.6 km) Cache Camper.

W 6.1 (9.8 km) **P 4** (6.4 km) Tesoro gas station and grocery at **Four Corner junction** with Trunk Road. Turn north for access to Bogard Road and **Finger Lake State Recreation Site**; go north on Trunk Road 1 mile/1.6 km to Bogard Road; turn west and drive 0.8 mile/1.3 km to park entrance; drive in 0.3 mile/0.5 km on gravel road. A scenic spot with 41 campsites, wheelchair-accessible toilets, picnic tables, water, hiking trails and boat launch, $10 camping fee, 7-day limit. Use the life jackets provided! Finger Lake is on the **7-Mile Canoe Trail.** Public access to the canoe trail is also from Wasilla Lake and Cottonwood Lake. ♿▲

W 6.7 (10.8 km) **P 3.4** (5.5 km) Business Park; pizza.

W 7.2 (11.6 km) **P 2.9** (4.7 km) Moffit Road; access to 49th Street, Colony middle school and refuse dump.

W 7.9 (12.7 km) **P 2.2** (3.5 km) Eagle View Car Wash. Animal Control to south.

W 8.2 (13.2 km) **P 1.9** (3.1 km) Loma Prieta Drive. Access to **Crevasse–Moraine Trails**; 0.7 miles/1.1 km south to trailhead parking. This loop trail system is used for cross-country skiing in winter and hiking, mountain biking and horseback riding in summer.

W 8.6 (13.8 km) **P 1.5** (2.4 km) Equestrian Acres subdivision.

W 8.8 (14.2 km) **P 1.3** (2.1 km) Country store.

W 9.7 (15.6 km) **P 0.4** (0.6 km) Alaska Tsunami Warning Center; phone (907) 745-4212.

W 10.1 (16.3 km) **P 0 Junction** with Glenn Highway at **Milepost A 41.8** in Palmer; Carrs Mall (24-hour supermarket) and fast-food outlet.

**Return to Milepost A 41.1
Parks Highway or A 41.8
Glenn Highway**

The Windbreak. See display ad this section.

A 41 (66 km) **F 317** (510.1 km) Cottonwood Creek bridge.

A 41.1 (66.1 km) **F 316.9** (510 km) Cottonwood Mall, 24-hour supermarket and gas station at turnoff.

Junction with Palmer–Wasilla Highway, which leads east 10 miles/16 km to the Glenn Highway at Palmer. See PALMER–WASILLA HIGHWAY side road log this section.

Cottonwood Creek Mall. "We Do What We Do For You"! The area's only enclosed mall is located in Wasilla with ample parking—RVs welcome! Offering 24-hour grocery, Alaskan gifts, banking, family apparel and shoes, hair and nail salons, health store, family dining, free entertainment events. Hours Monday–Friday 10 A.M.–6 P.M.; Saturday 10 A.M.–6 P.M.; Sunday noon to 5 P.M. (907) 376-6802. [ADVERTISEMENT]

A 41.7 (67 km) **F 316.3** (509 km) **Wasilla Lake Park** with picnic shelter, restrooms, playground and swimming beach; limited parking. Monument to George Parks.

A 41.8 (67.3 km) **F 316.2** (508.9 km) Fastfood outlet at Crusey Street intersection.

Junction with Bogard Road. See BOGARD ROAD side road log this section.

A 42 (67.6 km) **F 316** (508.5 km) Supermarket and gas stations.

A 42.1 (67.8 km) **F 315.9** (508.4 km) Boundary Street, Lake Lucille Park.

A 42.2 (67.9 km) **F 315.8** (508.2 km) Wasilla's Main Street; visitor center and museum 1 block north; post office 2 blocks north (ZIP code 99687). Access to Hatcher Pass and Knik from this intersection. Turn south across railroad tracks for Knik Road to Knik, the "Dog Mushing Center of the World" (see KNIK ROAD log on page 392). Turn north on Wasilla's Main Street for downtown Wasilla and Hatcher Pass. Description of Wasilla follows.

Wasilla–Fishhook Road leads northeast about 10 miles/16 km to junction with the Hatcher Pass (Fishhook–Willow) Road to Independence Mine State Historical Park; see the map on page 389. (The Hatcher Pass Road is logged on page 326 in the GLENN HIGHWAY section.)

Wasilla

A 42.2 (67.9 km) **F 315.8** (508.2 km). Located between Wasilla and Lucille lakes in the Susitna Valley, about an hour's drive from Anchorage. **Population:** 5,134. **Emergency Services: City Police,** phone (907) 745-2131, emergency only phone 911. **Fire Department** and **Ambulance,** phone (907) 376-5320, emergency only phone 911. **Hospital,** in Palmer. **Doctor** on Seward Meridian Road, **Milepost A 39.5,** phone (907) 376-1276, and at West Valley Medical Center, E. Bogard Road, phone (907) 376-5028. Chiropractic clinics, phone (907) 373-2022.

Visitor Information: At the Dorothy Page Museum and Historical Townsite on Main Street just off the Parks Highway, phone (907) 373-9071, fax 373-9072. Or contact the chamber of commerce, Box

Bogard Road Log

This 7.6 mile/12.2 km road provides access to Wasilla businesses and Finger Lake State Recreation Site.
Distance from junction with Parks Highway (J) is shown.

J 0 Junction with Parks Highwat at Crusey Street intersection, **Milepost A 41.8**; turn on Crusey Street.

J 0.5 (0.8 km) Wasilla High School; turn east on Bogard Road.

J 1.4 (2.3 km) Turnoff for **Mat-Su Resort** on Wasilla Lake; dining and lodging.

J 1.7 (2.7 km) Special Feet Studio of Alaskan artist Sabine Becker.

J 3 (4.8 km) Junction with Seward–Meridian Road.

J 4.6 (7.4 km) Intersection with E. Selden Road; gas station.

J 4.6 (7.4 km) West Cottonwood Drive.

J 5.4 (8.7 km) East Cottonwood Drive; public access to Cottonwood Lake.

J 6.7 (10.7 km) Greentree Street; **Tollers' Timbers** private chalets for rent.

J 6.8 (10.9 km) Finger Lake State Recreation Site; drive in 0.3 mile/0.5 km

on gravel road. A scenic spot with 41 campsites, wheelchair-accessible toilets, picnic tables, water, hiking trails and boat launch, $10 camping fee, 7-day limit. Use the life jackets provided! Finger Lake is on the **7-Mile Canoe Trail.** Public access to the canoe trail is also from Wasilla Lake and Cottonwood Lake. &▲

J 7.6 (12.2 km) Junction with Trunk Road, which leads south 1 mile/1.6 km to Palmer–Wasilla Highway and north 2.3 miles/3.7 km to Palmer-Fishhook Road.

Return to Milepost A 41.8 Parks Highway

871826, Wasilla 99687, phone (907) 376-1299. Mat–Su Visitors Center at **Milepost A 35.5**, write Mat–Su Convention & Visitors Bureau, HC 01, Box 6166J21-MP, Palmer, AK 99645; phone (907) 746-5000.

Radio and **Television** via Anchorage stations; KNBZ-FM 99.7. **Newspapers:** *The Valley Sun* (weekly); *The Frontiersman* (semiweekly). **Transportation: Air**—Charter service available. **Railroad**—Alaska Railroad. **Bus**—Matanuska Valley commuter to Anchorage.

Private Aircraft: Wasilla municipal airport, 4.8 miles/7.7 km north on Neuser Drive; elev. 348 feet/ 106m; length 3,700 feet/1,128m; gravel; unattended. Wasilla Lake seaplane base, 0.9 mile/1.4 km east; elev. 330 feet/100m. Numerous private

WASILLA ADVERTISERS

Knik Road Log

Distance is measured from the junction (J) with Parks Highway.

J 0 Junction with Parks Highway, Milepost A 42.2 at Main Street (Wasilla).

J 0.1 (0.2 km) *CAUTION: Road crosses railroad tracks.*

J 0.2 (0.3 km) VFW Post No. 9365.

J 0.7 (1.1 km) Glenwood Avenue, senior center.

J 1.5 (2.4 km) Gas station.

J 2 (3.2 km) Smith ball fields.

J 2.2 (3.5 km) Turnoff for **Iditarod Trail Sled Dog Race® headquarters** and visitor center; historical displays, films, dogs and musher, souvenir shop. Open 8 A.M. to 5 P.M., daily in summer, weekdays the rest of the year.

J 2.3 (3.7 km) **Lake Lucille Park** (Mat–Su Borough) campground and day-use area 0.6 mile/1 km north via gravel road just past Iditarod headquarters parking lot. There are 64 campsites in a heavily wooded area on a gravel loop road; picnic pavilion; firewood, firepits, restrooms. Camping fee charged. Fishing for landlocked silver salmon. Boardwalk trail to lake (non-motorized access only). ◄▲

J 4.1 (6.6 km) **Junction** with Fairview Loop Road, which joins the Parks Highway at **Milepost A 38**; access to Palmer Hay Flats State Game Refuge. Shopping center with gas and groceries at this junction.

J 7 (11.3 km) Knik fire hall.

J 8 (12.9 km) **Settlers Bay**, a residential development built around an 18-hole golf course (phone 907/376-5466); 4-star restaurant with scenic view; airstrip.

J 10.1 (16.3 km) Turnoff for **Homestead Museum**, with a large collection of early Alaskan memorabilia, and gift shop. **Knik Knack Mud Shack.** See display ad this section.

J 11.1 (17.9 km) Laurence airport.

J 13 (20.9 km) Knik Kennels.

J 13.3 (21.4 km) **KNIK** (area pop. 462) on **Knik Lake.** There is a bar here with a pay phone, a liquor store, gas station and private campground. Lake fishing for rainbow; inquire at the Knik Bar. Knik is a checkpoint on the Iditarod Trail Sled Dog Race® route and is often called the "Dog Mushing Center of the World"; many famous Alaskan dog mushers live in this area. ◄▲

J 13.9 (22.4 km) Knik Museum and Sled Dog Mushers' Hall of Fame, open noon to 6 P.M. Wednesday through Sunday, from June 1 through Aug. 31. The museum is housed in 1 of 2 buildings remaining from Knik's gold rush era (1898–1916). Regional memorabilia, artifacts, archives, dog mushing equipment, mushers' portraits and historical displays on the Iditarod Trail. Admission fee $2 for adults, $1.50 for seniors, free for children under 18. Phone (907) 376-7755, from September through May call 376-2005.

Traditional Athabascan graveyard with fenced graves and spirit houses next to Knik Museum. The gravesite can be observed from the Iditarod Trail. **Knik Museum and Sled Dog Mushers' Hall of Fame.** See display ad this section.

J 16.1 (25.9 km) **Fish Creek** bridge; parking, fishing for silver salmon. ◄►

J 17.2 (27.7 km) Goose Bay Point Road to Little Susitna River public-use facility at **Susitna Flats State Game Refuge** (12 miles/19.3 km); 83 parking spaces, 65 campsites, boat ramps, dump station, water, tables, toilets. Also access to Point Mackenzie. Daily parking $5; boat launch, $5 (includes parking); overnight camping, $10. State parks annual pass not accepted here. For more information phone (907) 745-3975. ▲

Acord Guide Service. See display ad on page 394.

J 18.5 (29.8 km) Pavement ends at small bar beside road. Road continues into rural area.

Return to Milepost A 42.2 Parks Highway

airstrips and lakes in vicinity.

Wasilla is one of the Matanuska–Susitna Valley's pioneer communities, supplying mines and farms in the area. Long before the Parks Highway was built, local residents and visitors bound for Lake Lucille, Wasilla Lake, Big Lake and Knik drove over the valley roads from Palmer to the village of Wasilla. Wasilla became a station on the Alaska Railroad about 1916.

Today, Wasilla is the largest community on the Parks Highway between Anchorage and Fairbanks. Shopping malls and businesses here offer a wide assortment of services. There are no banks between Wasilla and Fairbanks, but ATMs are available and noted in the log.

ACCOMMODATIONS/VISITOR SERVICES

All visitor facilities are available here, including sporting goods stores, post office, gas stations, tire and RV repair, laundromats and other services. Mat–Su Ice Arena, at Bogard Road and Crusey Street, has ice skating, picnic area and fitness court. Swimming and showers are available at Wasilla High School.

Alaska Kozey Cabins & RV Rental. Modern, hand-crafted log cabins set in the state's No. 1 recreation area. Cabins feature queen and full beds, fully equipped kitchens, bath and living rooms. Cross-country skiing, snow machining, hiking, fishing, and hunting abound. Near the official Iditarod restart. Open year-round. Phone (907) 376-3190. See display ad this section. [ADVERTISEMENT] *MP*

Country Lakes B&B. These cozy accommodations nestled on the shores of Lake Wasilla, 40 miles east of Anchorage, include a hearty homemade breakfast prepared by 35-year Alaska resident, Louise Carswell. Conveniently located for fishing, hiking and

Mount Denali flightseeing. Laundry facilities and freezer space available. Families welcome. Reasonable rates. Special requests accommodated. The coffee is on...we look forward to meeting you! P.O. Box 876694, Wasilla, AK 99687. Toll-free 1-877-373-5868. www.countrylakes.net. ADVERTISEMENT]

Lake Lucille Inn. Located 45 miles north of Anchorage on the shores of beautiful Lake Lucille. 54 deluxe rooms, suites with Jacuzzi, health club with sauna and hot tub. Boat and float plane dock, water craft rentals and lighted gazebo. Winter activities include lighted ice rink. Fine dining restaurant and lounge with pristine view. Convention and meeting facilities. [ADVERTISEMENT]

Special Feet Studio. A must-see on your way to Denali. Meet foot artist Sabine Becker in her studio and gift shop. Right in front of you she will create her famous Alaskan spirit dolls. Born without arms, Sabine uses her feet to create her artwork. Open from Memorial Day to Labor Day, 10 A.M.–6 P.M. Tuesday through Sunday. (907) 376-5397. [ADVERTISEMENT]

Valley Chiropractic Clinic Inc. Phone (907) 373-2022. 24-hour emergency service. Complete modern facility, same-day emergency care. Reasonable fees with VISA and MasterCard accepted. We're accustomed to treating travelers' needs. We're located at 400 N. Main St., in Wasilla. Turn north on to Main Street from the Parks Highway and go up 2 blocks on the left, directly across the street from the post office. [ADVERTISEMENT]

ATTRACTIONS

On the town's Main Street, north of the Parks Highway, are the **Dorothy Page Museum and Historical Townsite**, the library and the post office. The museum and historical townsite are open daily year-round, 10 A.M. to 6 P.M. in summer, 8 A.M. to 5 P.M. in winter; admission fees are $3 adults, $2.50 senior citizens; under 18 years free. Picnic tables and museum shop on site. Local Farmer's Market on Wednesdays in summer. The historical park has 7 renovated buildings

Mat-Su Visitors Center on Welcome Way near the Glenn Highway junction.
(© Barbara Willard)

www.themilepost.com

from before, during and after Wasilla's pioneer days, including Wasilla's first schoolhouse (built in 1917). Adjacent to the park is the Herning/Teeland Country Store, which is

Finger Lake forms a 7-mile canoe route with Mud, Cottonwood and Wasilla lakes.
(© Kris Graef, staff)

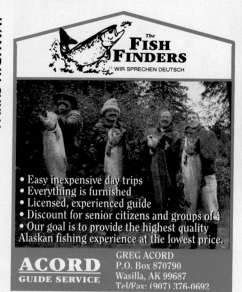
currently under restoration. The log museum building, school, store and nearby railroad depot are on the National Register of Historic Sites.

Wasilla is home to the **Iditarod Trail Sled Dog Race® Headquarters**. The internationally known 1,150-mile Iditarod Trail Sled Dog Race® between Anchorage and Nome takes place in March. The Iditarod Headquarters and Visitors Center is located at Mile 2.2 Knik Road. The center has historical displays on the Iditarod, videos, an Iditarod musher and dog team, and a gift shop with unique souvenirs. Open daily in summer, weekdays in winter. Large tours are welcome, phone (907) 376-5155 in advance. Circular drive for buses and motor-homes, camping at adjacent Lake Lucille campground. No fee for museum or film. Fee charged for rides on wheeled dogsled.

Historical displays on Alaskan mushers and sled-dog trails can be found at the Knik Museum at Mile 13.9 Knik Road (see KNIK ROAD log this section). The museum is open from noon to 6 P.M. daily except Monday and Tuesday in summer. Admission fee $2

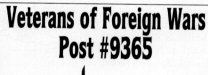

adults.

Iditarod Days is held in conjunction with the Iditarod Race in March. Other area winter events include ice golf at Mat–Su Resort and ice bowling at Big Lake. Check with the chamber of commerce about summer events.

Town Square Art Gallery. Representing the best of Alaskan and national artists—prints and originals distinctively custom framed. Local jewelry, pottery, unique gifts, porcelain collectibles, plates, books, cards. Open Monday–Friday 10 A.M.–6 P.M., Saturday 10 A.M.–5 P.M., seasonally Sundays 12–4 P.M. We pack and ship. We welcome credit cards. Carrs Mall. (907) 376-0123. [ADVERTISEMENT]

Parks Highway Log
(continued)

A 42.5 (68.4 km) **F 315.5** (507.7 km) **The Deli Restaurant & Bakery.** See display ad this section.

A 42.7 (68.7 km) **F 315.3** (507.4 km) Shoprite Mall, Wasilla Shopping Center.

The Rock Shop. Rough rock to finished gemstones. Handmade Alaskan jewelry. Original and custom designs. Native art and artifacts. Huge bead selection. Leather, feathers, furs. Hours Monday–Friday 10 A.M.–6 P.M., Saturday 10 A.M.–5 P.M. Day phone (907) 373-3094. 443 W. Parks Highway, DBA Shoprite Mall. [ADVERTISEMENT]

A 43.5 (70 km) **F 314.5** (506.1 km) Lucas Road; Hallea Lane access to Lake Lucille. Best Western Lake Lucille Inn.

A 44.2 (71.1 km) **F 313.8** (505 km) Deskas Road. Divided highway ends northbound.

A 44.4 (71.4 km) **F 313.6** (504.7 km) Church Road. Access to Bumpus ball fields.

A 45 (72.4 km) **F 313** (503.7 km) Wasilla city limits. Shopping and services are located along the highway to **Milepost A 39.5** and at Main Street in Wasilla city center.

Wasilla Car Wash. See display ad this section.

A 45.4 (73.1 km) **F 312.6** (503.1 km) Welcome to Meadow Lakes Community signed (incorporated).

A 45.5 (73.2 km) **F 312.5** (502.9 km) **Trading Post & Gifts.** Mile 45.5 Parks Highway, (907) 376-1327 or (907) 376-2327. Blue building with moose, bears and sheep in front. Safe bear encounters in our wildlife studio with your camera or ours. 9 A.M.–7 P.M. or appointment. Group discounts and prices available. Gifts, ice cream, espresso and more. Taxidermist available. [ADVERTISEMENT]

A 47 (75.6 km) **F 311** (500.5 km) Neuser Drive. Turnoff for Wasilla municipal airport and the Museum of Alaska Transportation and Industry. The museum features historic aircraft, railroad equipment, old farm machinery and heavy equipment. Steam train rides on selected Saturdays. Admission fees in summer are $5 adults, $12 families. Group tours by arrangement.

Museum of Alaska Transportation & Industry. See display ad this section.

Moose are the largest member of the deer family. — ALASKA A to Z

Watch for moose browsing along the Parks Highway. (© Susan Cole Kelly)

A **48.8** (78.5 km) F **309.2** (497.6 km) Tesoro/7-Eleven at **junction** with Pittman Road to Rainbow Lake.

A **49** (78.9 km) F **309** (497.3 km) Meadow Lakes Road **junction**. B&J Center; Mile 49 Cafe.

Mile 49 Cafe. See display ad this section.

A **49.8** (80.1 km) F **308.2** (496 km) Rainbow Street.

A **50.1** (80.6 km) F **307.9** (495.5 km) Sheele Road.

A **50.2** (80.8 km) F **307.8** (495.3 km) **Ice Worm RV Park & Country Store.** See display ad this section. ▲

A **51** (82 km) F **307** (494 km) Veterinary hospital.

A **51.3** (82.6 km) F **306.7** (493.6 km) **Earth'N Art Studio and Gift Shop.** Located 1 block east of the Parks Highway on Spring Drive, you will find the workshop of Michael Stanelle. Michael, a craftsman, ceramist and master mold maker creates individually handcrafted "Down to Earth" wind chimes and displays them in his showroom. Michael's wife, Ann, a designer, seamstress and mom creates polar fleece clothing and accessories for adults, children and infants under the Finishing Touch Designs

label. She uses Polartec™ fabrics from Malden Mills, including the new Polartec 1000™ windbloc series. Other local artists are also featured in this unique, quality gift shop. Open year-round. Easy RV access. VISA and MasterCard accepted. (907) 892-7516. [ADVERTISEMENT]

A **52.3** (84.2 km) F **305.7** (492 km) Meadowood shopping mall, service station, hardware store, ATM, grocery and emergency phone (dial 911) at Big Lake turnoff.

Junction with Big Lake Road. See BIG LAKE ROAD log this section.

Houston city limits; fireworks outlets. Begin bike trail next 4.6 miles/7.4 km northbound. (The bike trail also extends down Big Lake Road.)

A **53.3** (85.8 km) F **304.7** (490.4 km) Turnoff for Houston High School, Wasilla Senior Center and dog kennels.

A **54.1** (87.1 km) F **303.9** (489.1 km) Truck lane begins northbound.

A **54.3** (87.5 km) F **303.7** (488.7 km) **Alaska Explorers & Fisherman.** See display ad this section.

A **55.4** (89.2 km) F **302.6** (487 km) Truck lane ends northbound.

A **56.1** (90.3 km) F **301.9** (485.8 km) Miller's Reach Road. Alaska's most destructive wildfire began here in June 1996. The Big Lake wildfire burned some 37,000 acres and more than 350 homes.

A **56.4** (90.8 km) F **301.6** (485.4 km) Alaska Railroad overpass.

A **56.6** (91.1 km) F **301.4** (485 km) King Arthur Road; public access to Bear Paw, Loon lakes to east (no camping).

A **56.8** (91.4 km) F **301.2** (484.7 km) Bike route ends northbound.

A **57.1** (91.9 km) F **300.9** (484.2 km) Bridge over the **Little Susitna River**; a very popular fishing and camping area.

The Little Susitna River has a tremendous king salmon run and one of the largest silver salmon runs in southcentral Alaska. Kings to 30 lbs. enter the river in late May and June; use large red spinners or salmon eggs. Silvers to 15 lbs. come in late July and August, with the biggest run in August; use small weighted spoons or fresh salmon roe. Artificials are required during the early weeks of the fishery in the first part of August. Also red salmon to 10 lbs.; in mid-July, use coho flies or salmon eggs. Charter boats nearby. This river heads at Mint Glacier in the Talkeetna Mountains to the northeast and flows 110 miles/177 km into Upper Cook Inlet.

A **57.3** (92.4 km) F **300.7** (483.9 km) Turnoff to east to Houston City Hall, fire station, emergency phone and city-operated **Little Susitna River Campground** (follow signs). Large, well-maintained campground with 86 sites (many wide, level gravel sites);

picnic tables, firepits; restrooms, water pump, playground large covered picnic area; 10-day limit, camping fee charged. Off-road parking lot near river with access to river. Follow signs to camping and river. Day-use area with water and toilets west side of highway. ▲

A 57.5 (92.5 km) F 300.5 (483.6 km) HOUSTON (pop. 874) has a grocery store, restaurant (open daily), laundromat, gift shop, inn with food, lodging and pay phone, a campground and gas station. Post office located in the grocery store. Fishing charter operators and marine service are located here. Emergency phone at Houston fire station. ▲

Homesteaded in the 1950s, incorporated as a city in 1966. Houston is a popular fishing center for anglers on the Little Susitna River.

A 57.6 (92.7 km) F 300.4 (483.4 km)

Miller's Place. Don't miss this stop! Groceries, post office, laundry, RV parking, cabin rentals, tenting on riverbank. Gift shop, fishing tackle and licenses, fresh salmon eggs. Ice, sporting goods sales and rental, pay phone. Fishing charters available; full day only $45. Probably the best soft ice cream and hamburgers in Alaska. Clean restrooms. Visitor information

Big Lake Road Log

The 6.5-mile/10.5-km Big Lake Road leads south from the Parks Highway junction at **Milepost A 52.3** to **BIG LAKE** (pop. 2,228), a resort destination for Alaskans since the 1940s. Summer recreation includes swimming, camping, boating, fishing, jet skiing and tour boat rides in summer. Winter sports include snow machining, ice skating, cross-country skiing and ice fishing. Special events include the Big Lake Regatta and 4th of July fireworks. Businesses are found along Big Lake Road and along North Shore Drive, which forks off Big Lake Road at **Mile J 3.6.**

Distance is measured from the junction (J) with the Parks Highway.

Road construction was under way along Big Lake Road in summer 1998. Actual mileages may vary from log due to road improvement. Road widened and paved to junction with Burma Road. There is also a bike path along Big Lake Road.

J 0 Junction with Parks Highway. Meadowood Mall and gas station; ATM.

J 3.4 (5.5 km) Beaver Lake Road turnoff. Turn right here for public and private campgrounds. Drive 0.5 mile/0.8 km on Beaver Lake Road (gravel) for **Rocky Lake State Recreation Site**; 10 campsites, $10 nightly fee or annual pass, toilets, firepits, water and boat launch. ▲

J 3.5 (5.6 km) Gas station, ATM.

J 3.6 (5.8 km) Fisher's Y; gas station and Big Lake post office (ZIP code 99652). Big Lake Road forks here: Go straight ahead for North Shore Drive (description follows); keep to left for South Big Lake Road businesses and Big Lake South state recreation site (continue with this log).

North Shore Drive provides access to Klondike Inn and restaurant (1.4 miles/2.3 km) and **Big Lake North State Recreation Site** (1.6 miles/2.6 km), which has parking for 120 vehicles, overnight RV parking, tent sites, $10 nightly fee per vehicle or annual pass, covered picnic tables, water, toilets, dumpsters, boat launch ($5 fee) and sandy beach. Day-use parking $2. Pay phone. ▲

J 3.7 (6 km) Shopping mall.

J 3.9 (6.3 km) Big Lake fire station.

J 4 (6.4 km) East Lake Mall; numerous gift shops, espresso shop, family-style restaurant, pizza parlor, grocery and liquor stores. Studio/gallery of celebrated Alaskan artist James Belcher.

Gallery of the Lakes. Meet Alaskan legend James Belcher at his studio/gallery in the East Lake Mall. Museum-quality art and atmosphere, featuring original works by 19th and 20th century masters. Exclusive gift shop. Seasonal themes, shows

and events. Call (907) 892-98579 or 892-8357. Fax (907) 892-8589. Tour reservations recommended. [ADVERTISEMENT]

J 4.7 (7.6 km) Aero Drive and Big Lake airport. Big Lake is a 15-minute flight from Anchorage.

Private Aircraft: 1 mile/1.6 km southeast; elev. 150 feet/46m; length 2,400 feet/732m; gravel; fuel 100LL.

J 5 (8 km) **Big Lake Motel.** Bridge over Fish Creek. Fish Creek park picnic area; fish weir with salmon spawning view area. Fishing prohibited.

J 5.2 (8.4 km) **Big Lake South State Recreation Site**; 13 campsites, 6 picnic sites, toilets, water, dumpsters, boat ramp ($5 fee). Camping fee $10/night per vehicle or annual pass. Day-use fee $2. Nearby South Port Marina has boat slips, equipment rentals and a restaurant. ▲

J 6.5 (10.5 km) Pavement ends. Burma Road continues into rural area, providing access to the south Big Lake area, former Point MacKenzie dairy project and the Little Susitna River public-use facility at Susitna Flats State Game Refuge (also accessible via Knik Road); parking, camping, boat ramps. Fee charged, state parks annual pass not accepted. See description and fee schedule at **Milepost J 17.2** Knik Road this section. ▲

Big Lake is connected with smaller

lakes by dredged waterways. It is possible to boat for several miles in the complex. Fish in Big Lake include lake trout, Dolly Varden, rainbow, red and coho salmon, and burbot.

Return to Milepost A 52.3 Parks Highway

experts. Family-run Christian business. Gary and Debbie Miller. (907) 892-6129. [ADVERTISEMENT] ▲

A 57.7 (92.9 km) **F 300.3** (483.3 km) **Riverside Camper Park.** See display ad this section. ▲

A 57.8 (93 km) **F 300.2** (483.1 km) **Fisherman's Choice Charters.** We know where the fish are; we go where the fish are. Trophy kings, silvers, sockeye and trout. We fish the Little Susitna, Deshka and Talkeetna Rivers giving us over 200 miles of fishing

waters to choose from and a better than 90 percent succcess rate in 1998! 1-800-980-8707. P.O. Box 940276, Houston, AK 99694. E-mail: fish@matnet.com. Internet: www.alaskan.com/fishermanschoice. See display ad. [ADVERTISEMENT]

A 64.5 (103.8 km) **F 293.5** (472.3 km) Turnoff to west for Nancy Lake Resort.

Nancy Lake Resort. See display ad this section.

A 64.7 (104.1 km) **F 293.3** (472 km) *NOTE: No passing; drive with headlights on.*

A 66.5 (107 km) **F 291.5** (469.1 km) **Alaskan Host Bed & Breakfast.** See display ad this section.

A 66.7 (107.3 km) **F 291.3** (468.8 km) Highway crosses Alaska Railroad tracks. Turnoff for **Nancy Lake State Recreation Site**; 30 campsites, 30 picnic sites, toilets, boat launch, horseshoe pits. Camping fee $10/night or annual pass. ▲

A 67.2 (108.1 km) **F 290.8** (468 km) Wide gravel road leads southwest into **Nancy Lake Recreation Area** in the mixed birch and spruce forest of the Susitna River valley (good mushroom hunting area): Mile 2.5 (4 km) Tulik Nature Trail, toilets and parking area; Mile 4.7 (7.6 km) Tanaina Lake canoe trail, canoe launch, toilet and parking area; Mile 5.1 (8.2 km) Rhein Lake trailhead; Mile 6.2 (10 km) South Rolly Lake Overlook day-use area with barbecues, picnic tables, litter barrels and toilets; Mile 6.6 (10.6 km) **South Rolly Lake** Campground, 106 campsites,

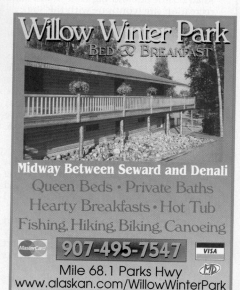

firepits, toilets, water, canoe rental (phone Tippecanoe Rentals 907/495-6688) and boat launch; firewood sometimes is provided. Camping fee $10/night or annual pass. South Rolly Lake has a small population of rainbow, 12 to 14 inches. ◀▲

A 68.1 (109.6 km) **F 289.9** (466.5 km) **Willow Winter Park Bed & Breakfast.**

Overlooking peaceful Winter Park Lake, 1/2 mile off Parks Highway. Beautiful smoke-free rooms decorated with flannel sheets and antiques. Laundry. Paddleboats and canoeing. A great place to stop and relax going to or from Mount McKinley. Phone (907) 495-7547; fax (907) 495-7638. E-mail: winterpark@matnet.com. See display ad. [ADVERTISEMENT]   MP

A 68.8 (110.7 km) **F 289.2** (465.4 km) Miner's Last Stand Museum of Hatcher Pass, gas, diesel and gift shop.

Newman's Hilltop Service. See display ad this section.

A 69 (111 km) **F 289** (465.1 km) Entering Willow, northbound. Gas station, grocery and hardware store to west. Willow extends about 2.5 miles/4 km north along the Parks Highway.

Willow True Value Hardware, Willow Creek Grocery and **Willow Creek Service.** See display ad this section.

A 69.2 (111.4 km) **F 288.8** (464.8 km) Long Lake Road.

A 69.4 (111.7 km) **F 288.6** (464.4 km) Gas station, convenience store. Willow elementary school.

Townsite Texaco Foodmart. See display ad this section.

A 69.5 (111.8 km) **288.5** (464.3 km) Turnoff to east on Willow Station Road for **WILLOW** (pop. 430) post office, trading post with cabins and camper spaces, Alaska Railroad depot and access to Ruth Lake Lodge.

Willow had its start about 1897, when gold was discovered in the area. In the early 1940s, mining in the nearby Talkeetna Mountains slacked off, leaving Willow a virtual ghost town. The community made a comeback upon completion of the Parks Highway in 1972. In 1976, Alaska voters selected the Willow area for their new capital site. However, funding for the capital move from Juneau to Willow was defeated in the November 1982 election.

The community is also a stop on the Alaska Railroad. The Willow civic organization sponsors an annual Winter Carnival in January.   ▲

Ruth Lake Lodge. See display ad this section.

Willow Trading Post Lodge. See display ad this section.   ▲

A 69.7 (112.2 km) **F 288.3** (464 km) Willow Community Center, open daily, has a large parking area, commercial kitchen, showers, covered picnic pavilion, grills, ball court, boat launch and pay phone. (Available for rent to groups, 500-person capacity; phone 907/495-6633). Willow library.

A 69.9 (112.5 km) F 288.1 (463.6 km) Fire station.

A 70 (112.7 km) F 288 (463.5 km) **Private Aircraft:** Willow airport; elev. 220 feet/67m; length 4,400 feet/1,341m; gravel; fuel 100LL. Unattended.

Willow Air Service Inc. See display ad this section.

A 70.8 (113.9 km) F 287.2 (462.2 km) Willow Creek Parkway (Susitna River access road) west 4 miles/6.4 km to **Willow Creek State Recreation Area**; camping $10/night, parking, litter barrels, water, toilets, dump station, trail to mouth of creek. Access to Deshka Landing boat launch. Fishing for king and silver salmon, rainbow trout. ◀▲

A 71 (114.3 km) F 287 (461.9 km) Willow DOT/PF highway maintenance station.

A 71.2 (114.6 km) F 286.8 (461.5 km) Turnoff to **Willow Creek State Recreation Area** 1.2 miles/1.9 km east via Hatcher Pass Road; camping, tables, firepits and toilets. Camping fee $10/night or annual pass. Bed and breakfast located 2 miles/3.2 km east of highway past the campground. ▲

Alaska Creekside Bed & Breakfast. See display ad this section.

Junction with Hatcher Pass (Fishhook–Willow) Road, which leads east and south across Hatcher Pass 49 miles/79 km to junction with the Glenn Highway. Independence Mine State Historical Park is 31.8 miles/51.2 km from here. Turn to the Hatcher Pass Road Log on page 326 in the GLENN HIGHWAY section and read log back to front.)

A 71.4 (114.9 km) F 286.6 (461.2 km) Pioneer Lodge to west on south side of **Willow Creek** bridge. Excellent king salmon fishing; also silvers, rainbow. Inquire at either lodge or resort for information. ▬◀

Entering Game Management Subunit 14B northbound, 14A southbound.

Pioneer Lodge. One of Alaska's oldest original log lodges. Restaurant with full bar

overlooking Willow Creek. Liquor store. Full RV hookups $18, campground—tent sites

$12, showers, laundromat, dump station. Rooms. Fishing, hunting charters, drop offs, wilderness tours, fly-ins, bank fishing—4 types of salmon, rainbows, grayling. Hiking trails. Boat launch. Bait, tackle, fishing rentals. Licenses, ice, gift shop. Phone (907) 495-1000. See display ad. [ADVERTISEMENT] ◄▲

A 71.5 (115.1 km) **F 286.5** (461.1 km) Willow Island campground resort to west on north side of Willow Creek bridge. Willow Creek heads in Summit Lake, west of Hatcher Pass on the Hatcher Pass Road. It is a favorite launch site for airboat enthusiasts.

Willow Island Resort. Scenic riverside RV park, cabins and campground. Great salmon and trout fishing from the banks of crystal clear Willow Creek. Full hookups on level riverbank sites. Hot showers, laundry, dump station, tackle, mini-grocery, good water. Excellent king and silver salmon fishing. Rainbows to 10 lbs. Scenic fishing and hunting charters. Guided fishing charters available. Close to Hatcher Pass; 3 hours from Denali National Park. Plan to stay awhile. Write: P.O. Box 85, Willow, AK

99688 or call (907) 495-6343. See display ad this section. [ADVERTISEMENT] ◄▲

A 74.7 (120.2 km) **F 283.3** (455.9 km) Bridge over **Little Willow Creek**. Parking on either side of creek; fishing for salmon and trout. ◄▲

A 75.2 (121 km) **F 282.8** (455.1 km) Speedway.

A 76.4 (122.9 km) **F 281.6** (453.2 km) Paved double-ended turnout to west by **Kashwitna Lake.** Stocked with rainbow trout. Small planes land on lake. Private floatplane base on east shore. Good camera viewpoints of lake and Mount McKinley (weather permitting).

A 76.6 (123.3 km) **F 281.4** (452.9 km) Air service.

A 78 (125.5 km) **F 280** (450.6 km) Great view of Mount McKinley northbound. From here to Denali National Park and Preserve watch for views of the Alaska Range to the east of the highway.

A 80 (128.7 km) **F 278** (447.4 km) **Lucky Husky.** Year-round "dog-gone" fun! Take an exciting summer dogsled ride! Tour the

A floatplane taxiing for takeoff from Kashwitna Lake. (© Loren Taft)

Adult loon and chick (© Mike Jones)

kennel and meet the Lucky Husky family. Get dressed in original musher's clothes at the Iditarod checkpoint display. Take pictures with your favorite husky. Wir sprechen

Deutsch. May–September: Open daily 10 A.M.–6 P.M. Winter: mushing adventures (drive your own dogteam), dogsled rides, mushing school. November–March: Reserva-

tion required. Phone: (907) 495-6470; fax (907) 495-6471; e-mail: infor@luckyhusky.com. Web: www.luckyhusky.com. Write: HC 89 Box 256, Willow, AK 99688. [ADVERTISEMENT]

A 81 (130.4 km) **F 277** (445.8 km) Campground.

A 81.3 (130.8 km) **F 276.7** (445.3 km) **Grey's Creek**, gravel turnouts both sides of highway. Fishing for salmon and trout. 🐟

A 82.5 (132.8 km) **F 275.5** (443.4 km) **Susitna Landing**, 1 mile/1.6 km west on side road; boat launch, camping, wheelchair-accessible restrooms, bank fishing, riverboat service. Concessionaire-operated (ADF&G land) boat launch on **Kashwitna River**, just upstream of the **Susitna River**; access to both rivers on site. The Susitna River heads at Susitna Glacier in the Alaska Range to the northeast and flows west then south for 260 miles/418 km to Cook Inlet. ♿🐟▲

A 83.2 (133.9 km) **F 274.8** (442.2 km) Bridge over the **Kashwitna River**; public parking area at north end of bridge. Salmon and trout fishing. The river heads in a glacier in the Talkeetna Mountains and flows westward 60 miles/ 96.5 km to enter the Susitna River 12 miles/19 km north of Willow. 🐟

A 84 (135.2 km) **F 274** (440.9 km) Gravel turnout to west. Public access (walk-in) for fishing at **Caswell Creek**; kings, silvers, pinks and rainbow. 🐟

A 85.1 (137 km) **F 272.9** (439.2 km) Caswell Creek.

A 85.5 (137.6 km) **F 272.5** (438.5 km) Gift shop and art gallery.

Willow Wildlife Art Gallery. Features Alaskan wildlife and sled dog art, as well as locally handcrafted gifts. Meet artist Dave

Totten in his home studio/gallery. "From Anchorage to Fairbanks ... best gallery,"

Jerry Griswold, *L.A. Times,* Aug. 1, 1993. Free coffee and wildberry muffins. Phone (907) 495-1090. Open all year. [ADVERTISEMENT]

A 86 (138.4 km) **F 272** (437.7 km) Public access road leads 1.3 miles/2.1 km west to mouth of Sheep Creek public boat launch and Bluffs on Susitna. **Sheep Creek** has parking, toilets, dumpster and wheelchair-accessible trail to mouth of creek; fishing for kings, silvers, pinks and rainbow. ♿🐟

A 86.9 (139.8 km) **F 271.1** (436.3 km) Native crafts store.

A 87.1 (140.2 km) **F 270.9** (436 km) Campground to east.

Camp Caswell RV Park. Open year-round. Located in the heart of Alaska's finest fishing and winter sports. We offer 15/30-amp pull-throughs, cabins, secluded RV and tent sites, groceries, ice, propane, fishing tackle, licensese, game tags, camp wood, phone and information. Free coffee and Alaska friendly! Phone (907) 495-7829. P.O. Box 333, Willow, AK 99688. [ADVERTISEMENT] ▲

A 88.1 (141.8 km) **F 269.9** (434.4 km) Signed turnoff for **Gigglewood Lakeside Inn.** See display ad this section.

A 88.2 (142 km) **F 269.8** (434.2 km) **Sheep Creek Lodge.** See display ad this section. ▲

A 88.5 (142.4 km) **F 269.5** (433.7 km) Bridge over **Sheep Creek**. Turnout on west side at north end of bridge. Fishing for salmon and trout.

A 89 (143.2 km) **F 269** (432.9 km) Gravel turnouts both sides of highway.

A 90.8 (146.1 km) **F 267.2** (430 km) **Mat-Su RV Park.** Clean full-service RV park conveniently located one block off the Parks Highway between Willow and Talkeetna junction. Good Sam's approved. Level pull-through gravel spaces, water, sewer and electric hookups. Picnic and secluded grassy tent sites. Store offers groceries, ice, propane, hot showers, laundromat, and fishing tackle. Fishing licenses sold on premises. We offer guided fishing charters on the Talkeetna and Susitna rivers as well as secluded canoe excursions. Open year-round. Phone (907) 495-6300; fax (907) 495-5550. www.mat survpark.com. [ADVERTISEMENT] ▲

A 91.5 (147.3 km) F 266.5 (428.9 km) Turnoff to west for dog tours and bed and breakfast (0.5 mile/0.8 km).

Susitna Dog Tours & Bed and Breakfast. Easy access to newly built log home offering a unique blend of Alaskan living and wilderness sled dog mushing or just a peaceful night's rest. Hot showers, sauna. Trails and seminars available for cross-country skiing, skijoring, dog mushing. Located within striking distance of Talkeetna and Denali National Park. Your hosts: Iditarod Veterans Bill and Rhodi Davidson and 50 sled dogs. Open year-round. Phone (907) 495-6324; e-mail: susdog@matnet.com. [ADVERTISEMENT]

A 91.7 (147.6 km) F 266.3 (428.5 km) *CAUTION: Railroad crossing.*

A 93.4 (150.3 km) F 264.6 (425.8 km) Gravel turnouts both sides of highway.

A 93.5 (150.5 km) F 264.5 (425.7 km) **Goose Creek** culvert; gravel turnout. Fishing.

A 93.6 (150.6 km) F 264.4 (425.5 km) Goose Creek community center; park pavilion, picnic tables, grills, litter barrels.

A 95.1 (153 km) F 262.9 (423.1 km) **Private Aircraft:** Montana Creek airstrip (private); elev. 250 feet/76m; length 2,300 feet/701m; dirt/gravel; no fuel. Current status unknown.

A 96.5 (155.3 km) F 261.5 (420.8 km) **Montana Creek Campground.** See display ad this section. ▲

A 96.6 (155.5 km) F 261.4 (420.7 km) Bridge over **Montana Creek.** Homesteaders settled in the area surrounding this creek in the 1950s. Today, about 200 families live in the area. Camping and picnic areas on both sides of Montana Creek (operated by concessionaire, state park annual pass not accepted). Water and parking. Excellent king salmon fishing, also silvers, pinks (even-numbered years), grayling, rainbow and Dolly Varden. ◄╾▲

A 97.8 (157.4 km) F 260.2 (418.7 km) Alaska State Troopers post (phone 907/733-2556 or 911 for emergencies).

A 98.4 (158.3 km) F 259.6 (417.8 km) Turnoff to west for Susitna Valley High School; 3.1-mile/5-km trail for running in summer, cross-country skiing in winter. Senior Center.

A 98.7 (158.8 km) F 259.3 (417.3 km) **Talkeetna junction.** Access to hardware, lumber and feed store with ATM. Turn east on paved spur road for Talkeetna, an interesting side trip. Talkeetna/Denali Visitor Center at junction with information on area attractions and lodging; restrooms, picnic area. Tesoro gas station just north of junction.

Mary Carey's Fiddlehead Fern Farm. See display ad this section.

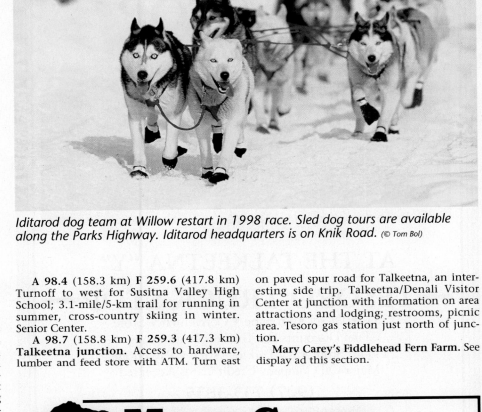

Iditarod dog team at Willow restart in 1998 race. Sled dog tours are available along the Parks Highway. Iditarod headquarters is on Knik Road. (© Tom Bol)

ATVers view of Mt. McKinley from the Peter Hills near Petersville. (© Mike Jones)

Moores' Mercantile. See display ad this section.

Junction with Talkeetna Spur Road. See TALKEETNA SPUR ROAD log this section.

Downtown Talkeetna is just 14 miles/23 km northeast of the Parks Highway via a paved spur road.

A 98.8 (159 km) **F 259.2** (417.1 km) **Sunshine One Stop/Tesoro Alaska.** See display ad this section.

A 99 (159.3 km) **F 259** (416.8 km) **Denali Way Auto.** See display ad this section.

A 99.3 (159.8 km) **F 258.7** (416.3 km) **Montana and Little Montana** lakes on

Alaska became the 49th state on Jan. 3, 1959, under President Dwight D. Eisenhower.

www.themilepost.com

View of Mt. McKinley from Milepost A 135.3. (© Loren Taft)

opposite sides of highway, stocked with rainbow. Watch for floatplanes. Double-ended gravel turnout to west. ◄

A 99.5 (160.1 km) **F 258.5** (416 km) **H&H Lakeview Restaurant & Lodge**, serving travelers since 1965. Feast your senses in our spacious lakeside dining room, hidden away from the busy highway by a birch grove. You'll love our omelettes. Great hamburgers and steaks. Prime rib and seafood and full-service lounge. Our bread pudding is famous statewide. Take home a taste of Alaska in jellies from our gift shop. We make the jellies from Alaska berries, each with its own distinct flavor. Lakeside RV parking and camping. Hear the loons and watch beavers from your motorhome. Gerald and Sherry Berryman, proprietors since 1977. See display ad for details. [ADVERTISEMENT] ▲

A 100.4 (161.6 km) **F 257.6** (414.6 km) *CAUTION: Railroad crossing.*

A 101.4 (163.2 km) **F 256.6** (412.9 km) Beaver lodge east side of highway.

A 101.8 (163.8 km) **F 256.2** (412.3 km) **Talkeetna Blue Grass Festival**, Aug.5, 6, 7, 8, 1999. Alaska's greatest musicians, arts, crafts and food. Good roads, outhouses, RV parking, no hookups. Great family weekend camping. Bring camping gear and cushions. $25 fee includes camping. Seniors and children 12 and under are free. No carry-in alcohol please. For information, phone (907) 495-6718. [ADVERTISEMENT]

A 102 (164.1 km) **F 256** (412 km) Large, paved double-ended turnout to east. Lakes both sides of highway.

A 102.6 (165.1 km) **F 255.4** (411 km) Turnout at Sunshine Road; access to **Sunshine Creek** for fishing via dirt road. ◄

A 104 (167.4 km) **F 254** (408.8 km) Lodge to east.

A 104.2 (167.7 km) **F 253.8** (408.4 km) Entering Game Management Unit 16A, northbound, Unit 14B southbound. Bridge over Big Susitna River. State rest area to west on south bank of river; loop road, parking area, tables, firepits, toilets, no drinking water. ▲

Some of the finest stands of white birch in Alaska may be seen for several miles on both sides of the river. This area is also noted for its fiddlehead ferns. The ferns (lady fern, ostrich fern and shield fern) are harvested in the spring, when their young shoots are tightly coiled, resembling a fiddle's head. Fiddleheads should be cooked before consumption.

A 104.6 (168.3 km) **F 253.4** (407.8 km) Rabideaux Creek access; parking, 0.3 mile/0.5 km trail to mouth of creek. Watch for seasonal flooding.

A 104.8 (168.7 km) **F 253.2** (407.5 km) Large dirt and gravel turnout west side of highway.

A 105.9 (170.4 km) **F 252.1** (405.7 km) Rabideaux Creek.

A 107.6 (173.2 km) **F 250.4** (403 km) View of Mount McKinley (weather permitting) for northbound travelers.

A 114.8 (184.7 km) **F 243.2** (391.4 km) **TRAPPER CREEK** (area pop. about 700); a
(Continues on page 412)

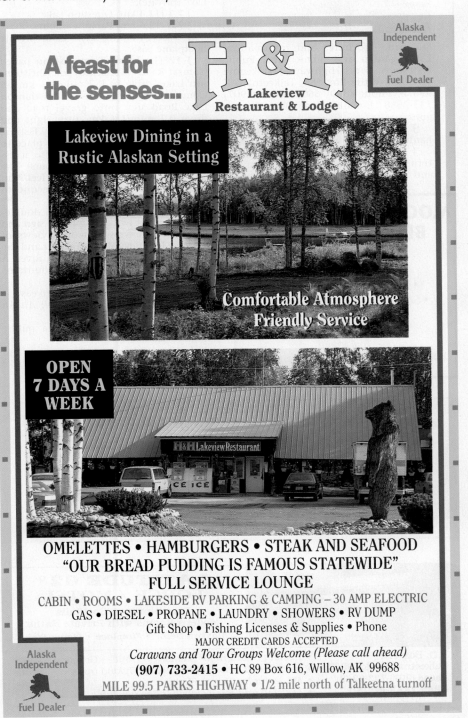

Talkeetna Spur Road Log

Distance from Parks Highway junction (J) at Milepost A 98.7 is shown.

J 0 Junction with the Parks Highway at Milepost A 98.7; visitor center.
Talkeetna/Denali Visitor Center. Staffed by knowledgeable local residents. Information and bookings of area recreational activities, including fishing, flightseeing, rafting, lodging and Denali Park.

Statewide brochures and information. Large garden and picnic area. Public restrooms. Parks Highway at Talkeetna Junction. Write Box 688, Talkeetna, AK 99676. Phone (800) 660-2688 or (907) 733-2688. E-mail: talkaero@alaska.net.
[ADVERTISEMENT]

J 0.3 (0.5 km) Moore's Mercantile hardware, lumber and feed store.
J 1 (1.6 km) Mary Carey's Fiddlehead Fern Farm and Moose Dropping Inn Bed and Breakfast.

Moose Dropping Inn Bed & Breakfast. See display ad this section.
J 2.2 (3.5 km) **Gold Pan Bed & Breakfast.** Turn left on Sunshine Road, continue for 1/4 mile to find Gold Pan Bed & Breakfast. Offering 2 new rooms With shared bath in a comfortable, quiet atmosphere. Featuring handpainted gold pans by owner/artist Kathy Reynolds. Located between Anchorage and Denali Park, 2 1/2 miles off the Parks Highway. (907) 733-4722. [ADVERTISEMENT]
J 3.1 (5 km) Turn west on Jubilee Road. Turn east on Yoder Road for Benka Lake (private).
J 7.1 (11.4 km) Question Lake.
J 7.8 (12.6 km) Paradise Cabins.
J 9.2 (14.8 km) Fish Lake private floatplane base.
J 12 (19.3 km) Turn east on paved Comsat Road (unmarked) for Christianson Lake; drive in 0.7 mile/1.1 km on Comsat Road, turn left at Christianson Lake Road sign onto gravel road and drive 0.7 mile/1.1 km, turn right and follow signs to floatplane base. Fishing for silvers and rainbow. Good place to observe loons and waterfowl. Also access to Alascom Earth Station (no tours). The dish-shaped antenna stands 98 feet/32m and can rotate 1 degree per second to receive satellite signals.
J 13 (20.9 km) Large gravel double-ended turnout with interpretive sign and viewpoint to west. Splendid views of Mount McKinley, Mount Foraker and the Alaska Range above the Susitna River. A must photo stop when the mountains are out.
Turnoff for Talkeetna Lodge to east.
J 13.3 (21.4 km) *CAUTION: Alaska Railroad crossing.*
J 13.5 (21.7 km) Talkeetna public library. Gas station.
J 13.8 (22.2 km) Restaurant and motel. VFW Post No. 3836 is 2 blocks west.

J 14 (22.5 km) East Talkeetna Road leads to state airport (Hudson Air, Doug Geeting and other air services), Swiss Alaska Inn, Mahay's Riverboat Service and McKinley Jetboat Safaris.,
J 14.2 (22.9 km) Talkeetna post office (ZIP code 99676).
J 14.3 (23 km) "Welcome to Beautiful Downtown Talkeetna" sign and Talkeetna Historical Society visitor center log cabin; walking tour brochures available. (Description of Talkeetna follows.)
Mountain Gift Shop/Visitor Information Cabin. Near the famous "Welcome to Beautiful Downtown Talkeetna" sign. Enjoy shopping for mountain theme items: books, maps, posters, T-shirts, flags, colorful gemstone necklaces and quill jewelry handmade in Alaska. Moose nugget items our specialty. Open summer 10–5:30. Free town map. Information, reservation (907) 733-1686.
[ADVERTISEMENT]
J 14.5 (23.3 km) Talkeetna Spur Road ends at Talkeetna River Park (camping).▲

Talkeetna

Located on a spur road, north of Milepost A 98.7 Parks Highway. **Population: 441. Emergency Services: Alaska State Troopers, Fire Department and Ambulance,** phone 911 or 733-2556. **Doctor,** phone 733-2708.

Visitor Information: Stop by the Talkeetna Historical Society Visitor Information Center cabin on entering Talkeetna. Or write the Chamber of Commerce, P.O. Box 334, Talkeetna, AK 99676.

The National Park Service maintains a ranger station that is staffed full time from mid-April through mid-September and intermittently during the winter. Mountaineering rangers provide information on Denali National Park and climbing within the Alaska Range. A reference library and video program are available to climbers. Mountaineering regulations and information may be obtained from Talkeetna Ranger Station, P.O. Box 588, Talkeetna, AK 99676; phone (907) 733-2231.

Elevation: 346 feet/105m. **Radio:** KSKA-FM (PBS). **Television:** Channels 4, 6, 9.

Private Aircraft: Talkeetna state airport, adjacent east; elev. 358 feet/109m; length 3,500 feet/1,067m; paved; fuel 100LL, Jet B.

A "Welcome to Beautiful Downtown

Talkeetna" sign is posted at the town park as you enter Talkeetna's old-fashioned Main Street, the only paved street in town. Log cabins and clapboard homes and businesses line Main Street, which dead-ends at the Susitna River.

Talkeetna is the jumping-off point for many climbing expeditions to Mount McKinley. Most climbing expeditions use the West Buttress route, pioneered by Bradford Washburn, flying in specially equipped ski-wheel aircraft to Kahiltna

TALKEETNA ADVERTISERS

Talkeetna Spur Road Log (continued)

Glacier. The actual climb on Mount McKinley is made from about 7,000 feet/2,134m (where the planes land) to the summit of the South Peak (elev. 20,320 feet/6,194m). Several air services based in Talkeetna specialize in the glacier landings necessary to ferry climbers and their equipment to and from the mountain. The climb via the West Buttress route usually takes 18 to 20 days. Flightseeing the mountain is also popular (and easier!).

ACCOMMODATIONS/VISITOR SERVICES

Talkeetna has 5 motels/hotels, several

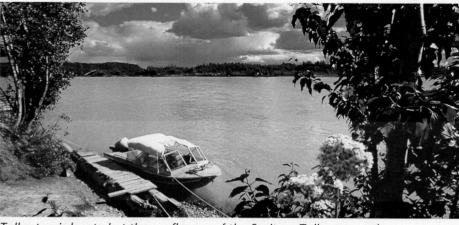

Talkeetna is located at the confluence of the Susitna, Talkeetna and Chulitna rivers. (© Gene & Judy Wright)

bed and breakfasts, 6 restaurants, 2 gas stations, laundromats, gift and clothing shops, grocery and general stores. A dump station is located at Three Rivers Tesoro.

RV and tent camping at River Park (located at the end of main street).

Hosted campground, $8 camping fee. Some people were tenting on the riverbank last summer (a short walk from River Park); inquire locally about permission.

Talkeetna Motel, Restaurant and Lounge. Built in 1964 by "Evil Alice" and Sherm Powell, the "Tee-Pee" (nicknamed by oldtimers) became known for its excellent food, fast service and sincere Alaskan hospitality. Today, we also offer private baths, color TV in rooms and lounge, full menu for casual and fine dining. MasterCard/VISA welcome. See display ad this section. [ADVERTISEMENT]

Talkeetna Roadhouse. Located on the edge of wilderness in a living pioneer village, the Talkeetna Roadhouse (Frank Lee cabin, circa 1917) has served the territory since early gold rush days. Still family owned and operated, this historic restaurant, lodge and bakery featuring 1902 sourdough is known worldwide for its fine home-style cooking, cinnamon rolls, and frontier hospitality. Slow down to "Talkeetna time," relax amidst the rustic charm and listen to the stories these old walls have to tell! Rooms start at $45, bunk spaces $21. Restaurant features classic roadhouse breakfast, daily soup and sandwich menu. Serving family-style supper by reservation. Phone (907) 733-1351, fax (907) 733-1353. E-mail: rdhouse@alaska.net. Internet: www.alaska.net/~rdhouse. [ADVERTISEMENT] MP

TRANSPORTATION

Air: There are several air taxi services in Talkeetna. Charter service, flightseeing and glacier landings are available. See ads this section.

Railroad: The Alaska Railroad.

Highway: At the end of a 14.5-mile/23.3-km spur road off the Parks Highway (Alaska Route 3).

ATTRACTIONS

Museums. Talkeetna boasts two museums, including a privately operated wax museum.

The Talkeetna Historical Society Museum is located 1 block off Main Street opposite the Fairview Inn. The original 1-room schoolhouse, built in 1936, exhibits historical items, local art, a historical library and a display on the late Don Sheldon, famous Alaskan bush pilot. In the Railroad Section House see the impressive 12-foot-by-12-foot scale model of Mount McKinley (Denali) with photographs by Bradford Washburn. A mountaineering display features pioneer and recent climbs of Mount McKinley. The Ole Dahl cabin, an early trapper/miner's cabin located on the museum grounds, is furnished with period items. Admission: $1 adult, under 12 free. Pick up a walking tour map of Talkeetna's historic sites here. Picnic area adjacent museum. Museum buildings open 10 A.M. to 5 P.M. daily in summer. Reduced hours other seasons. Phone

(907) 733-2487. Privately operated guided history tours.

Miners Day. Held the weekend before Memorial Day, this family event has a trade and craft fair, local cancan dancers, softball tournament, a thrilling outhouse race, street dance and parade.

Annual Moose Dropping Festival is held the second Saturday in July as a fund-raising project for the museum. Activities include a 5-km run and walk, a parade, entertainment, music, barbecue, food and game booths, and, of course, a moose dropping throwing contest.

Riverboat tours up Talkeetna Canyon, Devils Canyon, Chulitna River and Tokositna River are available. Several guides also offer riverboat fishing trips from Talkeetna. Commercial float trips and raft tours offer another popular way of exploring the roadless wilderness. Talkeetna is located at the confluence of the Susitna, Talkeetna and Chulitna rivers.

Inquire locally for details and see ads this section.

Crowley Guide Service. Main Street, Talkeetna. Guided fishing for salmon, rainbow trout and arctic grayling. River transportation and camp support. Scenic and wildlife charters. Mountain biking, rentals, sales and tours. Mount McKinley scenic flights and river rafting. International expeditions. Personalized service at reasonable rates. VISA, MasterCard. P.O. Box 431, Talkeetna, AK 99676. Phone (907) 733-1279; fax (907) 733-1278. [ADVERTISEMENT]

Hudson Air Service, Inc. is Talkeetna's "senior" air taxi; 50 years of experience and knowledge of Mount McKinley will make your flightseeing tour the highlight of your Alaskan adventure! Visit with pioneer aviator Cliff Hudson and fly with second generation Hudson pilots as you tour Denali National Park while enjoying narratives on the natural and local history. Fly over the Kahiltna Glacier and view base camp as climbers from all over the world prepare to ascend "The Great One." Include a landing on either the Ruth or Kahiltna Glacier for an experience you will never forget. We offer flights around the mountain, wildlife tours (bear, moose, caribou and sheep) and remote drop-off hunting/fishing. Open year-round.

Hudson Air Service Inc. is a National Park Service concessionaire. Office at Talkeetna State Airport. P.O. Box 648, Talkeetna, AK 99676. Phone (907) 733-2321, fax (907) 733-2333, e-mail: hasi@customcpu.com. Web site: www.alaskan.com/hudsonair/. See display ad in DENALI NATIONAL PARK section. [ADVERTISEMENT]

K-2 Aviation. Mount McKinley flightseeing tours starting at $95 per person. Land on a glacier, circle the mountain or fly to the summit. overnight fly/drive/rail Denali Park packages. Anchorage to Talkeetna day tours also available. Contact: P.O. Box 545, Talkeetna, AK 99676. Call (800) 764-2291 or (907) 733-2291. Visit our homepage at www.flyk2.com. [ADVERTISEMENT]

Mahay's Riverboat Service. Fish clear-water streams for all 5 species of Pacific salmon and trout. Custom-designed jet boats allow access to over 200 miles of prime fishing territory. Guided fishing charters include all equipment needed. Fishing packages are also available that include accommodations, meals and all the "extras." Drop-off fishing also available at reasonable rates. (800) 736-2210. www.alaskan.com/mahays. [ADVERTISEMENT]

Mahay's McKinley Jetboat Safari. The safari offers opportunities to view nesting bald eagles, beaver activity, moose and black bear in their natural habitat. Be sure to bring your camera so you can capture this unforgettable adventure. please dress warmly and wear comfortable walking shoes for the leisurely $1/4$-mile nature walk. (800) 736-2210. www.alaskan.com/mahays. [ADVERTISEMENT]

Museum of Northern Adventure. Highlighting Alaska's exciting history in 24 realistic dioramas, featuring life-sized figures and sounds. Entertaining and educational for all ages. Meander through the historic railroad building, experiencing Alaskana at every turn: homesteading, prospecting, wildlife, famous characters and more. Open daily year-round with special group/family rates. Clean restrooms. Gift shop featuring Eskimo dolls and totems. Carved grizzly and prospector outside to greet you. Main Street, Talkeetna. (907) 733-3999. Handicap accessible. [ADVERTISEMENT] ♿

Peak Dodger Flight Tours. Take flight with world renowned Doug Geeting Aviation. Look up at 14,000-foot rock and ice walls and land on a glacier—an Alaskan adventure highlight that will astound even the most experienced world traveler! We hold an NPS concession for Mount McKinley glacier landings, available only from the

Talkeetna State Airport. Planes are intercom equipped. Group rates available. Over-night accommodations available. For prices and reservations: Doug Geeting Aviation, P.O. Box 42MP, Talkeetna, AK 99676; (800) 770-2366. Fax (907) 733-1000. [ADVERTISEMENT]

Talkeetna Air Taxi. View Denali's most spectacular peaks and glaciers. Circle McKinley and land on a glacier, starting at $90. Anchorage–Denali Park–Talkeetna packages: Fly–Rail–Bus. Leave the logistics to us. Since 1947. Call 1-800-533-2219 or (907) 733-2218. http://www.alaska.net/~flytat. [ADVERTISMENT]

Talkeetna Gifts & Collectables. "One of the nicest and most complete gift shops in Alaska," located in a spacious log building with handmade keepsakes, souvenirs, jewelry, books, Alaskana, birch bowls, quilts and other treasures. Fur slippers/accessories, beautiful sweatshirts, sweaters, plush toys, puppets and huggable Eskimo dolls. Alaskan foods and sourdough. Suzy's exclusive "Alaska Map" cross-stitch pattern. Quality merchandise with friendly service. We mail purchases. Goldpanning, with gold guaranteed! Open daily year-round. Main Street, Talkeetna. (907) 733-2710. [ADVERTISEMENT]

Talkeetna River Guides. Fish with a recognized leader for salmon and trout in our exciting area streams and rivers. Guided charters available and include all equipment and use of our specialized jet boats. Drop-off fishing available as well. Also, join us on a wildlife, natural history float trip. 2-, 4- and 6-hour tours available daily. 1-800-353-2677. See display ad. [ADVERTISEMENT]

Fishing. A Calico (chum) Salmon Derby is held the first 3 weeks of August. The **Susitna River** basin offers many top fishing streams and lakes, either accessible by road, plane or riverboat.

Return to Milepost A 98.7
Parks Highway

Backpackers on the Kesugi Ridge Trail in Denali State Park. (© Bill Sherwonit)

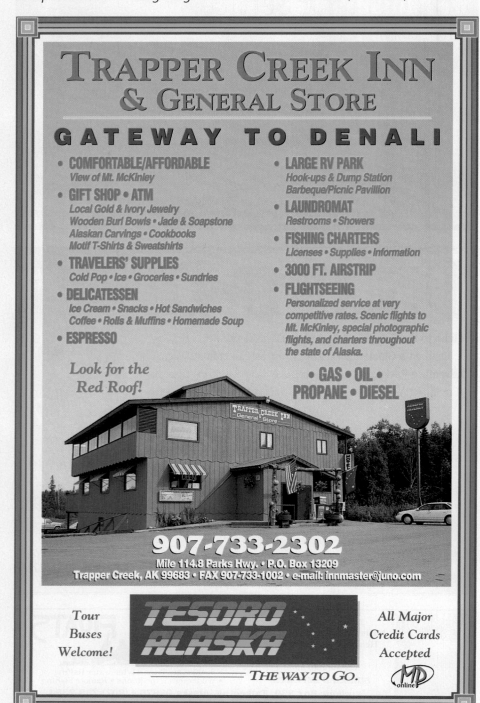

(Continued from page 405)
cluster of businesses around the junction with Petersville Road serves highway travelers.

Trapper Creek Inn & General Store. Gateway to Denali visitors information center. Tesoro gas, diesel, comfortable lodging with Mount McKinley view, large RV campground, full hookups, dump station, large barbecue/picnic pavilion, ATM, propane, showers, restrooms, laundry, pay phone, deli, espresso, groceries, coffee, ice, etc. Fishing and hunting licenses, supplies and charters. Flightseeing Mount McKinley. Major credit cards accepted. Phone (907) 733-2302. Fax (907) 733-1002. E-mail: innmaster@juno.com. Tour buses welcome. See large display ad this section. [ADVERTISEMENT] ▲

A 114.9 (184.9 km) **F 243.1** (391.2 km)

Junction with Petersville Road, which leads west 18.7 miles/30.1 km. See PETERSVILLE ROAD log this section.

Historic Trapper Creek post office (ZIP code 99683) north side of junction on east side of Parks Highway.

Trapper Creek's Old Historic Post Office. Come visit and bring your camera. See Alaskan artifacts and collectables you'll see nowhere else. Historian Mike Carpenter to greet you with 39 years of Alaskan tales. Some are true! Truly romantic Alaskan visitors center you can tell the folks back home about. Phone (907) 733-2637. [ADVERTISEMENT]

A 115.2 (185.4 km) **F 242.8** (390.7 km) Trapper Creek community park.

A 115.5 (185.9 km) **F 242.5** (390.2 km) **Trapper Creek Trading Post.** See display ad this section. ▲

A 115.6 (186 km) **F 242.4** (390.1 km) Highway crosses Trapper Creek.

Excellent views of Mount McKinley (weather permitting) northbound.

A 117.3 (188.8 km) **F 240.7** (387.4 km) Turnout east; vehicle weighing.

A 121.1 (194.9 km) **F 236.9** (381.2 km) Chulitna highway maintenance camp to west.

A 121.5 (195.5 km) **F 236.5** (380.6 km) Large paved double-ended rest area to east with tables, firepits, drinking water, toilet and interpretive bulletin board. Shade trees; cow parsnip grows lush here.

A 126.6 (203.7 km) **F 231.4** (371.7 km) Large paved parking area to east.

A 127 (204.4 km) **F 231** (372.1 km) Large unpaved turnout to west.

A 128.4 (206.6 km) **F 229.6** (369.5 km) Undeveloped parking area to east below highway on south side of creek.

A 132 (212.4 km) **F 226** (363.7 km) Boundary of Denali State Park (see description next milepost).

A 132.3 (212.9 km) **F 225.7** (363.2 km) **Denali State Park** entrance sign northbound. This 325,460-acre state park has 48 miles/77.2 km of hiking trails. Camping at Troublesome Creek (**Milepost A 137.3**), Byers Lake (**Milepost A 147**) and Denali View North (**Milepost A 162.7**). Hunting is permitted in the park, but discharge of firearms is prohibited within 0.3 mile of highway, 0.5 mile of a developed facility or 0.5 mile of trail around Byers Lake. ▲

A 132.8 (213.7 km) **F 225.2** (362.4 km) Middle of the **Chulitna River** bridge. *NOTE: Watch for bridge repair work in 1999.* Fishing for grayling, rainbow. ⤚

Entering Game Management Unit 13E, leaving unit 16A, northbound.

Miners built the Petersville Road in the 1920s and federal homesteading began here in 1948, with settlement continuing through the 1950s and 1960s. Petersville Road leads west and north from Trapper Creek through a homestead and gold mining area that also contains some new subdivisions. Berry picking in season. *Please respect private property.*

Distance from junction with the Parks Highway (J) is shown.

J 0 Junction with Parks Highway at Milepost A 114.9.

J 0.3 (0.5 km) **Trapper Creek B & B.** You will enjoy your stay with hosts Jim and Susan in a truly friendly Alaskan home. Clean, comfortable and new. Full breakfast with homemade bread. Walking distance to museum, general store, library, all on paved road. Excellent fishing, hunting, snowmachining. Beautiful views of Mount McKinley. Phone (907) 733-2234; fax (907) 733-2234. [ADVERTISEMENT]

J 0.7 (1.1 km) **Trapper Creek Museum and Gifts** to south. Visit historic homestead log cabin museum in view of Mount McKinley. Relive the local area's mining, trapping and homesteading eras, while browsing through local arts, crafts and authentic historic collectables on sale. Stroll around and pet miniature horses raised on the homestead. Pull-through parking for RVs. Phone (907) 733-2557. [ADVERTISEMENT]

J 2 (3.2 km) **Denali View Chalets.** Private, secluded, modern chalets with

spectacular views of Mount McKinley and the Alaska Range. Open year-round with access by paved road. Fully furnished with kitchenettes, microwave, gas grills and 2 twin and 2 double beds. Lots of area activities. The wilderness at your doorstep. Reasonable rates. E-mail address: denaliview@polarnet.com. Homepage address: http://www.alaskan.com/denaliviewchalets. P.O. Box 13245, Trapper Creek, AK 99683. Phone (907) 733-1333. [ADVERTISEMENT]

J 2.7 (4.3 km) Trapper Creek elementary school to south, bed and breakfast to north.

North Country Bed and Breakfast. Nestled on a lake with a spectacular view of Mount McKinley. Five first-class rooms with private bathrooms and private entries. Mount McKinley flightseeing trips available at the lake by appointment. Bird watching, wildlife, paddleboating and horseshoes available. Open

year-round. Your hosts—Mike and Sheryl Uher. Phone (907) 733-3981. See display ad this section. [ADVERTISEMENT]

J 3.1 (5 km) Pavement ends, gravel begins, westbound.

J 7 (11.3 km) Moose Creek; campground. Road narrows and climbs westbound.

J 10.5 (16.9 km) **Gate Creek Cabins** modern 1, 2 and 3-bedroom log cabins.

Located at Mile 10.5 on historic Petersville Road, with year-round access. Furnished with linens, dishes, utensils, stove, refrigerator, TV, VCR, showers, sauna, barbecue grill. Mountain viewing, hiking, biking, photography, fishing, berry picking. Free canoeing and paddleboating on our small lake; mountain bike and 4-wheeler rentals; snowmachine rentals in winter. Children 12 and under free. Weekly rate, 6th and 7th nights free. Family pets welcome. Your hosts, Gary and Dorothy Rawie. Reservations (907) 733-1393 or e-mail: gRawie@worldnet.att.net. Web page: alaskan.com/gatecreekcabins/. [ADVERTISEMENT]

J 13.4 (21.6 km) Steep grade and switchback.

J 13.9 (22.4 km) Kroto Creek. Narrow road climbs westbound. Slow down for some washboard.

J 17.2 (27.7 km) Turnoff for McKinley Foothills B&B (2.6 miles/4.2 km south).

McKinley Foothills B&B/Cabins. Off Mile 17.2 Petersville Road. Furnished, secluded log cabins, kitchenettes. Full breakfast. Great food, Alaskan hospitality. Great Mount McKinley views. Summer: gold panning tours, fishing

nearby, birding, hiking, mountain biking. Winter: skiing, snow machining, dog mushing tours. Major credit cards. Homepage: www. matnet.com/~mckinley. E-mail: mckinley@matnet.com. Phone/fax (907) 733-1454. P.O. Box 13089, Trapper Creek, AK 99683. [ADVERTISEMENT]

J 18.7 (30.1 km) Forks Roadhouse; food and lodging. Petersville Road forks

Children pet miniature horse at Trapper Creek Museum on Petersville Road. *(© Kris Graef, staff)*

here. Turn down the right fork for the former mining camp of Petersville (4-wheel drive only). The left fork leads 0.2 mile/0.3 km to **Peters Creek**; fishing for salmon and trout. ◄▲

The Forks Roadhouse. See display ad this section.

Return to Milepost A 114.9 Parks Highway

A 132.9 (213.9 km) **F 225.1** (362.2 km)
At north end of bridge, turn east uphill and
follow paved road approxiimately 1 mile/1.6
km for Mt. McKinley Princess Lodge. Trail
rides located on this access road.

D & S Alaskan Trail Rides, open mid-
May through mid-September, offers 1 1/2- to
8-hour nature trail rides with majestic views
of Mount McKinley and Ruth Glacier. You

View of Mount McKinley from the Princess Lodge access road at Milepost A 132.9. (© Mike Jones)

can only discover these views by riding the
best horses and mules in Alaska. It's the ride
of a lifetime! Ride our horse-drawn wagon to
view Mount McKinley, pan for gold and see
reindeer. Summer phone (907) 733-2207;
winter (907) 243-2589; fax (907) 243-7951.
[ADVERTISEMENT]

Mt. McKinley Princess Lodge. A stylish,
cozy riverside retreat bordering the south
side of Denali National Park featuring
incredible views of Mount McKinley and the
Alaska Range, expansive main lodge, finely
appointed guest rooms, array of dining
options, tour desk, gift shop. Open mid-May
through mid-September. Phone (800) 426-
0500 year round. [ADVERTISEMENT]

A 134 (215.6 km) **F 224** (360.5 km) Helicopter sightseeing service; private airstrip.

ERA Helicopters. Lift off over the banks
of the Chulitna River and see the numerous
glaciers covering the high mountain peaks

and the vast south slope of Denali, known
as "The Great One." Located at Milepost
134. May to September. For reservations
phone (800) 843-1947. Tours also available
in Juneau, Anchorage, Valdez and Denali
Park. [ADVERTISEMENT]

From here northbound for many miles
there are views of glaciers on the southern
slopes of the Alaska Range to the west. Ruth,
Buckskin and Eldridge glaciers are the most
conspicuous. Ruth Glacier trends southeast
through the Great Gorge for 31 miles/50 km.
The glacier was named in 1903 by F.A. Cook
for his daughter. The Great Gorge was

named by mountain climbers in the late
1940s. Peaks on either side of the gorge
tower up to 5,000 feet/1,500m above Ruth
Glacier. The gorge, nicknamed the Grand
Canyon of Alaska, opens into Don Sheldon
Amphitheater at the head of Ruth Glacier,

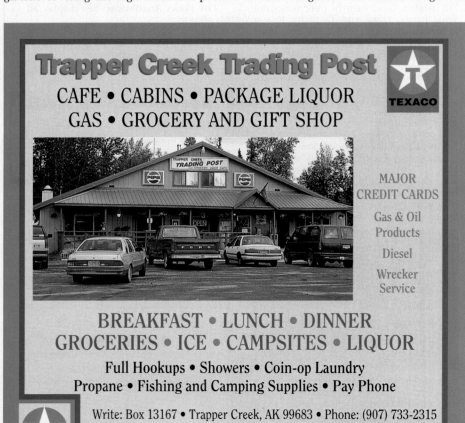

where the Don Sheldon mountain house sits. Donald E. Sheldon (1921–75) was a well-known bush pilot who helped map, patrol, and aid search and rescue efforts in this area.

Flightseeing trips can be arranged that take you close to Mount McKinley, into the Don Sheldon Amphitheater, through the Great Gorge and beneath the peak of The Mooses Tooth. Inquire with flightseeing oeprators along the Parks Highway and in the national park.

A 134.5 (216.5 km) **F 223.5** (359.7 km) **Mary's McKinley View Lodge.** Located on Mary Carey's original homestead. Spectacular view of McKinley from every room, especially the glass-walled restaurant. Mary, famous for Alaskan books, homesteaded before the state park was created. She fought for highway completion to share her magnificent view with travelers. Enjoy dining, browse the gift shop or spend a pleasant night in the modern rooms. Call (907) 733-1555. See display ad this page. [ADVERTISEMENT]

A 134.8 (216.9 km) **F 223.2** (359.2 km) Small turnout to east. Springwater piped to road. *CAUTION: Spring water is not treated. Use at own risk.*

A 135.2 (217.6 km) **F 222.8** (358.6 km) **Denali Viewpoint** (Denali State Park) is a large paved turnout overlooking the Chulitna River; toilet. A display board here points out peaks. View of 20,320-foot/6,194-m Mount McKinley. Peaks to be sighted, south to north, along the next 20 miles/32.2 km to the west are: Mount Hunter (elev. 14,573 feet/4,442m); Mount Huntington (elev. 12,240 feet/3,731m); Mount Barrille (elev. 7,650 feet/2,332m); and Mount Dickey (elev. 9,845 feet/3,001m).

A 137.3 (221 km) **F 220.7** (355.1 km) **Lower Troublesome Creek State Recreation Site** to west has 10 campsites, $6/night camping fee per vehicle or annual pass, day-use area with sheltered picnic sites, toilets, water and litter barrels. Lower Troublesome Creek trailhead. This is usually a clear runoff stream, not silted by glacial flour. The stream heads in a lake and flows 14 miles/22.5 km to the Chulitna River. ▲

Troublesome Creek bridge. Troublesome Creek, rainbow, grayling and salmon (king salmon fishing prohibited); June through September. ⮰

A 137.6 (221.4 km) **F 220.4** (354.7 km) Upper Troublesome Creek trailhead and parking area. Trails to Byers Lake (15 miles/24 km) and Tarn Point, elev. 2,881 feet/878m (10.8 miles/17.3 km). *NOTE: Trailhead and trail to Mile 5.5 closed from mid-July to Sept. 1 due to the high concentration of bears feeding on spawning salmon.*

A 139.9 (225.1 km) **F 218.1** (351 km) Paved turnout to west.

A 143.9 (231.6 km) **F 214.1** (344.6 km) Bridge over Byers Creek.

A 145.7 (234.5 km) **F 212.3** (341.6 km) Paved turnout to west.

A 147 (236.6 km) **F 211** (339.6 km) **Byers Lake State Campground** to east with 66 sites, $12/night camping fee or annual pass, picnic tables, firepits, water, toilets (wheelchair accessible) and access to Byers Lake (electric motors permitted). Fishing for grayling, burbot, rainbow, lake trout and whitefish. Remote campsite 1.8-mile/2.9-km hike from campground (see directions posted on bulletin board). Hiking trail to Curry Ridge and south to Troublesome Creek. *CAUTION: Bears frequent campground. Keep a clean camp.* ♿⮰▲

Susitna Expeditions offers canoe, kayak and boat rentals in Denali State Park. We also offer guided hiking, kayak and mountain bike tours, firewood bundles and visitor information. Experience Alaska with life-long Alaskans Kay and Toby Riddell. Our office is located at Byers Lake Campground. Phone (800) 891-6916. [ADVERTISEMENT]

A 147.2 (236.9 km) **F 210.8** (339.2 km) **Alaska Veterans Memorial** turnoff. This concrete memorial honoring the armed forces includes a park store, spotting scopes, viewing deck, visitor contact station, interpretive kiosk, picnic area and restrooms. Wheelchair accessible. The store is open 9 A.M. to 6 P.M. daily, Memorial Day to Labor Day. ♿

A 155.6 (250.4 km) **F 202.4** (325.7 km) For the next mile northbound, there are views of Eldridge Glacier to the west. The face of the glacier is 6 miles/9.7 km from the road. The Fountain River heads at the terminus of the glacier and flows into the Chulitna.

A 156.2 (251.4 km) **F 201.8** (324.8 km) Lodge.

A 156.5 (251.9 km) **F 201.5** (324.3 km) Large gravel turnout to east.

A 157.7 (253.8 km) **F 200.3** (322.3 km) Small paved turnout to west.

A 159.4 (256.5 km) **F 198.6** (319.6 km) Double-ended paved turnout to west.

A 161 (259.1 km) **F 197** (317 km) Large gravel turnout to east.

A 162.4 (261.4 km) **F 195.6** (314.8 km) **Denali Viewpoint** is a large paved turnout to west with a view of Mount McKinley.

A 162.7 (261.8 km) **F 195.3** (314.3 km) **Denali View North Campground** to west; 20 sites, $10/night, day-use parking, toilets (wheelchair accessible), water, interpretive kiosks, spotting scope, short loop trail. Overlooks Chulitna River. Views of Denali, Mooses Tooth, Mount Huntington and Alaska Range peaks above Hidden River valley. ♿▲

A 163.1 (262.5 km) **F 194.9** (313.6 km) Large double-ended paved turnout to west.

A 163.2 (262.6 km) **F 194.8** (313.5 km) Bridge over Little Coal Creek.

Coal Creek; rainbow, grayling and salmon, July through September. ⮰

A 163.8 (263.6 km) **F 194.2** (312.5 km) Little Coal Creek trailhead and parking area. According to park rangers, this trail offers easy access (1½-hour hike) to alpine country. It is a 27-mile/43.5-km hike to Byers Lake via Kesugi Ridge.

A 165.6 (266.5 km) **F 192.4** (309.6 km) Paved turnouts on both sides of highway. Good berry picking in the fall.

A 169 (272 km) **F 189** (304.2 km) *CAUTION: Railroad crossing.* A solar collector here helps power the warning signals.

Denali State Park boundary (leaving park northbound, entering park southbound).

A 170.3 (274 km) **F 187.7** (302.1 km) Paved turnout to west. Good glacier views to west.

A 170.5 (274.4 km) **F 187.5** (301.7 km) *CAUTION: Slow down for "bumps" next 1.2 miles/1.9 km northbound.*

A 174 (280 km) **F 184** (296.1 km) **Hurricane Gulch Bridge**; rest area. From the south end of the bridge, scramble through alders up the east bank of the gulch to find photographers' trail (unmarked). A 0.3-mile/0.4-km trail along edge of Hurricane Gulch offers good views of the bridge span and gulch. A pleasant walk, good berry picking in the fall. *Do not go too near the edge.*

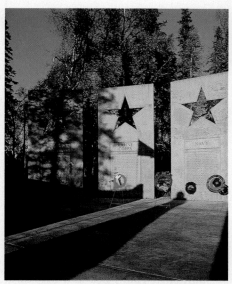

Alaska Veterans Memorial at Milepost A 147.2 Parks Highway. (© Mike Jones)

Parking areas at both ends of bridge.

Construction costs for the bridge were approximately $1.2 million. The 550-foot/168m deck of the bridge is 260 feet/79m above Hurricane Creek, not as high as the railroad bridge that spans the gulch near the Chulitna River. From this bridge the highway begins a gradual descent northbound to Honolulu Creek.

A 176 (283.2 km) **F 182** (292.9 km) Paved turnout to east. Highway descends long grade northbound.

A 176.5 (284 km) **F 181.5** (292.1 km) Rough, narrow, double-ended gravel turnout to west with view of the Alaska Range.

A 177.8 (286.1 km) **F 180.2** (290 km) Paved turnout and view of eroded bluffs to west.

A 178.1 (286.6 km) **F 179.9** (289.5 km) Bridge over Honolulu Creek. The highway begins a gradual ascent northbound to Broad Pass, the gap in the Alaska Range crossed by both the railroad and highway. Undeveloped parking areas below highway on the creek.

A 179.7 (289.2 km) **F 178.3** (286.9 km) Paved turnout to west by small lake. In early September blueberries are plentiful for the next 25 miles/40 km.

A 180 (289.7 km) **F 178** (286.5 km) Narrow double-ended paved turnout to west by small lake. Short trail to **Mile 180 Lake,** stocked with grayling. ⮰

A 183.2 (294.8 km) **F 174.8** (281.3 km) Paved double-ended turnout to west of highway. Look to the west across the Chulitna River for dramatic view of the Alaska Range (weather permitting).

A 184.5 (296.9 km) **F 173.5** (279.2 km) Paved turnout to west.

A 185 (297.7 km) **F 173** (278.4 km) East Fork DOT/PF highway maintenance station.

A 185.1 (297.9 km) **F 172.9** (278.3 km) Bridge over East Fork Chulitna River.

A 185.6 (298.7 km) **F 172.4** (277.4 km) East Fork rest area (no sign at turnoff) on right northbound. A 0.5-mile/0.8-km paved loop gives access to a gravel picnic area with overnight parking, 23 tables, concrete fireplaces and picnic shelter. The rest area is in a bend of the East Fork Chulitna River amid a healthy growth of Alaskan spruce and birch.

Cut wood is often available. ▲

A 187.5 (301.8 km) F 170.5 (274.4 km) Paved double-ended turnout to west; small paved turnout east side of highway.

A 188.5 (303.4 km) F 169.5 (272.8 km) **Igloo City**, an Alaskan landmark, 50 miles south of entrance to Denali National Park. New ownership. Unleaded, regular a nd diesel fuels, propane. Ask for 5-cent discount for cash fill-ups. Caravan discounts.Espresso, postcards, candy, snacks, soft drinks, ice, pay phone. Camping, lodging. Unique Alaskan art, gifts and souvenirs not sen elsewhere. Open 24 hours year-round. (907) 768-2622. See display ad. [ADVERTISEMENT]

A 189.9 (305.6 km) F 168.1 (270.5 km) Narrow gravel double-ended turnout to west. Watch for beaver dam to east northbound.

A 191 (307.4 km) F 167 (268.8 km) Large paved parking area to west. Look for cotton grass.

A 193 (310.6 km) F 165 (265.5 km) Bed and breakfast to west.

Sourdough Paul's Bed and Breakfast. Area attractions include a full day active gold mining tour, lake and creek fishing in view of Mount McKinley (boats are available), wildlife viewing, blueberry picking, camping. Enjoy a full sourdough breakfast. Pioneer hand-built log home complete with authentic Finnish log sauna, shower, 5-star

rated outhouse. Mount McKinley views. One hour to Denali National Park. Kids and pets stay free. Hunting and fishing parties welcome. Reservations (907) 768-2020 or (907) 892-6000. [ADVERTISEMENT]

A 194.3 (312.7 km) F 163.7 (263.4 km) *CAUTION: Railroad crossing.*

A 194.5 (313 km) F 163.5 (263.1 km) Bridge over Middle Fork Chulitna River.

CAUTION: Highway curves northbound. Windy area through Broad Pass.

A 195 (313.8 km) F 163 (262.3 km) Entering Broad Pass northbound. Good views of Broad Pass.

A 195.9 (315.3 km) F 162.1 (260.9 km) Large paved turnout east; mountain views.

A 201.1 (323.6 km) F 156.9 (252.5 km) Large paved parking area to east with mountain view.

A 201.3 (324 km) F 156.7 (252.2 km) **Broad Pass Summit** (not signed), 2,300 feet/701m. Broad Pass is one of the most

beautiful areas on the Parks Highway. A mountain valley, bare in some places, dotted with scrub spruce in others, and surrounded by mountain peaks, it provides a top-of-the-world feeling for the traveler, although it is one of the lowest summits along the North American mountain system. Named in 1898 by George Eldridge and Robert Muldrow, the 2,300-foot/701m pass, sometimes called Caribou Pass, marks the divide between the drainage of rivers and streams that empty into Cook Inlet and those that empty into the Yukon River.

Orange towers of weather service station building west of highway.

A 202.3 (325.6 km) F 155.7 (250.6 km) Boundary of Matanuska–Susitna and Denali boroughs.

A 203.1 (326.9 km) F 154.9 (249.3 km) *CAUTION: Railroad crossing.*

A 203.6 (327.7 km) F 154.4 (248.5 km) Paved parking area with view to east.

A 208 (334.7 km) F 150 (241.4 km) Turnout to west at end of bridge over Pass Creek; blueberries in season.

A 209.4 (337 km) F 148.6 (239.1 km) Large gravel parking area to east.

A 209.5 (337.1 km) F 148.5 (239 km) Bridge over Jack River; paved turnout.

A 209.7 (337.4 km) F 148.3 (238.7 km) **Reindeer Mtn. Lodge.** Lodging, gifts, snacks and furs. Beautiful view of Mount McKinley. Rooms have private baths and color TV. Beautiful log office has ornate wood carvings. Open year-round. Wildlife, scenery, skiing, snowmobiling, fishing, hunting, hiking or relaxing. Call (907) 768-2420 or fax (907) 768-2942. Write Box 7, Cantwell, AK 99729. [ADVERTISEMENT]

A 209.9 (337.8 km) F 148.1 (238.3 km)

Junction of the Parks Highway and the Denali Highway (Alaska Route 8). See the DENALI HIGHWAY section for log of highway east to Paxson.

Turn west on the Denali Highway for Cantwell (description follows), 1.8 miles/2.9 km from junction; turn east for Paxson.

Cantwell

Located 1.8 miles/2.9 km west of Parks Highway, end of the Denali Highway. **Population:** 145. **Emergency Services: Alaska State Troopers,** business phone (907) 768-2202. **Fire Department,** emergency only phone (907) 768-2240. **Ambulance,** phone (907) 768-2982.

Elevation: 2,190 feet/668m. Private Aircraft: Cantwell airport, adjacent north; elev. 2,190 feet/668m; length 2,100 feet/640m; gravel, dirt; fuel 100LL.

Cantwell began as a railroad flag stop on the Alaska Railroad. The village was named for the Cantwell River, the original name of the Nenana River, which was named by Lt. Allen in 1885 for Lt. John C. Cantwell of the Revenue-Cutter Service, who explored the Kobuk River region.

Many of Cantwell's businesses are clustered around the intersection of the Denali and Parks highways or on the way into downtown Cantwell. Services include food, gas, lodging and camping. ▲

George Parks Highway Log
(continued)

A 210 (338 km) **F 148** (238.2 km) Cantwell post office (ZIP code 99729).

A 210.3 (338.4 km) **F 147.7** (237.7 km) Gas station (diesel), food mart and gift shop.

Cantwell Food Mart and Parkway Gift Shop. See display ad this section.

A 210.4 (338.6 km) **F 147.6** (237.5 km) Gas and groceries.

Cotter's Quality Services. See display ad this section.

A 211.5 (340.4 km) **F 146.5** (235.8 km) Paved double-ended parking area to west.

A 212 (341.2 km) **F 146** (235 km) Slide area northbound.

A 212.7 (342.3 km) **F 145.3** (233.8 km) Gravel turnout to west by Nenana River. Watch for large beaver dam to west.

A 213.9 (344.2 km) **F 144.1** (231.9 km) Paved double-ended parking area to west among tall white spruce and fireweed.

A 215.3 (346.5 km) **F 142.7** (229.6 km) Access road to Nenana River on west side of highway, which parallels the highway northbound.

A 215.7 (347.1 km) **F 142.3** (229 km) First bridge northbound over the Nenana River. Highway narrows northbound.

A 216.2 (347.9 km) **F 141.8** (228.2 km) Entering Game Management Unit 20A and leaving unit 13E northbound.

A 216.3 (348.1 km) **F 141.7** (228 km) Paved double-ended turnout to west. Good

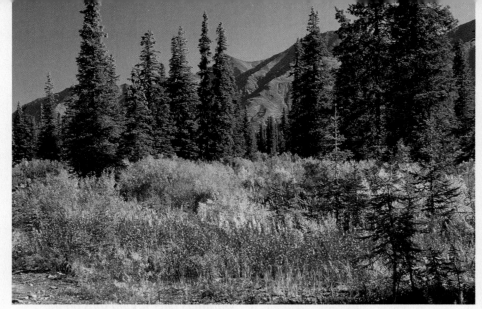

Autumn colors and the Alaska Range along the Parks Highway. (© Loren Taft)

spot for photos of Panorama Mountain (elev. 5,778 feet/1,761m), the prominent peak visible to the east.

A 218.6 (351.8 km) **F 139.4** (224.3 km)

Paved double-ended turnout to west with beautiful view of Nenana River.

A 219 (352.4 km) **F 139** (223.7 km) Slide area: Watch for rocks next 0.4 mile/0.6 km

Please support our MILEPOST® advertisers.

northbound.

A 219.8 (353.7 km) **F 138.2** (222.4 km) Paved double-ended parking area to west overlooking Nenana River.

A 220 (354 km) **F 138** (222.1 km) Slime Creek.

A 220.6 (355 km) **F 137.4** (221.1 km) Old alignment to west along Nenana River.

A 222.2 (357.6 km) **F 135.8** (218.5 km) Large paved double-ended turnout to west beside Nenana River. Watch for rafts on river.

A 222.5 (358.1 km) **F 135.5** (218.1 km) Snow poles beside roadway guide snowplows in winter.

A 223.9 (360.3 km) **F 134.1** (215.8 km) Carlo Creek Lodge to west.

Carlo Creek Lodge. Located 12 miles south of Denali Park entrance. 32 wooded acres bordered by beautiful Carlo Creek, the Nenana River and Denali National Park. Cozy creekside log cabins with own bathroom, showers. RV park, dump station, potable water, propane. Clean bathroom, showers. Dishwashing facility. Individual sheltered tent sites each with picnic table and firepit. Unique gift shop. Small store. Information. Pay phone. You won't be disappointed. It's a beautiful place to be. HC 2, Box 1530, Healy, AK 99743. (907) 683-2576, 683-2573. [ADVERTISEMENT] ▲

A 224 (360.5 km) **F 134** (215.7 km) The Perch Restaurant uphill to east.

The Perch. A beautiful, established restaurant-bar perched on a private hill. Spectacular dining, specializes in freshly

baked bread, seafood and steaks. Also, take-out giant cinnamon rolls. Breakfast 6 A.M. to 11:30 A.M.; lunch 11:30 A.M. to 2 P.M.; dinner 5 P.M. to 10 P.M., open daily mid-May through September; and Friday, Saturday, Sunday October through May. Sleeping cabins with central bath, some with private baths, beside Carlo Creek. Owners/operators, Duane and Leslie Watters. Phone (907) 683-2523. P.O. Box 53, Denali Park, AK 99755.

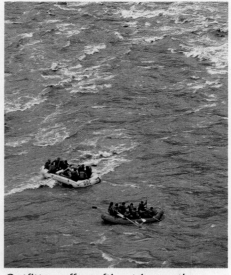

Outfitters offer rafting trips on the Nenana River at Denali National Park.
(© Rich Reid)

See display ad in the DENALI NATIONAL PARK section. [ADVERTISEMENT] ᴹᴾ

A 224 (360.5 km) **F 134** (215.7 km) Bridge over Carlo Creek. McKinley Creekside Cabins to east at north end of bridge.

McKinley Creekside Cabins. Scenic, peaceful setting on the banks of Carlo Creek. Large cabins with private bath; economy cabins with central bath. Home-style cafe and bakery, gourmet espresso bar, tour desk. Reservations: (888) 5-DENALI, or (907) 683-2277. Fax (907) 683-1558. P.O. Box 89, Denali National Park, AK 99755. Web: www.mckinleycabins.com. [ADVERTISEMENT]

A 224.1 (360.6 km) **F 133.9** (215.5 km) **Carlo Heights Bed and Breakfast and Rick Swenson's Denali Sled Dog School.** Share seclusion and spectacular views. Located on bluff overlooking Nenana River and Alaska Range. Accommodations include 2 double rooms and a private suite, full kitchen and laundry facilities. Ask about our sleeping cabin planned for summer 1999! Open year around, reservations recommended during summertime and required during off season. Sled dog school offers dog mushing courses

and tours. Box 86, Denali Park, AK 99755. Phone (907) 683-1615. Internet: www.mosquitonet.com/~birdsong/sbb.html. [ADVERTISEMENT]

A 225 (362.1 km) **F 133** (214 km) Beautiful mountain views southbound.

A 226 (363.7 km) **F 132** (212.4 km) Fang Mountain (elev. 6,736 feet/2,053m) may be visible to the west through the slash in the mountains.

A 229 (368.5 km) **F 129** (207.6 km) Lodge and cabins to east.

Denali Backcountry Lodge. Stop at Denali Cabins (located at **Milepost 229**) and visit the sales office for Denali Backcountry Lodge. The wilderness vacation lodge is for those who want to escape the park's crowded entrance and immerse themselves deep within Denali National Park for a few days. Located at the end of the 95-mile park road, Denali Backcountry Lodge features full-service accommodations, dining room and lounge. One- to 4-night stays include round-trip transportation from the train depot, all meals and lodging, guided hikes, wildlife viewing, bicycling, photography and natural history programs. Many famous naturalists are found staying at the lodge and occasionally they conduct special presentations. Credit cards accepted and discounts are given for last-minute bookings if space is available. P.O. Box 189, Denali National Park, AK 99755. Internet: www.denalilodge.com. Phone (800) 841-0692. [ADVERTISEMENT]

Denali Cabins. Private cabins with bath, outdoor hot tubs, complimentary coffee and extensive information about

Denali National Park. Restaurant on premises. Seasonal service mid-May through mid-September. VISA, MasterCard accepted. (907) 258-0134 (winter) or (907) 683-2643 (summer). Brochure: 200 W. 34th Ave., #362, Anchorage, AK 99503. Fax (907) 243-2062 or summer (907) 683-2595. Web: www.alaskan.com/deanlicabins. See display ad in DENALI NATIONAL PARK section. [ADVERTISEMENT]

A 229.2 (368.8 km) **F 128.8** (207.3 km) Private airstrip. Flightseeing service.

Denali Air, Inc. Fly closer to Denali's beauty on our 1-hour aerial tour of Mount McKinley/Denali National Park. Our private airstrip is the closest to Denali Park hotels

and the Alaska Range, offering the best tour and value. A pioneer service with the most experienced pilots. Two person minimum. Reservations: (907) 683-2261. See display ad in the DENALI NATIONAL PARK section. [ADVERTISEMENT]

A 229.7 (369.7 km) **F 128.3** (206.5 km) Double-ended paved turnout to west.

A 230.5 (370.9 km) **F 127.5** (205.2 km) *Steep grade northbound.*

A 231.1 (371.9 km) **F 126.9** (204.2 km) **McKinley Village Resort.** Convenient to all activities. Nestled on the banks of the Nenana River, this 150-room newly remodeled lodge is complete with dining room, lounge, gift shop, rafting and tour desk. Try gold panning at the Denali Mining Company. Call 1-800-276-7234 or in Anchorage phone (907) 276-7234. Internet: www.denalinationalpark.com. [ADVERTISEMENT]

Denali Grizzly Bear Cabins & Campground. South boundary Denali National Park. Denali's only AAA-approved campground. Drive directly to your individual kitchen, sleeping or tent cabin with its old-time Alaskan atmosphere overlooking scenic Nenana River. Two conveniently located buildings with toilets, sinks, coin-operated hot showers. Advance reservations suggested. Tenting and RV campsite available in peaceful wooded areas. Hookups. Propane, laundromat. Caravans welcome! Coffee and rolls, ice cream, snacks, groceries, ice, liquor store, Alaskan gifts, tour desk. VISA, Master-Card, Discover accepted. Owned and operated by pioneer Alaskan family. Reservations (907) 683-2696 (summer); (907) 683-1337 (winter). Internet: www.alaskaone.com/ dengrzly/index.htm. See display ad in DENALI NATIONAL PARK section. **MP ▲**

Denali River Cabins. Relax at Denali National Park. Charming destination resort five minutes from the Visitor Center. New cedar cabins and rooms, all with private bath, on the Nenana River, directly across from the Park. Enjoy homemade meals in our restaurant, indulge in our bakery, wine-taste at our bar, or sip hot chocolate and cappuccino in our cozy main lodge. We also feature an outdoor Jacuzzi, riverside sauna, and 3 large sundecks with grills. Our activities desk can help you with park tours (inquire about Kantishna—the complete park experience!), rafting, flightseeing, horseback riding, etc. Visit us at www.denalirivercabins.com or call us for reservations at 1-800-230-7275. Also ask us about our brand new luxury property— Hotel Edgewater—in Seward, gateway to the spectacular Kenai Fjords National Park. [ADVERTISEMENT] ▲

A 231.3 (372.2 km) **F 126.7** (203.9 km) **Crabb's Crossing**, second bridge northbound over the Nenana River. Small paved turnout with wide shoulders west side of highway.

At the north end of this bridge is the boundary of Denali National Park and Preserve. From here north for 6.8 miles/10.9 km

Park visitors view Mt. McKinley from Stoney Hill Overlook on the Park Road.

(© Craig Brandt)

the Parks Highway is within the boundaries of the park and travelers must abide by park rules. No discharge of firearms permitted.

A 234.1 (376.7 km) **F 123.9** (199.4 km) Double-ended scenic viewpoint with litter barrels to east. No overnight parking or camping. Mount Fellows (elev. 4,476 feet/ 1,364m) to the east. The constantly changing shadows make this an excellent camera subject. Exceptionally beautiful in the evening. To the southeast stands Pyramid Peak (elev. 5,201 feet/1,585m).

A 235.1 (378.4 km) **F 122.9** (197.8 km) *CAUTION: Railroad crossing.* Solar panels and wind generators provide power for crossing signals.

A 236 (379.8 km) **F 122** (196.3 km) Begin 55 mph/86 kmph speed zone northbound.

A 236.7 (380.9 km) **F 121.3** (195.2 km) Alaska Railroad crosses over highway. From this point the highway begins a steep descent northbound to Riley Creek.

A 237.2 (381.7 km) **F 120.8** (194.4 km) Riley Creek bridge.

A 237.3 (381.9 km) **F 120.7** (194.2 km) Turnoff to east for entrance to **DENALI NATIONAL PARK AND PRESERVE** (formerly Mount McKinley National Park) to west. Visitor Center is 0.5 mile/0.8 km from the highway junction.

Junction with Park Road. See DENALI NATIONAL PARK section for log of Park Road and details on the park.

Clusters of highway businesses north and south of the park entrance offer a variety of services to the highway traveler and park visitor including river running, gift shops, accommodations, restaurants and entertainment.

A 238 (383 km) **F 120** (193.4 km) Third bridge northbound over the Nenana River. Staging area for raft trips on the Nenana River at north end of bridge. Era Helicopters office is located here.

The 4.8 miles/7.7 km of road and 7 bridges in the rugged Nenana Canyon cost $7.7 million to build. Sugarloaf Mountain (elev. 4,450 feet/1,356m), to the east, is closed to the hunting of Dall sheep, which are regularly sighted in the early and late summer months. Mount Healy (elev. 5,716 feet/1,742m) is to the west.

Southbound for 6.8 miles/10.9 km the Parks Highway is within the boundaries of Denali National Park and Preserve and travelers must abide by park rules. No discharge of firearms.

A 238.1 (383.2 km) **F 119.9** (193 km) Public access to Nenana River; rafting trip oeprator (Denali Raft Adventures) located here.

Denali Raft Adventures. Come with the original Nenana River rafters! Paddleboats too! Age 5 or older welcome, 7 departures daily. Whitewater or scenic floats. Get away to untouched wilderness! 2-hour, 4-hour, full-day and overnight trips available. See

display ad in DENALI NATIONAL PARK section. Phone (907) 683-2234. Internet: www.dendiraft.com. E-mail: denraft@mtaonline.net. VISA, MasterCard accepted. [ADVERTISEMENT] **MP**

A 238.3 (383.5 km) **F 119.7** (192.6 km) Kingfisher Creek.

A 238.4 (383.6 km) **F 119.6** (192.5 km) **Denali Bluffs Hotel.** AAA approved. The newest and closest hotel to the Denali National Park and Preserve entrance. 112 rooms; each room features 2 double beds, TVs, phones, refrigerators, in-room coffee, cafe. Spectacular views of the Alaska Range. The lodge features a large stone fireplace and cathedral ceilings. There are comfortable sitting areas inside the lodge or outside on the deck to enjoy the panoramic views. Gift shop and coin-operated laundry. Shuttle service to all area facilities. Complete tour and activity desk. Wheelchair accessible. Open mid-May through mid-September. Credit cards accepted. P.O. Box 72460, Fairbanks, AK 99707. Phone (907) 683-7000. Fax (907) 683-7500. E-mail: denali@denalibluffs.com. Internet: wwwdenalibluffs.com. See display ad in the DENALI NATIONAL PARK section. [ADVERTISEMENT]   MP &

Denali River View Inn. Beautiful views of the park and sounds of the river. Private bath, attractive rooms, TVs, excellent service and transportation. Pay phone. Conveniently located. Major credit cards. For reservations and information write P.O. Box 49M, Denali Park, AK 99755. Phone (907) 683-2663. Fax (907) 683-7433. See display ad in the DENALI NATIONAL PARK section. [ADVERTISEMENT]

A 238.5 (383.8 km) F 119.5 (192.3 km) Alaska flag display features a 10-by-15-foot/3-by-5-m state flag and plaques detailing history of flag design and song.

A 238.5 (383.8 km) F 119.5 (192.3 km) **Denali Princess Lodge.** Riverside lodging near the entrance to Denali National Park featuring spectacular park and Nenana River views, several dining options including Mt. McK's dinner theatre, tour desk, gift shop, complimentary shuttle to rail depot and park activities. Open mid-May through mid-September. Phone (800) 426-0500 year-round. [ADVERTISEMENT]

Denali Wilderness Lodge. Alaska's historic fly-in wilderness lodge. Often called "the most remote hotel in America."

Authentic bush homestead, now intimate lodge, nestled in the pristine Wood River Valley just outside Denali National Park. Accessible only by spectacular bush plane flights over the mountains and glaciers of the Alaska Range. Comfortable accommodations, delicious meals, naturalist programs, flightseeing, horseback riding, river rafting, nature/photo walks and hikes, bird watching, wildlife museum. Experience all the beauty of wilderness Alaska! Overnight packages and day trips available. Free color brochure. Phone (800) 541-9779; e-mail: denwild@alaska.net. Internet: http://www.alaskaone.com/dwlodge. See display ad in DENALI NATIONAL PARK section. [ADVERTISEMENT]

A 238.7 (384.1 km) F 119.3 (192 km) **Denali Windsong Lodge.** Specialists at serving the highway traveler. 72 clean,

modern rooms with full bath, satellite TV and beautiful mountain views from every room. Located just north of park entrance, near all restaurants and activities. Our friendly staff and reasonable rates make this the place to stay. Phone (800) 208-0200 or

(907) 683-1240. See display ad in DENALI NATIONAL PARK section. [ADVERTISEMENT]

A 238.8 (384.3 km) F 119.2 (191.8 km) **Denali Sourdough Cabins.** Enjoy the beauty of Denali National Park from your individual cabin set in a spruce forest one mile from the park. The cabins offer comfortable accommodations in a warm atmosphere, all with private bath and within walking distance to all services. Courtesy transportation available. May to September. Phone (907) 683-2773, 1-800-354-6020; fax (907) 683-2357. www.denalisourdough cabins.com. VISA, MasterCard, American Express accepted. See display ad in DENALI NATIONAL PARK section. [ADVERTISEMENT]   ▲

A 238.9 (384.5 km) F 119.1 (191.7 km) **Denali Outdoor Center.** Denali's most diversified river outfitter! Oar rafts, paddle rafts, inflatable kayak tours and mountain bike rentals. 2-hour, 4-hour, and ¹/₂-day guided whitewater and scenic wilderness river trips. Custom "drysuits," professional guides and exceptional equipment provided. Ages 5 and up. Call for reservations (888) 303-1925 or (907) 683-1925. Major credit cards accepted. [ADVERTISEMENT]   MP

A 239 (384.6 km) F 119 (191.5 km) **Northern Lights Theatre and Gift Shop.** Come experience the Northern Lights on a 34-foot screen. This presentation is one-of-a-kind, entertaining and informative. Stop by for show times and tickets. Don't miss

Denali's largest gift shop in a beautiful, natural log building, specializing in quality Alaskan gifts. Full mount world-class polar bear on display. Located 1.5 miles north of park entrance. Large parking area. Don't miss this attraction! P.O. Box 65, Denali Park, AK 99755. (907) 683-4000. www.akpub.com/akht/lights.html. E-mail: lightstheatre@yahoo.com. [ADVERTISEMENT]

A 239.1 (384.8 km) F 118.9 (191.3 km) **McKinley Chalet Resort.** The original and largest—345 rooms. You'll find comfortable mini-suites and the largest rooms in Denali. Includes fine dining, lounge, relaxed dining, unique gifts, rafting, gold panning, tours and full-service tour desk. Home of the Famous Alaska Cabin Nite Dinner Theatre. Call 1-800-276-7234, or in Anchorage, 276-7234. www.denalinationalpark.com. [ADVERTISEMENT]

Alaska Raft Adventures. Rafting adventures with experienced guides. Our Wilderness Run floats through a glacial valley along the Park boundary. The Canyon Run offers exciting whitewater action. Courtesy transportation available between area hotels and the Train Depot. Stop by the tour desk at McKinley Chalet Resort or McKinley Village Resort. [ADVERTISEMENT]

A 240 (386.2 km) F 118 (189.9 km) Bridge over Iceworm Gulch.

CAUTION: Sharp curves, rock slide area, northbound. Do not park along the highway. Use the many parking areas provided. High winds in the Nenana Canyon can make this stretch of road dangerous for campers and motorhomes.

A 240.2 (386.6 km) F 117.8 (189.6 km) Riverside RV Park to west.   ▲

A 240.6 (387.2 km) F 117.4 (188.9 km) Paved double-ended turnout to west beside river.

A 241.6 (388.8 km) F 116.4 (187.3 km) Large gravel turnout to west.

A 242.1 (389.6 km) F 115.9 (186.5 km) Paved parking area to west.

A 242.3 (389.9 km) F 115.7 (186.2 km) Dragonfly Creek bridge; paved double-ended turnout to west.

A 242.6 (390.4 km) F 115.4 (185.7 km) Paved double-ended turnout to west.

CAUTION: Windy area next mile northbound.

A 242.9 (390.9 km) F 115.1 (185.2 km) Moody Bridge. This 4th bridge northbound over the Nenana River measures 174 feet/53m from its deck to the bottom of the canyon. Dall sheep can be spotted from the bridge. Entering Game Management Unit 20A northbound, 20C southbound.

A 243.5 (391.9 km) F 114.5 (184.3 km) Bridge over Bison Gulch. Sharp turn at north end to east for paved viewpoint.

Steep grade northbound. End windy area.

A 244.1 (392.8 km) F 113.9 (183.3 km) Large paved turnout to east. Watch for frost heaves next 1 mile/1.6 km northbound.

A 244.5 (393.5 km) F 113.5 (182.6 km) Bridge over Antler Creek.

A 245.1 (394.4 km) F 112.9 (181.7 km) **Denali RV Park & Motel.** 90 full and partial RV hookups, 30-amp electric, pull-throughs, level sites, easy access. RV rates $12–$26 (20 percent off extra RV nights). $12–$16 low-season rates. Caravans welcome! Private restrooms with pay showers, dump station. 14 motel rooms. Double with bath $69; family units with full kitchen and TV $99. Laundry, pay phones, outdoor cooking area, covered meeting area. Gift shop, tour booking, information. Beautiful panoramic mountain views, hiking trails. E-mail access line available. VISA/Mastercard/Discover. Web address: www.denaliRVpark.com. E-mail: stay@denaliRVpark.com. Located 8 miles north of park entrance. Box 155, Denali National Park, AK 99755. (800) 478-1501, (907) 683-1500. See dislay ad in the DENALI NATIONAL PARK section. [ADVERTISEMENT]   ▲

A 246.8 (397.2 km) F 111.2 (179 km) Paved turnout to east.

A 247 (397.5 km) F 111 (178.6 km) Side road leads 1 mile/1.6 km to Otto Lake, 5 miles/8 km to Black Diamond Coal Mine. Primitive parking area on lakeshore (0.8-mile/1.3-km drive in) with toilet, litter barrels, shallow boat launch. Stocked with rainbow and coho. Denali hostel. Access to bed and breakfasts, golf driving range and RV park.   ◄▲

Black Diamond Golf Course invites you to play golf on the northern threshold of the Alaska Range. Come enjoy a course sculpted amidst Alaska's mountains, lakes, wildflowers and wildlife. The course is just off the George Parks Highway at Mile 247, 10 miles north of the Denali Park entrance. We offer course, driving range, rentals, golf gift shop, transportation and food and beverage. (907) 683-GOLF. www.blackdiamongolf.com. [ADVERTISEMENT]

Homestead Bed and Breakfast, Mile 1.3 Otto Lake Road. Spectacular view overlooking Otto Lake. Old-fashioned comfort and hospitality. Very comfortable beds. Home-style hearty breakfasts. Smoke-free home. Hiking nearby. Paddle boats and canoes for rent locally. Host Evalyn Morrison. (907) 683-2575. P.O. Box 478, Healy, AK 99743. [ADVERTISEMENT]

Otto Lake Bed & Breakfast. Beautiful

lakeside Alaska Range views. Quilt-topped queen, double or twin beds. Private or shared baths. Sitting area with microwave, refrigerator, TV/VCR, library. Open year-round. VISA, MasterCard accepted. Phone (907) 683-2339. Fax (907) 683-2336. Your hosts, Lyle and Beth Westphal, P.O. Box 45, Healy, AK 99743. [ADVERTISEMENT]

Otto Lake R.V. Park and Campground. Beautiful mountain views from wooded lakeside RV and tent sites, 1/2 mile west of Parks Highway on Otto Lake Road. Spacious and secluded sites with picnic tables, firepits, firewood, potable water, toilets, dump station and pay phone. Boat rentals. Family camping at its best, not a gravel strip. Located 9.7 miles north of Denali National Park entrance. [ADVERTISEMENT] ▲

A 248 (399.1 km) **F 110** (177 km) Speed zone begins 45 mph/72 kmph northbound.

A 248.2 (399.4 km) **F 109.8** (176.7 km) Gas station.

A 248.3 (399.6 km) **F 109.7** (176.5 km) Auto and truck repair and parts.

Evans Industries Inc. See display ad this section.

A 248.4 (399.8 km) **F 109.6** (176.4 km) **McKinley RV & Campground.** One of the nicest campgrounds around; 89 sites and utilities available. We book area activities. We offer free showers, dump station, wooded landscape, nightly movie, fax service and

propane. Caravans/groups welcome. Reservations recommended. Write Box 340MP, Healy, AK 99743. Phone: (907) 683-2379. Fax: (907) 683-2281. National (800) 478-2561. See display ad in the DENALI NATIONAL PARK section. [ADVERTISEMENT] ▲

A 248.5 (399.9 km) **F 109.5** (176.2 km) Paved turnout to east. River rafting service office.

Nenana Raft Adventures. Raft Denali with the *first* raft company in Alaska to outfit every client in a full drysuit. Day trips as well as multi-day expeditions on the Talkeetna River. Oar rafts and paddle rafting both available. Our riverfront office is directly next door to ERA Helicopters. 1-800-7899-RAFT in Denali (907) 683-RAFT. See display ad on this page. [ADVERTISEMENT]

A 248.7 (400.2 km) **F 109.3** (175.9 km) **Junction** with spur road to community of Healy (see description following **Milepost A 248.8**). Homes and businesses of this Alaska community are dispersed along the highway from here north to **Milepost A 249.6** and in the first mile east along the spur road toward the Nenana River. Hotel and motel accommodations are available at the highway junction, and several bed and breakfasts are located along the spur road.

Totem Inn. Full-service facility year-round. Deluxe, mid-range and economy rooms, restaurant, lounge and gift shop. Satellite TV and laundry facilities for guests. 24-hour access to pay telephones. Good food, reasonable rates, Alaskan hospitality. MasterCard/VISA/Discover. Restaurant (907) 683-2420. Motel/fax (907) 683-2384. [ADVERTISEMENT]

A 248.8 (400.4 km) **F 109.2** (175.7 km) North side of Healy Spur Road intersection.

Denali North Star Inn is a full-service year-round hotel located in Healy, 10 miles north of Denali National Park at Milepost

248.8 George Parks Highway (Route 3). Amenities offered to our guests include comfortable, reasonably priced rooms; finest food and cocktail lounge in the Denali Park area. Alaskan gifts, self-service laundry, hair salon, and recreation and exercise areas with tanning beds and saunas. Information and reservations for Denali Park tours and other activities; courtesy shuttle service. (8800) 684-1560. [ADVERTISEMENT]

Stampede Lodge and Bushmaster Grill. Historic Alaskan lodge and restaurant recently remodeled. Warm, comfortable atmosphere, located 10 minutes from the park entrance. Private baths and phones in all rooms. Free train station pickup. Restaurant open 6 A.M.–10 P.M. Denali's best value—all rooms $79–89. Phone (800) 478-2370, fax (907) 683-2243. [ADVERTISEMENT] MP

Healy

Located on a spur road just east of the Parks Highway **junction**. **Population:** 605. **Emergency Services: Alaska State Troopers**, phone (907) 683-2232. **Fire Department**, Tri–Valley Volunteer Fire Dept., phone 911 or (907) 683-2223. **Clinic**, Healy Clinic, located on 2nd floor of Tri–Valley Community Center at Mile 0.5 Healy Spur Road, phone (907) 683-2211 or 911 (open

24 hours).

Visitor Information: Available at the Healy Senior Center, located on Healy Spur Road behind the grocery store. Open 11 A.M. to 7 P.M., year-round; phone (907) 683-1317.

Elevation: 1,294 feet/394m. **Radio:** KUAC-FM 101.7. **Private Aircraft:** Healy River airstrip adjacent north; length 2,800 feet/853m; paved; unattended.

Healy's power plant has the distinction of being the largest coal-fired steam plant in Alaska, as well as the only mine-mouth power plant. This plant is part of the Golden Valley Electric Assoc., which furnishes electric power for Fairbanks and vicinity. The Fairbanks–Tanana Valley area uses primarily coal and also oil to meet its electrical needs.

Across the Nenana River lie the mining settlements of Suntrana and Usibelli. Dry Creek, Healy and Nenana river valleys comprise the area referred to as Tri–Valley. Coal mining began here in 1918 and has grown to become Alaska's largest coal mining operation. Usibelli Coal Mine, the state's only commercial coal mine, mines about 800,000 tons of coal a year, supplying South Korea, the University of Alaska, the military and other Fairbanks-area utilities. The Usibelli Coal Mine began a successful reclamation program in 1971; Dall sheep now graze where there was once evidence only of strip mining.

From the highway, you may see a 33-cubic-yard walking dragline (named Ace in the Hole by local schoolchildren in a contest) removing the soil, or overburden, to expose the coal seams. This 4,275,000-lb. machine, erected in 1978, moves an average of 24,000 cubic yards each 24 hours. Private vehicles are not allowed into the mining area and no tours are available.

Denali Suites. Located 15 minutes north of entrance to Denali National Park on Healy Spur Road. Units include 2 or 3 bedrooms, kitchen and dining area, living room with queen-sized hide-a-bed, TV and VCR, and private baths. Coin-operated laundry facilities. Clean, comfortable, affordable. Each unit accommodates up to 6 people, one accommodates 8, with 2 private baths; families welcome. VISA, MasterCard, Discover. Open all year. Call (907) 683-2848 or write Box 393, Healy, AK 99743. E-mail: bharris@mail.denali.k12.ak.us. Internet: www.alaskaone.com/densuites. See display ad in the DENALI NATIONAL PARK section. [ADVERTISEMENT]

Dry Creek Bed & Breakfast is also home to D & J Kennels. Open year-round. Dogsled rides and demonstrations also available by appointment. Complete breakfast, clean rooms, reasonable rates with Alaskan hospitality. VISA and MasterCard accepted. For reservations phone (907) 683-2386 (also fax) or write Dry Creek B&B, Box 371, Healy, AK 99743. [ADVERTISEMENT]

GrandView Bed & Breakfast. Located 12 miles from the entrance to Denali National Park. Relax and enjoy the spectacular view of the Alaska Range. Deluxe suites, kitchens, peaceful wilderness setting. Affordable. VISA/MasterCard. (907) 683-2468. P.O. Box 109, Healy, AK 99743. Internet: www.mtaonline.net/~grndview. E-mail: grndview@mtaonline.net. See our ad in the DENALI NATIONAL PARK section. [ADVERTISEMENT]

Greyfox Manor, located at Mile 0.75 Healy Spur Road, is a comfortable, spacious, smoke-free home with a family atmosphere, conveniently situated near Denali National Park. Offering a peaceful respite for weary travelers. Full breakfast served daily. Early continental breakfasts available. Open year-round. Credit cards accepted. Phone (907) 683-2419 for reservations. [ADVERTISEMENT]

Parks Highway Log
(continued)

A 248.8 (400.4 km) **F 109.2** (175.7 km) Healy spur road junction, north side of intersection; food and lodging.

A 249 (400.7 km) **F 109** (175.4 km) Suntrana Road, post office and Tri–Valley School.

A 249.2 (401 km) **F 108.8** (175.1 km) **Larry's Healy Tesoro.** See display ad this section.

A 249.3 (401.2 km) **F 108.7** (174.9 km) Dry Creek Bridge No. 1.

A 249.4 (401.4 km) **F 108.6** (174.8 km) Lester Road. Dry Creek Bed and Breakfast and D&J Kennels.

A 249.5 (401.5 km) **F 108.5** (174.6 km) **Motel Nord Haven.** Built in 1994 with your motoring family in mind. West side of highway in the trees. Peaceful and secluded. 12 miles north of Denali National Park entrance. All rooms have queen beds, private bath, television and telephone. Open year-round. MasterCard, VISA, American Express. Phone (907) 683-4500. Fax (907) 683-4503. E-mail: nordhavn@ptialaska.net. Internet: www.ptialaska.net/~nordhavn/. [ADVERTISEMENT]

A 249.8 (402 km) **F 108.2** (174.1 km) Dry Creek Bridge No. 2. Good berry picking area first part of August.

Speed limit 65 mph northbound. Speed zone begins 45 mph/72 kmph southbound.

A 251.1 (404.1 km) **F 106.9** (172 km) Stampede Road to west. Lignite Road to east.

Earth Song Lodge, Denali's natural retreat. Enjoy the Denali Park area without the crowds. Ten charming log cabins with private baths. Evening programs by staff naturalist at comfortable central lodge. Dog sled demonstrations and rides. Continental breakfast available. Located on scenic and historic Stampede Road, just north of the park. Wonderful views of Denali and wildlife. Open year-round. Phone/fax (907) 683-2863. P.O. Box 89-MP, Healy, AK 99743. Internet: www.earthsonglodge.com. E-mail: earthsong@mail.denali.k12.ak.us. See display ad in the DENALI NATIONAL PARK section. [ADVERTISEMENT]

A 251.2 (404.3 km) **F 106.8** (171.9 km) Paved turnout to west. Coal seams visible in bluff to east.

A 252.4 (406.2 km) **F 105.6** (169.9 km) Gravel turnout to west.

A 252.5 (406.4 km) **F 105.5** (169.8 km) Bridge over **Panguingue Creek**; turnout at end. Moderate success fishing for grayling. This stream, which flows 8 miles/13 km to the Nenana River, was named for a Philippine card game.

A 258 (415.2 km) **F 100** (160.9 km) CAUTION: Watch for rough road northbound.

A 259.4 (417.5 km) **F 98.6** (158.7 km) Large paved turnout to east. Views of Rex Dome to the northeast. Walker and Jumbo domes to the east. Liberty Bell mining area lies between the peaks and highway.

A 261.1 (420.2 km) **F 96.9** (155.9 km)

Gravel turnout to east. Look for bank swallows, small brown birds that nest in clay and sand banks near streams and along highways. Pond with beaver dam to west.

A 262.8 (422.9 km) **F 95.2** (153.2 km) Large gravel turnout to east.

A 264.5 (425.7 km) **F 93.5** (150.5 km) Paved turnout to west.

A 269 (432.9 km) **F 89** (143.2 km) June Creek rest area and picnic spot to east; large gravel parking area. Gravel road leads down to lower parking area on June Creek (trailers and large RVs check turnaround space before driving down). Wooden stairs lead up to the picnic spot and a view of the Nenana River. There are picnic tables, fireplaces, toilets, a litter bin and a sheltered table. Cut wood may be available.

A 269.4 (433.5 km) **F 88.6** (142.6 km) Gravel turnout to east. Bridge over Bear Creek.

A 271.4 (436.8 km) **F 86.6** (139.4 km) Paved turnout to west. Highway northbound leads through boggy area with few turnouts.

A 275.6 (443.5 km) **F 82.4** (132.6 km)

Entering Game Management Unit 20A northbound, 20C southbound.

A 275.8 (443.9 km) **F 82.2** (132.3 km) Rex Bridge over Nenana River.

A 276 (444.2 km) **F 82** (132 km) **Tatlanika Trading Co.** Located in a beautiful pristine wilderness setting. Tent sites and RV parking with electricity, water, dump station, showers. 39 miles from Denali National Park on the Nenana River. Our gift shop features a gathering of handmade art/crafts/artifacts from various villages. See the rare Samson fox, along with relics and antiques from Alaska's colorful past in a museum atmosphere. Many historical and educational displays. Nothing sold from overseas. Visitor information. Coffee, pop, juice, snacks. Clean restrooms. This is a must stop. See display ad this section. [ADVERTISEMENT] ▲

A 276.5 (445 km) **F 81.5** (131.2 km) CAUTION: Railroad crossing.

A 280 (450.6 km) **F 78** (125.5 km) Lodge with dining and a cafe/grocery.

Clear Sky Lodge. See display ad this section.

A 280.1 (450.8 km) F 77.9 (125.4 km) **Rochester Lodge.** See display ad this section.

A 283.5 (456.2 km) F 74.5 (119.9 km) Access road west to 6 miles/9.6 km **ANDERSON** (pop. 1,906) and 1 mile/1.6 km for access to **CLEAR.** Clear is a military installation (ballistic missile early warning site), and a sign at turnoff states it is unlawful to enter without permission. However, you can drive into Anderson without permission. Located 6 miles/9.7 km northwest of Clear, Anderson has a city campground in a 616-acre park with 40 sites on the Nenana River. RV dump station, toilets, showers. The community also has churches, a restaurant, softball fields and shooting range. For more information call the city office at (907) 582-2500. Emergency aid is available through the Clear Air Force Site Fire Department; phone (907) 585-6321. ▲

Anderson Riverside Park. Come enjoy our city's 616 beautiful acres located along the bank of the Nenana River! Featuring restrooms, showers, RV dump station, electrical hook-ups. Riverside campsites, rustic campsites with barbecue pits, picnic area with covered pavilion, fireplace. Shooting range, bandstand, telephone. Home of the annual Anderson Bluegrass Festival, held the last weekend in July. City of Anderson, P.O. Box 3100, Anderson, AK 99744. Phone

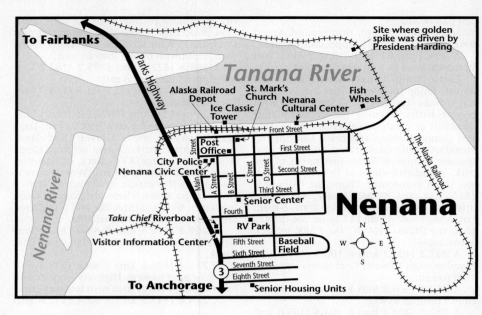

Map of Nenana showing: To Fairbanks, Parks Highway, Tanana River, Site where golden spike was driven by President Harding, Alaska Railroad Depot, St. Mark's Church, Nenana Cultural Center, Fish Wheels, Ice Classic Tower, Front Street, Post Office, First Street, City Police, Second Street, Nenana Civic Center, Third Street, Senior Center, Nenana, Taku Chief Riverboat, Fourth, RV Park, Visitor Information Center, Fifth Street, Baseball Field, Sixth Street, Seventh Street, Eighth Street, To Anchorage, Senior Housing Units, Nenana River, The Alaska Railroad

(907) 582-2500; fax (907) 582-2496.
[ADVERTISEMENT] ▲

Private Aircraft: Clear airstrip, 3 nm SE; elev. 552 feet/168m; length 4,000 feet/1,219m; asphalt; unattended. Clear Sky Lodge airstrip, 4 nm S; elev. 650 feet/198m; length 2,500 feet/762m; gravel, earth.

A 285.7 (459.8 km) F 72.3 (116.3 km) Julius Creek bridge.

A 286.3 (460.7 km) F 71.7 (115.4 km) View of Mount McKinley southbound.

A 286.8 (461.5 km) F 71.2 (114.6 km) Large double-ended paved parking area to east.

A 288.2 (463.8 km) F 69.8 (112.3 km) Denali Borough boundary.

A 288.7 (464.6 km) F 69.3 (111.5 km) Roadhouse.

A 292 (469.9 km) F 76 (122.3 km) Watch for pavement breaks and loose gravel northbound to Nenana.

A 296.7 (477.5 km) F 61.3 (98.7 km) Bridge over **Fish Creek.** Small gravel turnout with litter barrels by creek. Access to creek at south end of bridge; moderate success fishing for grayling. ➤

A 298 (479.6 km) F 60 (96.5 km) Tamarack Inn.

A 301.4 (485 km) F 56.6 (91.1 km)

Nenana city limits.

A 302.9 (487.4 km) F 55.1 (88.7 km) Nenana municipal rifle range.

A 303 (487.6 km) F 55 (88.5 km) Begin 45 mph/72 kmph speed zone northbound.

A 303.7 (488.7 km) F 54.3 (87.4 km) Nenana airport (see Private Aircraft information in Nenana).

A 304.5 (490 km) F 53.5 (86.1 km) Chevron gas station, diesel, food mart to west.

A Frame Service. See display ad this section.

Nenana

A 304.5 (490 km) F 53.5 (86.1 km) Located at the confluence of the Tanana and Nenana rivers. **Population:** 422. **Emergency Services:** Emergency only (fire, police, ambulance), phone 911. **Alaska State Troopers,** phone (907) 832-5554, at Milepost A 310 Parks Highway. **City Police,** phone (907) 832-5448. **Fire Department/EMT,** phone (907) 832-5632.

Visitor Information: In a picturesque log cabin with sod roof at junction of the highway and A Street, phone (907) 832-9953. Open 8 A.M. to 6 P.M., 7 days a week, Memorial Day to Labor Day. Pay phone and ice for sale. Ice Classic tickets may be purchased here.

Marge Anderson Senior Citizen Center, located on 3rd Street between Market and B streets, also welcomes visitors.

Elevation: 400 feet/122m. **Radio:** KIAM

www.themilepost.com

630, KUAC-FM 91.1. **Transportation: Air—** Nenana maintains an FAA-approved airport. **Railroad—**The Alaska Railroad.

Private Aircraft: Nenana Municipal Airport, 0.9 mile/1.4 km south; elev. 362 feet/110m; length 5,000 feet/1,524m; asphalt; fuel 100, Jet B. Floatplane and skiplane strip.

The town was first known as Tortella, a white man's interpretation of the Athabascan word *Toghottele*. A 1902 map indicates a village spelled Tortilli on the north bank of the Tanana River, on the side of the hill still known as Tortella. In the same year Jim Duke built a roadhouse and trading post, supplying river travelers with goods and lodging. The settlement became known as Nenana, an Athabascan word meaning, "a good place to camp between the rivers." The town thrived as a trading center for Natives of the region and travelers on the vast network of interior rivers.

Nenana boomed during the early 1920s as a construction base for the Alaska Railroad. On July 15, 1923, Pres. Warren G. Harding drove the golden spike at Nenana signifying the completion of the railroad. The depot, located at the end of Main Street, is on the National Register of Historic Places. Built in 1923 and renovated in 1988, the depot houses the state's Alaska Railroad Museum, open 9 A.M. to 6 P.M. daily.

The location "where rail and river meet" led to—in addition to occasional seasonal flooding—the town's vital role in the tugboat/barge shipping industry that traverses the rivers of the interior, providing goods to numerous villages. Tons of fuel, freight and supplies move from the docks at Nenana from late May through September each year. Because the rivers are shallow and silt-laden, the barges move about 12 mph downstream and 5 mph upstream. The dock area is to the right of the highway northbound. Behind the Nenana visitor information center is the dry-docked *Taku Chief*, a proud little tugboat that, with its loaded barges, plied the waters of the Tanana, Yukon and Koyukuk rivers for many years.

One block from the depot is **St. Mark's Mission Church.** In 1905 the Episcopal Church founded a boarding home and school upriver from the town. Many Native children from interior villages lived and were educated at the mission. Erosion of the riverbank threatened and in some cases destroyed mission buildings, and the church was relocated. The school and boarding home closed in the 1950s. The church, still serving a small but active congregation, is all that remains today of the once extensive mission property. The little log building, sometimes open to the public, is graced with hand-hewn pews and a raised altar decorated with Native beaded moosehide frontal and dossal hangings.

Nenana is perhaps best known for the **Nenana Ice Classic,** an annual event that awards cash prizes to the lucky winners who guess the exact minute of the ice breakup on the Tanana River. Ice Classic festivities begin the last weekend in February with the Tripod Raising Festival and culminate at breakup time (late April or May) when the surging ice on the Tanana River dislodges the tripod. A line attached to the tripod stops a clock, recording the official breakup time. The contest has been a spring highlight throughout the state since 1917.

The famous serum race in 1925, when the city of Nome was threatened with a

Freight leaves Nenana by barge on the Tanana River. *(© Laurent Dick)*

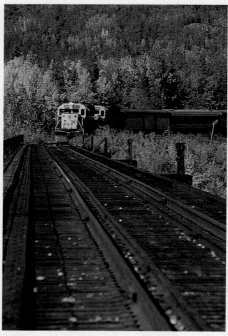

The Alaska Railroad parallels the Parks Highway. (© Beth Davidow)

diphtheria epidemic, started in Nenana when the serum was delivered by the Alaska Railroad to the first of the mushers who relayed the package by dog teams 600 miles to the stricken city on Norton Sound in western Alaska. (The sled dog "Balto"—featured in a popular animated film—led the final relay into Nome.) The achievement was re-enacted in a 1995-1996 Nenana-to-Nome relay. The annual Iditarod Trail Sled Dog Race between Anchorage and Nome also commemorates the event. Nenana celebrates River Daze the first weekend in June, welcoming summer's activities. The main event is "The Annihilator," the toughest 10-km footrace in Alaska, over Tortella Hill.

Nenana has an auto repair shop, radio station, several churches, a library, restaurants, a cultural center (new in 1998), a laundromat, a seniors' social center and senior housing units, gift shops, and Coghill's, a grocery/general store that has served the community for 83 years. Accommodations are available at motel, inn and bed and breakfast. RV park with hookups. Picnic tables and restrooms are beside the restored *Taku Chief* near the visitor information center. ▲

Alfred Starr Nenana Cultural Center and **Captain Alphonse Demientieff Wheelhouse Gift Shop.** New facility! Learn of the Natives who made their camp here and of their struggle to regain control of their land. See how the Ice Classic got its start and how the railroad was built. Alaskan and Native handcrafted items can be purchased in our gift shop. Book a river or dog mushing tour at our tour desk. Located on the bank of the Tanana River next to the new Nenana Salmon Bake that is scheduled to open in summer 1999. [ADVERTISEMENT]

Bed & Maybe Breakfast. Step back in time and charm yourself in the atmosphere of the old railroad depot built for President Harding's historic visit in 1923. Oak or brass beds, hardwood floors and braided rugs enhance the decor of these rooms. Overlook the hustling loading dock area of the barge lines on the Tanana River. View the Native cemetery and the historic railroad bridge from your window. Credit cards accepted. Reservations: (907) 832-5272 or 832-5556. [ADVERTISEMENT]

Tripod Gift Shop and Mini Mall. "Take time to smell the flowers." Over 19,000 flowers are planted each year to enhance the beauty of one of the loveliest gift shops in Alaska. A fun stop! Enjoy old-time concertina music played by Joanne Hawkins. Take the boardwalk to our Art Lovers' Gallery; Trapper's Cabin stocked with a wide selection of local furs; king- and queen-sized shop; Bargain Corner with special prices on T-shirts, souvenirs and mugs. Enjoy ice cream or snacks at our Sweets and Treats Shoppe and purchase our fine canned smoked salmon. Also available: ice, world-wide postcard stamps, assorted camera batteries and wildflower seeds. Complimentary gold panning with $5 purchase in any of these shops. The shops are a must, a high

light of any vacation. Interesting displays include record-size moose antlers, Kodiak grizzly bear trap (largest ever manufactured), antique ice saw, working fish wheel, trapper's steam boiler, dog salmon drying rack and authentic 1977 Ice Classic tripod. Be sure to have your picture taken with Sourdough Pete and rub his head for luck. Tour operators may call ahead to reserve a guided tour of Nenana, compliments of Tripod Gift Shop. Joanne Hawkins has hosted tour groups for over 20 years at no charge. Allow 30–45 minutes if the tour is to be included with your rest stop. A little history, a little fact, a little music and a lot of fun are packed into this tour. Have a picture taken of your coach, escort and driver for our display board. Over 15 years of tour operator photos are on display. This tour is a must! Remember, reservations are necessary. Tour operators thinking about lunch can call ahead for reservations at Two Choice Cafe (907) 832-5272. Ask about our soup and sandwich special for groups of 25 or more. Complimentary RV parking for self-contained vehicles. [ADVERTISEMENT]

Parks Highway Log
(continued)

A 305.1 (491 km) F 52.9 (85.1 km) **Tanana River** bridge. Large paved turnout to west at north end of bridge. The Tanana is formed by the joining of the Chisana and the Nabesna rivers near Northway and flows 440 miles/708 km westward to the Yukon River. From the bridge, watch for freight-laden river barges bound for the Yukon

River. North of this bridge, fish wheels may sometimes be seen in action and occasionally fish may be purchased from the owners of the wheels.

Entering Game Management Unit 20B northbound, 20A southbound.

A 305.5 (491.6 km) **F 52.5** (84.5 km) Turnout to east and to west by Tanana River.

A 305.6 (491.8 km) **F 52.4** (84.3 km) Paved turnout to west overlooking Tanana River.

A 305.9 (492.3 km) **F 52.1** (83.8 km) Double-ended gravel turnout to east. Paved turnout to west.

A 306.2 (492.8 km) **F 51.8** (83.4 km) RV parking. ▲

A 308.7 (496.8 km) **F 49.3** (79.3 km) *CAUTION: Railroad crossing.*

A 308.9 (497.1 km) **F 49.1** (79 km) Restaurant.

A 314.6 (506.3 km) **F 43.4** (69.8 km) Paved double-ended turnout to west.

A 314.8 (506.6 km) **F 43.2** (69.5 km) Bridge over Little Goldstream Creek.

A 315.4 (507.6 km) **F 42.6** (68.6 km) Truck lanes next 4 miles/6.4 km northbound to **Milepost A 319.5**.

A 318.8 (513 km) **F 39.2** (63.1 km) Paved double-ended turnout to west with scenic view. The view is mostly of bogs, small lakes and creeks, with names like Hard Luck Creek, Fortune Creek, All Hand Help Lake and Wooden Canoe Lake.

Southbound travelers will see the Tanana River on both sides of the highway. It follows a horseshoe-shaped course, the top of the closed end being the bridge at Nenana.

A 321 (516.6 km) **F 37** (59.5 km) *NOTE: Several long winding grades and intermittent truck lanes northbound to Fairbanks.*

A 324.5 (522.2 km) **F 33.5** (53.9 km) Double-ended turnout to east on old alignment.

A 325 (523 km) **F 33** (53.1 km) This stretch of highway is often called Skyline Drive; views to west. Downgrade northbound; truck lane southbound.

A 325.7 (524.1 km) **F 32.3** (52 km) Entering Fairbanks North Star Borough northbound.

A 328 (527.8 km) **F 30** (48.3 km) **Skinny Dick's Halfway Inn.** See display ad this section.

A 328.3 (528.3 km) **F 29.7** (47.8 km) Truck lane next 3 miles/4.8 km southbound.

A 331.6 (533.6 km) **F 26.4** (42.5 km) Double-ended turnout to east on old alignment.

A 338.2 (544.3 km) **F 19.8** (31.9 km) Wide views to east. Look for Murphy Dome (elev. 2,930 feet/893m) with white communication installations on summit to west.

A 339.3 (546 km) **F 19.7** (30.1 km)

Viewpoint and sign to east. This is the south end of a 1-mile/1.6-km scenic loop road that rejoins the highway at **Milepost A 339.9**. Highway begins downgrade northbound.

A 339.9 (547 km) **F 18.1** (29.1 km) Turnoff (unmarked) for Bonanza Experimental Forest via 1-mile/1.6-km loop road east; scenic viewpoint.

A 340.9 (548.6 km) **F 17.1** (27.5 km) Long double-ended gravel turnout to west.

A 342.2 (550.7 km) **F 15.8** (25.4 km) Rosie Creek Road to east.

A 342.4 (551 km) **F 15.6** (25.1 km) Old Nenana Highway to west.

A 344.2 (553.9 km) **F 13.8** (22.2 km) Monument in honor of George Alexander Parks (1883-1984) the territorial governor of Alaska from 1925 to 1933, for whom the Parks Highway is named. Also here is a Blue Star Memorial highway plaque honoring the armed forces. Viewpoint to east. The Tanana River can be seen below the Parks monument.

A 349 (561.6 km) **F 9** (14.5 km) Cripple Creek Road to south, Park Ridge Road to north. Truck lane next 4.2 miles/6.8 km southbound.

NOTE: Watch for rough road and dips northbound.

A 350 (563.3 km) **F 8** (12.9 km) Alder Creek.

A 350.1 (563.4 km) **F 7.9** (12.7 km) Welcome to Fairbanks North Star Borough sign.

A 351.2 (565.2 km) **F 6.8** (10.9 km) Old gold dredges visible to the east.

A 351.7 (566 km) **F 6.3** (10.1 km) Turnoff to west for Ester (description follows); weigh station. Fire station to east.

Ester

Located 0.6 mile/1 km west of highway. **Population:** 211. **Emergency Services:** Emergency only, phone 911. **Fire Department,** phone (907) 479-6858. A former gold mining camp and current visitor attraction, Ester has a hotel, RV camping, 2 saloons, 3 gift shops and a post office. A village sign on Main Street locates these services.

ESTER ADVERTISERS

Ester Gold Camp...............Ph. (907) 479-2500
Ester Hatworks.................Ph. (907) 479-5525
Judie Gumm Design..........Ph. (907) 479-4568

Tundra Swan Pin with Moonstone

Noted for her silver sculptural interpretations of northern images, **Judie Gumm's** work has been featured in many national publications. Priced moderately; easy to pack, her jewelry makes a perfect remembrance of your adventure North. Visit her showroom at the Ester turnoff mile 351.7. Follow the signs once in Ester. Weekdays 10-6 and Sat. 12-5. **Catalog available.**

Judie Gumm Designs, POB 169, Ester, AK 99725. (800) 478-4568
e-mail rjgumm@compuserve.com

Judie's work can be found in many fine gift stores and galleries at these Alaskan locations:

Anchorage
Anchorage Museum Gift Shop
Artique
Yankee Whaler
Jewels of the North
Once in a Blue Moose
Remember Alaska (3 locations)

Eagle River
Picture This

Chitina
Spirit Mountain

Denali Park
Denali Wilderness Center
Kantishna Roadhouse

Dutch Harbor
Grand Aleutian Hotel

Fairbanks
AK Riverways, Discovery Trading Post
Alaska House of Fine Art
Arctic Travelers
The Artworks
Cache Creek Mercantile
FMH Gift Shop
Fairbanks Princess Hotel
Matrix
Twigs
UAF Museum

Girdwood
Kobuk Valley Jade

Haines
Windspirit

Homer
Art Shop Gallery
Landing Gear

Juneau
Ad Lib
Glacier Gardens, Rainforest Adventures
Rie Munoz
Plumb Gold
Northern Nook
Annie Kaill

Ketchikan
Scanlons

Kodiak
Norman's Nickel & Dime

Petersburg
Berthiel's
Diamante

Seward
Bardarson's
Once in a Blue Moose

Sitka
Fairweather Prints

Soldotna
North Country Fair

Talkeetna
Talkeetna Gift

Valdez
Alaskan Fine gifts
Sandra's Gold & Silversmith
Stan Stephens Charters

Wasilla
Town Square Art Gallery

Skinny Dick's HALFWAY INN
SNACKS GIFTS

Phone (907) 452-0304
Rooms, Camping
Free Parking and Coffee
No Hookups *"But"* No Charge

Dick and Mable, Hosts

20 Miles from Fairbanks
Mile 328 Parks Highway
P.O. Box 88, Nenana, Alaska 99760

Parks Highway near Fairbanks offers spectacular views to the west. (© Laurent Dick)

Ester was a raucous mining camp in 1906, with a population of some 5,000 miners. Today a quiet bedroom community of Fairbanks, Ester's heydays are relived in music, song and dance at the Malemute Saloon. Active gold mining is still under way in the area. One of the best preserved gold dredges from the gold rush days can be seen from **Milepost A 351.2.**

Ester Gold Camp. At the turn of cen-

tury, discovery of gold in the Ester region drew hundreds of prospectors to seek their fortunes. In 1936, the Fairbanks Exploration Company built Ester Camp to support a large-scale gold dredge operation. After 20 years of operation, the camp was closed. It opened again in 1958, but this time as a summer visitor attraction. Today, Ester Gold Camp, on the National Register of Historic Places, provides services for another kind of

prospector: those seeking accommodations, excellent food and a fun-filled night of entertainment. Open late May through early September. See display ad in FAIR-BANKS section. [ADVERTISEMENT] ▲

Ester Hatworks. Inspired by 3 decades of living in Alaska's Interior, Judy Stauffer handcrafts headgear suitable for every weather extreme. Classic, fun, practical designs are available at her shop nestled beneath the birches, next to Ester Gold Camp Hotel. Open daily, May 28–Sept. 4, 5–9 P.M.; year-round by appointment. Phone/fax (907) 479-5525. Brochure available; P.O. Box 146, Ester, AK 999725. [ADVERTISEMENT]

Parks Highway Log
(continued)

A 351.8 (566.2 km) F 6.2 (10 km) Weigh stations.

A 352.5 (567.3 km) F 5.5 (8.8 km) Gold Hill Road. Gas stations, truck stop; diesel, groceries, liquor. Access to Inua Wool Shoppe.

Gold Hill. See display ad this section.

PHTS (Parks Highway Truck Stop). See display ad this section.

Inua Wool Shoppe. Turn on Gold Hill Road, go 0.3 mile left to Henderson, 1 mile to 202 Henderson Road. Inua Wool Shoppe is Interior Alaska's most complete knitting shoppe. Fabulous selection of qiviuq and other fine wool yarns. Large selection of Alaskan, Norwegian and American patterns, needlepoints, buttons, books and needles. Come enjoy a unique knitting shoppe. Open 10–5 Monday–Saturday. (907) 479-5830 (Alaska 1-800-478-9848). VISA and Master-Card welcome. [ADVERTISEMENT]

A 353.5 (568.9 km) F 4.5 (7.2 km) Gas station and store. Public dumpster.

A 355.8 (572.6 km) F 2.2 (3.5 km) Sheep Creek Road and Tanana Drive. Road to Murphy Dome (a restricted military site).

A 356.8 (574.2 km) F 1.2 (1.9 km) Turnoff to University of Alaska, Geist Road, Chena Ridge Loop and Chena Pump Road to Chena Pump House Historical Site (restaurant).

A 357.6 (575.5 km) F 0.4 (0.6 km) Bridge over Chena River.

A 357.7 (575.6 km) F 0.3 (0.5 km) West Airport Way exit to Fairbanks International Airport and access to *Discovery* sternwheeler.

A 358 (576.1 km) F 0 East Airport Way exit to River's Edge RV Park and University Avenue to Chena River State Recreation Site; access to Johansen Expressway. (See FAIR-BANKS section following for description of city and Fairbanks Vicinity map.)

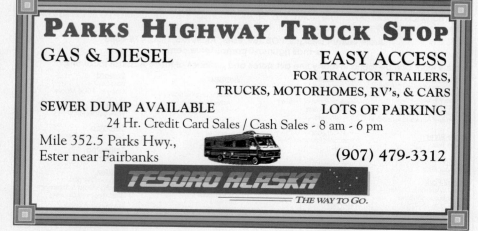

FAIRBANKS

(See maps, page 434)

Fairbanks lies in the Tanana River valley on the banks of the Chena River. The Alaska Range is to the south. *(© Laurent Dick)*

Located in the heart of Alaska's Great Interior country. By highway, it is approximately 1,488 miles/2,395 km north of Dawson Creek, BC, the start of the Alaska Highway (traditional milepost distance is 1,523 miles); 98 miles/158 km from Delta Junction (official end of the Alaska Highway); 358 miles/576 km from Anchorage via the Parks Highway; and 2,305 miles/3,709 km from Seattle.

Population: Fairbanks–North Star Borough, 84,380. **Emergency Services: Alaska State Troopers,** 1979 Peger Road, phone (907) 451-5333; for nonemergencies, (907) 451-5100; and using TTY service, (907) 451-5344. **Fairbanks Police,** 656 7th Ave., phone 911 or, for nonemergencies, phone (907) 459-6500. **Fire Department** and **Ambulance Service,** phone 911. **Hospitals,** Fairbanks Memorial, 1650 Cowles St., phone (907) 452-8181; Bassett Army Hospital, Fort Wainwright, phone (907) 353-5143; Eielson Clinic, Eielson AFB, phone (907) 377-2259. **Women's Crisis Line,** phone (907) 452-2293. **Emergency Management,** phone (907) 459-1481 or (907) 474-7721 (24-hour line). **Borough Information,** phone (907) 459-1000.

Visitor Information: Fairbanks Visitor Information Center at 550 1st Ave. (at Cushman Street, where a riverside marker reads "Mile 1523, Official End of the Alaska Highway"); phone (907) 456-5774 or 1-800-327-5774. In summer, open 8 A.M. to 8 P.M. daily; in winter, open 8 A.M. to 5 P.M. weekdays, closed weekends. Phone (907) 456-INFO for daily recorded information.

Visitor information is also available at Fairbanks International Airport in the baggage claim area and at the Alaska Railroad depot.

For information on Alaska's state parks, national parks, national forests, wildlife refuges and other outdoor recreational sites, visit the Alaska Public Lands Information Center downstairs in historic Courthouse Square at 250 N. Cushman St. The center is a free museum featuring films on Alaska, interpretive programs, lectures, exhibits, artifacts, photographs and short video programs on each region in the state. The exhibit area and information desk are open 7 days a week in summer; Tuesday through Saturday in winter. Phone (907) 456-0527. For recorded information on Denali National Park, phone (907) 456-0510. TDD information line is (907) 456-0532.

Elevation: 436 feet/133m at Fairbanks International Airport. **Climate:** January temperatures range from -2°F/-19°C to -19°F/-28°C. The lowest temperature ever recorded was -66°F/-54°C on January 14, 1934. July temperatures average 62°F/17°C, with a record high of 99°F/37°C in July 1919. In June and early July daylight lasts 21 hours—and the nights are really only twilight.

Annual precipitation is 10.9 inches, with an annual average snowfall of 65 inches. The record for snowfall is 147.3 inches, set the winter of 1990–91. **Radio:** KSUA-FM, KFAR, KCBF, KAKQ, KWLF-FM, KIAK, KIAK-FM, KJNP-AM and FM (North Pole), KUAC-FM 104.7. **Television:** Channels 2, 4, 7, 9, 11, 13 and cable. **Newspapers:** *Fairbanks Daily News–Miner.*

Private Aircraft: Facilities for all types of aircraft. Consult the *Alaska Supplement* for information on the following airports: Eielson AFB, Fairbanks International, Fairbanks International Seaplane, Chena Marina Air Field and Fort Wainwright. For more information phone the Fairbanks Flight Service Station at (907) 474-0137.

HISTORY

In 1901, Captain E.T. Barnette set out from St. Michael on the stern-wheeler *Lavelle Young*, traveling up the Yukon River with supplies for his trading post, which he proposed to set up at Tanana Crossing (Tanacross), the halfway point on the Valdez–Eagle trail. But the stern-wheeler could not navigate the fast-moving, shallow Tanana River beyond the mouth of the Chena River. The stern-wheeler's captain finally dropped off the protesting Barnette on the Chena near the present site of 1st Avenue and Cushman Street. A year later, Felix Pedro, an Italian prospector, discovered gold about 16 miles/26 km north of Barnette's temporary trading post. The opportunistic Barnette quickly abandoned his original plan to continue on to Tanana Crossing.

In September 1902, Barnette convinced the 25 or so miners in the area to use the name "Fairbanks" for the town that he expected would grow up around his trading post. The name had been suggested that summer by Alaska Judge James Wickersham, who admired Charles W. Fairbanks, the senior senator from Indiana. The senator later became vice president of the United States under Theodore Roosevelt.

The town grew, largely due to Barnette's promotion of gold prospects and discoveries in the area, and in 1903 Judge Wickersham moved the headquarters of his Third Judicial District Court (a district which encompassed 300,000 square miles) from Eagle to Fairbanks.

Thanks to Wickersham, the town gained government offices and a jail. Thanks to Barnette, it gained a post office and a branch of the Northern Commercial Company, a large Alaska trading firm based in San Francisco. In addition, after Barnette became the first mayor of Fairbanks in 1903, the town acquired telephone service, set up fire protection, passed sanitation ordinances and contracted for electric light and steam heat. In 1904, Barnette started a bank.

The town of "Fairbanks" first appeared in *(Continues on page 436)*

RIVERBOAT DISCOVERY • A most memorable adventure

The Riverboat Discovery is the one adventure you won't want to miss when you travel to Fairbanks. Owned and operated by the Binkley family, whose river boating experience in Alaska spans four generations and more than 100 years, the Riverboat Discovery tour has been rated the top boating attraction in North America in Travel Weekly Magazine. Captain Jim Binkley and his crew of children, grandchildren and native Alaskans takes you back to the heyday of sternwheelers, to an era when prospectors, fur traders and Native people of the Interior relied on rivers as their only link to the outside world.

Passengers relax in the comfort of glass enclosed or open decks as the Discovery III winds its way down the Chena and Tanana Rivers. Drawing on their knowledge of Alaskan history, the Binkley family entertains listeners with witty descriptions of Alaskan life during the four hour narrated cruise. The Discovery makes a brief stop at the river front home of veteran Iditarod Dog Musher Susan Butcher, where visitors hear tales of Susan's Iditarod adventures and are introduced to her champion sled dogs.

One of the highlights of the trip is a stop ashore at the Old Chena Indian Village. Here passengers disembark for a guided tour. Alaskan Natives share their culture as they recount how their ancestors hunted, fished, sewed clothing and built shelters to survive for centuries in the harsh Alaskan wilderness. At the village a dog mushing distance racing team gives passengers a "close-up" view of an actual mushing kennel.

The Discovery departs Steamboat Landing, off Dale Road, daily at 8:45 AM and 2:00 PM

mid-May through mid-September. Reservations are required. For further information call 907-479-6673.

Before or after your cruise step into the past at Steamboat Landing, one of the finest gift stores in Alaska. Stroll along the picturesque boardwalk beside the Chena River and enter any of four turn-of-the-century shops. Discovery Trading Post offers unique Alaskan gifts at great low prices. The Susan Butcher Dog Mushing gallery features mementos of the Iditarod champion's lifestyle and an exclusive line of sportswear. Susan's winning Iditarod dogsled and Iditarod trophies are conveniently located so you can take photos you'll always treasure. The Binkley and Barrington Gift Shop offers Alaskan made

products, and the Pioneer Hotel is replica of Fairbanks' first luxury hotel featuring authentic Native handicrafts. Be sure not to miss this cultural treat between Discovery III departures - you'll find an impressive selection of gifts at some of the best prices in Alaska. Open 7 days a week.

The two hour tour to a working gold mine begins when passengers board the Tanana Valley Railroad for a narrated trip through the original gold fields of the Interior that were once part of Alaska's richest mining district on record.

Passengers ride the narrow gauge rails through a permafrost tunnel where miners with head lamps and pick-axes seek out the rich gold veins, reminiscent of mining days gone by. Winding through the valley, the train comes to a halt as a prospector crouches down to dip his gold pan into cold, clear waters of Fox Creek in search of the sparkle of gold.

At El Dorado Camp, local miners "Yukon Yonda" and her husband Dexter Clark are on hand to conduct a guided tour through a working gold mine. Visitors gather around to watch the operation of a modern day sluice box and enjoy stories about life in Alaskan mining camps.

A crash course in gold panning is followed by the real thing. Visitors grab a poke filled with pay dirt right from the sluice box and try their hand at panning for gold. And when they strike it rich, they keep the gold!

The next stop is the assay office where visitors, while enjoying complimentary homemade cookies and coffee, weigh their gold and assay its market value. The "all aboard" call gathers everyone onto the train for the short ride back to the station.

Daily tours for the El Dorado Gold Mine depart from the old train station at 1.3 mile Elliott Highway, just past Fox, Alaska, nine miles north of Fairbanks. For reservations call 907-479-7613.

EL DORADO GOLD MINE • Gold Mining History

PAN for GOLD
You're guaranteed to find it!

Pan for gold at the El Dorado Gold Mine. Join the Binkley family for another Alaskan experience that can't be missed! El Dorado Gold Mine is an exciting hands-on adventure for the whole family. Visitors learn about the history of mining in Alaska, experience a modern day mining operation and pan for gold, while enjoying El Dorado Gold Mine's famous Alaskan hospitality.

Fairbanks

To the University
of Alaska

Farmers Loop Rd.

College Rd.

Tanana Valley
Fairgrounds

Creamers Field Wildlife Refuge

Department of
Fish and Game

Esquire Ave.

Noyes Slough

College Rd.

Danby St.

Aurora Dr.

Aspen St.

Bentley
Mall

Deadman
Slough

Johansen Expressway

Old Steese Highway

Minnie St.

Illinois St.

Graehl Street
Boat Landing

Geist
Rd.

Johansen Expressway

Hanson Rd.

The Alaska Railroad

Gavora
Mall

Chena River

Phillips Field Rd.

Chena River

1 Ave.

Alaska
Railroad
Depot

Visitor
Information
Center

Griffin
Park

Wendell

Steese Expressway

2 Ave.

Front
St.

Slater Dr. W.

University Ave.

2 Ave.

Lathrop St.

5 Ave.

6 Ave.

3 Ave.
4 Ave.

Post
Office

Police
& Fire
Depts.

Rampart—
Mini Mall

Dunkle

Clay

Noble
Lacey

Cushman St.

10 Ave.

9 Ave.

7 Ave.

8 Ave.

9 Ave.

11 Ave.

12 Ave.

Peger Rd.

Alaskaland
■ Tourist
Information

Crosson Ave.

Airport Way

Cowles St.

Mary Siah
Recreation
Center

10 Ave.

Federal
Building

University Center Mall

Rewak Dr.

Kiana St.

17 Ave.

18 Ave.

19 Ave.

■ Alaska State
Troopers

Hamme
Pool

Cowles St.

Wickersham St.

14 Ave.

15 Ave.

16 Ave.

Gaffney Rd.

Eielson St.

Entrance
to Fort
Wainwright

16 Ave.

18 Ave.

Alaska-
Richardson
Highway

University Ave. S.

Hez Ray Recreation
Complex and Parks &
Recreation Offices

Hospital

Gillam

Way

Gillam
Park

19 Ave.

21 Ave.

22 Ave.

18 Ave.

21 Ave.

Cushman St.
Ladd

2

Davis Road

Davis Road

23 Ave.

To Metro Field

To Delta
Junction

N W E S

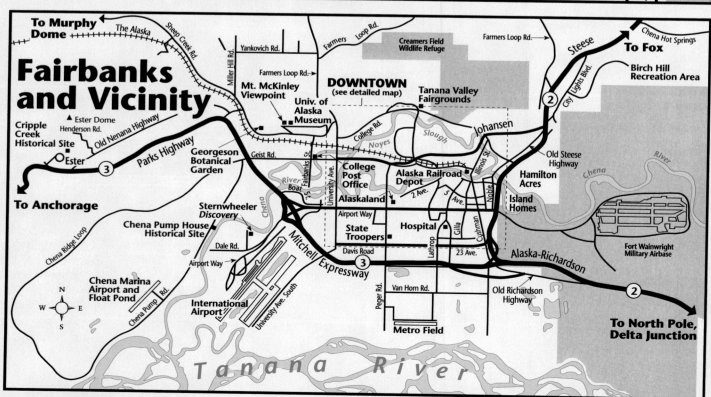

To Murphy
Dome

The Alaska

Sheep Creek Rd.

Yankovich Rd.

Farmers Loop Rd.

Creamers Field
Wildlife Refuge

Farmers Loop Rd.

Steese

Chena Hot Springs

To Fox

Fairbanks
and Vicinity

Miller Hill Rd.

Farmers Loop Rd.

Mt. McKinley
Viewpoint

Univ. of
Alaska
Museum

DOWNTOWN
(see detailed map)

Tanana Valley
Fairgrounds

College Rd.

Noyes

Slough

Johansen

2

City Lights Blvd.

Birch Hill
Recreation Area

Cripple
Creek
Historical Site

▲ Ester Dome

Henderson Rd.

Old Nenana Highway

Parks Highway

Georgeson
Botanical
Garden

Geist Rd.

Fairbanks St.

University Ave.

College
Post
Office

Alaska Railroad
Depot

Alaskaland

2 Ave.

S
Ave.

Noble

Illinois St.

Old Steese
Highway

Hamilton
Acres

Island
Homes

Chena

River

Ester

3

River
Boat

To Anchorage

Sternwheeler
Discovery

Chena Pump House
Historical Site

Dale Rd.

Airport Way

Mitchell Expressway

Airport Way

State Troopers

Hospital

Davis Road

Lathrop

Gilla

23 Ave.

Cushman

3

Alaska-Richardson

Fort Wainwright
Military Airbase

Chena Ridge Loop

Chena Marina
Airport and
Float Pond

Chena Pump Rd.

International
Airport

University Ave. South

Peger Rd.

Van Horn Rd.

Old Richardson
Highway

Metro Field

Old Richardson
Highway

2

To North Pole,
Delta Junction

N W E S

T a n a n a   R i v e r

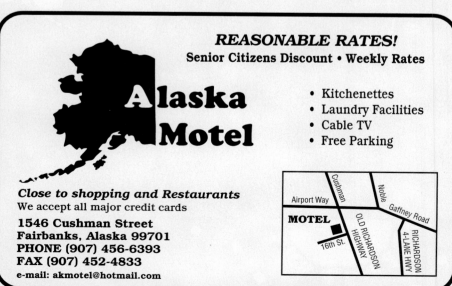
(Continued from page 429)
the U.S. Census in 1910 with a population of 3,541. Miners living beside their claims on creeks north of town brought the area population figure to about 11,000.

Barnette stayed in Fairbanks until late 1910, when he resigned the presidency of the Washington–Alska Bank and moved to California. When the bank collapsed early in 1911, the people of Fairbanks blamed Barnette. The tale of the "most hated man in Fairbanks" is told in *E.T. Barnette, The Strange Story of the Man Who Founded Fairbanks*.

ECONOMY

The city's economy is linked to its role as a service and supply point for Interior and Arctic industrial activities. Fairbanks played a key role during construction of the trans-Alaska pipeline in the 1970s. The Dalton Highway (formerly the North Slope Haul Road) to Prudhoe Bay begins about 75 miles/121 km north of town. Extractive industries such as oil and mining continue to play a major role in the economy.

Government employment contributes significantly to the Fairbanks economy. Including military jobs, 50 percent of employment in Fairbanks is through the government. Fort Wainwright (formerly Ladd Field) was the first Army airfield in Alaska, established in 1938. The fort currently employs 4,600 soldiers and 1,600 civilians, and it houses 6,200 family members. Fort Wainwright also provides emergency services by assisting with search and rescue operations. Eielson Air Force Base, located 25 miles/40 km southeast of Fairbanks on the Richardson–Alaska Highway, also has a strong economic impact on the city. Eielson has about 2,700 military personnel and approximately 4,200 family members assigned, with about 1,200 military personnel and family members living off base.

Also boosting the Fairbanks economy are the University of Alaska–Fairbanks, and trade and service industries such as retail sales and tourism.

DESCRIPTION

Alaska's second largest city and the administrative capital of the Interior, Fairbanks lies on the flat valley floor of the Tanana River on the banks of the Chena River. Good views of the valley are available from Chena Ridge Road to the west and Farmers Loop Road to the north.

The city is a blend of old and new: Modern hotels and shopping malls stand beside log cabins and historic wooden buildings.

Fairbanks is bounded to the north, east and west by low rolling hills of birch and white spruce. To the south is the Alaska Range and Denali National Park, about a 2 1/2-hour drive via the Parks Highway. The Steese and Elliott highways lead north to the White Mountains.

ACCOMMODATIONS/VISITOR SERVICES

Fairbanks has more than 100 restaurants, about 2 dozen hotels and motels and more than 100 bed and breakfasts during the summer. Rates vary widely, from a low of about $40 for a single to a high of $150 for a double. Reservations for accommodations are suggested during the busy summer months.

There are several private campgrounds in the Fairbanks area. Chena River recreation site, a state campground, is located on University Avenue by the Chena River bridge.

The campground has 57 sites, tables, firepits, toilets, water and a dump station. Camping fee $15/night or annual pass; $3 for use of dump station; and $5 for use of boat launch.

There is overnight camping at Alaskaland for self-contained RVs only with a 4-night limit, $12 fee and use of the borough dump station on 2nd Avenue. ▲

Ah, Rose Marie Downtown Bed and Breakfast. Historic 1928 Fairbanks home. Very centrally located. Full hearty breakfasts. Friendly cat. Outdoor smoking areas. Singles, couples, triples, families welcomed. Open year-round. Extraordinary hospitality. Single $50 up, doubles $65 up. Wow! John E. Davis, 302 Cowles St., Fairbanks, AK 99701. Phone (907) 456-2040; fax (907) 456-6193; website: www.akpub.com/akbb/rv/ahrose html. [ADVERTISEMENT]

A-1 Yankovich Inn Bed & Breakfast and Gift Shop. Located on a 2-acre estate adjoining the musk-ox farm; warm, relaxing atmosphere. University hiking/skiing trails with aurora viewing. Bedrooms have queen beds, shared bath, rollaway for x-tra person. Alaska blueberry waffles, house specialty. $75 double, $65 single. VISA, MC. 2268 Yankovich Road, Fairbanks, AK 99709. Phone: (907) 479-2861; e-mail: tundra @ptialaska.net. [ADVERTISEMENT]

Chena Marina RV Park guests speak: "RV having fun? Yes—Thanks to folks like you!...'Dankeschon' services really special... One of the best—location, spacious, landscaped...First-rate." Extra-wide, long pull-throughs (slide-outs welcome). Free Klondinental breakfast; on floatplane pond (fishing); laundry, free guest showers, electric, water, TV, dump, tour tickets, free RV/car wash. Mile 2.8 Chena Pump Road, watch for signs. (907) 479-GOLD (4653), 1145 Shypoke Dr., Fairbanks, AK 99709. See map in display ad for directions. Open May 1. [ADVERTISEMENT] MP ▲

Country Comforts Bed and Breakfast. Stay Free! Ask how! Quiet spacious home located near Birch Hill recreation area 5 minutes from downtown. Alaskan art. Queen/ twin beds, Jacuzzi, sauna, full breakfasts. Hosts Audrey and Ken Dunshie, 30-year residents. Open year-round. (907) 457-6867; toll free (888) 401-3232; pin 1761. 174 Creat Dr., Fairbanks 99712. Web site: www.bbhost./ countrycomforts. [ADVERTISEMENT]

Eleanor's Northern Lights Bed and Breakfast: Conveniently located, a 5-minute walk from downtown Fairbanks. Hearty, full, all-you-can-eat "home cooked breakfasts," a selection of six clean rooms, very reasonable rates. Energetic and bright hosts—Stella and Mike—have created a warm, cozy "home away from home." 360 State St. (corner of 4th Ave. and State St., Fairbanks, AK 99701. Phone: (907) 452-2598; fax: (907) 452-7247; e-mail: nlightsb@eagle.ptialaska.net; web page: www.akpub.com/akbbrv/elean.html. [ADVERTISEMENT]

Fairbanks Bed and Breakfast. Barbara Neubauer, hostess and 26-year resident, has many bear and gold mining tales. The quiet historical neighborhood is walking distance to town on bus route. Our home has many interesting ivory artifacts and Alaskan art. Private bath, large yard and deck. Deck smoking. Hearty breakfast and laundry facilities for fee plus ample parking. 902 Kellum St. (907) 452-4967, fax (907) 451-6955. [ADVERTISEMENT]

Fairbanks Princess Hotel. Interior Alaska's finest accommodations located on the Chena River. Featuring an array of

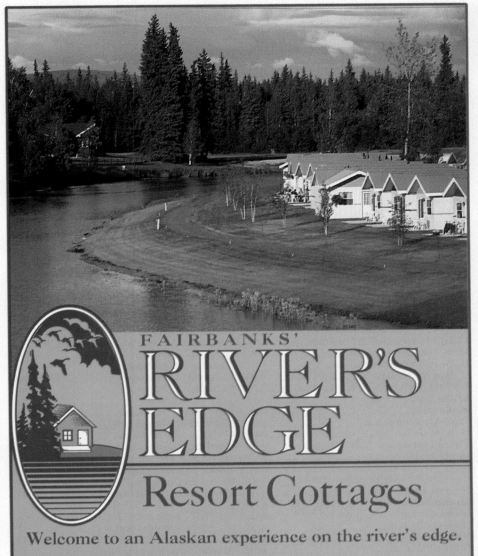

FAIRBANKS'
RIVER'S EDGE
Resort Cottages

Welcome to an Alaskan experience on the river's edge.

PHOTOS BY LYNN NELSON

Each cottage is charmingly decorated and features a private full bath with private vanity, two queen beds, phone, television, and patio doors that open to gardened courtyards or landscaped riverbank.

River's Edge Resort Cottages . . . for a delightful change of pace

Fairbank's newest and only riverfront guest cottage resort. It's like a 4-star hotel in a private cottage setting.

Located just minutes from the airport and downtown Fairbanks, these cottages are nestled along the banks of the Chena River.

Breakfast and dinner served daily in our beautiful Riverfront Dining Room.

Stroll along the river's edge, canoe the Chena River, fish for grayling or seasonal king salmon.

Also providing tour bookings to Pt. Barrow and local attractions.

4200 Boat St.
Fairbanks, Alaska 99709

e-mail: landersn@ptialaska.net
web site: www.riversedge.net

For reservations or information:
1-800-770-3343
(907) 474-0286, fax: (907) 474-3665

dining options, lounge, terraced riverside deck, tour desk, gift shop, health club with steam rooms, complimentary airport shuttle, meeting facilities for groups up to 435. Open year-round. Call (800) 426-0500 for reservations. [ADVERTISEMENT]

Fairbanks Private Vacation Homes Network. Peaceful, quiet, wooded settings, all within 12 minutes of city center. All have clean and modern kitchens and bathrooms, phones, TV/VCRs and stock breakfast fixings. Smoking outdoors. Reasonable rates. Brochures available. *Beth's Vacation Home, 1 bedroom house sleeps four, 1000 Bennett Road., Fairbanks, AK 99712, (907) 457-2725; e-mail:jimsamp@mosquitonet.com. *Cedar Creek Vacation Home, custom-built 2-story, 2½ bedrooms, pets on approval, P.O. Box 10355, Fairbanks, AK 99710, (907) 457-3392; within Alaska 1-800-764-3392; fax (907) 457-3332; e-mail: appleinn@ mosquitonet. com. Web site: http://www.akpub.com/ak. bbrv/apple.html. *Gram's Cabin, on 3 river-

front acres, pets on approval. P.O. Box 58034, Fairbanks, AK 99711, phone (907) 488-6513; fax: (907) 488-6513; e-mail: braniff@mosquitonet.com. Web site: http://www.mosquitonet.com/~braniff. [ADVERTISEMENT]

Fountainhead Hotels. Three of Fairbanks' finest hotels: Sophie Station, Wedgewood Resort, and the Bridgewater Hotel. Each property varies in design, personality and location, assuring you that we have exactly what you're looking for! Call our Reservations Department; we'll be happy to help you find the hotel most suited to your needs. For additional information call (800) 528-4916. You can write to us at 1501 Queens Way, Fairbanks, AK 99701, or e-mail us: fountain@mosquitonet.com. [ADVERTISEMENT]

Geni's Bed & Breakfast. Country hospitality May to September. Large bedroom, private bath. Two bedrooms with queen-sized beds, shared full bath. No pets, smoking on deck only. Continental or full country

breakfast. Affordable accommodations in woodland setting 15 minutes from Fairbanks

at Mile 5.3 Chena Hot Springs Road. Handmade Alaska crafts available. George and Nila Lyle, P.O. Box 10352, Fairbanks, AK 99710; phone (907) 488-4136. [ADVERTISEMENT]

River's Edge RV Park & Campground. Beautiful setting on the Chena River and within walking distance of major shopping centers. 180 spacious wooded sites. Wide pull-throughs; 30-amp electric; dump station; full and partial hookups; free showers; gifts; free shuttle to Riverboat *Discovery* and Alaskaland Salmon Bake. Tour arrangements

FAIRBANKS ADVERTISERS

featuring Point Barrow and Arctic Circle. Immaculate facilities. [ADVERTISEMENT] MP ▲

Riverview RV Park & Cookout is one of the top-rated RV parks in Alaska. It is situated on 20 acres adjoining the beautiful Chena River. Total atmosphere and only 10 minutes from downtown Fairbanks. Room for your convenience. It is the only RV park with cable TV in the Fairbanks area. Call Riverview RV Park (888) 488-6392 or (907) 488-6281. Telephones and e-mail. See display ad. [ADVERTISEMENT] ▲

7 Gables Inn. Central to major attractions, this remodeled fraternity house is between the University campus and the airport. The spacious Tudor-style house features a floral solarium, stained-glass foyer with indoor waterfall, cathedral ceilings, banquet/conference facilities. Gourmet breakfast served daily. Cable TV, VCR, phone in each room, laundry, bikes, canoes and skis. Rates $50–$120; 4312 Birch Lane, Fairbanks, AK 99709. Phone (907) 479-0751. [ADVERTISEMENT]

Uebernachtung und Fruehstueck, Bed & Breakfast. English and German speaking with German hospitality. Pets in house. Queen beds, private and shared bath, full breakfast. German TV. Robert and Sylvia Harris, 2402 Cowles St., Fairbanks,

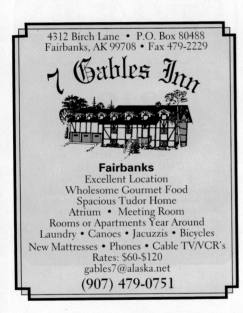

4312 Birch Lane • P.O. Box 80488
Fairbanks, AK 99708 • Fax 479-2229

7 Gables Inn

Fairbanks
Excellent Location
Wholesome Gourmet Food
Spacious Tudor Home
Atrium • Meeting Room
Rooms or Apartments Year Around
Laundry • Canoes • Jacuzzis • Bicycles
New Mattresses • Phones • Cable TV/VCR's
Rates: $60-$120
gables7@alaska.net

(907) 479-0751

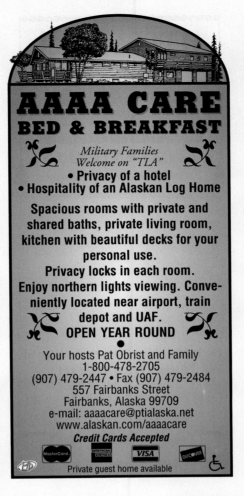

AAAA CARE BED & BREAKFAST

Military Families Welcome on "TLA"
• Privacy of a hotel
• Hospitality of an Alaskan Log Home
Spacious rooms with private and shared baths, private living room, kitchen with beautiful decks for your personal use.
Privacy locks in each room.
Enjoy northern lights viewing. Conveniently located near airport, train depot and UAF.
OPEN YEAR ROUND

Your hosts Pat Obrist and Family
1-800-478-2705
(907) 479-2447 • Fax (907) 479-2484
557 Fairbanks Street
Fairbanks, Alaska 99709
e-mail: aaaacare@ptialaska.net
www.alaskan.com/aaaacare
Credit Cards Accepted
MasterCard AMERICAN EXPRESS VISA DISCOVER
Private guest home available

The Captain Bartlett Inn
"For a Taste of Real Alaska"

Centrally located
Near Shopping & Major Attractions
Comfortable, Alaskan decor rooms

Slough Foot Sue's Dining Hall
Breakfast, Lunch, Dinner
Outdoor Dining

Dog Sled Saloon
Honky Tonk piano music nightly
World Renowned Alaskan
Decor & Hospitality

1411 Airport Way, Fairbanks, AK 99701
1-800-544-7528 (outside Alaska)
1-800-478-7900 (inside Alaska)
cbi@polarnet.com
http://www.akpub.com/akbbrv/cbinn.html

PRIVATE BATHS • OPEN YEAR ROUND
5 MIN. DRIVE NORTH OF TOWN • FULL OR CONTINENTAL BREAKFAST
A FAMILY HOMESTAY WITH THREE FRIENDLY FELINES
Applesauce Inn B&B
(907) 457-3392 • Fax (907) 457-3332 • 800-764-3392 (In Alaska)
119 Gruening Way • Fairbanks, Alaska 99712
http://www.akpub.com/akbbrv/apple.html • appleinn@mosquitonet.com

On Dec. 21, 1999 (winter solstice) the sun rises at 10:58 A.M. and sets at 2:40 P.M. in Fairbanks.

FAIRBANKS, ALASKA

GOLDEN NORTH MOTEL

✓ Near the International Airport
✓ Minutes from downtown
✓ Color TV
✓ Tub & Shower in Each Room
✓ 24 Hour Switchboard
✓ 62 Attractive Units
✓ Courtesy Car Available
✓ Fine Restaurant Nearby
✓ Open Year-Round
✓ Free Continental Breakfast
✓ Summer Rates Start at $69.
✓ Close to shopping

All Major Credit Cards Welcome

1-800-447-1910
(In Fairbanks call 479-6201)
4888 Old Airport Way
Fairbanks, Alaska 99709

Take Airport Way or Mitchell Express to Old Airport Way.

TRANSPORTATION

Air: Several international, interstate and intra-Alaska carriers serve Fairbanks.

Air charter services are available for flightseeing, fly-in fishing and hunting, and trips to bush villages; see ads.

Railroad: Alaska Railroad passenger depot at 280 N. Cushman St. in the downtown area. Daily passenger service in summer between Fairbanks and Anchorage with stop-overs at Denali National Park; less frequent service in winter. For details, phone (800) 544-0552.

Train to Denali (Gray Line of Alaska). Ride the luxurious private-domed railcars of the *McKinley Explorer* to Denali National Park from either Anchorage or Fairbanks. Overnight packages in Denali with round-trip train service are available from $405 for 3 days/2 nights, ppdo. Pre-overnight in either Anchorage or Fairbanks is included. Prices subject to change. Call Gray Line of Alaska at (907) 451-6835 for train and package tour options. [ADVERTISEMENT]

Bus: Local daily bus service is provided by the Metropolitan Area Commuter System (MACS). MACS service is available from Fairbanks to the University of Alaska, North Pole, Hamilton Acres, Davis Road and the International Airport daily Monday through Saturday (limited scheduled on Saturdays); no service on Sundays and six major holidays. Drivers do not carry change so exact change or tokens must be used. Fares: $1.50 or 1 token for adults; grade K-12, senior citizens or disabled, $0.75. All-day passes are $3, purchased from the drivers. Tokens are available at Transit Park, UAF Wood Center, Fred Meyer West, Bentley Mall and North Pole Plaza. Information is available via the Transit Hotline at (907) 459-1011 or from MACS office at 3175 Peger Road, phone (907) 459-1002 or on the internet at

www.co.fairbanks.ak.us/transit/ transit.htm.

Tours: Local and area sightseeing tours are available from several companies; see ads in this section.

Taxi: 9 cab companies.

Car and Camper Rentals: Several companies rent cars, campers and trailers; see ads in this section.

ATTRACTIONS

Get Acquainted: A good place to start is the visitor information center at 550 1st Ave., where you'll find free brochures, maps and tips on what to see and how to get there. Phone (907) 456-5774 or 1-800-327-5774. For a recording of current daily events phone (907) 456-INFO.

Next to the log cabin visitor information center is **Golden Heart Park**, site of the 18-foot/5-m bronze monument, "Unknown First Family." The statue, by sculptor Malcolm Alexander, and park were dedicated in July 1986 to celebrate Fairbanks' history and heritage.

Fairbanks has a number of public parks that make good stops for a picnic. **Graehl**

Famous for its history and hospitality, Fairbanks is known as the "Golden Heart City."

Creamer's Field Migratory Waterfowl Refuge on College Road. *(© Laurent Dick)*

Park has a boat launch and is a good place to watch traffic on the river.

Alaska Bird Observatory at Creamer's Refuge. Observe migratory bird research and Alaska's songbirds up close. Bird banding demonstrations are at 9 A.M. and 11 A.M. (May 1-June 10) and 9:15 A.M. and 11:15 A.M. (July 15-Sept. 20). Call for June 11-July 14 schedule. Guided birdwatching also available. Donation requested. (907) 451-7059.

[ADVERTISEMENT]

The Alaska Public Lands Information Center, located in the lower level of historic Courthouse Square at 3rd Avenue and Cushman Street, is a free museum and information center featuring Alaska's natural history, cultural artifacts and recreational opportunities. In addition to detailed information on outdoor recreation in the state, the center offers films, interpretive programs, lectures and a book shop.

Tours Starting At
$20
Per Person, Including Gold

Historic Landmark

Gold Dredge No. 8

A piece of history to experience.
A piece of gold to remember it by.

Prospectors used to travel for weeks through ice and snow in hopes of coming across a mere trace of gold. Today, Gray Line of Alaska has made prospecting much easier with tours to Gold Dredge No. 8, the only gold dredge in Alaska still open to the public. Gold Dredge No. 8 offers a truly authentic gold mining experience, including a tour of the site that unearthed millions of ounces of gold, as well as the opportunity to pan for guaranteed gold yourself. Afterwards enjoy the Miner's lunch for an additional $8, and visit the museum or gift shop for a large variety of mining souvenirs.

Open 9 a.m. to 6 p.m. every day from mid May through mid September.
From Fairbanks, take the Steese Highway north to Goldstream Road, then follow the signs.
Gold Dredge No. 8 is approximately 10 minutes from Fairbanks.
Please contact Gray Line of Alaska at (907) 451-6835.

GRAY LINE **Gray Line of Alaska**
A DIVISION OF HOLLAND AMERICA LINE-WESTOURS

Tour the University of Alaska–Fairbanks. Situated on a 2,250-acre ridge overlooking Fairbanks and the Alaska Range, UAF has the best view in town! With all the amenities of a small town, including a fire station, post office, radio and TV stations, medical clinic and a concert hall, it boasts a world-class faculty and a unique blend of students from around the world.

The new **International Arctic Research Center** (IARC) at University of Alaska Fairbanks is a 100,000-square-foot building located adjacent the Geophysical Institute on the West Ridge of the campus. The IARC, a joint effort of the U.S. and Japanese governments, will house scientists from around the world who will work together on global climate research.

UAF offers special tours and programs from June through August. Free guided walking tours of campus are offered Monday through Friday at 10 A.M. Tours begin at the UA Museum (see below). Several other summer tours are available, including a musk-oxen and caribou farm, rocket range, botanical garden and supercomputing

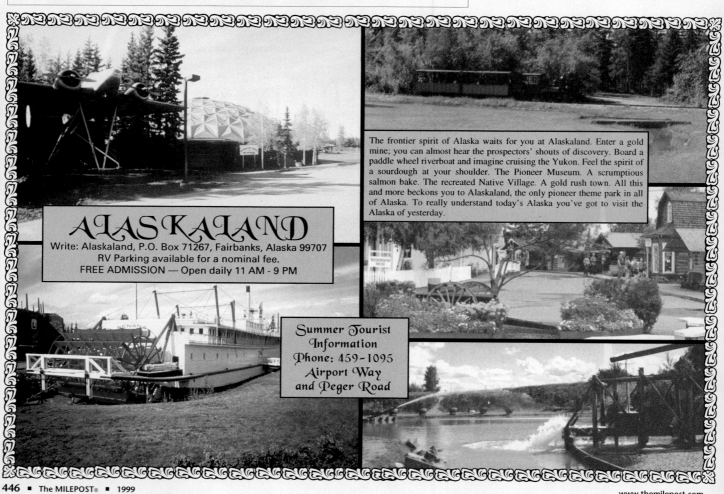

center. Call (07) 474-7581 for information on any tour; or visit our website: www.uaf.edu.

Consider UAF when you or someone you know is thinking about college. Guided tours of campus for prospective students can be arranged throughout the year by calling the Office of Admissions, (907) 474-7500 or (800) 478-1823.

The University of Alaska Museum is a must stop for Fairbanks visitors. The museum features cultural and natural history displays from all the state's regions. The 5 galleries explore Alaska's history, Native culture, art, natural phenomena, wildlife, birds, geology and prehistoric past. Highlights include a 36,000-year-old Steppe bison mummy, the state's largest gold display, the trans-Alaska pipeline story and a special section on the northern lights. The museum grounds hold sculptures, totem poles, a Russian blockhouse and a nature trail with signs identifying local vegetation.

The museum's special summer exhibit in 1999 is called "Not Just a Pretty Face," showing dolls and human figurines from Alaska Native cultures. Free summer programs include presentations on natural and cultural history topics discussing traditional and contemporary lifestyles. Summer shows include "Northern Inua," a 50-minute show of northern athletic games, dance and creation stories, produced in conjunction with the World Eskimo-Indian Olympics, and "Dynamic Autora," a 50-minute show on the scientific and Alaska Native understanding of the northern lights. Admission is charged for these shows; call for times.

Museum hours: May and September, 9

A.M. to 5 P.M.; June through August, 9 A.M. to 7 P.M.; October through April, weekdays, 9 A.M. to 5 P.M., weekends, noon to 5 P.M. museum admission fees: adults, $5; seniors, $4.50; youth (7-17), $3; children under 67, free. For 24-hour information, call (907) 474-7505, or check our website: www.uaf.edu/museum.

See Gold Displays. In addition to the large gold display at the university museum, visitors will find many exotic gemstones, a knowledgeable gemologist and staff, and rock specimens from around the world at Taylor's Gold-N-Stones on Cushman Street in downtown Fairbanks. A combination museum and old-fashioned working jewelry store, where skilled goldsmiths create gold-nugget and other jewelry, Taylor's is a fascinating stop for rockhounds. See display ad this section.

Celebrate Summer Solstice: Fairbanks has several unique summer celebrations associated with summer solstice in in June, when residents celebrate the longest day of the year (summer solstice is June 21). The Midnight Sun Baseball Game will be played at 10:30 P.M. on June 21, 1999, without artificial lights. For details, phone (907) 451-0095. The Midnight Sun 10K Fun Run begins at 10 P.M. on June 19, 1999; phone (907) 452-7211 for further information.

Golden Days, when Fairbanksans turn out in turn-of-the-century dress and celebrate the gold rush, is July 15-25, 1999. Golden Days starts off with a Felix Pedro look-alike taking his gold to the bank and includes a parade and rededication of the Pedro Monument honoring the man who started it all when he discovered gold in the Tanana Hills. Other events include pancake breakfasts, a dance, canoe and raft races, and free outdoor concerts. For additional information, phone (907) 452-1105.

The World Eskimo and Indian Olympics, with Native competition in such events as the high kick, greased pole walk, stick pull, fish cutting, parka contest and muktuk-eating contest will be held July 14-17, 1999. Phone (907) 452-6646.

The Ice Art Carnival, scheduled for March 3-13, 1999, draws thousands of people to admire ice sculptures created by artists from around the world. An ice castle, an ice gold tournament and all-ice children's play area are popular features.

Captain Kai Binkley pilots The Discovery III. *(© Lee Foster)*

The Tanana Valley State Fair will be held Aug. 6-14, 1999. Alaska's oldest state fair, the Tanana Valley State Fair features agricultural exhibits, arts and crafts, food booths, a rodeo and other entertainment. Phone (907) 452-3750 for more information.

The Fairbanks Summer Arts Festival, 2 weeks of workshops and concerts including music from jazz to classics, dance, theater and the visual arts, will be held July 24-Aug. 8, 1999 on the University of Alaska Fairbanks campus. Phone (907) 474-8869 for more information.

Check with the Fairbanks visitor information center for more information on all local events.

Besides these special events, summer visitors can take in a semipro baseball game at Growden Park where the Fairbanks Gold-panners take on other Alaska league teams.

Visit Creamer's Field. Follow the flocks of waterfowl to Creamer's Field Migratory Waterfowl Refuge. Located 1 mile/1.6 km from downtown Fairbanks, this 1,800-acre refuge managed by the Alaska Dept. of Fish and Game offers opportunities to observe large concentrations of ducks, geese, shore-birds and cranes in the spring and fall. Throughout the summer, sandhill cranes eat in the planted barley fields.

Explore the 2-mile/3.2-km self-guided nature trail and the renovated historic farm-house that serves as a visitor center. Stop at 1300 College Road to find the trailhead, viewing areas and brochures on Creamer's Field. For more information, phone (907) 452-5162.

Creamer's Field Migratory Waterfowl Refuge—where nature is at its best. Summer visitor center hours, 10 A.M. to 5 P.M., closed Sunday and Monday. June through August, guided walks begin at Farmhouse Visitor Center Tuesday and Thursday at 7 P.M.; Wednesday and Saturday at 9 A.M. No charge and the refuge is always open. Phone (907) 452-5162. [ADVERTISEMENT]

Tanana Valley Farmers Market. Visit Alaska's premier Farmers Market, located next to the Fairgrounds on College Road, open from mid-May to mid-September. Vendors offer "thousands of miles fresher"

Alaska grown vegetables; blue-ribbon florals; Alaskan meats, fish, honey, jams and syrups; made-in-Alaska handcrafts and baked goods. Look for our brochure at local Visitor's Centers. Market hours are Wednesdays 11 A.M. to 4 P.M. and Saturdays 9 A.M. to 4 P.M.; there's plenty of parking. Stop by the Market and enjoy Alaska made and grown products ... "Meet You At The Market!" [ADVERTISEMENT]

The Alaska Rag Co. A must-see for Fairbanks travelers. This unique Alaskan gift shop manufactures beautiful handwoven rag rugs from 100 percent recycled clothing. The store also features works from 70-plus Alaskan artists. Items include jewelry, pottery, Polarfleece, stained glass, qiviut, dog hair hats, mittens and much more. Stop in, meet our weavers and see their work. 552 2nd Ave., Fairbanks, AK 99701. Phone (907) 451-4401. ("A part of FCMHC's vocational unit.") [ADVERTISEMENT]

Chena Pump House National Historic Site. Built in 1931–33 by the Fairbanks Exploration Co. to pump water from the Chena River to dredging operations at Cripple Creek, the pump house was remodeled in 1978 and now houses a restaurant and saloon. The sheet metal cladding, interior roof and some equipment (such as the intake ditch) are from the original pump house, which shut down in 1958 when the F.E. Co. ceased its Cripple Creek dredging operations. The pump house is located at Mile 1.3 Chena Pump Road.

See the Pipeline: Drive about 10 miles/ 16 km north from downtown on the Steese Highway to see the trans-Alaska pipeline. Clearly visible are the thermal devices used to keep the permafrost frozen around the pipeline support columns.

See Bank Displays: Key Bank, at 1st Avenue and Cushman Street, has a display of gold nuggets and several trophy animals. Mount McKinley Mutual Savings Bank features a display of McKinley prints and the original cannonball safe used when the bank opened. The bank is at 531 3rd Ave.

Visit Historic Churches: St. Matthew's Episcopal Church, 1029 1st Ave., was originally built in 1905, but burned in 1947 and was rebuilt the following year. Of special interest is the church's intricately carved altar, made in 1906 of Interior Alaska birch and saved from the fire. **Immaculate Conception Church**, on the Chena River at Cushman Street bridge, was drawn by horses to its present location in the winter of 1911 from its original site at 1st Avenue and Dunkel Street.

View Mount McKinley: The best spot to see Mount McKinley is from the University of Alaska–Fairbanks campus (on Yukon

www.themilepost.com

Historic Gold Dredge #8 is just outside Fairbanks on the Steese Highway. *(© Lee Foster)*

Drive, between Talkeetna and Sheenjek streets) where a turnout and marker define the horizon view of Mount Hayes (elev. 13,832 feet/4,216m); Hess Mountain (elev. 11,940 feet/3,639m); Mount Deborah (elev. 12,339 feet/3,761m); and Mount McKinley (elev. 20,320 feet/6,194m). Distant foothills are part of the Wood River Butte.

Cruise Aboard the Riverboat *Discovery*: Every day at 8:45 A.M. and 2 P.M. in summer, the riverboat *Discovery* departs for a half-day cruise on the Chena and Tanana rivers. Drive out Airport Road, turn south at Dale Road and continue 0.5 mile/0.8 km on Dale to Discovery Drive. Reservations are required, as this is one of the most popular attractions in town. For the first leg of the trip, the *Discovery* winds its way down the meandering Chena River, its banks lined by old homesteads, modern homes and bush planes. The Chena River also joins with Cripple Creek, the Interior's richest gold rush stream. On the Tanana River, fish wheels turn in the swift glacial water, scoop-

ing up salmon to be dried and smoked for winter food. Returning up the Tanana River, the boat stops at Old Chena Indian Village, where passengers have the opportunity to see Susan Butcher's Iditarod-champion dog team in action. After the demonstration, passengers disembark for a tour of the village. Guides from the *Discovery*, who are of Indian or Eskimo heritage, are on hand to explain past and present Native culture. For more information on the riverboat *Discovery*, contact Alaska Riverways, Inc., 1975 Discovery Dr., Fairbanks, AK 99709; phone (907) 479-6673, fax 479-4613.

Play Tennis: There are 6 outdoor asphalt courts at the Mary Siah Recreation Center, 1025 14th Ave. No fees or reservations. For more information phone (907) 459-1070.

Play Golf: Maintaining a scenic 9-hole course with natural greens, the Fairbanks Golf and Country Club (public is invited) is west of the downtown area at 1735 Farmers Loop Road; phone (907) 479-6555 for information and reservations. The 18-hole Chena Bend Golf Course is located on Fort Wainwright; phone (907) 353-6223. North Star Golf Club, located 10 minutes north of downtown on the Old Steese Highway, offers a regulation 9-hole course; phone (907) 457-4653 or (907) 452-2104.

Ride Bikes Around Fairbanks: There are many day-touring choices in Fairbanks. A round-trip tour of the city, the University of Alaska and the college area can be made by leaving town on Airport Way and returning on College Road. The Farmers Loop Road or a ride out the Old Steese Highway toward Fox are easy tours.

Visit Alaskaland Pioneer Park. Visitors will find a relaxed atmosphere at Alaskaland, a pleasant park with historic buildings, small shops, food, entertainment, playgrounds and 4 covered picnic shelters. The park— which has no admission fee—is open year-round.

To drive to Alaskaland (at Airport Way and Peger Road), take Airport Way to Wilbur, turn north onto Wilbur, then immediately west onto access road, which leads to Alaskaland enclosure.

The 44-acre historic park was created in 1967 as the Alaska Centennial Park to commemorate the 100th anniversary of U.S. territorial status and provide a taste of interior Alaska history. Visitors may begin their visit at the information center, which is located just inside the park's main gate. Walk through Gold Rush Town, a narrow, winding street of authentic old buildings that once graced downtown Fairbanks and now house gift shops. Here you will find the Kitty Hensley and Judge Wickersham houses, furnished with turn-of-the-century items; the First Presbyterian Church, constructed in 1906; and the Pioneers of Alaska Museum, dedicated to those who braved frontier life to found Fairbanks. Free guided historical walking tours take place each afternoon.

The park is home to the newly renovated SS *Nenana*, a national landmark. Cared for by the Fairbanks Historical Preservation Foundation, the *Nenana* is the largest sternwheeler ever built west of the Mississippi, and the second largest wooden vessel in existence. The Foundation also displays a 300-foot/91-m diorama of life along the Tanana and Yukon rivers in the early 1900s.

The top level of the Civic Center houses an art gallery featuring rotating contemporary exhibits and paintings; 11 A.M. to 9 P.M. daily, Memorial Day through Labor Day; noon to 8 P.M. daily, except Monday, during the rest of the year.

Behind the Civic Center, you'll find the Pioneer Air Museum, which features antique aircraft and stories of their Alaskan pilots, with displays from 1913–48. Phone (907) 451-0037, Memorial Day through Labor Day, for information. Admission is $1.

At the rear of the park is the Native Village Museum and Kashims with Native wares, artifacts and crafts. Across from the Native Village is Mining Valley, with displays of gold-mining equipment. The

ALASKA SALMON BAKE

ALASKALAND

Pleasant Outdoor and Heated Indoor Seating!

OPEN DAILY IN ALASKALAND 5-9pm

SALMON • HALIBUT • RIBS • PORTERHOUSE STEAK

Our SALMON Fresh from Sitka cooked over an open pit

Our HALIBUT From the icy waters of Kachemak Bay

Our BARBECUED RIBS Barbecued over alder wood till tender.

Our PORTERHOUSE STEAK A 19 ounce selection grilled to your specification.

Includes: Salad Bar, Sourdough Rolls, Baked Beans, Blueberry Cake, Lemonade, Ice Tea, & Coffee.

ALASKA SALMON BAKE
☞ AND ☜
The Palace Theatre & Saloon

MUSICAL COMEDY Revue About Life In Fairbanks

The PALACE THEATRE's version of Fairbanks life style-The Golden Heart Revue, is known for its light hearted charm and delightful music. The story and songs tell the 90-year history of our "arctic" Tanana Valley.

Showtime 8:15pm Nightly

After a Salmon Bake dinner stroll across Alaskaland, to Gold Rush Town for an evening of sparkling entertainment and refreshments at The Palace Theatre and Saloon. Nightly Fun!

Alaskaland GOLD RUSH TOWN

THE PALACE THEATRE & SALOON

907-456-5960
Reservations Recommended

Alaska Salmon Bake & The Palace Theatre & Saloon
800-354-7274
call our offices: 907-452-7274 fax 907-456-6997
or write: 3175-MP College Rd., Fairbanks, AK 99709

Salmon Bake, with both outdoor and heated indoor seating areas, is also part of Mining Valley. A popular feature, the Salmon Bake is open daily for lunch from noon to 2 P.M. (June 10 to Aug. 15), and for dinner from 5–9 P.M. (end of May to mid-September). Salmon, barbecued ribs, halibut and 18-oz. porterhouse steaks are served, rain or shine.

There's entertainment 7 nights a week starting at 8 P.M. at the Palace Theatre & Saloon, featuring a musical comedy review about life in Fairbanks titled "Golden Heart Review." The Big Stampede show in Gold Rush Town is a theater in the round, pre-

Bronze statue of "Unknown First Familiy" at Golden Heart Park.
(© Bruce M. Herman)

senting the paintings of Rusty Heurlin, depicting the trail of '98; narrative by Ruben Gaines.

The Crooked Creek & Whiskey Island Railroad, a 30-gauge train, takes passengers for a 12-minute ride around the park. Other types of recreational activities available at Alaskaland include miniature golf, an antique carousel and picnicking in covered shelters. A public dock is located on the Chena River at the rear of the park.

Visitors are welcome to take part in square and round dances year-round at the Alaskaland Dance Center. Phone (907) 452-5699 evenings for calendar of events. For more information about Alaskaland, phone (907) 459-1087.

Area Attractions: Fairbanks is a good jumping-off point for many attractions in Alaska's Interior. Head out the Steese Highway for swimming at Chena Hot Springs or Circle Hot Springs. At Fox, 11 miles/17.7 km north of Fairbanks, the Steese Highway intersects with the Elliott Highway, which leads to the start of the Dalton Highway (formerly the North Slope Haul Road). Popular attractions in this area include Gold Dredge Number 8 (take Goldstream Road exit to Old Steese Highway), a historic 5-deck, 250-foot dredge, and El Dorado Gold Mine at Mile 1.3 Elliott Highway. Both offer gold mining demonstrations and gold panning. See detailed information on page XXX.

Denali National Park is a 2^{1}/$_{2}$-hour drive, or a 3^{1}/$_{2}$-hour train trip via the Alaska Railroad, from Fairbanks. Once there, take the shuttle bus or guided tour through the park. For road conditions on the Parks Highway between Fairbanks and Denali, phone the Dept. of Transportation at (907) 451-2226.

Eielson Air Force Base, 25 miles/40 km southeast of Fairbanks on the Richardson–Alaska Highway, was built in 1943. Originally a satellite base to Ladd Field (now Fort Wainwright) and called Mile 26, it served as a storage site for aircraft on their way to the Soviet Union under the WWII Lend–Lease program. Closed after WWII, the

On summer solstice (June 21, 1999) in Fairbanks, sunrise is at 2:59 A.M.,
sunset is at 12:47 A.M. the following day.

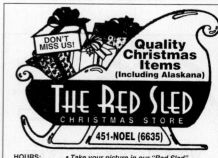

base was reactivated in 1946 and renamed Eielson AFB, after Carl Ben Eielson, the first man to fly from Alaska over the North Pole to Greenland. A tour of the base is offered every Friday during the summer months from 9–10 A.M.; phone the public affairs office at (907) 377-2116 for reservations and more information.

There are 1-day or longer sightseeing trips to Point Barrow, Prudhoe Bay, Fort Yukon and other bush destinations. See ads in this section or consult local travel services.

Historic Gold Dredge No. 8 (Gray Line of Alaska). Gold Dredge No. 8 is a monument to the miners who used the machinery to produce more than 7.5 million ounces of gold, and to the engineers who built it. Visitors tour the only dredge in Alaska open to the public. Gold panning and a Miner's lunch are also available at this national historic site. See advertisement on page 445 in this section. [ADVERTISEMENT]

Go Swimming. Fairbanks North Star Borough Parks and Recreation Dept. offers 3 pools: Mary Siah Recreation Center, 1025 14th Ave., phone (907) 459-1082; Robert Hamme Memorial Pool, 901 Airport Way, phone (907) 459-1086; and Robert Wescott Memorial Pool, 8th Avenue in North Pole, phone (907) 488-9402.

Chena Lakes Recreation Area. This 2,178-acre park, located 17.3 miles/27.8 km southeast of Fairbanks on the Richardson–Alaska Highway, offers a wide assortment of outdoor recreation. There are 86 campsites for both RV and tent camping, including campsites on an island; canoe, sailboat and rowboat rentals; bike paths and trails for nature hikes, skiing, skijoring and dog mushing; and boat ramp access to the nearby Chena River. Admission to the park, maintained by the Fairbanks North Star Borough, is $3 per vehicle between Memorial Day and Labor Day. No admission is charged the rest of the year. For more information, call (907) 488-1655.

Visit a Gold Mine: Travel professionals describe this tour at the **El Dorado Gold Mine**, which was featured nationally on NBC television, as "the best 2 hours you will spend in the State." The tour begins with a ride on the Tanana Valley Railroad and takes you through the gold fields of Interior Alaska. Along the way you'll see demonstrations of early mining techniques, including a stop in a permafrost tunnel where underground mining is explained. Upon arrival at the camp, Alaskan gold miners give you a brief but informative course in mining, and then you receive your own "poke" of paydirt to pan. The experienced crew will help you pan your own gold—and they guarantee that everyone finds gold. This interesting and entertaining tour is great fun for the whole family. It's a "must do" for everyone who visits Fairbanks. Tours depart daily at 9:45 A.M. and 3 P.M. in summer, *except* for Saturday and Monday, when there are afternoon tours only. Reservations are required (907) 479-7613. Take the Steese Expressway to Fox (about 10 miles north of Fairbanks)

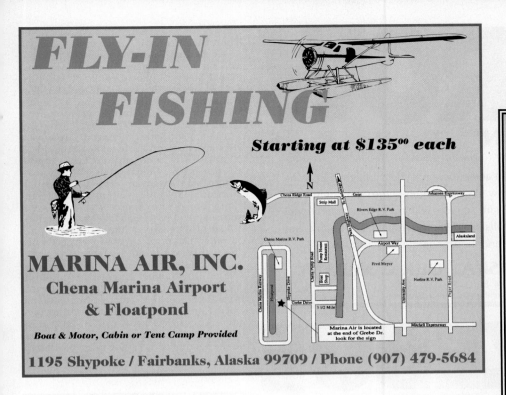

FLY-IN FISHING

Starting at $135⁰⁰ each

MARINA AIR, INC.
Chena Marina Airport & Floatpond

Boat & Motor, Cabin or Tent Camp Provided

1195 Shypoke / Fairbanks, Alaska 99709 / Phone (907) 479-5684

Chena Ridge Road · Geist · Johansen Expressway
Strip Mall
Rivers Edge R.V. Park
Chena Marina R.V. Park · Pump House Restaurant
Airport Way · Alaskaland
Chena Marina Runway · Float pond · Fred Meyer
Shypoke Drive · University Ave.
Boat Shop
Norlite R.V. Park · Peger Road
Grebe Drive
3 1/2 Mile
Mitchell Expressway

Marina Air is located at the end of Grebe Dr. look for the sign

The Arctic Circle lies at approximately 66°33'N latitude.
Fairbanks lies at approximately 64°08' N latitude

TUNDRA TOURS, INC.
TOP OF THE WORLD HOTEL

Don' Dare Stop Until You Reach The Top... Barrow, Alaska

An Experienced You Will Never forget

Experience...the ancient Inupiaq Eskimo culture: dancing, demonstrations, the famous blanket toss and a native craft sale.

Experience... the most northern point on North America, the Arctic Ocean, the

Experience It All...
With Us At The Top Year-Round

The Top Of The World Hotel is a full service hotel with legendary hospitality. Tundra Tours offers a very comprehensive ground tour.

For Instant Reservations Call:
Alaska Airlines 1-800-468-2248
Or 1-800-426-0333
P.O. Box 189, Barrow, Alaska 99723
(907) 852-3900
A SUBSIDIARY OF ARCTIC SLOPE REGIONAL CORPORATION

TOURS AND TRANSPORTATION

ARCTIC CIRCLE ADVENTURE®

Arctic Circle DRIVE

A one day guided journey by land across the Arctic Circle.

Travel the famous Dalton Highway and view the 800-mile long Trans Alaska pipeline.

Visit the Arctic Circle Trading Post situated in the rural community of Joy, Alaska.

Pass over the mighty Yukon River and enjoy a riverside picnic lunch.

Walk out on the delicate arctic tundra and feel the frozen ground beneath the surface.

Cross the Arctic Circle and receive an official Arctic Circle Adventure® Certificate.

Arctic Circle FLY / DRIVE

A one day guided journey by land and air.

All the highlights of the Arctic Circle Drive plus:

Fly north from Fairbanks across the Arctic Circle and receive an aerial view of the vast Alaska wilderness.

Experience the Yukon River. Enjoy a meal on your own *OR* climb aboard for an *OPTIONAL* cruise on the northland's most famous waterway, the Yukon River.

Travel the famous Dalton Highway under the Midnight Sun on the return journey to Fairbanks.

Arctic Circle NATIVE CULTURE

A one day guided journey highlighting the Native culture of Alaska's Arctic.

All the highlights of the Arctic Circle Fly/Drive plus:

Fly the wilderness airways of the rugged and magnificent Brooks Mountain Range.

Visit the Nunamiut Eskimo village of Anaktuvuk Pass nestled in the pristine and scenic Gates of the Arctic National Park.

Learn of the local Nunamiut Eskimo culture and history.

Arctic Circle AIR

A roundtrip journey by air across the Arctic Circle.

Fly north from Fairbanks. View interior gold fields, the Trans Alaska Pipeline, the Dalton Highway and the Yukon River.

Experience the Brooks Mountain Range while overflying the southern boundary of the Gates of the Arctic National Park.

Participate in an Arctic Circle landing at the wilderness outpost of Bettles and receive an official Arctic Circle Adventure® Certificate.

Enjoy the Midnight Sun on the return flight to Fairbamks.

NORTHERN ALASKA TOUR COMPANY

800-474-1986, 907-474-8600 Fax 907-474-4767

Box 82991-MF, Fairbanks, AK 99708 · e-mail adventure@alaskasarctic.com · www.alaskasarctic.com

BARROW
A D V E N T U R E ™

A one day roundtrip journey by air to the farthest north Eskimo village

Explore the shores of the Arctic Ocean and experience the Midnight Sun at the ancient Inupiat Eskimo village of Barrow •Witness sights of the community with a village tour •Learn of local Inupiat Eskimo culture with a program of traditional dance and song •Marvel at age old skills in a demonstration of skin sewing and traditional games •Meet local artisans and shop for unique native crafts.

NORTHERN ALASKA TOUR COMPANY
800-474-1986, 907-474-8600 Fax 907-474-4767
Box 82991-MF, Fairbanks, AK 99708   e-mail adventure@alaskasarctic.com   www.alaskasarctic.com

KOTZEBUE NOME
A D V E N T U R E ™

Single or multiple-day excursion by air to the remote Bering Sea Coast

Experience Inupiat Eskimo culture above the Arctic Circle at the Bering Sea village of Kotzebue •Participate in a village tour highlighted by a fascinating visit to the Museum of the Arctic and unique Culture Camp, where village elders teach ancestral heritage to Kotzebue's youth •Enjoy demonstrations of Inupiat dance, song, and traditional skills •At Nome, relive Gold Rush history and excitement •Pan for gold near the Discovery Claim •Enjoy a dogsled demonstration on the Iditarod Trail •Excursions range from 1 to 3 days.

NORTHERN ALASKA TOUR COMPANY
800-474-1986, 907-474-8600 Fax 907-474-4767
Box 82991-MF, Fairbanks, AK 99708   e-mail adventure@alaskasarctic.com   www.alaskasarctic.com

and then continue straight ahead on the Elliott Highway for 1.3 miles. [ADVERTISEMENT]

Go Skiing: Fairbanks has several downhill ski areas: Cleary Summit, **Milepost F 20.3** Steese Highway; Skiland, **Milepost F 20.9** Steese Highway; Eielson AFB, Fort Wainwright ski hills and Moose Mountain Ski Resort, Spinach Creek Road on Murphy Dome.

Chena Hot Springs Resort at **Milepost J 56.5** Chena Hot Springs Road has over 20 miles of cross-country ski trails, as well as cross-country ski rentals. Other cross-country ski trails are at Birch Hill Recreation Area; drive 2.8 miles/4.5 km north of Fairbanks via Steese Expressway to a well-marked turnoff, then drive in 2.3 miles/ 3.7 km. University of Alaska–Fairbanks has 26 miles/42 km of cross-country ski trails. The trail system is quite extensive: you may ski out to Ester Dome.

Sled Dog Racing. The Alaska Dog Mushers' Assoc. (ADMA) hosts a series of dog races from December to March, ending with the Open North American Championship, a 3-day event with 3 heats (of 20, 20 and 30 miles). The "Open" is considered by many to be the "granddaddy of dog races." Fairbanks also hosts the 1,000-mile/1,609-km Yukon

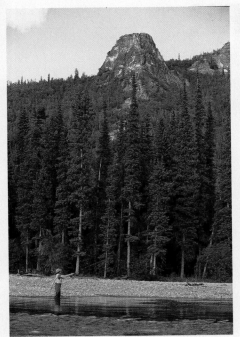

Fly-fishing for grayling on the Chena River near Angel Rocks. *(© Robin Brandt)*

Quest Sled Dog Race between Fairbanks and Whitehorse, YT, with the start and finish alternating between the 2 cities. For more information, contact the ADMA at (907) 457-MUSH, or the Yukon Quest office at (907) 451-8985. The ADMA has a Mushers Hall at 4 mile Farmers Loop Road where people can see dog teams train and race.

Go Fishing: There are several streams and lakes within driving distance of Fairbanks, and local fishing guides are available. **Chena Lake,** about 20 miles/32 km southeast of the city via the Richardson–Alaska Highway at Chena Lakes Recreation Area, is stocked with rainbow trout, silver salmon and arctic char. The **Chena River** and its tributaries offer fishing for sheefish, whitefish, northern pike and burbot. The Chena River flows through Fairbanks. Grayling fishing in the upper Chena is very good, with some large fish. Grayling fishing in the Chena is restricted to catch-and-release year-round. Chena Hot Springs Road off the Steese Highway provides access to fisheries in the Chena River Recreation Area (see the STEESE HIGHWAY section). The Steese Highway also offers access to the **Chatanika River.** Special regulations apply in these waters for grayling and salmon fishing. Phone the ADF&G Division of Sport Fish office at (907) 459-7207.

Air taxi operators and guides in Fairbanks offer short trips from the city for rainbow trout, grayling, northern pike, lake trout and sheefish in lakes and streams of the Tanana and Yukon river drainages. Some operators have camps set up for overnight trips while others specialize in day trips. The air taxi operators usually provide a boat and motor for their angling visitors. Rates are reasonable and vary according to the distance from town and type of facilities offered.

Visit www.themilepost.com

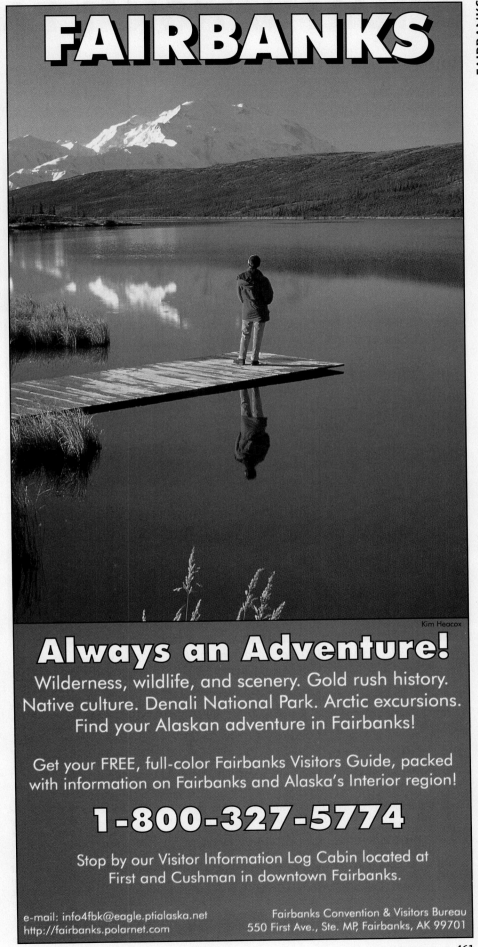

DENALI NATIONAL PARK

(formerly Mount McKinley National Park)

Includes log of Park Road

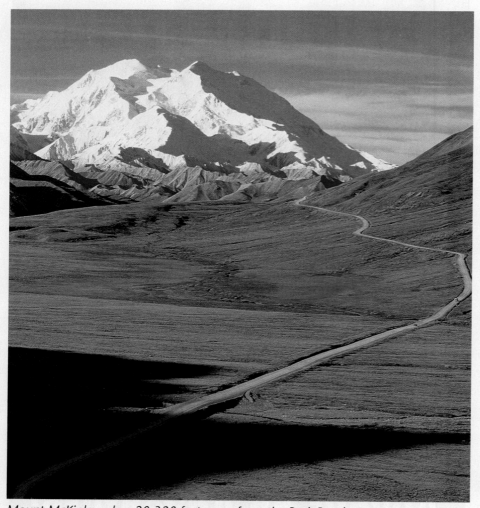

Mount McKinley, elev. 20,320 feet, seen from the Park Road. (© Mike Jones)

Denali National Park and Preserve lies on the north flank of the Alaska Range, 250 miles/402 km south of the Arctic Circle. The park entrance, accessible by highway, railroad and aircraft, is 237 highway miles/381 km north of Anchorage, and about half that distance from Fairbanks.

An admission fee of $5 per person ($10 per vehicle/family) is charged to visitors traveling the park road. The fee is collected when visitors obtain shuttle bus tickets, campground permits or stop at the Visitor Center. Persons between the ages of 16 and 62 are charged the entrance fee. U.S. citizens 62 and older may purchase a $10 lifetime Golden Age Passport. Children 16 years of age or under are exempt from the admission fee. (A $20 annual park pass and the $50 Golden Eagle Pass are valid for admission.)

For detailed information about the park, write Denali National Park and Preserve, Box 9, Denali Park, AK 99755; winter phone (907) 683-2294, summer phone (907) 683-1266 or 1267. The park's web site (www.nps.gov/dena) has current information and reservation forms.

The park is open year-round to visitors, although the hotel, most campgrounds, and food and shuttle bus service within the park are available only from late May or early June to mid-September. Opening dates for facilities and activities for the summer season are announced in the spring by the Park Service and depend mainly on snow conditions in May. Closing dates for facilities and activities at the park are announced in the fall. Last year, shuttle bus service ended and most park campgrounds (except for Riley Creek) closed for the season the first week in September; the visitor center closed Sept. 30.

When you arrive be sure to stop at the Visitor Center, near the park entrance. The center offers information and limited reservations for campgrounds in the park; maps, brochures and schedules of events; details on ranger talks, hikes, nature walks, sled dog demonstrations and wildlife tours; and shuttle bus schedules and ticket reservations. Also available are National Park entrance passes. The center is open daily in summer, generally from early morning into the evening.

Parking space is limited at the Visitor Center. Day parking is available at Riley Creek Campground (walk or mini-shuttle to Visitor Center).

Lodging and camping are available outside the park on the George Parks Highway, and there are many activities—river rafting, hikes and ranger programs—to enjoy. Check with operators outside the park and with personnel at the Visitor Center about programs and activities.

First-time visitors should be particularly aware of the controlled-access system for Park Road use. Private vehicle traffic on the 92-mile/148-km road into the park is restricted beyond the Savage River check station (**Milepost J 14.8**) to registered campers. Campers may reserve campsites by phone or at the Visitor Center. The shuttle bus system and concessionaire-operated tours are available to allow visitors a means of viewing the park without disturbing the wildlife. See Accommodations/Visitor Services this section for details on the shuttle bus service and campsite reservations system.

There is no policy restricting access by bicycle on the Park Road, although cyclists must stay on the road and overnight at one of the established campgrounds.

In an effort to preserve wildlife viewing opportunities for the public, the National Park Service has set road traffic limits. Traffic will be held to the 1984 averages. Consequently, there are limited bus seats available. When planning trips to the park, visitors should reserve shuttle bus tickets in advance by phone or plan activities in the entrance area—such as attending ranger-led interpretive programs—for the first 1 or 2 days, until bus seats can be obtained.

Each summer the park issues permits to a limited number of individuals, selected by lottery, to drive their vehicles through the park on one day of a specific weekend in early September. It is not unusual for these late-season visitors, the majority of whom are Alaskans, to have their tour curtailed because of early snows within the park. Information on how to apply for this popular lottery appears during the summer in local newspapers.

The crown jewel among the park's attractions is Mount McKinley, North America's highest mountain at 20,320 feet/6,194m. On a clear day, Mount McKinley is visible from Anchorage and many points along the Parks Highway; however, summer's often overcast

DENALI NATIONAL PARK AND PRESERVE

© 1999 The MILEPOST®

To Fairbanks

To Paxson

Park Entrance
(See detail map below)

Parks Highway

Denali Highway

Nenana River

Permit required to drive
beyond this point

Savage River

Sanctuary River

Fang Mountain
6,736 ft./2,053m

Cantwell

8

3

The Alaska Railroad

To Anchorage

Sable Mountain
5,923 ft./1,805m

Mount Eielson
5,802 ft./1,768m

Sunset Peak
7,865 ft./2,397m

Eldridge Glacier

Buckskin Glacier

Chitsia Mountain
1,180 ft./360m

Mount Sheldon
5,670 ft./1,728m

Park Road
(Limited Access)

Muldrow Glacier

Mount Deception
11,826 ft./3,605m

Mount Silverthrone
13,220 ft./4,029m

Mount Hunter
14,573 ft./4,442m

Ruth Glacier

Tokositna Glacier

N
E
S
W

Scale

0   10   Miles
0   10   Kilometres

Roads
Paved
Unpaved

Map Location

Kankona Peak
1,512 ft./461m

Wonder Lake

Kantishna

Clearwater Creek

Stony Creek

Peters Glacier

Mount McKinley
20,320 ft./6,194m

Mount Foraker
17,400 ft./5,304m

Foraker Glacier

Herron Glacier

Glacier

Mount Russell
11,670 ft./3,557m

Chedotlothna Glacier

Yenna Glacier

Kahiltna Glacier

East Fork

Ventna River

McKinley River

Slippery Creek

Birch Creek

Foraker River

Kuskokwim River

Swift Fork

Sumber Creek

West Fork

Park Entrance Area

Nenana River

Parks Highway

To Fairbanks

Horseshoe Lake

Visitor Center

The Alaska Railroad

Riley Creek Campground

Railroad Station

3

To Anchorage

Store
Hotel

Park Road

To Kantishna

Park Headquaters

Scale

0   2   Miles
0   2   Kilometres

Look for Dall sheep on the hillsides along the Park Road. (© Mike Jones)

or rainy weather frequently obscures the mountain, and travelers have about a 30 percent chance of seeing it in summer.

First mention of "the mountain" was in 1794, when English explorer Capt. George Vancouver spotted a "stupendous snow mountain" from Cook Inlet. Early Russian explorers and traders called the peak *Bolshaia Gora,* or "Big Mountain." The Athabascan Indian name for the mountain is *Denali,* "the High One." In 1896 a prospector named William A. Dickey named the mountain for presidential nominee William McKinley of Ohio, although McKinley had no connection with Alaska. Even today, the mountain is known by two names: Mount McKinley according to USGS maps, and Denali according to the state Geographic Names Board.

The history of climbs on McKinley is as intriguing as its names. In 1903, Judge James Wickersham and party climbed to an estimated 8,000 feet/2,438m, while the Dr. Frederick A. Cook party reached the 11,000-foot/3,353-m level. In 1906, Cook returned to the mountain and made 2 attempts at the summit—the first unsuccessful, the second (according to Cook) successful. Cook's vague description of his ascent route and a questionable summit photo led many to doubt his claim. The exhaustive research of McKinley expert Bradford Washburn has proven quite conclusively the exaggeration of Cook's claims. Tom Lloyd, of the 1910 Sourdough Party (which included Charles McGonagall, Pete Anderson and Billy Taylor), claimed they had reached both summits (north and south peaks) but could not provide any photographic evidence. (Much later it was verified that they had reached the summit of the lower north peak.) The first complete and well documented ascent of the true summit of Mount McKinley was made in June 1913 by the Rev. Hudson Stuck, Episcopal archdeacon of the Yukon, accompanied by Harry Karstens, Robert Tatum and Walter Harper. Harper, a Native Athabascan, was the first person to set foot on the higher south peak. The story of their achievement was colorfully recorded in Stuck's book, *The Ascent of Denali*.

Today, more than a thousand people attempt to climb Mount McKinley each year between April and June, most flying in to base camp at 7,000 feet/2,134m. (The first airplane landing on the mountain was flown in 1932 by Joe Crosson.) Geographic features of McKinley and its sister peaks bear the names of many early explorers: Eldridge and Muldrow glaciers, after George Eldridge and Robert Muldrow of the U.S. Geographic Service who determined the peak's altitude in 1898; Wickersham Wall; Karstens Ridge; Harper Icefall; and Mount Carpe and Mount Koven, named for Allen Carpe and Theodore Koven, both killed in a 1932 climb.

The National Park Service maintains a ranger station in Talkeetna that is staffed full time from mid-April through mid-September and intermittently during the winter. Mountaineering rangers provide information on climbing within the Alaska Range. A reference library and slide/tape program are available for climbers. Mountaineering regulations and information may be obtained from Talkeetna Ranger Station, P.O. Box 588, Talkeetna, AK 99676; phone (907) 733-2231.

Timberline in the park is at 2,700 feet/823m. The landscape below timberline in this subarctic wilderness is called taiga, a term of Russian origin that describes the scant tree growth. Black and white spruce, willow, dwarf birch and aspen grow at lower elevations. The uplands of alpine tundra are carpeted with lichens, mosses, wildflowers and low-growing shrubs. Wildflowers bloom in spring, usually peaking by early July.

Denali National Park is one of the last intact ecosystems in the world, according to the National Park Service. Here visitors have the opportunity to observe the natural behavior of wild animals. Grizzly bears, caribou, wolves and red foxes wander freely over the tundra. Moose wade through streams and lake shallows. Lynx pursue snowshoe hare in taiga forests. Marmots, pikas and Dall sheep inhabit high, rocky areas. The arctic ground squirrel's sharp warning call is heard throughout the park.

Migratory bird life encompasses species from 6 continents, including waterfowl, shorebirds, songbirds and birds of prey. Ptarmigan, gray jays and magpies are year-round residents.

The park's silty glacial rivers are not an angler's delight, but grayling, Dolly Varden and lake trout are occasionally caught in the clear streams and small lakes.

Emergency Services: Within Denali National Park, phone (907) 683-2294 or 911.

ACCOMMODATIONS/VISITOR SERVICES

There is only 1 hotel within the park, but several motels are on the highway, clustered around the park entrance (turn to **Milepost A 237.3** in the PARKS HIGHWAY section). Accommodations are also available in the Kantishna area. *NOTE: Visitors should make reservations for lodging far in advance.* The park hotel and area motels are often filled during the summer. Visitors must book their own accommodations. See ads for accommodations this section.

Visitor services are available from late May to mid-September, depending on weather. The Denali National Park Hotel has a gift shop, restaurant, snack bar and saloon. Limited groceries and showers are available at a small store near the hotel. Gas is no longer available inside the park. Gas service 1 mile/1.6 km north of the Park Road junc-

www.themilepost.com

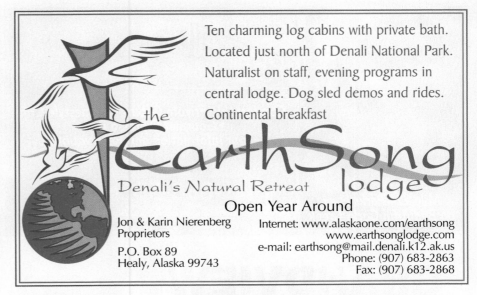
DENALI NATIONAL PARK

Please support our MILEPOST© advertisers.

Campground	Spaces	Tent	Trailer	Pit toilets	Flush toilets	Tap water	Fee
Morino	60	•		•			$12
Riley Creek	102	•	•		•	•	$12
Savage River	33	•	•		•	•	$12
Sanctuary River	7	•		•		•	$12
Teklanika River	50	•	•		•	•	$12
Igloo Creek	7	•		•		•	$12
Wonder Lake	28	•			•	•	$12

tion, May to mid-September. The post office is near the hotel. There is a dump station near Riley Creek Campground.

NOTE: There are no food services in the park after you leave the headquarters entrance area.

Campers should bring rain gear and a tent or waterproof shelter because of frequent rains; also a gasoline or propane stove, or be prepared to purchase firewood from concessionaire.

There are 7 campgrounds in the park along the 92-mile/148.1-km Park Road (see log of Park Road in this section for most locations). Wonder Lake, Sanctuary River and Igloo Creek campgrounds are tent camping only and accessible only by shuttle bus. Riley Creek, Savage River and Teklanika are available for both RV and tent camping. Morino is only for those without vehicles and is not on the reservation system. ▲

The campgrounds are open from about late May to early September, except for Riley Creek, which is open year-round (snow-covered and no water, flush toilets or dump station in winter). There is a fee and a 14-day limit at all campgrounds in summer. Reservations for campsites at Riley Creek, Teklanika River and Savage River campgrounds are available; see Reservation System following. There is a 3-night minimum stay requirement at Teklanika River Campground, and also a limit of one roundtrip to this campground for registered campers with vehicles. Additional travel to and from Teklanika is by shuttle bus. See chart for facilities at each campground. *(NOTE: Campground fees are subject to change!)*

Several private campgrounds are located outside the park along the George Parks Highway. See display ads this section.

For area accommodations, also turn to pages 416-421 in the PARKS HIGHWAY section.

Shuttle bus: The National Park Service concessionaire (Denali Park Resorts) provides shuttle bus service from the Visitor Center to Toklat, Eielson Visitor Center and Wonder Lake. During peak season, bus tickets for the next day's shuttles are generally gone by mid-morning. Up to 8 tickets may be reserved in advance; see Reservation System following. Shuttle buses pick up and drop off passengers along the Park Road on a space-available basis, and stop for scenic and wildlife viewing as schedules permit. The buses generally depart the Visitor Center on the hour and half-hour between 7 A.M. and 2 P.M., May 24 to Sept. 11.

Ticket prices are $12 adult, $6 youth (13–16 years) to Toklat; $20 adult, $10 youth to Eielson; $26 adult, $13 youth to Wonder Lake; and $30 adult, $15 youth to Kantishna. Children 12 and under are free.

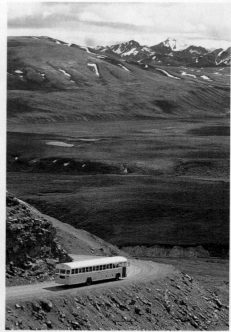

Park shuttle bus along Polychrome Pass. (© Rich Reid)

A round-trip between the Visitor Center and Eielson Visitor Center takes approximately 8 hours. The round-trip to Wonder Lake takes about 11 hours. Bring a lunch, camera, binoculars, extra film, warm clothes and rain gear. Buses run daily from approximately Memorial Day through Labor Day, weather permitting.

Reservation System: Park shuttle bus tickets and campsites may be reserved through a nationwide, toll-free number, 1-800-622-7275 (PARK). Advance reservations (more than 2 days before departure) are available for 40 percent of the bus tickets and campsites. The remaining 60 percent are available 2 days in advance. Anchorage residents and residents of foreign countries phone (907) 272-7275 for reservations. The phone-in reservation system opens in February. The call center is open 7 A.M. to 5 P.M. (Alaska time), 7 days a week. A maximum of 8 shuttle bus tickets may be requested with each call. Shuttle bus and campsite reservations may also be faxed (907/264-4684) or mailed to Denali Park Resorts, Visitor Transportation System, 241 W. Ship Creek Ave., Anchorage, AK 99501, between Dec. 1 and Sept. 1. Mail-in requests must include a check or credit card number with expiration date, and must be received by Denali Park Resorts 30 days prior to your scheduled departure. Tickets that have been requested and paid for prior to the date of departure can be picked up at a dedicated window at the park visitor center. For travel prior to 7 A.M. each day, unclaimed, prepaid reserved tickets will be in the possession of the bus drivers. During peak season, campgrounds fill up by midmorning for the following day and, on occasion, the day after. *NOTE: This reservation system may be revised in 1999.*

Alaskan Chateau Bed and Breakfast. Set on 2 wooded acres with hiking and biking trails. Just minutes to Denali National Park entrance. Private baths, entrances and sun decks, mini kitchens. Satellite TV available. Continental-plus breakfast. Families wel-

Rafting the Nenana River is a popular activity for park visitors. (© Loren Taft)

come. Hosts Teresa Chepoda and Alaskan-born John Usibelli will provide an environ-ment of elegance, hospitality and congenialaity. Call (907) 683-1377; fax (907) 683-1380, or write P.O. Box 187, Healy, AK 99743. [ADVERTISEMENT]

Alaska Raft Adventures. Rafting adven-tures with experienced guides. Our Wilder-ness Run floats through a glacial valley along the park boundary. The Canyon Run offers exciting whitewater action. Courtesy

transportation available between area hotels and the train depot. Stop by the tour desk at McKinley Chalet Resort or McKinley Village Resort. [ADVERTISEMENT]

At Timberline Bed & Breakfast. The view is simply spectacular. Just minutes from Denali. We have 3 rooms with queen beds. Continental breakfast included. The hospitality is warm and our comfortable rooms are very affordable. Your hosts are Dick and Kim White. Dick was born and raised in Alaska and Kim relocated here in 1987 from Wisconsin. Open year round with fantastic viewing of the Northern Lights from our 16-by-32-foot deck. Reservations strongly suggested, but not required. Box 13 Healy, AK 99743. Phone (907) 683-2757. Fax (907) 683-2767. E-mail: white@mail.denali.k12.ak.us. Internet: www.alaskaone.com/. [ADVERTISEMENT]

Carlo Heights Bed and Breakfast and Rick Swenson's Denali Sled Dog School. Share seclusion and spectacular views. Located on bluff overlooking Nenana River and Alaska Range. Accommodations include 2 double rooms and a private suite, full kitchen and laundry facilities. Ask about our sleeping cabin planned for summer 1998! Open year around, reservations recommended during summertime and required during off season. Sled dog school offers dog mushing courses and tours. Box 86, Denali Park, Alaska 99755. (907) 683-1615. www.mosquitonet.com/~birdsong/sbb.html. [ADVERTISEMENT]   MP

Denali Backcountry Lodge. Don't pass up a visit to this lodge if you want to escape the park's crowded east entrance and immerse yourself deep within Denali National Park for a few days. The lodge is located at the end of the 95 mile park road. Full service accommodations feature a comfortable wilderness vacation lodge, cozy cedar cabins, dining room and lounge. One to 4-night stays include round-trip transportation from the train depot, all meals and lodging, guided hikes, wildlife viewing, bicycling, photography and natural history programs. Many famous naturalists are found staying at the lodge and occasionally they

Adult grizzly on the tundra. (© Beth Davidow)

ters—Camp Denali. Since 1951, Alaska's premier small wilderness lodge and nature center. Log cabin lodging with unparalleled views of Mount McKinley. Natural history emphasis, guided backcountry hiking, wildlife observation, canoeing, biking. Special Emphasis series with guest lecturers. Three- and 4-night stays or longer include lodging, all meals and activities, round-trip transportation from park entrance. Brochure: P.O. Box 67, Denali National Park, AK 99755. (907) 683-2290. E-mail: dnpwild@alaska.net. Web site: www.gorp.com/dnpwild. [ADVERTISEMENT]

Denali National Park Wilderness Centers—North Face Lodge. Small, well-appointed inn with spectacular Mount McKinley view. Located in the remote heart of the park near the end of the 90-mile park road. Natural history emphasis, guided backcountry hiking, wildlife observation, canoeing, biking. Two- and three-night stays or

conduct special presentations. Credit cards accepted. P.O. Box 189, Denali National Park, Alaska 99755. www.denalilodge.com. Phone (800) 841-0692. [ADVERTISEMENT]

Denali Crow's Nest Log Cabins and The Overlook Bar & Grill. Open mid-May to mid-September, offering the finest view in area. Close to park entrance. Authentic Alaska log cabins with hotel comforts; all

rooms with private bath. Courtesy transportation. Hot tub, tour bookings. Dine on steaks, seafood, burgers, salmon and halibut indoors or on the deck at The Overlook Bar & Grill. 64 varieties of beer, 9 draft beers; meals 11 A.M. to 11 P.M. Bar open till midnight. For restaurants courtesy shuttle from all local hotels, call (907) 683-2723; fax (907) 683-2323. See display ad in this section. [ADVERTISEMENT]

Denali National Park Hotel. The only hotel in the park is the center for visitor activities. A short walk from the train depot, it provides a dining room, snack shop, gift shop, railcar lounge and grocery store which sells propane. The auditorium hosts National Park Service programs. Tours, rafting and transportation can be arranged. Call (800) 276-7234 or in Anchorage (907) 276-7234. www.denalinationalpark.com. [ADVERTISEMENT]

Denali National Park Wilderness Cen-

longer include lodging, all meals and activities, round-trip transportation from park entrance. Brochure: P.O. Box 67, Denali National Park, AK 99755. (907) 683-2290. E-mail: dnpwild@alaska.net. Web site: www.gorp.com/dnpwild. [ADVERTISEMENT]

Denali Princess Lodge. Riverside lodging near the entrance to Denali National Park featuring spectacular park and Nenana River views, several dining options including Mt. McK's dinner theatre, tour desk, gift shop, complimentary shuttle to rail depot and park activities. Open mid-May through mid-September. Phone (800) 426-0500 year-round. [ADVERTISEMENT]

Denali RV Park and Motel. 90 full and partial RV hookups, 30-amp electric. Pull-throughs, level sites, easy access. RV rates $12-$26 (20% off extra RV nights). $12-$16 low season rates. Caravans welcome! Private restrooms with pay showers, dump station. 14 motel rooms. Double with bath $69; family units with full kitchen and TV $99. Laundry, pay phones, outdoor cooking area, covered meeting area. Gift shop, tour booking, information. Beautiful panoramic mountain views, hiking trails. E-mail access line available. VISA/Mastercard/Discover. Web address: www.denaliRVpark.com. E-mail: stay@denaliRVpark.com. Located 8 miles north of park entrance. (245.1 George Parks Highway) Box 155, Denali National Park, AK 99755. (800) 478-1501, (907) 683-1500. See display ad this section.(907) 683-1500. 1-800-478-1501. See display ad this section. [ADVERTISEMENT] ▲

Denali Wilderness Lodge. Alaska's historic fly-in wilderness lodge. Often called "the most remote hotel in America." Authentic bush homestead, now intimate lodge, nestled in the pristine Wood River Valley. Accessible only by spectacular bush plane flights. Comfortable accommodations, delicious meals, naturalist programs, flight-seeing, horseback riding, river rafting, nature/photo walks and hikes, bird watching, wildlife museum. This will be your best memory of Alaska! Overnight packages and day trips available. Free brochure. Phone (800) 541-9779. E-mail: denwild@alaska.net. Internet: http://www.AlaskaOne.com/dwlodge. See display ad this section. [ADVERTISEMENT] ▲

Kantishna Roadhouse. Premier wilderness lodge located at the quiet west end of Denali National Park offers opportunities to view, photograph and explore the park. Packages include comfortable log cabins with private baths, guided hiking, gold panning, horses, fishing, fine meals and Alaskan hospitality. P.O. Box 130, Denali Park, AK 99755. Phone (800) 942-7420. E-mail: kantshna@polarnet.com. Internet address: www.alaskaone.com/krhouse/. [ADVERTISEMENT] MP

Kantishna Wilderness Trails. The ultimate tour through Denali National Park. 95 miles each way with breathtaking mountain vistas and the likelihood of seeing some of Denali's wildlife en route. Arrive at the Kantishna Roadhouse in time for lunch in the dining room, followed by gold panning or an interpretive program. For reservations phone (800) 942-7420; e-mail: kantshna@polarnet.com. [ADVERTISEMENT]

Lynx Creek Pizza. "The Best Pizza in Alaska!" Hand-dipped ice cream, beer/wine selections. Across the highway from the Park Mart with gas, groceries and liquor store. One mile north of national park entrance (at Mile 238.6 Parks Highway). Phone (907)

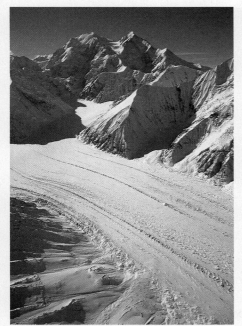

Flightseeing Mt. McKinley is a popular activity. (© Beth Davidow)

683-2547. [ADVERTISEMENT]

McKinley Chalet Resort. The original and largest. 345 rooms. You'll find comfortable mini suites and the largest rooms in Denali. Includes fine dining, lounge, relaxed dining, unique gifts, rafting, gold panning, tours and full-service tour desk. Home of the famous Alaska Cabin Nite Dinner Theatre. Call 1-800-276-7234 or in Anchorage (907) 276-7234. www.denalinationalpark.com. [ADVERTISEMENT]

McKinley Village Resort. Convenient to all activities. Nestled on the banks of the Nenana River, **Milepost A 231.3**, this 150-room, newly remodeled lodge is complete with dining room, lounge, gift shop, rafting and tour desk. Try gold panning at the Denali Mining Company. Call 1-800-276-7234 or in Anchorage (907) 276-7234. www.denalinationalpark.com. [ADVERTISEMENT]

TRANSPORTATION

Highway: Access via the George Parks Highway and the Denali Highway.

The Park Road runs westward 92 miles/148.1 km from the park's east boundary to Kantishna. The road is paved only to Savage River (**Milepost J 14.7**). Private vehicle travel is restricted beyond the Savage River checkpoint at Mile 14.8. Mount McKinley is first visible at about **Milepost J 9** Park Road, but the best views begin at about **Milepost J 60** and continue with few interruptions to Wonder Lake. At the closest point, the summit of the mountain is 27 miles/43.5 km from the road. See log this section.

Air: Charter flights are available from most nearby towns with airfields, and flightseeing tours of the park are offered by operators from the park area or out of Talkeetna,

**Beaver are the largest rodent in
North America.**

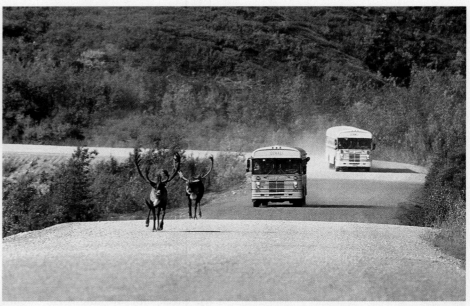

Park tour buses slow down for 2 bull caribou on the Park Road. (© Beth Davidow)

Anchorage or Fairbanks. A round-trip air tour of the park from Anchorage takes 3 to 4 hours. See ads this section.

Era Helicopters. Enjoy an up close eagle-eye view of the grandeur of Denali National Park. Look for wildlife in the valleys and mountainsides below. Glide by numerous glaciers as Mount McKinley towers on the horizon. Guided heli-hiking tours are also available. Located at Milepost 238. Phone (800) 843-1947 or (907) 683-2574, May to September. [ADVERTISEMENT]

Pere Air. Air tours the way they should be! Flightseeing with Pere Air may be your most memorable vacation highlight. Specializing in around the mountain and to the top of Mount McKinley tours. Soar among massive mountain peaks while classical music plays in the background. Two-way headsets allow communication between the pilot and passengers. Record both the sights and sounds of Denali with our modified intercom system for video cameras. Pere Air also offers charter services around the state, dinner tours and fly-in backpacking and biking tours. Twenty years accident-free flying in the Alaskan wilderness. Toll free reservations: 1-877-683-6033. E-mail: pereair@rmci.net. [ADVERTISEMENT]

Railroad: The Alaska Railroad offers daily northbound and southbound trains between Anchorage and Fairbanks, with stops at Denali Park Station, during the summer season. For reservations and information, phone (800) 544-0552.

Midnight Sun Express®. Ultra Domes feature glass-domed ceilings, meals freshly prepared by on-board chefs, and exclusive outdoor viewing platforms. Daily service between Anchorage, Talkeetna, Denali National Park and Fairbanks. Rail packages include overnights at the new Mt. McKinley Princess Lodge and/or Denali Princess Lodge, May through September. Phone (800) 835-8907. [ADVERTISEMENT]

Bus: Daily bus service to the park is available from Anchorage and Fairbanks, and special sightseeing tours are offered throughout the summer months. A 6- to 8-hour guided bus tour of the park is offered by the park concessionaire. Tickets and information are available in the hotel lobby at the front desk tour window. For details on the park shuttle bus system, see Accommodations/Visitor Services this section.

Tours by plane, bus and van are available. See ads this section.

ATTRACTIONS

Organized activities put on by the Park Service include ranger-led nature hikes; sled dog demonstrations at park headquarters; campfire programs at Riley Creek, Savage River, Teklanika River and Wonder Lake campgrounds; and interpretive programs at the hotel auditorium.

Private operators in the park offer flightseeing tours, bus tours, raft tours and wintertime dogsled tours. Cross-country skiing and snowshoeing are also popular in winter.

There are few established trails in the park, but there is plenty of terrain for cross-country hiking. Free permits are required for any overnight hikes.

Permits and information on ranger-led hikes and other activities are available at the Visitor Center near the park entrance.

A FEW SPECIAL NOTES FOR VISITORS

The 1980 federal legislation creating a much larger Denali National Park and Preserve also changed some rules and regulations normally followed in most parks. The following list of park rules and regulations apply in the Denali Wilderness Unit—the part of the park that most people visit. Contact the Superintendent at Denali (Box 9, Denali Park, 99755) for more information on regulations governing the use of aircraft, firearms, snow machines and motorboats in the park additions and in the national preserve units.

For those driving: The Park Road was built for scenic enjoyment and not for high speed. Maximum speed is 35 mph/56 kmph except where lower limits are posted.

Your pets and wildlife don't mix. Pets are allowed only on roadways and in campgrounds and must be leashed or in a vehicle at all times. Pets are not allowed on shuttle buses, trails or in the backcountry.

Backcountry camping permits are

required for hikers who stay overnight and can be obtained only at the Visitor Center, no more than 1 day in advance. A camper bus pass ($15) must be purchased in order to reach most backcountry camping units.

Professional photographer permits are available to qualified applicants, Contact the Chief Ranger at (907) 683-2294.

Mountaineering expeditions are required to acquire a permit and pay a $150 fee before climbing Mount McKinley or Mount Foraker. Permit applications must be received at least 60 days prior to the start of the expedition. Contact the Talkeetna Ranger Station, Box 588, Talkeetna, AK 99676; phone (907) 733-2231.

Natural features: The park was established to protect a natural ecosystem. Destroying, defacing or collecting plants, rocks and other features is prohibited. Capturing, molesting, feeding or killing any animal is prohibited.

Firearms and hunting are not allowed in the wilderness area.

Fishing licenses are not required in the wilderness area; state law is applicable on all other lands. Limits for each person per day are: lake trout—2 fish; grayling and other fish—10 fish or 10 lbs. and 1 fish. Fishing is poor because most rivers are silty and ponds are shallow.

Motor vehicles of any type, including trail bikes, motorcycles and mopeds, may not leave the Park Road.

Feeding wildlife is prohibited. Wild animals need wild food; your food will not help them.

Park Road Log

Distance from the junction (J) with Parks Highway is shown.

J 0 Junction. Turn west off the Parks Highway (Alaska Route 3) at **Milepost A 237.3** onto the Park Road. The Park Road is paved to the Savage River bridge.

J 0.2 (0.3 km) Turnoff for **Riley Creek Campground** and overflow parking area. Make sure you use the dump station located here and get all necessary supplies before prooceeding to campgrounds west of the checkpoint. ▲

J 0.5 (0.8 km) **Visitor Center** has information on all visitor activities as well as shuttle bus tickets and camping and overnight hiking permits. A park orientation program is available in the theater. The center is open daily. This is also the shuttle bus departure point.

J 1.2 (1.9 km) Alaska Railroad crossing. Horseshoe Lake trailhead; length, 1.5 miles/2.4 km round trip, allow about 1 hour..

J 1.4 (2.3 km) Convenience store, showers.

J 1.5 (2.4 km) Denali Park Hotel; post office. Taiga Loop Trail begins and ends at hotel parking lot; length 1.3 miles/2.1 km, allow 1-hour round trip.

J 1.6 (2.6 km) Denali Park Station (elev. 1,730 feet/527m), where visitors can make train connections to Anchorage and Fairbanks; daily service during the summer. Denali Park Hotel is across from the depot.

Private Aircraft: McKinley Park airstrip, 1.7 miles/2.7 km northeast of park headquarters; elev. 1,720 feet/524m; length 3,000

feet/914m; gravel; unattended.

J 3.5 (5.6 km) Park headquarters. This is the administration area for Denali National Park and Preserve. In winter, information on all visitor activities can be obtained here. Report accidents and emergencies to the rangers; phone (907) 683-9100 or 911, or outside Alaska (907) 474-7722. NOTE: There are no telephones west of this point.

J 5.5 (8.9 km) Paved turnout with litter barrel. Sweeping view of countryside. There are numerous small turnouts along the Park Road.

J 12.8 (20.6 km) **Savage River Campground** (elev. 2,780 feet/847m); 3 group tent sites (9 to 20 people each); advance reservations required. ▲

J 14.7 (23.7 km) Bridge over the Savage River. Blacktop pavement ends. Access to river, toilet and picnic tables at east end of bridge.

J 14.8 (23.8 km) Savage River check station. PERMIT OR SHUTTLE/BUS TICKET REQUIRED BEYOND THIS POINT.

NOTE: Road travel permits for access to the Kantishna area are issued at park headquarters only under special conditions; however, the road may be open to all vehicles to Milepost 30 in early May and late September, weather permitting.

J 17.3 (27.8 km) Viewpoint of the Alaska Range and tundra.

J 21.3 (34.3 km) Hogan Creek bridge.

J 22 (35.4 km) Sanctuary River bridge, ranger station and **Sanctuary River Campground** (tents only). ▲

J 29.1 (46.8 km) **Teklanika River Campground**, elev. 2,580 feet/786m; 3-night minimum stay. Grizzly bears may sometimes be seen on the gravel bars nearby. ▲

J 30.7 (49.4 km) Rest area with chemical toilets.

J 31.3 (50.4 km) Bridge over Teklanika River.

J 34.1 (54.9 km) **Igloo Creek Campground** (tents only); accessible by shuttle

Willow ptarmigan in winter. (© Nancy Faville)

bus only. ▲

J 37 (59.5 km) Igloo Creek bridge. *NOTE: The area within 1 mile/1.6 km of each side of the Park Road from Milepost J 38.3 to J 42.9 is closed to all off-road foot travel as a special wildlife protection area.* Toklat grizzlies are often seen in the area.

J 39.1 (62.9 km) **Sable Pass** (elev. 3,900 feet/1,189m).

J 43.4 (69.8 km) Bridge over East Fork Toklat River. Views of Polychrome Mountain, the Alaska Range and several glaciers are visible along the East Fork from open country south of the road.

J 45.9 (73.9 km) Summit of **Polychrome Pass** (elev. 3,700 feet/1,128m); rest stop with toilets. The broad valley of the Toklat River is visible below to the south. Good hiking in alpine tundra above the road.

J 53.1 (85.5 km) Bridge over the Toklat River. The Toklat and all other streams crossed by the Park Road drain into the Tanana River, a tributary of the Yukon River.

J 53.7 (86.4 km) Ranger station.

J 58.3 (93.8 km) Summit of **Highway Pass** (elev. 3,980 feet/1,213m). This is the highest point on the Park Road.

J 61 (98.2 km) Stony Hill (elev. 4,508 feet/1,374m). A good view of Mount McKinley and the Alaska Range on clear days.

J 62 (99.8 km) Viewpoint.

J 64.5 (103.8 km) **Thorofare Pass** (elev. 3,900 feet/1,189m).

J 66 (106.2 km) **Eielson Visitor Center**. Ranger-led hikes, nature programs, displays, restrooms and drinking water. Film, maps and natural history publications for sale. Report accidents and emergencies here.

Excellent Mount McKinley viewpoint. On clear days the north and south peaks of Mount McKinley are visible to the southwest. The impressive glacier, which drops from the mountain and spreads out over the valley floor at this point, is the Muldrow.

For several miles beyond the visitor center the road cut drops about 300 feet/91m to the valley below, paralleling the McKinley River.

J 84.6 (136.1 km) Access road leads left, westbound, to **Wonder Lake Campground** (elev. 2,090 feet/637m). Tents only; campground access by shuttle bus only. An excellent Mount McKinley viewpoint. ▲

The road continues to Wonder Lake, where rafting and canoeing are permitted (no rental boats available).

J 85.6 (137.8 km) Reflection Pond, a kettle lake formed by a glacier.

J 86.6 (139.4 km) Wonder Lake ranger station.

J 87.7 (141.1 km) Moose Creek bridge.

J 88 (141.6 km) North Face Lodge.

J 88.2 (141.9 km) Camp Denali.

J 91 (146.4 km) **KANTISHNA** (pop. 2 in winter, 135 in summer; elev. 1,750 feet/533m). Established in 1905 as a mining camp at the junction of Eureka and Moose creeks. Most of the area around Kantishna is private property and there may be active mining on area creeks in summer. Kantishna Roadhouse, which consists of a dozen log guest cabins and a dining hall, comprises the townsite of Kantishna.

Private Aircraft: Kantishna airstrip, 1.3 miles/2.1 km northwest; elev. 1,575 feet/480m; length 1,850 feet/564m; gravel; unattended, no regular maintenance.

J 91.8 (147.7 km) Mt. McKinley Gold Camp.

J 92 (148.1 km) Denali Backcountry Lodge.

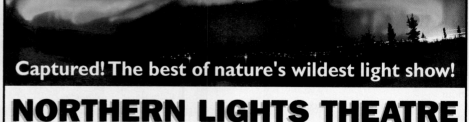

DENALI HIGHWAY ⑧

Connects: Paxson to Cantwell, AK   **Length:** 136 miles
Road Surface: Gravel   **Season:** Closed in winter
Highest Summit: Maclaren Summit 4,086 feet
Major Attraction: Tangle Lakes–Delta River Canoe Trail
(See map, page 482)

	Cantwell	Delta Junction	Denali Park	Paxson
Cantwell		217	27	136
Delta Junction	217		244	81
Denali Park	27	244		163
Paxson	136	81	163	

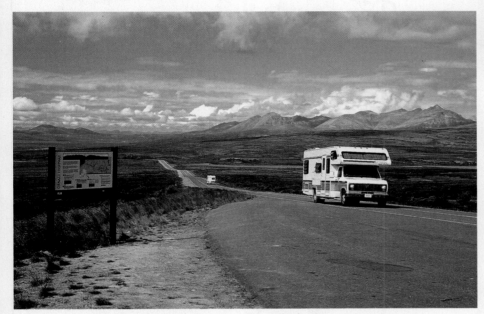

The Denali Highway offers broad vistas of the Alaska Range (© Craig Brandt)

The Denali Highway extends 135.5 miles/218.1 km from Paxson at Milepost V 185.5 on the Richardson Highway to Cantwell, about 2 miles/3.2 km west of Milepost A 209.9 on the Parks Highway. The first 21 miles/33.8 km from Paxson are paved and the rest is gravel. *NOTE: Watch for paving in summer 1999.* The highway is closed from October to mid-May. Do not attempt to drive this highway in the off-season.

The condition of the gravel portion of the highway varies, depending on highway maintenance, weather and the opinion of the driver. The road surface is rough; washboard can develop quickly. Much of the road is in need of gravel, but the roadbed is solid. This can be a dusty and bumpy drive in dry weather. Watch for potholes in wet weather. The Denali Highway becomes progressively narrower and more winding from east to west.

There are dozens of primitive campsites and turnouts along the highway (heavily used by hunters during caribou and moose seasons). Excellent fishing in lakes and streams accessible on foot or via designated off-road vehicle trails. Highway access to the Delta River canoe trail through the Tangle Lakes, headwaters of the Delta National Wild, Scenic and Recreational River System, is at **Milepost P 21.5**. The Denali Highway is popular with mountain bikers. There are also many unmarked trails leading off into the Bush. Inquire locally and carry a good topographic map when hiking off the highway.

The Denali Highway has very beautiful scenery and some interesting geography. Glacier-formed features visible from the road include: moraines (drift deposited by glaciers); kames (conical hills or terraces of gravel and sand); kettle lakes (holes formed by blocks of ice melting); and eskers (ridges of gravel formed by streams flowing under glaciers).

Tangle Lakes Archaeological District lies between **Milepost P 17** and **P 35**. Within this 226,000-acre area, more than 400 archaeological sites chronicle man's seasonal exploitation of the local natural resources. For more than 10,000 years, hunter-gatherers have dug roots, picked berries, fished and hunted big game (primarily caribou) in this area. You may hike along the same high, gravel ridges once used by prehistoric people and used today by modern hunters, anglers and berry pickers.

Off-road vehicles are permitted within the district, although some restrictions are in effect spring through fall.

Information on Tangle Lakes Archaeological District and off-road vehicle use is available at the lodges along the Denali Highway and at the Bureau of Land Management office in Glennallen. Write BLM, Box 147, Glennallen, AK 99588; or phone (907) 822-3217.

The Denali Highway was the only road link to Denali National Park and Preserve (formerly Mount McKinley National Park) prior to completion of the Parks Highway in 1972. Before the Denali Highway opened in 1957, Denali National Park was accessible only via the Alaska Railroad.

Emergency medical services: Between Paxson and **Milepost P 77.5** (Susitna Lodge), phone 911 or the state troopers at (907) 822-3263. Between **Milepost P 77.5** and Cantwell, phone the Cantwell ambulance at (907) 768-2982 or the state troopers at (907) 768-2202.

Denali Highway Log

Distance from Paxson (P) is followed by distance from Cantwell (C).

P 0 C 135.5 (218.1 km) PAXSON (pop. 33; elev. 2,650 feet/808m). Paxson Lodge with restaurant, gas station and post office at junction of Denali Highway and Richardson Highway.

Private Aircraft: Paxson airstrip, adjacent south; elev. 2,653 feet/809m; length 2,800 feet/853m; gravel; emergency fuel; attended.

Paxson Inn & Lodge. See display ad this section.

Junction of the Richardson Highway (Alaska Route 4) with the Denali Highway (Alaska Route 8). Turn to **Milepost V 185.5** in the RICHARDSON HIGHWAY section for log.

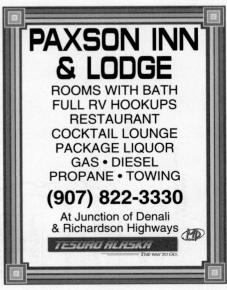

DENALI HIGHWAY *Paxson, AK, to Cantwell, AK*

© 1999 The MILEPOST®

To Tok
(see ALASKA HIGHWAY
section, page 83)

Icefall Peak ▲

Trans-Alaska
Pipeline

Delta Junction

To Fairbanks
(see RICHARDSON HIGHWAY section, page 509)

P-0
C-136/218km
DJ-80/129km
G-71/113km

N63°02'
W145°29'

Paxson

♠ P-0 Paxson Inn &
Lodge CDgGILMPT

To Glennallen
(see RICHARDSON
HIGHWAY section,
page 509)

P-0.2/0.3km Paxson
Alpine Tours L

P-18.5/29.8km Denali
Highlands Adventures

Gulkana River

Summit
Lake

Fielding
L

Sevenmile
Lake

Long Tangle Lake

Round
Tangle L

Little
Swede
Lake

Swede Lake

Lower Tangle Lake

Landmark
Gap
Lake

Upper Tangle
Lake

P-20/32.2km Tangle River Inn GLM

P-22/35.4km Tangle Lakes Lodge LM

Maclaren Summit
4,086 ft./1,245m

Maclaren Glacier

Rock Creek

Mount Hayes
13,832 ft./4,216m ▲

Glaciated

Area

Hess Mountain ▲
11,940 ft./3,639m

Mount Deborah ▲
12,339 ft./3,761m

West Fork Glacier

Susitna Glacier

East Fork

ALASKA

RANGE

Yanert Fork

Nenana River

Susitna River

Clearwater
River

Maclaren
River

P-42/68km
C-94/151km

Creek

Roosevelt Lake

Windy Creek

○ Denali

P-82/132km Gracious House CGILMr

Hatchet
Lake

Closed in Winter

Susitna
River

Susitna River

P-99.5/160.1km Adventures
Unlimited Lodge CLM

Butte Lake

Snodgrass Lake

P-80/128km
C-56/90km

Bruchkana

Stikkwan Creek

Seattle

Lily Cr.

Creek

To Fairbanks
(see PARKS HIGHWAY section)

The Alaska Railroad

Park Road

Denali National
Park and Preserve

P-136/218km
C-0
A-210/338km
F-148/238km

N63°23'
W148°56'
Cantwell

To Anchorage
(see PARKS HIGHWAY
section)

N W—E S

Key to mileage boxes
miles/kilometres
miles/kilometres
from:

P-Paxson
C-Cantwell
DJ-Delta Junction
A-Anchorage
F-Fairbanks
G-Glennallen

**Key to Advertiser
Services**
C -Camping
D -Dump Station
d -Diesel
G -Gas (reg., unld.)
I -Ice
L -Lodging
M-Meals
P -Propane
R -Car Repair (major)
r -Car Repair (minor)
S -Store (grocery)
T -Telephone (pay)

Map Location

Principal Route
Paved   Unpaved
Other Roads
Paved   Unpaved
Ferry Routes **Hiking Trails**
······· Refer to Log for Visitor Facilities

Scale
0   10 Miles
0   10 Kilometres

www.themilepost.com

ALASKA ROUTE 8

P 0.2 (0.3 km) C 135.3 (217.7 km) **Paxson Alpine Tours.** See display ad this section.

Gulkana River bridge; parking at west end. In season, spawning salmon may be seen here. This portion of the Gulkana River is off-limits to salmon fishing.

P 0.3 (0.5 km) C 135.2 (217.6 km) Entering Paxson Closed Area westbound. This area is closed to the taking of all big game. Side road leads south to Mud Lake.

Westbound, there are many long steep upgrades and many turnouts the next 21 miles/33.8 km. Wildflowers carpet the tundra in the spring and summer. Watch for nesting swans.

P 1.1 (1.8 km) C 134.4 (216.3 km) **Mud Lake** below highway; early grayling fishing.

P 3.6 (5.8 km) C 131.9 (212.3 km) Paved turnout to south. Several more turnouts next 3 miles/5 km westbound with views of Summit Lake to the north. Gakona Glacier to the northeast and Icefall Peak to the west of the glacier; and Gulkana Glacier west of Icefall Peak.

P 6.8 (10.9 km) C 128.7 (207.1 km) Access to **Sevenmile Lake** 0.8 mile/1.3 km north; excellent fishing for lake trout in summer.

P 7.1 (11.4 km) C 128.4 (206.6 km) Paved turnout to south.

P 7.3 (11.7 km) C 128.2 (206.3 km) Gravel turnout overlooking Sevenmile Lake. Two Bit Lake is the large lake to the north; Summit Lake is to the northeast.

P 7.5 (12.1 km) C 128 (206 km) Paved turnout to north overlooking Sevenmile Lake. Summit Lake visible to east.

P 8.7 (14 km) C 126.8 (204.1 km) Entering BLM lands westbound; federal hunting regulations apply.

P 9 (14.5 km) C 126.5 (203.6 km) Gravel turnout. Entering BLM public lands westbound.

P 10.1 (16.3 km) C 125.4 (201.8 km) Paved turnout to south overlooking **Ten Mile Lake.** Short hike downhill to outlet. Fishing for lake trout, grayling and burbot in summer.

P 10.6 (17.1 km) C 124.9 (201 km) Paved turnout overlooking **Teardrop Lake** to south. Short hike down steep hill to lake; lake trout, grayling and burbot in summer.

For the next 4 miles/6.4 km westbound, there are wide-open spaces with magnificent views of the great Denali country. Look for kettle lakes and kames.

P 11.1 (17.9 km) C 124.4 (200.2 km) Paved turnout and trail to **Octopus Lake** 0.3 mile/0.5 km south; lake trout, grayling,

whitefish.

P 11.8 (19 km) C 123.7 (199.1 km) Paved turnout to south.

P 13.1 (21.1 km) C 122.4 (197 km) Viewpoint at summit; interpretive plaque. In the spring from this spot a traveler can count at least 40 lakes and potholes. To the southeast are Mount Sanford, Mount Drum and Mount Wrangell in the Wrangell Mountain range.

Highway begins descent westbound to Tangle Lakes area. Lupine blooms alongside the road in late June.

P 14.5 (23.3 km) C 121 (194.7 km) Paved turnout and small lakes to north.

P 15 (24.1 km) C 120.5 (193.9 km) Swede Lake trail, 3 miles/4.8 km long, to south; **Little Swede Lake**, 2 miles/3.2 km. This trail connects with the Middle Fork Gulkana River branch trail (access to Dickey Lake and Meier Lake trail) and the Alphabet Hills trail. **Big Swede Lake** has excellent fishing for lake trout, grayling, whitefish and burbot. Little Swede Lake is excellent for lake trout. Inquire at Tangle River Inn for directions.

P 16.5 (26.6 km) C 119 (191.5 km) Entering Tangle Lakes Archaeological district westbound.

P 16.8 (27 km) C 118.7 (191 km) **16.8 Mile Lake** to north (walk up creek 200 yards); lake trout and grayling. **Rusty Lake**, 0.5 mile/0.8 km northwest of 16.8 Mile Lake; lake trout and grayling.

P 17 (27.4 km) C 118.5 (190.7 km) **17 Mile Lake** to north, turnout at west end of lake; lake trout and grayling fishing.

P 17.7 (28.5 km) C 117.8 (189.6 km) Paved turnouts both sides of highway.

P 18.1 (29.1 km) C 117.4 (188.9 km)

Hoary marmot. (© Craig Brandt)

Paved turnouts both sides of highway.

P 18.2 (29.3 km) C 117.3 (188.8 km) Paved turnout with lake access on both sides of highway.

P 18.4 (29.6 km) C 117.1 (188.4 km) Gravel turnout by **Denali–Clearwater Creek;** grayling fishing.

P 18.5 (29.8 km) C 117 (188.3 km) **Denali Highlands Adventures.** See display ad this section.

P 18.8 (30.2 km) C 116.7 (187.8 km) Paved turnout to north.

P 19.6 (31.5 km) C 115.9 (186.5 km) Paved turnout to south.

P 20 (32.2 km) **C 115.5** (185.9 km) **Tangle River Inn**, known for our cleanliness and warm atmosphere. Restaurant with full menu featuring delicious home-style cooking. Karaoke bar, liquor store, game room. Cozy cabins, log cabin with 5 rooms, 10 beds and private bath—wonderful for groups or families. Newly remodeled rooms with bathrooms. Great fishing, hunting, hiking, berry picking and bird watching. Jack and Naidine Johnson, original owners for over 28 years. Come, meet our friendly crew that's been here for years—a memorable experience. See display ad. [ADVERTISEMENT]

P 20.1 (32.3 km) **C 115.4** (185.7 km) Large paved turnout to north overlooking lake.

P 20.6 (33.2 km) **C 114.9** (184.9 km) Paved parking area with toilet to north.

P 21 (33.8 km) **C 114.5** (184.3 km) The Nelchina caribou herd travels through this area, usually around the end of August or early in September.

P 21.3 (34.3 km) **C 114.2** (183.8 km) Pavement ends westbound.

NOTE: Watch for road paving westbound in summer 1999.

P 21.4 (34.4 km) **C 114.1** (183.6 km) One-lane bridge over Tangle River.

P 21.5 (34.6 km) **C 114** (183.5 km) Tangle Lakes BLM campground and wayside, 0.7 mile/1.1 km north from highway on shore of Round Tangle Lake; 13 sites, toilets, boat launch, picnicking, hiking (no thick brush, good views). Blueberry picking in August. ▲

Easy access to boat launch for Delta River canoe trail, which goes north through Tangle Lakes to the Delta River. The 2- to 3-day float to the take-out point on the Richardson Highway requires 1 portage. The Delta National Wild, Scenic and Recreational River system is managed by the BLM. For details on this river trail or the Gulkana River trail, contact the BLM, Box 147, Glennallen, AK 99588; phone (907) 822-3217.

Watershed divide. The Gulkana River joins the Copper River, which flows into Prince William Sound. The Delta River joins the Tanana River, which flows into the Yukon River. The Yukon flows into the Bering Sea.

P 21.7 (34.9 km) **C 113.8** (183.1 km) Tangle River BLM campground to south; toilets, water pump, boat launch. Watch for caribou on surrounding hills. Watch for arctic warblers nesting along the Tangle River. ▲

The name Tangle is a descriptive term for the maze of lakes and feeder streams contained in this drainage system. Access to Upper Tangle Lakes canoe trail, which goes south through Tangle Lakes (portages required) to Dickey Lake, then follows the Middle Fork to the main Gulkana River.

AREA FISHING: Tangle Lakes system north and south of the highway (**Long Tangle**, **Round Tangle**, **Upper Tangle** and **Lower Tangle Lake**). Good grayling, burbot and lake trout fishing. Fishing begins as soon as the ice goes out, usually in early June, and continues into September. Good trolling, and some fish are taken from the banks. Early in season, trout are hungry and feed on snails in the shallows at the outlet. Inquire at Tangle Lakes Lodge or Tangle River Inn for information and assistance in getting to where the fish are.

P 22 (35.4 km) **C 113.5** (182.6 km) **Tangle Lakes Lodge**, built in 1952, was the first lodge on the Denali Highway. Owned for the last 8 years by longtime Alaska residents Rich and Linda Homstrom, it has become well known for its fine food and friendly atmosphere. In addition to being the best Arctic grayling fishery you can drive to in Alaska, Tangle Lakes also provides incredible birding opportunities (arctic warbler, Smith's longspur, gyrfalcon, long-tailed jaeger and many more). The Nelchina caribou herd, 50,000 strong, roams throughout the region, which is also a moose calving area, providing excellent wildlife viewing opportunities. Cozy log cabins, canoe rentals, fine food, accurate local information and a friendly lodge staff makes a stop at Tangle Lakes Lodge a most memorable one. Phone: (907) 688-9173 (winter) or (907) 259-7302 (summer). [ADVERTISEMENT]

P 22.3 (35.9 km) **C 113.2** (182.2 km) Trail to south along esker.

P 24.8 (39.9 km) **C 110.7** (178.1 km) Landmark Gap BLM trail to north open to ORVs to **Landmark Gap Lake**. Grayling in stream at trail end; trout in main lake. Mountain biking is also popular on this trail. Double-ended turnout to south.

P 24.9 (40.1 km) **C 110.6** (178 km) **Rock Creek** 1-lane bridge; parking and informal campsites at both ends of bridge. Fair grayling fishing. Landmark Gap Lake lies north of highway between the noticeable gap in the mountains (a caribou migration route).

P 28.1 (45.2 km) **C 107.4** (172.8 km) Downwind Lake north side of road.

P 30.6 (49.2 km) **C 104.9** (168.8 km) Cat trail leads 2 miles/3.2 km north to **Glacier Lake**; lake trout, grayling.

P 32 (51.5 km) **C 103.5** (166.6 km) Amphitheater Mountains rise above High Valley to the north. Glacier Lake is visible in the gap in these mountains. Turnout to north.

P 32.1 (51.6 km) **C 103.4** (166.4 km) Rough side road to turnout to north.

P 35.2 (56.6 km) **C 100.3** (161.4 km)

Gravel turnout. A profusion of flowers: various heaths, frigid shooting star, dwarf fireweed.

P 36 (57.9 km) **C 99.5** (160.1 km) **36 Mile Lake** 0.5-mile/0.8-km hike north; lake trout and grayling.

P 36.4 (58.6 km) **C 99.1** (159.5 km) Entering Clearwater Creek controlled-use area westbound. Closed to motorized hunting. Small turnouts to north and south.

P 36.6 (58.9 km) **C 98.9** (159.2 km) Osar Lake ORV trail leads 5 miles/8 km south toward the Alphabet Hills. Osar Lake was first named Asar Lake, the Scandinavian word for esker. (An esker is a ridge of sand and gravel marking the former stream channel of a glacier.)

P 36.9 (59.4 km) **C 98.6** (158.7 km) Maclaren Summit trail leads 3 miles/4.8 km north to good view of Alaska Range; mountain biking.

P 37 (59.5 km) **C 98.5** (158.5 km) **Maclaren Summit** (elev. 4,086 feet/1,245m). Highest highway pass in Alaska (not including 4,800-foot/1,463-m Atigun Pass on the Dalton Highway). Turnout with view of Susitna River valley, Mount Hayes and the Alaska Range.

P 37.8 (60.8 km) **C 97.7** (157.2 km) Leaving Tangle Lakes Archaeological district westbound.

P 39.8 (64.1 km) **C 95.7** (154 km) Sevenmile Lake ORV trail to north; 6.5 miles/10.5 km long, parallels Boulder Creek, crosses peat bog.

P 42 (67.6 km) **C 93.5** (150.5 km) **Maclaren River Bridge**, a 364-foot/111-m multiple span crossing this tributary of the Susitna River. Parking and litter barrels. Maclaren River Lodge to south on west side of bridge; boat launch (pay fee at lodge). Look for cliff swallows nesting under bridge.

P 43.3 (69.7 km) **C 92.2** (148.4 km) Maclaren River Road leads north 12 miles/19.3 km to Maclaren Glacier; mountain biking. Maclaren River trailhead to south. The Maclaren River rises in the glaciers surrounding Mount Hayes (elev. 13,832 feet/4,216m). For the next 60 miles/96.6 km westbound, the highest peaks of this portion of the mighty Alaska Range are visible, weather permitting, to the north. From east to west: Mount Hayes, Hess Mountain (elev. 11,940 feet/3,639m) and Mount Deborah (elev. 12,339 feet/3,761m). Mount Hayes, first climbed in August 1941, is named after Charles Hayes, an early member of the U.S. Geological Survey. Mount Deborah, first climbed in August 1954, was named in 1907 by Judge Wickersham after his wife.

P 44.6 (71.8 km) **C 90.9** (146.3 km) Highway crosses Crazy Notch gap.

P 46.9 (75.5 km) **C 88.6** (142.6 km) Road north to **46.9 Mile Lake**; fishing for grayling in lake and outlet stream.

P 47 (75.6 km) **C 88.5** (142.4 km) Beaver dam. Excellent grayling fishing in **Crooked Creek**, which parallels the highway.

P 48.6 (78.2 km) **C 86.9** (139.8 km) Informal campsite by small lake.

P 49 (78.8 km) **C 86.5** (139.2 km) The road follows an esker between 4 lakes. Parts of the highway are built on eskers. Watch for ptarmigan, swans, arctic terns, ducks and beaver. Look for a pingo (earth-covered ice hill) at lakeshore.

P 49.6 (79.8 km) **C 85.9** (138.2 km) Turnout to north.

P 49.7 (80 km) **C 85.8** (138.1 km) Turnout to north overlooks 50 Mile lake. Interpretive plaque on glacial topography

Susitna River bridge on the Denali Highway. (© Tom Culkin)

and wildlife, including trumpeter swans and loons. Road access to north.

P 51.8 (83.4 km) **C 83.7** (134.7 km) Private hunting camp to south. Trail to north.

P 56.1 (90.3 km) **C 79.4** (127.8 km) **Clearwater Creek** 1-lane bridge. Rest area with toilet west side of bridge; informal camping. Grayling fishing in summer.

P 57.8 (93 km) **C 77.7** (125 km) Clearwater Creek walk-in (no motorized vehicles) hunting area north of highway.

P 58.8 (94.6 km) **C 76.7** (123.4 km) Road winds atop an esker flanked by kames and kettle lakes. Watch for moose.

P 60 (96.5 km) **C 75.5** (121.5 km) Hunting trail to south.

P 64 (103 km) **C 71.5** (115.1 km) Road descends westbound into Susitna Valley. Highest elevation of mountains seen to north is 5,670 feet/1,728m.

P 70 (112.6 km) **C 65.5** (105.4 km) Great view westbound of Susitna Valley and lakes (moose habitat).

P 74 (119.1 km) **C 61.5** (99 km) Side road north to lakes; informal camping.

P 75 (120.7 km) **C 60.5** (97.4 km) Clearwater Mountains to north; watch for bears on slopes. View of Susitna River in valley below.

P 77 (123.9 km) **C 58.5** (94.1 km) **Private Aircraft:** Private airstrip, adjacent west; elev. 2,675 feet/815m; length 2,000 feet/610m; gravel.

P 77.5 (124.7 km) **C 58** (93.3 km) Lodge; current status of services unknown.

P 78.8 (126.8 km) **C 56.7** (91.2 km) Valdez Creek Road. Former mining camp of Denali, about 6 miles/10 km north of the highway via a gravel road, was first established in 1907 after the discovery of gold in 1903. The Valdez Creek Mine operated at this site from 1990 to 1995. The mine pit was converted into a lake in 1996 as part of a reclamation project. Area mining equipment was donated to the Museum of Transportation and Industry (see **Milepost A 47** in the PARKS HIGHWAY section). Do not trespass on private mining claims. Fair fishing reported in **Roosevelt Lake** and area creeks. Watch for bears.

P 79.3 (127.6 km) **C 56.2** (90.4 km) **Susitna River Bridge** (1-lane), a combination multiple span and deck truss, 1,036 feet/316m long. Butte Creek trailhead.

The Susitna River heads at Susitna Glacier in the Alaska Range (between Mounts Hess and Hayes) and flows southwest 260 miles/418 km to Cook Inlet. Downstream through Devil's Canyon it is considered unfloatable. The river's Tanaina Indian name, said to mean "sandy river," first appeared in 1847 on a Russian chart.

Entering Game Management Unit 13E westbound, leaving unit 13B eastbound.

P 80.3 (129.2 km) **C 55.2** (88.8 km) Turnout to north (used by hunters in season; watch for ATVs on road).

P 81 (130.4 km) **C 54.5** (87.7 km) Gracious House campground on lake to north.

P 82 (132 km) **C 53.5** (86.1 km) **Gracious House.** Centrally located on the shortest, most scenic route to Denali National Park. 27 modern units including a large den with

There's camping and fishing along the Denali Highway. (© Craig Brandt)

adjoining rooms for groups, most with private baths. Bed and breakfast atmosphere. Bar and cafe featuring ice cream and home-baked pies. Tent sites, parking for self-contained RVs overlooking lake. Water, restrooms and showers available at lodge. Gas, towing, welding, mechanical repairs, tire service. Air taxi, for the most beautiful scenic flights in Alaska. Guide service available for birding, hiking, biking, fishing, hunting and photography tours. Northern Lights viewing and winter snowmobiling. Same owners/operators for 42 years. Reasonable rates. For brochure on hunting and fishing trips, write to the Gracious Family. Summer address: P.O. Box 88, Cantwell, AK 99729. Winter address: P.O. Box 212549, Anchorage, AK 99521. Message phone (907) 333-3148 or phone (907) 822-7307 (let ring, radio phone). E-mail: crhoa36683@aol.com/. Internet: www.alaskaone.com/gracious. [ADVERTISEMENT]

MP ▲

P 83 (133.6 km) C 52.5 (84.5 km) Visible across the Susitna River is Valdez Creek mining camp at the old Denali townsite. Valdez Creek Mine is operated by Cambior Alaska Inc. *CAUTION: Watch for truck traffic.*

P 84 (135.2 km) C 51.5 (82.9 km) **Stevenson's Lake** 0.5 mile/0.8 km south; grayling fishing. ⬤➤

P 90.5 (145.6 km) C 45 (72.4 km) A major water drainage divide occurs near here. East of the divide, the tributary river system of the Susitna flows south to Cook Inlet. West of the divide, the Nenana River system flows north to the Yukon River, which empties into the Bering Sea.

P 93.8 (151 km) C 41.7 (67.1 km) **Butte Lake**, 5 miles/8 km south of highway. Motorized access by all-terrain vehicle from lodge at **Milepost P 99.5**. Best fishing June through September. Lake trout to 30 lbs., troll with red-and-white spoons or grayling remains; grayling to 20 inches, small flies or spinners; burbot to 12 lbs., use bait on bottom. ⬤➤

P 94.3 (151.8 km) C 41.2 (66.3 km) Short road north leads to parking area above pond. View of Monahan Flat and Alaska Range to the north. Interpretive plaque on earthquakes.

P 94.8 (152.6 km) C 40.7 (65.5 km) Bridge over Canyon Creek.

P 96.3 (155 km) C 39.2 (63.1 km) Rough narow side road north up to viewpoint of the West Fork Glacier. Looking north up the face of this glacier, Mount Deborah is to the left and Hess Mountain is in the center.

P 97 (156.1 km) C 38.5 (62 km) Looking at the Alaska Range to the north, Mount Deborah, Hess Mountain and Mount Hayes are the highest peaks to your right; to the left are the lower peaks of the Alaska Range and Nenana Mountain.

P 99.5 (160.1 km) C 36 (57.9 km) **Adventures Unlimited Lodge.** Only $55/double includes breakfast! Very popular stopover before or after visiting Denali Park. Remote, hike-in cabin with great fishing and boat available. Cafe serving great food and fresh pies. Phone (907) 561-0132, fax (907) 561-2093, e-mail mis@goalaska.com. Web site: http://www.goalaska.com. See display ad. [ADVERTISEMENT]

P 100 (160.9 km) C 35.5 (57.1 km) Residents of this area say it is a wonderful place for picking cranberries and blueberries in August. Numerous turnouts and some patches of rough road next 3 miles westbound.

P 103 (165.8 km) C 32.5 (52.3 km) Highway is built on an esker between kettle lakes.

P 104.6 (168.3 km) C 30.9 (49.7 km) **Brushkana River** Bridge. BLM campground to north at west end of bridge; 12 sites beside river, tables, firepits, toilets, litter bar-

rels and water. Fishing for grayling and Dolly Varden. Watch for moose. ⬤▲

P 106.6 (171.6 km) C 28.9 (46.5 km) **Canyon Creek**, grayling fishing. ⬤➤

P 107.2 (172.5 km) C 28.3 (45.5 km) **Stixkwan Creek** flows under highway in culvert. Grayling. ⬤➤

P 110.5 (177.8 km) C 25 (40.2 km) *CAUTION: Steep downgrade westbound; trucks use low gear.*

P 111.2 (179 km) C 24.3 (39.1 km) **Seattle Creek** 1-lane bridge. Fishing for grayling and Dolly Varden. ⬤➤

P 111.5 (179.4 km) C 24 (38.6 km) Turnout with vista.

P 112 (180.2 km) C 23.5 (37.8 km) Lily Creek. Matanuska–Susitna Borough boundary.

P 113.2 (182.2 km) C 22.3 (35.9 km) View to east of the Alaska Range and extensive rolling hills grazed by caribou.

P 115.7 (186.2 km) C 19.8 (31.9 km) Large gravel turnout with beautiful view of the Nenana River area.

P 116 (186.7 km) C 19.5 (31.4 km) Turnout with interpretive sign. *Steep downgrade westbound.*

P 117.1 (188.4 km) C 18.4 (29.6 km) Highway parallels the Nenana River, which flows into the Tanana River at the town of Nenana.

P 117.5 (189.1 km) C 18 (29 km) Leaving BLM public lands westbound.

P 120.7 (194.2 km) C 14.8 (23.8 km) Large gravel turnout.

P 121 (194.7 km) C 14.5 (23.3 km) Turnout at gravel pit.

P 122.3 (196.8 km) C 11.3 (18.2 km) View westbound (weather permitting) of Mount McKinley.

P 125.7 (202.3 km) C 9.8 (15.8 km) **Joe Lake**, about 0.5 mile/0.8 km long (large enough for floatplane), is south of highway. **Jerry Lake** is about 0.2 mile/0.3 km north of the highway. Two small turnouts provide room for campers and fishermen. Both lakes have grayling. ⬤➤

P 128.1 (206.2 km) C 7.4 (11.9 km) Fish Creek bridge. Access to creek and informal campsite at east end of bridge.

Beautiful view (weather permitting) of Talkeetna Mountains to the south.

P 132 (212.4 km) C 3.5 (5.6 km) Good grayling fishing in stream beside road. Large turnouts in slide area.

P 133 (214 km) C 2.5 (4 km) Cantwell Station highway maintenance camp.

P 133.1 (214.2 km) C 2.4 (3.9 km) **Junction** with old Anchorage–Fairbanks Highway; turn right westbound for Alaska State Troopers complex located approximately 0.2 mile/0.3 km north on left side of road.

P 133.7 (215.2 km) C 1.8 (2.9 km) Cantwell post office and school, a lodge, rental cabins, RV park with hookups, 2 restaurants, mini-grocery, gas stations and gift shop are clustered around this intersection with the Parks Highway. Continue straight ahead 1.8 miles/2.9 km for the original town of Cantwell. ▲

Junction of Denali and Parks highways (Alaska Routes 8 and 3). See **Milepost A 209.9** in the PARKS HIGHWAY section for log.

P 134.5 (216.5 km) C 1 (1.6 km) Jack River bridge.

P 135.5 (218.1 km) C 0 CANTWELL. See description on page 416 in the PARKS HIGHWAY section.

STEESE HIGHWAY ② ⑥

Connects: Fairbanks to Circle, AK **Length:** 162 miles
Road Surface: 30% paved, 70% gravel **Season:** Open all year
Highest Summit: Eagle Summit, 3,624 feet
Major Attractions: Hot Springs, Gold Dredge No. 8
(See map, pages 488)

	Central	Chena Hot Springs	Circle	Circle Hot Springs	Fairbanks
Central		180	35	8	128
Chena Hot Springs	180		214	188	61
Circle	35	214		43	162
Circle Hot Springs	8	188	43		136
Fairbanks	128	61	162	136	

Top of the world view at Twelvemile Summit on the Steese Highway. (© Laurent Dick)

The Steese Highway connects Fairbanks with Chena Hot Springs (61.4 miles/98.8 km) via Chena Hot Springs Road; the town of Central (127.5 miles/205.2 km); Circle Hot Springs (136.1 miles/219 km) via Circle Hot Springs Road; and with Circle, a small settlement 162 miles/260.7 km to the northeast on the Yukon River and 50 miles/80.5 km south of the Arctic Circle. The scenery alone makes this a worthwhile drive.

The first 44 miles/70.8 km of the Steese Highway are paved. Beyond this it is wide gravel road into Central, where there is a stretch of paved road. From Central to Circle, the highway is a narrow, winding road with gravel surface.

The highway is open year-round; check with the Dept. of Transportation in Fairbanks regarding winter road conditions. The Steese Highway was completed in 1927 and named for Gen. James G. Steese, U.S. Army, former president of the Alaska Road Commission.

Among the attractions along the Steese are Eagle Summit, highest pass on the highway, where there is an unobstructed view of the midnight sun at summer solstice (June 21); the Chatanika River and Chena River recreation areas; and Chena and Circle Hot Springs.

Emergency medical services: Between Fairbanks and Circle, phone the state troopers at 911 or (907) 452-1313. Use CB Channels 2, 19, 22.

Steese Highway Log

Distance from Fairbanks (F) is followed by distance from Circle (C).

ALASKA ROUTE 2

F 0 C 162 (260.7 km) **FAIRBANKS.** Junction of Airport Way, Richardson–Alaska Highway and the Steese Expressway. Follow the 4-lane Steese Expressway north.

F 0.4 (0.6 km) **C 161.6** (260.1 km) Tenth Avenue exit.

F 0.6 (1 km) **C 161.4** (259.7 km) Expressway crosses Chena River.

F 0.9 (1.4 km) **C 161.1** (259.3 km) Third Street exit.

F 1 (1.6 km) **C 161** (259.1 km) College Road exit to west and access to Bentley Mall and University of Alaska.

F 1.4 (2.3 km) **C 160.6** (258.5 km) Trainer Gate Road; access to Fort Wainright.

F 2 (3.2 km) **C 160** (257.5 km) Johansen Expressway (Old Steese Highway) to west; access to Fairbanks shopping. City Lights Boulevard to east.

F 2.8 (4.5 km) **C 159.2** (256.2 km) Gas station with foodmart at junction of Farmers Loop Road (to west) and Fairhill Road (to east). Access to Birch Hill Recreation Area, 2.3 miles/3.7 km from the highway via a paved road.

F 4.9 (7.9 km) **C 157.1** (252.8 km) Chena Hot Springs Road underpass, exits both sides of highway. Turn east at exit for Chena Hot Springs Road.

See CHENA HOT SPRINGS ROAD log beginning on page 489.

F 6.4 (10.3 km) **C 155.6** (250.4 km) Steele Creek Road. Exit for Bennett Road, Hagelbarger Road, Old Steese Highway and Gilmore trail. Exit to left northbound for scenic view of Fairbanks.

F 7 (11.3 km) **C 155** (249.4 km) View of pipeline from top of hill.

F 8 (12.9 km) **C 154** (247.8 km) End 4-lane divided highway, begin 2 lanes, northbound. *CAUTION: Watch for moose.*

F 8.4 (13.5 km) **C 153.6** (247.2 km) **Trans–Alaska Pipeline Viewpoint** with interpretive displays. Excellent opportunity for pipeline photos. Alyeska Pipeline Service Co. visitor center open May to September, 7 days a week. Free literature and information; phone (907) 456-9391. Highway parallels pipeline.

F 9.5 (15.3 km) **C 152.5** (245.4 km) Goldstream Road exit to Old Steese Highway and **Gold Dredge Number 8 National Historic Site.** The dredge, built in 1928, was added to the list of national historic sites in 1984 and designated a National Historical Mechanical Engineering Landmark in 1986. The 5-deck, 250-foot-long dredge operated until 1959; it is now privately owned and open to the public for tours (admission fee).

Historic Gold Dredge No. 8. Gold Dredge No. 8 is a monument to the miners who used the machinery to produce more than 7.5 million ounces of gold and the engineers who built it. Visitors tour the only dredge in Alaska open to the public. Gold panning and a Miner's lunch are also available at this national historic site. See advertisement in FAIRBANKS section.
[ADVERTISEMENT]

F 10.4 (16.7 km) **C 151.6** (244 km) Road to Permafrost Tunnel Research Facility to east (not open to public). Excavated in the early 1960s, the tunnel is maintained cooperatively by the University of Alaska–Fairbanks and the U.S. Army Cold Regions Research and Engineering Laboratory.

F 11 (17.7 km) **C 151** (243 km) End of Steese Expressway at junction of Alaska Routes 6 and 2; weigh station with pay phone. Access to Fox (description follows).

STEESE HIGHWAY   Fairbanks, AK to Circle, AK

© 1999 The MILEPOST®

Key to mileage boxes from:
miles/kilometres
miles/kilometres
F-Fairbanks
C-Circle
J-Junction
A-Anchorage
D-Dalton Highway
DJ-Delta Junction

Key to Advertiser Services
C - Camping
D - Dump Station
d - Diesel
G - Gas (reg., unld.)
I - Ice
L - Lodging
M - Meals
P - Propane
R - Car Repair (major)
r - Car Repair (minor)
S - Store (grocery)
T - Telephone (pay)

Principal Route
Paved
Unpaved
Other Roads
Paved
Unpaved
Ferry Routes   Hiking Trails
Refer to Log for Visitor Facilities

Scale
0   10 Miles
0   10 Kilometres

Map Location

Yukon River

Circle ✈ △
N65°49'
W144°03'

C-0
F-162/261km

⑥

F-162/260.7km H.C. Company Store dGrST
Yukon Trading Post CGIMPST

Birch Creek

F-127.7/205.5km Crabb's Corner CdGIMPST
F-127.5/205.2km Central Motor Inn & Campground CGILMT

Central
N65°34'
W144°48'

Albert Cr.

Medicine Lake

Circle Hot Springs △ ✈
N65°29'
W144°38'

J-8/13km

J-8.3/13.4km Circle Hot
Springs Resort CLM

South Fork

Harrison Creek

Deadwood Creek

Mammoth Creek

C-35/56km
J-0
F-128/205km

Crooked Creek

Porcupine Creek

Eagle Summit
3,624 ft./1,105m

North Fork

South Fork

Birch Creek

Porcupine Dome
4,915 ft./1,498m

Pinnell Mountain
4,721 ft./1,439m

Ptarmigan Fork

North Fork

Twelvemile Summit
2,982 ft./909m

Twelvemile Cr.

C-76/123km
F-86/138km

TANANA HILLS

Chena Hot Springs △ ✈
J-56.5/90.9km Chena Hot Springs Resort CDILMPT

J-57/91km

East Fork

Chena Hot Springs Road

Monument Creek

North Fork

West Fork

McManus Cr.

Faith Cr.

Angel Cr.

Colorado Cr.

Chena River

Little Chena River

Jenny M Creek

J-25.9/41.7km Snowy River Bed & Breakfast L
J-23.9/38.5km Pleasant Valley RV Park CDT
J-23.5/37.8km Tack's General Store and Greenhouse Cafe dGIMST

WHITE MOUNTAINS

Sourdough Cr.

Cripple Cr.

Davidson Ditch

Chatanika River

F-45.4/73.1km Long Creek Trading Post CDILrST

Table Top Mountain

U.S. Creek Road

Ptarmigan Creek

Grouse Cr.

Long Cr.

Moose Cr.

Nome Creek

McKay Cr.

Belle Cr.

F-28.6/46km Chatanika Lodge CILMPT

Chatanika

Cleary Summit
2,233 ft./681m

C-151/243km
F-11/18km
D-73/118km

F-9.5/15.3km Historic Gold Dredge No. 8 M

Steese Expressway

Little Chena River

Badger Road

Nordale Road

North Pole

To Delta Junction
(see RICHARDSON HIGHWAY section)

Trans-Alaska Pipeline

Chatanika River

Pedro Dome
2,600 ft./792m

⑥

Fox

F-11/17.7km
Fox General Store G3

C-157/253km
J-0
F-5/8km

Old Steese Highway

To Dalton Highway
(see ELLIOTT HIGHWAY section)

②

Crooked Cr.

Kokomo Cr.

To Anchorage
(see PARKS HIGHWAY section)

③

Fairbanks ✈ △

C-162/261km
F-0
DJ-198/158km
A-358/576km

Tanana River

Chena Hot Springs Road Log

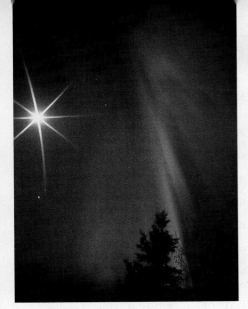

Aurora borealis over Fairbanks.

(© Craig Brandt)

Dalton Highway information sign. Turn east at this junction for continuation of Steese Highway, which now becomes Alaska Route 6 (log follows). Distance marker shows Chatanika 17 miles; Central 118 miles; Circle 152 miles.

Junction with Elliott Highway (Alaska Route 2) which continues northeast to the Dalton Highway and Manley Hot Springs See ELLIOTT HIGHWAY section for log.

Turn west for Old Steese Highway and for **FOX**, a once-famous mining camp established before 1905 and named for nearby Fox Creek. Gas, food and lodging.

Fox General Store. Located at the crossroads of Steese Expressway and Elliott Highway; the gateway to fishing, camping, hunting and mining. Last gas for 117 miles when traveling north on Steese, and next to last gas for 150 miles when traveling north on Elliott. Gas, grocery, beer, liquor, Alaskana gifts and hunting and fishing licenses. See display ad this section.
[ADVERTISEMENT]

This good all-weather paved road leads 56.5 miles/90.9 km east to Chena Hot Springs, a private resort open daily year-round. Chena Hot Springs Road passes through the middle of Chena River Recreation Area, 254,000 acres of mostly undeveloped river bottom and alpine uplands. This is an exceptional year-round recreation area with picnic sites, campgrounds, hiking trails and easy access to the Chena River, one of the most popular grayling fisheries in the state. *IMPORTANT: Check current ADF&G regulations regarding the taking of any fish.*
Distance is measured from junction with the Steese Highway (J).

J 0 Chena Hot Springs Road exit at **Milepost F 4.9** Steese Expressway. (*NOTE: Road construction was under way on the first 7 miles/11.3 km of this road in summer 1998.*)
J 4 (6.4 km) Turnoff for Grizzly Lodge (0.4 miles/0.6 km).
J 6.4 (10.3 km) Nordale Road, connects with Badger Road to Richardson Highway.
J 8.3 (13.4 km) Paved double-ended turnout to south. North Pole Borough welcome sign.
J 10.3 (16.6 km) Mini-mart, gas.
J 11.8 (19 km) Bridge over Little Chena River. Water gauging station in middle of bridge. This Army Corps of Engineers flood control project, completed in 1979, was designed to prevent floods such as the one which devastated Fairbanks in 1967.
J 15 (24.1 km) *Rough road next 2 miles/3.2 km eastbound. Watch for moose.*
J 18.3 (29.5 km) Two Rivers Road. Access to Two Rivers Elementary School.
J 20.1 (32.3 km) Jenny M. Creek.
J 22 (35.4 km) Baptist church.
J 23.4 (37.7 km) Grocery with gas; public dumpster.
J 23.5 (37.8 km) Tacks' General Store; groceries, ice, cafe. Two Rivers post office is in store.
Tacks' General Store and Greenhouse Cafe. See display ad this section.
J 23.8 (38.3 km) Pleasant Valley Plaza; laundry, showers, store, pay phones.

J 23.9 (38.5 km) **Pleasant Valley RV Park** next to Pleasant Valley Plaza. Quiet country setting, gateway to upper Chena Valley. Fishing, hiking, biking, ATV trails, canoe rentals. All pull-throughs. Water and electric hookups, restrooms, dump station, propane and pay phone. Tent sites, firepits, free firewood. Coin-operated laundry and showers available. Convenient to local amenities. P.O. Box 16019, Two Rivers, AK 99716. Phone (907) 488-8198. MasterCard, VISA accepted. [ADVERTISEMENT] ▲
J 25.6 (41.2 km) HIPAS Observatory, UCLA Plasma Physics Lab (Geophysical Institute Chena Radio Facility).
J 25.9 (41.7 km) **Snowy River Bed & Breakfast.** Mile 25.9. Attractive, clean log cabin. 35 minutes from Fairbanks in a private setting on the Chena River. Fishing, guided/unguided, hiking trails, float trips, canoe/raft rentals, wildlife viewing, photography and northern lights viewing. Available year-round. No smoking/pets. B&B in a true Alaskan setting. Full breakfast available. (907) 488-7517. [ADVERTISEMENT]
J 26.1 (42 km) Entering **Chena River Recreation Area**. No shooting except at target range. Grayling fishing (check current regulations).
J 26.7 (43 km) Turnout to north. Unmaintained gravel turnout to south for picnic area with tables and toilets.
J 27 (43.5 km) Large turnout to south at entrance to Rosehip state campground;

25 level, shaded sites, picnic tables, firepits, toilets, water, water nature trail. $8 nightly fee or annual pass. Large gravel pads and an easy 0.7-mile/1.1-km

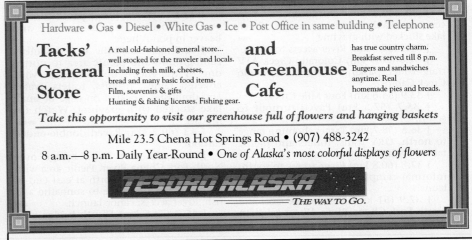

Chena Hot Springs Road Log (continued)

Fishing for grayling in the Chena River along Chena Hot Springs Road.

(© Robin Brandt)

loop road make this a good campground for large RVs and trailers. Firewood available, $5. Beautifully situated on the Chena River. *CAUTION: Steep, eroded riverbank; supervise small children.* ▲

This is a canoe exit point. The Chena is popular with paddlers, but should not be underestimated: The river is cold and the current very strong. Watch for river-wide logjams and sweepers. Secure your gear in waterproof containers. Local paddlers suggest a float from **Milepost J 39.5** to J 37.9 for easy paddling; J 44 to J 37.9 for a longer float; and J 52.3 to J 47.3 for paddlers with more skill. Allow about an hour on the river for each road mile traveled.

J 27.5 (44.3 km) Paved turnout to south.

J 28 (45.1 km) River access to south (0.9 mile/1.4 km); large parking area with picnic tables, dumpster, loop turnaround. Canoe exit point.

J 28.6 (46 km) River access to south (0.7 mile/1.1 km); canoe launch, picnic table, toilet, dumpster, parking.

J 29.4 (47.3 km) Long double-ended paved turnout to south on Chena River; picnic table.

J 30 (48.3 km) Outdoor education camp (available for rent by groups). Small lake stocked with grayling. ◄

J 31.4 (50.5 km) River access to south.

J 31.6 (50.9 km) Colorado Creek ATV trail. Toilet, parking, access to Colorado Creek Cabins.

J 33.9 (54.6 km) Four Mile Creek.

J 35.7 (57.5 km) Paved turnout to south.

J 36.5 (58.7 km) Target shooting range to north. ORV trails, toilets and picnic tables. Cathedral Bluffs view.

J 37.8 (60.8 km) River access to south; informal camping on gravel bar, canoe launch.

J 37.9 (61 km) First bridge over the **North Fork Chena River**. Water gauge in center of bridge (not visible to motorists). There are 3 stream flow meters on the upper Chena. Grayling fishing (check current special regulations). ◄

J 38.2 (61.5 km) River access to north; large parking area on gravel levee.

J 39.2 (63.1 km) Paved turnout to south.

J 39.5 (63.6 km) Second bridge over North Fork Chena River. Loop road through Granite Tors state campground; 20 large sites among tall spruce trees, parking area, water, toilets, tables, firepits, $8 nightly fee or annual pass. Canoe launch. Picnic area on loop road along river. ▲

Trailhead (west side of bridge) for **Granite Tors Trail**; follow dike (levee) on west side upstream 0.3 mile/0.5 km to trail sign. It is a 6-mile/9.7-km hike to the nearest tors, 8 miles/12.9 km to the main grouping. Tors are isolated pinnacles of granite jutting up from the tundra.

A 0.2-mile/0.3-km side road leads south to Chena River picnic area with tables, toilets and a riverbank of flat rocks ideal for sunbathing.

J 39.8 (64.1 km) Granite Tors Campground loop road exit.

J 42.1 (67.8 km) Large paved turnout south of road. Watch for muskrats and beaver in ponds here.

J 42.8 (68.9 km) Mile 43 Red Squirrel campground and picnic area to north, one of the nicest on this road, with covered tables, firepits, toilets, water and dumpster. Located on edge of small lake stocked with grayling. Watch for moose. ◄▲

J 43 (69.2 km) Paved double-ended turnout.

J 44.1 (71 km) Third bridge over North Fork Chena River. Picnic area with tables and toilets to north at east end of bridge. A favorite place to sunbathe and fish. River access; canoe launch. ◄

J 45.7 (73.5 km) Fourth bridge over North Fork Chena River.

J 46 (74 km) Paved turnout to south.

J 46.8 (75.3 km) **Chena River** flows alongside the road; good access point for fishermen. Paved parking to south opposite river. ◄

J 47.9 (77.1 km) Side road leads 0.1 mile/0.2 km south to **48-Mile Pond**. Stocked with grayling; picnic tables, informal campsites. ◄

J 48.8 (78.5 km) Watch for people and horses next mile eastbound.

J 48.9 (78.7 km) Angel Rocks trailhead to south; table, toilet, dumpster. Angel Rocks trail is a 3.5-mile/5.6-km loop trail to spectacular rock outcroppings; strenuous hike.

J 49 (78.9 km) Fifth bridge over **North Fork Chena River;** parking. Excellent fishing from here. ◄

J 49.1 (79 km) Lower Chena Dome trailhead. Side road leads 0.2 mile/0.3 km north to trailhead, parking, water, dumpster and toilets.

J 49.7 (80 km) Angel Creek Lodge..

J 49.9 (80.3 km) **Angel Creek,** grayling 12 to 17 inches. ◄

J 50.5 (81.3 km) Paved turnout to north. Chena Dome trailhead. This 29-mile/47-km loop trail exits at **Milepost J 49.1.** Angel Creek Cabin ATV trailhead (6 miles/10 km). Parking, toilets. Bring mosquito repellent!

J 52.3 (84.2 km) Bridge over West Fork Chena River. Gravel side road leads south to parking area along the river.

J 55.3 (89 km) North Fork Chena River bridge.

J 55.4 (89.2 km) Double-ended parking area to south.

J 56.5 (90.9 km) **CHENA HOT SPRINGS:** food, lodging, camping, bar and swimming. There is an airstrip at the lodge. Large parking area at end of road, one-lane wooden bridge. ▲

Chena Hot Springs Resort, Interior Alaska's year-round visitor destination. Relax, refresh and rejuvenate in the natural spring-fed pool and whirlpools. Enjoy the cozy lodge, comfortable hotel rooms, rustic cabins, spacious campground and RV parking (electric hookups, dump station and water available). Each season offers recreational opportunities. Enjoy the scenic 1-hour drive from Fairbanks. Summer solstice brings gold panning, hiking, horseback riding, flightseeing, ATV 4-wheel tours and mountain biking. Plus other activities like basketball, volleyball, horseshoes and picnicking. Fishing and boating areas are conveniently nearby. Massage therapy sessions available all year. Winter activities feature aurora viewing, dogsled rides, cross-country skiing, flightseeing, ice skating, snowshoeing and guided snow machine rides. P.O. Box 73440-MP, Fairbanks, AK 99707; phone (907) 452-7867 or (800) 478-4681. Internet: www.chenahotsprings.com. See display ad in FAIRBANKS section. [ADVERTISEMENT] ▲MP

Return to Milepost F 4.9
Steese Highway

ALASKA ROUTE 6

F 13.6 (21.9 km) **C 148.4** (238.8 km) Eisele Road; turnoff on right northbound for NOAA/NESDIS Command and Data Acquisition Station at Gilmore Creek. This facility tracks and commands multiple NOAA polar orbiting, environmental satellites. Tours of the satellite tracking station are available 9 A.M. to 4 P.M., Monday through Saturday, from June through August or by appointment September through May. Phone (907) 451-1200 for more information.

F 16.5 (26.6 km) **C 145.5** (234.2 km) Paved parking area to west with monument to Felix Pedro, the prospector who discovered gold on Pedro Creek in July 1902 and started the rush that resulted in the founding of Fairbanks.

F 17.5 (28.2 km) **C 144.5** (232.5 km) Paved parking area to east.

Winding ascent (8 1/2 percent grade) northbound to Cleary Summit area.

F 19.5 (31.4 km) **C 142.5** (229.3 km) Large paved parking area to east.

F 20.5 (33 km) **C 141.5** (227.7 km) **Cleary Summit** (elev. 2,233 feet/681m) Named for early prospector Frank Cleary. View of current mining operation and old buildings from early mining and dredging on Cleary Creek below. On a clear day there are excellent views of the Tanana Valley and Mount McKinley to the south and the White Mountains to the north.

Highway descends steep winding grade northbound. Watch for road construction.

F 21 (33.8 km) **C 141** (226.9 km) Cleary Summit Ski Area; open weekends in winter.

F 27.6 (44.4 km) **C 134.4** (216.3 km) Tailings (gravel and boulders of dredged streambeds) from early mining activity which yielded millions of dollars in gold. There is quite a bit of mining in the Chatanika area now.

F 27.9 (44.9 km) **C 134.1** (215.8 km) Sharp right turn up hill for historic old F.E. Camp (Fairbanks Exploration Co. gold camp) at CHATANIKA, built in 1925 to support gold dredging operations in the valley. Between 1926 and 1957 the F.E. Co. removed an estimated $70 million in gold. The gold camp is on the National Register of Historic Places.

F 28.6 (46 km) **C 133.4** (214.7 km) Old gold dredge behind tailing piles to west *(private property, DO NOT TRESPASS)*. Lodge to east with meals and lodging.

Chatanika Lodge. Cafe open 9 A.M. daily (year-round). Halibut/catfish fry Friday and Saturday, country-fried chicken on Sunday, served family-style, all you can eat. Diamond Willow Lounge. Rustic atmosphere, Alaska artifacts. Historic Alaska gold dredge across from lodge, plus aurora borealis videos on big-screen TV. Good grayling fishing. Great winter snow machining on groomed trails; snow machine rentals. Rooms available. See display ad this section. [ADVERTISEMENT]

F 29.5 (47.5 km) **C 132.5** (213.2 km) Neal Brown Road to Poker Flat rocket facility; off-limits except to authorized personnel. The Poker Flat rocket range, operated by the Geophysical Institute, University of Alaska, is dedicated to unclassified auroral and upper atmospheric research. It is the only university-owned sounding rocket range in the world and the only high latitude and auroral zone launch facility on U.S. soil. Tours for interested groups may be arranged by calling (907) 474-7798.

F 30.6 (49.2 km) **C 131.4** (211.5 km) Public fishing access east to **Mile 30.6 Pond.**

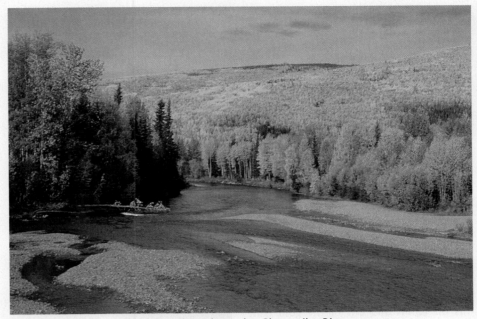

Autumn colors in early September along the Chatanika River. (© Craig Brandt)

F 31.3 (50.4 km) **C 130.7** (210.3 km) **Imaging Riometer Antenna Array** is a joint 10-year study of polar middle and upper atmosphere by CRL of Japan and UAF's Geophysical Institute. "The Aurora Borealis makes the atmosphere opaque to radio noise from our galaxy at altitudes of 60–100 km, reducing the intensity of the noise received at the ground. The imaging riometer works like a camera, taking a picture of the radio noise once a second."

F 31.4 (50.5 km) **C 130.6** (210.2 km) Public fishing access to west; pond stocked with grayling.

F 32.1 (51.6 km) **C 129.9** (209 km) *CAUTION: Slow down for rough road.*

F 32.3 (52 km) **C 129.7** (208.7 km) Captain Creek bridge.

F 34.6 (55.7 km) **C 127.4** (205 km) **Mile 34.6 Pond**; public fishing access.

F 34.8 (56 km) **C 127.2** (204.7 km) Double-ended paved turnout to west.

F 35.8 (57.6 km) **C 126.2** (203.1 km) **Mile 35.8 Pond** to east; public fishing access.

F 36.4 (58.6 km) **C 125.6** (202.1 km) Weltown.

F 36.6 (58.9 km) **C 125.4** (201.8 km) Gravel turnout alongside **Mile 36.6 Pond** to west; stocked with grayling.

F 36.8 (59.2 km) **C 125.2** (201.5 km) *CAUTION: Rough road.*

F 37.3 (60 km) **C 124.7** (200.7 km) Kokomo Creek bridge.

F 39 (62.8 km) **C 123** (197.9 km) Chatanika River bridge. **Upper Chatanika River State Recreation Site**, just north of the bridge, is a beautiful state campground with river access and rocky beach. There are 25 sites with fireplaces and a gravel parking area with toilets and a water pump at the entrance. Firewood is usually available during the summer. Camping fee $8/night or annual pass. Campground host. Look for wild roses here in June.

Boats can be launched on the gravel bars by the river. Bring your mosquito repellent and suntan lotion. This is an access point to the Chatanika River canoe trail. See **Milepost F 60** for more information on canoeing this river.

Chatanika River, grayling 8 to 20 inches, use flies or spinners, May to September.

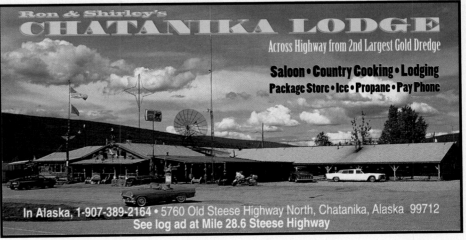

F 39.3 (63.2 km) C 122.7 (197.5 km) 39.3 Mile Pond, to west, is stocked with grayling.

F 40.2 (64.7 km) C 121.8 (196 km) *CAUTION: Rough road.*

F 40.4 (65 km) C 121.6 (195.7 km) Bridge over Crooked Creek.

F 41.5 (66.8 km) C 120.5 (193.9 km) Bridge over Belle Creek.

F 42.7 (68.7 km) C 119.3 (192 km) Gravel turnout to west; sled dog unloading area. McKay Creek trailhead.

F 42.8 (68.9 km) C 119.2 (191.8 km) Bridge over McKay Creek..

F 43.9 (70.6 km) C 118.1 (190.1 km) *Pavement ends; gravel road begins, northbound.*

Highway parallels the Chatanika River for the next 10 miles/16 km.

F 45.4 (73.1 km) C 116.6 (187.6 km) Long Creek bridge. Long Creek Trading Post to west at north end of bridge; gold panning equipment (and advice), groceries, liquor store, camping. D'nae Bolt at Long Creek suggests amateur gold panners headed to Nome Creek (see **Milepost F 57.3**) use dishwashing detergent (biodegradable) to keep oils off hands and out of the gold pan, because oils cause the gold to float to the surface and out of the pan. Fishing (and gold panning) in **Long Creek**; grayling 8 to 14 inches, use spinners or flies, May to September.

Long Creek Trading Post. See display ad this section. ▲

F 49 (78.9 km) C 113 (181.9 km) Views down Chatanika River valley to east.

F 57.1 (91.9 km) C 104.9 (168.8 km) Entering **White Mountains National Recreation Area** (BLM) northbound. Access to this area's trails and cabins is from **Milepost F 57.3**.

F 57.3 (92.2 km) C 104.7 (168.5 km) Turnoff for Nome Creek via U.S. Creek Road to west (description below). **Davidson Ditch Historical Site** immediately west on U.S. Creek. The large pipe was built in 1925 by the Fairbanks Exploration Co. to carry water to float gold dredges. The 83-mile/133.6-km-long ditch, designed and engineered by J.B. Lippincott, begins near **Milepost F 64** on the Steese Highway and ends near Fox. A system of ditches and inverted siphons, the pipeline was capable of carrying 56,100 gallons per minute. After the dredges closed, the water was used for power until 1967, when a flood destroyed a bridge and flattened almost 1,000 feet/305m of pipe.

U.S. Creek Road is a good hard-packed dirt and gravel road (steep, few turnouts) that winds up and over the hills to the northwest 6.9 miles/11.1 km to **Nome Creek Gold Panning Area**; large gravel parking area, outhouse and signs about White

Mountain National Recreation Area and the Nome Creek Gold Panning Area. Continue on Nome Creek Road for Mt. Prindle Campground and Quartz Creek Trail (4 miles/6.4 km) and Ophir Creek Campground and Beaver Creek National Wild River put-in point (12 miles/19.3 km).

F 59 (94.9 km) C 103 (165.8 km) Wide double-ended parking area to east.

F 60 (96.6 km) C 102 (164.1 km) Cripple Creek BLM campground to east (watch for dip in access road); 7-day limit, 6 tent, 12 level trailer sites; water pumps, firepits, outhouses, bear-proof dumpsters, picnic tables, nature trail. Camping fee $6. Parking for walk-in campers. Firewood is usually available all summer. Recreational gold panning permitted. *Bring mosquito repellent!* ▲

Access to Cripple Creek BLM recreation cabin. Preregister and pay $10 fee at BLM office, 1150 University Ave., Fairbanks, AK 99709; phone (907) 474-2200.

Cripple Creek bridge is the uppermost access point to the Chatanika River canoe trail. Follow side road near campground entrance to canoe launch site; parking area, outhouses. *CAUTION: This canoe trail may not be navigable at low water.* The Chatanika River is a clear-water Class II stream. The Steese Highway parallels the river for approximately 28 miles/45 km and there are many access points to the highway downstream from the Cripple Creek bridge. No major obstacles on this canoe trail, but watch for overhanging trees. Downstream pullout points are Perhaps Creek, Long Creek and Chatanika Campground.

F 62.3 (100.3 km) C 99.7 (160.4 km) Scenic viewpoint to east overlooking Chatanika River.

F 63.4 (102 km) C 98.6 (158.7 km) View of historic Davidson Ditch pipeline to west (see **Milepost F 57.3**).

F 63.8 (102.7 km) C 98.2 (158 km) Old Steese Highway alignment visible to west.

F 64.8 (104.3 km) C 9.27 (156.41 km) Side road east to scenic viewpoint. Large parking area.

F 65.6 (105.6 km) C 96.4 (155.1 km) Sourdough Creek bridge.

F 65.7 (105.7 km) C 96.3 (155 km) Mile 66. Davidson Ditch trailhead.

F 69 (111 km) C 93 (149.7 km) Faith Creek bridge and road. Creek access to east at north end of bridge; large parking area to west.

Highway climbs 7 percent grade northbound.

F 72 (115.9 km) C 90 (144.8 km) View ahead for northbound travelers of highway route along mountains, McManus Creek below.

F 79.1 (127.3 km) C 82.9 (133.4 km) Road widens for parking next 500 feet/152m.

F 80.1 (128.9 km) C 81.9 (131.8 km) Montana Creek state highway maintenance station. Montana Creek runs under road and into McManus Creek to the east. McManus Dome (elev. 4,184 feet/1,275m) to west.

F 81.2 (130.7 km) C 80.8 (130 km) Turnout to east. Spring water (untested) piped to roadside. Wide gravel highway begins ascent to Twelvemile Summit. Avalanche gates.

F 83 (133.6 km) C 79 (127.1 km) *CAUTION: Slow down for sharp turn.*

Watch for snowshoe hares.

F 85.5 (137.6 km) C 76.5 (123.1 km) Large parking area and viewpoint to east at **Twelvemile Summit** (elev. 2,982 feet/909m) on the divide of the Yukon and Tanana river drainages. Wildflowers carpet the alpine tundra slopes. Entering Game Management Unit 25C, leaving unit 20B, northbound. Fairbanks–North Star Borough limits. This is caribou country; from here to beyond Eagle Summit (**Milepost F 108**) migrating bands of caribou may be seen from late July through mid-September.

Access to Pinnell Mountain national recreation trail (Twelvemile Summit trailhead). The trail is also accessible from **Milepost F 107.1**. Named in honor of Robert Pinnell, who was fatally injured in 1952 while climbing nearby Porcupine Dome. This 27-mile-/43-km-long hiking trail winds through alpine terrain, along mountain ridges and through high passes. Highest elevation point reached is 4,721 feet/1,439m. The trail is marked by rock cairns. Shelter cabins at Mile 10.7 and Mile 17.7. Vantage points along the trail with views of the White Mountains, Tanana Hills, Brooks Range and Alaska Range. Watch for willow ptarmigan, hoary marmot, rock pika, moose, wolf and caribou. Mid-May through July is the prime time for wildflowers, with flowers peaking in mid-June. Carry drinking water and insect repellent at all times. Additional information on this trail is available from the Bureau of Land Management, 1150 University Ave., Fairbanks, AK 99708-3844; phone (907) 474-2350.

F 90.5 (145.6 km) C 71.5 (115.1 km) Double-ended turnout to east.

F 93.4 (150.3 km) C 68.6 (110.4 km) Bridge over the North Fork Twelve Mile Creek. Nice picnic spot to west below bridge.

F 94 (151.3 km) C 68 (109.4 km) Birch Creek access. Side road leads 0.2 mile/0.3 km down to north fork of Birch Creek; parking area and canoe launch for Birch Creek canoe trail. This is the main put-in point for canoeing Birch Creek, a Wild and Scenic River. Undeveloped campsite by creek. Extensive mining in area. **Birch Creek**, grayling to 12 inches; use flies, June to October. ●

F 95.8 (154.2 km) C 66.2 (106.5 km) Bridge over Willow Creek.

F 97.6 (157.1 km) C 64.4 (103.6 km) Bridge over Bear Creek. Private land holdings to east.

F 98 (157.7 km) C 64 (103 km) Much gold mining activity in streams along this part of the highway. These are private mining claims. *IMPORTANT: Do not trespass. Do not approach mining equipment without permission.*

F 99.7 (160.4 km) C 62.3 (100.3 km) Bridge over Fish Creek. Private land holdings to west.

F 101.5 (163.3 km) C 60.5 (97.4 km) Bridge over Ptarmigan Creek (elev. 2,398 feet/731m). Alpine meadows carpeted with wildflowers in spring and summer for next 9 miles/14.5 km.

NOTE: Avalanche gates may be closed if road conditions are hazardous over the summit.

F 103 (165.7 km) C 59 (94.9 km) Highway climbs to summit northbound. Good view to east of mining activity down in valleys.

F 105 (169 km) C 57 (91.7 km) Snowpoles guide snowplows in winter.

F 107.1 (172.4 km) C 54.9 (88.4 km) Parking area to west with wheelchair-accessible toilet, trail, bear-proof litter container. Pinnell Mountain trail access (Eagle Summit trailhead); see description at **Milepost F 85.5.**

F 107.5 (173 km) C 54.5 (87.7 km) **Eagle Summit** (elev. 3,685 feet/1,123m). This is the third and highest of 3 summits (including Cleary and Twelvemile) along the Steese Highway. Favorite spot for local residents to observe summer solstice (weather permitting) on June 21. Best wildflower viewing on Alaska highway system. Wildflowers found here include: dwarf forget-me-nots, alpine rhododendron or rosebay, rock jasmine, alpine azalea, arctic bell heather, mountain avens, Jacob's ladder, anemones, wallflowers, Labrador tea, lupine, oxytropes, gentians and louseworts. The museum in Central has a photographic display of Eagle Summit alpine flowers to help highway travelers identify the wildflowers of this area.

F 108 (173.8 km) C 54 (86.9 km) Steep, narrow, rocky side road leads from the highway 0.8 mile/1.3 km to Eagle Summit.

Scalloped waves of soil on hillsides to west are called solifluction lobes. These are formed when meltwater saturates the thawed surface soil, which then flows slowly downhill.

F 109.2 (175.7 km) C 52.8 (85 km) Large parking area to east; no guardrails. View down into Miller Creek far below.

Highway begins steep descent northbound.

F 111.3 (179.1 km) C 50.7 (81.6 km) Parking area to east.

F 114.2 (183.8 km) C 47.8 (76.9 km) Parking area to east looking down onto the Mastodon, Mammoth, Miller and Independence creeks area. Avalanche gates.

F 116.2 (187 km) C 45.8 (73.7 km) Road east to creek.

F 116.4 (187.3 km) C 45.6 (73.4 km) Bridge over Mammoth Creek. Near here fossil remains of many species of preglacial Alaskan mammals have been excavated and may be seen at the University of Alaska museum in Fairbanks and at the museum in Central.

F 117 (188.3 km) C 45 (72.4 km) Highway crosses over Stack Pup Creek. From here the highway gradually descends to Central.

F 117.5 (189.1 km) C 44.5 (71.6 km) Parking area to west.

F 119.1 (191.7 km) C 42.9 (69 km)

Circle Hot Springs Road Log

This wide, mostly flat gravel road, leads 8.3 miles/13.4 km to Circle Hot Springs resort.

Distance is measured from junction (J) at Milepost F 127.8 Steese Highway.

J 0 Pavement extends first 0.3 mile/0.5 km of road.

J 0.9 (1.4 km) Cemetery Road.

J 2.8 (4.5 km) Bridge over Deadwood Creek.

J 4.7 (7.6 km;) Ketchem Creek Road (1-lane dirt and gravel) leads to private mining claims and rock formations (keep right at forks in road). Road deteriorates at about Mile 3.4.

J 5.7 (9.2 km) Bridge over Ketchem Creek. Primitive camping at site of former Ketchem Creek BLM campground to south on west side of bridge. *Mosquitoes!*

J 8.3 (13.4 km) **CIRCLE HOT SPRINGS** (pop. 33). This resort offers year-round swimming, lodging, food and RV parking. A popular spot with Alaskans.

According to research done by Patricia Oakes of Central, the hot springs were used as a gathering place by area Athabascans before the gold rush. Local prospectors probably used the springs as early as the 1890s. Cassius Monohan homesteaded the site in 1905, selling out to Frank Leach in 1909. Leach built the airstrip, on which Noel Wien landed in 1924. (Wien pioneered many flight routes between Alaska communities.)

Colorful flower pots at Circle Hot Springs. (© Kris Graef, staff)

Private Aircraft: Circle Hot Springs state-maintained airstrip; elev. 956 feet/291m; length 3,600 feet/1,097m; gravel; lighted, unattended.

Return to Milepost F 127.8 Steese Highway

Bedrock Creek.

F 120 (193.1 km) C 42 (67.6 km) View northbound through foliage of mining operations to west.

F 121 (194.7 km) C 41 (66 km) Bridge over Sawpit Creek.

F 122.5 (197.1 km) C 39.5 (63.6 km) Road west to parking space by pond.

F 125.4 (201.8 km) C 36.6 (58.9 km) Bridge over Boulder Creek.

F 126.2 (203.1 km) C 35.8 (57.6 km) *CAUTION: Road narrows; slow down for curves northbound.*

F 126.8 (204.1 km) C 35.2 (56.6 km) Paved highway begins and continues through Central.

F 127.1 (204.5 km) C 34.9 (56.2 km) Central elementary school.

F 127.5 (205.2 km) C 34.5 (55.5 km) **CENTRAL** (pop. 61; elev. 965 feet/294m). **Radio:** KUAC-FM 91.7. This small community has a post office (ZIP code 99730), airstrip and park with picnic area. Gas, bar and restaurant, laundry and showers, rooms and other services at Central Motor Inn and Crabb's Corner.

Formerly called Central House, Central is situated on Crooked Creek along the Steese Highway. Central is the central point in the huge Circle Mining District, one of the oldest and still one of the most active districts in the state. The annual Circle Mining District Picnic for local miners and their families is held in August.

The **Circle District Historical Society Museum** has displays covering the history of

the Circle Mining District and its people. Also here are a photo display of wildflowers, fossilized remains of preglacial mammals, a minerals display, library and archives, gift shop and visitor information. Admission is $1 for adults, 50¢ for children under 12; members free. Open daily noon to 5 P.M., Memorial Day through Labor Day.

Central Motor Inn and Campground. See display ad this section. ▲

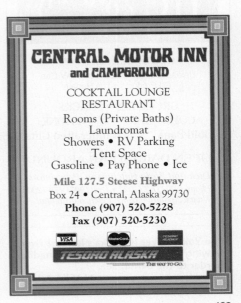

F 127.7 (205.5 km) **C 34.3** (55.2 km) **Crabb's Corner.** Jim and Sandy welcome you to Central with a host of roadhouse services—motel rooms, restaurants, bar, package store, convenience store, gas, diesel, propane, laundromat, self-contained RV parking, public telephone. As an official checkpoint for the Yukon Quest, we are happy to answer questions on the race, Central and gold panning. Open year-round. Phone (907) 520-5599. [ADVERTISEMENT]

F 127.8 (205.7 km) **C 34.2** (55 km)

Junction with Circle Hot Springs Road; see CIRCLE HOT SPRINGS ROAD log on page 493.

F 127.9 (205.8 km) **C 34.1** (54.9 km) Bridge over Crooked Creek. Site of Central House roadhouse on north side of bridge.

F 128.1 (206.2 km) **C 33.9** (54.6 km) Central DOT/PF highway maintenance station.

F 128.2 (206.3 km) **C 33.8** (54.4 km) Pavement ends, gravel begins, northbound.

Watch for ptarmigan and snowshoe hares between Central and Circle.

F 128.4 (206.6 km) **C 33.6** (54.1 km) **Private Aircraft:** Central state-maintained airstrip, adjacent north; elev. 932 feet/284m; length 2,700 feet/823m; gravel; unattended.

F 130.5 (210 km) **C 31.5** (50.7 km) Pond frequented by a variety of ducks.

F 131.1 (211 km) **C 30.9** (49.7 km) Albert Creek bridge.

F 138 (222.1 km) **C 24** (38.6 km) *NOTE: Winding road to Circle. Road narrows northbound.*

F 140.4 (225.9 km) **C 21.6** (34.8 km) Birch Creek access; large turnout with toilets, bear-proof litter containers.

F 147.1 (236.7 km) **C 14.9** (24 km) One-lane bridge over Birch Creek; clearance 13 feet, 11 inches. Spur roads at south and north ends of bridge lead to turnouts on creek; primitive camping. Usual takeout point for the **Birch Creek Canoe Trail.**

F 147.6 (237.5 km) **C 14.4** (23.2 km) Turnout to east.

The Yukon River is Alaska's longest river, flowing 1,400 miles from the Canadian border to the Bering Sea.
—ALASKA A TO Z

Aerial view of Circle and the many channels of the Yukon River. (© Laurent Dick)

F 148.7 (239.3 km) **C 13.3** (21.4 km) Gravel pit to west.

F 156.7 (252.2 km) **C 5.3** (8.5 km) Large turnout opposite gravel pit to east. Look for bank swallow nests in cliffs.

F 158.5 (255.1 km) **C 3.5** (5.6 km) *NOTE: Slow for 25 mph/40 kmph speed zone northbound.*

F 159.5 (256.7 km) **C 2.5** (4 km) Old Indian cemetery to east.

F 161 (259.1 km) **C 1** (1.6 km) Circle post office (ZIP code 99733); airstrip (see **Private Aircraft** in Circle); school.

Circle

F 162 (260.7 km) **C 0** Located on the banks of the Yukon River, 50 miles/80.5 km south of the Arctic Circle. The Yukon is Alaska's largest river; the 2,000-mile/3,219-km river heads in Canada and flows west into Norton Sound on the Bering Sea. **Population:** 86.

Elevation: 610 feet/186m. **Climate:** Mean monthly temperature in July 61.4°F/16.3°C, in January -10.6°F/-23.7°C. Record high 91°F/32.8°C July 1977, record low -69°F/-56°C in February 1991. Snow from October (8 inches) through April (2 inches). Precipitation in the summer averages 1.45 inches a month.

Private Aircraft: Circle City state-maintained airstrip, adjacent west; elev. 610 feet/186m; length 3,000 feet/914m; gravel; fuel 100LL.

Before the Klondike Gold Rush of 1898, Circle City was the largest gold mining town on the Yukon River. Prospectors discovered gold on Birch Creek in 1893, and the town of Circle City (so named because the early miners thought it was located on the Arctic Circle) grew up as the nearest supply point to the new diggings on the Yukon River.

Today, Circle serves a small local population and visitors coming in by highway or by river. The post office is at **Milepost F 161** just before the airstrip and school. Gas, groceries, snacks and sundries are available at the H.C. Company Store and Yukon Trading Post. The trading post houses the post office, cafe and liquor store. Hunting and fishing licenses are also available at the trading post. A motel is located just beyond the trading post. There's a lot of summer river traffic here: canoeists put in and take out.

The old Pioneer Cemetery, with its markers dating back to the 1800s, is an interesting spot to visit. Walk a short way upriver (past the old machinery) on the gravel road to a barricade: You will have to cross through a private front yard (please be respectful of property) to get to the trail. Walk straight ahead on the short trail, which goes through dense underbrush (many mosquitoes), for about 10 minutes. Watch for a path on your left to the graves, which are scattered among the thick trees.

Camping on the banks of the Yukon at the end of the road; tables, toilets, parking area. In 1989, when the Yukon flooded, water covered the bottom of the welcome sign at the campground entrance. From the campground you are looking at one channel of the mighty Yukon. ▲

H.C. Company Store. See display ad this section.

Yukon Trading Post. Visit Circle City...50 miles from the Arctic Circle on the mighty Yukon River. One of the northernmost points you can reach by road in the

United States. General store, cafe, liquor store, saloon. Free campground. Hunting and fishing licenses, ice, propane, tire repair. Gas and aviation gas. Owners Dan and Virginia. Phone (907) 773-1217. Write Yukon Trading Post, Circle, Alaska 99733. [ADVERTISEMENT]

ELLIOTT HIGHWAY ②

Connects: Fox to Manley Hot Springs, AK   **Length:** 152 miles
Road Surface: 20 % paved, 80 % gravel   **Season:** Open all year
Major Attraction: Minto Lakes, Manley Hot Springs

(See map, pages 496)

	Dalton Hwy	Fairbanks	Manley	Minto
Dalton Hwy		84	79	48
Fairbanks	84		163	132
Manley	79	163		53
Minto	48	132	53	

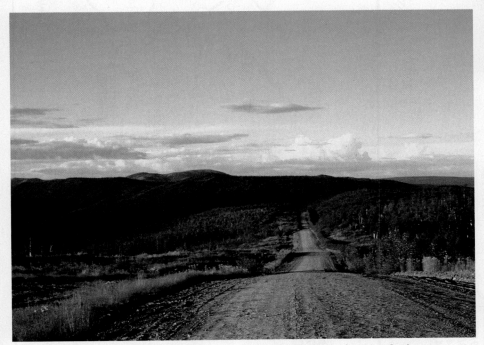

The Elliott Highway travels the ridges and hills toward Manley Hot Springs.

(© Kris Graef, staff)

The Elliott Highway leads 152 miles/244.6 km from its junction with the Steese Highway at Fox (11 miles/17.7 km north of Fairbanks) to Manley Hot Springs, a small settlement with a natural hot springs near the Tanana River. The first 73.1 miles/117.6 km of the Elliott Highway provide access to the Dalton Highway to Prudhoe Bay. The highway was named for Malcolm Elliott, president of the Alaska Road Commission from 1927 to 1932.

This is a great drive to a pocket of pioneer Alaska. The road travels the ridges and hills, providing a "top of the world" view of hundreds of square miles in all directions.

The first 30.4 miles/48.9 km of the Elliott Highway are paved; the remaining 121.6 miles/195.7 km are gravel. The highway is wide, hard-based gravel to the Dalton Highway junction. (The road is treated with calcium chloride for dust control; wash your vehicle after travel to prevent corrosion.) From the Dalton Highway junction to Manley, the road is narrower and the surface is rougher. Gas is available at **Milepost F 5.5, F 66** and at Manley.

Watch for heavy truck traffic. Drivers pulling trailers should be especially cautious when the road is wet. The highway is open year-round; check with the Dept. of Transportation in Fairbanks regarding winter road conditions.

The Elliott Highway also provides access to 4 trailheads in the White Mountains National Recreation Area. These hiking trails lead to recreation cabins; the trails and cabins are managed by the BLM in Fairbanks. For more information and cabin registration, contact the BLM office in Fairbanks at 1150 University Ave., Fairbanks, AK 99709; phone (907) 474-2350.

Emergency medical services: Between Fox and Manley Hot Springs, phone the state troopers at 911 or (907) 452-1313. Use CB channels 9, 14, 19.

Elliott Highway Log

Distance from Fox (F) is followed by distance from Manley Hot Springs (M).

ALASKA ROUTE 2

F 0 M 152 (244.6 km) **FOX. Junction** of the Steese Highway with the Elliott Highway. Weigh station.

F 0.2 (0.3 km) **M 151.8** (244.3 km) Private RV park. ▲

F 0.4 (0.6 km) **M 151.6** (244 km) Fox Spring picnic area; 2 tables, spring water.

F 1.2 (1.9 km) **M 150.8** (242.7 km) Turnoff for **El Dorado Gold Mine**, a commercial gold mine offering tours and gold panning to the public; admission charged.

F 1.7 (2.9 km) **M 150.3** (241.9 km) Fort Knox gold mine. Tours were available in summer 1998. Check with Fairbanks visitor center or phone the gold mine office about tours in 1999.

F 3.2 (5.1 km) **M 148.8** (239.5 km) Old Murphy Dome Road, very rough but passable, leads southwest around Murphy Dome to Murphy Dome Road.

F 5.5 (8.9 km) **M 146.5** (235.8 km) Hilltop 24-hour gas, diesel, phone and food.

F 7.5 (12.1 km) **M 144.5** (232.5 km) Views to the east of Pedro Dome and Dome Creek. Buildings of Dome and Eldorado camps are in the valley below to the east (best view is southbound).

F 8.6 (13.8 km) **M 143.4** (230.8 km) Dome Creek Road to east.

F 9.2 (14.8 km) **M 142.8** (229.8 km) Olnes, former railroad station of Tanana Valley Railroad and mining camp. Old tailings and abandoned cabins.

F 10.6 (17.1 km) **M 141.4** (227.6 km) Lower Chatanika River State Recreation Area **Olnes Pond Campground**, 1 mile/1.6 km west of highway on side road (watch for potholes and slow down for creek crossing).

Open camping area around pond (good swimming); 50 campsites, toilets, water, tables, group area with campfire ring and benches. Camping fee $8/night or annual pass. Campground host. ▲

F 11 (17.7 km) **M 141** (226.9 km) Chatanika River bridge. Lower Chatanika River State Recreation Area **Whitefish Camp-**

ground to west at north end of bridge. Picnic area (wheelchair accessible) with covered

ELLIOTT HIGHWAY *Fox, AK, to Manley Hot Springs, AK*

© 1999 The MILEPOST®

N
W E
S

WHITE MOUNTAINS

To Circle (see STEESE HIGHWAY section)

Pedro Dome 2,600 ft./792m

M-152/245km
F-0
C-151/243km
FB-11/218km

Fox

To Chena Hot Springs (see STEESE HIGHWAY section)

Chena River

To Delta Junction

Little Chena R.

Willow Creek

Wickersham Dome 3,207 ft./977m

Cleftman Creek

To Circle

River

2

2

Old Steese Highway

Fairbanks

River

Tanana

3

(see RICHARDSON HIGHWAY section, page 509)

F-49.5/79.7km The Arctic Circle Trading Post

Snowshoe Creek

Washington Creek

Murphy Dome 2,930 ft./893m

M-124/200km
F-28/45km

Amy Dome 2,317 ft./706m

M-81/131km
F-71/114km

Livengood

F-66/106.2km North Country Mercantile CGIST

Tolovana River

To Anchorage (see PARKS HIGHWAY section)

Minto Lakes

The Alaska Railroad

Trans-Alaska Pipeline

Hess Creek

Lost Creek

To Deadhorse/Prudhoe Bay (see DALTON HIGHWAY section)

11

M-79/127km
F-73/118km
D-414/666km
FB-84/135km

West Fork

Sawtooth Mountain 4,494 ft./1,370m

Tatalina River

Chatanika River

former Minto

Yukon River

Raven Creek Hill 2,388 ft./728m

Troublesome Creek

Wolverine Mountain 4,580 ft./1,396m

M-42/68km
F-110/177km

Cooper Lake

Minto

Ray River

Trout Creek

Elephant Mountain 3,661 ft./1,116m

Pioneer Cr.

Goff Cr.

Applegate Cr.

Eureka Cr.

2

Globe Creek

Hutlinana

Cooper Lake

Tolovana River

Tanana River

Eureka Dome 2,393 ft./729m

Eureka

Baker Lake

Baker Creek

Manley Roadhouse LM Manley Trading Post GS

M-152/244.6km

Hot Springs Slough

Tofty

M-0
F-152/245km

Manley Hot Springs

N65°00'
W150°38'

picnic tables and campsites along the Lower Chatanika River; toilets, firepits, water, litter barrels, river access and boat launch. Camping fee $8/night or annual pass. Campground host.   ♿▲

F 11.5 (18.5 km) **M 140.5** (226.1 km) 11 1/4 Mile Grocery uphill to northeast.

F 13.1 (21.1 km) **M 138.9** (223.5 km) Willow Creek bridge.

F 13.4 (21.6 km) **M 138.6** (223 km) Landmark old log cabin to west.

F 18.3 (29.5 km) **M 133.7** (215.2 km) Double-ended paved turnout to west.

F 18.5 (29.8 km) **M 133.5** (214.8 km) Washington Creek. Parking area below bridge east of road; undeveloped campsite.

F 20.1 (32.3 km) **M 131.9** (212.3 km) Beaver pond with dam and lodge to east. Paved double-ended parking area.

F 23.5 (37.8 km) **M 128.5** (206.8 km) Large double-ended parking area with view of forested valley to west.

F 24.7 (39.7 km) **M 127.3** (204.9 km) Long double-ended turnout to east on curve.

F 27.7 (44.6 km) **M 124.3** (200 km) Large double-ended paved turnout to west. Highway winds around the base of Wickersham Dome (elev. 3,207 feet/977m). Views of the White Mountains, a range of white limestone mountains (elev. 5,000 feet/1,524m). Entering Livengood/Tolovana Mining District northbound, Fairbanks Mining District southbound.

Trailhead for White Mountains–Wickersham Creek trail and White Mountains–Summit trail to Borealis–LeFevre BLM cabin. The Wickersham Creek route is 20 miles/32 km in length; ATVs are permitted. The Summit route is 22 miles/35.4 km long and ATVs are prohibited.

Pipeline access restricted to ensure public safety and security, and to protect the reseeding and restoration of construction areas.

F 28.9 (46.5 km) **M 123.1** (198.1 km) Sled Dog Rocks ahead northbound. Double-ended gravel turnout to west.

F 29.5 (47.5 km) **M 122.5** (197.1 km) Long double-ended gravel alignment to east.

F 29.8 (48 km) **M 122.2** (196.7 km) Turnouts to west. Spring water piped to road.

F 30.4 (48.9 km) **M 121.6** (195.7 km) Large rough double-ended turnout to west. Fairbanks–North Star Borough boundary.

Pavement ends, gravel begins, northbound.

F 31 (49.9 km) **M 121** (194.7 km) Long double-ended gravel turnout to east.

F 31.8 (51.2 km) **M 120.2** (193.4 km) Large turnout to west.

F 32.7 (52.6 km) **M 119.3** (192 km) Steep downgrade and first good view of pipeline northbound.

F 34 (54.7 km) **M 118** (189.9 km) Good view of pipeline going underground; creek.

F 36.4 (58.6 km) **M 115.6** (186 km) Large double-ended turnout to east.

F 37 (59.5 km) **M 115** (185.1 km) Globe Creek bridge. Steep access road to parking area next to bridge.

F 38 (61.2 km) **M 114** (183.5 km) Highway follows pipeline. View of Globe Creek canyon. Grapefruit Rocks ahead, northbound.

F 39 (62.8 km) **M 113** (181.9 km) Double-ended turnout to east.

F 39.3 (63.2 km) **M 112.7** (181.4 km) Double-ended turnout to west.

F 40.6 (65.3 km) **M 111.4** (179.3 km) Scenic view from double-ended parking area to east at top of hill.

F 42.8 (68.9 km) **M 109.2** (175.7 km) Pipeline pump station No. 7 to west.

F 43 (69.2 km) **M 109** (175.4 km) *Steep downgrade (signed) northbound.*

F 44.8 (72.1 km) **M 107.2** (172.5 km) Tatalina River bridge; parking area to east at south end of bridge. The Tatalina is a tributary of the Chatanika.

F 49.5 (79.7 km) **M 102.5** (165 km) **The Arctic Circle Trading Post.** See display ad this section.

F 49.9 (80.3 km) **M 102.1** (164.3 km) Northern Lights School. This 2-room public school has an enrollment of 22 students.

F 51.9 (83.5 km) **M 100.1** (161.1 km) Double-ended parking area, paved. View of White Mountains to northeast and the Elliott Highway descending slopes of Bridge Creek valley ahead. Bridge Creek flows into the Tolovana River.

Steep downgrade (signed) northbound.

F 57 (91.7 km) **M 95** (152.9) **Colorado Creek Winter Trailhead**; wheelchair-accessible toilet; litter container. Colorado Creek trail leads to Colorado Creek and Windy Gap BLM cabins.

F 57.1 (91.9 km) **M 94.9** (152.7 km) **Tolovana River** bridge. Grayling to 11 inches; whitefish 12 to 18 inches; northern pike.   ⏴

F 58 (93.3 km) **M 94** (151.3 km) Highway climbs northbound as it winds around Amy Dome (elev. 2,317 feet/706m) to east. The Tolovana River flows in the valley to the southwest, paralleling the road.

F 59.3 (95.4 km) **M 92.7** (149.2 km) Parking area to west by stream; informal camping.

F 59.9 (96.4 km) **M 92.1** (148.2 km) Double-ended turnout to west.

F 62.3 (100.3 km) **M 89.7** (144.4 km) Access to Fred Blixt BLM cabin, east side of road. Preregister at BLM office in Fairbanks.

F 66 (106.2 km) **M 86** (138.4 km) **North Country Mercantile.** Located in the beautiful historic Livengood, Tolovana Mining District. Cigarettes, groceries, hunting and fishing licenses. Ice, gas and tire repair. Notary public and pay phone available. Soft ice cream and espresso with Kaladi Brothers coffee coming soon. Watch for our signs. Open year-round. 11 A.M.–11 P.M. summer; 9 A.M.–9 P.M. winter. Phone (907) 295-6500. [ADVERTISEMENT]

F 70.1 (112.8 km) **M 81.9** (131.8 km) Livengood Creek, 2-lane bridge. Money Knob to northeast.

F 70.8 (113.9 km) **M 81.2** (130.7 km) Double-ended turnout at **junction** with Livengood access road. Drive 2 miles/3.2 km to former mining camp of **LIVENGOOD** (area pop. about 100); state highway maintenance station. No visitor services

The settlement of Livengood began in July 1914 with the discovery of gold by Nathaniel R. Hudson and Jay Livengood. A lively mining camp until 1920, it yielded some $9.5 million in gold. Large-scale mining was attempted in the late 1930s and again in the 1940s, but both operations were eventually shut down and Livengood became a ghost town. A mining corporation acquired much of the gold-rich Livengood Bench. *NO TRESPASSING* on mining claims.

F 71.1 (114.4 km) **M 80.9** (130.2 km) Large double-ended turnout to south. Overnight parking allowed.   ▲

F 73.1 (117.6 km) **M 78.9** (127 km)

Junction with the Dalton Highway (Alaska Route 11). See DALTON HIGHWAY section for log.

Turn southwest to continue on Elliott Highway to Minto and Manley Hot Springs.

NOTE: Road narrows (no shoulders) and becomes noticeably rougher westbound.

F 74.3 (119.6 km) **M 77.7** (125 km) Site of old Livengood pipeline camp.

F 74.7 (120.2 km) **M 77.3** (124.4 km) Camping spot at west end of **Tolovana River** bridge; grayling to 15 inches, use spinners or flies   ⏴▲

F 76.3 (122.8 km) **M 75.7** (121.8 km) Cascaden Ridge (low hills to north).

F 79 (127.1 km) **M 73** (117.5 km) Travelers may notice the abundance of dragonflies seen along the Elliott Highway: their main food is mosquitoes.

F 86.3 (138.9 km) **M 65.7** (105.7 km) Highway climbs westbound (no guard rails). Looking south toward the Tolovana River valley, travelers should be able to see Tolovana Hot Springs Dome (elev. 2,386 feet/727m).

F 93.7 (150.8 km) **M 58.3** (93.8 km) Wide spot in road with view of Minto Lakes and the highway winding along the top of hills ahead westbound.

F 94.5 (152.1 km) **M 57.5** (92.5 km) Long double-ended turnout to south. Good vantage point to view Minto Flats, Tanana River and foothills of the Alaska Range to south.

F 97 (156.1 km) **M 55** (88.5 km) The mountains to the north are Sawtooth (elev. 4,494 feet/1,370m); Wolverine (elev. 4,580 feet/1,396m); and Elephant (elev. 3,661 feet/1,116m). To the south are Tolovana River flats and Cooper Lake.

F 98.3 (158.2 km) **M 53.7** (86.4 km) Turnout to southwest with view of Minto Lakes.

F 106.8 (171.9 km) **M 45.2** (72.7 km) Turnout with view of Sawtooth Mountains to north.

F 110 (177 km) **M 42** (67.6 km) **Junction** with Minto Road which leads south 11 miles/17.7 km to the Indian village of **MINTO** (pop. 233). The village was moved to its present location on the Tolovana River from the east bank of the Tanana River in 1971 because of flooding.

Minto has a gas station and the Village End Cafe (7998-7373). Most Minto residents make their living by hunting and fishing. Some local people also work in the arts and crafts center, making birch-bark baskets, beaded skin and fur items. Temperatures here range from 55°F/13°C to 90°F/32°C in summer, and from 32°F/0°C to -50°F/-46°C in winter. Minto Flats is one of the most popular duck hunting spots in Alaska, according to the ADF&G.

Private Aircraft: Minto airstrip 1 mile/1.6 km east; elev. 460 feet/140m; length 2,000 feet/610m; gravel; unattended.

Minto Lakes, name refers to all lakes in this lowland area. Accessible only by plane or boat; best to fly in. Pike to 36 inches; use wobblers, bait, red-and-white spoons, good all summer. Also grayling, sheefish and whitefish.

F 113 (181.9 km) **M 39** (62.8 km) Evidence of 1983 burn.

F 119.5 (192.3 km) **M 32.5** (52.3 km) Eureka Dome (elev. 2,393 feet/729m) to north.

F 123.2 (198.3 km) **M 28.8** (46.3 km) Large turnouts both sides of highway, scenic views to north.

CAUTION: Road descends westbound; slow down for curves.

F 129.3 (208.1 km) **M 22.7** (36.5 km) Hutlinana Creek bridge. *CAUTION: One-lane bridge.*

F 131.3 (211.3 km) **M 20.7** (33.3 km) Eureka Road turnoff. Active mining is taking place in this area. *NO TRESPASSING* on private claims. A trail leads to the former mining camp of Eureka, at the junction of Pioneer and Eureka creeks, 3 miles/4.8 km south of Eureka Dome.

NOTE: Road construction (new alignment) was under way next 7 miles/11.3 km westbound in summer 1998. Driving distances may vary from log.

F 137.4 (221.1 km) **M 14.6** (23.5 km) Bridge over **Baker Creek.** Grayling 5 to 20 inches, use flies, black gnats, mosquitoes, May 15 to Sept. 30.

F 150 (241.4 km) **M 2** (3.2 km) Walter Woods Park to west.

NOTE: This part of the road can be

View of Minto Lakes from village of Minto. (© Kris Graef, staff)

extremely slick after heavy rains. Drive with caution.

F 151.2 (243.3 km) **M 0.8** (1.3 km) Tofty Road, which leads 16 miles/25.7 km to former mining area of Tofty, founded in 1908 by pioneer prospector A.F. Tofty. Mining activity in area.

F 151.7 (244.1 km) **M 0.3** (0.5 km) Turn uphill for hot springs, which are contained in 3 concrete baths inside a greenhouse. Check in at the house on the hill (phone 907/672-3171) for reservations; $5/person.

F 151.9 (244.5 km) **M 0.1** (0.2 km) One-lane bridge over Hot Springs Slough.

Manley Hot Springs

F 152 (244.6 km) **M 0** Located at the end of the Elliott Highway on Hot Springs Slough. **Population: 94. Elevation:** 330 feet/101m. **Climate:** Mean temperature in July is 59°F/15°C, in January -10.4°F/-23.6°C. Record high 93°F/33.9°C in June 1969, record low -70°F/-56.7°C in January 1934. Precipitation in summer averages 2.53 inches a month. Snow from October through April, with traces in September and May. Greatest mean monthly snowfall in January (11.1 inches). Record snowfall 49 inches in January 1937.

Private Aircraft: Manley Hot Springs civil airstrip (open year-round), adjacent southwest; elev. 270 feet/82m; length 2,900 feet/884m; gravel; fuel avgas.

A pocket of "Pioneer Alaska." J.F. Karshner homesteaded here in 1902, about the same time the U.S. Army Signal Corps established a telegraph station nearby. The location soon became known as Baker Hot Springs, after nearby Baker Creek. Frank Manley built a 4-story resort hotel here in 1907. The settlement's name was changed to Manley Hot Springs in 1957. Once a busy trading center during peak activity in the nearby Eureka and Tofty mining districts, Manley Hot Springs is now a quiet settlement with a trading post, roadhouse, airfield

and hot springs resort. Many residents are enthusiastic gardeners, and visitors may see abundant displays of vegetables and berries growing around homes and businesses. Outstanding display of wild irises at the airstrip in June.

A restaurant, bar and overnight accommodations are at the roadhouse. The post office, gas station and grocery are at the trading post. There is an air taxi service here and scheduled service from Fairbanks.

Manley Trading Post. See display ad this section.

Manley Roadhouse. Come visit one of Alaska's oldest original roadhouses from the gold rush era. See the many prehistoric and Alaskana artifacts on display. New rooms with private baths added 1997. Private cabins. The Manley Roadhouse is a great place to meet local miners, dog mushers, trappers or fishermen. We specialize in traditional Alaska home-style hospitality, fresh-baked pies, giant cinnamon rolls and good food. Largest liquor selection in Alaska. Stop by and see us. See display ad this section. [ADVERTISEMENT]   *MP*

Grassy picnic area, playground and camping at park on the slough across from Manley Roadhouse.   ▲

Manley Hot Springs Slough; pike 18 to 36 inches, use spinning and trolling lures, May through September. Follow the dirt road from the old Northern Commercial Co. store out of town for 2.5 miles/4 km to reach the Tanana River; king, silver and chum salmon from 7 to 40 lbs., June 15 to Sept. 30. Fish wheels and nets are used.

DALTON HIGHWAY ⑪

Connects: Elliott Hwy. to Deadhorse, AK   **Length:** 414 miles
Road Surface: Gravel   **Season:** Open all year
Steepest Grade: 12 percent
Highest Summit: Atigun Pass 4,800 feet
Major Attraction: Trans-Alaska Pipeline

(See map, page 500)

	Coldfoot	Deadhorse	Fairbanks
Coldfoot		239	259
Deadhorse	239		498
Fairbanks	259	498	

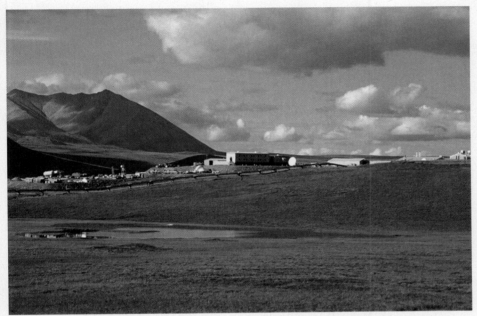

Pump Station No. 3 on the North Slope along the Dalton Highway. (© Ruth Fairall)

and was completed 5 months later. The road is 28 feet/9m wide with 3 to 6 feet/1 to 2m of gravel surfacing. Some sections of road are underlain with plastic foam insulation to prevent thawing of the permafrost.

Construction of the 800-mile-/1,287-km-long pipeline between Prudhoe Bay and Valdez took place between 1974 and 1977. The 48-inch-diameter pipeline, of which slightly more than half is above ground, has 10 operating pump stations. The control center is in Valdez. Design, construction and operation of the pipeline are managed by Alyeska Pipeline Service Company, a consortium of 7 oil companies (BP, ARCO, Exxon, Mobil, Amerada Hess, Phillips and Unocal). For more information, contact Public Affairs Dept., Alyeska Pipeline Service Co., 1835 S. Bragaw St., Anchorage, AK 99512.

The Bureau of Land Management (BLM) manages 2.1 million acres of public land along the Dalton Highway between the Yukon and Pump Station No. 3. For information on BLM lands, contact Arctic District, BLM, 1150 University Ave., Fairbanks, AK 99709; phone (907) 474-2301.

The 414-mile/666.3-km Dalton Highway (still referred to as the "Haul Road") begins at **Milepost F 73.1** on the Elliott Highway and ends—for the general public—at Deadhorse, a few miles from Prudhoe Bay and the Arctic Ocean. (Access to the Arctic Ocean is available only through commercial tour operators; private vehicles are not permitted on the oil field.) Permits are no longer required to drive the highway to Deadhorse.

The Dalton Highway is unique in its scenic beauty, wildlife and recreational opportunities, but it is also one of Alaska's most remote and challenging roads.

Road conditions vary depending on weather, maintenance and time of year, but in general the road surface ranges from acceptable to rough. Watch for ruts, rocks,

dust, soft shoulders and trucks. Calcium chloride is used on the road to control dust;

it is corrosive to vehicles and slippery when wet. There are several steep (10 to 12 percent) grades. Drive with your headlights on at all times. Slow down and pull over to the side of the road when meeting oncoming trucks. Stop only at turnouts. Carry spare tires; flat tires are a common occurrence on this road.

Services along the Dalton Highway are limited. Shop for groceries before departing Fairbanks. There are no convenience stores or grocery stores along the highway. Gas, diesel fuel, tire repair, restaurant, motel, phone and emergency communications are available at **Milepost J 56**, just past the Yukon River bridge, and at Coldfoot, **Milepost J 175**. The last dump station northbound is also located at Coldfoot. (Please do NOT dump holding tanks along the road.) Phones at both locations are for credit card and collect calls only. Public phone at Wiseman. Alyeska pump stations do not provide any public services. Although noted on the map, former pipeline camps have been removed.

The highway is named for James William Dalton, an arctic engineer involved in early oil exploration efforts on the North Slope. It was built as a haul road between the Yukon River and Prudhoe Bay during construction of the trans-Alaska pipeline, and was originally called the North Slope Haul Road. Construction of the road began April 29, 1974,

Travelers are requested to stay on the road and to use the formal turnouts and campgrounds provided to avoid permanently scarring the fragile tundra.

There are 4 formal campgrounds on the Dalton, and several informal campsites for self-contained RVs. All are noted in the log. There is overnight parking at the Tesoro in Deadhorse. ▲

For emergency services contact the Alaska State Troopers via CB radio, Channel 19, or contact any state highway maintenance camp along the highway. Highway maintenance camps can provide help only in the event of an accident or medical emergency; they cannot fix flat tires nor do they provide gas. Keep in mind that towing fees by private wrecker service can cost $5 a mile, each way.

Report wildlife violations to Fish and Game at Coldfoot.

All waters between the Yukon River bridge and Dietrich River are part of the Yukon River system, and most are tributaries of the Koyukuk River. Fishing for arctic grayling is especially good in rivers accessible by foot from the highway. The large rivers also support burbot, salmon, pike and whitefish. Small Dolly Varden are at higher elevations in streams north of Coldfoot. Fishing for salmon is closed within the trans-Alaska pipeline corridor. According to the Dept. of Fish and Game, anglers should expect high, turbid water conditions throughout much of June as the snowpack melts in the Brooks Range, with the best fishing occurring during July and August. ⬟

Dalton Highway Log

Distance from junction with Elliott Highway (J) is followed by distance from Deadhorse (D).

ALASKA ROUTE 11

J 0 D 414 (666.3 km) Sign at start of Dalton Highway: "Heavy Industrial Traffic. All vehicles drive with headlights on. Speed 50 mph next 416 miles."

Junction with Elliott Highway to Fairbanks and Manley Hot Springs. Turn to **Milepost F 73.1** in the ELLIOTT HIGHWAY section for log of that route.

J 1 (1.6 km) **D 413** (664.6 km) Distance marker shows Yukon River 56 miles, Coldfoot 75 miles, Deadhorse 414 miles.

J 2 (3.2 km) **D 412** (663 km) Pipeline passes under highway.

J 2.9 (4.7 km) **D 411.1** (661.6 km) Turnout to west.

J 4 (6.4 km) **D 410** (659.8 km) Highway descends steeply into the Lost Creek valley. Lost Creek flows into the West Fork Tolovana River. Pipeline is visible stretching across the ridge of the distant hill.

J 5 (8 km) **D 409** (658 km) Yellow numbered signs mark oil spill containment site. Materials are stockpiled here for use in case of an oil spill.

J 5.6 (9 km) **D 408.4** (657.2 km) Lost Creek culvert. APL pipeline access road; no public admittance. There are many of these

pipeline access roads along the highway; most are signed with the milepost on the pipeline. Because they are so numerous, most APL pipeline access roads are not included in *The MILEPOST* log unless they occur along with another feature. All these access roads are closed to the public for security and safety concerns. Do not block road access.

J 6.2 (10 km) **D 407.8** (656.3 km) Large informal gravel parking area.

Road narrows northbound; muddy in wet weather.

J 8.3 (13.4 km) **D 405.7** (652.9 km) Entering Game Management Unit 20 northbound.

J 10.6 (17.1 km) **D 403.4** (649.2 km) Turnout to east.

J 11 (17.7 km) **D 403** (648.5 km) *Begin steep (12 percent) downgrade northbound.*

J 12 (19.3 km) **D 402** (646.9 km) Turnout to west. Begin upgrade northbound.

J 20.7 (33.3 km) **D 393.3** (632.9 km) Long turnout west side of road with sweeping view.

J 21 (33.8 km) **D 393** (632.5 km) Descent to Hess Creek begins northbound.

J 23.6 (38 km) **D 390.4** (628.3 km) Pipeline access road, pond.

Very rough road surface north to Milepost J 28.

J 23.8 (38.3 km) **D 390.2** (627.9 km) **Hess Creek** bridge. Campsite in trees. Large gravel bar along creek at north end of bridge. Sandpit at entrance to gravel bar is an easy place to get stuck. Bring your mosquito repellent. Whitefish and grayling fishing. Hess Creek, known for its colorful mining history, is the largest stream between the junction and the Yukon River bridge. ◄▲

J 23.9 (38.5 km) **D 390.1** (627.8 km) Road to west leads 0.2 mile/0.3 km to pond with parking space adequate for camping.

J 25 (40.2 km) **D 389** (626 km) Double-ended rough turnout. Good view of pipeline and remote-operated valve site as the highway crosses Hess Creek and valley.

Highway climbs northbound; steep curve.

J 26.5 (42.6 km) **D 387.5** (623.6 km) APL access. Pipeline parallels highway about 250 feet/76m away.

J 27 (43.4 km) **D 387** (622.8 km) Evidence of lightning-caused forest fires.

J 28.2 (45.4 km) **D 385.8** (620.9 km) Large turnout opposite APL access. Downgrade northbound.

J 32.7 (52.6 km) **D 381.3** (613.6 km) Turnout to east.

J 33.7 (54.2 km) **D 380.3** (612 km) Turnout at tributary of Hess Creek. Chiming bells bloom in June.

J 35.5 (57.1 km) **D 378.5** (609.1 km) Turnout to east.

J 38 (61.2 km) **D 376** (605.1 km) Mile 38 Dalton Highway Crossing: pipeline goes under road. APL access road.

J 40.7 (65.5 km) **D 373.3** (600.7 km) Double-ended turnout. Overview of Troublesome and Hess creeks areas. Brush obscures sweeping views.

J 42 (67.6 km) **D 372** (598.7 km) Large turnout. Outcrop of dark gabbroic rock.

Begin steep descent northbound.

J 43.1 (69.4 km) **D 370.9** (596.9 km) Isom Creek culvert.

J 44 (70.8 km) **D 370** (595.4 km) *Steep, winding road northbound to Milepost J 46; 35 mph.*

J 44.6 (71.8 km) **D 369.4** (594.5 km) Turnout.

J 47.3 (76.1 km) **D 366.7** (590.1 km) Summit; sweeping view of mountains.

J 47.5 (76.4 km) **D 366.5** (589.8 km) Yukon radio repeater tower.

J 47.9 (77.1 km) **D 366.1** (589.2 km) Highway begins descent to Yukon River.

J 48.5 (78.1 km) **D 365.5** (588.2 km) APL pipeline access road. Goalpost-like structures, called "headache bars," guard against vehicles large enough to run into and damage the pipeline.

J 50.4 (81.1 km) **D 363.6** (585.1 km) Turnout; pond to east.

J 51.1 (82.2 km) **D 362.9** (584 km) Rough side road leads east 5.4 miles/8.7 km to Yukon River.

J 53 (85.6 km) **D 360.8** (580.6 km) First view northbound of the Yukon River. As road drops, you can see the pipeline crossing the river. Fort Hamlin Hills are beyond the river.

J 53.8 (86.6 km) **D 360.2** (579.7 km) **Pump Station No. 6.** Alyeska pump stations monitor the pipeline's oil flow on its journey from Prudhoe Bay to Valdez. No public facilities.

J 54.3 (87.4 km) **D 359.7** (578.9 km) Highway passes over pipeline.

J 54.5 (87.7 km) **D 359.5** (578.5 km) APL access (Milepost 354.2 on the pipeline).

J 55.6 (89.5 km) **D 358.4** (576.8 km) **Yukon River Bridge** (formally the E.L. Patton Bridge, named for the president of

the Alyeska Pipeline Service Co. after his death in 1982). This wood-decked bridge, completed in 1975, is 2,290 feet/698m long and has a 6 percent grade. The deck was replaced in 1993.

J 56 (90.1 km) **D 358** (576.1 km) Gas, diesel, tire repair, restaurant, motel, phone and emergency communications available at Yukon Ventures Alaska. Next services north

bound: 120 miles/193 km. Tours and charters of the Yukon River aboard the *Yookene Spirit*.

Yukon Ventures Alaska. See display ad this section.

This is the southern boundary of BLM-managed lands. BLM Yukon Crossing Visitor Contact Station here is open daily, June through August. **Alyeska Pipeline Interpretive Display** here with information on the Yukon River, pipeline construction and related subjects. Hunter check station trailer in season.

East of the highway is a camping area with litter barrels. ▲

J 60.5 (97.4 km) **D 353.5** (568.9 km) Turnoff to west for loop road to Hot Spot Cafe and RV parking and water pump at former Five Mile pipeline construction camp.

Hot Spot Cafe & Arctic Circle Gifts. Favorite stop for truckers and locals. Best BBQ in Alaska. Huge hamburgers, daily specials. The best coffee, ice cream and homemade pies and cakes. Arctic Circle Gifts—local Native crafts. Lowest prices on the road. Easy entrance and exit for motorhomes. [ADVERTISEMENT]

J 60.6 (97.5 km) **D 353.4** (568.7 km)

Highway crosses over buried pipeline.

J 60.8 (97.8 km) **D 353.2** (568.4 km) Five Mile airstrip (length 3,500 feet/1,067m); controlled by Alyeska Security. *CAUTION: Be prepared to stop at control gates at both ends of airstrip.*

J 61.3 (98.7 km) **D 352.7** (567.6 km) Airstrip control tower.

J 61.6 (99.1 km) **D 352.4** (567.1 km) View of Fort Hamlin Hills to north, pump station No. 6 to south.

J 61.8 (99.5 km) **D 352.2** (566.8 km) Seven Mile Station (DOT/PF highway maintenance) to east; APL access to west.

J 66.8 (107.5 km) **D 347.2** (558.7 km) Turnout to west.

J 68 (109.4 km) **D 346** (556.8 km) Dalton Pipeline Crossing: Highway crosses over buried pipeline.

J 69 (111 km) **D 345** (555.2 km) Turnout at crest of hill overlooking the Ray River to the north. Pipeline goes underground.

J 70 (112.7 km) **D 344** (553.6 km) View of Ray River and Ray Mountains to the west.

J 72.5 (116.7 km) **D 341.5** (549.6 km) Fort Hamlin Hills Creek bridge.

J 73.5 (118.3 km) **D 340.5** (548 km) *Begin steep 0.5-mile/0.8-km ascent of Sand Hill northbound.*

J 74.8 (120.4 km) **D 339.2** (545.9 km) *Steep descent northbound followed by steep ascent; dubbed the "Roller Coaster."*

J 79.1 (127.3 km) **D 334.9** (539 km) Steep descent northbound to **No Name Creek** bridge (narrow). Fishing for burbot, grayling and whitefish. ☞

Bow hunting only area.

J 81.6 (131.3 km) **D 332.4** (534.9 km) Fort Hamlin Hills are visible to the southeast. Tree line on surrounding hills is about 2,000 feet/610m.

J 86.5 (139.2 km) **D 327.5** (527 km) Scenic overlook 1 mile/1.6 km west with view of tors to northeast, Yukon Flats Wildlife Refuge to east and Fort Hamlin Hills to southeast. Tors are high, isolated pinnacles of jointed granite jutting up from the tundra and are a residual feature of erosion.

J 87 (140 km) **D 327** (526.2 km) *Long, steep ascent of Mackey Hill northbound; slippery in wet weather.*

J 88.5 (142.4 km) **D 325.5** (523.8 km) Road descends Mackey Hill northbound.

Entering Game Management Unit 25D northbound, Unit 20F southbound.

J 90.2 (145.2 km) **D 323.8** (521.1 km) Parking areas on both sides of highway at crest of hill. A good photo opportunity of the road and pipeline to the north. The zig-zag design allows the pipeline to flex and accommodate temperature changes. The small green structure over the buried pipe is a radio-controlled valve, allowing the pipeline oil flow to be shut down when necessary.

J 94 (151.3 km) **D 320** (515 km) Turnout at former gravel pit road to west.

J 96 (154.5 km) **D 318** (511.8 km) The road lies above tree line for about 5 miles/8 km. Northbound, the terrain becomes more rugged and scenic.

J 97.1 (156.3 km) **D 316.9** (510 km) Turnout to east.

J 97.6 (157.1 km) **D 316.4** (509.2 km) Good view northbound of **Finger Rock**, a tor, visible east of the road. Tors are visible for the next 2 miles/3.2 km. Prehistoric hunting sites are numerous in this region. Please do not collect or disturb artifacts.

J 98.1 (157.9 km) **D 315.9** (508.4 km) Finger Mountain wayside at crest of hill; toilet, parking, interpretive trail. Good

opportunities for photos, berry picking (blueberries, lowbush cranberries), wildflower viewing and hiking.

Caribou Mountain is in the distance to the northwest. Olsens Lake, Kanuti Flats, Kanuti River drainage and site of former Old Man Camp are visible ahead northbound.as the road descends and passes through several miles of valley bottom. Excellent mountain views.

J 102.3 (164.6 km) **D 311.7** (501.6 km) Arctic Circle Bed and Breakfast on west side of highway.

Arctic Circle Bed & Breakfast. See display ad this section.

J 105.8 (170.3 km) **D 308.2** (496 km) Large turnout to east. Narrow bridge over **Kanuti River**; burbot and grayling fishing. ☞

J 107 (172.2 km) **D 307** (494.1 km) Site of Old Man Camp, a former pipeline construction camp; no structures remain.

J 108.4 (174.4 km) **D 305.6** (491.8 km) Highway crosses pipeline.

J 109.8 (176.7 km) **D 304.2** (489.5 km) Turnout at Beaver Slide.

CAUTION: Road descends 9 percent grade northbound. Watch for soft spots. Slippery when wet.

J 110 (177 km) **D 304** (489.2 km) Sweeping view northbound of Brooks Range.

J 111 (178.6 km) **D 303** (487.6 km) *NOTE: Road surface deteriorates northbound.*

J 112.2 (180.6 km) **D 301.8** (485.7 km) Turnout at pipeline access road. Moose and bear frequent willow thickets here.

J 113.9 (183.3 km) **D 300.1** (483 km) Evidence of old winter trail to Bettles is visible here.

J 114 (183.5 km) **D 300** (482.8 km) Turnouts at both ends of **Fish Creek** bridge; grayling 12 to 18 inches. ☞

J 115.3 (185.5 km) **D 298.7** (480.7 km) Loop road east to **Arctic Circle** BLM Wayside with tables, grills, toilets and interpretive display. Stop and have your picture taken with the sign showing you are at the latitude (N 66°33′) at which the sun never sets on summer solstice (June 20 or 21) and never rises on winter solstice (December 21 or 22). A third of Alaska lies within the Arctic Cirlce, the only true polar region in the state. This is also a good photo point, with views to the south and to the west. Follow road off turnout 0.6 mile/1 km for primitive campsites (pull-throughs, nice views). If you reach the Alyeska access gate you've gone too far.▲

J 116.2 (187 km) **D 297.8** (479.2 km) Turnout to east (can be soft).

J 120.7 (194.2 km) **D 293.3** (472 km) Connection Rock (signed); north and south road-building crews linked up here.

J 124.7 (200.7 km) **D 289.3** (465.6 km) Turnout to east at **South Fork Bonanza Creek**; burbot, grayling, whitefish. ☞

J 125.7 (202.3 km) **D 288.3** (464 km) Turnout to east at **North Fork Bonanza**

Arctic Circle Bed & Breakfast

Gift Shop • Hand Crafted Items
Coffee • Food • Lodging • Canoes • Fishing
Midnight Sun / Northern Lights Viewing

Open Daily May thru Sept.

Write For Brochure, Winter Schedule
P.O. Box 9080, Coldfoot, AK 99701
Ph. **(907) 452-0081** • Fax **(907) 479-7306**

Creek; historic gold mining area; burbot, grayling, whitefish. ☞

J 127.7 (205.5 km) **D 286.3** (460.7 km) Paradise Hill (not signed); blueberries and lowbush cranberries in season.

J 130 (209.2 km) **D 284** (457 km) *Long, steep, ascent northbound.*

J 131.3 (211.3 km) **D 282.7** (454.9 km) Solar-powered communications tower to west.

J 131.5 (211.6 km) **D 282.5** (454.6 km) View of Pump Station No. 5 to north.

J 132 (212.4 km) **D 282** (453.8 km) Large turnout with litter barrels and toilet at Gobblers Knob (elev. 1,500 feet/457m) overlooking the Jack White Range, Pope Creek Dome (the dominant peak to the northwest), Prospect Creek drainage, Pump Station No. 5, Jim River drainage, South Fork Koyukuk drainage and the Brooks Range on the northern horizon.

CAUTION: Begin long, steep descent southbound.

J 135.1 (217.4 km) **D 278.9** (448.8 km) Narrow bridge over **Prospect Creek**; grayling, whitefish and pike. Active gold mining area. ☞

CAUTION: Steep uphill grade northbound; watch for trucks on blind hill.

J 135.7 (218.4 km) **D 278.3** (447.9 km) Turnout. Old winter road goes up creek to mines. Turn left for site of **PROSPECT CAMP**, which holds the record for lowest recorded temperature in Alaska (-80°F/-62°C, Jan. 23, 1971). Rough road leads 0.5 mile/0.8 km to Claja Pond; beaver, ducks. Undeveloped campsite on Jim River. Old winter road to Bettles crosses river here. ▲

J 137.1 (220.6 km) **D 276.9** (445.6 km) APL access road at Milepost 274.7 on the pipeline at **Pump Station No. 5**. Pump station No. 5 is not actually a pump station, but a "drain down" or pressure relief station to slow the gravity-fed flow of oil descending from Atigun Pass in the Brooks Range. Glacial moraine marks the southern boundary of Brooks Range glaciers during the most

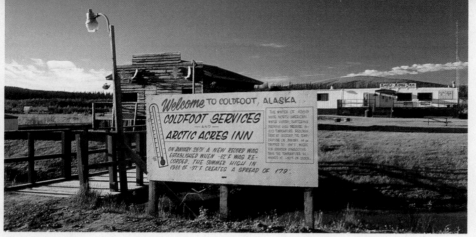

Sign at Coldfoot's Sourdough Services just east of the Dalton Highway at Milepost 175. (© Harry M. Walker)

recent ice age.

Private Aircraft: Airstrip; length 5,000 feet/1,524m; lighted runway. This airstrip is used as a BLM fire fighting staging area.

J 138.1 (222.2 km) **D 275.9** (444 km) Jim River Station (DOT/PF highway maintenance).

J 139 (223.7 km) **D 275** (442.6 km) Road to gravel pit.

J 140.1 (225.5 km) **D 273.9** (440.8 km) **Jim River No. 1** crossing (narrow bridge); turnouts. Burbot, chum and king salmon, grayling, pike, whitefish. *CAUTION: Bears here for fall salmon run.*

J 141 (226.9 km) **D 273** (439.3 km) **Jim River No. 2** crossing (narrow bridge); turnouts, fishing.

J 141.8 (228.2 km) **D 272.2** (438.1 km) Douglas Creek crossing.

J 144.1 (231.9 km) **D 269.9** (434.4 km) Parking area at APL access road south of **Jim River No. 3** crossing of main channel (narrow bridge). Fishing.

J 145.6 (234.3 km) **D 268.4** (431.9 km) Pipeline passes under road. First views northbound of Brooks Range foothills to the north.

J 150.3 (241.9 km) **D 263.7** (424.4 km) **Grayling Lake** to east has good grayling fishing in open water season.

J 150.8 (242.7 km) **D 263.2** (423.6 km) Turnout on Grayling Lake. The road is passing through the foothills of the Brooks Range. There is an active gold mining area behind the hills to the west.

J 156 (251.1 km) **D 258** (415.2 km) Large parking area with toilet and litter barrels at the **South Fork Koyukuk River** bridge. Self-contained RV camping in turnout. Fishing for grayling, whitefish, chum and king salmon. Active gold mining downstream.

This large river flows past the villages of Bettles, Allakaket, Hughes and Huslia before draining into the Yukon River near Koyukuk.

J 159.1 (256 km) **D 254.9** (410.2 km) Bridge over pipeline; large animal crossing over pipeline. Road narrows northbound.

J 160 (257.5 km) **D 254** (408.8 km) Good view of Chapman Lake west of road as highway descends steeply northbound. Old mine trail is visible from the road.

The 2 mountains visible to the north are Twelvemile Mountain (elev. 3,190 feet/972m), left, and Cathedral Mountain (elev. 3,000 feet/914m), on right. The foothills of the Brooks Range are also to the north.

J 161.2 (259.4 km) **D 252.8** (406.8 km) Road to west leads to gold claim. Many side roads off the Dalton Highway lead to private mining claims.

J 163.3 (262.8 km) **D 250.7** (403.5 km) Turnout to west.

J 164.6 (264.9 km) **D 249.4** (401.3 km) Example of a "sag bend," a short section of buried pipeline that allows large animals to cross.

J 165.1 (265.7 km) **D 248.9** (400.6 km) Turnout to west. APL access road to east.

J 165.7 (266.7 km) **D 248.3** (399.6 km) Turnout on west side of road overlooking Middle Fork Koyukuk River.

J 167.2 (269.1 km) **D 246.8** (397.2 km) Old winter trail to Tramway Bar. "River training structures" in place direct water away from the pipeline and highway during floods.

J 175 (281.6 km) **D 239** (384.6 km) Turnoff to east for Soughdough Services, Coldfoot (DOT) Station and visitor center at **COLDFOOT**, a former mining camp at the mouth of Slate Creek on the east bank of the Middle Fork Koyukuk River.

NOTE: Next services northbound are 244 miles/392.7 km from here.

Coldfoot Services (phone 907/678-5201) offers motel lodging and 24-hour restaurant. The "trucker's table" at the restaurant is a good place to get news on the highway. There is also a gift shop, general store, trading post, laundromat, fuel facility with gas, diesel and avgas; tire repair, minor vehicle repair; RV park with hookups and dump station; post office, phone and emergency medical service. It is also home of the "farthest North saloon in North America" with "readable walls." Area tours and guided hunting and fishing trips available. ▲

There is a 3,500-foot/1,067-m runway to west, maintained by the state. An Alaska State Trooper, a Fish and Wildlife officer and BLM field station are located at Coldfoot. A visitor center here, operated by the BLM, USF&WS and National Park Service, offers travel information and nightly presentations on the natural and cultural history of the Arctic. It is open from June 1 through Labor Day. Topographic maps for sale.

Originally named Slate Creek, Coldfoot reportedly got its name in 1900 when gold stampeders got as far up the Koyukuk as this point, then got cold feet, turned and departed. The old cemetery still exists. Emma Dome (elev. 5,680 feet/1,731m) is to the west.

Sourdough Fuel, Coldfoot Slate Creek Inn. See display ad this section. ▲

J 175.1 (281.8 km) **D 238.9** (384.5 km) Narrow bridge over Slate Creek.

J 175.7 (282.8 km) **D 238.3** (383.5 km) Radio repeater site on mountains to east.

J 179.7 (289.2 km) **D 234.3** (377.1 km) Turnoff to east for **Marion Creek Campground** (BLM); 27 sites on gravel loop road, $6 camping fee, tables, grills, firepits, water, toilets, bear-proof litter containers, resident

campground host, information kiosk, RV parking. Good berry picking (blueberries, lowbrush cranberries) in season. Marion Creek trailhead. ▲

J 179.9 (289.5 km) **D 234.1** (376.7 km)

Marion Creek.

J 181 (291.3 km) **D 233** (375 km) Entering BLM public lands.

J 186.8 (300.6 km) **D 227.2** (365.6 km) Turnouts both sides of highway.

J 187.3 (301.4 km) **D 226.7** (364.8 km) Parking area to west at **Minnie Creek**; burbot, grayling, whitefish.

J 188.5 (303.4 km) **D 225.5** (362.9 km) **Middle Fork Koyukuk River No. 1** crossing (narrow bridge); turnout. Dolly Varden, grayling, whitefish. ✦

J 188.6 (303.5 km) **D 225.4** (362.7 km) Improved access road leads 3 miles/4.8 km south to **WISEMAN** (pop. 25), a historic mining town on the Koyukuk River established in 1908. The heyday of Wiseman came in about 1910, after gold seekers abandoned Coldfoot. This is still an active mining area.

Several interesting historic buildings (all privately owned). The post office is located in an original log cabin. The Historic Pioneer Hall Igloo No. 8 is a bed and breakfast. The **Wiseman Historical Museum** is located in the historic Carl Frank Cabin. The museum contains old miner's journals, hotel registers and historical photos; limited gift items are for sale. Well worth a stop; watch for signs as you enter town. Follow the road south across the river for Wiseman Trading Co. Inquire locally about camping. ▲

Arctic Getaway Bed & Breakfast. See display ad this section.

Wiseman Museum. See display ad this section.

J 189 (304.2 km) **D 225** (362.1 km) Spur (finger) dikes keep river away from highway and pipeline.

J 190.5 (306.6 km) **D 223.5** (359.7 km) Narrow bridge over Hammond River; gold mining area upstream.

J 190.8 (307.1 km) **D 223.2** (359.2 km) **Middle Fork Koyukuk River No. 2** crossing (narrow bridge). "Guide banks," another example of river training structures.

J 192.8 (310.3 km) **D 221.2** (356 km) Link Up (not signed), where 2 sections of road constructed by different crews were joined.

J 193.6 (311.5 km) **D 220.4** (354.7 km) Pavement next 1.2 miles/1.9 km northbound.

J 194 (312.2 km) **D 220** (354 km) First view northbound of **Sukakpak Mountain**

www.themilepost.com

(elev. 4,000 feet/1,219m) to north. Sukakpak Mountain is sometimes said to mark a traditional boundary between Eskimo and Athabascan Indian territories. Wiehl Mountain (elev. 4,000 feet/1,219m) is east of Sukakpak. The high mountain just to the west of the road is unnamed.

J 195 (313.8 km) **D 219** (352.4 km) Pipeline close to road is mounted on sliding shoes to allow flexing.

J 197 (317 km) **D 217** (349.2 km) Gold Creek bridge (narrow).

J 197.2 (317.3 km) **D 216.8** (348.9 km) Turnout to east.

J 197.3 (317.5 km) **D 216.7** (348.7 km) Cat trail to gold mining area.

J 197.5 (317.8 km) **D 216.5** (348.4 km) Linda Creek in culvert.

J 197.7 (318.2 km) **D 216.3** (348.1 km) Turnout east and view of Wiehl Mountain.

J 200 (321.9 km) **D 214** (344.4 km) View of the Middle Fork Koyukuk River, a typical braided river exhibiting frequent changes of the streambed during high water.

J 203.5 (327.5 km) **D 210.5** (338.7 km) Park on shoulder for 0.5-mile/0.8-km footpath to Sukakpak Mountain. The short mounds of earth between the road and Sukakpak are palsas, formed by ice beneath the soil pushing the vegetative mat and soil upward.

J 203.8 (328 km) **D 210.2** (338.3 km) Turnouts next 0.6 mile/1 km northbound.

J 204.3 (328.8 km) **D 209.7** (337.5 km) **Middle Fork Koyukuk River No. 3** bridge. Large turnout with toilet (last public toilet northbound to Deadhorse) and litter barrels to east at north end of bridge. Self-contained RV camping in turnout. ▲

J 204.5 (329.1 km) **D 209.5** (337.1 km) **Middle Fork Koyukuk River No. 4** crossing (narrow bridge).

J 205.3 (330.4 km) **D 208.7** (335.9 km) Turnout to west. Good view of north side of Sukakpak Mountain.

J 206 (331.5 km) **D 208** (334.7 km) View of Wiehl Mountain.

J 207 (333.1 km) **D 207** (333.1 km) **Dietrich River** bridge. Half-way mark on the Dalton highway. Turnout to west at south end of bridge. Access to river to west at north end. Fishing for burbot, grayling, whitefish and Dolly Varden. ✦

J 209.1 (336.5 km) **D 204.9** (329.7 km) **Dietrich** 1 mile/1.6 km west, a former pipeline construction camp.

J 210.9 (339.4 km) **D 203.1** (326.8 km) Large turnout with bear-proof litter container to east.

J 211 (339.6 km) **D 203** (326.7 km) Disaster Creek.

J 216.2 (347.9 km) **D 197.8** (318.3 km) Snowden Creek culvert. Panorama of Dietrich River valley and Brooks Range north and west of the road.

J 217.1 (349.4 km) **D 196.9** (316.9 km) Rock spire to east is Snowden Mountain (elev. 5,775 feet/1,760m). Cirque above highway was carved by a glacier; hike up to waterfall.

J 218.3 (351.3 km) **D 195.7** (314.9 km)

Turnout to west.

J 221.6 (356.6 km) **D 192.4** (309.6 km) Quarry of black marble with white calcite veins to east.

J 224 (360.5 km) **D 190** (305.8 km) Turnout at gravel pit to east.

J 225.9 (363.5 km) **D 188.1** (302.7 km) Pipeline remote valve just west of road. The arch-shaped concrete "saddle weights" keep pipeline buried in areas of possible flooding.

J 228 (366.9 km) **D 186** (299.3 km) Highway parallels Dietrich River.

J 229.5 (369.3 km) **D 184.5** (296.9 km) Turnout to east next to stream in rock culvert.

J 231.4 (372.4 km) **D 182.6** (293.9 km) Small turnouts both sides of highway. Pipeline is buried under river.

J 232.8 (374.6 km) **D 181.2** (291.6 km) Turnout to west.

J 234.6 (377.5 km) **D 179.4** (288.7 km) Pipeline emerges from under river.

J 234.9 (378 km) **D 179.1** (288.2 km) Entering North Slope Borough—"the world's largest municipality"—northbound. North Slope Borough offices are located in Barrow.

J 235.3 (378.7 km) **D 178.7** (287.6 km) Large turnout with litter barrel at foot of Chandalar Shelf. Truck chain-up area.

Begin long, steep (10 percent) grade northbound. Give trucks plenty of room. Do not stop on road. Dirt road surface can be slippery in wet weather. Watch for soft spots.

J 237.1 (381.6 km) **D 176.9** (284.7 km) Narrow turnout to west at top of Chandalar Shelf; former checkpoint when a permit was required to drive beyond this point.

Headwaters of the Chandalar River are to the east. Table Mountain (elev. 6,425 feet/1,958m) is to the southeast. Dietrich River valley to south.

J 239.2 (384.9 km) **D 174.8** (281.3 km) Site of Chandalar Camp, a former pipeline construction camp, now used as a BLM field station.

J 239.4 (385.3 km) **D 174.6** (281 km) Chandalar Station (DOT/PF highway maintenance) to west; no visitor services.

J 242.1 (389.6 km) **D 171.9** (276.6 km) Avalanche gun emplacement.

J 242.2 (389.8 km) **D 171.8** (276.5 km) West Fork of the North Fork Chandalar River bridge.

Begin long, steep (12 percent) grade northbound toward Atigun Pass. Winter avalanche

Caribou range across the North Slope. (© Craig Brandt)

area. Slide area next 5 miles/8 km northbound.

J 243.4 (391.7 km) **D 170.6** (274.5 km) Turnout with spectacular view south of valley and pipeline.

J 244 (392.6 km) **D 170** (273.6 km) Turnout.

J 244.7 (393.8 km) **D 169.3** (272.5 km) Turnout at top of **Atigun Pass** (elev. 4,800 feet/1,463m), highest highway pass in Alaska; Continental Divide. A Wyoming Gauge to measure moisture is located here. Nice example of a cirque, an amphitheater-shaped bowl or depression caused by glacier erosion, in mountain east of road. Endicott Mountains are to the west, Philip Smith Mountains to the east. James Dalton Mountain is to the left ahead northbound.

J 245 (394.3 km) **D 169** (272 km) Turnout.

J 245.3 (394.8 km) **D 168.7** (271.5 km) Avalanche gun emplacement. Large turnouts. Look for Dall sheep (they were on the road here in summer 1998).

J 245.5 (395.1 km) **D 168.5** (271.2 km) Highway descends steeply toward the North Slope. Many mountains in the area exceed 7,000 feet/2,134m in elevation. The pipeline is in a buried, insulated concrete cribbing to the east to protect it from rock slides and avalanches, and to keep the ground frozen. Construction in this area was extremely complex, difficult and dangerous.

J 248.4 (399.8 km) **D 165.6** (266.5 km) Turnouts both sides of highway. Good spot to view Dall sheep.

J 250 (402.3 km) **D 164** (263.9 km) Bridge over Spike Camp Creek. Highway follows the Atigun River.

J 250.2 (402.6 km) **D 163.8** (263.6 km) Site of Atigun Camp, a former pipeline construction camp. Turnouts both sides of highway. View of Atigun River valley.

J 251.5 (404.7 km) **D 162.5** (261.5 km) Turnouts; wide shoulder next 1.5 miles/2.4 km northbound.

J 253.1 (407.3 km) **D 160.9** (258.9 km) Atigun River crossing No. 1. Highway crosses buried pipeline..

J 254 (408.8 km) **D 160** (257.5 km) Mountains to north exhibit extreme folding of sedimentary rock layers.

J 257.6 (414.6 km) **D 156.4** (251.7 km) Check valves on the pipeline keep oil from flowing backwards in the event of a leak.

J 258.4 (415.8 km) **D 155.6** (250.4 km) Trevor Creek bridge.

J 258.6 (416.2 km) **D 155.4** (250.1 km) Turnout to west. Good spot to hike up to rocks. *CAUTION: Grizzly bears in area.*

J 261.4 (420.7 km) **D 152.6** (245.6 km) Turnout.

J 265 (426.5 km) **D 149** (239.8 km) Roche Mountonee Creek bridge; turnout.

J 266.9 (429.5 km) **D 147.1** (236.7 km) Turnout.

J 267.5 (430.5 km) **D 146.5** (235.8 km) Bridge over Holden Creek.

J 268 (431.3 km) **D 146** (235 km) Good view of Pump Station No. 4.

J 269.3 (433.4 km) **D 144.7** (232.9 km) **Pump Station No. 4**. This station has the highest elevation of all the pipeline stations (2,760 feet/841m), and is also a launching and receiving station for special measuring and cleaning devices called "pigs." A scraper pig consists of spring-mounted scraper blades and/or brushes on a central body which moves through the pipe, cleaning accumulated wax from interior walls and monitoring conditions inside the pipe. There are "dumb" pigs and "smart" pigs. Dumb pigs clean out wax deposits in the line. Smart pigs scan the pipeline to check welds, wall thickness and other properties to help insure the integrity of the piping and identify maintenance needs.

J 269.5 (433.7 km) **D 144.5** (232.5 km) Highway bridge passes over pipeline.

J 270.9 (436 km) **D 143.1** (230.3 km) Atigun River crossing No. 2. The Arctic National Wildlife Refuge boundary is located 3 miles/4.8 km east along the Atigun gorge. Galbraith Lake may be seen to the west. There are a large number of archaeological sites in this vicinity.

J 274 (440.9 km) **D 140** (225.3 km) View of Galbraith Lake and Galbraith camp.

J 274.7 (442.1 km) **D 139.3** (224.2 km) Road access leads southwest 1 miles/1.6 km to **GALBRAITH CAMP**; airstrip. Self-contained RV camping available at the public campsite. USF&WS field station. Nice wildflowers in season. ▲

J 276.5 (445 km) **D 137.5** (221.3 km) Island Lake.

J 283 (455.4 km) **D 131** (210.8 km) View of Toolik Camp (see next milepost). Watch for caribou.

J 284.3 (457.5 km) **D 129.7** (208.7 km) Toolik Lake west of road. A former construction camp, it is now the site of Toolik Lake Research Camp, run by the Institute of Arctic Biology of the University of Alaska–Fairbanks. The field station conducts global warming studies and has no public facilities or services.

J 286.2 (460.6 km) **D 127.8** (205.7 km) Turnout to east at high point in road. View

of Brooks Range south and east. Philip Smith Mountains to west. Panoramic views of incredible beauty.

J 288.8 (464.8 km) **D 125.2** (201.5 km) Highway descends northbound to Kuparuk River bridge. Informal camping at turnout.

J 289.3 (465.6 km) **D 124.7** (200.7 km) Pipeline crossing. Short buried section of pipeline to west is called a sag bend and is to allow for wildlife crossing. Watch for caribou northbound.

J 290.4 (467.3 km) **D 123.6** (198.9 km) Turnout to east; road to materials site.

J 290.6 (467.7 km) **D 123.4** (198.6 km) Toolik Creek.

J 295 (474.7 km) **D 119** (191.5 km) *Watch for caribou crossing the highway.* (They were in the middle of the road here in summer 1998.)

J 297 (478 km) **D 117** (188.3 km) Pullout used by hunters in caribou season.

J 297.8 (479.2 km) **D 116.2** (187 km) Oksrukukuyik Creek culvert. Small turnout to east.

J 298.2 (479.9 km) **D 115.8** (186.4 km) Turnout to west. First view northbound of Sagavanirktok River valley.

J 301 (484.4 km) **D 113** (181.8 km) "Lucan Rock" (sign). APL access road. Slope Mountain (elev. 4,010 feet/1,222m) to west. Watch for Dall sheep. This is the northern boundary of BLM-managed land. Land north of here is managed by the state.

J 303 (487.6 km) **D 111** (178.6 km) *CAUTION: Slow for blind hill northbound. Watch for soft spots in road.*

J 305.7 (492 km) **D 108.3** (174.3 km) Sag River Station (DOT/PF highway maintenance). Slope Mountain Camp, a former pipeline construction camp, 1 mile/1.6 km east.

J 306 (492.4 km) **D 108** (173.8 km) *NOTE: Extremely rocky road surface northbound in summer 1998.*

J 309 (497.3 km) **D 105** (169 km) Highway parallels Sagavanirktok River northbound.

J 311.8 (501.8 km) **D 102.2** (164.5 km) **Pump Station No. 3**; mobile construction camp facility.

J 313.7 (504.8 km) **D 100.3** (161.4 km) Oksrukukuyik Creek in culvert.

J 319.8 (514.7 km) **D 94.2** (151.6 km) Turnout to east at Oil Spill Hill.

J 320 (515 km) **D 94** (151.3 km) The long range of hills east of the road is the Kakuktukruich Bluff. Nice views northbound of Sagavanirktok River.

J 325.3 (523.5 km) **D 88.7** (142.7 km) Turnout to east at the top of a steep and rocky grade called Ice Cut.

J 326.2 (525 km) **D 87.8** (141.3 km) Pipeline crossing on bridge.

CAUTION: Blind hills. Rocky road surface northbound to Milepost J 338.

J 327.7 (527.4 km) **D 86.3** (138.9 km) There was a grizzly bear here in summer 1998 digging for food around the pipeline supports.

J 330.7 (532.2 km) **D 83.3** (134.1 km) Dan Creek bridge. *Bump!*

J 334.4 (538.1 km) **D 79.6** (128.1 km) Site of **Happy Valley**, a former pipeline construction camp, now a Fish and Game field station; airstrip

J 350.5 (564.1 km) **D 63.5** (102.2 km) View of Sagwon Bluffs to the east.

J 355.1 (571.5 km) **D 58.9** (94.8 km) Turnout with litter barrel to east at crest of hill. Panoramic view..

J 358.8 (577.4 km) **D 55.2** (88.8 km)

Pump Station No. 2 to the east.

J 363 (584.2 km) **D 51** (82.1 km) Snow poles mark highway for motorists. *The worst winter weather conditions on the Dalton Highway are experienced the next 38 miles/61 km northbound. Blowing snow may obscure visibility and block road.*

J 364 (585.8 km) **D 50** (80.5 km) Low hills to the north are the Franklin Bluffs. East of the road, the Ivishak River empties into the Sagavanirktok River on its journey to the Arctic Ocean.

J 365.1 (587.6 km) **D 48.9** (78.7 km) Turnout to west. Watch for nesting waterfowl in ponds to west northbound along highway.

J 376 (605.1 km) **D 38** (61.2 km) The small hill that rises abruptly on the horizon about 5 miles/8 km west of the road is called a pingo. Pingos often form from the bed of a spring-fed lake that has been covered by vegetation. Freezing of the water can raise the surface several hundred feet above the surrounding terrain.

J 377.3 (607.2 km) **D 36.7** (59.1 km) Large turnout to east at Franklin Bluffs, a former pipeline construction camp where winter equipment is stored in summer.

J 383 (616.4 km) **D 31** (49.9 km) Franklin Bluffs to the east and a pingo to the west.

J 389 (626 km) **D 25** (40.2 km) Dalton Highway snakes across the flat coastal plain northbound.

J 398.7 (641.6 km) **D 15.3** (24.6 km) Underground pipeline crossing.

J 411 (661.4 km) **D 3** (4.8 km) Pavement to **Milepost J 413.3.** Oil field activity and equipment become visible along the horizon.

J 414 (666.3 km) **D 0** Northern end of Dalton Highway. Security gate; travel beyond this point is on oil company roads. About 2 miles/3.2 km ahead is the Deadhorse Airport and the public-access portion of the Prudhoe Bay oil field. A number of oil fields make up the Prudhoe Bay industrial area: Kuparuk, Milne Point, Point McIntyre, Prudhoe Bay, Niakuk and Endicott.

Deadhorse

End of the Dalton Highway. **Population:** 25 permanent; 2,500 part-time. **Visitor Information:** Try the Prudhoe Bay General Store, Arctic Caribou Inn or Prudhoe Bay Hotel. **Climate:** Arctic, with temperatures ranging from -56°F/-49°C in winter to 78°F/26°C in summer. Precipitation averages 5 inches; snowfall 20 inches. **Transportation:** Scheduled jet service to Deadhorse/Prudhoe Bay from Anchorage (flying time from Anchor-

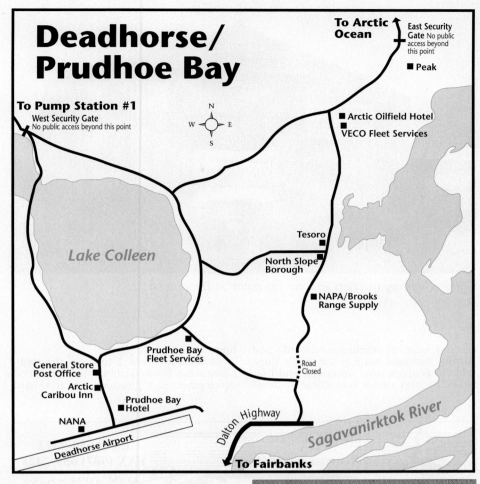

Deadhorse/ Prudhoe Bay

To Pump Station #1
West Security Gate
No public access beyond this point

To Arctic Ocean

East Security Gate No public access beyond this point

■ Peak

■ Arctic Oilfield Hotel
■ VECO Fleet Services

Tesoro ■

North Slope Borough ■

■ NAPA/Brooks Range Supply

Lake Colleen

Road Closed

Prudhoe Bay Fleet Services ■

General Store Post Office
Arctic Caribou Inn
Prudhoe Bay Hotel ■
NANA

Deadhorse Airport

Dalton Highway

Sagavanirktok River

To Fairbanks

DEADHORSE/PRUDHOE BAY ADVERTISERS

Arctic Caribou Inn............Ph. (907) 659-2368
Deadhorse–Pudhoe
  Bay Tesoro ....Ph. (907) 659-3198
Prudhoe Bay General
  Store ....Ph. (907) 659-2412

Dalton Highway travelers wait for tire repair in Deadhorse.
(© Kris Graef, staff)

age is 1 hour, 35 minutes), Fairbanks and Barrow. Packaged tours of the North Slope area are available from Anchorage and Fairbanks. Air taxi service is available at Deadhorse Airport.

Deadhorse is not a town in the traditional sense. It was established to support oil development in the surrounding area. Most buildings are modular, pre-fab-type construction, situated on gravel pads on tundra bog. Virtually all the businesses here are engaged in oil field or pipeline support activities, such as drilling, construction, maintenance, telecommunications, warehousing and transportation. Oil field employees work a rotation, such as 2 weeks on the job, then 2 weeks off. While on rotation, workers typically work 7 days a week, 10 to 12 hours each day. The largest employers are Arco, BP Exploration and Alyeska Pipeline Services.

According to Deborah Bernard in an article in the *Prudhoe Bay Journal*, there is more than one version of how Deadhorse got its name, but basically is was named after Deadhorse Haulers, a company hired to do the gravel work at the Prudhoe Bay airstrip. (How the company came to be called Deadhorse Haulers is another story.) Everybody began calling the airstrip "Deadhorse" and the name stuck—too well for those who prefer the name Prudhoe Bay. Some people were surprised when Prudhoe Bay got its own ZIP code on June 3, 1982, and was listed as "Deadhorse AK 99734," not Prudhoe Bay.

Visitor accommodations are available at the Arctic Caribou Inn. Prudhoe Bay Hotel accommodates both oil field workers and visitors. Both serve meals. Prudhoe Bay Hotel's cafeteria serves breakfast from 5:30 to 8 A.M., lunch from noon to 1 P.M., and dinner from 5 to 8 P.M., with self-serve snacks available inbetween.

Prudhoe Bay General Store carries everything from postcards and snacks to Arctic survival gear. About the only exceptions are alcohol, ammunition and weapons, which are not available in Deadhorse. The store houses the post office and issues fishing and hunting licenses. (You can also get "Dalton Highway Survivor" certificates here.)

There is no bank and no ATM in Deadhorse. Credit cards and traveler's checks are generally accepted, but fish and game licenses and postage must be paid for in cash.

Regular unleaded gasoline and No. 1 diesel are available at NANA (Chevron) or the local Tesoro station. Tesoro is a 24-hour self-serve station; an attendant is available and cash accepted from 7 A.M. until 6 P.M. There are a public phone, toilet and overnight parking with limited services available at Tesoro.

Tire and vehicle repairs are available. Arctic Tire Recycling carries a wide assortment of tires and does tire repair. The local auto parts store has an assortment of filters, oil, windshield wipers, headlights, etc.

Public access beyond Deadhorse is restricted. For security reasons, travel north of Deadhorse, including visits to the Arctic Ocean, is limited to commercial tours. Tour information is available at either the Arctic Caribou Inn or the Prudhoe Bay Hotel.

CAUTION: Beware of bears in the area.

Arctic Caribou Inn invites you to tour Prudhoe Bay, May 25–Sept. 8. Providing guided tours since 1975. Tour includes Milepost 0 at Pump Station 1. See oil rigs and Oilfield Visitor Center, and oil field informative video presentation and exhibits. Walk on the beach at the Arctic Ocean. Arctic Caribou Inn. Clean comfortable rooms. Buffet service, laundry and shower facilities. Summer phone (907) 659-2368. Winter phone (907) 659-2840. Tour Arctic/Arctic Caribou Inn, fax (907) 659-2289. Mailing address: P.O. Box 340112, Prudhoe Bay, AK 99734. [ADVERTISEMENT]

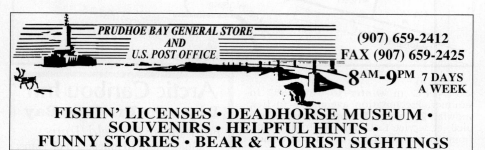

RICHARDSON HIGHWAY ④

Connects: Valdez to Fairbanks, AK   **Length:** 368 miles
Road Surface: Paved   **Season:** Open all year
Highest Summit: Isabel Pass 3,000 feet
Major Attractions: Trans-Alaska Pipeline, Worthington Glacier

(See maps, pages 510–511)

	Delta Jct.	Fairbanks	Glennallen	Paxson	Valdez
Delta Jct.		98	151	80	270
Fairbanks	98		249	179	368
Glennallen	151	249		71	119
Paxson	80	179	71		190
Valdez	270	368	119	190	

Motorcyclist on the Richardson Highway near Worthington Glacier. (© Rich Reid)

Richardson Highway Log

Distance from New Valdez (NV) is followed by distance from Old Valdez (OV).
Mileposts on the Richardson Highway were erected before the 1964 Good Friday earthquake and therefore begin 4 miles/6.4 km from present-day downtown Valdez near the Old Valdez townsite (destroyed during the earthquake).

ALASKA ROUTE 4

NV 0 OV 4 (6.4 km) Intersection of Meals Avenue and the Richardson Highway.

NV 0.4 (0.6 km) **OV 3.6** (5.8 km) Paved double-ended turnout to north with Valdez information kiosk, maps, brochures, pay phones.

NV 0.5 (0.8 km) **OV 3.5** (5.6 km) DOT/PF district office.

NV 0.6 (1 km) **OV 3.4** (5.5 km) Valdez highway maintenance station.

NV 0.9 (1.4 km) **OV 3.1** (5 km) Double-ended turnout to north at Crooked Creek salmon spawning area and hatchery. Viewing platform offers close-up look at salmon spawning in midsummer and fall. U.S. Forest Service information station is staffed Memorial Day through Labor Day; interpretive displays, history and recreation. Migrating birds such as Canada geese and various ducks are often here. It is a game sanctuary; no shooting is allowed. Good spot for pictures.

NV 1.3 (2.1 km) **OV 2.7** (4.3 km) Paved turnout to south.

NV 2 (3.2 km) **OV 2** (3.2 km) Paved turnout to south.

NV 2.1 (3.4 km) **OV 1.9** (3.1 km) Mineral Creek Loop Road through business and residential area on outskirts of Old Valdez comes out at **Milepost NV 3.4.** Access to Port of Valdez container terminal and grain elevators.

NV 3.4 (5.5 km) **OV 0.6** (1 km) Gas station at Airport Road turnoff; deli, market, liquor store, laundromat. Turn off to north for **Valdez Airport** (0.6 mile/1 km), Valdez Glacier campground (2 miles/3.2 km) and **Valdez Glacier** (3.9 miles/6.3 km). Parking area next to glacial moraine; good views of the glacier area are *not* available from this spot, nor is Valdez Glacier a very spectacular

---

The Richardson Highway (Alaska Route 4) extends 368 miles/592 km from Valdez to Fairbanks. It was Alaska's first road, known to gold seekers in 1898 as the Valdez to Eagle trail. Gold stampeders started up the trail again in 1902, this time headed for Fairbanks, site of a big gold strike. The Valdez to Fairbanks trail became an important route to the Interior, and in 1910 the trail was upgraded to a wagon road under the direction of Gen. Wilds P. Richardson, first president of the Alaska Road Commission. The ARC updated the road to automobile standards in the 1920s. The Richardson Highway was hard-surfaced in 1957.

Today, the Richardson is a wide paved highway in good condition except for sporadic frost heaving. A scenic route through the magnificent scenery of the Chugach Mountains and Alaska Range, the Richardson passes many fine king salmon streams, including the Gulkana and Tonsina rivers.

The Richardson Highway also offers good views of the Trans-Alaska pipeline. Completed in 1977, the 48-inch-diameter pipe carries oil 800 miles—from Prudhoe Bay on the Arctic Ocean to the pipeline terminus at Port Valdez. Along the Richardson Highway, the pipeline crests the Alaska Range at 3,420 foot/1,042m at Isabel Pass, before descending into the Copper River basin. It crosses the Chugach Mountains at Thompson Pass and descends through the Keystone Canyon to Valdez, where it is fed by gravity into tanks or directly into waiting oil tankers at the marine terminal.

Because of varying soil conditions along its route, the pipeline is both above and below ground. Where the warm oil would cause icy soil to thaw and erode, the pipeline goes above ground to avoid thawing. Where the frozen ground is mostly well-drained gravel or solid rock, and thawing is not a problem, the line is underground.

The line was designed with 12 pump stations (although Pump Station 11 was never built). Public tours are available of Pump Station No. 9, located at **Milepost V 258.3** on the Richardson Highway. There are several pipeline interpretive viewspoints on the Richardson Highway.

Emergency medical services: Phone 911 anywhere along the highway.

RICHARDSON HIGHWAY *Valdez, AK, to Delta Junction, AK*

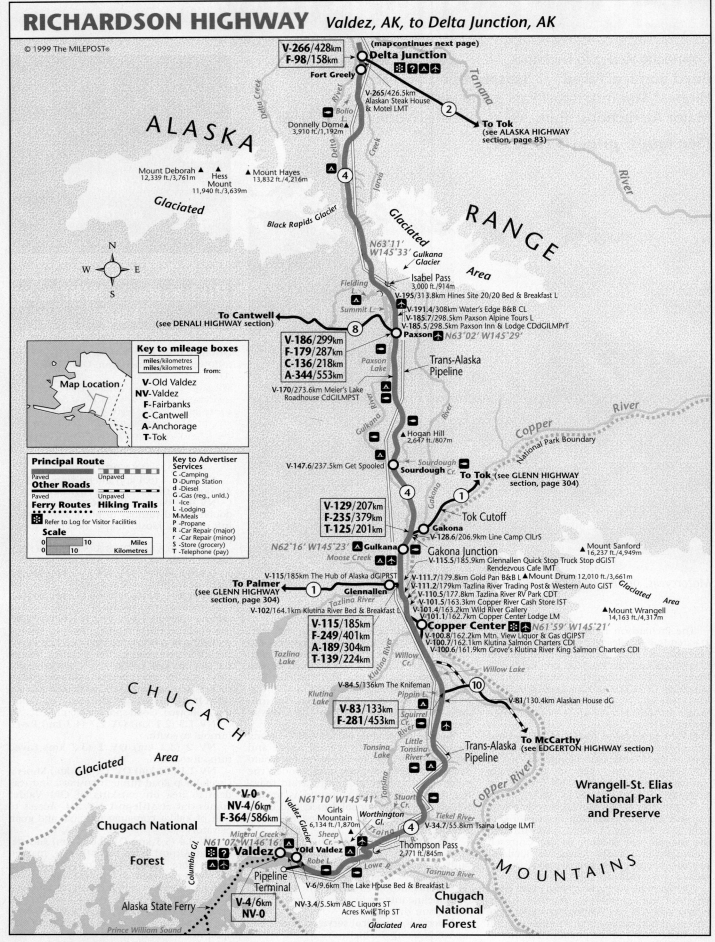

© 1999 The MILEPOST®

(map continues next page)

V-266/428km
F-98/158km
Delta Junction

Fort Greely

V-265/426.5km
Alaskan Steak House
& Motel LMT

To Tok
(see ALASKA HIGHWAY
section, page 83)

ALASKA

Bolio

Donnelly Dome▲
3,910 ft./1,192m

Mount Deborah ▲
12,339 ft./3,761m

▲ Hess
Mount
11,940 ft./3,639m

▲ Mount Hayes
13,832 ft./4,216m

Glaciated

Black Rapids Glacier

RANGE

Glaciated

Area

N63°11'
W145°33'

Gulkana
Glacier

Fielding L.

Isabel Pass
3,000 ft./914m

V-195/313.8km Hines Site 20/20 Bed & Breakfast L
V-191.4/308km Water's Edge B&B CL
V-185.7/298.5km Paxson Alpine Tours L
V-185.5/298.5km Paxson Inn & Lodge CDdGILMPrT

To Cantwell
(see DENALI HIGHWAY section)

Summit L.

Paxson   N63°02' W145°29'

V-186/299km
F-179/287km
C-136/218km
A-344/553km

Paxson
Lake

Trans-Alaska
Pipeline

V-170/273.6km Meier's Lake
Roadhouse CdGILMPST

Gulkana River

▲ Hogan Hill
2,647 ft./807m

Copper   *River*

National Park Boundary

V-147.6/237.5km Get Spooled

Sourdough
Cr.

Sourdough

To Tok (see GLENN HIGHWAY
section, page 304)

Gakona R.

V-129/207km
F-235/379km
T-125/201km

Tok Cutoff

N62°16' W145°23'   Gulkana

Gakona
V-128.6/206.9km Line Camp CILrS

▲ Mount Sanford
16,237 ft./4,949m

Moose Creek

Gakona Junction

V-115.5/185.9km Glennallen Quick Stop Truck Stop dGIST
Rendezvous Cafe IMT

V-115/185km The Hub of Alaska dGIPRST

To Palmer
(see GLENN HIGHWAY
section, page 304)

Glennallen

Tazlina River

V-102/164.1km Klutina River Bed & Breakfast L

V-111.7/179.8km Gold Pan B&B L   ▲ Mount Drum 12,010 ft./3,661m
V-111.2/179km Tazlina River Trading Post & Western Auto GIST
V-110.5/177.8km Tazlina River RV Park CDT
V-101.5/163.3km Copper River Cash Store IST
V-101.4/163.2km Wild River Gallery
V-101.1/162.7km Copper Center Lodge LM

▲ Mount Wrangell
14,163 ft./4,317m

V-115/185km
F-249/401km
A-189/304km
T-139/224km

Copper Center   N61°59' W145°21'

V-100.8/162.2km Mtn. View Liquor & Gas dGIPST
V-100.7/162.1km Klutina Salmon Charters CDI
V-100.6/161.9km Grove's Klutina River King Salmon Charters CDI

CHUGACH

Tazlina
Lake

Klutina River

Willow
Cr.

Willow Lake

V-84.5/136km The Knifeman

Klutina
Lake

Pippin L.

V-81/130.4km Alaskan House dG

V-83/133km
F-281/453km

Squirrel
Cr.

Little Tonsina
River

To McCarthy
(see EDGERTON HIGHWAY section)

Tonsina Lake

Tonsina
River

Trans-Alaska
Pipeline

Glaciated   *Area*

Copper River

**Wrangell-St. Elias
National Park
and Preserve**

Glaciated   *Area*

V-0
NV-4/6km
F-364/586km

N61°10' W145°41'

Girls
Mountain
6,134 ft./1,870m

Worthington
Gl.

Stuart
Cr.

Tiekel River

V-34.7/55.8km Tsaina Lodge ILMT

Chugach National

Mineral Creek

N61°07' W146°16'

Valdez

▲ Old Valdez

Sheep
Cr.

Tsaina R.

Thompson Pass
2,771 ft./845m

4

Forest

Valdez Glacier

Pipeline
Terminal

Robe L.

Lowe R.

V-6/9.6km The Lake House Bed & Breakfast L

Tasnuna River

MOUNTAINS

Columbia Gl.

Alaska State Ferry

V-4/6km
NV-0

NV-3.4/5.5km ABC Liquors ST
Acres Kwik Trip ST

**Chugach
National
Forest**

Glaciated Area

Prince William Sound

Key to mileage boxes

| miles/kilometres |
| miles/kilometres | from: |

V-Old Valdez
NV-Valdez
F-Fairbanks
C-Cantwell
A-Anchorage
T-Tok

Map Location

Principal Route

Paved — Unpaved
Other Roads
Paved — Unpaved
Ferry Routes •••• **Hiking Trails**

▣ Refer to Log for Visitor Facilities

Scale

0 ————— 10 Miles
0 ————— 10 Kilometres

Key to Advertiser Services

C -Camping
D -Dump Station
d -Diesel
G -Gas (reg., unld.)
I -Ice
L -Lodging
M -Meals
P -Propane
R -Car Repair (major)
r -Car Repair (minor)
S -Store (grocery)
T -Telephone (pay)

RICHARDSON HIGHWAY *Delta Junction, AK to Fairbanks, AK*

© 1999 The MILEPOST®

To Manley Hot Springs
(see ELLIOTT HIGHWAY section)

The Alaska Railroad

To Circle
(see STEESE HIGHWAY section)

**V-364/586km
F-0
M-163/262km
C-162/261km
CH-61/298km
A-358/576km**

To Chena Hot Springs
(see STEESE HIGHWAY section)

Fairbanks
N64°50'
W147°43'

To Anchorage
(see PARKS HIGHWAY section)

V-356/572.9km Road's End RV Park CDT

Chena River

Moose Creek

North Pole
V-349/561.6km Santa Claus House
V-348.7/561.2km Santaland RV Park CDIT

V-346/556.8 km North Pole VFW Post 10029
Eielson Air Force Base

Piledriver Slough

Salcha R.

Salcha River

Little Salcha R.

V-332.3/534.8km The Knotty Shop
V-328.3/528.3km Salcha Store and Service dGIPST

**V-326/524km
F-39/62km**

Salcha
V-322.2/518.5km Salcha River Lodge GILMST

Harding Lake

V-314.8/506.6km Midway Lodge ILMT

Birch Lake

Trans-Alaska Pipeline

Shaw Creek

Tanana River

Quartz Lake

V-275.4/443.2km The Fur Shack
V-275/442.6km

Big Delta
V-273.9/440.8km Big D B&B L
Rika's Roadhouse at Big Delta State Historical Park CDM
Tanana Trading Post dGI

V-270.3/435km Alaska 7 Motel L

Tanana River

V-268/431.3km Smith's Green Acres RV Park & Campground CDLT

Delta Junction
N64°00' W145°07'

**V-266/428km
F-98/158km
G-151/243km
T-108/2174km**

Fort Greely

Pump Station No. 9

Clearwater Creek

Little Delta Creek

Delta Creek

West Fork

East Fork

Sawmill Creek

Gerstle River

Little Gerstle River

Johnson River

Dry Cr.

Lisa L.

Moosehead L.

Sears Cr.

To Tok
(see ALASKA HIGHWAY section)

Berry Cr.

Bear Creek

Mount Deborah ▲
12,339 ft./3,639m

▲ Hess Mountain
11,940 ft./3,761m

▲ Mount Hayes
13,832 ft./4,216m

(map continues previous page)

Glaciated Area

ALASKA RANGE

Glaciated Area

Principal Route
Paved
Other Roads
Paved

Unpaved
Unpaved

Ferry Routes

Hiking Trails

Refer to Log for Visitor Facilities

Scale
0 — 10 Miles
0 — 10 Kilometres

Key to Advertiser Services
C -Camping
D -Dump Station
d -Diesel
G -Gas (reg., unld.)
I -Ice
L -Lodging
M -Meals
P -Propane
R -Car Repair (major)
r -Car Repair (minor)
S -Store (grocery)
T -Telephone (pay)

Map Location

Key to mileage boxes
miles/kilometres
miles/kilometres from:
F-Fairbanks
V-Valdez
A-Anchorage
G-Glennallen
M-Manley Hot Springs
C-Circle
CH-Chena Hot Springs
T-Tok

glacier. Valdez Glacier campground has 101 sites, tent camping, covered picnic area, litter barrels, water, toilets and fireplaces; 15-day limit, camping fee. *CAUTION: Beware of bears.* ▲

ABC Liquors. See display ad this section.

Acres Kwik Trip. See display ad this section.

Mineral Creek Loop Road leads south to the original townsite of Valdez, destroyed during the Good Friday earthquake on March 27, 1964. A few homes and businesses are here now; there is little evidence of the earthquake's destruction.

NV 4 (6.4 km) **OV 0** Former access road to Old Valdez, remains of the old dock and memorial for 1964 earthquake. **Milepost 0** of the Richardson Highway is located here.

Distance from Old Valdez (V) is followed by distance from Fairbanks (F).
Physical mileposts begin northbound showing distance from Old Valdez. (Southbound travelers note: Physical mileposts end here; it is 4 miles/6.4 km to downtown Valdez.)

V 0 F 364 (585.8 km) **Milepost 0** of the Richardson Highway is located here at the former access road to Old Valdez.

V 0.9 (1.4 km) **F 363.1** (584.4 km) The highway passes over the terminal moraine of the Valdez Glacier, bridging several channels and streams flowing from the melting ice.

V 1.4 (2.3 km) **F 362.6** (583.5 km) Valdez Sportsmans Trap Club.

V 1.5 (2.4 km) **F 362.5** (583.4 km) City of Valdez Goldfields Recreation Area; trails, ponds, swimming, picnic sites, baseball field.

V 2.2 (3.5 km) **F 361.8** (582.2 km) Dylen Drive.

V 2.4 (3.9 km) **F 361.6** (581.9 km) Paved turnout to west.

V 2.7 (4.3 km) **F 361.3** (581.5 km) River Road. Large paved double-ended turnout to west beside Robe River. During August and early September watch for pink and silver salmon spawning in roadside creeks and sloughs. *DO NOT* attempt to catch or otherwise disturb spawning salmon. *CAUTION: Beware of bears.*

V 2.9 (4.7 km) **F 361.1** (581.1 km) Turnoff for Old Dayville Road to **Trans-Alaska Pipeline Valdez Marine Terminal** and access to Allison Point fishery. This 5.4-mile/8.7-km paved road (open to the public) crosses the Lowe River 4 times. At Mile 2.4/3.9 km the road parallels the bay, and there is excellent fishing in season at Allison Point, especially for pink and silver salmon; also watch for sea otters and bald eagles along here. At Mile 4.1/6.6 km is the Solomon Gulch water project and a spectacular view of Solomon Gulch Falls; a fish hatchery is located across from the water project. Entrance to the pipeline terminal is at the end of the road. Supertankers load oil pumped from the North Slope to this facility via the trans-Alaska pipeline. Bus tours of the terminal are available; see the VALDEZ section for details. 🐟

V 3 (4.8 km) **F 361** (581 km) Weigh station.

V 3.4 (5.5 km) **F 360.6** (580.3 km) A 0.5-mile/0.8-km gravel road to Robe Lake and floatplane base. Watch for cow parsnip and river beauty (dwarf fireweed). Also watch for bears!

V 4.7 (7.5 km) **F 359.3** (578.2 km) Turnout to east. Access to **Robe River**; Dolly Varden, red salmon (fly-fishing only, mid-May to mid-June). 🐟

V 6 (9.7 km) **F 358** (576.1 km) **The Lake House Bed & Breakfast**. Comfortable and quiet, this very large home is located only 10 minutes from Valdez's city center and overlooks beautiful Robe Lake. Excellent bird and wildlife viewing and dramatic alpine scenery. Spacious rooms, most with private bath. Canoe/paddleboat. Brochure available. P.O. Box 1499, Valdez, AK 99686; phone (907) 835-4752. Mile 6 Richardson Highway. [ADVERTISEMENT].

V 11.6 (18.7 km) **F 352.4** (567.1 km) Large paved turnout to east.

V 12.8 (20.6 km) **F 351.2** (565.2 km) Here the Lowe River emerges from **Keystone Canyon**. The canyon was named by Captain William Ralph Abercrombie, presumably for Pennsylvania, the Keystone State. In 1884, Abercrombie had been selected to lead an exploring expedition up the Copper River to the Yukon River. Although unsuccessful in his attempt to ascend the Copper River, he did survey the Copper River Delta and a route to Port Valdez. He returned in 1898 and again in 1899, carrying out further explorations of the area (see **Milepost V 13.7**). The Lowe River is named for Lt. Percival Lowe, a member of his expedition. Glacier melt imparts the slate-gray color to the river.

V 13.5 (21.7 km) **F 350.5** (564.1 km) Horsetail Falls; large paved turnout to west.

CAUTION: Watch for pedestrians.

V 13.7 (22 km) **F 350.3** (563.7 km) Large turnout across from Bridal Veil Falls is the trailhead for the **Valdez Goat Trail**; scenic overlook ¼ mile, trail end 2 miles. Gold Rush Centennial interpretive sign at

Bridal Veil Falls is a favorite photo stop on the Richardson Highway.

(© Kris Graef, staff)

turnout. This is a restored section of the Trans-Alaska Military Packtrain Trail through Keystone Canyon that led to the first glacier-free land route from Valdez to the Interior. The first gold rush trail led over the treacherous Valdez Glacier, then northeast to Eagle and the Yukon River route to the Klondike goldfields. Captain W.R. Abercrombie and the U.S. Army Copper River Exploring Expedition of 1899 rerouted the trail through Keystone Canyon and over Thompson Pass, thus avoiding the glacier. As the Klondike Gold Rush waned, the military kept the trail open to connect Fort Liscum in Valdez with Fort Egbert in Eagle. In 1903, the U.S. Army Signal Corps laid the trans-Alaska telegraph line along this route.

V 13.8 (22.2 km) **F 350.2** (563.6 km) **Bridal Veil Falls**; large paved turnout to west.

V 14.9 (24 km) **F 349.1** (561.8 km) Lowe River bridge (first of 3 bridges northbound); view of Riddleston Falls. About 175 yards east of this bridge and adjacent to the highway is an abandoned hand-drilled tunnel. Large paved turnout with historical marker. Sign reads: "This tunnel was hand cut into the solid rock of Keystone Canyon and is all that is left of the railroad era when 9 companies fought to take advantage of the short route from the coast to the copper country. However, a feud interrupted progress. A gun battle was fought and the tunnel was never finished."

V 15.2 (24.5 km) **F 348.8** (561.3 km) Gravel turnout to east just south of bridge. Horse and Sled Trail (sign) reads: "On the far side just above the water are the remains of the old sled trail used in the early days. This trail was cut out of the rock just wide enough for 2 horses abreast. 200 feet above, the old goat trail can be seen. This road was used until 1945."

V 15.3 (24.6 km) **F 348.7** (561.2 km) Lowe River bridge No. 2, built in 1980, replaced previous highway route through the long tunnel visible beside highway.

Turnout at south end of bridge. Spectacular waterfalls.

V 15.9 (25.6 km) **F 348.1** (560.2 km) Leaving Keystone Canyon northbound, entering Keystone Canyon southbound.

V 16.2 (26.1 km) **F 347.8** (559.7 km) Avalanche gun emplacement.

V 16.3 (26.2 km) **F 347.7** (559.6 km) Lowe River bridge No. 3.

V 16.4 (26.4 km) **F 347.6** (559.4 km) Rafting outfitter cabin.

V 18 (29 km) **F 346** (556.8 km) Large paved turnouts both sides of highway; pay phone to west.

V 18.6 (29.9 km) **F 345.4** (555.8 km) Sheep Creek bridge.

Truck lane begins northbound as highway ascends 7.5 miles/12 km to Thompson Pass. This was one of the most difficult sections of pipeline construction, requiring heavy blasting of solid rock for several miles. The pipeline runs under the cleared strip beside the road. Low-flying helicopters often seen along the Richardson Highway are usually monitoring the pipeline.

V 21.6 (34.8 km) **F 342.4** (551 km) Paved turnout to east.

V 22.2 (35.7 km) **F 341.8** (550.1 km) Snow poles along highway guide snow plows in winter.

V 23 (37 km) **F 341** (548.8 km) Large gravel turnout to east.

V 23.4 (37.7 km) **F 340.6** (548.1 km) Large paved turnout to east with view.

V 23.6 (38 km) **F 340.4** (547.8 km) Loop road past Thompson Lake to Blueberry Lake and state recreation site; see **Milepost V 24.1.**

V 23.8 (38.3 km) **F 340.2** (547.5 km) Small paved turnout to east.

V 24.1 (38.8 km) **F 339.9** (547 km) Loop road to **Blueberry Lake State Recreation Site**; drive in 1 mile/1.6 km. Tucked into an alpine setting between tall mountain peaks, this is one of Alaska's most beautifully situated campgrounds; 10 campsites, 4 covered picnic tables, toilets, firepits and water. Camping fee $10/night or annual pass. ▲

Blueberry Lake and **Thompson Lake** (formerly Summit No. 1 Lake). Good grayling and rainbow fishing all summer. ◄

V 24.4 (39.3 km) **F 339.6** (546.5 km) Large paved turnout to west. Bare bone peaks of the Chugach Mountains rise above the highway. Thompson Pass ahead; Marshall Pass is to the east.

During the winter of 1907, the A.J. Meals Co. freighted the 70-ton river steamer *Chitina* (or *Chittyna*) from Valdez over Marshall Pass and down the Tasnuna River to the Copper River. The ship was moved piece by piece on huge horse-drawn freight sleds and assembled at the mouth of the Tasnuna. The 110-foot-/34-m-long ship navigated 170 miles/274 km of the Copper and Chitina rivers above Abercrombie Rapids, moving supplies for construction crews of the Copper River & Northwestern Railway. Much of the equipment for the Kennicott mill and tram was moved by this vessel.

V 25.5 (41 km) **F 338.5** (544.7 km) Large paved turnout to west. Entering Game Management Unit 13D, leaving unit 6D, northbound.

V 25.7 (41.4 km) **F 338.3** (544.4 km) Large paved turnout to west with view; Keystone Glacier to the south.

V 26 (41.8 km) **F 338** (543.9 km) **Thompson Pass** (elev. 2,678 feet/816m) at head of Ptarmigan Creek. Truck lane ends northbound; begin 7.5-mile/12-km descent southbound.

Thompson Pass, named by Captain Abercrombie in 1899, is comparatively low elevation but above timberline. Wildflower lovers will be well repaid for rambling over the rocks in this area: tiny alpine plants may be in bloom, such as Aleutian heather and mountain harebell.

The National Climatic Center credits snowfall extremes in Alaska to the Thompson Pass station, where record measurements are: 974.5 inches for season (1952–53); 298 inches for month (February 1953); and 62 inches for 24-hour period (December 1955). Snow poles along the highway mark the road edge for snow plows.

Private Aircraft: Thompson Pass airstrip; elev. 2,080 feet/634m; length 2,500 feet/762m; turf, gravel; unattended.

V 27 (43.5 km) **F 337** (542.3 km) Thompson Pass highway maintenance station.

V 27.5 (44.3 km) **F 336.5** (541.5 km) Steep turnout to east by **Worthington Lake**; rainbow fishing. ◄

V 27.7 (44.6 km) **F 336.3** (541.2 km) Good viewpoint of 27 Mile Glacier.

V 28 (45.1 km) **F 336** (540.7 km) Paved turnout to east. Entering winter avalanche area southbound.

V 28.6 (46 km) **F 335.4** (539.8 km) Paved turnout to west.

V 28.7 (46.2 km) **F 335.3** (539.6 km) **Worthington Glacier State Recreation Site**; large viewing shelter, interpretive displays, toilets, picnic sites, parking and pay phone. According to state park rangers, this is the most visited site in the Copper River Basin. The glacier, which heads on Girls Mountain (elev. 6,134 feet/1,870m), is accessible via a short road (upgraded in 1998) to the west. It is possible to drive almost to the face of the glacier. Care should be exercised when walking on ice because of numerous crevasses.

V 30.2 (48.6 km) **F 333.8** (537.2 km) Large paved turnout both sides of highway. Excellent spot for photos of Worthington Glacier. Gold Rush Centennial interpretive sign about freighting gold over Thompson Pass.

V 32 (51.5 km) **F 332** (534.3 km) Highway parallels Tsaina River northbound. Long climb up to Thompson Pass for southbound motorists.

V 34.7 (55.8 km) **F 329.3** (529.9 km) **Tsaina Lodge.** Treat yourself to a fine dining experience in the comforting, rustic charm of the hand-hewn log interior. View the spectacular Worthington Glacier surrounded by snow-capped peaks while relaxing in a museum of treasured relics from times long past. Modern gourmet food prepared the old-fashioned way, using fresh local ingredients. Specialties include Alaska seafood, homemade pastas, soups, "supercalifragilisticexpialidocious" desserts and fresh baked goods daily. Full-service bar and wine list. The spring helicopter ski operation attracts the world's finest skiers. Summer activities are many, ranging from berry picking and fishing to rafting and paragliding. Real Alaskan hospitality. New hand-crafted log cabins, yurts and a bunkhouse. (907) 835-3500. See display ad this section. [ADVERTISEMENT]

V 36.5 (58.7 km) **F 327.5** (527 km) Pipeline runs under highway.

V 37 (59.5 km) **F 327** (526.2 km) Entering BLM public lands northbound.

V 37.3 (60 km) **F 326.7** (525.8 km) Tsaina River bridge at Devil's Elbow. Large paved turnout at south end of bridge.

V 39 (62.8 km) **F 325** (523 km) Crest of hill; beautiful mountain views.
Highway descends northbound.

V 40.8 (65.7 km) **F 323.2** (520.1 km) Large gravel turnout to west.

V 42 (67.6 km) **F 322** (518.2 km) Gravel turnout to west side. Spruce bark beetles have killed many of the trees in the forest here. Buried pipeline. View of waterbars (ridges on slope designed to slow runoff and control erosion).

V 43.3 (69.7 km) **F 320.7** (516.1 km) Long double-ended turnout.

V 45.6 (73.4 km) **F 318.4** (512.4 km) Large paved turnout to east at north end of Stuart Creek bridge.

V 45.8 (73.7 km) **F 318.2** (512.1 km) Copper River Valley welcome sign. Watch for moose next 20 miles/32 km northbound.

V 46.9 (75.5 km) **F 317.1** (510.3 km) **Tiekel River** bridge; small Dolly Varden. Small turnout at north end of bridge. ◄

V 47.9 (77.1 km) **F 316.1** (508.7 km) Large paved rest area to west by Tiekel River; covered picnic sites, toilets, no drinking water. Viewpoint and historical sign for **Mount Billy Mitchell.**

Lieutenant William "Billy" Mitchell was a member of the U.S. Army Signal Corps, which in 1903 was completing the trans-Alaska telegraph line (Washington–Alaska Military Cable and Telegraph System) to connect all the military posts in Alaska. The 2,000 miles/3,200 km of telegraph wire included the main line between Fort Egbert in Eagle and Fort Liscum at Valdez, and a branch line down the Tanana River to Fort Gibson and on to Fort St. Michael near the mouth of the Yukon and then to Nome. Mitchell was years later to become the "prophet of American military air power."

V 50.7 (81.6 km) **F 313.3** (504.1 km) Bridge over Tiekel River. Dead spruce trees in this area were killed by beetles.

V 53.8 (86.6 km) **F 310.2** (499.2 km) Squaw Creek culvert.

V 54.1 (87.1 km) **F 309.9** (498.7 km) Large paved turnout to east. Look for lupine in June, dwarf fireweed along the Tiekel River in July.

V 54.5 (87.7 km) **F 309.5** (498.1 km) Moose often seen here in the evenings.
CAUTION: Watch for moose.

V 55.1 (88.7 km) **F 308.9** (497.1 km) Large paved turnout to east.

V 56 (90.1 km) **F 308** (495.7 km) Tiekel River Lodge; food, gas, lodging.

V 56.3 (90.6 km) **F 307.7** (495.2 km) Large paved turnout to east.

V 57 (91.7 km) **F 307** (494.1 km) Old beaver lodge and dams in pond to east. Old beaver lodge. Beaver may inhabit the same site for generations.

Tireless and skillful dam builders, beavers construct their houses in the pond created by the dam. Older beaver dams can reach 15 feet in height and may be hundreds of feet long. The largest rodent in North America, beavers range south from the Brooks Range. They eat a variety of vegetation, including aspen, willow, birch and poplar.

V 58.1 (93.5 km) **F 305.9** (492.3 km) Wagon Point Creek culvert.

V 60 (96.6 km) **F 304** (489.2 km) Large paved turnout to east. Highway parallels **Tiekel River**; fishing for small Dolly Varden.

V 62 (99.7 km) **F 302** (486 km) Ernestine Station (DOT/PF highway maintenance).

V 62.4 (100.4 km) **F 301.6** (485.4 km) Boundary for Sport Fish Management areas. Entering Upper Susitna/Copper River Area N northbound, Prince William Sound southbound.

V 64.7 (104.1 km) **F 299.3** (481.7 km) **Pump Station No. 12 Interpretive Viewpoint** to west, Pump Station 12 to east. Gravel drive leads west to parking area; short boardwalk trail to the viewpoint with interpretive signs about the station and the pipeline.

V 65 (104.6 km) **F 299** (481.2 km) Little Tonsina River.

V 65.1 (104.8 km) **F 298.9** (481 km) **Little Tonsina River State Recreation Site** to west on loop road; 10 campsites, firepits, water pump, litter barrels and toilets.

Camping fee $10/night or annual pass. Dolly Varden fishing. Good berry picking in fall. *CAUTION: Beware of bears!*

V 66.2 (106.5 km) **F 297.8** (479.2 km) Double-ended gravel turnout to west.
Watch for moose next 20 miles/32 km southbound.

V 71.2 (114.6 km) **F 292.8** (471.2 km) Long double-ended paved turnout to east.

V 72 (115.9 km) **F 292** (469.9 km) Double-ended paved turnout to west with view across valley of Trans-Alaska pipeline following base of mountains.

Leaving BLM public lands northbound.

V 74.4 (119.7 km) **F 289.6** (466.1 km) Paved double-ended turnout to west.

V 78.6 (126.5 km) **F 285.4** (459.3 km) Tonsina Controlled Use Area (sign); closed to vehicles and pack animals August and September.

V 79 (127.1 km) **F 285** (458.7 km) Tonsina Lodge (closed in 1998; current status unknown).

V 79.2 (127.5 km) **F 284.8** (458.3 km) Bridge over Tonsina River, which rises in Tonsina Lake to the southwest.

V 79.6 (128.1 km) **F 284.4** (457.7 km) Bridge and **Squirrel Creek State Recreation Site**. Pleasant campsites on the bank of Squirrel Creek, some pull-through spaces; $10/night or annual pass; dumpster, boat launch, water, toilets and firepits. Rough access road through campground; low-clearance vehicles use caution. Large vehicles note: Limited turnaround on back loop road.

Mouth of **Squirrel Creek** at Tonsina River. Some grayling and salmon; grayling, small, use flies or eggs, all season; salmon, average size, egg clusters and spoons, all season. Also try the gravel pit beside the campground; according to state park rangers, some fishermen have good luck catching rainbow and grayling here using flies, eggs and spinners.

V 79.7 (128.3 km) **F 284.3** (457.5 km) Begin 1.3-mile/2.1-km truck lane northbound up Tonsina Hill. *CAUTION: Steep hill, watch for bumps; road can be slippery in winter.*

V 81 (130.4 km) **F 283** (455.4 km) Gas station (diesel), coffee shop, gold nuggets.
Alaskan House. See display ad this section.
CAUTION: Begin steep descent southbound; watch for bumps.

V 82.6 (132.9 km) **F 281.4** (452.9 km)

Junction with the Edgerton Highway east to Chitina and McCarthy Road to McCarthy in Wrangell–St. Elias National Park and Preserve. See EDGERTON HIGHWAY section for log of that route.

V 83 (133.6 km) **F 281** (452.2 km) Small paved turnout to west beside Pippin Lake.
"Hill"; highway descends next 3 miles/4.8 km northbound.

V 84.5 (136 km) **F 279.5** (449.8 km) **The Knifeman.** See display ad this section.

rolling hills of homestead country and heavy thickets of birch and spruce.

V 100.2 (161.2 km) **F 263.8** (424.5 km) IMPORTANT: South *junction* with Copper Center Bypass (New Richardson Highway). Northbound travelers TURN OFF onto Old Richardson Highway for scenic route through historic Copper Center (log and description follow). The MILEPOST® does not log the bypass route (New Richardson Highway), which is the same distance as the old highway (6.5 miles/10.5 km) with no notable features. The old highway rejoins the bypass route at Milepost V 106.

V 100.6 (161.9 km) **F 263.4** (423.9 km) **Grove's Klutina River King Salmon Charters**. See display ad this section.

V 100.7 (162.1 km) **F 263.3** (423.7 km) Klutina River bridges. Excellent fishing in the **Klutina River** for red (sockeye) and king (chinook) salmon. Also grayling and

Dolly Varden. Kings to 50 lbs., average 30 lbs.; from June 15 to Aug. 10, peaking in mid-July. Red's peak run is from late June to early August; fish from either bank downstream from the new bridge to the mouth of the Copper River. NOTE: Most riverfront property is privately owned. Inquire at the tackle shop about river access. Two campgrounds and fishing charter services are located here.　　　　　　　　　　◄▲

Klutina Salmon Charters. See display ad this section.　　　　　　　　　　　　　▲

V 100.8 (162.2 km) **F 263.2** (423.6 km) Copper Center (description follows). Turn on loop road opposite gas station for access to Copper Center Lodge, George I. Ashby Memorial Museum.

Mtn. View Liquor & Gas. See display ad this section.

Copper Center

V 100.8 (162.2 km) **F 263.2** (423.6 km) Located on the Klutina River, 1 mile/1.6 km west of its junction with the Copper River; 104.8 miles/168.6 km north of Valdez via Alaska Route 4. An inner loop road leads through Copper Center and rejoins the Richardson Highway at **Milepost V 101.1**. **Population:** 525. **Emergency Services:** Phone 911. **Ambulance** in Glennallen, phone 911. **Elevation:** 1,000 feet/305m.

Private Aircraft: Copper Center NR 2 airstrip, 1 S; elev. 1,150 feet/351m; length 2,200 feet/671m; gravel; unattended.

Facilities include lodging, private campgrounds, meals, groceries, liquor store, gas station, general store, post office, laundromat and gift shops. Fishing charters, tackle,

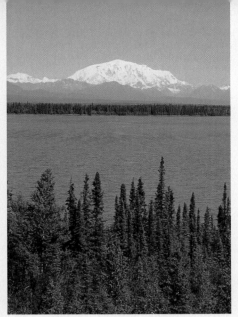

Willow Lake and the Wrangell Mountains from scenic viewpoint at Milepost V 87.7. (© Bruce M. Herman)

V 87.7 (141.1 km) **F 276.3** (444.6 km) Paved double-ended scenic viewpoint to east at **Willow Lake**. On a clear day this lake mirrors the Wrangell Mountains to the east, which lie within Wrangell–St. Elias National Park and Preserve. Gold Rush Centennial interpretive sign about Copper Mining on the Bonanza Ridge in the Wrangell Mountains.

V 88.5 (142.4 km) **F 275.5** (443.4 km) APL pipeline access road leads west to **Pipeline Interpretive Viewpoint**, 1 of 3 Alyeska pipeline displays along the Richardson Highway. Gravel loop turnout; pedestrian access.

V 90.8 (146.1 km) **F 273.2** (439.7 km) Large paved turnout to west by Willow Creek culvert; thick patches of diamond willow in woods off highway (and thick clouds of mosquitoes!).

V 91.1 (146.6 km) **F 272.9** (439.2 km) Turnoff to east is an 8-mile/12.9-km gravel cutoff that intersects Edgerton Highway at **Milepost J 7.3**. This is a drive through the riverboat services and guides available.

With the influx of gold seekers following the trail from Valdez to the Klondike, a trading post was established in Copper Center in 1898. Gold Rush Centennial interpretive signs here recount the difficulty of the journey over the Valdez Glacier Trail and the ordeal of the several hundred stampeders who overwintered in Copper Center in 1898-99. A telegraph station and post office were established in 1901, and Copper Center became the principal settlement and supply center in the Nelchina–Susitna region.

Copper Center Lodge on the inner loop road, selected by the Alaska Centennial Commission as a site of historic importance (a plaque is mounted to the right of the lodge's entrance), had its beginning as the Holman Hotel and was known as the Blix Roadhouse during the gold rush days of 1897–98. It was the first lodging place in the Copper River valley and was replaced by the Copper Center Lodge in 1932.

The **George I. Ashby Memorial Museum**, operated by the Copper Valley Historical Society, is housed in the bunkhouse annex at the Copper Center Lodge. It contains early Russian religious articles, Athabascan baskets, telegraph and mineral displays, copper and gold mining memorabilia, and trapping articles from early-day Copper Valley. Hours vary. Donations appreciated.

Historic buildings in Copper Center are located on private property. *Please do not trespass.*

The Copper River reportedly carries the highest sediment load of all Alaskan rivers. The river cuts through the Chugach Mountains and connects the interior of southcentral Alaska with the sea; it is the only corridor of its kind between Cook Inlet and the Canadian border.

Richardson Highway Log

(continued)

V 101 (162.5 km) **F 263** (423.3 km) A visitor attraction in Copper Center is the log **Chapel on the Hill** built in 1942 by Rev. Vince Joy with the assistance of U.S. Army volunteers stationed in the area. The chapel is open daily and there is no admission charge. A short slide show on the Copper River area is usually shown to visitors in the chapel during the summer. A highway-level parking lot is connected by stairs to the Chapel on the Hill.

V 101.1 (162.7 km) **F 262.9** (423 km) Inner loop road to historic Copper Center Lodge George I. Ashley Memorial Museum and other businesses.

Copper Center Lodge. Beautifully rustic historic landmark, serving the public since 1898; 21 rooms, private or shared baths. Century-old sourdough starter hotcakes, homemade pies. Restaurant serving breakfast, lunch, dinner. Wine and beer served.

Located near the base of the Wrangell–St. Elias National Park and next to the Copper and Klutina rivers. See display ad. [ADVERTISEMENT]

V 101.4 (163.2 km) **F 262.6** (422.6 km) Post office to east; outside mailbox. Wild River Gallery.

Wild River Gallery. All Alaskan handmade art and gifts, paintings, ceramics, beaded and ivory jewelry, furs, paper creations, baskets, beadwork, weaving, dolls, clothing and cards. Open 10 A.M. to 6 P.M. Monday through Saturday in Historic Copper Center, Alaska. Old Richardson Highway Loop Road. Major credit cards accepted. Phone (907) 822-5344. [ADVERTISEMENT]

V 101.5 (163.3 km) **F 262.5** (422.4 km) **Copper River Cash Store**, established in 1896, sits on part of the first farm started in Alaska. The center of the building is the original structure. Behind the store is the old jail, bars still on windows. Open 6 days a week, all year. Complete line of groceries, general merchandise, RV supplies, video rentals. [ADVERTISEMENT]

V 101.9 (164 km) **F 262.1** (421.8 km) Parking area. Historical marker about Copper Center reads: "Founded in 1896 as a government agriculture experiment station, Copper Center was the first white settlement in this area. The Trail of '98 from Valdez over the glaciers came down from the mountains and joined here with the Eagle Trail to Forty Mile and Dawson. 300 miners, destitute and lonely, spent the winter here. Many suffered with scurvy and died. Soon after the turn of the century, the Washington–Alaska Military Cable and Telegraph System, known as WAMCATS, the forerunner of the Alaska communications system, operated telegraph service here between Valdez and Fairbanks."

V 102 (164.1 km) **F 262** (421.6 km) Brenwick–Craig Road. Access to Klutina River Bed & Breakfast.

Klutina River Bed & Breakfast. See display ad this section.

V 102.2 (164.5 km) **F 261.8** (421.3 km) Copper Center Community Chapel and Indian graveyard.

V 102.5 (165 km) **F 261.5** (420.8 km) Fish wheel may sometimes be seen here operating in Copper River to east. The old school is a local landmark.

V 103.4 (166.4 km) **F 260.6** (419.4 km) Klutikaah Memorial park to east; community ball field.

V 104 (167.4 km) **F 260** (418.4 km) Ahtna building houses Copper River Native Assoc.

V 104.3 (167.8 km) **F 259.7** (417.9 km) Laundromat, showers.

V 104.5 (168.2 km) **F 259.5** (417.6 km)

Silver Springs Road. Copper Center school.

V 104.8 (168.7 km) **F 259.2** (417.1 km) Paved turnout to east. Watch for horses.

V 105.1 (169.1 km) **F 258.9** (416.6 km) **Wrangell–St. Elias National Park and Preserve Visitor Center** and National Park Service headquarters to west. Ranger on duty, general information available. A 10-minute video is shown; additional video programs shown on request. Copper ore samples on display. Maps and publications for sale. Open 8 A.M. to 6 P.M. daily, Memorial Day through Labor Day. Winter hours are 8 A.M. to 5 P.M. weekdays. For more information write P.O. Box 439, Copper Center, AK 99573; or phone (907) 822-5234. A new visitor center is under construction near **Milepost V 107.**

Access to Wrangell–St. Elias National Park and Preserve is via the Edgerton Highway and McCarthy Road and the Nabesna Road off the Tok Cutoff.

V 106 (170.6 km) **F 258** (415.2 km) *IMPORTANT: North junction with Copper Center Bypass (New Richardson Highway). Southbound travelers TURN OFF on to Old Richardson Highway for scenic route through historic Copper Center (see description this section). The MILEPOST® does not log the bypass route (New Richardson Highway), which is the same distance as the old highway (6.5 miles/10.5 km) but without notable features. The old highway rejoins the bypass route at Milepost V 100.2.*

V 110 (177 km) **F 254** (408.8 km) Dept. of Highways Tazlina station and Dept. of Natural Resources office. Report forest fires here or phone (907) 822-5533.

V 110.5 (177.8 km) **F 253.5** (408 km) Pipeline storage area. Turn west on pipeline storage area road and take second right for private RV park.

V 110.5 (177.8 km) **F 253.5** (408 km) **Tazlina River RV Park.** See display ad this section. ▲

V 110.6 (178 km) **F 253.4** (407.8 km) Rest area to east on banks of Tazlina River; large paved surface, 2 covered picnic tables, water, toilets.

V 110.7 (178.2 km) **F 253.3** (407.6 km) Tazlina River bridge. *Tazlina* is Indian for "swift water." The river flows east from Tazlina Glacier into the Copper River.

V 111 (178.6 km) **F 253** (407.2 km) Trading post; groceries and gas.

Tazlina River Trading Post & Western

Auto. See display ad this section.

V 111.7 (179.8 km) **F 252.3** (406 km) Copperville access road. Developed during pipeline construction, this area has a church and private homes. Glennallen fire station.

Gold Pan B&B. See display ad this section.

V 112.3 (180.7 km) **F 251.7** (405 km) Steep grade southbound from Tazlina River to the top of the Copper River bluffs.

V 112.6 (181.2 km) **F 251.4** (404.6 km) Scenic viewpoint to east; paved parking area, with historical information sign on the development of transportation in Alaska. Short (0.1 mile) walk to good viewpoint on bluff with schematic diagram of Wrangell Mountains: Mount Sanford (elev. 16,237 feet/4,949m); Mount Drum (elev. 12,010 feet/3,661m); Mount Wrangell (elev. 14,163 feet/4,317m); and Mount Blackburn (elev. 16,390 feet/4,996m).

Sign at viewpoint reads: "Across the Copper River rise the peaks of the Wrangell Mountains. The 4 major peaks of the range can be seen from this point, with Mount

---

Drum directly in front of you. The Wrangell Mountains, along with the St. Elias Mountains to the east, contain the most spectacular array of glaciers and ice fields outside polar regions. The Wrangell Mountains are part of Wrangell–St. Elias National Park and Preserve, the nation's largest national park. Together with Kluane National Park of Canada, the park has been designated a World Heritage site by the United Nations."

Visitor information for Wrangell–St. Elias National Park is available at **Milepost V 105.1** Old Richardson Highway.

V 114.1 (183.6 km) **F 249.9** (402.2 km) Double-ended turnout to west.

V 115 (185 km) **F 249** (400.7 km) **South junction** of Richardson and Glenn highways at GLENNALLEN; pay phone, gas and groceries at Hub of Alaska. **Greater Copper Valley Visitor Information Center** at junction is open daily in summer. The town of Glennallen extends west along the Glenn Highway from here.

The Hub of Alaska and Maxi Mart. See display ad this section.

Junction of the Richardson Highway (Alaska Route 4) and the Glenn Highway (Alaska Route 1). Anchorage- or Tok-bound travelers turn to **Milepost A 189** in the GLENN HIGHWAY section for log.

Valdez- or Fairbanks-bound travelers continue with this log. For the next 14 miles/22.5 km northbound the Richardson and Glenn highways share a common alignment. They separate at **Milepost V 128.6.**

V 115.5 (185.9 km) **F 248.5** (399.9 km) Rendezvous Cafe and Glennallen Quick Stop Truck Stop with gas, diesel and convenience store.

Rendezvous Cafe. See display ad this section.

Glennallen Quick Stop Truck Stop. Stop for friendly family service. Gas, diesel. Convenience store contains ice, pop, snacks,

postcards, ice cream, specialty items, pay phone and free coffee. Senior citizen, truck and caravan discounts. Several interesting items on display include an authentic Native Alaskan fish wheel. Full-service restaurant adjacent. [ADVERTISEMENT]

V 118 (189.9 km) **F 246** (395.9 km) **Dry Creek State Recreation Site**; 51 campsites, walk-in tent camping, water, tables, toilets, firepits, 15-day limit. Camping fee $10/night or annual pass. *Bring mosquito repellent!* Old ore car here was once used to haul gravel to Tonsina. ▲

V 118.1 (190.1 km) **F 245.9** (395.7 km) **Private Aircraft**: Gulkana airport; elev. 1,579 feet/481m; length 5,000 feet/1,524m; asphalt; fuel 100LL. Flying service located here.

V 123.2 (198.3 km) **F 240.8** (387.5 km) Large paved turnout to east and well-defined 1.5-mile/2.4-km trail east side of road to the mouth of the **Gulkana River.** (Inquire locally about permits and check special regu-

lations before fishing the Gulkana River.) Excellent fishing mid-June to mid-July for king salmon to 50 lbs. (average is 30 lbs.), and red salmon to 6 lbs. Use bright colored yarn or flies, half-inch hook. Heavy tackle with 25- to 30-lb.-test line recommended for kings. ⌐●

V 126 (202.8 km) **F 238** (383 km) Paved double-ended turnout to west.

V 126.2 (203.1 km) **F 237.8** (382.7 km) Bear Creek Inn.

V 126.8 (204.1 km) **F 237.2** (381.7 km) **Gulkana River** bridge. Large gravel parking areas at both ends of bridge provide access to river. Camping permitted. Grayling fishing and good king and sockeye salmon fishing (June and July). The Gulkana River flows 60 miles from the Gulkana Glacier in the Alaska Range to the Copper River. ⌐●▲

Entering Game Management Unit 13B eastbound, 13A westbound.

V 126.9 (204.2 km) **F 237.1** (381.6 km) Access road to **GULKANA** (pop. 96) on the bank of the Gulkana River. Most of the Gulkana River frontage in this area is owned by Gulkana village and managed by Ahtna, Inc. Ahtna lands are closed to the public for hunting, fishing and trapping.

V 128.6 (206.9 km) **F 235.4** (378.8 km) **North junction** (Gakona Junction) of the Richardson Highway and Tok Cutoff (Glenn Highway), known locally as Gulkana Junction. Gas, food and lodging.

Line Camp (at junction with Tok Cutoff). Groceries, ice, sporting goods, minor repairs, welding. 2 bed and breakfast units (2 bedrooms and kitchen in each). RV parking. Tourist information, guided king salmon on the Gulkana River. Specialized tours available. Phone (907) 822-3508 or (907) 822-5723; P.O. Box 255, Glennallen, AK 99588. [ADVERTISEMENT]

Junction of the Richardson Highway and Tok Cutoff. Tok-bound travelers turn to **Milepost A 203** in the GLENN HIGHWAY section for log.

Valdez- or Fairbanks-bound travelers continue with this log.

V 129.4 (208.2 km) **F 234.6** (377.5 km) Paved turnout to west. Sailor's Pit (gravel pit opposite lake to west); BLM trail across to **Gulkana River.** Fishing for rainbow trout,

grayling, king and red salmon. Highway follows the Gulkana River.

V 132.1 (212.6 km) **F 231.9** (373.2 km) Paved turnout to west.

V 134.6 (216.6 km) **F 229.4** (369.2 km) Paved double-ended turnout with view of Gulkana River to west.

V 135.5 (218.1 km) **F 228.5** (367.7 km) Watch for caribou.

V 135.8 (218.5 km) **F 228.2** (367.2 km) Paved turnout to east. Old beaver pond; 1 mile/1.6 km winter trail to Gulkana River.

V 136.4 (219.5 km) **F 227.6** (366.3 km) Coleman Creek bridge.

V 136.7 (220 km) **F 227.3** (365.8 km) Side road west to **Gulkana River** fishing access: Poplar Grove/Gulkana River BLM-marked vehicle trail, 1 mile/1.6 km. Informal campsites along river. ⌐●

V 138.1 (222.2 km) **F 225.9** (363.5 km) **Poplar Grove Creek** bridge; spring grayling fishing. Paved turnout to west at north end of bridge. ⌐●

V 139 (223.7 km) **F 225** (362.1 km) Watch for frost heaves.

V 139.4 (224.3 km) **F 224.6** (361.4 km) Paved turnout to west with view of Gulkana River.

V 140.6 (226.3 km) **F 223.4** (359.5 km) Paved turnout to east.

V 141.2 (227.2 km) **F 222.8** (358.6 km) Side road west to Gulkana River fishing access. Informal campsites along river. ⌐●

V 141.4 (227.6 km) **F 222.6** (358.2 km) Paved double-ended scenic viewpoint to west. One-mile/1.6-km trail to Gulkana River.

V 146 (234.9 km) **F 218** (350.8 km) Lakes and potholes next 9 miles/14.5 km northbound; watch for waterfowl and water lilies. Views of Chugach Mountains southbound.

V 146.4 (235.6 km) **F 217.6** (350.2 km) Entering BLM public lands northbound.

V 147.1 (236.7 km) **F 217** (349.1 km) Double-ended paved scenic viewpoint. Fishing trail to Gulkana River.

V 147.6 (237.5 km) **F 216.4** (348.3 km) **SOURDOUGH.** BLM Sourdough Creek Campground; 60 sites, good king salmon fishing. Access to **Gulkana River,** marked trail to Sourdough Creek. Across the bridge (load limit 8 tons) and to the right a road leads to parking, toilets and boat launch on river. Guided fishing trips available. Watch for potholes in access roads. Native lands; check for restrictions. ⌐●▲

Get Spooled. See display ad this section.

The Sourdough Roadhouse, destroyed by fire in December 1992, stood next to the creek. It was established in 1903. A gas station was operating here in 1996. The old Valdez trail runs 150 yards/137m behind the few buildings left standing.

The Gulkana River is part of the National Wild and Scenic Rivers System managed by the BLM. A popular float trip for experienced canoeists begins at Paxson Lake and ends at Sourdough Campground. See description at **Milepost V 175.**

Gulkana River above Sourdough Creek, grayling 9 to 21 inches (same as Sourdough Creek below), rainbow 10 to 24 inches, spinners, June through September; red salmon 8 to 25 lbs. and king salmon up to 62 lbs., use streamer flies or spinners, mid-June through mid-July. **Sourdough Creek,** grayling 10 to 20 inches, use single yellow eggs or corn, fish deep early May through first week in June, use spinners or flies mid-June until freezeup.

V 150.7 (242.5 km) **F 213.3** (343.3 km) Large gravel turnout to east.

V 151 (243 km) **F 213** (342.8 km) Private gravel driveway to west by large pond; please do not trespass.

V 153.8 (247.5 km) **F 210.2** (338.3 km) Highway passes through boggy terrain; watch for caribou. *CAUTION: No turnouts, little shoulder. Watch for dips and rough patches in highway next 10 miles/16 km northbound.*

V 154.2 (248.2 km) **F 209.8** (337.6 km) Double-ended gravel turnout to east.

V 156.4 (251.7 km) **F 207.6** (334.1 km) As the highway winds through the foothills of the Alaska Range, over a crest called Hogan Hill (elev. 2,647 feet/807m), there are magnificent views of 3 mountain ranges: the Alaska Range through which the highway leads, the Wrangell Mountains to the southeast and the Chugach Mountains to the southwest. To the west is a vast wilderness plateau where the headwaters of the Susitna River converge to flow west and south into Cook Inlet, west of Anchorage.

V 156.7 (252.2 km) **F 207.3** (333.6 km) Good view of pothole lakes to west.

V 157 (252.7 km) **F 207** (333.1 km) Good long-range viewpoints from highway. Moose and other game may be spotted from here (use binoculars).

V 158.9 (255.7 km) **F 205.1** (330.1 km) Sweeping view of the Glennallen area to the south.

V 160.7 (258.6 km) **F 203.3** (327.2 km) **Haggard Creek** BLM-marked trailhead; grayling fishing. Access to Gulkana River 7 miles/11.3 km to west.

V 162.2 (261 km) **F 201.8** (324.8 km) Double-ended gravel turnout to east.

V 166.5 (267.9 km) **F 197.5** (317.8 km) June Lake trail; 1 mile/1.6 km to west. Fishing access 1/4 mile to west.

V 168.1 (270.5 km) **F 195.9** (315.3 km) **Gillespie Lake** trailhead and parking to west. Walk up creek 0.3 mile/0.5 km to lake; grayling fishing.

V 169.3 (272.5 km) **F 194.7** (313.3 km) Large gravel pit. Turnout to west.

V 169.4 (272.6 km) **F 194.6** (313.2 km) Middle Fork BLM-marked trail to Meier's Lake and Middle Fork Gulkana River.

V 170 (273.6 km) **F 194** (312.2 km) Roadhouse with gas, food, lodging and camping. **Meier's Lake;** parking area, good grayling fishing.

Meier's Lake Roadhouse. See display ad this section.

V 171.6 (276.2 km) **F 192.4** (309.6 km) Gravel turnout by river to west. Long upgrade begins northbound.

V 172.7 (277.9 km) **F 191.3** (307.9 km) Small turnout to west, view of pipeline to east.

V 173.3 (278.9 km) **F 190.7** (306.9 km) **Dick Lake** to the east via narrow side road (easy to miss); no turnaround space. Good grayling fishing in summer. View of trans-Alaska oil pipeline across the lake. Good spot for photos.

V 175 (281.6 km) **F 189** (304.2 km) BLM Paxson Lake Campground turnoff. Wide gravel road (full of potholes if not recently graded) leads 1.5 miles/2.4 km to large camping area near lakeshore; 50 campsites, some pull-throughs, spaces for all sizes of vehicles but some sites on slope (RVs may need leveling boards); toilets, water, tables, firepits, dump station and concrete boat launch. Parking for 80 vehicles. Bring mosquito repellent. *CAUTION: Watch for bears.* Fishing in **Paxson Lake** for lake trout, grayling and red salmon.

This is the launch site for floating the Gulkana River to Sourdough Campground at **Milepost V 147.6.** Total distance is about 50 miles/80 km and 4 days travel, according to the BLM, which manages this national wild river. While portions of the river are placid, the Gulkana does have Class II and III rapids, with a gradient of 38 feet/mile in one section. Canyon Rapids may be Class IV depending on water levels (there is a portage). Recommended for experienced boaters only. For further information on floating the Gulkana, contact the BLM at Box 147, Glennallen, AK 99588, or phone (907) 822-3217.

V 177.1 (285 km) **F 186.9** (300.8 km) Small gravel turnout to west with view of Paxson Lake.

V 178.7 (287.6 km) **F 185.3** (298.2 km) Small gravel turnout to east.

V 179 (288.1 km) **F 185** (297.7 km) Gravel turnout overlooking Paxson Lake. The lake was named for the former owner of the roadhouse (still Paxson Lodge) about 1906. (See interpretive sign at **Milepost V 188.3.**)

V 179.2 (288.4 km) **F 184.8** (297.4 km) Gravel turnout to west overlooking Paxson Lake.

V 182.1 (293 km) **F 181.9** (292.7 km) Large gravel turnout at head of Paxson Lake. Rough gravel trail to lake.

V 183.2 (294.8 km) **F 180.8** (291 km) Entering Paxson Closed Area northbound (closed to taking of all big game).

V 184.4 (296.8 km) **F 179.6** (289 km) Large gravel turnout to west.

V 184.7 (297.2 km) **F 179.3** (288.6 km) One Mile Creek bridge.

V 185.5 (298.5 km) **F 178.5** (287.3 km) **PAXSON** (pop. 33), site of a lodge with gas station (open year-round) and restaurant. Arctic Man snowmachine race second weekend in April. Paxson Mountain (elev. 5,200 feet/1,585m) is 3 miles/4.8 km west-southwest.

Paxson Inn & Lodge. See display ad this section.

Private Aircraft: Paxson airstrip (Hufman Field), adjacent south; elev. 2,653 feet/809m; length 2,800 feet/853m; gravel; emergency fuel; attended.

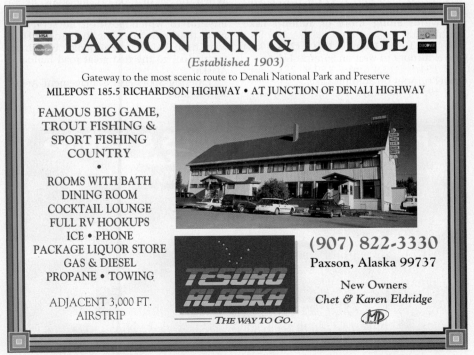

Junction with Denali Highway (Alaska Route 8) to Cantwell and the Parks Highway. See DENALI HIGHWAY section for log.

V 185.7 (298.9 km) **F 178.3** (286.9 km) Site of original Paxson Lodge.

Paxson Alpine Tours. See display ad this section.

V 185.8 (299 km) **F 178.2** (286.8 km) Paxson Station highway maintenance camp.

V 186.4 (300 km) **F 177.6** (285.8 km) Leaving BLM public lands northbound, entering BLM lands southbound.

V 188.3 (303 km) **F 175.7** (282.8 km) Large paved double-ended rest area to east across from Gulkana River; tables, fireplaces, toilets, dumpster and water. The Gulkana River flows south to the Copper River.

Gold Rush Centennial interpretive sign about Alvin J. Paxson's Timberline Tent Roadhouse established near here in 1906.

V 189.5 (305 km) **F 174.5** (280.8 km) Long paved double-ended turnout to west.

V 190.4 (306.4 km) **F 173.6** (279.4 km) Paved parking area by Gulkana River to west with picnic table and interpretive sign about spawning red salmon. Fishing for salmon prohibited. Public fishing access to **Fish Creek** across highway from turnout; grayling fishing.

V 191 (307.4 km) **F 173** (278.4 km) Summit Lake to west; rough, narrow drive to head of stream.

V 191.4 (308 km) **F 172.6** (277.8 km) **Water's Edge B&B** on Summit Lake. Extra-nice cabins and rooms, some with cooking facilities. Tent and motorhome spaces, showers. Quiet setting, breathtaking view. Good fishing, birding, berry picking, wildflowers, lots of wildlife, unique flower garden. Excellent winter snowmobiling. Hosts are longtime Alaskans. HC 72 Box 7196, Paxson, AK 99737-9203. Phone/fax (907) 482-9001. [ADVERTISEMENT]

V 192.2 (309.3 km) **F 171.8** (276.5 km) Gravel turnout with public access boat launch on **Summit Lake**; lake trout, grayling, burbot and red salmon.

V 192.6 (310 km) **F 171.4** (275.8 km) Large gravel turnout on Summit Lake. Highway winds along shore of Summit Lake northbound.

V 193.3 (311.1 km) **F 170.7** (274.7 km) Gravel turnout to west on Summit Lake.

V 194.1 (312.4 km) **F 169.9** (273.4 km) Gravel turnout on Summit Lake.

V 195 (313.8 km) **F 169** (271.9 km) Large

gravel turnout at **Summit Lake** (elev. 3,210 feet/978m). There are a number of homes in the area and a bed and breakfast. Summit Lake, 7 miles/11.3 km long, is named for its location near the water divide between the Delta and Gulkana rivers. The Gulkana River flows into the Copper River, which flows into Prince William Sound. The Delta River is part of the Yukon River drainage. Fishing for lake trout, grayling, red salmon and burbot.

Hines Site 20/20 Bed and Breakfast overlooks Summit Lake. Five new beautifully decorated non-smoking view rooms with private baths. Queen-size bed. Full breakfast. Quiet, peaceful environment. Good fishing

and snow machining. Open year around. Your host: "Boots" Hines, HC 72 Box 7195, Delta Junction, AK 99737. Reservation phone (907) 388-8299. Or just truck on in. [ADVERTISEMENT]

V 196.8 (316.7 km) **F 167.2** (269.1 km) Gunn Creek bridge. View of Gulkana Glacier to the northeast. This glacier, perched on 8,000-foot/2,438m Icefall Peak, feeds streams that drain into both Prince William Sound and the Yukon River.

V 197.6 (318 km) **F 166.4** (267.8 km) Summit of **Isabel Pass** (elev. 3,000 feet/914m). Large gravel turnout to east. Gold Rush Centennial interpretive sign about women in the gold rush, including Isabelle Barnette for whom Isabel Pass is named.

Memorial monument honoring Gen. Wilds P. Richardson, for whom the highway is named. Sign here reads: "Captain Wilds P. Richardson presented the need for roads to Congress in 1903. His familiarity with Alaska impressed Congress with his knowledge of the country and his ability as an engineer. When the Act of 1905 became a law, he was placed at the head of the Alaska Road Commission in which position he served for more than a decade. The Richardson Highway, from Valdez to Fairbanks, is a fitting monument to the first great road builder of Alaska."

Entering Sport Fish Management Area C southbound.

V 198.4 (319.3 km) **F 165.6** (266.5 km) Rough gravel turnout to west.

V 200.4 (322.5 km) **F 163.6** (263.3 km) Gravel side road leads west 1.5 miles/2.4 km to **Fielding Lake** Campground. Pleasant area above tree line; 7 campsites, no water, no camping fee, picnic tables, pit toilets, large parking areas and boat ramp. Good fishing for lake trout, grayling and burbot.

Snow poles along highway guide snow-plows in winter.

V 201.5 (324.3 km) **F 162.5** (261.5 km) Phelan Creek bridge. Phelan Creek heads near Gulkana Glacier and flows 16 miles to the Delta River.

V 202 (325.1 km) **F 162** (260.7 km) Entering BLM public lands northbound, leaving BLM lands southbound.

V 202.5 (325.9 km) **F 161.5** (259.9 km) McCallum Creek bridge, highway follows Phelan Creek northbound. This stream heads in Gulkana Glacier and flows northwest to the Delta River.

V 203.5 (327.5 km) **F 160.5** (258.3 km) Watch for beaver ponds (and beaver); lupine in June.

V 204 (328.3 km) **F 160** (257.5 km) Springwater piped to east side of highway; paved turnout.

V 204.7 (329.4 km) **F 159.3** (256.4 km) Large gravel turnouts both sides of highway.

V 205.3 (330.4 km) **F 158.7** (255.4 km) Small gravel turnout by stream. Good place for pictures of the pipeline climbing a steep hill.

V 205.6 (330.9 km) **F 158.4** (254.9 km) Snow poles along highway. Gravel turnout. *CAUTION: Slow down for sharp curve.*

V 206.4 (332.2 km) **F 157.6** (253.6 km) Double-ended parking area to west with picnic table and view of mineralized **Rainbow Ridge** to northeast. Wildflowers include yellow arnica and sweet pea.

V 207 (333.1 km) **F 157** (252.7 km) Good gravel turnout to west.

V 207.8 (334.4 km) **F 156.2** (251.4 km) Turnout. Rock slide and avalanche area next mile northbound; watch for rocks on road.

V 208.1 (334.9 km) **F 155.9** (250.9 km) Turnout to west.

V 208 4 (335.4 km) **F 155.6** (250.4 km) Large gravel turnout to west.

V 209.5 (337.1 km) **F 154.5** (248.6 km) Wide gravel shoulder along Phelan Creek.

V 211.7 (340.7 km) **F 152.3** (245.1 km) Wide gravel shoulders and turnouts to west beside Phelan Creek next 0.5 mile/0.8 km northbound.

V 213.6 (343.7 km) **F 150.4** (242 km) Gravel turnout and road to gravel pit to east. Avalanche area ends northbound.

V 214 (344.4 km) **F 150** (241.4 km) Double-ended paved turnout to east with picnic tables and litter barrels. Highway follows Delta River northbound, Phelan Creek southbound.

V 215.1 (346.2 km) **F 148.9** (239.6 km) Miller Creek bridge; parking at both ends. Pipeline crosses creek next to bridge.

V 215.9 (347.4 km) **F 148.1** (238.3 km) Pipeline interpretive viewpoint with information sign to west.

V 216.7 (348.7 km) **F 147.3** (237 km) Lower Miller Creek bridge. Turnouts at both ends of bridge.

V 217.2 (349.5 km) **F 146.8** (236.2 km) Castner Creek; parking at both ends of bridge, west side of road.

V 218.2 (351.1 km) **F 145.8** (234.6 km) Trims Station (DOT/PF highway maintenance).

V 218.8 (352.1 km) **F 145.2** (233.7 km) Bridge over Trims Creek, parking. Wildflowers in the area include lupine, sweet pea and fireweed. Watch for caribou on slopes.

V 219.2 (352.8 km) **F 144.8** (233 km) Access road west to Pump Station No. 10.

V 219.9 (353.9 km) **F 144.1** (231.9 km) Michael Creek bridge; shoulder parking at both ends of bridge.

V 220.9 (355.5 km) **F 143.1** (230.3 km) Flood Creek bridge; parking.

Southbound drivers have a spectacular view of Pump Station No. 10 and the surrounding mountains.

V 223 (358.9 km) **F 141** (226.9 km) Whistler Creek bridge; parking.

V 223.8 (360.2 km) **F 140.2** (225.6 km) Boulder Creek bridge.

V 224.5 (361.3 km) **F 139.5** (224.5 km) Lower Suzy Q Creek bridge; parking.

V 224.8 (361.8 km) **F 139.2** (224 km) Suzy Q Creek bridge; parking area.

V 225.2 (362.4 km) **F 138.8** (223.4 km) Large gravel turnout to east.

V 225.4 (362.7 km) **F 138.6** (223.1 km) Double-ended paved scenic viewpoint with picnic table and litter barrels to west. Historical marker here identifies the terminal moraine of Black Rapids Glacier to the west. Currently a retreating glacier with little ice visible, this glacier was nicknamed the Galloping Glacier when it advanced more than 3 miles/4.8 km during the winter of 1936–37.

Black Rapids Lake trail begins across from historical sign (0.3 mile/0.4 km to lake). Look for river beauty and wild sweet pea blooming in June.

V 226 (363.7 km) **F 138** (222.1 km) Large gravel turnouts to west above Delta River. The Delta River heads at Tangle Lakes and flows 80 miles north to the Tanana River.

V 226.3 (364.2 km) **F 137.7** (221.6 km) Falls Creek bridge.

View of Black Rapids Glacier to west.

V 226.7 (364.8 km) **F 137.3** (221 km) Black Rapids U.S. Army training site at Fall Creek.

Boundary between Game Management Units 20D and 13.

V 227 (365.3 km) **F 137** (220.5 km) Gunnysack Creek.

V 227.4 (366 km) **F 136.6** (219.8 km) Ruins of old Black Rapids Lodge, once the "farthest north of the old-time Richardson trail hostelries."

V 228.4 (367.6 km) **F 135.6** (218.2 km) One Mile Creek bridge; large gravel parking areas.

V 229.8 (369.8 km) **F 134.2** (216 km) Wide shoulder pull-offs west side of highway.

V 230.4 (370.8 km) **F 133.6** (215 km) Large paved turnout to west overlooks Delta River.

V 231 (371.7 km) **F 133** (214 km) Darling Creek; gravel turnout to east at south end.

V 232.2 (373.7 km) **F 131.8** (212.1 km) Gravel turnout to west. Highway climbs southbound.

V 233.3 (375.5 km) **F 130.7** (210.3 km) Bear Creek bridge; gravel turnout with access to creek. Wildflowers include pale oxytrope, yellow arnica, fireweed, wild rhubarb and cow parsnip.

V 234.2 (376.9 km) **F 129.8** (208.9 km) Double-ended gravel turnout to east.

V 234.5 (377.4 km) **F 129.5** (208.4 km) Paved turnout to west.

V 234.8 (377.9 km) **F 129.2** (207.9 km) Ruby Creek bridge; parking area to west at

View along the Richardson Highway near Donnelly Dome. (© *Laurent Dick*)

north end.

Distance marker shows Paxson 53 miles, Glennallen 127 miles.

V 237.9 (382.9 km) **F 126.1** (202.9 km) Loop road (watch for potholes) to east through **Donnelly Creek State Recreation Site**; 12 campsites, tables, firepits, toilets and water. Camping fee $8/night or annual pass. ▲

V 239.1 (384.8 km) **F 124.9** (201 km) Small gravel turnout to east.

V 241.3 (388.3 km) **F 122.7** (197.5 km) Large paved turnout to west at top of hill with view of Delta River.

V 242.1 (389.6 km) **F 121.9** (196.2 km) Coal Mine Road (4-wheel-drive vehicles only) leads east to fishing lakes; **Last Lake**, arctic char; **Coal Mine No. 5 Lake**, lake trout; **Brodie Lake** and **Pauls Pond**, grayling and lake trout. Check with the ADF&G for details. ◂

V 243.1 (391.2 km) **F 120.9** (194.6 km) Weasel Lake trail (not signed) to west.

V 243.4 (391.7 km) **F 120.6** (194.1 km) Pipeline viewpoint to east with interpretive signs. Good photo stop. The trans-Alaska oil pipeline snakes along the ground and over the horizon. Zigzag design of pipeline converts pipe thermal expansion, as well as movement from other forces (like earthquakes), into a controlled sideways movement.

V 243.9 (392.5 km) **F 120.1** (193.3 km) Paved double-ended scenic viewpoint to east. A spectacular view to the southwest of 3 of the highest peaks of the Alaska Range. From west to south they are: Mount Deborah (elev. 12,339 feet/3,761m); Hess Mountain (elev. 11,940 feet/3,639m), center foreground; and Mount Hayes (elev. 13,832 feet/4,216m).

V 244.3 (393.2 km) **F 119.7** (192.6 km) Public fishing access to **Donnelly Lake**; king and silver salmon, rainbow trout. ◂

Donnelly Dome ahead northbound.

V 246 (395.9 km) **F 118** (189.9 km) **Donnelly Dome** immediately to the west (elev. 3,910 feet/1,192m), was first named Delta Dome. For years the mountain has been used to predict the weather: "The first snow on the top of the Donnelly Dome means snow in Delta Junction within 2

weeks."

Great view southbound of peaks in the Alaska Range.

V 247 (397.5 km) **F 117** (188.3 km) Cutoff to Old Richardson Highway loop (dirt road) to west; access to fishing lakes.

V 247.3 (398 km) **F 116.7** (187.8 km) From here northbound the road extends straight as an arrow for 4.8 miles/7.7 km.

Distance marker southbound shows Paxson 65 miles, Glennallen 139 miles.

V 249.3 (401.2 km) **F 114.7** (184.6 km) Bear Drop Zone. Military games area. Controlled access road: No trespassing.

V 252.8 (406.8 km) **F 111.2** (179 km) Paved, double-ended rest area to west with picnic tables and litter barrels.

V 257.6 (414.6 km) **F 106.4** (171.2 km) Entrance to U.S. Army Cold Regions Test Center at Fort Greely.

Meadows Road (4-wheel-drive vehicles only) leads west to fishing lakes. Access to **Bolio Lake**; grayling, rainbow, lake trout. Rainbow-producing **Mark Lake** is 4.5 miles/7.2 km along this road. Meadows Road junctions with the Old Richardson Highway loop. Check with the ADF&G for details on fishing lakes. ◂

V 258.3 (415.7 km) **F 105.7** (170.1 km) **Alyeska Pipeline Pump Station No. 9** to east. Tours of Pump Station 9 are offered daily, except Sundays, from June through August. Tour times in 1998 were 9 A.M., 10 A.M., 11 A.M., 1:30 P.M., 2:30 P.M. and 3:30 P.M. Limited to 10 people per tour; children must be at least 9 years old. Reservations recommended; phone (907) 869-3270 or 456-9391.

V 261.2 (420.3 km) **F 102.8** (165.4 km)

End of the Alaska Highway monument at Delta Junction. (© Kris Graef, staff)

FORT GREELY (restricted area) main gate to east. Fort Greely was named for A.W. Greely, arctic explorer and author of *Three Years of Arctic Service*. Fort Greely is scheduled for phased reduction and closure by 2001.

V 262.6 (422.6 km) **F 101.4** (163.2 km) Double-ended paved rest area to west with scenic view. Watch for bison.

CAUTION: Wind area northbound.

V 264.9 (426.3 km) **F 99.1** (159.5 km) Jarvis Creek. "Welcome to Delta Junction" sign northbound. Bike trail begins northbound.

CAUTION: Wind area southbound.

V 265 (426.5 km) **F 99** (159.3 km) **Alaskan Steak House & Motel.** Comfortable rooms with cable TV at reasonable rates. Open daily year-round, 5 A.M.–10 P.M. for breakfast, lunch, dinner. Family-style dinners. Banquet room. Beer and wine available. Dinner special: All-you-can-eat barbecued ribs. Phone (907) 895-5175. Fax (907) 895-5048. HC 60 Box 4570, Delta Junction, AK 99737. [ADVERTISEMENT]

V 265.2 (426.8 km) **F 98.8** (159 km) **V 266** (428 km) **F 98** (157.7 km) Delta Fire Department to east.

ALASKA ROUTE 2

V 266 (428 km) **F 98** (157.7 km) Stop sign at intersection of the Richardson and Alaska highways in **DELTA JUNCTION** (see description beginning on page 192). **Delta Junction Visitor Information Center** to east; End of Alaska Highway monument, pipeline display, water, brochures, restrooms.

Junction of the Richardson Highway (Alaska Route 4) and Alaska Highway (Alaska Route 2). Turn to **Milepost DC 1422** (page 191) in the ALASKA HIGHWAY section for log of that route to Tok and the Canadian border (read log back to front).

The Richardson Highway continues north to Fairbanks as Alaska Route 2, and south to Valdez as Alaska Route 4.

V 266.3 (428.6 km) **F 97.7** (157.2 km) Delta Junction post office.

V 266.5 (428.9 km) **F 97.5** (156.9 km) Delta Junction library and city hall. Library hours are 11 A.M. to 6 P.M. Monday through Thursday and 11 A.M. to 4 P.M. Friday and Saturday; free paperback book and magazine exchange, Alaska videos, public fax and copier service. City Hall is open 9 A.M. to 5 P.M. weekdays; pay phone and public restrooms.

V 266.8 (429.4 km) **F 97.2** (156.4 km) Alaska Dept. of Fish and Game office.

V 267 (429.7 km) **F 97** (156.1 km) Airstrip.

V 267.1 (429.8 km) **F 96.9** (155.9 km) Delta state campground to east; 24 sites, water, tables, shelter with covered tables, toilets, $8 nightly fee or annual pass. Large turnout at campground entrance. Turnout on west side of highway on bank of the Delta River offers excellent views of the Alaska Range. ▲

V 267.2 (430 km) **F 96.8** (155.7 km) Alaska Division of Forestry office.

V 267.3 (430.2 km) **F 96.7** (155.6 km) Medical clinic.

V 267.6 (430.6 km) **F 96.4** (155.1 km) Delta laundry and fuel.

V 268 (431.3 km) **F 96** (154.5 km) RV park to east.

Smith's Green Acres RV Park & Campground & Nightly Lodging. Avoid the rush and the crowds, stay with us. One of Alaska's finest RV parks. 9.5 Good Sam rating. From a guest: "One of the best we've seen in Alaska." Nightly wildlife tours available. Great trout and grayling fishing nearby. See display ad in Delta Junction section. [ADVERTISEMENT] ▲

V 268.3 (431.7 km) **F 95.7** (154 km) **Junction** with Jack Warren Road (paved); see

Delta Vicinity map this section. Turn here for access to Clearwater state campground (10.5 miles/16.9 km). Clearwater campground has toilets, tables, water and boat launch; pleasant campsites on bank of river. Camping fee $8/night or annual pass. ▲

Driving this loop is a good opportunity to see local homesteads. Note that mileposts on these paved side roads run backward from Mile 13 at this junction to Mile 0 at the junction of Clearwater Road and the Alaska Highway.

V 270.3 (435 km) **F 93.7** (150.8 km) **Alaska 7 Motel**, 16 large, clean, comfortable rooms with full bath and showers. Color TV and courtesy coffee in each room. Kitchenettes and phone available. Comfort at a comfortable price. Open year-round. Major credit cards accepted. **Milepost 270.3** Richardson Highway. Phone (907) 895-4848. See display ad in Delta Junction section. [ADVERTISEMENT]

V 271.7 (437.2 km) **F 92.3** (148.5 km) Tanana Loop Road (gravel). Turn here for Delta Junction youth hostel. To make a loop drive through farmlands, follow Tanana Loop Road 1.3 miles/2.1 km, turn south on Tanana Loop Extension and drive 7.8 miles/12.5 km to Jack Warren Road (unsigned). Go west on Jack Warren Road (paved) for 2.9 miles/4.7 km to junction with Alaska Highway north of Delta Junction (see Delta Vicinity map this section).

V 272.1 (437.9 km) **F 92** (148 km) Big D Fire station.

V 273.9 (440.8 km) **F 90.2** (145.2 km) **Big D B&B.** Beautifully landscaped pioneer property features hand-hewn log and rock strutures, vegetable and flower gardens and greenhouse. Sourdough hosts give you the most Alaskan savvy for your buck. Great beds, private rooms, fresh bread baked daily and satellite TV. P.O. Box 1330, Delta Junction, AK 99737. Phone (907) 895-4148. [ADVERTISEMENT]

V 275 (442.6 km) **F 89** (143.2 km) Tanana Trading Post (Tesoro) gas station on west side of highway, turnoff to east for

Rika's Roadhouse (a worthwhile stop). Gold Rush Centennial interpretive sign on Big Delta's beginning as a trading post and roadhouse known first as Bates Landing and later as Rika's Landing, then McCarty.

Rika's Roadhouse was built in 1910 by John Hajdukovich. In 1923, Hajdukovich sold it to Rika Wallen, a Swedish immigrant who had managed the roadhouse since 1917. Rika ran the roadhouse into the late 1940s and lived there until her death in 1969. Rika's Roadhouse is now part of **Big Delta State Historical Park**. Drive in on gravel access road to large parking area; it is a short walk through trees to Rika's Roadhouse complex. The parking area also accommodates overnight RV parking; camping fee $8/vehicle, dump station ($3), toilets and phone. ▲

Rika's Roadhouse at Big Delta State Historical Park. Turn northeast at Rika's Road for Rika's Roadhouse and Landing on the banks of the Tanana River. Tour buses welcome. Parking areas with restrooms at both park entrances. The newly renovated Rika's Roadhouse offers worldwide postal service and gift shop specializing in furs, leather, gold and Alaska-made gifts. Meals served 9 A.M. to 5 P.M. in our Packhouse Restaurant which offers homemade soups, fresh salads and sandwiches. Guests love the homemade baked goods of the Alaska

Baking Co. Try our famous edible souvenir—the Bear Claw. We are also well-known for our pies: Strawberry-rhubarb, blueberry, pecan, coconut cream and chocolate truffle. Take a walk and visit the many historic buildings including the Roadhouse where you can also shop. After the dust of the highway, the green gardens of this 10-acre park are a welcome haven. Overnight parking and dump station available. P.O. Box 1229, Delta Junction, AK 99737. Phone (907) 895-4201 or 895-4938 anytime. Free admission. Handicapped access. See display ad in the ALASKA HIGHWAY section. [ADVERTISEMENT] ♿▲

The Tanana Trading Post. See display ad this section.

V 275.4 (443.2 km) **F 88.6** (142.6 km) Big Delta Bridge; **Tanana River/Pipeline Crossing**. Spectacular view of pipeline suspended across river. Slow down for parking area to east at south end of bridge with litter barrels and interpretive sign about pipeline.

BIG DELTA (pop. 519) is an unincorporated community at the junction of the Delta and Tanana Rivers. The Fur Shack is located here.

The Fur Shack. See display ad in the ALASKA HIGHWAY section.

V 277.7 (446.9 km) **F 86.3** (138.9 km) Turnoff to east for **Quartz Lake Recreation Area**. Drive in 2.5 miles/4 km on gravel road to intersection: turn left for Lost Lake, continue straight ahead for Quartz Lake (another 0.3 mile/0.5 km). Lost Lake, 0.2 mile/0.3 km from intersection, has 8 campsites with picnic tables, toilet, and a large parking area with tables and litter barrels. A shallow, picturesque lake with no fish. Quartz Lake has more developed campsites on good loop road, firepits, water, tables, toilet and 2 boat launches. Boat launch fee $3 or annual boat launch pass. Camping fees at both campgrounds: $8/night or annual pass. A trail connects Lost Lake and Quartz Lake camping areas.

Private cabins are scattered along the northern and eastern shorelines of Quartz Lake. About half the land along the lake is undeveloped and there is no road access beyond the campground. The lake covers 1,500 acres, more than 80 percent of which are less than 15 feet/5m deep. Maximum depth is 40 feet/12m. Aquatic vegetation covers most of the lake surface, hampering swimmers and waterskiers. Boat and motor rentals available from Black Spruce Lodge. **Quartz Lake** offers excellent fishing for stocked rainbow to 18 inches, silver salmon to 13 inches and Arctic char; use spinners, plugs and artificial flies. Ice fishing in winter. For more information phone the ADF&G office in Delta at (907) 895-4632. ⚓ ▲

The wide Tanana River flows west of the Richardson Highway between Delta Junction and Fairbanks. (© Ruth Fairall)

CAUTION: Rough road northbound. Watch for moose.

V 310 (498.9 km) **F 54** (86.9 km) Double-ended paved parking area to west.

V 313 (503.7 km) **F 51** (82.1 km) Paved double-ended turnout to west on Tanana River. Gold Rush Centennial interpretive sign about gold strikes in the Tanana Valley.

V 314.8 (506.6 km) **F 49.2** (79.2 km) **Midway Lodge** is open 7 A.M. to 11 P.M. daily. Bar open till ? Breakfast anytime, famous homemade chili, royal ½-pound hamburgers, fresh pies. Clean rooms starting

at $35. Showers. Gifts. We are a family-oriented stop on the Alaska Highway and welcome your visit. 11191 Richardson Highway, Salcha, AK 99714. Phone (907) 488-2939. [ADVERTISEMENT]

V 317.9 (511.6 km) **F 45.4** (73.1 km) Double-ended gravel parking area to west.

V 319.8 (514.7 km) **F 44.2** (71.1 km) Access road east to Harding Lake summer homes. Access to **Little Harding Lake**, king salmon fishing.

V 321.5 (517.4 km) **F 42.5** (68.4 km) **Harding Lake State Recreation Area** turnoff; drive east 1.5 miles/2.4 km on paved road to campground. Park headquarters, drinking water fill-up and dump station ($3 charge) at campground entrance. Picnic grounds on lakeshore, swimming, boat ramp ($5 launch fee or annual boat launch pass), ball fields and about 80 campsites. Camping fee $8/night or annual pass. Fishing for lake trout, arctic char, burbot, northern pike and salmon. Lake is reported to be "hard to fish." Worth the drive! *Bring your insect repellent. You may need it!*

V 322.2 (518.5 km) **F 41.8** (67.3 km) **SALCHA** (pop. 390). Post office (ZIP code 99714) and Salcha River Lodge; food, gas and lodging.

Salcha River Lodge. Alaskan hospitality. Gas, diesel, propane, clean showers, modern motel, groceries, restaurant, gift shop, post office. Ice cream cones, shakes, sundaes, homemade pie. Close to rivers and lakes; excellent fishing. 9162 Richardson Highway, Salcha, AK 99714. Phone (907) 488-2233. [ADVERTISEMENT]

V 323.1 (520 km) **F 40.9** (65.8 km) **Salcha River State Recreation Site** to east; large parking area with 75 sites, boat ramp ($3 launch fee or annual boat launch pass), picnic area, toilets and water. Camping fee $8/night per vehicle or annual pass. Fishing for king and chum salmon, grayling, sheefish, northern pike and burbot.

V 323.4 (520.4 km) **F 40.6** (65.3 km) Salcha River bridge.

V 323.7 (520.9 km) **F 40.3** (64.8 km) Snoshu Inn.

V 324.1 (521.6 km) **F 39.9** (64.2 km) Clear Creek bridge.

V 324.6 (522.4 km) **F 39.4** (63.4 km) Double-ended gravel turnout to east.

V 324.8 (522.7 km) **F 39.2** (63.1 km) **Munsons Slough** bridge; fishing.

V 325.6 (523.7 km) **F 38.6** (62.1 km) Salcha Elementary School.

V 326.4 (525.3 km) **F 37.6** (60.5 km) Salcha Baptist log church to west.

V 277.9 (447.2 km) **F 86.1** (138.6 km) Former U.S. Army petroleum station, now closed. Pay phone beside highway.

V 280.3 (451.1 km) **F 83.7** (134.7 km) Gravel turnout to east.

V 286.6 (461.2 km) **F 77.4** (124.6 km) Shaw Creek bridge; boat launch and snack shop. Excellent wildflower displays of sweet peas blooming in June.

V 286.7 (461.4 km) **F 77.3** (124.4 km) **Shaw Creek** road. Good to excellent early spring and fall grayling fishing; subject to closure (check locally).

Good view northbound of Tanana River which parallels the highway.

V 287.2 (462.2 km) **F 76.8** (123.6 km) Turnout and road to slough to east.

V 288.1 (463.6 km) **F 75.9** (122.1 km) Scenic viewpoint at parking area to west with panoramic view to the south of 3 great peaks of the Alaska Range: Mount Hayes, elev. 13,832 feet/4,216m, almost due south; Hess Mountain, elev. 11,940 feet/3,639m, to the west (right) of Mount Hayes; and Mount Deborah, elev. 12,339 feet/3,761m, to the west (right) of Hess Mountain. Mount Hayes is named for Charles Hayes, an early member of the U.S. Geological Survey. Mount Deborah was named in 1907 by the famous Alaskan Judge Wickersham for his wife.

V 289.8 (466.4 km) **F 74.2** (119.4 km) Long paved double-ended turnout to east in trees.

V 291.8 (469.6 km) **F 72.2** (116.2 km) Northbound truck lane begins. Southbound truck lane ends.

V 292.8 (471.2 km) **F 71.2** (114.6 km) Northbound truck lane ends.

View of Tanana River valley.

V 294 (473.1 km) **F 70** (112.7 km) Paved double-ended turnout to west.

V 294.2 (473.5 km) **F 69.8** (112.3 km) Southbound truck lane begins.

V 294.9 (474.6 km) **F 69.1** (111.2 km) Game Management Unit boundary between 20B and 20D. Fairbanks North Star Borough boundary.

V 295.4 (475.4 km) **F 68.6** (110.4 km) Banner Creek bridge; historic placer gold stream.

V 296.4 (477 km) **F 67.6** (108.8 km) Paved parking area to west; view of Alaska Range and Tanana River to south.

CAUTION: Rough road, watch for frost heaves northbound.

V 297.7 (479.1 km) **F 66.3** (106.7 km) Large gravel parking area to west below highway. Paved access road to Tanana River.

V 298.2 (479.9 km) **F 65.8** (105.9 km) Paved parking area to west.

V 301.7 (485.5 km) **F 62.3** (100.3 km) South end of long double-ended turnout.

V 304.3 (489.7 km) **F 59.7** (96.1 km) Parking area to east.

V 305.2 (491.2 km) **F 58.8** (94.6 km) Birch Lake Road to east; access to military recreation area (restricted).

V 306 (492.4 km) **F 58** (93.3 km) Large parking area east side of highway overlooks **Birch Lake**; unimproved gravel boat launch and beach; fish from shore in spring, from boat in summer, for rainbow and silver salmon. Many Fairbanks residents have summer homes at Birch Lake.

V 307.2 (494.3 km) **F 56.8** (91.4 km) Birch Lake highway maintenance station.

V 308 (495.7 km) **F 56** (90.1 km)

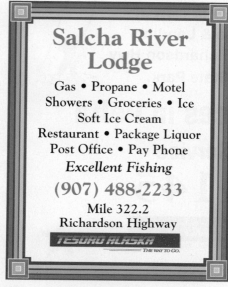

V 327.7 (527.4 km) **F 36.3** (58.4 km) Little Salcha River bridge.

V 328.3 (528.3 km) **F 35.7** (57.4 km) Salcha Store and gas station to east.

Salcha Store and Service. See display ad this section.

V 331.7 (533.8 km) **F 32.3** (52 km) Salcha Fairgrounds. Salcha Fair is held in late June.

V 332.2 (534.6 km) **F 31.8** (51.2 km) Access east to **31-Mile Pond**; stocked with arctic char.

V 332.3 (534.8 km) **F 31.7** (51 km) The Knotty Shop to west; gifts and wildlife museum.

The Knotty Shop. Stop and be impressed by a truly unique Alaskan gift shop and wildlife museum. Jim and Paula have attempted to maintain a genuine Alaskan flavor—from the unusual burl construction to the Alaskan wildlife displayed in a natural setting to the handcrafted Alaskan gifts. Don't miss the opportunity to stop and browse. See display ad this section. Show us *The MILEPOST®* advertisement for a free small ice cream cone. [ADVERTISEMENT]

V 334.7 (538.6 km) **F 29.3** (47.2 km) South boundary of Eielson AFB.

V 335.1 (539.3 km) **F 28.9** (46.5 km) Access east to **28-Mile Pond**; stocked with rainbow and silver salmon.

V 338 (543.9 km) **F 26** (41.8 km) View of Eielson AFB airstrip to northeast. Watch for various military aircraft taking off and landing to the east. Aircraft include Air Force F-16s, F-15s, KC-135s, C-130s, C-141s, OA-10s, Navy A-6s, F-14s and others.

V 340.7 (548.3 km) **F 23.3** (37.5 km) Divided highway begins northbound, ends southbound. *CAUTION: Watch for heavy traffic southbound turning east into the base, 7–8 A.M., and merging northbound traffic, 3:45–5:30 P.M., weekdays.*

V 341 (548.8 km) **F 23** (37 km) Entrance to east to **EIELSON AIR FORCE BASE**, constructed in 1943 and named for Carl Ben Eielson, a famous Alaskan bush pilot. A weekly tour is offered for groups of 10 or more. Phone the Public Affairs office at (907) 377-1410 for reservations and more information.

V 342.3 (550.9 km) **F 21.7** (34.9 km) North boundary of Eielson AFB.

V 343.7 (553.1 km) **F 20.3** (32.7 km) Moose Creek Road and general store; diesel, gas, propane.

Piledriver Slough parallels the highway from here north, flowing into the Tanana River. It is stocked with rainbow trout. Check with general store for access and fishing information. **Bathing Beauty Pond**, stocked with rainbow, arctic char and grayling, is accessible via Eielson Farm Road off Moose Creek Road.

V 344.7 (554.7 km) **F 19.3** (31 km) Moose Creek bridge.

V 345.5 (556 km) **F 18.5** (29.8 km) *CAUTION: Highway crosses Alaska Railroad tracks.*

V 346 (556.8 km) **DC 1502** (2417.2 km) **F 17.9** (28.8 km) Chena Flood Channel bridge. Upstream dam is part of flood control project initiated after the Chena River left its banks and flooded Fairbanks in 1967.

The **Moose Creek Dam Bikeway** is a 5-mile paved trail on the Chena Flood Project. The bikeway extends from a park-and-ride lot at Laurence and Nelson Roads to the damsite on the Chena River.

V 346.7 (558 km) **F 17.3** (27.8 km) Laurance Road; park-and-ride, Conkle's Automotive (towing, repair). Moose Creek Dam Bikeway.

North Pole VFW Post. See display ad this section.

Turn east for **Chena Lakes Recreation Area** (follow signs, 2.2 miles/3.5 km to entrance). Constructed by the Army Corps of Engineers and run by Fairbanks North Star Borough, the recreation area has 80 campsites, 92 picnic sites (some with wheelchair access), pump water, volleyball courts and a 250-acre lake with swimming beach. Chena Lake Bike Trail begins at Chena Lake swim beach and intersects with the Moose Creek Dam Bikeway. **Chena Lake** is stocked with silver salmon, arctic char, grayling and rainbow trout. Nonmotorized boats may be rented from a concessionaire. The **Chena River** flows through part of the recreation area and offers good grayling fishing and also northern pike, whitefish and burbot. Hiking and self-guiding nature trails. Open year-round. Fee charged Memorial Day to Labor Day; day use $3 per vehicle, camping $6 per day.

V 347.1 (558.6 km) **F 16.9** (27.2 km) Newby Road.

V 347.7 (559.6 km) **F 16.3** (26.2 km) Exit west for St. Nicholas Drive, east for Dawson Road.

V 348.7 (561.2 km) **F 15.3** (24.6 km) Exit northeast for **North Pole Visitor Information Center** (open 8 A.M. to 7 P.M. daily, Memorial Day to mid-September) and for Mission Road to radio station KJNP.

Exit southwest for 5th Avenue businesses, RV park and Santa Claus House.

Santaland RV Park. Good Sampark.

The ubiquitous arctic ground squirrel is is a favorite bear food.

(© Craig Brandt)

Center of North Pole, next to Santa Claus House, home of Dancer and Prancer, North Pole's resident reindeer. City water, full service pull-throughs, car wash. Free private showers, laundry, pay phones. Cable TV. 50-amp available. E-mail access. Handicapped accessible. Tour sales and reservations. Daily shuttle bus to Fairbanks points of interest.

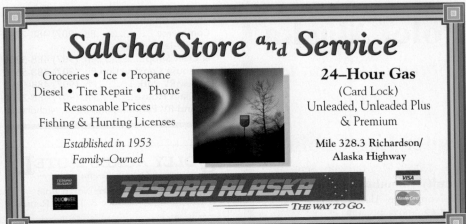

See display ad, or call (888) 488-9123 or (907) 488-9123. &♿▲ [ADVERTISEMENT]

V 349 (561.6 km) F 15 (24.1 km) Santa Claus House. In 1949, Con Miller began wearing a Santa Claus suit on business trips throughout the territory, bringing the spirit of St. Nicholas to hundreds of children for the first time. Here, the Miller family continues this tradition. Ask about Santa's Christmas letter. Mail your cards and letters here for authentic North Pole postmark. Enjoy the unique gift shop and exhibits. Summer hours: 8 A.M.–8 P.M. daily, Memorial Day through Labor Day. Ride the Snowy River Railroad daily except Sunday, summers only. Visit with Santa Claus summers and Christmas season only. Santa's reindeer, Dancer and Prancer, live on the grounds all summer long. Santa Claus House winter hours: 10 A.M.–6 P.M. (closed January and February for Santa's annual vacation). See display ad in this section. [ADVERTISEMENT]

V 349.5 (562.3 km) F 14.5 (23.3 km) North Pole and North Pole Plaza to southwest via Santa Claus Lane; access to Santa Claus House. Badger Road to the northeast.

Santa Claus Lane has several businesses along it, and connects with 5th Avenue, which loops back to the highway at **Milepost V 348.6.**

Truck stop with diesel, 2 small shopping malls, motel and other businesses are located on Badger Road. Badger Road is a

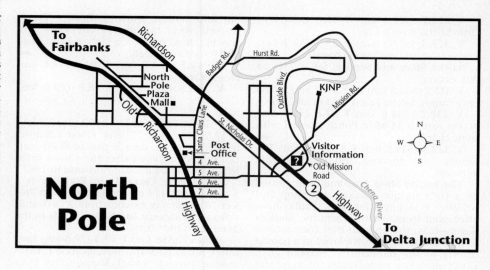

loop road leading 12 miles/19.3 km along Badger Slough and providing access to an RV park, salmon bake, convenience store with gas, and several bed and breakfasts. It also

junctions with Nordale Road to Chena Hot

Springs Road. It re-enters the Alaska Highway 7 miles/11.3 km outside of Fairbanks at **Milepost V 357.1.**

North Pole

V 349.5 (562.3 km) F 14.5 (23.3 km) The home of Santa Claus. **Population:** 1,619. **Emergency Services:** Emergencies only phone 911. **Police,** phone (907) 488-6902. **Alaska State Troopers,** phone (907) 452-2114. **Fire Department/Ambulance,** phone (907) 488-0444.

Visitor Information: At **Milepost V 348.7.** Open 8 A.M. to 7 P.M. daily, Memorial Day to mid-September. North Pole Chamber of Commerce, P.O. Box 55071, North Pole, AK 99705; phone (907) 488-2242, fax (907) 488-0366.

Elevation: 500 feet/152m. **Radio:** KJNP-AM 1170, KJNP-FM 100.3; also Fairbanks stations.

Private Aircraft: Bradley Sky Ranch, 1 NW; elev. 483 feet/147m; length 4,100

Fur-trimmed parka is typical Alaska winter clothing. (© Craig Brandt)

feet/1,250m; gravel; fuel 100.

North Pole has many services, including restaurants, a motel, bed and breakfasts, campgrounds, laundromats, car wash, grocery and gas stops, gift stores, library, churches, a public park, pharmacy and supermarket. The post office is on Santa Claus Lane.

North Pole has an annual Winter Carnival with sled dog races, carnival games, food booths and other activities. There's a big summer festival weekend celebration with carnival rides, food booths, arts and crafts booths, and a parade.

In 1944 Bon V. Davis homesteaded this area. Dahl and Gaske Development Co. bought the Davis homestead, subdivided it and named it North Pole, hoping to attract a toy manufacturer who could advertise products as being made in North Pole.

North Pole is the home of many Fairbanks commuters. It has an oil refinery that produces heating fuel, jet fuel and other products. Eielson and Wainwright military bases are nearby.

Radio station KJNP, operated by Calvary's Northern Lights Mission, broadcasts music and religious programs on 1170 AM and 100.3 FM. They also operate television station KJNP Channel 4. Visitors are welcome between 8 A.M. and 10 P.M.; tours may be arranged. KJNP is located on Mission Road about 0.6 mile/1 km northeast of the Alaska Highway. The missionary project includes a dozen hand-hewn, sod-roofed homes and other buildings constructed of spruce logs.

Full-service campgrounds at Santaland RV Park downtown, Road's End RV Park at **Milepost V 356.2** and Riverview RV Park at **Milepost V 357.1** Richardson Highway. North Pole Public Park, on 5th Avenue, has tent sites in the trees along a narrow dirt road; no camping fee. Dump station available at North Pole Plaza. ▲

Richardson Highway Log
(continued)

V 350.2 (563.6 km) **F 13.8** (22.2 km) Peridot Street.

V 350.6 (564.2 km) **F 13.4** (21.6 km) *CAUTION: Highway crosses Alaska Railroad tracks.*

V 351 (564.9 km) **F 13** (20.9 km) Twelvemile Village exit to south.

V 354.4 (570.3 km) **F 9.6** (15.4 km) Old Richardson Highway exit.

V 356.2 (573.2 km) **F 7.8** (12.6 km) **Road's End RV Park.** See display ad this section. ▲

V 357.1 (574.7 km) **F 6.9** (11.1 km) Badger Road exit; access to Riverview RV Park other businesses. Badger Road also junctions with Nordale Road to Chena Hot Springs Road and access to the Chena River.

V 357.6 (575.5 km) **F 6.4** (10.3 km) Weigh stations both sides of highway.

V 358.6 (577.1 km) **F 5.4** (8.7 km) Entrance to U.S. Army Fort Wainwright.

V 359.2 (578.1 km) **F 4.8** (7.7 km) *CAUTION: Highway crosses Alaska Railroad tracks.*

The Chena River and its tributaries are popular canoeing waters in the Fairbanks area. *(© Robin Brandt)*

V 359.6 (578.7 km) **F 4.4** (7.1 km) West truck route (Old Richardson Highway); northbound-only exit.

V 360.6 (580.3 km) **F 3.4** (5.5 km) Denali Park/Parks Highway (Alaska Route 3) exit northbound to bypass Fairbanks via the Robert J. Mitchell expressway. Hospital this exit.

V 361 (581 km) **F 3** (4.8 km) Exit via 30th Avenue to Big Bend business area for east- and westbound traffic. Access to motels, restaurants, Old Richardson Highway, Van Horn Road, South Cushman Street and downtown Fairbanks.

V 361.3 (581.4 km) **F 2.7** (4.3 km) 30th Avenue overpass; exits both sides of highway. A heart-shaped picture created from plantings of yellow flowers represents the Golden Heart of Fairbanks.

V 363 (584.2 km) **F 1** (1.6 km) Northbound exit to Gaffney Road for Fort Wainwright; turn left on Airport Way for downtown Fairbanks, University of Alaska, Alaskaland and Parks Highway (Alaska Route 3). Follow city center signs to downtown Fairbanks and visitor information center.

V 363.3 (584.7 km) **F 0.7** (1.1 km) 10th Avenue exit to downtown Fairbanks.

V 363.6 (585.1 km) **F 0.4** (0.6 km) Steese Expressway crosses Chena River.

V 363.9 (585.6 km) **F 0.1** (0.2 km) 3rd Street exit; access to Gavora Mall.

V 364 (585.8 km) **F 0 FAIRBANKS.** College Road exit to University of Alaska, Bentley Mall and city center (turn left). For details see FAIRBANKS section.

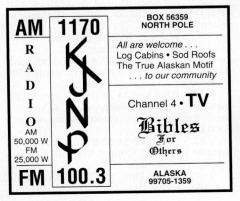

EDGERTON HIGHWAY / McCARTHY ROAD ⑩

Connects: Richardson Highway Junction to McCarthy, AK
Length: 93 miles   **Road Surface:** 40% paved, 60% gravel
Season: McCarthy Road not maintained in winter
Major Attraction: Wrangell–St. Elias National Park & Preserve

	Chitina	McCarthy	Richardson Hwy.
Chitina		60	33
McCarthy	60		93
Richardson Hwy.	33	93	

The Edgerton Highway cuts a straight swath east from the Richardson Highway toward the Wrangell Mountains. *(© Kris Graef, staff)*

Copper River EMS in Glennallen, phone 911 or (907) 822-3203.

Edgerton Highway Log

Distance from junction with Richardson Highway (R) is followed by distance from junction with McCarthy Road (M).

ALASKA ROUTE 10

R 0 M 35.1 (56.5 km) The Edgerton Highway leads east from the Richardson Highway.

Junction of the Edgerton Highway (Alaska Route 10) and the Richardson Highway (Alaska Route 4). Turn to **Milepost V 82.6** in the Richardson HIGHWAY for log of that route

Edgerton Highway begins long downgrade eastbound. Excellent view of Mount Drum (to the northeast), a 12,010-foot/3,661-m peak of the Wrangell Mountains. Mount Wrangell (elev. 14,163 feet/4,317m) and Mount Blackburn (elev. 16,390 feet/4,996m) are visible straight ahead.

R 5.2 (8.4 km) **M 29.9** (48.1 km) Kenny Lake School to the south.

R 5.3 (8.5 km) **M 29.8** (48 km) Paved turnout to north.

R 7.2 (11.6 km) **M 27.9** (44.9 km) Kenny Lake Mercantile & RV Park to north with grocery store, cafe, gas, laundromat, showers, camping and pay phone.

Kenny Lake Mercantile & RV Park. See display ad this section.

R 7.3 (11.7 km) **M 27.8** (44.7 km) Old Edgerton Loop Road (gravel) leads from here 8 miles/12.9 km through homestead and farm country to the Richardson Highway at **Milepost V 91.1.**

R 7.5 (12.1 km) **M 27.6** (44.4 km) Kenny Lake community hall, fairgrounds.

R 7.7 (12.4 km) **M 27.4** (44.1 km) Long double-ended paved rest area to south with picnic table on shore of Kenny Lake.

R 12.3 (19.8 km) **M 22.8** (36.7 km) Paved turnout to south. Tonsina River BLM trailhead, 2 miles/3.2 km (marked, brushed trail; good hike).

R 12.5 (20.1 km) **M 22.6** (36.4 km) Paved turnout to north. Copper River BLM trailhead, 5 miles/8 km.

R 13 (20.9 km) **M 22.2** (35.7 km) **Tonsina Native Arts & Crafts.** See display

The Edgerton Highway, known locally as the Edgerton Cutoff, is a scenic paved road leading 35.1 miles/56.5 km east from its junction with the Richardson Highway to Chitina, then across the Copper River bridge to the start of the McCarthy Road. Total driving distance from the Richardson Highway turnoff to the end of the McCarthy Road is 93.4 miles/ 150.3 km. The Edgerton Highway is named for U.S. Army Maj. Glenn Edgerton of the Alaska Territorial Road Commission.

The gravel McCarthy Road leads 58.3 miles/93.8 km east from Chitina and dead ends at the Kennicott River, about 1 mile/1.6 km west of the settlement of McCarthy. The Kennicott River crossing is by 2 foot bridges. There is no vehicle access across the river.

The McCarthy Road follows the right-of-way of the old Copper River & Northwestern Railway. Begun in 1907, the CR&NW (also referred to as the "can't run and never will") was built to carry copper ore from the Kennecott Mines to Cordova. It took 4 years to complete the railway. The railway and mine ceased operation in 1938.

The McCarthy Road is recommended for the adventurous traveler and only in the summer. Maximum speed is about 25

mph/40 kmph. Motorists with large vehicles or trailers should exercise caution, especially in wet weather. Watch for old railroad spikes in the roadbed. Unless recently graded, watch for potholes, soft spots and severe washboard. Tire repair and mechanical light-towing service are available at Silver Lake Campground, **Milepost J 9.3.**

Most land along the McCarthy Road is either privately or publicly held. Local residents have asked that visitors please help protect water sources from contamination.

The solitude and scenery of McCarthy, along with the historic Kennecott Mine and surrounding wilderness of Wrangell–St. Elias National Park and Preserve, have drawn increasing numbers of visitors to this area. It is a 126-mile/202-km drive from Glennallen to McCarthy, 315 miles/507 km from Anchorage.

The National Park Service ranger station in Chitina has information on current road conditions and also on backcountry travel in Wrangell–St. Elias National Park and Preserve.

Emergency medical services: Between the junction of the Richardson and Edgerton highways and McCarthy, contact the

EDGERTON HIGHWAY/McCARTHY ROAD

Richardson Highway to McCarthy, AK

To Glennallen
(see RICHARDSON HIGHWAY section, page 509)

Copper Center

National Park Boundary

▲ Mount Wrangell
14,163 ft./4,317m

WRANGELL

MOUNTAINS

Old Edgerton
Loop Road

R-7.2/11.6km Kenny Lake Mercantile & RV Park CDGIPST

R-13/20.9km Tonsina Native Arts & Crafts

Mount Blackburn ▲
16,390 ft./4,996m

Glaciated Area

Kennicott Glacier

Key to mileage boxes

miles/kilometres
miles/kilometres

from:

J-Junction
M-McCarthy Road Jct.
R-Richardson Highway Jct.
RE-Road End
G-Glennallen
V-Valdez

Map Location

10

4

**R-0
M-35/57km
RE-93/150km
G-32/151km
V-83/133km**

**R-35/57km
M-0
J-0
RE-58/94km**

R-9.3/15km Silver Lake Campground CIR

R-58.2/93.7km Copper Oar Rafting

Kennicott ❄

Chitina
N61°31' W144°26'

R-33/53.1km Chitina Fuel & Grocery
& Chitina Motel dGILPS
Spirit Mountain Artworks

**R-33/53km
M-2/3km**

The McCarthy Road

**J-58/94km
RE-0**

McCarthy ❄ ✈
N61°326' W142°55'

J-58/93.3km Glacier View Campground
and Glacier Wings Helicopter Tours CMrST

Trans-Alaska
Pipeline

To Valdez
(see RICHARDSON HIGHWAY
section, page 509)

J-55.2/88.8km Willow Herb
Mountain Depot Lr

Wrangell-St. Elias National Park and Preserve

Liberty Creek

Twomile L.

Strelna L.

Van Lake

Silver Lake

Sculpin Lake

Chitina River

Long Lake

Copper River

Kuskulana River

Glaciated

Area

Principal Route

Paved	Unpaved

Other Roads

Paved	Unpaved

Ferry Routes **Hiking Trails**

❄ Refer to Log for Visitor Facilities

Scale

0   10 Miles
0   10   Kilometres

Key to Advertiser Services
C -Camping
D -Dump Station
d -Diesel
G -Gas (reg., unld.)
I -Ice
L -Lodging
M-Meals
P -Propane
R -Car Repair (major)
r -Car Repair (minor)
S -Store (grocery)
T -Telephone (pay)

N
W   E
S

R 18 (29 km) **M 17.1** (27.5 km) Steep downhill grade eastbound. Views of the Copper River and bluffs to north.

R 19.4 (31.2 km) **M 15.7** (25.3 km) Tonsina River bridge. Highway climbs eastbound; winding road.

R 19.5 (31.4 km) **M 15.6** (25.1 km) Turnout to north.

R 19.6 (31.5 km) **M 15.5** (24.9 km) Double-ended turnout at lake to north.

R 21.6 (34.8 km) **M 13.5** (21.7 km) Paved viewpoint to north above Copper River.

R 22 (35.4 km) **M 13.1** (21.1 km) Top of hill. Steep winding descents both directions.

R 23.5 (37.8 km) **M 11.6** (18.7 km) Liberty Falls Creek BLM trailhead to south.

R 23.7 (38.1 km) **M 11.4** (18.3 km) Liberty Creek bridge (8-ton load limit) and **Liberty Falls State Recreation Site.** The campground is just south of the highway on the banks of Liberty Creek, near the foot of the thundering falls. Scenic spot. Loop road through campground (large RVs and trailers check road before driving in); 5 sites, no water, no camping fee. Berry picking; watch for bears.

R 28.5 (45.9 km) **M 6.6** (10.6 km) Side road north to Chitina DOT/PF maintenance station and Chitina Airport. ADF&G office (dip net permits).

Private Aircraft: Chitina Airport; elev. 556 feet/169m; length 2,800 feet/853m; gravel; unattended.

R 29.5 (47.5 km) **M 5.7** (9.2 km) Small gravel turnout by Three Mile Lake.

R 29.7 (47.8 km) **M 5.4** (8.7 km) Paved turnout by **Three Mile Lake**; good grayling and rainbow trout fishing.

www.themilepost.com

In 1914, Chitina had a tinsmith, 5 hotels, bars, dance halls, restaurants, a pool hall and movie theater. Few buildings remain today. *(© Kris Graef, staff)*

R 30.6 (49.2 km) M 4.5 (7.2 km) Large paved parking area to south at east end of **Two Mile Lake**; good grayling and rainbow trout fishing.

R 31.9 (51.3 km) M 3.2 (5.1 km) One Mile Lake (also called First Lake). Access road to boat launch at east end of lake.

Chitina

R 33 (53.1 km) M 2.1 (3.4 km). Located about 120 miles/193 km northeast of Valdez, and about 66 miles/106 km southeast of Glennallen. **Population:** 84. **Emergency Services:** Copper River EMS, phone (907) 822-3203.

Visitor Information: National Park Service ranger station for Wrangell–St. Elias National Park and Preserve is housed in a historic cabin in Chitina. Open daily, Memorial Day to Labor Day. A slide show on the McCarthy Road and video programs are available. Write Box 439, Copper Center, AK 99573, or phone (907) 822-5234 (park headquarters); Chitina ranger station, phone (907) 823-2205.

Chitina has a post office, grocery, gas, motel, restaurant, tire repair service and phone service. Public restrooms at Chitina Wayside. One of the first buildings in Chitina, a hardware and sheet metal shop now on the National Register of Historic Places, houses Spirit Mountain Artworks. Pay phone next to highway between the ranger station and Town Lake.

Chitina (pronounced CHIT-na) was established about 1908 as a railroad stop on the Copper River & Northwestern Railway and as a supply town for the Kennecott Copper Mines at McCarthy. The mine and railroad were abandoned in 1938. The McCarthy Road east of town follows the old railroad bed, which is listed on the National Register of Historic Places.

A big attraction in Chitina for fishermen and spectators is the seasonal salmon run (reds, kings or silvers), which draws hundreds of dip-netters to the **Copper River**. The dip-net fishery for salmon runs June through September (depending on harvest levels), and it's worth the trip to see fish wheels and dip nets in action. This fishery is open only to Alaska residents with a personal-use or subsistence permit. Check with

the Chitina ADF&G office for details and current regulations.

O'Brien Creek Road provides a state right-of-way access to popular fishing areas on large sandbars along the Copper River. Access to the Copper River is not permitted across private land. Access is permitted only at O'Brien Creek and Haley Creek and prohibited elsewhere unless official signs indicate access is allowed. Do not trespass, litter or disturb private lands in anyway. O'Brien Creek river access and camping (litter barrels, outhouse) is 2.7 miles/4.3 km from Chitina (steep and narrow downhill to O'Brien Creek). A DOT travel advisory at Mile 2.8 O'Brien Creek Road warns of *"narrow road, rock slides, creek crossings, sharp curves and steep dropoffs."* According to local residents, vehicles can drive in about 17 miles/27.4 km, but the road is very rough.

O'Brien Creek Road follows a portion of the old railroad grade to Cordova. The line shacks along this old right-of-way have been restored by the DOT and are available for public use on a first-come, first-served basis.

Chitina Fuel & Grocery and Chitina Motel. See display ad this section.

Spirit Mountain Artworks. See display ad this section.

Edgerton Highway Log

(continued)

R 33.5 (53.9 km) M 1.7 (2.7 km) **Chitina Wayside**; paved parking area and restrooms.

R 33.6 (54.1 km) M 1.6 (2.6 km) Pavement ends eastbound. No road maintenance east of here between Oct. 15 and May 15.

R 33.8 (54.4 km) M 1.4 (2.3 km) Turnout overlooking the Copper River.

R 34.1 (54.9 km) M 1.1 (1.8 km) Turnout overlooking the Copper River. Access to river.

R 34.7 (55.8 km) M 0.5 (0.8 km) Copper River bridge. Completed in 1971, this 1,378-foot/420-m steel span was designed for year-round use. The $3.5 million bridge reestablished access across the river into the McCarthy–Kennicott area.

Game Management Unit 11. Wrangell–St. Elias National Park and Preserve boundary. Sign reads: "Much of the land along the road is private owned. For land ownership information, contact Chitina Village Corp. (907/823-2223), Ahtna Inc. (907/822-3476) or the National Park Service (907/822-5234).

R 35.1 (56.5 km) M 0 **Junction** with McCarthy Road (log follows). Access to fishing and camping on the **Copper River**; red and king salmon.

McCarthy Road Log

Distance from junction with the Edgerton Highway (J) is followed by distance from road end (RE).

Traditional mileposts used by local residents are indicated in the log.

ALASKA ROUTE 10

J 0 RE 58.3 (93.8 km) **Junction** with the Edgerton Highway.

J 3.7 (6 km) **RE 54.6** (87.9 km) Turnout overlooking the Chitina River.

J 8.3 (13.4 km) **RE 50** (80.5 km) **Milepost 10.** Physical mileposts indicate distance from Chitina. Trail opposite homestead leads 0.3 mile/0.5 km north to **Strelna Lake**; rainbow trout and silver salmon. (Private property adjacent trail.)

J 9.3 (15 km) **RE 49** (78.9 km) **Milepost 11.** Private campground on **Silver Lake** to south; rainbow trout fishing, boat and canoe rentals, boat launch, tire repair. Trail access to **Van Lake**, located south of Silver Lake; good rainbow trout fishing.

Silver Lake Campground. Gene and Edith Coppede invite you to fish for rainbow trout or just relax at beautiful Silver Lake. Bring your camera. RV or tent spaces, motorboat, rowboat and canoe rentals. New tires, tire repairs, fishing tackle, cold pop and candy, ice, bottled drinking water. See display ad. [ADVERTISEMENT] ▲

J 14.5 (23.3 km) **RE 43.8** (70.5 km) Milepost 16.

J 15.5 (24.9 km) **RE 42.8** (68.9 km) Turnout with view of Kuskulana River and bridge. People were bungee jumping off the bridge in summer 1998.

J 15.8 (25.4 km) **RE 42.5** (68.4 km) **Kuskulana Bridge** (1-lane). This old railroad bridge (built in 1910) is approximately 525 feet/160m long and 385 feet/117m above the river. It is a narrow 3-span steel railway bridge with wood decking. Rehabilitated in 1988 for vehicle traffic. Road access to river at west end.

J 17.1 (27.5 km) **RE 41.2** (66.3 km) CAUTION: *Very narrow road next mile eastbound.*

J 22.3 (35.9 km) **RE 36** (57.9 km) Large gravel turnout to south with view of Wrangell Mountains. There are several turnouts between here and the Kennicott River.

J 22.5 (36.2 km) **RE 35.8** (57.6 km) Boundary between park and preserve lands (unmarked). Wrangell–St. Elias National Park and Preserve allows sport hunting with a valid Alaska state license.

J 23.5 (37.8 km) **RE 34.8** (56 km) **Lou's Lake** to north; silver salmon and grayling fishing.

J 25.5 (41 km) **RE 32.8** (52.8 km) Milepost 27. Chokosna River bridge.

J 27.7 (44.6 km) **RE 30.6** (49.2 km) Gilahina River bridge (1-lane). Old railroad trestle and parking.

J 28.2 (45.4 km) **RE 30.1** (48.4 km) Turnout to south.

J 34 (54.7 km) **RE 24.3** (39.1 km) Turnout by lake.)

J 36.5 (58.7 km) **RE 21.8** (35.1 km) Milepost 38.

J 40.3 (64.9 km) **RE 18** (29 km) Crystal Lake.

J 40.5 (65.2 km) **RE 17.8** (28.6 km) Milepost 42.

J 42.9 (69 km) **RE 15.4** (24.8 km) One-lane wood-plank bridge (max. height 13'2")

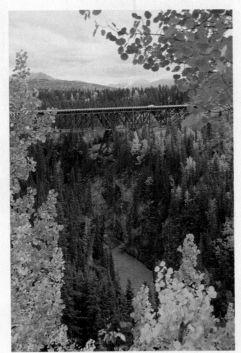

View of the Kuskulana Bridge from turnout at Milepost J 15.5. (© Kris Graef, staff)

over Lakina River. Access to river at east end.

Long Lake Wildlife Refuge sign; shooting prohibited eastbound.

J 43.2 (69.5 km) **RE 15.1** (24.3 km) Long Lake Wildlife Refuge sign; shooting prohibited westbound.

J 44.2 (71.1 km) **RE 14.1** (22.7 km) Watch for salmon spawning in Long Lake outlet (no fishing at outlet within 300 feet/91m of weir).

J 44.7 (71.9 km) **RE 13.6** (21.9 km) Turnout on **Long Lake**; a beautiful spot. Fishing for lake trout, silver salmon, grayling, Dolly Varden, burbot.

J 55.2 (88.8 km) **RE 3.1** (5 km) **Willow Herb Mountain Depot.** Experience Alaskan hospitality at our arts and crafts gallery or stay in our guest cabin. Stop and chat about log building or winter life with year-round McCarthy residents. Our new addition contains a bookstore and card shop. Rent a private, handscribed log cabin with a woodstove and cook-top. Experienced tire repair service. Terry and Dee Frady. MasterCard, VISA. (907) 554-4420. [ADVERTISEMENT]

J 57.3 (92.2 km) **RE 1** (1.6 km) National Park Information cabin to north; airstrip to south.

J 57.5 (92.5 km) **RE 0.8** (1.3 km) **Glacier View Resort and Glacier Wings Helicopter Tours.** Just ¹/₂ mile from the bridge, our scenic and private campsites offer breath-

taking views of the Root Glacier and surrounding Wrangell Mountains. Take a "thrill-a-minute" helicopter ride over timeless ice or just relax on the sun deck with your favorite beverage and a savory selection from our new barbecue menu. At Glacier View we strive to make your ultimate road trip unforgettable. Mountain bikes available. Phone (907) 554-4490, winter (907) 345-7121. [ADVERTISEMENT]

J 58 (93.3 km) **RE 0.3** (0.5 km) **Kennicott River Lodge and Hostel.** Road accessible. Your choice of accommodations include dormitory-style cabins, wall tents or lodge bunkroom. A 2-story log building provides common area for kitchen and dining. The upstairs sitting lounge with large deck offers views of the Kennicott Glacier. $25 per person. Phone (907) 554-4441. Open May 20–September 20. Internet: www2.polarnet.com/~grosswlr. [ADVERTISEMENT]

J 58.2 (93.7 km) **RE 0.1** (0.2 km) Parking lot for visitors crossing Kennicott River; Two pedestrian-only footbridges cross the channels of the Kennicott River. There is no vehicle access across the river. Until the state constructed the new footbridge across the Kennicott River in 1997, travelers had to haul themselves across the river using a hand-pulled, open-platform cable tram.

CAUTION: *Do not attempt to wade across this glacial river; strong currents and cold water make it extremely treacherous.* ▲

The Tram Station houses the parking concession, tour booking service, snack shop and gift shop. A CB radio at the Tram Station has instructions for calling businesses in McCarthy and Kennicott (they monitor Channel 5 when the Tram Station is closed).

Parking on the riverbank is not recommended in July or early August because of sudden flooding when an ice-dammed lake breaks free upstream.

Copper Oar Rafting. See display ad this section.

J 58.3 (93.8 km) **RE 0** McCarthy Road dead ends at Kennicott River. On the east side of the river, follow the road for about ¹/₂ mile to a fork, where there's a public restroom. The right fork leads to McCarthy, about another ¹/₂ mile, and the left fork goes to Kennicott, about 5 miles/8 km (shuttle bus service available in McCarthy).

McCarthy

Located across the Kennicott River and about 1 mile/1.6 km by road from the end of the McCarthy Road; within Wrangell–St. Elias National Park and Preserve; approximately 60 miles/96.5 km east of Chitina. **Population:** 28. **Transportation: Air**—Charter service between Chitina, McCarthy and Kennicott. **Van**—Scheduled service between Glennallen and McCarthy via Backcountry Connection; phone (907) 822-5292. Shuttle service between McCarthy and Kennicott via Wrangell Mountain Bus from Wrangell Mountain Air office; 1-way fare $5/adults, $2/dogs; phone (907) 554-4411.

Climate: Temperature extremes from -58° F/-50° C to 91° F/33° C; average snowfall 52 inches; annual precipitation 12 inches. **Radio:** KCAM (Glennallen).

Private Aircraft: McCarthy NR 2, 1 NE; elev. 1,531 feet/467m; length 3,500 feet/1,067m; gravel; unattended, unmaintained.

Lodging is available in McCarthy at the McCarthy Lodge, which also offers food service and a bar. The McCarthy area has flightseeing services, a bed and breakfast, a pizza restaurant and an operating gold mine. Check with lodges about activities in the area. Two wilderness guide services operate here. McCarthy has cellular phone service and some businesses can send and receive e-mail and faxes. McCarthy does not have a post office, school or television.

The town of McCarthy is in a beautiful area of glaciers and mountains. The Kennicott River flows by the west side of town and joins the Nizina River which flows into the Chitina River. The local museum, located in the railway depot, has historical artifacts and photos from the early mining days.

McCarthy lies within **WRANGELL–ST.**

ELIAS NATIONAL PARK AND PRESERVE. This 13.2 million acre park encompasses the southeast corner of the Alaska mainland, stretching from the Gulf of Alaska to the Copper River basin. Access to the park is by way of the McCarthy Road, the Nabesna Road (off the Tok Cutoff) and out of Yakutat. This vast unspoiled wilderness offers backpacking, mountaineering, river running, hunting and sportfishing. For more information, contact: Superintendent, Wrangell–St. Elias National Park and Preserve, P.O. Box 439, Copper Center, AK 99573; phone (907) 822-5234.

Wrangell Mountain Air provides twice daily, scheduled air service to McCarthy/Kennicott as a time saving alternative to driving the McCarthy Road. Park your car or RV in Chitina at the end of the paved road and enjoy a spectacular flight through the Wrangell–St. Elias Mountains. Affordable fly–drive day trips to Kennicott are also available from Chitina. Wrangell Mountain Air specializes in world-class flightseeing, fly-in alpine hiking, river rafting, glacier trekking. Aircraft are high wing for great viewing and equipped with intercom and headsets for each passenger. Phone free for reservations and information, (800) 478-1160 or (907) 554-4411. E-mail: flywma@aol.com. Internet: www.AlaskaOne.com/wma. See display ad. [ADVERTISEMENT]

It is about 5 miles/8 km from McCarthy to the old mining town of **KENNICOTT.** Perched on the side of a mountain next to Kennicott Glacier, the town was built by Kennecott Copper Corp. between 1910 and 1920. (An early-day misspelling made the mining company Kennecott, while the region and settlement are Kennicott.) The

Downtown McCarthy has a lodge, restaurant and flightseeing service. (© Bill Sherwonit)

richest copper mine in the world until its closure in 1938, Kennicott processed more than 591,535 tons of copper ore and employed some 800 workers in its heyday. Today, a lodge is located here. The 3 dozen barn-red mine buildings are on private land. Kennecott Copper Mine is a National Historic Site. Businesses include the Kennicott Glacier Lodge (ask about their special barbecues), a bed and breakfast and flightseeing service in Kennicott.

Kennicott Cottage, 16 Silk Stocking Row. Stay in the National Historic District of a scenic wilderness community. Charming 3-bedroom cottage sleeps 8 to 10. Discounts are available for stays of 3 days or more. Room rental includes shared kitchen, shower and outhouse. Reservations: phone (907) 242-1392 or 345-7961. E-mail: kenncott@alaska.net. Web page: www.alaska.net/~kenncott/kcc.htm. [ADVERTISEMENT]

Kennicott Glacier Lodge, located in the ghost town of Kennicott, offers the area's finest accommodations and dining. Built in 1987, this new lodge has 25 clean, delightful guest rooms, 2 living rooms, a spacious dining room, and a 180-foot front porch with a spectacular panoramic view of the Wrangell Mountains, Chugach Mountains and Kennicott Glacier. The homemade food, served family-style, has been called "wilderness gourmet dining." Guest activities at this destination resort include glacier trekking, flightseeing, photography, alpine hiking, historical and nature tours, rafting. May 15 to Sept. 20. (800) 582-5128. See display ad. [ADVERTISEMENT]

Porch at Kennicott Lodge overlooks old mine buildings and terminal moraine of Kennicott Glacier. (© James D. Ronan, Jr.)

PRINCE WILLIAM SOUND

Star attraction of Prince William Sound is Columbia Glacier. (© Rich Reid)

Southcentral Alaska's Prince William Sound lies at the northern extent of the Gulf of Alaska. In addition to its spectacular scenery, comparable to that of southeastern Alaska's Inside Passage, the area is also rich in wildlife. Visitors may see Dall sheep, mountain goats, sea lions, sea otters, whales, harbor seals, bald eagles and other birds. The waters contain all species of Pacific salmon; king, Dungeness and tanner crab; halibut; and rockfish.

This section includes: Columbia Glacier; Whittier; Valdez, start of the Richardson Highway; and Cordova, start of the Copper River Highway.

There are several ways to explore Prince William Sound. From Anchorage, drive south on the Seward Highway 47 miles/ 75.6 km to Portage and board the Alaska Railroad shuttle train for a 35-minute ride to Whittier (a road connection to Whittier is scheduled to open May 1, 2000). You may also start your trip across Prince William Sound from Valdez. Drive 304 miles/498.2 km from Anchorage to Valdez via the Glenn and Richardson highways (see GLENN HIGHWAY and RICHARDSON HIGHWAY sections).

From Whittier, Valdez or Cordova, board the ferry or one of the privately operated excursion boats to tour Prince William Sound. Flightseeing trips are also available. Depending on your itinerary and type of transportation, you may see Columbia glacier and return to Anchorage the same day or have to stay overnight along the way. All-inclusive tours of Prince William Sound

are available out of Anchorage.

Plan your trip in advance. Reservations for the ferry or cruise boats are necessary. The Alaska Railroad does not take reservations, although passengers with confirmed ferry reservations are given first priority when loading.

Columbia Glacier

Star attraction of Prince William Sound is Columbia Glacier, one of the largest and most magnificent of the tidewater glaciers along the Alaska coast. The Columbia Glacier has an area of about 440 square miles/1140 square km. The glacier is more than 40 miles/64 km long; its tidewater terminus, which visitors to Prince William Sound will see, is about 3 miles/4.8 km across. Columbia Glacier has receded more than 5 miles/8 km since the early 1980s and is expected to leave behind a 26-mile/42-km-long fjord. A bay has formed between its face and terminal moraine (where it rested prior to retreat). This bay has been filled with ice during the retreat, keeping boats away from the glacier's face. In late 1995, the icebergs had cleared enough so that boats were able to approach and visitors could watch ice calving from the face. However, the bay again filled with ice in early 1996, blocking access to the glacier's face.

The face of the glacier varies in height

above sea level from 25 to 200 feet/8 to 61m, and reaches 1,000 feet/305m or more below sea level. An abundance of plankton thrives here, attracting great numbers of fish which in turn attract bald eagles, kittiwakes, gulls and harbor seals. Seals can usually be seen resting on ice floes or swimming in the icy waters.

The glacier was named by the Harriman Alaska expedition in 1899 for Columbia University in New York City. The glacier's source is Mount Einstein (elev. 11,552 feet/3,521m) in the Chugach Mountains.

There are daily and weekly charters by yacht or sailboat and flightseeing trips over the glacier. (See the ads in Whittier, Valdez and Cordova in this section for charter boats offering sightseeing trips and flying services offering flightseeing trips.)

Whittier

Located at the head of Passage Canal on Prince William Sound, 75 miles/121 km southeast of Anchorage. **Population:** 290. **Emergency Services: Police, Fire** and **Medical,** phone (907) 472-2340. **Visitor Information:** Information kiosk at the Harbor Triangle.

Elevation: 30 feet/9m. **Climate:** Normal daily temperature for July is 56°F/13°C; for January, 25°F/-4°C. Maximum temperature is 84°F/29°C and minimum is -29°F/-2°C. Mean annual precipitation is 174 inches, including 260 inches of snow. Winter winds can reach 60 mph.

Private Aircraft: Airstrip adjacent northwest; elev. 30 feet/9m; length 1,100 feet/335m; gravel; no fuel; unattended.

Named after the poet John Greenleaf Whittier, the community of Whittier is nestled at the base of mountains that line Passage Canal, a fjord that extends eastward into Prince William Sound. Whittier is connected to the Seward Highway by railroad and to other Prince William Sound communities by ferry and charter air service. No roads lead to Whittier at this time, although a road connection is scheduled for completion on May 1, 2000.

Whittier was created by the U.S. Army during WWII as a port and petroleum delivery center tied to bases farther north by the Alaska Railroad and later a pipeline. The railroad spur from Portage was completed in 1943, and Whittier became the primary debarkation point for cargo, troops and dependents of the Alaska Command. Construction of the huge buildings that dominate Whittier began in 1948, and the Port of Whittier, strategically valuable for its ice-free deep-water port, remained activated until 1960, at which time the population was 1,200. The city of Whittier was incorporated in 1969. The government tank farm is still located here.

The 14-story Begich Towers, formerly the Hodge Building, houses more than half of Whittier's population. Now a condominium, the building was used by the U.S. Army for family housing and civilian bachelor quarters. The building was renamed in honor of U.S. Rep. Nick Begich of Alaska, who, along with Rep. Hale Boggs of Louisiana, disappeared in a small plane in this area in 1972 while on a campaign tour.

The Buckner Building, completed in 1953, once the largest building in Alaska, was called the "city under one roof." It is now privately owned and is to be renovated.

Whittier Manor was built in the early 1950s by private developers as rental units for civilian employees and soldiers who were ineligible for family housing elsewhere. In early 1964, the building was bought by another group of developers and became a

View of Whittier harbor from the deck of the E.L. Bartlett. *(© Kris Graef, staff)*

condominium, which now houses the remainder of Whittier's population.

Since military and government activities ceased, the economy of Whittier rests largely on the fishing industry, the port and increasingly on tourism.

Annual events in Whittier include a Fourth of July parade, barbecue and fireworks; a Fish Derby, held Memorial Day weekend to Labor Day weekend; and Regatta, at the end of April or beginning of May, when residents boat to Valdez for Game Night and then bus or fly back to Whittier.

Whittier has 2 inns providing accommodations, a bed and breakfast, several restaurants, 2 bars, gift shops, laundry facilities, 2 general stores, video rental, gas station, post office, library and a school (preschool through grade 12), and a camper park for tents and self-contained RVs ($5 nightly fee). Fishing licenses may be purchased locally. There is no bank in Whittier. ▲

Whittier also has a harbor office, marine services and repairs, marine supply store, boat launch and lift, freight services, dry storage and self-storage units.

Alaska Trail and Sail Adventures. Morning, afternoon and full-day guided sailing and sea kayaking. Get up close with otters, eagles, glaciers, salmon and kittiwakes. All necessary gear and instruction is provided. Paddling is easy and fun! Beginners welcome. Kayak rentals for experienced paddlers. Group discounts are available. Phone/fax (907) 276-2628. [ADVERTISEMENT]

Phillips' Cruises & Tours. Enjoy Alaska's most popular one-day glacier and wildlife adventure through Prince William Sound. Marvel at the scenery and watch for sea otters, seals, whales and bird life that inhabit Prince William Sound, as we take you on this fully-narrated 5-hour cruise aboard a 420-passenger deluxe catamaran. See our ad in the ANCHORAGE section. Departs daily from Whittier. Mid-May to mid-September. Sales office: 519 W. 4th Avenue, Suite 100, Anchorage, AK 99501-2211. Phone (907) 276-8023; (800) 544-0529; fax (907) 265-5890. [ADVERTISEMENT]

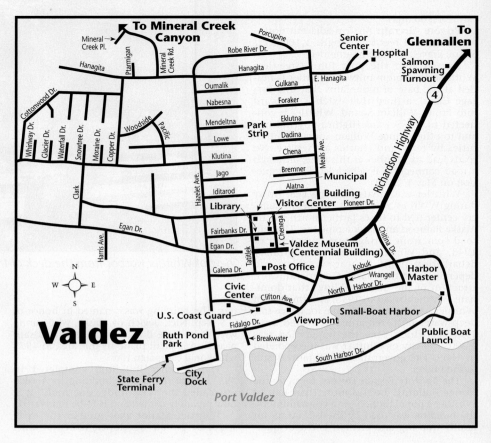

To Mineral Creek Canyon
Mineral Creek Pl.
Porcupine
Senior Center
Hospital
To Glennallen
Ptarmigan
Mineral Creek Rd.
Robe River Dr.
Salmon Spawning Turnout
Hanagita
Hanagita
E. Hanagita
4
Cottonwood Dr.
Oumalik
Gulkana
Nabesna
Foraker
Woodside
Pacific
Mendeltna
Eklutna
Park Strip
Whirlway Dr.
Glacier Dr.
Waterfall Dr.
Snowtree Dr.
Moraine Dr.
Copper Dr.
Lowe
Dadina
Chena
Richardson Highway
Klutina
Meals Ave.
Jago
Bremner
Municipal
Iditarod
Alatna
Building
Clark
Library
Visitor Center
Pioneer Dr.
Chitina Dr.
Hazelet Ave.
Fairbanks Dr.
Chenega
Egan Dr.
Egan Dr.
Valdez Museum (Centennial Building)
Tatitlek
Harbor Master
Harris Ave.
Galena Dr.
Post Office
Kobuk
Wrangell
North
Harbor Dr.
Civic Center
Clifton Ave.
Viewpoint
Small-Boat Harbor
U.S. Coast Guard
Fidalgo Dr.
Public Boat Launch
Valdez
Ruth Pond Park
Breakwater
South Harbor Dr.
State Ferry Terminal
City Dock
Port Valdez

Valdez

Located on Port Valdez (pronounced val-DEEZ), an estuary off Valdez Arm in Prince William Sound. Valdez is 115 air miles/ 185 km and 304 highway miles/489 km from Anchorage, 368 highway miles/592 km from Fairbanks. Valdez is the southern terminus of the Richardson Highway and the trans-Alaska pipeline. **Population:** 4,068.

Emergency Services: Alaska State Troopers, phone (907) 822-3263. **City Police, Fire Department** and **Ambulance,** emergency only phone 911. **Hospital,** Valdez Community, phone (907) 835-2249. **Maritime Search and Rescue,** dial 0 for Zenith 5555, toll free. Report oil spills to Dept. of Environmental Conservation, dial 0 and ask for Zenith 9300. **Fish and Wildlife Protection,** (907) 835-4307.

Visitor Information: The visitor information center, located opposite city hall at 200 Chenega St., is open 7 days a week from 8 A.M. to 8 P.M. The visitor center offers a self-guided tour map of homes moved from Old Valdez. Write: Valdez Convention and Visitors Bureau, Box 1603-MP, Valdez 99686; or phone (907) 835-2984, fax 835-4845. E-mail: valdezak@alaska.net. Visitors may also check the community calendar at the Valdez Civic Center by phoning the hotline

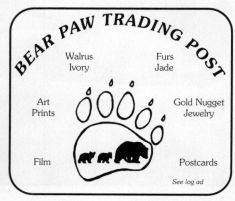

at (907) 835-3200.

Elevation: Sea level. **Climate:** Record high was 86°F/30°C in June 1997; record low -20°F/-29°C in January 1972. Normal daily maximum in January, 30°F/-1°C; daily minimum 21°F/-6°C. Normal daily maximum in July, 61°F/16°C; daily minimum 46°F/8°C. Average snowfall in Valdez from October to May is 329.7 inches, or about 25 feet. (By comparison, Anchorage averages about 6 feet in that period.) New snowfall records were set in January 1990, with snowfall for one day at 47¹/₂ inches. Record monthly snowfall is 180 inches in February 1996. Windy (40 mph/64 kmph) in late fall. **Radio:** KCHU 770, KVAK 1230. **Television:** Many channels via cable and satellite. **Newspapers:** *Valdez Vanguard* (weekly) and *Valdez Star* (weekly).

Private Aircraft: Valdez, 3 miles/4.8 km east; elev. 120 feet/37m; length 6,500 feet/1,981m; asphalt; fuel 100LL, Jet B; attended.

Situated in a majestic fjord, where the 5,000-foot-tall Chugach Mountains rise from Prince William Sound, Valdez is often called Alaska's "Little Switzerland." The city lies on the north shore of Port Valdez, an estuary named in 1790 by Spanish explorer Don Salvador Fidalgo for Antonio Valdes y Basan, a Spanish naval officer.

Valdez was established in 1897–98 as a port of entry for gold seekers bound for the Klondike goldfields. Thousands of stampeders arrived in Valdez to follow the All American Route to the Eagle mining district in Alaska's Interior, and from there up the Yukon River to Dawson City and the Klondike. The Valdez trail was an especially dangerous route, the first part of it leading over Valdez Glacier, where the early stampeders faced dangerous crevasses, snowblindness and exhaustion.

Copper discoveries in the Wrangell Mountains north of Valdez in the early 1900s brought more development to Valdez, and conflict. A proposed railroad from tidewater to the rich Kennicott copper mines at McCarthy began a bitter rivalry between Valdez and Cordova for the railway line. The Copper River & Northwestern Railway eventually went to Cordova, but not before Valdez had started its own railroad north. The Valdez railroad did not get very far: The only trace of its existence is an old hand-drilled railway tunnel at **Milepost V 14.9** on the Richardson Highway.

The old gold rush trail out of Valdez was developed into a sled and wagon road in the early 1900s. It was routed through Thompson Pass (rather than over the Valdez Glacier) by Captain Abercrombie of the U.S. Army, who was commissioned to connect Fort Liscum (a military post established in 1900 near the present-day location of the pipeline terminal) with Fort Egbert in Eagle. Colonel Wilds P. Richardson of the Alaska Road Commission further developed the wagon road, building an automobile road from Valdez to Fairbanks which was completed in the early 1920s.

Old photos of Valdez show Valdez Glacier directly behind the town. This is because until 1964 Valdez was located about 4 miles east of its present location, closer to the glacier. The 1964 Good Friday earthquake, the most destructive earthquake ever to hit southcentral Alaska, virtually destroyed Valdez. The quake measured between 8.4 and 8.6 on the Richter scale (since revised to 9.2) and was centered in Prince William Sound. A series of local waves caused by massive underwater landslides swept over Valdez

Prince William Sound tours depart from Valdez boat harbor. (© Tom Bol Photography)

wharf and engulfed the downtown area. Afterward, it was decided that Valdez would be rebuilt at a new townsite. By late August 1964, reconstruction projects had been approved and relocation was under way. The last residents remaining at "old" Valdez moved to the new town in 1968.

Since its days as a port of entry for gold seekers, Valdez has been an important gateway to Interior Alaska. As the most northerly ice-free port in the Western Hemisphere, and connected by the Richardson Highway to the Alaska highway system, Valdez has evolved into a shipping center, offering the shortest link to much of interior Alaska for seaborne cargo.

Construction of the trans-Alaska pipeline was begun in 1974 and completed in 1977 (the first tanker load of oil shipped out of Valdez on Aug. 1, 1977). The 1,000-acre site at Port Valdez was chosen as the pipeline terminus; tours of the marine terminal are available (see Attractions).

From Prudhoe Bay on the Arctic Ocean, the 48-inch-diameter, 800-mile-/1287-km-long pipeline follows the Sagavanirktok River and Atigun Valley, crossing the Brooks Mountain Range at 4,739-foot/1,444m Atigun Pass. South of the Brooks Range it passes through Dietrich and Koyukuk valleys and crosses the hills and muskeg of the Yukon–Tanana uplands to the Yukon River. South of the Yukon, the line passes through more rolling hills 10 miles/16 km east of Fairbanks, then goes south from Delta Junction to the Alaska Range, where it reaches an elevation of 3,420 feet/1,042m at Isabel Pass before descending into the Copper River basin. It crests the Chugach Mountains at Thompson Pass (elev. 2,812 feet/857m) and descends through the Keystone Canyon to Valdez, where it is fed by gravity into tanks or directly into waiting oil tankers at the marine terminal.

Because of varying soil conditions along its route, the pipeline is both above and below ground. Where the warm oil would cause icy sl to thaw and erode, the pipeline goes above ground to avoid thawing. Where the frozen ground is mostly well-drained gravel or solid rock, and thawing is not a problem, the line is underground.

The line was designed with 12 pump stations (although Pump Station 11 was never built) and numerous large valves to control the flow of oil. Since 1996, 4 pump stations have been placed on standby due to declining North Slope oil production. The entire system can operate on central computer control from Valdez or independent local control at each pump station.

National attention was focused on Valdez and the pipeline when the oil tanker *Exxon Valdez* ran aground on Bligh Reef in March 1989, causing an 11-million-gallon oil spill.

Valdez's economy depends on the oil industry, the Prince William Sound fishery, government and tourism. The city limits of Valdez comprise an area of 274 square miles and include all surrounding mountains to timberline. Valdez has long been known for its beautiful setting, with the Chugach Mountains rising behind the city, and the small-boat harbor in front. The town has wide streets and open spaces, with the central residential district built around a park strip which runs from the business district almost to the base of the mountains behind the town.

ACCOMMODATIONS/VISITOR SERVICES

Services in Valdez include several restaurants and bars, grocery store, sporting goods stores, gift shops, 3 gas stations (1 full-service), hardware, hair stylists, 1 drugstore, 2 pharmacies, 1 car rental agency and numerous churches.

Valdez has 7 motel/hotel facilities and numerous bed and breakfasts. You are advised to make reservations well in advance. Summer tourist season is also the

Passengers on the state ferry E.L. Bartlett *enjoy the view enroute to Valdez from* Whittier. *(© Kris Graef, staff)*

peak work season, and accommodations fill up quickly. Expect to pay $100 and up for a double motel room with bath, $55 to $85 for a bed and breakfast.

Blessing House B & B. Home-away-from-home. Walk to harbor, museum and shopping. Mountain views! See unique locking caribou horns; play piano or cook. Rates $55–$85. King beds, continental breakfast. Reservations phone (888) 853-5333 (*51 fax); (907) 835-5333, (907) 835-2259; P.O. Box 233, Valdez, AK 99686. Living units also available throughout year; Hursh Realtors, Diann Hursh, Broker. E-mail: bhousebb @alaska.net. Web site: www.valdezlink. com/bhousebb. [ADVERTISEMENT]

Downtown B & B Inn. Motel accommodations, 113 Galena Dr. Centrally located near small boat harbor, museum, ferry terminal, downtown shopping. View rooms, private and shared baths, coin-op laundry, TV and phones in rooms. Wheelchair accessible. Complimentary breakfast. Reasonable rates. Single, double, family rooms. Phone

(800) 478-2791 or (907) 835-2791. E-mail: onen2rs@alaska.net. Internet: www. alaskaone.com/downinn/index.htm. See display ad this section. [ADVERTISEMENT] MP &

Gussie's Lowe Street B & B. Quiet residential neighborhood a few blocks from downtown and ferry terminal. Clean rooms, queen or twin beds, homey atmosphere. Private or shared baths. In-room phones, cable TV, VCR. No stairs! Delicious hot breakfasts. Longtime Alaskan hosts, Joanne and Bob LaRue, and Gus Too, our lovable family pet. Phone (907) 835-4448. See display ad. [ADVERTISEMENT]

Keystone Hotel. Located downtown (corner of Egan and Hazelet) within walking distance to ferry terminal and shops. 106 rooms with private baths, cable TV, phones, nonsmoking or smoking, wheelchair access, coin-op laundry. Complimentary continental breakfast. Enjoy our casual seafood grill for dinner. Comfortable, clean rooms at reasonable rates. (888) 835-0665. E-mail: keyston@alaska.net. [ADVERTISEMENT] &

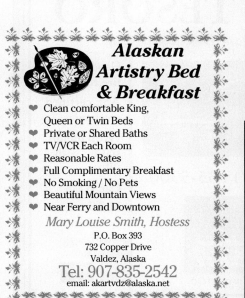

One Call Does It All. Whether it is a place to stay, a chance to catch the big one, something to do, or the means to get there, let us handle the logistics for your Alaskan adventure. VISA, MasterCard accepted. For the spectacular Prince William Sound, One Call Does It All (907) 835-4988. [ADVERTISEMENT]

Totem Inn. Motel and restaurant. Open for breakfast at 5 A.M. Famous for chicken fried steak and reindeer sausage. Lunches include burgers, salad bar and more. Fresh seafood specialties and family favorite dinners affordably priced make our restaurant the "locals' choice." Remodeled rooms include private baths, queen beds, TV, phone, fridge and microwave. Reservations suggested. Located downtown Valdez. Close

to harbor where the Richardson meets Egan Drive. Open year round. RV parking available. Phone (907) 835-4443, fax (907) 834-4430. E-mail: toteminn@alaska.net. [ADVERTISEMENT]

Valdez Village Inn, downtown Valdez: 100 modern rooms. Cable TV, private baths. Wheelchair access. Fitness center, sauna, Jacuzzi, beauty shop, espresso bar. Casa Valdez Restaurant & Sugarloaf Saloon. Room/Glacier Cruise packages. Phone (907) 835-4445, fax (907) 835-2437. See display ad this section. [ADVERTISEMENT]

There are 6 private RV parks with hookups near the small-boat harbor. Dump station and diesel at Valdez Tesoro and Capt'n Joe's Tesoro. Dump station at Bear Paw R.V.

Park for registered guests.

The nearest public campground is Valdez Glacier campground, at the end of the airport road, about 6 miles/9.7 km from town; turn left on Airport Road at **Milepost NV 3.4** Richardson Highway. This city-owned and privately operated campground has 101 sites, tent-camping areas, picnic areas, firepits, tables, litter barrels, water and toilets; 15-day limit, $10 fee charged. ▲

Bear Paw R.V. Park, centrally located on scenic North Harbor Drive overlooking the boat harbor, puts you within easy walking distance of museum, shops, restaurants, entertainment, charter boats—no need to

unhook and drive to grocery stores or points of interest. Full, partial or no hookups; immaculate private restrooms with hot, unmetered showers. Dump station and coin-operated launderette with irons and ironing boards available for guests. Also available, for adults only: waterfront full-hookup RV sites with cable TV, guest lounge, computer modem access line. Very nice, quiet wooded tent sites, some platforms, among the salmonberries on Porcupine Hill. Tables, fire pots and freezer available. Campfire wood for sale. Fuel discount coupons available. Let us book your glacier tour with Stan Stephens Cruises at the reservations desk in our spacious office lounge. We also book raft trips, flightseeing and pipeline terminal tours. Don't miss the Bear Paw Trading Post Gift Shop. Advance reservations recommended: (907) 835-2530. (Bear Paw does fill up!) The coffee pot is always on at Bear Paw. Let us know if you're coming in on the evening ferry and we'll be there to help you get parked. E-mail: bpawcamp@alaska.net. Internet: www.alaska.net/~bpawcamp/. See our large display ad this section. [ADVERTISEMENT] ▲

Eagle's Rest RV Park, the friendliest RV park in downtown Valdez, offers you Good Sam Park service with a smile. Let Herb, Jeff

or Laura take care of all your bookings on cruises, tours and charters. Enjoy the beautiful panoramic view of our mountains and glaciers right off our front porch! We also

can let you know where the hottest fishing spots are or the quietest walking trails! Fish-cleaning table and freezer available. 10-bay golf driving range. Capt'n Joe's Tesoro next door offers gas, diesel, propane; potable water, sewer dump. Parking with us puts you within walking distance of our museum, gift shops, banks and even the largest grocery store on our same block. Shuttle service for glacier cruises. No charge to wash your RV at your site. Phone us for reservations, 1-800-553-7275 or (907) 835-2373. Fax (907) 835-KAMP (835-5267). E-mail: rvpark@alaska.net. Internet: www.alaskaoutdoors.com/eagle/. Stay with us and leave feeling like family. See display ad this section.
[ADVERTISEMENT] MP ▲

TRANSPORTATION

Air: Daily scheduled service via Alaska Airlines and Era Aviation. Air taxi and helicopter services available.

Ferry: Scheduled state ferry service to Cordova, Whittier and Seward. Phone (907) 835-4436. Reservations are a must!

Bus: Regularly scheduled service to

Anchorage and Fairbanks.

Taxi: One local taxi service.

Car Rental: Two companies offer car rentals; available at airport terminal.

Highway: The Richardson Highway extends north from Valdez to the Glenn Highway and the Alaska Highway. See the RICHARDSON HIGHWAY section.

ATTRACTIONS

Celebrate Gold Rush Days. Held Aug. 4–8, 1999, this celebration includes a parade, contests and a game night. During the celebration cancan girls meet the cruise ships and a jail is pulled through town by "deputies" who arrest citizens without beards, and other suspects.

Visit Valdez Museum, located at 217 Egan Dr. Exhibits depict lifestyles and workplaces from 1898 to present. Displays include a beautifully restored 1907 Ahrens steam fire engine, the original Cape Hinchinbrook lighthouse lens, a Civil War-era field cannon and an illuminated model of the Alyeska Pipeline Marine Terminal. Interpretive exhibits explain the impact of the gold rush, the 1964 earthquake, the construction of the trans-Alaska oil pipeline and the 1989 *Exxon Valdez* oil spill cleanup. Visitors can touch Columbia Glacier ice and feel the luxurious softness of a sea otter pelt. The museum's William A. Egan Commons provides a showcase setting for the Ahrens steam fire engine, models of antique aircraft, and the lighthouse lens. Local quilts are on exhibit all summer (June-Aug.) in the Egan Commons. Outdoor exhibits include an oil

pipeline "pig" and a unique snow tractor. Valdez Museum is open year-round: daily 9 A.M. to 6 P.M. during summer months (May to September); Monday through Saturday during off-season (October to April). Children free; $3 for adults (18 and older); $2.50 for seniors, $2 for youth 14-18. Phone (907) 835-2764 for more information.

Tour the oil pipeline terminus. The marine terminal of the trans-Alaska pipeline is across the bay from the city of Valdez. Two-hour bus tours of the pipeline terminal are available several times daily, from May to September, from Valdez Tours; fee charged, reservations suggested, cameras welcome. Phone (907) 835-2686 for details.

While entry to the terminal is restricted to authorized bus tours only, the drive out to the terminal is worthwhile. From Meals Avenue drive 6.8 miles/10.9 km out the Richardson Highway and turn right on the terminal access road (Dayville exit). The 5.4-mile/8.7-km road leading to the terminal passes Solomon Gulch dam and a spectacular view of Solomon Gulch Falls. There is also excellent fishing in season at Allison Point for pink and silver salmon. Entrance to the pipeline terminal is at the end of the road.

Outside the marine terminal gate is a bronze sculpture commemorating the efforts of men and women who built the trans-Alaska oil pipeline. Dedicated in September 1980, the sculpture was created by Californian Malcolm Alexander. It is composed of 5 figures representing various crafts and skills employed in the construction project. The work is the focal point of a small park from which visitors can watch tankers loading Alaska crude oil at the terminal. A small parking lot accommodates about 30 cars, and a series of signs explains the pipeline and terminal operations.

Take a boat tour to see Columbia Glacier, Shoup Glacier and other Prince William Sound attractions. Columbia Glacier, a tidewater glacier in Columbia Bay 28 miles/45 km southwest of Valdez, has become one of Alaska's best-known attractions. See ads in this section.

Raft and kayak trips of Prince William Sound, Keystone Canyon and surrounding rivers are available.

Go flightseeing and see Columbia Glacier, spectacular Prince William Sound and the surrounding Chugach Mountains from the air. There are several air charter services and 1 helicopter service in Valdez; see ads in this section.

Our Point of View, an observation platform offering views of the original Valdez townsite, pipeline terminal and the town, is located by the Coast Guard office.

Valdez Consortium Library, located on Fairbanks Street, has a magazine and paperback exchange for travelers. A trade is appreciated but not required. The library also has music listening booths, public computers, typewriters and a photocopier. Wheelchair accessible. Open Monday and Friday 10 A.M. to 6 P.M., Tuesday through Thursday 10 A.M. to 8 P.M., Saturday noon to 5 P.M. and Sunday 1–5 P.M. when school is session. &

Visit Prince William Sound Community College, located at 303 Lowe St. Two huge wooden carvings on campus (1 located in front of the dorms on Pioneer Street), by artist Peter Toth, are dedicated to the Indians of America. Three Elderhostel programs are held at Prince William Sound Community College in July and August. This educational program (college credit given) is available for people over age 55. Subjects include Alaska history, wildlife and fisheries of Prince William Sound, and Alaska literature. Contact Elderhostel, 75 Federal St., Boston, MA 02110-1941, for more information on its Alaska programs. The 7th annual Edward Albee Theatre Conference, sponsored by the college, will be held June 20-27, 1999, at the Valdez Convention and Civic Center. Past visiting playwrights at the conference have included Edward Albee, Arthur Miller and August Wilson. For more information contact PWSCC, P.O. Box 97, Valdez, AK 99686.

View salmon spawning at Crooked Creek. From Meals Avenue drive 0.9 mile/1.4 km out the Richardson Highway to the Crooked Creek salmon spawning area and hatchery. A U.S. Forest Service information station, open Memorial Day to Labor Day, has interpretive displays and information on cultural history and recreation. An observation platform gives a close-up look at salmon spawning in midsummer and fall. This is also a waterfowl sanctuary and an excellent spot for watching various migrating birds.

Fish a Derby. The Valdez Chamber of Commerce holds a halibut, silver salmon and pink salmon derby every year, with cash prizes awarded to the first through third place winners for all 3 derbies. For further information contact the Valdez Chamber of Commerce at (907) 835-2330.

Drive Mineral Creek Road. A 5.5-mile/8.9-km drive behind town leading northwest through the breathtaking alpine scenery along Mineral Creek. *Drive carefully!* This is a narrow road; conditions depend on weather and how recently the road has been graded. Bears are frequently sighted here. To reach Mineral Creek Road drive to the end of Hazelet Street toward the mountains and

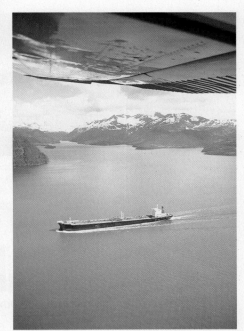

Aerial view of an oil tanker in Valdez Arm. (© Gene & Judy Wright)

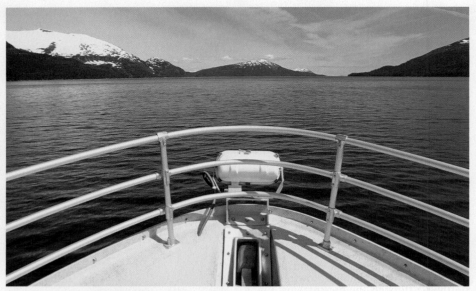

View of Prince William Sound from the bow of a tour boat. (© Bruce M. Herman)

turn left on Hanagita then right on Mineral Creek Road. Excellent view of the city from the water tower hill just to the right at the start of Mineral Creek Road.

Visit Dock Point Park. Located at the east end of the Valdez boat harbor, off North Harbor Drive, this park includes picnic tables, a restroom and a beautiful 1-mile hiking/walking trail with scenic overlooks of the Port of Valdez. The combination gravel and boardwalk trail provides easy access for people of all ability levels. Interpretive signs are planned for the summer of 1999.

Valdez Arm supports the largest sport fishery in Prince William Sound. Important species include pink salmon, coho (silver) salmon, halibut, rockfish and Dolly Varden. Charter boats are available in Valdez. A hot fishing spot near Valdez and accessible by road is the **Allison Point** fishery (or "Winnebago Point" as it is known locally) created by the Solomon Gulch Hatchery, which produces major pink and silver salmon returns annually. Turn off the Richardson

Highway at **Milepost V 2.9.** It is one of the largest pink salmon fisheries in the state. Pink salmon returns are best in odd years, but with hatchery production good pink runs are anticipated every year. Pinks average 3 to 5 lbs., from late June to early August. Silvers from 6 to 10 lbs., late July into September.

Bear Paw Trading Post Gift Shop, next to Bear Paw RV Park on Harbor Drive, features fine Alaska Native arts and crafts. Carved walrus ivory, scrimshaw, soapstone carvings, Native masks, fur items. Gold nugget jewelry, jade, hematite. Prints and books by Doug Lindstrand. Film, postcards, souvenirs, Alaska books. VISA, MasterCard accepted. Phone (907) 835-2530. [ADVERTISEMENT]

Era Helicopters. Fly over Valdez and the Prince William Sound with Alaska's most experienced helicopter company. Soar over the breathtaking Columbia Glacier. Land at the face of Shoup Glacier or take a heli-hiking adventure. Phone (800) 843-1947 or (907) 835-2595 locally. Tours also available in Anchorage, Juneau and Mount McKinley. [ADVERTISEMENT]

Ketchum Air Service, Inc. Alaska's outdoor specialists. Floatplane tours/charters into Prince William Sound, Wrangell–St. Elias park. Day fishing/fully equipped. Columbia Glacier tour. Drop-off cabins. Kennecott Mine visit! Floatplane tour office located small-boat harbor, Valdez. Call or write for brochure. VISA, MasterCard. Phone (907) 835-3789 or (800) 433-9114. Box 670, Valdez, AK 99686. [ADVERTISEMENT]

Glacier Wildlife Cruises/*Lu-Lu Belle*. The motor yacht *Lu-Lu Belle* is probably the cleanest, plushest tour vessel you will ever see! We cater to adult travelers. When you come aboard and see all the teak, mahogany and oriental rugs, you will understand why Captain Rodolf asks you to wipe your shoes before boarding. The *Lu-Lu Belle* has wide

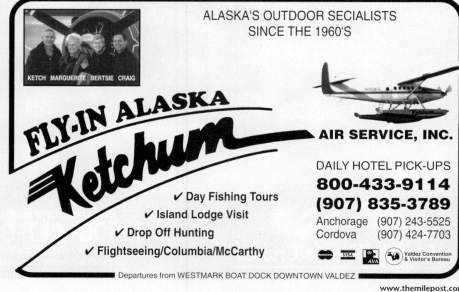

walk-around decks, thus assuring everyone ample opportunity for unobstructed viewing and photography, and is equipped with 110-volt outlets for your battery chargers. Captain Rodolf has logged over 2,950 Columbia Glacier cruises since 1979; he will personally guide and narrate every cruise. The Columbia Glacier wildlife cruise of Prince William Sound is awesome. The wildlife that is seen on the cruises will vary, depending upon the time of year and time of day, as the *Lu-Lu Belle* cruises from Valdez to Columbia Glacier on the calm, protected waters of the Sound. We guarantee no sea-sickness. Boarding time is 1 P.M. each day from Memorial Day to Labor Day. This "5 hour" cruise will vary in duration as much as an hour, because Captain Rodolf will run offshore, in search of whales and other wildlife. Cost is $70 per person (with a cash discount price of $65).During the busier part of the season, a 3-1/2- to 4-hour economy cruise, boarding at 7:45 A.M. is added for those with limited time. Cost is $60 per person (with a cash discount of $55). On the trip the crew prepares fresh-baked goods in the galley. Friendliness and gracious hospitality on a beautiful yacht with small intimate groups is the reason why people refer to the *Lu-Lu Belle* as "the limousine of Prince William Sound." Our best advertisement is our happy guests. Join us for an extra-special day and find out why Captain Rodolf refers to Switzerland as the "Valdez of Europe!" Phone (800) 411-0090 or (907) 835-5141 Web site: www.alaskan.com/lulubelle/. E-mail: lulubelle@uswest.net. [ADVERTISEMENT]

Northern Comfort Charters operates 2 boats designed for your fishing comfort and pleasure. For halibut (and a wide variety of other bottom-feeding fish) the 43-foot *Lady Luck* features a comfortable, warm, cabin, full restroom and a 360 degree all-around fishing deck. The 44-foot *Northern Comfort* is more suitable for 2-day overnight charters and is an excellent boat for silver salmon fishing, featuring a full fishing deck cover, large comfortable cabin and full restroom. Enjoy the excellent fishing and scenery of the Prince William Sound. Phone (800) 478-9884 or (907) 835-3070. See our display ad this section. [ADVERTISEMENT]

Prince William Sound Cruise. Experience the spectacular beauty of Prince William Sound aboard the *MV Nunatak*. This Gray Line of Alaska tour cruises past Columbia Glacier, the largest glacier in Prince William Sound. Watch for abundant marine life as you travel to picturesque Valdez and Whittier. Two meals are included. This all-day tour departs daily from Valdez and costs $115 per person. Prices subject to change. Phone (907) 835-4282. [ADVERTISEMENT]

Stan Stephens Cruises. This Alaskan business offers a variety of glacier and wildlife cruises in the protected waters of Prince William Sound. Tours depart from Valdez and Whittier. All of our tours are aboard comfortable vessels with heated

inner cabins and spacious outer decks. Our experienced and knowledgeable captains

Sea lions hauled out on rocky shore in Prince William Sound. (© Bruce M. Herman)

and crew will interpret and share the wonders of Prince William Sound with you: include the abundant wildlife spectacular glaciers and Growler Island Wilderness Camp. Growler Island is unique to Stan Stephens Cruises. We are pleased to share this pristine Prince William Sound location with visitors. Whether you come for the day or spend the night, Growler Island will be one of the highlights of your Alaskan experience. Our 2-hour trips stop at Growler Island for an all-you-can-eat Alaskan feast, featuring salmon, halibut, beef, chicken and a variety of salads and side dishes. Overnighting on Growler Island offers adventure travelers an opportunity to explore the peaceful beauty of a wilderness destination and is accessible from either Whittier or Valdez. Accommodations are in heated tent/cabins. All meals are provided. Overnight space at Growler Island is limited, so reservations are encouraged. Don't miss this opportunity for a truly Alaskan experience. We are successful at accommodating most physically challenged travelers. Phone toll free or write for

for more information: P.O. Box 1297, Valdez, AK 99686. Phone (800) 992-1297 or (907) 835-4731; fax (907) 835-3765; E-mail: info@princewilliamsound.com. Web site: www.princewilliamsound.com. See our full-page display ad on page 539. [ADVERTISEMENT]
&. MP

Cordova

porated in 1909.

One of the first producing oil fields in Alaska was located at Katalla, 47 miles/76 km southeast of Cordova on the Gulf of Alaska. The discovery was made in 1902 and the field produced until 1933.

The town was chosen as the railroad terminus and ocean shipping port for copper ore shipped by rail from the Kennecott mines near Kennicott and McCarthy. The railroad and town prospered until 1938 when the mine closed.

Commercial fishing has now supplanted mining as the basis of the town's economy. The fishing fleet can be seen at Cordova harbor, home port of the MV *Bartlett* and the USCG cutter *Sweetbrier*. Also at the harbor is the Cordova Fishermen's Memorial, *The Southeasterly*.

The fishing and canning season for salmon runs from about May to September, with red, king and silver (coho) salmon taken from the Copper River area, chum, red and pink salmon from Prince William Sound. Black cod, crab and shrimp season runs during winter. Dungeness crab season runs during the summer and early fall months. Halibut and herring are also processed.

ACCOMMODATIONS/VISITOR SERVICES

Cordova has 2 motels and 2 hotels, 11 bed and breakfasts, 8 restaurants, 2 laundromats and a variety of shopping facilities.

Cordova Rose Lodge. Historical 1924 landlocked barge and lighthouse. Former fishtrap setter, cannery, recluse home, machine shop and houseboat. Unique B&B in barge decor; nautical artifacts with a touch of whimsy. Guests from around the world "cruise" on the renovated barge. Alaskan ambiance and hospitality the moment you go on board. 1315 Whitshed Road. Phone: (907) 424-7673. E-mail: cordovarose@juno.com. See display ad. [ADVERTISEMENT]

Cordova has one campground, Odiak Camper Park, located on Whitshed Road and operated by the city. The camper park has 24 RV sites and a tenting area. Free shower tokens are available for paying campers. Contact Cordova's city hall at (907) 424-6200.

The historic Skater's Cabin on Eyak Lake is available for rent from the city. The rustic cabin has a woodstove and outhouse. The fee is $25 per night. Contact Bidarki Recreation Center, phone (907) 424-7282.

The U.S. Forest Service maintains 17 cabins in the Cordova district. Three are accessible by trail, the rest by boat or plane. Phone 1-877-444-6777 for current fees, reservations and information.

TRANSPORTATION

Cordova is accessible only by plane or boat.

Air: Scheduled service via Alaska Airlines and Era Aviation. Five air taxi services based at the municipal airport, Mile 13 airport and Eyak Lake offer charter and flightseeing service.

Ferry: The Alaska Marine Highway system ferries connect Cordova with Valdez, Whittier and Seward. Phone (907) 424-7333.

Taxi: Local service available.

Car Rental: Available locally.

Highways: The Alaska state highway system does not connect to Cordova. The Copper River Highway leads 48 miles/ 77 km east and north of Cordova, ending at the Million Dollar Bridge and Childs Glacier. (See the COPPER RIVER HIGHWAY section.)

Private Boats: Cordova has an 850-slip boat harbor serving recreational boaters as well as the commercial fishing fleet. Berth arrangements may be made by contacting the harbormaster's office at (907) 424-6400 or on VHF Channel 16.

View of fishing fleet in Cordova harbor. (© David Ranta, staff)

ATTRACTIONS

Cordova's **Museum and Library**, at 622 1st St., are connected by a central entryway. "Where Cultures Meet" is the theme of the museum. Native artifacts such as stone implements, a dugout canoe and skin bidarka (kayak) represent the rich Native culture. One display tells of early explorers to the area, including Vitus Bering, who claimed Alaska for Russia in 1741. Exhibits of the later mining and railroad era explain the development of the copper mines and of the town. Exhibits include a diorama of a vintage fishing vessel. The museum displays original work by Alaskan artists Sydney Laurence, Eustace Ziegler and Jules Dahlager, who all worked in Cordova. The Cordova Historical Society operates a small gift shop at the museum, featuring books of local interest and Alaskan crafts.

Admission to the museum is $1. Open Memorial Day to Labor Day, 10 A.M.–6 P.M. Monday through Saturday, 2–4 P.M. on Sunday; Tuesday–Friday, 1–5 P.M. and Saturday 2–4 P.M. the rest of the year. Tours can be arranged. Write P.O. Box 391 or phone (907) 424-6665 for more information. Library hours are 1–8 P.M. Tuesday through Saturday.

Swim in the Bob Korn Memorial Swimming Pool, Cordova's Olympic-sized pool, located on Railroad Avenue below Main Street. Open year-round to the public. Check locally for hours.

Mount Eyak Ski Area. Ski Hill is usually open for skiing mid-December to the end of April, depending on weather. Winter schedule is Wednesday, Saturday, Sunday and holidays, 9 A.M. to dusk. Phone (907) 424-7766 for further information. To reach the chair lift from 4th Avenue, take Council Avenue 1 block, then follow Ski Hill Road to top (about 1 mile/1.6 km from Main Street).

The single chair lift rises 880 feet/268m up Mount Eyak and overlooks the town and harbor from 1,600 feet/488km. Walk up, take a cab, take the tour bus or drive your own vehicle. A hiking trail from the base of the mountain to top of the chair lift and beyond connects with Forest Service Crater Lake trail.

Visit the USFS office at 612 2nd St. Erected in 1925, it is the original federal building for the town of Cordova. Natural history display in 2nd floor Interpretive Center. The USFS office is next to the old courtroom and jail. Open weekdays 8 A.M. to 5 P.M.

Copper River Delta Shorebird Festival, held May 5-9, 1999, offers 5 days of birding along the tidal mudflats and wetlands of the Copper River Delta and the rocky shoreline of Prince William Sound. The festival includes workshops, community activities and numerous field trip opportunities. Contact the Chamber of Commerce, Box 99, Cordova 99574, for details; or phone (907) 424-7260.

Attend the Iceworm Festival: Held the first full weekend of February, this festival offers a parade, art show, variety show, dances, craft show, ski events, survival suit race, beard judging and a King and Queen of Iceworm contest. Highlight is the 100-foot-/30-m-long "iceworm" that winds its way through the streets of Cordova. Contact Darrel Olsen, P.O. Box 768, Cordova, AK 99574; phone (907) 424-5756 for more information.

Whitshed Road leads out past the miniature lighthouse (Mile 0.4) to a large mudflat at Hartney Bay (Mile 5.5). The lighthouse is privately owned and maintained by the Gleins, who also operate a bed and breakfast in their home: a converted barge. Hartney Bay is part of the 300,000-acre Copper River Delta mudflats. The delta is one of the most important stopover places in the Western Hemisphere for the largest shorebird migration in the world. Birders can view up to 31 different species as millions of shorebirds pass through the delta each spring.

Power Creek Road, from the corner of Lake and Chase avenues, leads out past the municipal airport to Crater Lake trailhead and Skaters Cabin picnic area (Mile 1.2), continues to Hatchery Creek salmon spawning channel (Mile 5.7), and ends at the Power Creek trailhead (Mile 6.9). The Crater Lake trailhead is directly northwest of the Eyak Lake Skaters Cabin. The 2.4-mile/ 3.8-km trail climbs to 1,500 feet/457m. Excellent views, alpine lake with fishing for stocked rainbow trout. Watch for bears. Visitors may view spawning salmon at the Hatchery Creek channel in July and August. Power Creek trail, 4.2 miles/6.7 km long, accesses both the USFS public-use cabin in Power Creek Basin and a ridge that connects with the Crater Lake trail creating a 12-mile/19.3-km loop. Power Creek trail offers spectacular scenery, with waterfalls, hanging glaciers and views of Power Creek Basin (called "surprise valley" by locals), the Chugach Range and Prince William Sound. Excellent berry picking. Watch for bears.

Drive the Copper River Highway to see the Million Dollar Bridge, Childs Glacier and the Copper River Delta. The 48-mile/77-km highway leads east from Cordova through the Delta to the historic Million Dollar Bridge, built in 1909–10, and Childs Glacier. Viewing platform and picnic area at Childs Glacier. Wildlife seen along the highway includes brown and black bear, moose, beaver, mountain goats, trumpeter swans and numerous other species of birds. See COPPER RIVER HIGHWAY section for log of road.

AREA FISHING: According to the ADF&G, "Saltwater fishing in **Orca Inlet** and adjacent eastern Prince William Sound is accessible from Cordova. Species include halibut, rockfish and 5 species of salmon. Trolling for salmon is best for kings in the winter and spring, and silvers in the summer and fall. Boat charters are available locally. Road-accessible fishing opportunities exist for salmon in salt water at **Fleming Spit/ Lagoon**, near the ferry terminal off Orca Bay Road. Strong runs of hatchery-enhanced kings (in the spring) and silvers (August and September) return to this terminal fishery. Road-accessible freshwater fishing is also good in the Cordova Area. **Eyak River** supports strong returns of sockeye during June and July and silvers in August and September. The area at the outlet of the lake, where the road crosses, is fly-fishing only. Several streams along the **Copper River** Highway between Eyak Lake and the Million Dollar Bridge also support runs of sockeye and coho. These streams include **Clear Creek, Alaganik Slough, Eighteen-mile Creek** and **Twenty-mile Creek.** In addition, cutthroat trout and Dolly Varden are present in most of these streams. Lake fishing for sockeye salmon, Dolly Varden and cutthroat trout is available in **McKinley Lake** and the **Pipeline Lake** system. Fly-out fishing from Cordova is also popular for salmon, Dolly Varden and cutthroat trout. Charter operators are available locally." See also the COPPER RIVER HIGHWAY section for area fishing.

Connects: Cordova to Million Dollar Bridge, AK **Length:** 48 miles
Road Surface: 25% paved, 75% gravel
Season: Not maintained in winter
Major Attraction: Childs Glacier

(See map, page 556)

	Cordova	Alaganik Slough	Million Dollar Bridge
Cordova		17	48
Alaganik Slough	17		31
Million Dollar Bridge	48	31	

The Million Dollar Bridge at the end of Copper River Highway. (© David Ranta, staff)

The Copper River Highway leads 48.1 miles/77.4 km northeast from Cordova to the Million Dollar Bridge at the Copper River.

Construction of the Copper River Highway began in 1945. Built along the abandoned railbed of the Copper River & Northwestern Railway, the highway was to extend to Chitina (on the Edgerton Highway), thereby linking Cordova to the Richardson Highway.

Construction was halted by the 1964 Good Friday earthquake, which severely damaged the highway's roadbed and bridges. The quake also knocked the north span of the Million Dollar Bridge into the Copper River and distorted the remaining spans. The 48 miles of existing highway have been repaired and upgraded since the earthquake, with temporary repairs to the Million Dollar Bridge. Road work between the Million Dollar Bridge and the Allen River is planned as part of the development of the proposed Copper River hiking and biking trail connecting Cordova, Chitina and Valdez.

Copper River Highway Log

Distance is measured from Cordova (C).

C 0 CORDOVA. See description in the PRINCE WILLIAM SOUND section. The Copper River Highway starts at the ferry terminal and leads east through town.

C 0.4 (.64 km) Industrial Avenue.

C 0.5 (.80 km) Railroad Avenue.

C 0.8 (.13 km) Council Avenue, Main Street; access to post office and Cordova City Hall.

C 1.2 (1.9 km) Hollis Hendricks Park.

C 1.3 (2.1 km) Whitshed Road on right leads 0.5 mile/0.8 km to Odiak municipal camper park (24 sites, tenting area; obtain shower tokens at City Hall), 5.5 miles/8.9 km to **Hartney Bay.** Fishing from Hartney Bay bridge for Dolly Varden from May; pink and chum salmon, mid-July through August; closed for salmon upstream of bridge. Use small weighted spoons, spinners and eggs. Clam digging at low tide (license required). Shorebird migration in early spring.

C 1.5 (2.4 km) Cemetery on right side of road.

C 2.1 (3.4 km) Powder House Bar and Liquor Store (restaurant) overlooking Eyak Lake. Site of CR&NW railway powder house.

C 2.3 (3.7 km) Paved turnout to north by Eyak Lake. Heney Range to the south. Mount Eccles (elev. 2,357 feet/718m) is the first large peak. Pointed peak beyond is Heney Peak (elev. 3,151 feet/960m).

C 3.5 (5.6 km) Large paved turnout; Eyak Lake.

C 4.0 (6.4 km) Historical marker on left gives a brief history of the CR&NW railway. Also here is a monument erected by the railroad builder M.J. Heney in memory of those men who lost their lives during construction of the CR&NW. Begun in 1907 and completed in 1911, the CR&NW railway connected the port of Cordova with the Kennecott Copper Mines near Kennicott and McCarthy. The mine and railway ceased operation in 1938.

For the next 2 miles/3.2 km, watch for bears during early morning and late evening (most often seen in June). *CAUTION: Avalanche area.*

C 4.6 (7.4 km) Fireworks stand on left.

C 5.1 (8.2 km) Paved turnout at lake to north.

C 5.5 (8.8 km) Paved turnout at lake to north.

C 5.6 (9.0 km) Bridge over Eyak River; access to Eyak River trail. This is a good spot to see waterfowl feeding near the outlet of Eyak Lake. An estimated 100 trumpeter swans winter on Eyak Lake.

Eyak River trailhead is on the west bank of the river. The 2.2-mile/3.5-km trail, much of which is boardwalk over muskeg, is popular with fishermen.

C 5.9 (9.5 km) **Eyak River.** Toilet and boat launch. Dolly Varden; red salmon, June–July; silvers, August–September. Also pinks and chums. Use Vibrax spoon, spinner or salmon eggs. Fly-fishing only for salmon within 200 yards of weir.

C 6.5 (10.5 km) No shoulder on road.

C 7.0 (11.3 km) Small unpaved turnouts on either side of road.

C 7.3 (11.7 km) Paved turnout. *CAUTION: High winds for next 4 miles/6.4 km. In January and February, these winds sweep across this flat with such velocity it is safer to pull off and stop.*

C 7.4 (11.9 km) Bridge over slough.

C 7.5 (12.1 km) First bridge across Scott River.

C 8.0 (12.8 km) Bridge over slough waters. Gravel turnout; access to slough.

C 8.3 (13.4 km) Scott River bridge.

C 9.3 (14.9 km) Between **Mileposts 9** and **10** there are 4 bridges across the Scott River and the slough. Sloughs along here are from the runoff of the Scott Glacier, visible to the northeast. Bear and moose are often seen, especially in July and August. In May and August, thousands of dusky Canada geese nest here. This is the only known nesting area of the dusky geese, which winter in Oregon's Willamette Valley. Also watch for swans.

Moose feed in the willow groves on either side of the highway. Moose are not native to Cordova; the mountains and glaciers prevent them from entering the delta country. Today's herd stems from a

COPPER RIVER HIGHWAY — *Cordova, AK, to Million Dollar Bridge*

© 1999 The MILEPOST®

Principal Route

Paved — Unpaved

Other Roads

Paved — Unpaved

Ferry Routes — **Hiking Trails**

☒ Refer to Log for Visitor Facilities

Scale

0 — 5 Miles
0 — 5 Kilometres

Key to Advertiser Services

C - Camping
D - Dump Station
d - Diesel
G - Gas (reg., unld.)
I - Ice
L - Lodging
M - Meals
P - Propane
R - Car Repair (major)
r - Car Repair (minor)
S - Store (grocery)
T - Telephone (pay)

Map Location

Key to mileage boxes

miles/kilometres
miles/kilometres from:

C - Cordova

Allen Glacier

Copper River

Million Dollar Bridge

C-48/77km

Childs Glacier

Miles Lake

Miles Glacier

Area

Glaciated Area

CHUGACH MOUNTAINS

Scott Glacier

Chugach National Forest

Goodwin Glacier

Glaciated

▲ Mount Murchison
6,263 ft./1,909m

Sheridan Glacier

Sherman Glacier

▲ Goat Mountain
4,370 ft./1,332m

Cabin Lake

Eyak Lake

C-0

❄ ▲ ⊟ ⚓ **Cordova**
N60°33' W145°45'

Hawkins Island

Orca Bay

Orca Inlet

Hartney Bay

HENEY RANGE

▲ Mount Eccles
2,357 ft./718m

▲ Heney Peak
3,151 ft./960m

Eyak R.

10

⊟

✈

C-12/20km

⊟ ▲ ⚓
Alaganik Slough

Pipeline Lake

McKinley Lake

McKinley Peak
2,351 ft./717m

C-28/44km

Round Island

Long Island

Hotcake Channel

▼ Heart Island

Chugach National Forest

Copper River Delta

Castle Island Slough

Storey Slough

Castle Island

Martin River

Gulf of Alaska

N W E S (compass)

---

transplant of 26 animals made between 1949 and 1959.

C 10.2 (16.4 km) Scott River bridge. Watch for old and new beaver dams and lodges beside the highway.

C 10.5 (16.9 km) U.S. Forest Service information pavilion (8 interpretive plaques about Copper River Delta/Chugach National Forest areas) and large paved turnout with litter barrel to south. Game management area, 330,000 acres. Trumpeter swans and Canada geese. Look for arctic terns.

C 10.6 (17.0 km) Bridge, beaver lodge.

C 10.9 (17.5 km) Elsner River bridge.

C 11.5 (18.5 km) Look for brown bears feeding in the outwash plains of Scott Glacier. Thousands of salmon swim up nearby rivers to spawn. There are numerous beaver lodges on both sides of the highway.

C 11.6 (18.7 km) State of Alaska Cordova highway maintenance station to northeast. U.S. Coast Guard station.

C 11.9 (19.2 km) Cordova airport and access to **Cabin Lake Recreation Area**. Drive north 2.5 miles/4.0 km for recreation area (gravel access road forks 0.3 mile/0.5 km in; right fork leads to gravel pit, continue straight ahead for recreation area). *CAUTION: Narrow road, no directional signs, active logging and logging trucks.* Picnic tables, toilet, litter barrel and firepits at Cabin Lake; cutthroat fishing.

C 12.2 (19.6 km) Pavement ends, gravel begins. Watch for potholes.

C 12.9 (20.7 km) Keep a lookout for snowshoe hare and birds of prey.

C 13.5 (21.7 km) **Sheridan Glacier** access road leads 4.0 miles/6.4 km to the terminus

of Sheridan Glacier. At 1.8 miles (2.9 km) a road forks to the left; STAY RIGHT. The left fork connects to the Cabin Lake Access road. *CAUTION: Narrow road, watch for logging trucks.* The glacier was named by U.S. Army explorer Capt. Abercrombie for Gen. Philip H. Sheridan of Civil War fame. Sheridan Mountain trailhead, several picnic tables, litter barrels and a partial view of the glacier are available at the end of the access road. It is about a 0.5-mile/0.8-km hike to the dirt-covered glacial moraine.

C 14.6 (23.5 km) Bridge over Sheridan River. Raft takeout point. View of Sheridan Glacier. To the east of Sheridan Glacier is Sherman Glacier.

Winter moose range next 8 miles/13 km eastbound.

C 14.8 (23.8 km) Silver salmon spawn during September and October in the stream beside the highway.

C 15.7 (25.3 km) Beautiful view of Sheridan Glacier to the northeast.

C 16 (25.7 km) Second bridge over Sheridan River. Large unpaved turnout.

C 16.7 (26.9 km) Turnoff for **Alaganik Slough Chugach National Forest Recreation Area**. Drive south 3 miles/4.8 km via gravel road; picnic tables, firepits, wheelchair-accessible toilets, litter barrel, information kiosk and boat launch. Wheelchair-accessible interpretive boardwalk with viewing blind for watching birds and other wildlife. No water, informal camping. Fishing for Dolly Varden, sockeye (July) and silver salmon (Aug.–Sept.).

Interpretive plaque on side road reads: "Why are Delta moose the largest and

healthiest? This moose herd, first introduced in 1949, maintains its vitality primarily due to its abundant willow supply. As part of a normal cycle, accelerated by the 1964 earthquake, much of the willow is becoming unavailable to moose. As the willow grows tall, the moose can no longer reach the tender new shoots. In the future this could cause a decrease in the numbers of moose on the delta. To slow the cycle down, the Forest Service is experimenting in this area, cutting back the shrubs. This should increase the amount of available willow browse. Biologists will evaluate the response of moose to new willow growth."

C 17.2 (27.7 km) Trumpeter swans may be seen in pond beside highway. One of the largest of all North American waterfowl (6- to 8-foot wingspan), it has been almost completely eliminated in the Lower 48 and Canada. Alaska harbors more than 80 percent of breeding trumpeters, and more than 7 percent of the world's trumpeter population breeds in the Copper River Delta.

C 17.8 (28.6 km) For the next mile look for silver salmon spawning in streams during September. To the left and on the slopes above timberline mountain goats may be seen. The mountain to the left of the road ahead eastbound is McKinley Peak (elev. 2,351 feet/717m).

C 17.9 (28.8 km) Entering Chugach National Forest eastbound.

C 18.3 (29.5 km) Road narrows. *NOTE: Road not maintained in winter (after Nov. 1) beyond this point.*

C 18.5 (29.7 km) Turnout to north access to Muskeg Meander cross-country ski trailhead; length 2.5 miles/4 km. According to the USFS district office, this trail offers a beautiful view of the Copper River Delta.

C 18.8 (30.2 km) Haystack Trail trailhead to south. Easy 0.8-mile/1.2-km trail leads to delta overlook with interpretive signs. Excellent place to see moose and bear, according to the USFS district office in Cordova.

Several small turnouts next mile.

C 19.9 (32.0 km) Large gravel turnout to south; beaver dam, fishing. "Pay to park" area.

C 21.2 (34.1 km) Pipeline Lakes Trail trailhead to north, parking to south. The 1.8-mile/2.9-km trail was originally built as a water pipeline route to supply locomotives on the CR&NW railway. Segments of the pipeline are still visible. Fishing for cutthroat, fly or bait. Trail joins McKinley Lake trail. Rubber boots are necessary.

C 21.4 (34.4 km) McKinley Lake Trail to north; easy 2.1-mile/3.4-km hike with excellent fishing for sockeye, Dolly Varden and cutthroat. Access to USFS public-use cabins: McKinley Trail cabin (100 yards from highway) and McKinley Lake cabin (45-minute walk in from highway; also accessible by boat via Alaganik Slough).

C 21.9 (35.2 km) Alaganik Slough. Boat ramp, picnic tables, firepits, toilets, litter barrel, wildflowers, interpretive signs on local cultural history and fishing access to south at west side of Alaganik Slough river bridge. Sockeye (red) and coho (silver) salmon, July to September. Also boat access to McKinley Lake.

C 22.3 (35.8 km) Salmon Creek bridge, parking; creek access.

C 22.6 (36.4 km) Small turnout.

C 24.6 (39.6 km) One-mile/1.6-km road north leads to Saddlebag Glacier trailhead and parking area; access to canoe route. According to the USFS office in Cordova, this is an easy 3-mile/4.8-km trail to Saddlebag Lake. View of Saddlebag Glacier and icebergs; look for goats on surrounding mountains. *CAUTION: Watch for bears.*

C 24.8 (39.9 km) Channel to beaver pond for spawning salmon. A plaque here reads: "Pathway to salmon rearing grounds. Channel provided access to beaver pond (north side of road) for coho fry. Beaver pond can support up to 25,400 young salmon. Fallen trees and brush provide cover from predators."

C 25.4 (40.9 km) Small gravel turnout by 2 spawning channels with weirs. Interpretive signs along a short trail here explain the project: "Channel built by USDA Forest Service to provide high quality spawning habitat for coho and sockeye salmon. Before construction, the streambed was muddy and the stream dried up during low flow periods. Fish spawned in the streams but few eggs survived. Improved channel is deeper and ensures a consistent flow. Adjustable weirs control water depth. Clean gravels placed in

the channel make better spawning conditions while large rip-rap on streambanks prevent erosion.

"Can you see small circles of gravel which appear to have been turned over? These are salmon 'redds,' or nests in which female salmon lay their eggs. Female salmon create the redds by digging with their tails. Environmental conditions and predators take a heavy toll on salmon eggs and small fry. Of the 2,800 eggs which the average female coho salmon lays, only about 14 will survive to adulthood. Most of these will then be caught by commercial, sport or subsistence fishermen. Only 2 salmon from each redd will actually return to spawn and complete their life cycle."

Near here was the cabin of Rex Beach, author of *The Iron Trail*, a classic novel about the building of the CR&NW railway.

C 26.2 (42.2 km) Flag Point. Turnout with view of the Copper River which empties into the Gulf of Alaska. Downriver to the southwest is Castle Island Slough. Storey Slough is visible a little more to the south. Castle Island and a number of small islands lie at the mouth of the Copper River. Monument on the riverbank is dedicated to the men who built these bridges and "especially to the crane crew who lost their lives on July 21, 1971."

CAUTION: Extreme high winds next 10 miles/16 km in fall and winter. Stay in your vehicle.

C 26.4 (42.5 km) Two bridges cross the Copper River to Round Island, a small island with sand dunes and a good place to picnic.

In midsummer the Copper River has half a million or more red (sockeye) and king salmon migrating 300 miles/483 km upstream to spawn in the river's clear tributaries. There is no sportfishing in this stretch of the Copper River because of glacial silt.

Candlefish (eulachon) also spawn in the Copper River. Candlefish oil was once a significant trade item of the Coastal Indians. These fish are so oily that when dried they can be burned like candles.

C 27.3 (43.9 km) Copper River Bridge No. 3 from Round Island to Long Island. The 6.2 miles/10 km of road on Long Island pass through a sandy landscape dotted with dunes. Long Island is in the middle of the Copper River.

C 28.2 (45.4 km) Lake to south.

C 30.8 (49.5 km) Watch for nesting swans, other birds and beaver in slough to south of road. *NOTE: Use extreme caution if you drive off road: sandy terrain.*

C 31 (49.9 km) Lakes to south.

C 33 (53.1 km) View of 2 glaciers to the northwest; nearest is Goodwin, the other is Childs.

C 33.2 (53.4 km) First bridge leaving Long Island. View to south down Hotcake Channel to Heart Island. Road built on top of a long dike which stretches across the Copper River Delta. From here to **Milepost C 37.7** there are 7 more bridges across the delta. The Copper River channels have changed and many bridges now cross almost dry gulches. *NOTE: Watch for large potholes before and after bridges through this section.*

C 34.1 (54.8 km) Large gravel turnout to north.

C 34.2 (55.0 km) Copper River bridge.

C 35.6 (57.3 km) Large gravel turnout to north.

C 36.6 (58.9 km) Bridge crossing main flow of the Copper River (this is the 5th bridge after leaving Long Island eastbound).

Access to river at east end of bridge.

C 37.2 (59.8 km) Bridge, river access.

C 37.4 (60.2 km) Bridge, river access, large gravel turnout to north.

C 37.6 (60.5 km) Large gravel turnout.

C 38.8 (62.4 km) Childs Glacier directly ahead.

C 39.8 (64.0 km) Milky glacial waters of Sheep Creek pass through large culvert under road.

C 40.4 (65.0 km) Clear Creek. Dolly Varden, cutthroat, red salmon (July) and silvers (August–September). Use flies, lures, spinners or eggs. Watch for bears.

C 40.9 (65.8 km) Park on old railroad grade to south for access to Clear Creek.

C 41.7 (67.1 km) Goat Mountain (elev. 4,370 feet/1,332m) rises to the east of the highway. To the west, parts of the Sherman and Goodwin glaciers flow down the sides of Mount Murchison (elev. 6,263 feet/1,909m).

C 42.1 (67.7 km) Side road to gravel pit, pond, informal camping and picnic site by Goat Mountain.

C 48 (77.2 km) Access to **Childs Glacier Recreation Area** with 2 covered, wheelchair-accessible viewing areas, one at the bridge, the other 0.7 mile down access road. Picnic

sites, covered tables, toilets and trails. No water. Limited RV parking. U.S. Forest Service hosts on site in summer. Childs Glacier was named by Capt. W.R. Abercrombie (1884 expedition) for George Washington Childs of Philadelphia. The glacier face is approximately 350 feet/107m high and very active. In 1993 falling ice caused a 30-foot wave that crashed onto the viewing area. Car-sized icebergs were tossed onto the beach and viewing area. *CAUTION: Calving ice may cause waves to break over the beach and into the viewing area. Be prepared to run to higher ground!*

C 48.1 (77.4 km) The Million Dollar Bridge. Sign posted: Weight limit on bridge: 6,600 lbs. Viewing platform. The north span of the bridge collapsed during the 1964 earthquake. Temporary repairs were made and people have been driving across it, but driving across the bridge and beyond is definitely a "drive at your own risk" venture. Primitive road extends only about 10 miles/16 km beyond the bridge to the Allen River. Heavy snow blocks road in winter; road may not be open until June. Proposed extension of the Copper River Highway to Chitina is currently under debate.

From here there is a view of Miles Glacier to the east. This glacier was named by Lieutenant Allen (1885 expedition) for Maj. Gen. Nelson A. Miles.

C 48.2 (77.6 km) End of bridge.

C 48.8 (78.5 km) A 4X4 or 4-wheel-drive vehicle with very high clearance is a must to go any farther!

Drive with headlights on at all times.

SEWARD HIGHWAY ①⑨

Connects: Anchorage to Seward, AK   **Length:** 127 miles
Road Surface: Paved   **Season:** Open all year
Highest Summit: Turnagain Pass 988 feet
Major Attractions: Mount Alyeska; Portage Glacier; Kenai Fjords National Park

	Alyeska	Anchorage	Hope	Portage Glacier	Seward
Alyeska		42	56	22	95
Anchorage	42		88	54	127
Hope	56	88		46	75
Portage Glacier	22	54	46		85
Seward	95	127	75	85	

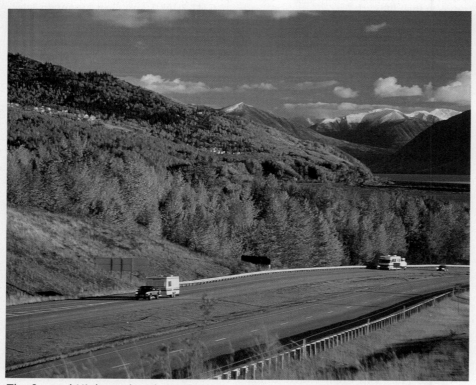

The Seward Highway heads south from Anchorage. (© Barbara Willard)

Seward Highway Log

Distance from Seward (S) is followed by distance from Anchorage (A).
Physical mileposts show distance from Seward. Many mileposts were missing in summer 1998.

ALASKA ROUTE 1

S 127 (204.4 km) **A 0** Gambell Street and 10th Avenue in Anchorage. The New Seward Highway (Gambell Street southbound, Ingra northbound)) connects with the Glenn Highway in Anchorage via 5th Avenue (westbound) and 6th Avenue (eastbound). (See map in the ANCHORAGE section.) Follow Gambell Street south.

S 126.7 (203.9 km) **A 0.3** (0.5 km) 15th Avenue.

S 126.6 (203.7 km) **A 0.4** (0.6 km) 16th Avenue; access to Sullivan sports arena, ice rinks and baseball stadium. Begin divided 4-lane highway southbound.

S 126 (202.8 km) **A 1** (1.6 km) Fireweed Lane. Shopping and services to west.

S 125.8 (202.4 km) **A 1.2** (1.9 km) Northern Lights Boulevard (one-way westbound). Access to Sears Mall from New Seward Highway. Shopping, services and 24-hour supermarket on Northern Lights Blvd. Fred Meyers east side of highway.

S 125.7 (202.3 km) **A 1.3** (2.1 km) Benson Boulevard (one-way westbound).

S 125.4 (201.8 km) **A 1.6** (2.6 km) Southbound access only to Old Seward Highway to 36th Ave..

S 125.3 (201.6 km) **A 1.7** (2.7 km) 36th Avenue; **Providence Hospital** approximately 2 miles east. Z.J. Loussac library and Midtown post office to west.

S 125.2 (201.5 km) **A 1.8** (2.9 km) Freeway begins southbound.

S 124.7 (200.7 km) **A 2.3** (3.7 km) Tudor Road overpass; exits both sides of highway to shopping and services.

S 124.2 (199.8 km) **A 2.8** (4.5 km) Highway crosses Campbell Creek; Campbell Creek Greenbelt. Views of Chugach Mountains to the east.

S 123.7 (199.1 km) **A 3.3** (5.3 km) Dowling Road underpass; exits on both sides of highway to shopping and services.

The 127-mile-/204-km-long Seward Highway connects Anchorage with the community of Seward on the east coast of the Kenai Peninsula. It has been called one of the most scenic highways in the country and has been designated a National Forest Scenic Byway. Leaving Anchorage, the Seward Highway follows the north shore of Turnagain Arm through Chugach State Park and Chugach National Forest, permitting a panoramic view of the south shore and the Kenai Mountains.

The Seward Highway provides access to Girdwood and Alyeska ski resort; the Hope Highway; the Whittier shuttle train, Portage Glacier; and Kenai Fjords National Park. The Seward Highway also junctions with the other major Kenai Peninsula route, the Sterling Highway (see STERLING HIGHWAY section).

The first 9 miles of the New Seward Highway are a major Anchorage thoroughfare (4-lane divided freeway), connecting South Anchorage with downtown. South of Anchorage, the Seward Highway is a paved, 2-lane highway with passing lanes. There are no gas stations on the Seward Highway between **Milepost S 90** (Girdwood turnoff) and **Milepost S 6.6**, just outside Seward.

The highway is open all year. Some sections of the highway are subject to avalanches in winter. Phone (907) 273-6037 or check Anchorage news sources for winter road conditions and avalanche road closures.

There is a bike trail between Alyeska and Bird Point. The bike route is marked by signs. This trail will link up with the Tony Knowles Coastal Trail from Anchorage. There is also a bike trail from the Hope "Y" to Quartz Creek campground.

CAUTION: The Seward Highway from Anchorage to just past Girdwood statistically has one of the highest number of traffic accidents in the state. DRIVE CAREFULLY! Motorists must drive with headlights on at all times.

Delay of 5 vehicles or more is illegal; use slow vehicle turnouts. Pass with care!

Emergency medical services: Phone 911 or use CB channels 9, 11 or 19. Cellular phone service is available as far south as Girdwood and is also available in Seward. Emergency call boxes are located at Turnagain Pass (**Milepost S 68.5**), Hope Highway junction (**S 56.3**), Summit Lake Lodge (**S 45.8**) and at the Sterling Highway junction.

SEWARD HIGHWAY
Anchorage, AK, to Seward, AK

© 1999 The MILEPOST®

Cook Inlet

To Palmer
(see GLENN HIGHWAY section, page 331)

Anchorage

S-127/204km
A-0

The Alaska Railroad

CHUGACH MOUNTAINS *Area*

Upper Lake George

State Park Boundary

Potter Point (Potter Marsh) State Game Refuge

Chugach State Park

McHugh Peak 4,298 ft./1,310m

Crow Creek Trail

Glaciated

Raven Glacier

National Forest Boundary

Potter Section House

National Forest Scenic Byway

Turnagain Arm

McHugh Cr.

Indian Cr.

Bird Creek

Indian

S-102.9/165.6km Mary Lou's Fun House l
S-100.8/162.2km Hush Puppy Kennel
Shoreside Texaco dGIPST
S-100.7/162.1km Bird Ridge Cafe & Bakery CILMT

Crow Creek Road Road not maintained in winter

Crow Creek Mine

Mount Alyeska 3,939 ft./1,201m

S-103.9/167.2km Indian Valley Meats

Alyeska Highway

Alyeska Resort

Girdwood

Twentymile R.

Twentymile Glacier

J-15.8/25.4km Henry's One Stop CDILPST
J-16/25.7km Discovery Cabins L

Hope Highway

J-18/29km

J-16.5/26.6km Discovery Cafe MT

Hope

S-90/144.8km Alpine Diner & Bakery M
Tesoro 7-Eleven dGIST

S-90/145km
A-37/60km

Chugach National Forest

S-80.3/129.2km Phillip's Cruises & Tours

Resurrection Creek Road

Palmer Creek Road

Chugach

Skilak Cr.

S-79/127.1km Big Game Alaska

S-80/129km
A-47/75km

Portage
(Alaska Railroad Loading)

Alaska State Ferry

National

Forest

Granite Cr.

S-79/127km
A-48/77km

Portage Glacier Road

Passage Canal

Whittier

S-57/91km
A-70/113km
J-0

S-56.8/91.4km Nenana Raft Adventures

Placer R.

The Alaska Railroad

Portage Glacier L.

Portage Glacier

Alaska Railroad Shuttle

Blackstone Bay

Resurrection

Resurrection Pass Trail

Resurrection Pass 2,600ft./792m

Canyon Cr.

Lower Summit Lake

Johnson Pass Trail

Bench Creek

Skookum Glacier

Glaciated

Kenai National Wildlife Refuge

Devils Summit 2,400ft./732m

S-45.8/73.7km Summit Lake Lodge CILM

Johnson Summit 1,450ft./442m

Area

MOUNTAINS

Swan L.

Devils Creek

Summit L.

Bench L.

Johnson L.

Quartz Creek

Tern Lake Junction

Johnson Cr.

National Forest Boundary

Juneau L.

To Sterling
(see STERLING HIGHWAY section)

Trout L.

Juneau Cr.

S-37/60km
A-90/145km
H-138/222km

S-35.7/57.5km Horseback Adventures Alaska

Upper Trail Lake

S-30.5/49.1km Alpenglow Cottage L
S-29.9/48.1km Pioneer's Lodge L

Moose Pass N60°29' W149°22'

Kings Bay

Cooper Landing

Crescent L.

Carter L.

S-29.4/47.3km Estes Brothers Groceries & Water Wheel IS
Lower Trail L. Trail Lake Lodge ILMT
S-29.1/46.8km Moose Pass RV Park C
S-28.9/46.5km Midnight Sun Log Cabins Lr
S-24.1/38.8km Crown Point Lodge LMT

Lower Russian Lake

Crescent Creek-Carter Lake Trail

Ptarmigan Creek Trail

Russian River

S-23/37km Alaska Nellie's Inn, Inc. B&B L

Ptarmigan Lake

Skilak Lake

Cooper Lake

S-19.9/32km I.R.B.I. Knives
S-19.5/31.4km Mrs. Leary's Alaskan Gallery and Senior B&B L
S-19.4/31.2km Renfro's Lakeside Retreat

National Forest Scenic Byway

Upper Russian Lake

Russian Lakes Trail

Resurrection River

KENAI

Primrose Trail

Grayling Lk.

Lost Lake

Chugach National Forest

The Alaska Railroad

Glaciated Area

S-6.6/10.6km A Creekside RV Park and Motel CDdGILPT
Bear Creek RV Park CDILPRST
Bear Lake Air

Bear Lk.

S-6.3/10.1km Eagle Song Bed & Breakfast L
0.2 Winterset Guest House L

S-5.4/8.7km Dave & Marie's Excellent Adventures

Exit Glacier Road

Grouse Lk.

S-3.7/6km Creekside Cabins Bed & Breakfast
Fjords RV Park CL
IdidaRide Sled Dog Tours
River Valley Cabins & Box Canyon Cabins L

S-2.3/3.7km Seward Resort (Military)
S-2/3.2km Seward Chamber of Commerce
N60°07' W149°26'

Seward

S-3.2/5.1km Camelot Cottages L
The Farm Bed and Breakfast Inn L
Mom Clock's Bed & Breakfast L
Rininger's Bed and Breakfast L

Harding Icefield

Kenai Fjords National Park

S-0
A-127/204km

Nash Road

Resurrection Bay

Alaska State Ferry

Doty Harbor

National Forest Boundary

Key to mileage boxes

miles/kilometres
miles/kilometres from:

S -Seward
A -Anchorage
H -Homer
J -Junction

Map Location

Principal Route

Paved ▬▬▬ Unpaved ▬▬▬

Other Roads

Paved ▬▬▬ Hiking Trails ▬▬▬

Ferry Routes

✳ Refer to Log for Visitor Facilities

Scale

0 ————— 5 Miles
0 ————— 5 Kilometres

Key to Advertiser Services

C -Camping
D -Dump Station
d -Diesel
G -Gas (reg., unld.)
I -Ice
L -Lodging
M -Meals
P -Propane
R -Car Repair (major)
r -Car Repair (minor)
S -Store (grocery)
T -Telephone (pay)

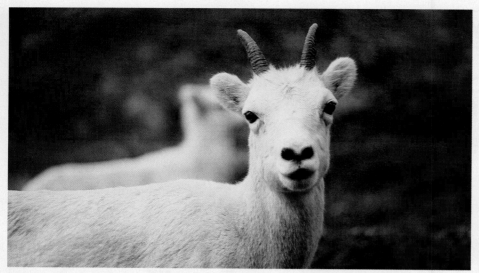

Use viewing turnouts to watch for Dall sheep along the Seward Highway.

(© Bill Sherwonit)

S 122.7 (197.5 km) **A 4.3** (6.9 km) 76th Avenue exit, southbound traffic only.

S 122.2 (196.7 km) **A 4.8** (7.7 km) Dimond Boulevard overpass; exits on both sides of highway. Access west to Dimond Mall, gas stations, fast-food and major shopping area. Gas station to east.

S 120.8 (194.4 km) **A 6.2** (10 km) O'Malley Road underpass; exits on both sides of highway. Turn east on O'Malley Road and drive 2 miles/3.2 km to reach the

Alaska Zoo. Continue east on O'Malley for Chugach State Park Upper Hillside hiking trails (follow signs).

Turn west for access to Minnesota Drive to **Anchorage International Airport.**

S 119.7 (192.6 km) **A 7.3** (11.7 km) Huffman Road underpass; exits on both sides of highway. Exit west for gas station, 24-hour supermarket and other services. Exit east for South Anchorage subdivisions.

S 118.5 (190.7 km) **A 8.5** (13.7 km)

De Armoun Road overpass, exits both sides of highway.

S 117.8 (189.6 km) **A 9.2** (14.8 km) Overpass: Exits both sides of highway for Old Seward Highway (west); access to Rabbit Creek Road (east) to South Anchorage subdivisions. The picturesque Chapel by the Sea overlooks Turnagain Arm. The church is often photographed because of its unique setting and its display of flowers.

View of Turnagain Arm and Mount Spurr southbound.

S 117.4 (188.9 km) **A 9.6** (15.4 km) Turnoff to west for **Rabbit Creek Rifle Range** (ADF&G); open to the public Feb–Nov. (closed Dec.–Jan.). Phone (907) 566-0130. Covered firing positions on handgun and rifle ranges. Shotgun range (shot shells only). Summer (June 15–Sept. 15) hours in 1998 were 11 A.M. to 6:50 P.M. Monday, Tuesday, Friday; 10 A.M. to 5:50 P.M. Saturday and Sunday; closed Wednesday and Thursday. Fees: $5/daily, $40/season (under 16 and 60 and over free); targets $1/6, ear plugs $1/pair.

Turnoff to east at Boardwalk Wildlife Viewing exit for **Potter Point State Game Refuge.** This is a very popular spot for bird watching. From the parking lot, an extensive boardwalk crosses Potter Marsh, a refuge and nesting area for waterfowl. The marsh was created when railroad construction dammed a small creek in the area. Today, the marsh is visited by arctic terns, Canada geese, trumpeter swans, many species of ducks and other water birds. Bring binoculars.

S 117.3 (188.8 km) **A 9.7** (15.6 km) *CAUTION: Highway narrows to 2 lanes southbound. Pass with care!*

S 117.2 (188.6 km) **A 9.8** (15.8 km) Small paved turnout east side of road at end of boardwalk.

S 116.1 (186.8 km) **A 10.9** (17.5 km) Paved double-ended turnout to east. Highway parallels Alaska Railroad southbound to **Milepost S 90.8.**

S 115.4 (185.7 km) **A 11.6** (18.7 km) **Junction** with Old Seward Highway; access to Potter Valley Road east to subdivision. Old Johnson trail begins 0.5 mile/0.6 km up Potter Valley Road; parking at trailhead. Only the first 10 miles/16 km of this state park trail are cleared. Moderate to difficult hike; watch for bears.

The natural gas pipeline from the Kenai Peninsula emerges from beneath Turnagain Arm here and follows the roadway to Anchorage.

WARNING: When the tide is out, the sand in Turnagain Arm might look inviting. DO NOT go out on it. Some of it is quicksand. You could become trapped in the mud and not be rescued before the tide comes in.

S 115.2 (185.4 km) **A 11.8** (19 km) Entering Chugach State Park southbound.

Turnoff to west for **Potter Section House, Chugach State Park Headquarters** (phone 907/345-5014); pay phone, large parking lot, wheelchair-accessible toilets. Open daily in summer, Monday to Friday 8 A.M. to 4:30 P.M. year-round. The renovated Potter Section House, dedicated in October 1986, was home to a small crew of railroad workers who maintained the Alaska Railroad tracks between Seward and Anchorage in the days of coal- and steam-powered locomotives. Displays here include photographs from the National Archives, a vintage snowblower and working model railroad.

S 115.1 (185.2 km) **A 11.9** (19.2 km) Turnoff to east for **Potter Creek Viewpoint**

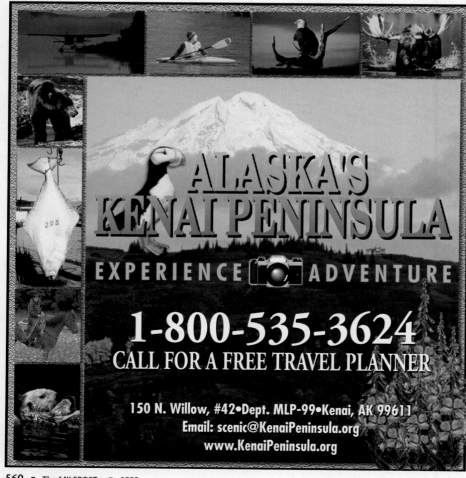

and Trail (Chugach State Park). Small parking area overlooking marsh with interpretive signs about wetlands and the railroad's role in creating these accidental marshes. Also an interpretive sign about the feeding habits of moose, who eat in marshes like these as well as in the backyards of Anchorage residents. Moose can eat the equivalent in twigs of a 50-lb. sack of dog food a day. Moose munch twigs and strip bark from willow, birch and aspen trees.

Drive up the hill via 2-lane paved road for large parking area, viewing platform with telescopes, interpretive signs and Potter Creek trailhead. The 0.4-mile nature trail examines the natural history of the surrounding forest, a blending of 2 climates: the continental climate (the boreal forest of Interior Alaska) and the wetter coastal climate (Sitka spruce, hemlock). Also access to Turnagain Arm trail to McHugh Creek Picnic Area and to Windy Corner (see trail information signs).

S 115 (185 km) **A 12** (19.3 km) Watch for rockfalls.

From here to **Milepost S 90** there are many turnouts on both sides of the highway, some with scenic views of Turnagain Arm. An easterly extension of Cook Inlet, **Turnagain Arm** was called Return by the Russians. Captain Cook, seeking the fabled Northwest Passage in 1778, called it Turnagain River, and Captain Vancouver, doing a more thorough job of surveying in 1794, gave it the present name of Turnagain Arm.

S 114.7 (184.6 km) **A 12.3** (19.8 km) Weigh station and pay phone to east.

S 114.5 (184.3 km) **A 12.5** (20.1 km) Double-ended gravel turnout to east (posted no camping).

S 113.3 (182.3 km) **A 13.7** (22.1 km) Slow vehicle turnout southbound.

S 113.1 (182 km) **A 13.9** (22.4 km) Informal gravel turnout to east at McHugh boulder area. Watch for rock climbers practicing on rock walls alongside the highway. The cliffs are part of the base of McHugh Peak (elev. 4,298 feet/1,310m).

S 111.9 (180.1 km) **A 15.1** (24.3 km) Paved side road to east goes up hill to **McHugh Creek Picnic Area**. Renovated in 1998, this state wayside on the flank of

McHugh Peak has restrooms, paved pathways, boardwalks, viewing platforms, picnic tables and a large parking area. McHugh Creek Scenic Overlook offers views of Turnagain Arm. McHugh Creek trailhead. &

S 111.6 (179.6 km) **A 15.4** (24.8 km) Informal turnout to east used by rock climbers.

S 111.2 (179 km) **A 15.8** (25.4 km) Rough gravel turnout to east.

S 110.9 (178.5 km) **A 16.1** (25.9 km) Gravel turnout to east.

S 110.4 (177.7 km) **A 16.6** (26.7 km) **Beluga Point** scenic viewpoint and photo stop to west is a large paved double-ended turnout with a commanding view of Turn-

again Arm. A good place to see bore tides and beluga whales. (The only all-white whale, belugas are easy to identify.) Tables, benches, telescopes and interpretive signs on orcas, bore tides, mountain goats, Captain Cook, etc.

Turnagain Arm is known for having one of the world's remarkably high tides, with a diurnal range of more than 33 feet/10m. A bore tide is an abrupt rise of tidal water just after low tide, moving rapidly landward, formed by a flood tide surging into a constricted inlet such as Turnagain Arm. This foaming wall of water may reach a height of 6 feet/2m and is very dangerous to small craft. To see a bore tide, check the Anchorage-area tide tables for low tide, then add approximately 2 hours and 15 minutes to the Anchorage low tide for the bore to reach points between 32 miles/51.5 km and 37 miles/59.5 km south of Anchorage on the Seward Highway. Visitors should watch for bore tides from Beluga Point south to Girdwood.

WARNING: Do not go out on the mud flats at low tide. The glacial silt and water can create a dangerous quicksand.

S 109.9 (176.9 km) **A 17.1** (27.5 km) Slow vehicle turnout southbound.

S 109.2 (175.7 km) **A 17.8** (28.6 km) Paved turnout to west.

S 109 (175.4 km) **A 18** (29 km) Gravel turnout to east.

S 108.7 (174.9 km) **A 18.3** (29.5 km) Paved double-ended viewpoint to west.

S 108.4 (174.4 km) **A 18.6** (29.9 km) Rainbow trailhead to east.

S 108.3 (174.3 km) **A 18.7** (30.1 km) Trailhead parking to west.

S 108.1 (174 km) **A 18.9** (30.4 km) Slow vehicle turnout southbound.

S 107.9 (173.6 km) **A 19.1** (30.7 km) Turnout to west.

S 107.3 (172.7 km) **A 19.7** (31.7 km) Rough gravel turnout to east is used by rock climbers practicing on the cliffs here.

S 106.9 (172 km) **A 20.1** (32.3 km) Scenic viewpoint to west; double-ended paved turnout. Watch for Dall sheep near road. *NOTE: DO NOT FEED WILDLIFE.*

S 106.7 (171.7 km) **A 20.3** (32.7 km) Windy Corner trailhead to east.

S 106.6 (171.5 km) **A 20.4** (32.8 km) Trailhead parking area to west.

S 106.2 (170.9 km) **A 20.8** (33.5 km) Slow vehicle turnout southbound.

S 105.9 (170.4 km) **A 21.1** (34 km) Slow vehicle turnout southbound.

S 105.7 (170.1 km) **A 21.3** (34.3 km) Falls Creek trailhead and parking to east; moderate 1.5-mile/2.4-km hike along creek.

S 104.9 (168.8 km) **A 22.1** (35.6 km)

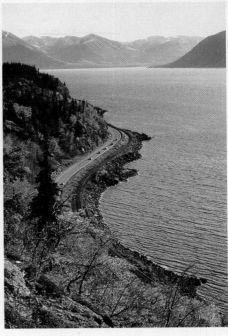

View from McHugh Creek Overlook of Seward Highway along Turnagain Arm.

(© David Ranta, staff)

Single-vehicle turnout to east under rock overhang by small waterfall.

S 104.4 (168 km) **A 22.6** (36.4 km) Slow vehicle turnout northbound.

S 104.3 (167.8 km) **A 22.7** (36.5 km) Slow vehicle turnout southbound.

S 104 (167.4 km) **A 23** (37 km) Indian Valley Mine National Historic Site.

S 103.9 (167.2 km) **A 23.1** (37.2 km) Indian Road to Indian Valley Meats.

Indian Valley Meats. Reindeer sausage and much more from this federally inspected processor of exotic game and fish. Fish boxes ready for shipping, gift packs with game jerky, smoked salmon and much more. Newly expanded retail area for 1999. Great buys! In business 23 years. Please stop in, meet our pet reindeer and tour the stunning grounds, featuring flowers, rock walls, B&B, log conference hall and trophy animal mounts. Just 1/2 mile up Indian Road. See display ad. [ADVERTISEMENT]

S 103.6 (166.7 km) **A 23.4** (37.7 km) **INDIAN.** Indian House motel, restaurant, gift shop (closed in 1998; current status unknown).

S 103.1 (165.9 km) **A 23.9** (38.5 km) Bore

Watch for spawning salmon in Kenai Peninsula streams. (© *Barbara Willard*)

Tide Road, also called Ocean View Road. Access to Indian Valley trailhead (1.4 miles), a 6-mile/10-km moderately steep hike to Indian Pass. Turnagain House restaurant.

S 103 (165.8 km) A 24 (38.6 km) Bridge over Indian Creek; rest area to west at south end of bridge. Bar and liquor store to east. Pay phone. &

Mary Lou's Fun House. See display ad this section.

Indian Creek is heavily fished for pink salmon, sea-run Dolly Varden, few coho

(silver) salmon and rainbow, June to September; pink salmon run from latter part of July to mid-August in even-numbered years. 🐟

S 102.1 (164.3 km) A 24.9 (40.1 km) Bird Ridge trailhead and parking to east.

S 101.5 (163.3 km) A 25.5 (41 km) Bridge over Bird Creek; parking. Very busy fishing area in season. *CAUTION: Watch for pedestrians next mile southbound.*

Bird Creek has a heavy run of pink salmon in July and August; sea-run Dolly Varden, few coho (silver) salmon and rainbow, June to September.. 🐟

S 101.2 (162.9 km) A 25.8 (41.5 km) Bird Creek fishing access to east; campground to west. **Bird Creek State Recreation Site** flats has picnic sites and 19 campsites, firepits, pay phone, covered picnic tables, toilets and water. Firewood is sometimes available. Camping fee $10/night or annual pass. A pleasant campground densely wooded but cleared along the high banks of Turnagain Arm. Paved bike trail goes through campground; a nice 3-mile/5-km ride along Turnagain Arm to Indian. Great spot for sunbathing. This campground is full most weekends in the summer. ▲

WARNING: Do not go out on the mud flats at low tide. The glacial silt and water can create a dangerous quicksand.

S 100.8 (162.2 km) A 26.2 (42.2 km) Gas station with diesel and grocery to east. Sled dog rides at kennel.

Shoreside Texaco. See display ad this section.

Husky Puppy Kennel offers a fun ride with a local Iditarod musher and his Alaskan huskies in Bird Valley (farthest north stand of Sitka spruce). Learn about the Iditarod Trail, the hearty dogs and the famous race. Located next to the Texaco Station. Mush!

[ADVERTISEMENT]

S 100.7 (162.1 km) A 26.3 (42.3 km) **Bird Ridge Cafe & Bakery**. See display ad this

section.

S 99.8 (160.6 km) A 27.2 (43.8 km) Paved turnout to west. Southbound traffic entering avalanche area. "Avalanche alley" is a 9-mile corridor from here south to the Girdwood turnoff that is prone to avalanches.

S 99.4 (160 km) A 27.6 (44.4 km) Large gravel turnout to west with view across Bird Flats on Turnagain Arm to the cut in the mountains where Sixmile Creek drains into the arm; the old mining settlement of Sunrise was located here. The town of Hope is to the southwest. The peak visible across Turnagain Arm between here and Girdwood is Mount Alpenglow in the Kenai mountain range. Avalanche gates.

S 99.2 (159.6 km) A 27.8 (44.7 km) Avalanche gun emplacement (motorists will notice several of these along the highway). The guns fire 105mm shells at Penguin Ridge above the highway south from Bird Hill to knock down potential slides and stabilize the slopes in winter.

S 96.7 (155.6 km) A 30.3 (48.8 km) Improved highway begins southbound. The new "Bird to Gird" segment of the Seward Highway, completed in 1998, is the result of a 5-year project to replace the narrow, winding road over Bird Hill. The approximately 7 miles of new alignment lies on the water side of the railroad tracks along the shore of Turnagain Arm. Plans call for the old Bird Hill road to be turned into a trail.

S 96.5 (155.3 km) A 30.5 (49.1 km) Southbound-only turnoff follows old alignment to large paved parking area overlooking Turnagain Arm.

S 95.7 (154 km) A 31.3 (50.4 km) Passing lane begins southbound.

S 95.3 (153.4 km) A 31.7 (51 km) Turnout No. 5; large paved parking area to west overlooking Turnagain Arm.

S 95.2 (153.2 km) A 31.8 (51.2 km) Watch for waterfalls cascading down the huge rock cuts blasted out of the mountainside during construction of this new stretch of highway.

S 93.7 (150.8 km) A 33.3 (53.6 km) End passing lane southbound.

S 93.3 (150.1 km) A 33.7 (54.2 km) Turnout No. 3; large paved parking area to west overlooking Turnagain Arm.

S 92.5 (148.9 km) A 34.5 (55.5 km) Turnout No. 2; large paved parking area to west overlooking Turnagain Arm.

S 92.3 (148.5 km) A 34.7 (55.8 km) Turnout No. 1A; large paved parking area to east.

S 92.1 (148.2 km) A 34.9 (56.2 km) Slow vehicle turnout to east.

S 91.5 (147.3 km) A 35.5 (57.1 km) Turnout No. 1; large paved parking area to west overlooking Turnagain Arm.

S 90.5 (145.6 km) A 36.5 (58.7 km) Bridge crosses Tidewater Slough.

S 90.4 (145.5 km) A 36.6 (58.9 km)
(Continues on page 567)

The 3-mile/4.8-km Alyeska Highway provides access to Crow Creek Road, Girdwood, Mount Alyeska ski area and Alyeska Resort. There are many restaurants, gift shops and accommodations in the Girdwood/Alyeska area. Major attractions include the Alyeska Aerial Tramway and rainforest hiking trails. Well worth the drive.

Distance is measured from junction with Seward Highway (J).

J 0 Junction with Seward Highway at **Milepost S 90.** Girdwood Station Mall: 24-hour convenience store and gas station, medical clinic with emergency services, restaurant and a bakery.

J 0.2 (0.3 km) Bridge over Alaska Railroad tracks.

Paved bike trail to Alyeska Resort begins.

J 0.4 (0.6 km) Forest Station Road. Chugach National Forest Glacier Ranger District office (P.O. Box 129, Girdwood, AK 99587; phone 907/783-3242). Open 8 A.M. to 5 P.M. Monday to Friday year-round; also 9 A.M. to 5 P.M. weekends Memorial Day through Labor Day. Maps and information available here.

J 0.5 (0.8 km) **Alaska Candle Factory.** One-half mile off Seward Highway on Alyeska Highway. Home of handcrafted candles made in the form of Alaska wild

animals. Hand-dipped tapers and molded candles made daily. All candles have unique individual designs. Open 7 days a week, 10 A.M. to 6 P.M., in summer until 7 P.M. Visitors welcome. Phone (907) 783-2354. P.O. Box 786, Girdwood, AK 99587. [ADVERTISEMENT]

J 1.5 (2.4 km) Bike rentals.

J 1.9 (3.1 km) **Junction** with Crow Creek Road (1-lane dirt and gravel). The Carriage House B&B at Mile 0.2; **Crow Creek Mine National Historic Site** (description follows) at Mile 3.1/5 km; Crow Pass Trailhead at Mile 7/11.3. In winter, the road is not maintained past Mile 0.6.

Crow Creek Mine. Visit this historic 1898 mining camp located in the heart of Chugach National Forest. Drive 3 miles up Crow Creek Road (Old Iditarod trail). Eight original buildings.

Pan for gold. Visit our gift shop. Enjoy beautiful grounds, ponds, flowers. Animals and friendly people. Campground

for tents and self-contained vehicles. Open May 15–Sept. 15, 9 A.M. to 6 P.M. daily. Phone (907) 278-8060 (messages). [ADVERTISEMENT] ▲

Crow Pass and Old Iditarod trailhead at Mile 7 Crow Creek Road. Crow Pass trail climbs steeply 3 miles/4.8 km to ruins of an old gold mine and a USFS public-use cabin at Crow Pass near Raven Glacier; hiking time approximately 2¹⁄₂ hours. The Old Iditarod trail extends 22.5 miles/36.2 km north from Crow Pass down Raven Creek drainage to the Chugach State Park Visitor Center on Eagle River Road. All of the hiking trail, from Crow Creek Road trailhead to the state park visitor center, is part of the Iditarod National Historic Trail used in the early 1900s. Trail is usually free of snow by mid-June. Closed to motorized vehicles; horses prohibited during early spring due to soft trail conditions.

J 2 (3.2 km) California Creek bridge.

Girdwood

J 2.1 (3.4 km) At the junction of Alyeska Highway and Hightower Road. **Population:** 1,935. **Emergency Services: Alaska State Troopers, EMS** and **Fire Department**, phone 911 or (907) 783-2704 (message only) or 269-5711.

The town was named after Col. James Girdwood, who established a mining operation near here in 1901. Today, Girdwood has a substantial year-round community and a flourishing seasonal population, thanks to its appeal as both a winter and summer resort destination.

Located here are a post office, restaurants, vacation rental offices, grocery

store with gas, a rafting business, small shops and fire hall. Flightseeing services located at Girdwood airport.

Girdwood Community Center offers tennis courts, pay phone, Kinder Park day-care center and picnic area. This is site of the Girdwood **Forest Fair**, a mid-summer (July) crafts fair.

Area hiking trails include Glacier Creek, Alyeska Basin, Iditarod, Beaver Pond and Winner Creek trails. The Winner Creek trail is a good one to experience Girdwood's rainforest. The

trail starts near the Alyeska Aerial Tramway ticket office. Girdwood averages 67 inches of rainfall a year. Inquire at Ranger Station at **Milepost J 0.4** Alyeska Highway for more information on area hiking trails.

Chair Five Restaurant. Favorite of locals and travelers since 1983. This is a must stop fun place to dine and drink. Daily offerings include fresh Alaskan halibut and salmon, the famous tundra steak

Girdwood

.... Hiking Trail
— — — Bike Path

Beaver Pond Trail

Crow Creek Rd.

Girdwood School

Hightower

Glacier Creek

Girdwood Airport

Winner Creek Trail

Tram
Westin Alyeska Prince Hotel

Lindblad Ave.

Tahoe Cir.

Mt. Hood Dr.

Aspen

Brighton

Cortina

Alpine

Davos

Alyeska Ave.

Arlberg

Alyeska Ski Resort

Olympic Circle Dr.

J 1.9

Girdwood Pl.

Alyeska Highway

J 2.1

California Creek

To Seward Highway

Glacier Creek Trail

Glacier Creek

Alta Dr.

Alpina Way

Timberline Dr.

Vail Dr.

Garmisch
Inssbruck
Kitzbuhel
Loveland

Megeve

Northland
Okemo

Andre

Lower Terrace

Higher Terrace

Alpine Ave.

Timberline Dr.

Virgin Creek

Day Lodge & Parking

N
W   E
S

The Girdwood/Alyeska area offers biking trails. (Courtesy Alyeska Resort)

(reindeer and buffalo) or try the gourmet fresh dough pizza that gets rave reviews. One of Alaska's largest single malt scotch selections and over 60 microbrews round out the menu. House rules are strictly enforced: 1) Use the little fork for the salad and 2) No fist, gun or food fights allowed. Open daily 11 A.M.–midnight. AX/MC/Visa. (907) 783-2500. See Girdwood on Mount Alyeska webcamera www.chair5.com. [ADVERTISEMENT]

Alyeska Mountain Views. Private homes with breathtaking views of Mt. Alyeska and the surrounding Girdwood Valley. Choose from 2 private homes, each with fireplaces, complete kitchens, hot tubs and laundry facilities. 35 miles south of Anchorage along scenic Turnagain Arm. Local attractions include alpine skiing in winter; hiking, gold pan-

ning, flightseeing and kayaking in summer, as well as fine dining year-round. Book in advance for daily or weekly accommodation: (907) 262-7249, (907) 274-4819, Fax (907) 222-2720.
[ADVERTISEMENT]

Alyeska Highway Log
(continued)

J 2.3 (3.7 km) Glacier Creek bridge.

J 2.5 (4 km) Donner access to Girdwood airstrip (follow signs); flightseeing.

Private Aircraft: Girdwood airstrip; elev. 150 feet/46m; length 2,100 feet/640m; gravel; unattended.

Alpine Air Inc. Home of ZIP the wonder dog! Scenic flights in spacious, intercom-equipped wheel/ski planes and floatplanes into Prince William Sound,

the Chugach Mountains and Mount McKinley area. Glacier and floatplane landings are our specialty. Guided and unguided fishing trips. Statewide charters available. Federally licensed and fully

Alyeska Highway Log (continued)

insured. Visitors welcome year-round to stop in at our hangar/office at the Girdwood airport, last blue hangar on the airport road. Phone (907) 783-2360. Internet address: www.alaska.net/~alpinair; e-mail: alpinair@alaska.net. [ADVERTISEMENT]

Alyeska Air Service. Flightseeing at its best. Minutes away from Alaska's most awe-inspiring sights: Mount McKinley, Prince William Sound and Turnagain Arm. Gaze in amazement at the mighty mountain peaks, massive glaciers and sparkling lakes. Marvel at wildlife in natural habitat and live a full Alaskan experience, starting at $99 per person. Statewide charter and air support year-round. Phone (888) 262-1345 or (907) 783-2163, http://www.alyeskaair.com. [ADVERTISEMENT]

J 2.6 (4.2 km) Timberline Drive. Access to bed and breakfasts.

A Cross Country Meadows B&B located in Alyeska Basin (¹/₂ mile down Timberline; turn right onto Alta Drive) caters to those who seek quiet, deluxe accommodations with a private atmosphere and bath; spectacular mountain and glacier views. Reservations (907) 783-3333 or write to P.O. Box 123, Girdwood, AK 99587. E-mail: XCountryBB@aol.com or www.AlaskaOne.com/crosscountry. [ADVERTISEMENT]

J 2.9 (4.7 km) Alyeska Highway ends at **junction** with Arlberg Avenue, road forks; Welcome to Alyeska Resort sign.

Turn west for Alyeska day lodge (ski school, rentals). Turn east for Alyeska Prince Hotel and tram. Bike and walking path continues to hotel.

Alyeska Resort is Alaska's largest ski area and Alaska's premier year-round resort destination. Owned and operated by Seibu Alaska Inc. since 1980. Ski season is generally from mid-November through mid-April. Facilities include the 60-passenger aerial tramway (departs from Alyeska Prince Hotel), a high-speed detachable bubble quad, 2 fixed-grip quads, 3 double chair lifts and 2 pony tows. Night skiing available during holiday periods in December, and Friday through Saturday from January through March. Ski school, ski rental shop and sports shops are available. Phone (907) 754-7669 for snow conditions and mountain information. Other activities include heli and snowcat skiing, Nordic skiing, dog sledding, snowshoeing and snowmobiling.

J 3 (4.8 km) Olympic Circle; Kobuk Valley Jade shop, The Bake Shop and other businesses.

The Bake Shop at Alyeska Resort is a MUST stop for food and flower lovers alike! Turn off the Seward Highway onto Alyeska Highway. Follow the road until you come to the "T" at Alyeska Resort. Turn left onto Arlberg and take the first right onto Olympic Circle. Don't be confused by a sign for another bakery and

coffee shop at the bottom of the road! Continue to drive to the very top of the gravel road, use the parking lot to your right and walk up to the front of the condo building and the boardwalk. Here you'll find the annual display of summer flowers such as dazzling begonias, giant ferns and many all-time favorites. Then step inside the Bake Shop to enjoy the heartwarming aroma of freshly baked breads and buns. The Bake Shop creates these with the original sourdough starter which was once the "prized" possession of a fortune-seeking gold miner in this valley over 80 years ago. Now look at the large menu board and you will find a variety of egg dishes and pancakes for breakfast. For lunch choose between a great selection of sandwiches made with sourdough buns; pizzas and homemade soups. Don't forget to leave room for our "famous" sweet rolls. Bring your breakfast or lunch outside for a garden picnic, enjoy the beauty of the flowers and the valley and remember to take some of our bread and handcrafted preserves for the road! [ADVERTISEMENT]

J 3.2 (5.1 km) Alyeska Field and Moose Meadow Park (Stumpy Faulkner Early Winter Trail).

J 3.9 (6.3 km) Entrance to Alyeska Prince Hotel; follow signs for parking and shuttle bus to hotel and tram.

J 4.1 (6.6 km) The Westin Alyeska Prince Hotel and Aerial Tramway Glacier Terminal; no parking. The 307-room deluxe chateau-style hotel has a cafe, Japanese steakhouse, 2 lounges, 2 retail shops and a fitness center with indoor swimming pool, sauna, whirlpool and exercise room.. For information phone (907) 754-1111 or (800) 880-3880; www.alyeskaresort.com.

The **Alyeska Aerial Tramway** is a state-of-the-art 60-passenger aerial tramway that transports skiers in winter

and visitors in summer up to the top of Mount Alyeska (elev. 3,939 feet/1,201m) and a mountaintop complex featuring fine dining at Seven Glaciers Restaurant and the Glacier Express cafeteria.

Winner Creek Trail (foot travel only) trailhead behind tram ticket office. Follow gravel path ¹/₄ mile for easy walk through rainforest. Continue on the Access Trail (easy 1.5 miles) to Winner Creek and trailhead junction with the Gorge Trail and the Upper Winner Creek Basin trail. Check bulletin board at trailhead for bear alerts.

Return to Milepost S 90 Seward Highway

Rusting truck and a few ruins are all that remain of Portage. (© Susan Cole Kelly)

(Continued from page 562)

Single-vehicle turnout to east. Leaving Chugach State Park southbound.

The 1964 Good Friday earthquake caused land to sink in the Turnagain Arm area, particularly apparent from here to **Milepost S 74.** As a result, many trees had their root systems invaded by salt water, as seen by the stands of dead spruce trees along here. Good bird watching, including bald eagles, arctic terns and sandhill cranes.

S 90.2 (145.2 km) **A 36.8** (59.2 km) Girdwood highway maintenance station. End avalanche area southbound..

S 90 (144.8 km) **A 37** (59.5 km) This intersection is "old" Girdwood: railroad station, school, and mall. Girdwood Station Mall houses a 24-hour Tesoro 7–Eleven gas station; medical clinic, and Alpine Diner & Bakery (breakfast, lunch, dinner). After the 1964 earthquake, Girdwood moved up the access road 2.1 miles/3.4 km.

Alpine Diner & Bakery. See display ad this section.

Tesoro 7–Eleven. See display ad this section.

Junction with 3-mile/4.8-km Alyeska Highway to Crow Creek road and mine, Girdwood and Alyeska (pronounced al-ee-ES-ka) Recreation Area. Worth the drive! See ALYESKA HIGHWAY log beginning on page 563.

NOTE: *Next gas available southbound on the Seward Highway is at* **Milepost S 6.6;** *next gas available westbound on Sterling Highway is at* **Milepost S 45** *(Sunrise).*

S 89.8 (144.5 km) **A 37.2** (59.9 km) Glacier Creek bridge.

S 89.2 (143.5 km) **A 37.8** (60.8 km) Virgin Creek bridge. View of 3 glaciers to east.

S 86.1 (138.6 km) **A 40.9** (65.8 km) Parking area. Chugach National Forest boundary sign.

S 84.1 (135.3 km) **A 42.9** (69 km) Peterson Creek. View of Blueberry Mountain.

S 82.3 (132.4 km) **A 44.7** (71.9 km) Turnout to east.

S 81 (130.4 km) **A 46** (74 km) BLM observation platform with informative plaques on Twentymile River wetlands and wildlife. Watch for dip-netters in the spring fishing for hooligan (also known as eulachon or candlefish), a species of smelt. Road access east to Twentymile River.

Twentymile River, good hooligan fishing in May. These smelt are taken with long-handled dip nets. Pink, red and silver (coho) salmon 4 to 10 lbs., use attraction lures, best in August. Dolly Varden 4 to 10 lbs., eggs best, good all summer in clear-water tributaries.

S 80.7 (129.9 km) **A 46.3** (74.5 km) Bridge over Twentymile River, which flows out of the Twentymile Glacier and other glaciers through a long green valley at the edge of the highway. Twentymile Glacier can be seen at the end of the valley to the northeast. Twentymile River is a popular windsurfing area in summer. Gravel turnout west side of highway.

S 80.3 (129.2 km) **A 46.7** (75.2 km) First of 3 turnoffs southbound for the **Alaska Railroad Whittier Shuttle.** Turn here for the vehicle loading area if you have tickets. Check in at the blue and yellow trailer before getting in line.

The Portage–Whittier shuttle train carries passengers and vehicles from here to Whittier on Prince William Sound. Whittier is the port for the state ferry MV *Bartlett,* which provides ferry service to Cordova and Valdez, and is also home port for a number of tour boats and charters cruising Prince William Sound. (See description of Whittier in the PRINCE WILLIAM SOUND section.) A road to Whittier is under construction and scheduled to open in May 2000.

S 80.1 (128.9 km) **A 46.9** (75.5 km) **PORTAGE.** No facilities here. The 1964 earthquake caused the land to drop between 6 and 12 feet along Turnagain Arm. High tides then flooded the area, forcing the estimated 50 to 100 residents of Portage to move. Some old buildings are visible; more evidence of trees killed by the invading salt water. Leaving Game Management Unit 14C, entering unit 7, southbound.

S 80 (128.7 km) **A 47** (75.6 km) Second turnoff southbound to Alaska Railroad Whittier Shuttle. Turn here for the ticket office, parking and pay phone. Small visitor infor-

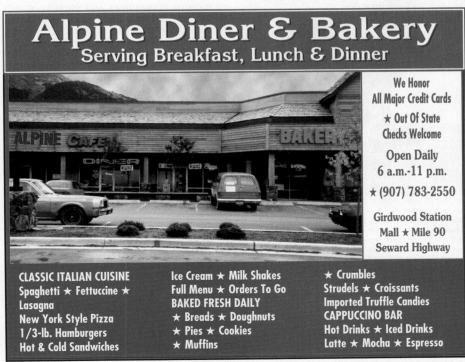

mation center, gift shop and tour boat office.

Phillip's Cruises and Tours. Enjoy Alaska's most popular, 1-day glacier and wildlife adventure through Prince William Sound. Park at the Portage rail station and ride the train to Whittier. Watch for sea otters, seals, whales and bird life that inhabit Prince William Sound as we take you on this fully-narrated, 5-hour cruise aboard a 420-passenger deluxe catamaran. See our ad in the Anchorage section. Departs daily from Whittier, mid-May–mid-September. Sales office: 519 W. 4th Avenue, Suite 100, Anchorage, AK 99501-2211. Phone (907) 276-8023; (800) 544-0529; fax (907) 265-5890. [ADVERTISEMENT]

S 79.8 (128.4 km) **A 47.2** (76 km) Third turnoff southbound, first turnoff northbound, to Alaska Railroad Whittier Shuttle; ticket office and parking.

S 79.4 (127.8 km) **A 47.6** (76.6 km) Portage Creek No. 2 bridge. Parking and interpretive sign to west at south end of bridge. This gray-colored creek carries the silt-laden glacial meltwater from Portage Glacier and Portage Lake to Turnagain Arm. Mud flats in Turnagain Arm are created by silt from the creek settling close to shore.

S 79 (127.1 km) **A 48** (77.2 km) Portage Creek No. 1 bridge.

Turnoff to west for Big Game Alaska, a drive-through wildlife park and gift shop. The park has taken care of a number of orphaned wild animals.

Big Game Alaska. See display ad this section.

S 78.9 (127 km) **A 48.1** (77.4 km)

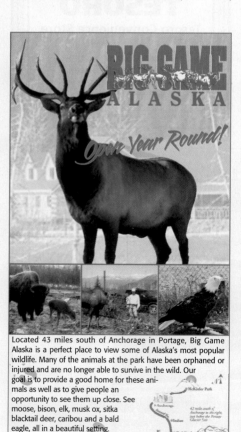

Junction with Portage Glacier access road. Portage Glacier is one of Alaska's most popular attractions. See PORTAGE GLACIER ROAD log opposite page.

S 78.7 (126.6 km) **A 48.3** (77.7 km) Large gravel turnout.

S 78.4 (126.1 km) **A 48.6** (78.2 km) **Placer River** bridge; parking and access at south end of bridge. The Placer River has good hooligan fishing in May. These smelt are taken with long-handled dip nets. Silver salmon may be taken in August and September.

Between Placer River and Ingram Creek, there is an excellent view on clear days of Skookum Glacier to the northeast. To the north across Turnagain Arm is Twentymile Glacier. Arctic terns and waterfowl are often seen in the slough here.

S 77.9 (125.4 km) **A 49.1** (79 km) Placer River overflow bridge. Paved turnout to west at south end of bridge.

S 77 (123.9 km) **A 50** (80.5 km) Boundary of Chugach National Forest.

S 75.5 (121.5 km) **A 51.5** (82.9 km) Paved double-ended Scenic Byway turnouts both sides of highway.

S 75.2 (121 km) **A 51.8** (83.4 km) Bridge over **Ingram Creek**; pink salmon fishing (even years).

S 75 (120.7 km) **A 52** (83.7 km) Paved turnout to west; Welcome to the Kenai Peninsula sign. *Highway begins ascent to Turnagain Pass southbound.*

Passing lane begins southbound.

S 74.5 (119.9 km) **A 52.5** (84.5 km) Long paved double-ended turnout to east.

S 72.5 (116.7 km) **A 54.5** (87.7 km) Double-ended paved turnout to east.

S 71.5 (115.1 km) **A 55.5** (89.3 km) Long paved double-ended turnout to west.

S 71.2 (114.6 km) **A 55.8** (89.8 km) Double-ended paved turnout to west.

S 71 (114.3 km) **A 56** (90.1 km) Slow vehicle turnout to east.

S 69.9 (112.5 km) **A 57.1** (91.9 km) Scenic viewpoint with double-ended parking area to west. The highway traverses an area of mountain meadows and parklike stands of spruce, hemlock, birch and aspen interlaced with glacier-fed streams. The many flowers seen in surrounding alpine meadows here include lupine, wild geranium, yellow and purple violets, mountain heliotrope, lousewort and paintbrush.

S 69.3 (111.5 km) **A 57.7** (92.8 km) Passing lane ends southbound.

S 69 (111 km) **A 58** (93.3 km) Slow vehicle turnout to east.

S 68.9 (110.9 km) **A 58.1** (93.5 km) Divided highway begins southbound, ends northbound.

S 68.5 (110.2 km) **A 58.5** (94.1 km) **Turnagain Pass Recreation Area** (elev. 988 feet/301m). Parking area, restrooms and dumpster (southbound lane). *Emergency call box.* U-turn. Turnagain Pass Recreation Area is a favorite winter recreation area for snowmobilers (west side of highway) and cross-country skiers (east side of highway). Snow depths here frequently exceed 12 feet/4m.

S 68.1 (109.6 km) **A 58.9** (94.8 km) Parking area, restrooms and dumpster for northbound traffic. U-turn.

S 67.8 (109.1 km) **A 59.2** (95.3 km) Bridge over Lyon Creek.

S 67.6 (108.8 km) **A 59.4** (95.6 km) Divided highway ends southbound, begins northbound.

Passing lane on an upgrade as Seward Highway climbs through Turnagain Pass. (© Barbara Willard)

S 66.8 (107.5 km) **A 60.2** (96.9 km) Paved double-ended turnout to east.

S 65.5 (105.4 km) **A 61.5** (99 km) Bridge over Bertha Creek. Bertha Creek USFS campground; 12 sites, water, toilets, firepits, table, dumpsters and $9 fee.

S 65.4 (105.2 km) **A 61.6** (99.1 km) Parking area to west.

S 65.2 (104.9 km) **A 61.8** (99.4 km) Passing lane begins southbound.

S 64.8 (104.3 km) **A 62.2** (100.1 km) Bridge over Spokane Creek.

S 64.1 (103.1 km) **A 62.9** (101.2 km) Pete's Creek. Passing lane ends southbound.

S 63.7 (102.5 km) **A 63.3** (101.9 km) Johnson Pass (Chugach National Forest) north trailhead. This 23-mile-/37-km-long trail is a good, fairly level family trail, which follows a portion of the Old Iditarod trail which went from Seward to Nome. See **Milepost S 32.6.**

Johnson Pass trail leads to **Bench Lake,** which has arctic grayling, and **Johnson Lake,** which has rainbow trout. Both lakes are about halfway in on trail.

S 63.3 (101.9 km) **A 63.7** (102.5 km) Bridge over Granite Creek. Traditional halfway point on highway between Anchorage and Seward.

S 63 (101.4 km) **A 64** (103 km) Granite Creek USFS campground, 0.8 mile/1.3 km east of highway; 19 sites (most beside creek), water, toilets, dumpsters, tables, firepits and $9 fee. **Granite Creek,** small Dolly Varden.

S 62.8 (101.1 km) **A 64.2** (103.3 km) Passing lane next mile southbound.

S 62 (99.8 km) **A 65** (104.6 km) Bridge over East Fork Sixmile Creek.

CAUTION: Watch for moose next 4 miles southbound.

S 61.5 (99 km) **A 65.5** (105.4 km) Passing lane next 0.7 mile southbound.

S 61 (98.2 km) **A 66** (106.2 km) Bridge over Silvertip Creek.

Portage Glacier Road Log

Distance is measured from junction with the Seward Highway (J).

J 0 Junction with Seward Highway at **Milepost S 78.9.**
CAUTION: Alaska Railroad tracks, rough crossing.

J 2.4 (3.8 km) Paved turnout. Explorer Glacier viewpoint on right.

J 3.1 (5 km) Bridge. Beaver dam visible from road.

J 3.7 (5.9 km) Black Bear USFS campground; 12 sites (2 will accommodate medium-sized trailers), toilets, water, firepits, dumpsters, tables, $9 fee. Pleasant wooded area. ▲

J 4.1 (6.6 km) Bridge over Williwaw Creek. USFS campground, south of road below Middle Glacier; 38 campsites, toilets, dumpsters, water, firepits, tables, $10 single, $15 double (reservations available, phone 1-877-444-NRRS). Beautiful campground. Campfire programs in the amphitheater; check bulletin board for schedule. Spawning red salmon and dog salmon can be viewed (from late July to mid-September) from Williwaw Creek observation deck near campground entrance. Self-guided Williwaw nature trail off the campground loop road goes through moose and beaver habitat. ▲

J 5.2 (8.4 km) Paved road forks at Portage Glacier Lodge (description follows); left fork leads to visitor center (see **Milepost J 5.5**). Take right fork 0.8 mile/ 1.3 km to parking lot; 1.2 miles/1.9 km to Byron Glacier overlook; and 1.5 miles/ 2.4 km to MV *Ptarmigan* sightseeing boat cruise dock and passenger waiting facility.

Visible from Portage Glacier Road and Beggich, Boggs Visitor Center is the **Whittier Access Road**, currently under construction and scheduled to open in May 2000. This major engineering project includes new road tunnels through the mountain side. Whittier is currently accessible by vehicle only via the Alaska Railroad shuttle from **Milepost S 80.3** Seward Highway.

Portage Glacier Lodge, a family-owned day lodge, open daily from 9 A.M. to 7 P.M., year-round. Located in Chugach National Forest, across the street from Begich, Boggs Visitor Center. A great place for lunch! A wonderful place to shop! The cafeteria serves

Portage Glacier Road offers camping and glacier viewing. (© Ruth von Spalding)

hearty soups, sandwiches and desserts. Espresso Bar! It's a must to sample the fudge, made daily on site. The gift shop is not a typical gift shop. You'll find an art gallery approach, presenting Alaskan

Indian and Eskimo carvings, masks and jewelry. Friendly, knowledgeable local staff will answer any questions. You'll also find Limited Edition Collectibles, made in Alaska souvenirs, and a huge postcard and card display featuring Alaskan photographers. Mail orders welcome. We will ship your purchase anywhere. P.O. Box 469, Girdwood, AK 99587; (907) 783-3117; Fax (907) 783-3004. E-mail: portageldg@aol.com.
[ADVERTISEMENT]

J 5.5 (8.8 km) **Begich, Boggs Visitor Center** at Portage Glacier and Portage Lake. Open daily in summer (9 A.M.–6 P.M.); weekends in winter (10 A.M.–4 P.M.). Phone the visitor center at (907) 783-2326 or the U.S. Forest Service district office at (907) 783-3242 for current schedule.

Forest Service naturalists are available to answer questions and provide information about Chugach National Forest resources. There are displays on glaciers and on the natural history of the area. The award-winning film *Voices from the Ice* is shown in the theater hourly. Schedules of hikes and programs led by naturalists are posted at the center. One of the most popular activities is the iceworm safari. (Often regarded as a hoax, iceworms actually exist; the small, black worms thrive at temperatures just above freezing.) A self-guided interpretive trail about glacial landforms begins just south of the visitor center.

Large paved parking area provides views of Portage Lake. There are several excellent spots in the area to observe salmon spawning (August and September) in Portage Creek and its tributaries.

**Return to Milepost S 78.9
Seward Highway**

S 59 (94.9 km) **A 68** (109.4 km) Paved parking area to west overlooking Granite Creek. Excellent place to photograph this glacial stream.

A bike trail and walking path leads south to the Hope Highway junction.

S 58.5 (94.1 km) **A 68.5** (110.2 km) Double-ended parking area.

S 57.7 (92.8 km) **A 69.3** (111.5 km) Viewpoint to west; access to bike trail.

S 56.7 (91.2 km) **A 70.3** (113.1 km) Rest area to west; access to bike trail and Old Canyon Creek bridge.

S 56.5 (90.9 km) **A 70.5** (113.4 km) Canyon Creek bridge; overlook.

Staging area for raft trips on Sixmile Creek.
Nenana Raft Adventures, Inc. See display ad this section.

S 56.3 (90.6 km) **A 70.7** (113.8 km)

Junction with Hope Highway to historic mining community of Hope. See HOPE HIGHWAY log on page 570.

S 56.2 (90.4 km) **A 70.8** (113.9 km) Passing lane begins southbound as highway climbs.

S 54.8 (88.2 km) **A 72.2** (116.2 km) Paved parking area to east.

S 53.5 (86.1 km) **A 73.5** (118.3 km) Turnout to east.

S 53.4 (85.9 km) **A 73.6** (118.4 km) Passing lane ends southbound.

S 52.7 (84.8 km) **A 74.3** (119.6 km)

Hope Highway Log

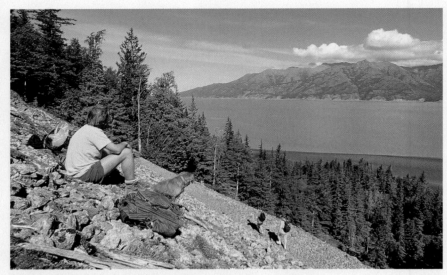

Hikers on Gull Rock Trail near Hope. (© Beth Davidow)

The paved 17.7-mile/28.5-km Hope Highway leads northwest to the historic community of Hope on the south side of Turnagain Arm and provides access to the Resurrection Creek area.
Distance is measured from junction with the Seward Highway (J).

J 0 Junction with Seward Highway at **Milepost S 56.7.**
J 0.1 (0.2 km) Silvertip highway maintenance station.
J 0.7 (1.1 km) Double-ended paved turnout to east; road access to creek.

J 0.9 (1.4 km) Highway parallels Sixmile Creek, a glacial stream. There are many paved turnouts along the Hope Highway, some with views of Turnagain Arm.
J 1 (1.6 km) **Nova River Runners**. See display ad this section.
J 1.4 (2.3 km) Beaver marsh to east.
J 2.3 (3.7 km) Large paved turnout to east. Moose may often be seen in Sixmile Creek valley below. The old gold mining town of Sunrise City, with a population of 5,000, was founded in 1895 at the mouth of Sixmile Creek. The present community of Sunrise has a population of about 20.

J 3.4 (5.5 km) Large paved turnout to east; trail access to creek.
J 3.9 (6.3 km) Large paved turnout to east; trail access to creek.
J 10 (16.1 km) Double-ended paved turnout to east overlooking Turnagain Arm.
J 11.1 (17.9 km) Large paved turnout to east overlooking Turnagain Arm.
J 11.8 (19 km) Double-ended paved turnout to east overlooking Turnagain Arm.
J 15.8 (25.4 km) **Henry's One Stop.** See display ad this section.   ▲
J 15.9 (25.6 km) Bear Creek Lodge.
J 16 (25.7 km) **Discovery Cabins.** See display ad this section.
J 16.2 (26 km) Turnoff to south for Hope airport; USFS Resurrection Pass trailhead, 4 miles/6.4 km south on Resurrection Creek Road; Resurrection Trail Resort, 4.6 miles/7.4 km; and Coeur d'Alene Campground on Palmer Creek Road, 7.6 miles/12.2 km.   ▲
The 38-mile-/61-km-long **Resurrection Pass Trail** climbs from an elevation of 400 feet/122m at the trailhead to Resurrection Pass (elev. 2,600 feet/792m) and down to the south trailhead at **Milepost S 53.1** on the Sterling Highway. There are 8 cabins on the trail. Parking area at the trailhead.
Coeur d'Alene, USFS primitive campground has 5 sites (not recommended for large RVs or trailers); toilets, tables, firepits; no water, no garbage service, no camping fee. Palmer Creek Road continues past the campground to alpine country above 1,500 feet/457m elevation, and views of Turnagain Arm and Resurrection Creek valley. The road past the campground is rough and narrow and not recommended for low-clearance vehicles. ▲

Cafe in downtown Hope
(© Susan Cole Kelly)

J 16.5 (26.6 km) Paved Hope Highway ends; turnoff onto Old Hope Highway loop for Hope businesses.

Discovery Cafe. See display ad this section.

HOPE (pop. 224); post office, motel, bed and breakfast, cafe, grocery store and gift shop. **Visitor Information:** Hope Chamber of Commerce, P.O. Box 89, Hope, AK 99605, www.advenalaska.com/hope.

This historic mining community was founded in 1896 by gold seekers working Resurrection Creek and its tributary streams. Today, many Anchorage residents have vacation homes here. The waterfront here is a favorite fishing spot.

Hope Gold Rush B&B. Next right past post office. Enjoy a delicious home-style breakfast along with the pioneer ambiance of this historic log cabin built by gold prospector John Hirshey in 1916. The charming guest cabin provides a living room and a full bath with sleeping accommodations for up to 5 persons. MasterCard/VISA accepted. p.O. Box 36, Hope, AK 99605. Phone (907) 782-3436. E-mail: Fayrene@alaska.net. [ADVERTISEMENT]

J 17 (27.3 km) Road to historic Hope townsite. Interpretive sign at intersection. The original townsite of Hope City was founded in 1896. Portions of the town destroyed by the 1964 earthquake are marked with dotted lines on the map sign.

J 17.1 (27.5 km) Resurrection Creek bridge.

J 17.7 (28.4 km) Gas station.

J 17.8 (28.6 km) Hope Highway ends at Porcupine USFS campground; 24 sites, tables, tent spaces, toilets, firepits, dumpster, drinking water and $9 fee. Gull Rock trailhead. ▲

**Return to Milepost S 56.7
Seward Highway**

Scenic Byway turnout.

S 52.4 (84.3 km) **A 74.6** (120.1 km) Passing lane begins southbound as highway climbs toward Summit Lake.

S 52 (83.7 km) **A 75** (120.7 km) Scenic viewpoint to east.

S 48 (77.2 km) **A 79** (127.1 km) Fresno Creek bridge; paved double-ended turnout to east at south end of bridge.

S 47.6 (76.6 km) **A 79.4** (127.8 km) Double-ended paved turnout to east on lake.

S 47.2 (76 km) **A 79.8** (128.4 km) Paved double-ended turnout to east next to Lower Summit Lake; a favorite photo stop. Extremely picturesque with lush growth of wildflowers in summer.

Upper and Lower Summit lakes, good spring and fall fishing for landlocked Dolly Varden (goldenfins), ranging in size from 6 to 11 inches, flies and single salmon eggs. ►

S 46 (74 km) **A 81** (130.4 km) Colorado Creek bridge. Tenderfoot Creek USFS campground 0.6 mile/0.9 km from highway; 28 sites, water, toilets (wheelchair accessible), dumpsters, tables, firepits, boat launch, $9 fee. &▲

S 45.8 (73.7 km) **A 81.2** (130.7 km) Summit Lake Lodge; open year-round. *Emergency call box*. Winter avalanche area begins southbound.

Summit Lake Lodge. Genuine hospitality on the north shore of Summit Lake in

Alaska's most beautiful log lodge. Located in the heart of Chugach National Forest, it is a landmark for many. The view is spectacular and the food excellent. Complete menu from eye-opening omelettes to mouth-watering steaks. Enjoy our cozy motel and relaxing lounge. Open year-round. Fishing, hiking, photography, cross-country skiing, snowmobiling. It's a must stop for every visitor in the last frontier. See display ad this section. [ADVERTISEMENT] ▲

S 45.5 (73.2 km) **A 81.5** (131.2 km) Upper Summit Lake. Paved turnout to east.

S 44.5 (71.6 km) **A 82.5** (132.7 km) Large

paved double-ended turnout with interpretive sign to east at end of Upper Summit Lake.

S 44.3 (71.3 km) **A 82.7** (133.1 km) Beaver dams.

S 44 (70.8 km) **A 83** (133.6 km) Gravel turnout to east. Avalanche gun emplacement.

S 43.8 (70.5 km) **A 83.2** (133.9 km) Winter avalanche area begins northbound. Avalanche gates.

S 43.7 (70.3 km) **A 83.3** (134.1 km) Paved double-ended turnout to east.

S 42.6 (68.6 km) **A 84.4** (135.8 km) Summit Creek bridge.

S 42.2 (67.9 km) **A 84.8** (136.5 km) Quartz Creek bridge.

S 41.4 (66.6 km) **A 85.6** (137.8 km) Passing lane next 1 mile/1.6 km northbound.

S 39.6 (63.7 km) **A 87.4** (140.7 km) Avalanche gates.

S 39.4 (63.4 km) **A 87.6** (141 km) Devils Pass trailhead; parking area and toilets to west. This USFS trail starts at an elevation of 1,000 feet/305m and follows Devils Creek to Devils Pass (elev. 2,400 feet/732m), continuing on to Devils Pass Lake and Resurrection Pass trail. Hiking time to Devils Pass is about 5^1/2 hours.

S 39 (62.8 km) **A 88** (141.6 km) Truck lane extends northbound to **Milepost S 39.3**.

S 38.6 (62.1 km) **A 88.4** (142.3 km) Paved turnout to west adjacent **Jerome Lake**, rainbow and Dolly Varden to 22 inches, use salmon egg clusters, year-round, still fish. ►

S 38.4 (61.6 km) **A 88.6** (142.6 km) Paved double-ended Scenic Byway turnout to west overlooking Jerome Lake.

S 38.2 (61.5 km) **A 88.8** (142.9 km) Truck lane ends northbound.

S 37.7 (60.7 km) **A 89.3** (143.7 km) Southbound-only exit for Sterling Highway (Alaska Route 1) to west. Continue straight ahead on Alaska Route 9 for Seward.

First **junction** southbound with Sterling Highway to Soldotna, Homer and other Sterling Highway communities. Turn to **Milepost S 38.3** in the STERLING HIGHWAY for log.

ALASKA ROUTE 9

S 37.2 (59.9 km) **A 89.8** (144.5 km) Paved turnout to west overlooking Tern Lake for Seward-bound travelers.

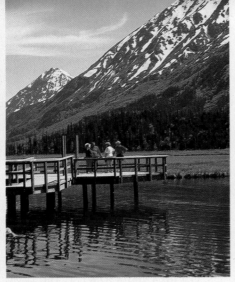

Tern Lake viewing area at Sterling Highway junction. (© Loren Taft)

S 37 (59.5 km) **A 90** (144.8 km) **Tern Lake Junction.** Turnoff to west (2-way road) on Sterling Highway for access to Tern Lake and **Tern Lake USFS Wildlife Viewing Platform.** Interpretive signs and ranger talks in summer. This is a good spot to see nesting birds, mountain goats, sheep and occasion-

ally moose and bear. Continue around the lake to the Tern Lake picnic area; walk-in picnic sites with water, tables, toilets and fire grates. Salmon-spawning channel with a viewing platform and interpretive signs. Tern Lake is a good spot for bird watching in summer. ▲

Second turnoff southbound and first junction northbound of the Seward Highway with the Sterling Highway (Alaska Route 1) to Soldotna, Kenai and Homer. Turn to **Milepost S 37** in the STERLING HIGHWAY section for log.

Continue straight ahead on Alaska Route 9 for Seward.

S 36.7 (59.1 km) **A 90.3** (145.3 km) Truck lane begins northbound.

S 36.4 (58.6 km) **A 90.6** (145.8 km) Avalanche gates.

S 35.7 (57.5 km) **A 91.3** (146.9 km) Outfitter for guided horse pack trips.

Horseback Adventures Alaska. See display ad this section.

S 35.3 (56.8 km) **A 91.7** (147.6 km) End avalanche area southbound.

S 35 (56.3 km) **A 92** (148 km) For the next 3 miles/4.8 km, many small waterfalls tumble down the brushy slopes. Winter avalanche area between **Milepost S 35.3** and **34.6.** You are driving through the Kenai mountain range.

S 34.1 (54.9 km) **A 92.9** (149.5 km) Turnout to west; large beaver dam.

S 33.1 (53.3 km) **A 93.9** (151.1 km) Carter Lake USFS trailhead No. 4 to west; parking and toilets. Trail starts at an elevation of 500 feet/152m and climbs 986 feet/300m to **Carter Lake** (stocked with rainbow trout). Trail is good, but steep; hiking time about 1 1/2 hours. Good access to sheep and mountain goat country. Excellent snowmobiling area in winter. ⌒

S 32.6 (52.5 km) **A 94.4** (151.9 km) Johnson Pass USFS south trailhead with parking area, toilet. North trailhead at **Milepost S 63.7.**

S 32.5 (52.3 km) **A 94.5** (152.1 km) Large

paved double-ended turnout; USFS information sign on life cycle of salmon; short trail to observation deck on stream where spawning salmon may be seen in August.

S 32.4 (52.1 km) **A 94.6** (152.2 km) Cook Inlet Aquaculture Association. **Trail Lake Fish Hatchery** on Moose Creek; display room. Open 8 A.M. to 5 P.M. daily; phone (907) 288-3688.

S 31.8 (51.1 km) **A 95.2** (153.2 km) Paved double-ended rest area to east on Upper Trail Lake; toilets.

S 30.5 (49.1 km) **A 96.5** (155.3 km) **Alpenglow Cottage.** A view from every window and exclusively yours. Two bedrooms, sleeps 4–6. Equipped custom kitchen; private bath. Enjoy the comfortable atmosphere with spacious deck and flowers. Annie's fresh fruit scones served each morning. Open year-round. Credit cards accepted. Minutes to hiking trails, boating, winter skiing. (907) 288-3142. E-mail: gaule@ptialaska.net. [ADVERTISEMENT]

S 30 (48.3 km) **A 97** (156.1 km) Short side road to large undeveloped gravel parking area on Upper Trail Lake; boat launch.

S 29.9 (48.1 km) **A 97.1** (156.3 km) Gravel turnout by Trail Lake.

Pioneers Lodge, featuring private colonial-style cabins with oil heat, electricity, outdoor facilities and hot showers, laundry. Art gallery and gift store all in a pristine setting at Mile 29.9 Seward Highway. Budget rates, some with kitchenettes. Look for the "Open" sign. Serving since 1956. General Delivery, Moose Pass, AK 99631. Phone (907) 288-3645. [ADVERTISEMENT]

S 29.7 (47.8 km) **A 97.3** (156.6 km) Highway maintenance station.

S 29.4 (47.3 km) **A 97.6** (157.1 km) Large working waterwheel that turns a grindstone, built by the late Ed Estes, on way into Moose Pass. Parking area and sign at waterwheel which reads: "Moose Pass is a peaceful little town. If you have an ax to grind, do it here."

MOOSE PASS (pop. 134) has a motel, bed and breakfast, log cabins for rent, RV park, general store, gift shop, restaurant, salmon bake, post office and highway maintenance station. Pay phone outside GTE building. Alaska State Troopers, emergency only phone 911. This mountain village on Upper Trail Lake was a construction camp on the Alaska Railroad in 1912. Local resident Ed Estes attributed the name Moose Pass to a 1904 observation by Nate White of the first moose recorded in this area. Another version holds that "in 1903, a mail carrier driving a team of dogs had considerable trouble gaining the right-of-way from a giant moose." A post office was established in 1928. ▲

Moose Pass has a 1.3-mile-/2.1-km-long paved bike trail which winds along Trail Lake from the Moose Pass ball diamond to the McFadden house on the south. Gravel turnout by lake.

The main street of town is the site of the Annual Moose Pass Summer Festival, a community-sponsored event which takes place the weekend nearest summer solstice (June 21). The festival features a triathlon, arts and crafts booths, a barbecue, auction and other events.

Estes Brothers Groceries & Water Wheel. See display ad this section.

Trail Lake Lodge. Home cooking, reasonable rates, friendly staff and clean facilities welcome you to this landmark lodge. Conveniently located in the heart of the Chugach National Forest trail system on the shores of scenic Trail Lake, a short drive to

Seward and Kenai Fjords National Park. Phone (800) 208-0200 or (907) 288-3101. See display ad this section. [ADVERTISEMENT]

S 29.1 (46.8 km) **A 97.9** (157.6 km) **Moose Pass RV Park.** 30 spaces. Electric hookups. Scenic campground-like setting. Close to restaurant, post office, small store, telephone. Rural area in beautiful surroundings. Convenient to Seward, but away from the crowds. Just off main highway. [ADVERTISEMENT] ▲

S 28.9 (46.5 km) **A 98.1** (157.9 km) **Midnight Sun Log Cabins.** See display ad this section.

S 26 (41.8 km) **A 101** (162.5 km) Lower Trail Lake. Timbered slopes of Madson Mountain (elev. 5,269 feet/1,605m) to the west. Crescent Lake lies just west of Madson.

S 25.8 (41.5 km) **A 101.2** (162.9 km) Gravel turnout to west.

S 25.4 (40.9 km) **A 101.6** (163.5 km) Bridge over Trail River. Floatplane base.

S 25 (40.2 km) **A 102** (164.1 km) Bridge over Falls Creek.

S 24.2 (38.9 km) **A 102.8** (165.4 km) Side road leads 1.2 miles/1.9 km to Trail River USFS campground; 64 sites, picnic tables, firepits, dumpsters, toilets, and volleyball and horseshoe area. Day-use group picnic area. Spacious, wooded campsites in tall spruce on shore of Kenai Lake and Lower Trail River. Pull-through sites available. Fee $9 single, $13 double, reservations available; phone 1-877-444-NRRS. Campground host may be in residence during summer, providing fishing and hiking information. Good spot for mushrooming and berry picking in August. ▲

Lower Trail River, lake trout, rainbow and Dolly Varden to 25 inches, July, August and September, use salmon eggs, small spinners. Access via Lower Trail River campground road. **Trail River,** Dolly Varden 12 to 20 inches, spring and fall, and rainbow 12 to 20 inches, spring; use fresh eggs. ⬿

S 24.1 (38.8 km) **A 102.9** (165.6 km) **Crown Point Lodge.** See display ad this section.

S 23.4 (37.7 km) **A 103.6** (166.7 km) *CAUTION: Railroad crossing.* USFS Kenai Lake work center (no information services available). Report forest fires here.

Private Aircraft: Lawing landing strip; elev. 475 feet/144m; length 2,200 feet/671m; gravel; unattended.

S 23.1 (37.1 km) **A 103.9** (167.2 km) **Ptarmigan Creek** bridge and USFS picnic area and campground with 16 sites, water, toilets, tables, firepits and dumpsters, $9 fee (reservations phone 1-877-444-NRRS). Fair to good fishing in creek and in lake outlets at **Ptarmigan Lake** (hike in) for Dolly Varden. Watch for spawning salmon in Ptarmigan Creek in August. ⬿◂

Ptarmigan Creek USFS trail No. 14 begins at campground (elev. 500 feet/152m) and leads 3.5 miles/5.6 km to Ptarmigan Lake (elev. 755 feet/230m). Trail is steep in spots; round-trip hiking time 5 hours. Good chance of seeing sheep, goats, moose and bears. Carry insect repellent. Trail is poor for winter use due to avalanche hazard.

S 23 (37 km) **A 104** (167.3 km) Turnoff for Alaska Nellie's Homestead. The late Nellie Neal–Lawing arrived in Alaska in 1915. Her colorful life included cooking for the railroad workers and big game hunting and guiding.

Alaska Nellie's Inn, Inc. B&B. See display ad this section.

S 22.9 (36.9 km) **A 104.1** (167.5 km)

Paved viewpoint to west overlooking Kenai Lake. This lake (elev. 436 feet/132m) extends 24 miles/39 km from the head of the Kenai River on the west to the mouth of Snow River on the east. A sign here explains how glacier meltwater gives the lake its distinctive color.

Winter avalanche area next 3 miles/4.8 km southbound.

S 22.5 (36.2 km) **A 104.5** (168.2 km) Rough gravel double-ended turnout to east.

S 21.3 (34.3 km) **A 105.7** (170.1 km) Gravel turnout to east overlooking lake.

S 20.2 (32.5 km) **A 106.8** (171.9 km) Avalanche gun emplacement.

S 20.1 (32.3 km) **A 106.9** (172 km) Gravel turnout. Avalanche area ends southbound.

S 19.9 (32 km) **A 107.1** (172.4 km) I.R.B.I. Knife Shop; open year-round.

I.R.B.I. Knives. See display ad this section.

S 19.5 (31.4 km) **A 107.5** (173 km) Victor Creek bridge. Victor Creek USFS trail No. 23 begins here. A 2-mile/3.2-km hike with good view of mountains.

Mrs. Leary's Alaskan Gallery and Senior B&B, located just south of the Victor Creek Bridge at Milepost 19.5 (27066 Seward Highway), in our 3 generation hand-built country home. Our delightful all-Alaska gift shop features books, art work and crafts by locals. Our guest bedroom is located on the second floor with queen-size bed (satin bedding for sensitive skin) and adjoins the bathroom, dining area and parlour. We serve a heart-friendly breakfast of salmon, sliced fresh fruit, toasted bagels and coffee or herbal tea. Smoking allowed in parlour area. $50 per

night. (907) 288-3168. [ADVERTISEMENT]

S 19.4 (31.2 km) **A 107.6** (173.2 km) **Renfro's Lakeside Retreat** offers the best of Alaska, beautiful cabins and a wilderness setting. Log cabins constructed from local trees feature a fully-equipped kitchen, modern bathroom and comfortably sleep 5–6 guests. Situated on the shores of Kenai Lake and surrounded by mountains, the magnificent scenery and wilderness setting lends itself to great wildlife viewing and fishing. RV sites offer easy access to the lake and each site has water, electricity and a beautiful view. A convenience store is planned for the spring of 1999. 27121 Seward Highway, Seward, AK 99664. Toll-free (877) 288-5059. See display ad. [ADVERTISEMENT] ▲

S 17.7 (28.5 km) **A 109.3** (175.9 km) Bridge over center channel of Snow River. This river has 2 forks that flow into Kenai Lake.

S 17 (27 km) **A 110** (177 km) Primrose Road. Access to bed and breakfast. Turn west for Primrose USFS campground, 1 mile/1.6 km from the highway. (Campground access road leads past private homes. Drive carefully!) The campground, overlooking Kenai Lake, has 10 sites, toilets, dumpsters, tables, firepits, boat ramp, water, $9 fee. Primrose trail (6.5 miles/10.5 km) starts from the campground and connects with Lost Creek trail (7 miles/11.2 km). High alpine hike to **Lost Lake**, rainbow fishing (stocked); trail is posted. ▲

Bridge over south channel of Snow River.

S 16.2 (26.1 km) **A 110.8** (178.3 km) Gravel turnout to east.

S 16 (25.7 km) **A 111** (178.6 km) Snow River hostel.

S 15 (24.1 km) **A 112** (180.2 km) Watch for moose in ponds and meadows.

S 14.9 (24 km) **A 112.1** (180.4 km) Gravel turnout to east.

S 14 (22.5 km) **A 113** (181.9 km) *CAUTION: Railroad crossing.*

S 13.3 (21.4 km) **A 113.7** (183 km) Grayling Lake USFS trailhead to west, large paved parking area to east. Grayling Lake trail No. 20, 1.6 miles/2.6 km, connects with trails to Meridian and Leech lakes. Good spot for photos of Snow River valley. Watch for moose. **Grayling Lake**, 6- to 12-inch grayling, use flies, May to October. ⚓

S 12 (19.3 km) **A 115** (185.1 km) Alaska Railroad crosses under highway.

S 11.6 (18.6 km) **A 115.4** (185.7 km) Gravel parking area to west and trail to **Golden Fin Lake**, Dolly Varden averaging 8 inches. This is a 0.6-mile/1-km hike on a very wet trail: wear rubber footwear. Ski trails in winter. ⚓

S 10.8 (17.4 km) **A 116.2** (187 km) Large gravel turnout to east.

S 8.5 (13.6 km) **A 118.5** (190.7 km) Gravel turnout to west.

S 8.3 (13.4 km) **A 118.7** (191 km) Paved turnout by creek to east. Leaving Chugach National Forest land southbound.

S 8 (12.9 km) **A 119** (191.5 km) **Grouse Creek** bridge. Dolly Varden fishing. ⚓

S 7.4 (11.9 km) **A 119.6** (192.5 km) **Grouse Lake** access road. Good ice fishing for Dolly Varden in winter. ⚓

S 7.1 (11.4 km) **A 119.9** (193 km) Old Mill subdivision.

S 6.6 (10.6 km) **A 120.4** (193.7 km) Bear Creek bridge and Bear Lake Road; access to gas station, RV parks, bed and breakfast, and a flying service. Drive in 0.7 mile/1.1 km on Bear Lake Road to see a state-operated fish weir. Silver and red (sockeye) salmon are trapped to provide life-cycle data and also eggs for the state's salmon stocking program.

A Creekside RV Park & Motel. See display ad this section. ▲

Bear Lake Air. See display ad this section.

Bear Creek RV Park, drive ¹/₂ mile on Bear Lake Road. Good Sam Park has full and partial hookups, dump station, 4 private restrooms with showers, cable TV, travelers lounge, propane, laundry, convenience store, ice, video rentals. 2 free showers per site. Pay phone inside. Excellent water. (907) 224-5725. Fax service available. Bunkhouse for rent. Free shuttle when reservations are booked through our office for glacier and fishing trips. Auto and RV repair and service. RV and boat storage. High pressure wash. Short walk to fish weir. Bear Creek RV Park is not to be mistaken for A Creekside RV Park located at the gas station on the corner of the Seward Highway and Bear Lake Road. Internet: http://www.alaska.net/~bear. E-mail: Hettick@alaska.net. See display ad this section. [ADVERTISEMENT] ▲

S 6.3 (10.1 km) **A 120.7** (194.2 km) Lake Drive; access to bed and breakfasts.

Eagle Song Bed & Breakfast is located in a peaceful country settting in the shadow

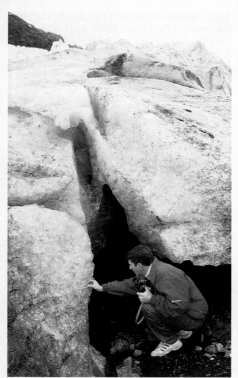

Visitor gets a very close-up view of Exit Glacier. (© David Foster, staff)

Windsong Lodge, restaurant, cabins, RV park, IdidaRide dogsled rides, and bed and breakfasts; turn right onto loop road (old Exit Glacier Road) immediately after turning off highway.

The 9-mile/14.5-km Exit Glacier Road (maintained by DOT/PF May to September, depending on snow) is paved for the first 4 miles/6.4 km. The road ends at a parking lot with toilets and picnic area next to Exit Glacier ranger station in Kenai Fjords National Park. Look for bears high on the hillside opposite the ranger station. Walk-in campground with 9 sites (no fee, reservations). A public-use cabin is available; access in winter by cross-country skis, dogsled or snow machine; permit required, phone (907) 224-3175. ▲

The National Park Service operates a visitor center at the ranger station (seasonal). The flat, easy 0.8-mile Lower Loop trail leads through alder forest to outwash plain; pick your own route to base of glacier. The longer half-mile Upper Loop trail offers excellent views of the glacier. The first 0.2 mile/0.3 km of this trail is paved and wheelchair accessible. There is also an easy 0.8 mile/1.3 km nature trail loop with 10 interpretive signs on forest succession. A strenuous 3.5-mile/5.6-km trail leads to Harding Icefield from the parking lot (a ranger patrols this trail). Summer activities include ranger-led nature walks at 10 A.M. and 2 P.M. daily. Park Information Line: (907) 224-2132. Worth the drive to see an active glacier up close. *CAUTION: Falling ice at face of glacier, stay behind warning signs.* ♿

The trailhead for Resurrection River trail is located just before crossing the Resurrection River bridge on the access road. The 16-mile/25.7-km USFS trail ties in with the Russian Lakes trail. It is part of the 75-mile/121-km Hope-to-Seward route. *CAUTION: Black and brown bears also use this trail.*

Creekside Cabins Bed & Breakfast. See display ad this section.

IdidaRide Sled Dog Tours. See display ad this section.

of an active bald eagle's nest. Easy 15-minute commute from Seward. We offer 3 bedrooms with queen-size beds, 1 bedroom with twin beds, 2 shared baths. Full country breakfast, smoking outside, adults only. VISA and MasterCard. (907) 224-8755. P.O. Box 2231, Seward, AK 99664. E-mail: eaglesng@ptialaska.net. [ADVERTISEMENT]

0.2 Winterset Guest House. First-class accommodations at $85/DO. Land's End down comforters on all our beds and quality mattresses for a good night's sleep. Hearty continental breakfast buffet. All rooms have private baths, cable TV. Laundry facilities, refrigerator, microwave, phone, coffee maker available to guests. Open year-round. (Discounted winter rates.) Smoke-free environment, wooded area with great mountain view. We will assist you with all your activity plans and book Fjord tours, fishing charters at discounted prices. Long-time Alaskan hosts. (907) 224-5185. [ADVERTISEMENT]

S 5.9 (9.4 km) **A 121.1** (194.8 km) **Salmon Creek** bridge. Good fishing in stream for sea-run Dolly Varden averaging 10 inches, use single salmon eggs, begins about Aug. 1. ◗

S 5.4 (8.7 km) **A 121.6** (195.7 km) **Dave & Marie's Excellent Adventures** (west side of highway). Visitor information center, fishing, sightseeing, kayaking, dinner cruises, gifts, snacks. We can help you choose the tour or adventure that suits you. We specialize in deep-sea halibut and silver salmon fishing. Personalized service, early reservations recommended. (907) 224-2030. E-mail: dmea@arctic.net. Visit our web site: www.AlaskaOne.com/dmexcell. [ADVERTISEMENT]

S 5.2 (8.4 km) **A 121.8** (196 km) Bear Creek volunteer fire department.

S 3.8 (6.1 km) **A 123.2** (198.3 km) Clear Creek bridge.

S 3.7 (6 km) **A 123.3** (198.4 km) Turnoff for **Exit Glacier Road**. Access to Seward

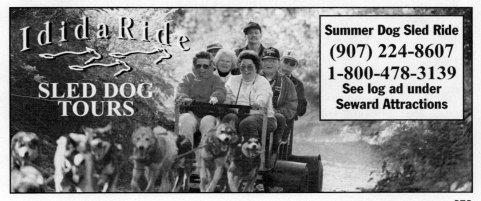

River Valley Cabins & Box Canyon Cabins. See display ad this section.

Fjords RV Park. Nestled in towering trees at Mile 1 of Exit Glacier Road, Gateway to Kenai Fjords National Park. Large open sites with water and electric hookups. Easy access.

Caravans, large groups and tenters welcome. Local activity information, glacier tour boats and fishing trips booked. Call (907) 362-3683. E-mail: Fjordstp@ptialaska.net.
[ADVERTISEMENT]   ▲

S 3.2 (5.1 km) **A 123.8** (199.2 km) Nash

Road, access to bed and breakfasts: Camelot Cottages, The Farm, Rininger's and Mom Clock's. It is a scenic 5-mile/8-km drive out Nash Road to Seward's Marine Industrial Center in the Fourth of July Creek valley. Fine views along the way and from Kertulla Point of Resurrection Bay and the city of Seward. At Mile 2.1 Nash Road is the trailhead for the Iditarod Trail, which begins at the ferry terminal in downtown Seward. Hike to Bear Lake; from north end of lake, trail continues to Mile 12 on the Seward Highway..

The Farm Bed & Breakfast Inn. Turn off Seward Highway onto Nash Road, cross the railroad tracks, turn left immediately onto Salmon Creek Road, follow signs to "The Farm." Tranquil country setting on acres of trees and lawn. Choose from our Main House ... Cottages ... Economy Bungalow ... or Kitchenette Units. Enjoy cable TV, decks, barbecue, private baths. Freezer space, laundry facilities. Families welcome. Continental breakfast. Open year-round. VISA, MasterCard, Discover. Long-time Alaskan host Jack Hoogland, Box 305, Seward, AK 99664. Reservations suggested. (907) 224-5691. Fax (907) 224-5698. E-mail: thefarm@ptialaska.net. Internet: www.alaskan.com/thefarm/. See display ad this section. [ADVERTISEMENT]

Mom Clock's Bed and Breakfast. See display ad this section.

Rininger's Bed & Breakfast (Mile 1.6 Nash Road) is located on Rabbit Run Road (left at fork). Open year-round. Large, sunny room with skylights and handcrafted furnishings. Private bath and kitchenette; sleeping loft, separate entrance. Breakfast in room at your leisure. Outdoor wood-heated sauna. Hiking and cross-country ski trails nearby. A perfect weekend getaway. Families welcome. Sleeps up to 8. Kent and Lisa Rininger, P.O. Box 548, Seward, AK 99664. (907) 224-5918.
[ADVERTISEMENT]

Camelot Cottages. See display ad this section

S 3 (4.8 km) **A 124** (199.6 km) Resurrection River; 3 channels, 3 bridges. This river flows from the Harding Icefield into Resurrection Bay just northeast of Seward. Seward city limits.

S 2.7 (4.3 km) **A 124.3** (200 km) Turnoff for Seward airport.

S 2.5 (4 km) **A 124.5** (200.4 km) Hemlock Street. Forest Acres municipal campground; water, flush toilets, 14-day limit. No tables.▲

S 2.3 (3.7 km) **A 124.7** (200.7 km) Sea Lion Drive. U.S. Air Force and U.S. Army Seward Recreation Area.

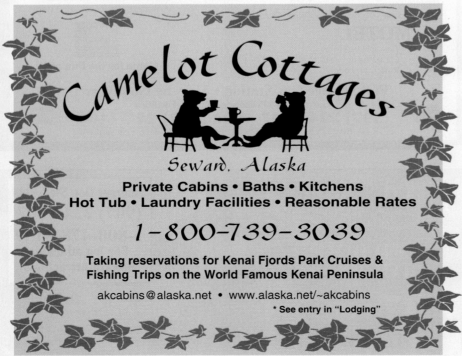

Seward Resort (Military). See display ad this section.

S 2.1 (3.4 km) A 124.9 (201 km) Dimond Boulevard.

S 2 (3.2 km) A 125 (201.1 km) Seward Chamber of Commerce–Convention and Visitors Bureau visitor center.

Seward Chamber of Commerce. See display ad this section.

S 1.8 (2.9 km) A 125.2 (201.5 km) Gas station.

S 1.7 (2.7 km) A 125.3 (201.6 km) Bear Drive; access to bed and breakfasts.

S 1.5 (2.4 km) A 125.5 (202 km) Resurrection Blvd., Seward High School.

S 1.2 (1.9 km) A 125.8 (202.4 km) Dairy Hill Lane to west. Large parking area to west with memorial to Benny Benson, who designed the Alaska state flag. Port Avenue to east, access to cruise ship and ferry dock.

S 1 (1.6 km) A 126 (202.8 km) South Harbor Street and main entrance to boat harbor.

S 0.4 (0.6 km) A 126.6 (203.7 km) Madison Street. Post office one block east.

S 0.3 (0.5 km) A 126.7 (203.9 km) Intersection of 3rd Avenue (Seward Highway) and Jefferson. Hospital 2 blocks west. Information Cache railcar at intersection.

S 0 A 127 (204.4 km) Alaska SeaLife Center/Seward Marine Education Center.

Seward

S 0 A 127 (204.4 km) Located on Resurrection Bay, east coast of Kenai Peninsula; 127 miles/204.4 km south of Anchorage by road, or 35 minutes by air. **Population: 3,040. Emergency Services: Police, Fire Department** and **Ambulance**, emergency only, phone 911. **State Troopers**, phone (907) 224-3346. **Hospital**, Providence Seward Medical Center, 1st Avenue and Jefferson Street, phone (907) 224-5205. **Maritime Search and Rescue**, phone (800) 478-5555.

Visitor Information: Available at 2 locations, operated by the Seward Chamber of Commerce–Convention and Visitors Bureau. The visitor center at **Milepost S 2** Seward Highway (2001 Seward Highway) is open 7 days a week from Memorial Day through Labor Day, weekdays the rest of the year;

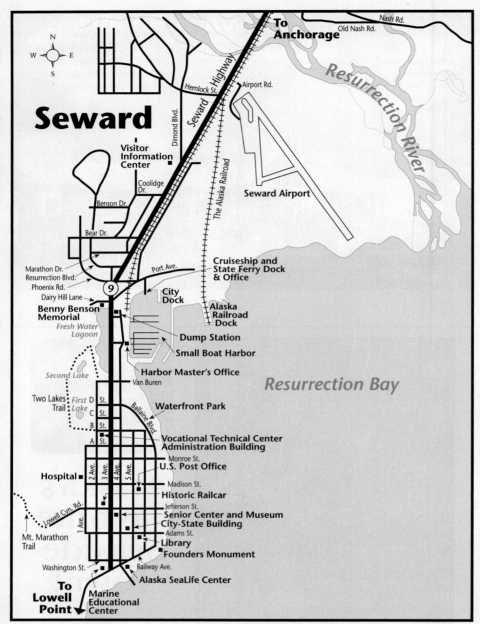

Seward

phone (907) 224-8051. The Information Cache, located in the historic railroad car *Seward* at 3rd and Jefferson Street, is open daily from 9 A.M. to 5 P.M., June through August; write Box 749, Seward, AK 99664.

Kenai Fjords National Park Visitor Center, 1212 4th Ave. (in the Small Boat Harbor), is open 8 A.M. to 7 P.M. daily, Memorial Day to Labor Day; 8:30 A.M. to 5 P.M. weekdays the remainder of the year. Information on the park, slide show, interpretive programs and bookstore. Phone (907) 224-3175 or the Park Information Line (907) 224-2132. Or write P.O. Box 1727, Seward, AK 99664.

Chugach National Forest, Seward Ranger District office, is located at 334 4th Ave. USFS personnel can provide information on hiking, camping and fishing opportunities on national forest lands. Open weekdays, 8 A.M. to 5 P.M. Mailing address: P.O. Box 390, Seward, AK 99664. Phone (907) 224-3374.

Elevation: Sea level. **Climate:** Average daily maximum temperature in July, 62°F /17°C; average daily minimum in January, 18°F/-7°C. Average annual precipitation, 67 inches; average snowfall, 80 inches. **Radio:** KSKA-FM 92, KWAVE 104.9, KPEN 102.3. **Television:** Several channels by cable. **Newspaper:** *Seward Phoenix Log* (weekly).

Private Aircraft: Seward airport, 1.7 miles/2.7 km northeast; elev. 22 feet/7m; length 4,200 feet/1,280m; asphalt; fuel 100LL, jet.

Seward—known as the "Gateway to Kenai Fjords National Park"—is a picturesque community nestled between high mountain ranges on a small rise stretching from Resurrection Bay to the foot of Mount Marathon. Thick groves of cottonwood and scattered spruce groves are found in the immediate vicinity of the city, with stands of spruce and alder growing on the surrounding mountainsides.

Downtown Seward (the main street is 4th Avenue) has a frontier-town atmosphere with some homes and buildings dating back to the early 1900s. The town was established in 1903 by railroad surveyors as an ocean terminal and supply center. The 470-mile/756-km railway connecting Fairbanks in the Interior with Seward was completed in 1923.

The city was named for U.S. Secretary of State William H. Seward, who was instrumental in arranging the purchase of Alaska from Russia in 1867. Resurrection Bay was named in 1791 by Russian fur trader and explorer Alexander Baranof. While sailing from Kodiak to Yakutat he found unexpected shelter in this bay from a storm and named the bay Resurrection because it was the Russian Sunday of the Resurrection.

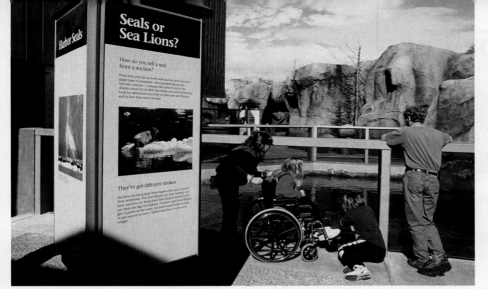

The Alaska SeaLife Center offers educational displays and close-up views of marine life. (© Ken Graham)

Resurrection Bay is a year-round ice-free harbor, and Seward is an important cargo and fishing port. The Alaska state ferry MV *Tustumena* calls at Seward.

Seward's economic base includes tourism, a coal terminal, marine research, fisheries and government offices. The Alaska Vocational Technical Center is located here. The new (1998) marine educational center—the Alaska SeaLife Center—is

SEWARD ADVERTISERS

A Cabin On The Cliff..........Ph. (907) 224-8001
Alaska Ferry........................Ph. (800) 720-4414
Alaska Kayak Camping Co.Ph. (907) 224-6056
Alaska Railroad Corp. ....Ph. (800) 544-0552
Alaska Renown Charters...Ph. (907) 224-3806
Alaska Saltwater Lodge ....Lowell Point
Alaska Sealife Center ....Ph. (800) 224-2525
Alaska Sunrise Fishing
   Adventures ....Ph. (907) 262-1250
Allen Marine Tours ....Ph. (888) 305-2515
Angels Rest on
   Resurrection Bay ....Lowell Point
Aurora Charters ....Ph. (907) 224-3968
Backlash Charters ....Ph. (907) 224-3979
Bardarson Studio ....Ph. (907) 224-5448
Bay Vista Bed
   & Breakfast.............................Phoenix Dr.
Beach House, The ....Ph. (907) 224-7000
Bear Creek RV Park...........Ph. (907) 224-5725
Bear's Den Bed &
   Breakfast.....................Ph. 1-800-232-7099
Benson Bed & Breakfast ...Ph. (907) 224-5290
Best Western Hotel
   Seward........................Ph. (907) 224-2378
Breeze Inn ....Small Boat Harbor
Brown & Hawkins................................4th Ave.
Camelot Cottages ....Ph. (907) 224-3039
Captain's Choice B&B...................519 5th Ave.
Charter Option, The ....Ph. (800) 224-2026
Clear Creek Cottage ....Ph. (907) 224-3968
Creekside Cabins Bed &
   Breakfast.....................Ph. (907) 224-3834
Crows Nest Cottages ....Ph. (907) 224-3979
Downtown Seward ....See ad page 586
Fish House, The ....Small Boat Harbor
Glacier's Edge Charters ....Ph. (907) 227-3151
Harborview Inn ....Ph. (907) 224-3217
Harmony Bed & Breakfast ..Ph. (907) 224-3661
Helly Hansen....................Ph. (907) 224-3041
Hertz Car Rental ....Ph. (907) 224-4378
Hotel Edgewater...............Ph. (907) 224-2700
IdidaRide Sled Dog Tours..Ph. (907) 224-8607

Kayak & Custom Adventures
   Worldwide ....Ph. (907) 258-3866
Kenai Fjords Tours ....Ph. (800) 478-8068
Kenai Fjords Wilderness
   Lodge ....Ph. 1-800-478-8068
Major Marine Tours..........Ph. (907) 224-8030
Mariah Tours ....Ph. (800) 270-1238
Marina Motel....................Ph. (907) 224-5518
Miller's Landing ....Mile 2.5 Lowell Point Rd.
Murphy's Motel ....4th Ave. & D St.
New Seward Hotel
   & Saloon ....Ph. (907) 224-8001
Northern Nights Bed &
   Breakfast......................Ph. (907) 224-5688
Northland Book & Charts ....201 3rd Ave.
Ocean Front B&B..............Ph. (907) 224-5699
Park Connection ....Ph. (888) 277-2757
Ray's Waterfront ....Small Boat Harbor
Renown Charters &
   Tours............................Ph. (907) 224-3806
Resurrect Art Coffee
   House Gallery.........................320 3rd Ave.
Resurrection Roadhouse...Ph. (800) 208-0200
Sablefish Charters.............Ph. (907) 224-3283
Sauerdough Lodging ....225 4th Ave.
Sea Treasures Inn ....Ph. (907) 224-7667
Seward Chamber ....Ph. (907) 224-8051
Seward Drug Co. ....Downtown
Seward Laundry ....806 4th Ave.
Seward Reservation Information
   Line ....Ph. (800) 844-2424
Seward Resort (Military).....Ph. 800-770-1858
Seward Waterfront
   Lodging ....Ph. (907) 224-5563
Seward Windsong
   Lodge Ph.1-800-208-0200
Sweet Darlings.................Ph. (907) 224-7313
Taroka Inn........................Ph. (907) 224-8975
Topsail Sailing
   Adventures ....Small Boat Harbor
Trail Lake Lodge ....Ph. (888) 395-3624
Van Gilder Hotel, the...............308 Adams St.

located here; see Attractions this section for more details.

ACCOMMODATIONS/VISITOR SERVICES

All visitor facilities, including hotels, motels, bed and breakfasts, cafes and restaurants, post office, grocery stores, drugstore, travel agencies, gift shops, gas stations, bars, laundromats, churches, bowling alley and theater.

The Harbormaster Building has public restrooms and pay showers, mailbox and pay phones. Weather information is available here during the summer. Public restrooms and pay showers on Ballaine Boulevard along the ocean between the boat harbor and town. Dump station and drinking water fill-up at the Small Boat Harbor at the end of 4th Avenue (see city map). There are picnic areas with covered tables along Ballaine Blvd., just south of the harbor, and at Adams Street.

Seward has made a good effort to provide overnight parking for self-contained RVs. There are designated camping areas along the shore south of Van Buren; camping fee charged. RV parking is marked by signs. Restrooms with coin-operated showers; water and electric hookups available at some sites. (Caravans: contact the City Parks and Recreation Dept. for reservations, phone 907/224-3331.) Forest Acres municipal campground is at **Milepost S 2.4** Seward Highway. Private RV parks at Small Boat Harbor, at **Milepost S 6.6** and on Lowell Point Road. Tent camping also available at Exit Glacier (turnoff at **Milepost S 3.7** Seward Highway). ▲

Alaska Saltwater Lodge. Seward's only drive-to oceanfront lodge. Experience sea otters, sea lions, seals, eagles and whale viewing. Scenic mountain and glacier setting. Enjoy beachcombing and fishing, coastal nature trail, on-site kayaking, guided saltwater fishing and daily small group Kenai Fjords National Park wildlife and glacier tours. private baths. (907) 224-5271. www.alaskasaltwaterlodge.com. See display ad. [ADVERTISEMENT]

Angels Rest on Resurrection Bay; opening in 1999. Charming deluxe beachside cabins with private baths, on private beach. Rest and relax amongst spectacular views of scenery and extensive wildlife from beachfront deck. Limited RV parking available. Call/e-mail for pricing and availability. Lowell Point, Box 1741, Seward, AK 99664. (907) 224-7378. E-mail: LYNANGEL@ ptialaska.net. [ADVERTISEMENT]

Bay Vista Bed & Breakfast, is nestled at the bottom of Mount Marathon in Seward, with a spectacular panoramic view of Resurrection Bay. Quiet wooded setting. We serve

a healthy and hearty continental breakfast. Our 4 beautifully appointed rooms have shared and private baths. The spacious common area provides guests with phone, TV/VCR, refrigerator, microwave and private entrances to guest area. Smoke-free environment. Rates: $89–99. Close to all Seward attractions. Host: Life-long Seward resident. P.O. Box 1232, Seward, AK 99664. (907) 224-5880. www.seward.net/bayvista. E-mail:

bayvista@arctic.net. [ADVERTISEMENT]

Bear Creek RV Park. Good Sam Park. Full and partial hookups, dump station, 4 private restrooms with showers, cable TV, traveler's lounge, propane, laundry, convenience store, ice, video rentals, pay phone. Fax service available. Bunkhouse for rent. Shuttle service available. Caravans and large groups welcome. Reservations encouraged. Internet: http://www.alaska.net/~bear. E-mail: hettick@alaska.net. Phone (907) 224-5725. [ADVERTISEMENT] ▲

Best Western Hotel Seward. Enjoy being in the center of activity, yet in a quiet setting overlooking Resurrection Bay. Our rooms include breathtaking views with in-room coffee and your own refrigerator. One floor all nonsmoking rooms. And check this out! For your in-room entertainment, all rooms include (1) remote control TVs with cablevision, (2) remote control VCRs with videotape rental available and (3) 2 channels of free in-room movies featuring the latest hits! Complimentary scheduled shuttle bus service for our guests to boat harbor, train depot and airport. One block to the Alaska SeaLife Center. We accept all major credit cards.

Reservations (907) 224-2378 or (800) 811-1191 inside Alaska. Fax (907) 224-3112. See display ad this section. [ADVERTISEMENT]

Camelot Cottages. Clean, cozy, affordable furnished cabins in a natural woodland setting. Beautiful chalet available for families or large groups. All units are heated and have private baths, fully equipped kitchens, linens provided. Open air hot tub, laundry facilities and fish freezer available for guest use. Private, family-owned and operated by longtime Alaskans. We also make reservations for Kenai Fjords Park tours and halibut and salmon fishing charters with the best operators in Seward! See display ad at Mile 3.2 Seward Highway. (800) 739-3039; (907) 346-3039 Anchorage; (907) 224-3039 Seward. akcabins@alaska.net and www.alaska.net/~akcabins. [ADVERTISEMENT]

Clear Creek Cottage. Fully furnished smoke-free 2-bedroom cabin, full kitchen. Sleeps up to 8. Clean, comfortable, affordable rates. Perfect hideaway for couples, families, small groups. On the banks of Clear Creek, on Resurrection River Road to Exit Glacier, Mile 3.7 Seward Highway. 7 minutes to downtown Seward. (907) 224-3968. Fax

(907) 224-7230. P.O. Box 241, Seward, AK 99664. [ADVERTISEMENT]

Creekside Cabins Bed & Breakfast. Clean, cozy cabins nestled in the trees, along peaceful Clear Creek. Continental breakfast. Central heated restrooms. Toasty log sauna on the creek; tent sites. Peaceful country setting for a relaxing stay. Nonsmoking. Phone (907) 224-3834. See display ad in Seward section. Take first right off Exit Glacier Road, 0.3 mile on right. [ADVERTISEMENT] ▲

Harborview Inn. 804 Third Avenue. New: 23 rooms with private entrances, private baths, cable TV in room, telephone, Alaska Native fine art. Just 10-minute walk to tour boats, fishing charters, downtown and Alaska SeaLife Center. Also "Seaview," our newly remodeled 2-bedroom apartments on the beachfront, breathtaking view of snowcapped mountains and bay. All nonsmoking. $109. Early reservations advised. Alaska Native hostess. Phone (907) 224-3217; fax (907) 224-3218. P.O. Box 1305MP, Seward, AK 99664. E-mail: harbrinn@ptialaska.net. Internet: www.alaskan.com/harborviewinn. See display ad. [ADVERTISEMENT]

Harmony Bed & Breakfast, nestled

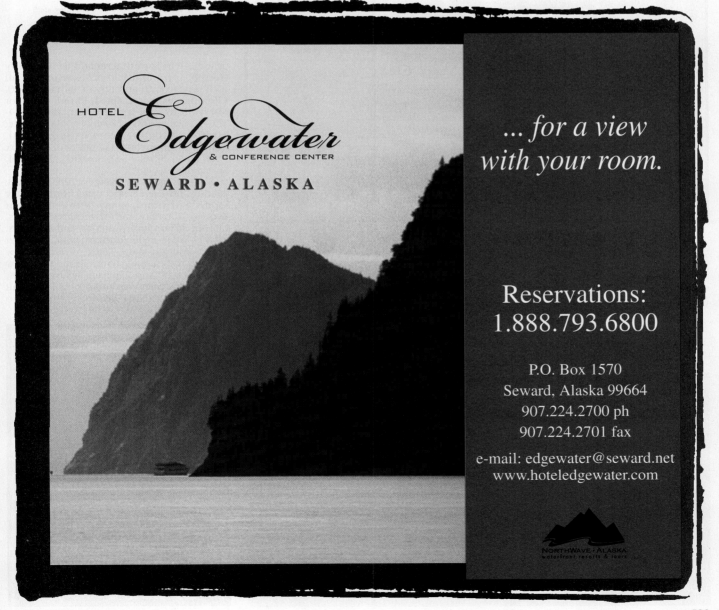

HOTEL *Edgewater* & CONFERENCE CENTER

SEWARD • ALASKA

... *for a view with your room.*

Reservations:
1.888.793.6800

P.O. Box 1570
Seward, Alaska 99664
907.224.2700 ph
907.224.2701 fax

e-mail: edgewater@seward.net
www.hoteledgewater.com

NORTHWAVE • ALASKA
waterfront resorts & tours

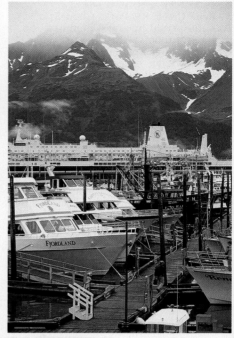

Seward Boat Harbor. (© David Foster, staff)

peacefully in Forrest Acres and conveniently close to town and harbor. New rooms, all with private bath and private entrance. $80. VISA/MasterCard accepted. Phone Carol for reservations and information, (907) 224-3661. Fax (907) 224-8740. Web site: http://www.bnbweb.com/harmony.html. E-mail: harmonyb@ptialaska.net. P.O. Box 1606 (2411 Spruce St.), Seward, AK 99664.
[ADVERTISEMENT]

Hotel Edgewater. New for 1999—luxury getaway on the Seward waterfront. Deluxe rooms and suites, many with spectacular Resurrection Bay and/or mountain views. Interior atrium with waterfall and skylights, classic lodge-style lounge room, fine art gallery and gift shop. Relax in our bayview Jacuzzi and sauna room. Enjoy the new Alaska SeaLife and Chugach Native centers, local shops, cafes, restaurants, galleries—all within easy walking distance. Allow us to

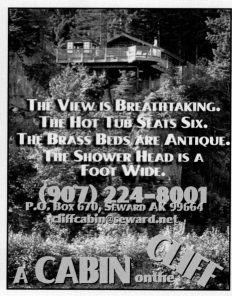

help you with your Seward visit—plan a tour of Kenai Fjords National Park, visit Exit Glacier, charter a halibut or salmon fishing charter. Visit us at www.hoteledgewater.com and call us at 1-888-793-6800 to make reservations. Planning a Denali trip? Inquire about our riverfront property—Denali River Cabins. [ADVERTISEMENT]

Miller's Landing is a campground with down-home Alaskan atmosphere, neighboring Caines Head State Park and hiking trail. Services include: fishing charters, water taxi service, kayak/skiff rentals and boat launching. Owned and operated by the Miller family on their Resurrection Bay homestead, this scenic campground offers beach and forested sites. Electric RV sites, 20/30 amp ($20), large tent sites ($15), cozy cabins ($30–up), hot showers and flush restrooms centrally located and included. Laundry planned for spring of 1999. Free launch access for our campers. Book a fishing charter for halibut or salmon (full and half-day) on heated cabin boats with gear and bait provided. Our water taxi service takes you to remote camping, kayaking, fishing and hunting sites throughout Kenai Fjords National Park and Resurrection Bay. Those without sea legs can rent a rod and reel to fish from our beaches while watching sea life, birds and the occasional whale. The country store sells bait, tackle, ice, fishing licenses, gifts, wood for campfires and farm fresh eggs. The coffee's always free. Mike Miller, who homesteaded here and survived the 1964 earthquake, is an expert on fishing and visitor information. Fishing advice 5¢. Guaranteed effective or your nickel back! Reservations encouraged for guaranteed site.

Mile 3 Lowell Point Road. Look for the blue road sign near the SeaLife Center. Phone (907) 224-5739. Fax (907) 224-5975. Box 81, Seward, AK 99664. [ADVERTISEMENT] ▲

Murphy's Motel. On Main Street, 2 blocks to Fjords tour departure/fishing charters at the Small Boat Harbor. 3 minutes to SeaLife Center. Quiet, private baths, cable

TV, queen beds, free local calls, coffee maker, fridge, microwave, data ports, parking in front of room. Smoking/nonsmoking rooms. (907) 224-8090. Fax (907) 224-5650. murphys@seward.net. See display ad. [ADVERTISEMENT]

New Seward Hotel & Saloon. Centrally located in downtown Seward, one block to

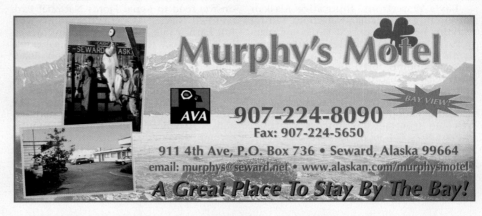

Murphy's Motel
907-224-8090
Fax: 907-224-5650
911 4th Ave, P.O. Box 736 • Seward, Alaska 99664
email: murphys@seward.net • www.alaskan.com/murphysmotel
A Great Place To Stay By The Bay!

SEWARD WATERFRONT LODGING
Bed and Breakfast
Downtown ✳ Open Year-Round
550 Railway • Overlooking The Bay
Hosted By 30-Year Alaskans
(907) 224-5563 ✳ Fax (907) 224-2397
VISA   PO Box 618, Seward, AK 99664   MasterCard

The Beach House
(907) 224-7000
OPEN YEAR-ROUND
200' From Bay On Magical Lowell Pt.
True Family Value—Sleeps 7

EXPERIENCE SEWARD – THE REAL ALASKA!

"Seward's finest lodging and dining experience."

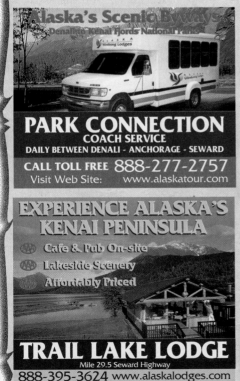

PARK CONNECTION
COACH SERVICE
DAILY BETWEEN DENALI - ANCHORAGE - SEWARD
CALL TOLL FREE **888-277-2757**
Visit Web Site: www.alaskatour.com

EXPERIENCE ALASKA'S KENAI PENINSULA
🆎 Cafe & Pub On-site
🆎 Lakeside Scenery
🆎 Affordably Priced

TRAIL LAKE LODGE
Mile 29.5 Seward Highway
888-395-3624 www.alaskalodges.com

SEWARD
Windsong Lodge

🆎 On The Road To Kenai Fjords National Park
🆎 Lovely Forest Setting Near Resurrection River
🆎 Modern Rooms With Queen Beds, Cable, VCR & Phone

RESURRECTION
ROADHOUSE

Alaskan Specialties In A Casual Atmosphere
Wide Variety Of Alaskan Ales On Tap
Scenic Views of the Resurrection River Valley

Visit our website at:
www.sewardlodging.com   **800-208-0200**   Mile 1/2 Exit Glacier Rd.
Just North Of Seward

Alaska SeaLife Center, within walking distance of shops, beach, boat harbor; 35 rooms featuring TV, phones, free videos. Some kitchenettes. Salmon and halibut fishing charters or Kenai Fjords tours available. Year-round service. Brochure. All major credit cards accepted. Reservations (907) 224-8001. Fax (907) 224-3112. See display ad this section. [ADVERTISEMENT]

Ray's Waterfront. Innovative Alaskan cuisine in a spectacular waterfront setting featuring fresh local seafood, steaks and vegetarian selections. Specialties include macadamia nut crusted halibut with Thai curry sauce, cioppino, brandied pepper steak, oven-roasted Tuscan vegetables, king crab and daily specials. Serving lunch and dinner daily. Full bar service with excellent wine selections. Group reservations in advance are welcome. Gourmet box lunches available. Phone (907) 224-5606, fax (907) 224-5631. E-mail: janaska@msn.com. [ADVERTISEMENT]

Seward Resort (Military). hotel, townhouses, RV and tent sites. Charter fishing, Resurrection Bay wildlife boat tours. Open year-round. Authorized patrons: active duty military; retirees; National Guard and Reserves; DOD/NAF civilians, families and guests; federal governmental agencies. Phone (800) 770-1858; DSN 384-3474/5463. Internet: www.usarak.army.mil/framwr/seward.htm. See display ad, **Mile 2.3** Seward Highway. [ADVERTISEMENT] MP ▲

Seward Windsong Lodge. Seward's newest lodge, overlooks Resurrection River, on the road to Kenai Fjords National Park and Exit Glacier. Modern, clean units with full bath, cable, VCRs, phone, and queen beds in a quiet, forested setting. Great casual dining on site at the Resurrection Roadhouse. One-half mile up Exit Glacier Road. Phone (800) 208-0200 or (907) 224-7116. See display ad this section. [ADVERTISEMENT]

Taroka Inn. We don't pretend to be fancy. We're not. We're just clean, comfortable, convenient and affordable. Family-owned, operated and oriented. We offer kitchen units with private bathroom, cable TV, in-room phone, data ports. Couples traveling together have a little more privacy. One queen bed in the bedroom and another in the living room (not a fold-out). Our larger units accommodate up to 9 persons. Great for family on a budget! Two blocks to Alaska SeaLife Center. One block to restaurants, shops, museum. ³/₄ mile to Small Boat Harbor. Nonsmoking available. Pets upon approval only. Phone (907) 224-8975. E-mail: taroka@arctic.net. Internet: www.alaskaone.com/taroka. See display ad. [ADVERTISEMENT] MP

Van Gilder Hotel. Seward's favorite small hotel, built in 1916 and completely renovated for the 1990s. Now a National Historic Site, it retains its original Edwardian charm. Located downtown 308 Adams Street within easy walking distance to shopping and SeaLife Center. For hotel reservations phone (800) 204-6835. P.O. Box 2, Seward, AK, 99664. Fax (907) 224-3689. E-mail: vangilderhotel@seward.net. See display ad this section. [ADVERTISEMENT]

TRANSPORTATION

Air: Seward airport is reached by turning east on Airport Road at **Milepost S 2.7** on the Seward Highway. Scheduled daily service to Anchorage; charters also available.

Ferry: Alaska Marine Highway office on Cruise Ship Dock; phone (907) 224-5485. The Alaska ferry MV *Tustumena* departs Seward for Kodiak and Valdez.

Railroad: The Alaska Railroad connects Seward to Anchorage and Fairbanks.

Bus: Scheduled service to Anchorage.

Taxi: Service available.

Highway: Seward is reached via the 127-mile/203.2-km Seward Highway from Anchorage.

Tours: Seward Trolley offers city tours 10 A.M. to 7 P.M. daily, Memorial Day through Labor Day.

ATTRACTIONS

The Railcar *Seward* houses the chamber of commerce information center. Located at 3rd and Jefferson Street, this railcar was the Seward observation car on the Alaska Railroad from 1936 until the early 1960s. Information and detailed map of the city are available.

Walking Tour of Seward encompasses more than 30 attractions including homes and businesses that date back to the early

Racers' view of Seward during the Mount Marathon Race in July. (© Bill Sherwonit)

municipal harbor, built after the 1964 earthquake, is home port to fishing boats, charter boats and sightseeing boats. The harbor is also home to sea otters—watch for them! Visitors may notice the great number of sailboats moored here: many are members of the William H. Seward Yacht Club, which sponsors an annual sailboat and yacht show.

Seward Museum, at Jefferson and 3rd Avenue, is operated by the Resurrection Bay Historical Society (Box 55, Seward 99664). The museum features artifacts and photographs from the 1964 earthquake, WWII, the founding days of Seward and other highlights of Seward's history. Also on display is a collection of Native baskets and ivory carvings. The museum is open daily, 10 A.M. to 5

1900s; some are still being used, while others have been restored as historic sites. A brochure containing details on all the attractions of the tour is available at the railcar information center. The complete tour covers about 2 miles/3.2 km and takes about 1 to 2 hours, depending upon how much time you wish to spend browsing.

Seward Marine Science Education Center, across from the Alaska SeaLife Center, has laboratories, aquaculture ponds and the research vessel *Alpha Helix.* In 1999, the Pratt Museum's *Darkened Waters* exhibit—which chronicles the impact of the Exxon *Valdez* grounding 10 years ago—will be featured here. Open daily in summer, 10 A.M. to 5 P.M. Admission is $3 adults, $1 for children. For group rates and tours, phone (907) 224-5261.

Alaska SeaLife Center. This 7-acre waterfront site combines research facilities with wildlife rehabilitation and public education. Construction of the SeaLife Center was funded by the Exxon Valdez Oil Spill Restoration fund and private donations.

The Center allows you to come face-to-face with Alaska's exciting marine wildlife, explore their undersea world and experience the wonder of nature in a one-of-a-kind marine science and visitor facility. This $50 million, 115,000-square-foot center opens windows to the sea—above and below the surface. Indoors, view the distinct habitats of marine birds, Steller sea lions, seals, fish and otters. Outdoors, step right to the edge of Resurrection Bay, teeming with Alaska marine wildlife. Open daily 9 A.M.–9:30 P.M. Admission $12.50 adults, $10 youth.

Visit the Small Boat Harbor. This

P.M., May 1 to Sept. 30. Open reduced hours remainder of year; check locally, or phone (907) 224-3902. A modest admission fee is charged.

Seward Community Library, across from the City–State Building, presents (on request) short slide/sound shows on a variety of subjects and has some informative displays. A program on the 1964 earthquake is shown daily at 2 P.M. (except Sunday) from June 15 through the first Saturday in September. Library hours are 1–8 P.M. Monday through Friday, 1–6 P.M. Saturday.

St. Peter's Episcopal Church is 3 blocks west of the museum at the corner of 2nd Avenue and Adams Street. It was built in 1906 and is considered the oldest Protestant church on the Kenai Peninsula. One feature is the unique painting of the Resurrection, for which Alaskans were used as models and Resurrection Bay as the background. Well-known Dutch artist Jan Van Emple was commissioned to paint the picture in 1925 when he was living in Seward. Obtain key to church from the Information Cache in season.

Hiking Trails. Two Lakes trail is an easy mile-long loop trail along the base of Mount Marathon. The trail passes through a wooded area and follows what used to be Hemlock Street. Beautiful view of marina below and north end of Resurrection Bay. Start at First Lake, behind the Alaska Vocational and Technical Center Administration Building at 2nd Avenue and B Street.

The **National Historic Iditarod Trail** begins at the ferry terminal and follows a marked course through town, then north on the Seward Highway. At Mile 2.1 Nash Road (turn off at **Milepost S 3.2** Seward Highway), the trail continues from a gravel parking area on the east side of Sawmill Creek north to Bear Lake. The trail eventually rejoins the Seward Highway at **Milepost S 12.**

Caines Head State Recreation Area, 6 miles/9.6 km south of Seward, is accessible by boat or via a 4.5-mile/7.2-km beach trail (low tide only). The trailhead/parking is located about Mile 2 Lowell Point Road. The Caines Head area has bunkers and gun emplacements that were used to guard the entrance to Resurrection Bay during WWII.

Mount Marathon Race™, Seward's annual Fourth of July endurance race to the top of Mount Marathon (elev. 3,022 feet/921m) and back down, is a grueling test for athletes. The race is said to have begun in 1909 with a wager between 2 sourdoughs as to how long it would take to run up and down Mount Marathon. The first year of the official race is uncertain: records indicate either 1912 or 1915. Fastest recorded time is 43 minutes, 23 seconds set in 1981 by Bill Spencer, who broke his own 1974 record. The descent is so steep that it's part run, part jump and part slide. The race attracts competitors from all over, and thousands of spectators line the route each year.

Annual Seward Silver Salmon Derby™ in August is one of the largest sporting events in Alaska. It is held over 9 days, starting the second Saturday in August and continuing through Sunday of the following weekend. 1999 will be the derby's 44th year. Record derby catch to date is a 20.59-lb. salmon caught off Twin Rocks by John Westlund of Anchorage.

There are more than $225,000 in prizes

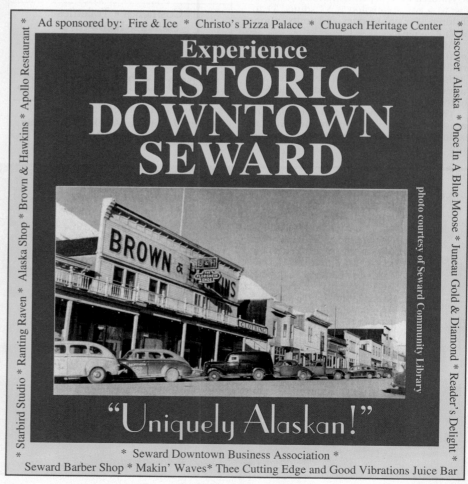

for the derby, including $10,000 in cash for the largest fish. Also part of the derby are the sought-after tagged silvers worth as much as $100,000. Prizes are sponsored by various merchants and the chamber of commerce.

The town fills up fast during the derby: Make reservations! For more information contact the Seward Chamber of Commerce; phone (907) 224-8051.

Kenai Fjords National Park. Seward is the gateway to this popular 605,000-acre national park. Dominant feature of the park is the Harding Icefield, a 300-square-mile vestige of the last ice age. Harding Icefield can be reached by a strenuous all-day hike from the base of Exit Glacier or by a charter flightseeing trip out of Seward.

The fjords of the park were formed when glaciers flowed down to the sea from the ice field and then retreated, leaving behind the deep inlets that characterize the coastline here. Substantial populations of marine mammals inhabit or migrate through the park's coastal waters, including sea otters, Steller sea lions, dolphins and whales. Icebergs from calving glaciers provide ideal refuge for harbor seals, and the rugged coastline provides habitat for more than 100,000 nesting birds. The park's spectacular scenery and wildlife may be viewed by daily private tour and charter boats or by charter planes. Four public-use cabins along the coast are available in summer by reservation; phone (907) 271-2737. Kayakers and boaters can also camp on beaches but must be aware ahead of time of land status; 45,000 acres of coastline are owned by Native corporations and are *not* available for public camping. Maps indicating land ownership are available from the park visitor center. NOTE: *Private boaters should consult with local outfitters and charter operators for detailed information on boating conditions.*

Exit Glacier is the most accessible of the park's glaciers. Turn at **Milepost S 3.7** on the Seward Highway and follow Exit Glacier Road to the visitor center parking area.

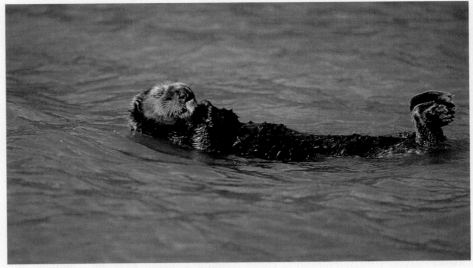

Sea otters are common in Resurrection Bay. *(© Tom Bol)*

There are several trails through the outwash plain of Exit Glacier that afford excellent views of the ice and surrounding mountains. A 0.2-mile paved trail is wheelchair accessible and leads from the parking lot to an information display. Ranger-led nature walks are available in summer at Exit Glacier, where there is a picnic area and walk-in

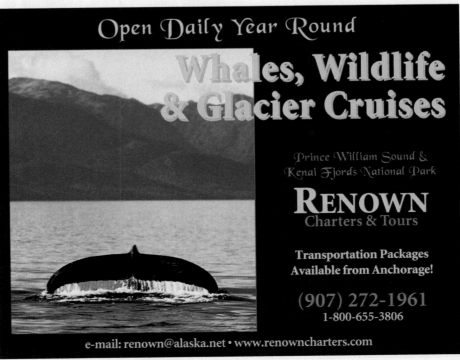

campground. Visitor information is available at the Exit Glacier ranger station and visitor center; open summer only. Exit Glacier is accessible in winter by skis, dogsled or snow machine. A public-use cabin is available by permit; phone (907) 224-3175 or the Park Information Line (907) 224-2132. *CAUTION: Active glacier with unstable ice. Do not walk past warning signs!*

Slide programs, videos, exhibits and information on Kenai Fjords National Park and organized activities at the park are available at the park visitor center on 4th Avenue in the Small Boat Harbor area next to the Harbormaster's office. The center is open daily from Memorial Day to Labor Day; hours are 9 A.M. to 6 P.M. The remainder of the year hours are 8 A.M. to 5 P.M. (subject to change) weekdays. Phone (907) 224-3175 or write the park superintendent, Box 1727, Seward 99664.

Alaska Renown Charters & Tours "Alaska's favorite daily, year-round cruise company" offers wildlife and glacier cruises in the Kenai Fjords and in Prince William Sound. Our comfortable vessels have heated cabins with plenty of viewing space. Calving glaciers, whales, puffins, otters and much more. Fully-narrated by a professional and friendly crew. Phone (800) 655-3806. E-mail: renown@alaska.net. Internet: www.renowncharters.com. See display ad. [ADVERTISEMENT] MP

Alaska SeaLife Center. Come face to face with Alaska's exciting marine wildlife and explore their undersea world. Experience the wonder of nature in all its grandeur at this new and unique marine science and visitor facility. View the distinct habitats of puffins, sea lions and seals. The Alaska SeaLife Center opens windows to the sea—above and below the surface. [ADVERTISEMENT]

Bardarson Studio. In Seward find Bardarson Studio on the prettiest boardwalk in the boat harbor area, with the best selection of Alaska art and fine crafts set to music. Bardarson Studio recognizes that shopping is entertainment for travelers, providing a Kiddie-Kave for children, and a video room for your non-shopper. Public restroom and postal service available. 1317

4th Avenue. Phone (800) 354-0141. E-mail: bardarson@seward.net. Internet: www.seward.net/bardarson. [ADVERTISEMENT] MP

The Fish House. First and finest fishing charter service in Seward! Record-class halibut and silver salmon fishing charters available now. While fishing, enjoy the scenic beauty of the Kenai Fjords National Park—glaciers, mountains, puffins, whales, sea otters and seals. The Fish House also supplies a complete line of fishing tackle, bait, ice and outboard motor repairs. Call now for

reservations or information on fishing the scenic waters surrounding Seward, Alaska. 1-800-257-7760 or (907) 224-3674. E-mail: fishhous@ptialaska.net. Internet: ptialaska. net/~fishhous/. Halibut charters: April 1–Oct. 1. Salmon charters: June 1–Sept. 20. P.O. Box 1209, Seward, AK 99664. See display ad this section. [ADVERTISEMENT]　MP

IdidaRide Sled Dog Tours. Experience dog mushing, summer style, on a 2-mile wilderness dog sled ride at 4th Place Iditarod racer Mitch Seavey's training location. Informative tour includes 60-husky kennel, cuddly puppies, arctic equipment demonstration. Reservations recommended. P.O. Box 2906, Seward, AK 99664. (907) 224-8607, fax (907) 224-8608. Internet: www.alaskaone.com/ididaride. Off Exit Glacier Road. See display ad Mile 3.7 Seward Highway. [ADVERTISEMENT]

Kayak & Custom Adventures Worldwide. Coastal kayaking excursions in Alaska include unforgettable wilderness experiences. Glaciers calving, whales breaching, icebergs floating, otters frolicking, waterfalls cascading and wildflowers blooming. Take home memories you can't get standing on the shore. Adventures available worldwide. Call now for a free brochure. Toll free (800) 288-3134 or (907) 258-FUNN. In Seward: (907) 224-3960. E-mail: kayak@arctic.net. Internet: www.alaskan.com/kayak. [ADVERTISEMENT]

Northland Books & Charts is "Alaska's foremost nautical boutique." Chart your Alaska cruise memories on Northland's NOAA and Alaska specialty maps, including USGS topographical, national park and recreational guides. The latest bestsellers, children's books, Alaska historical editions, cookbooks, outdoor guides and one-of-a-kind Alaska-made clocks and barometers await you in this maritime specialty gift shop. Located at the corner of Third Avenue and Washington Street, one block north of the Alaska SeaLife Center. E-mail: northlandbks@attmail.com. Open daily from 9 A.M. to 6 P.M. Phone (907) 224-3102. See display ad. [ADVERTISEMENT]

Kenai Fjords Tours. The excitement begins the moment you pull away from the Seward boat harbor! You'll be greeted by playful sea otters, view boisterous Steller

sea lions, look for whales and porpoises, photograph colorful puffins and bald eagles, and watch a calving glacier. Cruising since 1974, Kenai Fjords Tours is the original Kenai Fjords National Park tour and continues to be the most popular. Our new, comfortable boats have walk-around decks so you can easily watch and photograph the magnificent scenery. Our captains are experienced naturalists averaging more than 12 years in Kenai Fjords National Park, so you'll learn about this coastal wilderness from guides who really know the area. All cruises include a meal and many include a special stop at Fox Island for our delicious all-you-can-eat salmon bake at Kenai Fjords Wilderness Lodge. Don't miss it! Call today for reservations. Toll free (800) 478-8068 or (907) 224-8068. Located at the Seward Small Boat Harbor. See display ad this section. [ADVERTISEMENT]　MP

Major Marine Kenai Fjords National Park Tours. Join us for Seward's world-class wildlife and glacier cruises of the Kenai Fjords. We offer 2 wonderful cruise options: 1) a half-day wildlife cruise of the Kenai Fjords, and 2) a full-day wildlife and glacier cruise of the Kenai Fjords National Park and Chiswell Islands National Wildlife Refuge. Both cruises are hosted by a uniformed

National Park Ranger. During the cruise you'll generally see otters, sea lions, puffins, eagles, porpoises, whales, bird colonies and more. You'll also pull up close to some of Alaska's most awe-inspiring glaciers. The large tour boats feature reserved table seating, inside heated cabins and multiple outside decks. A freshly prepared all-you-can-eat salmon and roasted chicken buffet is available on both cruises for only $10. The food is consistently rated as the best of any daycruise company. Both cruises sail from Seward's boat harbor May to late September. The full-day cruise departs at 11:45 A.M. and costs $99. The half-day cruise departs at 1 P.M. and 6 P.M. and costs $64. For reservations or a free brochure, call: (800) 764-7300 or (907) 274-7300. Major Marine Tours, 411 West 4th, Anchorage, AK 99501. Ticket office also located on Seward boardwalk: (907) 224-8030 (May to September). Inter-

Kayakers in Aialik Bay at Aialik Glacier in Kenai Fjords National Park.
(© Bill Sherwonit)

net: www.majormarine.com. [ADVERTISEMENT]

Mariah Tours. Join us for a memorable day to the Chiswell Islands and Kenai Fjords National Park on the small ship alternative. You'll enjoy close-up viewing of whales, sea

lions and seabirds. You'll appreciate the personalized attention on our 43-foot vessel, with a limit of 16 passengers only on board. Featuring tours to spectacular Northwestern Glacier via Granite Passage, the most scenic area within Kenai Fjords National Park. Popular exclusive tours for birding and naturalist groups. Operating mid-May–September.

For reservations: (800) 270-1238. In Seward: (907) 224-8623. See display ad this section. [ADVERTISEMENT]

Wildlife Quest in Kenai Fjords National park. Enjoy the park's famous tidewater glaciers, sea lion rookeries, seabird colonies, whale watching waters and more. Our smooth-sailing, high-speed catamaran gets you to the park faster thhan any other vessel. That means you'll enjoy more sights—including more glaciers—in less time than other cruises. So call today and discover the most relaxing way to get wild. Also, ask about our relaxing Resurrection Bay Cruise, unique transportation packages and earning 500 Alaska Airlines Miles. Call Allen Marine Tours, 1321 4th Ave., Seward, AK 99664. 1-888-305-2515 or (907) 224-2282. [ADVERTISEMENT]

AREA FISHING: Resurrection Bay, coho (silver) salmon to 22 lbs., use herring, troll or cast, July to October; king salmon to 45 lbs., May to August; also bottom fish, flounder, halibut to 300 lbs. and cod, use weighted spoons and large red spinners by jigging, year-round. Charter and rental boats are available.

oceans away from ordinary

Where puffins fly through liquid skies – inches from your fingertips.
Seals give you curious, sidelong glances.
And sea lions perform an underwater ballet.
Only one place combines science and scenery,
to create a natural setting for viewing marine wildlife –
above *and* below the waves.
In this unique environment, where snowy mountains meet the
pristine waters of Resurrection Bay, the wildlife is *this* close.
And the experience is far from tame.

Alaska SeaLife Center©
w i n d o w s   t o   t h e   s e a

1-800-224-2525
(907) 224-6300 in Seward, Alaska
Located at Mile 0 of the
Seward Highway
http://www.alaskasealife.org

Photo ©Chris Arend

Kenai Peninsula
STERLING HIGHWAY ①

Connects: Seward Highway to Homer, AK   **Length:** 143 miles
Road Surface: Paved   **Season:** Open all year
Major Attractions: Kenai National Wildlife Refuge,
Russian Orthodox Churches, Homer Spit

(See maps, pages 595–596)

	Anchorage	Homer	Kenai	Seward	Soldotna
Anchorage		233	158	127	147
Homer	233		96	180	85
Kenai	158	96		105	11
Seward	127	180	105		94
Soldotna	147	85	11	94	

A camper at sunset overlooking Cook Inlet on the Sterling Highway. (© Tom Bol)

The Sterling Highway (Alaska Route 1) begins 90 miles/145 km south of Anchorage at its junction with the Seward Highway and travels 142.5 miles/229.3 km west and south to the community of Homer. The Sterling Highway junctions with several major Kenai Peninsula side roads (see logs this section): Skilak Lake Loop Road, Swanson River Road, Kenai Spur Highway, Kalifornsky Beach Road, Cohoe Loop Road and Anchor River Beach Road.

From its junction with the Seward Highway at Tern Lake (see SEWARD HIGHWAY section), the Sterling passes through Chugach National Forest and Kenai National Wildlife Refuge. The Kenai Mountains are home to Dall sheep, mountain goats, black and brown bears, and caribou. The many lakes, rivers and streams of the Kenai Peninsula are famous for their sportfishing. The highway also provides access to the Resurrection Pass Trail System.

From Soldotna south, the Sterling Highway follows the west coast of the peninsula along Cook Inlet. There are beautiful views of peaks on the Alaska Peninsula.

Physical mileposts on the Sterling Highway show distance from Seward. The Sterling Highway is a paved 2-lane highway, open year-round.

Emergency medical services: phone 911 or use CB channels 9, 11 or 19.

Sterling Highway Log

Distance from Seward (S) is followed by distance from Anchorage (A) and distance from Homer (H).
Physical mileposts show distance from Seward.

S 37 (59.5 km) **A 90** (144.8 km) **H 142.5** (229.3 km) **Tern Lake Junction.** Tern Lake day-use area (see description next milepost). Gravel turnout beside Tern Lake with interpretive boardwalk and viewing platforms. Information signs on area birds and wildlife.

Junction with Seward Highway (Alaska Route 9) to Seward and Anchorage. Turn to **Milepost S 37** in the SEWARD HIGHWAY section for log.

S 37.4 (60.2 km) **A 90.4** (145.5 km) **H 142.1** (228.7 km) USFS Tern Lake day-use picnic area; toilets, water, picnic tables. USFS spawning channel for king salmon on Daves Creek at outlet of Tern Lake. Short viewing trail with information signs illustrating use of log weirs and stream protection techniques.

S 38 (61.1 km) **A 91** (146.4 km) **H 141.5** (227.7 km) Avalanche gates. Gravel turnouts.

S 38.3 (61.6 km) **A 91.3** (146.9 km) **H 141.2** (227.2 km) Gravel turnout. *Emergency call box.*

S 39 (62.8 km) **A 92** (148 km) **H 140.5** (226.1 km) **Daves Creek,** an unusually beautiful mountain stream which flows west into Quartz Creek. Dolly Varden and rainbow averaging 14 inches, June through September. A good place to view spawning salmon in late July and August. ➤

S 40.5 (65.2 km) **A 93.5** (150.5 km) **H 139** (223.7 km) Double-ended gravel turnout to south.

S 40.9 (65.8 km) **A 93.9** (151.1 km) **H 138.6** (223 km) Bridge over Quartz Creek. This stream empties into Kenai Lake.

Westbound travelers are now entering one of Alaska's best-known lake and river fishing regions, across the center of the Kenai Peninsula. *NOTE: The diversity of fishing conditions and frequent regulation changes in all Kenai waters make it advisable to consult locally for fishing news and regulations.*

S 41.1 (66.1 km) **A 94.1** (151.4 km) **H 138.4** (222.7 km) Cooper Landing Closed Area. This area is closed to the hunting of Dall sheep. The ridges to the north are a lambing ground for Dall sheep.

STERLING HIGHWAY
Soldotna, AK, to Homer, AK

© 1999 The MILEPOST®

Map Location

Key to mileage boxes

miles/kilometres
miles/kilometres
from:
S-Seward
A-Anchorage
H-Homer
K-Kasilof
SY-Soldotna Y
SJ-Soutn Junction

Principal Route
Paved
Unpaved
Other Roads
Paved
Unpaved
Ferry Routes　**Hiking Trails**
❄ Refer to Log for Visitor Facilities

Key to Advertiser Services
C -Camping
D -Dump Station
d -Diesel
G -Gas (reg., unld.)
I -Ice
L -Lodging
M-Meals
P -Propane
R -Car Repair (major)
r -Car Repair (minor)
S -Store (grocery)
T -Telephone (pay)

Scale
0　　　　5 Miles
0　　　5 Kilometres

N　W　E　S

(map continues previous page)

Kenai Spur Highway

SY-0
S-94/152km
A-147/237km
H-85/137km

SY-11/18km
❄?⛺🏕✈ Kenai
Beaver Loop Road

(map continues previous pagee)

K-14.5/23.3km Robinson's Mini Mall CDGIST
K-16.5/26.6km Diamond M Ranch B&B,
Cabins & RV Spaces CDL
K-17.5/28.2km Salmon Ron B&B L
Kalifornsky Beach Road

? Soldotna ❄?⛺🏕✈

N60°29'
W151°03'　Funny River Road

Ski Hill Road

K-22/36km
S-96/154km
A-149/240km
H-83/134km

K-0
S-109/175km
A-162/260km
H-71/114km

K-2.8/4.5km Ingrid's Inn L

SJ-9.7/5.6km Kasilof River Kabins L

Kasilof

Cohoe Loop Road

S-109.2/175.7km Kasilof Riverview dGIPST
S-110.8/178.3km Tustumena Lodge IL
S-111/178.6km Crooked Creek RV Park and Guide Service CDILM
Kasilof RV Park CD
Tustumena Ridge Cabins L

SJ-0
S-114/184km
A-167/296km
H-65/105km

Johnson
Lake

Kenai National Wildlife Refuge

Clam Gulch
N60°14' W151°23'

S-119.6/192.5km Clam Gulch Lodge Bed & Breakfast L

S-127.1/204.5km Scenic View RV Park C
S-128.3/206.5km Ninilchik Cabins & Fish Camp L

S-130.1/209.4km Caribou Creek Cabins L
S-130.5/210km Ninilchik Point Overnighter CL
S-135.1/217.4km Ninilchik Village Cache
Ninilchik Village Cabins L
S-135.4/217.9km Alaskan Angler RV Resort CDILT
A FISHUNT Charters
S-135.7/218.4km Ninilchik General Store IST
S-135.8/218.5km Bull Moose Gifts
Ninilchik Saltwater Charters & Lodge L
S-135.9/218.7km Country Boy Campground CD
O'Fish'ial Charters of Alaska
Reel'Em Inn/Cook Inlet Charters CILT
S-140/225.3km Salty Dog Charters and Deep Creek B&B L
Solitudes Bed & Breakfast
S-140.5/226.1km Double Eagle Lodge L

S-132.2/212.7km Heavenly Sights Charters & Campground CL
S-134.5/216.4km Inlet View Lodge LM
S-133.9/215.5km
Black Goat's
Bluff RV Camp C

S-136/218km
A-189/303km
H-44/71km

Ninilchik ❄⛺🏕

S-136/218.9km Chinook Tesoro dGIPR

S-136.1/219km Chihuly's Charters and Porcupine Shop L
S-136.2/219.2km Deep Creek View Campground CDIL
S-137/220.4km Deep Creek Custom Packing, Inc. IT
Fishward Bound Adventures ILST
S-137.3/220.9km D&M RV Park & Charters CD
S-137.4/221.1km Roe's Charter Service L

S-145.5/234.2km King of Kings Guide Service and Lodge L

Happy Valley

S-150/241km Cooper's B&B L

S-152.7/245.7km Eagle Crest RV Park & Cabins CDILP

Cook Inlet

Ninilchik

Starlski　Creek

River

Deep Creek

National Refuge Boundary

Crooked Creek

Tustumena Lake

Harding Icefield

Anchor Point
N59°46' W151°49'

Old Sterling Highway

Anchor

East End Road

Homer

N59°38'
W151°33'

S-172.7/277.9km Oceanview RV Park CT

Homer Spit

Kachemak Bay

Halibut Cove ❄
N59°37'
W151°14'

S-180/289km
A-233/374km
H-0

KENAI

National Park Boundary

Kenai Fjords National Park

Cook Inlet

Alaska State Ferry

Seldovia ❄⛺🏕✈
N59°26' W151°42'

National Refuge Boundary

Glaciated

Area

MOUNTAINS

S **42.8** (68.9 km) A **95.8** (154.2 km) H **136.7** (220 km) Gravel turnouts on Quartz Creek.

S **43.1** (69.4 km) A **96.1** (154.6 km) H **136.4** (219.5 km) Double-ended gravel turnout to south on Quartz Creek.

S **43.5** (70 km) A **96.5** (155.3 km) H **136** (218.9 km) Gravel turnout to south.

S **44** (70.8 km) A **97** (156.1 km) H **135.5** (218.1 km) Gravel turnout on Quartz Creek.

S **44.3** (71.3 km) A **97.3** (156.6) H **135.2** (217.6 km) Solid waste transfer site to east; public dumpsters.

S **44.9** (72.3 km) A **97.9** (157.5 km) H **134.6** (216.6 km) Sunrise Inn (open year-round); food, gas and lodging. **Junction** with Quartz Creek Road.

Sunrise Inn. See display ad this section.

Quartz Creek Road leads south to **Quartz Creek Recreation Area.** Quartz Creek Campground, at Mile 0.3, has 45 sites, boat launch and parking lot, flush toilets, water system, firepits and a $10 camping fee. **Quartz Creek**, rainbow, midsummer; Dolly Varden to 25 inches, late May through June. ⬥▲

Crescent Creek Campground, at Mile 3, was closed for renovation in 1998, scheduled to reopen June 1999; 9 sites, toilets, firepits and water. Crescent Creek Trail (USFS), trailhead parking at Mile 3.4 Quartz Creek Road, is a popular trail with mountains bikers. Nice 6.2-mile/10-km hike through hemlock forest to subalpine **Crescent Lake**; stocked with grayling. *Watch for bears.* A public-use cabin is located at the lake; permit required for use; accessible in summer only. ⬥▲

S **45** (72.4 km) A **98** (157.7 km) H **134.5** (216.5 km) Beautiful views of Kenai Lake next 3 miles/4.8 km westbound. The lake's unusual color is caused by glacial silt.

Kenai Lake, lake trout, May 15 to Sept. 30; trout, May to September; Dolly Varden, May to September. Kenai Lake and tributaries are closed to salmon fishing. ⬥

S **45.6** (73.4 km) A **98.6** (158.7 km) H **133.9** (215.5 km) Large turnout to south with toilet. This is an observation point for Dall sheep on Near Mountain and mountain goats on Cecil Rhode Mountain (directly across Kenai Lake); use binoculars.

S **46.3** (74.5 km) A **99.3** (159.8 km) H **133.2** (214.4 km) Small gravel turnout to south.

S **47** (75.6 km) A **100** (160.9 km) H **132.5**

(213.2 km) Turnout to south.

S **47.1** (75.8 km) A **100.1** (161.1 km) H **132.4** (213.1 km) **Kenai Lake Cabins.** See display ad this section.

S **47.4** (76.3 km) A **100.4** (161.6 km) H

132.1 (212.5 km) **Kenai Grill.** See display ad this section.

S **47.6** (76.6 km) A **100.6** (161.9 km) H **131.9** (212.3 km) Laundromat and showers; towing.

S 47.7 (76.8 km) A 100.7 (162 km) H 131.8 (212.1 km) Bean Creek Road, access to Bruce Nelson's fishing guide service (0.3 mile), Alaskan Sourdough Bed and Breakfast (0.7 mile) and the Kenai Princess Lodge and RV Park on the Kenai River (2 miles). The lodge's lobby has an interesting chandelier made from antlers. ▲

Alaskan Sourdough Bed & Breakfast. See display ad this section.

Bruce Nelson's Float Fishing Service and Eid's Cabin. See display ad this section.

Kenai Princess Lodge. A wilderness retreat overlooking the salmon-rich Kenai River featuring 70 cozy bungalow-style rooms with sun porches, wood stoves, televisions and telephones. Spacious view deck, fine restaurant, lounge, gift shop, tour desk, hot tubs, exercise room. Meeting facilities. Open year-round. Call (800) 426-0500. [ADVERTISEMENT]

Kenai Princess RV Park. At Cooper Landing on the salmon-rich Kenai River. Featuring 35 sites with water and power, general store, showers, laundry, septic. Use of facilities at adjacent Kenai Princess Lodge. Open year-round. $20 per night. Phone (907) 595-1425 for reservations. [ADVERTISEMENT] ▲

S 47.8 (76.9 km) A 100.8 (162.2 km) H 131.7 (211.9 km) Kenai River bridge.

Cooper Landing boat launch facility, adjacent to the Kenai River Bridge, contains a concrete boat launch, day-use parking, restrooms, viewing decks, informational panels and telescopes. $5 launching fee or $5 parking fee for vehicles not launching boats.

The Kenai River flows directly alongside the highway for the next 10 miles/16 km with several gravel turnouts offering good views. (A proposed plan to reroute this portion of the Sterling Highway away from the Kenai River and into the mountains is under consideration.)

Upper Kenai River, from **Kenai Lake** to **Skilak Lake,** including Skilak Lake within a half mile of the Kenai River inlet, special regulations apply. For current recorded fishing forecast, phone (907) 267-2502. Silver salmon 5 to 15 lbs., August through October; pink salmon 3 to 7 lbs., July and August; red salmon 3 to 12 lbs., June 11 through mid-August; rainbow and Dolly Varden, June 11 through October. *IMPORTANT: Be familiar with current regulations and closures. Dates given here are subject to change!* ✍

S 47.9 (77.1 km) A 100.9 (162.4 km) H 131.6 (211.8 km) Snug Harbor Road. This side road leads 12 miles/19.3 km to Cooper Lake and trailhead for 23-mile/37-km USFS trail to Russian River Campground (see Mile-post S 52.6). A Baptist church and the St. John Neumann Catholic Church, named after one of the first American saints, are on Snug Harbor Road.

St. John Neumann Catholic Church. See display ad this section.

S 48.1 (77.4 km) A 101.1 (162.7 km) H 131.4 (211.7 km) **Ingram's Sport Fishing Cabins.** See display ad this section.

S 48.2 (77.6 km) A 101.2 (162.9 km) H 131.3 (211.3 km) **Troutfitters Alpine Motel.** See display ad this section.

S 48.3 (77.7 km) A 101.3 (163 km) H 131.2 (211.1 km) **Kenai River Drifter's Lodge.** When life offers you the best, take it! On the bank of the Kenai River, enjoy comfortable, first-class, tastefully furnished new chalets which include your own large private bath, fridge, microwave, coffee/tea, or your own lodge room. Mesmerizing views of the world-class Kenai River or Chugach Mountains can be seen from every window of your accommodations. Join in on the Alaskan tales during the evening campfires after a day of activities such as: fishing, hiking, rafting, cross-country skiing, snowmobiling or just plain relaxing. Chalets accommodate 5 people or the entire lodge can host 35 plus. Reservations encouraged, all seasons. (907) 595-5555. Web site: Driferslodge.com. See display ad. [ADVERTISEMENT]

S 48.4 (77.9 km) A 101.4 (163.2 km) H 131.1 (211 km) COOPER LANDING (pop. 283) stretches along several miles of the Sterling Highway at the west end of Kenai Lake. All visitor facilities available. **Emergency services:** Cooper Landing ambulance, phone (907) 595-1255.

Private Aircraft: Quartz Creek (Cooper Landing) airstrip, 4 miles/6.4 km west; elev. 450 feet/137m; length 2,200 feet/671m; gravel; unattended. Floatplanes land at Cooper Lake.

Cooper Landing was named for Joseph Cooper, a miner who discovered gold here in 1898. A school and post office opened in the 1920s to serve the miners and their families living in the area. Cooper Landing was connected to Kenai by road in 1948, and to Anchorage in 1951. According to the Alaska Dept. of Community and Regional Affairs, the population of the area nearly doubles each summer to support tourism businesses and activities.

The Shrew's Nest, Last Resort RV Park and Landing Latté. See display ad this section. ▲

S 48.5 (78.1 km) **A 101.5** (163.3 km) **H 131** (210.8 km) **Alaska River Adventures.** See display ad this section.

Hamilton's Place river resort, only complete stop on the upper Kenai River. Information center for the famous Russian River and surrounding area. Centrally located for day trips to Seward, Soldotna/Kenai, Homer. Make us your Kenai Peninsula headquarters. Tesoro services, 24-hour recovery and transport (flatbed) service, 24-hour locksmith, propane. (All-emergency road service providers.) General store, groceries, licenses, tackle, ice, liquor store. Restaurant, lounge.

RV hookups, modern B&B cabins with cooking facilities, laundromat, phone. Fish freezing, storage, Federal Express shipping. Hamilton's Place, serving the public since

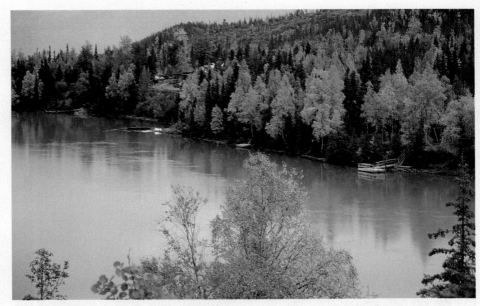

View of Kenai River from Bean Creek Road. (© Kris Graef, staff)

Sport Fishing INGRAM'S Cabins

KITCHENETTES • PRIVATE BATHS • FISHING FROM DOCK
• CABINS SLEEP UP TO 5 GUESTS
• DAILY AND WEEKLY RATES
• GUIDED DRIFT BOAT TRIPS
• TROPHY FISHING
P.O. BOX 748 • COOPER LANDING, AK 99572
MILE S 48.1 STERLING HIGHWAY FAX: (907) 595-1213
PHONE: (907) 595-1213

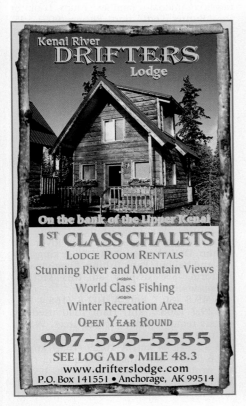

Kenai River DRIFTERS Lodge
On the bank of the Upper Kenai
1ST CLASS CHALETS
LODGE ROOM RENTALS
Stunning River and Mountain Views
World Class Fishing
Winter Recreation Area
OPEN YEAR ROUND
907-595-5555
SEE LOG AD • MILE 48.3
www.drifterslodge.com
P.O. Box 141551 • Anchorage, AK 99514

TROUTFITTERS ALPINE MOTEL
TROPHY TROUT DOLLY VARDEN
Troutfitters Alpine Motel
Located at the headwaters of the Kenai River. We have 12 modern units which include TV - VCR - Phones - Kitchenettes Full Bath & A Wonderful View
Fly Fish The Kenai River
Experienced fly fishing guides. Catch and release trophy Rainbow Trout and Dolly Varden. Raft and Drift Boat Rental Available
(907) 595-1212 • Fax (907) 595-1593
P.O. Box 570 Cooper Landing, Alaska 99572
aktrout@arctic.net

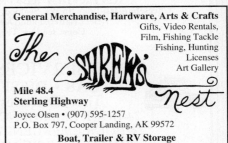

General Merchandise, Hardware, Arts & Crafts
Gifts, Video Rentals, Film, Fishing Tackle Fishing, Hunting Licenses Art Gallery
The SHREW'S nest
Mile 48.4 Sterling Highway
Joyce Olsen • (907) 595-1257
P.O. Box 797, Cooper Landing, AK 99572
Boat, Trailer & RV Storage
"LAST RESORT" RV PARK
Secluded, Wooded Sites
Electric Hookups • (907) 595-1257
Day - Week - Month Rates
LANDING LATTÉ
Cappuccino • Espresso • Latté
Fine Coffees • Pastries
Alaska Specialties • (907) 595-1606

SCENIC FLOAT TRIPS $39
KENAI NATIONAL WILDLIFE REFUGE
Alaska River Adventures
Mile 48.5 Sterling Highway PO Box 725, COOPER LANDING, AK 99572
907-595-2000 fishin@alaska.net 888-836-9027

MILE 48.5 STERLING HIGHWAY
100 MILES SOUTH OF ANCHORAGE
OVERLOOKING THE KENAI RIVER

"THE ONLY STOP FOR ALL YOUR TRAVEL NEEDS!"

GENERAL STORE
MUNCHIES, JUNK FOOD, SNACKS

Tackle Shop
LURES, NETS, POLES, HIP BOOTS, CAMP SUPPLIES
"Killer Coho Flies" and "Russian River Riggins"
FISHING LICENSES

FISH FREEZING, STORAGE & SHIPPING
WE NEVER RUN OUT OF CUBE ICE!

PACKAGE LIQUOR STORE

DINE AND RELAX
RIVERVIEW RESTAURANT & LOUNGE
Cheeseburgers, Juicy Steaks, Seafood, Fries, Homemade Soups, Chili and Pies
(Beer Battered and Deep Fried Halibut Chunks)
Come see Our Trophy Animal Display!

AUTO SERVICES • (907) 595-1260
GAS • DIESEL • PROPANE
Tires, Batteries & Oil Products
24-HOUR EMERGENCY RECOVERY/TOWING
24-HOUR EMERGENCY LOCKSMITH SERVICE
MINOR CAR REPAIR SERVICE • PARTS

Yes, we still have the Bunnies!

STAY OVERNIGHT
RV & Trailer Facilities

MODERN B&B CABINS WITH COOKING FACILITIES
LOCAL LAUNDROMAT AND PUBLIC SHOWERS
CALL WELL IN ADVANCE FOR RESERVATIONS
(907) 595-1260 • FAX (907) 595-1530
BOX 569, COOPER LANDING, AK 99572
hamspl@arctic.net

THE WAY TO GO.

MasterCard
VISA
DISCOVER

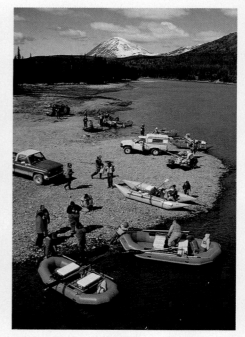

River rafting and fishing from rafts are popular on the Kenai River.

(© Barbara Willard)

1952, hopes to make your stay enjoyable. Phone (907) 595-1260; fax (907) 595-1530. E-mail: hamspl@arctic.net. See display ad this section. [ADVERTISEMENT]

The Hutch B&B. 12 clean smoke-free rooms with private baths at very reasonable rates. Continental breakfast served until 10 A.M. Common area TVs. View mountain goats, Dall sheep and Kenai River from our covered decks. Our parking area accommodates boat trailers and large vehicles. Also, new self-contained cabin with cooking facilities accommodates families/groups. Look for the "Bunny Trail" sign. Phone (907) 595-1270, fax (907) 595-1829. See display ad. [ADVERTISEMENT]

S 48.7 (78.4 km) **A 101.7** (163.7 km) **H 130.8** (210.5 km) Cooper Landing post office, located in resort; open 9 A.M. to 5 P.M. weekdays and Saturday morning. Pay phone.

S 48.8 (78.5 km) **A 101.8** (163.8 km) **H 130.7** (210.3 km) **Kenai Lake Air Service.** See display ad this section.

S 49.4 (79.5 km) **A 102.4** (164.8 km) **H 130.1** (209.4 km) Large paved turnout to north by Kenai River. The highway winds along the Kenai River.

S 49.7 (80 km) **A 102.7** (165.3 km) **H 129.8** (208.9 km) **The Miller Homestead Bed & Breakfast RV Park.** Make us your vacation headquarters for Kenai Peninsula adventures. We can arrange fishing for trophy rainbow trout, Russian River red salmon, Dolly Varden, Kenai River kings, silvers and halibut. Bank fishing. River-viewing platform. See display ad this section. [ADVERTISEMENT]

S 49.8 (80.1 km) **A 102.8** (165.4 km) **H 129.7** (208.7 km) Haul road used by loggers removing dead spruce trees. Watch for trucks.

S 49.9 (80.4 km) **A 102.9** (165.7 km) **H 129.6** (208.6 km) **Alaska Rivers Co.,** right side westbound. Rafting daily on the beautiful Kenai River. Half-day scenic float, or full-day canyon trip with exhilarating rapids.

Both trips include homemade picnic lunch, excellent viewing of wildlife, professional guides, all equipment provided. All ages welcome. Personalized guided drift boat fishing for all species of fish. Overnight accommodations available. Family-owned and operated by Cooper Landing residents. Gary Galbraith, owner. (907) 595-1226 for reservations or just stop by. E-mail: lrg@arctic.net. [ADVERTISEMENT]

S 50.1 (80.6 km) **A 103.1** (165.9 km) **H 129.4** (208.2 km) **Kenai Backcountry Lodge.** See display ad this section.

Alaska Wildland Adventures. Don't pass up taking a rafting or fishing trip with Alaska Wildland Adventures. You'll enjoy this facility's unique and scenic setting on the Kenai River. They offer daily guided raft trips along with a delicious Alaskan picnic lunch. You can expect to see wildlife and

The Kenai has many lakes for fishing and camping. (© Susan Cole Kelly)

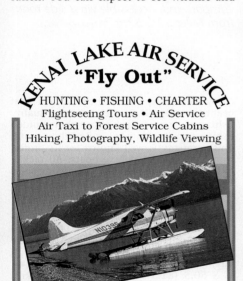
All 5 species of Pacific salmon are found in Alaska: King (chinook), silver (coho), pink (humpy), chum (dog) and red (sockeye).

Fish cleaning station at Russian River campground, accessible via a side road from Milepost S 52.6. (© Susan Cole Kelly)

enjoy the scenery of one of the world's most beautiful rivers. If you're seeking a quality fishing experience, ask about their guided fishing trips for salmon and rainbow trout. This company is well known for its professional guides and deluxe boats. All tackle, rods and reels are furnished. Operating since 1977. Phone toll free (800) 478-4100 for more information or reservations. See "Kenai River Trips" display ad. Internet address: www.alaskawildland.com. [ADVERTISEMENT] MP

S 50.4 (81.1 km) **A 103.4** (166.4 km) **H 129.1** (207.8 km) **Juneau Creek**, Dolly Varden and rainbow, mid-June through July.

S 50.5 (81.3 km) **A 103.5** (166.6 km) **H 129** (207.6 km) Bridge over Cooper Creek. USFS Cooper Creek Campground. Camping area on the river side of highway (second entrance westbound) has 7 sites, several on the riverbank. Camping area on the other side of the highway has 23 sites. Both have tables, water and firepits. Fee is $9 single, $13 double. Reservations available, phone 1-877-444-NRRS. ▲

S 52 (83.7 km) **A 105** (169 km) **H 127.5** (205.2 km) **Gwin's Lodge, Restaurant and Bar**, left side southbound. One of Alaska's few remaining traditionally built log roadhouses where Alaskans and visitors alike always stop for homemade "Alaska"-sized portions and fast courteous service. Selected by the "Best of Alaska" tour guide as the top restaurant in the northern Kenai Peninsula area. Gwin's specialties include delicious homemade chili, soups, chowders, quiches, pies and cheesecakes as well as steaks, seafood and our world-famous burger line-up. Gwin's Store & Tackle Shop features a full-array of fishing gear and tackle, licenses, rental gear and boots, groceries, Alaska cards/gifts, pizzeria, ice cream shop, espresso/latte, fish freezing and "Trapper's Creek Smoking Company" fish processing/

Fishing for salmon at Russian River campground, Milepost S 52.6. (© Susan Cole Kelly)

smoking/shipping drop-off service site. Gwin's exclusive line of "Kenai River," "Russian River," and "Alaska" embroidered shirts, hats, jackets and polar fleece are the Peninsula's finest. Gwin's charter booking service's wide array of excursions include Upper Kenai River rainbow trout; Lower Kenai River king and silver salmon; Cook Inlet Pacific halibut; fly-in trips to remote lakes and streams for rainbow trout and/or arctic grayling; Upper Kenai River scenic and wildlife viewing raft trips; and scenic flightseeing. VISA, MasterCard and Discover accepted. (907) 595-1266 (voice); (907) 595-1681 (fax). See display ad. [ADVERTISEMENT] ▲

Kenai Cache. See display ad this section.

S 52.6 (84.6 km) **A 105.6** (169.9 km) **H 126.9** (204.2 km) K'BEQ Footprints Heritage Site (Kenaitze Indian Tribe) north side of highway; USFS Russian River Campground to south (description follows).

K-Beq Footprints. See display ad this section.

Follow paved 2-mile/3.2-km road south for Russian River USFS camping units, parking areas and trailheads. Phones and overflow parking at exit to highway. Dump station at Mile 1.3 on the access road. Campground host at Mile 1.7. The Russian River

Campground is often full during the summer, particularly during the Russian River red salmon runs. Arrive early! There are 84 sites, toilets, water, tables and firepits. Fish cleaning stations. Fees: $11 single RV occupancy, $18 double RV occupancy, $5 12-hour day-use parking, $6 dump station. Concessionaire-operated. For reservations phone 1-877-444-NRRS. ▲

CAUTION: Bears attracted by the salmon are frequent visitors to this campground.

Upper Russian Lake USFS trailhead parking at Mile 1 on campground road. Lower Russian Lake trailhead parking at Mile 2.6. Lower Russian Lakes Trail: elev. 500 feet/152m; hiking time 1½ hours; good trail first 3 miles;.spur trail to Russian River Falls viewing platform. A good place to view jumping salmon, and a nice family hike. Upper Russian Lake: elev. 690 feet/210m, 12 miles/19.3 km. Trail continues to Cooper Lake at end of Snug Harbor Road (see **Milepost S 47.9**). Public-use cabins along trail. Winter use: good snowmobiling to lower lake only, avalanche danger beyond.

The **Russian River:** Closed to all fishing April 15 through June 10. Bait prohibited at all times in Russian River drainage. Check regulations for limits and other restrictions. Red (sockeye) salmon run starts mid-June. Second run begins July 20–25 and lasts about 3 weeks. Must use flies prior to Aug. 21. Silver (coho) salmon to 15 lbs., run begins mid-August. Catch-and-release only for rainbow trout in lower part of river at all times that season is open. ⌐≈

S 53 (85.3 km) **A 106** (170.6 km) **H 126.5** (203.6 km) Bridge over Kenai River.

Well-marked entry point to **Resurrection Pass Trail** USFS just west of bridge; large parking area to north at trailhead. This 38-mile-/61-km-long trail climbs to Resurrection Pass (elev. 2,600 feet/792m) and descends to north trailhead near Hope on Turnagain Arm.

S 53.7 (86.4 km) **A 106.7** (171.7 km) **H 125.8** (202.5 km) Kenaitze Indian Interpre-

Skilak Lake Loop Road Log

The 19.1-mile/30.7-km Skilak Lake Loop Road (good gravel) loops south through the Skilak Wildlife Recreation Area to campgrounds, trails and fishing spots. *CAUTION: Do not leave valuables in unattended boats or vehicles.*

Distance from east junction (EJ) with Sterling Highway at Milepost S 58 is followed by distance from **west junction (WJ) with Sterling Highway at Milepost S 75.2.**

EJ 0 WJ 19.1 (30.7 km) **Junction** with Sterling Highway at **Milepost S 58.**

EJ 0.1 (0.2 km) **WJ 19** (30.5 km) Jim's Landing Day-use area on Kenai River, 0.2 mile/0.3 km from road; toilets, tables, firepits, water, boat launch, parking area. Pavement ends westbound.

EJ 0.6 (1 km) **WJ 18.5** (29.7 km) East entrance parking area for Kenai River trail; map and trail chart (6.3-mile/10.1-km hike).

EJ 2 (3.2 km) **WJ 17.1** (27.5 km) Pothole Lake Overlook; gravel parking area overlooks scene of Pothole Lake forest fire of 1991. Interpretive sign on fire.

EJ 2.4 (3.9 km) **WJ 16.7** (26.8 km) West entrance parking area for Kenai River trail (6.3-mile/10.1-km hike).

EJ 3.6 (5.8 km) **WJ 15.5** (24.9 km) Located 0.5 mile/0.8 km in from the road on the lakeshore is Hidden Lake Campground, an exceptionally nice camping area with 44 sites on paved loop roads. It has picnic pavilions, a dump station, wheelchair-accessible toilets, tables, water, firepits and boat launch. Campfire programs Friday and Saturday evenings in summer at the amphitheater. Observation deck for viewing wildlife. Campground hosts in residence. Camping fee $10 for vehicles. Trailer parking area, interpretive exhibits and kitchen shelter with barbecue. ♿▲

Hidden Lake, lake trout average 16 inches and kokanee 9 inches, year-round, best from May 15 to July 1, use spoon, red-and-white or weighted, by trolling, casting and jigging. This lake is a favorite among local ice fishermen from late December through March. ◄

EJ 4.7 (7.6 km) **WJ 14.4** (23.1 km) Hidden Creek trail (1.5-mile/2.4-km hike); parking area and information sign.

EJ 5.3 (8.5 km) **WJ 13.8** (22.2 km) Hidden Creek Overlook double-ended turnout with sweeping view of one arm of Skilak Lake; forest fire damage from 1996 fire visible.

EJ 5.5 (8.9 km) **WJ 13.6** (21.8 km) Skilak Lookout trail (2.6-mile/4.2-km hike); parking area for 6 cars, 3 RVs.

EJ 6.2 (10 km) **WJ 12.9** (20.7 km) Bear Mountain trail (1-mile/1.6-km hike); parking area across from small lake.

EJ 6.9 (11.1 km) **WJ 12.2** (19.6 km) Scenic viewpoint of Skilak Lake.

EJ 8.5 (13.6 km) **WJ 10.6** (17 km) Upper Skilak Lake Campground, drive 2 miles/3.2 km along Lower Ohmer Lake; 0.2-mile/0.3-km loop road through campground. There are 25 campsites (some sites on lakeshore), boat launch, toilets and tables; similar facilities to Hidden Lake Campground (**Milepost EJ 3.6**). Camping fee $10/vehicle, $6/tent site (walk-in). ▲

Lower Ohmer Lake, rainbow 14 to 16 inches, year-round. **Skilak Lake** offers rainbow and Dolly Varden. Red (sockeye) salmon enter lake in mid-July.

EJ 8.6 (13.8 km) **WJ 10.5** (16.9 km) Lower Ohmer Lake, short side road to parking area on lake; 3 campsites, toilet, boat launch, firepits, tables. ▲

EJ 9.4 (15 km) **WJ 9.7** (15.6 km) Turnout overlooking Engineer Lake.

EJ 9.5 (15.2 km) **WJ 9.6** (15.4 km) Short side road to **Engineer Lake,** boat launch and Seven Lakes trail; turnaround and parking area with firepits. Stocked silver salmon to 15 inches, best in July. ◄

EJ 9.6 (15.4 km) **WJ 9.5** (15.3 km) Engineer Lake wayside; gravel turnout.

EJ 11.5 (18.5 km) **WJ 7.6** (12.2 km) Dump station on paved double-ended turnout to east.

EJ 13.8 (22.2 km) **WJ 6.3** (8.5 km) Well-marked 1-mile/1.6-km side road to Lower Skilak Lake Campground; 14 sites, tables, toilets, firepits, boat launch. ▲

CAUTION: Skilak Lake is cold; winds are fierce and unpredictable. Wear life jackets!

EJ 14.2 (22.8 km) **WJ 4.9** (7.8 km) Fire guard station.

EJ 18.7 (30.1 km) **WJ 0.4** (0.6 km) Bottinentnin Lake; well-marked side road leads 0.3 mile/0.5 km to parking area on lakeshore. Shallow lake: No sport fish, but nice area for recreational canoeing.

EJ 19.1 (30.7 km) **WJ 0 Junction** with Sterling Highway at **Milepost S 75.2.**

Return to Milepost S 58 or S 75.2 Sterling Highway

---

tive Site to south has a walking trail along the Kenai River; fishing, parking (no RVs or trailers)

S 54.7 (88 km) **A 107.7** (173.3 km) **H 124.8** (200.8 km) Leaving Chugach National Forest lands westbound. Many turnouts with recreation access signs on the Kenai River between here and **Milepost S 58.**

S 55 (88.5 km) **A 108** (173.8 km) **H 124.5** (200.4 km) Leaving Game Management Unit 7, entering Unit 15 westbound. Entering **Kenai National Wildlife Refuge** westbound, administered by the USF&WS; contains more than 1.97 million acres of land set aside to preserve the moose, bear, sheep and other wildlife found here.

Russian River Ferry entrance to southeast. New (1999) 60-space outer parking lot, boat launch, toilets and gatehouse. During salmon season this recreation area and campground are heavily used. Fees charged for boat launch, parking and camping. Privately operated 28-person ferry crosses the Kenai River to opposite bank and to the mouth of the Russian River. Ferry fee is $6 adults round-trip, $4 children. ◄▲

S 56.4 (90.8 km) **A 109.4** (176.1 km) **H 123.1** (198.1 km) Gravel turnout to southeast.

S 57.1 (91.9 km) **A 110.1** (177.2 km) **H 122.4** (197 km) Double-ended turnout to southeast. Fuller Lake trailhead (well marked), parking. **Lower Fuller Lake,** arctic grayling; **Upper Fuller Lake,** Dolly Varden. ◄

S 58 (93.3 km) **A 111** (178.6 km) **H 121.5** (195.5 km) Kenai National Wildlife Refuge visitor contact station to northwest, Skilak Road to southeast. The information cabin is open Memorial Day through Labor Day; brochures and information on Kenai National Wildlife Refuge recreation opportunities. Large gravel parking area, water pump, toilets, trailer parking (no camping).

Junction with Skilak Lake Loop Road. See SKILAK LAKE LOOP ROAD log this section.

S 59 (94.9 km) **A 112** (180.2 km) **H 120.5** (193.9 km) **Milepost S 59.** Actual driving distance between here and **Milepost S 61** is 2.6 miles/4.2 km or 0.6 mile/1 km more than the posts indicate.

S 60 (96.5 km) **A 113** (181.9 km) **H 119.5** (192.3 km) Large gravel turnout to north.

S 60.6 (97.5 km) **A 113.6** (182.8 km) **H 118.9** (191.3 km) **Jean Lake** campground (no sign in 1998); 3 sites, picnic area; boat launch, rainbow fishing. ◄▲

S 60.8 (97.8 km) **A 113.8** (183.1 km) **H 118.7** (191 km) Skyline trail to north; double-ended gravel parking area to south.

S 62.3 (100.3 km) **A 115.3** (185.6 km) **H 117.2** (188.6 km) Large gravel turnout to north. Mystery Hills to the north and Hideout Hill to the south.

S 64.5 (103.8 km) **A 117.5** (189.1 km) **H 115** (185.1 km) Highway straightens westbound. *CAUTION: Winding road eastbound.*

S 68.3 (109.9 km) **A 121.3** (195.2 km) **H 111.2** (179 km) Turnoff to south for Peterson Lake (0.5 mile/0.8 km) and Kelly Lake (1 mile/1.6 km) public campgrounds. Both have tables and firepits for 3 camping parties, water and boat launch, and parking space for self-contained RVs. **Kelly** and **Peterson** lakes have rainbow population. Access to Seven Lakes trail. ◄▲

S 70.4 (113.3 km) **A 123.4** (198.6 km) **H 109.1** (175.6 km) Egumen Lake gravel parking area to southeast. East Fork Moose River trailhead. Half-mile marshy trail to **Egumen Lake** (lake not visible from highway); good rainbow population. ◄

S 71.3 (114.7 km) **A 124.3** (200 km) **H 108.2** (174.1 km) Parking area at entrance to Watson Lake public campground; 0.4-mile/0.6-km drive from highway to small campground with 3 sites, toilets, picnic tables, fire grates, water, dumpsters and steep boat launch (suitable for canoes or hand-carried boats). **Watson Lake,** rainbow. ◄▲

S 72.8 (117.2 km) **A 125.8** (202.4 km) **H 106.7** (171.7 km) Paved double-ended turnout to south, lake to north.

S 75.2 (121 km) **A 128.2** (206.3 km) **H 104.3** (167.8 km) **Kenai River from**

Skilak Lake to Soldotna. Consult regulations for legal tackle, limits and seasons. King salmon 20 to 80 lbs., use spinners, excellent fishing June to August; red salmon 6 to 12 lbs., many, but hard to catch, use flies, best from July 15 to Aug. 10; pink salmon 4 to 8 lbs., abundant fish on even years Aug. 1 to Sept. 1, spoons; silver salmon 6 to 15 lbs., use spoons, Aug. 15 to Nov. 1; rainbow, Dolly Varden 15 to 20 inches, June through September, use spinners, winged bobber, small-weighted spoon.

NOTE: The Kenai River Special Management Area is managed by the Alaska Division of Parks and Outdoor Recreation (DPOR), and includes the waters of Kenai and Skilak lakes and the Kenai River. Motors are limited to maximum 35 horsepower on the river, and prohibited on some sections. For more information, contact DPOR at P.O. Box 1247, Soldotna, AK 99669, phone (907) 262-5581.

West junction with Skilak Lake Loop Road. See SKILAK LAKE LOOP ROAD log on page 605.

S 78.5 (126.3 km) **A 131.5** (211.6 km) **H 101** (162.5 km) **Alaskan Saddle Safaris.** For an unforgettable experience, step back in time, camping and riding through the spectacular, rugged Alaska wilderness to the site of a glacier. We offer 3–5 day trail rides and guided and unguided hunts into the breathtakingly beautiful Kenai National Wildlife Refuge. Wildlife abounds: Brown bear, moose, caribou, Dall sheep, wolves and much more. P.O. Box 1246, Sterling, AK 99672. For bookings and information call (907) 260-3843. [ADVERTISEMENT]

S 79.5 (127.9 km) **A 132.5** (213.2 km) **H 100** (160.9 km) Kenai Keys Road.

Begin 4-lane divided highway westbound.

S 80.3 (129.2 km) **A 133.3** (214.5 km) **H 99.2** (159.6 km) Turnoff for Peninsula Furs and **Bing's Landing State Recreation Site** with RV and tent camping at 36 sites, picnic area, water, boat launch, toilets (wheelchair accessible), dumpster and access to Kenai River. Camping fee $8/night or annual pass. Boat launch fee $5 or annual boat launch pass. $5 day-use parking fee. &🅰

Peninsula Furs. See display ad this section.

S 80.5 (129.5 km) **A 133.5** (214.8 km) **H 99** (159.3 km) **Diamond Willow.** See display ad this section.

S 81 (130.3 km) **A 134** (215.6 km) **H 98.5** (158.5 km) **STERLING** (pop. 5,888; elev. 150 feet/45m). This unincorporated community, located on the Sterling Highway at the confluence of the Moose and Kenai Rivers, serves the summer influx of sportfishermen, campers and others. The name was formalized in 1954 when a post office was established. Sterling has one school.

Traveler services include 2 gas stations, 2 motels, several restaurants and cafes; gift, grocery, hardware, antique, fur and furniture stores, laundromat and several campgrounds. Post office at **Milepost S 81.6.** (Businesses with a Sterling mailing address extend west to **Milepost S 85.**) Nearby recreational opportunities include fishing and the extensive canoe trail system (see description at **Milepost S 82**). Moose River Raft Race and Sterling Days held in July.

Bing Brown's RV Park & Motel. See display ad this section. ▲

S 81.1 (130.5 km) **A 134.1** (215.8 km) **H 98.4** (158.4 km) Gift shop and grocery store.

S 81.4 (131 km) **A 134.4** (216.3 km) **H 98.1** (157.9 km) **Weigner's Backcountry Guiding.** See display ad this section.

S 81.6 (131.3 km) **A 134.6** (216.6 km) **H 97.9** (157.6 km) Sterling post office (ZIP code 99672).

Sterling Auto Parts & Repair. See display ad this section.

S 81.7 (131.5 km) **A 134.7** (216.8 km) **H 97.8** (157.4 km) **Vacation Cabins.** See display ad this section.

Cook's Corner. See display ad this section.

S 82 (132 km) **A 135** (217.3 km) **H 97.5** (156.9 km) Pay phone on highway just before turnoff for **Izaak Walton State Recreation Site**, located at the confluence of the Kenai and Moose rivers. Paved access road, 25 campsites, parking, tables, toilets, water and dumpster. Camping fee $10/night or annual pass. Boat launch ($5 fee or annual boat launch pass) and good access to Kenai River. A small log cabin, totem pole and an information sign about Moose River archaeological site. ▲

Sterling Chevron & Food Mart. See display ad this section.

Bridge over Moose River. *CAUTION: Drive carefully during fishing season when fishermen walk along bridge and highway.*

Canoe rentals and shuttle bus service to the Kenai National Wildlife Refuge canoe trail system are available by the Moose River bridge. This is one terminus of the Swan Lake canoe trail. There are 2 canoe routes in Kenai National Wildlife Refuge: Swan Lake route, a 60-mile/97-km route connecting 30 lakes; and the Swanson River route, an 80-mile/129-km route linking 40 lakes. Guided canoe tours and fishing charters are available. Portions of the canoe system may be traveled, taking anywhere from 1 to 4 days. Contact Kenai National Wildlife Refuge, Box 2139, Soldotna, AK 99669 for details. See SWANSON RIVER/SWAN LAKE ROAD log this section.

Moose River, 0.3 mile/0.4 km of fishing down to confluence with Kenai River. Sockeyes here in June. Big summer run of reds follows into August; silvers into October. ◄━

Kenai and **Moose rivers** (confluence), Dolly Varden and rainbow trout, salmon (king, red, pink, silver). June 15 through October for trout; year-round for Dolly Varden. King salmon from May through July, pink salmon in August and silver salmon from August through October. This is a fly-fishing-only area from May 15 through Aug. 15; closed to fishing from boats, May 15 until the end of the king salmon season or July 31, whichever is later. ◄━

Killey River Lodge. See display ad this section.

S 82.3 (132.4 km) **A 135.3** (217.7 km) **H 97.2** (156.4 km) **Alaska Adventure Reservations.** Charters, fly-ins, bear-viewing camp; 5 or 7 days. Canoe outfitting. Budget camp and fish trips; salmon, halibut and trout. Budget camping trips. We do it all! Phone (800) 544-2261; fax (907) 262-8797; web page: www.greatalaska.com; e-mail: greatalaska@greatalaska.com. See display ad this section. [ADVERTISEMENT]

S 82.5 (132.8 km) **A 135.5** (218.1 km) **H 97** (156.1 km) Keystone Road. Big Sky

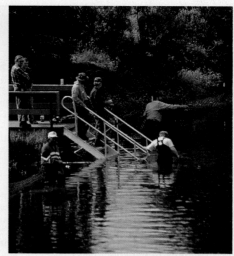

Salmon fishing at Izaak Walton State Recreation Area. (Susan Cole Kelly)

Swanson River/Swan Lake Road Log

Swanson River Road leads north 17.2 miles/27.7 km, where it junctions with Swan Lake Road, which leads east 12.7 miles/20.4 km and dead ends at Paddle Lake. Both roads provide access to fishing, hiking trails and canoe trails. *CAUTION: Do not leave valuables in vehicles at canoe trailheads.*

Distance from junction with the Sterling Highway (J) is shown.

J 0 Junction with Sterling Highway at **Milepost S 83.4.** Swanson River Road is a good gravel road but can be rough in spots; slow speeds are advised. There are numerous turnouts suitable for overnight camping in self-contained RVs.

J 0.7 (1.1 km) Robinson Loop Road; rejoins Sterling Highway at **Milepost S 87.5.**

J 1.3 (2.1 km) Airstrip.

J 4.4 (7.1 km) Entering Kenai National Wildlife Refuge.

J 7.9 (12.7 km) **Mosquito Lake,** turnout; 0.5-mile trail to lake. Rainbow trout.

J 9.1 (14.6 km) **Silver Lake** trailhead and parking: 1-mile/1.6-km hike to lake. Rainbow trout and arctic char. Arctic char are most easily caught in spring when the surface water is still cool. Once summer temperatures warm the surface, the char descend to deeper waters and are much harder to catch.

J 9.8 (15.8 km) **Finger Lake** trailhead: 2.3-mile/3.7-km hike to lake. Good arctic char fishing (spring).

J 10.6 (17.1 km) **Forest Lake** wayside, parking: 0.3-mile/0.5-km trail to lake. Rainbow trout; best fished from canoe or raft.

J 13 (20.9 km) **Weed Lake** wayside: small turnout by lake. Rainbow trout.

J 13.3 (21.4 km) **Drake** and **Skookum lakes** trailhead and parking; 2-mile/ 3.2-km trail. Rainbow trout and arctic char (spring).

J 14 (22.5 km) Access to Breeze Lake.

J 14.2 (22.9 km) **Dolly Varden Lake** Campground; 15 sites, water, toilets, boat launch. Large RVs and trailers note: 0.5-mile/0.8-km access road to campground is narrow and bumpy; check turnaround space before driving in. Fishing for Dolly Varden and rainbow; best in late August and September.

J 14.9 (24 km) Access road to canoe trails to east. Oil field road to west closed to private vehicles. The Swanson River Road was originally built as an access road to the Swanson River oil field. Chevron operated the field from 1958 to 1986; it is currently operated by Unocal.

J 15.7 (25.2 km) **Rainbow Lake** Campground; small 3-unit camping area on lakeshore with toilets, water and boat launch. Fishing for Dolly Varden and rainbow trout. *CAUTION: Steep road; difficult turnaround. Large RVs: check visually before driving in.*

J 17.2 (27.7 km) **Junction** with Swan Lake Road. Continue north 0.5 mile/ 0.8 km for Swanson River Landing at end of Swanson River Road; camping area with picnic tables, firepits, water, toilets, boat launch, large gravel parking area. This is the terminus of the Swanson River canoe route, which begins at Paddle Lake at the end of Swan Lake Road. Log now follows Swan Lake Road east.

J 17.3 (27.8 km) Kenai National Wildlife Refuge Outdoor Environmental Education Center. Reservation required. Educational group-use permits obtained at Kenai National Wildlife Refuge Visitor Center in Soldotna.

J 20.2 (32.5 km) **Fish Lake;** 3 sites, tables, firepits, toilets. Fishing for Dolly Varden.

Trumpeter swans.
(© Loren Taft)

J 21.2 (34 km) **Canoe Lake,** parking. West entrance to Swan Lake canoe route. Fishing for Dolly Varden.

J 21.8 (35.1 km) Sucker Creek wayside; campsite, table, fireplace. **Sucker Lake,** rainbow trout.

J 23.3 (37.5 km) **Merganser Lakes,** 0.5 mile/0.8 km south; rainbow trout.

J 25.4 (40.9 km) Nest Lakes trail, 0.5-mile/0.8-km hike north.

J 26.9 (43.3 km) Large turnout and toilet to west.

J 27 (43.5 km) **Portage Lake.** East entrance to Swan Lake canoe route. Lake is stocked with coho salmon.

J 27.3 (43.9 km) Informal pullout on lake.

J 29.4 (47.3 km) Y in road; bear left.

J 29.9 (48.1 km) End of road. **Paddle Lake** entrance to Swanson River canoe route; parking, picnic table, water and toilet. Fishing for rainbow and Dolly Varden.

Return to Milepost S 83.4 Sterling Highway

Charter & Fish Camp 0.5 mile north.

Big Sky Charter & Fish Camp. See display ad this section.

S 82.6 (132.9 km) **A 135.6** (218.2 km) **H 96.9** (155.9 km) Airstrip. Restaurant and bar.

S 82.8 (133.3 km) **A 135.8** (218.5 km) **H 96.7** (155.6 km) Truck weigh station; senior center across highway.

Highway narrows to 2 lanes westbound. Begin divided 4-lane highway eastbound.

S 83.2 (133.9 km) **A 136.2** (219.2 km) **H 96.3** (155 km) Log Cabin Maps, Books and Bookings. This interesting log cabin with circular driveway is your source for recreational, topographic, nautical and gift maps of Alaska and Kenai Peninsula. Also available are books and field guides to heighten your

Alaska experience. It's a good place to buy fishing licenses and make your reservations for salmon/halibut fishing trips, guided canoe adventures, Kachemak Bay sailboat charters, bear flightseeing, local and wilderness cabin rentals. E-mail/fax/copying services available. Phone/fax (907) 260-9283. Box 894, Sterling, AK 99672. E-mail: mapsAK@alaska.net. [ADVERTISEMENT]

S 83.4 (134.2 km) **A 136.4** (219.5 km) **H 96.1** (154.7 km) Swanson River Road to north, Scout Lake Road to south. Scout Lake Loop Road rejoins the Sterling Highway at **Milepost S 85** (see milepost for description). Swanson River Road leads north to canoe trails. Convenience store with gas, and church located on Swanson River Road, just off highway. Sterling elementary school.

Sterling Baptist Church. See display ad this section.

ZIPMART. See display ad this section.

Junction with Swanson River Road. See SWANSON RIVER/SWAN LAKE ROAD log this section.

S 84.3 (135.7 km) A 137.3 (221 km) H 95.2 (153.2 km) **Scout Lake Inn and Nicki's Restaurant**, located near the Kenai and Moose rivers. Good fishing May to September 30. Clean, modern rooms with phones, satellite TV, and in-room coffee. Guaranteed lower rates than Soldotna. Nicki's specializes in homemade cinnamon rolls, breads and pies. We have the "locals" stamp of approval for the best food. Visit our Alaskan gift shop. Phone (907) 262-5898, 1-800-829-5898. E-mail: akmunnzo@ptialaska.net. [ADVERTISEMENT]

S 84.9 (136.6 km) A 137.9 (221.9 km) H 94.6 (152.2 km) Scout Lake Loop Road leads south to Cast Away Riverside RV Park (2.5 miles) and **Scout Lake State Recreation Site**. The state recreation site has 12 campsites, water, toilets, covered picnic shelter. Camping fee $8/night or annual pass. Scout Lake Loop Road loops south of the Sterling Highway for 7 miles/11.3 km and rejoins the Sterling Highway at **Milepost S 83.4**. Turn here and drive down Scout Lake Loop Road 1.6 miles/2.6 km to turnoff for Morgan's Landing: follow side road 2.4 miles/3.9 km to reach **Morgan's Landing State Recreation Area**; $10 nightly fee per vehicle or annual pass, 42 developed campsites with 10 pull-through sites and some double sites, toilets and water. $5 day-use fee or annual pass. Alaska State Parks area headquarters is located here. ▲

Cast Away Riverside RV Park. See display ad this section. ▲

Good access from Morgan's Landing to the **Kenai River**, king salmon from mid-June through July, average 30 lbs. Red (sockeye) salmon average 8 lbs., use flies in July and August; silver (coho) salmon to 15 lbs., August and September, use lure; pink salmon average 4 lbs. with lure, best in July, even-numbered years only; rainbow and Dolly Varden, use lure, June through August. ◄•

S 87.5 (140.8 km) A 140.5 (226.1 km) H 92 (148.1 km) Robinson Loop Road to northwest. Tustumena Loop Road to southeast.

S 88 (141.6 km) A 141 (226.9 km) H 91.5 (147.3 km) St. Theresa's Drive southeast to Longmere Lake Lodge B&B.

Longmere Lake Lodge B&B. AAA-approved. Look for blue highway sign. Follow St. Theresa's/Edgington to Ryan. Beautiful lakeside setting. Comfortable, spacious accommodations. Large stone fireplace, Alaskan artifacts. Enjoy our hearty continental breakfast. Master bedrooms with full private baths, or large apartment

Camping and fishing along the Kenai River. (© Barbara Willard)

with kitchen. Guided salmon, halibut, hiking, bird watching, flightseeing arranged. Longtime Alaskan hosts. P.O. Box 1707, Soldotna, AK 99669. Phone (907) 262-9799. www.ptialaska.net/ bblodge. E-mail: bblodge@ptialaska.net. [ADVERTISEMENT] MP

S 88.3 (142.1 km) A 141.3 (227.4 km) H 91.2 (146.8 km) **Alaska Horn & Antler.** See display ad this section.

S 89.6 (144.2 km) A 142.6 (229.5 km) H 89.9 (144.7 km) **The Blue Moose Lakeside Lodge,** just outside Soldotna, is a picturesque lodge in a wilderness setting overlooking Longmere Lake. Guests are provided with enchanting lodging and various outdoor activities to participate in. Enjoy coffee and a homemade breakfast before you head off with one of the specialty guides for a day of adventure—it's a must on your Alaskan itinerary! Bedroom/bath suite, private rooms and cabin available. Call today. (877) BL-MOOSE. bluemoos@alaska.net. [ADVERTISEMENT]

Moose may be seen browsing in marshy areas along the road. (© Harry M. Walker)

S 91.3 (146.9 km) A 144.3 (232.2 km) H 88.2 (141.9 km) Gas stations and convenience store.

S 91.4 (147.1 km) A 144.4 (232.4 km) H 88.1 (141.8 km) **Silvertip Lair.** Stopping at the Silvertip Lair, you'll picture yourself wrapped in the arms of a big brown bear.

Saddle gigantic fish or make an Alaskan wish. Our boardwalks are handicap accessible. Strolling from shop to shop and talking to our friendly Alaskan Artists, you'll be glad you made this stop. Look for the 15-foot bear waiting for you at the Silvertip Lair. See display ad. (907) 262-2234. [ADVERTISEMENT]

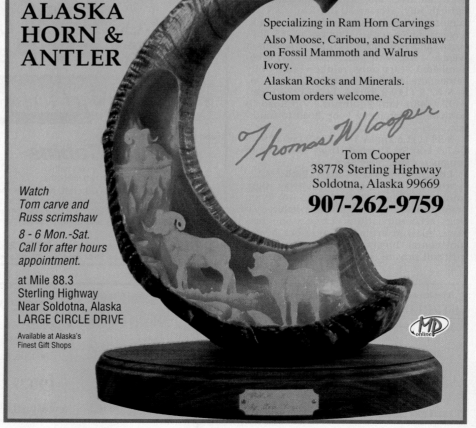

S 91.6 (147.4 km) **A 144.6** (232.7 km) **H 87.9** (141.4 km) **American Trophy Taxidermy.** Long-time Alaskans and 18 years of applied study have enabled us to refine the art and science of Alaskan fish and game taxidermy, guaranteeing a trophy that will enhance your adventure here. We book fishing/hunting charters and lodging. Expediting services. We will ship your trophy fish and game anywhere. Stop in and visit our trophy display studio. (907) 2627950. E-mail: fishart@alaska.net. See display ad. [ADVERTISEMENT]

S 91.8 (147.7 km) **A 144.8** (233 km) **H 87.7** (141.1 km) **Aurora Alaska Premium Smoked Salmon and Seafoods.** Home of the best gourmet-Alaskan smoked salmon and halibut products in the world. We offer a wide variety of products, from refrigerated to non-refrigerated (shelf stable). All our products are low in salt and contain no artificial colors, flavors, or preservatives. They are all-natural. Got your own fish to smoke? We will custom smoke (kipper) or pickle your sport-caught salmon or halibut for you. We will also vacuum pack, freeze, store, box and ship your fish. No luck fishing? Come in and choose from our own specially prepared smoked products. Choose from our world-famous smoked salmon jerky, which is available in 4 delicious flavors, smoked salmon or halibut fillets, canned smoked salmon and halibut, pickled salmon and halibut, smoked salmon and cream cheese spread, or our assorted retort products. Gift packs also available. Remember, whether it is a gift of appreciation or for something grand, we can help in selecting the right gift for that special someone or important client, even if that someone is you. Come in to try our free samples. Two locations to choose from. Box 4085, Soldotna, AK 99669. Phone or fax (907) 262-7007, or dial toll free at (800) 653-FISH (3474). [ADVERTISEMENT]

S 91.9 (147.9 km) **A 144.9** (233.2 km) **H 87.6** (141 km) Soldotna city limits.

S 92 (148 km) **A 145** (233.3 km) **H 87.5** (140.8 km) Birch Ridge public golf course, driving range and cottages.

S 92.4 (148.7 km) **A 145.4** (234 km) **H 87.1** (140.2 km) State Division of Forest, Land and Water Management. Fire danger indicator sign.

S 92.7 (149.1 km) **A 145.7** (234.5 km) **H 86.8** (139.7 km) Mackey Lake Road. Private lodging is available on this side road.

Bill Slemp's Cabin Rentals. See display ad this section.

S 93.7 (150.8 km) **A 146.7** (236.1 km) **H 85.8** (138.1 km) Four-lane highway begins southbound and continues through Soldotna; speed zone.

S 94.1 (151.6 km) **A 147.1** (236.7 km) **H 85.4** (137.4 km) Turn on East Redoubt Street (between Mapco and the Ford dealer) and follow signs 0.8 mile via gravel road to

Swiftwater Park Municipal Campground. The municipal campground has 20 spaces

Snow geese on the Kenai Flats, a popular birdwatching spot. (© Bill Sherwonit)

(some pull-throughs) on loop road above the Kenai River; tables, firepits, firewood ($4), phone, dump station($10), 2-week limit, litter barrels, toilets, boat launch ($6). Camping fee $8; day-use fee $3. No camping Sept. 30–May 1. Steep stairway down to **Kenai River**; good fishing. ◄▲

S 94.2 (151.6 km) **A 147.2** (236.9 km) **H 85.3** (137.3 km) Soldotna Y.

Junction with Kenai Spur Highway to city of Kenai. See KENAI SPUR HIGHWAY log beginning on page 621.

There are 2 ways to reach the city of Kenai: Turn right souththbound on Kenai Spur Highway, or continue on the Sterling Highway to **Milepost S 96.1** and turn right southbound on the Kalifornsky Beach Road.

S 94.4 (151.9 km) **A 147.4** (237.2 km) **H 85.1** (137 km) Soldotna DOT/PF highway

maintenance station, gas station. Turn east here for access to Soldotna Creek Park (day use only). Follow road behind restaurant.

S 95 (152.9 km) **A 148** (238.2 km) **H 84.5** (136 km) Soldotna city center; Peninsula Center shopping mall. Turn on Binkley Street for access to fire station, police station and post office.

Homer-bound travelers continue south across the Kenai River bridge past visitor center. Turn west on Kalifornsky Beach Road for Centennial Park, the Soldotna city campground, and Soldotna Historical Society Museum. The Slikok Valley School, the last of the Alaska Territory log schools, built in 1958, is one of the attractions at the museum's log village. Turn east off the Sterling Highway on Funny River Road for airport. See description at **Milepost S 96.1.**

Log of the Sterling Highway continues on page 628.

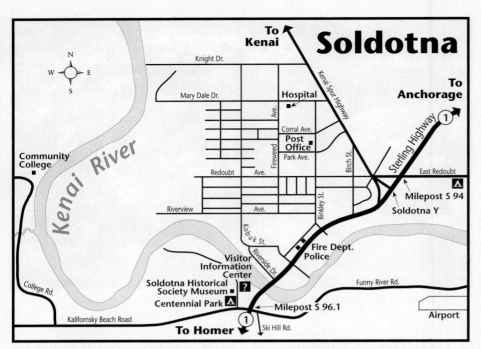

To Kenai

Soldotna

To Anchorage

Knight Dr.

Mary Dale Dr.

Hospital

Kenai Spur Highway

Corral Ave.

Post Office

Park Ave.

Sterling Highway

Ave.

Fireweed

Birch St.

East Redoubt

Redoubt Ave.

Milepost S 94

Community College

Kenai River

Riverview Ave.

Binkley St.

Soldotna Y

Kobuk St.

Riverside Dr.

Fire Dept. Police

Visitor Information Center

Soldotna Historical Society Museum

Funny River Rd.

College Rd.

Centennial Park

Milepost S 96.1

Airport

Kalifornsky Beach Road

To Homer

Ski Hill Rd.

Soldotna

S 95.2 (153.2 km) A 148.2 (238.5 km) H 84.3 (135.7 km) On the western Kenai Peninsula, the city stretches over a mile southwest along the Sterling Highway and northwest along the Kenai Spur Highway. **Population:** 4,134; Kenai Peninsula Borough 44,411. **Emergency Services:** Phone 911 for all emergency services. **Alaska State Troopers** at Mile 22 Kalifornsky Beach Road just off Sterling Highway, phone (907) 262-4453. **City Police,** phone (907) 262-4455. **Fire Department,** phone (907) 262-4792. **Ambulance,** phone (907) 262-4500. **Hospital,** Central Peninsula General, 1 mile/1.6 km north of Public Safety Building off Marydale Drive, phone (907) 262-4404.

Visitor Information: The Soldotna Visitor Information Center is located in downtown Soldotna on the Sterling Highway south of the Kenai River bridge. River access to walkway built for bank and fish-habitat protection. The center is open 7 days a week, May through September, 9 A.M. to 7 P.M. The

Welcome to the North Country!

Food cache displayed at historic log village on Centennial Park Road.
(Courtesy of Soldotna Historical Society)

remainder of the year the center is open weekdays from 9 A.M. to 5 P.M. Write: Greater Soldotna Chamber of Commerce, 44790 Sterling Highway, Soldotna, AK 99669; phone (907) 262-1337 or 262-9814, fax (907) 262-3566. E-mail: solchmbr@ptialaska.net.

Elevation: 115 feet/35m. **Climate:** Average daily temperature in July, 63°F to 68°F/17°C to 20°C; January, 19°F to 23°F/-7°C to -5°C. Annual precipitation, approximately 18 inches. **Radio:** KGTL 620, KFQD 750, KSRM 920, KZXX 980, KSLP 1140, KDLL-FM 91.9 (Pickle Hill Public Radio) KGTL-FM 100.9/103.5, MBN-FM 95.3/97.7, KWHQ-FM 1001, KPEN-FM 101.7. **Television:** Channels 2, 4, 9, 12 and 13 via booster

SOLDOTNA ADVERTISERS

Alaska Recreational
 Rentals ....Ph. (907) 262-2700
Alaskan Holiday Suites......Ph. (907) 262-9635
Alaskan Hospitality Bed and
 Breakfast......................Ph. (907) 260-5388
Beemun's Variety
 Store ....35277 Kenai Spur Hwy.
Best Western King Salmon
 Motel, Restaurant
 & RV Park..........................Kenai Spur Hwy.
Big Eddy Campground .....End of Big Eddy Rd.
Blazy's B&B ....Ph. (907) 262-4591
Bo's Fishing Guide
 Service ....Ph. (800) 699-5154
Centennial Campground..Ph. (907) 262-5299
Craftsman Hobbies...........Ph. (907) 262-2839
Custom Seafood
 Processors......................Ph. (907) 262-9691
Dan's Alaskan Sport-
 fishing Ventures ....Ph. (907) 337-5390
Diamond M Ranch, B&B
 Cabins, RV Spaces........Ph. (907) 283-9424
Donna's Country & Victorian
 Gifts ....Blazy's Soldotna Mall
Edgewater RV park...........Ph. (907) 262-7733
EZ Limit Guide Service......Ph. (907) 262-6169
Fenton Bros. Guided
 Sportfishing.................Ph. (907) 262-2502
Gull's Landing B&B...........Ph. (907) 262-6668
Greater Soldotna Chamber of
 Commerce ....Sterling Hwy.
Harry Gaines Kenai River
 Fishing Guide................Ph. (907) 262-5097
Iliamna Lock & Key ....Ph. (907) 262-5012
Jeff King's Budget
 Charters ....Ph. (907) 262-4564
Johnson Bros. Guides &
 Outfitters ....Downtown
Kenai Custom
 Seafoods ....Mile 14.4 Kalifornsky Beach Rd.

Kenai Peninsula Condos ...Ph. (907) 262-1383
Kenai River Lodge ....Kenai River Bridge
Kings Kitchen
 Bed & Breakfast...........Ph. (907) 262-2973
Klondike City...............Mile 95.5 Sterling Hwy.
MACtel ....Ph. 1-800-808-8083
Moose Creek Lodge..........Ph. (907) 260-3380
Moose Hollow Bed &
 Breakfast......................Ph. (907) 262-7526
Mykel's Restaurant
 & Lounge ....Mile 0.2 Kenai Spur Hwy.
Northland Gallery &
 Wildlife Studio ....At the 'Y'
Oil Exchange, The.............Ph. (907) 262-3954
Peninsula Center Mall....................Downtown
Poppy Ridge Bed
 & Breakfast ....Ph. (907) 262-4230
Posey's Kenai River
 Hideaway ....Ph. (907) 262-7430
River City Books................Ph. (907) 260-7722
River Quest RV Park..........Ph. (907) 283-4991
River Terrace RV Park ....Ph. (907) 262-5593
Riverside Auto
 Supply Inc.......................Kenai River Bridge
Robin Place Fabrics...........Ph. (907) 262-5438
Rod 'N Real Charters ....Ph. (907) 262-6064
Salmon Haus ....Ph. (907) 262-2400
Sal's Klondike Diner ....Mile 95.5 Sterling Hwy.
Skyline Bed & Breakfast....Ph. (907) 262-9890
Soldotna Bed &
 Breakfast Lodge...........Ph. (907) 262-4779
Soldotna Chamber of
 Commerce ....Ph. (907) 262-9814
Soldotna Inn.............Mile 0.2 Kenai Spur Hwy.
Soldotna Wash & Dry ....At the 'Y'
Sweeney's Clothing ....Ph. (907) 262-5916
Swiftwater Campground ..Ph. (907) 262-3151
Tom's Cabins &
 Guide Service...............Ph. (907) 262-3197

Please support our MILEPOST® advertisers.

line from Anchorage, cable and KANG public education channel. **Newspapers:** *Peninsula Clarion* (daily), *The Dispatch* (weekly).

Private Aircraft: Soldotna airstrip, 0.9 mile/1.4 km southeast; elev. 107 feet/32m; length 5,000 feet/1,524m; asphalt; fuel 100LL; unattended.

The town of Soldotna was established in the 1940s because of its strategic location at the Sterling–Kenai Spur Highway junction. (Visitors may see the homestead cabin, which became Soldotna's first post office in 1949, at its original location on the Kenai Spur Highway at Corral Street.) Soldotna was named for a nearby stream; it is a Russian word meaning "soldier," although some believe the name came from an Indian word meaning the "stream fork."

Soldotna was incorporated as a first-class city in 1967. It has a council–manager form of government. Kenai Peninsula Borough headquarters and state offices of the Departments of Highways, Public Safety, Fish and Game, and Forest, Land and Water Management are located here. Soldotna is also headquarters for the Kenai Peninsula Borough school district. There are 3 elementary schools, a junior high school and 2 high schools. University of Alaska–Kenai Peninsula College is also located in Soldotna.

Area terrain is level and forested, with many streams and lakes nearby. Large rivers of the area are the Swanson River, the Moose River and the Kenai River, which empties into Cook Inlet just south of Kenai. The area affords a majestic view of volcanic mountains across Cook Inlet. Always snow-covered, they are Mount Spurr (elev. 11,100 feet/3,383m), which erupted in 1992; Mount Iliamna (elev. 10,016 feet/3,053m), which has 3 smaller peaks to the left of the larger one; and Mount Redoubt (elev. 10,197 feet/3,108m), which was identified by its very regular cone shape until it erupted in December 1989.

ACCOMMODATIONS/VISITOR SERVICES

All modern conveniences and facilities are available, including supermarkets, banks, hotels/motels, restaurants and drive-ins, medical and dental clinics, bowling alley, golf course, veterinarians, churches and a library. Two shopping malls are located on the Sterling Highway near the center of town. Bed-and-breakfasts, cabin rentals and lodges also offer accommodations.

Alaskan Holiday Suites. Two-bedroom, 2-bath suites with fully equipped kitchens. Suites accommodate up to 6. Convenient location, close to all services and just a short walk to the famous Kenai River. Continental breakfast. Free local calls. Cable TV. Guide reservations available. VISA/MasterCard accepted. Reservations: (907) 242-2387 or (907) 262-9635. See display ad. [ADVERTISEMENT]

Best Western King Salmon Motel, Restaurant and RV Park, downtown Soldotna on Kenai Spur Highway. Large rooms, queen beds, some kitchenettes, cable TV, phones. Free in-room coffee. Restaurant serves early fisherman's breakfast, lunch, dinner. Steaks, seafood, salad bar. Beer and wine available. Fishing licenses, ice. Fish processing close by. RV park with 39 pull-through spaces, full hookups, restrooms, coin-operated showers and laundry. Phone (907) 262-5857; fax (907) 262-9441. See display ad this section. [ADVERTISEMENT] ▲

For Swiftwater Campground, turn on East Redoubt Street at **Milepost S 94.1** Sterling

Highway. Centennial Park Campground is
0.1 mile/0.2 km from the Sterling Highway
just south of the Kenai River bridge on Kalifornsky Beach Road; turn west at **Milepost
S 96.1**. Both campgrounds are owned by the
City of Soldotna. Register for camping at
either park; camping fees charged.
Wheelchair accessible. Dump station available at Centennial Park Campground.
Campsites for both tents and RVs (no
hookups). These campgrounds are heavily
used; good idea to check in early. There are
several private campgrounds located in and
near Soldotna; see ads this section and contact the chamber of commerce.　　　&▲

Edgewater RV Park on the banks of
world famous Kenai River, across from the
Soldotna visitors' center. Full and partial
hookups, laundry, showers, grassy sites,
picnic tables, local guide service and fish
cleaning facilities. Bank fishing. Walk to
stores, restaurants. Reservations and information: (907) 262-7733. P.O. Box 976,
Soldotna, AK 99669. [ADVERTISEMENT]　　　▲

River Terrace RV Park features a prime
Kenai River location near the Soldotna

bridge. Easy, comfortable, riverfront access
on the 1000-ft. boardwalk with steps right
into the river. Handicapped accessible with
fishing platform. A great place to fish or view

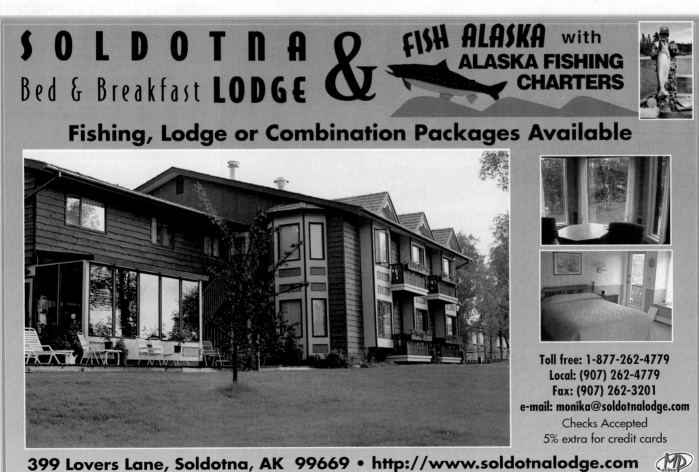

the exciting action. 28-ft. spaces, full hookups, riverfront sites, 20-30-50 amp, heated restrooms, free showers, unlimited hot water, laundry. Ice, fish processing and taxidermy available on premises. Local guides provide custom king and silver salmon charters. For a true Alaskan experience book remote fly-out fishing or spectacular bear watching. Remember, early and late season dates are easier to get and very enjoyable. (907) 26205593; Fax (907) 260-4775. P.O. Box 322, Soldotna, AK 99669. [ADVERTISEMENT] ▲

TRANSPORTATION

Air: Charters available. Soldotna airport is south of Soldotna, 2 miles/3.2 km off the Sterling Highway; at **Milepost S 96.1**, just after crossing Kenai River bridge, turn left (east) on Funny River (Airport) Road and continue 2 miles/ 3.2 km.

Local: Taxi service, car rentals, vehicle leasing, boat rentals and charters.

Highway: Accessible via the Sterling Highway (Alaska Route 1), 148.2 miles/ 238.5 km from Anchorage.

ATTRACTIONS

Join in Local Celebrations. July's big event is the annual Soldotna Progress Days, held during the 4th weekend of the month. Activities include a parade, 2 days of rodeo, car show, barbecues, dance, arts and crafts show, and other events.

The Peninsula Winter Games take place in February in Soldotna. Activities include an ice sculpture contest, cross-country ski race, ice bowling and snow volleyball. Games, booths, concessions and demonstrations are held throughout the weekend. The Alaska State Championship Sled Dog Races and Dog Weight Pull Contest take place during the Winter Games.

Donna's Country & Victorian Gifts at Blazy's Soldotna Mall. A shopper's delight, a

fisherman's wife's revenge. This is the perfect place to spend an afternoon while your

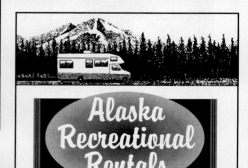

more remote fishing spot—or for visitors who want to see wildlife and glaciers—there are fly-in fishing trips for rainbow, grayling, salmon and Dolly Varden, and flightseeing trips to see Tustumena Lake, the Harding Icefield and wildlife, through local outfitters.

In Soldotna, the early run of kings begins about May 15, with the peak of the run occurring between June 12 and 20. The late run enters the river about July 1, peaking between July 23 and 31; season closes July 31. The first run of red salmon enters the river during early June and is present in small numbers through the month; the

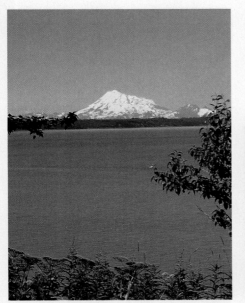

View of Mount Redoubt across Cook Inlet. (© Loren Taft)

husband goes fishing. Roomfuls of wonderful things, constantly changing. Enjoy our cozy, relaxing atmosphere. Don't miss our Santa room! You'll find things in our shoppe you never thought you'd find in Alaska! [ADVERTISEMENT]

River City Books is a locally owned, full-service bookstore with books for every taste. If you have Alaska books on your list or simply want to snuggle up with a good novel, you will enjoy browsing this delightful book shop. We happily serve up expresso, teas, and local information. Turn left at the second traffic light in town. Phone (907) 260-7722. 43977 Sterling Highway, Soldotna, AK 99669. Opening April 1999. [ADVERTISEMENT]

Fish the Kenai River. Soldotna is one of Alaska's best-known sportfishing headquarters, and many claim that some of the world's best fishing is here at the Kenai River, which flows next to town. Many charter boats and fishing guides for Kenai River fishing are located in the Soldotna area. In May 1985, Les Anderson of Soldotna landed a 97-lb., 4-oz. king salmon, a new world's record. The mounted fish is on display at the visitor center.

Soldotna gets very busy during fishing season, and for those fishermen who want a

Male mallard. There's good birdwatching at Kenai National Wildlife Refuge Center's Headquarters Lake. (© Loren Taft)

second run enters about July 15 and is present through early August. In even years pink salmon are present from early through mid-August. The early silver salmon run arrives in early August, peaks in mid-August, and is over by the end of the month. Late run silver salmon enter the Kenai in early September, peak in mid- to late-September, and continue to enter the river through October. Dolly Varden and rainbow trout can be caught all summer.

Day-use Parks. Soldotna Creek Park, located off the Sterling Highway on the Kenai River, behind Hutchings Chevrolet at the Y, has covered picnic tables, grills, playground and trails. Facilities include wheelchair-accessible toilets and a boardwalk with wheelchair accessibility for bank fishing. Airport Rotary Park, at Mile 4 Funny River Road, also has a wheelchair-accessible boardwalk with excellent bank fishing

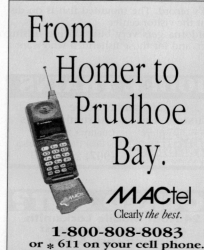

during the red salmon run.

Central Peninsula Sports Center, on Kalifornsky Beach (K-Beach) Road, has an Olympic-sized hockey rink, a jogging track, 2 racquetball/volleyball courts, a weight and exercise room, dressing rooms and showers. The Sports Center also has convention facilities and meeting rooms. Phone (907) 262-3150 for more information.

Soldotna Historical Society Museum, located on Centennial Park Road, features a wildlife museum and historic log village. Among the log buildings is the last territorial school (built in 1958). Soldotna's founding settlers arrived in 1947. The "habitable dwellings" that entitled 2 of these first homesteaders to 160 acres from what is now mid-town Soldotna are part of the village. How these latter-day pioneers lived is revealed in a collection of homestead artifacts and photos in the former Soldotna Chamber of Commerce log tourist center. Damon Hall, a large building constructed for the Alaska Centennial, features an outstanding display of wildlife mounts with a background mural of these species' natural habitat. Open 10 A.M. to 4 P.M., Tuesday through Saturday; noon to 4 P.M. Sunday; closed Monday.

Joyce Carver Memorial Library offers temporary cards for visitors; large sunlit reading areas for both adults and children; Alaska videos on summer Saturday afternoons at 2 P.M. Open 9 A.M. to 8 P.M. Monday through Thursday, noon to 6 P.M. Friday, and 9 A.M. to 6 P.M. Saturdays. 235 Binkley St., Soldotna, phone (907) 262-4227.

St. Nicholas Memorial Chapel in Kenai.
(© Susan Cole Kelly)

Kenai National Wildlife Refuge Visitor Center, located at the top of Ski Hill Road (see **Milepost S 97.9**) and also accessible from Funny River Road (see **Milepost S 96.1**), hosts some 25,000 visitors annually. This modern center has dioramas containing lifelike mounts of area wildlife in simulated natural settings. Free wildlife films are shown on the hour daily from noon to 4 P.M. Information available here on canoeing, hiking and camping. There is a 1-mile-/1.6-km-long nature trail with an observation platform and spotting scope on Headquarters Lake. In winter, the refuge visitor centre are hosts 8 miles of cross-country ski trails. The Alaska Natural History Assoc. has a sales outlet here with books, posters and videos. Pay phone located in center. Open weekdays 8 A.M. to 4:30 P.M., and weekends 10 A.M. to 6 P.M. No admission fee.

The refuge was created in 1941 when President Franklin D. Roosevelt set aside 1,730,000 acres of land (then designated the Kenai National Moose Range) to assure that the large numbers of moose, Dall sheep and other wild game would remain for people to enjoy. With the passage of the Alaska National Interest Lands Conservation Act in 1980, the acreage was increased to 1.97 million acres and redesignated Kenai National Wildlife Refuge. The area is managed by the U.S. Dept. of the Interior's Fish and Wildlife Service. Write: Refuge Manager, Kenai National Wildlife Refuge, P.O. Box 2139, Soldotna, AK 99669-2139; phone (907) 262-7021.

Take a Canoe Trip on one of several routes available in Kenai National Wildlife Refuge. Enjoyment of wildlife in their natural habitat, true wilderness scenery, camping, and fishing for trout and salmon are a few highlights of a canoe trip.

Established canoe trails include the Swanson River route (80 miles/129 km) and Swan Lake route (60 miles/97 km). Complete information on Kenai Peninsula canoe trails is available at the Kenai National Wildlife Refuge visitor contact station at Mile 58 Sterling Highway, the Kenai NWR visitor center in Soldotna and at chamber of commerce visitor centers in Kenai and Soldotna.

Log of the Sterling Highway continues on page 628.

Kenai Spur Highway Log

The Kenai Spur Highway junctions with the Sterling Highway at the Soldotna Y. **Distance from Soldotna Y (SY) is shown.**

SY 0 Junction with Sterling Highway at **Milepost S 94.2.**
SY 0.6 (1 km) Soldotna City Hall.
SY 0.7 (1.1 km) Soldotna High School.
SY 1 (1.6 km) Marydale Ave. Access to Central Peninsula General Hospital. 24-hour gas.
Tesoro 7–Eleven. See display ad this section.
SY 1.8 (2.8 km) Big Eddy Road to west. Access to Big Eddy recreational site on Kenai River with wheelchair-accessible toilets, fishing guides, private camping, moorage, boat launches and rental facilities.
SY 4.2 (6.7 km) Silver Salmon Drive leads 0.5 mile west to The **Pillars Boat Launch** (Alaska State Park) on the Kenai River; large gravel parking area, toilets, boat ramp, fishing dock, fee station. Fees: $10/launch, $5/day-use.
SY 5.6 (9 km) Gas station.
SY 6.1 (9.8 km) Beaver Creek Park day use only to west; parking, toilets, picnic tables, playground, basketball court, covered table, litter barrels.
SY 6.4 (10.3 km) Twin City Raceway to east. South **junction** with Beaver Loop Road: Drive 2.5 miles/4 km on Beaver Loop Road and turn south (left fork), crossing Warren Ames Memorial Bridge, to connect with Kalifornsky Beach Road. Turn north (right fork) for return to Kenai Spur Highway at Mile 10.9.
SY 8.2 (13.2 km) Begin divided 4-lane highway, 35-mph/56-kmph. Paved bike trails both sides of highway to Kenai.
SY 8.8 (14.2 km) Gas station (diesel)
SY 9 (14.5 km) Beaver Loop Road
SY 9.4 (15.1 km) Tinker Lane. Access to Peninsula Oilers baseball park, municipal golf course
SY 9.7 (15.6 km) Kenai Central High School.

SY 10.1 (16.2 km) Welcome to Kenai sign and turnoff for City of Kenai tent campground to east; $8 camping fee.
SY 10.2 (16.4 km) Motel and fast-food at intersection with Airport Road and Walker Lane.
SY 10.4 (16.7 km) Kenai Plaza shopping.
SY 10.5 (16.9 km) Carr's/K-Mart shopping.
SY 10.6 (17.1 km) Main Street Loop to east. Bridge Access Loop to west. Bridge Access Loop crosses Warren Ames Bridge and junctions with Kalifornsky Beach Road. Kenai River Flats state recreation site south of bridge is a good spot to see migrating waterfowl.
SY 10.7 (17.2 km) Lief Hanson Memorial Park.
SY 10.9 (17,5 km) Willow Street access to Kenai Municipal Airport 1 mile northeast.

Kenai

SY 11.2 (18 km). Main Street in Kenai; 159 miles/255 km from Anchorage, 89 miles/144 km from Homer. **Population:** 7,058. **Emergency Services:** Phone 911 for all emergency services. **Alaska State Troopers** (in Soldotna), phone (907) 262-4453. **Kenai City Police,** phone (907) 283-7879. **Fire Department** and **Ambulance,** phone 911. **Hospital** (in Soldotna), phone (907) 262-4404. **Maritime Search and Rescue,** dial 0 for Zenith 5555, toll free.

Visitor Information: The Kenai Visi-

Holy Assumption of the Virgin Mary Russian Orthodox Church.
(© Kris Graef, staff)

tors and Cultural Center, located at Main Street and Kenai Spur Highway, provides brochures and other visitor information; restrooms. The center features a cultural museum, wildlife displays and movies. Write the Kenai Visitors and Cultural Center, 11471 Kenai Spur Highway, Kenai, AK 99611; phone (907) 283-1991, fax 283-2230. E-mail: kvcb@alaska.net. Web site: www.visitkenai.com.

Elevation: 93 feet/28m. **Climate:** Average daily maximum temperature in July, 61°F/16°C; January temperatures range from 11° to -19°F/-12° to -28°C. Lowest recorded temperature in Kenai was -48°F/-44°C. Average annual precipitation, 19.9 inches (68.7 inches of snowfall). **Radio:** KCSY 1140, KENI 550, KGTL 620, KSRM 920, KWVV 105, KGTL

KENAI ADVERTISERS

100.9/103.5, KDLL-FM 91.9, MBN-FM 95.3/97.7, KENY 980, KWHQ-FM 100.1, KPEN-FM 101.7. **Television:** Several channels and cable. **Newspaper:** *Peninsula Clarion* (daily).

Private Aircraft: Kenai Municipal Airport, adjacent north; elev. 92 feet/28m; length 7,575 feet/2,309m; asphalt; fuel 100LL; attended. Transient tie-down fees $2/day. Adjacent floatplane base offers 3,500-foot/1,067-m basin with 35 slips.

Kenai is situated on a low rise overlooking the mouth of the Kenai River where it empties into Cook Inlet. It is the largest city on the Kenai Peninsula. Prior to Russian Alaska, Kenai was a Dena'ina Native community. The Dena'ina people fished, hunted, trapped, farmed and traded with neighboring tribes here. In 1791 it became the second permanent settlement established by the Russians in Alaska, when a fortified post called Fort St. Nicholas, or St. Nicholas Redoubt, was built near here by Russian fur traders. In 1848, the first Alaska gold discovery was made on the Russian River. In 1869 the U.S. Army established Fort Kenai (Kenay); in 1899 a post office was authorized.

Oil exploration began in the mid-1950s, with the first major discovery in this area, the Swanson River oil reserves, 20 miles/32.2 km northeast of Kenai in 1957. Two years later, natural gas was discovered in the Kalifornsky Beach area 6 miles/9.6 km south of the city of Kenai. Extensive exploration offshore in upper Cook Inlet has established that Cook Inlet's middle-ground shoals contain one of the major oil and gas fields in the world.

The industrial complex on the North Kenai Road is the site of Unocal Chemicals, which produces ammonia and urea for fertilizer. Phillips Petroleum operates a liquid natural gas plant. Tesoro has a refinery here.

Offshore in Cook Inlet are 15 drilling platforms, all with underwater pipelines bringing the oil to the shipping docks on both sides of Cook Inlet for loading onto tankers.

Federal and state agencies based in and around Kenai contribute to the local economy. Next to oil, tourism, fishing and fish processing are the leading industries.

ACCOMMODATIONS/VISITOR SERVICES

Kenai has all shopping facilities and conveniences. Medical and dental clinics, banks, laundromats, theaters, pharmacies, supermarkets, and numerous gift and specialty shops are located on and off the highway and in the shopping malls. Several motels and hotels and about a dozen restaurants and drive-ins are located in Kenai. Local artists are featured at the Kenai Fine Arts Center on Cook Street. Showers, sauna, weight room, racquetball courts and gym at Kenai Recreation Center, on Caviar Street. Open 6 A.M. to 10 P.M. Monday through Saturday, Sunday 1 to 10 P.M. Phone (907) 283-3855. For joggers there's the Bernie Huss Memorial Trail, a 0.5-mile jogging and exercise course located just off the Kenai Spur Highway on Main Street Loop. Dump stations located at several local service stations and city dock.

City of Kenai public boat ramp on Boat Launch Road off Bridge Access Road has 24-hour parking, restrooms with flush toilets, pay phone.

Kenai City Park has covered picnic tables and fireplaces. Arrangements for caravan camping may be made in advance through the Kenai Visitors and Cultural Center. Tent camping and private RV parks available in and near shopping areas. Ask at the visitors center for directions. ▲

Drive north of town on the Kenai Spur Highway for more lodging and camping. Municipal park at the end of Forest Drive has wheelchair-accessible trails, firepits, picnic tables and playground. &

Beluga Lookout RV Park, 2 blocks from Kenai Visitors Center in historic Old Town, downtown Kenai. Overlooking bluff with fantastic view of beluga whales, Kenai River, Cook Inlet, Mount Redoubt. Historic Russian Orthodox Church, Fort Kenay next door. Log lodge office, private bathrooms, hot showers, laundry. 75 full-hookup spaces, cable TV, picnic tables, instant private phone hookups, pull-throughs, 30–50 amp power. Caravans welcome. VISA, MasterCard. Reservations (800) 745-5999 or (907) 283-5999. E-mail: beluga@ptialaska.net. See display ad. [ADVERTISEMENT] ▲

Kenai's Old Town Village. Dine in the beautifully refurbished 1918 cannery building, featuring Alaska seafood, steaks, home cooking, beer and wine. Banquet space available for 150. Fantastic view of Kenai River, Cook Inlet and mountains. Visit log shops as they might have been in the early 1900s, featuring local artists and craftspersons. Book charters and sightseeing. Located 2 blocks from visitor center. Phone (907) 283-4515. E-mail: oldtown@ptialaska.net. See display ad. [ADVERTISEMENT]

Tanglewood Bed & Breakfast. Fish king salmon from our backyard, on lower Kenai River. View moose, caribou, bears, wolves, eagles, ducks, seals, beluga whales on regular basis. Rooms $75. Common room with fireplace. Fully equipped private suite with Jacuzzi, $125. Full breakfast. Laundry facilities. (907) 283-6771. Open year-round. Life-long Alaskans. See display ad. [ADVERTISEMENT]

The City of Kenai

Do It All From Kenai

All-America City
Kenai
1791-1991
BICENTENNIAL
VILLAGE WITH A PAST - CITY WITH A FUTURE

Discover the Alaska you've dreamed about.

For a 1,000 years, Kenai has been attracting people to its shores. Discover our natural beauty and diverse cultural history. Experience one of Alaska's best recreational areas. View beluga whales feeding on salmon, grazing caribou, swooping eagles, and active volcanoes. Stop by the Kenai Visitors & Cultural Center and see why the City of Kenai is the place to be.

Kenai Visitors & Convention Bureau, Inc.
11471 Kenai Spur Hwy. - MP • Kenai, AK 99611
Phone: (907) 283-1991 • Fax: (907)283-2230
Web Site: www.visitkenai.com • E-mail: kvcb@alaska.net

Toyon Villa. Suites at motel rates; $85 to $125. Studios and one- and 2-bedroom suites. Fully-equipped kitchens, cable TV, private phones, maid service. Located at Kenai River and Cook Inlet, in historic Old Town, across from Old Town Village Restaurant and gift shops. Phone (907) 283-4221. E-mail: tva@alaska.net. See display ad. [ADVERTISEMENT]

TRANSPORTATION

Air: Kenai Municipal Airport is served by Era Aviation (scheduled passenger service) and Southcentral Air (charter and cargo service) as well as other charter services.

Local: Limousine and taxi service is available as well as car rentals, vehicle leasing, boat rentals and charters.

Highway: On the Kenai Spur Highway, 11 miles/17.7 km north of Soldotna.

ATTRACTIONS

Get Acquainted. Pick up a brochure at the Kenai Visitors and Cultural Center. The center houses a cultural museum, which has wildlife displays, and information on local activities. The center also shows films on Alaska, daily year-round.

Old Town Kenai self-guided walking tour. Take a leisurely stroll through Old Town and read about the Native and Russian history on informational signs posted along the way. Check with the Kenai Visitors and Cultural Center for information.

Kenai River Flats is a must stop for bird-watchers. Great numbers of Siberian snow geese and other waterfowl stop to feed on this saltwater marsh in the spring. The state recreation site on Bridge

Historic Fort Kenay was established in 1868. (© Susan Cole Kelly)

Access Road at Warren Ames Bridge has parking and interpretive signs. Boardwalk for wildlife-watchers. Also watch for caribou on the Kenai Flats.

Beluga Whale Watching on the Kenai River beach at the west end of Spruce Street. Beluga whales are the only all-white whale. The beach also offers a good view of Kenai's fish-processing industry and volcanoes.

Watch Baseball or Play Golf. Some fine semipro baseball is played at the Peninsula Oilers ball park on Tinker Lane. Golfers may try the 18-hole Kenai

golf course on Lawton Drive.

Fort Kenay was the first American military installation in the area, established in 1868. More than 100 men were stationed here in the $1\frac{1}{2}$ years it officially served to protect American citizens in the area. A replica of the fort's barracks building was built as an Alaskan Purchase Centennial project by Kenai residents in 1967.

Holy Assumption of the Virgin Mary Russian Orthodox Church is across from Fort Kenay. The original church was founded in 1844 by a Russian monk, Igumen Nicholai. The present church was built some 50 years after the original and with its 3 onion-shaped domes is considered one of the finest examples of a Russian Orthodox church built on a vessel or quadrilateral ground plan. It is one of the oldest Russian Orthodox churches in Alaska. In 1971 it was designated a national historic landmark. An 1847 edition of the book of the Holy Gospel of the 4 evangelists— Matthew, Mark, Luke and John—with 5 enameled icons on the cover, is awaiting restoration (not on display). Regular church services are held here, and tours are available; inquire at the church. Donations accepted.

St. Nicholas Chapel, built in 1906, west of the Russian church, marks the burial location of Father Igumen Nicholai and other Russian Orthodox Church workers.

Kenai Spur Highway Log
(Continued)

SY 11.8 (19 km) Spruce Drive; beach access; toilets.

SY 12.1 (19.5 km) Forest Drive. Scenic viewpoint overlooking Cook Inlet. Municipal day-use park; covered picnic tables; trails.

SY 12.4 (20 km) C Plaza; shopping.

Inlet Card & Craft. See display ad this section.

SY 15 (24.1 km) Kenai city limits.

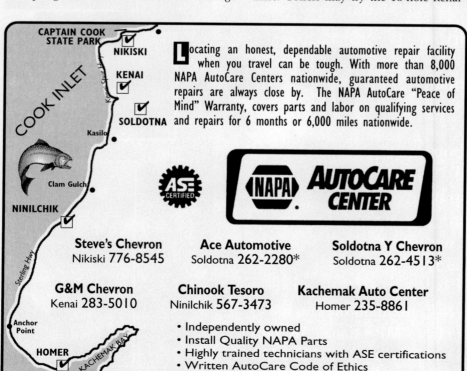

SY 21 (33.8 km) Unocal Manufacturing Facility.

SY 21.2 (34.1 km) Miller Loop Road, connects with Island Lake Road.

SY 21.6 (34.8 km) Kenai Point Phillips 66 LNG Plant.

SY 22.1 (35.5 km) **NIKISKI** (pop. 3,060). **Emergency Services**, phone 911 for fire and paramedics. Also known as Port Nikiski and Nikishka, this area was homesteaded in the 1940s and grew with the discovery of oil on the Kenai Peninsula in 1957. By 1964, oil-related industries here included Unocal Chemical, Phillips LNG, Chevron and Tesoro. Oil docks serving offshore drilling platforms today include Rigtenders, Standard Oil, Phillips 66 and Unocal Chemical. Commercial fishing is still a source of income for some residents.

SY 22.5 (36.2 km) Access to Nikiski Rigtenders dock; tankers may be seen next to dock.

SY 23.4 (37.6 km) North Peninsula Recreation and Nikiski elementary school. Dome-shaped building in trees near highway is the Nikiski recreational swimming pool, with indoor slide and hot tub; visitor observation area at pool; wheelchair-access, children's swimming area. Other facilities include an ice rink, hiking and ski trails, a picnic area and ball fields. Phone (907) 776-8800. &

North Peninsula Recreation/Nikiski Pool. See display ad this section.

SY 25.8 (41.5 km) Island Lake Road.

SY 26.6 (42.8 km) Nikishka Mall shopping, restaurants, grocery, gas station and Nikiski branch Kenai post office.

SY 26.7 (43 km) Nikiski Beach Road offers a good view of area industry (limited parking) Nikiski Fire Station No. 2. Access to Nikiski High School, heliport and Arness Dock, built on a base of WWII Liberty ships (still visible). Scenic view of Mount Spurr, Alaska Range, Nikishka Bay and oil platforms in Cook Inlet.

SY 29.7 (47.8 km) Halbouty Road.

Daniels Lake Lodge Bed & Breakfast. See display ad this section.

Grouchy Old Woman B&B. See display ad this section.

SY 30 (48.2 km) Daniels Lake.

SY 32.5 (52.3 km) Turnout west opposite Twin Lakes.

SY 35.6 (57.3 km) Entering Captain Cook State Recreation Area.

SY 35.9 (57.8 km) **Bishop Creek State Recreation Site**; 15 campsites, parking, toilets, water, picnic area and trail to beach. Camping fee $8/night or annual pass. Watch for spawning red salmon in creek in July and August, silvers August to September. Closed to salmon fishing. ▲

SY 36.5 (58.7 km) Access to **Stormy**

Lake swimming area, change house, toilet, water, parking, and rainbow and arctic char fishing. ✦

SY 36.7 (59.1 km) Stormy Lake overlook, a large paved turnout to east, offers a panoramic view.

SY 36.9 (59.4 km) Stormy Lake picnic area (not on lake); water, toilets, covered tables.

SY 37.8 (60.8 km) Stormy Lake boat launch; water, toilets, parking.

SY 38.6 (62.1 km) Swanson River canoe landing area; drive 0.6 mile/1 km east to parking and toilets, river access. End of the Swanson River canoe trail system.

SY 38.7 (62.3 km) Clint Starnes Memorial Bridge crosses **Swanson River**; parking next to bridge for fishing access, toilets, view of Mount Spurr. Fishing for silver and red salmon, and rainbow. ✦

SY 39 (62.8 km) Pavement ends at T. Take left fork for Discovery Picnic Area and Campground (Captain Cook SRA); 53 campsites, picnic area, Maggie Yurick Memorial hiking trail, water, beachcombing for agates, campfire circle, scheduled fireside programs in season.

Right fork leads to additional parking and toilets. No motorized vehicles. Camping fee $10/night or annual pass. ▲

SY 39.6 (63.7 km) Day-use picnic area at end of second fork (fork to beach is signed as "unsafe due to high tides and loose sand"); tables and toilets on bluff overlooking ocean at end of Kenai Spur Highway. *CAUTION: Steep cliffs; supervise children!*

Return to Milepost S 94.2 Sterling Highway

Sterling Highway Log

(continued from page 611)

S 95.9 (154.3 km) **A 148.9** (239.6 km) **H 83.6** (134.5 km) Kenai River bridge. Soldotna City limits.

S 96 (154.5 km) **A 149** (239.8 km) **H 83.5** (134.4 km) Soldotna visitor center at south end of Kenai River bridge.

S 96.1 (154.7 km) **A 149.1** (239.9 km) **H 83.4** (134.2 km) Funny River Road to east; access to airport and state recreation site (description follows). Kalifornsky Beach Road to west; access to Centennial Park campground (description follows). Kalifornsky Beach Road rejoins the Sterling Highway at **Milepost S 108.8**, or drive 9.3 miles/ 14.9 km to Kenai via the Warren Ames Memorial Bridge.

Junction with Kalifornsky Beach Road. See KALIFORNSKY BEACH ROAD log this section.

Centennial Park Municipal Campground, 0.1 mile/0.2 km west, on the banks of the Kenai River. There are 126 campsites (some on river), tables, firepits, firewood provided, water, restrooms, dump station, pay phone, 2-week limit. Register at entrance. Boat launch and favorite fishing site at far end of campground. ●◢▲

Funny River (Airport) Road leads east 2 miles/3.2 km to Soldotna airport, 4 miles/ 6.4 km to Airport Rotary Park (day-use only) and 11.5 miles/18.5 km to **Funny River State Recreation Site**; 12 campsites, $8 nightly fee per vehicle or annual pass, picnic tables, water, toilets, river access. Salmon and trout fishing at the confluence of the **Kenai** and **Funny** rivers. Turn on Funny River Road and take first right (Ski Hill Loop Road) for USF&WS visitor center. Funny River Road dead ends 17.2 miles/27.7 km from the highway. Private RV park located at Mile 13.8. ●◢▲

S 97.9 (157.6 km) **A 150.9** (242.8 km) **H 81.6** (131.3 km) Sky View High School. The school's Tsalteshi Trails System is 7 miles/12 km of loop trails, used in summer for walking, running and mountain biking; groomed in winter for cross-country skiing. Trails start behind the school.

Easy-to-miss turnoff for **Kenai National Wildlife Refuge Visitor Center**: Turn east off

Kalifornsky Beach Road Log

Also called K–Beach Road, Kalifornsky Beach Road leads west and south from the Sterling Highway at Soldotna, following the shore of Cook Inlet to Kasilof. **Distance from the Sterling Highway junction at Milepost S 96.1 at Soldotna (S) is followed by distance from Sterling Highway junction at Milepost S 108.8 at Kasilof (K).**

Mileposts run south to north and reflect mileage from Kasilof.

S 0 K 22.2 (35.7 km) **Junction** with Sterling Highway at **Milepost S 96.1**.

S 0.1 (0.2 km) **K 22.1** (35.6 km) Soldotna Alaska Purchase Centennial Park Campground, operated by the city of Soldotna. Kenai River access for bank fishing, boat launch (fee charged). ●◢▲

S 0.2 (0.3 km) **K 22** (35.4 km) Alaska State Troopers.

S 0.4 (0.6 km) **K 21.8** (35.1 km) Rodeo grounds.

S 0.6 (1 km) **K 21.6** (34.8 km) Central Peninsula Sports Center; hockey, ice skating, jogging track and other sports available; phone (907) 262-3150 for more information.

S 1.7 (2.7 km) **K 20.5** (33 km) Kenai Peninsula Community College access road. Also access to Slikok Creek State Recreation Site, 0.7 mile/1.1 km north; day use only with 12-hour parking, wheelchair-accessible toilets, picnic tables, information kiosk and trails. No fires or ATVs. ♿

S 2.9 (4.7 km) **K 19.3** (31.1 km) K–Beach center. ADF&G office; stop in here for current sportfishing information.

S 3.1 (5 km) **K 19.1** (30.7 km) Poppy Lane, access to community college. Grocery and gas.

S 3.5 (5.6 km) **K 18.7** (30.1 km) Red Diamond shopping center, Duck Inn Motel and restaurant. Motor Vehicle Dept. and Fish and Wildlife offices.

S 4.6 (7.4 km) **K 17.6** (28.3 km) Firehouse.

S 4.7 (7.6 km) **K 17.5** (28.2 km) Ciechansky Road leads 2.2 miles/3.5 km to **Ciechansky State Recreation Site**, a day-use only picnic area with tables, toilets, dumpster and Kenai River access. Also access to private campgrounds with RV hookups on the Kenai River. ▲

Salmon Run B&B. See display ad this section.

S 5.7 (9.2 km) **K 16.5** (26.6 km) **Diamond M Ranch B&B, Cabins & RV Spaces.** Hosts: Longtime Alaskans, JoAnne and Carrol Martin family. Nestled in the trees. Full hookups, central shower, dump station, shop vac. Magnificent view, wildlife, hiking trails and Kenai River access. Secluded, yet minutes from airport, shopping, restaurants, churches. Credit cards. (907) 283-9424. P.O. Box 1776, Soldotna, AK 99669. www.alaska.net/ diamonm. Display ad Soldotna section. [ADVERTISEMENT] ▲

S 6 (9.7 km) **K 16.2** (26.1 km) Turnoff for city of Kenai, 3.1 miles/5 km north via the Warren Ames Memorial Bridge.

S 6.8 (10.9 km) **K 15.4** (24.8 km) Magnificent beaver dam and lodge, lupine display in June.

S 7.6 (12.2 km) **K 14.6** (23.5 km) **Robinsons Mini-Mall.** See display ad this section.

S 7.8 (12.5 km) **K 14.4** (23.2 km) VIP Drive; Kenai Custom Seafoods.

S 8 (12.9 km) **K 14.2** (22.9 km) Cafe.

S 8.8 (14.2 km) **K 13.4** (21.6 km) K-Beach Fire Station.

S 13 (20.9 km) **K 9.2** (14.8 km) Paved, scenic viewpoint overlooking Cook Inlet.

S 17.4 (28 km) **K 4.8** (7.7 km) Kasilof Beach Road; access to beach, harbor, river.

S 19.4 (31.2 km) **K 2.8** (4.5 km) **Ingrid's Inn Bed & Breakfast.** See display ad this section.

S 20.1 (32.3 km) **K 2.1** (3.4 km) Kasilof Airfield Road.

S 22.1 (35.6 km) **K 0.1** (0.2 km) Kasilof post office.

S 22.2 (35.7 km) **K 0 Junction** with Sterling Highway at **Milepost S 108.8** at Kasilof.

Return to Milepost S 96.1 or S 108.8 Sterling Highway

highway and drive 1 mile/1.6 km on Ski Hill Road, which loops back to Funny River Road (see preceding milepost). Nature trail with wildlife observation platform and spotting scope on Headquarters Lake. The center is open 8 A.M. to 4:30 P.M. on weekdays, 10 A.M. to 6 P.M. weekends.

S 108.8 (175 km) **A 161.8** (260.4 km) **H 70.7** (113.8 km) South **junction** with Kalifornsky Beach Road. Drive west 4.8 miles/7.7 km to Beach Road for access to beach, Kasilof small-boat harbor and Kasilof River. This loop road rejoins Sterling Highway at **Milepost S 96.1.**

KASILOF (kuh-SEE-lawf; pop. 558; elev. 75 feet/23m) was originally a settlement established in 1786 by the Russians as St. George. An Indian fishing village grew up around the site, but no longer exists. Native inhabitants of the peninsula are mostly Kanai Indians, a branch of the great Athabascan family. The population is spread out over the general area which is called Kasilof. The area's income is derived from fishing and fish processing.

Kasilof River. The red salmon dip-net fishery here is open by special announcement for Alaska residents only. Check with the ADF&G for current regulations.

Private Aircraft: Kasilof airstrip, 1.7 miles/2.7 km north; elev. 125 feet/38m; length 2,100 feet/640m; gravel; unattended.

S 109 (175.4 km) **A 162** (260.7 km) **H 70.5** (113.5 km) Grocery store.

S 109.2 (175.7 km) **A 162.2** (261 km) **H 70.3** (113.1 km) **Kasilof Riverview.** See display ad this section.

S 109.4 (176.1 km) **A 162.4** (261.3 km) **H 70.1** (112.8 km) Bridge over Kasilof River, which drains Tustumena Lake, one of the largest lakes on the Kenai Peninsula. **Kasilof River State Recreation Site**; 10 campsites, $8 nightly fee or annual pass, 5 picnic sites on riverbank, picnic tables, toilets and water are on the south side of the bridge. Boat launch $5 fee or annual pass; $5 day-use fee or annual pass.

Entering Game Management Subunit 15C southbound, 15B northbound.

S 110 (177 km) **A 163** (262.3 km) **H 69.5**

(111.8 km) Tustumena Elementary School and north end of Tustumena Lake Road. This is the first turnoff southbound for access to Johnson and Tustumena lakes. Also turn off here for picnic area with covered picnic tables, toilets (wheelchair accessible), firepits, water and dumpster. There is a huge metal T at Tustumena Lake Road, just beyond the picnic area: Turn east at the T for Johnson and Tustumena lakes. **Johnson Lake** is 0.3 mile/0.5 km from the highway. Johnson Lake state campground has 50 sites (some double and some pull-throughs), $10 nightly fee or annual pass, water, toilets, boat launch and firewood. Lake is stocked with rainbow. Watch for beaver, moose and king salmon migrating up Crooked Creek. **Tustumena Lake** is 6.4 miles/10.3 km from the highway; a campground on the Kasilof River near the lake has 10 sites, toilets and boat launch. Fishing for lake trout and salmon. Tustumena Lake is closed to king and sockeye salmon fishing.

CAUTION: This lake is 6 miles/10 km wide and 25 miles/40 km long and subject to severe winds.

S 110.5 (177.8 km) **A 163.5** (263.1 km) **H 69** (111 km) Double-ended paved parking by Crooked Creek.

S 110.8 (178.3 km) **A 163.8** (263.6 km) **H 68.7** (110.6 km) **Tustumena Lodge.** Phone (907) 262-4216. E-mail: suzieq@ptialaska.net. Motel, cocktail lounge, outdoor patio, volleyball, horseshoes, fishing guides. Clean, affordable rooms at half the price of town. Some kitchenettes. Friendly Alaskan atmosphere where a cold drink, light snack and good fish stories are always available.

Home of the $8 dinner: Monday—prime rib; Friday—New York Steak; Saturday—halibut. See the world's largest razor clam and look for a hat from your hometown among the over 16,000 hats in our pending Guinness record collection. [ADVERTISEMENT]

S 111 (178.6 km) **A 164** (263.9 km) **H 68.5** (110.2 km) **Crooked Creek State Recreation Site** (camping and fishing) 1.8 miles/2.8 km west on Cohoe Loop Road. South end of Tustumena Lake Road (to east) for Johnson and Tustumena lakes (see description at **Milepost S 110**). Cohoe Loop Road rejoins the Sterling Highway at **Milepost S 114.3**

Just east of the highway on the Johnson and Tustumena lakes access road is Crooked Creek fish hatchery; a sign explains the chinook and sockeye salmon operation here. For further information, contact Cook Inlet Aquaculture Assoc., phone (907) 283-5761. The hatchery-produced salmon create a popular fishery at the confluence of Crooked Creek and the Kasilof River, accessible via the Cohoe Loop Road. Just past the hatchery is Crooked Creek Road, and just beyond is a huge metal T at Tustumena Lake Road. Continue past this monument for a picnic area, and return to Sterling Highway at **Milepost S 110**; turn at the T for lakes and camping.

Crooked Creek RV Park & Guide Service. See display ad this section.

Cohoe Loop Road Log

The Cohoe Loop Road loops south 15.3 miles/24.7 km from **Milepost S 111** on the Sterling Highway. The popular Crooked Creek fishing and camping area is at the top or north end of the loop. The bottom (or south) 10 miles of the Cohoe Loop Road travels through mostly undeveloped parcels of land; no services, views or recreation. Motorists may wish to use the north junction approach.

Distance from north junction with the Sterling Highway (NJ) at Milepost S 111 is followed by distance from south junction (SJ) at Milepost S 114.3.

Mileposts run south to north.

NJ 0 SJ 15.3 (24.6 km) **Junction** with Sterling Highway at **Milepost S 111.**

NJ 1.8 (2.9 km) **SJ 13.5** (21.7 km) Crooked Creek/Rilinda Drive; access to private RV park and Crooked Creek State Recreation Site at the confluence of Crooked Creek and the Kasilof River. The recreation site has 83 campsites, 36 day-use sites, toilets and water trails to Kasilof River for fishermen. Camping fee $8/night or annual pass, day-use fee $5/vehicle or annual pass. ▲

Fishing in **Crooked Creek** closed to king salmon fishing and closed to all fishing near hatchery. Fishing access to confluence of Crooked Creek and Kasilof River is through the state recreation site. *NOTE: Fishing access to Crooked Creek frontage above confluence is through a private RV park; fee charged.* Fishing in the **Kasilof River** for king salmon, late May through July, best in mid-June; coho salmon, mid-August to September, use salmon egg clusters, wet flies, assorted spoons and spinners. ◄═

NJ 2.4 (3.9 km) **SJ 12.9** (20.7 km) Webb–Ramsell Road. Kasilof River access across private property, fee charged.

NJ 5.3 (8.5 km) **SJ 10** (16 km) Cohoe Spur Road **junction**. A post office was established in 1950 at **COHOE** (area pop. 508), originally an agricultural settlement.

NJ 5.6 (9 km) **SJ 9.7** (15.6 km) T inter-

Spawning salmon at Crooked Creek.
(© Nancy Faville)

section; go west 0.8 mile/1.3 km for beach and boat launch. Private campground on Madsen Road. Cabins for rent on St. Elias Road to right. Cohoe Loop Road continues north. Pavement begins northbound. ▲

Kasilof River Kabins. See display ad this section.

NJ 15.3 (24.6 km) **SJ 0 Junction** with Sterling Highway at **Milepost S 114.3.**

Return to Milepost S 114.3 or Milepost S 111 Sterling Highway

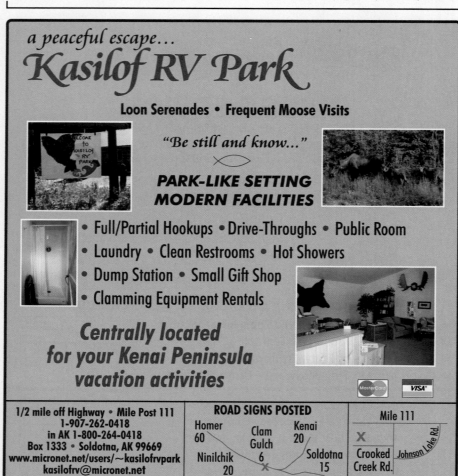
Kasilof RV Park. Modern, clean facilities in a park-like setting make this one of the Kenai Peninsula's favorite RV parks. The traveler is offered a great alternative from the parking lot-style RV parks and a peaceful retreat from the combat fishing campgrounds. The peaceful setting boasts wildflowers, beavers, moose, eagles and a variety of small birds. Enjoy walking, fishing for trout in Johnson Lake, salmon in the nearby Kasilof and Kenai rivers, halibut in Cook Inlet, or clamming on Alaska's famous razor-clam beaches. Level gravel sites, picnic tables, full/partial hookups, spotless restrooms, free showers and friendly owners make for "two thumbs up." Open Memorial weekend to Labor Day. See display ad. [ADVERTISEMENT] ▲

Tustumena Ridge Cabins. See display ad this section.

S 114.3 (183.9 km) **A 167.3** (269.2 km) **H 65.2** (104.9 km) Cohoe Loop Road loops 13 miles/21 km north to **Milepost S 111.**

South **junction** with Cohoe Loop Road. See COHOE LOOP ROAD log this section.

S 117.4 (188.9 km) **A 170.4** (274.2 km) **H 62.1** (99.9 km) **Clam Gulch State Recreation Area** is 0.5 mile/0.8 km from highway; picnic tables, picnic shelter, toilets, water, 116 campsites, $8 nightly fee or annual pass. $5 day-use fee or annual pass. *CAUTION: High ocean bluffs are dangerous.* Short access road to beach (recommended for 4-wheel-drive vehicles only, limited turnaround space). ▲

Clam digging for razor clams on most of the sandy beaches of the western Kenai

Peninsula from Kasilof to Anchor Point can be rewarding. Many thousands of clams are dug each year at Clam Gulch. You must have a sportfishing license to dig, and these are available at most sporting goods stores. The bag limit is 60 clams regardless of size (always check current regulations). There is no legally closed season, but quality of the clams varies with month; check locally. Good clamming and fewer people in March and April, although there may still be ice on the beach. Any tide lower than minus 1-foot is enough to dig clams; minus 4- to 5-foot tides are best. The panoramic view of Mount Redoubt, Mount Iliamna and Mount Spurr across Cook Inlet and the expanse of beach are well worth the short side trip even during the off-season. ⊷

S 118.2 (190.2 km) **A 171.2** (275.5 km) **H 61.3** (98.7 km) CLAM GULCH (pop. 108) consists of the lodge and the post office, which was established in 1950.

S 119.6 (192.5 km) **A 172.6** (277.8 km) **H 59.9** (96.4 km) **Clam Gulch Lodge B&B**, home of Captain J Charters. Continental breakfast buffet with mountain view from our fireplace lounge. We guide for salmon and halibut on fresh and saltwater and offer guided clam trips on the best clam beaches in Alaska. Call for tides. We offer a smoke-free environment, large rooms, twin and king-size beds with shared baths. Four RV sites with full hookups. Box 499, Clam Gulch, AK 99568. Phone/fax (907) 260-3778, 1-800-700-9555. Internet: www.clamgulch. com. E-mail: eviej@ptialaska.net. See display ad. [ADVERTISEMENT] ▲

S 122.8 (197.6 km) **A 175.8** (282.9 km) **H 56.7** (91.2 km) Paved, double-ended turnout oceanside (no view).

S 124.8 (200.8 km) **A 177.8** (286.1 km) **H 54.7** (88 km) Paved, double-ended turnout oceanside with view of Cook Inlet.

S 126.8 (204.1 km) **A 179.8** (289.4 km) **H 52.7** (84.8 km) Double-ended paved scenic wayside overlooking upper Cook Inlet. Polly Creek, due west across Cook Inlet, is a popular area for clam diggers (fly in). Across the inlet is Mount Iliamna; north of Iliamna is Mount Redoubt.

S 127.1 (204.5 km) **A 180.1** (289.8 km) **H 52.4** (84.3 km) Double-ended paved scenic viewpoint to west with interpretive display on Mount Redoubt and Mount Spurr volcanoes. Private RV park. ▲

Scenic View RV Park. Full hookups with electric, water, dump station and low monthly/weekly rates on 40-foot-by-20-foot pads. Located between Soldotna and Homer overlooking Cook Inlet and Mt. Redoubt. Fish for halibut and king salmon with Elby Charters and dig for razor clams on nearby beaches. E-mail: scenicrv@ alaska.net. Phone (907) 567-3909. See display ad. [ADVERTISEMENT] ▲

S 128.3 (206.5 km) **A 181.3** (291.8 km) **H 51.2** (82.4 km) **Ninilchik Cabins & Fish Camp.** See display ad this section.

S 130.1 (209.4 km) **A 183.1** (294.7 km) **H 49.4** (79.5 km) **Caribou Creek Cabins.** See display ad this section.

S 130.5 (210 km) **A 183.5** (295.3 km) **H 49** (78.9 km) **Ninilchik Point Overnighter.** Spacious, comfortable home-grown log cabins. Scenic getaway. Cook Inlet view. Economy camping, with showers. One cabin self-contained with kitchen. 3-cabins served by shower house. 2-burner electric units. Bedding, linens provided. Outdoor grill. Close to famous fishing, clam beaches. Local charters. (907) 567-3423. See display ad. [ADVERTISEMENT]. ▲

S 132.2 (212.7 km) **A 185.2** (298 km) **H 47.3** (76.1 km) **Heavenly Sights Charters & Camping.** See display ad this section. ▲

S 133.9 (215.5 km) A 186.9 (300.8 km) H 45.6 (73.4 km) **Black Goat's Bluff RV Park.** Panoramic view: Cook Inlet, Alaska Range, volcanoes. 5 minutes to fishing and clam beds. RV hookups, picnic tables, firepits surrounded by peaceful wilderness. At Quick Stop, turn right onto Banta Drive, left onto Barbara Drive, follow to Camp entrance. P.O. Box 39731, Ninilchik, AK 99639; (907) 567-7395. E-mail: s2d@alaska.net. [ADVERTISEMENT]▲

S 134.5 (216.4 km) A 187.5 (301.7 km) H 45 (72.4 km) **Ninilchik State Recreation Area.** Ninilchik River Scenic Overlook: $8/camping fee, $5/day-use fee or annual pass. Ninilchik River Campground: $10 camping fee, 43 sites, water, toilets and tables. Trail to **Ninilchik River**; fishing for king and silver salmon, steelhead and Dolly Varden. Ninilchik Beach Campground: $8 camping fee, 35 campsites, toilets, water. $5 day-use fee or annual pass. Popular beach for razor clamming. *CAUTION: Drownings have occurred here. Be aware of tide changes when clam digging. Incoming tides can quickly cut you off from the beach.* Access to the clamming beds adjacent to the campgrounds during minus tides. ◄▲

Inlet View Lodge. See display ad this section.

S 134.7 (216.8 km) A 187.7 (302 km) H 44.8 (72.1 km) Coal Street; access west to Ninilchik's historic **Russian Orthodox Church** at top of hill; plenty of parking and turnaround space; scenic overlook.

S 134.8 (216.9 km) A 187.8 (302.2 km) H 44.7 (71.9 km) Large double-ended gravel turnout; scenic overlook.

S 135.1 (217.4 km) A 188.1 (302.7 km) H 44.4 (71.4 km) Double-ended gravel turnout and dumpsters at north end of Ninilchik River bridge. Side road leads to NINILCHIK VILLAGE, the original village of Ninilchik, and to the beach. Access to mouth of **Ninilchik River**; fishing. A short road branches off this side road and leads into the old village of Ninilchik. Continue straight on side road for motel, beach, overnight RV parking, camping and toilets (follow signs). Sea breezes here keep the beach free of mosquitoes. Historic signs near beach and at village entrance tell about Ninilchik Village, which includes several old dovetailed log buildings. A walking tour brochure is available from businesses in the village and along the highway. Present-day Ninilchik is located at **Milepost S 135.5.** ◄▲

A beautiful white Russian Orthodox

Side road leads to Ninilchik Village and beach. (© Ruth von Spalding)

church sits on a hill overlooking the sea above the historic old village. Trail leads up to it from the road into town (watch for sign just past the old village store). The church and cemetery are still in use. You are welcome to walk up to it, but use the well-defined path behind the store (please do not walk through private property), or drive up using the Coal Street access at **Milepost S 134.7.**

Ninilchik Village Cache. See display ad this section.

Ninilchik Village Cabins. See display ad this section.

S 135.3 (217.7 km) A 188.3 (303 km) H 44.2 (71.1 km) Gravel turnout to west.

S 135.4 (217.9 km) A 188.4 (303.2 km) H 44.1 (71 km) Kingsley Road; access to Ninilchik post office and 2 private campgrounds. Ninilchik View state campground is across the highway overlooking the village and sea; 12 campsites, water, toilets, litter disposal, 2 dump stations ($5 fee), drinking water fill-up. Camping fee $10/night or annual pass. Foot trail from campground down to beach and village. DOT/PF road maintenance station. ▲

Alaskan Angler RV Resort (formerly Hylen's) and **AFISHUNT Charters.** Newly remodeled park and cabins at great central Ninilchik location on the corner of Kingsley Road and highway. Walk to old village, downtown, clamming beaches, salmon fishing, post office. Fifty new 50-, 30-, 20-amp full hookups; 10 partial; cable TV with HBO, telephone lines, tenting. One-, 2- and 3-bedroom furnished cabins. New public showers/laundry. We specialize in local fishing and clamming, with licenses, cleaning tables, smoker, vacpak, freezing, shipping and tackle. Experience Alaska's best fishing for succulent halibut and king salmon with on-site AFISHUNT Charters, departing from the park. Good Sam discounts. Owners on-site. Reservations (800) 347-4114, (907) 567-3393. www.afishunt.com. See display ad in Ninilchik section. [ADVERTISEMENT] ▲

Ninilchik

S 135.5 (218 km) A 188.5 (303.4 km) H 44 (70.8 km) Pronounced Nin-ILL-chick. **Population:** 675. **Emergency services:** Phone 911. **Visitor Information:** At Kiosk, Milepost S 136.1. Local businesses are also very helpful. **Private Aircraft:** Ninilchik airstrip, 6.1 miles/9.8 km southeast; elev. 276 feet/84m; length 2,400 feet/732m; dirt; unattended.

Restaurant, lodging and charter service east side of road are part of the community of Ninilchik. Ninilchik extends roughly from Ninilchik State Recreation Area to the north to Deep Creek to the south, with services (grocery stores, gas stations, campgrounds, etc.) located at intervals along the highway. The original village of Ninilchik (signed Ninilchik Village) is reached by a side road from **Milepost S 135.1.**

On Memorial Day weekend, Ninilchik is referred to as the third biggest city in Alaska, as thousands of Alaskans arrive for the fishing (see Area Fishing following). The Kenai Peninsula Fair is held at Ninilchik the third weekend in August. Dubbed the "biggest little fair in Alaska," it features a parade, horse show, livestock competition and exhibits ranging from produce to arts and crafts. Pancake breakfasts, bingo and other

NINILCHIK ADVERTISERS

Digging for razor clams on Cook Inlet beaches offers fine views. (© Nancy Faville)

events, such as the derby fish fry, are held at the fairgrounds throughout the year. The king salmon derby is held from May to June 15. A halibut derby, sponsored by the Ninilchik Chamber of Commerce, runs from Father's Day through Labor Day. There is an active senior center offering meals and events. Swimming pool at the high school.

AREA FISHING: Well-known area for saltwater king salmon fishing and record halibut fishing. Charter services available. (Combination king salmon and halibut charters are available and popular.) Salt water south of the mouth of **Deep Creek** has produced top king salmon fishing in late May, June and July. Kings 50 lbs. and over are frequently caught. "Lunker" king salmon are available 1 mile/1.6 km south of Deep Creek in **Cook Inlet** from late May through July. Trolling a spinner or a spoon from a boat is the preferred method. Silver, red and pink salmon are available in salt water between Deep Creek and the Ninilchik River during July. A major halibut fishery off Ninilchik has produced some of the largest trophy halibut found in Cook Inlet, including a 466-lb. unofficial world record sport-caught halibut.

Sterling Highway Log
(continued)

S 135.6 (218.2 km) A 188.6 (303.5 km) H 43.9 (70.6 km) Ninilchik High School. Ninilchik Library, open 10 A.M. to 4 P.M. daily in the summer.

S 135.7 (218.4 km) A 188.7 (303.7 km) H 43.8 (70.5 km) **Ninilchik General Store.** Open every day for all your travel needs. Offering groceries, bait, tackle, licenses, rain gear, ice, film, gifts, Beanie Babies, books, T-shirts, gold nugget jewelry, hardware and a snack bar. Try our Fisherman's Bag Lunch. Stop in for free information packet on the Ninilchik area. You'll like our prices and service. Ask your friends who have met us. We compete for your business, we don't just wait for it to happen. See display ad this section. [ADVERTISEMENT]

S 135.8 (218.5 km) A 188.8 (303.7 km) H 43.7 (70.3 km) **Ninilchik Saltwater Charters & Lodge.** See display ad this section.

Bull Moose Gifts. One of the nicest gift shops on the Kenai Peninsula, offering a wide selection of gifts, souvenirs and Beanie Babies. Alaskan and Russian arts and crafts, fine art prints, jewelry, including Alaskan gold nuggets, caps, postcards, notecards, and over 50 Alaskan designs of T-shirts and sweatshirts. Easy access for large RVs, lots of parking and clean restroom. See display ad this section. [ADVERTISEMENT]

S 135.9 (218.7 km) **A 188.9** (304 km) **H 43.6** (70.2 km) **Junction** with Oilwell Road; post office, airstrip, camping and charter services east on Oilwell Road (descriptions follow). Tesoro gas station on Sterling Highway south side of junction.

The O'Fish'ial Charters of Alaska. See display ad this section.

Reel'Em Inn/Cook Inlet Charters. East 1 mile on Oilwell Road at the Chinook Tesoro. Owned and operated by Alaskan family with the knowledge to show you how to experience the area's attractions. Full-service facility. Fishing charters, lodging, RV hookups. Equipment rental—fishing poles, raingear, boots, clam shovels. Check us out, you will not be sorry! Reservations welcome. Phone (907) 567-7335. See display ad. [ADVERTISEMENT]

Country Boy Campground. , just 3.1 miles down Oilwell Road. Turn at Chinook Tesoro. 44 full hookups, immaculate shower/laundry facility. Fish cleaning table, clam shovels. Fishing charters arranged and shuttle service. Potlucks every Sunday. At Country Boy, friends are family and family are friends. We want you to enjoy Alaska. (907) 567-3396. See display ad. ▲

S 136 (218.9 km) **A 189** (304.1 km) **H 43.5** (70 km) **Chinook Tesoro.** Ninilchik. 24-hour card lock. Open year-round. Self-serve gasoline, propane, on-road and dyed diesel. We install quality NAPA Auto Parts. Auto/RV mechanics, tire sales and repair, water/air for RVs. Bait, ice, market items. Free tide books, visitor information on clamming and guided fishing. Tesoro, VISA, MasterCard, Discover. All major oil company cards welcome. See display ad this section. [ADVERTISEMENT]

S 136.1 (219 km) **A 189.1** (304.3 km) **H 43.4** (69.8 km) **Chihuly's Charters** and **Porcupine Shop.** See display ad this section.

S 136.2 (219.2 km) **A 189.2** (304.5 km) **H 43.3** (69.7 km) **Peninsula Fairgrounds.** Visitor Information Kiosk opposite the fairgrounds.

Deep Creek View Campground. See display ad this section. ▲

S 136.7 (219.9 km) **A 189.7** (305.3 km) **H 42.8** (68.9 km) Bridge over Deep Creek.

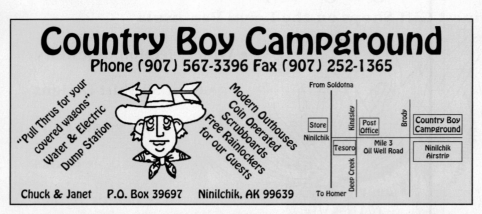

Country Boy Campground
Phone (907) 567-3396 Fax (907) 252-1365

"Pull Thrus for your covered wagons"
Water & Electric
Dump Station

Modern Outhouses
Coin Operated Scrubboards
Free Rainlockers for our Guests

Chuck & Janet   P.O. Box 39697   Ninilchik, AK 99639

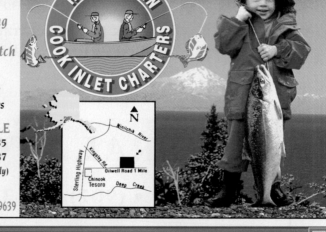

COMBINATION SALTWATER SALMON & HALIBUT FISHING

IN BEAUTIFUL NINILCHIK & DEEP CREEK

Lodging & RV Parking
Freezing & Storage
& Shipping of Your Catch

Rental Equipment
Clam Shovels • Raingear
Boots • River Fishing Poles

BROCHURES AVAILABLE
May - Sept. (907) 567-7335
Oct. - April (907) 345-3887
1-800-447-7335 (Alaska only)

Bruce & Charlene McLean
P.O. BOX 39292 NINILCHIK, AK 99639

REEL 'EM INN COOK INLET CHARTERS

CHINOOK TESORO
See log ad at MILE 136 (Ninilchik) • 24-Hour Gas (Card Lock)

Gasoline • Diesel
Propane • Ice
Snacks • Bait
Clean Restrooms
Tire Repair
NAPA AutoCare Center
Paved Parking
Guided Fishing Information

(907) 567-3473

TESORO ALASKA — THE WAY TO GO.

• Halfway between Deep Creek and Ninilchik Beaches

• Easy Access for Motorhomes, 5th Wheels, and Caravans

• Major Credit Cards and Traveler's Checks Welcome - Same as Cash. We honor all Major Oil Company Credit Cards.

Deep Creek View Campground

- Family Campground
- Spectacular Views
- Electric Hookups
- Bathrooms & Showers new in '99

Mile 136.2 Sterling Highway
P.O. Box 23, Ninilchik, Alaska 99639
(907) 567-3320
http://www.alaskaoutdoors.com/Smart
smart@alaska.net

1-888-HALIBUT
1-888-425-4288

- Halibut & Salmon Fishing
- 28 Foot Alumaweld Boat
-- Coast Guard Licensed Captains
-- Bathroom Facility On-Board

J & J Smart Charters
1-888-HALIBUT
Seasonal Operation

Developed sites on both sides of creek: Deep Creek North Scenic Overlook and Deep Creek South Scenic Overlook. Both have $8/camping fee, $5/day-use fee or annual pass, restrooms, water, interpretive kiosks, tables and fireplaces. Deep Creek South offers camping May and June only, day-use only rest of summer. ▲

Freshwater fishing in **Deep Creek** for king salmon up to 40 lbs., use spinners with red bead lures, Memorial Day weekend and the 4 weekends following; Dolly Varden in July and August; silver salmon to 15 lbs., August and September; steelhead to 15 lbs., late September through October. No bait fishing permitted after Aug. 31. Mouth of Deep Creek access from Deep Creek State Recreation Area turnoff at **Milepost S 137.3.** ◄

S 137 (220.4 km) **A 190** (305.8 km) **H 42.5** (68.4 km) Cannery and sports shop with tackle and clam shovel rentals west side of road.

Fishward Bound Adventures. See display ad this section.

Deep Creek Custom Packing, Inc. Just south of Deep Creek bridge in Ninilchik. Home of the finest gourmet smoked salmon and halibut in the world. Free samples and coffee. Seafood display includes locally caught scallops, razor clams, crab, halibut and salmon. Sport fishermen take their own catch in to be hand-packed, frozen, canned or smoked to their specifications. Mail order service available for gift packs, fresh Alaskan seafood, canned salmon, smoked salmon and halibut. State-of-the-art insulated packaging. Overnight delivery, door-to-door, anywhere in the U.S. Visitor information on the best charters, clam digging and fishing. Stop in and see this truly traditional Alaskan business. See display ad this section. [ADVERTISEMENT]

S 137.3 (220.9 km) **A 190.3** (306.2 km) **H 42.2** (67.9 km) **Deep Creek State Recreation Area** on the beach at the mouth of Deep Creek; parking for 300 vehicles, overnight camping, water, tables, dumpsters, toilets and fireplaces. Drive 0.5 mile/0.8 km down paved road. Camping fee $10/night per vehicle or annual pass, day-use fee $5 or annual pass. Favorite area for surf fishing and to launch boats. Boat launch $5 fee or annual pass. Private boat launch service here uses tractors to launch boats from beach into Cook Inlet. Seasonal checks by U.S. Coast Guard for personal flotation devices, boating safety. Good bird watching in wetlands behind beach; watch for eagles. Good clamming at low tide. The beaches here are lined with coal, which falls from the exposed seams of high cliffs. ◄▲

CAUTION: Rapidly changing tides and weather. Although the mouth of Deep Creek affords boaters good protection, low tides

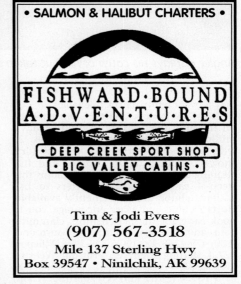

• SALMON & HALIBUT CHARTERS •

FISHWARD·BOUND A·D·V·E·N·T·U·R·E·S
· DEEP CREEK SPORT SHOP ·
· BIG VALLEY CABINS ·

Tim & Jodi Evers
(907) 567-3518
Mile 137 Sterling Hwy
Box 39547 • Ninilchik, AK 99639

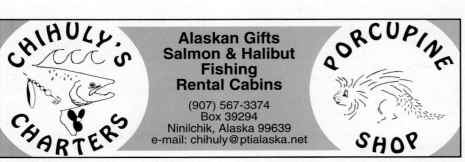

CHIHULY'S CHARTERS

Alaskan Gifts Salmon & Halibut Fishing Rental Cabins

(907) 567-3374
Box 39294
Ninilchik, Alaska 99639
e-mail: chihuly@ptialaska.net

PORCUPINE SHOP

DEEP CREEK CUSTOM PACKING, INC.

Same Day Processing

RETAIL SEAFOOD
FRESH & SMOKED
Halibut
Salmon
Scallops
King Crab
Prawns
Canned Salmon

CUSTOM PACKING
VACUUM PACKING
Freezing
Smoking
Canning
Shipping
Storage

Gift Packs

Mail Orders

Huge RV Access Two Driveways

OPEN 7 DAYS A WEEK 24 HRS-PEAK SEASON

MILE 137 STERLING HWY
BOX 229, NINILCHIK, AK 99639
Overlooking Campground at Deep Creek

907-567-3395

Angler displays his catch of halibut taken in Cook Inlet. (© Bill Sherwonit)

may prevent return; check tide tables.

D&M RV Park & Charters. Our park site on the bluff overlooking Cook Inlet has a million dollar view. We have 38 sites, 24 with water and electric hookups. Laundry, showers, dump station, storage and fish cleaning facilities on site. Heated cabins that sleep 4 each and daily charters to fish halibut/salmon are conveniently available. Hosts Debbie and Marc encourage you to book early for the best fishing, clamming dates and to reserve your spot. Year-round: (800) 479-4368. Fax (907) 349-3996. Milepost 127.3. Sterling Highway. Visit our Website. ▲ [ADVERTISEMENT]

S 137.4 (221.1 km) **A 190.4** (306.4 km)

H 42.1 (67.8 km) **Roe's Charter Service.** Family owned, operated by year-round residents. Halibut, salmon combo charters, April–September. Friendly, personalized service at our quiet location. Circle drive for RV convenience. Fish from custom built 26-foot offshore, heated-cabin boat, or 20-foot open boat. Both boats outfitted with enclosed marine bathroom, comfortable seating, state-of-the-art electronics, custom made rods, top quality gear. Free filleting. Further processing, shipping services nearby. Lodging, etc. available. Phone (888) 567-3496, (907) 567-3496. Internet: www.alaskaone.com/roe. See display ad. [ADVERTISEMENT]

S 140 (225.3 km) **A 193** (310.6 km)

H 39.5 (63.5 km) **Salty Dog Charters and Deep Creek B&B.** See display ad this section.

Solitudes Bed & Breakfast. See display ad this section.

S 140.3 (225.8 km) **A 193.3** (311.1 km) **H 39.2** (63.1 km) Double-ended turnout with scenic view to west.

S 140.5 (226.1 km) **A 193.5** (311.4 km) **H 39** (62.8 km) **Double Eagle Lodge.** Modern, deluxe cabins, adult setting, with spectacular Inlet view. Each has coffee, microwave, refrigerator and private bathrooms, one with kitchen and laundry. Centrally located on Kenai Peninsula within minutes to charters, rivers, clamming and stores. Full hearty breakfast at your convenience in Alaska-style cook shack included. Phone (907) 567-3492. [ADVERTISEMENT]

S 142.7 (229.6 km) **A 195.7** (314.9 km) **H 36.8** (59.2 km) Double-ended paved turnout with dumpster, view of Mount Iliamna across the inlet.

S 143.8 (231.4 km) **A 196.8** (316.7 km) **H 35.7** (57.4 km) Happy Valley Creek. The area surrounding this creek is known locally as the Happy Valley community.

S 145.5 (234.2 km) **A 198.5** (319.4 km) **H 34** (54.7 km) **King of Kings Guide Service and Lodge** on the shores of Cook Inlet. Full-service lodge. Fish 2 tides each day: one for salmon and one for halibut. Licensed and insured guides; all equipment furnished. We have 3-day and 6-day packages. 24715 Sterling Highway, Anchor Point, AK 99556. (907) 567-3667. E-mail: kings@ptialaska.net. [ADVERTISEMENT]

S 148 (238.1 km) **A 201** (323.5 km) **H 31.5** (50.7 km) Scenic viewpoint. Sign here reads: "Looking westerly across Cook Inlet, Mt. Iliamna and Mt. Redoubt in the Chigmit Mountains of the Aleutian Range can be seen rising over 10,000 feet above sea level. This begins a chain of mountains and islands known as the Aleutian Chain extending west over 1,700 miles to Attu beyond the International Date Line to the Bering Sea, separating the Pacific and Arctic oceans. Mt. Redoubt on the right, and Iliamna on the left, were recorded as active volcanoes in the mid-18th century. Mt. Redoubt had a minor eruption in 1966."

Mount Redoubt had a major eruption in December 1989. The eruptions continued through April 1990, then subsided to steam plumes. Mount Redoubt is still considered active.

S 150 (241 km) **A 203** (326.7 km) **H 29.5** (47.8 km) **Cooper's Bed & Breakfast.** See display ad this section.

S 150.9 (242.8 km) **A 203.9** (328.1 km) **H 28.6** (46 km) Bridge over Stariski Creek.

S 151.9 (244.4 km) **A 204.9** (329.7 km) **H 27.6** (44.4 km) **Stariski Creek State**

Recreation Site on bluff overlooking Cook Inlet; 16 campsites, $10 nightly fee or annual pass, toilets (wheelchair accessible) and well water. &▲

S 152.7 (245.7 km) A 205.7 (331 km) H 26.8 (43.1 km) **Eagle Crest RV Park & Cabins.** See display ad this section. ▲

Anchor Point

S 154 (247.8 km) A 207 (333.1 km) H 25.5 (41 km) Located along the Sterling Highway. **Population:** 1,188. **Emergency services:** Phone 911. **Visitor Information:** Located in the log cabin at the "Y" of the New and Old Sterling Highways at **Milepost S 156.9.** Anchor Point Chamber of Commerce, P.O. Box 610, Anchor Point, AK 99556; phone (907) 235-2600, fax (907) 235-2600.

The main business area of this small community stretches along the Sterling Highway and the banks of the Anchor River west to Cook Inlet via Anchor River Road (see **Milepost S 156.9**). Anchor Point is a full-service community with a variety of businesses, including lodging, restaurants, gas stations, fishing charters, tackle shops, auto repair, RV parks, groceries, lundries and gift shops.

Anchor Point was named in the summer

of 1778 by Captain James Cook when the *Resolution* and *Discovery* sailed into Cook Inlet looking for the Northwest Passage and lost a kedge anchor to the tidal currents. A post office was established here in 1949.

Anchor Point post office is located at the intersection of the Sterling Highway and Milo Fritz Road and North Fork Road (**Milepost S 156.7**). The post office is open 9 A.M. to 5 P.M. weekdays, 9 A.M. to noon Saturday.

The Anchor Point area is noted for seasonal king and silver salmon, steelhead and rainbow fishing. Saltwater trolling for king salmon to 80 lbs., halibut to 200 lbs., spring through fall. **Anchor River**, king salmon fishing permitted only on 5 consecutive weekends, beginning Memorial Day weekend; trout and steelhead from July to October; closed to all fishing Dec. 31 to June 30, except for king salmon weekends. Excellent

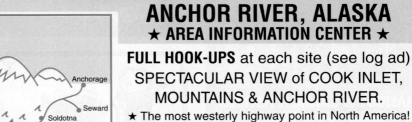

fishing for 12- to 24-inch sea-run Dollies in July and late summer. During August silver runs, fish high tides. Anchor River King Salmon Derby is usually held the last week-end in May and the first 4 weekends in June. A silver salmon derby is held in August. ⌐●

Anchor Point Lodging, Clive's Fishing Guide Service. Just off highway. Walking trails to river and beach. Large rooms with private bath. Central lounge with TV, coffee and phone. Combination salmon/halibut trips. All equipment furnished. Call (907) 235-1236 fax (907) 235-1905. E-mail: clives@ptialaska.net. Hosts: Clive and Marilyn Talkington, Box 497, Anchor Point, AK 99556. [ADVERTISEMENT]

Bear Paw Charters. This Anchor Point location is only minutes from trophy halibut and salmon fishing. All equipment provided plus free filleting. Small groups and personalized service are the focus of this family-owned and operated business. Lodging also available in private, fully equipped log cabins. You'll like the gift shop. Phone (907) 235-5399. See display ad this section. E-mail: bearpaw@xyz.net; Web address: www.xyz.net/~bearpaw. [ADVERTISEMENT]

Sterling Highway Log
(continued)

S 156.9 (252.5 km) A 209.9 (337.8 km) H 22.6 (36.4 km) Anchor Point "Y" junction with Old Sterling Highway; access to Anchor River businesses, **Anchor Point Visitor Information Center** (open year-round, 10 a.m. to 5 p.m. daily in summer), Anchor

Anchor River (Beach) Road Log

Turn off the Sterling Highway at **Milepost S 156.9** on to the Old Sterling Highway and continue past the Anchor River Inn to the Anchor River. Just beyond the bridge is the turnoff for Anchor River (Beach) Road, a 1.2-mile/1.9-km spur road providing access to Anchor River recreation area.

Distance from junction (J) is shown.

J 0 Junction of Old Sterling Highway and Sterling Highway at **Milepost S 156.9**.

J 0.1 (0.2 km) School Road. Anchor Point visitor information center. A plaque across from the visitor center marks the westernmost point on the contiguous North American Highway system.

Anchor River Inn, overlooking beautiful Anchor River and in business for 35 years, has the finest family restaurant on the peninsula, where you can see one of the largest displays of collectible plates in Alaska. Serving breakfast, lunch and dinner. Large cocktail lounge has a wide-screen TV, pool tables, dance floor and video games. 20 modern motel units with phones; 10 spacious units with color TV and 2 queen-sized beds, and 10 smaller units overlooking the river. Our fully stocked liquor, grocery store and gift shop serve the Anchor Point area year-round. Write: Box 154, Anchor Point, AK 99556; phone 1-800-435-8531 in USA, or (907) 235-8531; fax (907) 235-2296. Your hosts: Bob and Simonne Clutts. [ADVERTISEMENT]

J 0.3 (0.5 km) Anchor River bridge, also known as "the erector set bridge."

J 0.4 (0.6 km) Road forks: Old Sterling Highway (gravel) continues south through rural residential area and rejoins Sterling Highway at **Milepost S 164.8**. Turn right for Anchor River (Beach) Road. Tackle shop at intersection across from

Private tractor boat launch at Anchor Point. (© Susan Cole Kelly)

Silverking parking and campground (Anchor River State Recreation Area); toilets, dumpster, $8 nightly fee or annual pass.

J 0.6 (1 km) Coho campground and parking (Anchor River SRA); toilets, $8 nightly fee or annual pass.

J 0.7 (1.1 km) Anchor Point Chamber of Commerce Salmon Derby Weigh-in and information. Tackle shop.

J 0.8 (1.3 km) Steelhead campground and parking (Anchor River SRA); toilets, $8 nightly fee or annual pass.

J 1.1 (1.8 km) Slidehole campground and parking (Anchor River SRA); 30 campsites, $10 nightly fee or annual pass, shelter with tables, public water source for campers, special senior/wheelchair camping area, large day-use parking lot, trail access to river.

J 1.3 (2.1 km) **Kyllonen's RV Park**, a few steps from famous Anchor River and picturesque Cook Inlet. Providing spring water, electricity and sewer. Additional amenities include fish cleaning station, BBQ pits, free firewood and picnic tables. Showers, restrooms and laundry. Gift shop and Espresso Bar. Fishing licenses. We book fishing charters. May through September. Year-round area

information center, phone/fax (907) 235-7762, fax (907) 235-6435. E-mail: susank@xyz.net. See display ad this section. [ADVERTISEMENT]

J 1.5 (2.4 km) Halibut campground and parking (Anchor River SRA); toilets, $8 nightly fee or annual pass.

J 1.6 (2.6 km) Road deadends on shore of Cook Inlet; beach access, 12-hour parking. Private tractor boat launch service. Signs here mark the most westerly

point on the North American continent accessible by continuous road system and depict outlines of Cook Inlet volcanoes.

Return to Milepost S 156.9 Sterling Highway

River Inn and Anchor River (Beach) Road.

Junction with Old Sterling Highway and access to Anchor River (Beach) Road. See ANCHOR RIVER (BEACH) ROAD log this section.

S 157.1 (252.8 km) **A 210.1** (338.1 km) **H 22.4** (36 km) Anchor River bridge.

S 160.9 (258.9 km) **A 213.9** (344.2 km) **H 18.6** (29.9 km) Side road to artist Norman Lowell's studio and KWLS radio station.

S 161 (259.1 km) **A 214** (344.4 km) **H 18.5** (29.8 km) Anchor River bridge.

S 162.4 (261.4 km) **A 215.4** (346.6 km) **H 17.1** (27.5 km) Gravel turnout to east by Anchor River.

S 164.3 (264.4 km) **A 217.3** (349.7 km) **H 15.2** (24.5 km) North Fork Loop Road to Anchor River.

S 164.8 (265.2 km) **A 217.8** (350.5 km) **H 14.7** (23.7 km) **Junction** with Old Sterling Highway which leads 9.4 miles/15.1 km northwest to connect with Anchor River (Beach) Road, (see **Milepost S 156.9**).

S 167.1 (268.9 km) **A 220.1** (354.2 km) **H 12.4** (20 km) Diamond Ridge Road.

S 168.5 (271.2 km) **A 221.5** (356.5 km) **H 11** (17.7 km) Alaska State Parks' South District office is located on the bluff here. A

small parking lot is adjacent to the log office where visitors may obtain information on Kachemak Bay state park, as well as other southern Kenai Peninsula state park lands.

S 169.3 (272.5 km) **A 222.3** (357.7 km) **H 10.2** (16.4 km) Homer DOT/PF highway maintenance station. RV park.

S 169.6 (272.9 km) **A 222.6** (358.2 km) **H 9.9** (15.9 km) Two viewpoints overlooking Kachemak Bay. Double-ended turnout.

S 170 (273.6 km) **A 223** (358.9 km) **H 9.5** (15.3 km) Bay View Inn. Homer demonstration forest.

S 171.2 (275.5 km) **A 224.2** (360.8 km) **H 8.3** (13.4 km) Land fill road.

S 171.9 (276.6 km) **A 224.9** (361.9 km) **H 7.6** (12.2 km) West Hill Road; access to bed and breakfasts. Connects to Skyline Drive and East Hill Road for scenic drive along Homer Bluff.

S 172.5 (277.6 km) **A 225.5** (362.9 km) **H 7** (11.3 km) Hotel.

S 172.6 (277.8 km) **A 225.6** (363 km) **H 6.9** (11.1 km) Homer Junior High School.

S 172.7 (277.9 km) **A 225.7** (363.2 km) **H 6.8** (10.9 km) **Oceanview RV Park.** See display ad this section. ▲

S 172.8 (278.1 km) **A 225.8** (363.4 km) **H 6.7** (10.8 km) Exit onto Pioneer Avenue for downtown **HOMER** (description follows). Drive 0.2 mile/0.3 km on Pioneer Avenue and turn left on Bartlett Avenue for the Pratt Museum (see Attractions in the Homer section) and Homer city campground (follow signs). Pioneer Avenue continues through downtown Homer to Lake Street

Fishing for salmon on Homer Spit. (© Bill Sherwonit)

and to East Hill Road. ▲

S 173.1 (278.6 km) **A 226.1** (363.9 km) **H 6.4** (10.3 km) Homer Chamber of Commerce Visitor Center at Main Street; access to food, lodging, dump station and other services. Bishop's Beach Park.

S 173.5 (279.2 km) **A 226.5** (364.5 km) **H 6** (9.7 km) Eagle Quality Center; shopping, groceries.

S 173.7 (279.5 km) **A 226.7** (364.8 km) **H 5.8** (9.3 km) Heath Street. Post office (ZIP code 99603).

S 173.9 (279.9 km) **A 226.9** (365.2 km) **H 5.6** (9 km) Lake Street. Access to downtown Homer and Lakeside Center.

S 174 (280 km) **A 227** (365.3 km) **H 5.5** (8.9 km) Beluga Lake floatplane base.

S 174.4 (280.7 km) **A 227.4** (366 km) **H 5.1** (8.2 km) Lambert Lane, access to floatplane base.

S 174.7 (281.1 km) **A 227.7** (366.4 km) **H 4.8** (7.7 km) Alaska Dept. of Fish and Game office. The ADF&G Division of Sport Fish issues 5 different regulation booklets for each of the 5 different sportfishing regions in Alaska. For a current copy of the Kenai Peninsula–Cook Inlet Salt Water–Susitna–West Cook Inlet regulations, stop by the ADF&G office.

S 174.8 (281.3 km) **A 227.8** (366.6 km) **H 4.7** (7.6 km) Homer Tesoro.

S 175 (281.6 km) **A 228** (366.9 km) **H 4.5** (7.2 km) Airport Road. Sterling Highway crosses onto Homer Spit.

A series of boardwalks along the Spit houses shops, charter services, food outlets, etc. Also on the Spit: a resort hotel, restaurants, seafood markets, private campgrounds, and public camping areas (check in with camping registration office on the Spit); the harbormaster's office, small boat basin, shore fishing for salmon in the Fishing Hole, Alaska Marine Highway ferry terminal and a boat ramp. ▲

S 179.5 (288.9 km) **A 232.5** (374.2 km) **H 0** Sterling Highway ends at Land's End Resort and Campground at the tip of Homer Spit.

Homer

Located on the southwestern Kenai Peninsula on the north shore of Kachemak Bay at the easterly side of the mouth of Cook Inlet; 226 miles/364 km by highway or 40 minutes by jet aircraft from Anchorage. **Population:** 4,155. **Emergency Services:** Phone 911 for all emergency services. **City Police,** phone (907) 235-3150. **Alaska State Troopers,** in the Public Safety Bldg., phone (907) 235-8239. **Fire Department** and **Ambulance,** phone (907) 235-3155. **Coast Guard,** phone Zenith 5555. (Coast Guard Auxiliary, phone (907/235-7277.) **Hospital,** South Peninsula, phone (907) 235-8101. **Veterinary Clinic,** phone (907) 235-8960.

Visitor Information: Chamber of Commerce Visitor Center is located on the Homer Bypass at Main Street. Open year-round. Contact the Homer Chamber of Commerce, Box 541, Homer 99603; phone during business hours (907) 235-7740 or 235-5300.

The Pratt Museum is open daily 10 A.M. to 6 P.M. from May through September; open noon to 5 P.M. Tuesday through Sunday from October through April; closed in January. Contact the Pratt Museum, 3779 Bartlett St., Homer 99603. Phone (907) 235-8635.

Elevation: Sea level to 800 feet/244m. **Climate:** Winter temperatures occasionally fall below zero, but seldom colder. The Kenai Mountains north and east protect Homer from severe cold, and Cook Inlet provides warming air currents. The highest temperature recorded is 81°F/27°C. Average annual precipitation is 27.9 inches. Prevailing winds are from the northeast, averaging 6.5 mph/10.5 kmph. **Radio:** KGTL 620, KWAV 103.5/104.9/106.3, MBN-FM 107.1/96.7/95.3, KBBI 890, KPEN-FM 99.3/100.9/102.3, KWHQ-FM 98.3. **Television:** KTUU, KTBY, KTVA, KAKM, KIMO. **Newspaper:** *Homer News* (weekly), *Homer Tribune* (weekly).

Private Aircraft: Homer airport, 1.7 miles/2.7 km east; elev. 78 feet/24m; length 7,400 feet/2,255m; asphalt; fuel 100LL, Jet A; attended.

In the late 1800s, a coal mine was operating at Homer's Bluff Point, and a railroad carried the coal out to the end of Homer Spit. (The railroad was abandoned in 1907.) Gold seekers debarked at Homer, bound for the goldfields at Hope and Sunrise. The community of Homer was established about 1896 and named for Homer Pennock.

Coal mining operations ceased around the time of WWI, but settlers continued to trickle into the area, some to homestead, others to work in the canneries built to process Cook Inlet fish.

Today, Homer's picturesque setting, mild climate and great fishing (especially for halibut) attract thousands of visitors each year. In addition to its tourist industry and role as a trade center, Homer's commercial fishing industry is an important part of its economy. Homer calls itself the "Halibut

Fishing Capital of the World." Manufacturing and seafood processing, government offices, trades and construction are other key industries.

Homer is host to a large artist community. Potters, sculptors, painters and jewelers practice their craft and sell their goods in local shops and galleries. The local theater group provides live performances year-round.

Rising behind the townsite are the gently sloping bluffs which level off at about 1,200 feet/366m to form the southern rim of the western plateau of the Kenai. These green slopes are tinted in pastel shades by acres of wildflowers from June to September; fireweed predominates among scattered patches of geranium, paintbrush, lupine, rose and many other species. Two main roads (East Hill Road and West Hill Road) lead from the Homer business section to the "Skyline Drive" along the rim of the bluffs, and other roads connect with many homesteads on the "Hill."

The name *Kachemak* (in Aleut dialect said to mean "smoky bay") was supposedly derived from the smoke which once rose from the smoldering coal seams jutting from the clay bluffs of the upper north shore of Kachemak Bay and the cliffs near Anchor Point. In the early days many of the exposed coal seams were slowly burning from causes unknown. Today the erosion of these bluffs drops huge fragments of lignite and bituminous coal on the beaches, creating a plentiful supply of winter fuel for the residents. There are an estimated 400,000,000 tons of coal deposit in the immediate vicinity of Homer.

Kachemak is a magnificent deep-water bay that reaches inland from Cook Inlet for 30 miles/48.3 km, with an average width of 7 miles/11.3 km. The bay is rich in marine life. The wild timbered coastline of the south shore, across from Homer, is indented with many fjords and inlets, reaching far into the rugged glacier-capped peaks of the Kenai Mountains.

Jutting out for nearly 5 miles/8 km from the Homer shore is the Homer Spit, a long, narrow bar of gravel. The road along the backbone of the Spit connects with the main road through Homer (all the Sterling Highway). The Spit has had quite a history, and it continues to be a center of activity for the town. In 1964, after the earthquake, the Spit sank 4 to 6 feet, requiring several buildings to be moved to higher ground. Today, the Spit is the site of a major dock facility for boat loading, unloading, servicing and refrigerating. The deep-water dock can accommodate up to 2 340-foot vessels with 30-foot drafts at the same time, making it accessible to cruise and cargo ships. It is also home port to the Alaska Marine Highway ferry MV *Tustumena*. The small-boat harbor on the Spit has a 5-lane load/launch ramp. Also in the small-boat harbor area are the harbormaster's office, canneries, parking/camping areas, charter services, small shops, live theatre, galleries, restaurants, motels and bed and breakfasts.

ACCOMMODATIONS/VISITOR SERVICES

Homer has hundreds of small businesses offering a wide variety of goods and services. There are many hotels, motels, bed and breakfasts, and private campgrounds (reservations advised in summer). Nearly 40 restaurants offer meals ranging from fast food to fine dining. Homer has a post office, library, museum, laundromats, gas stations with propane and dump stations, banks, a hospital and airport terminal. There are many boat charters, boat repair and storage facilities, marine fuel at Homer marina, bait, tackle and sporting goods stores, and also art galleries, gift shops and groceries. City campground accessed via Bartlett Avenue (follow signs).

Homer Spit has both long-term parking and camping. Camping and parking areas are well-marked. Camping fees are $7 per night for RVs and $3 per night for tents. Camping permits are available at the camper registration office on the Spit. There is a 14-day limit; restrooms, water and garbage available. Check with the harbormaster's office or the camper registration office on the Spit if you have questions on rules and regulations pertaining to camping, campfires, long-term parking, boat launching and moorage. ▲

Alaska's Pioneer Inn. 244 Pioneer Ave., in downtown Homer. Clean, comfortable 1-bedroom suites with private baths and furnished kitchens. Sleeps up to 4. Complimentary coffee. Single guest rooms available.

Year-round. Homer's best value. Credit cards accepted. Brochure: P.O. Box 1430, Homer, AK 99603. (907) 235-5670. Toll free from continental U.S., 1-800-782-9655. In Alaska, 1-800-478-8765. [ADVERTISEMENT]

Almost Home B&B/Cabins. Panoramic view of the mountains and the bay. B&B room has private entrance, mini-kitchen, private bath and continental breakfast. Or, choose our cabin with complete kitchen, living room, bath and 2 bedrooms. Clean, comfortable, affordable and friendly! Halibut fishing packages with hosts, Sorry

Charlie Charters. Clean boat with heated cabin and enclosed bathroom. For great fish pictures, see our website. Advance reservations recommended. West Hill Road, $1^1/_2$ miles to Highland, then follow the signs. Phone (907) 235-2553, fax (907) 235-0553. In Alaska: 1-800-478-2352; 1269 Upland Court, Homer, AK 99603. http://www.AlaskaOne.com/almosthome. E-mail: coates@xyz.netalmosthomeB&B. [ADVERTISEMENT]

Bay & Bluff Bed & Breakfast. Welcome to our beautiful cedar home. Panoramic bay, mountain, glacier views. The "Bay View" suite has a king-sized bed, private bath,

adjoining family room for five, private entrance. The "Kachemak" has a queen-size bed, shared bath. Beautifully decorated and clean. Satellite TV/VCR, phone, refrigerator, coffee service. Homemade breakfasts. Open year-round. 4510 Towne Heights, Homer, AK 99603. (907) 235-2859. E-mail: ltpatton@xyz.net. [ADVERTISEMENT]

Bay View Inn. Spectacular panoramic view, next to the scenic overlook at the top of the hill as you enter Homer. Every room overlooks the shimmering waters of Kachemak Bay and the Kenai Mountains. Immaculately clean rooms, non-smoking, firm comfortable beds, telephone, TV with HBO, private bathrooms, outside entrances and freshly brewed morning coffee. Options include kitchenettes, suite with fireplace and separate honeymoon cottage. Espresso bar, serene setting, picnic tables and Adirondack chairs on the lawn. Friendly staff with local activity recommendations. Phone: (907) 235-8485, Fax (907) 235-8716. In Alaska: 1-800-478-8485. P.O. Box 804, Homer, AK 99603. E-mail: bayview@alaska.net Internet:

Three
Moose
Meadow
Wilderness
B&B

YOUR OWN PRIVATE LOG CABINS
907/235-0755 SEE OUR LOG AD UNDER HOMER ACCOMMODATIONS

THE BETTER
SWEATER
☆ Let the stars be your guide! ☆

100% WOOL HANDKNITS & JEWELRY

Next to
Coal Pt Trading
on the Homer Spit

888-842-4140

SKYLINE BED AND BREAKFAST
60855 Skyline Drive • Homer, AK 99603 • 907/235-3832

Glaciers, Eagles, Moose, Beautiful Bay – See It All From Our Deck.
Five Rooms With Private Baths. Full Breakfast.
Children's Play Area. 10 Wooded Acres. Peaceful.

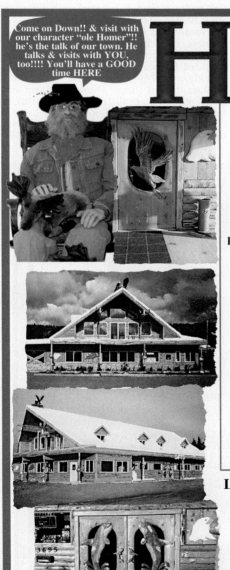

Come on Down!! & visit with our character "ole Homer"!! he's the talk of our town. He talks & visits with YOU, too!!!! You'll have a GOOD time HERE

HOMER'S FUN!!!

Begins with a VISIT & a GRIN !!
We'll SEE & GREET you Here !!
THIS place is REALLY SPECIAL!!

Whether you're a "Local" or a "Visitor", you'll enjoy Great service!

HOMER'S GOLD-MINE GIFTS & FINE JEWELRY
3695 Lake Street, Homer, Alaska 99603

Don'r Forget!!! Mail Orders ANYTIME. You can order Christmas Gift Packs with Salmon, Alaska Sausage, Jellies, Honeys, Fudges

Homer's largest, most unique gift shop!! You can TRY to define UNIQUE HERE!!!
From our hand carved Eagle and Killer Whale Doors, to our Snowy Roof (YEAR ROUND) with a pair of carved Eagles nesting on the peak (YEAR ROUND), and our Spectacular Log Gift Store with Acres of RV Parking, you'll see mounted Salmon, Trout, 410 LB. HALIBUT, and lots of EAGLES.
Coming in the spring of '99, is our LIFE-SIZE WHITE beluga whale sculpture with her Baby, museum, carvings, etc. LOTS to SEE for FREE!!!
GIFTS: Souvenirs Galore, Ornaments, Real Fur Teddy Bears, Eskimo Dolls & Slippers
Shirts: Homer's Largest Selection of Sweats & T's
Wild Alaskan Berry Jam, Jellies, Honeys, Syrups
★ Fresh Alaskan Fudge — It's Delicious
★ Alaska Supreme Ice Cream-Lip Smacking Good!!
★ Espresso Bar with Starbucks Coffee, Figurines, Ulus, Alaska Videos,
Alaskan Gold Nugget Jewelry, Jade, Ivory, Hematite, Scrimshaw
Alaskan Railroad Spike Trains, Hand Carved Moose Horns as Eagles
Fine Art Gallery: Original Jon Van Zyle, Annette Hartzell, Josephine Crumrine,
Doug Lindstrand, etc. Lots of Glass & Brass!! & More
Well Friend, you'll sure miss one of the high's of your trip, unless you stop & see some of our antiques; Elvis' "Throne", Alaska antique diving suit, 55-57 Chevys & classic Corvettes & more!!

Located on the Corner of Lake Street & the Bypass -
Look for the Eagle on our Snowy White Roof-Top

(Between McDonald's & the U.S. Post Office)

Homer's Gold-Mine Gifts
Lake Street
Sterling Highway
By-pass ►
McDonald's
To Homer Spit

Phone: (907) 235-6886
Message Center/Fax: **235-0105**
E-mail: homergm@alaska.net
Web site: http:///www.alaska.net/~homergm/index.html

Bucket of blueberries gathered in Kachemak Bay State Park. (© Bill Sherwonit)

and I welcome you to our home. Panoramic view of Kachemak Bay, from 1,200-foot elevation. Sandhill cranes, moose, coyotes visit regularly. Private and shared bath with twin to king beds. Continental breakfast. Ask about wheelchair access. Open year-round. Phone (907) 235-2969, (800) 338-2969. E-mail: crnscrst@xyz.net. See display ad. [ADVERTISEMENT]

Driftwood Inn and RV Park. Charming, historic beachfront inn with 21 rooms and full-hookup RV park. Both have spectacular view overlooking beautiful Kachemak Bay, mountains, glaciers. Quiet in-town location. Immaculately clean, charming rooms. Free

coffee, tea, local information. Comfortable common areas with TV, fireplace, library, microwave, refrigerator, barbecue, shellfish cooker, fish cleaning area, freezer, picnic and laundry facilities. Continental breakfast available. We are a smoke-free facility. The RV park has 20-/30-/50-amp electric, water, sewer, clean and comfortable laundry and shower room for RV guests. Phone and cable available. Friendly, knowledgeable staff, specializing in helping make your stay in Homer the best possible. Reasonable, seasonal rates. Open year-round. Write, call for brochure. 135 W. Bunnell Ave., MP, Homer, AK 99603. (907) 235-8019. (800) 478-8019. E-mail:

driftinn@xyz.net. Web site: http://www. See our display ad. [ADVERTISEMENT] ▲

Heritage Hotel-Lodge. One of Alaska's finest log hotels, conveniently located in the heart of Homer. Walking distance to beach, shops, museum. Accommodations: 36 rooms including suite with 2-person Jacuzzi. Reasonable rates. Color TV, movie channels. Phones, free local calls. Courtesy coffee. Restaurants adjacent. Alaskan hospitality. Open year-round. 147 E. Pioneer Ave., phone (907) 235-7787. Reservations 1-800-380-7787. Fax (907) 235-2804. See display ad this section. [ADVERTISEMENT]

Homer Alaska Referral Agency. We do it all with one phone call. Your reservation specialists for bed and breakfasts, lodging, halibut and salmon fishing, wildlife viewing, kayaking, bay excursions and adventures, and Kenai Fjords glacier trips. Bookings made at no expense to client for Anchorage, Seward, Homer and all the Kenai Peninsula. For free information, reservations (907) 235-8996 or fax (907) 235-2625. Box 1264, Homer, AK 99603. Established by Seekins, Alaskan residents since 1969. Your reliable source for making Alaskan dreams come true. Call today. E-mail: hara@alaska.net. Internet: www.homer-referral.com. [ADVERTISEMENT]

Homer Spit Campground and Lodging. "Where the land ends and sea begins." Beachfront and ocean-view campsites surrounded by beautiful mountains and bay. Weekly/monthly rates. Walk to harbor, restaurants and shops. Showers. Dump station, electric, pull-throughs, overnight rentals, supplies, gifts. Bookings for halibut charters, boat tours and all recreational needs. Satisfying visitors for 25 years. P.O.

Box 1196, Homer, AK 99603. Phone (907) 235-8206. Fax (907) 235-2595. E-mail: chap ple@xyz.net. [ADVERTISEMENT] ▲

Kachemak Shores Bed and Breakfast. Seven minutes from downtown Homer, you'll find us on a grassy bluff overlooking absolutely chin-dropping beauty of Kachemak Bay and the Kenai Mountains. Follow the bald eagles as they soar past your window which frames the bay and 5 icy-blue glaciers. Otters and seals play in the waters right in front of the deck. Our spacious suite includes a private bath, beautifully appointed sitting room chock full of original Alaskan art, extensive book collections, and a generous main living area. The kitchen is fully stocked with all the fixings of a do-it-your-way hearty continental breakfast and snacks. Return from sightseeing or fishing

Kachemak Bay and Homer Spit view from the hills behind Homer. (© Bill Sherwonit)

and relax on beautiful leather furniture, or maybe take a walk on our private beach. For the nautical-minded, nearby Northern Enterprises commercial boatyard offers a unique look at where those canned salmon really come from. At night you can cuddle up under handmade quilts or maybe watch one of our Alaskan videos in the library. Comfortably sleeps 1 to 7 folks. For reservations, call (907) 235-8234 or (907)

235-6864. E-mail: kshores@ptialaska.net. See display ad. [ADVERTISEMENT]

Land's End Resort. Open year-round! Beachfront spa and fitness area. Homer Spit's only hotel, on the water, at the tip of Homer Spit. Breathtaking views! Watch seals, otters, various seabirds and other sea life as you have lunch or cocktails on our spacious outdoor deck. The Chartroom restaurant is famous for its locally caught seafood. The Wheelhouse Lounge provides lighter meals. Truly an Alaskan landmark! (907) 235-2500 or (800) 478-0400 (AK). 4786 Homer Spit Rd., Homer, AK 99603. Internet: http//akms.com/landsend/. [ADVERTISEMENT]

Magic Canyon Ranch Bed & Breakfast, a 75-acre homestead, inhabits an enchanted canyon overlooking beautiful Kachemak Bay and glacier-filled Kenai Mountains. Visit the llamas, hike canyon rim trails, browse the

Alaskan library, or just relax on the sundeck. Guests enjoy hearty homemade breakfasts of favorite recipes. Guestroom decor is country elegance featuring heirloom antiques and quilts. Hosts: Davis, Betsy and Taber Webb. www.xyz.net/~mcalaska. E-mail: mcalaska@ xyz.net. 40275 Waterman Road, (907) 235-6077. [ADVERTISEMENT].

Ocean Shores Motel. 28 brand new, spacious seaside rooms located above our beautiful private beach. Each unit has a balcony and 7-foot picture window with spectacular views of the ocean, mountains and glaciers. Cable TV, phones, 5-star queen beds, kitchenette and handicap-accessible rooms. Three blocks to downtown Homer, adjacent to restaurants, quiet location and reasonable rates, all make this the best location in Homer. #451, #1 Sterling Highway, Homer, AK 99603. (907) 235-7775 or (800) 770-7775. E-mail: oceanshs@ptialaska.net. www. AKoceanshores.com. See display ad this section. [ADVERTISEMENT].

Oceanview RV Park just past Best Western Bidarka Inn on your right coming into Homer. Spectacular view of Kachemak Bay, beachfront setting. 85 large pull-through spaces in terraced park. Full/partial hookups, heated restrooms, free showers, laundry, pay phone, free cable TV, picnic area. Walking distance to downtown Homer. Special halibut charter rates for park guests. Phone (907) 235-3951. See display ad at Mile 172.7 Sterling Highway. [ADVERTISEMENT] ▲

3 Moose Meadow Wilderness B&B has taken the bed and breakfast to a new level. Understanding that travelers to Alaska want to experience Alaska, we offer you a newly constructed log cabin in a wilderness setting. Your cozy cottage is nestled in the woods and overlooks a meadow with snow-capped mountains beyond. It's very private, with a kitchen and bath, fireplace, large deck and even a porch swing. Cabin rates start at $95/night, $475/week, double occupancy, with breakfast included. Brochure or reservations call (907) 235-0755. E-mail: 3moose@ xyz.net; webpage: www.xyz.net/~3moose. See display ad this section. [ADVERTISEMENT]

Wild Rose Bed & Breakfast. Enjoy your own space in one of our four cozy cabins. Each different to accommodate your party. Queen and single beds, charmingly furnished with well stocked kitchens, bathrooms with showers and 1 has a Jacuzzi tub.. Lots of plants and antiques, books and TV. Decks or front porch for rockin' and talkin'. Slip into a complimentary pair of slippers, settle back and take in our breathtaking view while your catch of the day sizzles on the barbecue grill. P.O. Box 665, Homer, AK 99603. (907) 235-8780. E-mail: wildrose @xyz.net. [ADVERTISEMENT]

TRANSPORTATION

Air: Regularly scheduled air service to Anchorage. Several charter services also operate out of Homer.

Ferry: The Alaska State ferry *Tustumena* serves Seldovia, Kodiak, Seward, Port Lions, Valdez and Cordova from Homer with a limited schedule to Sand Point, King Cove and Dutch Harbor. Natural history programs offered on ferry in summer by Alaska Maritime National Wildlife Refuge naturalists. Contact the offices of the Alaska Marine Highway System at the City Dock, phone (907) 235-8449 for details. Tour boats offer passenger service to Seldovia and Halibut Cove.

Local: 3 rental car agencies and several taxi services.

ATTRACTIONS

The **Pratt Museum**, focusing on the natural and cultural history of southcentral Alaska, is located at 3779 Bartlett St. Exhibits range from artifacts of the area's first Native people, thousands of years ago, to those of homesteaders of the 1930s and 1940s. Excellent aquariums and a tide pool tank feature live Kachemak Bay sea creatures. Also exhibited are Alaskan birds and land and sea mammals, including the complete skeletons of a Bering Sea beaked whale and a beluga whale. Displays also feature local fish industry vessels and the restored Harrington homesteader cabin.

Summer visitors may take a self-guided tour through the botanical garden. This forest trail includes interpretive panels on local wild plants and the homesteader's

Halibut Cove

Halibut Cove is reached by private ferry from Homer. (© Steve Chopp)

Halibut Cove

Located 7 miles southeast of Homer on the east shore of Kachemak Bay. **Population:** 74. **Emergency Services:** In Homer. **Elevation:** 10 feet. **Climate:** Summer temperatures from 45° to 65°F; winter temperatures from 14° to 27°F; average annual precipitation, 24 inches.

Visitor Information: Welcome and information shack at the top of the ramp at the main dock. www.halibutcove.com.

The community of Halibut Cove is nestled along a 3-mile-wide bay on the east shore of Kachemak Bay. The bay was named Halibut Cove by W.H. Dall of the U.S. Coast & Geodetic Survey in 1880. The entrance to Halibut Cove is sheltered by 1.4-mile-long Ismailof Island, named in 1880 by Dall for Gerassiim Grigorovich Ismailov, IRN, who made explorations in Alaska in the late 18th century.

Between 1911 and 1928, Halibut Cove had 42 herring salteries and a population of about 1,000.

Today, the community of Halibut Cove is made up of self-employed artists, commercial fishermen and craftsmen. There are no state schools in the community.

ACCOMMODATIONS/VISITOR SERVICES

Overnight guests in Halibut Cove can stay in cabins or bed and breakfasts located on Ismailof Island (Cove Country Cabins, Highpoint B&B, the Cove House B&B and Halibut Cove Cabins); or on the mainland at Hideaway Cabins or Quiet Place Lodge. There is one restaurant (the Saltry). There is a post office. Banks, groceries and similar services are not available in Halibut Cove.

The Cove House is perfect for couples and larger groups. Stay for days or weeks in this spacious, fully furnished waterfront home. Shower/bath, laundry facilities, fully equipped kitchen, VCR, CD player and much more. Deep water tie-up available and skiff or kayak rentals. Advance reservations recommended. Summer: Phone (907) 2969-2255. Winter: (206) 542-8509. Fax (206) 645-7993. [ADVERTISEMENT]

Quiet Place Lodge. Enjoy a memorable wilderness experience in one of 5 beautifully appointed private cabins with shared baths on the waterfront of Quiet Place Lodge. As you arrive, have a homemade cookie from the "Bottomless Cookie Jar." The newly renovated Lodge and cabins house an eclectic collections of art, antiques and quilts. Spend your days hiking, kayaking, charter fishing and art gallery shopping. Relax on your deck viewing beautiful Halibut Cove or curl up with a book on the couch next to the woodstove in the oceanside library. You need 3–5 days to "take it all in." Don't forget a sauna before snuggling into your flannel sheets. Wake to fresh coffee and full hearty breakfast served in our guest dining area. Delightful Alaskan cuisine dinners offered 4 nights weekly. P.O. Box 6474 Halibut Cove, AK 99603. (907) 296-2212. [ADVERTISEMENT]

TRANSPORTATION

Air: Floatplane.

Boat: The private Kachemak Bay Ferry, M/V *Danny J*, departs Homer at noon and 5 P.M. daily in summer; reservations and tickets through Central Charters. Group charters through Narrows Charters & Tours. Board at the bottom of Ramp A at Homer boat harbor. The ferry ride is 4½ hours and includes Gull Island bird sanctuary.

ATTRACTIONS

There are no roads in Halibut Cove, but some 12 blocks of boardwalk run along the water's edge and provide a scenic and relaxing way to explore this charming community. Stroll the boardwalks for spectacular views of Kachemak Bay, access to the Saltry restaurant and to galleries displaying the work of local artists. Well-known artist Diana Tillion, who is famous for her octopus ink and watercolor paintings, has a gallery here. Other local artists include Alex Combs, Marian Beck, Sydney Bishop, Annette Bellamy, Jay Greene, Katherine Kochansky, Toni Maury, Jan Peyton, Kyle Rader, and Jan Thurston.

Visitors can also walk down to the floats to see several historic wooden boats.

Bird watching in the area is excellent and there are good hiking trails. Kachemak Bay State Park hiking trails are accessible from Halibut Cove. China Poot Lake Trail begins at Halibut Cove Lagoon. The Lagoon Trail winds along Halibut Cove to intersect with the China Poot Lake trail. The bay shoreline offers excellent kayaking, clamming, tide pooling and beach combing opportunities. Keep in mind that Kachemak Bay's tides are among the largest in the world and tidal currents can be substantial. A tide book is essential. Phone the district Alaska State Parks office at (907) 235-7024 for more information, or stop by the state park office outside Homer for more information on hiking Kachemak Bay State Park.

Walk to the end of the main boardwalk in Halibut Cove to reach the beach. Beachcomb, look at tide pools or have a picnic lunch at the tables provided. During salmon season, visitors may see seiners set out their nets.

Kachemak Bay is one of Alaska's most popular spots for halibut fishing, with catches often weighing 100 to 200 lbs. Halibut up to 350 lbs. are fished from June through September.

HALIBUT COVE ADVERTISERS

Central Charters Booking/
  Ferry............................Ph. (907) 235-7848
Cove Country Cabins........Ph. (888) 353-2683
Cove House, The...............Ph. (907) 296-2255
Diana Tillion's Cove
  Gallery ....Ph. (907) 296-2207
Halibut Cove Cabins.........Ph. (907) 296-2214
Halibut Cove Experience
  Gallery ....Ph. (907) 296-2215
High Point B&B.................Ph. (888) 320-5379
Quiet Place Lodge.............Ph. (907) 296-2212
Narrows Charters &
  Tours...........................Ph. (907) 296-2207
The Saltry Restaurant ....Ph. (907) 296-2223

charters are available locally. Halibut up to 350 lbs. are fished from June through September; fish the bottom with herring. Year-round trolling for king salmon is popular; use small herring. King salmon may also be taken during late May and June in area streams. Pink salmon (4 to 5 lbs.) may be caught in July and August; use winged bobbers, small weighted spoons and spinners. Similar tackle or fresh roe will catch silver salmon weighing 6 to 8 lbs. in August and September. Dolly Varden are taken throughout the area April to October; try single eggs or wet flies. Steelhead/rainbow are available in local streams, but for conservation purposes must be immediately released unharmed.

Fishermen have had great success in recent years casting from the shore of Homer Spit for king salmon. The Fishing Hole (also referred to as the Fishing Lagoon or Spit Lagoon) on the Homer Spit supports a large run of hatchery-produced kings and silvers beginning in late May and continuing to September. Kings range from 20 to 40 lbs. The fishery is open 7 days a week in season.

Regulations vary depending on species and area fished, and anglers are cautioned to consult nearby tackle shops or Fish and Game before fishing.

Take a Scenic Drive. East Road, a 20-mile/32-km drive from downtown Homer, climbs through hills and forests toward the head of Kachemak Bay; pavement ends at Mile 12.5, beautiful views of the bay. Or turn off East Road on to East Hill Road and drive up the bluffs to Skyline Drive; beautiful views of the bay and glaciers. Return to town via West Hill Road, which intersects the Sterling Highway at **Milepost S 167.1.**

The glaciers that spill down from the Harding Icefield straddling the Kenai Mountains across the bay create an ever-changing panorama visible from most points in Homer, particularly from the Skyline Drive. The most spectacular and largest of these glaciers is Grewingk Glacier in Kachemak Bay State Park, visible to the east directly across Kachemak Bay from Homer. The glacier was named by Alaska explorer William H. Dall in 1880 for Constantin Grewingk, a German geologist who had published a work on the geology and volcanism of Alaska. The Grewingk Glacier has a long gravel bar at its terminal moraine, behind which the water draining from the ice flows into the bay. This gravel bar, called Glacier Spit, is a popular excursion spot, and may be visited by charter plane or boat. (There are several charter plane operators and charter helicopter services in Homer.) Portlock and Dixon glaciers are also visible directly across from the spit.

Kachemak Bay State Park is located on the south shore of the bay and includes glaciers, alpine tundra, forests, fjords, bays and high-country lakes. The state enlarged this park by the purchase of 23,802 additional acres of land with funds from the settlement of the Exxon Valdez oil spill. The existing trail system offers hiking from Glacier Spit to China Poot Peak. An extensive new trail system is under construction. Campsites are currently available on Glacier Spit, Halibut Cove Lagoon and China Poot Lake. Additional campsites and public-use cabins are planned. Inquire locally about transportation to the park. Daily ferry service and water taxis are available to take you to trailheads. The bay shoreline offers excel-

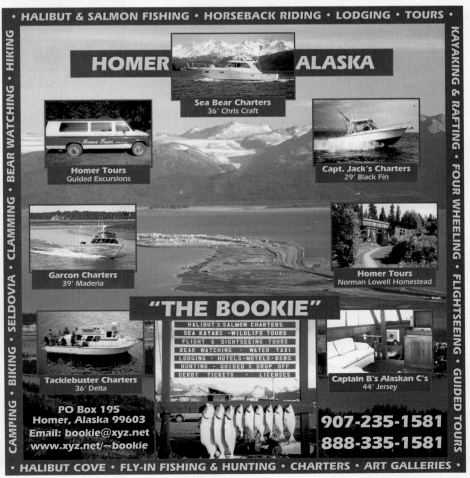

lent kayaking, clamming, tide pooling and beach combing opportunities. Phone the district office at (907) 235-7024 for more information, or stop by the state park office at **Milepost S 168.5.**

McNeil River State Game Sanctuary/ Katmai National Park. Homer is the main base for visitors flying across Cook Inlet to both locations, where the world's largest concentration of bears in a natural area this size is found. Brown bears congregate near the mouth of the McNeil River, where a falls slows down migrating salmon, making fishing easy for the bears. Visits to the game sanctuary are on a permit basis; a drawing for the limited number of permits is held in March each year. Permit applications are available from the Alaska Dept. of Fish and Game, Attn: McNeil River, 333 Raspberry Road, Anchorage 99518. Phone (907) 267-2100.

Katmai National Park offers viewing platforms for close (and safe!) brown bear viewing. Several area outfitters provide service, including overnight stays and access to remote areas of the park.

Study Marine Environment. The Center for Alaskan Coastal Studies is located across Kachemak Bay from Homer. Volunteer naturalists lead a day tour which includes Gull Island bird rookery, coastal forest and intertidal areas. Write the Center for Alaskan Coastal Studies, P.O. Box 2225-MP, Homer 99603; phone (907) 235-6667. Reservations, phone (907) 235-7272.

Alaska Wild Berry Products, celebrating more than 50 years in downtown Homer, invites you to see our wild berry jams, jellies and chocolates handmade the old-fashioned way. Delicious free samples at our taster's stand. Gift shop. Picnic area. Open year-round, 528 East Pioneer Avenue. See display ad this section. [ADVERTISEMENT]

Art Shop Gallery, where Homer shops for art. Open year-round. Original works, prints, posters by local, Alaskan and nationally recognized artists. Alaska Native art, jewelry, dolls, pottery, Christmas tree ornaments by Alaskan artists. Homer's premier gallery. A must see. World-wide shipping. Eagle Quality Center on the bypass. (907) 235-7076 or 1-800-478-7076. [ADVERTISEMENT]

(Continues on page 658)

Seldovia

Seldovia

Reached by air, tour boat or ferry. Located on the southwestern Kenai Peninsula on Seldovia Bay, an arm of Kachemak Bay, 16 miles/25.7 km southwest of Homer. **Population:** 281. **Emergency Services: City Police, Ambulance, Fire** and **Rescue,** emergency only, phone 911, monitor CB Channel 9. **Seldovia Medical Clinic,** phone (907) 234-7825. Seldovia has a resident doctor and visiting dentists.

Visitor Information: Seldovia Chamber of Commerce, Drawer F, Seldovia, AK 99663. Phone (970) 234-7612; Web page: www.xyz.net\~seldovia. Information cache at Synergy Art Works on Main Street, across from the boat harbor. Most Main Street businesses also provide visitor information.

RV parking is restricted along Main Street. Check with the Harbor Master (907/234-7643) for more information on parking.

Elevation: Sea level. **Climate:** Rather mild for Alaska, with a year-round average temperature of about 39°F/4°C. Annual precipitation, 28 inches. Wind is a small factor due to the protecting shield of the Kenai Mountains. **Radio:** Homer stations. **Television:** KENI Channel 2, KTVA Channel 4, KAKM Channel 7, KIMO Channel 13.

Private Aircraft: Seldovia airport, 0.6 mile/1 km east; elev. 29 feet/9m; length 2,000 feet/610m; gravel; unattended.

Seldovia is a small community connected to Homer by the Alaska Marine Highway Southwest ferry system. Because it is removed from Kenai Peninsula highways, Seldovia has retained much of its old Alaska charm and traditions (its historic boardwalk dates from 1931). The St. Nicholas Russian Orthodox Church was built in 1891 and is a national historic site. There are some areas just outside town, accessible by car, that have been called "Alaska's hidden paradises." A good place to observe bald eagles, seabirds and sea otters, Seldovia is included as a stop on some tour boat cruises out of Homer.

The name Seldovia is derived from Russian *Seldevoy,* meaning "herring bay."

SELDOVIA ADVERTISERS

The Alaska state ferry serves the scenic coastal community of Seldovia. (© Rich Reid)

Between 1869 and 1882, a trading station was located here. A post office was established in Nov. 1898.

ACCOMMODATIONS/VISITOR SERVICES

Seldovia has most visitor facilities, including 2 hotels, several bed and breakfasts, a lodge, general store, grocery/deli, restaurants and a variety of shops. The post office is in the center of town. Public restrooms, showers and pay phone in front of the boat harbor near town center. Pay phones are also located at the ferry dock outside ferry office, at the airport, and library.

Fantasy North Halibut Charters and B&B. We are family owned and operated. We believe in quality, personal, professional, friendly services at fair prices. Charters are for 3 to 6 people on our 34-foot Sports Fisherman twin-diesel yacht. Our B&B is a modern, clean, comfortable and spacious 2 bedroom, 1½ bath completely private apartment directly across from the Seldovia Boat Harbor. Phone or write for availability and rates (May–September). All travel arrangements can be handled. P.O. Box 211, Seldovia, AK 99663. Phone (907) 234-7557. [ADVERTISEMENT]

Gerry's Place B&B. Bed and breakfast one block from harbor. Convenient for fishermen and families. Freshly-baked continental breakfast. Three bedrooms accommodate 6 people with shared bath. Free airport pick-up. Close to shops, hiking trails, bike rentals, beachcombing. Open year-round. Box 33, Seldovia, AK 99663. Phone (907) 234-7471. E-mail: rolpat@xyz.net. [ADVERTISEMENT]

Seldovia Boardwalk Hotel. Waterfront view. 14 lovely rooms with private baths. Large harbor-view deck. In-room phones. Near bike rental and Otterbahn Trail. Free airport or harbor pickup. Friendly service. Romantic getaway. Package prices from Homer. P.O. Box 72, Seldovia, AK 99663. (907) 234-7816. E-mail: bbotler@alaska.net. [ADVERTISEMENT]

(Continues on page 658)

Seldovia (continued)

The Mad Fish Restaurant. Dine on fine gourmet cuisine by Chef Kate Fitzgerald-Haralson, as you overlook the picturesque Seldovia waterfront. We specialize in unique and delightful seafood specialties. "It's worth the trip just to eat here." Alaskan beers and fine wines available. Summer: 7 days a week. Winter: Limited hours. Reservations recommended. VISA/MasterCard. (907) 234-7676. E-mail: madfish@alaska.net. [ADVERTISEMENT]

RV camping at the city-owned Seldovia Wilderness Park located just outside the city. From downtown, drive 1 mile/1.6 km out via Anderson Way to fork in road; turn left and drive 0.9 mile/1.4 km to beach. ▲

TRANSPORTATION

Air: Scheduled and charter service available.

Ferry: Alaska's Southwestern Marine Highway system serves Seldovia, with connections to and from Homer, Port Lions, Kodiak, Valdez, Cordova and Seward.

Charter and Tour Boats: Available for passenger service; inquire locally and in Homer.

ATTRACTIONS

Explore Seldovia. Visitors can learn about Seldovia's cultural and natural history from a series of interpretive signs placed about the town. Guided driving tours of the area are available, and bicycles may be rented to explore the city at one's own pace. Seldovia's sheltered bay is ideal for kayaking. Kayak tours and rentals are available. The Otterbaun, a 1.2-mile hiking trail, is a popular way to get from town to Outside Beach. The trailhead is behind the Susan B. English School. Check the tidal charts before you go; access to the Outside Beach is cut off at high tide.

The community's historical artifacts are housed in 2 museums—the Seldovia Native Association Museum on Main Street and the Seldovia Historical Museum on Anderson Way.

Scenic Drives. Outside Beach, a beautiful spot with beachcombing, surf fishing, rockhounding, and a view of Kachemak Bay and the volcanoes St. Augustine, Mount Iliamna and Mount Redoubt, is 1.9 miles/3.1 km from town. Drive out Anderson Way from downtown 1 mile/1.6 km to a fork in the road by a gravel pit; turn left and drive 0.9 mile/1.4 km to beach.

Continue on Anderson Way (past the Outside Beach turnoff) to hilly and unpaved Jakolof Bay Road, which offers panoramic views of Kachemak Bay, McDonald Spit, Jakolof Bay and Kasitsna Bay. At Mile 7.5, steps lead down to 1.5-mile-long McDonald Spit, a favorite spot for seabirds and marine life. Spend an afternoon exploring the spit, or continue out to Jakolof Bay, where the road offers many opportunities to get onto the beach. The road becomes impassable to vehicles at Mile 13.

It is a pleasant drive out to Seldovia's refuse dump, with wonderful blueberry picking in the fall. From downtown, cross the bridge over Seldovia Slough; then turn right on North Augustine Avenue, then left on Rocky Street for the dump. This is a 1.4-mile/2.3-km drive.

Stairway Art Gallery meanders up the stairways of the Seldovia Rowing Club B&B on the original boardwalk. Professional artist Susan Mumma offers a spectacular view from her studio, where her original creations are for sale. She specializes in water colors and lovely remembrances of Seldovia. Gallery/studio hours: 1:30–5 P.M. daily. (907) 234-7614. www.ptialaska.net/~rowing. E-mail: rowing@ptialaska.net. [ADVERTISEMENT]

Herring Bay Mercantile. Fine Alaskan and natural history gifts on the Seldovia waterfront. Colorful kitchenwares and housewares, Alaskan books, elegant jewelry, creative toys, clothing, Alaska bath products, Christmas ornaments, original art. Many locally designed gifts. Featuring work by local artist and author Susan Woodward Springer, including the Seldovia History Book. Open dailiy. VISA/Mastercard. Phone (907) 234-7410. [ADVERTISEMENT]

Special Events. Just about the whole town participates in Seldovia's old-fashioned Fourth of July celebration. The holiday includes food booths, parade, games and contests. Check with the chamber of commerce for details.

Fishing: Kachemak Bay, king salmon January through August; halibut May through October; Dolly Varden June through September; silver salmon in August and September; red salmon July through August. **Seldovia Bay,** king, silver and red salmon, also halibut, May through September. Excellent bottom fishing. 🐟

Bald Mountain Air. All-day brown bear photo safari direct from Homer via floatplane landing in Katmai National Park. Let life-long Alaskans Gary and Jeanne Porter take you on an adventure you'll never forget. Scenic wildlife glacier tours. Expect the best from your Alaska vacation. P.O. Box 3134, Homer, AK 99603. (800) 478-7969. http://www.ptialaska.net/~baldmt. E-mail: baldmt@ptialaska.net. See display ad this section. [ADVERTISEMENT] MP

The Bookstore, located in Eagle Quality Center, is often acclaimed as one of the nicest bookstores in the state. The entire selection is hand-picked with a strong preference for Alaskana and paperback titles. Besides great reading, we have a wonderful card selection, many by local artists. Our hours are 10–7 or call us at (907) 235-7496. Come browse. [ADVERTISEMENT]

Coastal Outfitters: Experience the best wilderness adventure and photographic opportunity for all that Alaska has to offer. Choose from the following custom marine tours aboard our 66-foot vessel. April, May and June—Thrill to the whale migration through the Gulf of Alaska, along with seeing glaciers, volcanoes, a multitude of seabirds and sea mammals. June through September—World-class bear viewing along the coast of Katmai National Park. Stay on our 66-foot vessel with all the comforts of home while watching the magnificent Alaskan brown bears. All tours include unparalleled opportunities for halibut fishing. See display ad. (907) 235-8492; 1-888-235-8492; fax (907) 235-2967. E-mail: bear@xyz.net. Internet: http://www.xyz.net/~bear. [ADVERTISEMENT] MP

Homer's Gold-Mine Gifts & Fine Jewelry. Located on the corner of Lake Street and the Sterling Highway, across from McDonalds. Al and Jan Waddell, old-time Alaskans, offer a wonderful selection of Alaskan-made gifts, as well as fine jewelry, wild berry jams, jellies, syrups and honey. Also, they're cooking wonderful fudge candies with wild berries and nuts. Come and visit their store/museum and share their Alaskan hospitality. A visit to Homer isn't complete until you visit with "Ole' Homer" at Homer's Gold-Mine Gifts. He's the talk of the town! Visit us at www.alaska.net/~homergm/index.html. See display ad this section. [ADVERTISEMENT]

Kachemak Air Service, Inc. offers 2 unique opportunities: Fly over the glaciers across Kachemak Bay with Bill deCreeft in his 1929 Travel Air S6000B floatplane "Limousine of the Air," large, mahogany-framed windows for each passenger; or fly out for the day in Kachemak Air Service, Inc.'s deHavilland Otter floatplane with Chris Day for a day trip viewing brown bears. P.O. Box 1769, Homer, AK 99603. (907) 235-8924. Internet: www.xyz.net/~decreeft/fly1929.htm. [ADVERTISEMENT] MP

NOMAR® (Northern Marine Canvas Products) began business the summer of 1978 in a yellow school bus! Today, visit our manufacturing facility and retail store at 104 E. Pioneer Ave., downtown Homer. NOMAR® manufactures a wide variety of products for our Alaskan lifestyles. Warm NOMAR® fleece clothing to keep you warm, no matter what the adventure. Soft-sided 'Laska Luggage that's stuffable and floatplane friendly. Watertight bags and camp gear for kayak tours or whitewater expeditions. Plus, well-made, Homer-made, packable, mailable, useful gifts, for everyone on the "list." Park in our spacious, paved parking lot and walk around our town, it's a nice stroll. We'll gladly ship your purchases for you. See display ad this section. [ADVERTISEMENT]

North Country Charters, on the Homer Spit. Sean and Gerri Martin, original owners since 1979. We have an excellent catch record with prize-winning derby fish, bringing in some of the largest halibut in Homer. Three 6-passenger and one 16-passenger boat for halibut fishing along with a saltwater salmon trolling boat. All vessels are Coast Guard equipped, heated cabins, full restrooms. 1-800-770-7620. E-mail: norco@alaska.net. www.netalaska.com/northcountry. See display ad. [ADVERTISEMENT]

Pier One Theatre. Local talent lights up an intimate stage in an Alaskan-friendly waterfront atmosphere halfway out the Homer Spit. Plays, new productions, readings, dance theatre, musicals. Offered summer weekends, some midweek shows. Season information available locally. Phone (907) 235-7333. lance@xyz.net. [ADVERTISEMENT]

STERLING HIGHWAY • Homer

Eagles are abundant in Homer.
(© Terry Chick)

SeaFlight SportFishing Charters. Top of the line experience and bottom of the ocean fishing. 41' Hatteras Sportfisher leaving Homer Harbor daily for Kachemak Bay, Cook Inlet and Kodiak Island waters. Halibut fishing April through October; King salmon all year. Shark, rockfish, silver salmon, reds and pinks available in season. Deckhand and Captain experienced and willing to assist you for a unique and productive Alaskan fishing adventure. Reservations recommended. P.O. Box 2347, Homer, AK 99603. Phone (907) 235-7572, Fax: (907) 235-4962. E-mail: seaflight@xyz.net. [ADVERTISEMENT]

St. Augustine's Tours. Sea kayaking day trips out of Kachemak Bay includes water taxi, all equipment, lunch, instruction and guide service. Paddle in one of the world's richest estuaries and visit a bird rookery hosting over 10,000 seabirds. No experience necessary! Phone (907) 235-7568. Call (907) 299-1489. P.O. Box 2412, Homer, AK 99603. [ADVERTISEMENT]

Trail's End Horse Adventures. Horses and Alaska are my life. Join me in my 14th season offering trail rides in the Homer hills. Day trips and pack adventures to the head of Kachemak Bay. View mountains and glaciers. Gentle Alaskan horses. Located at **Mile 11.2** East End Road. Write Mark Marette, Box 1771, Homer, AK 99603, or phone (907) 235-6393. [ADVERTISEMENT]

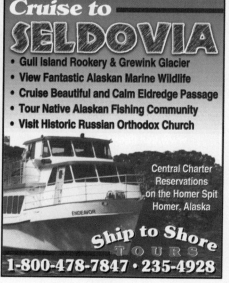

KODIAK

(See map, page 665)

Nootka lupine in bloom on Pillar Mountain above city of Kodiak. (© Marion Stirrup)

The Kodiak Island group lies in the Gulf of Alaska, southwest of Cook Inlet and the Kenai Peninsula. The city of Kodiak is located near the northeastern tip of Kodiak Island, at the north end of Chiniak Bay. By air it is 1 hour from Anchorage. By ferry from Homer it is 9½ hours.

Population: 13,848 Kodiak Island Borough. **Emergency Services in Kodiak:** Dial 911 for emergencies. **Alaska State Troopers,** phone (907) 486-4121. **Police,** phone (907) 486-8000. **Fire Department,** phone (907) 486-8040. **Harbor:** phone (907) 486-8080. **Hospital,** Providence Kodiak Island Medical Center, Rezanof Drive, phone (907) 486-3281. **Coast Guard,** Public Affairs Officer, phone (907) 487-5542. **Crime Stoppers,** phone (907) 486-3113.

Visitor Information: Located at 100 Marine Way; open year-round. Hours in June, July and August are 8 A.M. to 5 P.M. weekdays, 10 A.M. to 4 P.M. Saturday, 10-4 P.M. Sunday (and later for arriving ferries). Knowledgeable local staff will answer your questions and help arrange tours and charters. Free maps, brochures, hunting and fishing information. For information, contact the Kodiak Island Convention & Visitors Bureau, Dept. MP, 100 Marine Way, Kodiak 99615; phone (907) 486-4782 or 1-800-789-4782.

Elevation: Sea level. **Climate:** Average daily temperature in July is 58°F/15°C; in January 30°F/-1°C. September, October and January are the wettest months in Kodiak, with each month averaging more than 7 inches/17.8 cm of precipitation. **Radio:** KVOK 560, KMXT-FM 100.1, KRXX-FM 101. **Television:** Via cable and satellite. **Newspapers:** *The Kodiak Daily Mirror* (daily except Saturday and Sunday).

Private Aircraft: Kodiak state airport, 4.8 miles/7.7 km southwest; elev. 73 feet/22m; length 7,500 feet/2,286m; asphalt; fuel 100LL, Jet A-1. Kodiak Municipal Airport, 2 miles/3.2 km northeast; elev. 139 feet/42m; length 2,500 feet/762m; paved; unattended. Trident Basin seaplane base, on east side of Near Island, unattended, floats for 14 aircraft; fuel. Trident Basin has AVgas, (credit card or pre-pay).

Gravel airstrips at Akhiok, length 3,000 feet/914m; Karluk, length 1,900 feet/579m; Larsen Bay, length 2,400 feet/732m; Old Harbor, length 2,000 feet/610m; Ouzinkie, length 2,500 feet/762m; and Port Lions, length 2,600 feet/792m.

Kodiak Island, home of the oldest permanent European settlement in Alaska, is about 100 miles/161 km long. Known as "Alaska's Emerald Isle," Kodiak is the largest island in Alaska and the second largest island in the United States (after Hawaii), with an area of 3,588 square miles (9,292 sq. km) and about 87 miles/140 km of road (see logs this section). The Kodiak Island Borough includes some 200 islands, the largest being Kodiak, followed in size by Afognak, Sitkalidak, Sitkinak, Raspberry, Tugidak, Shuyak, Uganik, Chirikof, Marmot and Spruce islands. The borough has only one unincorporated townsite, **KARLUK** (pop. 48), located on the west coast of Kodiak Island, 75 air miles/121 km from Kodiak.

The 6 incorporated cities in the Kodiak Island Borough are: **KODIAK** (pop. 6,859) on Chiniak Bay, with all visitor services (see Visitor Services, Transportation and Attractions this section); **AKHIOK** (pop.109) at Alitak Bay on the south side of Kodiak Island, 80 miles/129 km southwest of Kodiak; **LARSEN BAY** (pop. 127) on the northwest coast of Kodiak Island, 62 miles/100 km southwest of Kodiak; **OLD HARBOR** (pop. 297) on the southeast side of Kodiak Island, 54 miles/87 km from Kodiak; **OUZINKIE** (pop. 252) on the west coast of Spruce Island; and **PORT LIONS** (pop. 242) on Settler Cove on the northeast coast of Kodiak Island.

Kodiak Island was originally inhabited by the Alutiiq people, who were maritime hunters and fishermen. More than 7,000 years later, the Alutiiq still call Kodiak home.

In 1763, the island was discovered by Stephen Glotov, a Russian explorer. The name Kodiak, of which there are several variations, was first used in English by Captain Cook in 1778. Kodiak was Russian Alaska's first capital city, until the capital was moved to Sitka in 1804.

Kodiak's turbulent past includes the 1912 eruption of Novarupta Volcano, on the nearby Alaska Peninsula, and the tidal wave of 1964. The Novarupta eruption covered the island with a black cloud of ash. When the cloud finally dissipated, Kodiak was buried under 18 inches/45.7 cm of drifting pumice.

On Good Friday in 1964 the greatest earthquake ever recorded in North America (9.2 on the Richter scale) shook the Kodiak area.

The tidal wave that followed virtually leveled downtown Kodiak, destroying the fishing fleet, processing plants, canneries and 158 homes.

Because of Kodiak's strategic location for defense, military facilities were constructed on the island in 1939. Fort Abercrombie, now a state park and a national historic landmark, was one of the first secret radar installations in Alaska. Cement bunkers still remain for exploration by the curious.

The Coast Guard occupies the old Kodiak Naval Station. Kodiak is the base for the Coast Guard's North Pacific operations; the U.S. Coast Guard cutters *Storis, Ironwood* and *Firebush* patrol from Kodiak to seize foreign vessels illegally fishing U.S. waters. (The 200-mile/322-km fishing limit went into effect in March 1977.) A 12-foot star, situated halfway up the side of Old Woman Mountain overlooking the base, was rebuilt and rededicated in 1981 in memory of military personnel who have lost their lives while engaged in operations from Kodiak. Originally erected in the 1950s, the star is lit every year between Thanksgiving and Christmas.

Kodiak's St. Paul and St. Herman harbors are home port to 800 local fishing boats and serve several hundred outside vessels each year.

Commercial fishing is the backbone of Kodiak's economy. Kodiak is one of the largest commercial fishing ports in the U.S. Some 1,000 commercial fishing vessels use the harbor each year, delivering salmon, shrimp, herring, halibut and whitefish, plus king, tanner and Dungeness crab to the 9 seafood processing companies in Kodiak. Cannery tours are not available. Kodiak's famous seafood is premarketed, with almost all the commercially caught seafood exported. You can celebrate Kodiak's main

View of downtown Kodiak from Near Island bridge. (© Marion Stirrup)

industry at the Kodiak Crab Festival, May 27-31, 1999.

Kodiak is also an important cargo port and transshipment center. Container ships stop twice weekly.

ACCOMMODATIONS/VISITOR SERVICES

There are 4 hotels/motels in Kodiak and more than 20 bed and breakfasts. A variety of restaurants offers a wide range of menus and prices. Shopping is readily available for gifts, general merchandise and sporting goods. There is a movie theater and 750-seat performing arts center.

There are 3 state campgrounds: Fort Abercrombie, north of town (see Rezanof–Monashka Bay Road log); Buskin River state recreation site, south of town (see Chiniak Road log); and Pasagshak River state recreation site at the end of Pasagshak Bay Road (see log).

Dump stations are located at the Petro Express station on Mill Bay Road, at the Union 76 service station in downtown Kodiak, and at Buskin River state recreation site at Mile 4.4 Chiniak Road.

There are 37 remote fly-in hunting and fishing lodges in the Kodiak area; several roadhouses on the island road system;

public-use cabins available within Kodiak National Wildlife Refuge, Shuyak Island and Afognak Island state parks; and private wilderness camps and cabin rentals available throughout the Kodiak area.

TRANSPORTATION

Air: Scheduled service via Era Aviation and Alaska Airlines.

Ferry: The Alaska state ferry MV *Tustumena* serves Kodiak from Homer (9½-hour ferry ride) and Seward (13 hours). It also stops at Port Lions. During the summer 1999 season the MV *Tustumena* will connect monthly with the 382-foot MV *Kennicott*, coming across the Gulf of Alaska from southeast Alaska. The MV *Kennicott* is the newest vessel of the Marine Highway fleet. Ferry terminal is downtown; phone (907) 486-3800 or toll free in the U.S. (800) 526-6731.

Highways: There are 4 roads on Kodiak Island (see logs this section). The 11.3-mile/18.2-km Rezanof–Monashka Bay Road leads from downtown Kodiak north to Fort Abercrombie and Monashka Bay. Chiniak

Road leads 42.8 miles/68.9 km south from Kodiak along the island's eastern shore to Chiniak Point and Chiniak Creek (it is a beautiful drive!). Anton Larsen Bay Road leads 11.8 miles/19 km from junction with Chiniak Road near Kodiak airport to Anton Larsen Bay. Pasagshak Bay Road branches off Chiniak Road and leads 16.5 miles/26.6 km to Fossil Beach at Pasagshak Point.

IMPORTANT: Most of the land along the road system is privately owned. Using land owned by Leisnoi, Inc. requires a non-fee user permit, available at the Leisnoi office in Kodiak at 3248 Mill Bay Rd.; phone (907) 486-8191.

Car Rental and Taxi: Available.

ATTRACTIONS

State Fair and Rodeo held Labor Day weekend, Sept. 4–6, 1999, at the fairgrounds in Womens Bay, includes all-state competitions in crafts, gardening, 4-H livestock raising and home products. Stock car races are held at the fairgrounds on weekends during the summer.

St. Herman's Day, Aug. 7–9, 1999, is of particular significance to the Kodiak community as Father Herman, the first saint of the Russian Orthodox Church in North America, was canonized in Kodiak in 1970. Father Herman arrived in Kodiak in 1794.

The Baranov Museum (Erskine House), maintained by the Kodiak Historical Society (101 Marine Way, Kodiak 99615; phone 907/486-5920), is open in summer, 10 A.M. to 4 P.M. Monday through Saturday; 12 noon to 4 P.M. Sunday. (Winter hours 10 A.M. to 3 P.M. weekdays, except Thursday and Sunday. Closed in February.) The building was originally a fur warehouse built in the early 1800s by Alexsandr Baranov. It is one of just 4 Russian-built structures in the United States today. Purchased by the Alaska Commercial Co. around 1867, the building was sold to W.J. Erskine in 1911, who converted it into a residence; it was then referred to as the Erskine House. In 1962 it was declared a national historic landmark. Many items from the Koniag and Russian era are on display. In the gift shop, Russian samovars, Russian Easter eggs, Alaska Native baskets and other items are for sale. Donations accepted, $2 per adult, children under 12 free.

Picnic on the Beach. There are some outstandingly beautiful beaches along Chiniak Road (see log this section). These unpopulated beaches are also good for beachcombing. Watch for Sitka deer and foxes.

Go for a Hike. Hiking trails around the Kodiak area provide access to alpine areas, lakes, coastal rainforests and beaches. Trail guide available for $5 at the visitors center, (907) 486-4782. Pay attention to notes regarding footwear and clothing, tides, bears, trailhead access and weather conditions.

Go Mountain Biking. Kodiak is fast becoming known for its premier mountain biking, attracting racers and enthusiasts from around the country.

Kodiak Bear Country Music Festival. An annual music festival (July 20-22, 1999) features bluegrass, folk, soft rock, country and Alaska music. More than 50 bands from around the state perform during this musical extravaganza. Contact (907) 486-6116.

Kodiak Tribal Council's Barabara Sod House is an authentic Alutiiq dwelling that features presentations of Alutiiq dancing. The Kodiak Alutiiq Dancers form the only Alutiiq dance group in Alaska. The dances have been re-created from stories passed down through generations of the Alutiiq people, who have inhabited Kodiak Island for more than 7,000 years. Dance performances are held in summer, 7 days a week at 3:30 P.M., at the barabara located at 713 Rezanof Drive. Phone (907) 486-4449 to confirm performance times.

Kodiak Whale Festival—A Migration Celebration. During the first and second week of April, whale watchers celebrate the return of migrating whales. Whale sightings reported daily, with special art, literature and performances scheduled throughout the festival. Contact (907) 486-4782.

City Parks and Recreation Department maintains a swimming pool year-round, and the school gyms are available on a year-round basis for community use. The town has 8 parks and playgrounds including the 7-acre Baranof Park with 4 tennis courts, baseball field, track, playgrounds and picnic areas. North End Park on Near Island has a scenic 1-mile/1.6 km improved trail. For more information phone (907) 486-8665.

Bear Valley Golf Course. The 9-hole Bear Valley Golf Course is located on the Anton Larsen Bay Road. Owned and operated by the U.S. Coast Guard, the course has a driving range, putting green and pro shack. The course is open to the public from approximately June until October, depending on weather. The pro shack carries golf clothing, items and rental equipment, and serves food and beer. Hours of operation vary according to weather and daylight hours. Call (907) 486-7561 or 487-5108.

Fort Abercrombie State Historic Park. Site of a WWII coastal fortification, bunkers and other evidence of the Aleutian campaign. The park is located north of Kodiak on scenic Miller Point. Picnicking and camping in a setting of lush rain forest, wildflowers, seabirds and eagles.

The U.S. Coast Guard Winter Recreation Area is located on the Anton Larsen Bay Road and has a lighted downhill ski slope with rope-tow lift, a separate sledding area and a ski chalet that serves refreshments. Open to the public, depending on weather and snow conditions. Call (907) 487-5108.

Alutiiq Museum Archaeological Repository Center in downtown Kodiak houses artifacts from coastal sites around Kodiak Island. The Alutiiq are descendants of the Pacific Eskimos, whom Russian explorers encountered and referred to as the Koniag people, many of whom lived in the Karluk area on Kodiak's west coast around 1200 A.D. However, some of the items found date to 3,000 and even 7,000 years ago. The Karluk area is billed as one of the most amazing archaeological finds in Alaska because of the level of preservation of the artifacts and because of the abundance of items used in daily life. Located at 215 Mission Road; phone (907) 486-7004.

Shuyak Island State Park encompasses 47,000 acres and is located 54 air miles north of Kodiak. Access is by boat or float plane only. Hunting, fishing and kayaking are the major recreational activities. Four public-use cabins are available, at $50 per night. Cabins are 12 feet by 20 feet and sleep up to 8 people. Reservations accepted up to 6 months in advance with a full nonrefundable payment. Call (907) 486-6339 or 269-8400.

Holy Resurrection Russian Orthodox Church. Orthodox priests, following Russian fur traders from Siberia, arrived in Kodiak and established the first Russian Orthodox Church in North America in September 1794. The original church was built on a bluff overlooking St. Paul Harbor in 1796. A second church was built on the same location. The bluff was leveled during reconstruction following the earthquake and tsunami in 1964.

Three churches have been built on the present site. The first appears on an 1869 map of Fort Kodiak. Another church was begun in 1874 and survived until destroyed by fire in 1943. The present church was built in 1945 and is listed on the National Register of Historic Places.

The church interior provides a visual feast, and the public is invited to attend services. The public may visit Thursday and Saturday at 6:30 P.M.; Sunday service at 8:30 A.M. Phone (907) 486-3854. A $1 donation is encouraged.

A scale replica of the original (1796) church building was completed in May 1994 and is located on the grounds of St. Herman's Theological Seminary on Mission Road.

Arrange a Boat or air charter, or guide for fishing and hunting trips, adventure tours, sightseeing and photography. There are several charter services in Kodiak.

See Kodiak by Kayak. One of the best ways to experience Kodiak's beautiful coastline, and view marine mammals and

Sunrise on Kodiak Island. (© Gene & Judy Wright)

seabirds, is from a kayak. Day tours around the nearby islands are available for all skill levels, or schedule an extended tour. Kayak rentals available.

Kodiak National Wildlife Refuge encompasses 2,812 square miles on Kodiak Island, Uganik Island, Afognak Island and Ban Island. The refuge was established in 1941 to preserve the natural habitat of the famed Kodiak bear and other wildlife. Biologists estimate that more than 3,000 bears inhabit Kodiak Island. Most bears enter dens by October and remain there until April. Bears are readily observable on the refuge in July and August when they congregate along streams to feed on salmon. At other times they feed on grasses or berries.

Native wildlife within the refuge includes the red fox, river otter, short-tailed weasel, little brown bat and tundra vole. Introduced mammals include the Sitka black-tailed deer, beaver, snowshoe hare and mountain goat. On Afognak Island, an introduced herd of elk share the island with the bears. The coastline of Kodiak refuge shelters a large population of waterfowl and marine mammals. Bald eagles are common nesting birds on the refuge.

Visitors to the refuge typically go to fish, observe/photograph wildlife, backpack, kayak, camp and hunt.

NOTE: The refuge is accessible only by float-plane or boat. There are primitive public-use cabins available; applications must be made in advance to the refuge manager. For more information contact the Kodiak National Wildlife Refuge Manager, 1390 Buskin River Road, Kodiak, AK 99615; phone (907) 487-2600. You may also stop by the U.S. Fish and Wildlife Service Visitor Center on Rezanof Road, a 1/2-mile from the state airport. The center features exhibits and films on Kodiak wildlife and is open weekdays year-round, and also Saturdays April through September; hours are variable.

Wildlife/Bird Watching. The best time to observe animals is when they are most active: at daybreak. At least 215 species of birds have been sighted around Kodiak Island archipelago. Kodiak is one of the best places in North America to view seaducks in the winter season. Bald eagles can be seen near the city of Kodiak from January through March, and nesting near water in the summer. Peregrine falcons are spotted frequently from the road in October. In the summer, puffins can be seen at Miller Point on calm days. Narrow Cape, Spruce Cape and Miller Point are good stakeout points in the

spring for those in search of gray whales; summer for humpback whales. Womens Bay is home to a variety of migrating geese in April.

Kodiak is a gateway to Katmai National Park and Preserve, well-known for its bear-viewing and sportfishing, as well as for an abundance of other wildlife and activities. There is a National Park Service information office in Kodiak, and local air taxi operators offer direct flights to King Salmon and also to the remote Katmai coast.

Bear-viewing Trips. To see brown bears, it's best to leave the road system and travel to the Bush by plane or boat. Almost all the air charter services offer some sort of bear-viewing excursion, ranging from half-day trips to multiple-day visits in cabins or tent-camps. Many lodge operations and licensed guides/outfitters also provide bear-viewing trips.

Adventure Charters and Marine Services Inc. Halibut charters, whale and bird watching, sightseeing, drop-off and pick-up in remote destinations for hunters, kayakers or other passengers. Experience the beauty of Kodiak waters aboard "The Boat," a 45-foot high-speed U.S. Coast Guard-approved ocean-going vessel. Fully enclosed cabin with 16-passenger capacity. Phone (907) 486-6400. [ADVERTISEMENT]

AREA FISHING: Kodiak Island is in the center of a fine marine and freshwater fishery and possesses some excellent fishing for rainbow, halibut, Dolly Varden and 5 species of Pacific salmon. Visiting fishermen will have to charter a boat or aircraft to reach remote lakes, rivers and bays, but the island road system offers many good salmon streams in season. Roads access red salmon fisheries in the Buskin and Pasagshak rivers. Pink and silver salmon are also found in the **Buskin** and **Pasagshak rivers**, and **Monashka, Pillar, Russian, Salonie, American, Olds, Roslyn** and **Chiniak creeks**.

Afognak and Raspberry islands, both approximately 30 air miles/48 km northeast of Kodiak, have lodges and offer excellent remote hunting and fishing. Both islands are brown bear country. Hikers and fishermen should make noise as they travel and carry a .30–06 or larger rifle. Stay clear of bears. If you take a dog, make sure he is under control. Dogs can create dangerous situations with bears.

CAUTION: A paralytic-shellfish-poisoning alert is in effect for all Kodiak Island beaches. This toxin is extremely poisonous. There are no approved beaches for clamming on Kodiak Island. For more current information, call the Dept. of Environmental Conservation in Anchorage at (907) 349-7343.

Rezanof–Monashka Bay Road Log

Distance is measured from the junction of Rezanof Drive and Marine Way in downtown Kodiak (K).

K 0.1 (0.2 km) Mill Bay Road access to library, post office and Kodiak businesses.

K 0.4 (0.6 km) Entrance to Near Island bridge to North End Park, a city park with trails and picnic areas; St. Herman Harbor, boat launch ramp, fish-cleaning station; and Fishery Industrial Technology Center (FITC), phone (907) 486-1500 for tours. Kodiak Fisheries Research Center, phone (907) 481-1800 for tours and information. Also access to Trident Basin seaplane base, located beyond FITC on Trident Way.

K 0.7 (1.13 km) Kodiak Auditorium

K 1.5 (2.4 km) Providence Kodiak Island Medical Center on left.

K 2 (3.2 km) Benny Benson Drive. Turnoff left to Kodiak College and beginning of paved bicycle trail, which parallels main road to Fort Abercrombie State Historic Park. Excellent for walking, jogging and bicycling.

K 3.4 (5.5 km) Turnout and gravel parking area to right for Mill Bay Park. Scenic picnic spot with picnic tables, barbecue grates. Good ocean fishing from beach. ⊷

K 3.8 (6.12 km) Bayside Fire Department

K 3.9 (6.3 km) Road right to Fort Abercrombie State Historic Park. Drive in 0.2 mile/0.3 km to campground; 13 campsites with 7-night limit at $10 per night, water, toilets, fishing, swimming and picnic shelter. Extensive system of scenic hiking trails. No off-road biking. View of bay and beach, WWII fortifications. Miller Point Bunker open Tuesday, Friday and Sunday at 2:30 P.M. for public viewing. Saturday evening naturalist programs June 1 to Aug. 30. Just beyond the campground entrance is the Alaska State Parks ranger station, open weekdays 8 A.M. to 5 P.M.; pay phone, public restrooms, park information. ⊷▲

K 4.6 (7.4 km) Monashka Bay Park left at junction with Otmeloi Way. Playground equipment, covered picnic area, barbecue grates.

K 6.4 (10.3 km) Kodiak Island Borough baler/landfill facility. Recycling center. Pavement ends. Excellent gravel road.

K 6.8 (10.9 km) Gravel turnout to right.

K 6.9 (11.1 km) Good view of Three Sisters mountains.

K 7.2 (11.6 km) Road on right leads to VFW RV park with camping facilities, scenic views, restaurant and lounge, (907) 486-3195; Kodiak Island Sportsman Association indoor shooting range, (907) 486-8566. ▲

K 7.6 (12.2 km) Pillar Creek bridge and Pillar Creek Hatchery to left.

K 8.3 (13.3 km) Road to right leads to Pillar Beach. Beautiful black-sand beach at mouth of creek. Scenic picnic area. Dolly Varden fishing. ⊷

K 8.5 (13.7 km) Pullout to right.

K 9.3 (14.9 km) Pullout to right. Scenic overlook and panoramic views of Monashka Bay and Monashka Mountain.

K 10.1 (16.3 km) Gravel pullout and parking to right. Access to North Sister trailhead directly across road.

K 11.2 (18 km) Bridge over Monashka Creek.

K 11.3 (18.2 km) Road ends. Large turnaround parking area. Paths to right lead through narrow band of trees to secluded Monashka Bay beach. Large, sweeping sandy beach. Excellent for picnics. Picnic tables, restrooms, improved beach access. Fishing

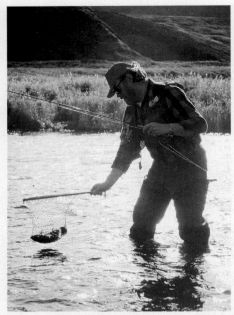

Netting a Dolly Varden in Kodiak Island waters. (© Marion Stirrup)

off beach for Dolly Varden, pink salmon and silvers. To north of parking area is trailhead for Termination Point hike, a beautiful 6-mile loop trail along meadows, ocean bluffs and dense Sitka spruce forest. *NOTE: Leisnoi user-permit required to hike this trail.*

Chiniak Road Log

Distance from Kodiak's U.S. post office building (K).

K 0 Kodiak U.S. post office building.

K 2.4 (3.9 km) Gravel turnout to left with panoramic view of Kodiak, Chiniak Bay and nearby islands.

K 3.8 (6.1 km) **Boy Scout Lake**, stocked; gravel turnout and parking to left.

K 4.4 (7.1 km) U.S. Fish and Wildlife Service Visitor Center and Kodiak National Wildlife Refuge headquarters. Exhibits and films on Kodiak wildlife. Open weekdays year-round, 8 A.M. to 4:30 P.M., in summer; weekends, noon to 4:30 P.M. Closed in off-season except for special events. Phone: (907) 487-2600. Road on left to **Buskin River State Recreation Site**; 15 RV campsites with a 14-night limit at $10/night, picnic tables and shelter, water, pit toilets, trails, beach access and dump station. Fishing along Buskin River and on beach area at river's mouth for red, silver and pink salmon and trout. Wheelchair-accessible fishing platform. Parking for fishermen.

K 5 (8 km) Unmarked turnoff on right for Anton Larsen Bay Road (see log this section).

K 5.1 (8.2 km) Kodiak airport.

K 5.5 (8.9 km) *CAUTION: Jet blast area at end of runway. Stop here and wait if you see a jet preparing for takeoff. Do not enter or stay in this area if you see a jet.*

K 5.7 (9.2 km) Gravel turnout and limited parking to access Barometer Mountain. Steep, straight, well-trodden trail to 2,500-foot peak. Beautiful panoramic views. To access trailhead, cross paved road and walk halfway back to jet blast area.

K 6.6 (10.6 km) Entrance to U.S. Coast Guard station.

K 7.2 (11.6 km) Road continues around Womens Bay. The drive out to Chiniak affords excellent views of the extremely rugged coastline of the island.

K 9.3 (15 km) Turnoff to right to Kodiak Island Fairgrounds. Excellent bird watching on tideflats to Salonie Creek.

K 10.1 (16.3 km) **Sargent Creek** bridge. Good fishing for pink salmon in August.

K 10.3 (16.6 km) Russian River and Bell Flats Road.

K 10.6 (17.1 km) Pavement ends; gravel begins. *NOTE: Be sure you have a spare tire. It is the law in Alaska to drive with headlights on at all times on all posted roads.*

K 10.7 (17.2 km) Grocery and liquor store, diesel and unleaded gas.

K 10.9 (17.5 km) Video store; tire repair.

K 12 (19.3 km) Salonie Creek. Pinks (early August), chums, silvers, Dolly Varden.

K 12.4 (20 km) Salonie Creek Rifle Range turnoff to right.

K 12.8 (20.6 km) Beach access. Remnants on beach of WWII submarine dock. Begin climb up Marine Hill. *NOTE: Very hazardous in winter when icy.*

K 13.6 (21.9 km) Good turnout to left with panoramic view of Mary Island, Womens Bay, Bell Flats, Kodiak. Mountain goats visible with binoculars in spring and fall in mountains behind Bell Flats.

K 14.4 (23.2 km) Pullout to right and limited parking at **Heitman Lake** trailhead. Beautiful views. Lake is stocked with rainbow trout.

K 15 (24.1 km) View of Long Island and Cliff Point..

K 16.2 (26 km) Turnout to left.

K 16.7 (26.9 km) Road east to Holiday Beach. Closed to public. Permission by USCG

required for access.

K 17.0 (27.4 km) USCG communication facility; emergency phone.

K 17.7 (28.5 km) View of Middle Bay.

K 19 (30.6 km) Undeveloped picnic area in grove of trees along beach of Middle Bay; easy access to beach. Watch for livestock.

K 19.6 (31.5 km) Small Creek bridge.

K 20 (32.2 km) Salt Creek bridge. Excellent bird watching on tideflats to left.

K 20.8 (33.5 km) American River bridge. River empties into Middle Bay.

K 20.9 (33.6 km) Unimproved road on right, marginal for 4-wheel-drive vehicles, leads toward Saltery Cove. *NOTE: Road is barely passable even for 4-wheel drive vehicles.*

K 21 (33.8 km) Felton Creek Bridge.

K 23.1 (37.2 km) Foot access to gravel beach; nice picnic site.

K 24.1 (38.8 km) *CAUTION: Steep switchbacks. Slow to 10 mph.*

K 24.5 (39.4 km) Pullout to right, limited parking. Access to Mayflower Lake. Stocked with landlocked silver salmon.

K 24.6 (39.6 km) Mayflower Beach.

K 25.3 (40.7 km) View of Kalsin Bay.

K 27.7 (44.6 km) Turnout to left. Great views.

K 28.1 (45.2 km) Improved pullout to left.

K 28.2 (45.4 km) Improved pullout to left. Steep road drops down to head of Kalsin Bay; sheer cliffs on both sides of road.

K 28.5 (45.9 km) Improved pullout to left

K 28.9 (46.5 km) Kalsin Bay Inn; food, bar, laundromat, showers, tire repair; open year-round.   D

K 29.2 (47 km) Deadman Creek Bridge.

K 29.9 (48.1 km) Improved pullout to left. Olds River.

K 30.2 (48.6 km) Kalsin River (creek) bridge.

K 30.6 (49.2 km) Road forks: Turn left for Chiniak, right for Pasagshak Bay. See Pasagshak Bay Road log this section.

K 30.9 (49.7 km) **Kalsin Pond** on right; excellent silver salmon fishing in fall.

K 31.1 (50 km) Turnoff to left; access to mouth of Olds River and beach.

K 31.5 (50.7 km) Highway maintenance station.

K 32 (51.5 km) Picnic area to left beside Kalsin Bay. Nice beach.

K 32.4 (52.1 km) Road to unimproved picnic area. Gravel beach. Fishing for pinks.

K 33.2 (53.4 km) Turnoff. Myrtle Creek, picnic site. Beach access.

K 34.9 (56.2 km) Thumbs Up Cove. Unimproved boat launch ramp.

K 35.1 (56.5 km) Chiniak post office. Window hours Tuesday and Thursday 4 to 6 P.M., Saturday noon to 2 P.M.

K 35.9 (57.8 km) Brookers Lagoon. Access to gravel beach.

K 36.4 (58.6 km) Chiniak Bakery to left.

K 36.9 (59.4 km) Roslyn River. Access to Roslyn Bay beach, a beautiful picnic area.

K 37.2 (59.9 km) Roslyn River Bridge.

K 37.6 (60.5 km) Access to mouth of Roslyn River.

K 39.5 (63.6 km) Access to a beautiful point overlooking the sea; site of WWII installations. Good place for photos. Sea otters in kelp beds year-round.

K 39.9 (64.2 km) Twin Creeks Beach, beautiful dark sand and rolling breakers. Park in pullout area. Do not drive onto soft beach sand.

K 40.4 (65 km) Twin Creek.

K 40.7 (65.5 km) Silver Beach.

K 40.8 (65.7 km) **Pony Lake** (stocked).

K 41.3 (66.4 km) Chiniak wayside, a

borough park; benches, beautiful setting.

K 41.5 (66.8 km) Chiniak school, public library, playground and ballfield. Baseball diamond, play area, picnic tables.

K 41.6 (66.9 km) Turnoff to right onto King Crab Way. Location of Tsunami Evacuation Center.

K 42.4 (68.2 km) Road's End lounge and restaurant. Excellent whalewatching for gray whales in April, across road from restaurant.

K 42.5 (68.4 km) **Chiniak Point**, also known as Cape Chiniak, is the south point of land at the entrance to Chiniak Bay. Capt. Cook named the point Cape Greville in 1778, but the name is now applied to that point of land 2 miles/3.2 km southeast of here. State road maintenance ends here. Unmaintained road continues as public easement across Leisnoi Native Corp. land. Public access discouraged beyond Chiniak Creek.

K 42.8 (68.9 km) Public road ends at **Chiniak Creek.** Pink salmon fishing in midsummer. View of Chiniak Point. Turnaround point.

A grizzly bear in the grass along a salmon stream near Karluk Lake. (© Tom Bol)

Pasagshak Bay Road Log

Distance is measured from junction with Chiniak Road (J).

J 0 Turn right at **Milepost K 30.6** Chiniak Road for Pasagshak Bay. Road leads up the valley of Kalsin Creek past a private ranch.

J 0.1 (0.2 km) Northland Ranch Resort; lodging, food, lounge.

J 1.2 (1.9 km) Turnout to right to access Kalsin River; good, unimproved picnic area.

J 3.4 (5.47 km) Turnout to unimproved picnic area by beautiful stream.

J 4.7 (7.6 km) Top of Pasagshak Pass; scenic views.

J 5.3 (8.5 km) Turnout to left.

J 6.8 (10.9 km) Road crosses Lake Rose Tead on causeway. Good fishing in river from here to ocean. Good place to view spawning salmon and eagles late summer through fall.

J 7.1 (11.4 km) Combined barn and single aircraft hangar to right. Remnant of Joe Zentner Ranch, established in the 1940s.

J 8.3 (13.4 km) Derelict wooden bridge once connected old road to Portage Bay, now an easy hiking trail. Trailhead begins across the river.

J 8.9 (14.2 km) **Pasagshak River State Recreation Site**: 7 campsites with a 14-night limit (no fee), toilets, water, picnic sites, fishing and beach access.

J 9.3 (15 km) Mouth of Pasagshak River, view of Pasagshak Bay.

J 9.5 (15.3 km) Turnout at Boat Bay, traditional gravel boat launch ramp and mooring area. Four-wheel drive vehicles required to use launch ramp.

J 10.3 (16.6 km) Turnoff to right takes you to Pasagshak Point, 2 trout lakes, nice vistas.

J 11.0 (17.7 km) Entrance to Kodiak Cattle Co. grazing lease. Public land—hunting, fishing, hiking, but keep vehicle on road.

J 11.3 (18.2 km) Turnout to right provides panoramas of Narrow Cape, Ugak Island, Pasagshak Point, Sitkalidik Island. Good beachcombing on sandy beaches.

J 12.0 (19.3 km) Bear Paw Ranch Youth Camp.

J 12.2 (19.6 km) Beach access to the

right. *CAUTION: Free-ranging buffalo sometimes block the road. Stop and wait; they will eventually move. Sounding your horn is not advised. Do not approach free-ranging buffalo on foot. They can be dangerous.*

J 14.4 (23.2 km) Entrance to Kodiak Cattle Co. Ranch; guided horseback riding, fishing, camping, hunting.

J 14.8 (23.8 km) Entrance at right to USCG Narrow Cape Loran Station. Emergency phone. No public access.

NOTE: Minimal road maintenance from here to end of road. Drive with caution and have a good spare tire.

J 15.7 (25.3 km) Kodiak Launch Complex, a 3,100-acre, low-earth-orbit launch complex developed by the Alaska Aerospace Development Corporation (AADC). Site includes support, payload and processing facilities and launch pad.

J 15.8 (25.4 km) Road splits; go to right for Fossil Beach.

J15.9 (25.6 km) Turnout to left. *NOTE: 4WD vehicles only beyond this point. Rental cars should park here and continue on foot.*

J 16.2 (26.1 km) **Twin Lakes** to the left and right of road. Trout in lake to the left.

J 16.5 (26.6 km) Road ends at Fossil Cliffs. Fossils imbedded in cliffs are visible along Fossil Beach to left and right (low tide only). *CAUTION: Cliffs are extremely unstable. Do not approach cliff face, and watch for falling rocks at all times.* Beautiful vistas and views of WWII observation bunkers on Narrow Cape to the left.

Anton Larsen Bay Road Log

Distance is measured from the turnoff (T) at Milepost K 5 Chiniak Road.

T 0 Unmarked turnoff for Anton Larsen Bay Road at **Milepost K 5** on Chiniak Road immediately before crossing the Buskin River bridge.

T 0.6 (1 km) **Buskin River** bridge No. 6. Parking area to left accessing fishing along river. Road to the right leads to good fishing holes.

T 0.7 (1.1 km) Pavement ends.

T 0.9 (1.4 km) Enter posted restricted-access area in USCG antenna field. Do not leave road for approximately next 1.5 miles.

T 1.4 (2.3 km) **Buskin River** bridge No. 7. Turnoff to left before crossing bridge accesses river and outlet of Buskin Lake. Good fishing for Dolly Varden, salmon.

T 1.6 (2.6 km) Immediately after crossing bridge, paved road to right leads to USCG communications site. Turn on gravel road to left to Anton Larsen Bay. Beautiful drive, berry picking, mountain views, wildflowers, boat launch ramp. Excellent kayaking in bay and around outer islands.

T 2 (3.2 km) High hill on right is Pyramid Mountain (elev. 2,420 feet/738m).

T 2.3 (3.7 km) End restricted access area.

T 2.9 (4.7 km) Bear Valley Golf Course. Pyramid Mountain in backdrop. Driving range, parking on left. Nine-hole course operated by USCG. Open to the public April to October, weather permitting. Phone (907) 486-7561 or 486-4782.

T 3.2 (5.1 km) Turnout to left to unimproved trailhead of Buskin Lake. *Watch for bears.*

T 4.1 (6.6 km) Steep switchback.

T 5.7 (9.2 km) Buskin Valley Winter Recreation Area. Phone (907) 487-5274 or 486-4782. To right is large parking area and trailhead to top of 2,400-foot/731.5m Pyramid Mountain. Trail follows ridgeline. Great vistas from top.

T 7.5 (12.1 km) Red Cloud River bridge. Small, unimproved campsite is adjacent to river on right.

T 8.9 (14.3 km) **Cascade Lake** trail to right. Approximately 5 miles round-trip. Rubber boots recommended to cross tidal areas. Watch for bears. Lake is stocked.

T 9.3 (15 km) Head of Anton Larsen Bay. Fox, land otters and deer can be seen in this area. Good bird watching along tidal flats.

T 10.3 (16.6 km) Public small-boat launch adjacent to road. Road continues on left side of bay for about 1.5 miles/2.4 km.

T 10.4 (16.7 km) Anton Larsen Bay public dock. Departure point for excellent sea kayaking.

T 11.7 (18.8 km) Road ends at turnaround. A foot-path continues beyond this point. Parking area to right.

INSIDE PASSAGE

Southeastern Alaska communities from Ketchikan to Skagway

(See maps, pages 669–673)

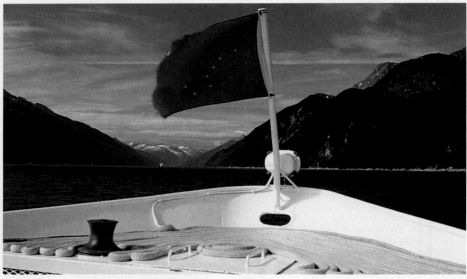

View of Lynn Canal from the MV Fairweather. *(© Susan Cole Kelly)*

Alaska's Inside Passage, located in the southeastern section of the state, is known by many residents simply as "Southeast." It is a unique region where industry, transportation, recreation and community planning are dictated by spectacular topography.

The region is accessible by air, land or sea. Jet service is available to Juneau, Ketchikan, Wrangell, Petersburg, Sitka and Gustavus. Smaller communities are served by local commuter aircraft. The port communities of Haines and Skagway offer road connections to the Alaska Highway system via the Haines Highway and Klondike Highway 2. The Alaska Marine Highway moves people and vehicles between ports, and connects the Inside Passage with Prince Rupert, BC, and Bellingham, WA. Several cruise ship lines ply the waterways of the Inside Passage and offer a variety of cruising opportunities.

Measuring about 125 by 400 miles/200 by 650 km, 60 percent of the region consists of thousands of islands covered with dense forests of spruce, hemlock and cedar, a result of the mild, moist coastal climate. These islands make up the Alexander Archipelago, and include Prince of Wales Island, the third largest island in the United States (the Big Island of Hawaii is first, followed by Kodiak). The Coast Mountains form the mainland portion of southeastern Alaska.

Southeastern Alaska lies between 54°40' and 60° north latitude, the same as Scotland, Denmark and southern Sweden. The latitude of Scotland's Loch Ness is slightly north of the latitude at Wrangell Narrows. Stockholm and Skagway share the same latitude, and Ketchikan's latitude is a little south of Copenhagen's.

Warmed by ocean currents, this region experiences mild, warm summers, with July temperatures averaging around 60°F/16°C. An occasional heat wave may reach the high 80s. Winters are cool, alternating snow, rain and sunshine; January temperatures average 20° to 40°F/-7° to 4°C. Sub-zero winter temperatures are uncommon. The region receives considerable annual rainfall, from 80 to more than 200 inches (heaviest in late fall, lightest in summer). Populated areas receive 30 to 200 inches of snow annually; the high mountains more than 400 inches a year.

The majority of southeastern Alaska lies within Tongass National Forest, the largest national forest in the United States. (Southeastern Alaska has over 5.6 million acres of wilderness lands.) The forests historically have provided one of the region's major industries; timber harvesting primarily supplies area sawmills.

Commercial fishing and fish processing is another major industry here. Numerous rivers and streams, mountains, valleys, melting glaciers and heavy rainfall create ideal spawning grounds for salmon. Local waters harbor abundant life, including crab, shrimp, halibut, herring and black cod.

Juneau is the state capital, and federal, state and local governments provide the majority of jobs throughout Southeast. Tourism, with its jobs and revenue, is another major contributor to the region's economy.

About 69,000 people live along the Inside Passage, according to 1990 U.S. Census figures. About 70 percent live in the 5 major communities of Juneau (29,755), Ketchikan (15,082), Sitka (9,194), Petersburg (3,350) and Wrangell (2,400). More than 20 percent are Native, mostly Tlingit (KLINK it) Indian, plus Haida (HI duh) and Tsimshian (SHIM shian).

Alaska's Natives, famous for their totem poles, weaving, beading, basketry and dancing, occupied the region long before Vitus Bering discovered Alaska in 1741.

Russia controlled Alaska from the turn of the 19th century until 1867, centering its extensive fur-trading empire in Sitka, the Russian capital of Alaska. Sitka was a port of international trade, controlling trading posts from California to the Aleutians, and was considered cultured because of European influence. At a time when San Francisco was a crude new boom town, Sitka was called the "Paris of the Pacific."

Commercial interest in southeastern Alaska declined with the fur trade, following Alaska's purchase by the United States. Interest in Southeast was rekindled by the salmon industry as canneries were established, the first at Klawock in 1878. Salmon canning peaked in the late 1930s and then declined from overfishing.

But the first significant white populations arrived because of gold. By the time thousands of gold seekers traveled through the Inside Passage in 1898 to Skagway and on to Canada's Klondike (sparking interest in the rest of Alaska), the largest gold ore mine of its day, the Treadwell near Juneau, had been in operation since 1884.

Juneau became Alaska's capital in 1906,
Continues on page 674

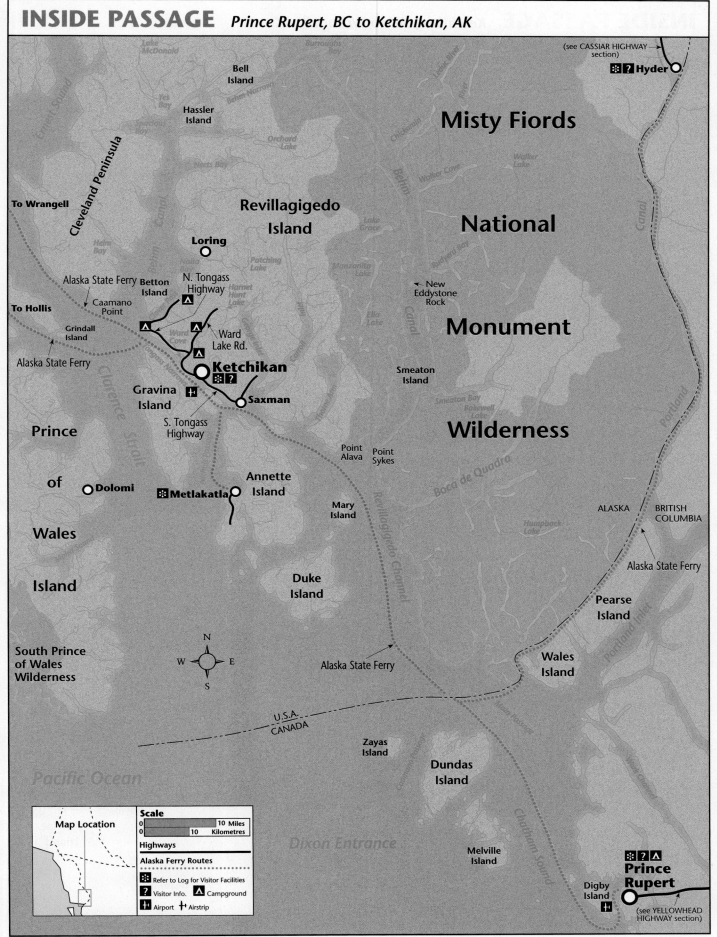

INSIDE PASSAGE
Prince Rupert, BC to Ketchikan, AK

(see CASSIAR HIGHWAY section)

Hyder

Misty Fiords

Bell Island

Hassler Island

Cleveland Peninsula

To Wrangell

Revillagigedo Island

National

New Eddystone Rock

Loring

Alaska State Ferry

Betton Island

N. Tongass Highway

To Hollis

Caamano Point

Ward Lake Rd.

Monument

Grindall Island

Alaska State Ferry

Ketchikan

Smeaton Island

Gravina Island

Saxman

S. Tongass Highway

Wilderness

Prince

Point Alava

Point Sykes

of

Dolomi

Metlakatla

Annette Island

Mary Island

ALASKA

BRITISH COLUMBIA

Wales

Alaska State Ferry

Island

Duke Island

Pearse Island

South Prince of Wales Wilderness

N
W   E
S

Alaska State Ferry

Wales Island

U.S.A.
CANADA

Zayas Island

Dundas Island

Pacific Ocean

Dixon Entrance

Melville Island

Prince Rupert

Digby Island

(see YELLOWHEAD HIGHWAY section)

Map Location

Scale
0 — 10 Miles
0 — 10 Kilometres

Highways
Alaska Ferry Routes
Refer to Log for Visitor Facilities
Visitor Info.   Campground
Airport   Airstrip

INSIDE PASSAGE Ketchikan, AK to Wrangell, AK

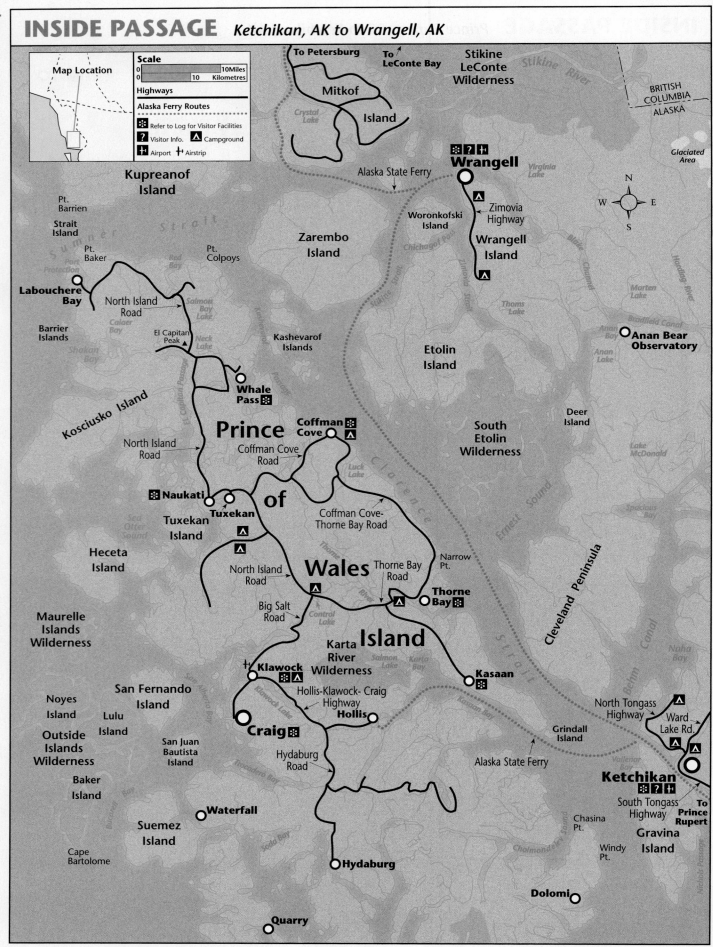

Map Location

Scale
0 — 10 Miles
0 — 10 Kilometres

Highways

Alaska Ferry Routes

⊞ Refer to Log for Visitor Facilities
? Visitor Info. ▲ Campground
✈ Airport ✈ Airstrip

To Petersburg

To LeConte Bay

Stikine LeConte Wilderness

Stikine River

BRITISH COLUMBIA
ALASKA

Mitkof Island

Crystal Lake

Kupreanof Island

⊞?✈ **Wrangell**

Alaska State Ferry

Woronkofski Island

Virginia Lake

▲ Zimovia Highway

Wrangell Island

▲

Glaciated Area

N
W E
S

Pt. Barrien

Strait Island

Summer Strait

Pt. Baker

Port Protection

Labouchere Bay

Barrier Islands

Shakan Bay

Red Bay

Calder Bay

North Island Road

Salmon Bay Lake

El Capitan Peak ▲

Neck Lake

Kosciusko Island

El Capitan Passage

Whale Pass ⊞

Pt. Colpoys

Kashevarof Islands

Zarembo Island

Zimovia Strait

Stikine Strait

Chichagof Pass

Etolin Island

Marten Lake

Hardings River

Bradfield Canal

Anan Bay

Anan Lake

⊙ **Anan Bear Observatory**

Coffman Cove ⊞▲

Coffman Cove Road

Prince

of

Luck Lake

Clarence

South Etolin Wilderness

Deer Island

Thoms Lake

Lake McDonald

North Island Road

⊞ **Naukati**

Tuxekan ▲

Tuxekan Island

Sea Otter Sound

Coffman Cove-Thorne Bay Road

Heceta Island

North Island Road

Wales

Thorne Bay Road

Thorne River

▲ **Thorne Bay** ⊞

Narrow Pt.

Ernest Sound

Spacious Bay

Big Salt Road

Control Lake

Island

Karta River Wilderness

Karta Lake

Salmon Lake

Karta Bay

Cleveland Peninsula

Strait

Maurelle Islands Wilderness

✈ **Klawock** ⊞▲

Klawock Lake

Hollis-Klawock-Craig Highway

San Fernando Island

San Alberto Bay

Kasaan ⊞

Kasaan Bay

Naha Bay

Noyes Island

Lulu Island

Outside Islands Wilderness

San Juan Bautista Island

Craig ⊞

Hollis

Hydaburg Road

Grindall Island

Alaska State Ferry

North Tongass Highway ▲

Ward Lake Rd.

Belm Canal

▲

Baker Island

Buccareli Bay

Trocadero Bay

Ketchikan
⊞?✈

South Tongass Highway

To Prince Rupert

Waterfall

Suemez Island

Soda Bay

Chasina Pt.

Cholmondeley Sound

Windy Pt.

Gravina Island

Cape Bartolome

Hydaburg

Vallenar Bay

Nichols Passage

Dolomi ⊙

Quarry ⊙

INSIDE PASSAGE *Coffman Cove, AK to Sitka, AK*

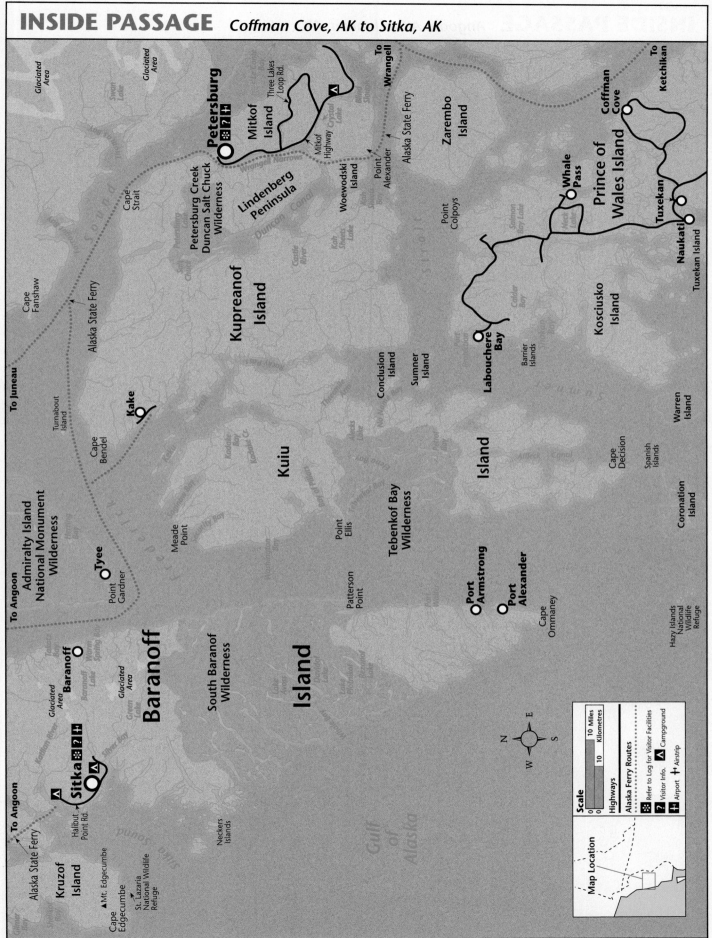

Glaciated Area

Swan Lake

Glaciated Area

To Wrangell

To Ketchikan

Three Lakes Loop Rd.

Petersburg ▦ ? ✚

Mitkof Island

Crystal Lake ⬛⃤

Blind Slough

Mitkof Highway

Alaska State Ferry

Zarembo Island

Coffman Cove ⬤

Wrangell Narrows

Point Alexander

Petersburg Creek Duncan Salt Chuck Wilderness

Lindenberg Peninsula

Woewodski Island

Kah Sheets Bay

Point Colpoys

Whale Pass ⬤

Prince of Wales Island

Tuxekan ⬤

Cape Strait

Duncan Canal

Kah Sheets Lake

Salmon Bay Lake

Naukati ⬤

Tuxekan Island

Castle River

Cape Fanshaw

Alaska State Ferry

Kupreanof Island

Conclusion Island

Summer Island

Calder Bay

Labouchere Bay ⬤

Kosciusko Island

To Juneau

Turnabout Island

Sand Spit

No Name Bay

Barrier Islands

Island

Kake ⬤

Cape Bendel

Kuiu

Jacks Lake

Warren Island

Thetis

Cape Decision

Spanish Islands

Coronation Island

To Angoon

Admiralty Island National Monument Wilderness

Meade Point

Point Ellis

Tebenkof Bay Wilderness

Affleck Canal

Tyee ⬤

Point Gardner

Patterson Point

Island

Port Armstrong ⬤

Port Alexander ⬤

Cape Ommaney

Hazy Islands National Wildlife Refuge

Trollers Cove Lake

To Angoon

Baranof ▦ ? ✚
Baranoff

Glaciated Area

Bennett Lake

Green Lake

Warm Spring Rd.

Silver Bay

South Baranof Wilderness

Island

⬛⃤

▦ ? ✚
Sitka ⬤

Halibut Point Rd.

Kruzof Island

▲ Mt. Edgecumbe

Cape Edgecumbe

St. Lazaria National Wildlife Refuge

Neckers Islands

Gulf of Alaska

To Angoon

Alaska State Ferry

Legend

Scale

| 0 | 10 Miles |
| 0 | 10 Kilometres |

Highways
━━ Alaska Ferry Routes

▦ Refer to Log for Visitor Facilities
? Visitor Info.   ⬛⃤ Campground
✚ Airport   ✚ Airstrip

Map Location

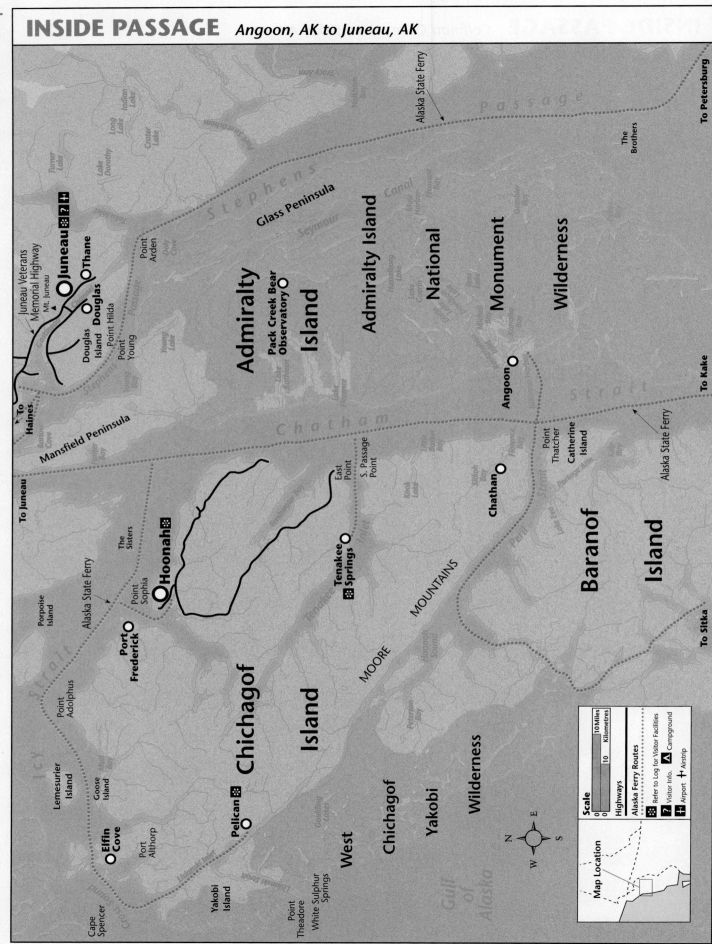

INSIDE PASSAGE *Angoon, AK to Juneau, AK*

To Petersburg

Tracy Arm

Alaska State Ferry

Passage

The Brothers

Timmer Lake

Indian Lake

Long Lake

Crater Lake

Lake Dorothy

Holkham Bay

Stephens

Glass Peninsula

Seymour

Admiralty Island

Mole Harbor

Hasselborg Lake

Windfall Harbor

National

Monument

Wilderness

To Kake

Juneau ▦ 🄬 ✚

Thane

Douglas

Douglas Island

Point Hilda

Point Young

Mt. Juneau ▲

Juneau Veterans Memorial Highway

Point Arden

Oliver Inlet

Admiralty

Island

Pack Creek Bear Observatory ○

Lake Kathleen

Young Lake

Young Bay

Canal

Swan Cove

Lake Guerin

Kanalku Bay

Mitchell Bay

Angoon ○

Strait

Point Thatcher

Catherine Island

Alaska State Ferry

To Haines

To Juneau

Barlow Cove

Mansfield Peninsula

Chatham

Hawk Inlet

To Sitka

The Sisters

East Point

S. Passage Point

Kootznahoo Inlet

Mitchell Bay

Favorite Bay

Kook Lake

Salt Lake Bay

Chatham ○

Peril

Baranof

Island

Saook Bay

Kelp Bay

Pauls Bay

Appleton Cove

Strait

Passage Arm

Alaska State Ferry

Porpoise Island

Hoonah ▦

Point Sophia

Tenakee Springs ○

Tenakee Inlet

▦

Alaska State Ferry

Port Frederick ○

Point Adolphus

Chichagof

Island

MOORE

MOUNTAINS

Hoonah Sound

Lemesurier Island

Goose Island

Icy

Pelican ▦

Port Althorp

West

Chichagof

Yakobi

Wilderness

Goulding Lakes

Pearson Bay

N
E
S
W

Strait

Elfin Cove ○

Yakobi Island

Point Theadore

White Sulphur Springs

Kimshan Cove

Gulf

of

Alaska

Cross Sound

Lisianski Inlet

Lisianski Strait

Cape Spencer

Scale
0	10 Miles
0	10 Kilometres

Highways

Alaska Ferry Routes

🄬 Refer to Log for Visitor Facilities
🄬 Visitor Info. ▲ Campground
✚ Airport ✈ Airstrip

Map Location

INSIDE PASSAGE
Juneau, AK to Skagway, AK

Scale

0   10 Miles
0   10   Kilometres

Highways

Alaska Ferry Routes

⊞ Refer to Log for Visitor Facilities

▲ Campground

? Visitor Info.   ✈ Airstrip

✈ Airport

Map Location

CANADA

Devils Paw

Mt. Nesselrode

Mt. Bressler

Mt. Ogilvie

U.S.A.

C o a s t   M o u n t a i n s

Mt. Poletica

Chilkoot Range

Mt. Canning

N
W   E
S

BRITISH COLUMBIA

ALASKA

Mt. Bagot

Meade Glacier

Muir Glacier

Juneau Icefield

Juneau Veterans' Memorial Highway

North Douglas Highway

Mendenhall Glacier

Windfall Lake

Auke Bay

Juneau ⊞ ?

Douglas

Echo Cove

Berners Bay

Shelter Island

Benjamin Cove

Lincoln Island

Point Retreat

Ralston Island

Admiralty Island

To Kake and Petersburg

To Hoonah and Angoon

Berners River

Point St. Mary

Kakuhan Range

L y n n   C a n a l

Alaska State Ferry

Eldred Rock

Sullivan Island

Chilkat Island

Seduction Point

Taiya Inlet

Chilkoot Inlet

Ferebee River

Skagway ⊞ ? ✈ ▲
(see KLONDIKE HIGHWAY 2 section, page 284)

Katzehin River

Chilkoot River

Chilkoot Lake

Chilkat Lake

Pyramid Harbor

Port Chilkoot

Haines ⊞ ? ✈ ▲

Chilkat Inlet

Lutak Inlet

Chilkat River

Haines Highway

(see HAINES HIGHWAY section, page 280)

Klehini River

Tsirku River

Takhin River

Takhinsha Mountains

▲Berg Mtn.

Endicott River Wilderness

C h i l k a t   R a n g e

Excursion Inlet

Porpoise Island

Pleasant Island

Gustavus ⊞ ✈

Bartlett Cove

Point Gustavus

Point Adolphus

Lemesurier Island

Chichagof Island

I c y   S t r a i t

G l a c i e r   Bay

National

Park

Glacier Bay

Muir Inlet

▲Mt. Wright

Queen Inlet

To Pelican

Taku Inlet

Turner Lake

Taku River

INSIDE PASSAGE ADVERTISERS

Activities and attractions include Russian and Tlingit dance performances; salmon bakes; historical melodramas; festivals; glaciers and icefield flightseeing; sportfishing and wilderness adventure tours by kayak, canoe and raft. Among other attractions are museums, totem poles, hiking trails, colorful saloons and fine dining.

The following sections describe the communities and attractions of Southeast with the exception of Hyder, which is accessible by highway from British Columbia and is included in the CASSIAR HIGHWAY section.

Ketchikan

(See map, pages 669–670)

Located on Revillagigedo Island, 235 miles/378 km south of Juneau, 90 miles/145 km north of Prince Rupert, BC. **Population:** Ketchikan Gateway Borough and city, 15,082. **Emergency Services: Alaska State Troopers**, phone (907) 225-5118. **City Police**, phone (907) 225-6631, or 911 for all emergency services. **Fire Department, Ambulance** and **Ketchikan Volunteer Rescue Squad**, phone (907) 225-9616. **Hospital**, Ketchikan General at 3100 Tongass Ave., phone (907) 225-5171. **Maritime Search and Rescue**, call the Coast Guard at (907) 225-5666.

Visitor Information: Ketchikan Visitors Bureau office is located on the downtown dock, open during daily business hours and weekends May through September. Write them at 131M Front St., Ketchikan 99901; phone (907) 225-6166 or (800) 770-2200; fax (907) 225-4250. U.S. Forest Service office for Misty Fiords National Monument and Ketchikan Ranger District is located at 3031 Tongass Ave.; open 8 A.M. to 4:30 P.M. weekdays; phone (907) 225-2148. The Southeast Alaska Visitor Center, located at 50 Main St., is open May 1 to Sept. 30, 8 A.M to 5 P.M. daily; Oct. 1 to April 30, 8:30 A.M. to 4:30 P.M., Tuesday through Saturday; phone (907) 228-6214, fax 228-6234.

Elevation: Sea level. **Climate:** Rainy. Yearly average rainfall is 162 inches and snowfall is 32 inches. Average daily maximum temperature in July 65°F/18°C; daily minimum 51°F/11°C. Daily maximum in January 39°F/4°C; daily minimum 29°F/-2°C. **Radio:** KTKN 930, KRBD-FM 105.9, KGTW-FM 106.7, KFMJ-FM 99.9. **Television:** CFTK (Prince Rupert, BC) and 27 cable channels. **Newspapers:** *Ketchikan Daily News* (daily); *Southeastern Log* (monthly); *New Alaskan* (monthly); *The Local Paper* (weekly).

Private Aircraft: Ketchikan International Airport on Gravina Island; elev. 88 feet/27m; length 7,500 feet/2,286m; asphalt; fuel 100LL, A. Ketchikan Harbor seaplane base downtown; fuel 80, 100, A.

Ketchikan is located on the southwest side of Revillagigedo (ruh-vee-uh-guh-GAY-doh) Island, on Tongass Narrows opposite Gravina Island. The name Ketchikan is derived from a Tlingit name, Kitschk-Hin, meaning the creek of the "thundering wings of an eagle." The creek flows through the town, emptying into Tongass Narrows.

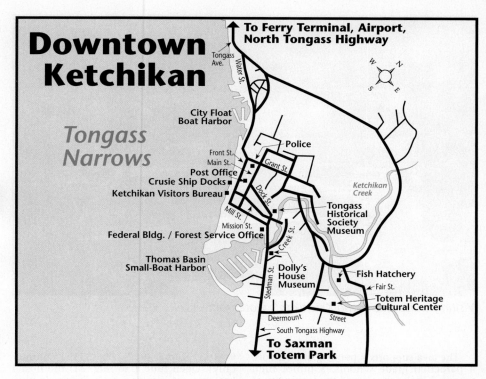

Downtown Ketchikan

Tongass Narrows

To Ferry Terminal, Airport, North Tongass Highway

Tongass Ave.

Water St.

City Float Boat Harbor

Police

Front St.

Main St.

Grant St.

Post Office

Crusie Ship Docks

Ketchikan Visitors Bureau

Dock St.

Mill St.

Mission St.

Federal Bldg. / Forest Service Office

Creek St.

Ketchikan Creek

Tongass Historical Society Museum

Thomas Basin Small-Boat Harbor

Stedman St.

Dolly's House Museum

Fish Hatchery

Fair St.

Totem Heritage Cultural Center

Deermount Street

South Tongass Highway

To Saxman Totem Park

Before Ketchikan was settled, the area at the mouth of Ketchikan Creek was a Tlingit Indian fish camp. Settlement began with interest in both mining and fishing. The first salmon cannery moved here in 1886, operating under the name of Tongass Packing Co. It burned down in August 1889. Gold was discovered nearby in 1898. This, plus residual effects of the gold, silver and copper mines, caused Ketchikan to become a booming little mining town. It was incorporated in 1901.

As mining waned, the fishing industry began to grow. By the 1930s more than a dozen salmon canneries had been built; during the peak years of the canned salmon industry, Ketchikan earned the title of "Salmon Capital of the World." Overfishing caused a drastic decline in salmon by the 1940s, and today only 4 canneries and a cold storage plant operate. Trident Seafoods Corp., owner of Ketchikan's oldest and largest cannery, provides lodging for 200-plus salmon processors in a floating bunkhouse. An industry under development is the commercial harvest of abalone near Ketchikan.

As fishing reached a low point, the timber industry expanded. The first sawmill was originally built in 1898 at Dolomi on Prince of Wales Island to cut timber for the Dolomi Mine. It was dismantled and moved to Ketchikan and rebuilt in 1903. A large pulp mill was constructed in 1953 at Ward Cove, a few miles northwest of town. It closed in 1997.

Tourism is an extremely important industry here; Ketchikan is Alaska's first port of call for cruise ships and Alaska Marine Highway vessels.

Ketchikan is Alaska's southernmost major city and the state's fourth largest (after Anchorage, Fairbanks and Juneau). The closest city in British Columbia is Prince Rupert. Ketchikan is a linear waterfront city, with much of its 3-mile/5-km-long business district suspended above water on pilings driven into the bottom of Tongass Narrows. It clings to the steep wooded hillside and has many homes perched on cliffs that are reached by climbing long wooden staircases or narrow winding streets.

Visiting cruise ship along Ketchikan's waterfront. (© James D. Ronan, Jr.)

The area supports 4 public grade schools, 4 parochial grade schools, a junior high school, 2 high schools and the University of Alaska Southeast campus.

ACCOMMODATIONS/VISITOR SERVICES

Accommodations in Ketchikan include bed and breakfasts (see ads following) and several motels/hotels. Major downtown lodgings include Best Western's The Landing (800/428-8304), Gilmore Hotel (800/275-9423), Ingersoll Hotel (800/478-2124), Super 8 Motel (800/800-8000) and the Westmark Cape Fox Lodge (800/544-0970). The major shopping areas are downtown and the west end.

Blueberry Hill Bed & Breakfast. Experience Ketchikan's historic past by staying in a charming historic home in downtown Ketchikan. Very spacious, comfortable rooms with relaxing ambiance. Super convenient to museums, galleries, shops and restaurants. Treat yourself to scrumptious homemade breads, scones and muffins. 500 Front Street, Ketchikan, AK 99901. Phone (907) 247-BLUE. See display ad this section.
[ADVERTISEMENT]

Ketchikan AYH hostel is located at the First United Methodist Church, Grant and Main streets; write Box 8515, Ketchikan, AK 99901; phone (907) 225-3319 (summer only). Open June 1 to Aug. 31, the hostel has showers, sleeping pads (bring sleeping bag) and kitchen facilities. Check-in time is 6 to 11 P.M. Reservations strongly recommended. Cost is $8 per night for members (AYH membership passes may be purchased at the hostel), $11 for nonmembers.

There are 5 campgrounds (4 public campgrounds and a private resort) north of the city on North Tongass Highway and Ward Lake Road. See highway logs in this section. Dump station located at Ketchikan Public Works office, 2 blocks north of state ferry terminal. Contact the visitors bureau for brochure on RV use and parking. ▲

TRANSPORTATION

Air: Daily scheduled jet service is provided from the Ketchikan International Airport by Alaska Airlines to other Southeast cities, Anchorage and Seattle, WA. Commuter and charter service to other Southeast communities is available via Taquan Air and Promech Air. Taquan Air (800/770-8800) has daily scheduled flights to Prince Rupert, BC. Air One, a branch of Taquan Air, services all of Southeast Alaska with a 19-passenger commuter jet plane.

Airport terminal, across Tongass Narrows on Gravina Island, is reached via shuttle ferry (10-minute ride, $2.50 per person, $5 per vehicle, one way) departing from the ferry terminal on North Tongass Avenue at half-hour intervals. Airport ferry terminal on Revillagigedo Island is 2.7 miles/4.3 km from downtown. Airporter service between downtown and airport is $11 to $12 (includes ferry fare). Shuttle and taxi service is also available between downtown and the airport.

Ferry: Alaska Marine Highway vessels connect Ketchikan with all mainline southeastern Alaska port cities, Prince Rupert, BC, and Bellingham, WA. There are also daily state ferry connections via the MV *Aurora* between Ketchikan and Metlakatla (1 hr. 15 min.), and Ketchikan and Hollis (2 hrs. 45 min.). The *Aurora* also sails between Ketchikan and Stewart/Hyder (11 hrs. 15 min.) 2 to 3 times a month in summer.

Terminal building with waiting room, ticket counter and loading area is on North Tongass Avenue (Highway), 2 miles/3.2 km north of downtown. Phone (907) 225-6181. Foot passengers can walk from the ferry to a post office, restaurant and grocery store if stopover time permits. Taxi service available.

Bus: Daily municipal bus service, stops at every stop within the city limits at half-hour intervals; schedules available at visitors bureau. Fare is $1/one way.

Car Rental: Available at airport and downtown locations from Alaska Car Rental (907) 225-5000 and Payless Car Rental (907) 225-6004.

Taxi: Taxi cabs meet ferry and airport arrivals.

Highways: North Tongass and South Tongass highways and Ward Lake Road (see logs this section).

Cruise Ships: Ketchikan is the first port of call for many cruise ships to Alaska. Cruises depart from U.S. West Coast ports and Vancouver, BC. Two cruise lines depart from Ketchikan.

Private Boats: Two public docks downtown, Thomas Basin and City Float, provide transient moorage. In the West End District, 1 mile/1.6 km from downtown, Bar Harbor has moorage, showers. No gas available. Permits required. Moorage space in Ketchikan is limited; all private boats should contact the harbormaster's office at (907) 225-3610 prior to arrival to secure a spot.

ATTRACTIONS

Ketchikan's waterfront is the center of the city. A narrow city on a mountainside, Ketchikan has a waterfront that runs for several miles and consists of docks, stores on pilings, seaplane floats, 3 picturesque boat harbors, a seaplane base and ferry terminal. There is constant activity here as seaplanes take off and vessels move in and out of the harbor. Walking-tour maps are available at the visitors bureau and at the ferry terminal.

The Plaza. Southeast Alaska's premier shopping center. Two comfort-controlled levels feature a variety of national and local retail shops and services for complete one-stop shopping. Plenty of free parking. Less than a mile south of the ferry terminal. Open every day except major holidays.
[ADVERTISEMENT]

Fish Pirate's Daughter, a well-done local musical-comedy melodrama, portrays Ketchikan's early fishing days, with some of the city's spicier history included. Performed 7 P.M. and 8:45 P.M. Fridays, July through August. Contact First City Players, 338 Main St., phone (907) 225-4792 or 225-2211, for more information. Admission fee.

Tongass Historical Museum, located on Dock Street, in central downtown, explores the rich culture of the Tlingit, Haida and Tsimshian people, as well as the early history and development of Ketchikan, Alaska's feisty "First City." Open in summer from 8 A.M. to 5 P.M. daily. Winter (October to mid-May) hours are 1-5 P.M. Wednesday through Friday, 1-4 P.M. Saturday and Sunday. The Raven Stealing the Sun totem stands just outside the entrance. Salmon viewing platforms. Admission fee is $3 for adults; free admission in off-season. Phone (907) 225-5600 for more information.

Creek Street is Ketchikan's famous "redlight district," where Black Mary, Dolly, Frenchie and others plied their trade for over half a century until 1954. Nearly 20 houses lined the far side of Ketchikan Creek; many have been restored. There are also several art and gift shops. Dolly's House, a former brothel, is open during the summer. Admission charged. Creek Street is a wooden street on pilings that begins just past the bridge on Stedman (South Tongass Highway). Watch for salmon in the creek below the bridge in late August. Also look for the metal sculpture paying tribute to the salmon; it's a local landmark.

Totem Heritage Center, at 601 Deermount St., houses 33 totem poles and fragments retrieved from deserted Tlingit and Haida Indian villages. This national landmark collection comprises the largest exhibit of original totems in the United States. Facilities include craft exhibits, craft classes for children and reference library. Gift shop, craft demonstrations and guided tours during summer months. Summer admission fee $4. No admission charged off-season. Summer hours are 8 A.M. to 5 P.M. daily. Winter hours (October through mid-May) are 1–5 P.M. Tuesday through Friday. Phone (907) 225-5900.

Deer Mountain Hatchery and Eagle Center is located in the city park within walking distance of downtown (take the bridge across Ketchikan Creek from the Totem Heritage Center). The hatchery produces about 100,000 king, 150,000 coho, 30,000 rainbow trout and 6,500 steelhead fingerlings annually. Observation platforms and information signs provide education on the life cycles of salmon. Also an opportunity photograph eagles up close at the Eagle Center. Open from 8 A.M. to 4:30 P.M. daily late May to late September.

The Ketchikan Mural on Stedman Street was created by 21 Native artists in 1978. The 125-by-18-foot/38-by-4-m design is collectively entitled *The Return of the Eagle.*

Fourth of July is a major celebration in Ketchikan. The Timber Carnival takes place over the Fourth of July with events such as ax throwing and chopping, power saw bucking and a tug-of-war. There are also fireworks, the Calamity Race (by canoe and kayak, bicycle and on foot), a parade and other events.

The Blueberry Arts Festival, in August, features arts and crafts, the performing arts and plenty of homemade blueberry pies, blueberry crepes, blueberry cheesecakes and other culinary delights. Events include a slug race, bed race, pie-eating contest, trivia contest and spelling bee. A juried art show, funrun and dance are also part of the festival. Sponsored and coordinated by the Ketchikan Area Arts and Humanities Council, Inc. (338 Main St., Ketchikan 99901; 907/225-2211).

Saxman Totem Park, Milepost 2.5 South Tongass Highway, is included in local sightseeing tours. Open year-round. There is

no admission charge, but there is a fee for guided tour (offered May through September). The totem park has 28 totems. The tour includes demonstrations at the Carving Center and performances by the Cape Fox Dancers at the Beaver Tribal House. For more information on hours, tours and events, phone the Cape Fox Tours office at (907) 225-5163, ext. 301 or 304.

Totem Bight community house and totem park, Milepost 9.9 North Tongass Highway, contains an excellent model of a Tlingit community house and a park with 13 totems.

Misty Fiords National Monument/ Ketchikan Ranger District, Tongass National Forest. 3.2 million acres surrounding Ketchikan and nearby communities. Pristine coastal rain forest, glacially carved fjords, waterfalls, wildlife, fishing, spectacular geologic features. Includes 2.3 million acres of the National Monument Wilderness. Forest Service maintains approximately 60 miles of trails. 30 cabins available for public rental. Most are accessible by floatplane or boat and can be reserved by calling toll free 1-877-444-6777 up to 180 days in advance. . Other recreational attractions include Ward Lake Recreation Area (3 campgrounds, dayuse area, trails), Naha Dock and Trail, Margaret Bay fish pass and bear viewing. Sea kayaking is a popular means of exploring the coastlines and venturing into remote areas. Cabin reservations, maps, brochures and trip planning assistance available from the Southeast Alaska Visitors Center, 50 Main St., Ketchikan, AK 99901. Phone (907) 228-6214, fax (907) 228-6234. Internet: www. fs.fed.us/r10/ketchikan.

Charter boats: About 120 vessels operate out of Ketchikan for half-day, all-day or overnight sightseeing or fishing trips and transport to USFS public-use cabins and outlying communities. See advertisements this section and check with the visitors bureau or at the marinas.

Fishing lodges and resorts in the area offer sportfishing for steelhead, salmon, halibut, trout, lingcod and red snapper. Resorts near Ketchikan include Misty Fiords Lodge, Salmon Falls Resort and Yes Bay Lodge. There are several fishing lodges on Prince of Wales Island, including Waterfall Resort, which is housed in a renovated fish cannery.

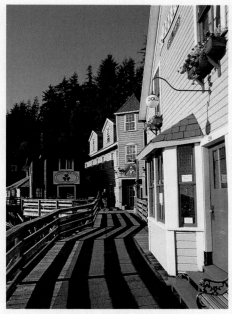

Creek Street is Ketchikan's historic redlight district. (© James D. Ronan, Jr.)

Charter planes operate from the airport and from the waterfront on floats and are available for fly-in fishing, flightseeing or service to lodges and smaller communities.

Picnic areas include Settlers Cove by Settlers Cove Campground, **Milepost 18.2** North Tongass Highway; Refuge Cove, **Milepost 8.7** North Tongass Highway; Rotary Beach at **Milepost 3.5** South Tongass Highway; and Grassy Point and Ward Lake, **Milepost 1.1** Ward Lake Road.

Hiking trails include Deer Mountain trail, which begins at the corner of Fair and Deermount streets. The 3-mile/4.8-km, 3,001-foot/915-m ascent gives trekkers an

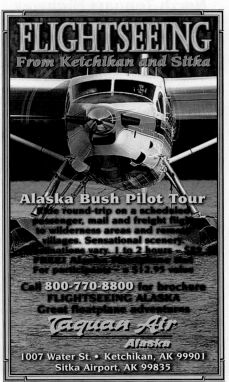

excellent vantage of downtown Ketchikan and Tongass Narrows. Good but steep trail. Access to Deer Mountain cabin, the only USFS public-use cabin accessible by trail from Ketchikan. Cabin reservations are required. Perseverance Lake trail, 2.4 miles/ 3.8 km from Ward Lake to Perseverance Lake. Connell Lake trail, about 2.0 miles/3.2 km along north shore of Connell Lake, is in good condition. Silvis Lakes trail, about 2 miles/3.2 km up to Lower Silvis Lake and picnic area. Trail continues to Upper Silvis Lake and Deer Mountain trail, but is very difficult. An easy and informative 1-mile/1.6-km nature trail circles Ward Lake.

Southeast Alaska Visitor Center, 50 Main St., features exhibits on Native cultures, ecosystems, resources and the rain forest in Southeast Alaska. Also 13-minute, award-winning "Mystical Southeast Alaska" audio visual program and Alaska Public Lands trip planning room. Admission charged May-Sept. Open 8 A.M. to 5 P.M. daily in summer, Tuesday through Saturday in winter.

AREA FISHING: Check with the Alaska Dept. of Fish and Game at 2030 Sea Level Dr., Suite 215, or phone (907) 225-2859 for details on fishing in the Ketchikan area. Good fishing spots range from Mountain Point, a 5-mile/8-km drive from Ketchikan on South Tongass Highway, to streams, lakes, bays, and inlets 50 miles/80 km away by boat or by air. Half-day and longer charters and skiff rentals available out of Ketchikan. There are fishing resorts at Yes Bay, Clover Pass and at the entrance to Behm Canal (Salmon Falls Resort); and 13 fishing resorts on Prince of Wales Island. Fish include salmon, halibut, steelhead, Dolly Varden, cutthroat and rainbow, arctic grayling, eastern brook trout, lingcod and rockfish; shellfish include dungeness crab and shrimp. Ketchikan has 2 king salmon derbies, a silver salmon derby and a halibut derby in summer. ◄◆

North Tongass Highway Log

The North Tongass Highway is 18.4 miles/29.6 km long with 15.2 miles/24.5 km paved. It begins at the corner of Mill Street and Stedman (at the Federal Bldg.) and proceeds north to Totem Bight, Clover Pass and Settlers Cove Campground.

0 Federal Building on left with area information display. Proceeding on Mill Street.

0.1 (0.2 km) Southeast Alaska Visitor Center with information on federal lands in Alaska.

0.2 (0.3 km) Turning right onto Front Street, cruise ship dock on left where passengers disembark from major ships. Ketchikan Visitors Bureau.

0.3 (0.5 km) Tunnel. North of this, Front Street becomes Water Street.

0.5 (0.8 km) City Float on left. Note older vessels.

0.7 (1.1 km) Highway turns left, then right, and becomes Tongass Avenue.

1.2 (1.9 km) West end shopping area begins.

1.7 (2.7 km) Bar Harbor boat basin on left.

2 (3.2 km) Ketchikan General Hospital on right, Ketchikan Ranger Station and Misty Fiords National Monument on left, north-bound.

2.3 (3.7 km) Ferry terminals for Alaska Marine Highway.

2.4 (3.9 km) Main branch post office.

2.6 (4.2 km) Carlanna Creek and bridge.

2.7 (4.3 km) Airport shuttle ferry.

3.2 (5.1 km) Almer Wolfe Memorial viewpoint of Tongass Narrows. Airport terminal is visible across the narrows on Gravina Island.

4 (6.4 km) Hillside on right is a logged area, an example of clear-cut logging method and regrowth.

4.4 (7.1 km) Alaska State Troopers and Highway Dept.

5.5 (8.8 km) Small paved viewpoint overlooking Tongass Narrows and floatplane dock.

6 (9.6 km) Ward Cove Cannery next to road. Cannery Creek and bridge.

6.8 (10.9 km) Ward Lake Road (see log this section); open to hikers and bikers only.

7 (11.3 km) Ward Creek and bridge; Ketchikan sawmill, owned by Ketchikan Pulp Co.; see **Mile 7.8.**

7.1 (11.4 km) **Junction** with Revilla Road (see log this section).

7.3 (11.7 km) **WARD COVE.** Post office, gas station and grocery.

7.8 (12.5 km) Ketchikan Pulp Co. pulp mill was built in 1953; it closed in 1997.

8.7 (14 km) **Refuge Cove State Recreation Site** with 14 picnic sites.

9.4 (15.1 km) Mud Bight; "float houses" rest on mud at low tide and float during high tide.

9.9 (15.9 km) **Totem Bight State Historical Park**; parking area, restrooms and phones. A short trail leads through the woods to Totem Bight community house and totem park. A striking setting. Don't miss this!

10.8 (17.4 km) Grocery store and gas station.

12.9 (20.8 km) Scenic viewpoint overlooking **Guard Island Lighthouse** built in 1903 and manned until 1969 when finally automated.

14.2 (22.9 km) Clover Pass Resort turnoff. Left, North Point Higgins Road leads 0.6 mile/1 km to turnoff to resort; food, lodging, camping.

Left, then immediately right, is Knudson Cove Road, leading 0.4 mile/0.6 km to Knudson Cove Marina with public float, boat launch and boat rentals. Road rejoins North Tongass Highway at **Milepost 14.8.** ▲

14.8 (23.8 km) Knudson Cove Marina to left 0.5 mile/0.8 km.

15.2 (24.5 km) Pavement ends.

16.6 (26.8 km) Salmon Falls Resort; private fishing lodge with restaurant and boat rentals.

18.2 (29.3 km) **Settlers Cove** state campground, parking area and picnic area; 13 tent/trailer campsites; 2 covered picnic pavilions flanked by 12 picnic units are along the beach on either side of the campground. Camping fee $6/night. Tables, water, pit toilets. Open year-round. Good gravel beach for kids and boats. To right of beach is **Lunch Creek** (pink salmon in August), falls and trail. ◄◆▲

18.4 (29.6 km) Road end.

Revilla Road Log

This 7.7-mile/12.4-km paved road off the North Tongass Highway provides access to Ward Lake Recreation Area, Harriet Hunt Lake (via Harriet Hunt Road at **Milepost 6.5**), Brown Mountains Logging Road and Council Lake. Motorists and hikers should be aware of private property boundaries, posted by Cape Fox Corp. (CFC), and logging and trucking activities.

Campers should be aware of USFS regulations in the Ward Lake Recreation Area: Camping is restricted to developed campgrounds and limited to 14 days.

0 Right turn northbound from North Tongass Highway at **Milepost 7.1.**

1.4 (2.3 km) **Junction** with Ward Lake Road (see log this section).

2.3 (3.8 km) Last Chance Campground on right; 19 spaces, paved road, gravel sites, tables, pit toilets, water. Camping fee charged. Open end of May to Sept. 30. Situated along Ward Creek among large old-growth trees. Stream fishing access from some sites along creek. Campsites can be reserved; phone 1-877-444-6777; internet: http://www.reserveusa.com.

2.4 (3.9 km) Connell Lake Road, on right, a narrow gravel road extending 0.6 mile/1 km to Connell Lake Reservoir. At Mile 0.4 Connell Lake Road, a bridge passes over large pipe which once carried water from the reservoir to the pulpmill (closed) at Ward Cove. Connell Lake Trail at reservoir.

2.7 (4.3 km) Turnout.

2.8 (4.4 km) Ward Creek Salvage Sale Interpretive Thinning Area on left. A 1.5-mile/2.4-km interpretive trail.

6.5 (10.4 km) **Junction** with 2.4-mile/3.9-km Harriet Hunt Lake Road, which deadends at **Harriet Hunt Lake Recreation Area**; parking, pit toilets, fishing (rainbow trout to 20 inches, May to November). Road is on Cape Fox Corp. lands. Watch for logging trucks. ◆

7.6 (12.2 km) Brown Mountain Logging Road, on right, a narrow gravel logging road 4.2 miles/6.8 km. Open to the public for dispersed camping. No services.

7.7 (12.3 km) End public highway. Private logging road begins.

Ward Lake Road Log

The Ward Lake Road turnoff at **Milepost 6.8** North Tongass Highway is open for bikers and hikers only. Motorists take Revilla Road turnoff from North Tongass Highway to **Milepost 1.4** for Ward Lake Road and access to Ward Lake Recreation Area. This log starts at that junction.

0 Junction with Revilla Road at **Milepost 1.4.**

0.5 (0.8 km) Ward Lake USFS picnic area on right; beach, parking area, picnic shelters and water. One end of nature trail around Ward Lake.

0.7 (1.1 km) Ward Creek bridge. Grassy Point picnic area on right. Several walk-in picnic sites with tables and shelters near road. Pit toilet at parking area. Footbridge across Ward Creek to Ward Lake Nature Trail. Good fly fishing for steelhead, salmon and Dolly Varden. ◆

0.8 (1.3 km) 3C's Campground (site of Civilian Conservation Corps camp and WWII Aleut relocation camp) entrance on left; 4 campsites, camping fee, open April to October. (Proposed group camping site.) ▲

0.9 (1.4 km) Beginning of **Perseverance**

Lake Trail on left. Trailhead is within 100 feet of 3C's Campground with parking across road. The 2.2 mile/3.5 km gravel and boardwalk trail leads to Perseverance Lake (elev. 518 ft/158 m); brook trout fishing. ⮜

1.1 (1.8 km) Signal Creek USFS campground on right; paved road, 24 gravel sites with tables, water and pit toilets. Open mid-May to Sept. 30. Camping fee charged. Situated among large trees on the shore of Ward Lake. The Ward Lake Nature Trail passes through the campground. The trail loops around Ward Lake, a 30–50-minute, 1.3-mile/2.1-km easy walk on a well-graveled path. Campsites can be reserved; phone 1-877-444-6777; internet: http://www.reserveusa.com. ▲

End of old Ward Lake Road, now open only for foot or bike traffic.

Ward Creek and Ward Lake, cutthroat and Dolly Varden year-round, best March to June; steelhead to 16 lbs.; silver salmon to 18 lbs. and pink salmon to 5 lbs., August to October. (Hatchery-raised coho salmon; bring head of tagged fish to ADF&G.) ⮜

Saxman Totem Park outside Ketchikan has 28 totems as well as a carving center and tribal house. (© James D. Ronan, Jr.)

South Tongass Highway Log

The 12.9-mile/20.8-km South Tongass Highway leads from the corner of Mill and Stedman streets south to Saxman Totem Park. First 8.5 miles/13.7 km are paved.

0 Federal Building on right.

0.1 (0.2 km) Ketchikan Creek and bridge. Beginning of Creek Street boardwalk on left next to bridge.

0.2 (0.3 km) Thomas Street begins on right, a boardwalk street where old-time businesses are located. Thomas Basin boat harbor.

0.5 (0.8 km) Cannery and cold storage plant.

0.9 (1.4 km) U.S. Coast Guard base.

2.5 (4 km) SAXMAN (pop. 389) was founded in 1896 by Tlingit Alaska Natives and named after a Presbyterian missionary who served the Tlingit people. The Native village of Saxman has a gas station and convenience store and is the site of Saxman Totem Park. Developed by Cape Fox Corp., this popular attraction includes a carving center and tribal house. Guided tours available from Cape Fox Tours.

2.7 (4.3 km) Gas station.

3.5 (5.6 km) Rotary Beach, public recreation area, contains a shelter and table.

5 (8.1 km) Mountain Point, suburb of Ketchikan. Parking area and access to good salmon fishing from shore in July and August. ⮜

5.6 (9 km) Boat ramp on right.

8.2 (13.2 km) Herring Cove bridge and sawmill. Private hatchery for chum, king and coho salmon on short road to left; no tours.

8.5 (13.7 km) Pavement ends.

8.8 (14.2 km) Whitman Creek and bridge.

9 (14.5 km) Scenic turnout on right. Note different shades of green on trees across the water. Light green are cedar; medium, hemlock; and the darker are spruce. Species grow intermixed.

10.3 (16.6 km) Left, scenic waterfall.

11 (17.7 km) Scenic turnout.

11.8 (19 km) Lodge.

12.9 (20.8 km) Road ends, view of power

plant, an experimental sockeye salmon hatchery (no tours) and an abandoned cannery. Two-mile/3.2-km walk up gravel road leads to Lower Silvis Lake picnic area. Trail continues to Upper Silvis Lake and joins Deer Mountain trail, which connects to John Mountain National Recreation trail. Trail between Upper and Lower Silvis lakes is very difficult.

Metlakatla

(See map, page 669)

Located on the west coast of Annette Island, 15 miles/24 km south of Ketchikan, Southeastern Alaska's southernmost community. **Population:** 1,673. **Emergency Services: Police, fire** and **ambulance**, emergency only, phone 911. **Visitor Information:** Tours to Metlakatla depart daily from Ketchikan; reservations are required. Contact the Community Tour Office at (800) 643-4898 for scheduling information. The Metlakatla tour and salmon bake operates from early-May to October. A permit from Metlakatla Indian Community is required for long-term visits to Annette Island.

Elevation: Sea level. **Climate:** Mild and moist. Summer temperatures range from 36°F/12°C to 65°F/18°C; winter temperatures from 28°F/-2°C to 44°F/7°C. Average annual precipitation is 115 inches; October is the wettest month with a maximum of 35 inches of rainfall. Annual snowfall averages 61 inches. **Radio:** KTKN 930 (Ketchikan). **Television:** 20 channels via cable.

Private Aircraft: Floatplane services.

Transportation: Air—Charter and scheduled floatplane service. **Ferry**—Daily state ferry service in summer via MV *Aurora* from Ketchikan; crossing time 1 hour 15 minutes.

Overnight accommodations, restaurant, groceries and banking services available.

Metlakatla was founded in 1887 by William Duncan, a Scottish-born lay minister, who moved here with several hundred Tsimshian Indians from a settlement in British Columbia after a falling-out with church authorities. Congress granted reservation status and title to the entire island in 1891, and the new settlement prospered under Duncan, who built a salmon cannery and sawmill.

Today, fishing and lumber continue to be the main economic base of Metlakatla. The community and island also retain the status of a federal Indian reservation, which is why Metlakatla has the only salmon fish traps in Alaska. (Floating fish traps were outlawed by the state shortly after statehood.)

The well-planned community has a town hall, a recreation center with an Olympic-sized swimming pool, a post office, 2 lumber mills and cold storage. The Metlakatla Indian Community is the largest employer in town, with retail and service trades the second largest. Many residents also are commercial fishermen. Subsistence activities remain an important source of food for residents, who harvest seaweed, salmon, halibut, cod, clams, dungeness crab and waterfowl.

There is a replica of the William Duncan Memorial Church here; the original was destroyed by fire in 1948. The Duncan Museum is located in the original cottage occupied by the Rev. William Duncan until his death in 1918.

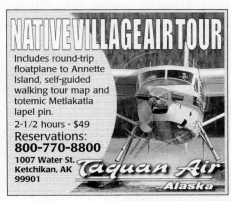

Prince of Wales Island

(See map, page 670)

Includes Coffman Cove, Craig, Hollis, Hydaburg, Kasaan, Klawock, Naukati, Thorne Bay and Whale Pass

About 15 miles/24.1 km west of Ketchikan. **Population:** Approximately 5,200. **Emergency Services:** Alaska State Troopers, in Klawock, phone (907) 755-2918. **Police,** in Craig, phone (907) 826-3330; in Klawock, phone (907) 755-2777; emergencies only, phone 911; **Village Public Safety Officers** in Thorne Bay, phone (907) 828-3905; in Hydaburg, phone (907) 285-3321; in Klawock, phone (907) 755-2906. **Ambulance,** Hydaburg emergency response team, phone 911. **Health Clinics** for all emergencies, phone 911; in Craig, phone (907) 826-3257; in Klawock, phone (907) 755-4800; in Thorne Bay, phone (907) 828-3906; in Hydaburg, phone (907) 285-3462. **Maritime Search and Rescue,** call the Coast Guard at (800) 478-5555.

Visitor Information: Prince of Wales Island Chamber of Commerce, P.O. Box 497, Craig, AK 99921; phone (907) 826-3870, fax (907) 826-2926.

Elevation: Sea level to 4,000 feet/1,219m. **Climate:** Mild and moist, but variable due to the island's size and topography. Rainfall in excess of 100 inches per year, with modest snowfall in winter at lower elevations. **Radio:** KRSA 580 (Petersburg), KTKN 930 (Ketchikan), KRBD-FM 90.1 (Ketchikan). **Television:** Via satellite. **Newspaper:** *Island News* (Thorne Bay, weekly).

Private Aircraft: Klawock airstrip, 2 miles/3.2 km northeast; elev. 50 feet/15m; length 5,000 feet/1,524m; lighted and paved. Seaplane bases adjacent to all the largest communities and in several bays.

Heavily forested with low mountains, Prince of Wales Island measures roughly 135 miles/217 km north–south by 45 miles /72 km east–west. The third largest island under the American flag (Kodiak is second, the Big Island of Hawaii is first), it is 2,231 square miles/5,778 square km. The 6 communities with city status on the island—Craig (the largest with 1,946 residents), Klawock, Thorne Bay, Hydaburg, Coffman Cove and Kasaan are connected by road, as are the other 3 smaller communities of Hollis, Naukati and Whale Pass. Not connected by road are **PORT PROTECTION** and **POINT BAKER,** both at the northwest tip of the island (see *The ALASKA WILDERNESS GUIDE* for details on these communities).

Prince of Wales Island has been the site of several lumbermills and mining camps since the 1800s. But it was salmon that led to permanent settlement on the island. Klawock was the site of one of Alaska's first canneries, built in 1878. In the following years, some 25 canneries were built on the island to process salmon. Today, logging is prevalent on the island.

Prince of Wales Island offers uncrowded backcountry, fishing for salmon and trout,

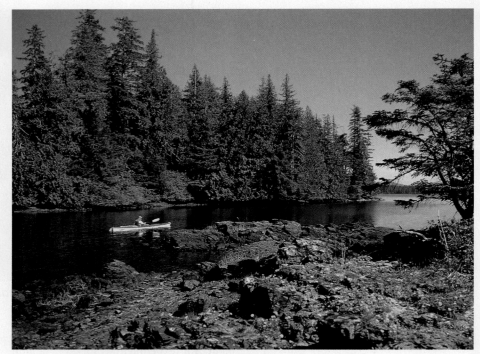

Kayaking in the islands of Prince of Wales Wilderness Area. (© David J. Job)

kayaking and canoeing waters, opportunities for viewing wildlife (black bears, Sitka black-tailed deer, bald eagles), adequate visitor facilities and some historical attractions. Most of the island is national forest land. The Forest Service manages 5 large, designated wilderness areas on Prince of Wales Island. There are also some Native corporation and private land holdings. Respect No Trespassing signs.

There are several roadside fishing spots on Prince of Wales Island. See the road logs in this section for details. Lakes and streams support red, pink and silver salmon, cutthroat, rainbow trout and Dolly Varden. ❧

ACCOMMODATIONS/VISITOR SERVICES

Prince of Wales Island has several hotels, lodges, rental cabins and bed and breakfasts. See community descriptions on pages 681–684.

There are also more than 20 USFS cabins (accessible by plane, boat or on foot) available for public use; reservations and a fee are required. Contact the USFS office in Ketchikan or the local ranger districts at Craig (907/826-3271) and Thorne Bay (907/828-3304).

There are private campgrounds with hookups at Coffman Cove and Klawock. There is one developed USFS campground on the island—Eagle's Nest on Thorne Bay Road ($8 camping fee)—and several undeveloped dispersed camping sites accessible via the island road system. See road logs this section. ▲

TRANSPORTATION

Air: All communities on the island are served by floatplane, most daily. Wheel planes land at Klawock. Daily scheduled service by Taquan Air (800/770-8800) and Pro–Mech Air (800/860-3845) from Ketchikan.

Ferry: Alaska state ferry MV *Aurora* from Ketchikan to Hollis; crossing time 2 hours, 45 minutes. Phone Craig office at (907) 826-

3432, Hollis terminal at (907) 530-7115.

Vehicle rental: Car rentals available in Craig at Wilderness Rent-A-Car (phone 800/949-2205) and Holiday Rentals (907/826-5388); in Coffman Cove from Kingfisher Charters (907/329-2235); in Klawock from Log Cabin RV Park & Resort (800/544-2205); in Thorne Bay from the Thorne Bay Company (907/828-3330) and Deer Creek Cottage (907/828-3393). RV rentals from Cast-a-Ways Alaskan Adventure in Thorne Bay, (907) 828-8220.

Highways: Prince of Wales Island has the most extensive road network in Southeast Alaska. Over 1,000 miles of road allow access to most areas of the island. The island's 8 main roads are logged in this section. See also the map on page 688. *DRIVER CAUTION: Watch for heavily loaded logging trucks while driving; they have the right-of-way.* CB radios are helpful. Carry a spare tire and spare gas. (Gas is available in Coffman Cove, Hydaburg, Craig, Klawock, Whale Pass and Thorne Bay.) Use turnouts and approach hills and corners on your side of the road. Spur roads are *NOT* recommended for large RVs or cars with trailers. Some side roads may be closed intermittently during logging operations or highway construction. Watch for signs posted when roads are closed and expect delays.

Taxi: No free public transport meets the ferry at Hollis, but arrangements can be made with taxis. According to the chamber of commerce, the fare ranges from about $25 per person to $50–$60 to charter a taxi (which is usually a van for several people). Available in Klawock from Irish Setter Cab (907/755-2217), Jackson Cab (907/755-2557) and Screaming Eagle (907/755-2699). Available in Craig from Chief Wiah Cab (907/826-3375) and Craig–Klawock Taxi (907/826-3077).

ATTRACTIONS

El Capitan Cave, located just north of Whale Pass off the North Island Road.

People have been visiting El Capitan Cave for many years. El Capitan's pit is one of the deepest known in the U.S. Northern Prince of Wales has extensive limestone cave systems. Significant scientific discoveries have been found in these caves, including grizzly bear bones dating back 12,295 years, and black bear bones dating back 11,565 years.

There is a steep trail (more than 365 steps) leading to the cave entrance. Because of damage to cave formations, a gate has been installed to regulate visitation. There is open visitation to the gate some distance within the cave; guided tours beyond the gate. The 2-hour guided tours depart several times a day, from mid-May to September; call for 1999 schedule. For guided tours, group size is limited to 6. For reservations write Thorne Bay Ranger District, Box 19001, Thorne Bay 99919; phone (907) 828-3304. There are vault toilets, a government dock and a floatplane and boat tie-up at this U.S. Forest Service-administrated site.

AREA FISHING: Most fish in streams on the island are anadromous (travel upstream to spawn). Try **Klawock Lake** for trout and salmon; **Klawock River** downstream from the hatchery is good for trout, steelhead and salmon; **Thorne River** for Dolly Varden, trout and salmon; and **Sarkar River** for trout, steelhead and salmon. Fresh and saltwater guiding services are available.

World-class saltwater sportfishing abounds immediately offshore and throughout the many smaller islands surrounding Prince of Wales Island. Most communities have boat ramps. For those traveling without a boat, quality half-, full- and multi-day fishing trips are available through many of the local charter operators. Ocean fishing for salmon is best in July and early August for kings (chinook), August and September for coho, July, August and September for pinks, and August and September for chum. 100-lb. halibut, 50-lb. king salmon and 15-lb. coho salmon are not considered uncommon in the sport season, usually May through August due to the weather and fish migration patterns. Abundant bottom fish, including lingcod and red snapper, reside throughout these waters year-round. ◂

COMMUNITY DESCRIPTIONS

COFFMAN COVE (pop. 254), 53 miles/ 85 km north of Klawock, a 2¹/₂-hour drive from Hollis. Formerly one of the largest independent logging camps in Southeast, Coffman Cove is now a small hamlet. Recreation includes hunting (deer and bear), good freshwater and saltwater fishing, boating, hiking. Charters for fishing and whalewatching available. Canoe Lagoon Oyster Co. here is the state's oldest and largest oyster producer; fresh oysters available locally.

Coffman Cove has a general store, liquor and gift shop (both open daily), gas pump, playground and ballfield, showers and laundry facilities, and a campground. Tire repair is available. There is a dock and a small beach with access to salt water for canoes and cartop boats. Oceanview RV Park has 14 full-hookup sites on the beach. Rental cabins are available. EMTs dispatch from Riggin' Shack. ▲

CRAIG (pop. 1,946), 31 miles/50 km from Hollis, is on the western shore of Prince of Wales Island. The original townsite, on Craig Island, is now connected to Prince of Wales by a short causeway. **Visitor information:** Craig City Hall, phone (907) 826-3275, open weekdays 8 A.M. to 5 P.M.;

Craig (pop. 1,946), is 31 miles from Hollis on the western shore of Prince of Wales Island. (© David J. Job)

U.S. Forest Service office, open weekdays 8 A.M. to 5 P.M., phone (907) 826-3271; Prince of Wales Chamber of Commerce, phone (907) 826-3870.

Craig has several hotels and lodges, including Haida Way Lodge downtown (800/347-4625); and Sunnahae Lodge (907/826-4000) and Shelter Cove Lodge (888/826-FISH), which specialize in fishing. There is also Dreamcatcher Bed and Breakfast (907/826-2238) and Bay View Inn apartment (907/826-3623). Sporting goods, fishing, hunting and camping supplies, gifts, seafood, grocery and health stores available. There are a laundromat and showers, liquor stores, bars, beauty and barber shops, a library and 2 banks (one with automatic teller machine). Craig has a school, grades K through 12, and an indoor community swimming pool.

Gas, propane, RV supplies, towing and auto repair available. Free RV dump facilities on Cold Storage Road. Contact City Public Works at (907) 826-3405 during business hours for key. Evenings and weekends, contact the police department at (907) 826-3330.

Craig Primary Health Care Facility, commonly known as the Craig clinic, is located just up the hill from the city municipal offices and is currently managed by the Craig Health Corp. The facility is approximately 4,300 square feet and is occupied by a physician and staff, public health nurses and the Craig Native health aide.

Physician services are generally available 24 hours a day except for brief periods of time when the physician is unavailable. An emergency room is provided at the clinic for treatment, minor surgery and stabilization of patients. Medications, emergency pharmaceuticals and medical supplies are available through the clinic (by doctor's prescription only; no retail pharmacies are located on the island). The clinic can take routine X-rays. Clinic hours are 9 A.M. to 5 P.M. Monday through Saturday in the summer; 9 A.M. to 5 P.M. weekdays in winter. Emergency Medical Services are available full-time at 911, or call Craig PD at (907)

826-3330. The Craig Native health aide and public health nurse are available weekdays from 9 A.M. to 4 P.M. Craig also has a chiropractic office and 2 dental clinics.

Craig has 2 modern boat harbors, North Cove and South Cove, located on either side of the causeway, a seaplane float, fuel dock, city dock and float, 2 fish-buying docks and an old cannery dock. The Craig harbormaster's office, with public showers and restrooms, is located on the corner close to South Cove; phone (907) 826-3404, VHF Channel 16.

Craig was once a temporary fish camp for the Tlingit and Haida Natives of the area. In 1907, with the help of local Natives, William D. Craig Millar established a mildcure station known as Fish Egg for nearby Fish Egg Island. The Tlingit name for Fish Egg Island is "Sheenda" and the townsite was "Sheensit," which is now used by the Native Shaan-Seet Corp. Between 1908 and 1911, a permanent saltery and cold storage facility, along with about 2 dozen homes, were built on the city's present location and named for founder Craig Millar. In 1912, the post office was established, E.M. Streeter opened a sawmill and Craig constructed a salmon cannery. Both businesses peaked during WWI. Craig was incorporated in 1922, and grew throughout the 1930s, with some families relocating from the Dust Bowl.

Although the salmon industry has both prospered and floundered over the years, fishing and fish processing still account for an important part of area employment. In recent years timber harvesting on the island has contributed many jobs in logging and timber processing. The Viking Lumber Co. mill, located between Craig and Klawock, provides year-round employment, producing moulding, window and door stock for the domestic market, and high-grade cants for export. The mill also produces wood chips for the manufacture of pulp. Despite recent legislation, timber will continue to be a viable though reduced economic influence on the island's economy for many years. Mining, transportation and tourism have the potential to become major employers in

□ Examine totem poles
□ Spelunk in one of the most extensive cave networks in North America
□ Explore sweeping beaches
□ Kayak unspoiled waterways and watch whales play
□ Hike into remote cabins or view panoramic mountains and pristine
   glacial lakes
□ Enjoy world class sport fishing both in fresh and salt water
□ Learn how salmon are reared at the hatchery or see them migrate
   upstream through various fish passes

Whatever your recreational desires, we can accommodate you, so begin *your*
Alaska wilderness experience on beautiful Prince of Wales, the island of contrasts.

**Prince
of Wales
Island**

Hydaburg was founded in 1911, and combined the populations of 3 Haida villages: Sukkwan, Howkan and Klinkwan. (© David J. Job)

the foreseeable future. Construction and government jobs will increase as the island and its economy develop.

Craig is the home port of many commercial fishing and charter sportfishing boats due to its proximity to the fertile fishing grounds off the west coast of the island. Halibut, coho and chinook salmon, lingcod and red snapper (yelloweye) are the primary target species. Craig and Klawock host the annual Craig–Klawock King Salmon Derby from April to July 3, followed by a big Fourth of July parade and celebration. In late July the P.O.W. Chamber of Commerce sponsors its annual fair and logging show with booths, fair entrants and a logging competition.

In 1996 the Healing Heart totem pole was raised in Craig. The totem was carved by Tsimshian master carver Stan Marsden in memory of his son. The totem is 46 1/2 feet/14m tall and is carved from a red cedar tree more than 500 years old.

HOLLIS (pop. 111), 25 road miles/40 km from Klawock, 35 nautical miles/56 km west of Ketchikan. Hollis was a mining town with a population of 1,000 from about 1900 to 1915. In the 1950s, Hollis became the site of Ketchikan Pulp Co.'s logging camp and served as the base for timber operations on Prince of Wales Island until 1962, when the camp was moved to Thorne Bay. Recent state land sales have spurred the growth of a small residential community here.

NOTE: Although Hollis is identified in the state ferry schedules as the port of call on Prince of Wales Island for the MV *Aurora* from Ketchikan, the ferry actually docks at Clark Bay, about 2 miles/3.2 km from Hollis.

HYDABURG (pop. 406), 36 miles/58 km from Hollis, 45 miles/72 km from Craig. Hydaburg was founded in 1911, and combined the populations of 3 Haida villages: Sukkwan, Howkan and Klinkwan. President William Howard Taft established an Indian reservation on the surrounding land in 1912, but, at the residents' request, most of the land was restored to its former status as part of Tongass National Forest in 1926. Hydaburg was incorporated in 1927, 3 years after its people became citizens of the United States.

Most of the residents are commercial fishermen, although there are some jobs in construction and the timber industry. Subsistence is also a traditional and necessary part of life here. Hydaburg has an excellent collection of restored Haida totems. The totem park was developed in the 1930s by the Civilian Conservation Corps, which brought in poles from the three abandoned Haida villages. There is also good salmon fishing here in the fall.

Four boardinghouses provide rooms and meals for visitors. Groceries, hardware and sundry items available locally. There are a gift shop, gas station, public telephones, video store and cafe. Cable television is available.

KASAAN (pop. 41), a small city located at the head of Kasaan Bay, was connected to the road system in 1996. It is approximately 16 miles/25.6 km south of Thorne Bay. There are a bed and breakfast, small cafe, a post office, a school and boat docks.

KLAWOCK (pop. 759), 24 miles/39 km from Hollis. Klawock originally was a Tlingit Indian summer fishing village; a trading post and salmon saltery were established here in 1868. Ten years later a salmon cannery was built—the first cannery in Alaska and the first of several cannery operations in the area. Over the years the population of Klawock, like other Southeast communities, grew and then declined with the salmon harvest. The local economy is still dependent on fishing, along with timber cutting and sawmilling. A fish hatchery operated by Prince of Wales Hatchery Assoc. is located on Klawock Lake, very near the site of a salmon hatchery that operated from 1897 until 1917. Visitors are welcome. Klawock Lake offers good canoeing and boating.

Recreation here includes good fishing for salmon and steelhead in Klawock River, saltwater halibut fishing, and deer and bear hunting. Klawock's totem park contains 21 totems—both replicas and originals—from the abandoned Indian village of Tuxekan (developed by the Civilian Conservation Corps in 1938–40). A 5-year restoration project to restore and replace totems in the park was begun in 1995.

Groceries and gas are available in Klawock. Automatic teller machine located in A&P grocery store. Accommodations available at Columbine Inn (907/755-2287) and Log Cabin Resort (800/544-2205). Log Cabin Resort also offers full-hookup RV sites on the beach. Meals at Dave's Diner. Charters for fishing and whalewatching from Lemire Charters (907/826-3007). ▲

NAUKATI (pop. 250). Located 61 miles/97.6 km north of Hollis, Naukati was established as a mining camp, and is currently a logging camp for Ketchikan Pulp Co. Naukati West is privately owned. The Naukati Connection has groceries, gas, propane, liquor, diesel, boat rentals, and tire repair; open daily (phone 907/629-4104). There is a school and a floatplane dock. The EMS squad can be reached on CB channel 16, VHF Channel 16 or phone (907) 629-4283 or 629-4234.

THORNE BAY (pop. 650), 59 miles/95 km from Hollis. Thorne Bay was incorporated in 1982, making it one of Alaska's newest cities. The settlement began as a logging camp in 1962, when Ketchikan Pulp Co. (a subsidiary of Louisiana Pacific Corp.) moved its operations from Hollis. Thorne Bay was connected to the island road system in 1974. Camp residents created the community—and gained city status from the state—as private ownership of the land was made possible under the Alaska Statehood Act. Employment here depends mainly on the lumber company and the U.S. Forest Service, with assorted jobs in municipal government and in local trades and services. Thorne Bay is centrally located between 2 popular Forest Service recreation areas: Eagle's Nest Campground and Sandy Beach picnic area. The Thorne River offers excellent canoeing and kayaking, and the bay offers excellent sailing and waterskiing (wet suit advised).

Accommodations available at Deer Creek Cottage (800) 830-3393, McFarland's Floatel (888) 828-3335 and several bed and breakfast establishments. Call City Hall for listings, (907) 828-3380. General merchandise and fishing and hunting supplies at the Thorne Bay Company (907/828-3330). Boat rentals available. Fuel for boats may be purchased at the Thorne Bay Co. float (unleaded) and JC's float (diesel, unleaded). The Thorne Bay Co. is open Monday through Saturday, 9 A.M. to 6 P.M., and 10 A.M. to 4 P.M. on Sunday. JC's is open daily, 7 A.M. to 6 P.M. Aviation fuel available through Petro Marine. City-operated RV dump station. Groceries available from Thorne Bay Market. Facilities include boat dock (with potable water, power, sewer pumpout station and fish cleaning facilities), cement boat-launch ramp, helicopter landing pad, and floatplane float and parking facilities. ▲

WHALE PASS (pop. 92), accessible by 7-mile/11.3-km loop road from **Milepost 39.7** North Island Road, was the site of a floating logging camp on Whale Passage. The camp moved out in the early 1980s, but new residents moved in with a state land sale. The community has a small grocery store and gas pump; cabins and freezer space available. There is also a school, post office and floatplane dock. Accommodations at Northend Cabin (907/846-5315). Good fishing on the loop road into Whale Pass.

Hollis–Klawock–Craig Highway Log

This highway, 31.5 miles/50.7 km long, begins at the ferry landing at Hollis and heads west through Klawock then south to Craig, taking motorists through the temperate rainforest environment typical of Southeast Alaska. It is a wide, paved road. Posted speed is 35 to 50 mph/56 to 80 kmph.

Many roads and trails off highway lead to private property; please respect barricades and No Trespassing signs. *CAUTION: Watch for logging trucks.*

Distance from Hollis (H) is followed by distance from Craig (C). Physical mileposts show distance from Craig.

H 0 C 31.5 (50.7 km) Alaska Marine Highway, Hollis ferry terminal at Clark Bay, open during ferry arrivals and departures only (phone 907/530-7115, or in Craig 826-3432). Pay phone; no other services.

H 0.2 (0.3 km) **C 31.3** (50.4 km) Clark Bay subdivision access to right.

H 1.4 (2.3 km) **C 30.1** (48.4 km) Left 0.3 mile to Hollis townsite. School and USFS office, city harbor and float, floatplane dock, post office, telephone; no other services.

H 2 (3.2 km) **C 29.5** (47.5 km) Alaska Power and Telephone power plant and Alascom satellite station to left. Hollis Fire Department and EMS garage to right.

H 2.4 (3.9 km) **C 29.1** (46.8 km) **Maybeso Creek**, cutthroat; Dolly Varden; pink and silver salmon; steelhead run begins in mid-April. Pools offer the best fishing. Walking good along streambed but poor along bank. Watch for bears.

H 4.2 (6.8 km) **C 27.3** (43.9 km) Turnout left, view of mouth of the Harris River.

H 4.8 (7.7 km) **C 26.7** (43 km) Head left for lower Harris subdivision.

H 5.2 (8.4 km) **C 26.3** (42.3 km) Turnout, one of several slide-damaged areas from October 1993 storm that dumped 11 inches of rain in 24 hours.

H 6.4 (10.3 km) **C 25.1** (40.4 km) Entering Tongass National Forest.

H 6.5 (10.5 km) **C 25** (40.2 km) Head left for upper Harris subdivision.

H 7.7 (12.4 km) **C 23.8** (38.3 km) Turnout, slide damage repaired.

H 8.4 (13.5 km) **C 23.1** (37.2 km) USFS hiking trail to **Harris River** fishing: cutthroat; steelhead run mid-April; salmon and Dolly Varden run beginning in mid-July. Easy walking on the gravel bars in the middle of 1.3-mile/2.1-km-long river.

H 8.5 (13.7 km) **C 23** (37 km) Turnout, slide damage repaired.

H 10.5 (16.9 km) **C 21** (33.8 km) **Junction** with Hydaburg Road; see log this section.

H 11.2 (18 km) **C 20.3** (32.7 km) USFS trailhead for 20 Mile Spur Trail (approximately 3 miles/4.8 km long).

H 11.3 (18.2 km) **C 20.2** (32.5 km) Harris River bridge.

H 12.4 (20 km) **C 19.1** (30.7 km) End of Harris River valley. Island divide is here at 500 feet/152m elev.; streams now flow west. Turnout state DOT gravel storage area.

H 12.6 (20.3 km) **C 18.9** (30.4 km) Leaving Tongass National Forest.

H 13.6 (21.9 km) **C 17.9** (28.8 km) East end of Klawock Lake, about 7 miles/11 km long and up to 1 mile/1.6 km wide. Lake borders the road on the left at several places. Private property; contact Klawock–Heenya Corp. in Klawock.

H 16.1 (25.9 km) **C 15.4** (24.8 km) Turnout left, boat launch for Klawock Lake.

H 16.2 (26.1 km) **C 15.3** (24.6 km) 35 mph/56 kmph curve; believe the sign.

H 17.6 (28.3 km) **C 13.9** (22.4 km) Turnout left, view of Klawock Lake.

H 20.1 (32.3 km) **C 11.4** (18.3 km) Turnout right, view of Klawock Lake.

H 22 (33.7 km) **C 9.5** (16.9 km) **Prince of Wales** *Hatchery*, operated by the Prince of

Klawock, 24 miles from Hollis, was originally a Tlingit Indian summer fishing village. (© David J. Job)

Wales Assoc. The hatchery produces sockeye, coho and steelhead. Visitors welcome; Daily tours, phone (907) 755-2231.

H 22.1 (35.6 km) **C 9.4** (15.1 km) Klawock-Heenya Trailer Court to right; turnout left for trail access to Klawock River sportfishing.

H 22.2 (35.7 km) **C 9.3** (15 km) Turnout left, access to Klawock River fishing.

H 22.3 (35.9 km) **C 9.2** (14.8 km) Turnout left, access to Klawock River fishing.

H 22.4 (36 km) **C 9.1** (14.6 km) Turnout left, access to Klawock River fishing.

H 23.3 (37.5 km) **C 8.2** (13.2 km) Belltower Mall, grocery store, liquor store, gift shop and Papa's Pizza.

H 23.4 (37.7 km) **C 8.1** (13 km) **Junction** with Big Salt Road; access to Thorne Bay, Kasaan, Coffman Cove, Naukati, Whale Pass and the north end of the island.

H 23.5 (37.8 km) **C 8** (12.9 km) Turnoff right, services available.

H 23.7 (38.1 km) **C 7.8** (12.6 km) Fireweed Lodge to left, St. John's by the Sea Catholic Church to right. St. John's was designed and built with local lumber and materials by the local church community. The stained-glass designs, representing all known Native tribes, were designed and built by local artists. This is a "must-see" structure. Father Jim Blaney and Sister Tish welcome the opportunity to show the church. Good eagle viewing in Klawock River estuary during salmon season.

H 23.8 (38.3 km) **C 7.7** (12.4 km) Loop road with 21 totem poles.

H 23.9 (38.5 km) **C 7.6** (12.2 km) Klawock-Heenya Corp. offices.

H 24.2 (38.9 km) **C 7.3** (11.7 km) **Klawock River** bridge spans tidal estuary where river meets salt water.

H 24.3 (39.1 km) **C 7.2** (11.6 km) Klawock Fuels (gas and diesel), Alaska State Troopers and Alaska Dept. of Fish and Game to left. Alesha Roberts Center.

H 24.5 (39.4 km) **C 7** (11.3 km) Leaving village of **KLAWOCK**. State troopers in building on left.

H 24.6 (39.6 km) **C 6.9** (11.1 km) Turnoff right to Phoenix log sort yard, Phoenix shop and Klawock Indian Corp. dock. Oceangoing vessels load locally harvested logs for

worldwide transport.

H 25 (40.2 km) **C 6.5** (10.5 km) Viking Lumber Co. mill; produces moulding, window and door stock for the domestic market and high-grade cants for export.

H 26.6 (42.8 km) **C 4.9** (7.9 km) Turnout right, scenic view of Klawock Inlet and San Alberto Bay.

H 27.9 (44.9 km) **C 3.6** (5.8 km) On left is landfill operated by city of Klawock. Bears can usually be seen here.

H 29.1 (46.8 km) **C 2.4** (3.9 km) Crab Creek subdivision.

H 29.3 (47.2 km) **C 2.2** (3.5 km) Crab Creek bridge.

H 29.8 (48 km) **C 1.7** (2.7 km) Shaan-Seet Trailer Court and St. Nicholas Road to left. St. Nicholas Road, which extends 14 miles/22.5 km around Port St. Nicholas, is scenic but in very poor condition.

H 30.1 (48.5 km) **C 1.4** (2.2 km) P.O.W. Chamber of Commerce on right.

H 30.2 (48.6 km) **C 1.3** (2.1 km) Craig schools to left, post office, bank and Thompson House supermarket on right.

H 30.3 (48.8 km) **C 1.2** (1.9 km) Cold Storage Road. Dump station on right, behind supermarket.

H 30.4 (48.9 km) **C 1.1** (1.8 km) North and South Cove Harbors operated by the city of Craig. Turn left for Cemetery Island, ballpark and archaeological dig.

H 30.7 (49.4 km) **C 0.8** (1.3 km) Stop sign, downtown **CRAIG**. Turn left 1 block for Craig municipal offices and city gym. Craig clinic is on left, half block past city office. End of highway is 3 blocks right.

H 31 (49.9 km) **C 0.5** (0.8 km) Road dead ends.

Big Salt Road Log

Big Salt Road begins at **Milepost C 8.1** on the Hollis–Klawock–Craig Highway and extends 17.1 miles/27.5 km, ending at its junction with Thorne Bay Road. It is a gravel road with much logging traffic; scheduled for seal coating. Top speed for much of the road is 25 mph/40 kmph. Good berry picking for blueberries and huckleberries along

the road.
Distance is measured from Klawock.

0 Black Bear Quick Stop: grocery store, laundromat and gas station. Dave's Diner/Restaurant.

0.1 (0.2 km) Klawock city trailer park on right with some overnight sites; obtain permits from the city clerk. A camping fee is charged. ▲

0.4 (0.6 km) Log Cabin R.V. Park & Resort: tackle store, skiff rentals, lodging and campground. ▲

0.9 (1.4 km) Airport turnoff. Pavement ends.

8.7 (14 km) Big Salt Lake, actually a saltwater body protected by small islands but permitting tidal flow in and out, is visible to the left from several spots along road. Waterfowl and bald eagles are often observed here. Wreckage of a military aircraft can be seen across lake. The plane crashed in 1969 en route to Vietnam; all on board survived.

8.9 (14.3 km) Boat ramp and canoe launching area on Big Salt Lake. If boating on this tidal lake, be aware of strong currents.

9.7 (15.6 km) **Black Bear Creek**, cutthroat; Dolly Varden; red, pink, dog and silver salmon, run mid-July to mid-September. Except for the lower 2 miles/3.2 km, creek can be fished from the bank. Best at the mouth of stream, 200 yards/183m upstream from the bridge or in large meadow, 1.5 miles/2.4 km from the mouth. Road on right leads to Black Lake. Watch for heavy equipment. ◄━

12.6 (20.3 km) **Steelhead Creek**, cutthroat; Dolly Varden; steelhead; pink, dog and silver salmon. Creek can be reached by boat through south entrance to Big Salt Lake. Lake should only be entered during high and low slack tides due to the strong tidal currents. High tide in lake is delayed 2 hours from outside waters. Bank fishing restricted by undergrowth. ◄━

15 (24.1 km) Lovely muskeg on right.

16.6 (26.7 km) Short boardwalk on right leads to **Control Lake**, cutthroat; Dolly Varden; pink and silver salmon; good red salmon stream in August. USFS cabin on other side is available for public use. Skiff docked at end of boardwalk is for registered cabin users. Wolf population in area. ◄━

17.1 (27.5 km) **Control Lake Junction.** Junction of Big Salt Road (SR 929) with Thorne Bay Road and North Island Road (FR 20). Road to Thorne Bay (log follows) to east. Road to Labouchere Bay, with access to Whale Pass and Coffman Cove, to north; see North Island Road log this section. Turn right for Eagle's Nest Campground. ▲

Thorne Bay Road Log

Thorne Bay Road extends 18 miles/29 km to Thorne Bay logging camp.
Physical mileposts show distance from Thorne Bay post office.

18 (29 km) **Control Lake Junction.** Junction with Big Salt Road and North Island Road.

16.6 (26.7 km) Eagle's Nest USFS campground; 12 sites, tables, water, hand pump, toilet and canoe launch. Camping fee $8. **Balls Lake**, cutthroat; Dolly Varden; red, pink and silver salmon. ◄━▲

13 (20.9 km) Bridge. **Rio Roberts** and **Rio Beaver creeks**, cutthroat; pink and silver

salmon. A 0.7-mile/1.1-km cedar-chip and double-plank boardwalk leads to a viewing deck overlooking falls and Rio Roberts Fish Pass. ◄━

10.7 (17.2 km) Rio Beaver Creek bridge.

6.7 (10.8 km) **Goose Creek**, cutthroat; pink and silver salmon. Excellent spawning stream. Good run of pink salmon in mid-August. Lake Ellen Road on right leads 4.5 miles/7.2 km south to Lake No. 3 USFS campsite; space to accommodate up to 2 RVs, pit toilet, 2 fire rings and 2 picnic tables. No water or garbage. Road continues beyond campsite to lake and hiking trail to Salt Chuck. Abandoned Salt Chuck Mine is located here. ◄━▲

6.5 (10.5 km) **Thorne River** runs beside road for the next 0.5 mile/0.8 km. Cutthroat; Dolly Varden; steelhead; rainbow; red, pink, dog and silver salmon. Excellent fishing reported from **Milepost 4.9** to **2.1**. ◄━

4.9 (7.9 km) Thorne River bridge. Thorne River now follows road on right.

4.1 (6.6 km) Falls Creek.

4 (6.4 km) **Gravelly Creek** USFS picnic area; walk in to picnic area on the bank of Thorne River at the mouth of Gravelly Creek; 3 tables, fire rings, vault toilet and open-sided shelter. This site was logged in 1918. Note the large stumps with notches. Notches were used by old-time loggers for spring boards to stand on while sawing or chopping.

3.7 (5.9 km) Gravelly Creek.

2.1 (3.4 km) Right, mouth of Thorne River.

1.3 (2.1 km) Log sorting area. Here different species of logs are sorted for rafting and transporting to mills or for export.

1.2 (1.9 km) Log raft holding area. After logs are sorted and tied into bundles, the bundles are chained together into a raft suitable for towing by tugboat.

0.7 (1.1 km) Dump station on Shoreline Drive just past Bayview Tire; $5 charge.

0 THORNE BAY. The road extends about 10 miles/16 km beyond the community to Sandy Beach day-use area with picnic shelter, 6 tables, fire rings, vault toilet and RV parking. Good view of Clarence Strait. Road then continues north to Coffman Cove.

Kasaan Road Log

This narrow road runs southeast 17.1 miles/27.3 km from Thorne Bay Road to Kasaan. Turnouts, occurring every 1/10 mile, are only noted if some other feature is present. A warning sign says to monitor CB channel 3.
Distance is measured from Thorne Bay Road Mile 6.7.

0 Turn off Thorne Bay Road just past Goose Creek. South to Kasaan.

0.4 (0.6 km) Road splits. Veer north for Kasaan, south for Forest Service campsite. Speed limit 20 mph/32 kmph. ▲

0.5 (0.8 km) Private drive next 1 mile/1.6 km. No hunting. Shake mill to south.

0.6 (1 km) Thorne Bay solid waste facility to north.

0.8 (1.3 km) Sawmill to south.

1.2 (1.9 km) Turnout north. Unnamed lake to north. Informal picnic site.

1.4 (2.2 km) Gravel pit to north.

2.1 (3.4 km) 15 mph/24 kmph curve. Turnout to north at the end of the curve.

Slide area.

3.0 (4.8 km) Turnout to north. First view of the waters of Thorne Bay.

4.1 (6.6 km) Road was built around a huge rock. Keep to the right. Note tree growing on top of the rock and splitting it in half.

4.4 (7 km) Water hose to the right.

4.6 (7.4 km) Turnout to south. Informal campsite in old gravel pit.

5.3 (8.5 km) Muskeg to north. Turnout to south.

5.4 (8.6 km) 15 mph/24 kmph curve. No Hunting sign. Road splits; keep north for Kasaan.

5.5 (8.8 km) Turnout to south. Road changes to packed shot-rock. Observe sign— "One lane road with pullouts."

5.6 (9 km) Turnouts to north and south. Informal campsite.

6.1 (9.8 km) Turnouts to north and south. Informal tent site.

6.5 (10.4 km) Turnout to north. Setter Lake to east.

6.7 (10.7 km) Turnout to north. View of small lake for next 0.2 mile/0.3 km.

6.9 (11 km) Turnout to south. Informal campsite.

7.1 (11.4 km) Turnout to north. Informal picnic site.

8.8 (14.1 km) Bridge over creek. Turnout to south.

9.2 (14.7 km) Turnout to north. Glimpse of Loon Lake to west.

10.2 (16.3 km) Beaver dam to south. Road crosses over a culvert.

10.5 (16.8 km) Informal picnic site to south.

10.8 (17.3 km) Good view of Tolstoi Bay. Beach access, boat portage. Informal picnic site. 10 mph/16 kmph, one-lane road for next 0.5 mile/0.8 km. Packed shot-rock ends and gravel begins.

11.6 (18.6 km) Bridges with stop signs over creek.

11.7 (18.7 km) Informal campsite to north in the old rock pit.

11.9 (19 km) Informal campsite to north in the old rock pit.

12.5 (20 km) Turnout to north. Informal campsite in the old rock pit.

12.8 (20.5 km) Turnout to north. Sign announces that surrounding forest was harvested in 1973 by Sealaska and thinned in 1993.

13 (20.8 km) Sign on a stump notes trap line 1993–94.

13.1 (21 km) Road splits. Veer south over the bridge for Kasaan. 2000 Road to north.

13.2 (21.1 km) Beaver dams can be seen along creek.

13.9 (22.2 km) Road crosses both north and south.

14.3 (22.9 km) 2300 Road to north.

14.5 (23.2 km) First view of Kasaan Bay and up Twelvemile Arm. Please remember this land is privately owned. Contact Sealaska for permission to camp.

15 (24 km) Turnout to south. Road to north.

15.2 (24.3 km) Road to north.

15.7 (25.1 km) Beautiful viewpoint of Kasaan Bay.

16.1 (25.8 km) Road to south. Note alpine ridge lines.

16.5 (26.4 km) Road to south.

16.9 (27 km) Wide turnout to south.

17.1 (27.4 km) Stop sign. Turn south for Kasaan and totem park, go straight for Dexter Wallace Harbor. To get to the totem park, turn south and head towards the waterfront, driving all the way to the end of the road. At the bed and breakfast ask Annette Thompson for permission to walk down the path and for a personal tour of the totem park.

Hydaburg Road Log

The Hydaburg Road is 24 miles/38.6 km long and begins 11 miles/17.7 km west of the Hollis main ferry terminal on the Hollis–Klawock–Craig Highway. Some sections of the road are heavily used by logging trucks.

0 Junction with Hollis–Klawock–Craig Highway at **Milepost H 10.5.**

1.1 (1.8 km) Harris River bridge.

2.6 (4.2 km) Trailhead for One Duck 1.3-mile/2.1-km-long trail to alpine area and shelter. Contact the USFS office for more information on all trails along the Hydaburg Road.

4.6 (7.4 km) Bridge over Trocadero Creek.

8.9 (14.3 km) Cable Creek fish pass. Boardwalk to viewing area overlooking stream.

9.3 (15 km) Trocadero trailhead, gravel pullout.

9.5 (15.2 km) Trocadero picnic area. Picnic tables and fire grills; no toilets, trash service or water. Good view of Trocadero Valley.

9.9 (15.9 km) Road on left leads to Twelvemile Arm. This logging road leads to Polk Inlet. Watch for logging and construction activity.

12.3 (19.8 km) Trailhead for Soda Springs trail, 2.5 miles/4 km long.

13.9 (22.4 km) North Pass.

15.6 (25.1 km) Natzuhini logging camp.

15.9 (25.6 km) Natzuhini River bridge.

16.8 (27 km) Road winds along Natzuhini Bay.

21.9 (35.2 km) Hydaburg River bridge.

22.3 (35.9 km) Quarry Road to right.

23.6 (38 km) T-junction: right to Hydaburg, left to Saltery Point. Private land. No trespassing.

24 (38.6 km) **HYDABURG.**

North Island Road Log

Signed as USFS Road No. 20, this narrow 2-lane road leads north 79.5 miles/127.9 km from its junction with Big Salt and Thorne Bay roads near Control Lake to Labouchere Bay on the northwest corner of the island. The road has a fair to excellent gravel surfacing and some steep grades. Slow down for approaching vehicles. Posted speed is 25 mph/40 kmph. Gas is available at Whale Pass and Coffman Cove.

0 Control Lake Junction, junction with Big Salt and Thorne Bay roads near Control Lake.

3.1 (5 km) Drinking water on right (from hose).

4.8 (7.7 km) USFS Road No. 2050 leads west to upper Staney Creek/Horseshoe Hole and loops back to Road No. 20. Access to Staney Bridge campsite. ▲

7.4 (11.9 km) Rock quarry to east.

10.9 (17.5 km) USFS Road No. 2054 leads west to Staney Creek campsite, Staney Creek cabin and access to salt water. ▲

15.5 (24.9 km) **Junction** with Coffman Cove Road (see log this section).

18.4 (29.6 km) Naukati Creek.

19.2 (30.9 km) View to west of Tuxekan Island and Passage.

21 (33.8 km) Logging road leads west to Naukati Bay.

21.4 (34.4 km) Yatuk Creek bridge.

23.3 (37.5 km) **NAUKATI**, established and operating as a mining camp, is 3 miles/4.8 km west. The population has grown due to a state land sale. Liquor, grocery, gas, boat rentals and boat repair available.

CAUTION: Road narrows northbound.

26.5 (42.6 km) **Sarkar Lake** to east. Fishing and boat launch. USFS public-use cabin at east end of lake. Public toilets. Skiff docked at end of dock for registered cabin users only. ◄

27.9 (44.9 km) Bridge over Sarkar Lake outlet to salt water. Good spot to see eagles and sea lions during salmon season.

39.7 (63.9 km) USFS Road No. 25 leads east 7 miles/11.3 km past Neck Lake to small settlement of **WHALE PASS**; groceries and gas available, 4 cabins, floatplane dock, post office and school (1 teacher, 13 grades). Whale Pass Road loops back to the main North Island Road at **Milepost 48.6.**

40 (64.4 km) View of Neck Lake to east.

48.6 (78.2 km) Whale Pass loop road to east. Whale Pass is 8 miles/12.9 km from here; Exchange Cove is 16 miles/25.7 km from here.

50.3 (80.9 km) View of El Capitan Passage and Kosciusko Island to west.

51 (82.1 km) Side road leads west 1 mile/1.6 km to USFS El Cap Work Center; access to El Capitan Cave. Public toilets.

55.6 (89.5 km) Summit of the North Island Road (elev. 907 feet/276m). Keep an eye out for highbush cranberries.

59.5 (95.8 km) Rough road, heavy truck traffic and 1-lane bridges north from here.

60.6 (97.5 km) Red Creek 1-lane bridge.

61.7 (99.3 km) Big Creek 1-lane bridge.

63.9 (102.8 km) View of Red Bay to north; Red Lake is to the south.

67.6 (108.8 km) Buster Creek 1-lane bridge.

68.3 (109.9 km) Shine Creek 1-lane bridge.

72 (115.9 km) Flicker Creek 1-lane bridge.

72.1 (116 km) Memorial Beach picnic area 1.7 miles/2.7 km north; follow signs to parking area. A short trail leads to picnic tables, pit toilet, memorial plaque and beach. Good view of Sumner Strait and Kupreanof Island. This site is a memorial to 12 victims of a 1978 air crash.

79.5 (127.9 km) **LABOUCHERE BAY**, a small logging camp (no facilities) owned and operated by Louisiana Pacific Corp. The road continues several miles and dead ends at the base of Mount Calder.

Coffman Cove Road Log

Coffman Cove Road branches off the North Island Road (No. 20) at **Milepost 15.5** and leads east and north 20.5 miles/33 km to the logging camp of Coffman Cove. Watch for heavy truck traffic; 25 mph/40 kmph. Slow down for approaching vehicles.

0 Junction with North Island Road.

4.4 (7.1 km) Side road on left (USFS Road No. 30) leads 5 miles/8 km through clear-cut and dead ends.

4.5 (7.2 km) **Logjam Creek** bridge; cut-

Killer whales are commonly sighted in Alaska waters. (© Robin Brandt)

throat and steelhead; Dolly Varden; pink, silver and sockeye salmon.

9.1 (14.6 km) **Hatchery Creek** bridge; fishing same as Logjam Creek. Trailhead for canoe route to Thorne Bay. ◄

9.4 (15.1 km) Bumpy road on right leads 13 miles/20.9 km to USFS parking area and canoe launch (no trailers) on Luck Lake, and junctions with the 3030 Road between Coffman Cove and Thorne Bay.

12.1 (19.5 km) View of Sweetwater Lake to left. USFS access site: parking area for Sweetwater public-use cabin, located 0.5 mile/0.8 km along west shore of lake.

17 (27.4 km) Coffman Creek bridge.

19.5 (31.4 km) Chum Creek bridge.

20.2 (32.5 km) **Junction** with Luck Lake loop road.

20.3 (32.7 km) Chum Creek bridge.

20.5 (33 km) **COFFMAN COVE**, a logging and fishing community; groceries, gas, cafe, rental cabins, gifts and local fresh oysters.

Coffman Cove–Thorne Bay Road Log

The 3030 Road travels 36.1 miles/57.8 km between Coffman Cove and Thorne Bay. Leaving Coffman Cove southbound, cross Dog Creek and begin on the 3030 Road. Turnouts are frequent but are noted here only if some other feature is present. A warning sign says to monitor CB channel 20.
Distance from Coffman Cove (C) is followed by distance from Thorne Bay (T).

C 0.6 (1 km) **T 35.5** (56.8 km) End of Muskeg Subdivision. Boardwalk to west is a private residence.

C 1.1 (1.8 km) **T 35** (56 km) Road crosses over a small creek.

C 1.7 (2.7 km) **T 34.4** (55 km) Rock pit to west. Grassy pullout to east; nice area for a picnic.

C 2.5 (4 km) **T 33.6** (53.8 km) Milepost 6. Road crosses over a small creek.

C 3.3 (5.3 km) **T 32.8** (52.5 km) Turnout to west. View of Clarence Strait, to the east, begins for next 0.6 mile/1 km.

C 3.6 (5.8 km) **T 32.5** (52 km) Turnout to east. Nice informal campsite.

C 3.9 (6.2 km) **T 32.2** (51.5 km) Turnout to east. Rock pit to west. Good view of Clarence Strait.

C 4.5 (7.2 km) **T 31.6** (50.6 km) Turnout to east. Room for a small camp. Last View of Clarence Strait for 10 miles/16 km.

C 5 (8 km) **T 31.1** (49.8 km) Turnout to east. Road veers to west.

C 7 (11.2 km) **T 29.1** (46.6 km) Turnout to east. Beginning of Luck Lake trailhead.

C 7.3 (11.7 km) **T 28.8** (46.1 km) Turnout to east. View of Luck Lake to east.

C 7.8 (12.5 km) **T 28.3** (45.3 km) Turnout to east. Good view of Luck Lake to east.

C 8.5 (13.6 km) **T 27.6** (44.2 km) Intersection. Turn east to Thorne Bay and Lick Creek. Turn west to Naukati (29 miles/46.4 km) and Hollis (74 miles/118.4 km). Southbound Forest Service Road 30 continues. Good informal campsite to west.

C 8.9 (14.2 km) **T 27.2** (43.5 km) Road crosses over Luck Creek. Turnouts both east and west. Good salmon-watching stream late August/early September.

C 9.2 (14.7 km) **T 26.9** (43 km) Milepost 45. Road crosses over creek. Road off to east.

C 9.5 (15.2 km) **T 26.6** (42.6 km) Steep, narrow climb begins for next 1.2 miles/1.9 km.

C 9.7 (15.5 km) **T 26.4** (42.2 km) Turnout to west. View to east of alder forest, view to west of alpine forest.

C 10.6 (17 km) **T 25.5** (40.8 km) Turnout to west. Heed warning sign of 15 mph/24 kmph curves for next 0.3 mile/0.5 km.

C 11.4 (18.2 km) **T 24.7** (39.5 km) Steep, narrow road continues to climb up mountainside. Good view to west of alpine forest.

C 11.6 (18.6 km) **T 24.5** (39.2 km) Turnout to west. Good informal campsite. Excellent view of mountainside.

C 12.2 (19.5 km) **T 23.9** (38.2 km) Turnout to west. Heed 15 mph/24 kmph curves warning.

C 12.5 (20 km) **T 23.6** (37.8 km) Turnout to west. Big gravel pit to east. Good view overlooking muskeg and alpine above.

C 13.2 (21.1 km) **T 22.9** (36.6 km) Milepost 41. Road crosses over a little creek. Good berry picking next 0.5 mile/0.8 km in season.

C 13.8 (22.1 km) **T 22.3** (35.7 km) Turnout to west. View of Little Lake to the east, next 0.5 mile/0.8 km.

C 14.2 (22.7 km) **T 21.9** (35 km) Turnout to east. Milepost 40.

C 14.5 (23.2 km) **T 21.6** (34.6 km) Turnout to west. Road leads to gravel pit and through muskeg. Southbound intersection sign: veer west on FS 30 for Sandy Beach (16 miles/25.6 km) and Thorne Bay (22 miles/35.2 km). East is FS 3026.

C 14.6 (23.4 km) **T 21.5** (34.4 km) Northbound intersection sign indicates Luck Lake (10 miles/16 km), Coffman Cove (15 miles/24 km) and Hollis (80 miles/128 km). West is FS 3026. First view of Clarence Strait.

C 15.3 (24.5 km) **T 20.8** (33.3 km) Turnout to east. View of Clarence strait.

C 15.6 (25 km) **T 20.5** (32.8 km) Turnout to east. Descent for next 0.3 mile/0.5 km.

C 16.3 (26.1 km) **T 19.8** (31.7 km) Turnouts both east and west. Bridge over small stream. Good salmon viewing in late August and early September.

C 16.4 (26.2 km) **T 19.7** (31.5 km) Turnout to east. Bridge over Big Ratz Creek.

C 17.5 (28 km) **T 18.6** (29.8 km) Turnout to the east. Road to the west.

C 17.6 (28.2 km) **T 18.5** (29.6 km) Turnout to west. Road to west.

C 18.2 (29.1 km) **T 17.9** (28.6 km) Turnout to west. First view of Clarence Strait at sea level, continues for next 0.3 mile/0.5 km. Ratz Harbor and beach to east. Road construction 2 miles/3.2 km.

C 18.5 (29.6 km) **T 17.6** (28.2 km) Road crosses over culvert. Turnout to east, with beach access. Road to west. Good informal campsite.

C 18.7 (29.9 km) **T 17.4** (27.8 km) Road runs through salt marsh estuary next 0.1 mile/ 0.2 km. Turnout to west.

C 20.3 (32.5 km) **T 15.8** (25.8 km) Truck crossing.

C 20.7 (33.1 km) **T 15.4** (24.6 km) Bridge over small creek. Good salmon-viewing stream in early September.

C 21 (33.6 km) **T 15.1** (24.2 km) Road to west. Road narrows next 1 mile/1.6 km.

C 21.6 (34.6 km) **T 14.5** (23.2 km) Road to east.

C 21.8 (34.9 km) **T 14.3** (22.9 km) Turnout to west. Curves for 2 miles/3.2 km. View of Clarence Strait.

C 22 (35.2 km) **T 14.1** (22.6 km) Viewpoint east. Possible to see humpback and orca whales and dall porpoise. Road runs along steep mountainside for next 2 miles/3.2 km.

C 22.4 (35.8 km) **T 13.7** (21.9 km) Viewpoint. In kelp beds otters may be visible.

C 24.8 (39.7 km) **T 11.3** (18.1 km) Turnouts to east and west. Road narrows next 0.3 mile/0.5 km.

C 25.5 (40.8 km) **T 10.6** (17 km) Road to west.

C 25.6 (41 km) **T 10.5** (16.8 km) 3020 Road intersects.

C 26.9 (43 km) **T 9.2** (14.7 km) Road crosses over a culvert. Turnout to east. Beach and view of Clarence Strait next 0.4 mile/0.6 km.

C 27.3 (43.7 km) **T 8.8** (14.1 km) Turnout to east. Beach access.

C 28.2 (45.1 km) **T 7.9** (12.6 km) Turnout to east. View of cove and beach access next 0.2 mile/0.3 km.

C 30.2 (48.3 km) **T 5.9** (9.4 km) Bridge over Barren Creek. Salmon viewing. Turnout to west after bridge.

C 30.3 (48.5 km) **T 5.8** (9.3 km) Turnout to west. Sandy Beach access. Firepit, outhouse, beach access, covered picnic area and trash cans. Parking to east.

C 30.9 (49.4 km) **T 5.2** (8.3 km) Bridge over Slide Creek. Salmon viewing. Turnout to east. Informal campsite.

C 32.7 (52.3 km) **T 3.4** (5.4 km) Milepost 22. Turnout to east. Informal campsite. Road to west.

C 35.4 (56.6 km) **T 0.7**(1.1 km) FS 3018 road to west.

C 35.6 (57 km) **T 0.5** (0.8 km) Road crosses over culvert and runs along marsh to the east for next 0.5 mile/0.8 km. Milepost 19. Turnout to east.

C 35.7 (57.1 km) **T 0.4** (0.6 km) Creek with natural dams to east. Turnout to west.

C 36 (57.6 km) **T 0.1** (0.2 km) No hunting begins southbound. Turnout to east.

C 36.1 (57.8 km) **T 0** Turnout to west. Veer east for Thorne Bay. Private land and city limits begin here.

Alaska state ferry approaches Wrangell ferry dock. (© Crystal Images, Kathleen Marie Menke)

Wrangell

(See map, page 670)

Located at northwest tip of Wrangell Island on Zimovia Strait; 6 miles/9.6 km southwest of the mouth of the Stikine River delta; 3 hours by ferry or 32 air miles/51 km southeast of Petersburg, the closest major community; and 6 hours by ferry or 85 air miles/136 km north of Ketchikan. **Population:** 2,400. **Emergency Services:** Phone 911 for all emergencies. **Police**, phone (907) 874-3304. **Fire Department** and **Ambulance**, phone (907) 874-2000. **Hospital**, Wrangell General, 310 Bennett St. just off Zimovia Highway, phone (907) 874-7000. **Maritime Search and Rescue**, contact the Coast Guard at (800) 478-5555.

Visitor Information: Center located in the Stikine Inn Building at 107 Stikine Ave., near the cruise ship dock; phone (800) 367-9745 or (907) 874-3901, fax (907) 874-3905, Internet: www.wrangell.com, e-mail: wrangell@wrangell.com. Write: Chamber of Commerce, Box 49MP, Wrangell, AK 99929. Information is also available at the Wrangell Museum, 318 Church St.; phone (907) 874-3770.

The U.S. Forest Service maintains several recreation sites and trails along the Wrangell Island road system, as well as remote cabins. Contact the USFS office in Wrangell, 525 Bennett St., phone (907) 874-2323.

Elevation: Sea level. **Climate:** Mild and moist with slightly less rain than other Southeast communities. Mean annual precipitation is 79.2 inches, with 63.9 inches of snow. Record monthly precipitation, 20.43 inches in October 1961. Average daily maximum temperature in June is 61°F/16°C; in July 64°F/18°C. Daily minimum in January is 21°F/-6°C. **Radio:** KSTK-FM 101.7. **Televi-**

sion: Cable and satellite. **Newspaper:** *Wrangell Sentinel* (weekly).

Private Aircraft: Wrangell airport, adjacent northeast; elev. 44 feet/13m; length 6,000 feet/1,829m; paved; fuel 100LL, A.

Wrangell is the only Alaskan city to have existed under 4 nations and 3 flags—the Stikine Tlingits, the Russians, Great Britain and the United States. Wrangell began in 1834 as a Russian stockade called Redoubt St. Dionysius, built to prevent the Hudson's Bay Co. from fur trading up the rich Stikine River to the northeast. The Russians, in a change of policy, leased the mainland of southeastern Alaska to Hudson's Bay Co. in 1840. Under the British the stockade was called Fort Stikine.

The post remained under the British flag until Alaska was purchased by the United States in 1867. A year later the Americans established a military post here, naming it Fort Wrangell after the island, which was named by the Russians after Baron von Wrangel, a governor of the Russian–American Co.

Its strategic location near the mouth of the Stikine River, the fastest free-flowing navigable river in North America, made Wrangell an important supply point not only for fur traders but also for gold seekers following the river route to the goldfields. Today, the Stikine River is a popular hunting and recreation area. Currently, there is an active hard rock mine on the largest tributary of the Stikine, the Iskut. They are extracting gold, silver, copper and traces of other minerals from the site.

Wrangell serves as a hub for goods, services and transportation for outlying fishing villages, and logging and mining camps. The town depended largely on fishing until Japanese interests arrived in the mid-1950s and established a mill (now closed). A small, locally owned mill is now in operation 2 miles/3.2 km beyond the end of Zimovia Highway, off Forest 6265. Fishing is one of Wrangell's largest industries, with salmon the major catch.

ACCOMMODATIONS/VISITOR SERVICES

Wrangell has several motels including the Stikine Inn (907/874-3388) and Hardings Old Sourdough Lodge (907/874-3613). There are also several bed and breakfasts.

The Wrangell Hostel is located in the Presbyterian church, about ¼ mile from the ferry terminal, next to the Wrangell Museum. Open from June 9 to Labor Day, 5 P.M. to 9 A.M.; $10/night; phone (907) 874-3534.

There are 4 restaurants downtown, as well as service stations, hardware and appliance stores, banks, drugstore, laundromat, grocery stores (1 with a bakery and deli), a fish market and gift shops. Bed-and-breakfasts are available. Lodges with restaurants are located on Peninsula Street and at **Mile 4.4** Zimovia Highway.

RV camping at Alaska Waters R.V. Park on Berger street. Camping and picnic area at Shoemaker Bay, **Milepost 4.9** Zimovia High-

way. Dump stations located at Shoemaker Bay and downtown. City Park, at **Milepost 1.9** Zimovia Highway, has tent sites, camping, picnic area with tables, flush toilets, shelters and playground. ▲

TRANSPORTATION

Air: Daily scheduled jet service is provided by Alaska Airlines to other Southeast cities with through service to Seattle and Anchorage. Scheduled commuter air service to Petersburg, Kake and Ketchikan. Charter service available.

Airport terminal is 1.1 miles/1.8 km from ferry terminal or 1.1 miles/1.8 km from Zimovia Highway on Bennett Street. Hotel courtesy vans are available from the airport to downtown. Taxi service is also available for about $5.

Ferry: Alaska Marine Highway vessels connect Wrangell with all Southeastern Alaska ports plus Prince Rupert, BC, and Bellingham, WA. Ferry terminal is at the north end of town at the end of Zimovia Highway (also named Church or 2nd Street at this point). Walk or take a taxi from terminal to town for approximately $4. Tours for independent travelers are available downtown. Terminal facilities include ticket office, waiting room and vehicle waiting area. Phone (907) 874-3711.

Car Rental: Available from Practical Rent-A-Car (907) 874-3975.

Taxi: Available to/from airport and ferry terminal. Approximate cost is $4 and $5.

Highways: Zimovia Highway (see log this section). Logging roads have opened up most of Wrangell Island to motorists. Check with the USFS office at 525 Bennett St. for a copy of the Wrangell Island Road Guide map. (Write USDA Forest Service, Wrangell Ranger District, Box 51, Wrangell, AK 99929; phone 907/874-2323.) City maps are also available at the Chamber of Commerce Visitor Center downtown.

Cruise Ships: Wrangell is a regular port of call in summer for several cruise lines.

Private Boats: Transient floats are

located downtown and 4.5 miles/7.2 km south of Wrangell on Zimovia Highway at Shoemaker Bay Harbor. Reliance Float is located near Shakes Tribal House.

If you are traveling to Wrangell by boat, radio ahead to the harbor master for tie-up space. Or phone (907) 874-3736 or 874-3051.

ATTRACTIONS

Shakes Island and Tribal House, in Wrangell Harbor, is reached by boardwalk. It is the site of several excellent totem poles. The replica tribal house contains Indian working tools, an original Chilkat blanket design carved on a house panel and other cultural items. It is listed on the National Register of Historic Places. Open irregular hours when cruise ships are in port during summer (May to September) or by appointment; phone (907) 874-3747 or 874-2023.

Chief Shakes Island Eagle Totem greets visitors. (© James D. Ronan, Jr.)

Admission $1.50.

Totem Poles. The last original totems standing in Wrangell were cut down in November 1981 and removed for preservation. A totem restoration project funded by both state and federal agencies was initiated, and replicas of original totems can be found at Kiksadi Totem Park at the corner of Front and Episcopal streets.

Wrangell Museum, at 318 Church St., features local history and includes displays representing Tlingit, Russian, British, Chinese, Japanese and American influences in Wrangell. Gold rush, trapping, logging and fishing industry exhibits depict Wrangell's boom and bust economy. May to September hours are: 10 A.M. to 5 P.M. weekdays, 1–5 P.M. Saturdays. October to April hours are: 10–11:30 A.M., 12:30–4 P.M. Tuesday through Friday, closed Saturday and Sunday. Open for cruise ships and ferries in port longer than one hour on Saturdays and Sundays when staffing available. Phone (907) 874-3770; fax (907) 874-3785. Admission for adults, $2; children 16 and under, free.

Our Collections Museum, located on Evergreen Avenue, is a private collection of antiques and Alaska memorabilia. Open when cruise ships and ferries are in port and by special request. Phone (907) 874-3646. Donations accepted.

Sightseeing Tours of attractions and fish bakes are available upon request. Sightseeing buses meet some ferries and cruise ships. Inquire at the visitor center or Wrangell Museum. Flightseeing and jetboat excursions available to Stikine River, Stikine Icefield, Anan Wildlife Observatory and other remote locations.

Celebrations in Wrangell include a big Fourth of July celebration which begins with a salmon bake. The annual Tent City Festival, celebrated the first weekend in February, commemorates Wrangell's gold rush days. The Garnet Festival, celebrated the third week of April, marks the arrival of spring and the annual bald eagle migration on the Stikine River. The festival celebrates the arts with family activities, and includes a golf tournament at Muskeg Meadows. A tree-lighting and Christmas celebration takes place in December.

Petroglyphs are ancient designs carved into rock faces, usually found between low and high tide marks on beaches. Petroglyph Beach is located 0.7 mile/1.1 km from the ferry terminal; a boardwalk trail leads to the head of the beach from the left of the road. Turn right as you reach the beach and look for petroglyphs between there and a rock outcrop several hundred feet away. This beach has the largest number of petroglyphs found anywhere in southeastern Alaska; at times as many as 40 can be seen. Petroglyphs are also located on the library lawn and are on display in the museum.

Muskeg Meadows. A new (1998) 9-hole, 36-acre regulation golf course and driving range is open in Wrangell. Annual tournaments have been inaugurated. Contact the Wrangell Golf Assoc., Box 2199, Wrangell, AK 99929, or association president Lloyd Hartshorn, phone (907) 874-3989.

Anan Wildlife Observatory, managed by the U.S. Forest Service, is located 35 miles/56 km southeast of Wrangell; accessible by boat or plane only. During July and August, visitors can watch bears catch pink salmon headed for the salmon spawning grounds. Bald eagles, ravens, crows and seals are frequently seen feeding on the fish. Contact the visitor center. (800) 367-9745, or the Forest Service office, (907) 874-2323, for list of guides permitted to transport visitors to Anan.

Wrangell Salmon Derby runs from mid-May to Memorial Day weekend. Kings weighing more than 50 lbs. are not unusual.

Garnet Ledge, a rocky outcrop on the right bank of the Stikine River delta at Garnet Creek, is 7.5 miles/12.1 km from Wrangell Harbor, reached at high tide by small boat. Garnet, a semiprecious stone, can be found embedded in the ledge here. The garnet ledge is on land deeded to the Southeast Council of the Boy Scouts of America and the children of Wrangell by the late Fred Hanford (former mayor of Wrangell). The bequest states that the land shall be used for scouting purposes and the children of Wrangell may take garnets in reasonable quantities (garnets are sold by children at the docks when ships and ferries are in port).

Contact the Wrangell Museum (Box 1050, Wrangell 99929; phone 907/874-3770) for information on digging for garnets.

The Stikine River delta lies north of Wrangell within the Stikine–LeConte Wilderness and is accessible only by boat or plane. The delta is habitat for migrating waterfowl, eagles, bears and moose. During the spring run, the second largest concentration of bald eagles in the world can be seen in the Stikine River delta.

Also watch for seals resting on ice floes from LeConte Glacier. The glacier is at the head of LeConte Bay, just north of the delta. It is the southernmost tidewater glacier in North America. It is also an actively calving glacier, known for its prodigious iceberg production.

The Stikine River is the fastest navigable river on North America, and can be rafted, canoed or run by skiff or jet boat from Telegraph Creek, BC, to Wrangell, AK, 165 miles/264 km one way.

USFS trails, cabins and recreation sites on Wrangell Island and in the surrounding area are a major attraction here. Nemo Campsites, for example, only 14 miles/22.5 km south of Wrangell, provides spectacular views of Zimovia Strait and north Etolin Island. No reservations or fees required. Parking areas, picnic tables, fire grills and outhouses at each campsite.

USFS public-use cabins in the Wrangell district are accessible by air or by boat. The 22 USFS cabins are scattered throughout the region.

For details on these sites and others, contact the Forest Service district office at (907) 874-2323, or stop by the USFS office at 525 Bennett St. You may also write the Wrangell Ranger District at Box 51, Wrangell, AK 99929. White courtesy phone located in the ferry terminal building. Reservations for all Forest Service cabins can be made through a national reservation system called Park.net. Park.net's toll free number is: 1-877-444-6777. This service is available 7 days/week, but business hours vary by season. Also, beginning in late spring 1999, cabin reservations can be made through Park.net over the internet at: ReserveUSA.com . ▲

AREA FISHING: The Wrangell Island forest road system provides access to several recreation sites and trails with fishing. For more information contact the USFS office in Wrangell at (907) 874-2323.

Fly in to **Thoms Lake, Long Lake, Marten Lake, Salmon Bay, Virginia Lake** and **Eagle Lake.** Thoms Lake and Long Lake are also accessible via road and trail. **Stikine River** near Wrangell (closed to king salmon fishing), Dolly Varden to 22 inches, and cutthroat to 18 inches, best in midsummer to fall; steelhead to 12 lbs., use bait or lures; coho salmon 10 to 15 lbs., use lures, September and October. Saltwater fishing near Wrangell for king salmon, 20 to 40 lbs., best in May and June. Stop by the Dept. of Fish and Game at 215 Front St. for details. 🐟

Zimovia Highway Log

Zimovia Highway leads south from the ferry terminal to Mile 14.2, where it connects with island's Forest Development roads.

0 Alaska Marine Highway ferry terminal, ticket office and waiting area. There is a bike path to Mile 4.4.

0.3 (0.5 km) St. Rose of Lima Catholic Church, the oldest Roman Catholic parish in Alaska, founded May 2, 1879.

0.4 (0.6 km) First Presbyterian Church has a red neon cross, 1 of 2 in the world that serve as navigational aids. This was the first church in Wrangell and is one of the oldest Protestant churches in Alaska (founded in 1877 and built in 1879).

Wrangell Museum interim location situated between the church and Wrangell High School.

0.6 (1 km) Bennett Street (Airport Road) loops north 2.2 miles/3.5 km to the airport and back to the ferry terminal.

0.7 (1.1 km) Public Safety Bldg.

1.9 (3.1 km) City park. Picnic area with shelters, firepits, restrooms, litter barrels. Tent camping only allowed; 24-hour limit. ▲

3.6 (5.8 km) Turnout with beach access. Several turnouts along the highway here offer beach access and good spots for bird watching.

4.4 (7.1 km) Lodge on left with restaurant and lounge. End of bike path.

4.9 (7.9 km) Shoemaker Bay small-boat harbor, boat launch, picnic, camping and parking area. Camping area has tent sites, 29 RV sites ($10 per night, with hookups), water, dump station and restrooms. Tennis court, horseshoe pits and children's playground nearby. Rainbow Falls trailhead; 0.7-mile/1.1-km trail to scenic waterfall. Institute Creek trail intersects with Rainbow Falls trail at Mile 0.6 and leads 2.7 miles/4.3 km to viewpoint and shelter overlooking Shoemaker Bay and Zimovia Strait. ▲

6.5 (10.5 km) Sawmill owned by Silver Bay Logging Inc. is operating.

7.3 (11.7 km) **Milepost 7**, scenic turnout.

8 (12.9 km) Turnout.

8.5 (13.7 km) Turnout, beach access (8 Mile Beach undeveloped recreation area).

10.8 (17.4 km) Access road west to Pat Creek Log Transfer Facility and small boat launch. Road east (Pat Creek Road) is a 1-lane, maintained, crushed rock road with turnouts. It leads 0.3 mile/0.5 km to Pat's Lake, and continues approximately 6 miles/10 km northeast through both old and active logging areas.

Pat Creek and **Pat's Lake**, cutthroat, Dolly Varden, pink and silver salmon, spinning gear or flies. ◄

11 (17.7 km) Pat Creek camping area (unmaintained, no facilities); parking for self-contained vehicles.

11.1 (17.9 km) Pavement ends. Begin 2-lane gravel road passing scattered houses. The next 3.1 miles /4.9 km of road are scheduled to be paved during summer 1999. Watch for trucks and paving equipment.

13.4 (21.6 km) McCormack Creek crossing on new concrete bridge. Trout and salmon fishing (in season) downstream at mouth of creek.

13.6 (21.8 km) **Junction** with Nemo Road, single-lane gravel FS road 6267, which leads to the Nemo Campsites. Spectacular views of Zimovia Strait and north Etolin Island; parking areas, picnic tables, fire grills and outhouses each site. Campground Host during summer. No reservations.

14.2 (22.8 km) Two-lane road ends at National Forest boundary; begin single-lane FS road with turnouts. Road 6265 connects with other FS roads. (A map showing island roads with recreation sites and trails is available from the USFS office in Wrangell.) Watch for log trucks and other heavy equipment. ▲

Petersburg

(See map, page 671)

Located on the northwest tip of Mitkof Island at the northern end of Wrangell Narrows, midway between Juneau and Ketchikan. **Population:** 3,400. **Emergency Services:** Phone 911. **Alaska State Troopers,** phone (907) 772-3100. **City Police, Poison Center, Fire Department** and **Ambulance,** phone (907) 772-3838. **Hospital,** Petersburg Medical Center, 2nd and Fram St., phone (907) 772-4291. **Maritime Search and Rescue:** contact the Coast Guard at (800) 478-5555. Harbormaster, phone (907) 772-4688, CB Channel 9, or VHF Channel 16.

Visitor Information: Petersburg Visitor Information Center located at 1st and Fram streets; open Monday–Saturday from 9 A.M. to 5 P.M., noon to 4 P.M. Sundays, spring and summer; 10 A.M. to 2 P.M. fall and winter. Write Petersburg Visitor Information Center, Box 649, Petersburg 99833. Clausen Memorial Museum, 2nd and Fram streets, open daily in summer, limited winter hours; phone (907) 772-3598. Alaska Dept. of Fish and Game, State Office Building, Sing Lee Alley; open 8 A.M. to 4:30 P.M., Monday through Friday, phone (907) 772-3801.

Elevation: Sea level. **Climate:** Average daily maximum temperature in July, 64°F/18°C; daily minimum in January, 20°F/-7°C. All-time high, 84°F/29°C in 1933; record low, -19°F/-28°C in 1947. Mean annual precipitation, 110 inches; mostly as rain. **Radio:** KRSA-AM 580, KFSK-FM 100.9. **Television:** Alaska Rural Communication Service, Channel 15; KTOO (PBS) Channel 9 and cable channels. **Newspaper:** *Petersburg Pilot* (weekly).

Private Aircraft: James A. Johnson Airport, 1 mile/1.6 km southeast; elev. 107 feet/33m; length 6,000 feet/1,829m; asphalt; fuel 100, A. Seaplane base 0.5 mile/0.8 km from downtown.

Petersburg was named for Peter Buschmann, who selected the present townsite for a salmon cannery and sawmill in 1897. The sawmill and dock were built in 1899, and the cannery was completed in 1900. He was followed by other Norwegian immigrants who came to fish and work in the cannery and sawmill. Since then the cannery has operated continuously (with rebuilding, expansion and different owners) and is now known as Petersburg Fisheries Inc., a division of Icicle Seafoods Inc. Petersburg Fish-

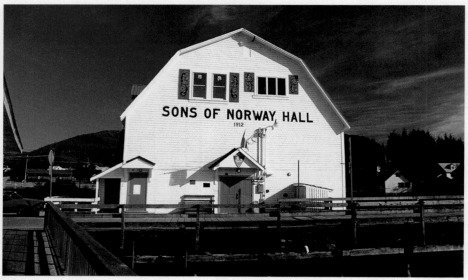

Petersburg's historic Sons of Norway Hall was built in 1912. (© James D. Ronan, Jr.)

eries shares the waterfront with two other canneries, two other cold storage plants and several other fish processing facilities.

Today, Petersburg boasts the largest home-based halibut fleet in Alaska and is also well known for its shrimp, crab, salmon, herring and other fish products. Most families depend on the fishing industry for livelihood. Sportfishing questions should be directed to the Alaska Dept. of Fish and Game's Division of Sportfishing in Petersburg. phone (907) 772-3801

ACCOMMODATIONS/VISITOR SERVICES

Petersburg has 3 hotels, including Scandia House (1-800-772-5006), Tides Inn (1-800-665-8433) and Narrows Inn. There are also numerous bed and breakfasts and guest houses, several restaurants and fast-food outlets located downtown. The 5-block-long commercial area on Main Street (Nordic Drive) has grocery stores, marine and fishing supply stores, hardware, a drugstore, travel agency, public showers, banks, gift and variety stores specializing in both Alaskan and

Scandinavian items, city hall, post office and cocktail bars. A community gym with racquetball courts and a public swimming pool are located a couple of blocks off Nordic Drive. Petersburg has 13 churches.

There are 2 RV parks, dump station, hookups, showers, laundry; fee charged. There is a tent campground (known locally as Tent City) on Haugen Drive; it is often filled to capacity in summer with young cannery workers. Public campgrounds (1 developed, several undeveloped) are located on Mitkof Highway some distance south of town. ▲

TRANSPORTATION

Air: Twice daily scheduled jet service by Alaska Airlines to major Southeast cities and Seattle, WA, with connections to Anchorage and Fairbanks. A scheduled regional carrier and several local carrier and charter services also serve the area.

The airport is located 1 mile/1.6 km from the Federal Building on Haugen Drive. It has a ticket counter and waiting room. There is no shuttle service to town; hotel courtesy vans and taxis are available for a fee.

Ferry: Alaska Marine Highway vessels connect Petersburg with all Southeastern Alaska cities plus Prince Rupert, BC, and Bellingham, WA. Terminal at Milepost 0.8 Mitkof Highway, includes dock, ticket office with waiting room, and parking area. Phone (907) 772-3855.

Car Rental: Avis Rent-A-Car at Tides Inn, (907/772-4716), and All Star, Scandia House, (907/772-4281).

Taxi: There are 2 taxi companies. Cab service to and from the airport and ferry terminal.

Highways: Mitkof Highway, Sandy Beach Road and Three Lakes Loop Road (see logs this section).

Cruise Ships: Smaller cruise ships dock ¼ mile from town. Vans take passengers to town.

Private Boats: Boaters must check with harbormaster for moorage assignment.

ATTRACTIONS

Little Norway Festival is scheduled for May 13–16, 1999, as a celebration for Norwegian Independence Day. Pageantry, old-country dress, contests, Vikings, a Viking ship, dancing and a Norwegian "fish feed" for locals and visitors are featured.

Clausen Memorial Museum, 203 Fram St., features Petersburg area history. On display are artifacts representing the cannery and fisheries, a world-record 126.5-lb. king salmon, the Cape Decision light station lens, a Tlingit canoe and the wall piece "Land, Sea, Sky." Open Wednesday and Saturday, 12:30–4:30 P.M., Oct. 1 to April 30. Open daily, 9:30 A.M. to 4:30 P.M., May 1 to Sept. 21. Phone (907) 772-3598 for programs, updated visitor information and to leave messages. Wheelchair accessible. &

The Fisk (Norwegian for fish), a 10-foot/3-m bronze sculpture commemorating Petersburg's fishing tradition, stands in a working fountain in front of the museum. It was completed during the Alaska centennial year of 1967 by sculptor Carson Boysen.

Sons of Norway Hall, on the National Register of Historic Places, was built in 1912. Situated on pilings over Hammer Slough (a favorite photography subject), its window shutters are decorated with rosemaling (Norwegian tole painting).

Fisherman's Memorial Park, next to the Sons of Norway Hall. Newly constructed in 1998, this park commemorates those townspeople lost at sea.

LeConte Glacier, in LeConte Bay, 25 miles/40 km east of Petersburg, is the continent's southernmost tidewater glacier. Fast-moving, the glacier continually "calves," creating icefalls from its face into the bay. Seals and porpoises are common; whales are often seen. Helicopters, small aircraft and boats may be chartered in Petersburg or Wrangell to see LeConte Glacier.

Whale Research and Whale-Watching.

Petersburg has become the center for humpback whale research in Southeast Alaska. Three feature documentaries have been filmed in adjacent waters in the past five years. The area attracts professional photographers from around the world.

Salmon migration and spawning are best observed in the Petersburg area July though September. Falls Creek bridge and fish ladder, at **Milepost 10.8** Mitkof Highway, is a good location. The ladder helps migrating salmon bypass difficult falls on the way to spawning grounds in Falls Creek. It can be observed from the creek bank just off the roadside. Other viewing areas include Blind Slough and the Blind River Rapids area, Petersburg Creek and Ohmer Creek.

Crystal Lake Fish Hatchery is at **Milepost 17.5** Mitkof Highway. This hatchery for coho, king and steelhead is operated by the state and used for fish-stocking projects in southeastern Alaska. It is open for visits, and hatchery personnel will explain the operation, though formal guided tours are not available. Best time to visit is between 8 A.M. and 4 P.M., Monday through Friday.

Petersburg King Salmon Derby is scheduled for Memorial Day weekend May 28–31, 1999. $30,000 in prizes are awarded. Check with the Chamber of Commerce for details.

Charter a Boat or Plane. There are charter boat services in Petersburg for guided saltwater sportfishing, glacier trips, access to remote cabins, kayak transfers and world-class whale watching. Inquire at the visitor information center. Charter floatplanes and helicopters are available for flightseeing, including fly-in fishing, the Stikine Ice Field and transportation.

Kaleidoscope Cruises. This tour is a must! Specializing in glacier ecology, whale watching and custom sightseeing and fishing. Professional biologist and naturalist Barry Bracken, skipper of the 28-foot *Island Dream*, has over 25 years experience in Southeast Alaskan waters, conducting research, exploring and sportfishing. Half-day, full-day, overnight tours. Phone (800) TO-THE-SEA. E-mail: bbsea@alaska.net. Internet: www.alaska.net/~bbsea.
[ADVERTISEMENT]

Viking Travel, Inc. 101 N. Nordic, phone (800) 327-2571, (907) 772-3818. Great selection of tours and activities around Petersburg. Whale-watching, sea kayaking day trips, LeConte Glacier Bay, halibut and salmon fishing charters, bear viewing, river rafting, Glacier Bay tours. Independent travel planning for all Alaska. Instant ferry and airline reservations and ticketing. E-mail: akres@viking1.attmail.com. [ADVERTISEMENT]

AREA FISHING: Salmon, steelhead, cutthroat and Dolly Varden at **Falls Creek**, **Blind Slough** and **Blind River Rapids**; see log of Mitkof Highway this section. Salmon can be caught in the harbor area and **Scow Bay** area. (Rapid tidal currents in front of the town necessitate the use of an outboard motor.) **Petersburg Creek**, directly across Wrangell Narrows from downtown within Petersburg Creek–Duncan Salt Chuck

Wilderness Area, also offers good fishing. Blind Slough, located 15 miles/24 km south of the ferry terminal, offers good fishing for king salmon. Dolly Varden can be caught from the beach north of town and from downtown docks. Sportfishing opportunities for halibut, crab and shrimp. Harvest of mussels, clams and other shellfish is not recommended because of the possibility of paralytic shellfish poisoning. Contact the Sport Fish Division of the Alaska Dept. of Fish and Game (907) 772-3801 for additional information.

Wrangell Narrows is a 23-mile-/37-km-long channel between Mitkof and Kupreanof islands. The channel was dredged in the 1940s to a depth of 26 feet/7.8m. Extremely narrow in places and filled with rocky reefs, islands and strong currents, the narrows is navigated by ships and ferries with the aid of dozens of markers and flashing lights. The 1 1/2-hour run through Wrangell Narrows begins immediately on ferries departing Petersburg southbound, or about 1 1/2 hours after departing Wrangell northbound.

Cabins, canoe/kayaking routes and hiking trails managed by the U.S. Forest Service are all within reach of Petersburg, which is the administrative center for the Stikine Area of Tongass National Forest. Stop by the USFS office in the Federal Building, or phone (907) 772-3871 for detailed information on cabins and trails or contact the Petersburg Visitor Information Center, (907) 772-4636. Also consult *The ALASKA WILDERNESS GUIDE* (to order, phone 800/726-4707). Information for canoers and kayakers interested in the Stikine River delta or Tebenkof Bay and Kuiu wilderness areas is also available here or at the USFS office in Wrangell.

Sandy Beach Road Log

From Federal Building, drive north through town; road leads to Sandy Beach Recreation Area.

0 Federal Building and post office.
0.1 (0.2 km) Petersburg boat harbor 1 block to left, contains one of Alaska's finest fishing fleets.
0.2 (0.3 km) Downtown Petersburg.
0.3 (0.5 km) Petersburg Fisheries Inc., the city's largest processing plant.

Eagles Roost Park. Eagles feed on beach at low tide; best viewing in early summer.
1.2 (1.9 km) Eagle observation point. Eagles can be seen resting nearby and fishing in Wrangell Narrows. To the northeast is Frederick Sound and the mainland.
2 (3.2 km) Bed and breakfast, sightseeing cruises.
2.8 (4.5 km) Sandy Beach Recreation Area on left; picnic tables, playground, volleyball court, shelter, toilets, limited parking, no camping. **Junction** with Haugen Drive, which loops to airport and back to town.
Just past Sandy Beach Recreation Area is Sound Drive, a 7.5-mile/12.1-km road completed in 1998 which links Petersburg to the USFS road system and the Three Lakes Loop Road. This is a 1 1/2-lane gravel road recommended for 4-wheel drive or mountain biking.

Mitkof Highway Log

The major road on the island, Mitkof Highway leads 33.8 miles/54.4 km south from the Federal Building to the Stikine River delta at the south end of Mitkof Island. The highway is paved to **Milepost 17.5**; good wide gravel to road end.

0 Federal Building and post office.
0.1 (0.2 km) Bridge over Hammer Slough, an intertidal estuary.
0.5 (0.8 km) Harbor parking.
0.6 (1 km) Pier and floatplane base.
0.8 (1.3 km) Alaska Marine Highway ferry terminal, office and waiting area on right.
2.9 (4.6 km) **Scow Bay**, a wide portion of Wrangell Narrows with king salmon fishing in spring. Scow Bay Loop Road rejoins highway at **Milepost 3.1**.
7.5 (12.1 km) Twin Creek RV Park, private campground, small store and phone. ▲
10.7 (17.2 km) North turnoff to Three Lakes Loop Road (see log this section).
10.8 (17.4 km) **Falls Creek** and fish ladder. Steelhead, April and May; pink salmon below falls in August; coho, August and September; Dolly Varden and cutthroat late summer and fall. No fishing within 300 feet/90m of fish ladder.
11 (17.7 km) Road on right leads 0.5 mile/0.8 km to Papke's Landing; transient boat moorage and boat ramp. USFS Log

A purse seiner hauls in salmon in Frederick Sound. (© James D. Ronan, Jr.)

Transportation Facility.

14.3 (23 km) Entering Tongass National Forest.

14.5 (23.3 km) Blind River Rapids parking area and trail; outhouse; handicap access. 0.3-mile/0.4-km boardwalk trail through muskeg meadow to **Blind River Rapids**, hatchery steelhead, mid-April to mid-May; king salmon, June to late July; coho, mid-August to October. Also Dolly Varden and cutthroat trout.

16.3 (26.2 km) Blind Slough waterfowl viewing area on right. Covered platform with interpretive sign on area waterfowl. Trumpeter swans winter in this area.

17.5 (28.2 km) Pavement ends; wide, hard-packed gravel to end of road. Short road leads to Crystal Lake Fish Hatchery and **Blind Slough Recreation Area** with picnic tables, shelter and pit toilets; no overnight camping. Hatchery is open for visiting, though no scheduled tours are available. Fishing for cutthroat and Dolly Varden in summer; coho salmon, mid-August to mid-September; king salmon in June and July.. Fishing in this area may be regulated. Check with ADF&G, (907) 772-3801.

20 (32.2 km) **Manmade Hole** picnic area with tables, firepits, swimming and short trail. Ice skating in winter. Fishing for cutthroat and Dolly Varden year-round; best in summer and fall.

20.6 (33.1 km) Three Lakes Loop Road begins on left leading to Three Lakes on other side of Mitkof Island, looping back to Mitkof Highway at **Milepost 10.7** near Falls Creek bridge.

21.4 (34.4 km) Woodpecker Cove Road (1-lane) leads about 15 miles/24 km along south Mitkof Island to Woodpecker Cove and beyond. Good views of Sumner Strait. Watch for logging trucks.

21.5 (34.6 km) Ohmer Creek nature trail, 1.5 mile/2.4 km loop; first 0.3 mile/0.5 km is barrier-free.

21.7 (34.9 km) Ohmer Creek Campground, 10 sites (2 are wheelchair accessible), toilets, parking area, picnic tables, drinking water and firepits. Set in meadow area among trees. Open spring to fall; small fee; accommodates RVs to 32 feet/9.6m.

24 (38.6 km) **Blind Slough** USFS Log Transportation Facility. Fishing from skiff for coho salmon, mid-August to mid-September. *NOTE: Kings have not returned to this system for several years.*

26.1 (42 km) Narrow 0.7-mile/1.1-km road on right to Sumner Strait Campground, locally called Green's Camp (undeveloped); must walk in, no facilities. May be inaccessible at high tide.

27 (43.4 km) View of city of Wrangell.

28 (45 km) Wilson Creek state recreation area (undeveloped); picnic tables, parking. Good view of Sumner Strait.

28.6 (46 km) Banana Point, boat ramp, outhouse.

31 (49.9 km) Stikine River mud flats, visible on right at low tide. Part of the Stikine River delta, this is the area where Dry Strait meets Sumner Strait.

33.8 (54.4 km) Road ends with turnaround.

Three Lakes Loop Road Log

Access to this 21.4-mile-/34.4-km-long, 1-lane loop road is from **Mileposts 10.7** and **20.6** on the Mitkof Highway. *CAUTION: No services; use turnouts.*

0 Junction at **Milepost 10.7** Mitkof Highway; turn east.

1.4 (2.3 km) View of Wrangell Narrows to west. Older clear-cuts; this area was logged between 1964 and 1968.

4.4 (7.1 km) Falls Creek bridge.

7 (11.3 km) Second-growth stand of spruce–hemlock. First growth was destroyed by fire or wind throw more than 180 years ago. This second-growth stand serves as an example of what a logging unit could look like a century or two after clear-cutting.

9.7 (15.6 km) Directly south is a 384-acre clear-cut logged in 1973 under a contract predating the current policy, which usually limits clear-cut tracts to 100 acres.

10.2 (16.4 km) **Bear Creek**; steelhead in April and May; coho late August and September; cutthroat and Dolly Varden, best late summer and fall.

12.3 (19.8 km) Muskeg; view of Frederick Sound.

12.8 (20.5 km) Turnoff on right to LeConte Glacier Overlook, a picnic site with spectacular view of the mainland. Limited turnaround space.

14.2 (22.8 km) Sand Lake trail. Short boardwalk trail leads to each of the Three Lakes. Tennis shoes are ideal for these short walks, but for areas around the lakes it is advisable to wear rubber boots. A 0.7-mile/1.1-km connecting trail to Hill Lake.

14.7 (23.6 km) Hill Lake trail.

15.1 (24.3 km) Crane Lake trail, 1.3 miles/2.1 km to lake; connecting trail to Hill Lake. USFS skiffs and picnic platforms are located at Sand, Hill and Crane lakes.

Sand, Hill and **Crane lakes**, cutthroat from May through September.

16.4 (26.4 km) Dry Straits Road.

21.4 (34.4 km) Second **junction** with Mitkof Highway, at **Milepost 20.6**.

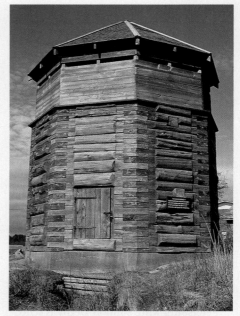

Replica of original Russian Blockhouse is beside the Pioneers' Home in Sitka.

(© Harry M. Walker)

Sitka

(See map, page 671)

Located on west side of Baranof Island, 95 air miles/153 km southwest of Juneau, 185 air miles/ 298 km northwest of Ketchikan; 2 hours flying time from Seattle, WA. **Population:** City and Borough, 9,194. **Emergency Services: Alaska State Troopers, City Police, Fire Department,** and **Ambulance,** phone 911. **Hospital,** Sitka Community, 209 Moller Ave., phone (907) 747-3241; Mount Edgecumbe, 222 Tongass Dr., phone (907) 966-2411. **Maritime Search and Rescue,** phone the Coast Guard at (800) 478-5555.

Visitor Information: Contact the Sitka Convention and Visitors Bureau at Box 1226-MP, Sitka, AK 99835; phone (907) 747-5940. Also available at the Isabel Miller Museum in Harrigan Centennial Hall on Harbor Drive. Museum hours are 8 A.M. to 5 P.M. in summer, extended hours to accommodate ferry passengers; phone (907) 747-6455. For USDA Forest Service information write the Sitka Ranger District, 201 Katlian, Suite 109, Sitka, AK 99835; phone (907) 747-4220. For information on Sitka National Historical Park, write 106 Metlakatla St., Sitka, AK 99835; phone (907) 747-6281.

Elevation: Sea level. **Climate:** Average daily temperature in July, 55°F/13°C; in January, 33°F/1°C. Annual precipitation, 95 inches. **Radio:** KIFW 1230, KRSA-FM 94.9, KSBZ-FM 103.1, KCAW-FM 104.7. **Television:** Cable channels. **Newspaper:** *Daily Sitka Sentinel.*

Private Aircraft: Sitka airport on Japonski Island; elev. 21 feet/6m; length 6,500 feet/1,981m; asphalt; fuel 100, A1. Sitka seaplane base adjacent west; fuel 80, 100.

One of the most scenic of southeastern Alaska cities, Sitka rests on the ocean shore protected at the west by myriad small islands and Cape Edgecumbe. Mount Edgecumbe, the Fuji-like volcano (dormant), is 3,201 feet/976m high.

The site was originally occupied by Tlingit Indians. Alexander Baranof, chief manager of the Russian–American Co. with headquarters in Kodiak, built a trading post and fort (St. Michael's Redoubt) north of Sitka in 1799. Indians burned down the fort and looted the warehouses. Baranof returned in 1804, and by 1808 Sitka was capital of Russian Alaska. Baranof was governor from 1790 to 1818. A statue of the Russian governor was unveiled in 1989; it is located outside of Centennial Hall. Castle Hill in Sitka is where Alaska changed hands from Russia to the United States in 1867. Salmon was the mainstay of the economy from the late 1800s until the 1950s, when the salmon population decreased. A pulp mill operated at nearby Silver Bay from 1960 to 1993. Today, tourism, commercial fishing, cold storage plants and government provide most jobs.

ACCOMMODATIONS/VISITOR SERVICES

Sitka has several hotels/motels, most with adjacent restaurants, including: Sitka Harborview Inn (907/747-8611), Sitka Hotel (907/747-3288), Super 8 Hotel (907/747-8804) and Westmark Shee Atika (907/747-6241). Bed and breakfasts include Alaska Ocean View (907/747-8310) and Helga's (907/747-5497).

Alaska Ocean View Bed & Breakfast. You'll enjoy casual elegance at affordable rates at this superior, quality B&B where guests experience a high degree of personal comfort, privacy and friendly, knowledgeable hosts. Open your day with the tantalizing aroma of fresh bread, fresh ground coffee and a delicious, generous breakfast, and close your day with a refreshing soak in the bubbling patio spa. Open year-round, credit cards, smoke-free, on airporter/ferry shuttle route. Business travelers and vacationers rate this lodging a 12 plus! "Delighted beyond our expectations!" Brochure and reservations: 1101 Edgecumbe Drive, Sitka, AK 99835; phone (907) 747-8310. See display ad this section. [ADVERTISEMENT]

Sitka Youth Hostel is located in the United Methodist Church, 303 Kimsham St. (1½ blocks north of McDonald's on Halibut Point Road). Send correspondence to Box 2645, Sitka, AK 99835. Open June 1 to Aug. 31; 20 beds, showers, kitchen facilities, sleeping pads required; $7/member; $10/nonmembers. Phone (907) 747-8661.

An array of businesses cluster in the downtown area, which saw its first traffic light installed in 1992. Services in Sitka's downtown area include restaurants, a laundromat, drugstore, clothing and grocery stores, and gift shops. Shopping and services are also available along Sawmill and Halibut Point roads. Dump stations are located at the Wastewater

Treatment Plant on Japonski Island.

Four campgrounds are available in the Sitka area. From the ferry terminal north they are Starrigavan, Sitka Sportsman's, Sealing Cove and Sawmill Creek. Starrigavan Campground (USFS), at **Milepost 7.8** Halibut Point Road, has 32 sites, 2 picnic sites, artesian water, tables, vault toilets, 14-day limit, $8 fee (fee rate subject to change), available first-come, first-served only; phone (907) 747-4216. (see information at end of this paragraph). Sitka Sportsman's Assoc. RV Park, located 1 block south of the ferry terminal on Halibut Point Road, has 16 RV sites, water and electrical hookups, $18.00 fee, reservations accepted; phone (907) 747-6033. Sealing Cove, operated by the City and Borough of Sitka, is located adjacent Sealing Cove Boat Harbor on Japonski Island; overnight parking for 26 RVs, water and electrical hookups, 15-night limit, $16 fee. Sawmill Creek Campground (USFS) is

located on Blue Lake Road, which is accessible at **Milepost 5.4** Sawmill Creek Road; 11 tent sites, vault toilet, boil water, no garbage service, no fee, 14-day limit. Phone (907)

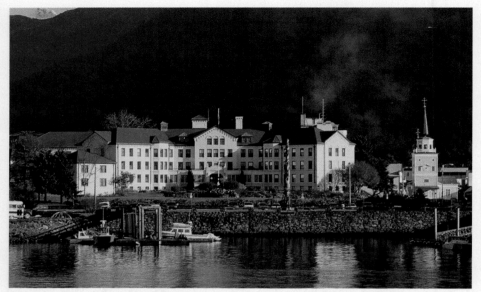

Sitka Pioneers' Home dominates the waterfront. (© Loren Taft)

747-4216. Starrigavan and Sawmill Creek campgrounds are both operated by the USDA Forest Service; phone (907) 747-4216 for more information, or contact them by e-mail: sitka.rd/r10_chatham@fs.fed.us. ▲

TRANSPORTATION

Air: Scheduled jet service by Alaska Airlines. Charter and commuter service also available. The airport is on Japonski Island, across O'Connell Bridge, 1.7 miles/2.7 km from downtown. Airport facilities include ticket counters, rental cars, small gift shop, restaurant and lounge. Van and taxi service to downtown hotels available.

Ferry: Alaska Marine Highway ferry terminal is located at **Milepost 7** Halibut Point Road; phone (907) 747-8737. Buses for downtown meet all ferries. Van and taxi service also available. Sitka is connected via the Marine Highway to other Southeast ports, Prince Rupert, BC, and Bellingham, WA.

Bus: Available to downtown hotels.

Car Rental: Available from A&A Car Rental–Baranof Motors Inc. (907/747-8228), Advantage Car Rentals (907/747-7557) and Avis Rent-A-Car (907/966-2404).

Taxi: Local service is available.

Highways: Halibut Point Road, 7.9 miles/12.7 km, and Sawmill Creek Road, 7.4 miles/11.9 km; see logs this section.

Cruise Ships: Sitka is a popular port of call for several cruise lines.

Private Boats: Transient moorage available at ANB Harbor, located downtown next to the fuel dock; Thomsen Harbor on Katlian Street, 0.6 mile/1 km from city center; and Sealing Cove on Japonski Island. Moorage is limited during the summer.

ATTRACTIONS

St. Michael's Cathedral is the focal point of Sitka's history as the capital of Russian Alaska. Built in 1844–48 under the direction of Bishop Innocent (Ioann Veniaminov) of the Russian Orthodox Church, one of the finest examples of rural Russian church architecture for 118 years. It was destroyed by fire on Jan. 2, 1966. Priceless icons, some predating 1800, were saved by townspeople and are now back in place in the rebuilt cathedral (an exact replica).

St. Michael's is located in the center of Lincoln Street downtown; a donation is requested when entering to view icons. Open daily June 1 to Sept. 30, 11 A.M. to 3 P.M. St. Michael's currently serves a Russian Orthodox congregation of about 100 families. Visitors are reminded that this is an active parish conducting weekly services.

Castle Hill (Baranof Castle Hill Historic Site) is where Alaska changed hands from Russia to the United States on Oct. 18, 1867. Castle Hill was the site of Baranof's castle. Walkway to site is located on the south side by the bridge (look for sign).

Sitka Pioneers' Home, near the waterfront at Lincoln and Katlian streets, was built in 1934. Pioneers welcome visitors, and handicrafts made by the residents are sold in the gift shop located on the first floor of the west wing.

Totem Square is across Katlian Street from the Pioneers' Home and contains a totem, petroglyphs, Russian cannon and 3 large anchors found in Sitka Harbor and believed to be 18th century English.

Russian Blockhouse beside Pioneers' Home is a replica of the blockhouse that separated Russian and Tlingit sections of Sitka after the Tlingits moved back to the area 20 years after the 1804 battle. (See model of early Sitka in Centennial Building.)

New Archangel Russian Dancers, a group of local women, perform authentic Russian dances in authentic costumes. Performances are scheduled to coincide with the arrival of cruise ships. Fee charged. Inquire at the Centennial Building for details.

Old Russian Cemetery is located behind Pioneers' Home and includes graves of such notables as St. Iahov Netsvetov, a recently canonized saint of the Russian Orthodox Church, who was a priest in Russian Alaska for over 40 years.

The Finnish Lutheran Cemetery, dedicated in 1841, is located on Princess Way next to the Russian cemetery. Just a few steps up the hill from Sitka Lutheran Church, it holds the grave of Princess Maskutov, wife of Alaska's last Russian governor, and other important personages.

Sitka National Cemetery, Milepost 0.5

Sawmill Creek Road, is open 8 A.M. to 5 P.M. daily (maintained by the Veterans Administration). It was known locally as Military Cemetery. In 1924 Pres. Calvin Coolidge designated the site as Sitka National Cemetery, and until WWII it was the only national cemetery west of the Rockies. Civil War veterans, veterans of the Aleutian Campaign in WWII and many notable Alaskans are buried here. One gravestone is dated December 1867, 2 months after the U.S. purchase of Alaska from Russia.

Whale Watching. During the summer, whales are often found in Sitka Sound. During the winter, up to 80 whales are near Sitka from mid-September to mid-January. Whale Park, 4.4 miles/7 km from town on Sawmill Creek Road, has stationary binoculars for whale viewing.

Alaska Day Celebration, Oct. 14–18, 1999, celebrates the transfer of Alaska from Russia to the United States with a reenactment of the event, complete with Sitka's own 9th (Manchu) Infantry, authentic uniforms and working muskets of the period. Period costumes and beards are the order of the day. Events ranging from pageant to costume ball and parade highlight the affair.

Annual Sitka Summer Music Festival (June 4–25, 1999). Concerts on Tuesday, Friday and some Saturday evenings in Centennial Hall, praised for its excellent acoustics. Emphasizing chamber music, an international group of professional musicians give evening concerts during the festival, plus open rehearsals. Advance tickets are a good idea; the concerts are popular. Dress is informal and concert-goers may have the opportunity to talk with the musicians. Children under 6 years not admitted.

Harrigan Centennial Hall, by the boat harbor on Harbor Drive, is used for Russian dance performances, music festivals, banquets and conventions. Its glass-fronted main hall overlooks Sitka Sound. The Isabel Miller Museum is located here. Nearby is a large hand-carved Tlingit canoe made from a single log.

Sheet'ka Kwaan Naa Kahidi (Sitka's Community House) is a northwest coast tribal "longhouse" constructed in traditional Nakaahidi design and aimed at preserving the Tlingit culture. The Community House is a performing arts center offering Tlingit story telling and dance performances. Exhibits on Native culture are also on display. Donations accepted. 200 Katlian St., Sitka, AK 99835; phone (907) 747-7290.

Isabel Miller Museum, located in the Centennial Building, has permanent exhibits highlighting the history of Sitka and its people. Russian tools, paintings from all eras, fishing, forestry, tourism, and Alaska Purchase exhibits, and an 8-foot-square scale model of Sitka in 1867 are among the displays. Operated by the Sitka Historical Society; hosts are available to answer questions. Open year-round; free admission. Hours are 9 A.M. to 5 P.M. daily in summer; 10 A.M. to 4 P.M. Tuesday through Saturday during the winter. Phone (907) 747-6455.

Saint Peter's-by-the-Sea Episcopal Church, at 611 Lincoln Street, was consecrated as "The Cathedral of Alaska" on Easter Sunday, 1900. The church building and See House are listed on the National Historic Register. The Rt. Rev. Peter Trimble Rowe, first Episcopal bishop of Alaska (1895-1942) is buried in the churchyard.

Sitka Lutheran Church, downtown on

Lincoln Street, has a small historical display. Established in 1840, it was the first Protestant church organized on the west coast of North America.

Sitka National Historical Park reflects both the community's rich Tlingit Indian heritage and its Russian-ruled past. The park consists of 2 units—the Fort Site, located at the end of Lincoln Street, 0.5 mile/0.8 km from town, and the Russian Bishop's House, located on Lincoln Street near Crescent Harbor.

At the Fort Site stood the Tlingit fort, burned to the ground by Russians after the 1804 Battle of Sitka; this was the last major stand by the Tlingits against Russian settlement. For Alexander Baranof, leader of the Russians, the battle was revenge for the 1802 destruction of Redoubt St. Michael by the Tlingits. There is a visitor center here with audiovisual programs and exhibits of Indian artifacts. The Southeast Alaska Indian Cultural Center has contemporary Tlingit artists demonstrate and interpret various traditional arts for visitors.

There is a self-guiding trail through the park to the fort site and battleground of 1804. The National Park Service conducts guided walks; check for schedule. The park's totem pole collection stands near the visitor center and along the trail. The collection includes original pieces collected in 1901–03, and copies of originals lost to time and the elements. The pieces, primarily from Prince of Wales Island, were collected by Alaska Gov. John Brady (now buried in Sitka National Cemetery). The originals were exhibited at the 1904 St. Louis Exposition.

The Russian Bishop's House was built by the Russian–American Co. in 1842 for the first Russian Orthodox Bishop to serve Alaska. It was occupied by the church until 1969, and was added to Sitka National Historical Park in 1972. The house is 1 of 2 Russian log structures remaining in Sitka, and 1 of 4 remaining in North America.

The park's visitor center is open daily, 8 A.M. to 5 P.M., June through September; weekdays, 8 A.M. to 5 P.M., October through May. The park grounds and trails are open daily, 6 A.M. to 10 P.M. in summer; shorter hours in winter. Russian Bishop's House open 9 A.M. to 5 P.M. daily, closed from 1–2 P.M. for lunch; other times by appointment; hours subject to change. The visitor center is closed Thanksgiving, Christmas and New Year's. Admission fee $2 per person and $5 per family. Tours are $3 per person. Students under 18 free with student identification. Phone (907) 747-6281 for more information.

Sheldon Jackson Museum, 104 College Dr., on the Sheldon Jackson College campus, contains some of the finest Native arts and crafts found in Alaska. Much of it was collected by missionary Sheldon Jackson and is now owned by the state of Alaska. Museum shop specializes in Alaska Native arts and crafts: ivory, dolls, masks, silver jewelry, baskets and beadwork. Admission $3, students under 18 free, annual pass $10. Open in summer 9 A.M. to 5 P.M. daily. Winter hours: Tuesday through Saturday, 10 A.M. to 4 P.M. Phone (907) 747-8981.

The Prospector is a 13½-foot/4-m clay and bronze statue in front of the Pioneers' Home. Sculpted by Alonzo Victor Lewis, the statue was dedicated on Alaska Day in 1949. Lewis's model was a genuine pioneer, William "Skagway Bill" Fonda.

Blarney Stone, across from Sheldon Jackson College. Believed to originally have been

St. Michael's Cathedral in downtown Sitka. (© Loren Taft)

called Baranof's stone and used as a resting stop by Russian–American Co. chief manager Alexander Baranof.

O'Connell Bridge, 1,225 feet/373m long, connecting Sitka with Japonski Island, was the first cable-stayed, girder-span bridge in the United States. It was dedicated Aug. 19, 1972. You'll get a good view of Sitka and the harbors by walking across this bridge.

Old Sitka, at **Milepost 7.5** Halibut Point Road, is a registered national historic landmark and the site of the first Russian settlement in the area in 1799, known then as Fort Archangel Michael. In 1802, in a surprise attack, the Tlingit Indians of the area destroyed the fort and killed most of its occupants, driving the Russians out until Baranof's successful return in 1804.

Visit the Alaska Raptor Rehabilitation Center, located at 1101 Sawmill Creek Road (**Milepost 0.9**) just across Indian River, within easy walking distance of downtown Sitka. This unique facility treats injured eagles, hawks, owls and other birds. Visitors will have the opportunity to see American bald eagles and other raptors close up, review case histories of birds treated at the center and observe medical care being administered to current patients. From May 15 through September the facility is open daily for tours and educational programs; limited hours October to May 15. Phone (907) 747-8662 or fax 747-8397 for times. Admission charged.

St. Lazaria Island is host to one of the largest seabird colonies in Southeast Alaska. This 65-acre volcanic island was set aside as a wildlife refuge in 1909. A half-million seabirds representing 11 different species breed here. Landing on the island or exploring the island is not advisable because foot traffic damages nesting burrows. Boat charters are available in Sitka for viewing from the water. The best time to visit is May–June. For more information, contact the Refuge Manager, Alaska Maritime National Wildlife Refuge, 2355 Kachemak Bay Dr., Suite 101, Homer, AK 99603; phone (907) 235-6546.

Hiking Trails. Sitka Ranger District office

at 201 Katlian, provides information sheets and maps for area trails and remote cabins. Trails accessible from the road include Harbor Mountain Ridge trail; Mount Verstovia trail; the easy 5-mile/8-km Indian River trail; and the short Beaver Lake trail off Sawmill Creek Road on Blue Lake Road.

AREA FISHING: Sitka holds an annual salmon derby Memorial Day weekend and the weekend following. Contact the Sitka Convention and Visitors Bureau for more information; phone (907) 747-5940. Saltwater fishing charters available locally. There are also many lakes and rivers on Baranof Island with good fishing; these range from **Katlian River**, 11 miles/17.7 km northeast of Sitka by boat, to more remote waters such as **Rezanof Lake**, which is 40 air miles/64 km southeast of Sitka. USFS public-use cabins at some lakes. Stop by the Dept. of Fish and Game office at 304 Lake St. for details on fishing. ✦

Sawmill Creek Road Log

Sawmill Creek Road is a 7.4-mile/11.9-km road, paved for the first 5.4 miles/8.7 km, which begins at Lake Street and ends beyond the pulp mill (closed) at Silver Bay.

0 Intersection of Lake Street (Halibut Point Road) and Sawmill Creek Road.

0.5 (0.8 km) Sitka National Cemetery.

0.6 (1 km) Entrance to Sheldon Jackson College.

0.7 (1.1 km) Indian River bridge. Beginning of Indian River trail on left.

0.9 (1.4 km) Alaska Raptor Rehabilitation Center.

1 (1.6 km) Post office.

1.7 (2.7 km) Mount Verstovia trail on left next to supper club. The trail extends 2.5 miles/4 km to summit of Mount Verstovia; strenuous hike, great views.

3.6 (5.8 km) Thimbleberry Creek bridge.

3.7 (6 km) On left past bridge is start of Thimbleberry Lake and Heart Lake trail. Hike in 0.5 mile/0.8 km to **Thimbleberry Lake**, brook trout to 12 inches, May–September. *NOTE: It is illegal to use bait in fresh water, except from Sept. 15–Nov. 15.* Trail continues 1 mile/1.6 km past Thimbleberry Lake to **Heart Lake**, brook trout. ✦

4.4 (7.1 km) Scenic Whale Park viewpoint turnout; stationary binoculars for whale watching.

5.3 (8.5 km) Alaska Pulp Corp. (closed).

5.4 (8.7 km) Blue Lake Road on left. Pavement ends on Sawmill Creek Road. Blue Lake Road (narrow dirt) leads 2.2 miles/3.5 km to small parking area and short downhill trail to Blue Lake (no recreational facilities; check with city for information). At Mile 1.5 on right is Sawmill Creek USFS campground. **Blue Lake**, rainbow, May–September; use flies or lure, do not use bait. Lightweight skiff or rubber boat recommended. ✦▲

5.7 (9.2 km) Sawmill Creek and bridge. Pavement ends; gravel begins.

7.2 (11.6 km) Public road ends at Herring Cove near mouth of Silver Bay (boat tours of the bay available in Sitka). City road to hydroelectric power plant continues.

7.4 (11.9 km) Gate marking boundary of city road. No vehicles beyond this point; access for hikers and bicyclists only. No guardrails or road signs to road end.

10.5 (16.9 km) Fish hatchery and gate.

Sitka Sound from Harbor Mountain Road. (© Ruth von Spalding)

13.7 (22 km) Road end. Green Lake Power Plant.

Halibut Point Road Log

Halibut Point Road (paved) leads northwest from the intersection of Harbor Drive and Lincoln Street past Old Sitka to Starrigavan Campground.

0 Harbor Drive and Lincoln Street. Proceed northwest (road is now Lake Street).

0.1 (0.2 km) Fire station. Intersection with Sawmill Creek Road; keep left.

0.3 (0.5 km) **Swan Lake** to right of road, rainbow from 12 to 14 inches.

0.6 (1 km) Katlian Street on left leads to boat ramp and then to downtown. Hospital to the right.

1.8 (2.9 km) Pioneer Park picnic and day-use area with beach access; parking available.

2.2 (3.5 km) Cascade Creek bridge.

2.3 (3.7 km) Tongass National Forest work center.

2.4 (3.9 km) Sandy Beach; good swimming beach, ample parking, view of Mount Edgecumbe. Whales are sometimes sighted.

3.8 (6.1 km) Viewpoint. On a clear day you can see for 50 miles/80 km.

4.2 (6.8 km) Harbor Mountain Road; steep gravel, accessible to cars. Road leads 5 miles/8 km to road end and Harbor Mountain Ridge trail to lookout at 2,300 feet/701m. Great view of Sitka Sound.

4.4 (7.1 km) Granite Creek bridge. Just beyond the bridge on left is Halibut Point state recreation site with swimming beach, shelters, tables, fireplaces and toilets.

7 (11.3 km) Alaska Marine Highway ferry terminal on left.

7.3 (11.7 km) Boat ramp, litter barrel and pit toilet to left.

7.5 (12.1 km) Old Sitka State Historical Site at left, and Starrigavan Creek bridge just ahead. Old Sitka was the site of the Russian Fort Archangel Michael, established in 1799. Commemorative plaque and historical markers. The site is a registered national historic landmark.

7.6 (12.2 km) Narrow road on right runs along the bank of Starrigavan Creek, where pink salmon spawn in August and September, and continues several miles through Starrigavan River valley. Off-road vehicles permitted on ATV trail only.

7.7 (12.4 km) USFS estuary life trail, Starrigavan Recreation Area; bird watching.

Wheelchair access, vault toilets, trails, parking adjacent.

7.8 (12.6 km) Turnoff for Starrigavan USFS campground and picnic area; artesian well with excellent drinking water. Forest and muskeg nature trail, across from boat ramp, connects with Estuary life trail. Access to beach. **Starrigavan Bay**, Dolly Varden; pink and silver salmon, May to October.

7.9 (12.7 km) Road ends.

Kake

(See map, page 671)

Located on the northwest coast of Kupreanof Island; Petersburg is 40 air miles/64 km or 65 miles/105 km by boat; Juneau is 95 air miles/153 km northeast. **Population:** 820 (approximately 85 percent Native). **Emergency Services:** for all emergencies, 911. **Police,** phone (907) 785-3393. **Public Health Center,** phone (907) 785-3333. **Maritime Search and Rescue,** phone the Coast Guard at (800) 478-5555 or (907) 785-3500.

Visitor Information: City of Kake, Box 500, Kake 99830.

Elevation: Sea level. **Climate:** Less than average rainfall for southeastern Alaska, approximately 50 inches annually. Mild temperatures. January average temperatures are around freezing. Slightly warmer than nearby Petersburg, Kake is noted for being in the "banana belt" of Southeast.

Private Aircraft: Kake seaplane base, located adjacent southeast; fuel 100. Airstrip 1 mile/1.6 km west; elev. 148 feet/45m; length 4,000 feet/1,219m; asphalt; unattended.

Transportation: Air—Scheduled service from Petersburg (15-minute flight), Juneau (45 minutes), Wrangell and Sitka. Scheduled daily charter service provided by Haines Air, Taquan Air and L.A.B. Flying Service. **Ferry**—Alaska Marine Highway vessel from Petersburg and Sitka.

Accommodations at local inns and bed and breakfasts. There are general, variety and video stores, a cafe and other services. Church groups include Baptist, Salvation Army, Presbyterian and Assembly of God.

Kake has an accredited high school, junior high school and elementary.

The town is a permanent village of the Kake (pronounced cake) tribe of the Tlingit Indians. In a series of incidents in the late 1860s, several white men were killed by Kake warriors in reprisal for the deaths of their clansmen. United States gunboats retaliated by shelling and destroying 3 Kake villages.

The tribe eventually settled at the present-day site of Kake, where the government established a school in 1891. Residents have historically drawn ample subsistence from the sea. However, with the advent of a cash economy, the community has come to depend on commercial fishing, fish processing (there is a cold storage) and logging. In recent years, the fish processing has expanded to include the production of value-added products such as smoked and dried fish, and pet treats made from dried salmon skins. The post office was established in 1904, and the city was incorporated in 1952. The city's claim to fame is its totem, reputedly the world's tallest one-piece pole at 132 feet, 6 inches. It was carved for the 1967 Alaska Purchase Centennial Celebration.

The annual Kake Dog Salmon Festival, held in July, celebrates Tlingit culture and the return of dog salmon, also known as chum salmon. Over 700 people joined the festivities in recent years, which included events such as a Tlingit canoe race called "The Challenge of the Chums," the Chum Run foot race and a dog salmon toss. Contact Kake Tribal Corp. for more information, phone (907) 785-3221.

Other area activities include a guided tour of the local salmon hatchery (907/785-6460) and watching black bear fish for salmon in Gunnuk Creek, which flows through the center of the village.

Angoon

(See map, page 672)

Located on the west coast of Admiralty Island on Chatham Strait, at the mouth of Kootznahoo Inlet. Peril Strait is across Chatham Strait from Angoon. Juneau is 60 air miles/97 km northeast. Sitka is 41 miles/66 km southwest. **Population:** 587. **Emergency Services: Police,** phone (907) 788-3631. **Clinic,** phone (907) 788-3633.

Visitor Information: Local people are happy to help. You may also contact the USFS Admiralty Island National Monument office in Angoon (phone 907/788-3166) or the city of Angoon (phone 907/788-3653).

Elevation: Sea level. **Climate:** Moderate weather with about 40 inches of annual rainfall and mild temperatures.

Private Aircraft: Angoon seaplane base; 0.9 mile/1.4 km southeast; unattended.

Transportation: Air—Scheduled seaplane service from Juneau. **Ferry**—Alaska Marine Highway service.

Accommodations available at a motel and 2 bed and breakfasts. There are 2 general stores. Fuel service available. There are no RV facilities. Canoes and 12 charter boats available. Transient moorage for private boats also available.

Angoon is a long-established Tlingit Indian settlement at the entrance to Kootznahoo Inlet. It is the only permanent community on Admiralty Island. On Killisnoo Island, across the harbor from the state ferry landing, a community of mostly summer homes has grown up along the island beaches. The lifestyle of this primarily Tlingit community is heavily subsistence: fish, clams, seaweed, berries and venison. Fishing, mostly hand trolling for king and coho salmon, is the principal industry.

The scenery of Admiralty Island draws many visitors. All but the northern portion of the island was declared a national monument in December 1980 and is jointly managed by the U.S. Forest Service and Kootznoowoo Inc., the local Native corporation. Kootznahoo Inlet and Mitchell Bay near Angoon offer a network of small wooded islands, reefs and channels for kayaking. Mitchell Bay and Admiralty Lakes Recreational Area are the 2 major recreational attractions within the monument. Pack Creek, on the east coast of the island, is a well-known bear viewing spot (best mid-July to late August); permit required. Admiralty Island's Indian name, *Kootznoowoo*, means "Fortress of Bears." There are 12 USFS cabins available for public use in the monument; contact the U.S. Forest Service in Angoon.

Local residents can provide directions to the interesting old Killisnoo graveyards, located both on the island and on the Angoon shore of the old Killisnoo settlement, which once was one of the larger communities in southeastern Alaska.

Fishing for salmon is excellent in the Angoon area. (Record kings have been caught in nearby Kelp Bay and in Angoon harbor.) There is also excellent halibut and other bottom fish fishing. Trout (cutthroat and Dolly Varden) fishing in the lakes and streams on Admiralty Island; fair but scattered. ⌑

Tenakee Spring

(See map, page 672)

Located on the north shore of Tenakee Inlet on Chichagof Island, 50 miles/81 km northeast of Sitka. **Population:** 101. **Visitor Information:** Can be obtained from city hall, phone (907) 736-2207, or from the town's store, phone (907) 736-2205. **Elevation:** Sea level. **Climate:** Average rainfall 63.2 inches annually, with moderate snowfall. **Private Aircraft:** Seaplane base.

Transportation: Air—Scheduled and

View of Kake on Kupreanof Island. (© Alan D. Musy/ADM PhotoGraphics)

charter service available through Wings of Alaska out of Juneau and by Taquan Air out of Sitka. **Ferry**—Alaska Marine Highway service from Sitka and Juneau.

Tenakee Springs has 1 street—Tenakee Avenue—which is about 1.7 miles/2.7 km long and 4 to 12 feet wide. At each end of town is a foot trail that runs 3 miles/5 km west and 5 miles/8 km east on which no motorized vehicles or bicycles are allowed. Many residents ride bicycles, some use 3-or 4-wheeled vehicles, but most walk the short distances between buildings. There are a store, cafe, bakery, clinic, post office, art co-op, library and city hall. Accommodations at 7 rental cabins (bring your sleeping bag) are available at Snyder Mercantile, and Tenakee Hot Springs Lodge offers guided sportfishing and sightseeing; phone (907) 736-2400. Tenakee Springs became a city in 1971 and has a mayor, council and planning commission.

The word Tenakee comes from the Tlingit word *tinaghu*, or "Coppery Shield Bay." This refers to 3 copper shields, highly prized by the Tlingits, which were lost in a storm.

The hot springs (temperatures from 106°F to 108°F/41°C to 42°C) brought people to Tenakee at the turn of the century. A bathhouse, completed in 1940, located on the waterfront posts times of use for men and women. The facility is maintained by contributions from residents and visitors.

The major industry at Tenakee might be described as relaxation, as many retirees have chosen to live here, away from the bustle of other Southeast cities. There are many summer homes along Tenakee Avenue. During the summer, watch for whales in Tenakee Inlet, which are sometimes spotted from town.

Some logging is under way in the area around Tenakee. Tenakee Inlet produces salmon, halibut, prawns, Dungeness and king crab, red snapper and cod. A small fleet of fishing vessels is home-ported in Tenakee's harbor, located about 0.5 mile/0.8 km east of the center of town. Although many visitors come to Tenakee to hunt and fish, there are no hunting guides or rental boats available locally. There are 3 fishing and sightseeing charter services.

Pelican

(See map, page 672)

Located on the east shore of Lisianski Inlet on the northwest coast of Chichagof Island; 70 air miles/113 km north of Sitka and 70 air miles/113 km west of Juneau. **Population:** 149. **Emergency Services: Public Safety Officer** and **Fire Department**, phone 911. **Clinic**, phone (907) 735-2250. **Elevation:** Sea level. **Climate:** Average winter temperatures from 21°F/-6°C to 39°F/4°C; summer temperatures from 51°F/11°C to 62°F/17°C. Total average annual precipitation is 127 inches, with 120 inches of snow.

Visitor Information: Contact the Pelican Visitor Assoc., Box 737, Pelican, AK 99832; phone (907) 735-2282 or 735-2259.

Private Aircraft: Seaplane base; fuel 80, 100. **Transportation: Air**—Scheduled air service from Juneau via Alaska Seaplane Services and Taquan Air. Scheduled service from Sitka via Taquan Air. Seaplanes land within walking distance to downtown. **Ferry**—Alaska Marine Highway serves Pelican; terminal is approximately 1/4 mile from downtown boardwalk. There are no cars or taxis in Pelican, which is fine, as the town is not very big. Bring good walking shoes. Four-wheels are available.

Pelican has 2 bar-and-grills (1 with 4 rooms for rent) and a cafe. Accommodations available at a lodge, 2 seasonal lodges, and bed and breakfast. There are a grocery and dry goods store, laundromat and 2 liquor stores. There are a small-boat harbor, marine repair and a fuel dock.

Established in 1938 by Kalle (Charley) Raataikainen, and named for Raataikainen's fish packer *The Pelican*, Pelican relies on commercial fishing and seafood processing. Pelican Seafoods processes salmon, halibut, crab, herring, black cod, rockfish, sea urchin and sea cucumber, and is the primary year-round employer. Pelican has dubbed itself "closest to the fish," a reference to its close proximity to the rich Fairweather salmon grounds. Salmon trolling season is from about June to mid-September, and the king salmon winter season is from October through April. Pelican's population increases greatly when nonresident fishers work during the salmon seasons. Pelican was incorporated in 1943. Most of Pelican is built on pilings over tidelands. A wooden boardwalk extends the length of the community, and there are about 2 miles/3.2 km of gravel road.

Local recreation includes kayaking, hiking, fishing, and watching birds and marine mammals.

Sweeping view of Mendenhall Glacier and Valley. (© David J. Job)

Hoonah

(See map, page 672)

Located on the northeast shore of Chichagof Island, about 40 miles/64 km west of Juneau and 20 miles/32 km south across Icy Strait from the entrance to Glacier Bay. **Population: 896. Emergency Services: Alaska State Troopers** and **Hoonah City Police,** phone (907) 945-3655; emergency only phone 911. **Maritime Search and Rescue,** call the Coast Guard at (800) 478-5555.

Visitor Information: Local business people, city office staff (907/945-3663, weekdays 8 A.M. to 4:30 P.M.) and the postmaster are happy to help. The U.S. Forest Service office in Hoonah (Box 135, Hoonah, AK 99829, phone 907/945-3631) also has visitor information, including a $4 Hoonah area road guide showing forest roads on Chichagof Island and a $4 Tongass National Forest map.

Elevation: Sea level. **Climate:** Typical Southeastern Alaska climate, with average annual precipitation of 70 inches. Average daily temperature in July, 57°F/13°C; in January, 35°F/1°C. Prevailing winds are southeasterly.

Private Aircraft: Hoonah airport, adjacent southeast; elev. 30 feet/9m; length 3,000 feet/914m; paved. Seaplane base adjacent.

Transportation: Air–Scheduled and charter service from Juneau. Airport is located about 3 miles/5 km from town. **Ferry**–Alaska Marine Highway vessel serves Hoonah.

Bed-and-breakfast lodging at Wind'n Sea Inn (907/945-3438). Accommodations also available at Hoonah Lodge. Hoonah has 2 restaurants, 2 grocery stores, a hardware store, a gift shop, a variety store, a fishing tackle supply store, a bank, marine fuel docks, a gas pump and 3 flying services. The marina, with showers and a laundromat, is a popular layover for boaters awaiting permits to enter Glacier Bay.

Hoonah is a small coastal community with a quiet harbor for the seining and trolling fleets. The most prominent structures are a cold storage facility, the lodge, bank, post office and the public school. The village has been occupied since prehistory by the Tlingit people. In the late 1800s, missionaries settled here. Canneries established in the area in the early 1900s spurred the growth of commercial fishing, which remains the mainstay of Hoonah's economy. During the summer fishing season, residents work for nearby Excursion Inlet Packing Co. or Hoonah Cold Storage in town. Halibut season begins in May, and salmon season opens in mid-summer and runs through September. Logging also contributes to the economy, with employment loading log ships and other industry-related jobs. Subsistence hunting and fishing remain an important lifestyle here, and many families gather food in the traditional way: catching salmon and halibut in summer, shellfish and bottom fish year-round; hunting deer, geese and ducks; berry picking in summer and fall.

Kayaking, sightseeing, hunting and fishing are the main attractions for visitors. Charter fishing is available locally, with good seasonal king and coho (silver) salmon and halibut fishing as well as crabbing. Guide services are available.

Hoonah is the starting point for an extensive logging and forest road system for northwest Chichagof Island. Island road maps ($4) are available through the USFS in Hoonah, Sitka and Juneau.

Juneau

(See maps, pages 672-673)

Located on Gastineau Channel; 900 air miles/1,448 km (2 hours, 10 minutes flying time) from Seattle, WA, 650 air miles/1,046 km (1 hour, 25 minutes by jet) from Anchorage. **Population:** Borough 29,755. **Emergency Services:** Phone 911 for all emergencies. **Police,** phone (907) 586-2780. **Fire Department,** phone (907) 586-5245. **Alaska State Troopers,** phone (907) 465-4000. **Poison Center** and **Hospital,** Bartlett Regional, 3260 Hospital Dr., phone (907) 586-2611. **Maritime Search and Rescue,** Coast Guard, phone (907) 463-2000 or (800) 478-5555.

Visitor Information: Juneau Convention & Visitors Bureau, Davis Log Cabin Information Center, 134 3rd St., phone (907) 586-2201 or (888) 581-2201; Internet: www.juneau.com; e-mail: jcub@ptialaska.net. Open year-round 8:30 A.M. to 5 P.M. Monday through Friday; additional hours during the summer, 9 A.M. to 5 P.M. Saturday and Sunday. Visitor information kiosk located in Marine Park on waterfront near Merchants

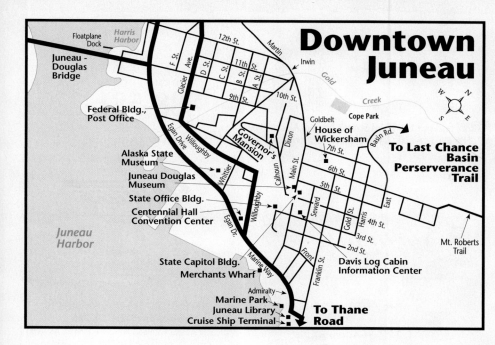

Downtown Juneau

Floatplane Dock
Harris Harbor
Juneau-Douglas Bridge
12th St.
11th St.
9th St.
10th St.
F St.
D St.
C St.
B St.
A St.
Glacier Ave.
Martin
Irwin
Gold Creek
Cope Park
Federal Bldg., Post Office
Governor's Mansion
Goldbelt
House of Wickersham
7th St.
Basin Rd.
To Last Chance Basin Perserverance Trail
Alaska State Museum
Juneau Douglas Museum
State Office Bldg.
Centennial Hall Convention Center
Egan Drive
Willoughby
Whittier
Calhoun
Main St.
Dixon
6th St.
5th St.
Seward
Gold St.
Harris
East
4th St.
3rd St.
2nd St.
Mt. Roberts Trail
Juneau Harbor
State Capitol Bldg.
Merchants Wharf
Egan Dr.
Willoughby
Marine Way
Front
Franklin St.
Davis Log Cabin Information Center
Admiralty
Marine Park
Juneau Library
Cruise Ship Terminal
To Thane Road

Juneau Vicinity

Point Bridget
Berners Bay
Echo Cove
Lynn Canal
Juneau Veterans' Memorial Highway
Eagle Glacier
Eagle River
Herbert Glacier
Favorite Channel
Shrine of St. Therese
Windfall Lake
Juneau Veterans' Memorial Highway
Shelter Island
Tee Harbor
Lena Cove
Peterson Lake
Mendenhall Lake Campground
Mendenhall Glacier
Montana Creek Rd.
Mendenhall Lake
Auke Bay Ferry Terminal
Auke Village Campground Rec. Area
Auke L.
Auke Bay
Glacier Hwy.
Univ. of Alaska SE Information Center
Mendenhall Loop Rd.
Mendenhall River
Airport
Mendenhall Peninsula
Fritz Cove
Old Glacier Highway
North Douglas Highway
Egan Dr.
Salmon Creek Reservoir
Hospital
Gastineau Salmon Hatchery
Tongass National Forest
Juneau-Douglas Bridge
Gastineau Channel
Downtown Juneau
Eaglecrest Ski Area
Douglas Highway
Cruise Ship Dock, Mt. Roberts Tram
Douglas Island
Douglas
Stephens Passage
Sandy Beach Rec. Area
Thane Rd.

Wharf, usually open daily 8:30 A.M. to 6 P.M., from about mid-May to mid-September. Information booth at the airport terminal. Visitor information is also available at the cruise ship terminal on S. Franklin Street when cruise ships are in port, and at the Auke Bay ferry terminal. Large groups contact the Davis Log Cabin Information Center in advance for special assistance.

USFS Information Center at Centennial Hall, 101 Egan Dr.; open 8 A.M. to 5 P.M. daily from mid-May to mid-September; 9 A.M. to 5 P.M. Monday through Friday the rest of the year. Phone (907) 586-8751. U.S. Park Service office here open in summer. The center has seasonal features of natural history films. USFS cabins may also be reserved here. The center issues permits for visiting Pack Creek, the bear preserve on Admiralty Island. Juneau Ranger District (USFS), **Milepost** 9.4 Glacier Highway (airport area), phone (907) 586-8800; open 8 A.M. to 5 P.M. weekdays. Mendenhall Glacier Visitor Center (USFS), phone (907) 789-0097, open 8:30 A.M. to 5:30 P.M. daily in summer, 9 A.M. to 4 P.M. weekends only in winter.

Elevation: Sea level. **Climate:** Mild and wet. Average daily maximum temperature in July, 63°F/17°C; daily minimum in January, 20°F/-7°C. Highest recorded temperature, 90°F/32°C in July 1975; the lowest -22°F/-30°C in January 1972. Average annual precipitation, 56.5 inches (airport), 92 inches

(downtown); 103 inches of snow annually. Snow on ground intermittently from mid-November to mid-April. Prevailing winds are east-southeasterly. **Radio:** KJNO 630, KINY 800, KTOO-FM 104.3, KTKU-FM 105.1, KSUP-FM 106. **Television:** KJUD Channel 8; JATV cable; KTOO (public television). **Newspapers:** Juneau Empire (Sunday through Friday) and Capital City Weekly.

Private Aircraft: Juneau International Airport, 9 miles/14.5 km northwest; elev. 18 feet/5m; length 8,456 feet/2,577m; asphalt; fuel 100LL, Jet A. Juneau harbor seaplane base, due east; restricted use, no fuel. International seaplane base, 7 miles/11.3 km northwest; 5,000 feet/1,524m by 450 feet/137m, avgas, Jet A. For more information, phone the Juneau Flight Service Station at (907) 789-6124.

HISTORY AND ECONOMY

In 1880, nearly 20 years before the great gold rushes to the Klondike and to Nome, 2 prospectors named Joe Juneau and Dick Harris found "color" in what is now called Gold Creek, a small, clear stream that runs

through the center of present-day Juneau. What they found led to the discovery of one of the largest lodes of gold quartz in the world. Juneau (called Harrisburg the first year) quickly boomed into a gold rush town as claims and mines sprang up in the area.

For a time the largest mine was the Treadwell, across Gastineau Channel south of Douglas (which was once a larger town than Juneau), but a cave-in and flood closed the mine in 1917. In 36 years of operation, Treadwell produced $66 million in gold. The Alaska–Gastineau Mine, operated by Bart Thane in 1911, had a 2-mile shaft through Mount Roberts to the Perseverance Mine

near Gold Creek. The Alaska–Juneau (A–J) Mine was constructed on a mountain slope south of Juneau and back into the heart of Mount Roberts. It operated until 1944, when it was declared a nonessential wartime activity after producing over $80 million in gold. Post–WWII wage and price inflation and the fixed price of gold prevented its reopening.

In 1900, the decision to move Alaska's capital to Juneau was made because of the city's growth, mining activity and location on the water route to Skagway and the Klondike; the decline of post-Russian Sitka, as whale and fur trading slackened, secured Juneau's new status as Alaska's preeminent city.

Congress first provided civil government for Alaska in 1884. Until statehood in 1959 Alaska was governed by a succession of presidential appointees, first as the District of Alaska, then as the Territory of Alaska. Between 1867 (when the United States purchased Alaska from Russia) and 1884, the military had jurisdiction over the District of Alaska, except for a 3-year period (1877–79) when Alaska was put under control of the U.S. Treasury Dept. and governed by U.S. Collectors of Customs.

With the arrival of Alaska statehood in 1959, Juneau's governmental role increased even further. In 1974, Alaskans voted to move the capital from Juneau to a site between Anchorage and Fairbanks, closer to the state's population center. In 1976, Alaska voters selected a new capital site near Willow, 65 road miles/105 km north of Anchorage on the Parks Highway. However, in November 1982, voters defeated funding for the capital move.

Today, government (federal, state and local) comprises an estimated half of the total basic industry. Tourism is the largest employer in the private sector.

DESCRIPTION

Juneau, often called "a little San Francisco," is nestled at the foot of Mount Juneau (elev. 3,576 feet/1,091m) with Mount Roberts (elev. 3,819 feet/1,164m)

rising immediately to the east on the approach up Gastineau Channel. The residential community of Douglas, on Douglas Island, is south of Juneau and connected by a bridge. Neighboring residential areas around the airport, Mendenhall Valley and Auke Bay lie north of Juneau on the mainland.

Shopping is in the downtown area and at suburban malls in the airport and Mendenhall Valley areas.

Juneau's skyline is dominated by several government buildings, including the Federal Building (1962), the massive State Office Building (1974), the State Court Building (1975) and the older brick, and marble-columned Capitol Building (1931). The modern Sealaska Plaza is headquarters for Sealaska Corp., 1 of the 13 regional Native corporations formed after congressional passage of the Alaska Native Claims Settlement Act in 1971.

To explore downtown Juneau, it is best to park and walk; distances are not great. The streets are narrow and congested with pedestrians and traffic (especially rush hours), and on-street parking is scarce. Visitors should check at the Davis Log Cabin and at the police station to see whether parking permits are available. Public parking lots are located across from Merchants Wharf Mall at Main Street and Egan Drive and south of Marine Park at the Marine Park parking garage; fee required.

The Juneau area supports 35 churches, a high school, 2 middle schools, several elementary schools and a University of Alaska Southeast campus at Auke Lake. There are 3 municipal libraries and the state library. The Perseverance Theatre, which was established in 1978, provides Juneau with classical and original works, September through May.

The area is governed by the unified city and borough of Juneau, which encompasses 3,108 square miles/8,060 square km. It is the first unified government in the state, combining the former separate and overlapping jurisdictions of the city of Douglas, city of Juneau and greater Juneau borough.

ACCOMMODATIONS/VISITOR SERVICES

Juneau has several hotels and motels, most of them downtown. These include: Alaska Hotel & Bar (907) 586-1000, Best Western Country Lane Inn (907) 789-5005, Breakwater Inn (907) 586-6303, Driftwood Lodge Motel (907) 586-2280, Prospector Hotel (907) 586-3737, Super 8 Motel (907) 789-4858, Travelodge (907) 789-9700, Westmark Baranof (907) 586-2660 and Goldbelt Hotel Juneau (907) 586-6900. There are also numerous bed and breakfasts as well as wilderness lodges; see ads this section.

The Juneau International Hostel is located at 614 Harris St. (Juneau 99801), 4 blocks northeast of the Capitol Bldg. All ages are welcome. Check-in time is 5–11 P.M.

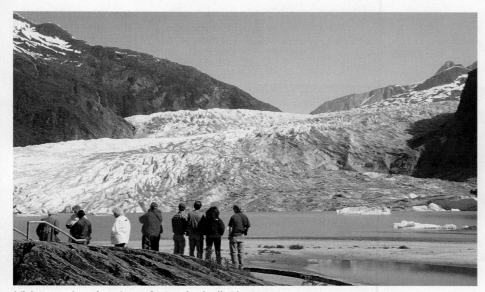

Visitors enjoy the view of Mendenhall Glacier. (© Susan Cole Kelly)

during summer, 5–10:30 P.M. the rest of the year. Showers, cooking, laundry and storage facilities are available. Cost for members is $7, nonmembers $10, children accompanied by parent $5. Groups welcome. Open year-round. Phone (907) 586-9559.

More than 60 restaurants offer a wide variety of dining. Also watch for sidewalk food vendors downtown in summer.

Juneau also has a microbrewery. The Alaskan Brewing Co., located at 5429 Shaune Dr. in the Lemon Creek area, produces Alaskan Amber Beer and Alaskan Pale Ale. Free tours available. Phone (907) 780-5866 for more information.

Cinnamon Inn, cheerful and congenial, is conveniently located near the Juneau airport and state ferries. The dramatic Mendenhall Glacier is 3 miles away. This charming Inn has five rooms, each with handmade quilts, embroidered linens and comfortable furnishings—a relaxed indulgence is found at the Cinnamon Inn. The master suite has a private bath, queen-sized bed, VCR, microwave and refrigerator. Four additional rooms, with new double beds, share two bathrooms. You'll enjoy a hearty hot breakfast each morning, with abundant gourmet coffee. The Cinnamon Inn is located near bus lines, 10 miles from downtown Juneau. The Cinnamon House, a cozy, private and delightfully decorated 2-bedroom guest home is right next door. With a new queen-sized bed, twin beds and a pull-out couch, it comfortably sleeps 6. The Cinnamon House

has well-stocked cupboards for breakfast, and homemade treats are delivered to you each morning. Children are welcome. Reasonable rates. Call today: (907) 789-INNS, fax (907) 789-5876; fax; www.wetpage.com/cinnamon. VISA, Mastercard, American Express. [ADVERTISEMENT]

Fireweed House Bed & Breakfast. If you are seeking the finest in private, plush accommodations and breakfast dining in the Juneau area, look no further than Fireweed House Bed & Breakfast. This fabulous 4-acre location on Douglas Island is just a few minutes from downtown Juneau; but when you are a guest at Fireweed House, you'll feel like you've stepped into a pampered world away from the vacation hustle and bustle. *What a find!* Although this is a destination by itself, a more ideal base for your Southeast Alaska experience would be difficult to locate. The accommodations are all first class and the breakfast dining experience is a *must!* The Thomas Glacier and the surrounding mountains are prominent from many of the windows. The 2-bedroom, cedar guest house on its own adjoining, 2-acre site is unsurpassed in its beauty, seclusion and spaciousness. In addition, the private Fireweed Apartment and guest rooms in the Main House are also extraordinarily appointed and comfortable. Many amenities. Several accommodations include King-size beds and Jacuzzi baths. Birds and other forms of wildlife grace the grounds surrounding this establishment. Complimentary arrangements for personal-

ized tours and charters. Non-smoking. Children welcome. AAA 3-diamond approved. Toll free (800) 586-3885; phone (907) 586-3885; fax (907) 586-3385. 8530 North Douglas Highway, Juneau, AK 99801; website with e-mail: http://fireweedhouse.com. Reserve early to assure space at this B&B! [ADVERTISEMENT]

Pearson's Pond Luxury Inn and Garden Spa. Looking for the perfect getaway? You'll find it here, nestled in the rainforest next to the Mendenhall Glacier. You'll be away from the crowds, yet conveniently located, at this breathtaking retreat on the banks of a peaceful pond. Enjoy a relaxing hot tub and massage amid lush gardens and sparkling fountains. Between naps on the dock, bike the adjacent nature trail, photograph wildlife, roast marshmallows, enjoy a workout or winter cross-country ski. Everything, including stocked kitchenettes, is provided for an exceptional value. Year-round, smoke and pet free. Ski, spa and wedding packages. 4541-MP Sawa Circle, Juneau, AK 99801-8723; phone (907) 789-3772, fax 789-6722, e-mail: pearsons.pond@juneau.com. Website: www.juneau.com/pearsons.pond. AAA/ABBA Excellence Awards. Recommended as a "Best B & B" in America

Colorful mural decorates a Juneau building. (© Lee Foster)

(Fodor's/Soule's) and Alaska (Frommer's). Book far ahead, as this place earns its excellent reputation. A definite 10! [ADVERTISEMENT]

The city and borough of Juneau offers limited RV overnight parking spaces at Savikko Park/Sandy Beach (**Milepost 2.5** Douglas Highway); $5 per space, per night, paid at the harbormaster's office. For parking at both yacht club and park, sign in at the harbormaster's office (across from high school on Egan Drive). Contact the visitor information center (907/586-2201) for a brochure on RV facilities. Dump stations are located at Mendenhall Lake campground, Valley Tesoro at Mendenhall Center shopping mall in the Mendenhall Valley, and Savikko Park in Douglas.

There are 2 USFS campgrounds and 1 private RV park north of Juneau via the Glacier Highway. The USFS campgrounds are Mendenhall Lake (turn off Glacier Highway

at **Milepost 9.4** or **12.2** and continue to Montana Creek Road) and Auke Village (**Milepost 15.4** Glacier Highway). Mendenhall Lake, closed for construction for the past two years. will have a limited number of campsites open in 1999. Both campgrounds are first come, first served. Auke Village Campground, 1.5 miles/2.4 km west of the ferry terminal, has 12 campsites, flush and pit toilets, water and firewood: first-come, first-served. The private RV park, with hookups, is located at **Milepost 12.3** Glacier Highway; phone (907) 789-9467. ▲

Spruce Meadow RV Park. (Planned to open in spring 1999.) 64 private, unique, full-service spaces located on 10.5 acres of virgin wetlands in spruce, alder and meadows. Services available: 30-amp electric, water, sewer, garbage, phone, cable TV, laundromat, showers, restrooms, recreation hall, gazebos, dump station, on-site management,

bicycle rental, tourist information and brochures. Only 5 minutes from Mendenhall Glacier and Auke Bay boat harbor. Reservations strongly recommended. Visit us at 10200 Mendenhall Loop Rd. E-mail: juneauRVer@aol.com. Phone (907) 789-1990. [ADVERTISEMENT] ▲

TRANSPORTATION

Air: Juneau Municipal Airport turnoff is at **Milepost 8.8** Egan Drive (Glacier Highway). Airport terminal contains ticket counters, waiting area, gift shop, rental cars, restaurant, lounge and information booth.

The city express bus stops at the airport weekdays from 8 A.M. to 5 P.M. A shuttle and taxi and van service to downtown are also available. Shuttle service $8 1-way per person, $5 each for groups of 3 or more. Taxi service approximately $15 to $20. Courtesy vans to some hotels.

Alaska Airlines serves Juneau daily from Seattle, WA, Anchorage, Fairbanks, Ketchikan, Sitka, Yakutat, Cordova, Petersburg and Wrangell. Scheduled commuter service to Haines, Skagway, Sitka, Angoon and other points via several air services. Scheduled service by Summit Air between Juneau and Whitehorse, YT, year-round and between Juneau and Atlin, BC, in summer. Air North serves Whitehorse/Juneau, and Air One provides regional air service.

Charter air service (wheel and floatplanes and helicopters) is available for hunting, fishing, sightseeing and transportation to other communities (see ads in this section).

Alaska Seaplane Service provides experienced floatplane service to wilderness cabins, villages, and fishing lodges in Southeast Alaska. Over 30 years of flying experience guarantees personalized, professional sightseeing and wildlife tours. Visit our ticket counter in the Juneau International Airport or phone (907) 789-3331 for further information. [ADVERTISEMENT]

Ferry: Juneau is served by Alaska Marine Highway ferries.

Alaska state ferries dock at the Auke Bay terminal at **Milepost 13.9** Glacier Highway; phone (907) 465-3941 or 789-7453. Taxi service and private shuttle bus is available from Auke Bay terminal to downtown Juneau. Shuttle service runs mid-May to mid-October; $5 each way. There is also a bus stop 1.5 miles/2.4 km toward town from the ferry terminal (see following).

Bus: Capital Transit city bus system runs from the cruise ship terminal downtown and includes Juneau, Douglas, Lemon Creek, Mendenhall Valley and airport area, Auke Bay (the community, which is about 1.5 miles/2.4 km south of the ferry terminal). Hourly service Monday through Saturday, year-round; limited service on Sundays. Route map and schedule available at the visitor information center. Flag buses at any corner except in downtown Juneau, where bus uses marked stops only. Fare: $1.25 anywhere.

Highways: Longest road is Glacier Highway, which begins in downtown Juneau and leads 40.5 miles/65.3 km north to Echo Cove. Other major roads are Mendenhall Loop Road and Douglas and North Douglas highways. See logs this section.

Taxi: Five companies.

Cruise Ships: Juneau is southeastern Alaska's most frequent port of call. There were 547 port calls by cruise ships in 1998.

Car Rental: Several car rental agencies are available at the airport and vicinity,

View of downtown Juneau from a hiking trail on Mount Jumbo. (© David J. Job)

including All Star/Practical Rent-A-Car (907/790-2414); Avis Rent-A-Car (907/789-9450), Evergreen/Ford–Lincoln–Mercury (907/789-9386), Hertz (907/789-9494), Mendenhall Auto Center (907/789-1386), National Car Rental (907/789-9814) and Rent-A-Wreck (907/789-4111).

There are no car rental agencies downtown, but most rental agencies will take you to their offices (sometimes at an extra charge). Best to reserve ahead of time because of the great demand for cars.

Private Boats: Transient moorage is available downtown at Harris and Douglas floats and at Auke Bay. Most boaters use Auke Bay. For more information call the Juneau harbormaster at (907) 586-5255 or hail on Channel 16 UHF.

ATTRACTIONS

Juneau walking-tour map (in English, French, Spanish, German, Chinese or Japanese) is available from the Davis Log Cabin Information Center at 134 3rd St. and from other visitor information sites and hotels. See Juneau's many attractions—the St. Nicholas Orthodox Church, totems, Capitol Building, Governor's Mansion, historic graves, monuments, state museum, city museum, hatchery and others.

Charter a Boat for salmon and halibut fishing or sightseeing. The visitor information center can provide a list of charter operators; also see ads in this section.

Charter a Plane for fly-in fishing, hunting, transportation to remote lodges and longer flightseeing trips.

Take a Tour. Tours of Juneau and area attractions—by boat, bus, plane and helicopter—can be arranged. These tours range from sightseeing trips out to Mendenhall Glacier to river trips on the Mendenhall River.

Era Helicopters. Soar over the massive Juneau Icefield, viewing 4 unique and distinctive glaciers. Land on a glacier and explore the ancient ice. Fly past historical gold mining areas. Personalized tour with Alaska's most experienced helicopter company. Phone (800) 843-1947 or (907) 586-2030 locally. Tours also available in Anchorage, Mount McKinley and Valdez. [ADVERTISEMENT]

Visit the Juneau Library. Built on top of the 4-story public parking garage in downtown Juneau, this award-winning library designed by Minch Ritter Voelckers Architects is well worth a visit. Take the elevator to the 5th floor and spend a morning or afternoon reading in this well-lit and comfortable space with a wonderful view of Juneau, Douglas and Gastineau Channel. Located at South Franklin and Admiralty Way, between Marine Park and the cruise ship terminal.

Juneau–Douglas City Museum, located in the Veteran's Memorial Building across from the State Capitol Building at 4th and Main streets, offers exhibits and audiovisual presentations on the Juneau–Douglas area, featuring gold mining and local cultural history. Displays include a turn-of-the-century store and kitchen, a large relief map, a hands-on history room that's fun for kids of all ages and a special summer exhibit. Free historical walking-tour maps of Juneau are available. Museum gift shop. Summer hours are 9 A.M. to 5 P.M. weekdays, 10 A.M. to 5 P.M. weekends, mid-May to mid-September. Limited hours in winter. Admission $2. Students free. Phone (907) 586-3572 or write Parks and Recreation, Attn: Juneau–Douglas City Museum, 155 S. Seward St., Juneau, AK 99801, for more information.

State Capitol Building, at 4th and Main streets, contains the legislative chambers and the governor's office. Free tours available from capitol lobby; most days in summer on the half-hour from 9 A.M. to 5 P.M. The **State Office Building,** one block west, houses the State Historical Library and Kimball theater organ (free organ concerts at noon Fridays).

Alaska State Museum is a major highlight of Juneau located downtown at 395 Whittier St. Exhibits include dioramas and contain materials from Alaska's Native groups; icons and other artifacts from Russian–America days; and a popular life-size

Juneau's Native Indian Theatre is designed after a traditional clan house.
(© Chris Sharp)

eagle nesting tree surrounded by a mural of a Southeast Alaska scene. A replica of Capt. George Vancouver's ship, *Discovery*, is located in the children's room for kids to explore. During the summer of 1999, there will be an exhibition entitled *Agayuliyararput (Our Way of Making Prayer): The Living Tradition of Yup'ik Masks*, featuring over 100 Yup'ik Eskimo masks gathered from around the world. This exhibit presents the traditions and heritage of the Yup'ik people using the masks in the context of the dances, the stories and the cosmology of the Yup'ik people. There will also be an exhibit of paintings by Eustace Ziegler, one of Alaska's most popular and influential artists who helped to forge the enduring image of Alaska. The museum store carries Alaska Native crafts and Alaska books and gifts for all ages. Summer hours are 9 A.M. to 6 P.M.

Monday through Friday and 10 A.M. to 6 P.M. weekends. Winter hours are 10 A.M. to 4 P.M. Tuesday through Saturday. General admission is $4. Visitors 18 and under and members of the Friends of the Alaska State Museum are admitted free. A $10 museum pass is also available. Phone (907) 465-2901; Internet:http://www.educ.state.ak.us/lam/museum/home.html. E-mail: bruce_kato@educ.state.ak.us.

The House of Wickersham, 213 7th St., has an important historical collection dating to the days of the late Judge James Wickersham, one of Alaska's first federal judges, who collected Native artifacts and baskets, as well as many photographs and historical documents concerning Native culture, during his extensive travels throughout the territory early in the century. Visiting hours in summer. Phone (907) 586-9001 for more

information. (Steep climb up to Seventh Street.)

The Governor's Mansion at 716 Calhoun Ave. has been home to Alaska's chief executives since it was completed in 1913. The 2½-story structure, containing 12,900 square feet of floor space, took nearly a year to build. Tours may be possible by advance arrangement. Phone (907) 465-3500.

The Gastineau Salmon Hatchery, operated by Douglas Island Pink and Chum, Inc., is located on Channel Drive 3 miles/4.8 km from downtown. The hatchery offers visitors a chance to see adult salmon, over 100 species of Southeast Alaska sea-life in saltwater aquariums, aquaculture displays, and other seasonal activities. A variety of salmon products is also available for purchase. Fishing available near the hatchery; buy licenses and rent gear at kiosk. Visitor center open in summer 10 A.M. to 6 P.M. Monday through Friday; 10 A.M. to 5 P.M. Saturday and Sunday. Incubation-room tours available May 15 through June 30; spawning salmon sights and hatchery operations tour July 1 through Oct. 1. Educational tours provided; $3 adult; $1 child. Group: 5 adults, $12; 12 children, $12. Phone (907) 463-5114.

See Old Mine Ruins. Remnants from the Treadwell Mine may be seen from a marked trail that starts just south of Sandy Beach on Douglas Island. The impressive remains of the A–J mine mill are located on the hillside along Gastineau Channel just south of downtown Juneau; good views from Douglas Island and from the water. Evidence of the Alaska–Gastineau Mine can be seen south of town along Thane Road. Walking-tour maps of the Treadwell area are available from the city museum.

Marine Park, located at foot of Seward Street, has tables, benches, information kiosk and lighterage facilities for cruise ship launches. The Ed Way bronze sculpture, "Hard Rock Miner," is located at Marine Park. Free concerts on Friday evenings in summer.

Thane Road is a wide, straight paved road beginning just south of downtown Juneau and extending 5.5 miles/8.9 km along Gastineau Channel. Good views of the channel and old mines. Excellent viewpoint for spawning salmon at Sheep Creek bridge and falls, Mile 4.3, in summer.

Mount Juneau Waterfall, scenic but difficult to photograph, descends 3,576 feet/1,091m from Mount Juneau to Gold Creek behind the city. Best view is from Basin Road. The waterfall is also visible from Marine Park.

Mount Roberts Tramway. A 60-passenger aerial tramway takes you from Juneau's downtown waterfront to a modern mountain complex at the 1800-foot level of Mount Roberts. The panoramic views of the town, harbor, waterways and surrounding mountains are a photographer's delight. The complex houses a theater, restaurant, bar, select gift shop and Native artists, and offers access to a nature center and alpine walking trails. Tickets valid all day and include viewing *Seeing Daylight*, an award-winning cultural film. [ADVERTISEMENT]

Mount Roberts Trail Observation Point offers an elevated view of Juneau. Though the trail extends to the 3,819-foot/1,164-m summit, an excellent observation point above Juneau is reached by a 20-minute hike from the start of Mount Roberts trail at the top of Starr Hill (6th Street).

Mendenhall Glacier is about 13 miles/

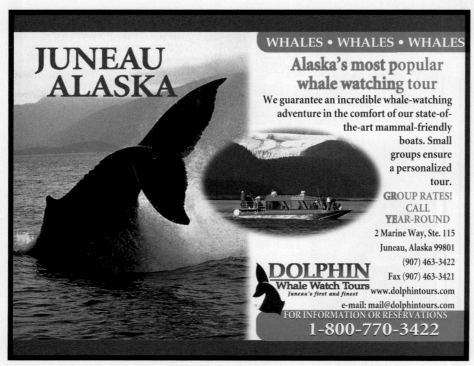

21 km from downtown Juneau at the end of Mendenhall Glacier Spur Road. Turn right northbound at **Milepost 9.4** Egan Drive (Glacier Highway), and then drive straight for 3.6 miles/5.8 km to the glacier and visitor center. There is a large parking area, and trails lead down to the edge of the lake (a sign warns visitors to stay back; falling ice can create huge waves). A 0.5-mile/0.8-km nature trail starts behind the visitor center. Trailheads for 2 longer trails—East Glacier and Nugget Creek—are a short walk from the visitor center. Programs and guided hikes with Forest Service interpreters are offered in summer. Recent renovations, including a new salmon-viewing area and salmon-viewing trail, are scheduled for completion in spring of 1999. The new center will feature an exhibit area with a model of a glacier and displays on glacial processes and the rebirth of landscape as glaciers retreat. The new center will also feature an expanded lobby area and a theatre seating 100 people; phone (907) 586-8751. There will be a nominal admission fee for the visitor center only; no charge for access to the lake, trail and parking lot.

Bike Paths. There are designated bike routes to Douglas, to Mendenhall Valley and Glacier, and to Auke Bay. The Mendenhall Glacier route starts at the intersection of 12th Street and Glacier Avenue; total biking distance is 15 miles/24.1 km. Bikes can be rented downtown and in the vicinity of the airport. Bike-route map and hiking information are available at the Davis Log Cabin.

Glacier Bay National Park contains some of the most impressive tidewater glaciers in the world. Juneau is located about 50 miles/80 km east of the bay and is subsequently the main jumping-off point for many Glacier Bay visitors. There are several local businesses offering 1- and 2-day or longer boat and air packages to the park. The state ferries do not service Glacier Bay, but there is a private ferry service available. Contact AUK NU Tours for information on the Glacier Bay Ferry; write 76 Egan Dr., Juneau, AK 99801, or phone 1-800-820-2628, (907) 586-8687, fax (907) 586-1337. See GLACIER BAY NATIONAL PARK and GUSTAVUS sections for more information.

Tracy Arm. Located 50 miles/80 km southeast of Juneau, Tracy Arm and adjoining Endicott Arm are the major features of the Tracy Arm–Fords Terror Wilderness Area. Both Tracy and Endicott arms are long, deep and narrow fjords that extend more than 30 miles/48 km into the heavily glaciated Coast Mountain Range. Active tidewater glaciers at the head of these fjords calve icebergs into the fjords.

Fords Terror, off of Endicott Arm, is an area of sheer rock walls enclosing a narrow entrance into a small fjord. The fjord was named in 1889 for a crew member of a naval vessel who rowed into the narrow canyon at slack tide and was caught in turbulent icy currents for 6 terrifying hours when the tide changed.

Access to this wilderness area is primarily by boat or floatplane from Juneau. Large cruise ships and small cruise ships and charter boats include Tracy Arm and Endicott Arm in their itineraries. It is also a popular destination for sea kayakers.

Tracy Arm Fjord–*Adventure Bound*, Alaska's greatest combination of mountains, wildlife, icebergs and tidewater glaciers. Tracy Arm could be called "cascade fjord" because of its many waterfalls or "icy fjord"

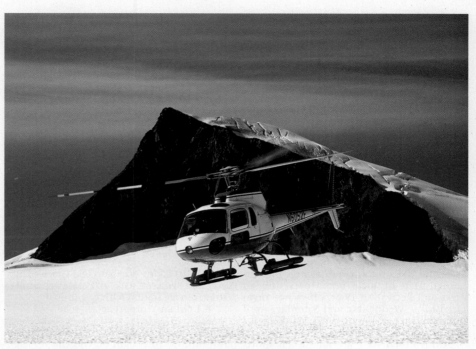
Flightseeing the Juneau Icefield is a popular attraction. (© David J. Job)

because it is the home of Alaska's largest icebergs. Best viewed from the *Adventure Bound.* Juneau's favorite because the Weber family doesn't overcrowd and they take the time to enjoy it all. For comfort, viewing time, elbow room and personal attention, this is the quality cruise that you are looking for. The *Adventure Bound* office is located in the Marine View Center. It is the 9-story building that stands across from Juneau's Marine Park. Street address: 215 Ferry Way. Mailing address: P.O. Box 23013, Juneau, AK 99802. Reservations: (907) 463-2509, (800) 228-3875. [ADVERTISEMENT]

Dolphin Jet Boat Tours, The Whale Watch Company—Juneau's first and finest whale watching company specializes in close encounter excursions on state-of-the-art, mammal-friendly jet boats. Small groups ensure a personalized tour with our local, friendly and knowledgeable crew. All boats are built for the comfort and safety of both passengers and wildlife. Each has a fully enclosed and heated cabin, restroom, big windows and plenty of deck space for viewing the majestic scenery and wildlife. For reservations and information, phone (800) 770-3422. 2 Marine Way, Suite 115, Juneau, AK 99801. Phone (907) 463-3422, fax (907) 463-3421. [ADVERTISEMENT]

Juneau Icefield, immediately to the east of Juneau, is a 1,500-square-mile/2,414 km expanse of glaciated mountains that is the source of all the glaciers in the area, including Mendenhall, Taku, Eagle and Herbert. Best way to experience and photograph it is via charter flightseeing. Flights usually take 30 to 60 minutes. Helicopter tours, which land on the glacier, are also available. Helicopter tours last from about 45 minutes to 1 1/2 hours.

Ski Eaglecrest, Juneau's downhill and cross-country ski area on Douglas Island. Built and maintained by the city of Juneau, the area features a day-lodge, cafeteria, ski school, ski patrol, ski rental shop, 2 chair lifts, a surface lift and runs for experienced, intermediate and beginning skiers. Three

miles/5 km of maintained cross-country trails available. Open 5 days a week, Dec. to mid-April. The view from the top of the chair lift (operating during ski season only) is worth the visit—Mendenhall Glacier, Juneau Icefield, Lynn Canal, Stephens Passage and more. Drive North Douglas Highway to turnoff left at Eaglecrest sign, then 5.3 miles/8.5 km up the Eaglecrest access road to the lodge. For more information, write Eaglecrest Ski Area, 155 S. Seward St., Juneau, AK 99801; phone (907) 586-5284 (790-2000 during ski season), or phone (907) 586-5330 for a recorded message about ski conditions. Internet: www.juneau.lib.ak.us/eaglecrest/eaglcrst.htm.

St. Nicholas Orthodox Church, 5th and Gold streets, a tiny structure built in 1894, is now the oldest original Russian Orthodox church in southeastern Alaska. Visitors are welcome to Sunday services; open daily for summer tours. Phone (907) 586-1023.

The Alaskan Brewing Company. Be sure to enjoy our international award-winning beers on your travels throughout Alaska. In Juneau, visit Alaska's oldest and largest operating brewery for a fascinating tour. Learn about modern and turn-of-the-century brewing techniques. Sample our gold-rush recipe Alaskan Amber and other award-winning brews. Tours every half hour. Gift shop and hospitality bar. Phone (907) 780-5866; Internet: www.alaskanbeer.com. [ADVERTISEMENT]

Glacier Gardens Rainforest Adventures. Nestled along the Inside Passage in picturesque Juneau is one of the world's finest garden tours. Visitors experience the lush tropical feel of an Alaskan rainforest through 100 acres of floral artistry. The gardens dazzle the senses with massive displays of color, fragrance and textures. Gently winding paths link each unique garden and lead to a spectacular view of the world-famous Mendenhall Glacier. Delightful surprises include a tunnel of flowers, unique hanging gardens, wildlife in their natural habitat and beautiful ponds and waterfalls. Educational displays of native plant uses are wheelchair accessible. Electric carts available. Phone (907) 789-5166, fax 789-5598 or write 7600 Old Glacier Hwy., Juneau, AK 99801. Located about ten minutes north of downtown on the city bus line. This is a "must see" for Alaska. [ADVERTISEMENT]　　　　&

Chapel-by-the-Lake (Presbyterian), **Milepost 11.6** Glacier Highway, is a log structure perched above Auke Lake. Its front, made entirely of glass, frames the scenic lake, Mendenhall Glacier and mountains. Popular marriage chapel.

Shrine of St. Therese (Roman Catholic), **Milepost 23.1** Glacier Highway, is a natural stone chapel on its own island, connected to shore by a gravel causeway. A 1 P.M. Sunday mass takes place during the summer.

Golden North Salmon Derby is a 3-day derby in late August.

Hiking Trails. *Juneau Trails*, a guidebook of 20-plus area hikes, can be purchased for $4 at the USFS Information Center in Centennial Hall or local bookstores. Juneau Parks and Recreation Dept. offers free organized hikes Wednesday and Saturday, April through October; phone (907) 586-5226 for information.

AREA FISHING: (Several special sportfishing regulations are in effect in the Juneau area; consult current regulations booklet.) Good Dolly Varden fishing available along most saltwater shorelines in Juneau area; king salmon best from mid-May to mid-June, pink salmon available about mid-July through August, silver salmon best August to mid-September. Good fishing by boat from Juneau, Auke Bay or Tee Harbor in **Favorite** and **Saginaw channels, Chatham Strait** and near mouth of **Taku Inlet** for salmon, Dolly Varden and halibut. USFS public-use cabins available.

For up-to-date angling data in the Juneau area, phone (907) 465-4116 for recorded Alaska Dept. of Fish and Game message (April through Oct.). For specific angling information or for a copy of the local sportfishing guide, contact the ADF&G, Division of Sport Fish, Area Management Biologist, P.O. Box 20, Douglas 99824; phone (907) 465-4320. A list of charter boats is available from the Juneau Convention and Visitors Bureau (phone 907/586-2201). Also see ads this section.　　　　◄►

Egan Drive and Glacier Highway/Juneau Veterans' Memorial Highway Log

Egan Drive from downtown Juneau proceeds north to **Milepost 9.4**, then becomes Glacier Highway. Egan Drive is named for William A. Egan (1914–84), first governor of the state of Alaska. From **Milepost 12.2** to road end, Glacier Highway has been renamed the Juneau Veterans' Memorial Highway. The highway ends 40.5 miles/65.3 km north of Juneau near Echo Cove on Berners Bay. It is a scenic drive northward along Favorite Channel.

0 Cruise ship terminal.

0.3 (0.5 km) Parking garage, 3-hour limit.

0.5 (0.8 km) Stoplight. Marine Way and Main Street. Egan Drive begins here.

0.7 (1.1 km) Alaska State Museum, exit east onto Whittier Street.

1.2 (1.9 km) Stoplight. Tenth Street exit

east. For access to Douglas Highway and North Douglas Highway, turn west across Juneau–Douglas bridge (see logs this section).

1.3 (2.1 km) Turn west (left northbound) for Harris Harbor for small boats.

1.5 (2.4 km) Juneau–Douglas High School to east (right northbound).

1.7 (2.7 km) Aurora Basin small-boat harbor to west (left northbound). Access to Juneau Yacht Club on Harbor Way Road.

3.9 (6.3 km) Stoplight. Picnic tables at Twin Lakes to east. Also exit east for Bartlett Memorial Hospital and Alaska Native Health Center; access to Old Glacier Highway and residential area. Gastineau Salmon Hatchery to west.

5.5 (8.9 km) Stoplight. Lemon Creek area.

5.9 (9.5 km) Lemon Creek passes beneath highway.

6.1 (9.8 km) Mendenhall Wetlands viewing area; great place to see eagles and waterfowl.

6.7 (10.7 km) Access to Old Glacier Highway and Switzer Creek; exit east. Department store; service station with gas, propane.

8.1 (13 km) Airport access road.

8.2 (13.2 km) Fred Meyer shopping center. Access to Glacier Gardens Rainforest Adventures. Turn right on Old Glacier Highway. What began as a project to generate hydro-electricity for commercial greenhouses has emerged as Juneau's newest attraction, scheduled to open in summer of 1998. Rainforest Gardens, natural and domestic, on Thunder Mountain. Guided and self-guided tours. Admission charged.

8.8 (14.2 km) Stoplight; McDonald's. Airport turnoff and access to Nugget Mall and Airport Shopping Center to west. A 0.3-mile/0.5-km loop road (Old Glacier Highway) provides access to malls and to Juneau International Airport. Access to Mendenhall Wetlands State Game Refuge dike trail via Berners Avenue. Loop road rejoins Egan Drive at **Milepost 9.4**.

9.4 (15.1 km) Stoplight. South **junction** with Mendenhall Loop Road. Turn west for airport. Turn east for Mendenhall Center shopping mall and post office (just east of junction), and Mendenhall Glacier and visitor center (3.6 miles/5.8 km from junction).

Mendenhall Loop Road is a paved 6.8-mile/10.9-km loop that rejoins Glacier Highway at **Milepost 12.2**. To reach Mendenhall Glacier from here, drive west 2.2 miles/3.5 km and take spur road another 1.4 miles/2.2 km to the glacier and visitor center. The visitor center is open daily in summer from 8:30 A.M. to 5:30 P.M.; weekends only in winter, 9 A.M. to 4 P.M.

Continue on Mendenhall Loop Road past glacier spur road turnoff for Montana Creek Road (3.7 miles/6 km from junction) and access to Mendenhall Lake USFS campground, at Mile 0.4 Montana Creek Road. The campground has 60 sites, tables, fireplaces, water, pit toilets and dump station. Reservations available for some sites; phone (800) 280-CAMP. $8 fee. Montana Creek Road dead ends 3.5 miles/5.6 km from Mendenhall Loop Road.　　　　▲

9.7 (15.6 km) Airport area access for southbound travelers via Old Glacier Highway.

9.9 (15.9 km) Mendenhall River and Brotherhood Bridge. The bridge was named in honor of the Alaska Native Brotherhood and is lined by bronze plaques symbolizing the Raven and Eagle clans.

10 (16.1 km) Mendenhall Glacier view-

point to east; parking area with sign about Brotherhood Bridge and short walking trail.

10.5 (16.9 km) State troopers office.

10.8 (17.4 km) The 2.1-mile/3.4-km Mendenhall Peninsula Road, a 2-lane gravel road, to west. About halfway along this road, Engineer's Cutoff leads 0.3 mile/0.5 km to Fritz Cove Road.

11.4 (18.3 km) Auke Lake scenic wayside to east. Good view of Mendenhall Glacier reflected in the lake. This is one of the most photographed spots in Alaska. Red, pink and coho salmon spawn in Auke Lake system July to September (only limited fishing, for coho in September). Chum salmon are primarily from Auke Creek hatchery program.

11.5 (18.5 km) Fritz Cove Road (paved) leads 2.6 miles/4.2 km west and dead ends at Smuggler's Cove; excellent small-boat anchorage. Scenic viewpoint on Fritz Cove Road at Mile 1.2; Engineer's Cutoff at Mile 1.9 extends 0.3 mile/0.5 km to Mendenhall Peninsula Road.

11.6 (18.7 km) Turnoff to east for Chapel-by-the-Lake and to southeastern branch of University of Alaska.

11.8 (19 km) Short road west to National Marine Fisheries Service biological laboratory (self-guided walking tours between 8 A.M. and 4:30 P.M. Monday through Friday).

12.2 (19.6 km) **North junction** with Mendenhall Loop Road to west. Glacier Highway becomes Juneau Veterans' Memorial Highway and curves around Auke Bay to west. A small-boat harbor with snack shop, skiff and tackle rentals, and boat launch located at the head of the bay. Private ferry service (AUK NU) to Glacier Bay departs from here.

The 6.8-mile/10.9-km Mendenhall Loop Road rejoins Glacier Highway at **Milepost 9.4**. Motorists may turn east here and follow loop road 3.1 miles/5 km to Montana Creek Road and access to Mendenhall Lake USFS campground, or drive 4.6 miles/7.4 km and turn off on Mendenhall Glacier spur road, which leads another 1.4 miles/2.2 km to the glacier and visitor center. Parking area at Mendenhall Glacier; short, steep path to visitor center. The center is open daily in summer from 8:30 A.M. to 5:30 P.M.　　　▲

12.3 (19.8 km) Private RV park.

12.4 (20 km) Auke Bay post office to west.

12.6 (20.3 km) Spaulding trailhead to east; 3.5 miles/5.6 km long. Access to John Muir USFS cabin.

12.8 (20.6 km) Waydelich Creek and bridge.

13.8 (22.2 km) Auke Bay ferry terminal vehicle exit.

13.9 (22.4 km) Auke Bay ferry terminal entrance. *LeConte* ferry passengers use adjacent parking area on right side of terminal building; all others use adjacent parking area on left of terminal. Visitor information counter staffed in summer; open only for ferry arrivals and departures.

15.1 (24.3 km) Auke Village Recreation Area begins northbound; 5 beachside picnic shelters accessible to west of highway (park on highway shoulder).

15.3 (24.6 km) Auke Village totem pole to east.

15.4 (24.8 km) Auke Village USFS campground; 14 picnic units, 12 campsites, tables, fireplaces, water, flush and pit toilets. $8 fee. Open May 1 to Sept. 30.　　　▲

16.5 (26.6 km) Lena Point Road, south entrance to loop road.

17 (27.3 km) Lena Point Road, north

entrance to loop road.

17.4 (28.1 km) Lena Beach picnic area.

18.4 (29.6 km) Tee Harbor–Point Stevens Road (gravel) leads 0.3 mile/0.6 km west to public parking area and a private marina and fuel float.

19.2 (30.9 km) Inspiration Point turnout to west with view of the Chilkat Range, and over Tee Harbor and Shelter Island across Favorite Channel. Once a bread-and-butter commercial fishing area, hence the name "The Breadline" for this stretch of shoreline, it is now a popular sportfishing area.

23.1 (37.3 km) Short road west to Catholic Shrine of St. Terese, located on a small island reached by a causeway.

23.3 (37.5 km) Turnout to west and view of island on which Shrine of St. Terese is situated.

23.9 (38.5 km) Peterson Lake trailhead to east; 4 miles/6.4 km long. Access to Peterson Lake USFS cabin. This trail connects with the Spaulding trail (see **Milepost 12.6**).

24.2 (39 km) **Peterson Creek** bridge. View spawning salmon here in late summer and early fall. Trout fishing. Black and brown bears in area. 🐟

24.8 (40 km) Gravel road leads 0.6 mile/1 km west to Amalga Harbor; dock, boat launch, bait-casting area. Fireplace and chimney near end of road are remains of an old trapper's cabin.

27.1 (43.7 km) Windfall Lake trailhead to east; 3 miles/4.8 km long.

27.2 (43.9 km) Herbert River bridge.

27.4 (44.2 km) Herbert Glacier trailhead to east; 4.5 miles/7.2 km long.

27.7 (44.7 km) Eagle River bridge. Amalga trailhead just across bridge to east; 5.5 miles/8.8 km long.

28 (45 km) Eagle Beach State Recreation Area; parking, trails along river and picnicking.

28.4 (45.8 km) Eagle Beach picnic area with beachside picnic shelter and 8 picnic sites. View of Chilkat Range across Lynn Canal. Duck hunting on flats in low tide during open season.

28.7 (46.2 km) Scenic viewpoint to west.

29.3 (47.2 km) Scenic viewpoint to west.

32.7 (52.8 km) Turnout to west with view of Benjamin Island to southwest; just beyond it is Sentinel Island lighthouse. Visible to the northwest is North Island and northwest of it is Vanderbilt Reef, site of a great sea disaster. The SS *Princess Sophia*, carrying 288 passengers and 61 crew, ran aground on Vanderbilt Reef early in the morning of Oct. 24, 1918. All aboard perished when a combination of stormy seas and a high tide forced the *Princess Sophia* off the reef and she sank early in the evening of Oct. 25. Walter Harper, in 1913 the first person to stand on the summit of Mount McKinley, was among the *Princess Sophia*'s casualties. Vanderbilt Reef is now marked by a navigation light.

32.8 (52.9 km) Pavement ends northbound; 2-lane gravel extension of the Glacier Highway begins.

33 (53.1 km) Scenic viewpoint to west. Yankee Cove and beach below this point.

35.4 (57.1 km) Sunshine Cove public beach access.

37.6 (60.7 km) North Bridget Cove beach access. The 2,850-acre park offers meadows, forests, rocky beaches, salmon streams and a trail system. Area is popular for cross-country skiing. Fires allowed on beach.

39 (62.8 km) Point Bridget State Park trailhead; 3.5-mile/5.6-km hike to Point Bridget (7 hours round-trip); panoramic view of Lynn Canal and Chilkat Mountains from point.

39.4 (63.5 km) Cowee Creek bridge. Large parking area to west.

40.4 (65 km) Access left to Echo Cove beach. Parking area.

40.5 (65.3 km) Road dead ends near Echo Cove on Berners Bay. Berners Bay is a popular destination for Juneau paddlers. It is 3 miles across and 34 miles northwest of Juneau.

Douglas Highway Log

Douglas Highway is a 3-mile/4.8-km paved road beginning on the Juneau side of the Douglas Bridge, crossing to Douglas Island, turning southeast, passing through the city of Douglas to road end and beginning of Treadwell Mine area.

0 Intersection of Egan Drive and Douglas Bridge.

0.5 (0.8 km) Right, Cordova Street leads to Dan Moller trail.

1.5 (2.4 km) Lawson Creek bridge.

2 (3.2 km) Tlingit Indian cemetery and grave houses.

2.5 (4 km) Turn left to boat harbor; dump station and Savikko Park with 4 overnight RV parking spaces without hookups. $5 per night, 3-day limit; obtain permit from Harbormaster's office at 1600 Harbor Way. Short gravel road leads to Juneau Island U.S. Bureau of Mines headquarters. Sandy Beach Recreation Area with water, toilets, play area, tennis courts, track, 2 ball fields, picnic tables, shelters and children's playground. Aptly named, this is one of the few sandy beaches in southeastern Alaska. Highway becomes St. Ann's Avenue.

3 (4.8 km) Road end.

North Douglas Highway Log

North Douglas Highway begins after crossing Douglas Bridge from Juneau and immediately turning right, northwest. **Milepost 1** appears at small bridge on this turn.

0 Douglas Bridge.

0.3 (0.5 km) **Junction** of Douglas Highway and North Douglas Highway.

4.4 (7.1 km) Heliport to right.

6.9 (11.1 km) Eaglecrest Ski Area turnoff on left; drive 5.3 miles/8.5 km on gravel road to ski area. Good blueberry picking in August.

8.3 (13.5 km) Fish Creek bridge. Large parking area on right of bridge. This is a popular roadside fishing spot.

8.6 (13.9 km) Ninemile trail on right; small parking area.

9.5 (15.3 km) Scenic turnout and parking area with excellent view of Mendenhall Glacier; litter barrel. Boat ramp; launch permit required (contact harbormaster before arrival).

10.3 (16.6 km) Small waterfall on left.

11.4 (18.4 km) False Outer Point public beach access. Scenic view of Favorite Channel and Lynn Canal; parking area on right. Near the northern tip of Douglas Island, this is an excellent spot to observe marine activity and eagles.

12.3 (19.8 km) Outer Point trailhead on right.

13.1 (21 km) Road end.

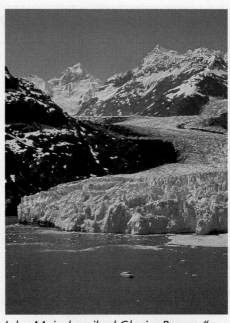

John Muir described Glacier Bay as "a picture of icy wildness unspeakably pure and sublime." (Courtesy of Glacier Bay Tours & Cruises)

Glacier Bay National Park and Preserve

What Tlingit Indians called "Big Ice-Mountain Bay" in naturalist John Muir's day (1879) is today one of southeastern Alaska's most dramatic attractions, Glacier Bay National Park and Preserve. Muir described Glacier Bay as "a picture of icy wildness unspeakably pure and sublime."

There are no roads to Glacier Bay National Park, except for a 10-mile/16-km stretch of road connecting Bartlett Cove with Gustavus airport. Bartlett Cove is the site of a ranger station and Glacier Bay Lodge. Park naturalists conduct daily hikes and other activities from the visitor center at the lodge, and the excursion boat departs from there. Airlines service Gustavus airport. See Accommodations/Visitor Services and

GLACIER BAY NATIONAL PARK AND PRESERVE

© 1999
The MILEPOST®

Tongass National Forest

Skagway

Tongass National Forest

Takhinsha Mountains

Haines

Mount Hay
8,870 ft./2,704m

Alsek Glacier

Grand Pacific Glacier

Grand Plateau Glacier

Alsek River

Dry Bay

National Park Boundry

Muir Glacier

McBride Glacier

Casement Glacier

Snow Dome
3,900 ft./1,189m

Gulf of Alaska

Mount Quincy Adams
13,650 ft./4,160m

Mount Fairweather
15,300 ft./4,663m

Mount Escures
4,377 ft./1,334m

National Park Boundry

Margerie Glacier

Rendu Glacier

Carroll Glacier

Toaro Inlet

Russell Island

Reid Inlet

Muir Inlet

Adams Inlet

Lynn Canal

Cape Fairweather

Johns Hopkins Glacier

Lamplugh Glacier

Reid Glacier

Chilkat Range

Fairweather Range

Mount Crillon
12,728 ft./3,879m

Brady Icefield

Geikie Inlet

Glacier Bay

Sandy Cove

Bartlett River

Harbor Point

Lituya Bay

Mount Divide
4,290 ft./1,308m

Beardslee Islands

Lodge

Bartlett Cove

Gustavus

Icy Point

Dundas Bay

Taylor Bay

Icy Strait

Point Adolphus

Excursion Inlet

Map Location

Scale
0   10 Miles
0   10 Kilometres

Unpaved Road

International Border

National Park Boundary

Cape Spencer

Pacific Ocean

Cross Sound

Elfin Cove

Chichagof Island

Hoonah

Tongass National Forest

Transportation under Gustavus this section.

Visitors should contact the Superintendent, Glacier Bay National Park and Preserve, Gustavus, AK 99826-0140, for more information, or check with Glacier Bay tour operators. The national park's headquarters is at Bartlett Cove; phone (907) 697-2230.

Glacier Bay National Park, at the northwest end of Alexander Archipelago, includes not only tidewater glaciers but also Mount Fairweather in the Fairweather Range of the St. Elias Mountains, the highest peak in southeastern Alaska, and also the U.S. portion of the Alsek River.

With passage of the Alaska National Interest Lands Conservation Act in December 1980, Glacier Bay National Monument, established in 1925 by Pres. Calvin Coolidge, became a national park. Approximately 585,000 acres were added to the park/preserve to protect fish and wildlife habitat and migration routes in Dry Bay and along the lower Alsek River, and to include the northwest slope of Mount Fairweather. Total acreage is 3,328,000 (3,271,000 in park, 57,000 in preserve) with 2,770,000 acres designated wilderness.

When the English naval explorer Capt. George Vancouver sailed through the ice-choked waters of Icy Strait in 1794, Glacier Bay was little more than a dent in the coastline. Across the head of this seemingly minor inlet stood a towering wall of ice marking the seaward terminus of an immense glacier that completely filled the broad, deep basin of what is now Glacier Bay. To the north, ice extended more than 100 miles/160 km into the St. Elias Mountains, covering the intervening valleys with

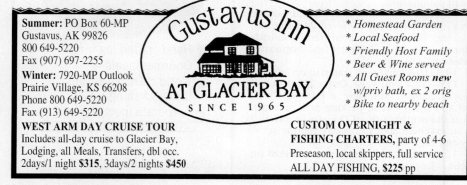

a 4,000-foot-/1,219-m-deep mantle of ice.

During the century following Vancouver's explorations, the glacier retreated some 40 miles/64 km back into the bay, permitting a spruce–hemlock forest to gradually fill the land. By 1916, the Grand Pacific Glacier, which once occupied the entire bay, had receded some 65 miles/105 km from the position observed by Vancouver in 1794. Nowhere else in the world have glaciers been observed to recede at such a rapid pace.

Today, few of the many tributary glaciers that once supplied the huge ice sheet extend to the sea. Glacier Bay National Park encloses 12 active tidewater glaciers, including several on the remote and seldom-visited western edge of the park along the Gulf of Alaska and Lituya Bay. Icebergs, cracked off from near-vertical ice cliffs, dot the waters of Glacier Bay.

A decline in the number of humpback whales using Glacier Bay for feeding and calf-rearing led the National Park Service to limit the number of boats visiting Glacier Bay from June to August. These regulations affect all motorized vessels. Check with the National Park Service for current regulations.

Glacier Bay National Park is approximately 100 miles/160 km from Juneau by boat. Park rangers at Bartlett Cove are available to assist in advising visitors who wish to tour Glacier Bay in private boats or by kayak. Guided kayak trips are available through park concessionaire, Alaska Discovery. Permits are required for motorized pleasure boats between June 1 and Aug. 31. The permits are free. A limited number are available. Permits must be obtained prior to entry into Glacier Bay and Bartlett Cove. Request permits no more than 2 months in advance by writing the National Park Service, Gustavus, AK 99826-0140. For more information, phone (907) 697-2627 (May 1 to Sept. 7).

Glacier Bay Lodge is the only accommodation within the national park, although nearby Gustavus (see description this section) has a number of lodges, inns, bed and breakfasts and rental cabins. Contact Glacier Bay Lodge Inc., (800) 451-5952, for more information on the concessionaire-operated Glacier Bay Lodge and excursion boat cruises offered from the lodge.

Gasoline and diesel fuel may be purchased at Bartlett Cove, where a good anchorage is available. There are no other public facilities for boats within park boundaries; Sandy Cove, about 20 miles/32 km from Bartlett Cove, is a popular anchorage.

Gustavus has a dock and small-boat harbor.

CAUTION BOATERS: No attempt should be made to navigate Glacier Bay without appropriate charts, tide tables and local knowledge. Floating ice is a special hazard. Because of the danger from waves caused by falling ice, small craft should not approach closer than 0.5 mile/0.8 km from tidewater glacier fronts.

Wildlife in the national park area is protected and hunting is not allowed. Firearms are illegal. *CAUTION: Brown and black bears are present.*

Fishing for silver and pink salmon, Dolly Varden and halibut is excellent. A valid Alaska fishing license is required. Charter fishing trips are available. ◄

There is an established campground at Bartlett Cove with 25 sites. Wilderness camping is also available throughout the park.

Gustavus

(See map, page 673)

Gateway to Glacier Bay National Park and Preserve, the small community of Gustavus is located just outside the park boundary at the mouth of the Salmon River on the north shore of Icy Passage, 48 miles northwest of Juneau. It is 10 miles/16 km by road from Gustavus to Bartlett Cove within the park. **Population:** 380. **Emergency Services:** Phone 911. **Visitor Information:** Gustavus

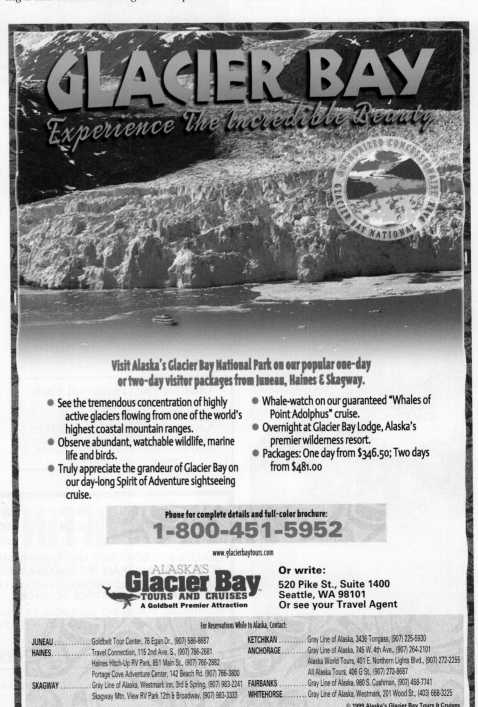

GLACIER BAY
Experience The Incredible Beauty

Visit Alaska's Glacier Bay National Park on our popular one-day or two-day visitor packages from Juneau, Haines & Skagway.

- See the tremendous concentration of highly active glaciers flowing from one of the world's highest coastal mountain ranges.
- Observe abundant, watchable wildlife, marine life and birds.
- Truly appreciate the grandeur of Glacier Bay on our day-long Spirit of Adventure sightseeing cruise.

- Whale-watch on our guaranteed "Whales of Point Adolphus" cruise.
- Overnight at Glacier Bay Lodge, Alaska's premier wilderness resort.
- Packages: One day from $346.50; Two days from $481.00

Phone for complete details and full-color brochure:
1-800-451-5952

www.glacierbaytours.com

ALASKA'S Glacier Bay
TOURS AND CRUISES
A Goldbelt Premier Attraction

Or write:
520 Pike St., Suite 1400
Seattle, WA 98101
Or see your Travel Agent

For Reservations While In Alaska, Contact:

JUNEAU . . . . Goldbelt Tour Center, 76 Egan Dr., (907) 586-8687	KETCHIKAN . . . . Gray Line of Alaska, 3436 Tongass, (907) 225-5930
HAINES . . . . Travel Connection, 115 2nd Ave. S., (907) 766-2681	ANCHORAGE . . . . Gray Line of Alaska, 745 W. 4th Ave., (907) 264-2101
Haines Hitch-Up RV Park, 851 Main St., (907) 766-2882	Alaska World Tours, 401 E. Northern Lights Blvd., (907) 272-2255
Portage Cove Adventure Center, 142 Beach Rd. (907) 766-3800	All Alaska Tours, 406 G St., (907) 272-8687
SKAGWAY . . . . Gray Line of Alaska, Westmark Inn, 3rd & Spring, (907) 983-2241	FAIRBANKS . . . . Gray Line of Alaska, 980 S. Cushman, (907) 458-7741
Skagway Mtn. View RV Park 12th & Broadway, (907) 983-3333	WHITEHORSE . . . . Gray Line of Alaska, Westmark, 201 Wood St., (403) 668-3225

© 1999 Alaska's Glacier Bay Tours & Cruises

A Three Sisters Enterprise
The Annie Mae Lodge
Old fashioned comfort and hospitality
❀ *Relax with us, enjoy wonderful food and lodgings. Experience the wilderness in the last frontier-Alaska.*

Call or write;
P.O. Box 80, Gustavus, Alaska 99826
Telephone (907) 697-2346
1-800-478-2346 • Fax (907) 697-2211
Glacier Bay, Alaska

Please support our MILEPOST® advertisers.

Visitors Assoc., Box 167, Gustavus 99826.

Private Aircraft: Gustavus airport, adjacent northeast; elev. 36 feet/11m; length 6,700 feet/2,042m; asphalt; fuel 100LL, A. Landing within the park is restricted to salt water. All wilderness/non-motorized waters are closed to aircraft landing between 5/1-9/15.

Surrounded on 3 sides by the snow-covered peaks of the Chilkat Range and the Fairweather Mountains, Gustavus offers miles of level land with expansive sandy beaches, open land and forest. Homesteaded in 1914 as a small agricultural community, the area was once named Strawberry Point because of its abundant wild strawberries. Today, most residents maintain gardens and make their living by fishing (commercial and subsistence), fish processing, tourism, arts and crafts, and working for the National Park Service and in various local trades.

Besides its proximity to the national park, Gustavus offers a number of attractions. Local charter boats—sometimes called "6 packs" because they carry about 6 passengers—are available for sportfishing (salmon, halibut), sightseeing Icy Strait and Glacier Bay, and whale watching. Whale sightings are almost guaranteed at Point

Charters for whale watching may be arranged at Gustavus. (© Robin Brandt)

Adolphous, where their food source is rich. A paved road in town is great for bike riding.

There are extensive beaches in Gustavus which are great for beachwalking. Flat land walking is possible in the fern wetland environment, which also offers good bird watching. Be sure to bring rubber boots.

ACCOMMODATIONS/VISITOR SERVICES

Accommodations in Gustavus include several inns, lodges, bed and breakfasts, and self-sufficient cabins. There is 1 restaurant. The lodges and inns serve meals for guests; drop-in customers check for space-available meal reservations.

Businesses in Gustavus include a grocery store, art gallery, cafe, gift shop, hardware/building supply store, gas station and fish-processing facilities. Fishing supplies and

licenses may be purchased locally.

Annie Mae Lodge. Old-fashioned good food and good company. Three fine family-style meals using home-baked bread and pastries, fresh caught seafood, berries off the bush, and garden vegetables. We offer beautiful comfortable rooms, peace, quiet, abundant wildlife, wilderness, sportfishing, kayak trips, whale watching. Glacier Bay boat/plane tours. Box 80, Gustavus, AK 99826. Phone (800) 478-2346 or (907) 697-2346, fax (907) 697-2211. [ADVERTISEMENT]

Bear Track Inn. This remarkable luxury inn must be seen to be believed. Offering complete packages—the inn's tour programs include world-class fishing, kayaking, whale watching, glacier viewing, wildlife and more. Enjoy this handcrafted log inn with inspiring views from wrap-around windows in the lobby as you relax beside a roaring fire. Feast on gourmet meals and sleep in large beautifully appointed guest rooms. Special corporate meeting facilities available. It's a worry-free vacation and a trip of a life time. Make tracks to the Bear Track Inn. Phone (907) 697-3017 or e-mail: beartrac@aol.com. [ADVERTISEMENT]

Grand Pacific Charters. Custom boating excursions in and around Glacier Bay. Personalized itinerary may include whale watching; renowned deep sea fishing for halibut and/or salmon. Many excellent angling and fly fishing opportunities in remote areas. P.O. Box 5, Gustavus, AK 99826. Phone (800) 628-0912. E-mail: gbci@thor.he.net. [ADVERTISEMENT]

Gustavus Inn. Country living, family-style gourmet local seafood meals, cozy bar, kitchen garden, bikes, trout fishing poles, courtesy van, afternoon park naturalist trip. Family-run since 1965. Custom fishing and Glacier Bay sightseeing packages arranged. For map, brochures, please write: Gustavus Inn, Box 60-MP, Gustavus, AK 99826 or call (800) 649-5220. [ADVERTISEMENT]

The Puffin. See nearby Glacier Bay and Icy Strait. Stay in your own modern, comfortable, attractively decorated cabin with electricity on quiet wooded homestead. Picturesque central lodge. Complete breakfast. Bicycles, children, pets welcome. Reservations for all charters, Glacier Bay tours. Qualified captains guide fishing, sightseeing charters. Friendly, personal attention. (907) 697-2260; fax (907) 697-2258; e-mail: puffin@compuserve.com. Homepage: http://www.puffintravel.com. [ADVERTISEMENT]

Spruce Tip Lodge—Stay in our hand-crafted log lodge and experience this part of Southeast Alaska in comfort and style. Included in our rates are three homecooked meals daily, room with bath and local ground transportation. We can arrange all activities in Gustavus/Glacier Bay. Phone (907) 697-2215, fax (907) 697-2236 or write Box 299–MP, Gustavus, AK 99826. [ADVERTISEMENT]

TRI Bed and Breakfast of Glacier Bay. Visit us in our secluded rainforest homesite. Full breakfast with daily fresh eggs, homemade bread/jam. Deluxe and spacious individual cottages with insuite bath. Hiking, kayaking, whale watching, beachcombing, sportfishing, the Glacier Bay day boat or just getting here from Juneau, let us arrange your trip to Glacier Bay/Gustavus. P.O. Box 214MP, Gustavus, AK 99826. Phone (907) 697-2425; fax (907) 697-2450; e-mail trig-bay@pluto.he.net. [ADVERTISEMENT]

Whalesong Lodge. Full-service lodge close to the beach and amenities. B&B accommodation with optional American plan. Also, condominium rental with full meal packages available. Unforgettable day or overnight tours of Glacier Bay, whale watching, sport fishing, kayaking, hiking. Airport transfers. Complimentary bicycles. Box 5-MP, Gustavus, AK 99826. Phone (800) 628-0912, fax (907) 697-2289. [ADVERTISEMENT]

TRANSPORTATION

Ferry: *NOTE: There is no state ferry service to Glacier Bay.* Closest port of call for state ferries is Hoonah. (Kayakers getting off at Hoonah can expect a 2-day paddle across Icy Strait.

Private ferry services Gustavus from Juneau; contact AUK NU Tours, 76 Egan Dr., Juneau, AK 99801; phone (907) 586-8687 or toll free (800) 820-2628, fax (907) 586-1337. One-way fare is $45.

Air: Glacier Bay may be reached by Alaska Airlines daily jet flights from Juneau; summer service begins early June. Air taxi and charter service available from Juneau, Sitka, Haines and Skagway to Gustavus airport; there are many scheduled air taxi flights daily. Bus service between the airport and Bartlett Cove is available for arriving jet flights. Taxi service to local facilities and courtesy van service for some lodges are also available.

Many Gustavus bed and breakfasts will make transportation arrangements for guests from Juneau, Haines and Skagway.

Rental Cars: There is one car rental company in Gustavus, BW Rent-A-Car, phone (907) 697-2403.

Boat Service: Excursion boats operated by the park concession depart daily from Bartlett Cove. You may also charter a boat in Gustavus for sightseeing or fishing. Overnight cruise tours are available from Juneau.

Cruise Ships: Several cruise ships include Glacier Bay cruising in their itineraries.

Yakutat

Located on the Gulf of Alaska coast where Southeastern Alaska joins the major body of Alaska to the west; 225 miles/362 km northwest of Juneau, 220 miles/354 km southeast of Cordova and 380 miles/611 km southeast of Anchorage. **Population:** 801. **Emergency Services: Dept. of Public Safety,** phone (907) 784-3206. **Fire Department,** phone 911. **Yakutat Health Center,** phone (907) 784-3275. **Maritime Search and Rescue,** contact the Coast Guard at (800) 478-5555.

Visitor Information: Inquire at one of the lodges, at the USFS and NPS office, or the chamber of commerce office (write Chamber of Commerce, Box 234, Yakutat, AK 99689). For sportfishing information, stop by the ADF&G office, 1/4 mile west of the airport, or write Sport Fish Division, Box 49, Yakutat 99689, phone (907) 784-3222. For information about the National Park Service, contact the visitor center at Box 137, Yakutat, AK 99689; phone (907) 748-3295. Interpretive programs are offered daily at 2 P.M. from June through August. City and Borough of Yakutat offices, (907) 784-3323.

Elevation: Sea level. **Climate:** Similar to the rest of coastal southeastern Alaska; mild in summer, winters are moderate. Average annual snowfall is 201 inches. Total annual precipitation is about 151 inches. Normal daily maximum in August, 60°F/16°C; minimum in January, 17°F/-8°C. Prevailing winds are southeasterly.

Private Aircraft: Yakutat airport, 5 miles/4.8 km southeast; elev. 33 feet/10m; length 7,700 feet/2,347m; asphalt; fuel 100, A1. Seaplane base 1 mile/1.6 km northwest; float only, no fuel.

Transportation: Air—Daily jet service from Seattle, Juneau, Anchorage and Cordova. Charter air service available. **Ferry**—The MV *Kennicott* makes a whistle stop at Yakutat. See the ALASKA STATE FERRY SCHEDULES section.

Yakutat has 4 lodges, 1 inn, 7 bed and breakfasts, a restaurant, cafe, 2 gift shops, bank, 2 grocery stores, 1 hardware store, ATM, post office, clinic and gas station. Boat rentals, car rentals and cab service are available.

Yakutat Bay is one of the few refuges for vessels along this long stretch of coast in the Gulf of Alaska. The site was originally

Yakutat is a popular sportfishing destination. (© David J. Job)

the principal winter village of the local Tlingit Indian tribe. Sea otter pelts brought Russians to the area in the 19th century. Fur traders were followed by gold seekers, who came to work the black sand beaches. Commercial salmon fishing developed in this century, and the first cannery was built here in 1904. Today's economy is based primarily on fishing and fish processing. Salmon, halibut, crab and black cod make up the fishery. Government and local businesses employ most residents. Subsistence activities are primarily fishing (salmon and shellfish), hunting (moose, bear, goats, ducks and small game), and gathering seaweed and berries. The soil is not suitable for agriculture, and a vegetable garden requires a great deal of preparation to produce small quantities.

While hunting and fishing in particular draw visitors to Yakutat, the surge of Hubbard Glacier in June 1986, which sealed off the mouth of Russell Fiord, drew national attention. Malaspina Glacier, largest on the North American continent, is northwest of town. Nearer to town, Cannon Beach has good beachcombing and a picnic area.

AREA FISHING: Yakutat is considered a world-class sportfishing destination. Steelhead fishing is among the finest anywhere. King and silver (coho) salmon run in abundance in Yakutat area, rivers and streams June through September. The area also boasts red and pink salmon and smelt in season. USFS cabins available on some rivers; check with the Forest Service (907/784-3359).

Lost River and **Tawah Creek,** 10 miles/16 km south of Yakutat on Lost River Road, silver (coho) salmon to 20 lbs., mid-August through September. **Situk River,** 12 miles/19.3 km south of Yakutat on the Lost River Road (also accessible by Forest Highway 10), is one of Alaska's top fishing spots spring and fall for steelhead and silver salmon and has one of the best sockeye (red) salmon runs in the state, late June through August; steelhead averaging 10 lbs., April 1 to May 30 for spring run, October and November for fall run; king salmon to 45 lbs., mid-June through July; silver salmon to 23 lbs., mid-August through September; pink salmon run in August, yields Dolly Varden also. **Yakutat Bay,** king salmon 30 to 50 lbs., May through June; silver salmon to 20 lbs., August through September.

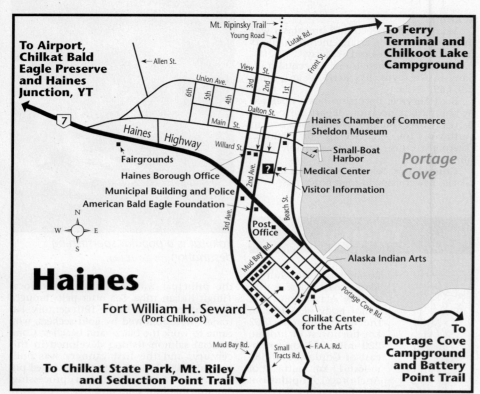

Haines

(See map, page 673)

Located on Portage Cove, Chilkoot Inlet, on the upper arm of Lynn Canal, 80 air miles/129 km northwest of Juneau; 151 road miles/243 km southeast of Haines Junction, YT. Southern terminus of the Haines Highway. *NOTE: Although Haines is only 13 miles/21 km by water from Skagway, it is 359 miles/578 km by road!* **Population:** Borough, 2,300. **Emergency Services: Alaska State Troopers,** phone (907) 766-2552. **City**

Police, phone (907) 766-2121. **Fire Department** and **Ambulance,** emergency only phone 911; business phone: (907) 766-2115.. **Doctor,** phone (907) 766-2521. **Maritime Search and Rescue,** contact the Coast Guard at 1-800-478-5555.

Visitor Information: At 2nd and Willard streets. There are free brochures for all of Alaska and the Yukon. Open daily, 8 A.M. to 8 P.M., June through August; 8 A.M. to 5 P.M. weekdays, September through May. Phone (907) 766-2234; toll free 1-800-458-3579; Internet: www.haines.ak.us; e-mail: hainesak@wwa.com.. Write the Haines Convention and Visitors Bureau at Box 530, Haines, AK 99827. Phone the Alaska Dept. of Transportation at (907) 766-2340.

Elevation: Sea level. **Climate:** Average daily maximum temperature in July, 66°F/19°C; average daily minimum in January, 17°F/-8°C; Extreme high summer temperature, 90°F/32°C; extreme winter low, -16°F/-27°C; average annual precipitation, 59 inches. **Radio:** KHNS-FM 102.3. **Television:** 24 cable channels. **Newspaper:** *Chilkat Valley News* (weekly), *Eagle Eye.*

Private Aircraft: Haines airport, 4 miles/6.4 km west;.elev. 16 feet/5m; length 3,000 feet/914m; asphalt; fuel 100; unattended.

The original Indian name for Haines was *Dei Shu,* meaning "end of the trail." It was an area where Chilkat and Chilkoot Indians met and traded with Russian and American ships. It was also their portage route for transporting canoes from the Chilkat River to Portage Cove and Lynn Canal. The first white man to settle here was George Dickinson, who came as an agent for the North West Trading Co.

In 1879 missionary S. Hall Young and naturalist John Muir came to the village of Yen Dustucky (near today's airport) to determine the location of a Presbyterian mission and school. The site chosen, Dei Shu, was on the narrow portage between the Chilkat River and Lynn Canal. The following year, George Dickinson established a trading post for the Northwest Trading Company, next to the mission site. His wife Sarah began a school for Tlingit children. By 1881, Eugene and Caroline Willard arrived to establish Chilkat Mission. Later, the mission and eventually the town were named for Francina E. Haines, secretary of the Presbyterian Women's Executive Society of Home Missions, who raised funds for the new mission.

In 1882 the Haines post office was established. The town became an important outlet for the Porcupine Mining District, producing thousands of dollars' worth of placer gold at the turn of the century. The Dalton Trail, which crossed the Chilkat mountain pass to the Klondike goldfields in the Yukon, started at Pyramid Harbor Cannery across the Chilkat River from Haines.

Just to the south of Haines city center is Fort Seward on Portage Cove. Named Fort William H. Seward, in honor of the secretary of state who negotiated the purchase of Alaska from Russia in 1867, this was established as the first permanent Army post in the territory. The first troops arrived in 1904 from Camp Skagway. In 1922, the fort was renamed Chilkoot Barracks, after the mountain pass and the Indian tribe on the Chilkoot River. (There are 2 tribes in this area: the Chilkat and the Chilkoot.)

Until WWII this was the only U.S. Army post in Alaska. Chilkoot Barracks was deactivated in 1946 and sold in 1947 to a group of enterprising U.S. veterans who had designs of creating a business cooperative on the site. Their original plans were never fully realized, but a few stayed on, creating the city of Port Chilkoot and converting some of the houses on Officers' Row into permanent homes.

In 1970, Port Chilkoot merged with Haines to become a single municipality, the city of Haines. Two years later, the post was designated a national historic site and became officially known, again, as Fort William H. Seward (although many people still call it Port Chilkoot).

Fishing and gold mining were the initial industries of the Haines area. Haines is also remembered for its famous strawberries, developed by Charles Anway about 1900. His Alaskan hybrid, *Burbank,* was a prize winner at the 1909 Alaska–Yukon–Pacific Exposition in Seattle, WA. A strawberry festival was held annually in Haines for many years, and this local event grew into the Southeast Alaska State Fair, which each summer draws thousands of visitors. Today, halibut and gill-net salmon fishing and tourism are the basis of the economy. Haines is an important port on the Alaska Marine Highway System as the southern terminus of the Haines Highway, 1 of the 2 year-round roads linking southeastern Alaska with the Interior.

ACCOMMODATIONS/VISITOR SERVICES

Haines offers travelers accommodations at one hotel and 5 motels. There are also 5 bed and breakfasts and 2 apartment/condo rentals. See ads this section.

There is a youth hostel (families welcome) with cabin accommodations on Small Tracts Road.

Haines has all traveler facilities, including hardware and grocery stores, gift shops and art galleries, automotive repair, laundry, post office and bank. Gift shops and galleries feature the work of local artisans. There are several restaurants, cafes and taverns. First National Bank of Anchorage and Howser's Supermarket, both on Main Street, have ATMs.

State campgrounds in the area include Portage Cove, Chilkat State Park, Chilkoot Lake and Mosquito Lake. ▲

Portage Cove State Recreation Site offers 9 tent sites, half-mile past Fort Seward on Portage Cove. Water and toilets available. Campers enjoy view of the Coast Range and Lynn Canal. Watch for cruise ships, ferries, eagles, whales and porpoises. *NOTE: This site is for walk-in and bicyclist camping only.* ▲

Chilkat State Park, with 32 RV sites and 3 tent sites, is about 8 miles/13 km from Haines on Mud Bay Road (from the Haines

Haines has a spectacular setting between the mountains and the sea. (© Rich Reid)

HAINES

© Cynthia L. Jones (CI)

THE ALASKA OF YOUR DREAMS

DRAMATIC MOUNTAIN SCENERY • HEART OF THE TLINGIT CULTURE
HISTORIC FORT WILLIAM H. SEWARD • VALLEY OF THE EAGLES

Sponsored by: Haines Chamber of Commerce 907-766-2202
http://seaknet.alaska.edu/~chamber

ATTRACTIONS & TOURS

1. ALASKA BALD EAGLE FESTIVAL November 11-14, 1999 Celebrate the world's largest gathering of bald eagles. Speakers, arts and crafts, family events, and much more. 907-766-2202 FAX 907-766-2271 P.O. Box1449, Haines, AK 99827 E-mail:chamber@seaknet.alaska.edu. http://seaknet.alaska.edu/~chamber

2. ALASKA4YOU by the TRAVEL CONNECTION Glacier Bay Headquarters, customized tours of Alaska including Denali, the Arctic, Pribilofs, and more. Ferry reservations. Local Haines sightseeing. 907-766-2681 FAX 907-766-2585 115 2nd Ave. S., PO Box 645,Haines, AK 99827 E-mail:randa@alaska4you.com www.alaska4you.com

3. ALASKA INDIAN ARTS/CHILKAT DANCERS Traditional Northwest Coast totem carvers, silversmiths & print makers. Home of the Chilkat Dancers performing several times weekly during the summer. Phone/FAX 907-766-2160 Historic Building #13 Fort Seward Dr., P.O. Box 271, Haines, AK 99827 E-mail: aiaio@seaknet.alaska.edu

4. ALASKA LLAMA GUIDES & TOURS Scenic trail hikes with meals prepared or Llama Limo Tours featuring natural history of Haines area: Llamas carry your gear. 1-888-76LLAMA 62 Helmsloop, P.O. Box 293, Haines, AK 99827 E-mail:alaskalama@aol.com http://kcd.com/alaskallama

5. ALASKA NATURE TOURS Wildlife viewing in and around the Chilkat Bald Eagle Preserve by experienced local naturalists. Photography. Bus and walking tours & hiking adventures. 907-766-2876 FAX 766-2844 123 Second Ave. S., P.O. Box 491, Haines, AK 99827 E-mail:aknature@kcd.com http://kcd.com/aknature

6. ALASKA STATE PARKS Parks include: Chilkat State Park (7 Mile Mud Bay Road), Chilkoot Lake State Recreation Site (10 Mile Lutak Road), Portage Cove State Recreation Site (Beach Road, tent and backpackers only), and Mosquito Lake State Recreation Site (27 Mile Haines Highway) 907-766-2292 FAX 907-766-2284

7. CHILKAT CRUISES Haines-Skagway Shuttle Ferry. Large comfortable vessel. Smooth sailing in any water! One hour between ports. 888-766-2103 FAX 907-766-2101 142 Beach Road, P.O. Box 509, Haines, AK 99827 E-mail:chilkat@klukwan.com http://www.chilkatcruises.com

8. CHILKAT RIVER ADVENTURES INC. Join us on a wilderness adventure in the heart of the Bald Eagle Preserve in the pristine Chilkat Valley 907-766-

2050 800-478-9827 (AK only) FAX 766-2051 1 1/2 mile Haines Hwy., P.O. Box 556, Haines, AK 99827 E-mail:k.hess@eudoramail.com.

9. HAINES AIRWAYS INC. Haines Airways offers Glacier Bay Tours and scheduled flights. We look forward to seeing that your Alaska vacation is unforgettable!!!! 907-766-2646 FAX 766-2780 108 Main St., P.O. Box 470, Haines, AK 99827

10. HAINES-SKAGWAY WATER TAXI The Sea Venture through Lynn Canal! See eagles, seals, and waterfalls aboard the Sea Venture II. $32 round-trip, $20 one-way 1-888-766-3395 Phone/FAX 907-766-3395 Small Boat Harbor, P.O. Box 246, Haines, AK 99827 E-mail:h2otaxi@kcd.com http://kcd.com/watertaxi

11. KEET GOOSHI TOURS Exclusive Tour thru Bald Eagle Preserve to Native Village of Klukwan. Learn history and Culture. View Tribal Houses and Totems. 907-766-2168 FAX 907-766-2513 32 Helms Loop, P.O. Box 997, Haines, AK 99827

12. L.A.B. FLYING SERVICE INC. Offering year-round daily scheduled flights, Flightseeing tours and charters. Cities served: Haines, Juneau, Skagway, Gustavus, Hoonah, Kake and Petersburg. Earn Alaska Airlines Miles! 800-426-0543 or 907-766-2222 FAX 907-766-2734 4th & Main St., P.O. Box 272, Haines, AK 99827 E-mail:labflying@aol.com http://www.haines.ak.us/lab

13. McCORMICK CHARTERS, INC. CUSTOM ADVENTURES: Fishing, Sightseeing, Whale watching (underwater microphone), Remote hiking & drops. "Wind Rider" single person sailing trimarans: Guided sailing eco-tours. Phone/FAX 907-766-2450 Small Boat Harbor D-28, P.O. Box 352, Haines, AK 99827 E-Mail: trimaran@sailak.com www.sailak.com

14. PORTAGE COVE ADVENTURE CENTER One stop shopping for all Haines tours & activities. Home of Haines-Skagway Shuttle Ferry and Fast Ferry to Juneau. Bike & Scooter Rentals. Toll Free 877-766-2800 FAX 907-766-3801 142 Beach Road, P.O. Box 509, Haines, AK 99827 E-mail:portage@klukwan.com http://www.portage.klukwan.com

15. SHELDON MUSEUM & CULTURAL CENTER Features Native Tlingit Art & Culture/ Pioneer History (Ft. Seward, Haines Mission, lighthouse lens, etc.) Featured. Alaskana Book & Gift Store 907-766-2366 FAX 766-2368 11 Main St., P.O. Box 269, Haines, AK 99827 E-mail:sheldmus@seaknet.alaska.edu http://seaknet.alaska.edu/~sheldmus/

16. SOCKEYE CYCLE CO. Daily 1-3 hour guided and multi day fully supported Mountain Bike Tours.

Two full service bike shops in Haines & Skagway. Rentals. Phone/FAX 907-766-2869 24 Portage St., P.O. Box 829, Haines, AK 99827 E-mail:cycleak@ibm.net http://www.haines.ak.us/sockeye/

17. SOUTHEAST ALASKA STATE FAIR, INC. August 11-15, 1999: Great Music, Parade, Horseshow, Logging Show, Exhibits, Kids Events, Food/Trade booths. For information call 907-766-2476 FAX 907-766-2478 296 Fair Drive, P.O. Box 385, Haines, AK 99827 E-mail:seasfair@seaknet.alaska.edu

18. WEEPING TROUT SPORTS RESORT Day tours & overnight accommodations for people seeking paradise. Trout & salmon fishing. Par 29 golf, fine food, spectacular scenery. 907-766-2827 FAX 766-2824 Chilkat Lake, P.O. Box 129, Haines, AK 99827 E-Mail: weepingt@kcd.com http://kcd.com/weepingt

GALLERIES GIFT SHOPS

19. ALASKAN LIQUOR STORE Micro Brew and Fine Wine Headquarters of Haines. Located on Main Street Across From Howsers IGA- Local Information 907-766-3131 FAX 907-766-3132 208 Main Street, P.O. Box 1309, Haines, AK 99827

20. ALASKAN SPIRIT SHOP Alcoholic and non-alcoholic beverages, tobacco and snacks. Great location, friendly service. Free ice with purchase! 907-766-3006 842 Main Street, PO Box 1689, Haines, AK 99827

21. BELL'S STORE Alaskan Seafood at it's Best, Alaskan gifts - Fresh Flowers. Clothing. OPEN ALL YEAR. A unique shopping experience. 907-766-2950 FAX 766-2958 18 Second Ave. N., P.O. Box 1189, Haines, AK 99827

22. EAGLE CLASSICS Not just another gift store! T-Shirts, Women's Clothing, Shoes, CD's & Tapes, Joe Boxer, & Lots of other groovy stuff! 907-766-3223 FAX 766-2787 209 Main Street, P.O. Box 1309, Haines, AK 99827

23. THE FAR NORTH Finest Alaska Native Art. Sculpture in Soapstone, Whalebone & Ivory. Hand carved silver jewelry. Across from Visitor Center. 907-766-3535 FAX 907-766-3090 111 Second Ave., P.O. Box 145, Haines, AK 99827

24. OUTFITTER LIQUOR STORE Best Deals In Town - Free Ice with Purchase. Widest Variety & Best Selection. Located next to Post Office. 907-766-3220 FAX 907-766-2787 Mile 0 Haines Hwy. P.O. Box 1709, Haines, AK 99827

25. OUTFITTER SPORTING GOODS Fishing, Hunting, Camping & Hiking Products. Fishing & Hunting Licenses, Bait. We carry Nike, Woolrich, Helly Hansen, Xtratuf Rubber Boots, & Rocky Brand Boots. 907-766-3221 FAX 907-766-2787 Mile 0 Haines Hwy., P.O. Box 1709, Haines, AK 99827

LODGING

26. ALASKAN EAGLE RV PARK Full service RV sites with cable TV. Discounts on area sightseeing & sport fishing tours. 907-766-2335. 755 Union Street., P.O. Box 43, Haines, AK 99827 E-mail: akeaglerv@aol.com website: http://haines.ak.us/akeaglerv

27. BEAR CREEK CABINS Family Cabins ~ $38. Centrally located, clean, modern kitchen and bath facilities. Campsites, laundry, bike rentals. 907-766-2259 1 Mile Small Tracts Road, P.O. Box 908, Haines, AK 99827 E-mail: hostel@kcd.com http://kcd.com/hostel

28. CAPTAIN'S CHOICE INC. MOTEL Haines finest and most comfortable lodging. Car rentals, courtesy transfers; centrally located. Tour Desk, Bus Terminal 907-766-3111 FAX 907-766-3332 108 2nd Ave., P.O. Box 392, Haines, AK 99827 E-mail:captchoice@usa.net http://www.kcd.com/captain

29. CHILKAT EAGLE BED & BREAKFAST Lovely historic residence, waterfront & mountain views, walk to local services, full breakfast, kitchen facilities, TV lounge. Open Year Round. 907-766-2763 FAX 766-3651 #69 Soap Suds Alley, P.O. Box 387, Haines, AK 99827 E-mail:eaglebb@kcd.com www.kcd.com/eaglebb

30. EAGLES NEST MOTEL Beautiful rooms, queen size beds, private baths, car rental. Featuring Chilkoot Lake Tours. Winter rates, packages available. See color ad. 907-766-2891 FAX 907-766-2848 1069 Haines Hwy., P.O. Box 250, Haines, AK 99827 E-mail:eagles_nest@wytbear.com

31. FORT SEWARD CONDOS Completely furnish 1 & 2 bedroom suites, full kitchen, bath & laundry. 2 day minimum---no pets. Reasonable. Phone/ FAX 907-766-2425 #3 Fort Seward Drive, P.O. Box 75, Haines, AK 99827

32. FORT SEWARD LODGE & RESTAURANT Affordable lodging, oceanview kitchenettes, restaurant, cocktail lounge. Full dinner menu, courtesy transfer, military & senior discounts. See our display ad. 800-478-7772 907-766-2009 FAX 907-766-2006 Mile 0 Haines Highway, P.O. Box 307, Haines, AK 99827

33. HAINES HITCH-UP RV PARK 92 Spacious Sites. 20 Pull Thrus. Cable TV sites available. Gift Shop. Laundromat (Guests Only). Tour Information & Ticket Sales Phone/FAX 907-766-2882 851 Main Street, P.O. Box 383, Haines, AK 99827 E-mail:HitchupRV@aol.com

34. THE SUMMER INN BED & BREAKFAST Charming, historical house. Open year round. Full homemade breakfast, centrally located, mountain & ocean views. Recommended by Alaska Best Places Guidebook. Phone/FAX 907-766-2970 117 Second Ave., P.O. Box 1198, Haines, AK 99827

RESTAURANTS GROCERIES

35. ALASKAN INTERNATIONAL CAFE A unique Alaskan dining experience, featuring a $9.95 Salmon Bake. Located at the Alaskan Eagle RV Park, 755 Union St., Haines, AK 99827. 907-766-2335

36. ALASKAN & PROUD Bagged ice and finest selection of groceries, freshest meats, produce, dairy products, sandwiches. Enjoy our Alaskan Hospitality! 907-766-2181 FAX 766-2182 3rd & Dalton, P.O. Box 1689, Haines, AK 99827

37. BAMBOO ROOM RESTAURANT Downtown. Famous Halibut Fish & Chips. Breakfast, Lunch, Dinner. Espresso. Senior & Kid's Menu. Pool, Darts, Pull Tabs, Sports Bar. 907-766-2800 FAX 766-2613 11-13 2nd Ave.N., P.O. Box 190, Haines, AK 99827 E-mail:bamboo@kcd.com http://kcd.com/bamboo

38. CHILKAT RESTAURANT & BAKERY Bakery Products fresh daily. Breakfast-Lunch-Dinner. Plenty of parking. 5th & Dalton Street 907-766-2920 FAX 766-2992, P.O. Box 591, Haines, AK 99827

39. HAINES QUICK SHOP Convenience Store-Snack Headquarters of Haines-Cold Pop–Ice-ATM-Day Phones OPEN 7 AM – MIDNIGHT Local Information Near Fort Seward 907-766-2330 FAX 907-766-2787 Mile 0 Haines Hwy., P.O. Box 709, Haines, AK 99827

40. HOWSERS IGA SUPERMARKET Howsers IGA, your one stop shopping supermarket. We have a variety of travelers needs: ATM cash machine, Block Ice, Coolers, Fresh Produce & Meats. 907-766-2040 FAX 766-2787 209 Main Street, P.O. Box 1309, Haines, AK 99827

41. "JUST FOR THE HALIBUT" FISH & CHIPS CAFE Affordable Dining with a view of Lynn Fjord! Enjoy Fish & Chips, Halibut Kabobs, Burgers, Espresso! At the Chilkat Cruises Dock. Toll Free 877-766-2800 FAX 907-766-3801 142 Beach Road, P.O. Box 509, Haines, AK 99827 E-mail: portage@klukwan.com http://www.portage.klukwan.com

42. KLONDIKE SALOON/ RESTAURANT May-October Located in Dalton City - Set of Walt Disney's "White Fang" - Outdoor Seating/ Horseshoe Pits. For Information - 907-766-2477 FAX 766-2478 296 Fair Drive, P.O.Box 385, Haines, AK 99827

43. MOUNTAIN MARKET Natural and Organic Foods, Fresh baked goods, and the best Espresso and Sandwiches in Southeast Alaska. Open Seven Days. 907-766-3340 FAX 907-766-3339 151 3rd Ave. S., P.O. Box 863, Haines, AK 99827

44. THE WILD STRAWBERRY Fresh-grilled Alaskan Seafood, Gourmet Salad Bar, Soup & Sandwiches, Outstanding Espresso, Belgian Waffles, Baked Goods, Fine Chocolates, Dreyer's Grand Ice Cream 907-766-3608 138 Second Ave.S., P.O. Box 770, Haines, AK 99827

SERVICES

45. BIGFOOT AUTO SERVICE INC Full service - cars, pick-ups, RVs, motorhomes - welding - 24 hour towing - Unleaded & Diesel - NAPA Parts - Tires 800-766-5406 907-766-2458 FAX 907-766-2460 987 Haines Hwy., P.O. Box 150, Haines, AK 99827

46. BUSHMASTER AUTO SERVICE Alignment/ Brakes/Engines/Transmissions/Electronic Controls. Cars, Light Trucks, RVs. Factory Warranty Service. Professional Workmanship 907-766-3217 FAX 766-2415 Fourth St. North, P.O. Box 1355, Haines, AK 99827 E-mail:Bushmasters@webtv.net

47. DELTA WESTERN Gas and diesel. Free coffee, RV water and dump. Propane. MasterCard/VISA accepted. At intersection of the Haines Hwy./Main Street 907-766-3190 FAX 766-3196 P.O. Box 1369, Haines, AK 99827

48. HAINES QUICK LAUNDRY OPEN 7 AM-MIDNIGHT DAILY Large Washers & Dryers. Pay Phone. Located next to the Post Office. 907-766-2330 FAX 907-766-2787 Mile 0 Haines Hwy. P.O. Box 1709, Haines, AK 99827

49. KRSA RADIO - Tune to 94.9 FM for Southeast Alaska's Only Full-Service Christian Radio Station. News, Weather, Sports, and More. 907-772-3891 FAX 907-772-4538 12th H. Streets, P.O. Box 650. Petersburg, AK 99833 E-mail:krsa@alaska.net www.krsa@fm.net

50. THE PARTS PLACE Auto-RV-Marine If you need it and we don't have it we will get it! 907-766-2940 104 3rd Avenue S., P.O. Box 9, Haines, AK 99827

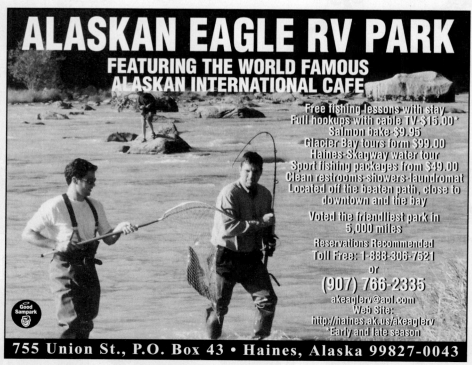
Highway: bear right at the Y by the Welcome to Haines sign; continue straight past the high school and up the hill; turn right on 3rd Ave., which becomes Mud Bay Road at the top of the Hill; then, where the road bends to the right, follow signs from hill to Chilkat State Park). See Mud Bay Road log this section.

Chilkoot Lake Campground (32 sites) is approximately 10 miles/16 km from Haines on Lutak Road (6 miles/10 km past the ferry terminal; turn right when exiting the ferry for Chilkoot Lake); see Lutak Road log this section. There are 5 private campgrounds in Haines.

Mosquito Lake State Recreation Site is located on Mosquito Lake Road, 3 miles/6.5 km north of Mile 27 Haines Highway. It has 6 campsites nestled in a wooded setting around Mosquito Lake. Toilets, drinking water, a picnic shelter, fishing and boat launch are available. Small store and softball diamond at Mile 27. See the HAINES HIGHWAY section. ▲

Eagle RV Park Alaska's finest-full service park offering free breakfast, fishing lessons and an on-site activities director. Good Sam and KOA cards honored. Convenient full- and partial-service RV sites, tent sites, clean restrooms and showers, dump station, laundry and public phones. Gift and bait shop Rod and reel rentals. Crab and shrimp pot rentals. Up to 30 percent discount on area sightseeing and sport-fishing tours. The only RV wash in town. Five star member of the North to Alaska RV Park Association. 755 Union Street, P.O. Box 43, Haines, AK 99827. For reservations and directions to the Eagle, phone toll tree (888) 306-7521 or (907) 766-2335. [ADVERTISEMENT] ▲

Haines Hitch-Up RV Park offers easy access to 92 full hookups (30 amps), spacious, grassy, level sites. 20 pull-throughs. Cable TV sites available. Immaculate restrooms for registered guests only. Gift shop and laundromat. Located at the junction of Haines Highway and Main Street. See map in ad this section. P.O. Box 383, Haines, AK 99827. Phone (907) 766-2882. [ADVERTISEMENT]

Salmon Run Adventures RV Campground, Cabins and Charters. "A true Alaska experience." Beautiful forested property overlooking Lutak Inlet with superb mountain and water vistas. Depending on season, watch for whales, porpoises, sea lions or eagles. Fish from the beach or book a fishing expedition on the owner's charter boat; guests have preference, but advance bookings are recommended. The facility has attractive private sites appointed with picnic tables, fire rings and firewood. Hot showers and restrooms. On Lutak Road, 1.8 miles north of ferry terminal. P.O. Box 1122, Haines, AK 99827. Phone (907) 723-4229. E-mail: salmon.run@wytbear.com. Recommended by U.S. News Travel Guide. [ADVERTISEMENT]

A Sheltered Harbor Bed & Breakfast. Waterfront accommodation in Haines, located in historic Fort Seward across from the cruise ship dock providing a panoramic view of the Lynn Canal. Five spacious rooms, each with a private bath, color cable TV with remote, phone and generous hot home-style breakfast. Charter fishing and sightseeing tours available, along with vacuum-packing and freezing of your catch. Browse our gift shop featuring Alaska-made and local arts and crafts. Open year-round. VISA/MasterCard accepted. Reservations: (907) 766-2741. [ADVERTISEMENT]

Chilkat Dancers interpret ancient Tlingit legends. *(© Crystal Images: Kathleen Marie Menke)*

TRANSPORTATION

Air: L.A.B. Flying Service, Haines Airways and Wings of Alaska offer several flights daily to and from Juneau, Skagway and other southeast Alaska communities. Haines airport is 3.5 miles/5.6 km from downtown. Commercial airlines provide transportation to and from motels, and some motels offer courtesy car pickup.

Bus: Local bus service to ferry terminal and guided sightseeing tours are available. Gray Line of Alaska serves Haines to and from the Alaska interior. Alaska Direct bus line connects the interior with Whitehorse, but does not come down to Haines.

Car Rental: Available at Avis Rent-A-Car, Halsingland Hotel (907/766-2733). Rental Car Service also available at Captain's Choice Motel (907/766-3111), and Eagle's Nest Motel (907/766-2891).

Taxi: 24-hour service to ferry terminal and airport.

Highways: The Haines Highway connects Haines, AK, with Haines Junction, YT. It is maintained year-round. See HAINES HIGHWAY section for details.

Ferry: Alaska Marine Highway vessels serve Haines from southeastern Alaska, Prince Rupert, BC, and Bellingham, WA. Alaska state ferries run year-round; phone (907) 766-2111. Ferries unload at the terminal on Lutak Road, 4.5 miles/7.2 km from downtown Haines. Bus/van service meets all ferries in summer.

Water-taxi: The Haines/Skagway Water Taxi and Chilkat Cruises provide daily water-taxi service to Skagway twice daily during the summer; phone (907) 766-3395.

Cruise Ships: Eleven cruise ships will regularly call in Haines in 1998, with a total of 17 different ships anticipated during the season.

Private Boats: Transient moorage is available at Letnikof Cove and at the small-boat harbor downtown. Contact the harbormaster, phone (907) 766-2448.

ATTRACTIONS

Take the walking tour of historic Fort William H. Seward; details and map are available at the visitor information center and at other businesses. Historic buildings of the post include the former cable office; warehouses and barracks; "Soapsuds Alley," the housing for noncommissioned officers whose wives did washing for the soldiers; the former headquarters building, now a residence, fronted by a cannon and a totem depicting a bear and an eagle; Officers' Row at the "Top O' the Hill," restored homes and apartments; the commanding officers' quarters, now the Halsingland Hotel, where Elinor Dusenbury (who later wrote the music for "Alaska's Flag," which became the state song) once lived; the fire hall; the guard house (jail); the former contractor's office, the plumber's quarters; the post exchange (now a lodge), gymnasium, movie house and the mule stables. Look for historic and interpretive signs.

Visit the Chilkat Center for the Arts at the auditorium. Here, the Chilkat Dancers interpret ancient Tlingit legends. Check with the visitor information center or Alaska Indian Arts Inc. for performance schedule.

Totem Village, on the former post parade ground, includes a replica of a tribal ceremonial house and a trapper's cabin and cache. There is a salmon bake, the Port Chilkoot Potlatch, held nightly in summer

next to the tribal house; reservations recommended.

See the Welcome Totems located at the Y on the Haines Highway. These poles were created by carvers of Alaska Indian Arts Inc. *The Raven* pole is symbolic of Raven, as founder of the world and all his great powers. The second figure is *The Whale,* representing Alaska and its great size. The bottom figure is the head of *The Bear,* which shows great strength. *The Eagle* pole tells of its feeding grounds (the Haines area is noted for eagles). Top figure is *The Salmon Chief,* who provides the late run of salmon to the feeding grounds. *The Eagle Chief,* head of the Eagle clan, is the third figure, and the bottom figure is *The Brown Bear,* which also feeds on salmon and is a symbol of strength. Inquire at the visitor information center and museum about location of poles.

The Sheldon Museum and Cultural Center is located on the old Haines Mission property at the end of Main Street by the boat harbor. Exhibits present the pioneer

Alaska Chilkat Bald Eagle Preserve is just outside Haines. (© Bill Sherwonit)

history of the Chilkat Valley and the story and culture of the Tlingit Native people. Chilkat blankets, Russian trunks, blue dishes, mounted eagles, Jack Dalton's sawed-off shotgun, photographs and a video on eagles make a fascinating history lesson. Children's "discovery" sheet available. Open daily 1–5 P.M. in summer, plus most mornings and evenings; winter, 1–4 P.M Sunday, Monday and Wednesday, 3–5 P.M. Tuesday, Thursday and Friday. Admission fee $3; children free. Phone (907) 766-2366.

Mountain Flying Service/Tickets & Tours. Located 3 doors south of the visitors' center, specializing in flights over and into Glacier Bay as well as Alaska ferry reservations and all Haines/Glacier Bay tour sales. We provide the highest quality high wing "Bush" aircraft and experienced pilots to give you the best flight in all of Alaska. Mountain Flying Service (907) 766-3007. Tickets & Tours 1-800-954-8747, Box 1404, Haines, AK 99827. [ADVERTISEMENT]

Enjoy the Fourth of July celebration, which includes canoe and kayak races on Chilkoot Lake, logging events, bicycle and foot races, pie-eating and other contests, parades and performances at the Chilkat Center for the Arts.

The Southeast Alaska State Fair, held at the fairgrounds in Haines (Aug. 11-15, 1999), features agriculture, home arts, and fine arts and crafts. A big event at the fair is the Bald Eagle Music Festival. There are exhibits of flowers, livestock, baked goods, beer and wine, needlework, quilting, woodworking and over a dozen other categories. There are also a parade, horse show and other events, including pig racing for cookies. Brochures available from the Fair offices or the visitor information center. Write to Box 385, Haines 99827, or (907) 766-2476.

Summer Solstice Celebration, sponsored by the Southeast Alaska State Fair, takes place on the Saturday closest to the June 21 summer solstice and features bands, dances, games, a beer garden and special activities. All (907) 766-2476 for more information.

American Bald Eagle Foundation is Haines' newest attraction. Interpretive center shows visitors how the bald eagle interacts with its environment through exhibits; mounted eagles, a wide variety of mammals, and fish and undersea life. Admission fee $2 for adults; $5 for families. Children under 12 are free. Open daily 10 A.M. to 6 P.M. in summer. Located at the Haines Highway and 2nd Street, just across 2nd Street from the city/municipal building.

Bald Eagle Festival. The festival includes release of wild rehabilitated eagles, live bird presentations, art exhibits, naturalist-guided tours to bald eagle preserve, exhibits and more. The events take place in November, and coincide with "the gathering," when eagles congregate to feed on late fall run salmon (see following). Contact the chamber of commerce at (800) 246-6268 for more information.

Alaska Chilkat Bald Eagle Preserve, where the world's greatest concentration of American bald eagles takes place late October through December on Chilkat River flats below Klukwan. The eagle viewing area begins at **Milepost H 17** on the Haines Highway. The 48,000-acre Alaska Chilkat Bald Eagle Preserve was established in 1982. The Chilkat Valley at Haines is the annual gathering site of more than 3,000 bald eagles, which gather to feed on the late run of chum and coho salmon in the Chilkat River. For information contact Alaska State Parks, (907) 465-4563.

Dalton City, opened in 1992, is housed in the "White Fang" Disney film set. It is located at the fairgrounds. The former movie set houses a few businesses and a Klondike restaurant open in summer.

Visit the small-boat harbor at the foot of Main Street for an interesting afternoon outing. Watch gill-net and crab fishermen setting out from here. Good views from Lookout Park and also from the shoreline between Haines and Portage Cove Campground. Land otters may sometimes be seen cavorting on the floating dock at the northeast corner of the harbor where commercial fishing nets are set out to dry.

Visit State Parks. Chilkoot Lake, at the end of Lutak Road, is worth a visit. Beautiful setting with a picnic area, campground and boat launch. Watch for brown bears in nearby waters in the fall, attracted by spawning salmon. (Private boat tours of Chilkoot Lake are available; check in town.) Chilkat State Park on Mud Bay Road is also a scenic spot with hiking trails, beach access, views of glaciers (Rainbow and Davidson), saltwater fishing (boat required), camping and picnick-

ing. Both parks are within 10 miles/16 km of downtown Haines.

Go Flightseeing. Local air charter operators offer flightseeing trips for spectacular close-up views of glaciers, ice fields, mountain peaks and bald eagles. The heart of Glacier Bay is just west of Haines.

Charter boat operators in Haines offer fishing, sightseeing and photography trips.

Watch totem carvers at the Alaska Indian Arts Inc. workshop, located in the restored hospital at Fort Seward. This non-profit organization is dedicated to the revival of Tlingit Indian art. Craftsmen also work in silver and stone, and sew blankets. Visitor hours 9 A.M. to noon and 1–5 P.M. weekdays year-round.

Hike Area Trails. Mount Ripinsky trail is a strenuous all-day hike, with spectacular views from the summit of mountains and tidal waters. Start at the north end of Young Road angling right at the top of the hill. Follow the upper road, then turn left at the water tower. Follow the pipeline right-of-way for 0.5 mile/0.3 km to the chain across the road. Turn left onto the trail which climbs 3.5 miles/5.8 km to the 3,610 foot/1,100m summit. Hikers should stop at the visitor information center for updates on wildlife sightings and to pick up a free copy of the pamphlet *Haines is for Hikers*, which

contains trail descriptions and maps. *CAUTION: This is an unmaintained trail, recommended for experienced hikers only.*

Battery Point trail starts 1 mile/1.6 km beyond Portage Cove Campground and leads about 1.5 miles/2.4 km to a primitive camping site on Kelgaya Point overlooking Lynn Canal.

Mount Riley (elev. 1,760 feet/536m) has 3 routes to the summit. The steepest and most widely used trail starts at Mile 3 Mud Bay Road and climbs 2.8 miles/4.5 km to the summit. A second route starts at the end of F.A.A. Road and leads 1.7 miles/2.7 km along the city water-supply route to connect with the trail from Mud Bay Road to the summit. A third route follows the Battery Point trail for approximately 0.9 mile/1.4 km, then forks right for a fairly steep climb 3.1 miles/5 km to the summit of Mount Riley.

Seduction Point, at the southern tip of the Chilkat Peninsula, is accessible from Chilkat State Park via a 6-mile/9.7-km trail; a rolling forest and beach walk. Views of Davidson and Rainbow glaciers.

AREA FISHING: Local charter boat operators and freshwater fishing guides offer fishing trips. Sportfishing lodges at Chilkat Lake offer good fishing in a semi-remote setting. Good fishing in the spring for king salmon in **Chilkat Inlet.** Halibut best in

summer in **Chilkat, Lutak** and **Chilkoot inlets.** Dolly Varden fishing good in all lakes and rivers, and along marine shorelines from early spring to late fall. Great pink salmon fishing every other year in August along the marine shoreline of **Lutak Inlet** and in the **Chilkoot River.** Sockeye salmon in the **Chilkoot River,** late June through August. Coho salmon in the **Chilkoot** and **Chilkat** rivers, mid-September through October. Cutthroat trout year-round at **Chilkat** and **Mosquito lakes. Herman Lake** is full of hungry grayling stocked there in the mid-1970s. The lake is located off the Sunshine Mountain Road (watch out for logging trucks) accessed from the steel bridge across the Klehini River at **Milepost H 26.3** Haines Highway; get directions locally. For more information, contact the Alaska Dept. of Fish and Game at (907) 766-2625. For web sportfishing information for Haines and Skagway: www.state.ak.us/local/akpages/ FISH.GAME/sportf/region1/geninfo/fishrpt/h ns9398.htm.

Mud Bay Road Log

Mileposts on Mud Bay Road measure distance from its junction with the Haines Highway near Front Street to road end at Mud Bay, a distance of 8 miles/13 km. This road, first paved, then wide gravel, leads to Chilkat State Park, following the shoreline of Chilkat Inlet to Mud Bay on Chilkoot Inlet. **Distance is measured from junction with Haines Highway.**

0.1 (0.2 km) Hotel on left, motel and private camper park on right. ▲

0.2 (0.3 km) **Junction** with 3rd Street, which leads back to town.

0.5 (0.8 km) Small Tracts Road on left, a 1.9-mile/3.1-km loop road which rejoins Mud Bay Road at **Milepost 2.3.** Small Tracts Road leads to private residences and to Bear Creek Camp and Youth Hostel (dorms, cabins and tent camping).

Mud Bay Road leads to the right, down Cemetery Hill (the old military cemetery was located here), then follows the shoreline of Chilkat Inlet, with views of Pyramid Island. Excellent area for eagle pictures.

2.3 (3.7 km) Stop sign at T intersection: go right for state park, left to return to town via Small Tracts Road.

3 (4.8 km) Mount Riley trail on left, parking area on right.

3.9 (6.3 km) View of Pyramid Island and Rainbow Glacier across Chilkat Inlet. Rainbow Glacier, is a hanging glacier. The ice field moved out over a cliff rather than moving down a valley to the sea. Davidson Glacier is about 2 miles/3.2 km south of Rainbow Glacier.

4.9 (7.9 km) Boat dock on right for small boats (summer tie-off only), boat ramp.

5.3 (8.5 km) Private road on right to cannery on Letnikof Cove.

6.7 (10.8 km) Pavement ends, gravel begins. Turn right and drive in 1.2 miles/1.9 km to entrance of Chilkat State Park (camping area 0.5 mile/0.8 km beyond entrance): 32 campsites, 3 tent sites on beach, $6 nightly fee or annual pass, picnic sites, pit toilets and boat launch. Access road paved and graveled, grades to 11 percent. Drive carefully. Beach access, view of glaciers and hiking trail to Seduction Point at southern tip of Chilkat Peninsula. ▲

8 (12.9 km) Mud Bay Road turns east and crosses Chilkat Peninsula to Flat Bay (commonly called Mud Bay) off Lynn Canal. Road ends at Mud Bay; short walk to rocky beach. These are private lands. No camping.

Lutak Road Log

Lutak Road begins at Front Street, and leads north along Chilkoot and Lutak inlets past the Alaska Marine Highway ferry terminal. Pavement ends at a fork in the road: the left fork leads straight along the Chilkoot River to Chilkoot Lake campground; the right crosses the the Chilkoot River and serves a residential area at the end of Lutak Inlet (no outlet or turnaround).
Distance is measured from the junction of Front Street with Lutak Road.

0 Junction, Front Street and Lutak Road.
0.1 (0.2 km) Turnout on right with view of Fort Seward and Lynn Canal.
1.6 (2.6 km) Turnouts along road from here to Mile 7 allow good view of gill-net fleet, July through September.
2.4 (3.9 km) Government tank farm, petroleum distribution terminal and beginning of an oil pipeline to Fairbanks. No entry.
3.2 (5.1 km) Dock for oil tankers on right.
3.6 (5.8 km) Alaska Marine Highway ferry terminal on right.
3.8 (6.1 km) City dock on right is used for shipping lumber and also for docking barges.
4.4 (7.1 km) Closed and partly dismantled sawmill. A small building for fish processing is also here.
8.3 (13.4 km) Road on left follows a wide stretch of the Chilkoot River for 1 mile/1.6 km to Chilkoot Lake picnic area and boat launch; state campground with 32 sites just beyond picnic area, 7-day limit, $10 nightly fee or annual pass. ▲
8.4 (13.5 km) Bridge over the mouth of the **Chilkoot River.** Good salmon fishing June through October. Watch for bears. ⚓

In 1983, the Chilkoot tribe dedicated Deer Rock here as a historic reminder of the original location of their village.

Road continues to private homes and dead ends; no turnaround.

Skagway

(See map, page 673)

Located on the north end of Taiya Inlet on Lynn Canal, 90 air miles/145 km northwest of Juneau; 108 road miles/174 km south of Whitehorse, YT. The northern terminus of the Alaska Marine Highway Southeast ferry system and southern terminus of Klondike Highway 2 which connects with the Alaska Highway. *NOTE: Although Skagway is only 13 miles/21 km by water from Haines, it is 359 miles/578 km by road!* **Population:** 816. **Emergency Services: Skagway Police Department**, phone (907) 983-2232. **Fire Department** and **Ambulance**, phone 911. **Clinic**, phone (907) 983-2255. **Maritime**

www.themilepost.com

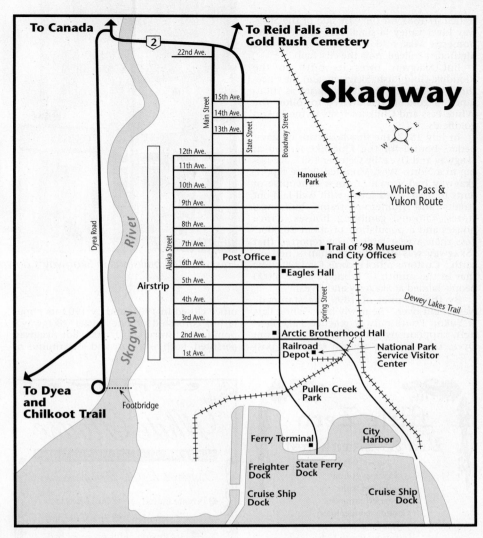

Search and Rescue, contact the Coast Guard at (800) 478-5555.

Visitor Information: Write the Skagway Convention and Visitors Bureau, Box 415MP, Skagway, AK 99840. Phone (907) 983-2854, fax 983-3854. Klondike Gold Rush National Historical Park Visitor Center has exhibits and films on the history of the area and information on hiking the Chilkoot Trail; write Box 517, Skagway, AK 99840; phone (907) 983-2921. Located in the restored railroad depot on 2nd Avenue and Broadway, it is open daily in summer.

Elevation: Sea level. **Climate:** Average daily temperature in summer, 57°F/14°C; in winter, 23°F/-5°C. Average annual precipitation is 29.9 inches. **Radio:** KHNS-FM 91.9.

Newspaper: *Skagway News* (biweekly).
Private Aircraft: Skagway airport, adjacent west; elev. 44 feet/13m; length 3,700 feet/1,128m; asphalt; fuel 100LL; attended.

The name Skagway (originally spelled Skaguay) is said to mean "home of the north wind" in the local Tlingit dialect. It is the oldest incorporated city in Alaska (incorporated in 1900). Skagway is also a year-round port and 1 of the 2 gateway cities to the Alaska Highway in Southeast Alaska: Klondike Highway 2 connects Skagway with the Alaska Highway. (The other gateway city is Haines, connected to the Alaska Highway via the Haines Highway.)

The first white residents were Capt. William Moore and his son, J. Bernard, who settled in 1887 on the east side of the Skagway River valley (a small part of the Moore homesite was sold for construction of a Methodist college, now the city hall).

But Skagway owes its birth to the Klondike Gold Rush. Skagway, and the once-thriving town of Dyea, sprang up as thousands of gold seekers arrived to follow the White Pass and Chilkoot trails to the Yukon goldfields.

In July 1897, the first boatloads of stampeders bound for the Klondike landed at Skagway and Dyea. By October 1897, according to a North West Mounted Police report, Skagway had grown "from a concourse of tents to a fair-sized town, with well-laid-out streets and numerous frame buildings, stores, saloons, gambling houses, dance houses and a population of about 20,000." Less than a year later it was reported that "Skagway was little better than a hell on earth." Customs office records for 1898 show that in the month of February alone 5,000 people landed at Skagway and Dyea.

By the summer of 1899 the stampede was all but over. The newly built White Pass & Yukon Route railway reached Lake Bennett, supplanting the Chilkoot Trail from Dyea. Dyea became a ghost town. Its post

False-fronted buildings in Skagway's downtown historical district. *(© Susan Cole Kelly)*

office closed in 1902, and by 1903 its population consisted of one settler. Skagway's population dwindled to 500. But Skagway persisted, both as a port and as terminus of

the White Pass & Yukon Route railway, which connected the town to Whitehorse, YT, in 1900. Cruise ships, and later the Alaska State Ferry System, brought tourism and business to Skagway. Scheduled state ferry service to southeastern Alaska began in 1963.

Today, tourism is Skagway's main economic base, with Klondike Gold Rush National Historical Park Skagway's major visitor attraction. Within Skagway's downtown historical district, false-fronted buildings and boardwalks dating from gold rush times line the streets. The National Park Service, the city of Skagway and local residents have succeeded in retaining Skagway's Klondike atmosphere.

Skagway has modern schools, churches, a clinic, bank and post office. U.S. customs office is located at Mile 6.8 Klondike Highway 2; phone or fax (907) 983-2325. The boat harbor and seaplane base has space for cruisers up to 100 feet/30m. Gas, diesel fuel and water are available.

ACCOMMODATIONS/VISITOR SERVICES

Skagway offers a variety of accommodations; see ads this section. Reservations advised in summer.

Historic Skagway Inn Bed & Breakfast, established 1897, located at 7th and Broadway in historic district. Once a gold rush brothel, Victorian-style rooms are comfortable. Hearty breakfast and fresh-ground coffee. Walking distance to shops, museums and trails. Friendly innkeepers can make your reservations for railroad, shows, tours plus arrange transportation to Chilkoot trailhead. Known for fine dining. Phone (907) 983-2289. (800) 478-2290 (inside Alaska), fax (907) 983-2713. [ADVERTISEMENT]

The White House, historic accommodations. Newly renovated 10-room inn features private baths and phones in each room, hand-made quilts on every comfortable bed, original woodwork, family antiques, high ceilings, spacious yard, delicious breakfast and bottomless cookie jar. Owner operated, we're open year-round. 475 8th Avenue, P.O. Box 41-MP, Skagway, AK 99840-0041. Phone (907) 983-9000, fax (907) 983-9010, e-mail: whitehse@ptialaska.net. [ADVERTISEMENT]

There are several restaurants, cafes and bars, grocery, hardware and clothing stores, and many gift and novelty shops offering Alaska and gold rush souvenirs, photos, books, records, gold nugget jewelry, furs and ivory. Propane, marine and automobile gas are available, as is diesel fuel.

There is 1 bank in town (National Bank of Alaska), located at 6th and Broadway; open 9:30 A.M. to 5 P.M. Monday through Friday in summer. Automatic teller machines at bank and next to the Trail Bench gift shop on Broadway between 2nd and 3rd avenues.

There are several private campgrounds in Skagway offering hookups, tent sites, restrooms and showers, dump stations and laundromats. A campground for backpackers is located at the Chilkoot Trail trailhead near Dyea. ▲

TRANSPORTATION

Air: Daily scheduled service between Skagway and Haines and Juneau via L.A.B. Flying Service, Skagway Air and Wings of Alaska. Charter service also available between towns and for flightseeing via Skagway Air. Temsco provides helicopter tours. Transportation to and from the airport is provided by the flight services and local hotels in the summer.

Bus: Bus/van service to Anchorage, Fairbanks, Haines and Whitehorse, YT.

Car Rental: Available from Avis Rent-A-Car (907/983-2247) and Sourdough Car & Van Rental (907/983-2523). Motorhomes available from ABC Motor Home Rentals (800/421-7456 or 907/983-3222).

Highway: Klondike Highway 2 was completed in 1978 and connects Skagway to the Alaska Highway. It is open year-round. See KLONDIKE HIGHWAY 2 section.

Railroad: White Pass & Yukon Route offers 3-hour excursions from Skagway to White Pass Summit and return. Through rail/bus connections are also available daily between Skagway and Whitehorse.

Ferry: Alaska Marine Highway vessels call regularly year-round, as Skagway is the northern terminus of the Southeast ferry system. The ferry terminal is in the large building on the waterfront (see city map this section); restrooms, pay phone and lockers inside. Ferry terminal office hours

vary: opening hours are usually posted at the front door. Phone (907) 983-2941 or 983-2229. It's an easy walk into town, but hotel and motel vans do meet ferries.

Water-taxi: Service is available between Haines and Skagway. For schedules and rates, phone (907) 983-2083 in Skagway; (907) 766-3395 in Haines.

Cruise Ships: Skagway is a regular port of call for cruise ships and the 17th most visited port in the world. Downtown is not far from the dock. Tours can be purchased dockside and at downtown offices.

Private Boats: Transient moorage is available at the Skagway small-boat harbor. Con-

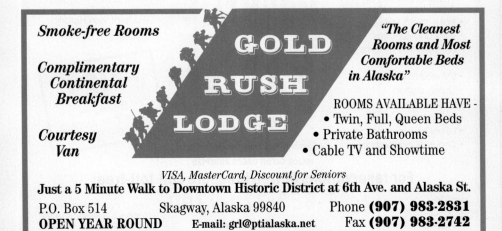

tact the harbormaster at (907) 983-2628.

ATTRACTIONS

Earth's Past. Experience nature's wonders at Skagway's exclusive prehistoric gallery. Fine fossil walrus and mammoth ivory carvings in Alaska themes. Unique jewelry, handcrafted from prehistoric ivory and rare, fiery, iridescent ammolite. Fine fossils, minerals, geodes, etc. Great gifts for all ages. 7th at Broadway, Skagway, AK 99840. Phone (907) 983-2880. [ADVERTISEMENT]

Trail of '98 Museum is temporarily relocated in the Arctic Brotherhood Hall on Broadway Street between 2nd and 3rd avenues, while its original home, McCabe College Building/City Hall, is being renovated. The Arctic Brotherhood Hall's facade has almost 10,000 pieces of driftwood sticks

Skagway's restored railroad depot houses Klondike National Historical Park visitor center. (© Susan Cole Kelly)

arranged in a mosaic pattern, with the brotherhood's AB letters and symbols, a gold pan with nuggets. The museum's primary interest is to help preserve Alaskan historical material and to display Alaskan pioneer life. The

museum is open daily May through October, 9 A.M. to 5 P.M.; contact the museum for winter hours. Phone (907) 983-2420.

McCabe College Building/City Hall is the first granite building constructed in

Linger awhile

Visit Historic Skagway:

Gateway to the Klondike

Garden City of Alaska

Northern Terminus of the
Alaska Marine Highway System

Home of the Klondike Gold Rush
National Historical Park

SKAGWAY CONVENTION AND VISITORS BUREAU
Toll Free: 888-762-1898 • (907) 983-2854 • Fax (907) 983-3854
P.O. Box 1025 • Skagway, AK 99840
http://www.skagway.org • E-mail: infoskag@ptialaska.net

Alaska. It was built by the Methodist Church as a school in 1899–1900 to be known as McCabe College, but public-school laws were passed that made the enterprise impractical, and it was sold to the federal government. For decades it was used as U.S. District Court No. 1 of Alaska, but as the population of the town declined, the court was abandoned, and in 1956 the building was purchased by the city. The main floor is occupied by City of Skagway offices. From the waterfront, walk up Broadway and turn right on 7th Avenue.

See the show *The Days of 1898 Show With Soapy Smith.* This show, produced by Gold Rush Productions, is put on several times a day; summer evening performances (subject to cruise ship arrivals) in Eagles Hall. Check the billboard in front of the hall for show times. The show relates the history of Skagway, from the days of the notorious Soapy Smith. Phone (907) 983-2545.

This show is good family entertainment; bring your camera, gamble with funny money (during evening show only), and enjoy this well-done historical musical comedy. Admission fee charged.

Alaska Wildlife Adventure displays Alaska wildlife mounts and has an extensive and eclectic collection of Alaskana memorabilia. Gift shop and donut shop. Admission fee charged.

Klondike Gold Rush National Historical Park was authorized in 1976 to preserve and interpret the history of the Klondike Gold Rush of 1897–98. In 1998 this became the nation's only International Historical Park, with units in Seattle, Skagway, British Columbia and the Yukon Territory. The park, managed by the National Park Service, consists of 4 units: a 6-block historical district in Skagway's business area; a 1-mile-/1.6-km-wide, 17-mile-/27.4-km-long corridor of land comprising the Chilkoot Trail; a 1-mile-/1.6-km-wide, 5-mile-/8-km-long corridor of land comprising the White Pass Trail; and a visitor center at 117 S. Main St. in Seattle, WA. The Skagway unit is the most visited national park in Alaska. For more information, phone (907) 983-2921; fax: (907) 983-2046; website: http://www.nps.gov/klgo.

In Skagway, the National Park Service offers a variety of free programs in summer. Visit the restored Mascot Saloon at Third Avenue and Broadway. There are daily, guided walking tours of the downtown Skagway historic district and ranger talks on a variety of topics. Films are also shown. Check with the Park Service's visitor center in the restored railroad depot on 2nd Avenue and Broadway. Summer (May through Sept.) hours are 8 A.M. to 6 P.M. The original Moore cabin and the restored J. Bernard Moore House at 5th Avenue and Spring Street provide insights into the Alaska pioneer lifestyle during Skagway's early years. Entrance to the Moore House and interpretation by National Park Service Rangers is provided for a nominal fee.

Hike the Chilkoot Trail. This 33-mile/53-km trail begins on Dyea Road (see log this section) and climbs Chilkoot Pass (elev. 3,739 feet/1,140m) to Lake Bennett, following the historic route of the gold seekers of 1897–98. The trail is arduous but offers both spectacular scenery and historical relics. There are several campgrounds and shelters along the route. Hikers planning to take the Chilkoot Trail should check with the Trail Center in Skagway, phone (907) 983-3655. Permits are required and reservations recommended for travel on the Canadian portion of the trail. Call (867) 667-3910, or from Canada and the U.>S. mainland call 1-800-661-0486. The Trail Center is open daily from 7:30 A.M. to 4:30 P.M., May through mid-September. Trail maps, local natural and cultural history guides, bear precaution and safety information, and other materials are available free or for sale. *The ALASKA WILDERNESS GUIDE* also has details on the Chilkoot Trail, and "Chilkoot Pass" by Archie Satterfield is a good hiking and history guide to the trail.

Corrington Museum of Alaska History, located at 5th and Broadway, offers a unique record of events from prehistory to the present. Each of the 40 exhibits at the museum features a scene from Alaska history hand-engraved (scrimshawed) on a walrus tusk. The museum is open in summer. Free admission.

Picnic at Pullen Creek Park. This attractive waterfront park has a covered picnic shelter, 2 footbridges and 2 small docks. It is located between the cruise ship and ferry docks, behind the White Pass & Yukon Route depot. Watch for pink salmon in the intertidal waters in August, silver salmon in September.

Helicopter and airplane tours of Skagway and White Pass are available in summer.

Gold Rush Cemetery is 1.5 miles/2.4 km from downtown and makes a nice walk. Go north on State Street to a sign pointing to the cemetery. Follow dirt road across tracks into railroad yard, follow posted direction signs, then continue about 0.4 mile/0.6 km farther to the cemetery. If you drive in, a circular road around the cemetery eliminates having to back up to get out. A path on left at the end of the road leads to the cemetery where the graves of both "bad guy" Soapy Smith and "good guy" Frank Reid are located (both men died in a gunfight in July 1898). Smith's original gravestone was whittled away by souvenir hunters, and the resting place of the feared boss of Skagway is now marked by a metal marker.

Reid Falls are located near Gold Rush Cemetery, and it is only a short hike from Frank Reid's grave to view them.

AREA FISHING: Local charter boat operators offer fishing trips. The ADF&G Sport Fish Division recommends the following areas and species. Dolly Varden: Fish the shore of **Skagway Harbor**, **Long Bay** and **Taiya Inlet**, May through June. Try the **Taiya River** by the steel bridge in Dyea in early spring or fall; use red and white spoons or salmon eggs. Hatchery-produced king salmon have been returning to the area in good numbers in recent years. Try fishing in salt water during June and July and in **Pullen Creek** in August. Pink salmon are also plentiful at Pullen Creek in August. Coho and chum

salmon near the steel bridge on the **Taiya River**, mid-September through October. Trolling in the marine areas is good but often dangerous for small boats. Trout: A steep trail near town will take you to Dewey lakes, which were stocked with Colorado brook trout in the 1920s. **Lower Dewey Lake**, 1/2-hour to 1-hour hike; heavily wooded shoreline, use raft. The brook trout are plentiful and grow to 16 inches but are well fed, so fishing can be frustrating. **Upper Dewey Lake**, a steep 2 1/2-hour to 4-hour hike to above tree line, is full of hungry brook trout to 11 inches. Use salmon eggs or size #10 or #12 artificial flies. **Lost Lake** is reached via a rough trail near Dyea (ask locals for directions). The lake lies at about elev. 1,300 feet/396m and has a good population of rainbow trout. Use small spinners or spoons. For more information, contact the ADF&G office in Haines at (907) 766-2625. For web sportfishing information: www.state.ak.us/local/akpages/FISH.GAME/sportf/region1/geninfo/fishrpt/hns9398.htm. ✦

Dyea Road Log

The Dyea Road begins at **Milepost S 2.3** on Klondike Highway 2. It leads southwest toward Yakutania Point, then northwest past Long Bay and the Taiya River to the beginning of the Chilkoot Trail and to a side road leading to the old Dyea townsite and Slide Cemetery. The Dyea Road is a narrow winding gravel road.

Distance is from the junction with Klondike Highway 2.

0 Junction.
0.1 (0.2 km) Old cemetery on right.
0.4 (0.6 km) View of Reid Falls east across the Skagway River.

The only building still standing in Dyea. (© David J. Job)

1.4 (2.3 km) A scenic wayside with platform on left southbound affords view of Skagway, Taiya Inlet and the Skagway River.

1.7 (2.7 km) A steep, primitive road on left southbound descends 0.4 mile/0.6 km toward bank of the Skagway River, with a view of the Skagway waterfront and Taiya Inlet.

Drive to parking area and walk 0.2 mile/0.3 km to Yakutania Point; horse trail beyond parking area. Bridge at base of hill leads to a short trail back to town. Dyea Road turns northwest along Long Bay at this point.

1.9 (3.1 km) Skyline trailhead (poorly signed). This trail leads to top of AB Mountain (elev. 5,000 feet/1,524m).

2.1 (3.4 km) Head of Long Bay.

4 (6 km) City dump.

4.3 (6.9 km) Taiya Inlet comes into view on left northbound as the road curves away from Long Bay.

5.1 (8.2 km) View of the old pilings in Taiya Inlet. The docks of Dyea used to stretch from the trees to beyond the pilings, which are still visible. These long docks were needed to reach deep water because of the great tidal range in this inlet.

5.7 (9.2 km) Hooligan (smelt) run here in the Taiya River in May and early June. Local swimming hole across the road.

6.5 (10.5 km) Dyea information display.

6.7 (10.8 km) Chilkoot Trail trailhead campground, parking area and ranger station.

7.2 (11.6 km) The Chilkoot Trail begins on right northbound. Bridge over Taiya River.

7.4 (11.9 km) A primitive road on left northbound leads southwest to Slide Cemetery (keep right at forks and follow signs) and old Dyea townsite. The cemetery, reached by a short unmarked path through the woods, contains the graves of men killed in the Palm Sunday avalanche, April 3, 1898, on the Chilkoot Trail. At Dyea townsite, covered with fireweed and lupine in summer, hardly a trace remains of the buildings that housed 8,000 people here during the gold rush. About 30 people live in the valley today.

8.4 (13.5 km) Steel bridge across West Creek. Four-wheel drive recommended beyond this point.

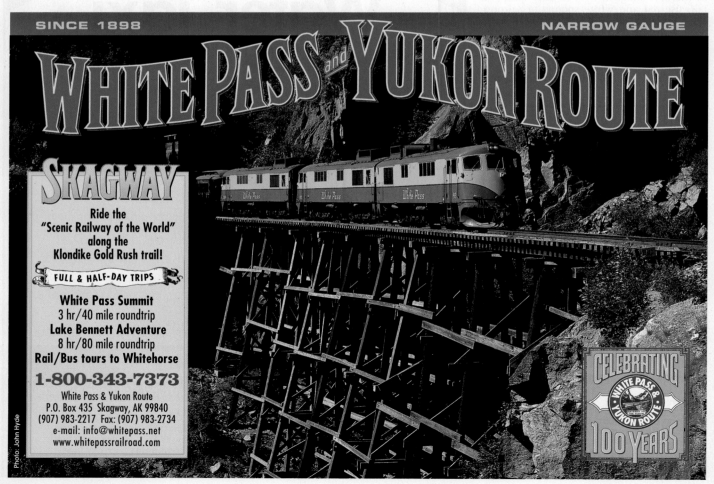

HAINES HIGHWAY

Connects: Haines, AK, to Haines Junction, YT   **Length:** 152 miles
Road Surface: Paved   **Season:** Open all year
Highest Summit: Chilkat Pass 3,493 feet
Major Attraction: Chilkat Bald Eagle Preserve

(See map, page 734)

	Alaska Hwy. Jct.	Atlin	Carcross	Skagway	Whitehorse
Alaska Hwy. Jct.		125	33	99	10
Atlin	125		92	158	81
Carcross	33	92		66	43
Skagway	99	158	66		109
Whitehorse	10	81	43	109	

The Haines Highway descends into Haines Junction, YT. (© Earl L. Brown, staff)

The paved 151.6-mile-/244-km-long Haines Highway connects Haines, AK (on the state ferry route), at the head of Lynn Canal with the Alaska Highway at Haines Junction, YT. The highway is open year-round. Allow about 4 hours driving time. Watch for logging and fuel trucks. *NOTE: In summer, gas is available along the highway only at 33 Mile Roadhouse and at Kathleen Lake Lodge, Milepost H 135.2.*

Noted for the grandeur and variety of its alpine scenery, the highway leads from coastal forests near Haines through the Chilkat Eagle Preserve up over the backbone of the St. Elias Mountains, skirting Tatshenshini–Alsek Wilderness Provincial Park, and running along the eastern border of Kluane National Park Reserve and down into the valleys of the Yukon basin. Information on Kluane National Park Reserve is available in Haines Junction, YT.

Part of what is now the Haines Highway was originally a "grease trail" used by the coastal Chilkat Indians trading eulachon oil for furs from the Interior. In the late 1880s, Jack Dalton developed a packhorse trail to the Klondike goldfields along the old trading route. The present road was built in 1943 as a military access highway during WWII to provide an alternative route from the Pacific tidewater into Yukon Territory.

This historic corridor is celebrated each year during Dalton Trail Days, July 1–4. Watch for bikes on the highway during the annual Kluane/Chilkat International Bike Race (June 19, 1999). Some 950 cyclists participated in recent years.

U.S. and Canada customs stations are located about 40 miles/64 km north of Haines. U.S. customs is open from 7 A.M. to 11 P.M. (Alaska time); Canada customs is open from 8 A.M. to midnight (Pacific time). There are no facilities or accommodations at the border. All travelers must stop.

A valid Alaska fishing license is required for fishing along the highway between Haines and the international border at **Milepost H 40.7.** The highway then crosses the northern tip of British Columbia into Yukon Territory. You must have valid fishing licenses for both British Columbia and Yukon Territory if you fish these areas, and a national park fishing license if you fish waters in Kluane National Park.

If you plan to drive the Haines Highway in winter, check road conditions before starting out. In Haines Junction, the maintenance garage (867/634-2227) or weigh scale station (867/634-2228) can help if they are in. (Flashing lights at the Haines Junction weigh scales indicate hazardous winter road conditions; travel not recommended.) Or phone (867) 667-8215 for the daily recorded road condition report.

Emergency medical services: Between Haines and the U.S.–Canada border at **Milepost H 40.7,** phone 911. Between the U.S.–Canada border and Haines Junction, phone the RCMP at (867) 634-5555.

Haines Highway Log

Driving distance is measured in miles from Haines, AK. Mileposts are up along the Alaska portion of the highway. The kilometre figures on the Canadian portion of the highway reflect the physical kilometreposts and are not an accurate metric conversion of the mileage figure.

Distance from Haines (H) is followed by distance from Haines Junction (HJ).

ALASKA ROUTE 7

H 0 HJ 151.6 (244 km) HAINES. See HAINES section for accommodations and facilities.

H 0.2 (0.3 km) HJ 151.4 (243.7 km) Front Street.

H 0.4 (0.6 km) HJ 151.2 (243.4 km) Second Street. Turn right northbound (left southbound) for visitor information center and downtown Haines.

H 0.5 (0.8 km) HJ 151.1 (243.2 km) Third Street. Turn right northbound (left southbound) for downtown Haines.

H 1 (1.6 km) HJ 150.6 (242.4 km) Haines Hitch-Up RV Park.   ▲

H 1.2 (1.9 km) HJ 150.4 (242.1 km) Main Street Y. If southbound, turn right to Fort William H. Seward, left to downtown Haines.

H 1.3 (2.1 km) HJ 150.3 (241.9 km) Eagle's Nest Motel.

H 3 (4.8 km) HJ 148.6 (239.1 km) Sign indicates Customs 38 miles/61 km.

H 3.5 (5.6 km) HJ 148.1 (238.3 km) Private Aircraft: Haines airport; elev. 16 feet/5m; length 4,000 feet/1,219m; asphalt; fuel 100; unattended.

H 4 (6.4 km) HJ 147.6 (237.5 km) Takhinsha Mountains to the southwest form a backdrop to the Chilkat River. Haines Highway (2-lanes, 50 mph) winds through the Chilkat River Valley. The Chilkat River flows into Chilkat Inlet of Lynn Canal, a massive fjord about 60 miles/96.5 km long. Lynn Canal was named by English explorer Captain Vancouver for his birthplace (King's Lynn) in England.

H 4.3 (6.9 km) HJ 147.3 (237 km) Turnout along river.

H 6 (9.6 km) HJ 145.6 (234.3 km) Picnic spot next to Chilkat River.

H 6.6 (10.6 km) HJ 145 (233.3 km) Mount Ripinski trailhead (not signed).

H 9.2 (14.8 km) HJ 142.4 (229.2 km) Entering Alaska Chilkat Bald Eagle Preserve northbound. *NOTE: Please use pullouts.* Established in 1982, the 48,000-acre preserve is the seasonal home to more than 3,000

HAINES HIGHWAY
Haines, AK, to Haines Junction, YT

© 1999 The MILEPOST®

To Beaver Creek
(see ALASKA HIGHWAY section, page 83)

Pine Lake

1

Dezadeash River

1

To Whitehorse
(see ALASKA HIGHWAY section, page 83)

Key to mileage boxes
miles/kilometres
miles/kilometres from:
H-Haines
HJ-Haines Junction
W-Whitehorse
B-Beaver Creek

Map Location

Haines Junction
N60°45'
W137°30'

HJ-0
H-152/246km
W-100/161km
B-183/295km

Kathleen R.

Jo Jo Lake

Sixmile Lake

Principal Route
Paved   Unpaved
Other Roads
Paved   Unpaved
Ferry Routes   **Hiking Trails**
Refer to Log for Visitor Facilities
Scale
0   10 Miles
0   10 Kilometres

Key to Advertiser Services
C -Camping
D -Dump Station
d -Diesel
G -Gas (reg., unld.)
I -Ice
L -Lodging
M -Meals
P -Propane
R -Car Repair (major)
r -Car Repair (minor)
S -Store (grocery)
T -Telephone (pay)

ST. ELIAS MOUNTAINS

Kluane National Park Reserve

3

Kathleen Lake

Dezadeash Lake

River

Kusawa Lake

Klukshu Lake

Klukshu

Klukshu R.

Takhanne R.

Dalton Post

Tatshenshini

Lake Bennett

N
W   E
S

HJ-64/103km
H-88/145km

3

YUKON TERRITORY
BRITISH COLUMBIA

National Park Boundary
Provincial Park Boundary

Blanchard R.
Stanley Cr.

Mount Mansfield
6,232 ft./1,900m

Alsek

River

Glaciated Area

Tatshenshini-Alsek Wilderness Provincial Park

4

Kelasil Lake

Nadahini Creek

Nadahini Mountain
6,809 ft./2,075m

Chilkat Pass
3,493 ft./1,065m

BRITISH COLUMBIA
ALASKA

Glaciated Area

Samuel Glacier

Stonehouse

Kelsol River

Chilkat River

To Carcross
(see KLONDIKE HIGHWAY 2 section)

2

Skagway

Three Guardsmen Pass
3,215 ft./980m

Copper Butte ▲

Three Guardsmen Mountain
6,300 ft./1,920m

Sellat Creek

Tatshenshini River

Pleasant Camp
Canada Customs

Mount McDonell
8,509 ft./2,594m

Jarvis Glacier

Dalton Cache
U.S. Customs

Mosquito Lake

Klehini River

Klukwan

HJ-152/244km
H-0

Provincial Park Boundary
National Park Boundary

Saksaia Glacier

H-27.3/43.9km
Swan's Rest RV Park C

Chilkat Lake

Chilkat River

7

Haines
N59°14'
W135°26'

BOUNDARY RANGE

Glaciated Area

TAKHINSHA MOUNTAINS

CANADA
UNITED STATES

Mount Krause ▲

Mount Emmerich ▲

Alaska State Ferry

Chilkoot Inlet

Lynn Canal

Glaciated Area

Glacier Bay National Park and Preserve

bald eagles, which gather each year to feed on the late run of chum salmon. Eagle-viewing area begins at **Milepost H 19**; best viewing is mid-October to January.

Of the 40,000 bald eagles in Alaska, most are found in Southeast. Eagles build nests in trees along the shoreline. Nests are added to each year and can be up to 7 feet across. (Nests the size of pickup trucks have fallen out of trees.) Nesting eagles have a second backup nest. Eagles lay their eggs in April; the eaglets fledge in August.

H 9.6 (15.4 km) **HJ 142** (228.5 km) Magnificent view of Takhinsha Mountains across Chilkat River. This range extends north from the Chilkat Range; Glacier Bay is on the other side. Prominent peaks are Mount Krause and Mount Emmerich (elev. 6,405 feet/1,952m) in the Chilkat Range.

H 10 (16 km) **HJ 141.6** (227.8 km) Watch for subsistence fish camps along the highway in June. Also watch for fish wheels on the river.

H 14.7 (23.6 km) **HJ 136.9** (220.3 km) Watch for mountain goats on the ridges.

H 15 (24.1 km) **HJ 136.6** (219.8 km) Milepost 17 (yellow sign) is one of several along the highway that indicate mileages on the U.S. Army oil pipeline. The pipeline formerly pumped oil from Haines over the St. Elias Mountains to the Alaska Highway at Haines Junction, YT. These signs were used for aerial checking and monitoring of the line.

H 17.6 (28.3 km) **HJ 134** (215.6 km) Decaying barn and cabins.

H 18.8 (30.3 km) **HJ 132.8** (213.7 km) Slide area.

H 19 (30.6 km) **HJ 132.6** (213.4 km) Turnout with parking, interpretive panels and restrooms; Chilkat Bald Eagle Preserve. Begin eagle viewing area (northbound) on Chilkat River flats. Best viewing is mid-October to January. Paved and gravel biking and walking trail along river. *CAUTION: Eagle watchers, use turnouts and park well off highway!*

H 20.5 (33 km) **HJ 131.1** (211 km) Turnout with parking area and interpretive panel; Chilkat Bald Eagle Preserve.

H 21.4 (34.4 km) **HJ 130.2** (209.5 km) Turnoff via paved access road to Indian village of **KLUKWAN**.

H 23.8 (38.3 km) **HJ 127.8** (205.6 km) Chilkat River bridge. Highway now follows Klehini River. Watch for eagles beginning in late summer. *CAUTION: Watch for moose.*

H 26.3 (42.3 km) **HJ 125.3** (201.6 km) Porcupine Road west leads across Klehini River; turn off here for jet boat landing on Tsirku River for Birch Island Lodge on Chilkat Lake.

H 27.3 (43.9 km) **HJ 124.3** (200 km) Turnoff for **Mosquito Lake State Recreation Site**; 10 campsites, tables, water, toilets, $6/night or annual pass. Mosquito Lake general store. Access to private RV park. ▲

Swan's Rest RV Park. Quiet location near eagle preserve. 12 large RV sites situated on lakeshore with full hookups. Hot showers. Coin laundry. Tenters welcome. Bed and breakfast cabin sleeps 4. Good fishing. Rowboats for rent. Nesting swans and eagles. Wildlife. Great photo opportunities. At end of road, just 3 miles from highway. (907) 767-5662. [ADVERTISEMENT] ▲

H 28.8 (46.3 km) **HJ 122.8** (197.6 km) Muncaster Creek bridge.

H 31 (49.8 km) **HJ 120.6** (194.1 km) Leaving Alaska Chilkat Bald Eagle Preserve northbound.

H 31.6 (50.9 km) **HJ 120** (193.1 km)

Bridge over Little Boulder Creek.

H 33.2 (53.4 km) **HJ 118.4** (190.5 km) 33 Mile Roadhouse; gas and phone. RV campground. Store. *NOTE: Last available gas northbound until Kathleen Lake Lodge. Check your gas tank.*

H 33.8 (54.4 km) **HJ 117.8** (189.6 km) Bridge over Big Boulder Creek. Watch for salmon swimming upstream during spawning season. Closed to salmon fishing.

H 36.2 (58.3 km) **HJ 115.4** (185.7 km) View of Saksaia Glacier.

H 40.4 (65 km) **HJ 111.2** (179 km) **U.S. Customs, Dalton Cache station.** All travelers entering United States MUST STOP. Open year-round 7 A.M. to 11 P.M., Alaska time. Phone (907) 767-5511. Restrooms, large parking area. Jarvis Glacier moraine is visible from the old Dalton Cache (on the National Register of Historic Places), located behind the customs building.

H 40.7 (65.5 km) **HJ 110.9** (178.5 km) U.S.–Canada border. Last milepost marker is Mile 40, first kilometrepost marker is Kilometrepost 74, northbound.

TIME ZONE CHANGE: Alaska observes Alaska time, Canada observes Pacific time.

BC HIGHWAY 4

H 40.8 (71.8 km) **HJ 110.8** (178.3 km) **Pleasant Camp Canada Customs and Immigration office.** All travelers entering Canada MUST STOP. Office is open daily year-round, 8 A.M. to midnight, Pacific time. Phone (907) 767-5540. No public facilities.

H 43.4 (76 km) **HJ 108.1** (174.1 km) Granite Creek bridge.

H 44.9 (78.5 km) **HJ 106.7** (171.7 km) Fivemile Creek bridge.

H 49.7 (87 km) **HJ 101.9** (164 km) Highway crosses Seltat Creek. This is eagle country; watch for them soaring over the uplands. Three Guardsmen Mountain (elev. 6,300 feet/1,920m) to the east.

H 53.9 (92 km) **HJ 97.7** (157.2 km) Three Guardsmen Lake to the east. Glave Peak, part of Three Guardsmen Mountain, rises directly behind the lake.

H 55.1 (94.6 km) **HJ 96.5** (155.3 km) Three Guardsmen Pass to the northeast, hidden by low hummocks along the road. Stonehouse Creek meanders through a pass at the base of Seltat Peak to join the Kelsall River about 6 miles/10 km to the east. To the north is the Kusawak Range; to the south is Three Guardsmen Mountain. The tall poles along the highway indicate the edge of the road for snowplows.

H 55.8 (95.8 km) **HJ 95.8** (154.2 km) Stonehouse Creek culvert.

H 56.2 (96.3 km) **HJ 95.4** (153.5 km) Clear Creek culvert.

H 59.8 (102.1 km) **HJ 91.8** (147.7 km) Double-ended paved turnout on west side of highway at **Chilkat Pass**, highest summit on this highway (elev. 3,493 feet/1,065m). White Pass Summit on Klondike Highway 2 is 3,290 feet/1,003m. The wind blows almost constantly on the summit and causes drift-

ing snow and road closures in winter. The summit area is a favorite with snow machine and cross-country ski enthusiasts in winter. Snow until late May.

The Chilkat Pass was one of the few mountain passes offering access into the Yukon from the coast. The Chilkat and the Chilkoot passes were tenaciously guarded by Tlingit Indians. These southern Yukon Indians did not want their lucrative fur-trading business with the coastal Indians and Russians jeopardized by white strangers. But the gold rush of 1898, which brought thousands of white people inland, finally opened Chilkat Pass, forever altering the lifestyle of the Interior Natives.

From the Chilkat Pass over Glacier Flats to Stanley Creek, the highway crosses silt-laden streams flowing from the Crestline Glacier. Nadahini Mountain (elev. 6,809 feet/2,075m) to the northwest. Three Guardsmen Mountain to the southeast.

H 63 (107 km) **HJ 88.6** (142.6 km) Chuck Creek culvert.

H 64.4 (109.3 km) **HJ 87.2** (140.3 km) Nadahini River culvert.

H 67.8 (114.7 km) **HJ 83.8** (134.8 km) **Private Aircraft:** Mule Creek airstrip; elev. 2,900 feet/884m; length 4,000 feet/1,219m; gravel. No services.

H 68.9 (116.4 km) **HJ 82.7** (133 km) Mule Creek. **Historic Milepost 75.**

H 73.6 (124.2 km) **HJ 78** (125.5 km) Goat Creek bridge. Watch for horses on road.

H 75.7 (127.3 km) **HJ 75.9** (122.1 km) Holum Creek.

H 77.6 (130.5 km) **HJ 74** (119 km) Twin Lakes.

H 79.8 (134 km) **HJ 71.8** (115.5 km) Turnout to west. Good viewpoint for Tatshenshini–Alsek Wilderness Provincial Park. This park encompasses the rugged northwest corner of British Columbia and is dominated by the St. Elias Mountains. It is also habitat for grizzly bears, Dall sheep, the rare "glacier" bear and also rare birds such as the king eider and Steller's eider. The Tatshenshini and Alsek rivers are famous for their river rafting and sightseeing opportunities.

H 80 (134.3 km) **HJ 71.6** (115.2 km) Mansfield Creek.

H 86.5 (144.3 km) **HJ 65.1** (104.8 km) Blanchard River bridge. The Blanchard River crosses the Yukon–BC boundary and joins the Tatshenshini River near Dalton Post. It was originally called the Kleheela River by local Native tribes. It was re-named in 1915 after G. Blanchard Dodge, DLS, who was in charge of survey parties which delineated much of the Yukon–BC boundary.

H 87.1 (144.5 km) **HJ 64.5** (103.8 km) Welcome to Kluane Country and Welcome to Yukon signs.

H 87.4 (145 km) **HJ 64.2** (103.3 km) Entering Kluane Game Sanctuary northbound.

H 87.5 (145.2 km) **HJ 64.1** (103.1 km) **BC–YT border.** Former U.S. Army Alaska–Blanchard River Petroleum pump station, now a highway maintenance camp.

YUKON HIGHWAY 3

H 96.2 (159.5 km) **HJ 55.4** (89.1 km) Turnoff for Yukon government **Million Dollar Falls** Campground on south side of Takhanne River bridge. Follow access road 0.7 mile/1.1 km west. Boardwalk trail and viewing platform of scenic falls. View of the St. Elias Mountains. Two kitchen shelters, tenting and group firepit, 27 campsites, 8 tent-only sites, $8 fee, playground and drinking water (boil water). Hiking trails in area. ▲

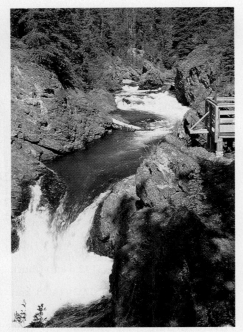

Million Dollar Falls viewing platform at Milepost H 96.2. (© Bruce M. Herman)

Good fishing below **Takhanne Falls** for grayling, Dolly Varden, rainbow and salmon. **Takhanne River**, excellent king salmon fishing in early July. ⚓

CAUTION: The Takhanne, Blanchard, Tatshenshini and Klukshu rivers are grizzly feeding areas. Exercise extreme caution when fishing or exploring in these areas.

H 96.4 (159.7 km) **HJ 55.2** (88.8 km) Parking area at Million Dollar Falls trailhead to west.

H 98.3 (162 km) **HJ 53.3** (85.8 km) Large paved photo viewpoint with view of Kluane Range; viewing platform, litter barrels, outhouse.

H 99.5 (164.5 km) **HJ 52.1** (83.8 km) Turnoff to historic Dalton Post, a way point on the Dalton Trail. Steep, narrow, winding access road; four-wheel drive recommended in wet weather. Road not recommended for large RVs or trailers at any time. Several old abandoned log cabins and buildings are located here. Indians once formed a human barricade at Dalton Post to harvest the Klukshu River's run of coho salmon. The river system here hosts seasonal runs of chinook, sockeye and coho salmon. Chinook are most visible in July, coho in late September and October, and sockeye from August to October. In fall, grizzly bears come here to feast on the fish. *Be alert to their presence.*

Fishing for chinook, coho, sockeye salmon in **Village Creek**. Grayling, Dolly Varden and salmon in **Klukshu River**. Fishing restrictions posted. *CAUTION: Watch for bears.* ⚓

H 103.4 (169.7 km) **HJ 48.2** (77.5 km) Viewpoint with information sign to west. Alsek Range and Tatshenshini River to southwest.

H 104 (171 km) **HJ 47.6** (76.6 km) Motheral Creek.

H 105.2 (173 km) **HJ 46.4** (74.6 km) Large gravel turnout; photo stop.

H 106.1 (174 km) **HJ 45.5** (73.2 km) Vand Creek.

H 110.8 (181.6 km) **HJ 40.8** (65.6 km) Klukshu Creek.

H 111.6 (183 km) **HJ 40** (64.4 km) **Historic Milepost 118** at turnoff for KLUKSHU, an Indian village, located 0.5 mile/0.8 km off the highway via a gravel road. This summer fish camp and village on the banks of the Klukshu River is a handful of log cabins, meat caches and traditional l fish traps. Steelhead, king, sockeye and coho salmon are taken here. Each autumn, families return for the annual catch. The site is on the old Dalton Trail and offers good photo possibilities. Museum, picnic spot, souvenirs for sale. Information panels on First Nations heritage and traditional fishing techniques.

Kluane National Park Reserve borders the highway to the west from here to Haines Junction (the visitor centre there has information on the park). Watch for signs for hiking trails, which are posted 3.1 miles/5 km before trailheads. For more information on the park, contact Kluane National Park Reserve, Parks Canada, Box 5495, Haines Junction, YT Y0B 1L0, phone (867) 634-7209, fax (867) 634-7208. Also visit the park information centre in Haines Junction. Open daily, May to September, the centre has excellent interpretive displays.

H 112.8 (185 km) **HJ 38.8** (62.4 km) Gribbles Gulch.

H 114 (187 km) **HJ 37.6** (60.5 km) Parking area at St. Elias Lake trailhead (4.5-mile/7.2-km round-trip). Novice and intermediate hiking trail winds through subalpine meadow. Watch for mountain goats.

H 117.8 (193 km) **HJ 33.8** (54.4 km) Dezadeash Lodge (closed in 1998, current status unknown). Historically, this spot was known as Beloud Post and is still noted as such on some maps. Mush Lake trail (13.4 miles/21.6 km long) begins behind lodge. It is an old mining road.

NOTE: Watch for horses on highway.

H 119.3 (195 km) **HJ 32.3** (52 km) Turnout along Dezadeash Lake, one of the earliest known features in the Yukon, which parallels the highway for 9 miles/14.5 km northbound, and Dezadeash mountain range. Dezadeash (pronounced DEZ-dee-ash) is said to be the Indian word describing their fishing method. In the spring, the Indians built small fires around the bases of large birch trees, peeled the heat-loosened bark and placed it, shiny white side up, on the bottom of the lake near shore, weighted with stones. From log wharfs built over the white bark, Indians waited with spears for lake trout to cross the light area. Another interpretation of Dezadeash relates that Chilkat Indians referred to it as *Dasar-ee-ASH*, meaning "Lake of the Big Winds." Entire tribes were annihilated during mid-19th century Indian wars here.

Dezadeash Lake offers good trolling, also fly-fishing along the shore where feeder streams flow into the lake. There are northern pike, lake trout and grayling in Dezadeash Lake. *CAUTION: This is a mountain lake and storms come up quickly.* ⚓

H 119.7 (195.7 km) **HJ 31.9** (51.3 km) Entrance to Yukon government Dezadeash Lake Campground, a very scenic spot on the lake; 20 campsites, $8 fee, kitchen shelter, picnic area, boat launch, no drinking water, pit toilets. ▲

H 123.9 (202.3 km) **HJ 27.7** (44.6 km) Rock Glacier trailhead to west; short 0.5-mile/0.8-km self-guiding trail, partially boardwalk. Interesting walk, some steep sections. Parking area and viewpoint.

H 126.2 (206.9 km) **HJ 25.4** (40.8 km) Dalton Trail Lodge to east.

H 134.7 (216.8 km) **HJ 16.9** (27.2 km) Access to bed and breakfast.

H 134.8 (219.5 km) **HJ 16.8** (27 km) Access road leads west less than a mile to **Kathleen Lake**, a glacier-fed turquoise-blue lake, nearly 400 feet/122m deep. Access to Kathleen Lake Campground, the only established campground within Kluane National Park; 42 campsites and a kitchen area; day-use area with picnic tables, restrooms; boat launch at lake; campfire programs by park staff. Fees charged for camping ($10). Campfire talks and backcountry registration. The 53-mile/85-km Cottonwood loop trail begins here. ▲

NOTE: National parks fishing license required. **Kathleen Lake** lake trout average 10 lbs., use lures, June and July; kokanee average 2 lbs., June best; grayling to 18 inches, use flies, June to September. **Kathleen River** rainbow to 17 inches, June to September; grayling to 18 inches, July and August; lake trout average 2 lbs., best in September. ⚓

H 135.2 (220.3 km) **HJ 16.4** (26.4 km) Kathleen Lake Lodge; food, gas and lodging.

NOTE: Last available gas southbound for next 102 miles. Check your gas tank.

H 135.8 (221 km) **HJ 15.8** (25.4 km) **Kathleen River** bridge; a popular spot for rainbow, lake trout and grayling fishing. Some kokanee. A turnout on the east side of the road provides access to Kathleen River. From here, you can canoe to Lower Kathleen Lake and Rainbow Lake. This is an easy half-day paddle, but do not attempt to go farther on Kathleen River, as there are many falls. Waterfowl in this area include harlequins, northern pintails and American wigeon. Lesser yellowlegs, spotted sandpiper, western wood-pewee and common yellowthroat are also present. ⚓

H 139.2 (226.5 km) **HJ 12.4** (20 km) Turnout to west. Good view of Kathleen Lake. Information plaque on Kluane and Wrangell–St. Elias national parks. (World Heritage Site).

H 143.4 (233.5 km) **HJ 8.2** (13.2 km) Quill Creek. Quill Creek trailhead (unsigned); 7-mile/11-km trail.

H 147.1 (239.1 km) **HJ 4.5** (7.2 km) Parking area to west at Auriol trailhead (9.3-mile/15-km loop trail); skiing and hiking.

H 148.8 (242 km) **HJ 2.8** (4.5 km) Rest stop to east with litter barrels and pit toilets. View of community of Haines Junction and Shakwak Valley.

H 151 (245 km) **HJ 0.6** (1 km) Dezadeash River Bridge; Dezadeash River Trail. This river is part of the headwaters system of the Alsek River, which flows into the Pacific near Yakutat, AK.

H 151.6 (246 km) **HJ 0 HAINES JUNCTION** (see description on page 159); turn left for Alaska, keep straight ahead for Whitehorse.

Junction of the Haines Highway (Yukon Highway 3) and Alaska Highway (Yukon Highway 1) at Haines Junction. Turn to **Milepost DC 985** on page 158 in the ALASKA HIGHWAY section for highway log. Whitehorse-bound travelers read log back to front, Alaska-bound travelers read log front to back.

Approximate driving distances from Haines Junction are: Whitehorse 100 miles/161 km; Tok 297 miles/475 km; Fairbanks 503 miles/805 km; and Anchorage 625 miles/1000 km.

KLONDIKE HIGHWAY 2

Connects: Skagway, AK, to Alaska Hwy., YT   **Length:** 99 miles
Road Surface: Paved   **Season:** Open all year
Highest Summit: White Pass 3,290 feet
Major Attraction: Klondike Gold Rush National Historical Park

(See map, page 738)

	Alaska Hwy. Jct.	Atlin	Carcross	Skagway	Whitehorse
Alaska Hwy. Jct.		125	33	99	10
Atlin	125		92	158	81
Carcross	33	92		66	43
Skagway	99	158	66		109
Whitehorse	10	81	43	109	

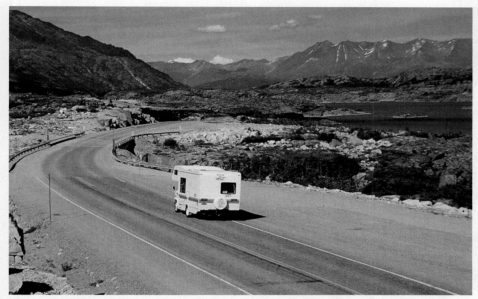

Turnout with historic information sign about Bove Island at Milepost S 59.5.
(© Harry M. Walker Photo)

The 98.8-mile-/159-km-long Klondike Highway 2 (also known as the Skagway–Carcross Road and South Klondike Highway) connects Skagway, AK, with the Alaska Highway at **Milepost 874.4** south of Whitehorse. The highway between Skagway and Carcross (referred to locally as the Skagway Road) was built in 1978 and formally dedicated on May 23, 1981. The highway connecting Carcross with the Alaska Highway (referred to locally as the Carcross Road) was built by the U.S. Army in late 1942 to lay the gas pipeline from Skagway to Whitehorse.

Klondike Highway 2 is a 2-lane, asphalt-surfaced road, open year-round. The road has been improved in recent years and is fairly wide. There is a steep 11.5-mile/18.5-km grade between Skagway and White Pass.

IMPORTANT: If you plan to cross the border between midnight and 8 A.M., inquire locally regarding customs stations' hours of operation or phone (907) 983-3144.

Klondike Highway 2 is one of the two highways connecting ferry travelers with the Alaska Highway; the other is the Haines Highway out of Haines. Klondike Highway 2 offers some spectacular scenery and adds only about 55 miles/89 km to the trip for Alaska-bound motorists, as compared to the Haines Highway. (The distance from Haines to Tok, AK, is approximately 445 miles/716 km; the distance from Skagway to Tok is 500 miles/805 km.) Klondike Highway 2, like the Haines Highway, crosses from Alaska into British Columbia, then into Yukon Territory.

Klondike Highway 2 continues north of Whitehorse, turning off the Alaska Highway to Dawson City. See KLONDIKE LOOP section for log of Klondike Highway 2 between the Alaska Highway and Dawson City.

Emergency medical services: Between Skagway and the BC–YT border, phone the Skagway Fire Department at (907) 983-2300. Between the border and the Alaska Highway, phone the Whitehorse ambulance at (867) 667-3333, RCMP at (867) 667-5555. Police monitor CB Channel 9.

Klondike Highway 2 Log

Mileposts in Alaska and kilometreposts in Canada reflect distance from Skagway. The kilometre distance from Skagway in *The MILEPOST®* log reflects the location of the physical kilometreposts, and is not necessarily an accurate conversion of the mileage figure.

Distance from Skagway (S) is followed by distance from Alaska Highway (AH).

S 0 AH 98.8 (159 km) Ferry terminal in **SKAGWAY**, northern terminus of the Alaska Marine Highway. Skagway owes its birth to the Klondike Gold Rush; see the description of Skagway in the INSIDE PASSAGE section.

S 1.6 (2.6 km) **AH 97.2** (156.4 km) Skagway River bridge.

S 2.3 (3.7 km) **AH 96.5** (155.3 km) Junction with Dyea Road.

S 2.6 (4.2 km) **AH 96.2** (154.8 km) Highway maintenance camp.

S 2.8 (4.5 km) **AH 96** (154.5 km) Plaque to east honoring men and women of the Klondike Gold Rush, and access to parklike area along Skagway River.

S 2.9 (4.7 km) **AH 95.9** (154.3 km) Access road east to Skagway River. Highway begins steep 11.5-mile/18.5-km ascent northbound from sea level to 3,290 feet/1,003m at White Pass.

S 4.7 (7.6 km) **AH 94.1** (151.4 km) Turnout to west.

S 5 (8 km) **AH 93.8** (151 km) Turnout to east with view across canyon of White Pass & Yukon Route railway tracks and bridge. The narrow-gauge WP&YR railway was completed in 1900.

S 5.5 (8.8 km) **AH 93.3** (150.1 km) Turnout to west with historical information signs.

S 6 (9.6 km) **AH 92.8** (149.3 km) Turnout to east.

S 6.8 (10.9 km) **AH 92** (148 km) **U.S. Customs** station; open 24 hours in summer (manned 8 A.M. to midnight, video camera reporting midnight to 8 A.M.). Phone (907) 983-3144 for border crossing (immigration); phone (907) 983-2325 for customs in Skagway. All travelers entering the United States must stop. Have identification ready. Residents of North America must present birth certificate, driver's license or voter registration. All other foreign visitors must have a passport. ID is also required for children.

S 7.4 (11.9 km) **AH 91.4** (147.1 km) View to east of WP&YR railway line.

S 7.7 (12.4 km) **AH 91.1** (146.6 km) Good photo stop for **Pitchfork Falls**, visible across the canyon. Pitchfork Falls flows from Goat Lake.

S 8.1 (13 km) **AH 90.7** (146 km) Turnout to east.

S 9.1 (14.6 km) **AH 89.7** (144.4 km) Paved turnout to east with historical interest signs about the Klondike Gold Rush trail. Viewpoint looks across the gorge to the WP&YR railway tracks.

S 9.9 (15.9 km) **AH 88.9** (143.1 km) Truck runout ramp to west for large transport units that may lose air brakes on steep descent southbound.

S 11.1 (17.9 km) **AH 87.7** (141.1 km) **Captain William Moore Bridge.** This unique cantilever bridge over Moore Creek spans a 110-foot-/34-m-wide gorge. Just

KLONDIKE HIGHWAY 2

Skagway, AK, to Junction with Alaska Highway (includes Tagish and Atlin Roads)

© 1999 The MILEPOST®

To Carmacks
(see KLONDIKE LOOP section, page 259)

To Haines Junction
(see ALASKA HIGHWAY section, page 83)

N60°43' W135°03'
Whitehorse
S-99/159km
AH-0
W-12/19km

White Pass & Yukon Route

Kookatsoon Lake

Cowley
Cowley Lake

Klondike Highway 2

Robinson

Two Horse Cr.
Bear Cr.
Lewes L.

Marsh Lake

The Alaska Highway

Needle Mountain ▲
Mount Gillam ▲
Annie L.

J-13.7/22km Tagish Stores, Cafe, Motel, RV CLS
J-24.7/39.7km Eagles Landing Bed & Breakfast LM
Caribou Mountain 5,645 ft./1,721m

Lewes Cr.
N60°18' W134°16'
Tagish
Tagish River

Jake's Corner

To Johnson's Crossing
(see ALASKA HIGHWAY section, page 83)

C-34/54km
J-0
W-49/79km

AH-33/53km
J-34/54km
C-0
S-66/106km

S-72.1/115km Spirit Lake Wilderness Resort CDdGILMT
S-71.9/115.7km Cinnamon Cache Bakery and Coffee Shop M
S-67.9/108.6km Frontierland M

Watson R.
Watson River
Spirit L.

Crag Lake
Chooutla Lake
Nares Lake
Bove Island

Tagish Lake

Little Atlin Lake

Atlin Road

Snafu Lake

N60°11' W134°43'
Carcross

S-66.2/106.5km Montana Services & RV Park CDdGIMPST
Top of the World Gold

Montana Mountain 7,280 ft./2,219m

J-8/13km Tagish Lake Resort

Lime Mountain 5,225 ft./1,593m

Lubbock River
Snafu Creek
Tarfu Lake
Tarfu River

Wheaton R.

Lake Bennett

YUKON TERRITORY
BRITISH COLUMBIA

Mount Racine ▲
Mount Conrad ▲

AH-49/78km
S-50/81km

Windy Arm

Mount Minto ▲ 6,913 ft./2,107m

Hitchcock Creek

Tutshi Lake

Jack Peak ▲ 7,050 ft./2,149m

J-33/53km

Taku Arm

Tagish Lake

Indian Lake
Indian Creek

Gladys Lake

White Pass & Yukon Route

Bennett

Chilkoot Trail

Log Cabin

Tutshi R.

Klondike Highway 2

Taku Arm

Atlin Lake

McDonald Lake
Fourth of July Cr.

Surprise Lake

CANADA
UNITED STATES

Fraser

Bernard Lake
N59°43' W135°03'
Summit Lake

Chilkoot Pass 3,739 ft./1,140m

Glaciated Area

AH-85/136km
S-14/23km

White Pass 3,290 ft./1,003m

White Pass Fork

White Pass & Yukon Route

Goat Lake
Skagway River

Dyea Road

Scotia
N59°35' W133°43'
Atlin

Discovery
Pine Creek
Discovery Road

Spruce Creek

J-58/93km

AH-99/159km
S-0

N59°27' W135°18'
Skagway

BRITISH COLUMBIA
ALASKA

To Haines Junction
(see HAINES HIGHWAY section)

Lutak Inlet

Taiya Inlet

COAST MOUNTAINS

Birch Mountain ▲ 6,755 ft./2,060m

McKee Creek
Palmer L.

Warm Bay Road

Teresa Island

Wilson Creek
O'Donnel River

Haines

Chilkat Inlet
Chilkoot Inlet

Lynn Canal

BOUNDARY RANGES

Atlin Provincial Park

Provincial Park Boundary

Alaska State Ferry

Llewellyn Glacier

Key to mileage boxes
miles/kilometres
miles/kilometres from:
S-Skagway
AH-Alaska Highway
J-Junction
C-Carcross
W-Whitehorse

Map Location

Principal Route
Paved   Unpaved
Other Roads
Paved   Unpaved
Ferry Routes   **Hiking Trails**
▨ Refer to Log for Visitor Facilities

Scale
0   10 Miles
0   10 Kilometres

Key to Advertiser Services
C -Camping
D -Dump Station
d -Diesel
G -Gas (reg., unld.)
I -Ice
L -Lodging
M -Meals
P -Propane
R -Car Repair (major)
r -Car Repair (minor)
S -Store (grocery)
T -Telephone (pay)

north of the bridge to the west is a large waterfall. The bridge is named for Capt. Billy Moore, a riverboat captain and pilot, prospector, packer and trader, who played an important role in settling the town of Skagway. Moore helped pioneer this route over White Pass into the Yukon and was among the first to realize the potential of a railroad across the pass.

S 11.6 (18.7 km) **AH 87.2** (140.3 km) Large paved turnouts to east with view of Skagway River gorge, Captain William Moore Bridge and waterfalls, next 0.1 mile/0.2 km northbound.

S 12 (19.3 km) **AH 86.8** (139.7 km) Truck runout ramp to west.

S 12.6 (20.3 km) **AH 86.2** (138.7 km) Posts on east side of road mark highway shoulders and guide rails for snowplows.

S 14.4 (23.2 km) **AH 84.4** (135.8 km) **White Pass Summit** (elev. 3,292 feet/ 1,003m). Turnout to west.

CAUTION: Southbound traffic begins steep 11.5-mile/18.5-km descent to Skagway.

Many stampeders on their way to the Klondike goldfields in 1898 chose the White Pass route because it was lower in elevation than the famous Chilkoot Pass trail, and the grade was not as steep. But the White Pass route was longer and the final ascent to the summit treacherous. Dead Horse Gulch (visible from the railway line) was named for the thousands of pack animals that died on this route during the gold rush.

The North West Mounted Police were stationed at the summit to meet every stampeder entering Canada and ensure that each carried at least a year's provisions (weighing about a ton).

S 14.5 (23.3 km) **AH 84.3** (135.7 km) Paved turnout to west.

S 14.9 (24 km) **AH 84** (135.2 km) **U.S.–Canada (AK–BC) border.** Turnout to west. Monument to east. *TIME ZONE CHANGE: Alaska observes Alaska time; British Columbia and Yukon Territory observe Pacific time.*

S 16.2 (26.1 km) **AH 82.6** (133 km) Highway winds through rocky valley of Summit Lake (visible to east). Several small gravel turnouts next 6 miles/9.6 km northbound.

S 18.1 (29.1 km) **AH 80.7** (129.9 km) Summit Creek bridge.

S 18.4 (29.6 km) **AH 80.4** (129.4 km) Summit Lake to east.

S 19.3 (31.1 km) **AH 79.5** (128 km) North end of Summit Lake.

S 21.4 (34.4 km) **AH 77.4** (124.5 km) Creek and railroad bridge to east. Railroad parallels highway next 6 miles.

S 22.5 (36.2 km) **AH 76.3** (122.8 km) **Canada Customs** at **FRASER** (elev. 2,400 feet/732m), open 24 hours Apr. 1-Nov. 1; 8 A.M.-midnight Nov. 1-Apr. 1; phone (867) 821-4111. Pay phone. All travelers entering Canada must stop. *Reminder: Have proper ID for all travellers, including children.*

Old railroad water tower to east, highway maintenance camp to west.

S 22.6 (36.4 km) **AH 76.2** (122.7 km) Beautiful deep-green Bernard Lake to east.

S 22.8 (36.7 km) **AH 76** (122.3 km) Large double-ended turnout with 2 interpretive panels on area attractions and the WP&YR.

S 24.2 (38.9 km) **AH 74.6** (120.1 km) Turnout to east.

S 25.1 (40.4 km) **AH 73.7** (118.6 km) Shallow Lake to east.

S 25.5 (41 km) **AH 73.3** (118 km) Old cabins and buildings to east.

S 26.6 (42.8 km) **AH 72.2** (116.2 km)

There are great views of beautiful Tutshi Lake along the highway. (© Susan Cole Kelly)

Turnout to east. Beautiful view of Tormented Valley, a rocky desolate "moonscape" of stunted trees and small lakes east of the highway.

S 27.3 (43.9 km) **AH 71.5** (115 km) Highway crosses tracks of the White Pass & Yukon Route at **LOG CABIN**. With completion of the railway in 1900, the North West Mounted Police moved their customs checkpoint from the summit to Log Cabin. There is nothing here today.

There are numerous turnouts along the highway between here and Carcross. Turnouts may be designated for either commercial ore trucks or passenger vehicles.

S 30.7 (49.4 km) **AH 68.1** (109.6 km) Tutshi (too-shy) River visible to east.

S 31.1 (50 km) **AH 67.7** (108.9 km) Highway parallels **Tutshi Lake** for several miles northbound. Excellent fishing for lake trout and grayling early in season. Be sure you have a British Columbia fishing license. 🐟

S 40.1 (64.5 km) **AH 58.7** (94.5 km) Short, narrow gravel access road to picnic area with pit toilet on Tutshi Lake. Large vehicles check turnaround space before driving in.

S 40.7 (65.5 km) **AH 58.1** (93.5 km) Good views of Tutshi Lake along here.

S 43.7 (70.5 km) **AH 55.1** (88.7 km) Turnout to east with view of Tutshi Lake.

S 46.4 (75.1 km) **AH 52.4** (84.3 km) To the east is the Venus Mines concentrator, with a capacity of 150 tons per day. A drop in silver prices caused the Venus mill's closure in October 1981.

S 48.5 (78.1 km) **AH 50.3** (81 km) South end of Windy Arm, an extension of Tagish Lake.

S 49.2 (79.2 km) **AH 49.6** (79.9 km) Viewpoint to east.

S 49.9 (80.5 km) **AH 48.9** (78.7 km) Dall Creek.

S 50.2 (81 km) **AH 48.6** (78.2 km) **BC–YT border.** Turnout with picnic table and litter barrel to east overlooking Windy Arm.

S 51.9 (83.5 km) **AH 46.9** (75.5 km) Large turnout to east with litter barrel, picnic table and historical information sign about Venus Mines.

The first claim on Montana Mountain was staked by W.R. Young in 1899. By 1904 all of the mountain's gold veins had been claimed. In 1905, New York financier Col. Joseph H. Conrad acquired most of the Montana Mountain claims, formed Conrad Consolidated Mines, and began exploration

and mining. A town of about 300 people sprang up along Windy Arm and an aerial tramway was built from the Conrad townsite up the side of Montana Mountain to the Mountain Hero adit. (This tramline, visible from the highway, was completed in 1906 but was never used to ship ore because the Mountain Hero tunnel did not find a vein.) More tramways and a mill were constructed, but by 1911 Conrad was forced into bankruptcy: The ore was not as rich as estimated and only a small quantity of ore was milled before operations ceased.

Small mining operations continued over the years, with unsuccessful startups by various mining interests. United Keno Hill Mines (Venus Division) acquired the mining claims in 1979, constructed a 100-ton-per-day mill and rehabilitated the old mine workings in 1980.

S 52.9 (85.1 km) **AH 45.9** (73.8 km) Pooly Creek and canyon, named for J.M. Pooly, who staked the first Venus claims in 1901.

Access road east to Pooly Point and Venus Mines maintenance garage, trailers and security station. No services, facilities or admittance.

S 54.2 (87.2 km) **AH 44.6** (71.8 km) Venus Mines ore storage bin and foundation of old mill to east. The mill was built in the late 1960s, then disassembled and sold about 1970. A sign here warns of arsenic being present: Do not pick or eat berries.

S 55.7 (89.6 km) **AH 43.1** (69.4 km) Tramline support just east of highway.

S 59.5 (95.8 km) **AH 39.3** (63.3 km) Turnout with historic information sign. Lt. F. Schwatka, US Army, renamed Tagish Lake in 1883 after Lt. Bove of the Italian navy, who had served with the Austro-Hungarian Expedition of 1872-74. Dr. G.M. Dawson, GSC, gave Tagish Lake its original name in 1887 and left Bove's name on the island. Magnificent views along here of Windy Arm and its islands (Bove is the larger island). Windy Arm is an extension of Tagish Lake. Lime Mountain (elev. 5,225 feet/1,593m) rises to the east beyond Bove Island.

S 63.5 (102.2 km) **AH 35.3** (56.8 km) Sections of the old government wagon roads that once linked Carcross, Conrad and other mining claims, visible on either side of the highway.

S 65.3 (105.1 km) **AH 33.5** (53.9 km) Private road west to homes, Carcross Tagish First Nation's Band office.

S 65.8 (104.3 km) AH 33 (53.6 km) Small Native-operated convenience store.

S 65.9 (106 km) AH 32.9 (52.9 km) Access road west to Montana Mountain.

S 66 (106.2 km) AH 32.8 (52.7 km) Nares Bridge crosses the narrows between Lake Bennett to the west and Tagish Lake to the east. Nares Lake remains open most winters, despite air temperatures that drop well below -40°F/-40°C. The larger lakes freeze to an ice depth of more than 3 feet/1m.

Caribou Mountain (elev. 5,645 feet/ 1,721m) is visible to the east.

S 66.2 (106.5 km) AH 32.6 (52.4 km) Turnoff west for Carcross (description follows).

Carcross

On the shore of Lake Bennett, 44 miles/71 km southeast of Whitehorse. **Population:** 431. **Emergency Services: Police,** phone (867) 821-5555. **Fire Department,** phone (867) 821-2222. **Ambulance,** phone (867) 821-3333. **Health Centre,** phone (867) 821-4444.

Visitor Information: Carcross Visitor Reception Centre, operated by Tourism Yukon, is located in the old White Pass & Yukon Route train station. Lifeboat display. The centre operates daily from 8 A.M. to 8 P.M., mid-May to mid-September; phone (867) 821-4431. Ferry schedules, maps and information on Yukon, British Columbia and Alaska available.

Elevation: 2,175 feet/663m. **Climate:** Average temperature in January, -4.2°F/ -20.1°C; in July, 55.4°F/13°C. Annual rainfall 11 inches, snowfall 2 to 3 feet. Driest month is April, wettest month August. **Radio:** 590-AM, CHON-FM 90.5, CKRW. **Television:** CBC. **Transportation: Bus**—Scheduled bus service by Atlin Express Service, between Atlin and Whitehorse via Tagish and Carcross, 3 times weekly. Chilkoot Trail hikers should check with visitor centre for boat and bus connections.

Private Aircraft: Carcross airstrip, 0.3 mile/0.5 km north of town via highway; elev. 2,161 feet/659m; length 2,000 feet/ 610m.

There are a hotel, general store, gift shops with Native handicrafts, snack bar and RV park. Gas station with gifts, groceries,

laundromat, showers, RV park and cafe located on the highway by the airstrip. ▲

Carcross was formerly known as Caribou Crossing because of the large numbers of caribou that traversed the narrows here between Bennett and Nares lakes. In 1903 Bishop Bompas, who had established a school here for Native children in 1901, petitioned the government to change the name of the community to Carcross because of confusion in mail services due to duplicate names in Alaska, British Columbia and the Klondike. The post office made the change official the following year, but it took the WP&YR until 1916 to change the name of its station.

Carcross became a stopping place for gold stampeders on their way to the Klondike goldfields. It was a major stop on the White Pass & Yukon Route railroad from 1900 until 1982, when the railroad ceased operation. Passengers and freight transferred from rail to stern-wheelers at Carcross. One of these stern-wheelers, the SS *Tutshi* (tooshy), was a historic site here in town until it burned down in July 1990.

A cairn beside the railroad station marks the site where construction crews laying track for the White Pass & Yukon Route from Skagway met the crew from Whitehorse. The golden spike was set in place when the last rail was laid at Carcross on July 29, 1900. The construction project had begun May 27, 1898, during the height of the Klondike Gold Rush.

Other visitor attractions include St. Saviour's Anglican Church, built in 1902; the Royal Mail Carriage; and the little locomotive *Duchess*, which once hauled coal on Vancouver Island. Frontierland, 2 miles/ 3.2 km north of town on the highway, is also a popular attraction. Ask at the Visitor Reception Centre for the brochure "101 Great Things to Do in the Carcross Tagish

Loop."

On sunny days you may sunbathe and picnic at Sandy Beach on Lake Bennett. Or swim at Carcross Pool; for information call (867) 821-3211. Isabelle Pringle Public Library presents programs and displays; phone (867) 821-3801.

Behind the post office there is a footbridge across Natasaheenie River. This small body of water joins Lake Bennett and Nares Lake. Check locally for boat tours and boat service on Bennett Lake. Fishing in **Lake Bennett** for lake trout, northern pike, arctic grayling, whitefish and cisco. ◄

Development was under way in 1998 of a waterfront arts and crafts project. Check with Chief Andy Carvill at the First Nation Office for information, (867) 821-4251.

Montana Services & RV Park. See display ad this section. ▲

Top Of The World Gold. Stroll down Bennett Avenue to our shop overlooking historic Lake Bennett. "It isn't Tiffany's, nor is it Birk's. We have no chandeliers, no well-dressed clerks. We do have the gold claims; we sluice and we pan. We make jewellery and souvenirs with our very own hands. So come in for a visit, have a browse, share our view. We have something for everyone, and yes, stories too." Open mid-June. VISA/Mastercard. Phone (867) 821-3702. [ADVERTISEMENT]

Eagles Landing Bed & Breakfast. In the mountains on the shores of scenic Crag Lake (Tagish Road). Open year-round. Home-cooked meals. Rustic cabins or cozy rooms in our log home. Sauna, hiking, swimming, great fishing in the area. Cross-country skiing. Rentals of boats, canoes, snowmobiles, ATV's arranged. Reasonable rates. Your hosts: the Barr family. Phone (867) 667-1057. PO Box 110, Carcross, YT Y0B 1B0. [ADVERTISEMENT]

Klondike Highway 2 Log
(continued)

S 66.4 (106.9 km) AH 32.4 (52.1 km) Airstrip to east. Turn on access road directly north of airstrip for Carcross Yukon government campground; 14 sites, picnic tables, firewood, drinking water, outhouses, camping fee. ▲

S 66.5 (107 km) AH 32.3 (52 km)

Junction with Yukon Highway 8, which leads east to Tagish, Atlin Road and the Alaska Highway at Jake's Corner (see TAGISH ROAD section).

Turn east here for alternate access to Alaska Highway and for Yukon government campground on Tagish Road.

S 67.3 (108.3 km) AH 31.5 (50.7 km) Turnout with point of interest sign about **Carcross Desert.** This unusual desert area of sand dunes, east of the highway between Kilometreposts 108 and 110, is the world's smallest desert and an International Biophysical Programme site for ecological studies. The desert is composed of sandy lake-bottom material left behind by a large glacial lake. Strong winds off Lake Bennett make it difficult for vegetation to take hold here; only lodgepole pine, spruce and kinnikinnick survive. (Kinnikinnick is a low trailing evergreen with small leathery leaves; used for tea.)

S 67.9 (108.6 km) AH 30.9 (49.7 km) Frontierland (formerly the Museum of Yukon Natural History) features a Yukon wildlife museum, gift shop and coffee house. Displays include a saber-toothed tiger and the world's largest mounted bear—a polar bear.

Frontierland. See display ad this section.

S 70.3 (112.3 km) **AH 28.5** (45.9 km) Dry Creek.

S 71.2 (113.8 km) **AH 27.6** (44.4 km) Carl's Creek.

S 71.9 (115.7 km) **AH 26.9** (43.3 km) **Cinnamon Cache Bakery Coffee Shop.** See display ad this section.

S 72.1 (115 km) **AH 26.7** (43 km) Spirit Lake Wilderness Resort east side of road with food, gas, propane, repairs, lodging, camping and ice cream. ▲

Spirit Lake Wilderness Resort. See display ad this section. ▲

S 73.2 (116.8 km) **AH 25.6** (41.2 km) Spirit Lake is visible to the east.

S 73.5 (117.3 km) **AH 25.3** (40.7 km) Large turnout with point of interest sign to west overlooking beautiful **Emerald Lake**,

also called **Rainbow Lake** by Yukoners. (Good view of lake by climbing the hill across from the turnout.) The rainbowlike colors of the lake result from blue-green light waves reflecting off the white sediment of the lake bottom. This white sediment, called marl, consists of fragments of decomposed shell mixed with clay; it is usually found in shallow, freshwater lakes that have low oxygen levels during the summer months.

S 75.4 (120.3 km) **AH 23.4** (37.7 km) Highway follows base of Caribou Mountain (elev. 5,645 feet/1,721m). View of Montana Mountain to south, Caribou Mountain to east and Gray Ridge Range to the west between Kilometreposts 122 and 128. Flora consists of jack and lodgepole pine.

S 79.8 (127.1 km) **AH 19** (30.6 km) Highway crosses Lewes Creek.

S 85.4 (136.3 km) **AH 13.4** (21.6 km) Access road west leads 1 mile/1.6 km to Lewes Lake.

S 85.6 (136.5 km) **AH 13.2** (21.2 km) Rat Lake to west.

S 86.7 (138.2 km) **AH 12.1** (19.4 km) Bear Creek.

S 87 (140 km) **AH 11.8** (19 km) Access to bed and breakfast and Bear Creek Dog Sled Kennels.

S 87.3 (139.1 km) **AH 11.5** (18.5 km) Access road west to large gravel pull-through

White Pass & Yukon Route at Fraser. (© Susan Cole Kelly)

with historic information sign about Robinson and view of Robinson. In 1899, the White Pass & Yukon Route built a railroad siding at Robinson (named for Stikine Bill Robinson). Gold was discovered nearby in the early 1900s and a townsite was surveyed. A few buildings were constructed and a post office, manned by Charlie McConnell, operated from 1909 to 1915. Low mineral yields caused Robinson to be abandoned, but postmaster McConnell stayed and established one of the first ranches in the Yukon. Robinson is accessible from Annie Lake Road (see next milepost).

S 87.5 (139.4 km) **AH 11.3** (18.2 km) Road west to Annie Lake (turn left after crossing the railroad tracks to reach Robinson).

Annie Lake Road (can be rough) leads 0.8 mile/1.4 km to Annie Lake golf course (18 holes, wilderness setting), 1.9 miles/3.1 km to McConnell Lake and 11 miles/17.7 km to Annie Lake. Beyond Annie Lake the road crosses the Wheaton River. The Wheaton Valley–Mount Skukum area has seen a surge of mineral exploration by private prospectors and mining companies in recent years. For the adventuresome, this is beautiful and

interesting country. There are no facilities along Annie Lake Road. *CAUTION: Annie Lake Road can be very muddy during spring breakup or during rain.*

S 93 (148.5 km) **AH 5.8** (9.4 km) Turnoff west for Cowley and for access to Cowley Lake (1.6 miles/2.6 km).

S 95.5 (154.2 km) **AH 3.3** (5.3 km) Turnoff east for Kookatsoon Lake. There is a Yukon government picnic area at Kookatsoon Lake (day use only). The lake is shallow and usually warm enough for swimming in summer. Picnic tables, firepits and pit toilets. Canoe launch.

S 98.4 (156.5 km) **AH 0.4** (0.7 km) Rock shop on east side of road.

S 98.8 (157.1 km) **AH 0** Turn left (north) for Whitehorse, right (south) for Watson Lake.

Junction with the Alaska Highway. Turn to **Milepost DC 874.4** on page 136 in the ALASKA HIGHWAY section: Whitehorse-bound travelers continue with that log; travelers heading south down the Alaska Highway read that log back to front.

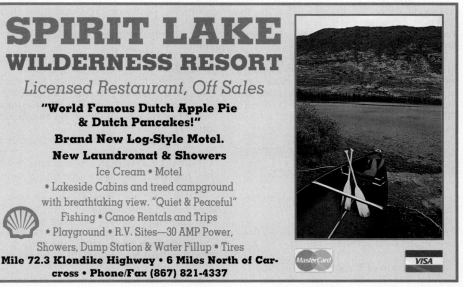

ATLIN ROAD

Connects: Tagish Road Jct. to Atlin, BC
Road Surface: 60% gravel, 40% paved
Major Attraction: Atlin Lake

Length: 58 miles
Season: Open all year

(See map, page 738)

	Atlin	Carcross	Jake's Corner	Skagway	Whitehorse
Atlin		92	59	158	106
Carcross	92		35	66	43
Jake's Corner	59	35		101	47
Skagway	158	66	101		109
Whitehorse	106	43	47	109	

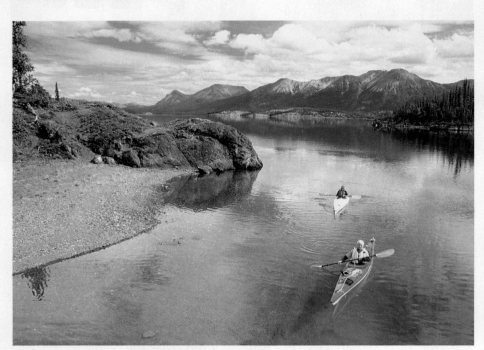

Kayakers on Atlin Lake, Atlin Provincial Park. (© David J. Job)

This 58-mile/93.3-km all-weather road leads south to the pioneer gold mining town of Atlin. Built in 1949 by the Canadian Army Engineers, Atlin Road is a good road, usually in excellent condition, with some winding sections. The first 40 miles/64.4 km are gravel, with the remaining 18 miles/29 km into Atlin paved. Watch for slippery spots in wet weather.

To reach Atlin Road, turn south at Jake's Corner, **Milepost DC 836.8** on the Alaska Highway; drive 1.1 miles/1.8 km to the junction of Atlin Road (Highway 7) and Tagish Road (Highway 8); turn left (south) for Atlin.

It is about a 2¹/₂-hour drive to Atlin from Whitehorse, and the lake scenery from the village is well worth the trip. For more information contact the Atlin Visitors Assoc., Box 365-M, Atlin, BC V0W 1A0; fax (250) 651-7721. Or phone the Atlin museum at (250) 651-7522 for visitor information.

Atlin Road Log

Distance from Tagish Road junction (J) is shown.
Physical kilometreposts in Yukon Territory and mileposts in British Columbia show distance from Tagish Road junction.

J 0 Junction of Tagish and Atlin roads.
J 1.4 (2.3 km) Fish Creek crossing. The road is bordered by many low-lying, boggy areas brilliant green with horsetail (*equisetium*).
J 1.8 (2.9 km) Side road west to Little Atlin Lake. Atlin Road descends along east shoreline of Little Atlin Lake approximately 7.6 miles/12.2 km southbound. During midsummer, the roadsides are ablaze with fireweed and wild roses.
J 2.4 (3.9 km) Large turnout to west on Little Atlin Lake; informal boat launch, dumpster, outhouse and camping area. Mount Minto (elev. 6,913 feet/2,107m) can be seen to the southwest. Road climbs southbound.
J 2.8 (4.5 km) Turnout to west. Watch for bald eagles.
J 5 (8 km) Information sign to east about 1983–84 mountain goat transplant. The 12 goats were brought from Kluane National Park. They may be observed on the mountainsides.
J 7.8 (12.6 km) Private campground, cabins and boat rentals.
J 8.1 (13 km) Greenhouse and farm, roadside vegetable stand in season. Haunka Creek. Turnout to west.
J 8.9 (14.3 km) Good view of Mount Minto ahead southbound.
J 13.8 (22.2 km) Unmarked side road leads 2.4 miles/3.9 km to **Lubbock River**, which connects Little Atlin Lake with Atlin Lake. Excellent for grayling from breakup to mid-September.
J 15.5 (24.9 km) Snafu Creek. Turnout to west, north of bridge. According to R. Coutts, author of "Yukon Places & Names," the creek name is an acronym bestowed by army crews who built the road. It stands for Situation Normal—All Fouled Up. (Mr. Coutts resides in Atlin.)
J 16.4 (26 km) Access road leads 0.7 mile/1.1 km to **Snafu Lake** Yukon government campground; 4 sites, $8 camping fee, pit toilets, tables, gravel boat ramp, good fishing.
J 18.6 (29.9 km) Tarfu Creek. Small turnout to east, north of bridge. Creek name is another army acronym. This one stands for Things Are Really Fouled Up.
J 18.7 (30 km) Abandoned cabin and turnout to west.
J 20.4 (32.8 km) Turnoff to east for **Tarfu Lake** Yukon government campground via 2.4-mile/3.8-km side road; 6 sites, $8 camping fee, pit toilets, fishing. Steep grade near campground; not recommended for large RVs or trailers.
J 20.5 (33 km) Short narrow side road leads east to Marcella Lake; good lake for canoeing.
J 21.8 (35.1 km) Turnout to west with view of Atlin Lake, which covers 307 square miles/798 square km and is the largest natural lake in British Columbia. Coast Mountains to the southwest.
J 25.8 (41.5 km) BC–YT border. Road follows east shoreline of Atlin Lake into Atlin.
J 27 (43.5 km) Mount Minto to west, Black Mountain to east, and Halcro Peak (elev. 5,856 feet/1,785m) to the southeast.
J 28.5 (45.8 km) Slow down for sharp curve.
J 32 (51.5 km) Excellent views of Coast Mountains, southwest across Atlin Lake, next 6 miles/9.7 km southbound.
J 32.7 (52.6 km) **Hitchcock Creek**, grayling to 2 lbs.
J 32.8 (52.7 km) Campground on Atlin Lake; 6 sites, pit toilets, tables, ramp for small boats.
J 36.3 (58.4 km) Turnout with litter barrel to west. Base Camp Creek.
J 36.8 (59.2 km) **Historic Milepost 38.**
J 40 (64.4 km) Indian River. Pull-through turnout south of creek. Highway is paved from here to Atlin.
J 40.2 (64.7 km) Big-game outfitter/guest ranch to east. Watch for horses.
J 45.3 (72.9 km) Turnout to west.
J 49.8 (80.1 km) Burnt Creek.
J 49.9 (80.3 km) Davie Hall Lake and

turnout to west. Waterfowl are plentiful on lake.

J 51.6 (83 km) Ruffner Mine Road leads east 40 miles/64.4 km. Access to **MacDonald Lake**, 2 miles/3.2 km east; bird watching and lake trout fishing from spit.

J 52.8 (85 km) Fourth of July Creek.

J 53.4 (85.9 km) Spruce Mountain (elev. 5,141 feet/1,567m) to west.

J 55.1 (88.7 km) Road skirts east shore of Como Lake next 0.6 mile/1 km southbound.

J 55.2 (88.8 km) Turnout with litter barrel to west on **Como Lake**; good lake for canoeing, also used by floatplanes. Stocked with rainbow.

J 55.7 (89.6 km) South end of Como Lake; boat ramp.

J 57.1 (91.9 km) Atlin city limits.

J 58 (93.3 km) Junction of Atlin Road with Discovery Road. Turn right (west) on Discovery Avenue for town of Atlin; description follows. Turn left (east) for Discovery Road and Warm Bay Road (see logs this section).

Atlin

The most northwesterly town in British Columbia, located about 112 miles/ 180 km southeast of Whitehorse, YT. **Population:** 500. **Emergency Services: Police**, phone (250) 651-7511. **Fire Department**, phone (250) 651-7666. **Ambulance**, phone (250) 651-7700. Red Cross outpost clinic, phone (250) 651-7677.

Visitor Information: Contact the Atlin Visitors Assoc., P.O. Box 365-M, Atlin, BC V0W 1A0, fax (250) 651-7721, phone (250) 651-7522, (250) 651-7522.

Elevation: 2,240 feet/683m. **Radio:** CBC on FM-band. **Television:** 3 channels (CBC, BCTV and the Knowledge Network).

Private Aircraft: Peterson Field, 1 mile/ 1.6 km northeast; elev. 2,348 feet/716m; length 3,950 feet/1,204m; gravel.

Transportation: Air—Regular service from Juneau via Summit Air, Apex Air and Tuchone Air. **Bus**—Service from Whitehorse 3 times a week.

Referred to by some visitors as Shangri-la, the village of Atlin overlooks the crystal clear water of 90-mile/145-km-long Atlin Lake and is surrounded by spectacular mountains. On Teresa Island in Atlin Lake is Birch Mountain (elev. 6,755 feet/2,060m), the highest point in fresh water in the world.

Atlin was founded in 1898. The name was taken from the Indian dialect and means Big Water. The Atlin Lake area was one of the richest gold strikes made during the great

Historic MV Tarahne *in Atlin, BC.*
(© David J. Job)

rush to the Klondike in 1897–98. The first claims were registered here on July 30, 1898, by Fritz Miller and Kenneth McLaren.

VISITOR SERVICES/ACCOMMODATIONS

The village has a hotel, inns, cottages, bed and breakfasts, laundromat (with showers), restaurants, gas station (propane, diesel and unleaded available), grocery, government liquor store and general stores, and a post office. Atlin branch of Bank of Montreal located at Government Agents Office on 3rd Street; open weekdays 10 A.M. to noon and 1–3 P.M. Dump station at Mile 2.3 Discovery Road. The museum and several shops feature local gold nugget jewelry, arts and crafts, and other souvenirs. Air charter service for glacier tours and fly-in fishing trips. Charter boats and fishing charters available. Bus tours are welcome, but phone ahead so this small community can accommodate you.

The Noland House. This historic home

has been restored to provide luxurious accommodations for 4 guests. Host residence is next door. Private baths and sitting rooms, complimentary wine and snacks, fully equipped kitchen, lake and mountain views, airport and floatplane dock pickup. Single $85, double $95, open May–October. Box 135, Atlin, BC V0W 1A0. Phone/fax: (250) 651-7585. [ADVERTISEMENT]

RV park with electric and water hookups, showers and laundry, pay phone and boat moorage downtown on lake. There are several camping areas on Atlin Road, Discovery Road and Warm Bay Road (see logs this section). Atlin community operates the Pine Creek campground at **Milepost J 1.6** Warm Bay Road; 14 sites, $5 fee (pay at any downtown business or at the museum). ▲

ATTRACTIONS

The MV *Tarahne* (Tah-ron) sits on the lakeshore in the middle of town. Tours daily in summer at 3 P.M.; admission by donation. Sunday brunch is served aboard the MV *Tarahne* and a highly recommended Murder Mystery Dinner Theatre is featured weekly, July and August; phone (250) 651-7709. Built at Atlin in 1916 by White Pass & Yukon Route, she carried passengers and

ATLIN ADVERTISERS

Atlin Inn, The	Ph. (250) 651-7546
Happy Trails	Ph. (250) 651-7662
Kirkwood Cottages	Ph. (250) 651-7546
M.V. *Tarahne*	Ph. (250) 651-0076
Noland House, The	Ph. (250) 651-7585
Norseman Adventures	
R.V. Park	Ph. (250) 651-7535
Pine Tree Serivces	Ph. (250) 651-2405
Quilts & Comforts	
Bed & Breakfast	Ph. (250) 651-7476
Simply Gold	Ph. (250) 651-7708

Guided tour of old mining equipment, Atlin Historical Museum. (Earl L. Brown, staff)

freight from Atlin to Scotia Bay until 1936. (Scotia Bay is across the lake from Atlin and slightly north.) A 2-mile/3.2-km railway connected Scotia Bay on Atlin Lake to Taku Landing on Tagish Lake, where passengers arrived by boat from Carcross, YT. The *Tarahne* was the first gas-driven boat in the White Pass fleet. After she was lengthened by 30 feet in 1927, she could carry up to 198 passengers. In recent years, Atlin residents have launched a drive to restore the boat; they hope to eventually refloat the vessel and offer tours of Atlin Lake.

Atlin Historical Museum, open weekends during June and September, daily July through August. Located in Atlin's original 1-room schoolhouse, the museum has mining artifacts and photo exhibits of the Atlin gold rush. Gift shop features northern and Atlin books and the work of local artisans. Admission fee; phone (250) 651-7522.

The Globe Theatre, built in 1917, was restored by the Atlin Historical Society and re-opened in 1998. Information is available from the Atlin Museum, (250) 651-7522.

Visit the mineral springs at the north end of town, where you may have a drink of sparkling cold mineral water. The gazebo-like structure over the springs was built by White Pass in 1922. Picnic area nearby.

The Pioneer Cemetery, located at Milepost J 1.1 Discovery Road, contains the weathered grave markers of early gold seekers, including Fritz Miller and Kenneth McLaren, who made the first gold discovery in the Atlin area in July 1898. Also buried here is Walter Gladstone Sweet, reputed to have been a card dealer for Soapy Smith

in Skagway.

Public Gold Panning Area has been set aside on Spruce Creek. Turn off Discovery Road at **Milepost J 3.6**. Check at the museum for details. Gold pans available locally for rent or purchase.

Take a Hike. At **Milepost J 2.3** Warm Bay Road are 2 trails: the 3-mile/4.8-km Monarch trail and the short, easy Beach trail. The Monarch trail is a moderately strenuous hike with a steep climb at the end to a bird's-eye view of the area. Hiking and fishing information is available at Atlin's Happy Trails, (250) 651-7662.

Weekend guided nature walks are available at Warm Bay and Warm Springs, late May to early September. Fee charged. Inquire locally for details.

Tours and Rentals. Motorbike rentals, houseboat rentals, boat tours of Atlin and Tagish lakes, guided fishing trips and marine gas are available. Helicopter service, float-planes for charter hunting and fishing trips and flightseeing trips of Llewellyn Glacier and the Atlin area are also available.

Atlin Provincial Park, accessible by boat or plane only (charters available in Atlin). Spectacular wilderness area; varied topography; exceptional wildlife habitat.

Take a Drive. 13-mile/21-km Discovery Road and 16.5-mile/26.5-km Warm Bay Road are both suitable for passenger cars and RVs, and both offer sightseeing and recreation. See side road logs this section for details.

Atlin Art Centre, located at **Milepost J 2** Warm Bay Road, offers alpine hiking, boating and canoeing adventures to the general public from June to September. The centre is also a summer school and retreat for artists and students, run by Gernot Dick. The centre is designed to allow participants to distance themselves from urban distractions and focus on the creative process. Contact Atlin Art Centre, Monarch Mountain, Atlin, BC V0W 1A0; (800) 651-8882 for more information. Currently, a number of talented artists, authors and other creative people make their home in Atlin.

AREA FISHING: The Atlin area is well known for its good fishing. Fly-in fishing for salmon, steelhead and rainbow, or troll locally for lake trout. Grayling can be caught at the mouths of most creeks and streams or off Atlin docks. Public boat launch on Atlin Lake, south of the MV *Tarahne*. Boat charters available. For information on fishing in the area, contact Atlin's Happy Trails (250) 651-7662 or other local businesses. British Columbia fishing licenses are available from the government agent and local outlets. Fresh and smoked salmon may be available for purchase locally in the summer. Annual fishing derby held in June.

Discovery Road Log

Discovery Road begins 0.4 mile/0.6 km from Atlin's business district at junction with Atlin Road and leads east 13 miles/20.9 km. This is a good, wide gravel road, bumpy in spots. Posted speed limit is 50 mph/80 kmph, but 40 mph/60 kmph or less is recommended. There is active gold mining under way along the road; watch for large trucks. Beyond Surprise Lake Dam bridge, the road becomes steep and winding for 1.2 miles/1.9 km to road end (large RVs use caution).
Distance is measured from junction with Atlin Road (J).

J 0 **Junction** of Atlin Road and Discovery Avenue.
J 0.3 (0.5 km) **Junction** with Warm Bay Road.
J 1.1 (1.8 km) Atlin airport to east. Pioneer cemetery to west contains grave markers and monuments to many of Atlin's historical figures.
J 2.3 (3.7 km) Dump station to south.
J 3.5 (5.6 km) Turnout to south with view of Pine Creek and falls.
J 3.6 (5.8 km) Spruce Creek Road leads south 0.9 mile/1.4 km to designated public recreational gold panning area and 1.5 miles/2.4 km to active gold mining on Spruce Creek (no tours but operations can be photographed from the road). This side road is signed as rough and narrow; suitable for cars, vans and pickups.
J 3.9 (6.3 km) Winding road next 1 mile/1.6 km.
J 5.4 (8.7 km) Former townsite of Discovery, originally called Pine Creek, now a ghost town. In its boom days, the

Pioneer building at former townsite of Discovery. (® Earl L. Brown, staff)

town supplied miners working in the area.
J 7 (11.2 km) Active gold mining operation to south can be photographed from the road.
J 8.6 (13.8 km) Slow down for Pine Creek 1-lane bridge. Road follows creek drainage from here to Surprise Lake.
J 9.2 (14.8 km) Small lake to east usually has waterfowl.
J 10.7 (17.2 km) View west of mining road switchbacks on mountainside.
J 11.2 (18 km) Road forks: bear to left. Small lake to west.
J 11.8 (19 km) Surprise Lake Dam bridge. Turnout east side of bridge with litter barrel and view of Surprise Lake.
CAUTION: Steep and winding road next 1.2 miles/1.9 km eastbound to road end.
J 12 (19.3 km) **Surprise Lake** recreation site. One campsite near main road. Steep, bumpy access road leads to more campsites near lake. Pit toilets, picnic tables, firepits. Boat launch for cartop boats and canoes. A gold mining operation is visible across the lake. Fishing for arctic grayling. ◄▲
J 13 (20.9 km) Road forks and both forks dead end along Boulder Creek. Ample turnaround space for vehicles.

Warm Bay Road Log

Warm Bay Road leads south 16.5 miles/26.5 km to numerous points of interest and 5 camping areas. Warm Bay Road begins at **Milepost J 0.3** Discovery Road, 0.7 mile/1.1 km east of Atlin business district.
Distance is measured from junction with Discovery Road (J).

J 0 **Junction** with Discovery Road.
J 0.3 (0.5 km) Atlin School.
J 1.5 (2.4 km) Pine Creek 1-lane bridge.
J 1.6 (2.6 km) Pine Creek Campground and picnic area; 14 campsites, tenting area, pit toilets, picnic tables, firepits, some firewood and water. Camping fee $5; pay at any Atlin business. Short trail to Pine Creek and Pine Creek Falls. ▲
J 2 (3.2 km) Atlin Art Centre (see Attractions in Atlin).
J 2.3 (3.7 km) Trailheads either side of road. Monarch trail is a moderately strenuous 3-mile/4.8-km hike through meadows to scenic vista of Atlin area. Some steep sections; summit of Monarch Mountain at elev. 4,723 feet/1,439m.

Beach trail is short and easy.
J 2.5 (4 km) Drinking water from pipe beside road.
J 5.7 (9.2 km) Lina Creek.

J 7 (11.2 km) Viewpoint with litter barrel. Llewellyn Glacier and Atlin Lake are to the southwest. Good photo spot.
J 7.3 (11.7 km) Bed and breakfast, canoe rentals.
J 9.5 (15.3 km) McKee Creek 1-lane bridge. The McKee Creek area has been mined since the 1890s. In July 1981, 2 area miners found what has been dubbed the "Atlin nugget," a 36.86-troy-ounce, hand-sized piece of gold.

J 11.3 (18.2 km) Palmer Lake to east.
J 11.9 (19.1 km) **Palmer Lake** recreation site to east; camping, fishing, picnic tables, pit toilets. No camping fee. ◄▲
J 13.9 (22.3 km) Warm Bay recreation site on **Atlin Lake**; camping, fishing, picnic tables, pit toilets. No camping fee. Boat launch for small boats. ◄▲
J 14.4 (23.2 km) Warm Springs to north. This is a small and shallow spring, good for soaking road-weary bones. Large grassy camping area, pit toilet. No camping fee. The meadow streams are lined with watercress. Guided nature walks available; inquire locally for details. ▲
J 16.3 (26.2 km) Grotto recreation site; 2 campsites, picnic tables, pit toilets, firepits, litter barrel. ▲
J 16.4 (26.4 km) "The Grotto" to north. Large turnaround. Water flows through a hole in the rocks from an underground stream. Locals report this is a good place to obtain drinking water.
J 16.5 (26.5 km) Maintained road ends. Steep, bumpy and narrow road continues beyond this point; not recommended for travel.

TAGISH ROAD

Connects: Alaska Hwy. to Carcross, YT
Road Surface: 40% gravel, 60% paved
Length: 34 miles
Season: Open all year

(See map, page 738)

Tagish Marina at Tagish River Bridge.
(© Susan Cole Kelly)

The Tagish Road was built in 1942 to lay a gas pipeline. It leads south from the Alaska Highway junction at Jake's Corner (**Milepost DC 836.8**) through the settlement of Tagish to Carcross. This was the original route of the Alaska Highway in 1942. This 33.8-mile/54.4-km road connects the Alaska Highway with Klondike Highway 2. The road is good gravel from the Alaska Highway junction to Tagish, asphalt-surfaced between Tagish and Carcross.

If you are traveling Klondike Highway 2 between Skagway and Whitehorse, Tagish Road provides access to Atlin Road and also makes a pleasant side trip. Travelers may wish to use Tagish Road as an alternate route if there is road construction on Klondike Highway 2 between Carcross and the Alaska Highway. This is also a very beautiful drive in the fall; good photo opportunities.

Emergency medical services: Phone the RCMP, (867) 667-5555; ambulance, phone (867) 667-3333.

Tagish Road Log

Kilometreposts measure east to west from Alaska Highway junction to Carcross turn-off; posts are up about every 2 kilometres. Distance from the junction (J) is followed by distance from Carcross (C).

J 0 C 33.8 (54.4 km) Jake's Corner.

Junction with the Alaska Highway. Turn to **Milepost DC 836.8** in the ALASKA HIGHWAY section.

Drive south 1.1 miles/1.8 km from the Alaska Highway to the junction of Tagish Road and Atlin Road (Highway 7).

J 1.1 (1.8 km) C 32.7 (52.6 km) Junction of Tagish and Atlin roads. Head west on Tagish Road.

Turn southeast for Atlin, BC. See ATLIN ROAD section for log.

J 8.8 (14.2 km) C 25 (40.2 km) For several miles, travelers may see the NorthwesTel microwave tower on Jubilee Mountain (elev. 5,950 feet/ 1,814m) to the south between Little Atlin Lake and Tagish River. Jubilee Mountain was named by Dr. G.M. Dawson in 1887 in honor of Queen Victoria's Jubilee.

J 12.8 (20.6 km) C 21 (33.8 km) Gravel ends, pavement begins, westbound. Tagish Yukon government campground, on **Six Mile River** between Marsh Lake to the north and Tagish Lake to the south. Good fishing, boatlaunch, picnic area, playground, kitchen shelter, 28 campsites with firepits and tables, drinking water and toilets. Camping fee $8. *CAUTION: Watch for black bears.*

J 13 (20.9 km) C 20.8 (33.5 km) Gas, oil, minor repairs, snacks and post office. Pay phone on road. Marina on north side of road at east end of Tagish bridge has bait, tackle, fishing licenses, boat rental.

J 13.1 (21 km) C 20.7 (33.3 km) Tagish Bridge. Good fishing is a tradition here; Tagish bridge has an anglers' walkway on the north side. **Tagish River,** lake trout, arctic grayling, northern pike, whitefish and cisco.

West end of bridge has a day-use area with parking, 4 picnic sites and water pump.

J 13.5 (21.7 km) C 20.3 (32.6 km) Improved gravel road leads through parklike area to settlement of **TAGISH** (pop. about 134) on Tagish River between Marsh and Tagish lakes. Express bus service between Atlin and Whitehorse stops here and in Carcross 3 times weekly. Tagish means "fish trap" in the local Indian dialect. It was traditionally an Indian meeting place in the spring on the way to set up fish camps and again in the fall to celebrate the catch. Post office at Tagish Service at east end of Tagish bridge. Wilderness lodge on Taku Arm of Tagish Lake.

Two miles/3.2 km south of Tagish on the Tagish River is **TAGISH POST,** originally named Fort Sifton, the Canadian customs post established in 1897. Two of the original 5 buildings still stand. The North West Mounted Police and Canadian customs collected duties on thousands of tons of freight carried by stampeders on their way to the Klondike goldfields between September 1897 and February 1898.

J 13.7 (22 km) C 20.1 (32.3 km) Tagish Stores, Cafe, Motel, RV, built 1996–98, is located in the greenbelt of the Tagish Road Km 22. The store offers groceries, non-food, hardware, gifts and movies. Cafe: breakfast, lunch, ice cream. Motel: 6 units, showers and luxury king-size beds, TV and VCR. RV: 9 sites including pull-throughs, 15-/30-amps, water, sani-dump

and shower house. Phone/fax (867) 399-3344. [ADVERTISEMENT]

J 16.3 (26.2 km) C 17.5 (28.1 km) Side road leads 1.2 miles/2 km to Tagish Lake and homes.

Tagish Lake, fishing for trout, pike and grayling.

J 23 (37 km) C 10.8 (17.4 km) Bryden Creek.

J 23.8 (38.3 km) C 10 (16 km) Tagish Lake Resort. Experience our unique wilderness resort. Fine dining in our panoramic view dining room. Casual ambiance. Swiss-Canadian cuisine. Accommodation in authentic lakefront cabins with bath. Enjoy

walking, hiking, canoeing, boating, fishing, mountain biking, floatplane tours, campfire romance. Stress release and winter activities too. Located 8 miles (13 km) drive south of Tagish Road on picturesque Tagish Lake and surrounded by spectacular mountain scenery. Web site: www.tagishlake.com. E-mail: tagishlake@yukon.net. Phone/fax: (867) 668-1009. [ADVERTISEMENT]

J 24.7 (39.7 km) C 9.1 (14.6 km) Eagles Landing Bed & Breakfast. In the mountains on the shores of scenic Crag Lake (Tagish Road). Open year-round. Home-cooked meals. Rustic cabins or cozy rooms in our log home. Sauna, hiking, swimming, great fishing in the area. Cross-country skiing. Rentals of boats, canoes, snowmobiles, ATV's arranged. Reasonable rates. Your hosts: the Barr family. Phone (867) 667-1057. P.O. Box 110, Carcross, YT Y0B 1B0. [ADVERTISEMENT]

J 24.8 (39.9 km) C 9 (14.4 km) Crag Lake. Road now enters more mountainous region westbound. Caribou Mountain (elev. 5,645 feet/1,721m) on right.

J 27.2 (43.8 km) C 6.6 (10.6 km) Porcupine Creek.

J 27.5 (44.3 km) C 6.3 (10.1 km) Historic Milepost 7.

J 28.4 (45.7 km) C 5.4 (8.7 km) Pain Creek.

J 30.2 (48.6 km) C 3.6 (5.8 km) Side road to Chooutla Lake.

J 31 (49.9 km) C 2.8 (4.5 km) First glimpse westbound of Montana Mountain (elev. 7,230 feet/2,204m) across narrows at Carcross.

J 33.8 (54.4 km) C 0 Tagish Road ends westbound; turn left for Carcross, right for Whitehorse.

Junction with Klondike Highway 2. See **Milepost S 66.5** in the KLONDIKE HIGHWAY 2 section for log.

Tent campers on stern of cabin deck. (© David Job)

On the following pages are summer schedules and rates—effective May 1 through September 30, 1999—provided by the Alaska Marine Highway office. NOTE: The state reserves the right to revise or cancel schedules and rates without prior notice and assumes no responsibility for delays and/or expenses due to such modifications. On-line updates on the Alaska state ferry system are available on the Internet at: http://www.dot.state.ak.us/amhshome.html. Or phone 1-800-642-0066 for more information. Copies of the Alaska Marine Highway summer schedules are available at all state ferry terminals or from the Alaska Marine Highway, 1591 Glacier Ave., Juneau, AK 99801-1427.

For additional information on Alaska State ferry travel, see "Ferry Travel" in the TRAVEL PLANNING section.

How to Determine Fares

Fares for passengers, vehicles and staterooms are all calculated separately and must be added together to determine the total cost of your travel. For a breakdown of rates, see the Tariff sections on pages 760-762 and 764.

The MV Bartlett *serves Whittier, Cordova and Valdez.* (© Kris Graef, staff)

One-way fares for passage, vehicles and alternate means of conveyance (bicycles, kayaks, and inflatable boats) are charged from the port of embarkation to the port of debarkation.

Stateroom fares are calculated according to the route taken, and may vary from the rates printed here depending on the ship and schedules.

Payments and Cancellations

Payment may be made by mail with certified or cashier's check, or money order in U.S. dollars. Mail payments to: Alaska Marine Highway, 1591 Glacier Ave., Juneau, AK 99801-1427. Personal checks will not be accepted unless written on an Alaskan bank. No counter checks are accepted. VISA, Mas-terCard, American Express and Discover credit cards are accepted at all terminals and by phone (some restrictions may apply).

Cancellation charges apply for changes made within 14 days of sailing. Unless other arrangements are made and noted in your itinerary, full payment is required on or before the due date.

Payment Due Date

If reservation is made 55 days or more before sailing, payment is due 30 days after booking.

If reservation is made less than 55 days before sailing, payment is due within 10 days of making the reservation.

If reservation is made 10 days or less before sailing, payment is due at time of booking

Bookings will be canceled if reservations are not paid for by the payment due date.

Call or Fax Reservations

Reservations are required on all vessels for passengers, vehicles and cabins. For reservations write the Alaska Marine Highway, 1591 Glacier Ave., Juneau, AK 99801-1427; phone toll free 1-800-642-0066, or fax (907) 277-4829; TDD 1-800-764-3779. Phone local reservation numbers in Juneau (907/465-3941) and Anchorage (907/272-7116).

To make a reservation, you will need to provide the following information: ports of embarkation/debarkation; full names of all travelers, and ages of those under 12 years; width, height and overall length of vehicles (including extensions such as trailer hitches, bike racks, and storage containers); mailing address and phone number; alternate travel dates (cabin or vehicle space may not be available on your first choice of travel dates); and approximate date you will be leaving your home.

Getting on our Waitlist

If the desired space is not available, reservation personnel may offer to place your request on a waitlist. A limited number of requests will be added to a waitlist, which is checked on a regular basis. If cancellations occur you will be notified of confirmation of space. If your cabin has not been confirmed, you must sign-up on the purser's "STANDBY" list on board. If your vehicle's waitlist space has not been confirmed, you must sign up on the "STANDBY" list at your boarding terminal. DO NOT SEND PAYMENT FOR WAITLISTED SPACE UNTIL CONFIRMED.

Check-in Times

For recorded arrival/departure information call the specific terminal/office number listed below. Your reservations may be canceled if you do not check in on time. Passengers without vehicles must check in at Bellingham 2 hours before departure; 1 hour before at all other ports. Check-in times are printed on all tickets. Vehicle check-in time is 3 hours before departure at Bellingham and Prince Rupert; 2 hours before at Ketchikan, Juneau, Haines, Skagway, Homer, Kodiak and Seward; 1 1/2 hours at Petersburg; and 1 hour at Wrangell, Cordova, Seldovia and Valdez. (For Sitka times, call terminal.)

Southeast Offices

	Recorded Arrival/ Departure Information	Locations and distance from city center
Bellingham	(360) 676-8445	I-5 Exit #250
	(360) 676-0212	(24-hour recorded info.)
Prince Rupert	(250) 627-1744	Yellowhead Hwy #16
Ketchikan	(907) 225-6181	2.5 miles north
Wrangell	(907) 874-3711	2.0 blocks north
Petersburg	(907) 772-3855	0.9 miles south
Sitka	(907) 747-3300	7.1 miles north
Juneau	(907) 465-3940	14.0 miles north
Haines	(907) 766-2113	5.0 miles north
Skagway	(907) 983-2229	3.0 blocks south

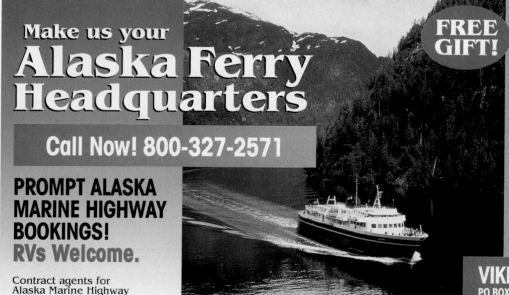

Southcentral/Southwest Offices

Anchorage	(907) 272-4482 Fax (907) 277-4829
Cordova	(907) 424-7333
Homer	(907) 235 -8449
Kodiak	(907) 486-3800
Seldovia	(907) 234-7868
Seward	(907) 224-5485
Valdez	(907) 835-4436

Ferry terminals are located within 1/2 mile of all Southcentral and Southwest city centers.

How To Estimate Arrival Times

Arrival times are not generally listed for interport stops. In-port times vary from 30 minutes to 6 hours. To calculate an approximate unlisted arrival time, add the running time listed in the table to the departure time from the port preceding your arrival city.

Please note that these running times are approximate and are listed for the convenience of those meeting passengers, and for travelers planning stopovers. For more accurate arrival times, please contact the local Marine Highway office on the day of arrival.

Due to traffic demands and tidal conditions, most Marine Highway vessels run continuously, docking at all hours of the day for brief transfers of passengers and vehicles. Passengers wishing to explore a particular community should consider a stopover and continuation on another Marine Highway vessel.

Running Time Table

INSIDE PASSAGE ROUTE:
Bellingham–Ketchikan ....37 hrs.
Prince Rupert–Ketchikan ....6 hrs.
Ketchikan–Wrangell ....6 hrs.
Wrangell–Petersburg ....3 hrs.

Petersburg–Juneau ....8 hrs.
Petersburg–Sitka ....10 hrs.
Sitka–Juneau/Auke Bay ....8 hrs. 45 min.
Juneau/Auke Bay–Haines ....4 hrs. 30 min.
Haines–Skagway ....1 hr.

SOUTHCENTRAL ROUTE:
Whittier–Valdez ....6 hrs. 45 min.
Valdez–Cordova ....5 hrs. 30 min.
Cordova–Whittier ....7 hrs.
Cordova–Seward ....11 hrs.
Valdez–Seward ....11 hrs.
Homer–Seldovia ....1 hr. 30 min.

GULF CROSSING ROUTE:
Juneau to Valdez ....32 hrs.

Valdez to Seward ....10 hrs.

SOUTHCENTRAL/SOUTHWEST:
Homer–Kodiak ....9 hrs. 30 min.
Homer–Port Lions ....10 hrs.
Seward–Kodiak ....13 hrs. 15 min.

SOUTHWEST ROUTES:
Kodiak–Port Lions ....2 hrs. 30 min.
Kodiak–Chignik ....18 hrs. 30 min.
Chignik–Sand Point ....9 hrs. 15 min.
Sand Point–King Cove ....6 hrs. 30 min.
King Cove–Cold Bay ....2 hrs.
Cold Bay–False Pass ....4 hrs. 15 min.
False Pass–Akutan ....10 hrs. 30 min.
Akutan–Unalaska ....3 hrs. 30 min.

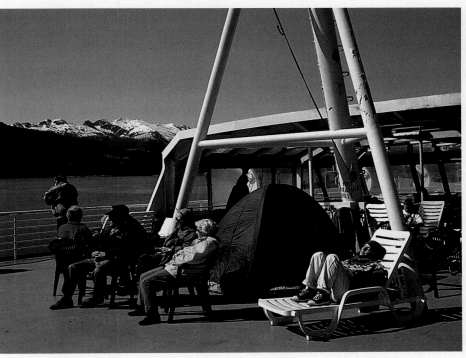

Tenters and other passengers share the solarium deck. (© Ruth von Spalding)

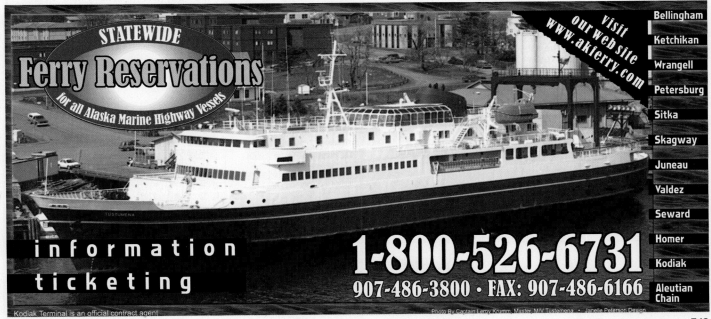

www.themilepost.com

MAY 1999 NORTHBOUND - INSIDE PASSAGE/SOUTHEAST ALASKA   1-800-642-0066

NO SAILINGS UNTIL JUNE

LEAVE BELLINGHAM	LEAVE PRINCE RUPERT	LEAVE STEWART/HYDER	METLAKATLA	KETCHIKAN	HOLLIS	WRANGELL	PETERSBURG	KAKE	ARRIVE SITKA	ANGOON	TENAKEE	HOONAH	JUNEAU/AUKE BAY	HAINES	ARRIVE SKAGWAY
								Lv. Sitka	S1 4:45P	S1 11:15P	SU2 2:30A	SU2 6:45A	SU2 10:00A		
	F30 1:00P			F30 7:30P		S1 2:15A	S1 6:15A		S1 8:30P				SU2 10:15A	SU2 3:45P	SU2 4:45P
F30 6:00P				SU2 10:30A		SU2 5:30P	SU2 10:30P						M3 9:30A	M3 3:30P	M3 4:30P
			T4 6:15P	T4 8:30P	T4 11:15P										
	T4 9:00A			T4 3:00P		T4 9:45P	W5 1:30A						W5 11:15A	W5 4:45P	W5 5:45P
			W5 8:15A	W5 10:30A	W5 1:15P										
				W5 6:00P			TH6 2:15A	TH6 7:15A		TH6 12:15P		TH6 5:15P	TH6 9:30P	F7 3:00A	F7 4:00A
	F7 10:15A			F7 4:15P		F7 11:00P	S8 2:45A		S8 1:30P				SU9 3:15A	SU9 9:15A	SU9 10:15A
								Lv. Sitka	S8 9:15A	S8 3:30P	S8 6:45P	S8 11:00P	SU9 2:15A		
F7 6:00P				SU9 10:30A		SU9 5:30P	SU9 10:30P						SU9 10:00P		
			T11 10:15P	W12 12:30A	W12 3:15A								M10 9:30A	M10 4:00P	M10 5:00P
	T11 8:00A			T11 2:00P		T11 8:45P	W12 12:30A								
			W12 10:00A	W12 12:15P	W12 3:00P								W12 10:15A	W12 3:45P	W12 4:45P
				W12 7:45P			TH13 4:00A	TH13 9:00A		TH13 2:00P		TH13 7:00P	TH13 11:15P	F14 4:45A	F14 5:45A
	F14 8:30A			F14 2:30P		F14 9:15P	S15 1:00A		S15 1:45P				SU16 3:00A	SU16 9:00A	SU16 10:00A
								Lv. Sitka	S15 3:45P	S15 10:00P	SU16 1:15A	SU16 5:30A	SU16 8:45A		
F14 6:00P				SU16 11:30A		SU16 7:30P	M17 12:30A						M17 10:30A	M17 4:30P	M17 5:30P
			T18 6:15P	T18 8:30P	T18 11:15P										
	T18 8:00A			T18 3:00P		T18 8:45P	W19 12:30A						W19 10:15A	W19 3:45P	W19 4:45P
			W19 6:15A	W19 8:30A	W19 11:15A										
				W19 4:00P			TH20 12:15A	TH20 5:15A		TH20 10:15A		TH20 3:15P	TH20 7:30P	F21 1:00A	F21 2:00A
	F21 9:30A			F21 3:30P		F21 10:15P	S22 2:00A		S22 1:45P				SU23 4:15A	SU23 10:15A	SU23 11:15A
								Lv. Sitka	S22 10:00A	S22 4:15P	S22 7:30P	S22 11:45P	SU23 3:15A		
F21 6:00P				SU23 9:30A		SU23 4:30P	SU23 9:30P			Lv. Pelican	SU23 3:30P		SU23 10:00P		
	M24 7:00P			T25 2:30A		T25 9:15A	T25 1:00P	T25 11:00P					M24 8:30A	M24 2:30P	M24 3:30P
				T25 5:15A	T25 8:00A								W26 12:15P	W26 6:15P	W26 7:15P
				T25 6:15P	T25 9:00P										
	T25 8:00A			T25 3:00P		T25 9:45P	T25 8:00A	T25 3:00P	T25 11:00P	W26 7:30A		W26 12:30P	W26 3:45P		
			W26 2:15P	W26 6:15P	W26 9:00P		W26 1:30A						W26 9:15A		
				TH27 6:15P	TH27 9:00P								F28 7:00A	F28 12:30P	F28 1:30P
	TH27 3:30P			TH27 11:30P		F28 7:00A	TH27 2:00P	TH27 7:00P		TH27 11:55P	F28 3:15A	F28 7:30A	F28 10:45A		
			F28 2:15P	F28 6:15P	F28 9:00P		F28 10:45A						F28 7:30P	F29 1:00A	F29 2:00A
	F28 6:15P			S29 1:45A		S29 8:30A	S29 12:15P						S29 7:00A	S29 12:30P	S29 1:30P
				S29 8:15A	S29 10:30A	S29 1:15P							S29 9:30P	SU30 3:00A	SU30 4:00A
				S29 8:45A	S29 11:00P	SU30 1:45A									
F28 6:00P				SU30 9:45A		SU30 5:15P	SU30 10:00P		Lv. Sitka S29 3:45P	S29 10:00P	SU30 1:15A	SU30 5:30A	SU30 8:45A	M31 2:45P	M31 3:45P
			SU30 2:15P	SU30 6:15P	SU30 9:00P								M31 8:45A		
													SU30 7:00A	SU30 12:30P	SU30 1:30P
F28 6:00P	SU30 7:45P			M31 5:15A		M31 11:55A	M31 3:45P	T1 2:30A					T1 4:00P	T1 9:30P	T1 10:30P
			M31 2:45P	M31 6:15P	M31 9:00P								M31 7:00A	M31 12:30P	M31 1:30P

ALL TIMES ARE LOCAL TIMES

HOW TO READ YOUR SCHEDULE

1. Reading across the top of each page, find the month you wish to travel, and refer to either the Northbound or Southbound schedule. (Using the example of traveling from Skagway to Juneau/Auke Bay, you would read the Southbound schedule on the right hand page.)

2. Reading across the top of the schedule, find the city from which you wish to depart. (e.g., Leave Skagway)

3. Read down the column to locate your desired departure date. For example: Leave Skagway T2 (Tuesday, the 2nd) 1:45 A.M.

4. Beginning with the departure date, read horizontally from left to right for dates and times of departure from various ports. For Example: After departing Skagway, the ferry will dock in Haines, and after a short time in port will depart Haines on T2, (Tuesday the 2nd) at 5:15 A.M. for Juneau/Auke Bay.

5. The color of the horizontal bars indicate the vessel on which you will travel.

LEAVE SKAGWAY	HAINES	JUNEAU/AUKE BAY	HOONAH	TENAKEE	ANGOON	ARRIVE SITKA	KAKE	PETERSBURG	WRANGELL	HOLLIS	KETCHIKAN	METLAKATLA	ARRIVE STEWART/HYDER	ARRIVE PRINCE RUPERT	ARRIVE BELLINGHAM
S30 5:30P	S30 8:00P	SU31 1:30A						SU31 10:30A	SU31 3:00P		SU31 10:30P			M1 6:00A	
SU31 8:30P		M1 1:30A													
M1 12:15P	M1 2:45P	M1 8:15P						T2 4:45A			T2 1:15P			T2 8:15P	
T2 1:45A	T2 5:15A	T2 11:45A				T2 8:00P		W3 11:45A	W3 3:45P		W3 10:15P				F5 7:15A
										M1 6:15A	M1 12:15P	M1 1:30P			
	M1 3:00A	M1 7:15A	M1 11:15A	M1 2:30P	M1 7:30P										

Day of Week — Day of Month (arrows pointing to schedule entries)
AM or PM — Time (arrows pointing to schedule entries)

VESSEL COLOR CODES   Aurora   Columbia   Le Conte   Malaspina   Matanuska   Taku   Kennicott

ALASKA STATE FERRY SCHEDULES

LEAVE SKAGWAY	HAINES	JUNEAU/ AUKE BAY	HOONAH	TENAKEE	ANGOON	ARRIVE SITKA	KAKE	PETERSBURG	WRANGELL	HOLLIS	KETCHIKAN	METLAKATLA	ARRIVE STEWART/HYDER	ARRIVE PRINCE RUPERT	ARRIVE BELLINGHAM
		F30 4:15P	F30 8:30P	S1 12:30A	S1 3:45A	S1 8:45A	M3 9:00P	T4 1:45A		T4 12:15P	T4 4:00P	T4 5:15P			
		SU2 5:00P	SU2 9:15P	M3 1:15A	M3 4:30A	M3 9:30A		M3 12:15P	M3 4:00P		M3 11:00P			T4 7:00A	
SU2 7:45P	SU2 9:45P	M3 3:45A						W5 6:45A	W5 12:15P		W5 7:15P				
M3 7:30P	M3 10:00P	T4 6:15A				T4 4:00P		TH6 1:45P	TH6 5:30P	W5 12:15A	W5 6:15A	W5 7:30A			F7 10:15A
		TH6 5:15A									F7 12:30A			F7 7:30A	
W5 8:45P	W5 10:45P	F7 2:00P	F7 6:15P	F7 10:15P	S8 1:30A	S8 6:30A				W5 2:15P	W5 5:00P				
F7 5:30A	F7 7:30A	SU9 9:45P						M10 6:15A	M10 10:00A		M10 11:00P				
SU9 1:15P	SU9 3:45P	SU9 7:00A	Ar. Pelican	SU9 1:30P										T11 6:00A	
		SU9 11:00P	M10 3:15A	M10 7:15A	M10 10:30A	M10 3:30P	T11 2:30A	T11 7:15A		T11 4:45P	T11 8:15P	T11 9:30P			
M10 8:00P	M10 11:00P	T11 7:00A				T11 4:45P		W12 7:30A	W12 11:30A		W12 6:30P				F14 10:30A
W12 7:45P	W12 9:45P	TH13 4:15A						TH13 12:45P	TH13 4:30P	W12 4:15A	W12 8:00A	W12 9:15A		F14 6:30A	
										W12 4:00P	TH13 11:30P				
											W12 6:45P				
F14 7:15A	F14 9:15A	F14 9:00P	S15 1:15A	S15 5:15A	S15 8:30A	S15 1:30P		M17 5:15A	M17 9:00A		M17 10:00P			T18 6:00A	
SU16 1:00P	SU16 3:15P	SU16 8:45P						T18 1:30A		T18 12:15P	T18 4:00P	T18 5:15P			F21 9:45A
		SU16 4:45P	SU16 9:00P	M17 1:00A	M17 4:15A	M17 9:15A	M17 8:45P	W19 7:00A	W19 11:15A		W19 6:45P				
M17 8:30P	M17 11:00P	T18 6:15A				T18 4:00P				W19 12:15A	W19 4:00A	W19 5:15A		F21 7:30A	
W19 5:45P	W19 8:30P	TH20 2:00A						TH20 1:45P	TH20 5:30P		F21 12:30A				
										W19 12:15P	W19 3:00P				
F21 3:30A	F21 5:30A	F21 3:15P	F21 7:30P	F21 11:30P	S22 2:45A	S22 7:45A								T25 6:00A	
SU23 2:15P	SU23 4:45P	SU23 11:15P						M24 8:00A	M24 11:55A		M24 11:00P				
		SU23 7:00A	Ar. Pelican	SU23 1:30P											F28 10:45A
		SU23 11:00P	M24 3:15A	M24 7:15A	M24 10:30A	M24 3:30P	T25 3:15A	T25 7:15A						F28 1:15P	
M24 6:30P	M24 9:00P	T25 5:45A				T25 4:30P		W26 8:00A	W26 12:15P		W26 7:45P				
W26 10:15P	TH27 12:30A	TH27 6:30A						TH27 3:00P	TH27 6:45P		F28 6:15A				
										T25 9:15A	T25 11:55A				
										W26 6:15A	W26 12:15P	W26 1:30P			
	W26 7:00P	W26 11:15P		TH27 4:15A			TH27 9:15A	TH27 1:15P		W26 6:45P	W26 10:30P				
		W26 10:15A									TH27 5:30A			TH27 12:30P	
										TH27 9:15A	TH27 11:55A				
F28 3:30P	F28 5:30P	F28 10:00P						F28 6:15A	F28 12:15P	F28 1:30P					
		F28 3:00P	F28 7:15P	F28 11:15P	S29 2:30A	S29 7:30A		S29 9:00A	SU30 1:45A		SU30 10:45A			SU30 5:45P	
S29 5:00A	S29 7:00A	S29 12:30P													
S29 3:30P	S29 5:30P	S29 10:00P								F28 10:00P	S29 6:15A	S29 7:30A			
SU30 6:30A	SU30 9:00A	SU30 3:15P						SU30 11:45P	M31 3:30A		M31 11:15A			M31 6:15P	
										S29 2:15P	S29 6:45P	S29 8:00P			
										SU30 6:15A	SU30 12:15P	SU30 1:30P			
		SU30 4:00P	SU30 8:15P	M31 12:15A	M31 3:30A	M31 8:30A	M31 8:00A	M31 11:55P							
M31 6:45P	M31 9:15P	T1 3:15A						T1 12:15P	T1 4:15P		T1 11:15P			W2 6:45A	
SU30 3:30P	SU30 5:30P	SU30 10:00P								M31 6:15A	M31 11:00A	M31 12:15P			
M31 3:30P	M31 5:30P	M31 10:00P								M31 10:00P	T1 12:45A				

ARRIVE STEWART/HYDER: **NO SAILINGS UNTIL JUNE**

ALL TIMES ARE LOCAL TIMES

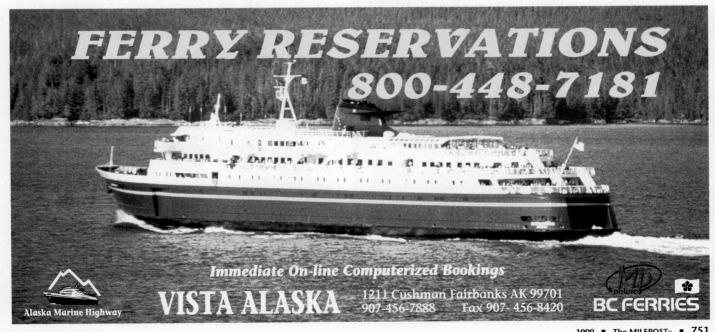

ALASKA STATE FERRY SCHEDULES

LEAVE BELLINGHAM	LEAVE PRINCE RUPERT	LEAVE STEWART/HYDER	METLAKATLA	KETCHIKAN	HOLLIS	WRANGELL	PETERSBURG	KAKE	ARRIVE SITKA	ANGOON	TENAKEE	HOONAH	JUNEAU/AUKE BAY	HAINES	ARRIVE SKAGWAY
	SU30 7:45P	SEE M/V AURORA SCHEDULE BELOW	SEE M/V AURORA SCHEDULE BELOW	M31 5:15A	SEE M/V AURORA SCHEDULE BELOW	M31 12:00P	M31 3:45P		T1 2:30A				T1 4:00P	T1 9:30P	T1 10:30P
	M31 9:00P			T1 6:15A		T1 1:00P	T1 5:00P		W2 3:00A				W2 5:00P	W2 10:30P	W2 11:30P
							T1 2:00A	T1 7:00A	T1 3:00P	T1 11:30P		W2 4:30A	W2 7:45A		
	W2 9:45A			W2 5:30P		TH3 12:30A	TH3 5:30A						TH3 1:30P		
							TH3 8:15A	TH3 1:15P		TH3 6:15P	TH3 9:30P	F4 1:45A	F4 5:00A		
	TH3 1:45P			TH3 10:45P		F4 5:30A	F4 9:15A		F4 11:00P				S5 11:15A		
	F4 4:45P			F4 10:45P		S5 5:30A	S5 9:15A						S5 6:30P	SU6 12:30A	SU6 1:30A
									Lv. Sitka						
	S5 5:00P			S5 11:45P		SU6 6:45A	SU6 11:30A		S5 7:15A	S5 1:30P	S5 4:45P	S5 9:00P	SU6 12:15A		
									M7 1:15A				M7 7:45P		
											Lv. Pelican SU6 3:30P		SU6 10:00P		
F4 6:00P	M7 11:45A			SU6 9:30A		SU6 4:30P	SU6 8:30P						M7 8:30A	M7 2:30P	M7 3:30P
	M7 7:45P			M7 6:15P		T8 1:15A							T8 1:00P		
	W9 8:15A			T8 2:15A		T8 9:00A	T8 12:45P		W9 3:30A				W9 5:00P	W9 11:15P	TH10 12:15A
							T8 2:30P	T8 7:30P	W9 3:30A	W9 11:55A		W9 5:00P	W9 8:15P		
	TH10 8:00A			W9 3:00P		W9 9:45P	TH10 2:30A						TH10 10:30A		
	F11 6:45P			TH10 2:30P		TH10 9:15P	TH10 4:15P	TH10 9:15P		F11 2:15A	F11 5:30A	F11 9:45A	F11 1:00P		
							F11 1:00A		F11 11:45A				S12 6:00A		
	S12 2:00P			S12 1:15A		S12 8:00A	S12 11:45A						S12 9:00P		
									Lv. Sitka / S12 2:45P	S12 9:00P	SU13 12:15A	SU13 4:30A	SU13 7:45A		
F11 6:00P				SU13 12:15A		SU13 7:45A	SU13 12:45P		M14 1:45A				M14 8:15P		
	M14 9:00A			SU13 10:30A		SU13 7:30P	SU13 11:30P						M14 10:00A	M14 4:00P	M14 5:00P
	M14 10:00P			M14 5:00P		M14 11:55P	T15 4:00A						T15 11:45A		
	W16 11:00A			T15 6:30A		T15 1:15P	T15 5:00P		W16 3:00A				W16 4:15P	W16 9:45P	W16 10:45P
							T15 2:00A	T15 7:00A	T15 3:00A	W16 5:00A		W16 10:00A	W16 1:15P		
	TH17 11:30A			W16 6:15P		TH17 1:15A	TH17 6:15A						TH17 2:15P		
							TH17 1:00P	TH17 6:00P		TH17 11:00P	F18 2:15A	F18 6:30A	F18 9:45A		
	F18 4:30P			TH17 8:00P		F18 3:00A	F18 7:00A	F18 5:45P					S19 6:00A		
				F18 11:00P		S19 5:45A	S19 9:30A						S19 6:45P	SU20 12:45A	SU20 1:45A
	S19 6:00P								Lv. Sitka / S19 8:15A	S19 2:30P	S19 5:45P	S19 10:00P	SU20 1:15A		
											Lv. Pelican SU20 2:30P		SU20 9:00P		
F18 6:00P	M21 9:00P			SU20 12:45A		SU20 8:15A	SU20 2:15P		M21 1:30A				M21 8:15P		
	M21 8:00A			SU20 9:30A		SU20 4:30P	SU20 8:30P						M21 9:30A	M21 3:30P	M21 4:30P
				T22 6:15A		M21 9:45P							W23 5:15A	*TO SE/SE INTER-TIE*	
	W23 1:15P			M21 3:00P			T22 1:30A						T22 9:15A		
							T22 6:45A	T22 1:30P	T22 9:30P	W23 6:00A		W23 11:00A	W23 2:15P		
	TH24 8:00A			W23 8:30P			TH24 8:30A						TH24 4:30P		
				TH24 2:00P			TH24 1:00P	TH24 6:00P		TH24 11:00P	F25 2:15A	F25 6:30A	F25 9:45P		
							F25 1:00A		F25 11:45A				S26 6:00A		
									Lv. Sitka / S26 2:30P	S26 8:45P	SU26 11:55P	SU27 4:15A	SU27 7:30A		
F25 6:00P	S26 6:00P			SU27 1:45A		SU27 8:45A	SU27 1:45P		M28 1:00A				M28 7:45P		
	M28 9:45A			SU27 10:15A		SU27 6:15P	SU27 10:15P						M28 9:15A	M28 3:15P	M28 4:15P
				M28 4:45P		M28 11:30P	T29 3:15A						T29 11:00A		
	M28 9:00P			T29 6:00A		T29 12:45P	T29 1:15A	T29 6:15A	T29 2:15P	T29 10:45P			W30 7:00A		
	W30 10:30A			W30 5:45P		TH1 12:45A	T29 4:30P		W30 2:30A			W30 3:45P	W30 3:30P	W30 9:00P	W30 10:00P
							TH1 5:45A						TH1 1:45P		

ALL TIMES ARE LOCAL TIMES

M/V MALASPINA
NORTH LYNN CANAL TRIPS

The M/V Malaspina operates on a daily schedule as indicated in the following table. To determine the best connection for your trip, use these schedules. Please allow enough time to make appropriate connections with the sailings listed above. (See tables above)

DAILY SCHEDULE MAY 28 - SEPTEMBER 12, 1999

Leave Juneau	7:00AM
Arrive Haines	11:30AM
Leave Haines	12:30PM
Arrive Skagway	1:30PM
Leave Skagway	3:30PM
Arrive Haines	4:30PM
Leave Haines	5:30PM
Arrive Juneau	10:00PM

M/V KENNICOTT
SOUTHEAST/SOUTHWEST INTER-TIE TRIPS

The M/V Kennicott for the month of June will depart from Juneau as indicated in the following table. To determine the best connection for your trip, use this schedule. Please allow enough time to make appropriate connections with the sailings listed above. (See tables above).

Leave Juneau	Wednesday	JUN 23	5:15AM
Arrive Valdez	Thursday	JUN 24	6:15PM
Leave Valdez	Thursday	JUN 24	9:15PM
Arrive Seward	Friday	JUN 25	7:15AM
Leave Seward	Friday	JUN 25	1:15PM
Arrive Valdez	Friday	JUN 25	11:15PM
Leave Valdez	Saturday	JUN 26	2:15AM
Arrive Juneau	Sunday	JUN 27	2:45PM

Whistle Stop service is provided to Yakutat on inter-tie trips in both directions between Juneau and Valdez. The vessel will stop ONLY if there are vehicle reservations.

Legend: Aurora · Columbia · Le Conte · Malaspina · Matanuska · Taku · Kennicott

ALASKA STATE FERRY SCHEDULES

LEAVE SKAGWAY	HAINES	JUNEAU/AUKE BAY	HOONAH	TENAKEE	ANGOON	ARRIVE SITKA	KAKE	PETERSBURG	WRANGELL	HOLLIS	KETCHIKAN	METLAKATLA	ARRIVE STEWART/HYDER	ARRIVE PRINCE RUPERT	ARRIVE BELLINGHAM
M31 6:45P	M31 9:15P	T1 3:15A						T1 12:15P	T1 4:15P		T1 11:15P			W2 6:45A	
											W2 4:30P				F4 7:00A
W2 1:30A	W2 3:30A	W2 9:00A						W2 5:30P	W2 9:15P		TH3 4:45A			TH3 11:45A	
TH3 2:30A	TH3 4:30A	TH3 10:30A						TH3 7:15P	TH3 11:15P		F4 6:45A			F4 1:45P	
		W2 10:15A	W2 5:30P		W2 10:30P		TH3 3:30A	TH3 7:30A							
		TH3 6:30P						F4 7:15P	F4 11:30P		S5 6:30A			S5 2:00P	
		F4 12:30P	F4 4:45P	F4 8:45P	F4 11:55P	F4 4:15A	S5 5:00A								
		S5 2:30P				SU6 12:15A									
SU6 4:30A	SU6 7:00A	SU6 1:30P						SU6 3:15P	SU6 7:15P		M7 2:45A			M7 9:45A	
		SU6 7:00A	Ar. Pelican SU6 1:30P					SU6 10:00P	M7 1:45A		M7 9:45A			M7 4:45P	
		M7 11:30P												W9 5:45A	
		M7 3:15A	M7 7:30A	M7 11:30A	M7 2:45P	M7 7:45P	T8 9:00A	T8 8:45A	T8 1:00P		T8 10:15P				
M7 6:30P	M7 9:00P	T8 5:30A				T8 2:45P		T8 1:00P							F11 8:30A
		W9 12:15A						W9 6:15A	W9 10:15A		W9 6:30P				
TH10 3:15A	TH10 5:45A	TH10 12:15P						W9 8:45A	W9 12:30P		W9 11:00P				F11 6:00A
		W9 9:15P	TH10 1:30A		TH10 6:30A		TH10 11:30A	TH10 9:15P	F11 1:15A		F11 8:45A				F11 3:45P
		TH10 1:30P						TH10 3:30P							
		F11 8:00P	S12 12:15A	S12 4:15A	S12 7:30A	TH10 11:15P		F11 2:15P	F11 6:30P		S12 3:30A				S12 11:00A
		S12 9:00A				S12 12:30P									
						S12 6:45P		SU13 11:00A	SU13 3:00P		SU13 11:00P				M14 6:00A
SU13 5:30A	SU13 8:00A	SU13 3:45P						M14 12:15A	M14 4:00A		M14 11:55A				M14 7:00A
		SU13 3:45P	SU13 8:00P	S13 11:55P	M14 3:15A	M14 8:15A	M14 7:45P	M14 11:45P							
		T15 3:30A						T15 12:45P	T15 5:30P		W16 12:30A				W16 8:00A
M14 8:00P	M14 11:15P	T15 6:15A			T15 2:30P			W16 3:45A	W16 7:45A		W16 4:00P				
		W16 4:45A						W16 8:45A	W16 5:00P		TH17 1:30A				TH17 8:30A
TH17 1:45A	TH17 3:45A	TH17 9:45A						TH17 6:30P	TH17 10:30P		F18 6:30A				TH17 1:30P
		W16 2:15P	W16 6:30P		W16 11:15P		TH17 4:15A	TH17 8:15A							
		TH17 7:15P				F18 5:00A		F18 7:45P	F18 11:55P		S19 7:30A				S19 3:00P
		F18 1:30P	F18 5:45P	F18 9:45P	S19 1:00A	S19 6:00A									
		S19 8:45P				S19 6:30P		SU20 9:00A	SU20 1:00P		SU20 11:00P				M21 6:00A
SU20 4:45A	SU20 7:15A	SU20 1:45P						SU20 10:15P	M21 2:00A		M21 10:00A				M21 5:00P
		SU20 6:00A	Ar. Pelican SU20 12:30P												
		SU20 10:00P	M21 2:15A	M21 6:15A	M21 9:30A	M21 2:30P	T22 2:00A	T22 6:00A			T22 10:30P				W23 6:00A
		M21 11:30P						T22 8:45A	T22 1:00P		W23 6:30P				
M21 7:30P	M21 10:00P	T22 7:00A				T22 3:30P		W23 6:30A	W23 10:30A						F25 8:45A
		T22 11:30P						W23 8:00A	W23 12:45P		W23 11:00P				TH24 6:00A
		W23 6:00P	W23 10:15P		TH24 3:15A		TH24 8:15A	TH24 12:15P							
		TH24 7:30P						F25 8:15P	F25 8:15P		S26 7:30A				S26 3:00P
		F25 1:45P	F25 6:00P	F25 10:00P	S26 1:15A	F25 5:15A			S26 12:30A						
		S26 8:30A			S26 6:15A	S26 6:15P		SU27 10:15A	SU27 2:15P		M28 12:45A				M28 7:45A
		SU27 3:15P	SU27 7:30P	SU27 11:30P	M28 2:45A	M28 7:45A	M28 7:15P	M28 11:15P							
FROM SE/SW INTER-TIE		SU27 4:45P									M28 10:45A				M28 5:45P
		T29 2:30A						T29 11:45A	T29 4:00P		T29 11:00P				W30 6:30A
M28 7:15P	M28 10:15P	T29 5:30A			T29 1:45P			W30 3:30A	W30 7:30A		W30 3:45P				F2 6:15A
		W30 3:30A						W30 11:55A	W30 3:45P		W30 11:00P				TH1 6:00A
		W30 11:55A	W30 4:15P		W30 9:15P		TH1 2:15A	TH1 6:15A							

Columns HOLLIS, METLAKATLA and ARRIVE STEWART/HYDER display the rotated note: SEE M/V AURORA SCHEDULE BELOW

ALL TIMES ARE LOCAL TIMES

M/V AURORA - SOUTHERN PANHANDLE SUMMER 1999
EFFECTIVE JUNE 1, 1999 THROUGH SEPTEMBER 14, 1999

SUN Lv Hollis 6:15AM
Ar Ketchikan 9:00AM
Lv Ketchikan 12:15PM
Ar Metlakatla 1:30PM
Lv Metlakatla 2:15PM
Ar Ketchikan 3:30PM
Lv Ketchikan 6:15PM
Ar Hollis 9:00PM

MON Lv Hollis 6:15AM
Ar Ketchikan 9:00AM
Lv Ketchikan 11:00AM
Ar Metlakatla 12:15PM
Lv Metlakatla 2:45PM
Ar Ketchikan 4:00PM
Lv Ketchikan 6:15PM
Ar Hollis 9:00PM

MON Lv Hollis 10:00PM
TUE Ar Ketchikan 12:45AM
Lv Ketchikan 1:45AM
Ar Hyder 12:30PM
Lv Hyder 3:45PM
WED Ar Ketchikan 12:30AM
Lv Ketchikan 1:30AM
Ar Hollis 4:15AM

WED Lv Hollis 6:15AM
Ar Ketchikan 9:00AM
Lv Ketchikan 12:15PM
Ar Metlakatla 1:30PM
Lv Metlakatla 2:15PM
Ar Ketchikan 3:30PM
Lv Ketchikan 6:15PM
Ar Hollis 9:00PM

THU Lv Hollis 9:15AM
Ar Ketchikan 11:55AM
Lv Ketchikan 6:15PM
Ar Hollis 9:00PM

FRI Lv Hollis 6:15AM
Ar Ketchikan 9:00AM
Lv Ketchikan 12:15PM
Ar Metlakatla 1:30PM
Lv Metlakatla 2:15PM
Ar Ketchikan 3:30PM

FRI Lv Ketchikan 6:15PM
Ar Hollis 9:00PM
Lv Hollis 10:00PM
SAT Ar Ketchikan 12:45AM

SAT Lv Ketchikan 6:15AM
Ar Metlakatla 7:30AM
Lv Metlakatla 8:15AM
Ar Ketchikan 9:30AM
Lv Ketchikan 10:30AM
Ar Hollis 1:15PM
Lv Hollis 2:15PM
Ar Ketchikan 5:00PM
Lv Ketchikan 6:45PM
Ar Metlakatla 8:00PM
Lv Metlakatla 8:45PM
Ar Ketchikan 10:00PM
Lv Ketchikan 11:00PM
SUN Ar Hollis 1:45AM

ALASKA STATE FERRY SCHEDULES

JULY 1999 NORTHBOUND – INSIDE PASSAGE/SOUTHEAST ALASKA 1-800-642-0066

Leave Bellingham	Leave Prince Rupert	Leave Stewart/Hyder	Metlakatla	Ketchikan	Hollis	Wrangell	Petersburg	Kake	Arrive Sitka	Angoon	Tenakee	Hoonah	Juneau/Auke Bay	Haines	Arrive Skagway
	W30 10:30A	SEE M/V AURORA SCHEDULE BELOW	SEE M/V AURORA SCHEDULE BELOW	W30 5:45P	SEE M/V AURORA SCHEDULE BELOW	TH1 12:45A	TH1 5:45A			TH1 5:00P	TH1 8:15P	F2 12:30A	TH1 1:45P		
	TH1 9:00A			TH1 6:15P		F2 1:15A	TH1 7:00A	TH1 11:55A					F2 3:45A		
	F2 3:00P			F2 9:30P		S3 4:15A	F2 5:15A			F2 4:00P			S3 4:15A		
							S3 8:00A		Lv. Sitka S3 12:30P	S3 6:45P	S3 10:00P	SU4 2:15A	S3 5:15P	S3 11:15P	SU4 12:15A
F2 6:00P	S3 3:30P			S3 9:45P		SU4 4:30A	SU4 9:30A	SU4 11:45P			Lv. Pelican SU4 3:30P		SU4 5:30A		
	M5 10:45A			SU4 9:30A		SU4 5:15P	SU4 10:15P		SU4 11:45P	SU4 11:45P			SU4 10:00P		
	M5 7:30P			M5 5:45P		T6 12:30A	T6 4:15A						M5 6:00P	M5 2:30P	M5 3:30P
				T6 1:30A		T6 8:15A	T6 3:00P						M5 8:30A		
	W7 11:15A			W7 6:15P		TH8 2:00A	T6 11:00A	T6 4:00P	W7 1:45A	W7 1:45A			T6 11:55A		
							TH8 7:00A	W7 1:45A		W7 10:15A		W7 3:15P	W7 3:30P	W7 9:30P	W7 10:30P
	TH8 8:00A			TH8 2:30P		TH8 9:30P	TH8 2:30P	TH8 7:30P					W7 6:30P		
	F9 4:45P			F9 11:45P			F9 2:30A		F9 4:30P	F9 12:30A	F9 3:45A	F9 8:00A	TH8 3:00P		
							S10 6:30A						F9 11:15A		
F9 6:00P	S10 4:45P			S10 11:30P		S10 6:30A	S10 10:15A		Lv. Sitka S10 7:30P	S10 7:30P			S10 4:45A	S10 1:30A	S10 2:30A
	M12 8:00A			SU11 9:30A		SU11 6:30A	SU11 11:30A		SU11 1:45A	SU11 1:45A	SU11 5:00A	SU11 9:15A	S10 7:30P		
	M12 8:45P			M12 3:00P		SU11 5:30P	SU11 10:15P	M12 12:30A	M12 12:30A				SU11 12:30P	SU11 1:30A	SU11 2:30A
				T13 5:30A		M12 10:00P	M12 10:00P						M12 7:15P	M12 3:15P	M12 4:15P
	W14 10:45A			W14 7:00P		T13 12:15P	T13 1:45A		W14 2:00A	W14 2:00A		W14 3:30A	M12 9:15A		
							T13 4:00P	T13 6:00A		T13 2:00P			T13 9:30A		
	TH15 8:30A			TH15 5:30P		TH15 2:00A	T13 12:30A		W14 3:45P	W14 10:30A			W14 3:45P	W14 9:30P	W14 10:30P
	F16 3:30P			F16 9:30P		F16 1:30A	TH15 7:00A	TH15 10:45A	TH15 10:45A	TH15 3:45P	TH15 7:00P	TH15 11:15P	W14 6:45A		
							TH15 5:45A						TH15 3:00P		
F16 6:00P	S17 4:00P			S17 10:15P		S17 4:15A	F16 5:30A						F16 2:30A		
	M19 10:45A			SU18 9:30A		SU18 5:00A	S17 8:00A		Lv. Sitka S17 12:45P	S17 7:00P	S17 10:15P	SU18 2:30A	S17 4:30A	S17 11:15P	SU18 12:15A
	M19 9:00P			M19 6:45P		SU18 5:30P	SU18 9:45A	SU18 11:55P	SU18 11:55P	Lv. Pelican SU18 3:30P	SU18 3:30P		S17 5:15P		
				T20 6:15A		T20 1:30A	SU18 10:00P					M19	SU18 5:45A		
	W21 10:30A			W21 5:15P		TH22 12:15A	T20 5:15A		W21 2:00A	W21 10:30A		W21 3:30P	SU18 10:00P		
							T20 6:00P	T20 6:00P					M19 6:30P	M19 2:30P	M19 3:30P
	TH22 9:45A			TH22 6:45P		F23 1:45A	TH22 5:15A	TH22 7:45P		F23 12:45A	F23 4:00A	F23 8:15A	M19 8:30A		
							TH22 2:45P		F23 4:30P				T20 1:00P		*TO SE/SW INTER-TIE*
F23 6:00P	S24 4:30P			S24 11:15P		SU25 6:15A	F23 5:45A	S24 9:45P	SU25 5:45A	SU25 2:15A	SU25 5:30P	SU25 9:45P	W21 5:15A		
	M26 10:00A			SU25 9:30A		SU25 4:30P	SU25 11:15A		M26 12:15A	M26 12:15A			W21 6:45P		
	M26 9:00P			M26 5:00P		M26 11:45P	SU25 8:30P						TH22 1:15P		
				T27 4:45A		T27 11:30A	T27 3:30A						F23 11:30A		
	W28 10:00A			W28 5:15P		TH29 12:15A	T27 3:15P	T27 5:30P	W28 1:15A	W28 1:15A		W28 3:00P	S24 4:45A		
							T27 12:30P			W28 10:00A			M26 1:00A		
	TH29 8:00A			TH29 5:00P		TH29 11:55P	TH29 5:15A	TH29 9:15P					M26 12:30P	M26 2:30P	M26 3:30P
	F30 2:30P			F30 8:30P		S31 3:15A	TH29 4:15P		F30 3:00P	F30 2:15A	F30 5:30A	F30 9:45A	M26 8:30A		
							F30 4:00A						T27 11:15A		
							S31 7:00A	S31 7:00A	Lv. Sitka S31 11:45A	S31 6:00P	S31 9:15P	SU1 1:30A	W28 2:30P	W28 8:30P	W28 9:30P
													W28 6:15P		
													TH29 1:15P		
													F30 1:00P		
													S31 3:15A	S31 10:00P	S31 11:00P
													S31 4:15P		
													SU1 4:45A		

ALL TIMES ARE LOCAL TIMES

M/V MALASPINA — NORTH LYNN CANAL TRIPS

The M/V Malaspina operates on a daily schedule as indicated in the following table. To determine the best connection for your trip, use these schedules. Please allow enough time to make appropriate connections with the sailings listed above. (See tables above)

DAILY SCHEDULE MAY 28 – SEPTEMBER 12, 1999

Leave Juneau	7:00AM
Arrive Haines	11:30AM
Leave Haines	12:30PM
Arrive Skagway	1:30PM
Leave Skagway	3:30PM
Arrive Haines	4:30PM
Leave Haines	5:30PM
Arrive Juneau	10:00PM

M/V KENNICOTT — **SOUTHEAST/SOUTHWEST INTER-TIE TRIPS**

The M/V Kennicott for the month of July will depart from Juneau as indicated in the following table. To determine the best connection for your trip, use this schedule. Please allow enough time to make appropriate connections with the sailings listed above. (See tables above)

Leave Juneau	Wednesday	JUL 21	5:15AM
Arrive Valdez	Thursday	JUL 22	6:15PM
Leave Valdez	Thursday	JUL 22	9:15PM
Arrive Seward	Friday	JUN 23	7:15AM
Leave Seward	Friday	JUL 23	1:15PM
Arrive Valdez	Friday	JUL 23	11:15PM
Leave Valdez	Saturday	JUL 24	2:15AM
Arrive Juneau	Sunday	JUL 25	2:45PM

Whistle Stop service is provided to Yakutat on inter-tie trips in both directions between Juneau and Valdez. The vessel will stop ONLY if there are vehicle reservations.

Legend: ▪ Aurora ▪ Columbia ▪ Le Conte ▪ Malaspina ▪ Matanuska ▪ Taku ▪ Kennicott

ALASKA STATE FERRY SCHEDULES

Note: The columns **Hollis**, **Metlakatla**, and **Arrive Stewart/Hyder** carry the vertical notice "SEE M/V AURORA SCHEDULE BELOW" across the body of the table.

Leave Skagway	Haines	Juneau/Auke Bay	Hoonah	Tenakee	Angoon	Arrive Sitka	Kake	Petersburg	Wrangell	Hollis	Ketchikan	Metlakatla	Arrive Stewart/Hyder	Arrive Prince Rupert	Arrive Bellingham
TH1 1:00A	TH1 3:00A	TH1 9:00A						TH1 5:45P	TH1 9:45P		F2 5:15A				F2 12:15P
		TH1 5:45P				F2 3:30A		F2 6:15P	F2 10:15P		S3 5:00A				S3 12:30P
		F2 11:45A	F2 4:00P	F2 8:00P	F2 11:15P	S3 4:15A									
		S3 1:00P				S3 10:45A		SU4 2:15P	SU4 6:15P		M5 1:45A				M5 8:45A
SU4 3:15A	SU4 5:45A	SU4 11:45A						SU4 8:15P	SU4 11:55P		M5 9:30A				M5 4:30P
		SU4 7:00A	Ar. Pelican	SU4 1:30P											
		M5 2:00A	M5 6:15A	M5 10:15A	M5 1:30P	M5 6:30P	T6 6:00A	T6 10:00A	T6 1:30P		T6 10:30P				
		M5 11:30P						T6 8:45A	W7 4:15A		W7 4:30P				W7 6:00A
M5 6:30P	M5 9:00P	T6 4:30A				T6 12:45P		W7 8:45A	W7 8:15A		W7 11:00P				TH8 6:00A
		W7 12:15A							W7 12:30P					F9 6:30A	F9 1:45P
TH8 1:30A	TH8 4:00A	TH8 10:00A					TH8 9:45A	TH8 1:45P	TH8 10:45P		F9 6:45A				
		W7 7:30P	W7 11:45P		TH8 4:45A	F9 4:15A		TH8 6:45P							S10 1:45P
		TH8 6:30P						F9 7:00P	F9 11:15P						
		F9 6:45P	F9 11:00P	S10 3:00A	S10 6:15A	S10 11:15A					S10 6:15A				
		S10 7:45A				S10 5:30P									
SU11 4:30A	SU11 7:30A	SU11 2:30P						SU11 10:00A	SU11 2:00P						M12 6:00A
		SU11 2:30P	SU11 6:45P	SU11 10:45P	M12 2:00A	M12 7:00A	M12 6:30P	SU11 11:00P	M12 2:45A		M12 10:45A				M12 5:45P
M12 7:15P	M12 10:15P	T13 2:30A						M12 10:30P							
		T13 5:15A				T13 1:45P		T13 11:45A	T13 4:30P						W14 7:45A
		W14 3:45A						W14 3:30A	W14 7:30A		W14 12:15A				
TH15 1:30A	TH15 3:45A	TH15 9:45A					TH15 1:00A	W14 12:15P	W14 4:00P		W14 3:45P				TH15 6:30A
		W14 10:45A	W14 3:00P		W14 8:00P			TH15 5:00A	TH15 10:30P		W14 11:30P				F16 12:30P
		TH15 6:00P				F16 3:45A		F16 6:30P	F16 10:45P		F16 5:30A			F16 6:00A	
		F16 11:55A	F16 4:15P	F16 8:15P	F16 11:30P	S17 4:30A					S17 5:45A				S17 1:15P
		S17 7:30A				S17 5:15P									
SU18 3:15A	SU18 5:45A	SU18 12:15P						SU18 7:30A	SU18 11:30A		SU18 10:45P				M19 5:45A
		SU18 7:00A	Ar. Pelican	SU18 1:30P				SU18 8:45P	M19 12:30A		M19 10:30A				M19 5:30P
		M19 2:15A	M19 6:30A	M19 10:30A	M19 1:45P	M19 6:45P	T20 6:15A	T20 10:15A	T20 1:30P						
		M19 11:30P						T20 8:45A	W21 8:15A						W21 6:00A
M19 6:30P	M19 9:00P	T20 5:15A				T20 1:30P		W21 4:15A	W21 1:30P						TH22 6:00A
		T20 11:55P						W21 9:45A							
		W21 7:45P	W21 11:55P		TH22 5:00A		TH22 10:00A	TH22 2:00P							
		TH22 6:15P				F23 4:00A		F23 6:45P	F23 11:00P		S24 6:00A			F23 6:30A	
		F23 4:15P	F23 8:30P	S24 12:30A	S24 3:45A		S24 7:45A								S24 1:30P
		S24 7:45A				S24 5:30P		SU25 9:00A	SU25 1:00P		SU25 11:00A				M26 6:00A
FROM SE/SW INTER-TIE		SU25 4:45P									M26 11:00A				M26 6:00P
		M26 2:30A	M26 6:45A	M26 10:45A	M26 2:00A	M26 7:00P	T27 7:00A	T27 11:00A	T27 3:30P		T27 10:30P				W28 6:00A
		T27 12:15A						T27 10:45A	W28 6:45A		W28 3:00P				TH29 6:00A
M26 5:30P	M26 8:00P	T27 3:00A				T27 1:00P		W28 2:45A	W28 2:45P		W28 11:00P				F30 6:00A
		W28 2:30A						W28 11:00A							
TH29 12:30A	TH29 3:00A	TH29 9:00A					TH29 11:30A	TH29 5:30P	TH29 9:30P		F30 4:30A				F30 11:30A
		W28 7:15P	TH29 1:30A		TH29 6:30A			TH29 3:30P							
		TH29 5:00P				F30 2:45A		F30 5:30P	F30 9:45P		S31 4:45A				S31 12:15P
		F30 5:00P	F30 9:15P	S31 1:15A	S31 4:30A	S31 9:30A									
		S31 6:00A				S31 3:45P		SU1 6:00A	SU1 11:00A		SU1 11:00P				M2 6:00A

ALL TIMES ARE LOCAL TIMES

M/V AURORA - SOUTHERN PANHANDLE SUMMER 1999
EFFECTIVE JUNE 1, 1999 THROUGH SEPTEMBER 14, 1999

SUN
Lv Hollis 6:15AM
Ar Ketchikan 9:00AM
Lv Ketchikan 12:15PM
Ar Metlakatla 1:30PM
Lv Metlakatla 2:15PM
Ar Ketchikan 3:30PM
Lv Ketchikan 6:15PM
Ar Hollis 9:00PM

MON
Lv Hollis 6:15AM
Ar Ketchikan 9:00AM
Lv Ketchikan 11:00AM
Ar Metlakatla 12:15PM
Lv Metlakatla 2:45PM
Ar Ketchikan 4:00PM
Lv Ketchikan 6:15PM
Ar Hollis 9:00PM

MON Lv Hollis 10:00PM
TUE Ar Ketchikan 12:45AM
Lv Ketchikan 1:45AM
Ar Hyder 12:30PM
Lv Hyder 3:45PM
WED Ar Ketchikan 12:30AM
Lv Ketchikan 1:30AM
Ar Hollis 4:15AM

WED
Lv Hollis 6:15AM
Ar Ketchikan 9:00AM
Lv Ketchikan 12:15PM
Ar Metlakatla 1:30PM
Lv Metlakatla 2:15PM
Ar Ketchikan 3:30PM
Lv Ketchikan 6:15PM
Ar Hollis 9:00PM

THU
Lv Hollis 9:15AM
Ar Ketchikan 11:55AM
Lv Ketchikan 6:15PM
Ar Hollis 9:00PM

FRI
Lv Hollis 6:15AM
Ar Ketchikan 9:00AM
Lv Ketchikan 12:15PM
Ar Metlakatla 1:30PM
Lv Metlakatla 2:15PM
Ar Ketchikan 3:30PM

FRI
Lv Ketchikan 6:15PM
Ar Hollis 9:00PM
Lv Hollis 10:00PM
SAT Ar Ketchikan 12:45AM

SAT
Lv Ketchikan 6:15AM
Ar Metlakatla 7:30AM
Lv Metlakatla 8:15AM
Ar Ketchikan 9:30AM
Lv Ketchikan 10:30AM
Ar Hollis 1:15PM
Lv Hollis 2:15PM
Ar Ketchikan 5:00PM
Lv Ketchikan 6:45PM
Ar Metlakatla 8:00PM
Lv Metlakatla 8:45PM
Ar Ketchikan 10:00PM
Lv Ketchikan 11:00PM
SUN Ar Hollis 1:45AM

ALASKA STATE FERRY SCHEDULES

LEAVE BELLINGHAM	LEAVE PRINCE RUPERT	LEAVE STEWART/HYDER	METLAKATLA	KETCHIKAN	HOLLIS	WRANGELL	PETERSBURG	KAKE	ARRIVE SITKA	ANGOON	TENAKEE	HOONAH	JUNEAU/ AUKE BAY	HAINES	ARRIVE SKAGWAY
								Lv. Sitka	S31 11:45A	S31 6:00P	S31 9:15P	SU1 1:30A	SU1 4:45A		
										Lv. Pelican	SU1 3:30P		SU1 10:00P		
F30 6:00P				SU1 9:30A		SU1 4:30P	SU1 8:30P						M2 8:30A	M2 2:30P	M2 3:30P
	S31 3:15P			SU1 12:15A		SU1 10:00A	SU1 2:45P		M2 4:30A				M2 4:45P		
	M2 10:00A			M2 5:00P		M2 11:45P	T3 3:30A						T3 11:15A		
	M2 8:15P			T3 3:30A		T3 12:15P	T3 4:15P						W4 8:00P	TH5 2:00A	TH5 3:00A
							T3 10:15A	T3 3:45P	W4 12:15A	W4 8:45A		W4 1:45P	W4 9:00P		
	W4 9:00A			W4 4:45P		TH5 12:15A	TH5 5:15A		W4 6:15A				TH5 1:15P		
							TH5 1:00P	TH5 6:00P		TH5 11:00P	F6 2:15A	F6 6:30A	F6 9:45A		
	TH5 8:00A			TH5 2:30P		TH5 9:30P	F6 1:30A		F6 3:00P				S7 3:15A		
	F6 8:15P			S7 2:45A		S7 9:30A	S7 1:15P						SU8 12:30A	SU8 6:00A	SU8 7:00A
								Lv. Sitka	S7 12:15P	S7 6:30P	S7 9:45P	SU8 2:00A	SU8 5:15A		
	S7 3:15P			S7 10:15P		SU8 5:15A	SU8 10:15A		SU8 11:30P				M9 6:00P		
F6 6:00P				SU8 9:30A		SU8 4:30P	SU8 8:45P						M9 8:30A	M9 2:30P	M9 3:30P
	M9 8:00A			M9 3:00P		M9 9:45P	T10 1:30A						T10 10:45A	T10 4:15P	T10 5:15P
	M9 10:15P			T10 6:15A		T10 1:00P	T10 5:30A		W11 7:30A				W11 9:00P	TH12 3:00A	TH12 4:00A
							M9 11:55P	T10 5:00A	T10 1:00P	T10 9:30P		W11 2:30A	W11 5:45A		
	W11 10:00A			W11 5:15P		TH12 12:15A	TH12 5:15A						TH12 1:15P		
							TH12 3:45A	TH12 8:45A		TH12 1:45P	TH12 5:00P	TH12 9:15P	F13 12:30A		
	TH12 9:00A			TH12 5:00P		TH12 11:55P	F13 4:15A		F13 3:00P				S14 3:15A		
	F13 9:45P			S14 3:45A		S14 10:45A	S14 2:30P						S14 11:45P	SU15 5:15A	SU15 6:15A
								Lv. Sitka	S14 11:30A	S14 5:45P	S14 9:00P	SU15 1:15A	SU15 4:30A		
	S14 3:15P			SU15 12:15A		SU15 10:00A	SU15 3:00P		M16 4:45A				M16 5:00P		
										Lv. Pelican	SU15 3:30P		SU15 10:00P		
F13 6:00P				SU15 9:30A		SU15 4:30P	SU15 8:30P						M16 10:30A	M16 4:30P	M16 5:30P
	M16 10:00A			M16 7:00P		T17 1:45A	T17 5:30A						T17 1:15P		
	M16 10:00P			T17 7:15A		T17 3:45P	T17 7:30A		W18 6:15A				W18 7:30P	TH19 1:00A	TH19 2:00A
							T17 11:15A	T17 4:15P	W18 12:15A	W18 8:45A		W18 1:45P	W18 9:00P		
	W18 9:00A			W18 4:45P		TH19 12:15A	TH19 5:15A						TH19 1:15P		
							TH19 1:00P	TH19 6:00P		TH19 11:00P	F20 2:15A	F20 6:30A	F20 9:45A		
	TH19 8:00A			TH19 5:00P		TH19 11:55P	F20 4:00A		F20 2:45P				S21 3:00A		
	F20 6:45P			S21 1:15A		S21 8:00A	S21 11:45A						S21 9:00P	SU22 2:30A	SU22 3:30A
								Lv. Sitka	S21 11:45A	S21 6:00P	S21 9:15P	SU22 1:30A	SU22 4:45A		
F20 6:00P	S21 2:45P			S21 10:30P		SU22 5:30A	SU22 10:30A		SU22 10:45P				M23 5:30P		
	M23 9:00A			SU22 9:30A		SU22 6:00P	SU22 10:00P						M23 8:15A	M23 2:00P	M23 3:30P
	M23 9:00P			M23 6:00P		T24 12:45A	T24 4:30A						T24 12:15P		
													W25 5:15A	*TO SE/SW INTER-TIE*	
					T24 6:15A		M23 11:15P	T24 4:15A	T24 12:15P	T24 8:45P		W25 1:45A	W25 5:30A		
	W25 10:00A			W25 5:15P		TH26 12:15A	TH26 5:15A						TH26 1:15P		
							TH26 3:00A	TH26 8:00A		TH26 1:00P	TH26 4:15P	TH26 8:30P	TH26 11:45P		
	TH26 9:00A			TH26 4:30P		TH26 11:30P	F27 3:30A		F27 2:15P				S28 2:30A		
								Lv. Sitka	S28 10:30A	S28 4:45P	S28 8:00P	SU29 12:15A	SU29 3:30A		
	S28 2:15P			SU29 12:15A		SU29 9:00A	SU29 2:00P		M30 3:30A				M30 9:45P		
											Lv. Pelican	SU29 3:30P		SU29 10:00P		
F27 6:00P				SU29 8:15A		SU29 3:00P	SU29 6:45P						M30 4:15A	M30 9:45A	M30 10:45A
	M30 10:00A			M30 6:00P		T31 12:45A	T31 4:30A						T31 12:15P		
	M30 9:00P			T31 6:15A		T31 1:15P	T31 5:15P		W1 5:00A				W1 6:30P	TH2 12:30A	TH2 1:30A
							T31 8:45A	T31 2:15P	T31 10:45P	W1 7:15A		W1 12:15P	W1 3:30P		

SEE M/V AURORA SCHEDULE BELOW (spanning Stewart/Hyder, Metlakatla, Ketchikan columns)

ALL TIMES ARE LOCAL TIMES

M/V MALASPINA
NORTH LYNN CANAL TRIPS

The M/V Malaspina operates on a daily schedule as indicated in the following table. To determine the best connection for your trip, use these schedules. Please allow enough time to make appropriate connections with the sailings listed above. (See tables above)

DAILY SCHEDULE MAY 28 - SEPTEMBER 12, 1999

Leave Juneau	7:00AM
Arrive Haines	11:30AM
Leave Haines	12:30PM
Arrive Skagway	1:30PM
Leave Skagway	3:30PM
Arrive Haines	4:30PM
Leave Haines	5:30PM
Arrive Juneau	10:00PM

M/V KENNICOTT
SOUTHEAST/SOUTHWEST INTER-TIE TRIPS

The M/V Kennicott for the month of August will depart from Juneau as indicated in the following table. To determine the best connection for your trip, use this schedule. Please allow enough time to make appropriate connections with the sailings listed above. (See tables above)

Leave Juneau	Wednesday	AUG 25	5:15AM
Arrive Valdez	Thursday	AUG 26	6:15PM
Leave Valdez	Thursday	AUG 26	9:15PM
Arrive Seward	Friday	AUG 27	7:15AM
Leave Seward	Friday	AUG 27	1:15PM
Arrive Valdez	Friday	AUG 27	11:15PM
Leave Valdez	Saturday	AUG 28	2:15AM
Arrive Juneau	Sunday	AUG 29	2:45PM

Whistle Stop service is provided to Yakutat on inter-tie trips in both directions between Juneau and Valdez. The vessel will stop ONLY if there are vehicle reservations.

▮ Aurora ▮ Columbia ▮ Le Conte ▮ Malaspina ▮ Matanuska ▮ Taku ▮ Kennicott

ALASKA STATE FERRY SCHEDULES

LEAVE SKAGWAY	HAINES	JUNEAU/ AUKE BAY	HOONAH	TENAKEE	ANGOON	ARRIVE SITKA	KAKE	PETERSBURG	WRANGELL	HOLLIS	KETCHIKAN	METLAKATLA	ARRIVE STEWART/HYDER	ARRIVE PRINCE RUPERT	ARRIVE BELLINGHAM
SU1 2:00A	SU1 4:30A	SU1 11:00A						SU1 7:30P	SU1 11:15P		M2 10:15A			M2 5:15P	
		SU1 7:00A	Ar. Pelican	SU1 1:30P											
		M2 12:30A	M2 4:45A	M2 8:45A	M2 11:55A	M2 5:00P	T3 4:30A	T3 8:30A	W4 11:00A		W4 7:30P				
M2 6:30P	M2 9:00P	T3 9:00A				T3 5:30P		W4 7:15A	T3 1:00P		T3 10:30P			W4 6:00A	F6 9:30A
		M2 11:30P						T3 8:45A	W4 8:00A		W4 11:00P			TH5 6:00A	
		T3 11:30P						TH5 11:15P	F6 3:15A		F6 10:15A			F6 5:15P	
TH5 6:00A	TH5 8:30A	TH5 2:30P			TH5 3:15A		TH5 8:15A	TH5 12:15P	F6 5:30P		F6 9:45P				
		W4 6:00P	W4 10:15P			F6 2:45A					S7 4:45A			S7 12:15P	
		TH5 5:00P				S7 4:00A									
		F6 11:30A	F6 3:45P	F6 7:45P	F6 11:00P	S7 4:15A		SU8 8:30A	SU8 12:30P		SU8 11:00P			M9 6:00A	
		S7 6:30A						M9 1:30A	M9 5:15A		M9 12:45P			M9 7:45P	
SU8 9:00A	SU8 11:00A	SU8 5:00P						M9 9:30P							
		SU8 1:30P	SU8 5:45P	SU8 9:45P	M9 1:00A	M9 6:00A	M9 5:30P	T10 10:30A	T10 2:45P		T10 10:30P			W11 6:00A	
		M9 11:30P						W11 11:00A	W11 6:45A		W11 3:00P			TH12 6:00A	
M9 6:00P	M9 8:30P	T10 3:00A			T10 12:30P			W11 11:00A	W11 2:45P		W11 11:00P			F13 6:45P	F13 6:00A
T10 6:15P	T10 8:15P	W11 2:30A						F13 12:15A	F13 4:15A		F13 11:45A				
TH12 6:30A	TH12 9:00A	TH12 3:30P					W11 11:00P	TH12 3:00A							
		W11 8:45A	W11 1:00P		W11 6:00P			F13 5:30P	F13 9:45P		S14 4:45A			S14 12:15P	
		TH12 5:00P				F13 2:45A									
		F13 10:45A	F13 3:00P	F13 7:00P	F13 10:15P	S14 3:15A		SU15 1:30P	SU15 5:30P		M16 1:00A			M16 8:00A	
		S14 12:15P				S14 10:00P		M16 1:45A	M16 5:30A		M16 12:30P			M16 7:30P	
SU15 9:00A	SU15 11:15A	SU15 5:15P													
		SU15 7:00A	Ar. Pelican	SU15 1:30P											
		M16 11:30P						T17 8:45A	T17 1:00P		T17 10:30P			W18 6:00A	
M16 8:30P	M16 11:00A	M16 12:45A	M16 5:00A	M16 9:00A	M16 12:15P	M16 5:15P	T17 4:45A	W18 7:00A	W18 11:00A		W18 7:15P				F20 9:15A
		T17 9:00A				T17 5:15P		W18 10:00A	W18 1:45P		W18 11:00P			TH19 6:00A	
		W18 1:30A						TH19 9:30P	F20 1:15A		F20 8:45A			F20 3:45P	
TH19 5:00A	TH19 7:00A	TH19 1:00P			TH19 3:15A		TH19 8:15A	TH19 12:15P							
		W18 6:00P	W18 10:15P			F20 2:15A		F20 5:00P	F20 9:15P		S21 4:15A			S21 11:45A	
		TH19 4:30P				S21 3:30A									
		F20 10:45A	F20 3:15P	F20 7:15P	F20 10:30P	S21 9:45A		SU22 12:30P	SU22 4:30P		SU22 11:55P			M23 7:00A	
		S21 11:55A						SU22 11:30P	M23 3:15A		M23 11:00A			M23 6:00P	
SU22 6:30A	SU22 8:30A	SU22 3:00P						M23 9:00P							F27 6:00A
		SU22 1:00P	SU22 5:15P	SU22 9:15P	M23 12:30A	M23 5:30A	M23 5:00P	T24 9:15A	T24 1:30P		T24 10:30P			W25 6:00A	
		M23 11:30P						W25 2:45A	W25 6:45A		W25 3:00P			TH26 6:00A	
M23 5:30P	M23 8:00P	T24 3:30P			T24 11:55A			W25 9:45A	W25 1:30P		W25 11:00P				
		T24 11:55P						TH26 2:15A	F27 4:30P	F27 8:45P	S28 3:45A			S28 11:15A	
		W25 8:00A	W25 12:15P		W25 5:15P		W25 10:15P	F27 1:45A							
		TH26 4:00P				F27 1:45A									
		F27 9:45A	F27 2:00P	F27 6:00P	F27 9:15P	S28 2:15A		SU29 12:30P	SU29 4:30P		SU29 11:55P			M30 7:00A	
		S28 11:00A				S28 8:45A					M30 10:45A			M30 5:45P	
		SU29 7:00A	Ar. Pelican	SU29 1:30P										W1 7:00A	
FROM SE/SW INTER-TIE		SU29 4:45P						T31 11:45A	T31 4:00P		T31 11:30P				
		M30 11:30P						T31 7:30A							
		SU29 11:30P	M30 3:45A	M30 7:45A	M30 11:00A	M30 4:00P	T31 3:30A	T31 1:30A	W1 6:15A		W1 2:30P				F3 6:00A
M30 1:15P	M30 4:15P	T31 1:30A				T31 10:00A			W1 2:00A						

ALL TIMES ARE LOCAL TIMES

M/V AURORA - SOUTHERN PANHANDLE SUMMER 1999
EFFECTIVE JUNE 1, 1999 THROUGH SEPTEMBER 14, 1999

SUN Lv Hollis 6:15AM
Ar Ketchikan 9:00AM
Lv Ketchikan 12:15PM
Ar Metlakatla 1:30PM
Lv Metlakatla 2:15PM
Ar Ketchikan 3:30PM
Lv Ketchikan 6:15PM
Ar Hollis 9:00PM

MON Lv Hollis 6:15AM
Ar Ketchikan 9:00AM
Lv Ketchikan 11:00AM
Ar Metlakatla 12:15PM
Lv Metlakatla 2:45PM
Ar Ketchikan 4:00PM
Lv Ketchikan 6:15PM
Ar Hollis 9:00PM

MON Lv Hollis 10:00PM
TUE Ar Ketchikan 12:45AM
Lv Ketchikan 1:45AM
Ar Hyder 12:30PM
Lv Hyder 3:45PM
WED Ar Ketchikan 12:30AM
Lv Ketchikan 1:30AM
Ar Hollis 4:15AM

WED Lv Hollis 6:15AM
Ar Ketchikan 9:00AM
Lv Ketchikan 12:15PM
Ar Metlakatla 1:30PM
Lv Metlakatla 2:15PM
Ar Ketchikan 3:30PM
Lv Ketchikan 6:15PM
Ar Hollis 9:00PM

THU Lv Hollis 9:15AM
Ar Ketchikan 11:55AM
Lv Ketchikan 6:15PM
Ar Hollis 9:00PM

FRI Lv Hollis 6:15AM
Ar Ketchikan 9:00AM
Lv Ketchikan 12:15PM
Ar Metlakatla 1:30PM
Lv Metlakatla 2:15PM
Ar Ketchikan 3:30PM

FRI Lv Ketchikan 6:15PM
Ar Hollis 9:00PM
Lv Hollis 10:00PM
SAT Ar Ketchikan 12:45AM

SAT Lv Ketchikan 6:15AM
Ar Metlakatla 7:30AM
Lv Metlakatla 8:15AM
Ar Ketchikan 9:30AM
Lv Ketchikan 10:30AM
Ar Hollis 1:15PM
Lv Hollis 2:15PM
Ar Ketchikan 5:00PM
Lv Ketchikan 6:45PM
Ar Metlakatla 8:00PM
Lv Metlakatla 8:45PM
Ar Ketchikan 10:00PM
Lv Ketchikan 11:00PM
SUN Ar Hollis 1:45AM

SEPTEMBER 1999 NORTHBOUND – INSIDE PASSAGE/SOUTHEAST ALASKA

ALASKA STATE FERRY SCHEDULES

Columns for STEWART/HYDER, METLAKATLA and HOLLIS all read: **SEE M/V AURORA SCHEDULE BELOW**

Leave Bellingham	Leave Prince Rupert	Ketchikan	Wrangell	Petersburg	Kake	Arrive Sitka	Angoon	Tenakee	Hoonah	Juneau/Auke Bay	Haines	Arrive Skagway
	M30 9:00P	T31 6:15A	T31 1:15P	T31 5:15P		W1 5:00A	W1 7:15A		W1 12:15P	W1 6:30P	TH2 12:30A	TH2 1:30A
				T31 8:45A	T31 2:15P	T31 10:45P				W1 3:30P		
	W1 11:15A	W1 6:00P	TH2 12:45A	TH2 5:30A						TH2 1:30P		
				TH2 11:30A	TH2 4:30P			TH2 9:30P	F3 12:45A			
	TH2 11:55A	TH2 9:45P	F3 4:45A	F3 8:45A		F3 7:30P			F3 5:00A	F3 8:15A		
	F3 7:15P	S4 1:45A	S4 8:30A	S4 12:15P						S4 8:15A		
F3 6:00P										S4 9:30P	SU5 3:45A	SU5 4:45A
						Lv. Sitka S4 5:00P	S4 11:15P	SU5 2:30A	SU5 6:45A	SU5 10:00A		
	S4 1:30P	S4 9:15P	SU5 4:15A	SU5 9:15A		SU5 10:30P				M6		
	M6 9:15A	SU5 8:15A	SU5 3:00P	SU5 6:45A						M6 8:30A	M6 2:30P	M6 3:30P
	M6 9:00P	M6 4:15P	M6 11:00P	T7 2:45A						T7 11:30A		
		T7 5:45A	T7 12:30P	T7 4:15A	T7 8:45A	T7 5:45P	W8 6:15A		W8 7:15A	W8 7:30P	TH9 1:00A	TH9 2:00A
	W8 10:00A	W8 5:00P	W8 11:55P	T7 3:45A			W8 2:15A			W8 10:30A		
	TH9 8:00A	TH9 2:30P	TH9 9:30P	TH9 5:00A	TH9 3:30P			TH9 8:30P	TH9 11:45P	TH9 1:00P		
	F10 8:15P	S11 2:45P	S11 9:30A	TH9 10:30A					F10 4:00A	F10 7:15A	F10 3:45P	F10 4:45P
F10 6:00P				F10 1:30A						F10 10:15A		
				S11 1:15P		S11 10:45A	S11 5:00P	S11 8:15P	SU12 12:30A	S11 10:30P	SU12 4:00A	SU12 5:00A
						Lv. Sitka		Lv. Pelican SU12 3:30P		SU12 3:45A		
	SU12 8:45A	SU12 3:15P	SU12 10:00P	SU12 1:45P						SU12 10:00P		
	S11 5:45P	SU12 1:45A	SU12 8:45A	SU12 6:45P			M13			M13 9:30A		
		SU12 8:00A	SU12 2:45P	M13 1:45A			M13 3:30A			T14 7:00A	T14 1:00P	T14 2:00P
	M13 10:15P	T14 7:30A	T14 2:45P	T14 6:45P						M13 5:45A	M13 11:15A	M13 12:15P
				T14 9:30A	T14 2:30P	W15 4:45A	W15 7:00A	W15 11:55A		W15 6:15P	TH16 12:15A	TH16 1:15A
				TH16 2:15P	TH16 7:15P			F17 3:30A	F17 7:45A	W15 3:15P		
	TH16 9:00A	TH16 3:45P	TH16 10:30P	F17 3:15A			F17 12:15A			F17 11:00A	F17 5:45P	F17 6:45P
	F17 7:30P	S18 2:00A	S18 8:45A	S18 12:30P						F17 12:15P	SU19 3:15P	SU19 4:15P
F17 6:00P						S18 3:45P	S18 10:00P	SU19 1:15A	SU19 5:30A	S18 9:45A		
	SU19 11:00A	SU19 9:00A	SU19 4:30P	SU19 8:30P		Lv. Sitka				SU19 8:45A		
	M20 10:30P	SU19 5:15P	M20 12:15A	M20 5:00A						M20 9:30A	M20 3:30P	M20 4:30P
		T21 7:30A			M20 4:15P					T21 6:00A	T21 11:55A	T21 1:00P
							W22 5:15A			W22 5:15A *TO SE/SW INTER-TIE*		
				T21 2:45A	T21 8:15A	T21 5:00P	W22 1:30A		W22 6:30A	W22 9:45A		
	TH23 9:00A	TH23 5:15P	TH23 11:55P	TH23 9:00A	TH23 2:00P		TH23 7:00P	TH23 10:15P	F24 2:30P	F24 5:45A	F24 7:45P	F24 8:45P
				F24 4:45A						F24 2:15P		
						S25 9:45A	S25 4:00P	S25 7:15P	S25 11:30P	SU26 2:45A		
F24 6:00P						Lv. Pelican		SU26 3:30P		SU26 10:00P	M27 3:15P	M27 4:15P
	SU26 1:15P	SU26 7:30A	SU26 2:00P	SU26 5:45P						M27 9:45A		
	M27 10:30P	SU26 7:30P	M27 2:15A	M27 7:00A		M27 9:00P				T28 10:45A	T28 4:45P	T28 5:45P
		T28 7:45A	T28 2:30P	T28 6:15P		W29 4:15A			W29 5:30P	W29 6:15P	W29 11:45P	TH30 12:45A
				T28 3:00P	T28 8:00P	W29 4:00A	W29 12:30P	F1 2:45A		W29 8:45P		
				TH30 4:45P	TH30 9:45P		F1 6:00A		F1 10:15A	F1 1:30P		

ALL TIMES ARE LOCAL TIMES

M/V MALASPINA NORTH LYNN CANAL TRIPS

The M/V Malaspina operates on a daily schedule as indicated in the following table. To determine the best connection for your trip, use these schedules. Please allow enough time to make appropriate connections with the sailings listed above. (See tables above)

DAILY SCHEDULE MAY 28 – SEPTEMBER 12, 1999

Leave Juneau	7:00AM
Arrive Haines	11:30AM
Leave Haines	12:30PM
Arrive Skagway	1:30PM
Leave Skagway	3:30PM
Arrive Haines	4:30PM
Leave Haines	5:30PM
Arrive Juneau	10:00PM

M/V KENNICOTT **SOUTHEAST/SOUTHWEST INTER-TIE TRIPS**

The M/V Kennicott for the month of September will depart from Juneau as indicated in the following table. To determine the best connection for your trip, use this schedule. Please allow enough time to make appropriate connections with the sailings listed above. (See tables above)

Leave Juneau	Wednesday	SEP 22	5:15AM
Arrive Valdez	Thursday	SEP 23	6:15PM
Leave Valdez	Thursday	SEP 23	9:15PM
Arrive Seward	Friday	SEP 24	7:15AM
Leave Seward	Friday	SEP 24	1:15PM
Arrive Valdez	Friday	SEP 24	11:15PM
Leave Valdez	Saturday	SEP 25	2:15AM
Arrive Juneau	Sunday	SEP 26	2:45PM

Whistle Stop service is provided to Yakutat on inter-tie trips in both directions between Juneau and Valdez. The vessel will stop ONLY if there are vehicle reservations.

Legend: Aurora ■ Columbia ■ Le Conte ■ Malaspina ■ Matanuska ■ Taku ■ Kennicott

SEPTEMBER 1999 SOUTHBOUND - INSIDE PASSAGE/SOUTHEAST ALASKA

Note: The columns **HOLLIS**, **METLAKATLA**, and **ARRIVE STEWART/HYDER** each read vertically: **SEE M/V AURORA SCHEDULE BELOW**.

LEAVE SKAGWAY	HAINES	JUNEAU/AUKE BAY	HOONAH	TENAKEE	ANGOON	ARRIVE SITKA	KAKE	PETERSBURG	WRANGELL	KETCHIKAN	ARRIVE PRINCE RUPERT	ARRIVE BELLINGHAM
M30 1:15P	M30 4:15P	T31 1:30A				T31 10:00A		W1 2:00A	W1 6:15A	W1 2:30P		F3 6:00A
		M30 11:30P						T31 11:45A	T31 4:00P	T31 11:30P	W1 7:00A	
		W1 12:30A						W1 9:00A	W1 12:45P	W1 11:55P	TH2 7:00A	
TH2 4:30A	TH2 7:00A	TH2 1:00P						TH2 9:45P		F3 9:15A	F3 4:15P	
		W1 4:30P	W1 8:45P		TH2 1:45A		TH2 6:45A	TH2 10:45P	F3 1:45A	S4 3:00A	S4 10:30A	
		TH2 3:15P				F3 1:00A		F3 3:45P	F3 8:00P			
		F3 4:00P	F3 8:15P	S4 12:15A	S4 3:30A	S4 8:30A						
		S4 11:15A				S4 9:00P					M6 6:15A	
SU5 7:00A	SU5 9:00A	SU5 3:15P						SU5 11:45A	SU5 3:45P	SU5 11:15P	M6 6:15P	
		SU5 6:30P	SU5 10:45P	M6 2:45A	M6 6:00A	M6 11:00A	M6 11:00P	SU5 11:45P	M6 3:30A	M6 11:15A		
		M6 11:30P						T7 3:00A	T7 1:30P	T7 10:30P		
M6 5:15P	M6 7:45P	T7 2:15A				T7 11:45A		T7 9:15A				
		W8 1:15A						W8 12:45A	W8 5:45A	W8 11:00P	W8 6:00A	
TH9 5:00A	TH9 7:00A	TH9 2:15P						W8 9:45A	W8 1:30P		TH9 6:00A	
		W8 11:30A	W8 7:45P		TH9 12:45A		TH9 5:45A	TH9 11:00P	F10 3:00A	F10 10:30A	F10 5:30A	
		TH9 4:00P				F10 1:45A		TH9 9:45A	F10 4:30P	F10 8:45P		
F10 7:45P	F10 9:45P	F10 4:00P	F10 8:15P	S11 12:15A	S11 3:30A	S11 8:30A		S11 12:15P	S11 4:15P	S11 11:45P	S11 11:15A	F10 6:00A
SU12 8:00A	SU12 10:00A	S11 3:45A						M13 12:45A	M13 4:30A	M13 12:15P	SU12 6:45A	
		SU12 4:15P										
		SU12 7:00A	Ar. Pelican	SU12 1:30P								
		SU12 11:15P	M13 3:30A	M13 7:30A	M13 10:45A	M13 3:45P	T14 3:15A	T14 7:15A			M13 7:15P	
		M13 12:30P				M13 10:15P		T14 12:15P				
T14 5:00P	T14 7:30P	T14 1:45A				T14 10:00A			T14 4:00P	T14 10:00P		
M13 2:15P	M13 4:45P	W15 1:30A						W15 10:30A	W15 2:30P	W15 10:30P		
TH16 4:15A	TH16 6:45A	W15 7:15P	W15 11:30P		TH16 4:30A		TH16 9:30A	W15 1:15A	W15 6:15A	W15 2:30P	TH16 6:00A	F17 6:00A
		TH16 12:45P	F17 7:15P	F17 11:15P	S18 2:30A	S18 7:30A		TH16 9:30P	F17 1:30A	F17 9:00A	F17 4:00P	
F17 9:45P	F17 11:45P	F17 3:00P						TH16 1:30P				
		S18 5:15A						S18 2:15P	S18 6:15P	SU19 1:15A	SU19 8:45A	
SU19 7:15A	SU19 9:45A	SU19 4:15P							M20 4:30A	M20 12:30P	M20 7:30P	
		SU19 6:00P	SU19 10:15P	M20 2:15A	M20 5:30A	M20 10:30A	M20 10:00P	T21 2:00A				
M20 7:30P	M20 10:00P	T21 7:30A						W22 8:30A	W22 12:30P	W22 8:00P		F24 10:00A
T21 4:00P	T21 6:30P	W22 12:30A				T21 5:00P		W22 9:30A	W22 1:30P	W22 10:30P	TH23 6:00A	
		W22 2:00P	W22 6:15P		W22 11:15P	TH23 4:15A	TH23 8:15A					
		F24 3:00P	F24 7:15P	F24 11:15P	S25 2:30A	S25 7:30A						
F24 11:45P	S25 1:45A	S25 7:15A						S25 4:15P	S25 8:15P	SU26 3:15A	SU26 10:45A	
		SU26 7:00A	Ar. Pelican	SU26 1:30P								
FROM SE/SW INTER-TIE		SU26 4:45P								M27 10:45A	M27 5:45P	
M27 7:15P	M27 9:45P	M27 4:30A	M27 8:45P	M27 12:45P	M27 4:00P	M27 9:00P	T28 8:30A	T28 12:30P				F1 7:00A
T28 8:45P	T28 11:15P	T28 5:15A				T28 3:00P		W29 5:15A	W29 9:00A	W29 5:00P		
TH30 2:15A	TH30 4:15A	W29 5:15A						W29 2:15P	W29 6:15P	TH30 1:45A	TH30 9:15A	
		TH30 9:45A	TH30 2:00A		TH30 7:00A	TH30 11:55A		TH30 6:30P	TH30 10:30P	F1 5:30A	F1 12:30P	
		W29 9:45P						TH30 4:00P				

ALL TIMES ARE LOCAL TIMES

M/V AURORA - SOUTHERN PANHANDLE SUMMER 1999
EFFECTIVE JUNE 1, 1999 THROUGH SEPTEMBER 14, 1999

SUN Lv Hollis 6:15AM
Ar Ketchikan 9:00AM
Lv Ketchikan 12:15PM
Ar Metlakatla 1:30PM
Lv Metlakatla 2:15PM
Ar Ketchikan 3:30PM
Lv Ketchikan 6:15PM
Ar Hollis 9:00PM

MON Lv Hollis 6:15AM
Ar Ketchikan 9:00AM
Lv Ketchikan 11:00AM
Ar Metlakatla 12:15PM
Lv Metlakatla 2:45PM
Ar Ketchikan 4:00PM
Lv Ketchikan 6:15PM
Ar Hollis 9:00PM

*MON Lv Hollis 10:00PM
TUE Ar Ketchikan 12:45AM
Lv Ketchikan 1:45AM
Ar Hyder 12:30PM
Lv Hyder 3:45PM
WED Ar Ketchikan 12:30AM
Lv Ketchikan 1:30AM
Ar Hollis 4:15AM

WED Lv Hollis 6:15AM
Ar Ketchikan 9:00AM
Lv Ketchikan 12:15PM
Ar Metlakatla 1:30PM
Lv Metlakatla 2:15PM
Ar Ketchikan 3:30PM
Lv Ketchikan 6:15PM
Ar Hollis 9:00PM

THU Lv Hollis 9:15AM
Ar Ketchikan 11:55AM
Lv Ketchikan 6:15PM
Ar Hollis 9:00PM

FRI Lv Hollis 6:15AM
Ar Ketchikan 9:00AM
Lv Ketchikan 12:15PM
Ar Metlakatla 1:30PM
Lv Metlakatla 2:15PM
Ar Ketchikan 3:30PM

FRI Lv Ketchikan 6:15PM
Ar Hollis 9:00PM
Lv Hollis 10:00PM
SAT Ar Ketchikan 12:45AM

SAT Lv Ketchikan 6:15AM
Ar Metlakatla 7:30AM
Lv Metlakatla 8:15AM
Ar Ketchikan 9:30AM
Lv Ketchikan 10:30AM
Ar Hollis 1:15PM
Lv Hollis 2:15PM
Ar Ketchikan 5:00PM
Lv Ketchikan 6:45PM
Ar Metlakatla 8:00PM
Lv Metlakatla 8:45PM
Ar Ketchikan 10:00PM
Lv Ketchikan 11:00PM
SUN Ar Hollis 1:45AM

SEP 15 THRU SEP 30, 1999

*TUE Lv Hollis 6:15AM
Ar Ketchikan 9:00AM
Lv Ketchikan 6:15PM
Ar Hollis 9:00PM

INSIDE PASSAGE/SOUTHEAST ALASKA PASSENGER & VEHICLE TARIFFS

ALASKA STATE FERRY SCHEDULES

BETWEEN ___ AND ___

ADULT 12 YEARS OR OVER (Meals and Berth NOT included) — ITEM ADT

	BELLINGHAM	PRINCE RUPERT	STEWART/HYDER	KETCHIKAN	METLAKATLA	HOLLIS	WRANGELL	PETERSBURG	KAKE	SITKA	ANGOON	HOONAH	JUNEAU	HAINES	SKAGWAY	PELICAN
KETCHIKAN	164	38	40													
METLAKATLA	168	42	44	14												
HOLLIS	178	52	54	20	22											
WRANGELL	180	56	58	24	28	24										
PETERSBURG	192	68	70	38	42	38	18									
KAKE	202	80	82	48	52	48	34	22								
SITKA	208	86	88	54	58	54	38	26	24							
ANGOON	222	100	102	68	72	68	52	40	28	22						
HOONAH	226	104	106	74	78	74	56	44	38	24	20					
JUNEAU	226	104	106	74	78	74	56	44	44	26	24	20				
HAINES	244	122	124	92	96	92	74	62	62	44	42	38	24			
SKAGWAY	252	130	132	98	102	98	82	70	70	50	48	46	32	17		
PELICAN	248	126	128	96	100	96	78	66	52	40	38	22	32	50	60	
TENAKEE	226	104	106	74	78	74	56	44	44	26	16	16	22	38	46	32

CHILD 2 THROUGH 11 YEARS (Under 2 Transported Free) — ITEM CHD

	BELLINGHAM	PRINCE RUPERT	STEWART/HYDER	KETCHIKAN	METLAKATLA	HOLLIS	WRANGELL	PETERSBURG	KAKE	SITKA	ANGOON	HOONAH	JUNEAU	HAINES	SKAGWAY	PELICAN
KETCHIKAN	82	18	20													
METLAKATLA	84	20	22	8												
HOLLIS	88	26	28	12	14											
WRANGELL	90	28	30	12	14	12										
PETERSBURG	96	34	36	20	22	20	10									
KAKE	102	40	42	24	26	24	18	12								
SITKA	104	42	44	26	28	26	20	14	12							
ANGOON	110	50	52	34	36	34	26	20	14	12						
HOONAH	114	52	54	38	40	38	28	22	20	12	10					
JUNEAU	114	52	54	38	40	38	28	22	22	12	12	10				
HAINES	122	62	64	46	48	46	38	32	32	22	22	20	12			
SKAGWAY	127	65	67	49	51	49	41	35	35	25	23	17	9			
PELICAN	126	64	66	48	50	48	40	34	28	22	20	12	16	26	31	
TENAKEE	114	52	54	38	40	38	28	22	16	12	8	8	12	20	23	16

ALTERNATE MEANS OF CONVEYANCE (Bicycles-Small Boats-Inflatables) — ITEM AMC

	BELLINGHAM	PRINCE RUPERT	STEWART/HYDER	KETCHIKAN	METLAKATLA	HOLLIS	WRANGELL	PETERSBURG	KAKE	SITKA	ANGOON	HOONAH	JUNEAU	HAINES	SKAGWAY	PELICAN
KETCHIKAN	28	10	11													
METLAKATLA	29	11	12	7												
HOLLIS	30	12	13	8	9											
WRANGELL	31	13	14	9	10	9										
PETERSBURG	32	14	15	11	12	11	8									
KAKE	34	16	17	12	13	12	10	8								
SITKA	35	17	18	13	14	13	11	9	8							
ANGOON	37	19	20	15	16	15	13	11	9	7						
HOONAH	38	20	21	16	17	16	14	12	11	8	8					
JUNEAU	38	20	21	16	17	16	14	12	12	9	9	8				
HAINES	41	24	25	20	21	20	18	16	16	12	12	10				
SKAGWAY	42	25	26	21	22	21	19	17	17	14	13	11	8			
PELICAN	41	23	24	19	20	19	17	15	13	11	10	8	10	14	15	
TENAKEE	38	20	21	16	17	16	14	12	10	8	7	7	9	12	13	10

TWO WHEELED MOTORCYCLES (No Trailers - Driver NOT included) — ITEM 705

	BELLINGHAM	PRINCE RUPERT	STEWART/HYDER	KETCHIKAN	METLAKATLA	HOLLIS	WRANGELL	PETERSBURG	KAKE	SITKA	ANGOON	HOONAH	JUNEAU	HAINES	SKAGWAY	PELICAN
KETCHIKAN	133	28	31													
METLAKATLA	140	32	35	8												
HOLLIS	146	40	44	16	17											
WRANGELL	150	45	47	20	23	20										
PETERSBURG	160	54	58	30	33	30	14									
KAKE	169	66	68	40	44	40	26	17								
SITKA	174	70	72	45	48	45	30	20	18							
ANGOON	186	82	84	56	60	56	43	32	22	16						
HOONAH	191	86	89	61	64	61	46	36	30	18	15					
JUNEAU	191	86	89	61	64	61	46	36	36	20	18	15				
HAINES	208	102	104	76	80	76	62	51	51	35	34	30	19			
SKAGWAY	213	109	110	82	86	82	67	58	58	41	40	36	25	10		
PELICAN	210	106	107	79	83	79	64	53	41	32	30	17	26	42	49	
TENAKEE	191	86	89	61	64	61	46	36	25	17	13	13	17	32	37	26

All motorcycles must be fully secured on the car deck with tie-downs. It is the responsibility of the owner to ensure this is completed properly. Rope may be obtained from car deck personnel for lashing purposes.

VEHICLES UP TO 10 FEET (Driver NOT Included) — ITEM 710

	BELLINGHAM	PRINCE RUPERT	STEWART/HYDER	KETCHIKAN	METLAKATLA	HOLLIS	WRANGELL	PETERSBURG	KAKE	SITKA	ANGOON	HOONAH	JUNEAU	HAINES	SKAGWAY	PELICAN
KETCHIKAN	218	45	50													
METLAKATLA	223	53	56	14												
HOLLIS	238	66	71	26	29											
WRANGELL	243	73	76	31	38	31										
PETERSBURG	259	89	94	49	54	49	23									
KAKE	275	105	110	65	71	65	43	28								
SITKA	284	114	118	73	79	73	49	33	30							
ANGOON	303	133	136	91	98	91	69	53	36	26						
HOONAH	310	140	144	99	105	99	75	59	49	30	25					
JUNEAU	310	140	144	99	105	99	75	59	59	33	30	24				
HAINES	336	166	169	124	130	124	100	82	82	57	55	49	31			
SKAGWAY	346	176	178	133	139	133	109	93	93	67	64	59	41	18		
PELICAN	341	171	174	129	134	129	104	86	68	53	49	29	43	69	79	
TENAKEE	310	140	144	99	105	99	75	59	41	28	20	20	28	51	61	43

VEHICLES UP TO 15 FEET (Driver NOT Included) — ITEM 715

	BELLINGHAM	PRINCE RUPERT	STEWART/HYDER	KETCHIKAN	METLAKATLA	HOLLIS	WRANGELL	PETERSBURG	KAKE	SITKA	ANGOON	HOONAH	JUNEAU	HAINES	SKAGWAY
KETCHIKAN	374	75	83												
METLAKATLA	372	84	95	21											
HOLLIS	394	107	119	41	46										
WRANGELL	405	117	129	51	61	51									
PETERSBURG	433	145	158	80	90	80	35								
KAKE	460	174	187	109	119	109	70	44							
SITKA	473	187	200	122	132	122	80	52	49						
ANGOON	505	220	233	155	164	155	116	86	60	41					
HOONAH	534	240	246	168	177	168	126	98	82	49	39				
JUNEAU	534	240	246	168	177	168	126	98	98	52	47	38			
HAINES	578	283	288	210	220	210	168	139	139	95	90	81	49		
SKAGWAY	594	299	304	226	237	226	185	156	156	112	107	98	66	26	
PELICAN	570	285	298	220	228	220	176	147	114	86	80	47	70	114	132
TENAKEE	(Unable to off-load vehicles longer than ten feet)														

VEHICLES UP TO 19 FEET (Driver NOT Included) — ITEM 719

	BELLINGHAM	PRINCE RUPERT	STEWART/HYDER	KETCHIKAN	METLAKATLA	HOLLIS	WRANGELL	PETERSBURG	KAKE	SITKA	ANGOON	HOONAH	JUNEAU	HAINES	SKAGWAY
KETCHIKAN	445	90	99												
METLAKATLA	443	100	113	25											
HOLLIS	470	128	141	49	55										
WRANGELL	482	139	153	61	73	61									
PETERSBURG	515	172	188	95	107	95	42								
KAKE	548	207	223	130	141	130	83	52							
SITKA	563	223	238	145	157	145	96	63	58						
ANGOON	602	261	277	184	196	184	138	103	71	49					
HOONAH	636	285	292	200	211	200	150	117	97	58	47				
JUNEAU	636	285	292	200	211	200	150	117	117	62	56	45			
HAINES	687	336	342	249	261	249	199	165	165	112	106	95	57		
SKAGWAY	707	356	362	269	282	269	220	186	186	132	127	116	78	31	
PELICAN	679	339	354	261	271	261	213	175	136	103	95	56	83	135	156
TENAKEE	(Unable to off-load vehicles longer than ten feet)														

VEHICLES UP TO 21 FEET (Driver NOT Included) — ITEM 721

	BELLINGHAM	PRINCE RUPERT	STEWART/HYDER	KETCHIKAN	METLAKATLA	HOLLIS	WRANGELL	PETERSBURG	KAKE	SITKA	ANGOON	HOONAH	JUNEAU	HAINES	SKAGWAY
KETCHIKAN	557	112	127												
METLAKATLA	572	129	145	31											
HOLLIS	606	164	182	62	70										
WRANGELL	622	179	197	78	93	78									
PETERSBURG	665	222	242	122	137	122	53								
KAKE	707	267	287	167	182	167	107	67							
SITKA	727	287	307	187	202	187	123	80	74						
ANGOON	777	337	357	237	252	237	177	132	91	63					
HOONAH	821	368	377	257	272	257	193	150	125	74	60				
JUNEAU	821	368	377	257	272	257	193	150	150	79	72	57			
HAINES	887	434	442	322	337	322	257	213	213	145	137	123	74		
SKAGWAY	913	460	467	347	364	347	284	240	240	171	164	150	101	39	
PELICAN	877	437	457	337	350	337	270	225	175	132	122	71	107	174	202
TENAKEE	(Unable to off-load vehicles longer than ten feet)														

TARIFFS — All fares are one-way. Fares for passengers, vehicles and staterooms are all calculated separately and must be added together to determine the total cost of your travel.

Passage and vehicle fares are charged from the port of embarkation to the port of debarkation. Stateroom fares are calculated according to the route taken, and may vary from the printed rates depending on the ship and schedules.

PETS - Dogs, cats, and other household pets are charged $25 to/from Bellingham, and $10 to/from Prince Rupert and Stewart/Hyder. There is no charge for a certified service animal traveling with a disabled person.

VEHICLE FARES — Vehicle fares are determined by the vehicle's overall length and width. Vehicles 8-1/2 to 9 feet wide will be charged approximately 125% of the listed fare. Vehicles over 9 feet wide will be charged approximately 150% of the listed fare. If you are towing a vehicle, the overall connected length is used to determine fares.

VEHICLES OVER 21 FEET — Contact any Marine Highway office for fares. Vessels in Southeast Alaska can load vehicles up to 70 feet long with special arrangements. Fares for towed vehicles or trailers are calculated at their combined connected length. Vehicles may not be disconnected for travel at separate rates on the same sailing.

MINIMUM 25' RATE — Vehicles with high centers of gravity (commercial highway vans, loaded flat bed trailers) are charged at the 25 ft. rate unless the vehicle is over 25 ft.in which case the appropriate rate for the vehicle length applies. Contact the commerical booking desk (907) 465-8816 for information and reservations.

ALL TARIFFS AND RATES ARE QUOTED IN U.S. DOLLARS

INSIDE PASSAGE/SOUTHEAST ALASKA CABIN TARIFFS

FOUR BERTH CABIN/SITTING ROOM - OUTSIDE/COMPLETE FACILITIES — ITEM 4BS
M/V COLUMBIA - M/V MALASPINA

BETWEEN / AND	BELLINGHAM	PRINCE RUPERT	KETCHIKAN	HOLLIS	WRANGELL	PETERSBURG	KAKE	SITKA	JUNEAU	HAINES
KETCHIKAN	272	63		N			N			
WRANGELL	300	89	58	O			O			
PETERSBURG	318	103	71		47					
SITKA	351	128	91	S	71	60	S			
JUNEAU	371	145	107	T	91	78	T	54		
HAINES	405	177	142	O	121	110	O	87	64	
SKAGWAY	405	177	142	P	121	110	P	87	64	39

FOUR BERTH CABIN - OUTSIDE/COMPLETE FACILITIES — ITEM 4BF
M/V COLUMBIA - M/V MALASPINA - M/V MATANUSKA - M/V TAKU - M/V KENNICOTT

BETWEEN / AND	BELLINGHAM	PRINCE RUPERT	KETCHIKAN	HOLLIS	WRANGELL	PETERSBURG	KAKE	SITKA	JUNEAU	HAINES
KETCHIKAN	248	58								
HOLLIS	266	71	48							
WRANGELL	274	80	53	50						
PETERSBURG	289	92	65	65	41					
KAKE	304	104	75	65	53	48				
SITKA	319	114	84	74	64	53	50			
JUNEAU	337	128	100	90	80	69	63	48		
HAINES	373	163	132	121	111	101	88	78	56	
SKAGWAY	373	163	132	121	111	101	88	78	56	44

FOUR BERTH CABIN - INSIDE/COMPLETE FACILITIES — ITEM 4BI
M/V COLUMBIA - M/V MALASPINA - M/V MATANUSKA - M/V TAKU - M/V KENNICOTT

BETWEEN / AND	BELLINGHAM	PRINCE RUPERT	KETCHIKAN	HOLLIS	WRANGELL	PETERSBURG	KAKE	SITKA	JUNEAU	HAINES
KETCHIKAN	210	50								
HOLLIS	229	57	42							
WRANGELL	233	69	48	43						
PETERSBURG	250	80	57	49	39					
KAKE	262	90	64	56	46	40				
SITKA	275	100	75	64	56	48	42			
JUNEAU	292	112	88	78	69	60	55	42		
HAINES	321	141	116	106	98	89	79	69	49	
SKAGWAY	321	141	116	106	98	89	79	69	49	39

TWO BERTH CABIN - OUTSIDE/NO FACILITIES — ITEM 2NO
M/V KENNICOTT

BETWEEN / AND	BELLINGHAM	PRINCE RUPERT	KETCHIKAN	HOLLIS	WRANGELL	PETERSBURG	KAKE	SITKA	JUNEAU	HAINES
KETCHIKAN	142	33		N			N			
WRANGELL	157	46	30	O			O			
PETERSBURG	165	53	37		23					
SITKA	182	65	48	S	37	31	S			
JUNEAU	193	73	57	T	46	39	T	27		
HAINES	213	93	75	O	63	57	O	44	31	
SKAGWAY	213	93	75	P	63	57	P	44	31	25

TWO BERTH - INSIDE/NO FACILITIES — ITEM 2NI
M/V KENNICOTT

BETWEEN / AND	BELLINGHAM	PRINCE RUPERT	KETCHIKAN	HOLLIS	WRANGELL	PETERSBURG	KAKE	SITKA	JUNEAU	HAINES
KETCHIKAN	128	30		N			N			
WRANGELL	141	41	27	O			O			
PETERSBURG	149	47	33		21					
SITKA	164	59	43	S	37	28	S			
JUNEAU	173	66	51	T	41	35	T	25		
HAINES	192	84	68	O	57	52	O	40	29	
SKAGWAY	192	84	68	P	57	52	P	40	29	23

THREE BERTH CABIN - OUTSIDE/COMPLETE FACILITIES — ITEM 3BF
M/V COLUMBIA - M/V MATANUSKA

BETWEEN / AND	BELLINGHAM	PRINCE RUPERT	KETCHIKAN	HOLLIS	WRANGELL	PETERSBURG	KAKE	SITKA	JUNEAU	HAINES
KETCHIKAN	202	45		N			N			
WRANGELL	222	63	44	O			O			
PETERSBURG	232	72	52		35					
SITKA	254	90	67	S	52	45	S			
JUNEAU	271	102	77	T	62	55	T	40		
HAINES	304	129	101	O	84	77	O	63	47	
SKAGWAY	304	129	101	P	84	77	P	63	47	38

TWO BERTH - OUTSIDE/COMPLETE FACILITIES — ITEM 2BF
M/V COLUMBIA - M/V MALASPINA - M/V MATANUSKA - M/V TAKU - M/V KENNICOTT

BETWEEN / AND	BELLINGHAM	PRINCE RUPERT	KETCHIKAN	HOLLIS	WRANGELL	PETERSBURG	KAKE	SITKA	JUNEAU	HAINES
KETCHIKAN	177	43								
HOLLIS	188	50	35							
WRANGELL	193	58	37	36						
PETERSBURG	204	67	46	44	33					
KAKE	216	76	54	46	40	34				
SITKA	227	84	61	58	47	40	36			
JUNEAU	243	97	72	70	58	50	45	37		
HAINES	271	121	92	90	77	70	68	56	42	
SKAGWAY	271	121	92	90	77	70	68	56	42	33

TWO BERTH CABIN - INSIDE/COMPLETE FACILITIES — ITEM 2BI
M/V COLUMBIA - M/V MALASPINA - M/V MATANUSKA - M/V TAKU

BETWEEN / AND	BELLINGHAM	PRINCE RUPERT	KETCHIKAN	HOLLIS	WRANGELL	PETERSBURG	KAKE	SITKA	JUNEAU	HAINES
KETCHIKAN	156	38								
HOLLIS	164	44	27							
WRANGELL	174	53	34	28						
PETERSBURG	180	61	41	36	29					
KAKE	189	68	48	42	36	30				
SITKA	199	74	53	47	41	35	32			
JUNEAU	211	83	63	60	51	44	40	33		
HAINES	234	105	83	80	70	64	63	51	38	
SKAGWAY	234	105	83	80	70	64	63	51	38	31

TWO BERTH ROOMETTE - OUTSIDE/NO FACILITIES/*NO LINEN — ITEM 2RO
M/V KENNICOTT

BETWEEN / AND	BELLINGHAM	PRINCE RUPERT	KETCHIKAN	HOLLIS	WRANGELL	PETERSBURG	KAKE	SITKA	JUNEAU	HAINES
KETCHIKAN	85	20		N			N			
WRANGELL	94	27	18	O			O			
PETERSBURG	99	32	22		14					
SITKA	109	39	29	S	22	19	S			
JUNEAU	116	44	34	T	27	24	T	16		
HAINES	128	56	45	O	38	35	O	27	19	
SKAGWAY	128	56	45	P	38	35	P	27	19	15

TWO BERTH ROOMETTE - INSIDE/NO FACILITIES/*NO LINEN — ITEM 2RI
M/V KENNICOTT

BETWEEN / AND	BELLINGHAM	PRINCE RUPERT	KETCHIKAN	HOLLIS	WRANGELL	PETERSBURG	KAKE	SITKA	JUNEAU	HAINES
KETCHIKAN	71	17		N			N			
WRANGELL	78	23	15	O			O			
PETERSBURG	83	26	19		12					
SITKA	91	33	24	S	18	16	S			
JUNEAU	96	37	29	T	23	20	T	14		
HAINES	106	46	38	O	32	29	O	22	16	
SKAGWAY	106	46	38	P	32	29	P	22	16	13

SOUTHEAST/SOUTHWEST INTER-TIE TARIFFS

	BELLINGHAM VALDEZ	KETCHIKAN VALDEZ	JUNEAU VALDEZ
Passengers (12 yrs & older)	328	164	90
Child (2 yrs through 11 yrs)	164	82	44
AMC (Bicycles-Kayaks-Inflatables)	56	28	12
2 Wheeled Motorcycles	266	133	72
Vehicles up to 10 feet	436	218	119
Vehicles up to 15 feet	748	374	206
Vehicles up to 19 feet	890	445	245
Vehicles up to 21 feet	1114	557	300
Vehicles up to 23 feet	1396	698	376
Vehicles up to 25 feet	1658	829	447
CABINS			
4 Berth - Outside/complete facilities	496	248	148
4 Berth -Inside/complete facilities	420	210	122
2 Berth Outside/no facilities	283	142	85
2 Berth - Inside/no facilities	255	128	76
2 Berth Roomette - Outside/no facilities*	170	85	51
2 Berth Roomette - Inside/no facilities*	142	71	42

*No linen - Linen may be rented separately.

	BELLINGHAM YAKUTAT	KETCHIKAN YAKUTAT	JUNEAU YAKUTAT
Passengers (12 yrs & older)	292	128	54
Child (2 yrs through 11 yrs)	146	64	26
AMC (Bicycles-Kayaks-Inflatables)	51	23	7
2 Wheeled Motorcycles	237	104	43
Vehicles up to 10 feet	388	170	71
Vehicles up to 15 feet	666	292	124
Vehicles up to 19 feet	792	347	147
Vehicles up to 21 feet	994	437	180
Vehicles up to 23 feet	1246	548	226
Vehicles up to 25 feet	1479	650	268
CABINS			
4 Berth - Outside/complete facilities	456	189	89
4 Berth -Inside/complete facilities	365	161	73
2 Berth Outside/no facilities	244	108	51
2 Berth - Inside/no facilities	219	97	46
2 Berth Roomette - Outside/no facilities*	147	65	31
2 Berth Roomette - Inside/no facilities*	121	54	25

*No linen - Linen may be rented separately.

	BELLINGHAM SEWARD	KETCHIKAN SEWARD	JUNEAU SEWARD
Passengers (12 yrs & older)	386	222	148
Child (2 yrs through 11 yrs)	194	112	74
AMC (Bicycles-Kayaks-Inflatables)	66	38	22
2 Wheeled Motorcycles	306	173	112
Vehicles up to 10 feet	504	286	187
Vehicles up to 15 feet	860	486	318
Vehcles up to 19 feet	1024	579	379
Vehicles up to 21 feet	1286	729	472
Vehicles up to 23 feet	1612	914	592
Vehicles up to 25 feet	1914	1085	703
CABINS			
4 Berth - Outside/complete facilities	587	339	239
4 Berth -Inside/complete facilities	496	286	198
2 Berth Outside/no facilities	337	196	139
2 Berth - Inside/no facilities	304	176	125
2 Berth Roomette - Outside/no facilities*	202	117	83
2 Berth Roomette - Inside/no facilities*	169	98	69

*No linen - Linen may be rented separately.

M/V TUSTUMENA CABIN TARIFFS

FOUR BERTH CABIN - OUTSIDE/COMPLETE FACILITIES — ITEM 4BF

BETWEEN AND	UNALASKA	AKUTAN	FALSE PASS	COLD BAY	KING COVE	SAND POINT	CHIGNIK	KODIAK	PORT LIONS	SELDOVIA	HOMER	SEWARD
AKUTAN	23											
FALSE PASS	80	57										
COLD BAY	109	86	29									
KING COVE	122	129	72	43								
SAND POINT	152	165	108	79	68							
CHIGNIK	194	210	153	124	113	80						
KODIAK	282	295	238	209	194	166	124					
PORT LIONS	282	295	238	209	194	166	124	43				
SELDOVIA	337	350	293	264	250	216	182	96	96			
HOMER	328	342	285	256	242	209	175	88	88	43		
SEWARD	349	362	305	276	262	228	194	98	98	163	155	
VALDEZ	(NO DIRECT SAILINGS)							164	164	216	209	91

FOUR BERTH CABIN - INSIDE/NO FACILITIES — ITEM 4NO

	UNALASKA	AKUTAN	FALSE PASS	COLD BAY	KING COVE	SAND POINT	CHIGNIK	KODIAK	PORT LIONS	SELDOVIA	HOMER	SEWARD
AKUTAN	19											
FALSE PASS	66	47										
COLD BAY	91	72	25									
KING COVE	102	108	61	36								
SAND POINT	127	138	91	66	57							
CHIGNIK	162	175	128	103	94	67						
KODIAK	235	246	199	174	162	138	103					
PORT LIONS	235	246	199	174	162	138	103	36				
SELDOVIA	281	292	245	220	208	180	152	80	80			
HOMER	274	285	238	213	202	174	146	73	73	36		
SEWARD	291	302	255	230	218	190	162	82	82	136	129	
VALDEZ	(NO DIRECT SAILINGS)							137	137	180	174	76

TWO BERTH CABIN - OUTSIDE/NO FACILITIES — ITEM 2NO

	UNALASKA	AKUTAN	FALSE PASS	COLD BAY	KING COVE	SAND POINT	CHIGNIK	KODIAK	PORT LIONS	SELDOVIA	HOMER	SEWARD
AKUTAN	13											
FALSE PASS	47	33										
COLD BAY	64	51	17									
KING COVE	75	79	45	28								
SAND POINT	100	97	63	46	40							
CHIGNIK	129	129	95	78	68	43						
KODIAK	179	192	158	141	130	110	76					
PORT LIONS	179	192	158	141	130	110	76	28				
SELDOVIA	213	226	192	175	164	140	115	56	56			
HOMER	208	221	187	170	159	136	111	52	52	28		
SEWARD	218	230	196	179	168	144	119	60	60	101	96	
VALDEZ	(NO DIRECT SAILINGS)							103	103	144	140	54

M/V TUSTUMENA ALEUTIAN CHAIN TRIPS

LV KODIAK	WED	4:55 PM		LV UNALASKA	SAT	11:45 AM
LV CHIGNIK	THU	1:00 PM		LV AKUTAN	SAT	4:00 PM
LV SAND POINT	FRI	12:30 AM		LV COLD BAY	SUN	4:45 AM
LV KING COVE	FRI	9:00 AM		LV KING COVE	SUN	7:15 AM
LV COLD BAY	FRI	11:55 AM		LV SAND POINT	SUN	3:00 PM
LV FALSE PASS	FRI	5:30 PM		LV CHIGNIK	MON	1:45 AM
AR UNALASKA	SAT	6:30 AM		AR KODIAK	MON	8:15 PM

REFER TO COLOR CODED BARS ON M/V TUSTUMENA SCHEDULE BEGINNING AND ENDING AT KODIAK

M/V BARTLETT / AK RAILROAD SCHEDULE
Effective May 1, 1999

The M/V BARTLETT serves the port of Whittier using the Alaska Railroad shuttle between Portage and Whittier. In Portage, passengers and their vehicles load on an Alaska Railroad flatcar for a 40 minute sight-filled trip through mountain tunnels to Whittier, a former military town. Ferry service from Whittier is available to Cordova and Valdez.

PORTAGE TO WHITTIER*

LV	PORTAGE	10:15 AM
AR	WHITTIER	10:55 AM
LV	PORTAGE	1:20 PM
AR	WHITTIER	2:00 PM

WHITTIER TO PORTAGE

LV	WHITTIER	3:30 PM
AR	PORTAGE	4:10 PM
LV	WHITTIER	6:15 PM
AR	PORTAGE	6:55 PM

*Check-in time in Portage is one hour earlier than departure.

THE STATE OF ALASKA RESERVES THE RIGHT TO ALTER, REVISE OR CANCEL SCHEDULES AND RATES WITHOUT PRIOR NOTICE AND ASSUMES NO RESPONSIBILITY FOR DELAYS AND/OR EXPENSES DUE TO SUCH MODIFICATIONS.

SOUTHCENTRAL/SOUTHWEST ALASKA - M/V BARTLETT SCHEDULE

EFFECTIVE MAY 1 — MAY 27, 1999 AND AUGUST 29 — SEPTEMBER 14, 1999

MON	LV CORDOVA	7:00 AM		FRI	LV VALDEZ	12:15 AM	
	AR WHITTIER	2:00 PM			AR CORDOVA	6:00 AM	
	LV WHITTIER	2:45 PM			LV CORDOVA	7:00 AM	
	AR CORDOVA	9:45 PM			AR WHITTIER	2:00 PM	
					LV WHITTIER	2:45 PM	
TUE	LV CORDOVA	12:30 AM			AR CORDOVA	9:45PM	
	AR VALDEZ	6:15 AM					
	LV VALDEZ	7:15 AM		*SAT	LV CORDOVA	12:30 AM	
	AR WHITTIER	2:00 PM			AR VALDEZ	6:15 AM	
	LV WHITTIER	2:45 PM			LV VALDEZ	7:15 AM	
	AR VALDEZ	9:30 PM			AR WHITTIER	2:00 PM	
					LV WHITTIER	2:45 PM	
WED	LV VALDEZ	6:45 AM **			AR VALDEZ	9:30 PM	
	AR CORDOVA	2:30 PM					
	LV CORDOVA	6:30 PM **		SUN	LV VALDEZ	7:15 AM	
THU	AR VALDEZ	2:15 AM			AR WHITTIER	2:00 PM	
					LV WHITTIER	2:45 PM	
THU	LV VALDEZ	7:15 AM			AR VALDEZ	9:30 PM	
	AR WHITTIER	2:00 PM			LV VALDEZ	11:45 PM ###	
	LV WHITTIER	2:45 PM		MON	AR CORDOVA	5:30 AM	
	AR VALDEZ	9:30 PM					

EFFECTIVE MAY 27, 1999 — AUGUST 29, 1999

MON	LV VALDEZ	7:15 AM		THU	LV VALDEZ	7:15 AM	
	AR WHITTIER	2:00 PM			AR WHITTIER	2:00 PM	
	LV WHITTIER	2:45 PM			LV WHITTIER	2:45 PM +++	
	AR CORDOVA	9:45 PM			AR VALDEZ	9:30 PM	
MON	LV CORDOVA	10:45 PM **		FRI	LV VALDEZ	5:00 AM **	
TUE	AR VALDEZ	6:15 AM			AR CORDOVA	12:45 PM	
	LV VALDEZ	7:15 AM			LV CORDOVA	6:30 PM	
	AR WHITTIER	2:00 PM		SAT	AR VALDEZ	12:15 AM	
TUE	LV WHITTIER	2:45 PM		SAT	LV VALDEZ	7:15 AM	
	AR VALDEZ	9:30 PM			AR WHITTIER	2:00 PM	
	LV VALDEZ	11:45 PM			LV WHITTIER	2:45 PM	
WED	AR CORDOVA	5:30 AM			AR VALDEZ	9:30 PM	
WED	LV CORDOVA	7:00 AM		SUN	LV VALDEZ	7:15 AM	
	AR WHITTIER	2:00 PM			AR WHITTIER	2:00 PM	
	LV WHITTIER	2:45 PM			LV WHITTIER	2:45 PM	
	AR VALDEZ	9:30PM			AR VALDEZ	9:30 PM	

* Schedule begins here May 1, 1999.
** Tatitlek Whistle Stops available by notifying Valdez or Cordova Terminal
+++ Switch to this schedule at Whittier, Thursday May 27.
Switch to this schedule at Valdez, Sunday August 29.

SOUTHCENTRAL/SOUTHWEST ALASKA M/V TUSTUMENA

MAY EASTBOUND

Leave SELDOVIA	Leave HOMER	PORT LIONS	Arrive KODIAK	Leave SEWARD	Arrive VALDEZ
SU2 6:00A	SU2 9:30A		SU2 7:00P		
	M3 9:30A		M3 7:00P		
T4 4:00P	T4 7:55P	W5 6:30A	Lv. W5 4:00P		Ar. TH6 5:15A
SU9 6:00A	SU9 9:30		SU9 7:00P		
	M10 9:30A		M10 7:00P		
T11 4:00P	T11 11:30P		W12 9:00A		
FROM ALEUTIAN CHAIN TRIP			M17 8:15P		
T18 4:00P	T18 7:55P	W19 6:30A	Lv. W19 4:00P	TH20 9:45A	TH20 11:00P
SU23 6:00A	SU23 9:30A		SU23 7:00P		
	M24 9:30A		M24 7:00P		
*T25 4:00P	W26 12:30A		Lv. W26 4:00P	TH27 9:45A	TH27 11:00P
SU30 6:00A	SU30 9:30A		SU30 7:00P		
	M31 9:30A		M31 7:00P		

* Kodiak King Crab Festival May 25 - 31

JUNE EASTBOUND

Leave SELDOVIA	Leave HOMER	PORT LIONS	Arrive KODIAK	Leave SEWARD	Arrive VALDEZ
T1 5:00P	T1 7:55P	W2 6:30A	Lv. W2 4:00P	TH3 9:45A	TH3 11:00P
SU6 6:00A	SU6 9:30A		SU6 7:00P		
	M7 9:30A		M7 7:00P		
T8 4:00P	T8 11:30P		W9 9:00A		
FROM ALEUTIAN CHAIN TRIP			M14 8:15P		
T15 4:00P	T15 7:55P	W16 6:30A	Lv. W16 4:00P	TH17 9:45A	TH17 11:00P
SU20 6:00A	SU20 9:30A		SU20 7:00P		
	M21 9:30A		M21 7:00P		
T22 4:00P	T22 7:55P	W23 6:30A	Lv. W23 4:00P	TH24 9:45A	TH24 11:00P
SU27 6:00A	SU27 9:30A		SU27 7:00P		
	M28 9:30A		M28 7:00P		
T29 4:00P	T29 7:55P	W30 6:30A	Lv. W30 4:00P	TH1 9:45A	TH1 11:00P

JULY EASTBOUND

Leave SELDOVIA	Leave HOMER	PORT LIONS	Arrive KODIAK	Leave SEWARD	Arrive VALDEZ
SU4 6:00A	SU4 9:30A		SU4 7:00P		
	M5 9:30A		M5 7:00P		
T6 4:00P	T6 7:55P	W7 6:30A	Lv. W7 4:00P	TH8 9:45A	TH8 11:00P
SU11 6:00A	SU11 9:30A		SU11 7:00P		
	M12 9:30A		M12 7:00P		
T13 4:00P	T13 11:30P		W14 9:00A		
FROM ALEUTIAN CHAIN TRIP			M19 8:15P		
T20 4:00P	T20 7:55P	W21 6:30A	Lv. W21 4:00P	TH22 9:45A	TH22 11:00P
SU25 6:00A	SU25 9:30A		SU25 7:00P		
	M26 9:30A		M26 7:00P		
T27 4:00P	T27 7:55P	W28 6:30A	Lv. W28 4:00P	TH29 9:45A	TH29 11:00P

AUGUST EASTBOUND

Leave SELDOVIA	Leave HOMER	PORT LIONS	Arrive KODIAK	Leave SEWARD	Arrive VALDEZ
SU1 6:00A	SU1 9:30A		SU1 7:00P		
	M2 9:30A		M2 7:00P		
T3 4:00P	T3 7:55P	W4 6:30A	Lv. W4 4:00P	TH5 9:45A	TH5 11:00P
SU8 6:00A	SU8 9:30A		SU8 7:00P		
	M9 9:30A		M9 7:00P		
T10 4:00P	T10 11:30P		W11 9:00A		
FROM ALEUTIAN CHAIN TRIP			M16 8:15P		
T17 4:00P	T17 7:55P	W18 6:30A	Lv. W18 4:00P	TH19 9:45A	TH19 11:00P
SU22 6:00A	SU22 9:30A		SU22 7:00P		
	M23 9:30A		M23 7:00P		
T24 4:00P	T24 7:55P	W25 6:30A	Lv. W25 4:00P	TH26 9:45A	TH26 11:00P
SU29 6:00A	SU29 9:30A		SU29 7:00P		
	M30 9:30A		M30 7:00P		

SEPTEMBER EASTBOUND

Leave SELDOVIA	Leave HOMER	PORT LIONS	Arrive KODIAK	Leave SEWARD	Leave CORDOVA	Arrive VALDEZ
T31 4:00P	T31 7:55P	Lv. W1 6:30A	Lv. W1 4:00P	TH2 9:45A		TH2 11:00P
SU5 6:00A	SU5 9:30A		SU5 7:00P			
	M6 9:30A		M6 7:00P			
T7 4:00P	T7 11:30P		W8 9:00A			
FROM ALEUTIAN CHAIN TRIP			M13 8:15P			
T14 4:00P	T14 7:55P	W15 6:30A	Lv. W15 4:00P	TH16 9:45A		*TH16 11:00P
				S18 9:55P	SU19 3:30A	
T21 1:00P	T21 7:55P	W22 6:30A	Lv. W22 4:55P	TH23 11:15A	TH23 11:45P	*F24 7:30A
				S25 9:55P	S26 3:30A	
T28 1:00P	T28 7:55P	W29 6:30A	Lv. W29 4:55P	TH30 11:45A	F1 1:15A	*F1 6:45A

MAY WESTBOUND

Leave VALDEZ	Leave SEWARD	Leave KODIAK	PORT LIONS	Leave HOMER	Arrive SELDOVIA
	F30 9:30P	S1 12:45P	S1 3:45P	SU2 3:30A	SU2 4:55A
		SU2 10:30P		Ar. M3 8:00A	
		M3 10:30P		T4 12:30P	T4 2:00P
	F7 9:30P	S8 12:45P	S8 3:45P	SU9 3:30A	SU9 4:55A
		SU9 10:30P		Ar. M10 8:00A	
		M10 10:30P		T11 12:30P	T11 2:00P
		W12 4:55P	***TO ALEUTIAN CHAIN TRIP***		
		M17 10:30P		T18 12:30P	T18 2:00P
F21 6:30A	F21 9:30P	S22 12:45P	S22 3:45P	SU23 3:30A	SU23 4:55A
		SU23 10:30P		Ar. M24 8:00A	
		M24 10:30P		T25 12:30P	T25 2:00P
F28 6:30A	F28 9:30P	S29 12:45P	S29 3:45P	SU30 3:30A	SU30 4:55A
		SU30 10:30P		Ar. M31 8:00A	
		*M31 11:55P		T1 2:00P	T1 3:30P

JUNE WESTBOUND

Leave VALDEZ	Leave SEWARD	Leave KODIAK	PORT LIONS	Leave HOMER	Arrive SELDOVIA
F4 6:30A	F4 9:30P	S5 12:45P	S5 3:45P	SU6 3:30A	SU6 4:55A
		SU6 10:30P		Ar. M7 8:00A	
		M7 10:30P		T8 12:30P	T8 2:00P
		W9 4:55P	***TO ALEUTIAN CHAIN TRIP***		
		M14 10:30P		T15 12:30P	T15 2:00P
F18 6:30A	F18 9:30P	S19 12:45P	S19 3:45P	SU20 3:30A	SU20 4:55A
		SU20 10:30P		Ar. M21 8:00A	
		M21 10:30P		T22 12:30P	T22 2:00P
F25 6:30A	F25 9:30P	S26 12:45P	S26 3:45P	SU27 3:30A	SU27 4:55A
		SU27 10:30P		Ar. M28 8:00A	
		M28 10:30P		T29 12:30P	T29 2:00P

JULY WESTBOUND

Leave VALDEZ	Leave SEWARD	Leave KODIAK	PORT LIONS	Leave HOMER	Arrive SELDOVIA
F2 6:30A	F2 9:30P	S3 12:45P	S3 3:45P	SU4 3:30A	SU4 4:55A
		SU4 10:30P		Ar. M5 8:00A	
		M5 10:30P		T6 12:30P	T6 2:00P
F9 6:30A	F9 9:30P	S10 12:45P	S10 3:45P	SU11 3:30A	SU11 4:55A
		SU11 10:30P		Ar. M12 8:00A	
		M12 10:30P		T13 12:30P	T13 2:00P
		W14 4:55P	***TO ALEUTIAN CHAIN TRIP***		
		M19 10:30P		T20 12:30P	T20 2:00P
F23 6:30A	F23 9:30P	S24 12:45P	S24 3:45P	SU25 3:30A	SU25 4:55A
		SU25 10:30P		Ar. M26 8:00A	
		M26 10:30P		T27 12:30P	T27 2:00P
F30 6:30A	F30 9:30P	S31 12:45P	S31 3:45P	SU1 3:30A	SU1 4:55A

AUGUST WESTBOUND

Leave VALDEZ	Leave SEWARD	Leave KODIAK	PORT LIONS	Leave HOMER	Arrive SELDOVIA
		SU1 10:30P		Ar. M2 8:00A	
		M2 10:30P		T3 12:30P	T3 2:00P
F6 6:30A	F6 9:30P	S7 12:45P	S7 3:45P	SU8 3:30A	SU8 4:55A
		SU8 10:30P		Ar. M9 8:00A	
		M9 10:30P		T10 12:30P	T10 2:00P
		W11 4:55P	***TO ALEUTIAN CHAIN TRIP***		
		M16 10:30P		T17 12:30P	T17 2:00P
F20 6:30A	F20 9:30P	S21 12:45P	S21 3:45P	SU22 3:30A	SU22 4:55A
		SU22 10:30P		Ar. M23 8:00A	
		M23 10:30P		T24 12:30P	T24 2:00P
F27 6:30A	F27 9:30P	S28 12:45P	S28 3:45P	SU29 3:30A	SU29 4:55A
		SU29 10:30P		Ar. M30 8:00A	
		M30 10:30P		T31 12:30P	T31 2:00P

SEPTEMBER WESTBOUND

Leave VALDEZ	Arrive CORDOVA	Leave SEWARD	Leave KODIAK	PORT LIONS	Leave HOMER	Arrive SELDOVIA
F3 6:30A		F3 9:30P	S4 12:45P	S4 3:45P	SU5 3:30A	SU5 4:55A
			SU5 10:30P		Ar. M6 8:00A	
			M6 10:30P		T7 12:30P	T7 2:00P
			W8 4:55P	***TO ALEUTIAN CHAIN TRIP***		
			M13 10:30P		T14 12:30P	T14 2:00P
F17 8:45A	F17 2:15P					
SU19 4:30A	*SU19 11:30A	M20 12:30A	M20 6:00P	M20 9:00P	T21 9:00A	T21 10:30A
F24 8:45A	F24 2:15P					
SU26 4:30A	*SU26 1:45P	M27 2:15A	M27 6:00P	M27 9:00P	T28 9:00A	T28 10:30A

Whistle stops at Chenega Bay are on Thursdays Between Seward and Valdez arriving Chenega Bay at 2:15PM. Vessel will not stop if there are no reservations.

* SEPTEMBER ONLY - Whistle stops at Tatitlek. Vessel will not stop if there are no reservations.

SOUTHCENTRAL/SOUTHWEST ALASKA PASSENGER & VEHICLE TARIFFS

ALASKA STATE FERRY SCHEDULES

PASSENGER 12 YEARS & OVER (Meals and Berths NOT included) — ITEM ADT

BETWEEN AND	UNALASKA	AKUTAN	FALSE PASS	COLD BAY	KING COVE	SAND POINT	CHIGNIK	KODIAK	PORT LIONS	SELDOVIA	HOMER	SEWARD	WHITTIER	VALDEZ	TATITLEK
AKUTAN	16														
FALSE PASS	46	34													
COLD BAY	62	50	18												
KING COVE	74	66	34	18											
SAND POINT	98	90	58	42	32										
CHIGNIK	132	124	92	76	66	42									
KODIAK	202	194	162	146	136	112	76								
PORT LIONS	202	194	162	146	136	112	76	20							
SELDOVIA	246	240	208	192	180	156	122	52	52						
HOMER	242	236	204	188	176	152	118	48	48	18					
SEWARD	250	242	210	194	184	160	124	54	54	100	96				
WHITTIER	316	308	276	260	250	226	190	120	120	166	162				
VALDEZ	292	286	254	238	226	202	168	98	98	142	138	58	58		
TATITLEK	292	286	254	238	226	202	168	98	98	142	138	58	58	30	
CORDOVA	292	286	254	238	226	202	168	98	98	142	138	58	58	30	30

CHILDREN 2 THROUGH 11 YEARS OLD (Under 2 Transported Free) — ITEM CHD

BETWEEN AND	UNALASKA	AKUTAN	FALSE PASS	COLD BAY	KING COVE	SAND POINT	CHIGNIK	KODIAK	PORT LIONS	SELDOVIA	HOMER	SEWARD	WHITTIER	VALDEZ	TATITLEK
AKUTAN	8														
FALSE PASS	24	18													
COLD BAY	32	26	10												
KING COVE	38	34	18	10											
SAND POINT	50	46	30	22	16										
CHIGNIK	66	62	46	38	34	22									
KODIAK	102	98	82	74	68	56	38								
PORT LIONS	102	98	82	74	68	56	38	10							
SELDOVIA	124	120	104	96	90	78	62	26	26						
HOMER	122	118	102	94	88	76	60	24	24	10					
SEWARD	126	122	106	98	92	80	62	28	28	50	48				
WHITTIER	158	154	138	130	126	114	96	60	60	84	82				
VALDEZ	146	144	128	120	114	102	84	50	50	70	70	30	30		
TATITLEK	146	144	128	120	114	102	84	50	50	70	70	30	30	16	
CORDOVA	146	144	128	120	114	102	84	50	50	70	70	30	30	16	16

ALTERNATE MEANS OF CONVEYANCE (Bicycles-Kyaks-Inflatables) — ITEM AMC

BETWEEN AND	UNALASKA	AKUTAN	FALSE PASS	COLD BAY	KING COVE	SAND POINT	CHIGNIK	KODIAK	PORT LIONS	SELDOVIA	HOMER	SEWARD	WHITTIER	VALDEZ	TATITLEK
AKUTAN	6														
FALSE PASS	10	8													
COLD BAY	12	10	8												
KING COVE	14	12	10	6											
SAND POINT	18	16	12	9	8										
CHIGNIK	23	18	14	15	13	9									
KODIAK	33	23	18	25	23	20	15								
PORT LIONS	33	23	23	25	23	20	15	6							
SELDOVIA	40	33	23	32	30	26	21	11	11						
HOMER	39	40	33	31	29	26	21	10	10	5					
SEWARD	40	39	40	32	30	27	22	11	11	18	17				
WHITTIER	50	44	42	42	40	37	31	21	21	28	27				
VALDEZ	47	54	52	38	37	33	28	18	18	24	24	10	8		
TATITLEK	47	54	52	38	37	33	28	18	18	24	24	10	8	8	
CORDOVA	47	54	52	38	37	33	28	18	18	24	24	10	8	8	8

TWO-WHEELED MOTORCYCLES (No trailers-Driver not included) — ITEM 705

(AKUTAN column reads vertically: "NO VEHICLES")

BETWEEN AND	UNALASKA	AKUTAN	FALSE PASS	COLD BAY	KING COVE	SAND POINT	CHIGNIK	KODIAK	PORT LIONS	SELDOVIA	HOMER	SEWARD	WHITTIER	VALDEZ	TATITLEK
FALSE PASS	38	N													
COLD BAY	52	O	14												
KING COVE	61		28	14											
SAND POINT	197	V	48	35	25										
CHIGNIK	227	E	78	64	55	35									
KODIAK	171	H	139	125	115	209	64								
PORT LIONS	171	I	139	125	115	209	64	15							
SELDOVIA	210	C	176	162	153	132	102	43	43						
HOMER	207	L	174	160	151	130	99	39	39	12					
SEWARD	213	E	178	164	155	135	105	45	45	84	81				
WHITTIER	265	S	232	219	209	189	160	100	100	139	135				
VALDEZ	246		213	199	190	169	139	82	82	121	118	40	29		
TATITLEK	246		213	199	190	169	139	82	82	121	118	40	29	24	
CORDOVA	246		213	199	190	169	139	82	82	121	118	40	29	24	24

All motorcycles must be fully secured on the car deck with tie-downs. It is the responsibility of the owner to ensure this is completed properly. Rope may be obtained from car deck personnel for lashing purposes.

VEHICLES UP TO 10 FEET (Driver NOT included) — ITEM 710

(AKUTAN column reads vertically: "NO VEHICLES")

BETWEEN AND	UNALASKA	AKUTAN	FALSE PASS	COLD BAY	KING COVE	SAND POINT	CHIGNIK	KODIAK	PORT LIONS	SELDOVIA	HOMER	SEWARD	WHITTIER	VALDEZ	TATITLEK
FALSE PASS	61	N													
COLD BAY	84	O	23												
KING COVE	99		45	23											
SAND POINT	133	V	79	56	41										
CHIGNIK	181	E	128	105	90	56									
KODIAK	279	H	225	203	188	154	105								
PORT LIONS	279	I	225	203	188	154	105	25							
SELDOVIA	341	C	286	264	249	215	166	69	69						
HOMER	335	L	281	259	214	210	161	64	64	19					
SEWARD	345	E	290	268	253	219	170	73	76	136	131				
WHITTIER	436	S	383	360	345	311	263	165	165	229	223				
VALDEZ	405		350	328	313	279	230	133	133	196	191	68	49		
TATITLEK	405		350	328	313	279	230	133	133	196	191	68	49	39	
CORDOVA	405		350	328	313	279	230	133	133	196	191	68	49	39	39

VEHICLES UP TO 15 FEET (Driver NOT included) — ITEM 715

BETWEEN AND	UNALASKA	AKUTAN	FALSE PASS	COLD BAY	KING COVE	SAND POINT	CHIGNIK	KODIAK	PORT LIONS	SELDOVIA	HOMER	SEWARD	WHITTIER	VALDEZ	TATITLEK
FALSE PASS	104	N													
COLD BAY	142	O	38												
KING COVE	168		72	34											
SAND POINT	226	V	131	93	67										
CHIGNIK	311	E	215	177	151	93									
KODIAK	480	H	384	346	320	262	177								
PORT LIONS	480	I	384	346	320	262	177	39							
SELDOVIA	587	C	492	454	428	369	285	116	116						
HOMER	577	L	482	444	418	359	275	106	106	29					
SEWARD	593	E	498	460	434	376	291	122	122	233	223				
WHITTIER	753	S	657	619	593	535	450	281	281	392	382				
VALDEZ	697		602	564	538	480	395	226	226	337	327	112	72		
TATITLEK	697		602	564	538	480	395	226	226	337	327	112	72	64	
CORDOVA	697		602	564	538	480	395	226	226	337	327	112	72	64	64

VEHICLES UP TO 19 FEET (Driver NOT included) — ITEM 719

BETWEEN AND	UNALASKA	AKUTAN	FALSE PASS	COLD BAY	KING COVE	SAND POINT	CHIGNIK	KODIAK	PORT LIONS	SELDOVIA	HOMER	SEWARD	WHITTIER	VALDEZ	TATITLEK
FALSE PASS	123	N													
COLD BAY	169	O	46												
KING COVE	200		87	41											
SAND POINT	269	V	156	110	80										
CHIGNIK	370	E	257	211	180	110									
KODIAK	571	H	458	412	381	312	211								
PORT LIONS	571	I	458	412	381	312	211	46							
SELDOVIA	699	C	586	540	509	439	339	138	138						
HOMER	687	L	574	528	497	428	327	126	126	35					
SEWARD	706	E	594	548	517	447	347	145	145	277	265				
WHITTIER	896	S	783	737	706	637	536	335	335	467	455				
VALDEZ	830		718	672	641	571	470	269	269	401	389	134	85		
TATITLEK	830		718	672	641	571	470	269	269	401	389	134	85	76	
CORDOVA	830		718	672	641	571	470	269	269	401	389	134	85	76	76

VEHICLES UP TO 21 FEET (Driver NOT included) — ITEM 721

BETWEEN AND	UNALASKA	AKUTAN	FALSE PASS	COLD BAY	KING COVE	SAND POINT	CHIGNIK	KODIAK	PORT LIONS	SELDOVIA	HOMER	SEWARD	WHITTIER	VALDEZ	TATITLEK
FALSE PASS	158	N													
COLD BAY	217	O	59												
KING COVE	257		111	52											
SAND POINT	347	V	201	142	102										
CHIGNIK	477	E	331	272	232	142									
KODIAK	737	H	591	532	492	402	272								
PORT LIONS	737	I	591	532	492	402	272	59							
SELDOVIA	902	C	756	697	657	567	437	177	177						
HOMER	887	L	741	682	642	552	422	162	162	44					
SEWARD	912	E	766	707	667	577	447	187	187	357	342				
WHITTIER	1157	S	1011	952	912	822	692	432	432	602	587				
VALDEZ	1072		926	867	827	737	607	347	347	517	502	172	110		
TATITLEK	1072		926	867	827	737	607	347	347	517	502	172	110	97	
CORDOVA	1072		926	867	827	737	607	347	347	517	502	172	110	97	97

ALL TARIFFS AND RATES ARE QUOTED IN U.S. DOLLARS

TARIFFS — All fares are one-way. Fares for passengers, vehicles and staterooms are all calculated separately and must be added together to determine the total cost of your travel.

Passage and vehicle fares are charged from the port of embarkation to the port of debarkation. Stateroom fares are calculated according to the route taken, and may vary from the printed rates depending on the ship and schedules.

VEHICLE FARES — Vehicle fares are determined by the vehicle's overall length and width. Vehicles 8-1/2 to 9 feet wide will be charged approximately 125% of the listed fare. Vehicles over 9 feet wide will be charged approximately 150% of the listed fare. If you are towing a vehicle, the overall connected length is used to determine fares.

VEHICLES OVER 21 FEET — Contact any Marine Highway office for fares. The M/V TUSTUMENA can load vehicles to a maximum length of 40 feet. The M/V BARTLETT will accept vehicles up to 60 feet in length. Please notify your reservation agent at the time of booking if your vehicle is over 6 foot 6 inches in height. Fares for towed vehicles or trailers are calculated at their combined connected length. Vehicles may not be disconnected for travel at separate rates on the same sailing.

MINIMUM 25' RATE — Vehicles with high centers of gravity (commercial highway vans, loaded flat bed trailers) are charged at the 25 ft. rate unless the vehicle is over 25 ft. in which case the appropriate rate for the vehicle length applies. Contact the commerical booking desk (907) 465-8816 for information and reservations.

Communities, Highways, National Parks (NP), National Wildlife Refuges (NWR) and other attractions. *(*Detailed map.)*

INDEX

Historic cabin at Kantishna, AK. (© Terry Chick)

Liard River Hotsprings Provincial Park. (© Earl L., Brown, staff)

View of Dawson City, YT, from Dome Mountain. (© Earl L., Brown, staff)